Recent Advances in Swarm Intelligence Algorithms and Their Applications

Recent Advances in Swarm Intelligence Algorithms and Their Applications

Editor

Jian Dong

MDPI • Basel • Beijing • Wuhan • Barcelona • Belgrade • Manchester • Tokyo • Cluj • Tianjin

Editor
Jian Dong
Central South University
Changsha
China

Editorial Office
MDPI
St. Alban-Anlage 66
4052 Basel, Switzerland

This is a reprint of articles from the Special Issue published online in the open access journal *Mathematics* (ISSN 2227-7390) (available at: https://www.mdpi.com/si/mathematics/Recent_Advances_Swarm_Intelligence_Algorithms_Their_Applications).

For citation purposes, cite each article independently as indicated on the article page online and as indicated below:

LastName, A.A.; LastName, B.B.; LastName, C.C. Article Title. *Journal Name* **Year**, *Volume Number*, Page Range.

ISBN 978-3-0365-8254-2 (Hbk)
ISBN 978-3-0365-8255-9 (PDF)

Contents

About the Editor

Jian Dong

Jian Dong received a B.S. degree in communication engineering at Hunan University in 2004, and a Ph.D. degree in information and communication engineering at the Huazhong University of Science and Technology (HUST) in 2010. He was a Research Assistant at the National Key Laboratory of Science and Technology on Multispectral Information Processing of HUST from 2006 to 2010. He was a Visiting Scholar at the Eledia Research Center of University of Trento in Italy from 2016 to 2017. He works as a Full Professor at the School of Computer Science and Engineering of Central South University. He has published 7 books and over 150 peer-reviewed academic papers in international journals and conferences. He owns 24 innovation patents. His research interests include antennas, metamaterials, radars, machine learning and its applications to electromagnetics. He is the director of Hunan Engineering Research Center for new-generation mobile communication RF inductive components. He is a member of the Young Talents Board of Zhejiang Lab, a member of the expert database of the Ministry of Science and Technology, the National Natural Science Foundation, and the Ministry of Education. He has served as a Guest Editor and Editorial Board member of some international journals, including Frontiers in Physics and Mathematics. He has served as a general co-chair of IoTCIT and 6GIoTT, as a technical program chair of CCPQT and EITCE, and as a Session chair for IEEE ICMMT/IWS/NEMO/ISAPE/ISAP/IWAT, ACES, and PIERS.

mathematics

MDPI

Editorial

Preface to the Special Issue on "Recent Advances in Swarm Intelligence Algorithms and Their Applications"—Special Issue Book

Jian Dong

School of Computer Science and Engineering, Central South University, Changsha 410075, China; dongjian@csu.edu.cn

Swarm intelligence algorithms represent a rapidly growing research domain and have recently attracted a great deal of attention. They have been successfully applied in engineering, transportation, planning and scheduling, logistics and supply chains, and a broad range of other domains. They often find high-quality solutions with less computational effort than other optimization methods.

With the advancement of swarm intelligence algorithms, new variants and improvements are continuously proposed to accommodate different types of problems and application domains. The research and application of these algorithms provide an efficient and flexible approach to tackling real-world problems, while also driving the development of optimization algorithms and advancing theoretical investigations.

This Special Issue aims to highlight the latest results on swarm intelligence and its combination with real-world problems and other fields, such as engineering problems, vehicle swarm motion, viscoelastic Maxwell-type DVA, deep learning, loss of the network, echo cancellation scenarios, etc.

Contribution [1] proposes a novel discrete differential evolution (DE) algorithm to calculate the deficiency number of the tiles. In detail, to decrease the difficulty of computing the deficiency number, some pretreatment mechanisms are first put forward to convert it into a simple combinatorial optimization problem with varying variables by changing its search space. Subsequently, employing the superior framework of DE, a novel discrete DE algorithm is specially developed for the simplified problem through devising proper initialization, a mapping solution method, a repairing solution technique, a fitness evaluation approach, and mutation and crossover operations. Contribution [2] introduces chaotic mapping into the PPE algorithm to propose a new algorithm, the Chaotic-based Phasmatodea Population Evolution (CPPE) algorithm, and apply CPPE to stock prediction. The results show that the predicted curve is relatively consistent with the real curve. In [3], the viscoelastic Maxwell-type DVA model with an inverter and multiple stiffness springs is investigated with the combination of the traditional theory and an intelligent algorithm, providing a theoretical and computational basis for the optimization design of DVA. An improved multi-strategy Harris Hawks optimization (MSHHO) algorithm is proposed in paper [4]. Through experiments on 33 benchmark functions and 2 engineering application problems, it has been shown that the improved algorithm performs well in terms of optimization accuracy, convergence speed, and stability. Contribution [5] proposes a new convex combination based on grey wolf optimization and LMS algorithms, to save area and achieve high convergence speed by maximally exploiting the best features of each algorithm, presenting a customized time-multiplexing control scheme to dynamically vary the number of search agents.

An enhanced moth-flame optimization algorithm named MFO-SFR is developed to solve global optimization problems in paper [6]. The MFO-SFR algorithm introduces an effective stagnation finding and replacing (SFR) strategy to effectively maintain population diversity throughout the optimization process. The high performance of the algorithm

Citation: Dong, J. Preface to the Special Issue on "Recent Advances in Swarm Intelligence Algorithms and Their Applications"—Special Issue Book. *Mathematics* **2023**, *11*, 2624. https://doi.org/10.3390/math11122624

Received: 5 June 2023
Revised: 7 June 2023
Accepted: 7 June 2023
Published: 8 June 2023

is verified through experiments on the CEC2018 benchmark and mechanical engineering problems in the CEC2020 test-suite. In paper [7], a partition-based random search method is proposed, in which the entire feasible domain is partitioned into smaller and smaller subregions iteratively. Promising regions are partitioned faster than unpromising regions, thus exploiting promising areas earlier than unpromising areas. By cooperating with local search to refine the obtained solutions, the proposed method demonstrates good performance in many benchmark functions with multiple global optima. Aiming at the characteristics of complex networks structure and multiple design variables of energy-harvesting non-orthogonal multiple-access cognitive relay networks (EH-NOMA-CRNs), the authors of [8] utilized the proposed hybrid strategy to improve the Bat algorithm (HSIBA) to optimize the performance of EH-NOMA-CRNs. Contribution [9] formulates the cooperative attack defence evolution of large-scale agents in high-dimensional environments as a multi-population high-dimensional stochastic mean-field game (MPHD-MFG), significantly reducing the communication frequency and computational complexity, and tractably solving the MPHD-MFG with a generative-adversarial-network (GAN)-based method using the MFGs underlying variational primal-dual structure. Contribution [10] proposes a tunicate swarm algorithm based on Tent–Lévy flight (TLTSA) to avoid converging prematurely or failing to escape from a locally optimal solution. The 16 unimodal benchmark functions, 14 multimodal benchmark functions, 6 fixed-dimension functions, and 3 constrained practical problems in engineering are selected to verify the performance of the TLTSA.

The authors in [11] propose an Oppositional Pigeon-Inspired Optimizer (OPIO) algorithm to overcome the drawback of premature convergence and local stagnation. The proposed algorithm would be used to determine the load demand of a power system, by sustaining the various equality and inequality constraints, to diminish the overall generation cost. To overcome unmanned aerial vehicle swarm motion error, a near-field array beam-forming model with array element position error is constructed in [12], and the Taylor expansion of the phase difference function is used to approximately simplify the model. The improved Newton maximum entropy algorithm is proposed to estimate and compensate for the phase errors. The maximum entropy objective function is established, and the Newton iterative algorithm is used to estimate the phase error iteratively. Contribution [13] studies the cavity morphology characteristics and proposes a deep learning (DL)-based morphology classification method using 3D ground-penetrating radar (GPR) data, and experimental results are validated using the 3D GPR road modelling data obtained from the gprMax3D system. Contribution [14] provides HHO-NN (Harris Hawk Optimization-Neural network), a novel algorithm based on Harris Hawk optimization (HHO) that is capable of fast convergence when compared to previous evolutionary algorithms that automatically search for meaningful multilayered perceptron neural network (MPNN) topologies for optimal bidding. Contribution [15] presents an efficient optimization technique named the honey badger algorithm (HBA) for specifying the optimum size and location of capacitors and different types of DGs to minimize the total active power loss of the network. The combined power loss sensitivity (CPLS) factor is deployed with the HBA to accelerate the estimation process by specifying the candidate buses for optimal placement of DGs and capacitors in an RDS.

To make the Whale Optimization algorithm compatible with several challenging problems, two major modifications are proposed in [16]: the first one is opposition-based learning in the initialization phase, while the second is the inculcation of the Cauchy mutation operator in the position-updating phase. The proposed variant is named the Augmented Whale Optimization Algorithm (AWOA) and tests over two benchmark suits. Contribution [17] proposes a contextual semantic-guided entity-centric graph convolutional network (CEGCN) model that enables entity mentions to obtain semantic-guided contextual information for more accurate relational representations. This model develops a self-attention-enhanced neural network to concentrate on the importance and relevance of different words to obtain semantic-guided contextual information, employs a dependency tree with entities as global nodes, and adds virtual edges to construct an entity-centric logical adjacency matrix (ELAM). The authors in [18] introduce a new approach to enhance optimization algorithms when solving the piecewise linearization problem of a given function. Eight swarm intelligence algorithms are selected to be experimentally compared. Contribution [19] introduces a strategy to enrich swarm intelligence algorithms with the preferences of the Decision Maker (DM) represented in an ordinal classifier based on interval outranking. The hybridizing strategy is applied to two swarm intelligence algorithms, i.e., Multi-objective Grey Wolf Optimization and Indicator-based Multi-objective Ant Colony Optimization for continuous domains. The resulting hybrid algorithms are called GWO-InClass and ACO-InClass. In the survey, Contribution [20] sheds light on population-based deep reinforcement learning (PB-DRL) algorithms, their applications, and general frameworks. They introduce several independent subject areas, including naive self-play, fictitious self-play, population-play, evolution-based training methods, and the policy-space response oracle family. These methods provide a variety of approaches to solving multi-agent problems and are useful in designing robust multi-agent reinforcement learning algorithms that can handle complex real-life situations.

This Special Issue has published a total of 20 articles, comprising 19 research articles and 1 review article. The collective body of work presented herein expands the application boundaries of swarm intelligence algorithms and fosters future research in swarm intelligence and its integration with real-world problems. We find the selection of papers in this Special Issue to be highly inspiring, and we extend our gratitude to the editors and reviewers for their dedicated efforts and valuable assistance throughout this process.

Funding: This research was funded in part by the National Natural Science Foundation of China under grant number 61801521 and 61971450, in part by the Natural Science Foundation of Hunan Province under grant number 2018JJ2533, 2022JJ30052 and 2023JJ40775, and in part by the Fundamental Research Funds for the Central Universities under grant number 2018gczd014 and 20190038020050.

Conflicts of Interest: The author declares no conflict of interest.

References

1. Yan, X.; Li, Y. A Novel Discrete Differential Evolution with Varying Variables for the Deficiency Number of Mahjong Hand. *Mathematics* **2023**, *11*, 2135. [CrossRef]
2. Wu, T.-Y.; Li, H.; Chu, S.-C. CPPE: An Improved Phasmatodea Population Evolution Algorithm with Chaotic Maps. *Mathematics* **2023**, *11*, 1997. [CrossRef]
3. Chen, Y.; Li, J.; Zhu, S.; Zhao, H. Further Optimization of Maxwell-Type Dynamic Vibration Absorber with Inerter and Negative Stiffness Spring Using Particle Swarm Algorithm. *Mathematics* **2023**, *11*, 1904. [CrossRef]
4. Tian, F.; Wang, J.; Chu, F. Improved Multi-Strategy Harris Hawks Optimization and Its Application in Engineering Problems. *Mathematics* **2023**, *11*, 1525. [CrossRef]
5. Pichardo, E.; Anides, E.; Vazquez, A.; Garcia, L.; Avalos, J.G.; Sánchez, G.; Pérez, H.M.; Sánchez, J.C. A Compact and High-Performance Acoustic Echo Canceller Neural Processor Using Grey Wolf Optimizer along with Least Mean Square Algorithms. *Mathematics* **2023**, *11*, 1421. [CrossRef]
6. Nadimi-Shahraki, M.H.; Zamani, H.; Fatahi, A.; Mirjalili, S. Nadimi-Shahraki, M.H.; Zamani, H.; Fatahi, A.; Mirjalili, S. MFO-SFR: An Enhanced Moth-Flame Optimization Algorithm Using an Effective Stagnation Finding and Replacing Strategy. *Mathematics* **2023**, *11*, 862. [CrossRef]
7. Lin, Z.; Matta, A.; Du, S.; Sahin, E. A Partition-Based Random Search Method for Multimodal Optimization. *Mathematics* **2023**, *11*, 17. [CrossRef]
8. Luo, Y.; Wu, C.; Leng, Y.; Huang, N.; Mao, L.; Tang, J. Throughput Optimization for NOMA Cognitive Relay Network with RF Energy Harvesting Based on Improved Bat Algorithm. *Mathematics* **2022**, *10*, 4357. [CrossRef]
9. Wang, G.; Li, Z.; Yao, W.; Xia, S. A Multi-Population Mean-Field Game Approach for Large-Scale Agents Cooperative Attack-Defense Evolution in High-Dimensional Environments. *Mathematics* **2022**, *10*, 4075. [CrossRef]
10. Cui, Y.; Shi, R.; Dong, J. CLTSA: A Novel Tunicate Swarm Algorithm Based on Chaotic-Lévy Flight Strategy for Solving Optimization Problems. *Mathematics* **2022**, *10*, 3045. [CrossRef]
11. Ramalingam, R.; Karunanidy, D.; Alshamrani, S.S.; Rashid, M.; Mathumohan, S.; Dumka, A. CLTSA: Oppositional Pigeon-Inspired Optimizer for Solving the Non-Convex Economic Load Dispatch Problem in Power Systems. *Mathematics* **2022**, *10*, 3315. [CrossRef]

12. Zhang, Y.; Wang, G.; Leng, Y.; Yu, G.; Peng, S. IN-ME Position Error Compensation Algorithm for the Near-Field Beamforming of UAVs. *Mathematics* **2022**, *10*, 3256. [CrossRef]
13. Hou, F.; Liu, X.; Fan, X.; Guo, Y. DL-Aided Underground Cavity Morphology Recognition Based on 3D GPR Data. *Mathematics* **2022**, *10*, 2806. [CrossRef]
14. Jain, K.; Jasser, M.B.; Hamzah, M.; Saxena, A.; Mohamed, A.W. Harris Hawk Optimization-Based Deep Neural Networks Architecture for Optimal Bidding in the Electricity Market. *Mathematics* **2022**, *10*, 2094. [CrossRef]
15. Elseify, M.A.; Kamel, S.; Abdel-Mawgoud, H.; Elattar, E.E. A Novel Approach Based on Honey Badger Algorithm for Optimal Allocation of Multiple DG and Capacitor in Radial Distribution Networks Considering Power Loss Sensitivity. *Mathematics* **2022**, *10*, 2081. [CrossRef]
16. Alnowibet, K.A.; Shekhawat, S.; Saxena, A.; Sallam, K.M.; Mohamed, A.W. Development and Applications of Augmented Whale Optimization Algorithm. *Mathematics* **2022**, *10*, 2076. [CrossRef]
17. Long, J.; Liu, L.; Fei, H.; Xiang, Y.; Li, H.; Huang, W.; Yang, L. Contextual Semantic-Guided Entity-Centric GCN for Relation Extraction. *Mathematics* **2022**, *10*, 1344. [CrossRef]
18. Škorupová, N.; Raunigr, P.; Bujok, P. Usage of Selected Swarm Intelligence Algorithms for Piecewise Linearization. *Mathematics* **2022**, *10*, 808. [CrossRef]
19. Castellanos, A.; Cruz-Reyes, L.; Fernández, E.; Rivera, G.; Gomez-Santillan, C.; Rangel-Valdez, N. Hybridisation of Swarm Intelligence Algorithms with Multi-Criteria Ordinal Classification: A Strategy to Address Many-Objective Optimisation. *Mathematics* **2022**, *10*, 322. [CrossRef]
20. Long, W.; Hou, T.; Wei, X.; Yan, S.; Zhai, P.; Zhang, L. A Survey on Population-Based Deep Reinforcement Learning. *Mathematics* **2022**, *10*, 2234. [CrossRef]

mathematics MDPI

Article

Hybridisation of Swarm Intelligence Algorithms with Multi-Criteria Ordinal Classification: A Strategy to Address Many-Objective Optimisation

Alejandro Castellanos [1], Laura Cruz-Reyes [1], Eduardo Fernández [2], Gilberto Rivera [3,*], Claudia Gomez-Santillan [1] and Nelson Rangel-Valdez [1]

1 Tecnológico Nacional de México, Instituto Tecnológico de Ciudad Madero, División de Estudios de Posgrado e Investigación, Madero 89440, Tamaulipas, Mexico; g14070628@itcm.tecnm.mx (A.C.); lauracruzreyes@itcm.edu.mx (L.C.-R.); claudia.gomez@itcm.edu.mx (C.G.-S.); nelson.rangel@itcm.edu.mx (N.R.-V.)
2 Facultad de Contaduría y Administración, Universidad Autónoma de Coahuila, Torreón 27000, Coahuila, Mexico; eduardo.fernandez@uadec.edu.mx
3 División Multidisciplinaria de Ciudad Universitaria, Universidad Autónoma de Ciudad Juárez, Ciudad Juárez 32579, Chihuahua, Mexico
* Correspondence: gilberto.rivera@uacj.mx

Abstract: This paper introduces a strategy to enrich swarm intelligence algorithms with the preferences of the Decision Maker (DM) represented in an ordinal classifier based on interval outranking. Ordinal classification is used to bias the search toward the Region of Interest (RoI), the privileged zone of the Pareto frontier containing the most satisfactory solutions according to the DM's preferences. We applied this hybridising strategy to two swarm intelligence algorithms, i.e., Multi-objective Grey Wolf Optimisation and Indicator-based Multi-objective Ant Colony Optimisation for continuous domains. The resulting hybrid algorithms were called GWO-InClass and ACO-InClass. To validate our strategy, we conducted experiments on the DTLZ problems, the most widely studied test suit in the framework of multi-objective optimisation. According to the results, our approach is suitable when many objective functions are treated. GWO-InClass and ACO-InClass demonstrated the capacity of reaching the RoI better than the original metaheuristics that approximate the complete Pareto frontier.

Keywords: preference incorporation; ant colony optimisation; grey wolf optimisation; interval outranking; multi-criteria decision analysis

Citation: Castellanos, A.; Cruz-Reyes, L.; Fernández, E.; Rivera, G.; Gomez-Santillan, C.; Rangel-Valdez, N. Hybridisation of Swarm Intelligence Algorithms with Multi-Criteria Ordinal Classification: A Strategy to Address Many-Objective Optimisation. *Mathematics* **2022**, *10*, 322. https://doi.org/10.3390/math10030322

Academic Editor: Jian Dong

Received: 13 December 2021
Accepted: 18 January 2022
Published: 20 January 2022

1. Introduction

Organisations from different sectors and domains often face problems with multiple conflicting objectives to optimise. The scientific literature classifies these problems according to the number of objectives as Multi-objective Optimisation Problems (MOPs) for problems with 2–4 objectives and Many-objective Optimisation Problems (MaOPs) for problems with more than four objectives. Typically, MOPs and MaOPs are addressed through the so-called a posteriori approach, which consists of the following two phases:

1. A set of efficient solutions is approximated (the Pareto optimal set).
2. The Decision Maker (DM) has to choose the best compromise: the solution that best matches their preferences.

Metaheuristic algorithms are promising alternatives to address Phase 1. Multi-objective Evolutionary Algorithms (MOEAs) and Multi-objective Swarm Intelligence Algorithms (MOSIAs) are quite popular because their application does not demand particular mathematical properties on the objective functions, the geometry of the Pareto frontier or the constraints of the problem [1–3].

Even though MOEAs and MOSIAs have been widely used in addressing MOPs, most of them cannot adequately approximate the Pareto frontier for MaOPS. They have to cope with severe difficulties as the number of objectives increases; remarkably, the number of dominance resistant solutions, the high cost to ensure diversity, and the low effectiveness of the genetic operators. Studies on the difficulties and challenges found by MOEAs in addressing MaOPs are discussed by Bechikh et al. [4], López Jaimes and Coello Coello [5], Sudeng and Wattanapongsakorn [6], and Ikeda et al. [7]. One of the main criticisms of the a posteriori approaches is that they require reaching a sufficiently representative approximation of the complete Pareto front before the multi-criteria decision making.

Even supposing a good approximation of the Pareto frontier, the DM has to solve a multi-criteria selection problem in this set to address Phase 2. An alternative is to make a heuristic selection; the DM is supposed to consistently compare solutions on the approximated Pareto frontier until the best compromise is identified. This task is likely to become pretty hard and impractical in problems with many objective functions because of the human mind cognitive limitations (as stated by Miller [8]). Another alternative is to apply a Multi-Criteria Decision Analysis (MCDA) method that articulates the preferences of the DM. Again, this approach assumes that the solution set effectively contains the most preferred solutions, which is questionable under the presence of many objective functions.

As a consequence of the above discussion, there has been an increasing interest in combining MOEAs and MCDA methods in recent years. One way is to consider the preferences to bias the search toward the Region of Interest (RoI). The RoI is the region of the Pareto frontier with the solutions that best match the DM's preferences; accordingly, the best compromise is a solution belonging to the RoI.

The preference incorporation requires considering non-trivial aspects such as defining the model of the DM's preferences, characterising the RoI, and determining the relevance of the solutions [9]. Most methods for preference incorporation admit at least one of the following kinds of information on the preferences [10,11]: weights, e.g., [12]; ranking of solutions, e.g., [13]; ranking of objective functions, e.g., [14]; reference points, e.g., [15]; trade-offs between objective functions, e.g., [16]; desirability thresholds, e.g., [17]; solution classification, e.g., [18]; and pairwise comparisons based on preference relations, e.g., [19,20].

The two alternatives to incorporate the above strategies are the interactive approach and the a priori approach, and both have advantages over the a posteriori one. On the one hand, better solutions are found because there is an increment in the selective pressure toward the RoI [21]. On the other hand, preference incorporation can alleviate the DM's cognitive effort to select the best compromise because the number of candidate solutions is relatively short. Still, the interactive approaches are strongly criticised because they require preference relations with full comparability and transitivity (as the dimensionality increases, these properties become unlikely) [22]. Contrastingly, the a priori preference incorporation does not mandatorily require such properties. However, it demands a model that reflects the DM's preferences about the solutions.

In many real-world MaOPs, the models should support imprecision and vagueness in the DM's preferences. For instance, if the DM is a heterogeneous group (e.g., a board of directors) or an ill-defined entity (e.g., a community in social networks). In those circumstances, the task of eliciting the parameters of a preference model is highly difficult and is only reachable with some level of imprecision. If such imperfect knowledge is not considered, the best compromise could hardly be identified among the existing alternatives. Interval mathematics is a straightforward but effective way to express imprecision [23].

Fernandez et al. [24] introduced an extension of the outranking method by incorporating interval numbers in the preference parameters. This MCDA method can handle incomparability, veto situations, and non-transitive preferences. These properties become critical to address real-world MaOPs because many DMs have non-transitive and non-compensatory preferences. Additionally, the DM feels more comfortable eliciting the values of the parameters as interval numbers than as precise values. If the DM cannot (or not want to) directly give a value for some required parameters, they may use an indirect elicitation method to infer them, e.g., [25].

In light of the above discussions, this paper presents a further analysis to observe how incorporating interval outranking in MOSIAs impacts the performance. We propose embedding multi-criteria ordinal classification based on interval outranking (strictly speaking, the INTERCLASS-nC method [26]) into many-objective optimisation algorithms. Similar to previous approaches based on ordinal classification, e.g., [11], our proposal also requires representative samples of solutions classified by the DM as 'Satisfactory' or 'Dissatisfactory'. However, we extended this notion with two artificial classes (for internal use of the algorithms) that increase the selective pressure toward the RoI. By applying this strategy, we introduce the a priori versions of two relevant a posteriori algorithms based on swarm intelligence; specifically, Multi-objective Grey Wolf Optimisation (MOGWO) [27] and Indicator-based Multi-objective Ant Colony Optimisation for continuous domains (iMOACO$_{\mathbb{R}}$) [28]. The a priori preference incorporation significantly increased the performance of the MOSIAs according to a non-parametric test (Mann–Whitney–Wilcoxon).

The remainder of this paper is organised as follows. Section 2 includes some preliminaries on multi-objective optimisation, interval outranking, ordinal classification, and the MOSIAs taken as baseline. Section 3 details the proposed algorithms with preference incorporation. Section 4 shows the experimental results. Lastly, Section 5 discusses the conclusions and provides some directions for future research.

2. Background

This section presents an overview of the theoretical foundations. Section 2.1 presents some preliminaries on optimisation with multiple objectives. Section 2.2 briefly describes the baseline versions of the MOSIAs used in this paper. Lastly, Section 2.3 presents the model for multi-criteria ordinal classification based on interval outranking.

2.1. Preliminaries on Multi-Objective Optimisation

Optimisation refers to finding the values in the decision variables (independent variables) that provoke extreme values of one or more objective functions (dependent variables). It is called 'mono-objective' optimisation if a single function is treated. In contrast, it is called 'multi-objective' optimisation if a few objective functions are treated (typically, up to four). Farina and Amato [29] recognised that most MOEAs are severely affected when they address problems with more than four objective functions, named them 'many-objective' optimisation problems.

Real-world applications often involve optimising several functions that are essentially conflicting [30]. As a consequence, no point is simultaneously optimal in all objective functions.

Here, $x = \langle x_1, x_2, x_3, \ldots, x_n \rangle$ represents a solution of a MOP/MaOP: a vector of decision variables that optimises a vector function $f(x)$ whose components represent the values of the objectives. Equation (1) defines $f(x)$, where m is the number of objectives (dimensionality of the problem), and n is the number of decision variables. Applied optimisation models usually add constraints to Equation (1) to reflect real situations.

$$f(x) = \langle f_1(x), f_2(x), f_3(x), \ldots, f_m(x) \rangle \quad f_k : \mathbb{R}^n \to \mathbb{R} \tag{1}$$

Pareto dominance is widely accepted to compare two solutions, determining which of them is better. Thus, Pareto dominance discriminates between solutions by comparing their $f(x)$. Without loss of generality, let us consider minimising the m objectives; the Pareto dominance relation, represented by the symbol $\preccurlyeq$, may be expressed as [31]

$$x \preccurlyeq y = \Big\{ (x,y) : \quad f_k(x) \leqslant f_k(y) \; \forall k \in \{1,2,3,\ldots,m\} \; \wedge \\ f_k(x) < f_k(y) \; \exists k \in \{1,2,3,\ldots,m\} \Big\}. \tag{2}$$

The non-dominated solutions make up the Pareto set, expressed as

$$PS = \{x \in R_F : y \preccurlyeq x \nexists y \in R_F\}, \tag{3}$$

where R_F is the feasible region.

The Pareto frontier, $PF = \{f(x) : x \in PS\}$, is the image of the Pareto set. In the absence of information on the preferences of the DM, a sufficiently representative sample of the Pareto frontier should be calculated.

Identifying a set of Pareto efficient solutions is indeed necessary to solve MOPs and MaOPS. Still, it is not sufficient since the DM must select the best compromise (the solution to implement). The DM chooses the best compromise according to their personal preferences about the objective functions. In practice, the best compromise is the ultimate solution to the problem.

2.2. An Overview of Two Swarm Intelligence Algorithms to Address MaOPs

In this section, we provide a brief description of MOGWO [27] and iMOACO$_{\mathbb{R}}$ [28].

2.2.1. Multi-Objective Grey Wolf Optimisation

Mirjalili et al. [27] proposed MOGWO—Multi-Objective Grey Wolf Optimiser—which extends the mono-objective algorithm Grey Wolf Optimiser (GWO) [32] to treat multiple objectives. This swarm intelligence algorithm is inspired by nature, specifically by the behaviour of grey wolves in tracking and hunting their prey. By analogy, the solution with the best value in the objective function is named the α wolf. The second-best and the third-best solutions are named β and δ wolves, respectively. The remaining solutions are known as Ω wolves. The leaders (α, β, and δ) guide the optimisation process, and the Ω wolves follow the leaders in the search for the global optimum.

Let n be the number of decision variables, ι be the number of the current iteration, $x_i^\iota = \left\langle x_{i,1}^\iota, x_{i,2}^\iota, x_{i,3}^\iota, \ldots, x_{i,n}^\iota \right\rangle$ be the n-dimensional location point of the ith wolf during the ιth iteration, and $x^\iota = \langle x_1^\iota, x_2^\iota, x_3^\iota, \ldots, x_\hbar^\iota \rangle$ be the positions of a pack with $\hbar$ wolves. The following equation simulates how the Ω wolves are relocated to siege their prey during hunt following the social leadership:

$$x_i^{\iota+1} = \frac{\mathfrak{r}_1^\iota + \mathfrak{r}_2^\iota + \mathfrak{r}_3^\iota}{3} \quad \forall i \in \{1, 2, 3, \ldots, \hbar\}, \tag{4}$$

where $\mathfrak{r}_1^\iota$, $\mathfrak{r}_2^\iota$, and $\mathfrak{r}_3^\iota$ are n-dimensional vectors reflecting the influence of the three leader wolves during the ιth iteration. Each component of them is calculated as

$$\mathfrak{r}_{1,j}^\iota = x_{\alpha,j} - A_j \cdot D_{\alpha,j} \;\; \forall j \in \{1, 2, 3, \ldots, n\}, \;\; \text{where } D_{\alpha,j} = \left| C_j \cdot x_{\alpha,j} - x_{i,j}^\iota \right|, \tag{5}$$

$$\mathfrak{r}_{2,j}^\iota = x_{\beta,j} - A_j \cdot D_{\beta,j} \;\; \forall j \in \{1, 2, 3, \ldots, n\}, \;\; \text{where } D_{\beta,j} = \left| C_j \cdot x_{\beta,j} - x_{i,j}^\iota \right|, \tag{6}$$

$$\mathfrak{r}_{3,j}^\iota = x_{\delta,j} - A_j \cdot D_{\delta,j} \;\; \forall j \in \{1, 2, 3, \ldots, n\}, \;\; \text{where } D_{\delta,j} = \left| C_j \cdot x_{\delta,j} - x_{i,j}^\iota \right|. \tag{7}$$

In Equations (4)–(7), $x_{\alpha,j}$, $x_{\beta,j}$ and $x_{\delta,j}$ are the positions of the leader wolves at the jth coordinate, $\iota + 1$ is the number of the next iteration, and A and D_α are coefficient vectors modelling the encircling behaviour of wolves as

$$A_j = 2a_j \cdot r_{1,j} - a_j \;\; \forall j \in \{1, 2, 3, \ldots, n\}, \tag{8}$$

and

$$D_{\alpha,j} = \left| C_j \cdot x_{\alpha,j} - x_{i,j}^\iota \right| \;\; \forall j \in \{1, 2, 3, \ldots, n\}, \;\; \text{where } C_j = 2 \cdot r_{2,j}. \tag{9}$$

In Equations (8) and (9), a is an n-dimensional vector whose elements linearly decrease from two to zero throughout the run of the algorithm, and r_1 and r_2 are random

n-dimensional vectors with values in $[0,1]$. The components of D_β and D_δ are similarly calculated as those of D_α in Equation (9).

Exploration is promoted by A with values greater than one (or less than –1); with that setting, the Ω wolves diverge from the leaders. C is another component of GWO that favours exploration, whose components represent weights and are generated at random to emphasise ($C_j > 1$) or de-emphasise ($C_j < 1$) the influence of the α, β and δ wolves in defining the distance in Equations (5)–(7). According to Mirjalili et al. [27], p. 109: "C is not linearly decreased in contrast to A. The C parameter was deliberately required to provide random values at all times in order to emphasise exploration not only during initial iterations but also final iterations".

GWO exploits the search space if $|A_j| < 1$ because, when the components of A are in $[-1,1]$, the position of the ith wolf in the next iteration will be located between its current position and the position of the leader. This setting assists Ω wolves to converge toward an estimated position of their prey, provided by x_α, x_β and x_δ.

GWO starts the optimisation process by generating solutions at random during the first population. Then, the three best solutions so far are considered as the α, β and δ wolves. In the next iteration, each Ω wolf updates its position by applying Equations (4)–(7). Simultaneously, the components of a are linearly decreased in each iteration. Therefore, the pack of wolves tends to widely explore the search space during the first iterations and intensively exploit it during the last iterations. The algorithm stops when a maximum number of iterations is reached, and x_α is returned as the best solution obtained throughout the optimisation process.

To treat MOPs via GWO, MOGWO integrates the following two extensions into GWO: (*i*) an archive with the Pareto optimal solutions obtained so far, and (*ii*) a criterion for picking the leaders (x_α, x_β and x_δ) from the archive.

If the archive is full of non-dominated solutions (note that there is a predefined size) and there is a new solution to be entered; then, a grid technique determines the region in the Pareto frontier that is the most crowded by the archive. A solution is removed from this region at random; then, the new solution may be added to the archive. Thus, the probability of a solution being deleted is proportional to the number of points in each hypercube (region).

Complementarily, the criterion to select x_α, x_β and x_δ favours the least crowded regions in the Pareto front. The selection is based on a roulette-wheel method with the following probability for each hypercube:

$$p_l = \frac{\mathcal{C}}{N_l}, \tag{10}$$

where $\mathcal{C}$ is a constant ($\mathcal{C} \geqslant 1$), and N_l is the number of solutions in the lth hypercube. The two extensions of MOGWO jointly promote the representativeness in the sample of the Pareto frontier.

2.2.2. Indicator-Based Multi-Objective Ant Colony Optimisation for Continuous Domains

Socha and Dorigo [33] proposed $ACO_{\mathbb{R}}$, an extension of Ant Colony Optimisation (ACO) [34] to optimise mono-objective problems with continuous decision variables. In $ACO_{\mathbb{R}}$, the pheromone matrix (τ) is an archive that stores the best-so-far solutions. Here, a vector $x_l = \langle x_{l,1}, x_{l,2}, x_{l,3}, \ldots, x_{l,n} \rangle$ represents a solution of a problem with n decision variables, and $f(x_l)$ is the objective function to minimise. The κ best-evaluated solutions are stored in τ, following the implicit order given by $f(x_l)$. The position in τ of each x_l determines a weight (ω_l) that measures the quality of x_l, defined in Equation (11).

$$\omega_l = \frac{e^{-\varphi(l)}}{\varsigma \cdot \kappa\sqrt{2\pi}}, \text{ where } \varphi(l) = \frac{(l-1)^2}{2\varsigma^2\kappa^2} \tag{11}$$

Equation (11) defines ω_l as a value of the Gaussian function with standard deviation $\varsigma \cdot \kappa$, mean 1.0, and argument l. Here, κ is the number of solutions in τ, and ς is a parameter ($0 \leqslant \varsigma \leqslant 1$). The effect of ς is to establish the proper balance between the pressures exerted by the best-so-far solution (with values close to one) and the iteration-best solutions (with values close to zero).

Furthermore, a Gaussian kernel (G_j) is calculated for each decision variable ($1 \leqslant j \leqslant n$) as

$$G_j(x) = \sum_{l=1}^{\kappa} \omega_l g_l^j(x), \tag{12}$$

where

$$g_l^j(x) = \frac{e^{-\phi_j(l)}}{s_l^j\sqrt{2\pi}}, \text{ where } \phi_j(l) = \frac{\left(x - x_{l,j}\right)^2}{2\left(s_l^j\right)^2}. \tag{13}$$

According to Equation (13), $g_l^j(x)$ is a normal distribution, where s_l^j is the standard deviation, and $x_{l,j}$ is the mean. The former is calculated in each iteration as ants construct solutions. Then, G_j in Equation (12) is a weighted sum of $g_l^j(x)\ \forall l \in \{1,2,3,\ldots\kappa\}$, which defines the one-dimensional Gaussian function for the jth decision variable of the lth solution in τ.

Ants construct solutions by performing n steps. The ith ant sets the value for the variable $x_{i,j}$ at the jth step. Here, only G_j—the resulting Gaussian kernel—is needed. Then, the weights ω_l are computed through Equation (11) and used to sample, by following two phases:

1. One Gaussian function is picked from the Gaussian kernel. The probability p_l of choosing the lth Gaussian function is given by

$$p_l = \frac{\omega_l}{\sum_{r=1}^{\kappa} \omega_r}. \tag{14}$$

   To exploit the synergy among decision variables, $g_l^j(x)$ is the single Gaussian function ants use to construct a solution incrementally during a complete iteration.
2. The chosen Gaussian function (l) is used to sample new solutions. At the jth step, the standard deviation (s_l^j) is required to calculate the Gaussian function, $g_l^j(x)$, picked in Phase 1 (de facto, the sampled Gaussian function will be different in each jth construction step). Here, s_l^j is dynamically calculated by Equation (15).

$$s_l^j = \xi \sum_{r=1}^{\kappa} \frac{\left|x_{r,j} - x_{l,j}\right|}{\kappa - 1} \tag{15}$$

   Equation (15) defines the standard deviation as the average distance from x_l (the picked solution) to other solutions (x_r) in τ. The parameter ξ weights this distance ($0 \leqslant \xi \leqslant 1$). The effect of the parameter ξ is similar to the pheromone evaporation in ACO, influencing the behaviour of the colony: with low values, exploitation is more promoted than exploration. The value of the jth decision variable is inferred by the ith ant by following

$$x_{i,j} \sim g_l^j(x). \tag{16}$$

2.3. Multi-Criteria Ordinal Classification Based on Interval Outranking

The notion behind outranking is that the credibility of the proposition 'x is at least as good as y'—represented as $\sigma(x,y)$—may be calculated by analysing each pair of their criteria scores [35]. ELECTRE is the most representative MCDA method of the outranking approaches. Typically, ELECTRE defines $\sigma(x,y) = c(x,y) \cdot d(x,y)$, where

- $c(x,y)$, the concordance index, cumulates the weights of the criteria in favour of the statement 'x is at least as good as y'; and
- $d(x,y)$, the discordance index, assesses the combined strength of the criteria against 'x is at least as good as y'.

Both indexes are calculated in function of a series of parameters that must be appropriately inferred so that σ models the preferences of the DM. Interval outranking generalises the classic outranking to the framework of interval numbers, providing support when the values of the preference parameters are imprecisely known.

If the reader is be unfamiliar with interval mathematics, Appendix A compiles the basic notions to understand interval outranking. Note that interval numbers in this paper are written in boldface italic letters.

Let O be a set of alternatives (solutions). Each $x \in O$ is evaluated with an m-dimensional objective function $f(x) = \langle f_1(x), f_2(x), f_3(x), \ldots, f_m(x) \rangle$. Without loss of generality, we suppose that each $f_k(x)$ is a minimising objective and, consequently, the preference of the DM increases as the value of $f_k(x)$ decreases. The parameters of the outranking model are:

- The vector of weights, $\boldsymbol{w_k} = \left[\underline{w_k}, \overline{w_k}\right]$ $\forall k \in \{1,2,3,\ldots,m\}$, where $\sum_{k=1}^{m} \underline{w_k} \leqslant 1$ and $\sum_{k=1}^{m} \overline{w_k} \geqslant 1$;
- The vector of veto thresholds, $\boldsymbol{v_k} = \left[\underline{v_k}, \overline{v_k}\right]$ $\forall k \in \{1,2,3,\ldots,m\}$;
- The majority threshold, $\boldsymbol{\lambda} = \left[\underline{\lambda}, \overline{\lambda}\right]$, where $0.5 \leqslant \underline{\lambda} \leqslant \overline{\lambda} \leqslant 1$; and
- The credibility threshold, β, where $0.5 \leqslant \beta \leqslant 1$.

The concordance coalition of two solutions (x,y), denoted as $C_{x,y} = \{k \in \{1,2,3,\ldots,m\} : P(f_k(y) \geqslant f_k(x)) \geqslant 0.5\}$, is the subset of objectives favouring the statement 'x is at least as good as y'. The concordance index for the statement 'x is at least as good as y' is the interval number $\boldsymbol{c(x,y)} = \left[\underline{c(x,y)}, \overline{c(x,y)}\right]$, defined as

$$\underline{c(x,y)} = \begin{cases} \sum\limits_{k \in C_{x,y}} \underline{w_k} & \text{if } \sum\limits_{k \in C_{x,y}} \underline{w_k} + \sum\limits_{k \in D_{x,y}} \overline{w_k} \geqslant 1, \\ 1 - \sum\limits_{k \in D_{x,y}} \overline{w_k} & \text{otherwise,} \end{cases} \tag{17}$$

and

$$\overline{c(x,y)} = \begin{cases} \sum\limits_{k \in C_{x,y}} \overline{w_k} & \text{if } \sum\limits_{k \in C_{x,y}} \overline{w_k} + \sum\limits_{k \in D_{x,y}} \underline{w_k} \leqslant 1, \\ 1 - \sum\limits_{k \in D_{x,y}} \underline{w_k} & \text{otherwise.} \end{cases} \tag{18}$$

Moreover, the discordance coalition consists of the objectives that are not in the concordance coalition, defined as $D_{x,y} = \{1,2,3,\ldots,m\} \setminus C_{x,y}$. These objectives justify arguments invalidating the outranking relation 'x is at least as good as y'. The value $P\big(f_k(x) - f_k(y) \geqslant \boldsymbol{v_k}\big)$ models the degree of credibility of the proposition 'the kth criterion alone vetoes the statement x *outranks* y'. The discordance index, $d(x,y)$, is calculated appraising the credibility of veto of each objective in $D_{x,y}$, and is expressed as

$$d(x,y) = 1 - \max_{k \in D_{x,y}} \left\{ P\big(f_k(x) - f_k(y) \geqslant \boldsymbol{v_k}\big) \right\}. \tag{19}$$

Accordingly, $\sigma(x,y)$ is redefined as

$$\sigma(x,y) = \min\left\{ P\big(\boldsymbol{c(x,y)} \geqslant \boldsymbol{\lambda}\big), d(x,y) \right\}. \tag{20}$$

By following Equation (20), Fernandez et al. [24] introduced a pair of binary preference relations. First, the crisp outranking relation (S) is presented in Equation (21), where β is a threshold on the credibility of 'x is at least as good as y'. Lastly, Equation (22) presents the crisp relation 'x is preferred to y'.

$$xSy = \{(x,y) : \sigma(x,y) \geqslant \beta\} \tag{21}$$

$$xPry = \{(x,y) : x \preccurlyeq y \vee (xSy \wedge \neg ySx)\} \tag{22}$$

Fernandez et al. [26] proposed INTERCLASS-nC, an extension of ELECTRE TRI-nC [36] in the framework of interval outranking to multi-criteria ordinal classification. INTERCLASS-nC is applicable in circumstances in which other MCDA methods fail, specifically when the DM does not want to (or cannot) set precise values for the model parameters (majority threshold, veto thresholds, and weights). INTERCLASS-nC is especially advantageous if the DM has only a vague idea about the boundaries between adjacent classes; nonetheless, they can quickly identify one representative solution at least in each category, which may be characterised by intervals.

INTERCLASS-nC considers the array of classes $C = \langle C_1, C_2, C_3, \ldots, C_\varpi \rangle$, increasingly sorted by preference ($\varpi \geqslant 2$), and the subset of reference solutions introduced to characterise each C_ℓ, $R_\ell = \left\{ r_{\ell,\jmath} \right\}$ (where $1 \leqslant \jmath \leqslant |R_\ell|$, and $1 \leqslant \ell \leqslant \varpi$). Additionally, $\langle r_0, R_1, R_2, R_3, \ldots, R_\varpi, r_{\varpi+1} \rangle$ is the array of all reference solutions sorted by preference, where r_0 is the anti-ideal point and $r_{\varpi+1}$ is the ideal point. Following the interval outranking, the following condition is true for $1 \leqslant \ell < \varpi$:

$$\neg xSy \;\; \forall x \in R_\ell,\; y \in R_{\ell+1}. \tag{23}$$

Then, Equations (24) and (25) are used to define the categorical credibility indices between an alternative x and the category C_ℓ.

$$\vartheta(x, R_\ell) = \max_{1 \leqslant \jmath \leqslant |R_\ell|} \left\{ \sigma\left(x, r_{\ell,\jmath}\right) \right\} \tag{24}$$

$$\vartheta(R_\ell, x) = \max_{1 \leqslant \jmath \leqslant |R_\ell|} \left\{ \sigma\left(r_{\ell,\jmath}, x\right) \right\} \tag{25}$$

The crisp relation of interval outranking is extended to compare actions with the sets of characteristic actions as

1. $xSR_\ell = \{(x, R_\ell) : \vartheta(x, R_\ell) \geqslant \beta\}$;
2. $R_\ell Sx = \{(R_\ell, x) : \vartheta(R_\ell, x) \geqslant \beta\}$.

To suggest a class for a new alternative x, INTERCLASS-nC uses the selection function $S_f(x, R_\ell) = \min\{\vartheta(x, R_\ell), \vartheta(R_\ell, x)\}$ and two heuristics—the ascending rule and the descending rule—that are conjointly used. Each one of these heuristics proposes a class for an alternative x. If the classes do not coincide, they define a range of assignments for x (any category within such a range is admissible as the class of x).

The steps of the ascending rule are the following

1. Compare x to R_ℓ for $\ell = 1, 2, 3, \ldots, \varpi + 1$ until the first ℓ such that $R_\ell Sx$;
2. If $\ell = 1$, select C_1 as a possible class for x;
3. If $1 < \ell < \varpi + 1$, select C_ℓ as a possible class for x if $S_f(x, R_\ell) \geqslant S_f(x, R_{\ell-1})$; otherwise, select $C_{\ell-1}$.
4. If $\ell = \varpi + 1$, select C_ϖ as a possible class for x.

The descending rule has the following steps

1. Compare x to R_ℓ for $\ell = \varpi, \varpi - 1, \varpi - 2, \ldots, 0$ until the first ℓ such that xSR_ℓ;
2. If $\ell = \varpi$, select C_ϖ as a possible class for x;
3. If $0 < \ell < \varpi$, select C_ℓ as a possible class for x if $S_f(x, R_\ell) \geqslant S_f(x, R_{\ell+1})$; otherwise, select $C_{\ell+1}$.

4. If $\ell = 0$, select C_1 as a possible class for x.

3. Proposed Algorithms

In this section, we describe how ordinal classification based on interval outranking was embedded in MOGWO and iMOACO$_{\mathbb{R}}$ to incorporate the preferences of the DM. The primary strategy is to measure the quality of the solutions in terms of the class suggested by INTERCLASS-nC. Consequently, the selective pressure increases toward the solutions the DM is highly satisfied with. Note that both proposed algorithms are not intended for searching representative approximations of the complete Pareto frontier; instead, they search for the RoI: a relatively short subset of Pareto optimal solutions that best match the DM's preferences. Here, we propose that the RoI is made of solutions classified as 'Highly Satisfactory', and the best compromise—the final prescription chosen by the DM—should be a solution belonging to the RoI. Section 3.1 introduces the Grey Wolf Optimiser with Interval outranking-based ordinal Classification, abbreviated as GWO-InClass. Section 3.2 introduces Ant Colony Optimisation with Interval outranking-based ordinal Classification, abbreviated as ACO-InClass.

3.1. The GWO-InClass Algorithm

GWO-InClass extends MOGWO by classifying the solutions in each iteration utilising INTERCLASS-nC before picking the leaders from the archive, keeping the solutions ranked in the following order: 'Highly Satisfactory', 'Satisfactory', 'Dissatisfactory', and 'Strongly Dissatisfactory'.

We suggest using an ordinal classifier that has already been validated in an evolutionary algorithm for many-objective optimisation [37]. In this approach, the DM should classify the reference solutions (input) in two classes, 'Dissatisfactory' and 'Satisfactory' (respectively, C_1 and C_2), the minimum number of classes to apply INTERCLASS-nC. Then, the model is extended by artificially adding the classes 'Highly Satisfactory' and 'Strongly Dissatisfactory'. Each new solution x generated during the evolutionary search is classified according to the following assumptions:

- If $x\text{Pr}y\ \forall y \in R_2$, then the DM is *highly satisfied* with x; otherwise, the DM is *satisfied* with x.
- If $y\text{Pr}x\ \forall y \in R_1$, then the DM is *strongly dissatisfied* with the solution x; otherwise, the DM is *dissatisfied* with x.

Algorithm 1 presents an outline of the ordinal classifier proposed by Balderas et al. [37].

A crucial process of GWO-InClass is to update the archive and select the α, β and δ wolves; this process is presented in Algorithm 2. Here, Lines 1–2 initialise the variables; Lines 3–12 rank the solutions according to the class suggested by Algorithm 1; Lines 13–15 make sure that the archive ($\mathcal{A}$) is not larger than the maximum size allowed by the parameter $\hbar$; and, lastly, Lines 16–20 pick three different solutions from the non-empty best-evaluated class to be the leader wolves.

Algorithm 3 provides an algorithmic outline of GWO-InClass. Unlike MOGWO, GWO-InClass needs information about the preferences of the DM, which is exploited to become closer to the RoI. The preferences of the DM are articulated through an interval outranking model. We suggest using the proposal by Fernandez et al. [25] to infer the model parameters that reflect the preferences of the DM. Furthermore, GWO-InClass also needs the reference sets with solutions labelled by the DM as 'Satisfactory' or 'Dissatisfactory'. Initially, synthetic solutions are helpful to perform this task; however, if the DM is not confident about those initial sets, they may additionally have some interactions with GWO-InClass throughout the optimisation process and directly classify the solutions in the archive, updating the reference sets. Binary classification of solutions is one of the least cognitively demanding ways to interact with the DM.

Algorithm 1 Ordinal classifier based on interval outranking

Input: Number of objectives (m), parameters of the outranking model (λ, β, v, w), a solution x, representative sets R_1 and R_2
Output: The class for x ($class$)

```
c_nc ← INTERCLASS-nC(x, R1, R2)                ▷ Descending and ascending rules
if c_nc = 'Satisfactory' then
    if xPry ∀y ∈ R2 then
        class ← 'Highly Satisfactory'
else
    if yPrx ∀y ∈ R1 then
        class ← 'Strongly Dissatisfactory'
return class
```

Algorithm 2 Selection of the leader wolves

Input: Archive ($\mathcal{A}$), solutions of the current iteration (x^t), maximum size of the archive ($\hbar$)
Output: The leader wolves ($x_\alpha, x_\beta, x_\delta$)

```
R ← ⟨∅,∅,∅,∅⟩
T ← PS(A ∪ x^t)                ▷ Filtering only Pareto efficient solutions, see Equation (3)
for x_i ∈ T do                 ▷ Main loop for ranking solutions
    class ← extended_INTERCLASS-nC(x_i)        ▷ Classifying by Algorithm 1
    if class = 'Highly Satisfactory' then
        R1 ← R1 ∪ {x_i}
    if class = 'Satisfactory' then
        R2 ← R2 ∪ {x_i}
    if class = 'Dissatisfactory' then
        R3 ← R3 ∪ {x_i}
    if class = 'Strongly Dissatisfactory' then
        R4 ← R4 ∪ {x_i}
if |T| > ħ then
    Remove the |T| − ħ worst solutions according to the ranking
A ← T
leaders ← ⟨x_α, x_β, x_δ⟩
for x_i ∈ leaders do           ▷ Main loop for picking the leaders
                  ⎧ R1  if R1 ≠ ∅
    topRanked ←   ⎨ R2  if R1 = ∅ ∧ R2 ≠ ∅
                  ⎨ R3  if R1 = R2 = ∅ ∧ R3 ≠ ∅        ▷ Choosing the best evaluated
                  ⎩ R4  otherwise
  set that is not empty
    x_i ← roulette_wheel(topRanked)    ▷ Probabilities calculated by Equation (10)
    Remove x_i from R                  ▷ To avoid selecting the same solution as x_α, x_β or x_δ
return x_α, x_β, x_δ
```

In Algorithm 3, Lines 1–5 initialise the parameters and generate the initial positions of the wolves. Line 6 picks the first leader wolves. Lines 7–12 present the iterated process of GWO-InClass; here, Line 8 applies Equations (4)–(9) to update the positions of the Ω wolves, following the social leadership of the α, β and δ wolves; Line 10 updates the archive and obtains the latest positions of the leader wolves; and lastly, Lines 11–12 update the parameters and variables to perform the next iteration.

Algorithm 3 The Grey Wolf Optimiser with Interval outranking-based ordinal Classification

Input Number of objectives (m), number of decision variables (n), parameters of the outranking model ($w_k, v_k\ \forall k \in \{1,2,3,\ldots,m\}, \lambda, \beta$), reference solution sets (R_1, R_2), maximum size of the archive ($\hbar$)
Output: An approximation of the RoI ($\mathcal{A}$)

Initialise the parameters of MOGWO (a, A, and C)
$x_i^0 \leftarrow$ `random_solution()` $\forall i \in \{1,2,3,\ldots,\hbar\}$ ▷ Generating the initial pack of wolves at random
Calculate $f_k(x_i^0)\ \forall k \in \{1,2,3,\ldots,m\}, i \in \{1,2,3,\ldots,\hbar\}$ ▷ Getting the values of the objective functions for each wolf
$\mathcal{A} \leftarrow \emptyset$
$\iota \leftarrow 1$
$(x_\alpha, x_\beta, x_\delta) \leftarrow$ `get_leaders`$(\mathcal{A}, x^0, \hbar)$ ▷ Algorithm 2
while $\iota \leqslant iter_{\max}$ **do** ▷ Main loop of the optimisation process
  $x_i^\iota \leftarrow \frac{\mathfrak{r}_1^{\iota-1}+\mathfrak{r}_2^{\iota-1}+\mathfrak{r}_3^{\iota-1}}{3}\ \forall i \in \{1,2,3,\ldots,\hbar\}$ ▷ Updating the pack of wolves by applying Equations (4)–(9)
  Calculate $f_k(x_i^\iota)\ \forall k \in \{1,2,3,\ldots,m\}, i \in \{1,2,3,\ldots,\hbar\}$
  $(x_\alpha, x_\beta, x_\delta) \leftarrow$ `get_leaders`$(\mathcal{A}, x^\iota, \hbar)$ ▷ Algorithm 2
  Update a, A, and C
  $\iota \leftarrow \iota + 1$
return $\mathcal{A}$

3.2. The ACO-InClass Algorithm

Like GWO-InClass, ACO-InClass stores the best solutions in the pheromone matrix τ—its archive—considering the class suggested by Algorithm 1. Figure 1 depicts the pheromone representation used in ACO-InClass; here, κ is the size of the archive, n is the number of decision variable, $x_l\ \ \forall l \in \{1,2,3,\ldots,\kappa\}$ is the vector of the lth solution in the archive, $x_{l,j}$ is the value of the jth decision variable of x_l, $G_j\ \ \forall j \in \{1,2,3,\ldots,n\}$ is the Gaussian kernel for the jth decision variable, and $\omega_l\ \ \forall l \in \{1,2,3,\ldots,\kappa\}$ is the weight of the lth solution.

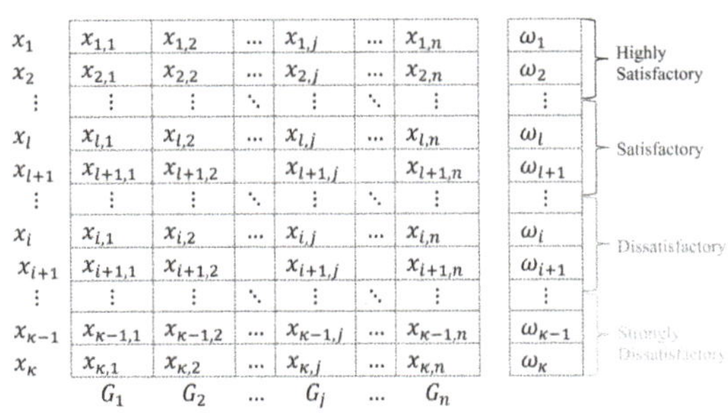

Figure 1. Pheromone matrix in ACO-InClass.

The chief difference between iMOACO$_{\mathbb{R}}$ and ACO-InClass is the criteria to sort τ. Falcón-Cardona and Coello Coello [28] suggested R_2 scores [38] as the primary criterion to rank the solutions in τ. Contrarily, in this paper, we propose the class indicated by Algorithm 1 as the primary criterion, and R_2 scores as the secondary criterion (intra-class solutions are sorted using the R_2 metric). The archive is set to store the κ top-ranked solutions.

Algorithm 4 provides an algorithmic outline of ACO-InClass. Lines 1 and 7 initialise the parameters and variables of the algorithm; Lines 2–6 generate and evaluate the initial random solutions of the colony. Lines 8–16 present the iterated process of ACO-InClass; here, Lines 9–10 generate the solutions of the colony by following the equations provided in Section 2.2.2, particularly Equations (14)–(16); Lines 11–14 evaluate and rank the solutions; and, lastly, Lines 15–16 update the data structures to perform the next iteration.

Algorithm 4 Ant Colony Optimisation with Interval outranking-based ordinal Classification

Input Number of objectives (m), number of decision variables (n), parameters of the outranking model ($\boldsymbol{w}_k, \boldsymbol{v}_k$ $\forall k \in \{1, 2, 3, \ldots, m\}$, $\boldsymbol{\lambda}$, $\boldsymbol{\beta}$), reference solution sets (R_1, R_2), maximum size of the archive (κ)
Output: An approximation of the RoI (τ)

Initialise the parameters of iMOACO$_{\mathbb{R}}$ (ξ and ς)
$x_i \leftarrow$ `random_solution()` $\forall x_i \in \tau$ ▷ Generating the initial solutions of the pheromone trail at random
Calculate $f_k(x_i)$ $\forall k \in \{1, 2, 3, \ldots, m\}, x_i \in \tau$ ▷ Getting the values of the objective functions for each ant
$\tau \leftarrow PS(\tau)$ ▷ Filtering only Pareto efficient solutions, see Equation (3)
`Normalise`(τ)
Rank solutions in τ ▷ See Algorithm 1
$\iota \leftarrow 1$
while $\iota \leqslant iter_{\max}$ **do** ▷ Main loop of the optimisation process
  for $x_i \in \Lambda$ **do** ▷ Λ is the colony (with κ ants)
    Generate a new solution based on τ ▷ Applying Equation (16)
  Calculate $f_k(x_i)$ $\forall k \in \{1, 2, 3, \ldots, m\}, x_i \in \Lambda$ ▷ Getting the values of the objective functions for each ant
  $\mathcal{O} \leftarrow PS(\Lambda \cup \tau)$ ▷ Filtering only Pareto efficient solutions, see Equation (3)
  `Normalise`$(\mathcal{O})$
  Rank solutions in $\mathcal{O}$ ▷ See Algorithm 1
  Copy into τ the κ first solutions of $\mathcal{O}$
  $\iota \leftarrow \iota + 1$
return τ

4. Experimental Validation

We implemented GWO-InClass and ACO-InClass in Java using OpenJDK 11.0.10, on a computer with an Intel Core i7-10510U CPU 1.80 GHz, 16 GB of RAM, and Manjaro 5.10 as operating system. This computer setting applies to all experiments reported in this section.

GWO-InClass has three main parameters to be adjusted: a, C, and $\hbar$. The components of the vector a are initially set in two, and are linearly decreased to reach zero in the last iteration. The vector C is dynamically generated during each iteration, providing random numbers (cf. [27]). The parameter setting of ACO-InClass is $\varsigma = 0.1$ and $\xi = 0.5$ (cf. [28]). The parameter settings of the reference algorithms—NSGA-III, MOGWO and iMOACO$_{\mathbb{R}}$—are also those originally published by the authors in the articles [27,28,39]. A particular case is the size of the population ($\hbar$ in GWO-InClass and κ in ACO-InClass), which depends on the number of objective functions (m): $\hbar = \kappa = 92$ for $m = 3$, $\hbar = \kappa = 212$ for $m = 5$, and $\hbar = \kappa = 276$ for $m = 10$. These values were inspired by the discussion of Deb and Jain [39] on suitable population sizes for evolutionary algorithms. The maximum number of iterations for all the algorithms reported in this section is $iter_{\max} = 1000$ for $m \in \{3, 5\}$ and $iter_{\max} = 1500$ for $m = 10$.

The adjective 'significant' is used in this section if a non-parametric U test (also know as Mann–Whitney test or Wilcoxon rank-sum test) with a 0.95-confidence level validates the difference as statistically significant. Furthermore, we performed all tests for statistical significance through STAC [40].

The rest of this section is organised as follows. Section 4.1 presents the test suite used to validate the results, as well as the indicators to measure the quality of the solutions. Section 4.2 describes the results obtained by GWO-InClass. Lastly, Section 4.3 presents the results by ACO-InClass.

4.1. Benchmark Problems and Performance Indicators

DTLZ [41] has become the standard test suite most broadly accepted to assess the performance of MOEAs and MOSIAs. Accordingly, we ran our algorithms on the nine problems in the DTLZ suite, named DTLZ1–DTLZ9. These problems have continuous decision variables, and are scalable regarding the number of decision variables and objective functions, offering Pareto frontiers with challenging properties (e.g., bias, concavity, convexity, degeneration, multi-frontality, and separability). We explored the dimensionality of each DTLZ problem by considering 3, 5, and 10 objective functions (m); accordingly, there are 27 different instances to validate our algorithms. The numbers of position-related variables (k) and decision variables (n) for each problem are the following:

- DTLZ1: $k = 5$ and $n = m + k - 1$.
- DTLZ2–DTLZ6: $k = 10$ and $n = m + k - 1$.
- DTLZ7: $k = 20$ and $n = m + k - 1$.
- DTLZ8 and DTLZ9: $k = m - 1$ and $n = 10m$.

As GWO-InClass and ACO-InClass consider the DM's preferences, each of the 27 test instances was validated using ten interval outranking models, representing different DMs. Some state-of-the-art studies [42–44] have proposed and used these synthetic DMs to validate a priori optimisation methods run on the DTLZ suite. The primary motivation behind this choice is that an acceptable approximation to the true RoI is known for these synthetic DMs, and these Approximated RoIs (abbreviated as 'A-RoI' from hereon) are in compliance with the interval outranking model described in Section 2.3, which is the keystone of the interval ordinal classifier GWO-InClass and ACO-InClass use (see Algorithm 1).

The A-RoI should contain the most preferred solutions in terms of interval outranking; Rivera et al. [44] followed this underlying principle to calculate the A-RoI as follows (cf. [42,43]):

1. A representative sample with 100,000 Pareto optimal points is generated, represented by the set $\mathcal{O}$.
2. Considering the preference relation $x\mathrm{Pr}y$, the set of the 'least weak' solutions is calculated as

$$NW(\mathcal{O}) = \arg\min_{y \in \mathcal{O}} \left\{ \sum_{x \in \mathcal{O} \setminus \{y\}} \varrho_{\mathrm{Pr}}(x, y) \right\}, \text{ where } \varrho_{\mathrm{Pr}}(x, y) = \begin{cases} 1 & \text{if } x\mathrm{Pr}y, \\ 0 & \text{otherwise.} \end{cases}$$

3. Then, the A-RoI is finally calculated as

$$A\text{-}RoI(\mathcal{O}) = \arg\max_{x \in NW(\mathcal{O})} \left\{ \sum_{y \in \mathcal{O} \setminus \{x\}} \varrho_{\mathrm{S}}(x, y) \right\}, \text{ where } \varrho_{\mathrm{S}}(x, y) = \begin{cases} 1 & \text{if } x\mathrm{S}y, \\ 0 & \text{otherwise.} \end{cases}$$

The proposed algorithms ran 30 times on each test instance using each synthetic DM (as a consequence, each algorithm was run 300 times per instance). The benchmark algorithms—NSGA-III, MOGWO and iMOACO$_{\mathbb{R}}$—were also run 300 times.

There are several indicators for evaluating the performance of a multi-objective optimiser that approximates the complete Pareto frontier (e.g., hypervolume, spacing, spread, and inverted generational distance). However, these indicators are inadequate for assessing the performance of preference-based multi-objective algorithms because no metric can be directly applied when only a partial Pareto frontier is considered [45]. Furthermore, some attempts to assess the quality of a preferred solution adapt these indicators in an oversimplified way, making the assessments misleading. In line with this notion, we measured the performance via three indicators that consider the solutions that maximise the preferences of the DM. Let X^* be the latest set of solutions of an algorithm, the following three indicators are utilised:

- Minimum Euclidian distance. The distance from the A-RoI to the closest point in X^*.

- Average Euclidian distance. The average distance from the points in the A-RoI to those in X^*.
- Satisfaction. The proportion of solutions in X^* belonging to the class 'Highly Satisfactory'.

On the one hand, the distance-based indicators measure the quality in terms of the similarity between X^* and the A-RoI; the minimum distance considers the best solution alone, and the average distance considers the overall trend. For these indicators, the lower the values, the closer the approximation. On the other hand, the satisfaction-based indicator measures the quality of the algorithm considering the number of solutions that could potentially become the best compromise solution. For this indicator, greater values are preferred.

4.2. On the Performance of GWO-InClass

Table 1 shows the results of GWO-InClass in comparison with MOGWO. Given a number of objectives (Column 1), Table 1 presents the average performance in terms of the indicators (referred to in Column 2) obtained by each algorithm (referred to in Column 3) on each DTLZ problem (referred to in Columns 4–12); here, the cells were shaded if the difference is statistically significant: in blue if it is in favour of GWO-InClass, in yellow if it is in favour of MOGWO.

Table 1. Average results obtained by GWO-InClass and MOGWO.

			Benchmark Problems								
m	Indicator	Algorithm	DTLZ1	DTLZ2	DTLZ3	DTLZ4	DTLZ5	DTLZ6	DTLZ7	DTLZ8	DTLZ9
3	Min. Euclid.	MOGWO	1164.89	4.99	606.87	11.94	0.91	3.73	0.25	0.04	5.39
		GWO-InClass	37.01	2.12	374.02	21.14	0.90	5.16	0.35	0.05	5.21
	Avg. Euclid.	MOGWO	1283.63	5.61	776.68	26.70	0.95	4.53	1.56	0.36	7.23
		GWO-InClass	74.11	2.85	487.44	21.69	0.93	6.06	1.66	0.40	6.98
	Satisfaction	MOGWO	1.28	25.17	1.89	23.22	0.00	2.71	48.59	48.37	1.60
		GWO-InClass	8.84	48.40	3.49	50.96	1.61	7.44	48.51	50.00	1.62
5	Min. Euclid.	MOGWO	131.74	693.38	8201.95	0.00	0.17	74.29	0.61	0.76	9.09
		GWO-InClass	24.04	1.61	193.63	6.37	0.00	2.64	0.56	0.76	9.05
	Avg. Euclid.	MOGWO	168.45	693.91	8226.69	0.64	5.73	76.75	2.81	2.68	9.45
		GWO-InClass	78.02	3.03	414.04	17.69	0.26	3.08	2.68	1.28	9.48
	Satisfaction	MOGWO	0.84	12.91	0.28	33.00	1.61	0.18	48.49	49.36	1.61
		GWO-InClass	14.05	48.92	19.84	50.26	49.83	31.84	51.39	50.63	1.61
10	Min. Euclid.	MOGWO	20.16	148.91	189.48	7.03	3.94	2.64	1.96	1.48	7.97
		GWO-InClass	14.12	1.64	186.59	6.26	0.02	0.02	1.89	1.48	8.25
	Avg. Euclid.	MOGWO	84.21	920.18	435.90	16.45	4.82	4.79	5.98	2.22	8.45
		GWO-InClass	87.16	4.67	425.63	16.86	0.08	0.11	5.79	2.22	8.73
	Satisfaction	MOGWO	4.32	0.15	30.69	49.14	1.61	0.00	47.93	48.61	1.59
		GWO-InClass	49.63	53.45	53.70	50.81	50.90	50.18	50.45	51.38	1.63

The information in Table 1 may be summarised in the following points:

- Considering the satisfaction-based indicator: The results of GWO-InClass were significantly better than those of MOGWO in DTLZ1, DTLZ2, and DTLZ6 regardless of the number of objectives. In other problems (DTLZ3, DTLZ5, and DTLZ7), the advantage of including ordinal classification only became significant when m increased. On the whole, our strategy had a greater impact on the 'satisfaction' indicator in many-objective optimisation ($m \in \{5, 10\}$) than in multi-objective optimisation ($m = 3$).
- Considering the Euclidean indicators: The results on DTLZ1–3 were particularly encouraging because the averages of GWO-InClass were consistently lower than those of MOGWO, having statistical significance in the great majority of the instances. In DTLZ5 and DTLZ6, GWO-InClass became closer to the RoI only in many-objective instances. Contrastingly, when $m = 3$, our strategy was inconvenient to treat DTLZ4 and DTLZ6.

- Considering DTLZ8 and DTLZ9: The embedding of ordinal classification in MOGWO does not yield any significant benefit. It is worth noting that they are the only problems with side constraints in this benchmark [46].

As a partial conclusion, we would recommend using GWO-InClass instead of MOGWO to address MaOPS. GWO-InClass was at least as good as MOGWO; what is more, it was significantly better on a regular basis. A test for statistical significance supports this hypothesis on the DTLZ test suit.

Additionally, we compared the results of GWO-InClass with NSGA-III, which has been widely accepted by the scientific community as a benchmark algorithm for evolutionary many-objective optimisation. Table 2 presents the results of both algorithms on the DTLZ test suit. Again, the three indicators—the average Euclidean distance, the minimum Euclidean distance, and satisfaction—are considered, and the cells with significant differences are shaded (blue in favour of GWO-InClass, yellow in favour of NSGA-III).

Table 2. Average results obtained by GWO-InClass and NSGA-III.

			Benchmark Problems								
m	**Indicator**	**Algorithm**	**DTLZ1**	**DTLZ2**	**DTLZ3**	**DTLZ4**	**DTLZ5**	**DTLZ6**	**DTLZ7**	**DTLZ8**	**DTLZ9**
3	Min. Euclid.	GWO-InClass	45.82	2.13	8589.97	21.14	0.01	56.40	0.1	0.05	8.83
		NSGA-III	0.55	0.01	0.17	0.0	0.0	0.00	0.0	0.00	0.17
	Avg. Euclid	GWO-InClass	80.58	2.85	8617.98	21.7	7.30	56.40	1.43	0.40	15.14
		NSGA-III	1.01	0.97	0.99	0.81	0.03	0.00	1.32	0.41	0.78
	Satisfaction	GWO-InClass	5.57	48.35	1.91	48	1.6	0.03	48.44	50.11	1.61
		NSGA-III	5.12	35.29	20.78	34.66	0.94	2.26	44.70	32.99	5.31
5	Min. Euclid.	GWO-InClass	35.86	1.61	400.36	16.43	0.0	2.91	0.56	0.76	38.57
		NSGA-III	0.31	0.04	0.33	0.01	0.0	0.44	0.20	0.84	1.69
	Avg. Euclid	GWO-InClass	102.66	3.03	627.42	27.26	0.26	3.18	2.68	1.28	39.05
		NSGA-III	0.80	0.98	1.10	0.8	0.13	0.58	2.53	1.33	2.15
	Satisfaction	GWO-InClass	7.07	48.74	5.26	48.55	49.93	22.54	50.01	48.97	1.61
		NSGA-III	14.49	3.06	10.97	1.12	10.46	0.83	48.35	51.02	27.30
10	Min. Euclid.	GWO-InClass	0.18	1.64	0.04	1.50	0.02	0.02	1.90	1.85	8.25
		NSGA-III	0.22	0.34	0.79	0.16	1.35	8.73	1.13	1.46	15.25
	Avg. Euclid	GWO-InClass	1.04	2.50	4.40	6.26	0.08	0.11	5.79	2.02	8.73
		NSGA-III	0.54	2.11	1.49	1.17	1.99	9.73	5.66	2.10	15.85
	Satisfaction	GWO-InClass	45.22	49.90	55.39	51.48	67.50	45.73	51.61	89.02	2.82
		NSGA-III	48.72	47.90	28.59	39.93	0.43	42.69	48.38	10.97	0.39

According to Table 2, the worst performance was observed when $m = 3$. Contrarily, GWO-InClass approximated the RoI significantly better than NSGA-III in most of the 10-objective instances. Considering the satisfaction-based indicator, DTLZ1, DTLZ7, and DTLZ9 are especially challenging for GWO-InClass. To conclude, the performance of GWO-InClass becomes competitive as the number of objectives increases according to this standard of the literature.

Lastly, we plotted the results of some single runs of GWO-InClass in Figure 2. We took those runs on the three-objective problems with the results closest to the A-RoI. Although such runs are not representative, they clearly depict how GWO-InClass biases the search toward a privileged region in the Pareto frontier. The best compromise would be a solution belonging to such region (coloured in red in Figure 2).

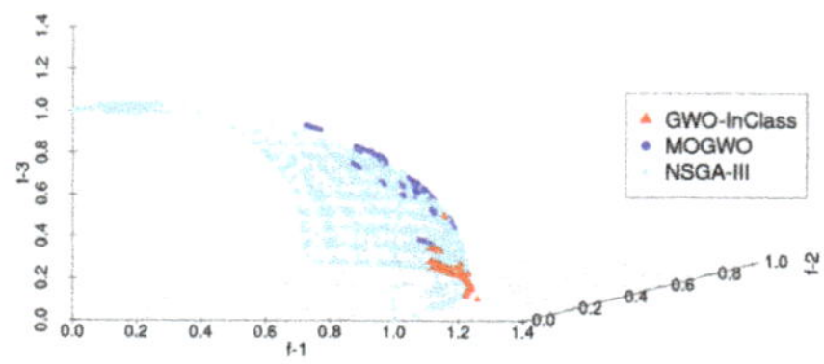

(**a**) Results of GWO-InClass on DTLZ2

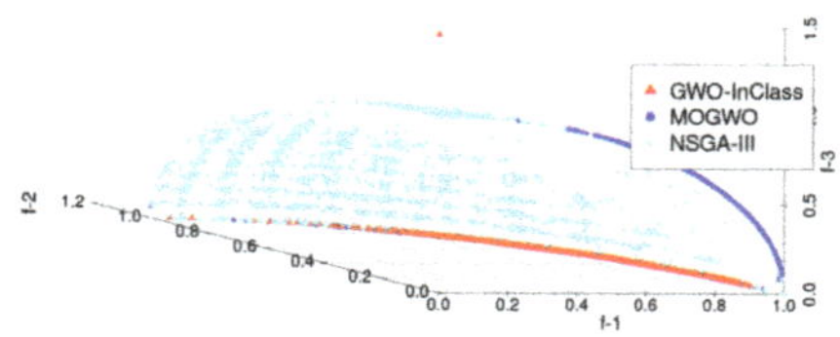

(**b**) Results of GWO-InClass on DTLZ4

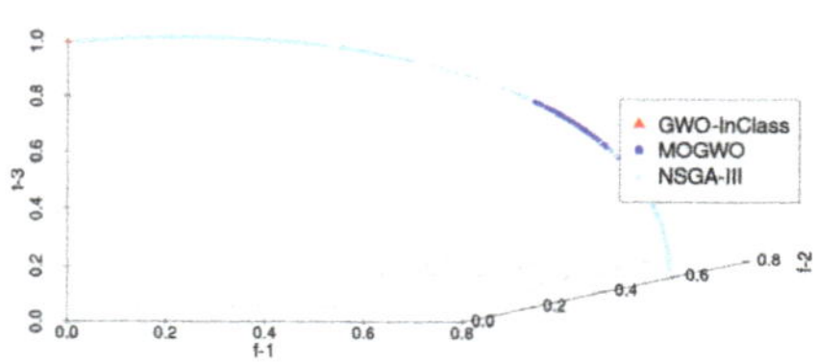

(**c**) Results of GWO-InClass on DTLZ5

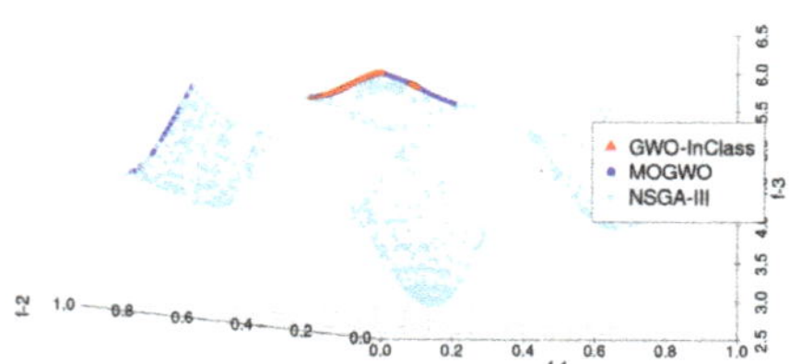

(**d**) Results of GWO-InClass on DTLZ7

Figure 2. Results of GWO-InClass on some 3-objective problems.

4.3. *On the Performance of ACO-InClass*

Table 3 presents the results of ACO-InClass in comparison with iMOACO$_\mathbb{R}$; its columns should be interpreted with the same meaning provided for Table 1. As a summary of the information provided, let us discuss the following remarks:

- Considering ten objective functions: The advantage of embedding ordinal classification became statistically significant only when $m = 10$. Taking DTLZ1–4 and DTLZ6–8, ACO-InClass outperformed iMOACO$_\mathbb{R}$ in at least one indicator, performing especially well in DTLZ1, DTLZ3, DTLZ6, and DTLZ8.

- Considering three and five objective functions: With the only exception of a specific setting (DTLZ6, average Euclidean distance, and $m = 5$), ACO-InClass was at least as good as iMOACO$_{\mathbb{R}}$ regardless of the number of objectives.
- Considering DTLZ5 and DTLZ9: Like in the case of GWO-InClass, no advantage was observed in DTLZ9. Additionally, this situation also occurred in DTLZ5.

We would strongly recommend using ACO-InClass instead of iMOACO$_{\mathbb{R}}$ to address MaOPS with about ten objective functions. This insight is relevant because the efficiency of MOSIAs and MOEAs is degraded as the number of objectives increases. The strategy proposed in this paper could become a viable means of mitigating this severe drawback. Still, the DM should be prepared to devote the necessary time to express their preferences.

Table 3. Average results obtained by ACO-InClass and iMOACO$_{\mathbb{R}}$.

			Benchmark Problems								
m	**Indicator**	**Algorithm**	**DTLZ1**	**DTLZ2**	**DTLZ3**	**DTLZ4**	**DTLZ5**	**DTLZ6**	**DTLZ7**	**DTLZ8**	**DTLZ9**
3	Min. Euclid.	iMOACO$_{\mathbb{R}}$	35.33	2.84	506.46	12.77	0.00	5.46	1.30	0.43	14.04
		ACO-InClass	47.72	0.19	497.91	7.28	0.00	5.70	1.21	0.44	13.61
	Avg. Euclid.	iMOACO$_{\mathbb{R}}$	73.25	3.70	633.16	6.21	3.26	5.74	8.16	0.91	14.71
		ACO-InClass	79.33	1.33	634.59	14.12	2.99	5.98	7.72	0.91	14.23
	Satisfaction	iMOACO$_{\mathbb{R}}$	11.62	28.51	24.42	32.82	1.37	2.47	23.37	46.21	0.00
		ACO-InClass	11.18	32.21	15.38	31.79	2.08	2.64	24.27	52.14	3.22
5	Min. Euclid.	iMOACO$_{\mathbb{R}}$	44.73	0.94	256.49	0.00	0.00	6.50	2.01	7.62	18.28
		ACO-InClass	30.93	1.19	200.61	4.29	0.00	6.78	1.88	11.95	17.74
	Avg. Euclid.	iMOACO$_{\mathbb{R}}$	93.16	3.73	305.69	0.81	0.15	7.59	13.75	51.32	19.28
		ACO-InClass	77.75	4.22	275.32	6.79	0.17	7.97	14.47	83.02	18.73
	Satisfaction	iMOACO$_{\mathbb{R}}$	21.26	18.22	24.56	23.50	16.63	3.99	33.71	60.70	0.00
		ACO-InClass	22.91	18.92	22.77	24.55	15.54	3.97	34.43	38.26	3.22
10	Min. Euclid.	iMOACO$_{\mathbb{R}}$	20.57	0.39	224.90	6.28	0.09	8.13	7.85	56.96	25.79
		ACO-InClass	6.44	0.19	148.08	7.59	0.16	7.09	2.34	1.16	26.22
	Avg. Euclid.	iMOACO$_{\mathbb{R}}$	53.85	1.23	308.24	6.95	0.21	9.45	26.70	217.89	26.82
		ACO-InClass	33.53	1.22	220.34	9.09	0.49	9.12	17.06	2.48	27.34
	Satisfaction	iMOACO$_{\mathbb{R}}$	28.47	28.61	22.27	40.27	16.13	15.19	48.16	12.24	3.22
		ACO-InClass	49.84	47.47	61.03	59.72	11.94	25.63	49.13	87.75	2.21

Furthermore, Table 4 shows the results of ACO-InClass in comparison with those of NSGA-III. The columns of Table 4 should be analogously interpreted as in Table 2. These results together with the statistical tests allow concluding that ACO-InClass is competitive to address 10-objective problems according to the standard established by NSGA-III; in fact, ACO-InClass outperformed NSGA-III in the vast majority of these instances. As a welcome side effect, ACO-InClass can also support the a posteriori decision analysis; this feature would reduce the DM's cognitive effort invested in identifying the best compromise. Adversely, these results clearly imply that ACO-InClass was unsuitable for treating three-objective instances.

Again, we plotted the results of some runs of ACO-InClass, which are shown in Figure 3. These runs presented the best results on the three-objective instances and clearly depicted how ACO-InClass biases the search toward the A-RoI. Here, the best compromise would be a solution obtained by ACO-InClass (coloured in red in Figure 3).

Table 4. Average results obtained by ACO-InClass and NSGA-III.

m	Indicator	Algorithm	Benchmark Problems DTLZ1	DTLZ2	DTLZ3	DTLZ4	DTLZ5	DTLZ6	DTLZ7	DTLZ8	DTLZ9
3	Min. Euclid.	ACO-InClass	1782.09	0.00	478.51	12.80	0.00	0.00	70.01	40.91	9.12
		NSGA-III	0.56	0.01	0.17	0.00	0.00	0.00	0.01	0.01	0.18
	Avg. Euclid	ACO-InClass	1786.36	0.93	612.73	16.15	3.18	0.12	78.33	53.03	15.64
		NSGA-III	1.02	0.98	0.99	0.82	0.04	0.01	1.32	0.42	0.79
	Satisfaction	ACO-InClass	0.27	28.04	2.80	31.89	1.86	0.00	1.11	0.03	0.00
		NSGA-III	5.48	37.86	20.59	33.40	0.44	2.18	88.27	66.34	6.49
5	Min. Euclid.	ACO-InClass	58.84	0.01	3.38	4.29	0.00	1.44	6.83	41.87	2.83
		NSGA-III	0.31	3.05	0.33	0.02	0.00	0.44	0.20	0.85	1.33
	Avg. Euclid	ACO-InClass	122.12	0.08	327.58	4.81	0.13	9.10	17.02	40.31	5.61
		NSGA-III	0.81	10.99	1.10	2.80	3.18	0.59	2.54	2.15	2.69
	Satisfaction	ACO-InClass	15.39	15.76	11.42	1.21	10.18	1.95	7.98	0.14	28.91
		NSGA-III	2.91	3.35	2.97	19.94	12.44	1.08	8.63	9.77	0.00
10	Min. Euclid.	ACO-InClass	0.45	0.20	0.79	0.17	0.00	7.04	2.70	1.46	25.25
		NSGA-III	0.23	0.35	5.06	7.59	22.54	8.94	1.13	25.30	26.22
	Avg. Euclid	ACO-InClass	0.72	1.23	1.49	1.17	0.25	9.04	5.66	2.10	25.85
		NSGA-III	0.55	1.11	33.26	9.10	26.48	9.68	16.85	71.46	27.35
	Satisfaction	ACO-InClass	85.44	54.43	77.10	55.70	24.74	44.58	68.46	96.62	0.00
		NSGA-III	10.38	35.42	4.31	32.38	0.00	28.60	29.24	3.38	3.23

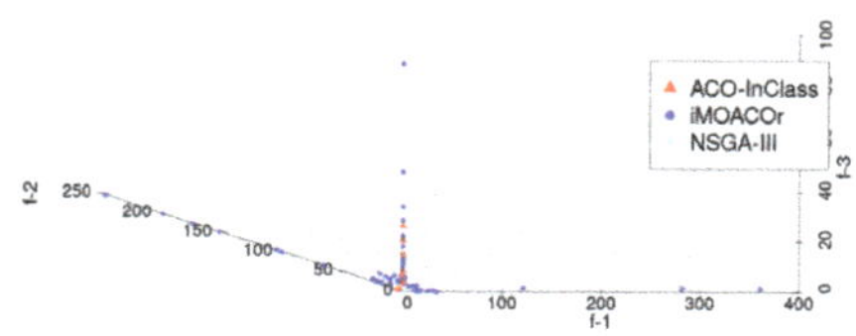

(**a**) Results of ACO-InClass on DTLZ1

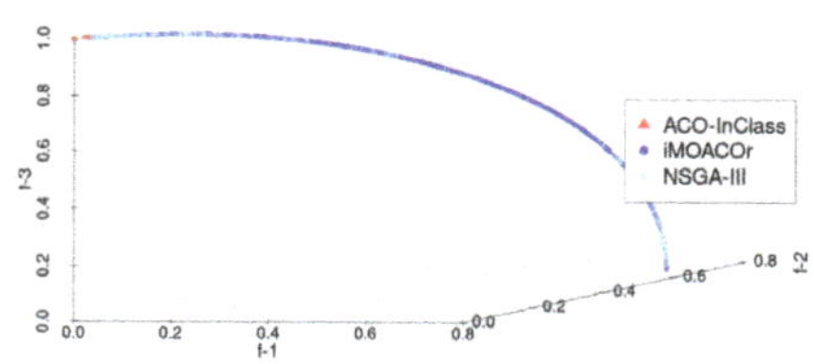

(**b**) Results of ACO-InClass on DTLZ5

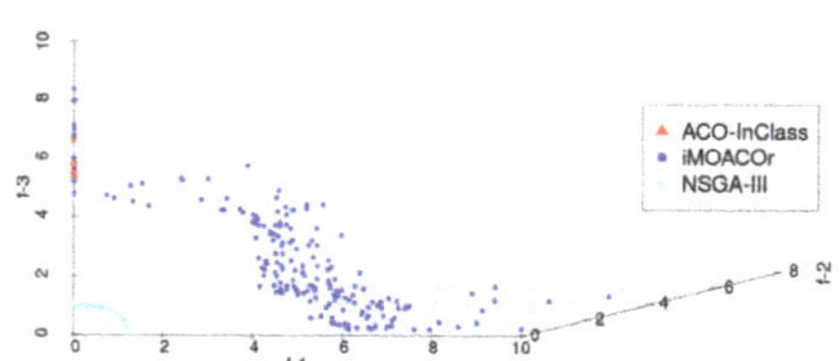

(**c**) Results of ACO-InClass on DTLZ6

Figure 3. *Cont.*

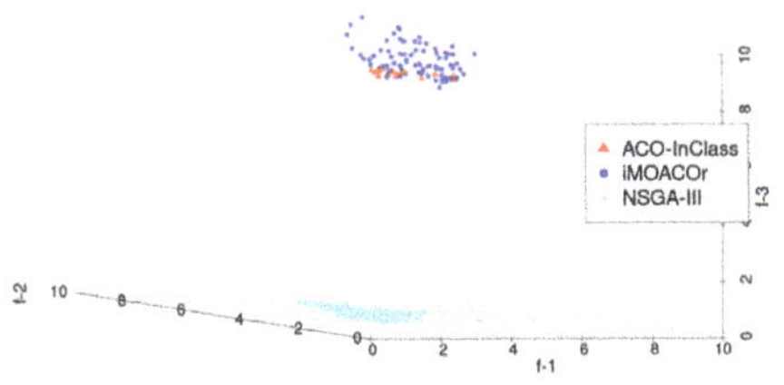

(**d**) Results of ACO-InClass on DTLZ9

Figure 3. Results of ACO-InClass on some 3-objective problems.

5. Conclusions and Directions for Future Research

This paper introduces a novel strategy to incorporate preferences into swarm intelligence algorithms. Following the taxonomy of Bechikh et al. [4], the proposed strategy falls into the category of 'solution classification'. Initially, the DM should express their preferences about the solutions by classifying them as 'Satisfactory' or 'Dissatisfactory'. The proposed strategy is one of the least cognitively demanding in the framework of solution classification because the DM must merely classify solutions into just two categories.

Then, we suggest that the optimisation algorithms additionally identify two artificial classes—'Highly Satisfactory' and 'Strongly Dissatisfactory'—through an ordinal classifier based on interval outranking to model different levels of intensity in the DM's preferences. Consequently, the classifier increases its ability to discriminate. Here, we hypothesised that swarm intelligence algorithms can obtain the edge by increasing the selective pressure toward the region of the Pareto frontier containing 'Highly Satisfactory' solutions. A straightforward way to achieve it is to consider ordinal classification as the major criterion to rank the solutions in the archive.

Typically, swarm intelligence algorithms use an archive with the best so-far approximation of the Pareto frontier. These solutions are sorted to pick the solution(s) whose patterns will be exploited in the next iteration, hence its relevance.

By applying this strategy, ordinal classification was embedded in two swarm intelligence algorithms, expressly Multi-objective Grey Wolf Optimisation and Indicator-based Multi-objective Ant Colony Optimisation for continuous domains. The extended versions were called Grey Wolf Optimiser with Interval outranking-based ordinal Classification (GWO-InClass) and Ant Colony Optimisation with Interval outranking-based ordinal Classification (ACO-InClass). We used ten synthetic DMs to validate the results; we also considered each problem in the DTLZ test suite and explored different numbers of objective functions (three, five, and ten). The algorithms ran 30 times for each setting.

The impact of our strategy depended on several factors: the number of objectives, the baseline algorithm, and the properties of the test problem. Despite this, our strategy conferred marked benefits when many objective functions were treated. In the case of GWO-InClass, such benefits became significant in six of the nine DTLZ problems when the number of objectives was at least five. In the case of ACO-InClass, the ordinal classifier impacted the performance in seven DTLZ problems only when ten objective functions were considered.

Although our strategy requires that the DM is well-disposed to spend the necessary time to elicit their preferences, such an effort can be favourably compensated when problems with many objective functions are treated; especially, keeping in mind that these problems are still highly challenging for a posteriori algorithms (that approximate the complete Pareto frontier). The embedding of ordinal classification based on interval outranking contributed to coping with these difficulties. Numerical results and tests for statistical significance supported these conclusions.

Perhaps, the major criticism of our approach is that it is only applicable when the preferences of the DM are compatible with the underlying principles of outranking. That is, the DM admits veto effects and has a non-compensatory preference about the objectives.

Further research is needed to draft conclusions with a greater generalisation. First, it is necessary to know the impact of this strategy on other swarm intelligence algorithms (e.g., particle swarm optimisation, artificial bee colony, and elephant herding optimisation). Second, it is also necessary to conduct more experimentation with a deeper analysis to connect the performance with the properties of the problem, providing plausible explanations for those problems in which no advantage was observed (e.g., DTLZ9).

Author Contributions: Conceptualization, L.C.-R. and E.F.; methodology, G.R. and C.G.-S.; software, A.C.; validation, A.C. and N.R.-V.; formal analysis, E.F. and G.R.; investigation, A.C. and N.R.-V.; resources, G.R.; data curation, N.R.-V.; writing—original draft preparation, G.R.; writing—review and editing, G.R.; visualization, C.G.-S.; supervision, L.C.-R. and E.F.; project administration, L.C.-R. and C.G.-S. All authors have read and agreed to the published version of the manuscript.

Funding: This research received no external funding.

Institutional Review Board Statement: Not applicable.

Informed Consent Statement: Not applicable.

Data Availability Statement: Not applicable.

Conflicts of Interest: The authors declare no conflict of interest.

Appendix A. Basic Notions of Interval Mathematics

An interval number represents a quantity whose precise value is uncertain; yet, the range in which the value lies is known [47]. Moore [48] defines an interval number $\boldsymbol{E}$ as $\boldsymbol{E} = [\underline{E}, \overline{E}]$, where $\underline{E}$ denotes the lower bound and $\overline{E}$ the upper bound of $\boldsymbol{E}$. Note that interval numbers are written in boldface italic letters in this paper.

Considering two interval numbers $\boldsymbol{E} = [\underline{E}, \overline{E}]$ and $\boldsymbol{D} = [\underline{D}, \overline{D}]$, the basic arithmetic operations are defined as follows:

- Addition: $\boldsymbol{E} + \boldsymbol{D} = [\underline{E} + \underline{D}, \overline{E} + \overline{D}]$.
- Subtraction: $\boldsymbol{E} - \boldsymbol{D} = [\underline{E} - \overline{D}, \overline{E} - \underline{D}]$.
- Multiplication: $\boldsymbol{E} \cdot \boldsymbol{D} = [\min\{\underline{E}\underline{D}, \underline{E}\overline{D}, \overline{E}\underline{D}, \overline{E}\overline{D}\}, \max\{\underline{E}\underline{D}, \underline{E}\overline{D}, \overline{E}\underline{D}, \overline{E}\overline{D}\}]$.
- Division: $\frac{\boldsymbol{E}}{\boldsymbol{D}} = [\underline{E}, \overline{E}] \cdot \left[\frac{1}{\underline{D}}, \frac{1}{\overline{D}}\right]$.

A realisation of an interval number $\boldsymbol{E}$ is any real number $e \in [\underline{E}, \overline{E}]$ [49]. Let e and d be realisations of $\boldsymbol{E}$ and $\boldsymbol{D}$, respectively, $\boldsymbol{E} > \boldsymbol{D}$ if the proposition 'e is greater than d' has greater credibility than 'd is greater than e,' which can be calculated through the possibility function:

$$P(\boldsymbol{E} \geqslant \boldsymbol{D}) = \begin{cases} 1 & \text{if } p_{ED} > 1, \\ 0 & \text{if } p_{ED} < 0, \\ p_{ED} & \text{otherwise,} \end{cases} \tag{A1}$$

where $p_{ED} = \frac{\overline{E} - \underline{D}}{(\overline{E} - \underline{E}) + (\overline{D} - \underline{D})}$. If $\boldsymbol{E}$ and $\boldsymbol{D}$ are real numbers E and D, then

$$P(E \geqslant D) = \begin{cases} 1 & \text{if } E \geqslant D, \\ 0 & \text{otherwise.} \end{cases} \tag{A2}$$

The possibility function $P(\boldsymbol{E} \geqslant \boldsymbol{D}) = \alpha$ is taken as the degree of credibility that the realisation d will be smaller than the realisation e [50]. The order relations are defined as:

- $\boldsymbol{E} = \boldsymbol{D}$ if $P(\boldsymbol{E} \geqslant \boldsymbol{D}) = 0.5$.
- $\boldsymbol{E} > \boldsymbol{D}$ if $P(\boldsymbol{E} \geqslant \boldsymbol{D}) > 0.5$.
- $\boldsymbol{E} \geqslant \boldsymbol{D}$ if $P(\boldsymbol{E} \geqslant \boldsymbol{D}) \geqslant 0.5$.

Let us consider $P(\boldsymbol{E} \geqslant \boldsymbol{D}) = \alpha_1$ and $P(\boldsymbol{D} \geqslant \boldsymbol{C}) = \alpha_2$, the possibility function is transitive because

$$\alpha_1 \geqslant 0.5 \wedge \alpha_2 \geqslant 0.5 \Rightarrow P(\boldsymbol{E} \geqslant \boldsymbol{C}) \geqslant \min\{\alpha_1, \alpha_2\}, \tag{A3}$$

as a consequence, the relations $\geqslant$ and $>$ also meet the transitivity property on interval numbers.

References

1. Chakraborty, A.; Kar, A.K., Swarm Intelligence: A Review of Algorithms. In *Nature-Inspired Computing and Optimization*; Springer: Berlin/Heidelberg, Germany, 2017; pp. 475–494. [CrossRef]
2. Ertenlice, O.; Kalyci, C.B. A survey of swarm intelligence for portfolio optimization: Algorithms and applications. *Swarm Evol. Comput.* **2018**, *39*, 36–52. [CrossRef]
3. Bansal, J.C.; Singh, P.K.; Pal, N.R. *Evolutionary and Swarm Intelligence Algorithms*; Springer: Berlin/Heidelberg, Germany, 2019. [CrossRef]
4. Bechikh, S.; Elarbi, M.; Said, L.B. Many-objective optimization using evolutionary algorithms: A survey. In *Recent Advances in Evolutionary Multi-Objective Optimization*; Springer: Berlin/Heidelberg, Germany, 2017; pp. 105–137. [CrossRef]
5. López Jaimes, A.; Coello Coello, C.A., Many-Objective Problems: Challenges and Methods. In *Springer Handbook of Computational Intelligence*; Springer: Berlin/Heidelberg, Germany, 2015; pp. 1033–1046. [CrossRef]
6. Sudeng, S.; Wattanapongsakorn, N., Finding Robust Pareto-optimal Solutions Using Geometric Angle-Based Pruning Algorithm. In *Intelligent Systems for Science and Information*; Springer: Berlin/Heidelberg, Germany, 2014; pp. 277–295. [CrossRef]
7. Ikeda, K.; Kita, H.; Kobayashi, S. Failure of Pareto-based MOEAs: Does non-dominated really mean near to optimal? In Proceedings of the 2001 Congress on Evolutionary Computation (IEEE Cat. No.01TH8546), Seoul, Korea, 27–30 May 2021. [CrossRef]
8. Miller, G.A. The magical number seven plus or minus two: Some limits on our capacity for processing information. *Psychol. Rev.* **1956**, *63*, 81–97. [CrossRef]
9. Goulart, F.; Campelo, F. Preference-guided evolutionary algorithms for many-objective optimization. *Inf. Sci.* **2016**, *329*, 236–255. [CrossRef]
10. Chapter Four-Preference Incorporation in Evolutionary Multiobjective Optimization: A Survey of the State-of-the-Art. *Adv. Comput.* **2015**, *98*, 141–207.
11. Cruz-Reyes, L.; Fernandez, E.; Sanchez-Solis, J.P.; Coello Coello, C.A.; Gomez, C. Hybrid evolutionary multi-objective optimisation using outranking-based ordinal classification methods. *Swarm Evol. Comput.* **2020**, *54*, 100652. [CrossRef]
12. Wang, R.; Purshouse, R.C.; Fleming, P.J. Preference-inspired co-evolutionary algorithms using weight vectors. *Eur. J. Oper. Res.* **2015**, *243*, 423–441. [CrossRef]
13. Yuan, M.H.; Chiueh, P.T.; Lo, S.L. Measuring urban food-energy-water nexus sustainability: Finding solutions for cities. *Sci. Total Environ.* **2021**, *752*, 141954. [CrossRef]
14. Kulturel-Konak, S.; Coit, D.W.; Baheranwala, F. Pruned Pareto-optimal sets for the system redundancy allocation problem based on multiple prioritized objectives. *J. Heuristics* **2008**, *14*, 335–357. [CrossRef]
15. Wang, Y.; Limmer, S.; Olhofer, M.; Emmerich, M.; Back, T. Automatic preference based multi-objective evolutionary algorithm on vehicle fleet maintenance scheduling optimization. *Swarm Evol. Comput.* **2021**, *65*, 100933. [CrossRef]
16. Branke, J.; Kaußler, T.; Schmeck, H. Guidance in evolutionary multi-objective optimization. *Adv. Eng. Softw.* **2001**, *32*, 499–507. [CrossRef]
17. He, Y.; He, Z.; Kim, K.J.; Jeong, I.J.; Lee, D.H. A Robust Interactive Desirability Function Approach for Multiple Response Optimization Considering Model Uncertainty. *IEEE Trans. Reliab.* **2020**, *70*, 175–187. [CrossRef]
18. Cruz Reyes, L.; Fernandez, E.; Sanchez, P.; Coello, C.; Gomez, C. Incorporation of implicit decision-maker preferences in Multi-Objective Evolutionary Optimization using a multi-criteria classification method. *Appl. Soft Comput.* **2017**, *50*, 48–57. [CrossRef]
19. Gomez, C.G.; Cruz-Reyes, L.; Rivera, G.; Rangel-Valdez, N.; Morales-Rodriguez, M.L.; Perez-Villafuerte, M. Interdependent Projects selection with preference incorporation. In *New Perspectives on Applied Industrial Tools and Techniques*; Springer: Berlin/Heidelberg, Germany, 2018; pp. 253–271. [CrossRef]
20. Rivera, G.; Porras, R.; Sanchez-Solis, J.; Florencia, R.; García, V. Outranking-based multi-objective PSO for scheduling unrelated parallel machines with a freight industry-oriented application. *Eng. Appl. Artif. Intell.* **2022**, *108*, 104556. [CrossRef]
21. Branke, J.; Corrente, S.; Greco, S.; Słowiński, R.; Zielniewicz, P. Using Choquet integral as preference model in interactive evolutionary multiobjective optimization. *Eur. J. Oper. Res.* **2016**, *250*, 884–901. [CrossRef]
22. French, S., Ed. Decision Theory: An Introduction to the Mathematics of Rationality. Halsted Press, 1986. Available online: https://www.amazon.com/Decision-Theory-Introduction-Mathematics-Applications/dp/0853126828 (accessed on 12 December 2021).
23. Balderas, F.; Fernandez, E.; Gomez-Santillan, C.; Rangel-Valdez, N.; Cruz, L. An Interval-Based Approach for Evolutionary Multi-Objective Optimization of Project Portfolios. *Int. J. Inf. Technol. Decis. Mak.* **2019**, *18*, 1317–1358. [CrossRef]

24. Fernandez, E.; Figueira, J.; Navarro, J. An interval extension of the outranking approach and its application to multiple-criteria ordinal classification. *Omega* **2019**, *84*, 189–198. [CrossRef]
25. Fernandez, E.; Navarro, J.; Solares, E.; Coello, C.C. Using evolutionary computation to infer the decision maker's preference model in presence of imperfect knowledge: A case study in portfolio optimization. *Swarm Evol. Comput.* **2020**, *54*, 100648. [CrossRef]
26. Fernandez, E.; Figueira, J.R.; Navarro, J. Interval-based extensions of two outranking methods for multi-criteria ordinal classification. *Omega* **2020**, *95*, 102065. [CrossRef]
27. Mirjalili, S.; Saremi, S.; Mirjalili, S.M.; Coelho, L.d.S. Multi-objective grey wolf optimizer: A novel algorithm for multi-criterion optimization. *Expert Syst. Appl.* **2016**, *47*, 106–119. [CrossRef]
28. Falcón-Cardona, J.G.; Coello Coello, C.A. A new indicator-based many-objective ant colony optimizer for continuous search spaces. *Swarm Intell.* **2017**, *11*, 71–100. [CrossRef]
29. Farina, M.; Amato, P. On the optimal solution definition for many-criteria optimization problems. In Proceedings of the 2002 Annual Meeting of the North American Fuzzy Information Processing Society Proceedings, NAFIPS-FLINT 2002 (Cat. No. 02TH8622), New Orleans, LA, USA, 27–29 June 2002; pp. 233–238. [CrossRef]
30. Coello Coello, C.A.; Lamont, G.B.; Van Veldhuizen, D.A. *Evolutionary Algorithms for Solving Multi-Objective Problems*; Springer: Berlin/Heidelberg, Germany, 2007; Volume 5. [CrossRef]
31. Emmerich, M.T.M.; Deutz, A.H. A tutorial on multiobjective optimization: Fundamentals and evolutionary methods. *Nat. Comput.* **2018**, *17*, 585–609. [CrossRef]
32. Mirjalili, S.; Mirjalili, S.M.; Lewis, A. Grey Wolf Optimizer. *Adv. Eng. Soft.* **2014**, *69*, 46–61. [CrossRef]
33. Socha, K.; Dorigo, M. Ant colony optimization for continuous domains. *Eur. J. Oper. Res.* **2008**, *185*, 1155–1173. [CrossRef]
34. Dorigo, M.; Di Caro, G. Ant colony optimization: A new meta-heuristic. In Proceedings of the 1999 Congress on Evolutionary Computation-CEC99 (Cat. No. 99TH8406), Washington, DC, USA, 6–9 July 1999; Volume 2; pp. 1470–1477. [CrossRef]
35. Roy, B. The outranking approach and the foundations of ELECTRE methods. In *Readings in Multiple Criteria Decision Aid*; Springer: Berlin/Heidelberg, Germany, 1990; pp. 155–183. [CrossRef]
36. Almeida-Dias, J.; Figueira, J.R.; Roy, B. A multiple criteria sorting method where each category is characterized by several reference actions: The Electre Tri-nC method. *Eur. J. Oper. Res.* **2012**, *217*, 567–579. [CrossRef]
37. Balderas, F.; Fernandez, E.; Cruz-Reyes, L.; Gomez-Santillan, C.; Rangel-Valdez, N. Solving group multi-objective optimization problems by optimizing consensus through multi-criteria ordinal classification. *Eur. J. Oper. Res.* **2021**, *297*, 1014–1029. [CrossRef]
38. Brockhoff, D.; Wagner, T.; Trautmann, H. On the properties of the R2 indicator. In Proceedings of the 14th Annual Conference on Genetic and Evolutionary Computation, Lille, France, 10–14 July 2012; pp. 465–472. [CrossRef]
39. Deb, K.; Jain, H. An Evolutionary Many-Objective Optimization Algorithm Using Reference-Point-Based Nondominated Sorting Approach, Part I: Solving Problems With Box Constraints. *IEEE Trans. Evol. Comput.* **2014**, *18*, 577–601. [CrossRef]
40. Rodríguez-Fdez, I.; Canosa, A.; Mucientes, M.; Bugarín, A. STAC: A web platform for the comparison of algorithms using statistical tests. In Proceedings of the 2015 IEEE International Conference on Fuzzy Systems (FUZZ-IEEE), Istanbul, Turkey, 2–5 August 2015; pp. 1–8. [CrossRef]
41. Deb, K.; Thiele, L.; Laumanns, M.; Zitzler, E. Scalable multi-objective optimization test problems. In Proceedings of the 2002 Congress on Evolutionary Computation, CEC'02, Honolulu, HI, USA, 12–17 May 2002; Volume 1; pp. 825–830. [CrossRef]
42. Castellanos-Alvarez, A.; Cruz-Reyes, L.; Fernandez, E.; Rangel-Valdez, N.; Gómez-Santillán, C.; Fraire, H.; Brambila-Hernández, J.A. A Method for Integration of Preferences to a Multi-Objective Evolutionary Algorithm Using Ordinal Multi-Criteria Classification. *Math. Comput. Appl.* **2021**, *26*, 27. [CrossRef]
43. Fernandez, E.; Rangel-Valdez, N.; Cruz-Reyes, L.; Gomez-Santillan, C.G.; Coello Coello, C.A. Preference Incorporation into MOEA/D Using an Outranking Approach with Imprecise Model Parameters. *Soc. Sci. Res. Netw.* **2021**, 1–24. [CrossRef]
44. Rivera, G.; Coello Coello, C.A.; Cruz-Reyes, L.; Fernandez, E.R.; Gomez-Santillan, C.; Rangel-Valdez, N. Preference Incorporation into Many-Objective Optimization: An Outranking-based Ant Colony Algorithm. *Swarm Evol. Comput.* **2022**, *69*, 101024. [CrossRef]
45. Li, K.; Deb, K.; Yao, X. R-metric: Evaluating the performance of preference-based evolutionary multiobjective optimization using reference points. *IEEE Trans. Evol. Comput.* **2017**, *22*, 821–835. [CrossRef]
46. Meneghini, I.R.; Alves, M.A.; Gaspar-Cunha, A.; Guimaraes, F.G. Scalable and customizable benchmark problems for many-objective optimization. *Appl. Soft Comput.* **2020**, *90*, 106139. [CrossRef]
47. Kearfott, R.B.; Kreinovich, V. Applications of interval computations: An introduction. In *Applications of Interval Computations*; Springer: Berlin/Heidelberg, Germany, 1996; pp. 1–22. [CrossRef]
48. Moore, R.E. *Methods and Applications of Interval Analysis*; Society for Industrial and Applied Mathematics: Philadelphia, PA, USA, 1979.
49. Fliedner, T.; Liesiöb, J. Adjustable robustness for multi-attribute project portfolio selection. *Eur. J. Oper. Res.* **2016**, *252*, 931–946. [CrossRef]
50. Balderas, F.; Fernandez, E.; Gómez, C.; Rivera, G.; Cruz-Reyes, L.; Rangel, N. Uncertainty modelling for project portfolio problem using interval analysis. *Int. J. Comb. Optim. Probl. Inf.* **2016**, *7*, 20–27.

mathematics

MDPI

Article

Usage of Selected Swarm Intelligence Algorithms for Piecewise Linearization

Nicole Škorupová [1,*,†], Petr Raunigr [2,†] and Petr Bujok [2,†]

1 CE IT4Innovations–IRAFM, University of Ostrava, 70103 Ostrava, Czech Republic
2 Department of Informatics and Computers, University of Ostrava, 30. dubna 22, 70103 Ostrava, Czech Republic; petr.raunigr@osu.cz (P.R.); petr.bujok@osu.cz (P.B.)
* Correspondence: nicole.skorupova@osu.cz
† These authors contributed equally to this work.

Abstract: The paper introduces a new approach to enhance optimization algorithms when solving the piecewise linearization problem of a given function. Eight swarm intelligence algorithms were selected to be experimentally compared. The problem is represented by the calculation of the distance between the original function and the estimation from the piecewise linear function. Here, the piecewise linearization of 2D functions is studied. Each of the employed swarm intelligence algorithms is enhanced by a newly proposed automatic detection of the number of piecewise linear parts that determine the discretization points to calculate the distance between the original and piecewise linear function. The original algorithms and their enhanced variants are compared on several examples of piecewise linearization problems. The results show that the enhanced approach performs sufficiently better when it creates a very promising approximation of functions. Moreover, the degree of precision is slightly decreased by the focus on the speed of the optimization process.

Keywords: swarm intelligence algorithms; piecewise linearization; optimization; parameter tuning; approximation; experimental comparison

MSC: 68T20

Citation: Škorupová, N.; Raunigr, P.; Bujok, P. Usage of Selected Swarm Intelligence Algorithms for Piecewise Linearization. *Mathematics* **2022**, *10*, 808. https://doi.org/10.3390/math10050808

Academic Editor: Jian Dong

Received: 30 January 2022
Accepted: 28 February 2022
Published: 3 March 2022

1. Introduction

Linearization is one of the most powerful methods that deal with nonlinear systems. One of the most important factors in piecewise linearization is the number of linear segments. Piecewise linear functions are often used to approximate nonlinear functions, and the approximation itself is an important tool for many applications. This method can be found in many applications, for example, dynamical systems, nonlinear non-smooth optimization, nonlinear differential equations, fuzzy ordinary differential equations and partial differential equations, petroleum engineering, and medicine [1–5].

Various existing approaches attempt to find a piecewise linear approximation of a given function. Classical mathematical methods based on differentiable nonlinear functions have been introduced, for example, the Newton–Kantorovich iterative method, analytical linearization, forward–difference approximation, or center-difference approximation [6,7]. Other types of classical transforms or approximations, e.g., Laplace, Fourier, or integral, are used for the construction of approximation models [8]. Methods based on fuzzy theory are called fuzzy approximation methods, and the most known method is called a fuzzy transform [9].

In [10], the authors introduced linearization methods that used the large deviation principle, utilizing the Donsker–Varadhan entropy of a Gaussian measure and the relative entropy of two probability measures. In [1], the author presented an easy and general method for constructing and solving linearization problems. A spline algorithm to construct the approximant and the interior point method to solve the linearization problem was created. In [11], the Wiener models were composed of a linear dynamical system together with a nonlinear static part. If the nonlinear part is invertible, the inverse function is approximated by a piecewise linear function estimated by the usage of the genetic algorithm and evolution strategy. The linear dynamic system part is estimated by the least square method.

In [12], the authors introduced a method to find the best piecewise linearization of nonlinear functions based on an optimization problem that is reduced to linear programming. Another algorithm that is used to find the optimal piecewise linearization for a predefined number of linear segments with particle swarm optimization (PSO), without the knowledge of the function and without ideal partitions, is introduced in [13]. Further, the authors of [14] introduced a genetic algorithm-based clustering approach to obtain the minimal piecewise linear approximation applied on nonlinear functions. The technique uses a trade-off between higher approximation accuracy and low complexity of the approximation by the least number of linearized sectors. Another piecewise linearization based on PSO is applied to piecewise area division; the control parameter optimization of the model was introduced in [15]. In [16], an effective algorithm to solve the stochastic resource allocation problem that designs piecewise linear and concave approximations of the recourse function of sample gradient information was introduced. In [17], the authors presented a range of piecewise linear models and algorithms that provided an approximation that fits well in their applications. The models involve piecewise linear functions using a constant maximum number of linear segments, border envelopes, strategies for continuity, and a generalization of the used models for stochastic functions.

We can already find some piecewise linearization problems solved by evolutionary algorithms, where specific kinds of functions or the number of piecewise linear parts are required. In this experiment, a kind of function is not restricted, and the number of linear segments does not need to be predefined. Nevertheless, only the 2D functions are used to be approximated in this experiment. Besides evolutionary algorithms, the traditional mathematical approaches were mentioned in this section to solve the piecewise linearization problems, however, these approaches will not be addressed in this paper, and a comparison with our methods will be mentioned in future work.

The aim of this paper is to contribute to the problem of piecewise linearization using popular swarm intelligence algorithms with automatic parameters tuning. The linearization of a given nonlinear function is an approximation problem leading to the determination of appropriate points. The goal is to find the best distribution of the points to minimize the distance between the original function and the approximated piecewise linear function. As there is no acceptable analytical solution of this optimization problem, using the stochastic-based (swarm intelligence) algorithms promises sufficient accuracy. Moreover, the selected swarm intelligence algorithms will be enhanced by the automatic parameter tuning approach and compared to provide an insight into the algorithm's performance.

The rest of the paper is arranged as follows. In Section 2, the basic terms used in this paper are introduced. In Section 3, swarm intelligence algorithms selected for the comparison are briefly described. In Section 4, the application of the original swarm intelligence algorithms on piecewise linearization with their parameters is proposed. Finally, in Section 5, the application of the newly proposed automatic parameter tuning of the swarm intelligence algorithms is introduced. A compendious discussion of the algorithm's efficiency and precision is assumed in Section 6.

2. Preliminaries

In this paper, we work with a real-value problem in a continuous search area. We consider the objective function $f(x)$, where $x = (x_1, x_2, \dots, x_\ell)$, $\ell \in \mathbb{N}$ is defined on the search domain $X = [a, b]$. The problems solved in a discrete search space could require some modifications of the presented methods. Through this paper, for the simplicity of the demonstrated method, the domain $[0, 1]$ is used, but the problem can be easily reduced to the more general domain.

2.1. Piecewise Linear Function

Through this paper, piecewise linear functions are used, therefore the piecewise linear function should be defined.

A *piecewise linear function* $f\colon [0,1] \to [0,1]$ given by finite number of points $(x_i, y_i) \in [0,1] \times [0,1]$ for $i = 1, \ldots, \ell$, is a function $f\colon [0,1] \to [0,1]$ such that $x_1 = 0, x_\ell = 1$, and $f(x_i) = y_i$ for each $i = 1, 2, \ldots, \ell$, and $f|_{[x_i, x_i+1]}$ is linear for every $i = 1, 2, \ldots, \ell - 1$. Points x are called *turning points*. More precisely,

$$f(x) = \begin{cases} y_1 + (y_2 - y_1)\frac{(x-x_1)}{(x_2-x_1)}, & x_1 \le x \le x_2, \\ y_2 + (y_3 - y_2)\frac{(x-x_2)}{(x_3-x_2)}, & x_2 \le x \le x_3, \\ \vdots & \\ y_{\ell-1} + (y_\ell - y_{\ell-1})\frac{(x-x_{\ell-1})}{(x_l-x_{\ell-1})}, & x_{\ell-1} \le x \le x_\ell. \end{cases}$$

2.2. Metrics

The difference between the original function and the approximated piecewise linear function is calculated with chosen metrics. In this paper, two different metrics are applied to achieve more complex results of compared methods.

Let $(\mathbf{x}, \mathbf{y})$ are vectors, where $\mathbf{x} = \{x_1, x_2, \ldots, x_n\}$, $\mathbf{y} = \{y_1, y_2, \ldots, y_n\}$. A *Manhattan metric* is a function $d_1\colon \mathbb{R}^n \times \mathbb{R}^n \to \mathbb{R}$ in n-dimensional space, which gives the distance between vectors $\mathbf{x}, \mathbf{y}$ by the sum of the line segments projection lengths between the points onto the coordinate system. More precisely,

$$d_1(\mathbf{x}, \mathbf{y}) = \sum_{i=1}^{n} |\mathbf{x_i} - \mathbf{y_i}|.$$

A metric defined on a vector space, induced by the supremum or uniform norm, where the two vectors distance is the biggest of the differences, is called *Maximum metric*. More precisely,

$$d_2(\mathbf{x}, \mathbf{y}) = \max_{\mathbf{i=1,2,\ldots,n}} |\mathbf{x_i} - \mathbf{y_i}|.$$

3. Selected Swarm Intelligence Algorithms

Now, the use of swarm algorithms for searching a global optima of an interval map $f\colon [0,1] \to [0,1]$ will be demonstrated. A population is represented as a finite set of $n \in \mathbb{N}$ randomly chosen points $x \in [0,1]$. Further, the population moves in the domain with the help of the given algorithm strategy. The processes are mostly combined with the help of stochastic parameters, adapted towards the required solution. These algorithms stop after a certain number of iterations or under some predefined condition. The algorithms were selected based on the popularity of the methods measured by the frequency of their real applications and also based on our previous experiments [18,19].

3.1. Swarm Intelligence Algorithms

Swarm intelligence algorithms are stochastic algorithms from the group of evolutionary algorithms. These algorithms are used for solving global optimization problems that model the social behaviors of a group of individuals. The inspiration comes mostly from nature, especially from biological systems inspired by biological evolution, such as selection, crossover, and mutation. Most swarm intelligence in nature-based systems involve algorithms of ant colonies, bird flocking, hawk hunting, animal herding, fish schooling, and others. The difference between evolutionary algorithms and swarm intelligence is that there is an interaction of more candidate solutions, but they differ in the model between individuals. In swarm intelligence algorithms, there is also a group (population), but its move in the domain is followed by the group behavior rules of a given population. In this section, the swarm algorithms used in this manuscript will be introduced.

3.1.1. Particle Swarm Optimization

A population in the PSO algorithm is composed of particles that move in a predefined search area according to evolutionary processes. In each step, several characteristics are computed and employed to illustrate how the particles are toward the solution [20–22].

The population is represented by a finite set of $n \in \mathbb{N}$ points $x \in [0,1]$ called *particles* is given randomly. Then, the population is evaluated, and each particle controls its movement in the search area according to its personal best position p_{best}, the best neighbour position $\mathbf{p}_g$ and with the stochastic parameters (acceleration coefficients Φ_1, Φ_2, constriction factor χ). There exist several variants of the PSO algorithm. In this paper, the original PSO algorithm from [21] with the modification by constriction factor χ is used. Parameter χ does not change during the algorithm's run and it has a restrictive impact on the result. When the PSO algorithm runs without restraining velocities, it can rapidly increase to unacceptable levels within a few iterations. The elements U_{Φ_1}, U_{Φ_2} are represented by random points from a uniformly distributed intervals $[0, \Phi_1]$, $[0, \Phi_2]$, where $\Phi_1, \Phi_2 \in \mathbb{R}$. At first, p_{best_i} and $f(\mathbf{x}_i)$ are compared, and if $p_{best_i} \leq f(\mathbf{x}_i)$, then $\mathbf{p}_i = \mathbf{x}_i$ and to the value of p_{best_i} is saved a value of the function ($p_{best_i} = f(\mathbf{p}_i)$). In the next step, it finds the best neighbour $\mathbf{p}_g$ of i-th position and assign it j-th position, if $f(\mathbf{p}_g) \geq f(\mathbf{x}_j)$, then $\mathbf{p}_g = \mathbf{x}_j$ and $f(\mathbf{p}_g) = f(\mathbf{x}_j)$. The main part of the calculation consists of computing the velocity and updating the new particle positions which are given by the following formulas:

$$\mathbf{v}_i = \chi(\mathbf{v}_i + \mathbf{U}_{\Phi_1}(\mathbf{p}_i - \mathbf{x}_i) + \mathbf{U}_{\Phi_2}(\mathbf{p}_g - \mathbf{x}_i)),$$

$$\mathbf{x}_i = \mathbf{x}_i + \mathbf{v}_i.$$

3.1.2. Self-Organizing Migrating Algorithm

A self-organizing migrating algorithm (SOMA) is a simple model of the hunting pack. The individuals move across the domain, such that each individual in each migration round goes straight to the leader of the pack, checks the place of each jump, and remembers the best-found place for the next migration round. SOMA has several strategies, we use the' AllToOne' strategy, where all individuals move towards the best one from the population. Each individual $x_i \in [0,1]$ is evaluated by the fitness, and the one with the highest fitness is chosen as a leader for the loop. Then the rest of the individuals jump towards the leader and each of them is evaluated by the cost function after each jump. SOMA has three numerical parameters defining a way of moving an individual behind the leader. These parameters are the relative size of the skipping leader, the size of each jump, and the parameter which determines the direction of movement of the individual behind the leader. The jumping approach continues until a new individual-position restricted by *PathLength* is reached. The new individual position at the end of each jump is determined by

$$x_i^{ML+1} = x_{i,start}^{ML} + (x_L^{ML} - x_{i,start}^{ML}) StepSize \cdot PRTVector.$$

Then each individual moves toward the best position on its jumping trajectory. Before an individual continues to jump towards the leader, a set of random numbers from the interval $[0,1]$ is generated, and each member of this set is compared with *PRT*, where $PRT \in [0,1]$. If the generated random number is greater than *PRT*, the corresponding ith coordinate will be taken from the new position ($PRTVector_j = 1$) otherwise it will be taken from the original individuals position ($PRTVector_j = 0$). During the process, each individual attempts to find its best position and the best position from all individuals [23].

3.1.3. Cuckoo Search

The Cuckoo search (CS) algorithm is inspired by brood parasitism of cuckoos which give eggs in the nests of the host birds. The host bird throws the egg away from the nest or abandons the nest whereas build a new nest by the fraction p_a. The idea of the algorithm is to create new and better solutions (cuckoos) that replace worse solutions from the nests.

Each egg represents one solution and a cuckoo egg gives a new possible solution. In our case, we use the easiest form of the algorithm when each nest has one egg.

Cuckoo search uses the Mantegna Lévy flight $Lévy(\beta)$, which is given by the following equation: $step = u/|v|^{1/\beta}$. The parameter β is taken from the interval $[0.3, 2)$, parameters u, v are normally distributed stochastic variables and u is calculated as $u \cdot \sigma$, where σ is the standard deviation. The main part of the algorithm is the application of Lévy flights and random walks in the equation that generates new solutions:

$$\mathbf{x}_i^{t+1} = \mathbf{x}_i^t + \alpha Lévy(\beta).$$

The parameter $\alpha > 0$ is the step size, and mostly, the value $\alpha = 1$ can be used. The total number of possible host nests is constant, where the probability that the host bird discovers a cuckoo's egg is $p_a \in [0, 1]$ [24].

3.1.4. Firefly Algorithm

Firefly algorithm (FFL) is inspired by the flashing behavior of fireflies that produce light at night. Fireflies are unisexual; therefore, they are attracted to each other no matter their sex. A new generation of fireflies is given by the random walk and their attraction. Fireflies can communicate with their light intensity that informs the swarm about its features as species, location, and attractiveness. Between any two fireflies i and j the Euclidean distance $r(i, j)$ at positions $\mathbf{x}_i$ and $\mathbf{x}_j$ is defined. The attractiveness function of a firefly j should be selected as any monotonically decreasing function with a distance to the selected firefly defined as $\beta = \beta_0 \cdot e^{-\gamma \cdot r_{ij}^2}$, where r_{ij} is the distance, β_0 is the initial attractiveness at a distance $r_{ij} = 0$, and γ represents an absorption coefficient characterizing the variation of the attractiveness value. The movement of each ith firefly attracted by a more firefly j with higher attractiveness is given by the equation

$$\mathbf{x}_i^{t+1} = \mathbf{x}_i^t + \beta(\mathbf{x}_j^t - \mathbf{x}_i^t) + \alpha(\sigma - 0.5).$$

The first component represents the ith firefly position, the second part enables the model of the attractiveness of the firefly, and the last part is randomization, with $\alpha \in [0, 1]$ represented by the problem of interest. The parameter σ represents a scaling factor that determines the distance of visibility, and mostly $\sigma \in [0, 1]$ that is given by a random uniform distribution in the space can be used [25].

3.1.5. Grey Wolf Optimizer

Grey wolf optimizer (GWO) is inspired by wolves living in a pack. In the mathematical model of the wolves' social hierarchy, the best solution is represented by α, the second-best solution is β, and δ represents the third-best solution. The rest of the candidate solutions are in a group ω. The optimization in this algorithm is guided by the best three wolves α, β, δ, and the wolves in ω follow these three wolves. The model is given by the following equations:

$$\mathbf{d} = |\mathbf{c} \cdot \mathbf{x}_p^{(t)} - \mathbf{x}^{(t)}|$$

and

$$\mathbf{x}^{(t+1)} = \mathbf{x}_p^{(t)} - \mathbf{a} \cdot \mathbf{d},$$

where t is the current iteration, variables $\mathbf{a}$ and $\mathbf{c}$ are coefficient vectors, $\mathbf{x}_p$ is the prey's position vector, and $\mathbf{x}$ represents the position vector of a grey wolf. The vectors $\mathbf{a}$ and $\mathbf{c}$ are determined as follows: $\mathbf{a} = 2ar_1 - a$, $\mathbf{c} = 2r_2$. Components of $\mathbf{a}$ are linearly decreased from 2 to 0 over the course of iterations by the formula $2 - (2\frac{FES}{maxFES})$, where $maxFES$ is a total count of fitness value evaluations, and r_1, r_2 are random values from interval $[0, 1]$ [26].

3.1.6. Artificial Bee Colony

The artificial bee colony (ABC) is inspired by the foraging behavior of honey bees, and it employs three types of bees: employed foraging bees, onlookers, and food sources. Employed foraging bees and onlookers search for food sources, and for one food source equals to one employed bee. It means the number of employed bees is the same as the number of food places around the hive. The algorithm randomly places a population of initial vectors, which is iteratively improved. The possible solution is represented by the position of the food, and the food source gives the quality (fitness) of a given problem [27]. The ABC algorithm is quite simple because it uses only three control parameters that should be determined (size of the population, limit of scout L, dimension of the problem).

The new solution is given by the following formula

$$\mathbf{v}_i = \mathbf{x}_i + \phi_i(\mathbf{x}_i - \mathbf{x}_k),$$

where k and j are randomly selected indexes and ϕ is random number from the range $[-1,1]$. Then, it computes the probability value p for the solutions x with the help of the fitness value. The next step is to produce and evaluate new onlookers solutions $\mathbf{v}_i$, which are based on the solutions $\mathbf{x}_i$ that depends on $\mathbf{p}_i$.

3.1.7. Bat-Inspired Algorithm

The inspiration of the bat-inspired algorithm (BIA) comes from the echolocation behavior of microbats, which use varying pulse rates controlled by emission and loudness. Each bat flies randomly with a given velocity, and it has its position with a varying frequency or wavelength and loudness. All bats use echolocation; thus, they know the distance and the difference between food.

The population of bats is placed randomly, and after that, they fly randomly with a given velocity $\mathbf{v}_i$ to the position $\mathbf{x}_i$ with a given frequency f_{min}, changing wavelength λ, and loudness parameter A_0. The bats automatically adjust the proper wavelength of the emitted pulses, and also the pulse emission rate $r \in [0,1]$. The loudness can vary, for example, between A_0 and a minimum value A_{min}. The frequency f is in a range $[f_{min}, f_{max}]$ and it corresponds to the range of wavelengths $[\lambda_{min}, \lambda_{max}]$. Here, the wavelengths are not used, instead, the frequency varies whereas the wavelength λ is fixed. This is caused by the relation between λ and f, where $\lambda \cdot f$ is constant. For simplicity, the frequency is set from $f \in [0, f_{max}]$. It is clear that higher frequencies give short wavelengths and provide a shorter distance. The rate of the pulse can be in the interval $[0,1]$, where 0 denotes no pulses, and 1 marks the maximum rate of pulse emission. The new solutions $\mathbf{x}_i^t$ and velocities $\mathbf{v}_i^t$ at current time t are given by

$$\begin{aligned} f_i &= f_{min} + (f_{max} - f_{min})\beta, \\ \mathbf{v}_i^t &= \mathbf{v}_i^{t-1} + (\mathbf{x}_i^t - \mathbf{x}_{best})f_i, \\ \mathbf{x}_i^t &= \mathbf{x}_i^{t-1} + \mathbf{v}_i^t, \end{aligned}$$

where $\beta \in [0,1]$ represents a uniformly distributed random vector, and value $\mathbf{x}_{best}$ demonstrates the current global best position detected after comparing all bat-solutions. The local search strategy generates a new solutions for each bat using random walk $\mathbf{x}_{new} = \mathbf{x}_{old} + \epsilon\mathbf{A}^t$, where $\epsilon \in [-1,1]$ is a random number, while $\mathbf{A}^t = \{A_i^t\}$ is the mean loudness of whole bats population in the current time step. The loudness parameter $\mathbf{A}_i$ and the pulse emission rate r_i are updated during the iterations proceed. Now we have $A_i^{t+1} = \alpha A_i^t, r_i^{t+1} = r_i^0[1 - e^{-\gamma t}]$, where α and γ are constants. For any $0 < \alpha < 1$ and $\gamma > 0$, we have $A_i^t \to 0, r_i^t \to r_i^0$, as $t \to \infty$ [28].

3.1.8. Tree-Seed Algorithm

The tree-seed algorithm (TSA) is based on the relationship observed between trees and seeds, where seeds gradually grow, and new trees are created from them. The trees' surface is represented by a search area, and the tree and seed locations are mentioned as possible solutions of the optimization problem. It employs two peculiar parameters as the total number of trees and the seed production. The main and important problem is to obtain the seed location produced from a tree. The first equation finds the tree location used for the production of the seed, whereas the second employs the locations of two different trees to produce a new seed for the tree:

$$s_{i,j} = t_{i,j} + \alpha_{i,j} \times (b_j - t_{r,j}),$$

$$s_{i,j} = t_{i,j} + \alpha_{i,j} \times (t_{i,j} - t_{r,j}),$$

where $s_{i,j}$ is jth dimension of ith seed position to produce ith tree and $t_{i,j}$ is the jth dimension of the ith tree, b_j represents the jth dimension of the best tree, where b is computed as $b = \min\{f(t_i)\}$, the jth dimension of rth tree $t_{r,j}$ is selected from the population randomly. The scaling factor α is produced randomly from $[-1,1]$, i and r are different indices.

First, the initial tree locations that give us trial solutions of the optimization problem are designed by using:

$$t_{i,j} = l_{j,min} + r_{i,j}(h_{j,max} - l_{j,min})$$

where, $l_{j,min}$ represents the lower bound of the search area, $h_{j,max}$ denotes the upper bound of the search area, and $r_{i,j} \in [0,1]$ is a uniformly distributed random number. The best solution is selected from the population using b where n represents the size of the trees population. The number of seeds can be higher than the number of trees [29].

3.1.9. Random Search

Random search (RS) is the simplest stochastic algorithm for global optimization, which was proposed by Rastrigin in 1963. In every iteration, it generates a new point from the uniform distribution in the search area. Then, the function value of this point is compared with the best point found so far. If the new trial point is better, it replaces the old best point. There is not used any learning mechanism or exploitation of knowledge from the previous search [30]. This algorithm does not belong to the group of swarm algorithms, but because it can have fast and good convergence to the given solution, it can be used as a comparing algorithm.

4. Piecewise Linearization Using Swarm Intelligence Algorithms

Our implementation of the swarm algorithms consists of searching for a linearization l_f (the piecewise linear function definition is above) of a fixed interval map $f\colon [0,1] \to [0,1]$. To allocate a suitable solution, the optimization function (objective function) is represented by a distance function given by the metric between f and its linearization l_f. Every possible linearization is represented by a finite number of points ($\ell \in \mathbb{N}$), every population contains n particles (ℓ-dimensional vectors), where the stochastic parameters are adapted.

In this section, we introduce the testing functions, provide the setting of the algorithm's parameters that can be used for the problem of linearization, and we look at which algorithm can give us the best results.

4.1. Test Functions

For testing, we chose continuous functions $f\colon [0,1] \to [0,1]$, where for simplicity, we work only in the space $[0,1]$. These functions were chosen from the most basic to the complicated ones (see Figure 1), to demonstrate the algorithm behavior on different levels of functions. The functions are given by the following formulas:

$$f_1(x) = 4x - 4x^2 \tag{1}$$

$$f_2(x) = \frac{1}{2}(\sin\left(\frac{\frac{3}{2}}{x+\frac{1}{10}}\right) + 1) \tag{2}$$

$$f_3(x) = \frac{1}{25}(\sin 20x + 20x \cdot \sin 20x \cdot \cos 20x) + \frac{1}{2} \tag{3}$$

$$
\begin{aligned}
f_4(x) = 0.9 + (-1 + x)(0.9 + (-0.16 + (5.4 + (-27 + \\
(36 + (510 + (-120 - 2560(-0.9 + x))(-0.1 + x)) \\
(-0.6 + x))(-0.2 + x))(-0.8 + x))(-0.4 + x))x)
\end{aligned} \tag{4}
$$

$$
f_5(x) = \sin\left(\frac{\frac{3}{2}}{x + \frac{13}{200}}\right) + 1 \tag{5}
$$

$$
f_6(x) = \left(x - \tfrac{1}{2}\right)\sin\left(\frac{1}{x - \frac{1}{2}}\right) + \frac{1}{2} \tag{6}
$$

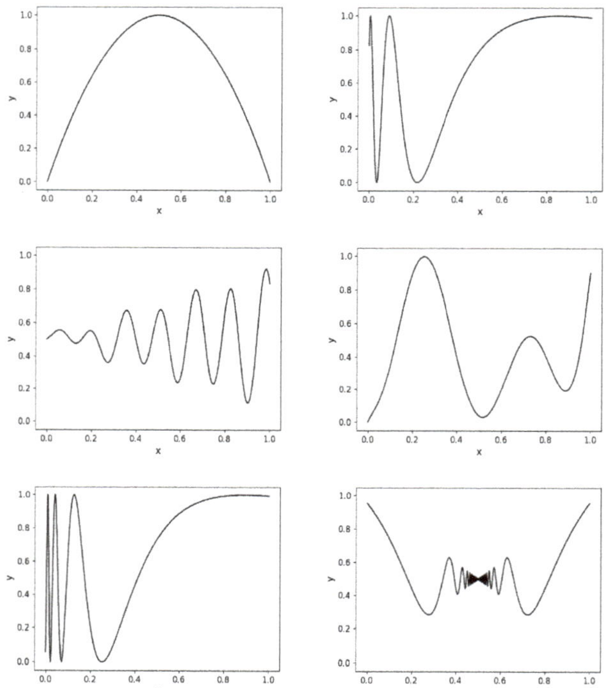

Figure 1. Graphs of the functions f_1, f_2, f_3, f_4, f_5, and f_6.

4.2. Parameter Settings of the Chosen Algorithms

The proper choice of parameters can have a large influence on the optimization performance and, therefore, for each algorithm, in comparison, we tested which parameters were suitable for our problem, in regard to searching for the best possible linearization. In this subsection, we will discuss the setting of parameters for the algorithms introduced in Section 3.1. Each algorithm proceeded 50 times with a fixed dimension $\ell = 16$ and also a fixed population size set to $n = 25$. Each algorithm runs as long as it takes to find a solution with a good enough $fitness\_value$, but it has to find it before $maxFES = 10{,}000$. This $fitness\_value$ threshold was set to value 0.2.

In PSO, the setting of acceleration coefficients Φ_1, Φ_2 and constriction factor χ should be set. Parameter Φ_1 controls the importance of the particle's personal best value, whereas the importance of the neighbor best value is controlled by parameter Φ_2. The algorithm can be unstable when these parameters are too high because the velocity can grow up faster. The equation $\Phi = \Phi_1 + \Phi_2$, where $\Phi > 4$, should be satisfied and the authors of the algorithm recommended Φ_1, Φ_2 set to 2.05. Parameter χ has a restrictive effect on the result, and it does not change in time. In the original version, PSO has $\chi = \frac{2}{(\Phi - 2 + \sqrt{\Phi^2 - 4\Phi})}$.

In SOMA, there are a few parameters in which the settings should be considered and tested. Parameter $PathLength \in (1,5]$ is a parameter that defines how far an individual stops behind the leader. The *StepSize* is from the interval $(0, PathLength]$ and step is from the interval $(0,1]$. One of the most sensitive parameters is $PRT \in [0,1]$, which represents the perturbation and decides if an individual will travel towards the leader directly or not [23].

In the original version of the cuckoo search algorithm, parameter β is taken from the interval $[0.3, 2)$. The step size $\alpha > 0$ is dependent on the scales of the problem, and mostly, the value $\alpha = 1$ is used. The total number of possible host nests is restricted, where the probability that the host bird discovers a cuckoo's egg is $p_a \in [0,1]$.

In the firefly algorithm, the parameter $\beta_0 = 1$ is the initial attractiveness for a distance $r_{ij} = 0$. Parameter of γ represents an absorption coefficient that characterizes the variation of the attractiveness value of a firefly. If $\beta_0 = 0$, it becomes a simple random walk.

All parameters used in the grey wolf optimizer are given by random values, so there is no need for more detailed parameter testing.

The control parameters in the ABC algorithm, which should be set, are the size of the population *CS* and the limit for scout ($L = \frac{(CS \cdot D)}{2}$, where D is the dimension of the problem).

In the original version of the bat-inspired algorithm, the values $f_{min} = 0$ and $f_{max} = 100$ depends on the size of the search area dimension. Each bat has a randomly assigned frequency with the uniform distribution of $[f_{min}, f_{max}]$. For simplicity, it can be used $\alpha = \gamma$, and in the original version author used $\alpha = \gamma = 0.9$, but for our case, we had to do experimental testing. For each bat individual, different values of loudness and pulse emission rate are recommended, based on randomization. In the tree-seed algorithm, importance is given to the selection of an equation that will produce a new seed location. Control parameter $ST \in [0,1]$, called search tendency, is used for the selection. The seed number of each tree is determined randomly, and it should not be less than 1. The recommended number of randomly generated seeds is between 10 and 25% of the number of trees.

For a better overview of the algorithm configuration, the settings of the numerical parameters are assumed in Table 1. The Optimal Interval column presents the intervals containing the achieved acceptable values of the parameters. In the Chosen Value column, the final values of the parameters are presented.

Table 1. Parameters setting.

Algorithm	Parameter	Optimal Interval	Chosen Value
PSO	χ	-	0.69
	ϕ_1	-	2.45
	ϕ_2	-	1.65
SOMA	$step$	$[0.11, 0.31]$	0.11
	$PathLength$	$[3.5, 5.0]$	4.7
	PRT	$[0.6, 0.9]$	0.6
CS	p_a	$[0.0, 1.0]$	0.25
	β_0	$[0.0, 1.66]$	1.5
FFL	α	$[0.0, 1.0]$	1.0
	γ	$[7, 10]$	10
	β_0	$[0.6, 1.0]$	0.8
ABC	L	-	50
BIA	α	-	0.9
	γ	-	0.9
	r_0	$[0, 0.2], [0.8, 1.0]$	0.8
	A_0	$[1.0, 1.6]$	1.6
TSA	$l_{j,min}$	$[0.05, 0.25]$	0.25
	$h_{j,max}$	$[0.5, 1.0]$	0.9
	ST	-	0.1

4.3. Examples of Piecewise Linearization

In this subsection, we will demonstrate an example of linearization for Function f_5 given by all chosen evolutionary algorithms. To demonstrate how the algorithm works, the graph of results for Function f_5 of each evolutionary algorithm is presented (Figure 2). Each evolutionary algorithm has set its input parameters in accordance with Section 4.2.

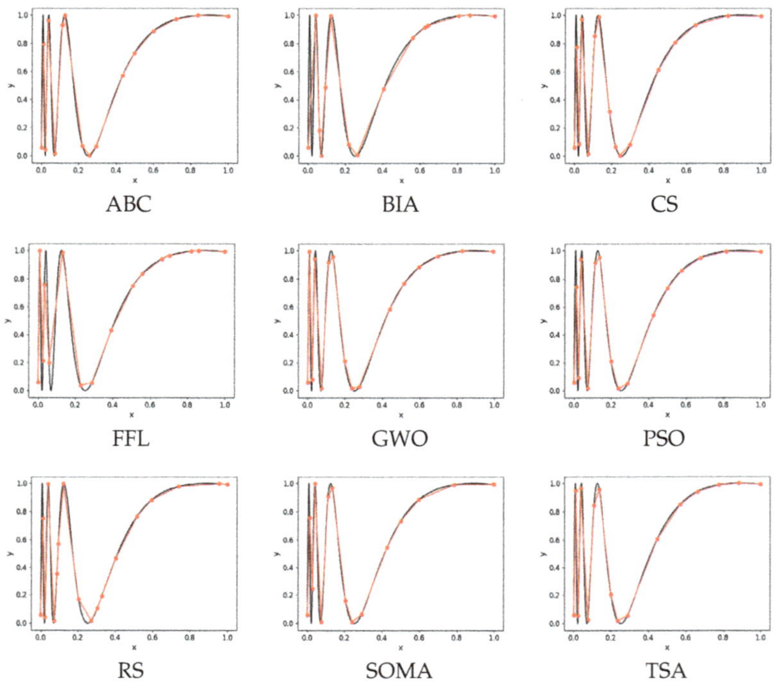

Figure 2. Each graph represents the best result of a specific algorithm. The total number of points was set to 16 and $maxFES = 10{,}000$.

4.4. Summary of Results

In this subsection, we will introduce a set of tables showing the results of each evolutionary algorithm, and to make the results clearer, we chose to use only the four testing functions introduced in Section 4.1.

The following tables (Tables 2–5) show results of min, max, mean, median, and standard deviation values computed from 50 independent runs for each function. The following functions run with the same settings of parameters as was introduced in Section 4.2. Figures 3 and 4 show graphs of distance convergence means for a selected *maxFES* where checkpoints are taken each 100th iteration.

Table 2. Comparison of algorithms for Function f_1.

	Mean	Median	SD	Min	Max
PSO	0.206	0.204	0.007	0.202	0.235
SOMA	0.211	0.209	0.005	0.204	0.234
CS	0.202	0.202	0.001	0.202	0.203
FFL	0.284	0.283	0.013	0.252	0.313
GWO	0.223	0.220	0.018	0.199	0.264
ABC	0.203	0.203	0.004	0.191	0.212
BIA	0.430	0.431	0.059	0.329	0.567
TSA	0.214	0.212	0.004	0.204	0.227
RS	0.231	0.231	0.011	0.204	0.258

Table 3. Comparison of algorithms for Function f_3.

	Mean	Median	SD	Min	Max
PSO	2.388	2.283	0.353	1.931	3.656
SOMA	2.377	2.352	0.256	1.973	3.309
CS	2.524	2.533	0.180	2.152	3.116
FFL	5.245	5.269	0.267	4.594	5.742
GWO	3.575	3.304	0.718	2.908	5.649
ABC	2.088	2.079	0.079	1.908	2.256
BIA	6.014	6.093	0.621	4.509	6.935
TSA	2.453	2.440	0.203	2.137	2.951
RS	3.372	3.389	0.227	2.831	3.830

Table 4. Comparison of algorithms for Function f_4.

	Mean	Median	SD	Min	Max
PSO	0.847	0.828	0.062	0.783	1.112
SOMA	0.892	0.881	0.052	0.820	1.024
CS	0.863	0.854	0.039	0.803	0.983
FFL	2.180	2.206	0.184	1.707	2.523
GWO	1.824	1.808	0.143	1.524	2.347
ABC	0.822	0.820	0.017	0.789	0.895
BIA	2.320	2.230	0.354	1.831	3.447
TSA	0.912	0.914	0.044	0.832	1.032
RS	1.187	1.184	0.077	0.981	1.335

Table 5. Comparison of algorithms for Function f_5.

	Mean	Median	SD	Min	Max
PSO	1.719	1.705	0.321	0.890	3.066
SOMA	1.927	1.966	0.132	1.426	2.140
CS	1.662	1.704	0.187	1.143	2.067
FFL	3.347	3.400	0.251	2.625	3.772
GWO	2.174	2.023	0.291	1.886	2.705
ABC	1.632	1.688	0.220	1.112	1.977
BIA	3.726	3.771	0.419	2.501	4.351
TSA	1.718	1.729	0.146	1.149	1.959
RS	2.144	2.159	0.139	1.499	2.383

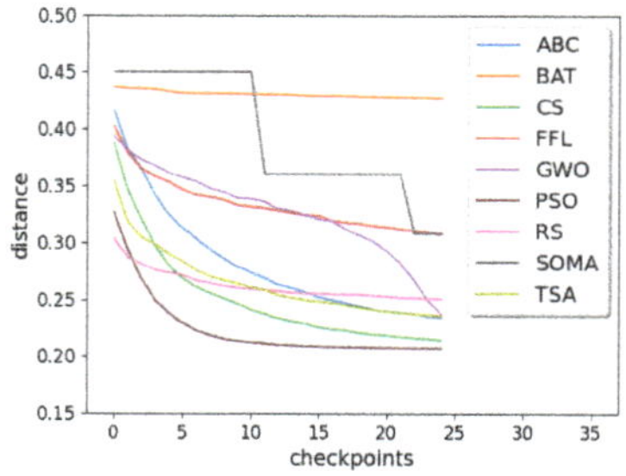

Function f_1

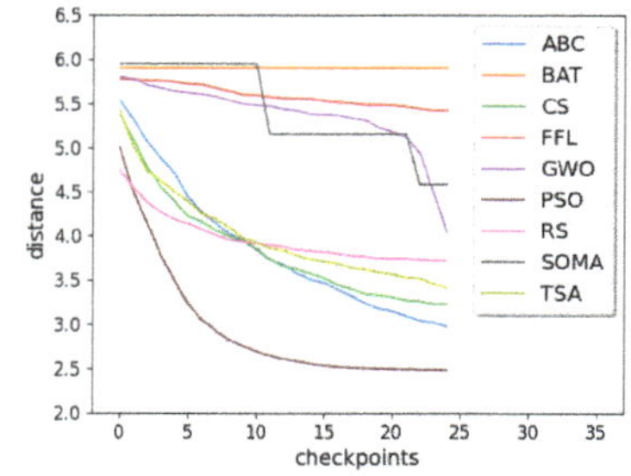

Function f_3

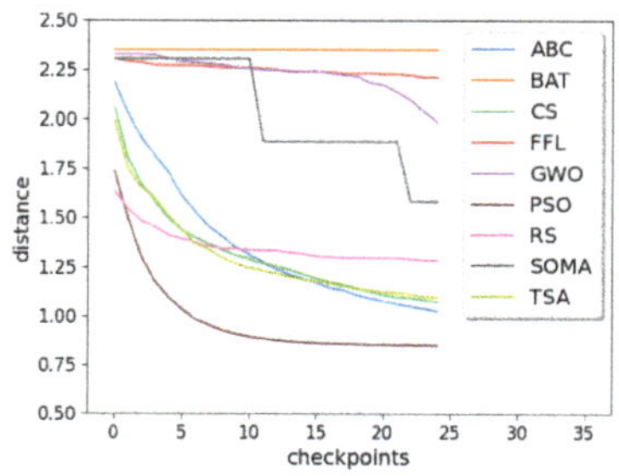

Function f_4

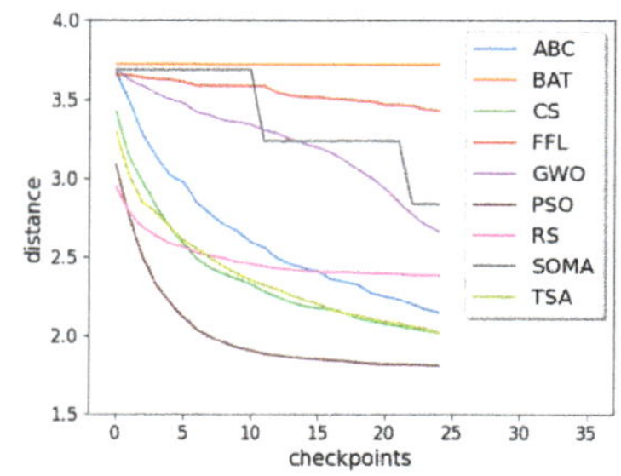

Function f_5

Figure 3. Graphs of distance convergence means for $maxFES = 2500$.

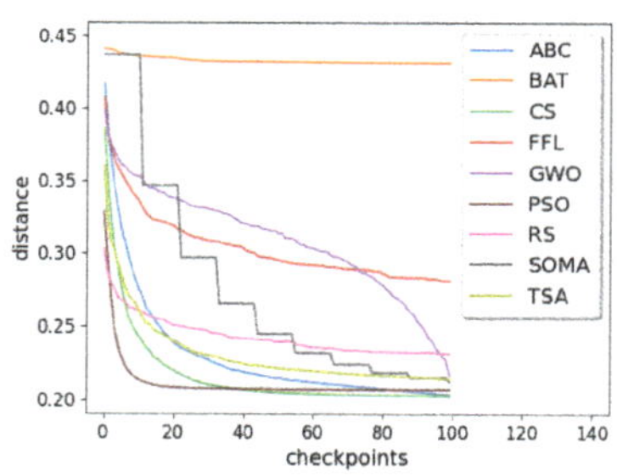

function F_1

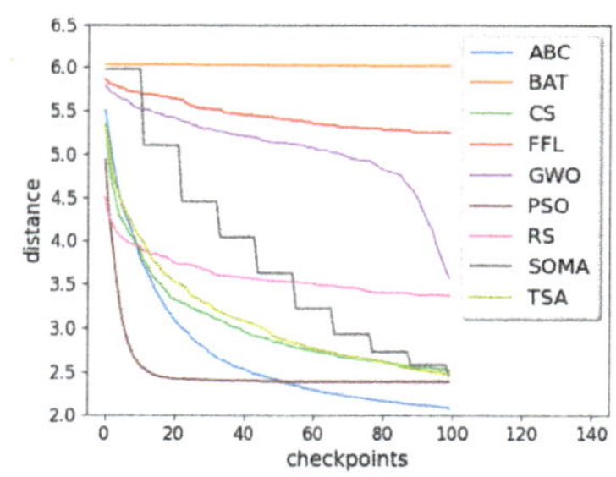

function F_3

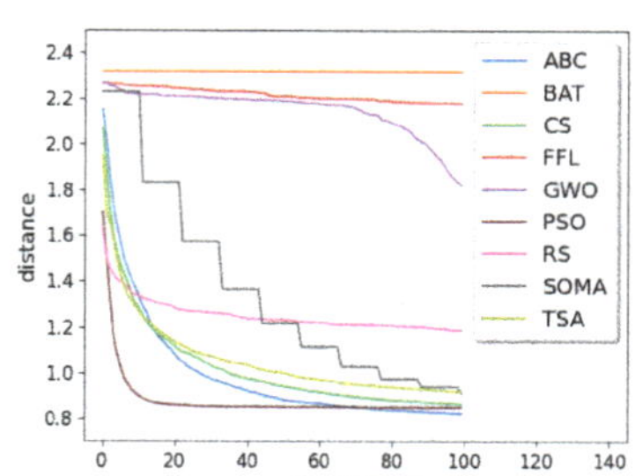

function F_4

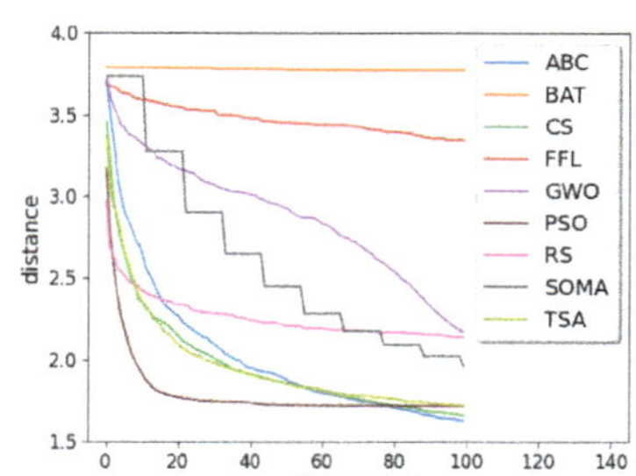

function F_5

Figure 4. Graphs of distance convergence means for $maxFES = 10{,}000$.

From the results (see Tables 2–5) it is obvious that there is simply no evolutionary algorithm suitable to use for linearization of all functions. Results show that for the function f_1 the best algorithm is CS. On the other hand, f_3 and f_4 are best handled by the ABC algorithm. In the case of f_5, there is no clear which method performs the best.

If we disregard the best values for each tested function, other evolutionary algorithms can get the job done with sufficient results. We are talking mainly about PSO, SOMA, and TSA algorithms, which have results across all tested functions similar to the best results. It means that we have some degree of freedom to choose which evolutionary algorithm to use.

5. Piecewise Linearization Using Swarm Intelligence Algorithms with Automatic Parameters Tuning

In this section, we introduce an algorithm that is used for automatic detection of points ℓ used for linearization, and automatic detection of discretization points *discr_step* representing the length between equidistant points. This algorithm tries to find the number of input points ℓ and a set of equidistant points given by a discretization step *disc_step* to achieve the best possible solution evaluated based on an algorithm output fitness function value.

The main goal of this algorithm is to run a total number of six evaluations of an evolutionary algorithm in every loop iteration using parallel computing as long as it is needed to find an optimal solution. We chose to use this approach because we need to try several combinations of ℓ and *discr_step* in each iteration.

In the beginning, our algorithm sets the input parameters for an evolutionary algorithm and default values for $\ell = 10$ and $discr\_step = 1/100$. Then, the loop starts where every iteration consists of setting up six different *discr_step* values and six different ℓ values, and each of the six parallel runs takes one *discr_step* and one ℓ. The six ℓ and *discr_step*, where ℓ_{i-1} and $discr\_step_{i-1}$ is a ℓ and *discr_step* of the best result from the previous iteration, can be seen in the Table 6.

Table 6. Six variants of ℓ and *discr_step*.

ℓ	*discr_step*
$\ell_{i-1} + 3$	$discr\_step_{i-1}/1.5$
$\ell_{i-1} + 6$	$discr\_step_{i-1}/1.5$
$\ell_{i-1} + 3$	$discr\_step_{i-1}/2$
$\ell_{i-1} + 6$	$discr\_step_{i-1}/2$
$\ell_{i-1} + 3$	$discr\_step_{i-1}$
ℓ_{i-1}	$discr\_step_{i-1}/1.5$

Each of these six parallel runs is processed, and then their results are evaluated. This evaluation is done by computing the linearization provided $final\_points$ of all six results given as an output of an evolutionary algorithm run and a fixed $discr\_step = 1/200$. We need to ensure that all six results are evaluated using the same evaluation criterion, which is done by setting up *discr_step* the same for all results. Based on this evaluation, it gives the results $final\_distance$ computed with Manhattan metric, and it keeps the result with the smallest $final\_distance$ value. The *distance* value serves as a $fitness\_value$ for all selected evolutionary algorithms. The best results *discr_step*, $final\_distance$, $final\_points$, and ℓ are saved to be used in the next iteration.

Next, we examine all linear segments created from $final\_points$. This examination consists of creating three equidistant points on a linear segment and calculating the distance of these points from the initial function. We always take the output of the maximum metric from all points of all linear segments. Linear segments whose slope value is too high and a maximum metric value of their equidistant points are under the set threshold are ignored. It is because they tend to get a high maximum metric output value even when these linear segments sufficiently overlap with the initial function part. The maximum of all linear segments illustrates whether the linearization is close enough to the real function or not.

At the end of every iteration, it checks whether the $fitness\_value$ value, and a maximum metric value are good enough. Thus, we check whether we should continue with the next iteration.

There is a special case when we set $\ell_{1,...,6} = \ell_i$ and $discr\_step_{1,...,6} = discr\_step_{i-1}$ before we process parallel runs. This special case occurs when the best result from the previous iteration has a good enough $fitness\_value$ (but not a good enough maximum metric value). The idea is that the previous iteration's best result was almost the optimal result, but the algorithm placed the final points a little off. Thus, for the next three iterations, we take all six parallel runs and use them to determine if the current $discr\_step$ and ℓ are sufficient to get an optimal solution.

It also keeps $final\_points$ of the best result and provides them to all six evolutionary algorithms run in parallel in the next iteration. This approach enables speeding-up the process of finding the optimal result by enabling an evolutionary algorithm in the next iteration to start from a position where the best result of the previous iteration ended up. The only scenario where we do not provide $final\_points$ is when the special case is triggered because we do not want to influence the parallel runs with the previous result because it was close but not close enough. Pseudocode of parameter tuning approach is in Algorithm 1.

Algorithm 1 Pseudocode of the parameter tuning algorithm.

```
def evaluate_evolutionary_algorithm
Set evolutionary algorithm input parameters
while the previous best results final_distance is not small enough OR the previous results
maximum metric value is not small enough do
    set ℓ_{1,...,6} and discr_step_{1,...,6}
    if special case AND special case count <3 then
        modify ℓ_{1,...,6} and discr_step_{1,...,6}
    end if
    run all six parallel runs
    collect all six results
    compute a final_distance for all six results
    select the best result of this iteration
    save the best results discr_step, final_points, final_distance, and ℓ
    get a maximum metric value of the best results linear segments
end while
```

5.1. Examples of Tuning Algorithm

In this subsection, the evolutionary algorithms selected in Section 3 will be applied to the algorithm introduced in Section 5 on Function f_5. Therefore, two sets of results were achieved, where the first one was achieved for $maxFES = 2500$ and the second for $maxFES = 10{,}000$. In both sets of results, each evolutionary algorithm optimal result should have a $final\_distance$ calculated with Manhattan distance to be equal or better than 2.0. All evolutionary algorithms use input parameter values from Section 4.2. Each experiment is executed 50 times in Python 3.8 on a computer with the CPU: AMD 2920X, RAM: 32 GB DDR4, GPU: AMD RX VEGA64. The time complexity of the compared algorithms of each run is estimated in seconds.

Example 1. *This example consists of the results of selected evolutionary algorithms with a value of $maxFES = 2500$. The graph of results for Function f_5 approximation of each algorithm is presented (Figure 5). The best result of each parallel run is saved as a checkpoint result. Then, we take the best run out of all 50 runs and illustrate its checkpoint results in graphs in Figure 6 and Table 7.*

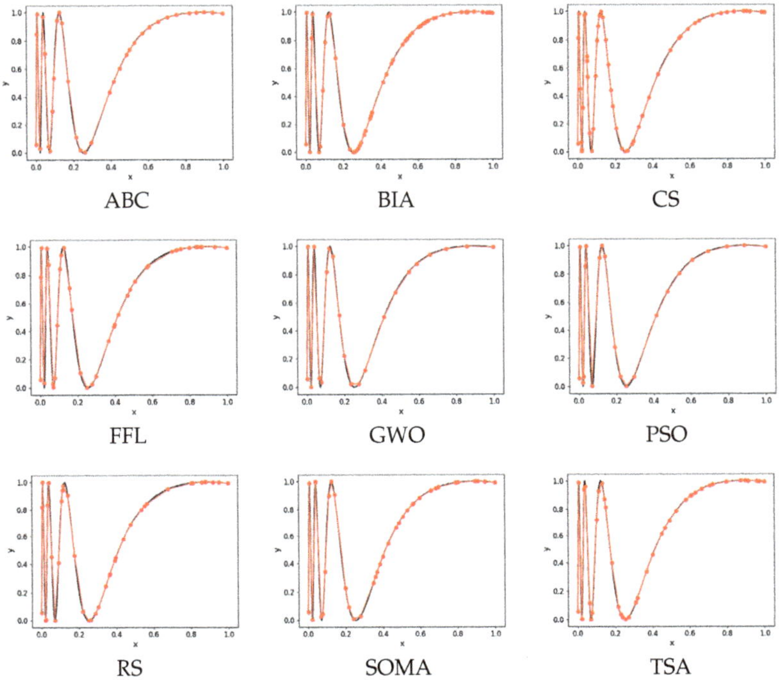

Figure 5. Graphs of algorithms with a value of $maxFES = 2500$.

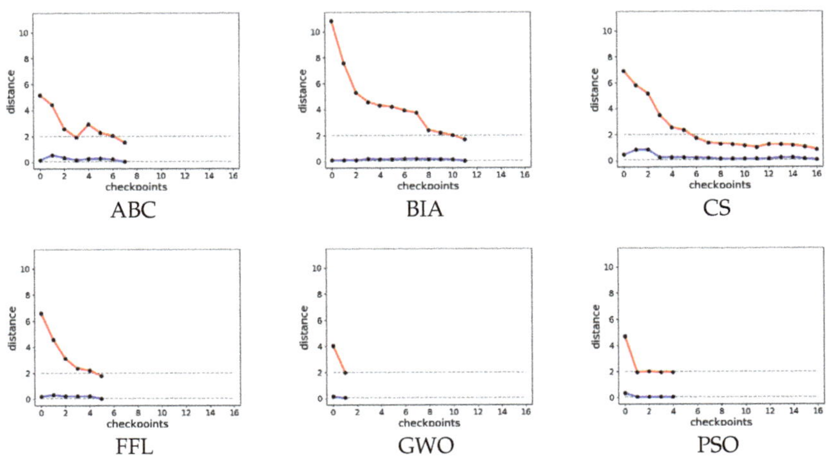

Figure 6. *Cont.*

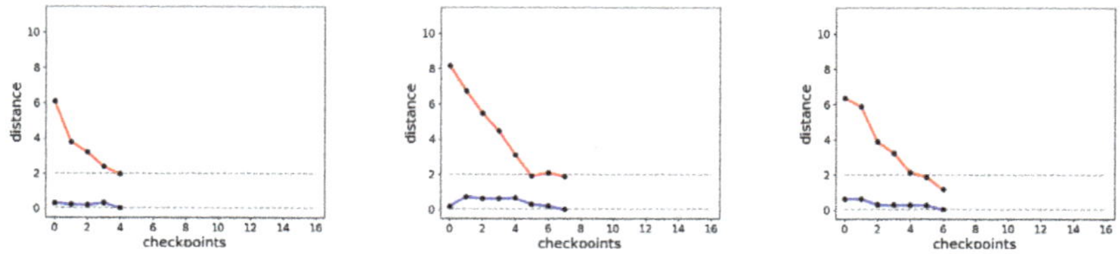

RS SOMA TSA

Figure 6. Checkpoints of each algorithm automatic parameter tuning with *maxFES* = 2500. Red lines are values of $final\_distance$ and blue ones show the maximum value of Manhattan distance. Grey dashed lines show values thresholds.

Table 7. The best results of evolutionary algorithms with a value of *maxFES* = 2500.

	ℓ	Discr_Step	Final_Distance	Time (s)
PSO	22	0.003	1.945	13.16
SOMA	43	0.001	1.886	31.03
CS	52	0.001	0.845	77.26
FFL	43	0.001	1.786	22.29
GWO	22	0.004	1.961	9.74
ABC	34	0.001	1.505	30.06
BIA	61	0.001	1.670	49.82
TSA	43	0.001	1.193	31.73
RS	37	0.002	1.965	15.44

Example 2. *The second example consists of results with maxFES = 10,000. The graph of results for Function f_5 approximation of each algorithm is presented (Figure 7). The best result of each parallel run is saved as a checkpoint result. Then, we take the best run out of all 50 runs and illustrate its checkpoint results in graphs in Figure 8 and Table 8.*

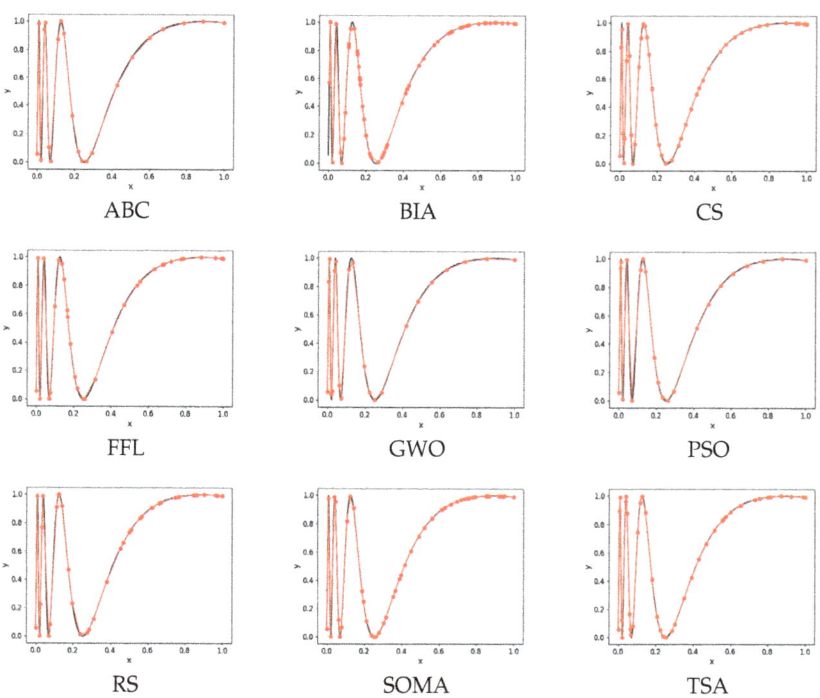

Figure 7. Graphs of algorithms with a value of *maxFES* = 10,000.

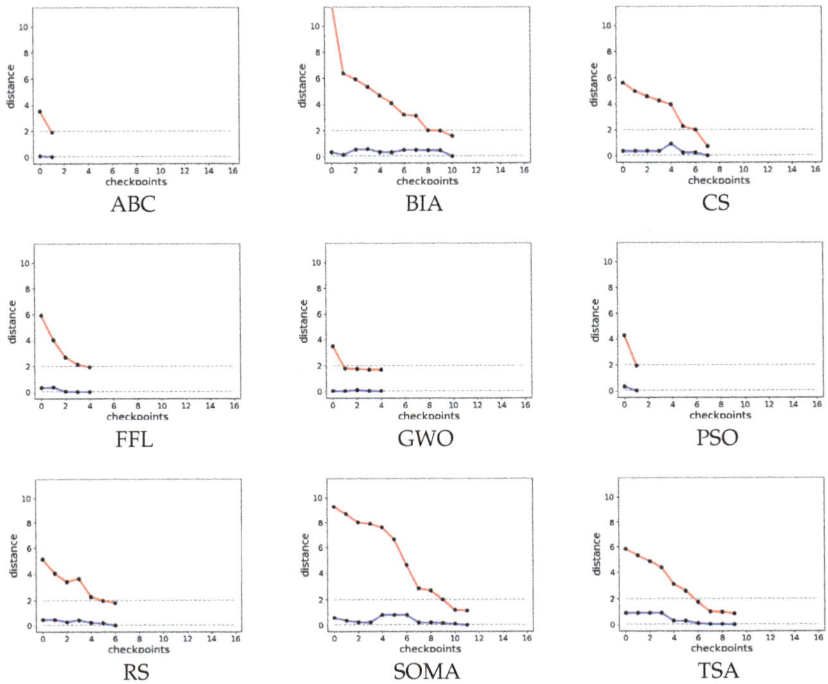

Figure 8. Checkpoints of each algorithm automatic parameter tuning with $maxFES = 10{,}000$. Red lines are values of $final\_distance$ and blue ones show the maximum value of Manhattan distance. Grey dashed lines show values thresholds.

Table 8. The best results of evolutionary algorithms with a value of $maxFES = 10{,}000$.

	ℓ	Discr_Step	Final_Distance	Time (s)
PSO	22	0.003	1.957	14.20
SOMA	49	0.001	1.149	151.99
CS	46	0.001	0.753	88.07
FFL	34	0.001	1.927	41.47
GWO	22	0.003	1.669	85.72
ABC	22	0.003	1.904	12.26
BIA	58	0.001	1.571	123.00
TSA	43	0.001	0.882	146.58
RS	37	0.001	1.827	69.51

5.2. Comparison Results Summary

The comparison of the algorithms mentioned in this section was done on all testing functions from Section 4.1. For demonstration, we chose only four functions, to not overwhelm readers with tables (see Functions f_1, f_3, f_4, and f_5).

We calculated the values of arithmetic mean of ℓ, $discr\_step$, $final\_distance$, and $time$ what has estimated time complexity measured in seconds from 50 runs for each testing function and each evolutionary algorithm. All 50 runs were calculated for $maxFES = 2500$ and $maxFES = 10{,}000$. Results show that the $maxFES = 10{,}000$ variant offers almost the same results as $maxFES = 2500$ variant or there is a slight decrease in a total number of points but at the expense of increasing time.

The most important value is always $final\_distance$, but we cannot decide which algorithm is the best one based only on this value. In general, we need to find the balance between $final\_distance$ and the time it takes to achieve this value where time is affected by ℓ (the higher, the worse) and $discr\_step$ (the lower, the worse). We even have to consider a situation when $final\_distance$ is good enough, but that is due to bad linearization, which results in taking longer to accomplish an optimal result. It also means that an evolutionary algorithm will need more iterations to get to this optimal result and, thus, it will have more points ℓ, which improves $final\_distance$, which takes more time. Finally, $final\_distance$ is so good thanks to the evolutionary algorithm's inability to create a good linearization. In some cases, it is recommended to favor an evolutionary algorithm with a worse $final\_distance$ but with significantly better ℓ, $discr\_step$, and $time$.

In Table 9, the best three algorithms for the testing functions f_1, f_3, f_4, and f_5 are presented.

Table 9. The three best evolutionary algorithms for each testing function.

Function	FES	1st	2nd	3rd
f_1	2500	PSO	RS	ABC
f_3	2500	PSO	ABC	CS
f_4	2500	PSO	ABC	FFL
f_5	2500	GWO	PSO	CS
f_5	10,000	PSO	ABC	GWO

Based on the finding, we decided to show only one set of results of $maxFES = 10{,}000$ variant (see Tables 10–14). It is obvious that the best overall evolutionary algorithm to use for linearization is PSO. Except for f_5 (variant $maxFES = 2500$) where PSO ended up the second best, it was always the best evolutionary algorithm to use. Based on the results, we can also see that the ABC algorithm can also be considered as a suitable evolutionary algorithm to overall use for linearization.

Table 10. The mean results for Function f_1 for 50 runs of evolutionary algorithms with a value of $maxFES = 2500$.

	ℓ	Discr_Step	Final_Distance	Time (s)
PSO	15	0.006	1.139	2.66
SOMA	15	0.005	1.413	3.21
CS	16	0.005	1.426	3.79
FFL	15	0.006	1.455	2.00
GWO	15	0.005	1.477	5.31
ABC	16	0.005	1.330	2.96
BIA	17	0.004	1.423	3.88
TSA	16	0.005	1.378	4.28
RS	15	0.006	1.283	3.01

Table 11. The mean results for Function f_3 for 50 runs of evolutionary algorithms with a value of $maxFES = 2500$.

	ℓ	Discr_Step	Final_Distance	Time (s)
PSO	68	0.001	1.536	74.17
SOMA	81	0.001	1.658	119.26
CS	74	0.001	1.540	74.49
FFL	88	0.001	1.727	81.51
GWO	95	0.001	1.615	345.76
ABC	61	0.001	1.711	54.77
BIA	85	0.001	1.704	79.29
TSA	73	0.001	1.562	114.93
RS	86	0.001	1.539	114.40

Table 12. The mean results for Function f_4 for 50 runs of evolutionary algorithms with a value of $maxFES = 2500$.

	ℓ	Discr_Step	Final_Distance	Time (s)
PSO	29	0.002	1.519	12.25
SOMA	34	0.001	1.682	18.02
CS	35	0.001	1.638	17.11
FFL	35	0.001	1.588	16.10
GWO	33	0.001	1.631	37.28
ABC	29	0.002	1.645	11.40
BIA	36	0.001	1.688	16.46
TSA	35	0.001	1.626	22.15
RS	35	0.001	1.666	20.64

Table 13. The mean results for Function f_5 for 50 runs of evolutionary algorithms with a value of $maxFES = 2500$.

	ℓ	Discr_Step	Final_Distance	Time (s)
PSO	28	0.002	1.489	15.52
SOMA	86	0.001	1.016	142.64
CS	74	0.001	0.615	76.08
FFL	69	0.001	1.346	149.29
GWO	28	0.002	1.374	32.87
ABC	53	0.001	1.156	98.07
BIA	91	0.001	1.055	168.31
TSA	75	0.001	0.619	91.78
RS	61	0.001	1.234	108.15

Table 14. The mean results for Function f_5 for 50 runs of evolutionary algorithms with a value of $maxFES = 10{,}000$.

	ℓ	Discr_Step	Final_Distance	Time (s)
PSO	27	0.002	1.463	41.41
SOMA	78	0.001	0.783	273.57
CS	73	0.001	0.422	207.79
FFL	63	0.001	1.305	331.04
GWO	25	0.002	1.495	101.53
ABC	29	0.002	1.499	53.39
BIA	94	0.001	1.021	538.83
TSA	72	0.001	0.500	280.39
RS	54	0.001	1.302	252.29

5.3. Statistical Results Summary

In this section, the results of the compared algorithms will be statistically assessed. We assess whether or not our proposed method of automatic parameters tuning algorithm proves itself successful or not.

The mean ranks from the Friedman tests [31] can be seen in Table 15. The results of the algorithms without tuning to the value $maxFES = 10{,}000$ are labeled without any upper/lower index. The tuning algorithm results using $maxFES = 10{,}000$ are labeled with an upper asterisk index. The tuning algorithm results where $maxFES = 2500$ was set are labeled with an upper asterisk index and lower s letter index. The best three performing algorithms are variants with $maxFES = 2500$ using a tuning algorithm. They also achieved similar results in the Friedman test, so it is a good indicator that they are all good to use for the piecewise linearization of functions.

Table 15. The mean ranks of all algorithms from the Friedman test.

Algorithm	**PSO_s^***	**RS_s^***	**TSA_s^***	**ABC**	**RS***	**SOMA***
m.rank	**9.5**	**9.75**	**9.75**	**10**	**10.5**	**11**
PSO*	PSO	ABC_s^*	CS_s^*	CS	ABC*	TSA*
11.5	11.5	11.75	11.75	11.75	12.375	12.75
SOMA	TSA	$SOMA_s^*$	CS*	FFL_s^*	BAT_s^*	RS
13	13.5	14.25	15	15.375	15.5	15.75
GWO_s^*	BAT*	GWO*	FFL*	GWO	FFL	BAT
16	16.5	16.5	19	19.75	21.5	22.5

In Table 16 are the median values for each algorithm and each setting. There are four different settings: O10 and O25 are the original algorithms with $maxFES = 2500$ (O25) and 10,000 (O10). The T10 and T25 settings represent the automatic-parameter-tuning versions with $maxFES = 2500$ (T25) and 10000 (T10). For O10, the best algorithm is ABC. On the other hand, O25 is the best to use with PSO. Results of setting variants T10 and T25 are not that straightforward, but it is obvious that the PSO algorithm is the overall best choice to use.

Table 16. The median values for each algorithm and each set.

SET	*f*	ABC	BAT	CS	FFL	GWO	PSO	RS	SOMA	TSA
O10	1	0.204	0.432	0.203	0.281	0.224	0.205	0.232	0.209	0.213
O10	3	2.080	6.093	2.534	5.269	3.305	2.284	3.390	2.352	2.441
O10	4	0.820	2.230	0.855	2.207	1.808	0.828	1.184	0.882	0.914
O10	5	1.688	3.828	1.704	3.401	2.024	1.705	2.160	1.966	1.729
T10	1	1.167	1.494	1.574	1.498	1.627	1.056	1.311	1.281	1.616
T10	3	1.654	1.742	1.666	1.862	1.703	1.613	1.517	1.643	1.561
T10	4	1.630	1.721	1.736	1.764	1.518	1.647	1.636	1.685	1.702
T10	5	1.529	1.014	0.410	1.238	1.699	1.412	1.266	0.774	0.457
T25	1	1.277	1.441	1.493	1.477	1.525	1.098	1.257	1.386	1.351
T25	3	1.741	1.725	1.603	1.840	1.654	1.553	1.516	1.702	1.604
T25	4	1.601	1.718	1.686	1.627	1.689	1.545	1.664	1.710	1.644
T25	5	1.110	1.029	0.596	1.355	1.352	1.521	1.201	1.027	0.555
O25	1	0.233	0.427	0.214	0.309	0.231	0.205	0.253	0.268	0.234
O25	3	2.996	5.969	3.233	5.447	3.818	2.339	3.725	4.138	3.322
O25	4	1.024	2.387	1.056	2.246	1.962	0.819	1.297	1.381	1.083
O25	5	2.129	3.726	2.025	3.457	2.652	1.785	2.399	2.480	1.987

The next level of statistical comparison provides the Kruskal–Wallis test [32] (see Table 17). This method provides us with the same results as Table 16. The variant O10 is the best to use together with the ABC algorithm. The variant O25, on the other hand, is the best to use together with the PSO algorithm. We cannot say which algorithm to use together with T10 and T25 variants because there is no straightforward choice suitable for all tested functions. Overall, the best choice would be the PSO algorithm which can be found in the first place most times compared to the rest of the algorithms.

Table 17. The first, second, third, and the last position of all algorithms and each setting from the Kruskal–Wallis tests.

SET	f	Sig.	1st	2nd	3rd	Last
O10	1	<0.001	CS	ABC	PSO	BAT
O10	3	<0.001	ABC	PSO	SOMA	BAT
O10	4	<0.001	ABC	PSO	CS	BAT
O10	5	<0.001	ABC	CS	TSA	BAT
T10	1	<0.001	PSO	ABC	SOMA	TSA
T10	3	<0.001	RS	TSA	PSO	FFL
T10	4	<0.01	GWO	ABC	PSO	CS
T10	5	<0.001	CS	TSA	SOMA	ABC
T25	1	<0.001	PSO	RS	ABC	GWO
T25	3	<0.001	RS	PSO	CS	FFL
T25	4	<0.05	PSO	FFL	GWO	BAT
T25	5	<0.001	CS	TSA	SOMA	PSO
O25	1	<0.001	PSO	CS	ABC	BAT
O25	3	<0.001	PSO	ABC	CS	BAT
O25	4	<0.001	PSO	ABC	CS	BAT
O25	5	<0.001	PSO	TSA	CS	BAT

Finally, the results of the Wilcoxon rank-sum statistical test [33] are presented (see Table 18). The variant T25 was selected as a reference method, and it is compared against variants T10 and O10. The symbol of '+' is used for significantly better results of counterpart, a symbol of '−' is used for significantly better results of reference method, and finally, the symbol of '≈' illustrates no significant difference between algorithms. The comparison of T25 and T10 shows only several significant differences between settings, so it is obvious that these two variants score very similarly. Both variants seem to find good results very quickly, and thanks to this, the importance of *maxFES* is not that high. Comparing T25 and O10, there are 15 cases where the O10 variant performs significantly better than the T25 variant (especially for problem f_1), but there are 21 cases in total when the O10 variant is significantly worse than the variant T25. We can interpret the results slightly different, though. The variant T25 delivers more consistent results across all cases, whereas the O10 variant delivers either very good or very bad results.

Results also show that the non-tuning algorithm suffers from lowering *maxFES* from 10,000 to 2500, and that is the reason we did not include the O10 variant at all. On the other hand, the automatic parameters tuning algorithm is resistant to the length of the optimization process, therefore, it does not matter if we choose the value of $maxFES = 2500$ or 10,000.

Table 18. The median values and significance of all algorithms from the Wilcoxon rank-sum tests.

f	alg	T25	T10	O10
1	ABC	1.2768	1.1673(++)	0.20377(+ + +)
1	BAT	1.4415	1.4942(≈)	0.43178(+ + +)
1	CS	1.4928	1.574(−)	0.20281(+ + +)
1	FFL	1.4774	1.4976(≈)	0.28131(+ + +)
1	GWO	1.5246	1.627(≈)	0.22386(+ + +)
1	PSO	1.098	1.0557(≈)	0.20484(+ + +)
1	RS	1.2572	1.3113(≈)	0.23168(+ + +)
1	SOMA	1.3856	1.2814(≈)	0.20902(+ + +)
1	TSA	1.3507	1.6165(− − −)	0.21299(+ + +)

Table 18. *Cont.*

f	alg	T25	T10	O10
3	ABC	1.7409	1.654(≈)	2.0797(− − −)
3	BAT	1.7248	1.7422(≈)	6.0932(− − −)
3	CS	1.603	1.6659(≈)	2.5338(− − −)
3	FFL	1.8396	1.8621(≈)	5.2694(− − −)
3	GWO	1.6536	1.7029(≈)	3.3049(− − −)
3	PSO	1.5535	1.6128(≈)	2.2837(− − −)
3	RS	1.5156	1.5173(≈)	3.3899(− − −)
3	SOMA	1.7017	1.6433(≈)	2.3522(− − −)
3	TSA	1.6039	1.5613(≈)	2.4407(− − −)
4	ABC	1.6015	1.6296(≈)	0.82008(+ + +)
4	BAT	1.7178	1.7211(≈)	2.2302(− − −)
4	CS	1.6855	1.7358(≈)	0.85474(+ + +)
4	FFL	1.6296	1.7641(−)	2.2069(− − −)
4	GWO	1.6887	1.5177(+)	1.808(− − −)
4	PSO	1.5454	1.6473(−)	0.82815(+ + +)
4	RS	1.6641	1.6358(≈)	1.1841(+ + +)
4	SOMA	1.7101	1.6848(≈)	0.88182(+ + +)
4	TSA	1.6438	1.7023(≈)	0.91401(+ + +)
5	ABC	1.1098	1.5286(− − −)	1.6882(− − −)
5	BAT	1.0294	1.0142(≈)	3.8278(− − −)
5	CS	0.5961	0.4104(+ + +)	1.7042(− − −)
5	FFL	1.3547	1.2379(≈)	3.4007(− − −)
5	GWO	1.3519	1.6986(≈)	2.0238(− − −)
5	PSO	1.5213	1.4122(≈)	1.7051(− − −)
5	RS	1.2013	1.2659(≈)	2.1597(− − −)
5	SOMA	1.0273	0.77375(+ + +)	1.9665(− − −)
5	TSA	0.5553	0.45704(++)	1.7291(− − −)

6. Conclusions

In this paper, we introduced two ways to solve the optimization of the piecewise linearization of a given function. In the first approach, the usage of optimization algorithms for searching piecewise linearization with a predefined number of piecewise linear parts and discretization points with the calculation of the distance between the original and piecewise linear function is proposed. The second method extends the previous approach by the automatic selection of the number of piecewise linear parts and discretization points.

Based on the experimental part of the paper, the following conclusions were achieved. Enhancing the swarm-based optimization algorithms by the proposed tuning approach enables a significant increase in the performance of the optimization process. When the algorithms were applied to the piecewise linearization problem with 2500 function evaluations, the variants of PSO and GWO provided sufficient results, where GWO performs substantially better (Table 7). For $maxFES$ = 10,000, GWO, PSO, and ABC provide results with a similar quality, where ABC was the fastest method (Table 8).

From the results of the optimization problems, it is obvious that the variant of PSO was always located on the best positions (Tables 10–14). Moreover, a variant of ABC provided an acceptable quality solution (Table 9). Studying the complexity of the compared algorithms, the variants of PSO and ABC achieved mostly low time demands.

Results of the application of the proposed tuning approach illustrate the substantially increasing performance of the compared swarm algorithms (Table 15). In eight algorithms out of nine, the better overall performance was achieved by the tuning approach, where the biggest difference was achieved in variant of RS, which provided second-best results. It is also obvious that several swarm methods provide worse results compared to the simple RS method, which generates random solutions (BAT, FFL, GWO).

Comparing the achieved median values in three out of four optimization problems, the best performance is provided with the proposed tuning approach (Table 16). Surprisingly, the best results of the piecewise linearization problem f_4 provided the RS algorithm with the tuning mechanism.

The main benefit of our tuning approach is the lower time complexity of the optimization process (measured by a number of function evaluations) with sufficient solutions. Using the PSO algorithm as the main swarm intelligence algorithm for solving piecewise linearization problems is, without a doubt, the best choice. This conclusion was clearly demonstrated in Section 5.3.

The proposed tuning approach performs worse than the original swarm intelligence algorithms, especially in problem f_1. This provides motivation to further study the approach settings. The first step in the research is to generalize the proposed algorithms for functions with higher dimensions and use them for solving other real problems.

The next natural step is to extend this algorithm into higher dimensions and to compare the swarm-based optimization algorithms with the classical mathematical approaches.

Author Contributions: Conceptualization, N.Š. and P.R.; methodology, N.Š.; software, P.R.; validation, N.Š., P.R. and P.B.; formal analysis, P.B.; investigation, N.Š.; resources, P.R.; data curation, P.B.; writing—original draft preparation, N.Š., P.R. and P.B.; writing—review and editing, N.Š., P.R. and P.B.; visualization, P.R.; supervision, P.B.; project administration, P.B.; funding acquisition, P.B. All authors have read and agreed to the published version of the manuscript.

Funding: This research was funded by the Department of Informatics and Computers, University of Ostrava and also by an Internal Grant Agency of the University of Ostrava grants, numbers SGS17/PřF-MF/2021 and SGS17/PřF-MF/2022.

Institutional Review Board Statement: Not applicable.

Informed Consent Statement: Not applicable.

Data Availability Statement: All data were measured in MATLAB during the experiments.

Conflicts of Interest: The funders had no role in the design of the study; in the collection, analyses, or interpretation of data; in the writing of the manuscript, or in the decision to publish the results.

References

1. Kontogiorgis, S. Practical piecewise-linear approximation for monotropic optimization. *INFORMS J. Comput.* **2000**, *12*, 324–340. [CrossRef]
2. Kupka, J.; Škorupová, N. On PSO-Based Simulations of Fuzzy Dynamical Systems Induced by One-Dimensional Ones. *Mathematics* **2021**, *9*, 2737. [CrossRef]
3. Kupka, J.; Škorupová, N. On PSO-Based Approximation of Zadeh's Extension Principle. In Proceedings of the International Conference on Information Processing and Management of Uncertainty in Knowledge-Based Systems, Lisbon, Portugal, 15–19 June 2020; pp. 267–280.
4. Bagwell, S.; Ledger, P.D.; Gil, A.J.; Mallett, M.; Kruip, M. A linearised hp–finite element framework for acousto-magneto-mechanical coupling in axisymmetric MRI scanners. *Int. J. Numer. Methods Eng.* **2017**, *112*, 1323–1352. [CrossRef]
5. Lifton, J.; Liu, T. Ring artefact reduction via multi-point piecewise linear flat field correction for X-ray computed tomography. *Opt. Express* **2019**, *27*, 3217–3228. [CrossRef] [PubMed]
6. Griewank, A. On stable piecewise linearization and generalized algorithmic differentiation. *Optim. Methods Softw.* **2013**, *28*, 1139–1178. [CrossRef]
7. Persson, J.; Söder, L. Comparison of threes linearization methods. In Proceedings of the PSCC2008, 16th Power System Computation Conference, Glasgow, Scotland, 14–18 July 2008.
8. Dyke, P. *An Introduction to Laplace Transforms and Fourier Series*; Springer: London, UK, 2014.
9. Perfilieva, I. Fuzzy transforms: Theory and applications. *Fuzzy Sets Syst.* **2006**, *157*, 993–1023. [CrossRef]
10. Bernard, P.; Wu, L. Stochastic linearization: The theory. *J. Appl. Probab.* **1998**, *35*, 718–730. [CrossRef]
11. Hatanaka, T.; Uosaki, K.; Koga, M. Evolutionary computation approach to Wiener model identification. In Proceedings of the 2002 Congress on Evolutionary Computation. CEC'02 (Cat. No. 02TH8600), Honolulu, HI, USA, 12–17 May 2002; Volume 1, pp. 914–919.
12. Mazarei, M.M.; Behroozpoor, A.A.; Kamyad, A.V. The Best Piecewise Linearization of Nonlinear Functions. *Appl. Math.* **2014**, *5*, 3270. [CrossRef]
13. Cleghorn, C.W.; Engelbrecht, A.P. Piecewise linear approximation of n-dimensional parametric curves using particle swarms. In Proceedings of the International Conference on Swarm Intelligence, Brussels, Belgium, 12–14 September 2012; Springer: Berlin/Heidelberg, Germany, 2012; pp. 292–299.

14. Ghosh, S.; Ray, A.; Yadav, D.; Karan, B. A genetic algorithm based clustering approach for piecewise linearization of nonlinear functions. In Proceedings of the 2011 International Conference on Devices and Communications (ICDeCom), Mesra, India, 24–25 February 2011; pp. 1–4.
15. Liu, L.; Fan, Z.; Wang, X. A Piecewise Linearization Method of Significant Wave Height Based on Particle Swarm Optimization. In Proceedings of the International Conference in Swarm Intelligence, Harbin, China, 12–15 June 2013; Springer: Berlin/Heidelberg, Germany, 2013; pp. 144–151.
16. Topaloglu, H.; Powell, W.B. An algorithm for approximating piecewise linear concave functions from sample gradients. *Oper. Res. Lett.* **2003**, *31*, 66–76. [CrossRef]
17. Camponogara, E.; Nazari, L.F. Models and algorithms for optimal piecewise-linear function approximation. *Math. Probl. Eng.* **2015**, *2015*, 876862. [CrossRef]
18. Bujok, P.; Tvrdik, J.; Polakova, R. Nature-Inspired Algorithms in Real-World Optimization Problems. *MENDEL* **2017**, *23*, 7–14. [CrossRef]
19. Bujok, P.; Tvrdik, J.; Polakova, R. Comparison of nature-inspired population-based algorithms on continuous optimisation problems. *Swarm Evol. Comput.* **2019**, *50*, 100490. [CrossRef]
20. Poli, R.; Kennedy, J.; Blackwell, T. Particle swarm optimization. *Swarm Intell.* **2007**, *1*, 33–57. [CrossRef]
21. Eberhart, R.; Kennedy, J. Particle swarm optimization. In Proceedings of the IEEE International Conference on Neural Networks, Perth, WA, Australia, 27 November–1 December 1995; Citeseer: Perth, WA, Australia, 1995; Volume 4, pp. 1942–1948.
22. Kennedy, J. Particle swarm optimization. *Encycl. Mach. Learn.* **2010**, 760–766. [CrossRef]
23. Zelinka, I. SOMA-Self-Organizing Migrating Algorithm. In *New Optimization Techniques in Engineering*; Springer: Berlin/Heidelberg, Germany, 2004; pp. 167–217.
24. Yang, X.S.; Deb, S. Cuckoo search via Lévy flights. In Proceedings of the 2009 World Congress on Nature & Biologically Inspired Computing (NaBIC), Coimbatore, India, 9–11 December 2009; pp. 210–214.
25. Yang, X.S. Firefly algorithm, Levy flights and global optimization. In *Research and Development in Intelligent Systems XXVI*; Springer: Berlin/Heidelberg, Germany, 2010; pp. 209–218.
26. Mirjalili, S.; Mirjalili, S.M.; Lewis, A. Grey wolf optimizer. *Adv. Eng. Softw.* **2014**, *69*, 46–61. [CrossRef]
27. Karaboga, D.; Basturk, B. Artificial bee colony (ABC) optimization algorithm for solving constrained optimization problems. In Proceedings of the International Fuzzy Systems Association World Congress, Cancun, Mexico, 18–21 June 2007; Springer: Berlin/Heidelberg, Germany, 2007; pp. 789–798.
28. Yang, X.S. A new metaheuristic bat-inspired algorithm. In *Nature Inspired Cooperative Strategies for Optimization (NICSO 2010)*; Springer: Berlin/Heidelberg, Germany, 2010; pp. 65–74.
29. Kiran, M.S. TSA: Tree-seed algorithm for continuous optimization. *Expert Syst. Appl.* **2015**, *42*, 6686–6698. [CrossRef]
30. Rastrigin, L. The convergence of the random search method in the extremal control of a many parameter system. *Autom. Remote Control* **1963**, *24*, 1337–1342.
31. Friedman, M. A Comparison of Alternative Tests of Significance for the Problem of *m* Rankings. *Ann. Math. Stat.* **1940**, *11*, 86–92. [CrossRef]
32. Kruskal, W.H.; Wallis, W.A. Use of Ranks in One-Criterion Variance Analysis. *J. Am. Stat. Assoc.* **1952**, *47*, 583–621. [CrossRef]
33. Wilcoxon, F. Individual Comparisons by Ranking Methods. *Biom. Bull.* **1945**, *1*, 80–83. [CrossRef]

mathematics

MDPI

Article

Contextual Semantic-Guided Entity-Centric GCN for Relation Extraction

Jun Long [1,2], Lei Liu [2], Hongxiao Fei [2], Yiping Xiang [2], Haoran Li [2], Wenti Huang [3,*] and Liu Yang [2,*]

1 School of Software, Xinjiang University, Urumqi 830046, China; junlong@csu.edu.cn
2 School of Computer Science and Engineering, Central South University, Changsha 410083, China; lei153@csu.edu.cn (L.L.); hxfei@csu.edu.cn (H.F.); 194712189@csu.edu.cn (Y.X.); 194712136@csu.edu.cn (H.L.)
3 School of Computer Science and Engineering, Hunan University of Science and Technology, Xiangtan 411201, China
* Correspondence: wthuang@hnust.edu.cn (W.H.); yangliu@csu.edu.cn (L.Y.)

Abstract: Relation extraction tasks aim to predict potential relations between entities in a target sentence. As entity mentions have ambiguity in sentences, some important contextual information can guide the semantic representation of entity mentions to improve the accuracy of relation extraction. However, most existing relation extraction models ignore the semantic guidance of contextual information to entity mentions and treat entity mentions in and the textual context of a sentence equally. This results in low-accuracy relation extractions. To address this problem, we propose a contextual semantic-guided entity-centric graph convolutional network (CEGCN) model that enables entity mentions to obtain semantic-guided contextual information for more accurate relational representations. This model develops a self-attention enhanced neural network to concentrate on the importance and relevance of different words to obtain semantic-guided contextual information. Then, we employ a dependency tree with entities as global nodes and add virtual edges to construct an entity-centric logical adjacency matrix (ELAM). This matrix can enable entities to aggregate the semantic-guided contextual information with a one-layer GCN calculation. The experimental results on the TACRED and SemEval-2010 Task 8 datasets show that our model can efficiently use semantic-guided contextual information to enrich semantic entity representations and outperform previous models.

Keywords: graph convolutional network; relation extraction; machine learning; natural language processing

MSC: 68T50

Citation: Long, J.; Liu, L.; Fei, H.; Xiang, Y.; Li, H.; Huang, W.; Yang, L. Contextual Semantic-Guided Entity-Centric GCN for Relation Extraction. *Mathematics* **2022**, *10*, 1344. https://doi.org/10.3390/math10081344

Academic Editor: Victor Mitrana

Received: 10 March 2022
Accepted: 13 April 2022
Published: 18 April 2022

1. Introduction

Relation extraction is an important task in natural language processing (NLP) which aims to predict the semantic relations between entities. It extracts special events or information in unstructured text. For example, it can extract events, institutions, and people relations from reports. Therefore, relation extraction is widely used in downstream natural language processing (NLP) tasks, such as information relation extraction [1,2], knowledge network construction [3,4], and intelligent question-answering systems [5,6].

In recent years, deep learning models have made remarkable progress in many research areas, such as convolutional neural networks (CNNs) [7], recurrent neural networks (RNNs) [8], and other neural network architectures [9], which are are widely used in relation extraction tasks. These models convert words or phrases in text into low-dimensional vectors through NLP processing tools and obtain the word-level or sentence-level semantic representation through a feature extractor. Finally, the relation between the entity pair is acquired through a specifically designed classifier. However, in entity relation extraction processing, predicates have significant meaning, which means long distances between entities and predicates will cause semantic information loss. To solve this problem, the dependency tree [10] is proposed to capture remote semantic information. To better obtain the semantic information from the dependency tree, the SDP-LSTM model [11] applies long short-term memory (LSTM) to obtain the shortest dependency path between entities. Zhang et al. [12] propose an extended graph convolutional network (GCN) to train a dependency tree with a pruning strategy to obtain important words in the shortest path. Compared with CNN and LSTM, GCN [12] can parallelly process non-Euclidean data and align trees for efficient batch training, which is used widely in image recognition [13], visual reasoning [14], and biological graph generation [15].

Although the previous results are obtained using GCN-based models, they treat textual contexts and entities equally with the graph convolutional operation. Entity representations cannot obtain semantic-guided contextual information from sentences, and the ambiguity of the entity mentions affect the relation extraction results. Therefore, the impact of semantic-guided contextual information on entity mentions in a sentence is still worth investigating. For example, in the following sentence (S1), "*Donald Trump* is the 45th president of the *United States*", the relation between entities is "*president_of*". However, in the follwoing sentence (S2), "*Donald Trump* was born in the *United States*", the relation between entities is "*born_in*". We can observe that the entity mentions (*Donald Trump* and *United States*) have ambiguity in different sentences. The textual context can guide the semantic information of entity mentions in a sentence, such as "the president of" in S1 and "was born in" in S2; these phrases are strongly semantic-guided. Focusing the semantic information of textual contexts on entity mentions can improve the precision of the relation extraction.

To address these problems, our paper proposes a novel GCN model for relation extraction. Firstly, we propose a self-attention enhanced neural network that consists of extended LSTM with a gate mechanism and a multi-head self-attention mechanism. Both mechanisms are arranged in a parallel manner. This model can capture the long-distance dependency and concentrate on the relevance and importance of different words in a sentence to highlight the semantic information of crucial words. By combing the output of both parallel modules, we can obtain semantic-guided contextual information. The latest GCN model based on a sentence dependency tree enables global nodes to aggregate the semantic information of all nodes. Therefore, we build a dependency tree with entities as global nodes and add virtual edges to construct an entity-centric logical adjacency matrix (ELAM). This matrix enables entities to aggregate semantic-guided contextual information. Finally, we model the association between the subject and object entities, and use a difference vector as a part of the relation extraction constraint.

We evaluated the performance of the model on two popular datasets: the Semeval-2010 Task 8 dataset [16] and the TACRED dataset [17]. Our model achieves satisfactory performance on both datasets.

The main contributions of this paper are summarized as follows:

- We propose a self-attention enhanced neural network that captures long-distance dependency and concentrates on the importance and relevance of different words in a sentence to obtain semantic-guided contextual information;
- We propose a novel entity-centric logical adjacency matrix that enables entities to aggregate contextual semantic information with a one-layer GCN calculation.
- Finally, we analyze the complementary semantic-feature-capturing effect of the extended LSTM, GCN, and multi-head self-attention mechanisms.

2. Materials and Methods

In this section, we will introduce our novel relation extraction model (CEGCN). This model proposes a self-attention enhanced neural network and an entity-centric logical adjacency matrix to focus semantic-guided contextual information on entity representations in relation extraction to produce more accurate results. Figure 1 illustrates the overview of the model. The model consists of four modules, including (1) a sequence encoding module, (2) a self-attention enhanced neural network module, (3) a semantic aggregation module, and (4) a relation extraction module.

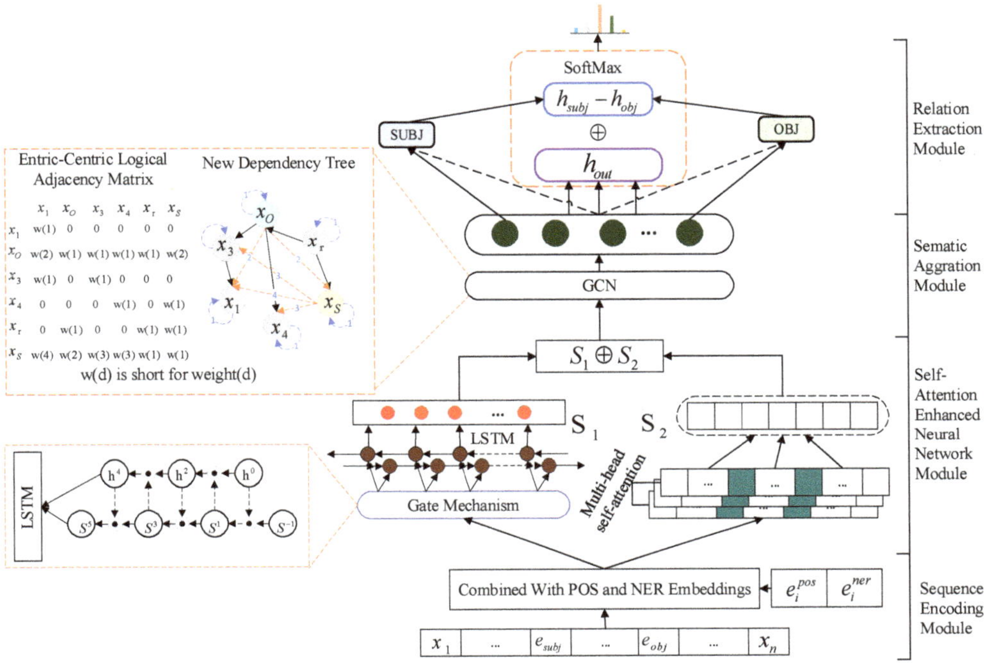

Figure 1. Model architecture diagram. The right side of the figure is the overall architecture of the model's algorithm. The left half describes the extended LSTM with a gate mechanism and an entity-centric logical adjacency matrix (ELAM). In the gate mechanism, S^i and h_i represent the output of the i-th gating interaction, S^{-1} represents the input sentence S, and h^0 represents an initialized hidden state. In the ELAM, the nodes of x_O and x_S represent the subject entity and object entity, respectively, and x_r represents the root node.

2.1. Sequence Encoding Module

We define a sentence as $S = [x_1, x_2, x_3, \ldots, x_n]$ with subject entity e_{subj} and object entity e_{obj}, where x_i is the i-th word and n is the length of the sentence.

First, we use GloVe [18] to map each word of the sentence to low-dimensional word vectors. The word embedding of the i-th word in S is denoted by $e_i^w \in R^{d^w}$, where d^w is the size of the word embeddings. Considering that the part of speech and the named entity recognition are the important features of each word or phrase in a sentence, we concatenate the word embedding, NER label embedding, and POS tag embedding of each word in a sentence. This approach can enrich the semantic features of each word or phrase in relation extraction models. Then, the representation of the i-th word is as follows:

$$e_i = \left[e_i^w, e_i^{pos}, e_i^{ner}\right], \tag{1}$$

where $e_i \in R^{d^w+d^p+d^n}$, d^w, d^p, and d^n denote the dimensions of the word, POS, and NER embeddings.

2.2. Self-Attention Enhanced Neural Network Module

This section introduces a self-attention enhanced neural network consisting of extended LSTM with a gate mechanism and a multi-head self-attention mechanism. Both mechanisms are arranged in a parallel manner. We employ an extended LSTM to capture the long-distance dependency and the multi-head self-attention mechanism to concentrate on the importance and relevance of different words in a sentence. Finally, we combine the output of both modules to obtain semantic-guided contextual information as the input of the following layer.

Extended LSTM: we concatenate forward and reverse LSTM to encode the sentence features. This can efficiently capture long-distance semantic information. However, the input sentence S and previous state h_{prev} are independent and only interact in the LSTM. This model results in contextual information loss. Inspired by Gábor Melis et al. [19], we add a gate mechanism before the LSTM to afford a richer space of interaction between input S and hidden state h_{prev}. In the gate mechanism, h_{prev} and S interactions are regulated several times through a sigmoid gate. This mechanism reduces information loss during encoding, as shown in Figure 2. That is, we define the extended LSTM as $\widetilde{\mathrm{LSTM}}(S, c_{prev}, h_{prev}) = \mathrm{LSTM}(S\uparrow, c_{prev}, h^{\uparrow}_{prev})$, where $S\uparrow$ and $h^{\uparrow}_{prev}$ are defined as the highest-indexed S^i and h^i_{prev}, respectively. The formula is as follows:

$$S^i = 2\sigma(Q^i h^s i - 1_{prev}) \odot S^{i-2} \qquad \text{for odd } i \in [1 \ldots r], \tag{2}$$

$$h^i_{prev} = 2\sigma(R^i S^{i-1}) \odot h^{i-2}_{prev} \qquad \text{for even } i \in [1 \ldots r], \tag{3}$$

where Q^i and R^i are learnable weight matrices, h_{prev} is the initialization vector, and the number of rounds, $r \in N$, is a hyperparameter. Then, we feed the sentence S into the $\widetilde{\mathrm{LSTM}}$ to obtain contextual semantic representations:

$$h_t = \widetilde{LSTM}(S, c_{prev}, h_{prev}) \in R^{d_l}, \tag{4}$$

where d_l denotes the LSTM hidden dimension. After concatenating the forward and reverse $\widetilde{\mathrm{LSTM}}$, we obtain the final hidden representation, as in Equation (4), and $\overleftrightarrow{h_1}$, $\overleftrightarrow{h_t}$, ..., and $\overleftrightarrow{h_n}$ as the output of the sequence encoding module, which obtains the semantic features:

$$\overleftrightarrow{h_t} = \left[\overrightarrow{h_t}, \overleftarrow{h_t}\right]. \tag{5}$$

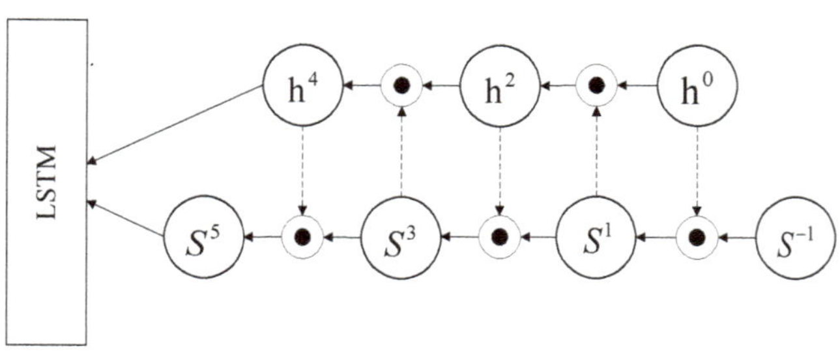

Figure 2. Gate mechanism of the extended LSTM. The previous state $h^0 = h_{prev}$ is transformed linearly, passing through the sigmoid and S^{-1} gates to produce S^1, where S^{-1} is the representation of the input sentence S. After repeating this gating interaction five times, the final representation of sentence S^5 and the previous state h^4 are fed to the LSTM.

Multi-Head Self-Attention Mechanism: in a text sentence, each word has different importance, especially entity mentions. In semantic feature extraction processing, the relevance between different words affects the semantic information of entity mentions.

In order to reflect the relevance and importance of different words in a sentence, this paper uses a multi-head self-attention mechanism to calculate the correlations of each word. Transformer model [20] shows that the multi-head self-attention mechanism could obtain better results in sentence encoding by learning internal semantic features.

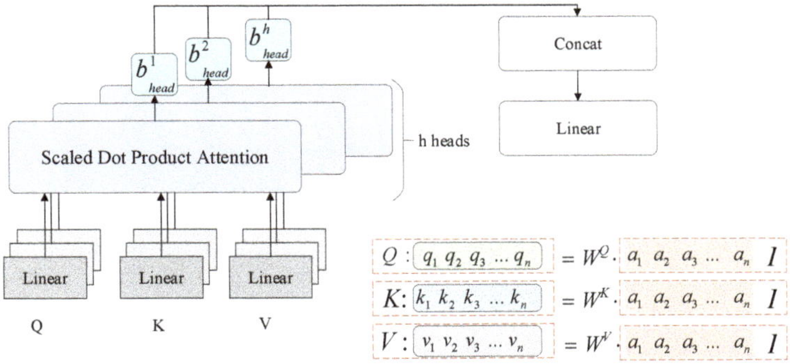

Figure 3. Multi-head self-attention module. The inputs $I = [a_1, a_2, a_3, \ldots, a_n]$ are multiplied by the learnable matrices W^Q, W^K, and W^V to obtain the novel matrices Q, K, and V. Then, Q, K, and V are fed into a scaled dot-product attention to obtain the attention matrix b_i. The multi-head self-attention module performs this scaled dot-product attention h times parallelly, and concatenates each output b_i with linear transforming.

In this paper, we use scaled dot-product attention to calculate the attention weight. The input of the scaled dot-product attention consists of a query (Q), key (K), and value (V). Formally, after the encoding layer, the input representation $S = [e_1^w, e_2^w, \ldots, e_n^w]$. We define $Q = K = V = S \in R^{n \times d_w}$. The hidden representation of a sentence obtained by self-attention is as follows:

$$H = Attention(Q, K, V) = softmax(\frac{QK^T}{\sqrt{d_w}}V). \tag{6}$$

In the multi-head self-attention module, we linearly transform Q, K, and V before inputting them into the scaled dot-product attention, as shown in Figure 3. Instead of conducting a single self-attention, we perform it h times parallelly to jointly extract semantic features from different positions in a sentence. The i-th head is obtained from:

$$H_i = Attention(QW_i^Q, KW_i^K, VW_i^V)(i = 1, ..., h), \tag{7}$$

where W_i^Q, W_i^K, and $W_i^V \in R^{(d \times d_m)}$ are learnable weight matrices; $d_m = m/h$. The multi-head attention module concatenates h outputs of each head's self-attention operation. The output is denoted by:

$$A = MultiHead(Q, K, V) = W^R Concat(H_1, H_2, \ldots, H_h), \tag{8}$$

where $W^R \in R^d \times d$ is a learnable weight matrix. The attention matrix A is the hidden represention of the input through the multi-head self-attention module.

We add a fully connected feed-forward network (FFN) to integrate the information extracted by the multi-head self-attention layer. The FFN consists of two linear transformations with a ReLU activation function between them. The feed-forward network is calculated as follows:

$$FFN(a_i) = \rho(a_i M_1 + \beta_1) M_2 + \beta_2, \tag{9}$$

where a_i is the output of the multi-head self-attention layer, M_1 and M_2 represent the linear transformation matrices, β_1 and β_2 are bias terms, d_q represents the dimension of the hidden layers, and ρ is the activation function (e.g., RELU). Inspired by Vaswani et al. [20], we employ layer normalization [21] and integrate the outputs of the multi-head self-attention layer and the FFN layer through a residual connection:

$$C = layerNorm(A' + FFN(A')), \tag{10}$$

where $A' = LayerNorm(A + S)$ represents the residual connection around the input sentence (S) embedding and the multi-head self-attention outputs (A). Finally, we employ a max pooling layer to obtain the final representation of S. The output is denoted by:

$$r = Max(C) = Max\{c_1, c_2, \ldots, c_n\}. \tag{11}$$

2.3. Semantic Aggregation Module

Firstly, we introduce the convolutional graph network (GCN) [12] in this module. The GCN is an adaption of a convolution neural network for efficiently processing graph-structured data. Let graph G = (V, E), where V represents a set of nodes and E represents a set of edges. The input of the GCN is an adjacency matrix A; if there is an edge from node i to node j, define $A_{ij} = 1$. The convolution formula is as follows:

$$h_i^{(l)} = \rho(\sum_{j=1}^{n} A_{ij} W^{(l)} h_j^{l-1} + b^{(l)}), \tag{12}$$

where $h_i^{(l)}$ denotes the output vector of the i-th node after the l-th convolution operation layer. $W^{(l)}$ is a weight matrix and $b^{(l)}$ is a bias vector.

In the graph convolutional network, each convolutional layer operation fuses each node with the features of neighbor nodes. However, entities and textual contexts are considered equally important in this process. Inspired by Guo et al. [22], this paper proposes an entity-centric logical adjacency matrix (ELAM) to emphasize the impact of textual context on the entities in the dependency tree. We construct a dependency tree with entities as global nodes and add virtual edges between the entity nodes and other nodes. Then, we parse a sentence as graph-structured data on the relation extraction task through the dependency tree. The proposed model can fuse the semantic features of all nodes to the entity nodes with only a one-layer GCN convolutional operation. In addition, the information of the node itself in $h^{(l-1)}$ cannot be transmitted to $h^{(l)}$; thus, we add a self-loop for each node. The algorithm for constructing the ELAM is shown as Algorithm 1.

Algorithm 1 Contruction of the entity-centric logical adjacency matrix (ELAM).

Input:
P: entity position in sentence; N: sentence length; S: target sequence.
Output:
Entity-centric logical adjacency matrix (ELAM);
1: Construct the sentence S as a dependency tree with entities as global nodes;
2: Initialize the entity-centric logical adjacency matrix (ELAM) with all elements set to 0; $ELAM \in R^{N \times N}$
3: Traverse all nodes of the subtree and calculate distance d between node i and root;
4: To each node itself, add a self-citation and set d = 1;
5: Set the value of the corresponding position in the matrix to $w(d)$ where $w(d) = Weight(d)$;
6: **return** $ELAM$.

The $w(d)$ in Algorithm 1 represents the weight coefficient of the feature fusion between the nodes, which is calculated by the *Weight* function. The greater the weight, the shorter the distance between nodes and the richer the semantic information. We define the *Weight* function as:

$$Weight(e) = \frac{1}{e^{d-1}}, \tag{13}$$

where e is the Euler's number and d is the distance from the node to the entity. The further the distance, the less semantic information, and the lower the weight. Figure 4 illustrates the construction process of the entity-centric logical adjacency matrix.

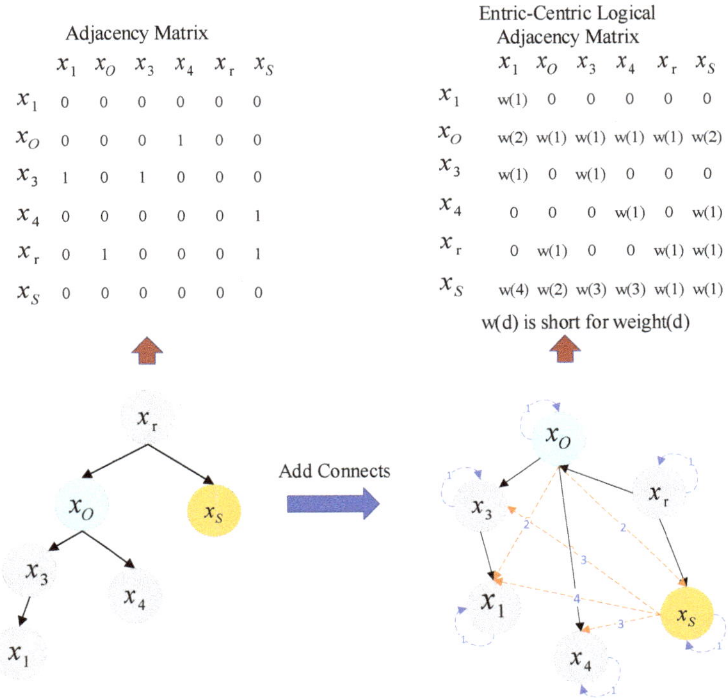

Figure 4. Construction process of the entity-centric logical adjacency matrix. The dashed lines represent the new connections between the entity nodes and the other established nodes, and the dashed line represents the self-loops of the nodes themselves. The number on the line represents the distance between the nodes. $w()$ is short for $weight()$ function. The nodes of x_O and x_S represent the subject entity and object entity, respectively.

This model has two advantages. First, it emphasizes the impact of the textual context on the semantic representation of the entities and uses enhanced semantic entity information to improve the accuracy of the relation extraction. Second, the entity-centric logical adjacency matrix can integrate k-order neighborhood information directly on a one-layer GCN and alleviate the tendency of over-smoothing in the multi-layer GCN calculation. Therefore, the paper modifies the convolution calculation as follows (Equation (14)):

$$h_i^{(l)} = \rho(\sum_{j=1}^{n} ELAM_{ij} W^{(l)} h_j^{l-1} / d_i + b^{(l)}) \in R^{d_w}, \tag{14}$$

where $h_1^0, h_2^0, \ldots, h_n^0 = S = [e_1^w, e_2^w, \ldots, e_n^w]$, d_i represents the out-degree of the node i, and d_w denotes the GCN hidden representation size; $W^{(l)} \in R^{2d_l \times d_w}$.

2.4. Relation Extraction Module

After the L-layer CEGCN calculation, the hidden representation of the sentence is $H^{(L)} = [h_1^{(l)}, h_2^{(l)}, \ldots, h_n^{(l)}]$. This paper employs a *maxpool* function to reduce the hidden representation matrix from two dimensions to one dimension as d_w. The formula is as follows:

$$h = maxpool[H^{(L)}]. \tag{15}$$

Embedding the semantic-guided contextual information into the subject and object entities can improve their association. To focus more semantic information of the textual context on the subject entity and the object entity, we combine hidden representations of entities and the textual context in the relation extraction module. In this module, the semantic-guided contextual information from a sentence can be concentrated on the semantic entity representations. We feed the hidden representation into a *softmax* function to calculate the attention weight α. Then, the final entity representation is given by:

$$h_{entity} = maxpool(H^{(L)}_{entity}), \tag{16}$$

$$y = WH^{(L)}h_{entity} + b, \tag{17}$$

$$\alpha = \frac{exp(y^L)}{\sum_{j=1}^{L} exp(y^j)}, \tag{18}$$

$$h'_{entity} = maxpool(\alpha H^{(L)}_{entity}). \tag{19}$$

We believe modeling the association between the subject and object entities to be a significant factor in determining their relation. Lin et al. [23] propose that the entity relation r in a sentence is a subject entity to the object entity transformation ($e_{sub} + r = e_{obj}$). Their models have thoroughly employed and evaluated the difference vector of the entity pair to represent the relation between the entity pair and achieve good results. Therefore, we calculate the difference vector of the entity pair ($r = h_{sub} - h_{obj}$) as a part of the relation extraction constraint, where h_{sub} and h_{obj} are the entity vectors obtained through Equations (16)–(19). Then, we join the difference vector of the entity pair (r) and hidden layer output of the context (h_{text}) to obtain the final vector representation. The formula is as follows:

$$h_{out} = [h_{text}; r]. \tag{20}$$

Finally, this paper feeds the final vector representation into the feed-forward network (FFN) and obtains the probability distribution of the relation between entity pairs through the $softmax$ function:

$$h_{final} = FFN(h_{out}), \tag{21}$$

$$p(y \mid h_{final}) = softmax(MLP(h_{final})) \in R^{|C|}, \tag{22}$$

where $|C|$ is the number of relation categories defined in the datasets. We train the model by back-propagation and employ the cross-entropy function as the loss function of the model. The cross-entropy function is defined as follows:

$$Loss = \textstyle\sum_{i\in[1,L]} -logP_\theta(c_i = C_i), \tag{23}$$

where c_i represents the predicted relation category and C_i represents the true relation category.

3. Experiment

3.1. Datasets

We evaluate the performance of our model on two popular relation extraction datasets: TACRED and SemEval-2010 Task 8.

TACRED: The TACRED dataset is a relation extraction dataset with 106,264 instances and 42 relation types (including 41 declared semantic relations and a "None" relation, which indicates that an entity pair has no defined relation) [17]. In the TACRED dataset, 79.5% of instances have been labeled as "no_relation"; the main predefined relations include "per:titled", "org:employ_of", "per:age", "org:founded_by", etc. Each TACRED instance is a sentence that contains an entity pair, 23 fine-grained types of entity mentions, and 1 of the 42 relation types. The type of entity mentions includes "organization", "time", "person", etc.

SemEval-2010 Task 8: The SemEval-2010 Task 8 [16] dataset consists of 10,717 examples, 9 relation types, and a specific "other" type, which has been widely used in relation extraction tasks. In the SemEval-2010 Task 8 dataset, 17.6% of instances are labeled as "Other"; the main predefined relations include "Cause–Effect", "Instrument–Agency", "Entity–Destination", etc. Each instance of this dataset contains two marked entities and the relation between the entity pair. The training set has 8000 instances, whereas the test set contains 2717 instances.

Based on these two datasets, we use a pre-trained 300-dimensional GloVe [18] vector to map each word of the sentence to word embeddings and initialize POS and NER label embeddings with a 30-dimension vector. The number of interactive computations in the gate mechanism is set to 5. The hidden GCN size is set to 200, the dropout rate is 0.5, and the prune k = 1 [12]. For the TACRED dataset, we set a learning rate of CEGCN 0.1 with a decay rate 0.95. For the SemEval-2010 Task 8 dataset, we set a learning rate of CEGCN 0.5 with a decay rate 0.9. We trained our model for 120 epochs on both datasets. We list the details of the hyperparameters of our model for both datasets in Table 1.

Table 1. Hyperparameters of the model for both datasets.

Parameters	Description	Value
d_w	word embedding	300
d_p	POS embedding	30
d_n	NER embedding	30
h_l	LSTM hidden size	100
h_g	GCN hidden size	200
d_l	CEGCN layers	3
h	attention heads	6
r	interaction rounds	5
batch	batch size	50

3.2. Performance Comparison

We use precision (P), recall (R), and F1 score (F1) to evaluate our model on the TACRED dataset and F1 score on the SemEval-2010 Task 8 dataset. For both datasets, we compare our model (CEGCN) against several competitive baselines, which contain logical regression models [24], sequence-based feature extraction models [8,25], the LSTM-based models [10,26], and graph-based models [27,28]. These baselines include the relation extraction model with a dependency tree as the input and the latest improved GCN models. To avoid effects from external enhancements, we do not employ BERT-based [29] models as the baseline.

The performance metrics of our model and all comparison models on the TACRED dataset are shown in Table 1. Four types of models are compared. (1) The logical regression (LR) models [24]: a traditional relation extraction model based on dependency trees combined with lexical information. (2) The CNN-based models [30]: these models use multi-window filters to capture the semantic features of sentences for relational extraction automatically. (3) The LSTM-based relation extraction models: these include the position-aware LSTM (PA-LSTM) [17] model, the tree-LSTM model [26], and the SDP-LSTM model [11]. The PA-LSTM model employs the position-aware attention mechanism combined with LSTM sequence encoder models. The SDP-LSTM model uses the shortest dependency path between the entity pair and the LSTM encoder. The tree-LSTM model encodes the entire tree structure to acquire the semantic information of words. (4) GCN-based relation extraction models: Zhang et al. [12] proposed the C-GCN model to apply a pruned dependency tree. The AGGCN model was proposed by Guo et al. [22] as a soft-pruning strategy based on the attention mechanism with the whole dependency tree as the GCN input. Chen et al. [27] proposed the DAGCN model, which automatically learned the neighbor importance of different points using multiple attentional components.

As shown in Table 2, we can observe that the F1 score of our model is significantly improved. Compared with other models, the precision of the CNN model achieves 75.6, but the lowest recall results in the lowest F1 score. We argue that the low recall score of the CNN-based model is because the CNN tends to classify pre-defined relations precisely, producing the wrong prediction of undefined relation types. Moreover, compared with GCN-based models, the F1 score of our model improved by at least 0.4. In particular, compared with AGGCN, our model has a specific improvement in all three evaluation standards. The AGGCN takes the whole dependency tree as the input and employs an attention mechanism to guide the GCN. In contrast, our model concentrates on the important context rather than the whole text, improving the semantic-guided relation between entity pairs. We believe this is because our model focuses the contextual semantic information on the entity mentions in a sentence, enriching the semantic features of the entities and reducing the ambiguity of the entity mentions. The experimental results show the effectiveness of the model.

Table 2. Results on the TACRED dataset.

Model	P	R	F1
LR [24]	73.5	49.9	59.4
CNN [30]	75.6	47.5	58.3
SDP-LSTM [11]	66.3	52.7	58.7
PA-LSTM [17]	66.0	59.2	62.4
C-GCN [12]	65.7	63.3	66.4
AGGCN [22]	69.9	60.9	65.1
DAGCN [27]	70.1	63.5	66.8
CEGCN (our model)	73.4	61.8	67.2

In addition, we conducted validation experiments on the SemEval-2010 Task 8 dataset to assess the versatility of our model. As indicated in Table 3, we conducted validation experiments on some relevant dependency models. The SDP-LSTM model calculates the shortest path to the common ancestor in the dependency tree, but this only focuses on the part of the information between entities, ignoring the important words in context. The F1 score of our model is 1.7 points higher than that of SDP-LSTM. By observing the experimental results, we find our model improved the F1 score by at least 0.4, compared to other GCN-based models. Compared with the latest C-MDR-GCN model, our model could focus on essential words in context to obtain a higher F1 score. The proposed model can achieve an 86.1 F1 score and thereby outperform other models.

Table 3. Results on the Semeval-2010 Task 8 dataset.

Model	F1
LR [24]	82.2
CNN [30]	83.7
SDP-LSTM [11]	84.4
PA-LSTM (2017) [17]	84.8
C-GCN (2018) [12]	84.8
C-AGGCN (2020) [22]	85.7
C-MDR-GCN (2021) [31]	84.9
CEGCN (our model)	86.1

3.3. Ablation Study

To demonstrate the contribution of each module in the proposed framework, we perform ablation experiments on the TACRED dataset and adopt the F1 score as the standard. The results of the ablation experiments are shown in Table 4. Based on the proposed model, we introduce three different ablation models, which are described below:

- "CEGCN w/o Entity" means that we mask the entities with random tokens in the proposed model;
- "CEGCN w/o Self-Attention Enhanced NN" means that the self-attention enhanced neural network is removed;

- "CEGCN w/o ELAM" means that the entity-centric logical adjacency matrix is replaced by the ordinary adjacency matrix.

Table 4. Results on the Semeval-2010 Task 8 dataset.

Model	Dev F1
CEGCN (our model)	67.2
CEGCN w/o Entity	65.4
CEGCN w/o Self-Attention Enhanced NN	66.3
CEGCN w/o ELAM	66.5

Figure 5 indicates that the performance of the proposed model significantly drops when removing different modules. We can observe that, compared with CEGCN, the performance of the CEGCN w/o Entity decreases by 1.8. This indicates that the entities are crucial in the model. Experiments demonstrate that entity mentions obtain essential semantic information, which is necessary for relation extraction. When we remove the self-attention enhanced neural network, the performance of the CEGCN w/o Self-Attention Enhanced NN decreases by 1.0. This demonstrates the effectiveness of the self-attention enhanced neural network module. This module can obtain the semantic information of relevance and importance between different words to enrich the contextual dependencies. When we replace the entity-centric logical adjacency matrix with an ordinary adjacency matrix, the F1 score of CEGCN w/o ELAM decreases from 67.2 to 66.5. This proves that the effectiveness of ELAM can focus the semantic-guided contextual information on entities to improve the accuracy of the relation extraction. The convergence results of different models are shown in Figure 6. The smaller the train_loss, the more accurate the prediction result. The CEGCN model converges faster and obtains a lower train_loss than variant ablation study models.

Effect of Mask-Entity. Figure 5 indicates that the performance of the proposed model with masking entities is lower than without masking entities under each epoch. We can also observe that, in Figure 6, CEGCN w/o Entity converges slowly and obtains a higher train_loss. This demonstrates that entity mentions obtain essential semantic information. Enhancing the semantic representations of entities is crucial for relation extraction.

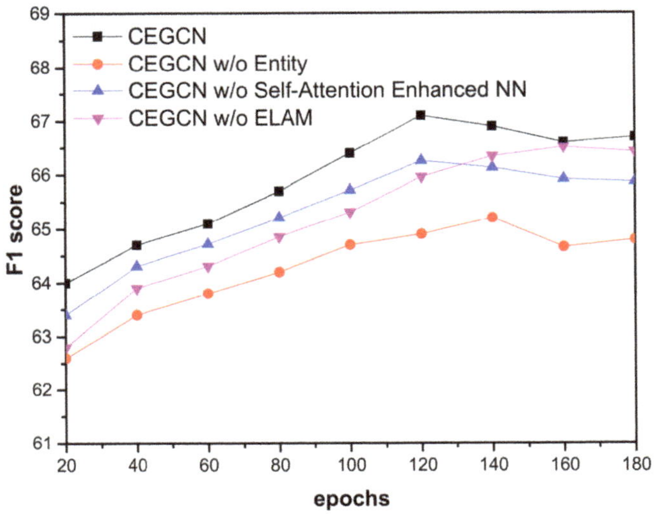

Figure 5. Experimental results in terms of F1 under different epochs for variant models of the ablation study.

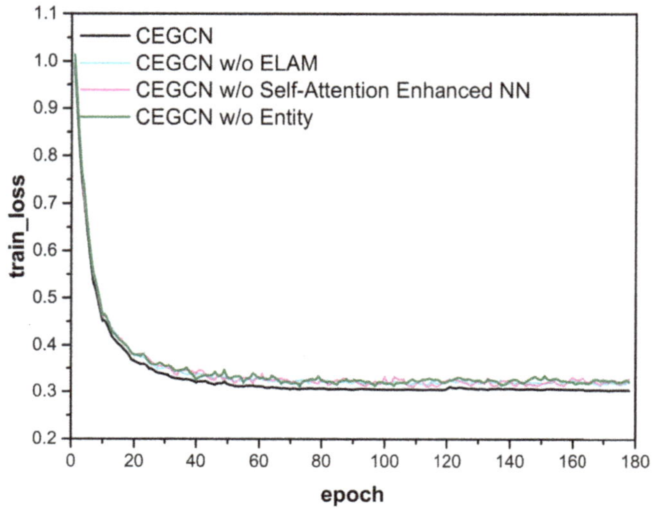

Figure 6. The train_loss for variant models of the ablation study.

Analysis of LSTM, Self-Attention, and GCN. Most natural language processing models based on deep learning use LSTM to obtain semantic information. The LSTM can capture the long-distance semantic information and enables each word to obtain the semantic features of the context. However, the input and previous state are independent and only interact in the LSTM, resulting in contextual information loss. In this model, we use a gate mechanism to solve this problem. The self-attention mechanism can help concentrate more on the relevance and importance of different words in a sentence to highlight the semantic information of key words. By combining them, we can obtain semantic-guided contextual information. Figure 7 indicates that the self-attention enhanced model can concentrate more on phrases containing predicates in different sentences; these context fragments are strong semantic-guided relations, such as "quit and later founded the hedge" in S1.

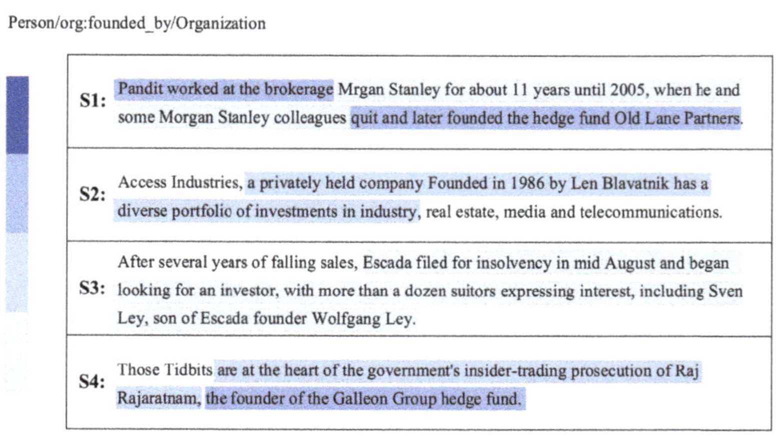

Figure 7. Self-attention weight distribution visualization. "Person/org:founded_by/Organization" means all sentences contain the same entity types (Person, Organization) and the same relation type (org:founded_by). The color depth expresses the degree of the attention weight distribution of the different text sequences to demonstrate the effectiveness of the self-attention enhanced model. The darker context fragments contain more important semantic information for relation.

The novel GCN models allow each word to capture the information of its dependent words directly. Focusing semantic-guided contextual information on entities can improve the representation of the relation between entities; these are complementary effects of LSTM, the self-attention mechanism, and GCN. Table 4 indicates that all three modules contribute the F1 score to the proposed model. Combining LSTM, the self-attention mechanism, and GCN enriches the representations of entities with semantic-guided information to obtain a more accurate relation between entities. Moreover, the entity-centric logical adjacency matrix enables entities to aggregate the semantic features of all nodes with a one-layer GCN. Furthermore, considering the distance of different words to entities, it calculates a fusion weight coefficient for each word to the entity; it can fuse the relevant information of the words and improve the accuracy of relation extractions.

Effect of ELAM. In our research, we insist that the entity-centric logical adjacency matrix can enrich the semantic representations of entities to improve the performance of our model. To demonstrate the effiectiveness of ELAM in relation extraction tasks, we replace it with an ordinary adjacency matrix in the proposed model. We compare the F1 score and train_loss of them under different epochs. Figure 5 indicates that the CEGCN outperforms the CEGCN w/o ELAM by at least 0.7 F1 scores and reaches a peak around the 120th epoch in terms of the final F1 score. Figure 7 indicates that the self-attention enhanced model can improve the weight of important phrases in feature extraction; it can improve the semantic impact on the relation representation between entity pairs in the convolution operation. Moreover, our model converged quicker than the CEGCN w/o ELAM, as shown in Figure 6. The above has proved that ELAM can effectively aggregate the semantic-guided contextual information on entities and obtain better results in relation extraction tasks.

3.4. Effect of Hyper-Parameters

This paper introduces some hypermeters to improve model performance. Compared with the other hypermeters, the number of attention heads h and rounds r has a more significant impact on model performance. This section discusses the influence of two hyperparameters that affect model performance through experiments, namely, the number of attention heads h and the number of interaction rounds r in the gate mechanism of the extended LSTM.

The multi-head attention mechanism can reflect the relevance and importance of different words in a sentence. It is of great significance to select the correct number of heads for model improvement. Figure 8 shows that the model achieves its optimal performance at six heads, and the performance degrades with each additional head when using over six heads. Then, we study the number of interaction rounds r in the gate mechanism of the extended LSTM. Extended LSTM with a gate mechanism can afford more space for modeling the long-distance dependency feature, and can reduce information loss during encoding. Choosing the different numbers of r affects the model performance. In Figure 8, the comparison shows that the performance of the CEGCN model is relatively close when the r is set to 4 or 5, that the model obtains the highest score when the r is set to 5, and that the F1 score decreases when it exceeds 5.

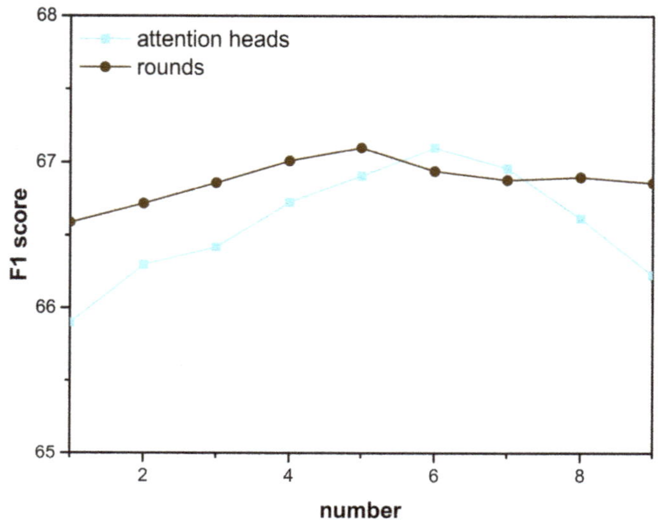

Figure 8. Experimental results on different numbers of attention heads h and different rounds r in extended LSTM.

4. Related Work

Traditional relation extraction tasks are based on feature extractors and rely on semantic features obtained from lexical resources. With the popularity of deep learning, deep learning models have been widely used in many research areas, such as intelligent Q&A systems [32], pattern recognition [33], and intelligent transportation systems [34]. In recent years, researchers mainly employed deep neural network models for relation extraction tasks [35]. Compared with classical machine learning models, the deep-learning-based models can automatically extract and learn from sentence features without complex feature extractors.

Initially, scholars tended to exploit CNN, RNN, and their improved deep learning models for relation extraction tasks. Zeng et al. [8] employed CNN to extract word-level and sentence-level features and took all of the per-trained word tokens as the input. Xu et al. [25] proposed a CNN model based on the dependency tree, parsing the sentence with a dependency tree as the input. Traditional RNNs have difficulty addressing long-term dependence; LSTM can solve this problem by adding a cell state, and gated operations can afford a richer space of interaction for the RNN. Xu et al. [11] proposed SDP-LSTM to obtain structure information through the shortest path between entities.

Dependency trees can convert text inputs into graph-structured data, and CNN and RNN models cannot efficiently process these data parallelly. Kipf and Welling et al. [12] proposed a graph convolutional network for supervised learning on graph-structured data. Hong et al. [28] proposed a relation-aware attention GCN for end-to-end relation extraction. Huang et al. [35] employed a GCN and knowledge graph enhanced transformer encoder for measuring semantic similarity between sentences and relation types. Guo et al. [22] proposed using soft attention to prune unimportant edges in the graph data dynamically. Huang et al. [36] proposed a knowledge-aware framework to highlight the keyword and relation clues and employed GCN for relation extraction. Our model exploits the advantages of GCN and enables entities to aggregate contextual semantic information with a one-layer GCN calculation.

5. Conclusions

This paper proposes a novel contextual semantic-guided entity-centric GCN model for relation extraction (CEGCN). This model combines the semantic information of relevance and importance between different words to obtain semantic-guided contextual information. To enable entity aggregate semantic-guided contextual information, we construct a dependency tree with entities as global nodes and connect global nodes directly with other nodes. It can aggregate information from the whole tree with only a one-layer GCN calculation. In addition, our model can combine the semantic representations of the text sequence and the difference vectors of entities to constrain the relation between the entity pair, improving its performance. The experimental results on the TACRED and SemEval-2010 Task 8 datasets illustrate that this model enables the entities to obtain the semantic-guided contextual information to reduce the ambiguity of entity mentions in a sentence and outperform previous models. Finally, we find that the extended LSTM with a gate mechanism can effectively reduce information loss and complement GCN and multi-head self-attention in capturing semantic features.

Author Contributions: Conceptualization: J.L. and L.L.; experimentation and data analysis: L.L.; writing—original draft preparation: L.L.; writing—review and editing: L.L., H.F., Y.X., and H.L.; funding acquisition: W.H. and L.Y. All authors have read and agreed to the published version of the manuscript.

Funding: This work was supported in part by the Joint Funds of the National Natural Science Foundation of China, under Grant No. U2003208, the National Natural Science Foundation of China, Grant No. 62177014, the Open Research Projects of Zhejiang Lab (Grant No. 2022KG0AB01), and the National Natural Science Foundation of China, under Grant No. 62172451.

Institutional Review Board Statement: Not applicable.

Informed Consent Statement: Not applicable.

Data Availability Statement: Not applicable.

Conflicts of Interest: The authors declare no conflict of interest.

Abbreviations

The following abbreviations are used in this manuscript:

CNN	Convolutional neural network
LSTM	Long short-term memory
GCN	Graph convolutional network
RNN	Recurrent neural network

References

1. Fader, A.; Soderland, S.; Etzioni, O. Identifying relations for open information extraction. In Proceedings of the 2011 Conference on Empirical Methods in Natural Language Processing, Edinburgh, UK, 27–31 July 2011; pp. 1535–1545.
2. Hobbs, J.R.; Riloff, E. Information Extraction. In *Handbook of Natural Language Processing*; Chapman & Hall/CRC Press: London, UK, 2010.
3. Aviv, R.; Erlich, Z.; Ravid, G.; Geva, A. Network analysis of knowledge construction in asynchronous learning networks. *J. Asynchronous Learn. Netw.* **2003**, *7*, 1–23. [CrossRef]
4. Chen, Z.; Li, H.; Kong, S.C.; Xu, Q. An analytic knowledge network process for construction entrepreneurship education. *J. Manag. Dev.* **2006**, *25*, 11–27. [CrossRef]
5. Yih, S.W.t.; Chang, M.W.; He, X.; Gao, J. Semantic parsing via staged query graph generation: Question answering with knowledge base. In Proceedings of the Joint Conference of the 53rd Annual Meeting of the Association for Computational Linguistics and the 7th International Joint Conference on Natural Language Processing, Beijing, China, 26–31 July 2015.
6. Dong, J.; Wu, R.; Pan, Y. A Low-Profile Broadband Metasurface Antenna with Polarization Conversion Based on Characteristic Mode Analysis. *Front. Phys.* **2022**, *10*, 860606. [CrossRef]
7. Hashimoto, K.; Miwa, M.; Tsuruoka, Y.; Chikayama, T. Simple customization of recursive neural networks for semantic relation classification. In Proceedings of the 2013 Conference on Empirical Methods in Natural Language Processing, Seattle, WA, USA, 18–21 October 2013; pp. 1372–1376.
8. Zeng, D.; Liu, K.; Lai, S.; Zhou, G.; Zhao, J. Relation classification via convolutional deep neural network. In Proceedings of the 25th International Conference on Computational Linguistics (COLING 2014), Dublin, Ireland, 23–29 August 2014; pp. 2335–2344.
9. Dong, J.; Qin, W.; Wang, M. Fast multi-objective optimization of multi-parameter antenna structures based on improved BPNN surrogate model. *IEEE Access* **2019**, *7*, 77692–77701. [CrossRef]

10. Zhou, P.; Shi, W.; Tian, J.; Qi, Z.; Li, B.; Hao, H.; Xu, B. Attention-based bidirectional long short-term memory networks for relation classification. In Proceedings of the 54th Annual Meeting of the Association for Computational Linguistics, Berlin, Germany, 7–12 August 2016; pp. 207–212.
11. Xu, Y.; Mou, L.; Li, G.; Chen, Y.; Peng, H.; Jin, Z. Classifying relations via long short term memory networks along shortest dependency paths. In Proceedings of the 2015 Conference on Empirical Methods in Natural Language Processing (EMNLP), Lisbon, Portugal, 17–21 September 2015; pp. 1785–1794.
12. Zhang, Y.; Qi, P.; Manning, C.D. Graph convolution over pruned dependency trees improves relation extraction. *arXiv* **2018**, arXiv:1809.10185.
13. Chen, Z.M.; Wei, X.S.; Wang, P.; Guo, Y. Multi-label image recognition with graph cosnvolutional networks. In Proceedings of the IEEE/CVF Conference on Computer Vision and Pattern Recognition (CVPR), Long Beach, CA, USA, 15–20 June 2019; pp. 5177–5186.
14. Li, L.; Gan, Z.; Cheng, Y.; Liu, J. Relation-aware graph attention network for visual question answering. In Proceedings of the IEEE/CVF International Conference on Computer Vision (ICCV), Seoul, Korea, 27 October–2 November 2019; pp. 10313–10322.
15. Babič, M.; Mihelič, J.; Calì, M. Complex network characterization using graph theory and fractal geometry: The case study of lung cancer DNA sequences. *Appl. Sci.* **2020**, *10*, 3037. [CrossRef]
16. Hendrickx, I.; Kim, S.N.; Kozareva, Z.; Nakov, P.; Séaghdha, D.O.; Padó, S.; Pennacchiotti, M.; Romano, L.; Szpakowicz, S. Semeval-2010 task 8: Multi-way classification of semantic relations between pairs of nominals. *arXiv* **2019**, arXiv:1911.10422.
17. Zhang, Y.; Zhong, V.; Chen, D.; Angeli, G.; Manning, C.D. Position-aware attention and supervised data improve slot filling. In Proceedings of the Conference on Empirical Methods in Natural Language Processing, Copenhagen, Denmark, 7–11 September 2017.
18. Santoro, A.; Raposo, D.; Barrett, D.G.; Malinowski, M.; Pascanu, R.; Battaglia, P.; Lillicrap, T. A simple neural network module for relational reasoning. In Proceedings of the 31st Annual Conference on Neural Information Processing Systems (NIPS 2017), Long Beach, CA, USA, 4–9 December 2017.
19. Melis, G.; Kočiský, T.; Blunsom, P. Mogrifier LSTM. *arXiv* **2019**, arXiv:1909.01792.
20. Vaswani, A.; Shazeer, N.; Parmar, N.; Uszkoreit, J.; Jones, L.; Gomez, A.N.; Kaiser, Ł.; Polosukhin, I. Attention is all you need. In Proceedings of the 31st Annual Conference on Neural Information Processing Systems (NIPS 2017), Long Beach, CA, USA, 4–9 December 2017.
21. Kim, M.; Park, S.; Lee, W. A robust energy saving data dissemination protocol for IoT-WSNs. *KSII Trans. Internet Inf. Syst.* **2018**, *12*, 5744–5764.
22. Guo, Z.; Zhang, Y.; Lu, W. Attention guided graph convolutional networks for relation extraction. *arXiv* **2019**, arXiv:1906.07510.
23. Lin, Y.; Liu, Z.; Sun, M.; Liu, Y.; Zhu, X. Learning entity and relation embeddings for knowledge graph completion. In Proceedings of the Twenty-Ninth AAAI Conference on Artificial Intelligence, Austin, TX, USA, 25–30 January 2015.
24. Tsukimoto, H. Logical regression analysis: From mathematical formulas to linguistic rules. In *Foundations and Advances in Data Mining*; Springer: Berlin/Heidelberg, Germany, 2005; pp. 21–61.
25. Xu, K.; Feng, Y.; Huang, S.; Zhao, D. Semantic relation classification via convolutional neural networks with simple negative sampling. *arXiv* **2015**, arXiv:1506.07650.
26. Tai, K.S.; Socher, R.; Manning, C.D. Improved semantic representations from tree-structured long short-term memory networks. *arXiv* **2015**, arXiv:1503.00075.
27. Chen, F.; Pan, S.; Jiang, J.; Huo, H.; Long, G. DAGCN: Dual Attention Graph Convolutional Networks. In Proceedings of the International Joint Conference on Neural Networks (IJCNN 2019), Budapest, Hungary, 14–19 July 2019.
28. Hong, Y.; Liu, Y.; Yang, S.; Zhang, K.; Wen, A.; Hu, J. Improving graph convolutional networks based on relation-aware attention for end-to-end relation extraction. *IEEE Access* **2020**, *8*, 51315–51323. [CrossRef]
29. Shi, P.; Lin, J. Simple bert models for relation extraction and semantic role labeling. *arXiv* **2019**, arXiv:1904.05255.
30. Nguyen, T.H.; Grishman, R. Relation extraction: Perspective from convolutional neural networks. In Proceedings of the 1st Workshop on Vector Space Modeling for Natural Language Processing, Denver, CO, USA, 5 June 2015; pp. 39–48.
31. Hu, Y.; Shen, H.; Liu, W.; Min, F.; Qiao, X.; Jin, K. A Graph Convolutional Network With Multiple Dependency Representations for Relation Extraction. *IEEE Access* **2021**, *9*, 81575–81587. [CrossRef]
32. Yu, M.; Yin, W.; Hasan, K.S.; Santos, C.D.; Xiang, B.; Zhou, B. Improved neural relation detection for knowledge base question answering. *arXiv* **2017**, arXiv:1704.06194.
33. Kong, Q.; Cao, Y.; Iqbal, T.; Wang, Y.; Wang, W.; Plumbley, M.D. PANNs: Large-scale pretrained audio neural networks for audio pattern recognition. *IEEE/ACM Trans. Audio Speech Lang. Process.* **2020**, *28*, 2880–2894. [CrossRef]
34. Shi, H.; Zhao, X.; Wan, H.; Wang, H.; Dong, J.; Tang, K.; Liu, A. Multi-model induced network for participatory-sensing-based classification tasks in intelligent and connected transportation systems. *Comput. Networks* **2018**, *141*, 157–165. [CrossRef]
35. Huang, W.; Mao, Y.; Yang, Z.; Zhu, L.; Long, J. Relation classification via knowledge graph enhanced transformer encoder. *Knowl.-Based Syst.* **2020**, *206*, 106321. [CrossRef]
36. Huang, W.; Mao, Y.; Yang, L.; Yang, Z.; Long, J. Local-to-global GCN with knowledge-aware representation for distantly supervised relation extraction. *Knowl.-Based Syst.* **2021**, *234*, 107565. [CrossRef]

mathematics

MDPI

Article

Development and Applications of Augmented Whale Optimization Algorithm

Khalid Abdulaziz Alnowibet [1], Shalini Shekhawat [2,*], Akash Saxena [2,*], Karam M. Sallam [3] and Ali Wagdy Mohamed [4,5,*]

1 Statistics and Operations Research Department, College of Science, King Saud University, P.O. Box 2455, Riyadh 11451, Saudi Arabia; knowibet@ksu.edu.sa
2 Swami Keshvanand Institute of Technology, Management & Gramothan, Jaipur 302017, Rajasthan, India
3 School of IT and Systems, University of Canberra, Canberra, ACT 2601, Australia; karam.sallam@canberra.edu.au
4 Operations Research Department, Faculty of Graduate Studies for Statistical Research, Cairo University, Giza 12613, Egypt
5 Department of Mathematics and Actuarial Science School of Sciences Engineering, The American University in Cairo, Cairo 11835, Egypt
* Correspondence: drshalini@skit.ac.in (S.S.); aakash.saxena@hotmail.com (A.S.); aliwagdy@gmail.com (A.W.M.)

Abstract: Metaheuristics are proven solutions for complex optimization problems. Recently, bio-inspired metaheuristics have shown their capabilities for solving complex engineering problems. The Whale Optimization Algorithm is a popular metaheuristic, which is based on the hunting behavior of whale. For some problems, this algorithm suffers from local minima entrapment. To make WOA compatible with a number of challenging problems, two major modifications are proposed in this paper: the first one is opposition-based learning in the initialization phase, while the second is inculcation of Cauchy mutation operator in the position updating phase. The proposed variant is named the Augmented Whale Optimization Algorithm (AWOA) and tested over two benchmark suits, i.e., classical benchmark functions and the latest CEC-2017 benchmark functions for 10 dimension and 30 dimension problems. Various analyses, including convergence property analysis, boxplot analysis and Wilcoxon rank sum test analysis, show that the proposed variant possesses better exploration and exploitation capabilities. Along with this, the application of AWOA has been reported for three real-world problems of various disciplines. The results revealed that the proposed variant exhibits better optimization performance.

Keywords: metaheuristic algorithms; Whale Optimization Algorithm

MSC: 68T01; 68T05; 68T07; 68T09; 68T20; 68T30

Citation: Alnowibet, K.A.; Shekhawat, S.; Saxena, A.; Sallam, K.M.; Mohamed, A.W. Development and Applications of Augmented Whale Optimization Algorithm. *Mathematics* **2022**, *10*, 2076. https://doi.org/10.3390/math10122076

Academic Editor: Jian Dong

Received: 13 May 2022
Accepted: 6 June 2022
Published: 15 June 2022

1. Introduction and Literature Review

Optimization is a process to fetch the best alternative solution from the given set of alternatives. Optimization processes are evident everywhere around of us. For example, to run a generating company, the operator has to take care of operating cost and to check and deal with various type of markets to execute financial transactions.The operator has to optimize the fuel purchase cost, sell the power at maximum rate and purchase the carbon credits at minimum cost to earn profit. Sometimes, optimization processes involve various stochastic variables to model the uncertainty in the process. Such processes are quite difficult to handle and often pose a severe challenge to the optimizer or solution provider algorithms. Evolution of modern optimizers is the outcome of these complex combinatorial multimodal nonlinear optimization problems. Unlike classical optimizers, where the search starts with the initial guess, these modern optimizers are based on the stochastic variables, and hence, they are less vulnerable towards local minima entrapment. These problems become the main source of emerging of metaheuristic algorithms, which are capable of finding a near-optimal solution in less computation time. The popularity of metaheuristic algorithms [1] has increased exponentially in the last two decades due to their simplicity, derivation-free mechanism, flexibility and better results providing capacity in comparison with conventional methods. The main inspiration of these algorithms is nature, and hence, aliased as nature-inspired algorithms [2].

Social mimicry of nature and living processes, behavior analysis of animals and cognitive viability are some of the attributes of nature-inspired algorithms. Darwin's theory of evolution has inspired some nature-inspired algorithms, based on the property of "inheritance of good traits" and "competition, i.e., survival of the fittest". These algorithms are Genetic Algorithm [3], Differential Evolution and Evolutionary Strategies [4].

The other popular philosophy is to mimic the behavior of animals which search for food. In these approaches, food or prey is used as a metaphor for global minima in mathematical terms. Exploration, exploitation and convergence towards the global minima is mapped with animal behavior. Most of the nature-inspired algorithms also known as population-based algorithms can further be classified as:

- Bio-inspired Swarm Intelligence (SI)-based algorithms: This category includes all algorithms inspired by any behavior of swarms or herds of animals or birds. Since most birds and animals live in a flock or group, there many algorithms that fall under this category, such as Ant Colony Optimization (ACO) [5], Artificial Bee Colony [6], Bat Algorithm [7], Cuckoo Search Algorithm [8], Krill herd Algorithm [9], Firefly Algorithm [10], Grey Wolf Optimizer [11], Bacterial Foraging Algorithm [12], Social Spider Algorithm [13], Cat Swarm Optimization [14], Moth Flame Optimization [15], Ant Lion Optimizer [16], Crow Search Algorithm [17] and Grasshopper Optimization Algorithm [18]. A social interaction-based algorithm named gaining and sharing knowledge was proposed in reference [19]. References pertaining to the applications of bioinspired algorithms affirm the suitability of these algorithms on real-world problems [20–23]. A timeline of some famous bio-inspired algorithms is presented in Figure 1.
- Physics- or chemistry-based algorithms: Algorithms developed by mimicking any physical or chemical law fall under this category. Some of them are Big bang-big crunch Optimization [24], Black Hole [25], Gravitational search Algorithm [26], Central Force [27] and Charged system search [28].

Other than these population-based algorithms, a few different algorithms have also been proposed to solve specific mathematical problems. In [29,30], the authors proposed the concept of construction, solution and merging. Another Greedy randomised adaptive search-based algorithm using the improved version of integer linear programming was proposed in [31].

The No Free Lunch Theorem proposed by Wolpert et al. [32] states that there is no one metaheuristic algorithm which can solve all optimization problems. From this theorem, it can be concluded that there is no single metaheuristic that can provide the best solution for all problems. It is possible that one algorithm may be very effective for solving certain problems but ineffective in solving other problems. Due to the popularity of nature-inspired algorithms in providing reasonable solutions to complex real-life problems, many new nature-inspired optimization techniques are being proposed in the literature. It is interesting to note that all bio-inspired algorithms are subsets of nature-inspired algorithms. Among all of these algorithms, the popularity of bio-inspired algorithms has increased exponentially in recent years. Despite of this popularity, these algorithms have also been critically reviewed [33].

Figure 1. Development timeline of some of the leading bio-inspired algorithms.

In 2016, Mirjalili et al. [34] proposed a new nature-inspired algorithm called the Whale optimization algorithm (WOA), inspired by the bubble-net hunting behavior of humpback whales. The humpback whale belongs to the rorqual family of whales, known for their huge size. An adult can be 12–16 m long and weigh 25–30 metric tons. They have a distinctive body shape and are known for their breaching behavior in water with astonishing gymnastic skills and for haunting songs sung by males during their migration period. Humpback whales eat small fish herds and krills. For hunting their prey, they follow a unique strategy of encircling the prey spirally, while gradually shrinking the size of the circles of this spiral. With incorporation of this theory, the performance of WOA is superior to many other nature-inspired algorithms. Recently, in [35], WOA was used to solve the optimization problem of the truss structure. WOA has also been used to solve the well-known economic dispatch problem in [36]. The problem of unit commitment from electric power generation was solved through WOA in [37]. In [38], the author applied WOA to the long-term optimal operation of a single reservoir and cascade reservoirs. The following are the main reasons to select WOA:

- There are few parameters to control, so it is easy to implement and very flexible.
- This algorithm has a specific characteristic to transit between exploration and exploitation phasesm as both of these include one parameter only.

Sometimes, it also suffers from a slow convergence speed and local minima entrapment due to the random size of the population. To overcome these shortcomings, in this paper, we propose two major modifications to the existing WOA:

- The first modification is the inculcation of the opposition-based learning (OBL) concept in the initialization phase of the search process, or in other words, the exploratory stage. The OBL is a proven tool for enhancing the exploration capabilities of meta-heuristic algorithms.
- The second modification is of the position updating phase, by updating the position vector with the help of Cauchy numbers.

The remaining part of this paper is organized as follows: Section 2 describes the crisp mathematical details of WOA. Section 3 is a proposal of the proposed variant; an analogy based on modified position update is also established with the proposed mathematical framework. Section 4 includes the details of benchmark functions. In Sections 5 and 6 show the results of the benchmark functions and some real-life problems that occur with different statistical analyses. Last but not the least, the paper concludes in Section 7 with a decisive evaluation of the results, and some future directions are indicated.

2. Mathematical Framework of WOA

The mathematical model of WOA can be presented in three steps: prey encircling, exploitation phase through bubble-net and exploration phase, i.e., prey search.

1. Prey encircling: Humpback whales choose their target prey through the capacity to finding the location of prey. The best search agent is followed by other search agents to update their positions, which can be given mathematically as:

$$\vec{P} = \left| \vec{Q}\, \vec{Y}^*(s) - \vec{Y}(s) \right| \tag{1}$$

$$\vec{Y}(s+1) = \vec{Y}^*(s) - \vec{R} \cdot \vec{P} \tag{2}$$

where Y^* denotes the position vector of the best obtained solution, $\vec{Y}$ is the position vector, s is the current iteration, $|\ |$ denotes the absolute value and $\cdot$ denotes the element to element multiplication.
The coefficients $\vec{R}$ and $\vec{Q}$ can be calculated as follows:

$$\vec{R} = 2\vec{p} \cdot \vec{r} - \vec{p} \tag{3}$$

$$\vec{Q} = 2\vec{r} \tag{4}$$

where $\vec{p}$ linearly decreases with every iteration from 2 to 0 and $\vec{r} \in [0,1]$. By adjusting the values of vectors $\vec{P}$ and $\vec{R}$, the current position of search agents shifted towards the best position. This position updating process in the neighborhood direction also helps in encircling the prey n dimensionally.

2. Exploitation phase through bubble-net: The value of $\vec{p}$ decreases in the interval $[-p,p]$. Due to changes in $\vec{p}$, $\vec{P}$ also fluctuates and represents the shrinking behavior of search agents. By choosing random values of $\vec{P}$ in the interval $[-1,1]$, the humpback whale updates its position. In this process, the whale swims towards the prey spirally and the circles of spirals slowly shrink in size. This shrinking of the spirals in a helix-shaped movement can be mathematically modeled as:

$$\vec{Y}(s+1) = \vec{Q}' \cdot e^{al} \cdot \cos(2\pi l) + \vec{Y}^*(s) \tag{5}$$

$$\vec{Q}' = \left|\vec{Y}^*(s) - \vec{Y}(s)\right| \tag{6}$$

where $\vec{a}$ is the constant factor responsible for the shape of spirals and l randomly belongs to interval $[-1,1]$.

In the position updating phase, whales can choose any model, i.e., the shrinking mechanism or the spiral mechanism. The probability of this simultaneous behavior is assumed to be 50 during the optimization process. The combined equation of both of these behavior can be represented as:

$$\vec{Y}(s+1) = \begin{cases} \vec{Y}^*(s) - \vec{P} \cdot \vec{Q} & p < 0.5 \\ \vec{Q}' e^{al} \cos(2\pi l) + Y^s & p > 0.5 \end{cases} \tag{7}$$

3. Exploration Phase

In this phase, $\vec{P}$ is chosen opposite to the exploitation phase, i.e., the value of $\vec{P}$ must be > 1 or < -1, so that the humpback whales can move away from each other, which increases the exploration rate. This phenomenon can be represented mathematically as:

$$\vec{Q} = \left|\vec{R} \cdot \vec{Y}_{rand} - \vec{Y}\right| \tag{8}$$

$$\vec{Y}(s+1) = \vec{Y}_{rand} - \vec{P} \cdot \vec{Q} \tag{9}$$

where $\vec{Y}_{rand}$ represents the position of a random whale.

After achieving the termination criteria, the optimization process finishes. The main features of WOA are the presence of the dual theory of circular shrinking and spiral path, which increase the exploitation process of finding the best position around the prey. Afterwards, the exploration phase provides a larger area through the random selection of values of $\left|\vec{A}\right|$.

3. Motivation and Development of the Augmented Whale Optimization Algorithm

It is observed in the previous reported applications that inserting mutation in the population-based schemes can enhance the performance of the optimization. Some noteworthy applications are reported in [39].

3.1. Augmented Whale Optimization Algorithm (AWOA)

By taking the motivation of the modified position update, we present the development of AWOA and the mathematical steps we have incorporated. To simulate the behavior of whale through modified position update and their connection to the position update mechanism for mating, we require two mechanisms:

1. The mechanism that puts the whales in diverse directions.
2. The mechanism that updates the positions of the whales by using a mathematical signal.

3.1.1. The Opposition-Based Position Update Method

For simulating the first mechanism, we choose the opposition number generation theory that was proposed by H. R Tizoosh. Opposition-based learning is the concept that puts the search agents in diverse (rather opposite directions) so that the search for optima can also be initiated from opposite directions. This theory has been applied in many metaheuristic algorithms, and now, it is a proven fact that the search capabilities of the optimizer can substantially be enhanced by the application of this opposition number generation technique. Some recent papers have provided evidence of this [40,41]. With these approaches, an impact of opposition-based learning can be easily seen. Furthermore, a rich review on the techniques related to opposition, application area and performance-wise comparison can be read in [42,43].

The following points can be taken as some positive arguments in favor of the application of the oppositional number generation theory (ONGT) concept:

1. While solving multimodal optimization problems, it is required that an optimizer should start a process from the point which is nearer to the global optima; in some cases, the loose position update mechanism becomes a potential cause for local minima entrapment. The ONGT becomes a helping hand in such situations, as it places search agents in diverse directions, and hence, the probability of local minima entrapment is substantially decreased.
2. In real applications, where the shape and nature of objective functions are unknown, the ONGT can be a beneficial tool because if the function is unimodal in nature, as per the research, the exploration capabilities of any optimizers can be substantially enhanced by the application of ONGT. On the other hand, if the function is multimodal in nature, then ONGT will help search agents to acquire opposite positions and help the optimizer's mechanism to converge to global optima.

For the reader's benefit, we are incorporating some definitions of opposite points in search space for a 2D and multidimensional space.

Definition 1. *Let $x \in [a, b]$ be a real number, where the opposite number of x is defined by:*

$$\bar{x} = a + b - x \tag{10}$$

The same holds for Q dimensional space.

Definition 2. *Let $A = (x_1, x_2, \ldots, x_Q)$ be a point in Q dimensional space, where $x_1, x_2, \ldots, x_Q \in R$ and $x_i \in [a, b], i=1, 2, \ldots, Q$; the opposite points matrix can be given by $\bar{A} = [\bar{x_1}, \bar{x_2}, \bar{x_3} \ldots, \bar{x_Q}]$. Hence:*

$$\bar{x_i} = [a_i + b_i - x_i] \tag{11}$$

where a_i and b_i are the lower limit and upper limit, respectively. Furthermore, Figure 2 illustrates the search process of ONGT, where A1 and B1 are the search boundaries, and it shrinks as the iterative process progresses.

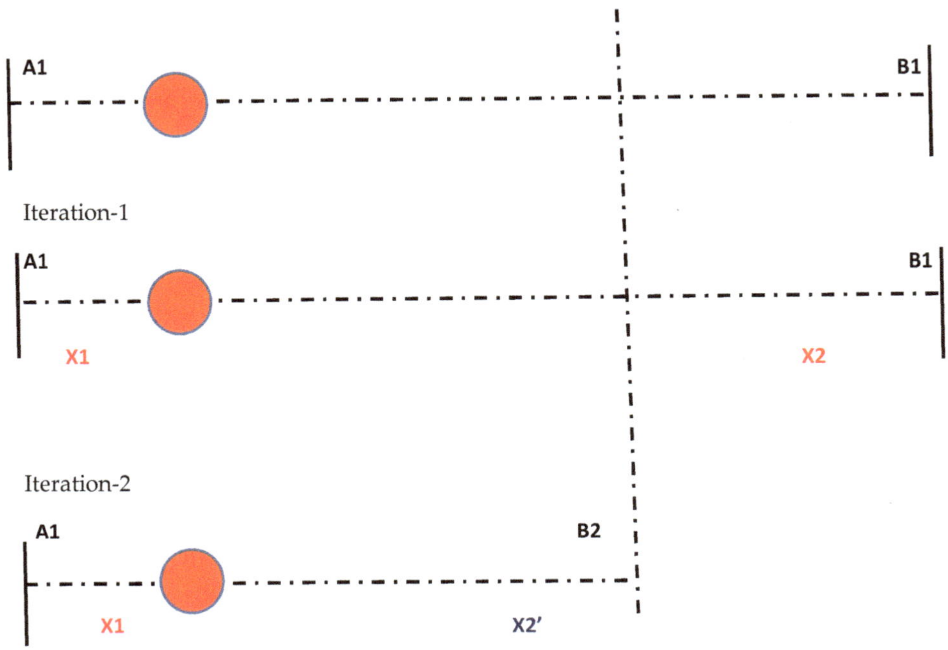

Figure 2. Solving the one-dimensional problem by recursive halving the search interval.

3.1.2. Position Updating Mechanism Based on the Cauchy Mutation Operator

For simulating the second mechanism, we require a signal that is a close replica of a whale song. In the literature, a significant amount of work has been done on the application of the Cauchy mutation operator due to the following reasons:

1. Since the expectation of the Cauchy distribution is not defined, the variance of this distribution is infinite; due to this fact, the Cauchy operators sometimes generate a very long jump as compared to normally distributed random numbers [44,45]. This phenomenon can be observed in Figure 3.
2. It is also shown in [44] that Cauchy distribution generates an offspring far from its parents; hence, the avoidance of local minima can be achieved.

In the proposed AWOA, the position update mechanism is derived from the Cauchy distribution operator. The Cauchy density function of the distribution is given by:

$$f_t(x) = \frac{1}{\pi} \frac{t}{t^2 + x^2} \quad -\infty < x < \infty \tag{12}$$

where t is the scaling parameter and the corresponding distribution function can be given as:

$$F_t(x) = \frac{1}{2} + \frac{1}{\pi} \arctan(\frac{x}{t}) \tag{13}$$

First, a random number $y \in (0,1)$ is generated, after which a random number α is generated by using following equation:

$$\alpha = x_0 + t\ \tan(\pi(y - 0.5)) \tag{14}$$

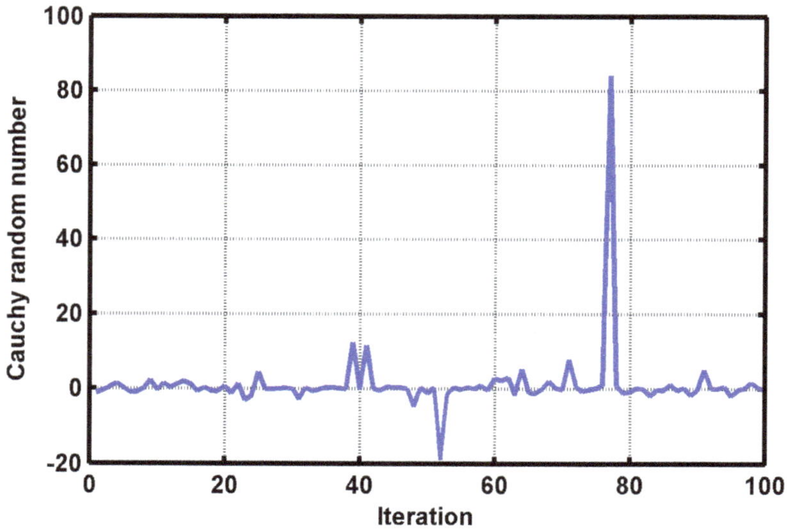

Figure 3. Whale position update inspired from Cauchy Distribution.

We assume that α is a whale position update generated by the search agents and on the basis of this signal, the position of the whale is updated. Furthermore, we define a position-based weight matrix of jth position vector of ith whale, which is given as:

$$W(j) = \frac{\left(\sum_{i=1}^{NP} x_{i,j}\right)}{NP} \tag{15}$$

where $W(j)$ is a weight vector and NP is the population size of whale. Furthermore, the position update equation can be modified as:

$$x'(j) = x(j) + W(j) * \alpha \tag{16}$$

Summarizing all the points discussed in this section, we propose two mechanisms for the improvement of the performance of WOA. The first one is the opposition-based learning concept that places whales in diverse directions to explore the search space effectively, and based on the whale behaviour(modified position update) is created by them, the position update mechanism is proposed. To simulate whale song, we employ Cauchy numbers. Hence, both of these mechanisms can be beneficial for enhancing the exploration and exploitation capabilities of WOA. In the next section, we will evaluate the performance of the proposed variant on some conventional and CEC-17 benchmark functions.

4. Benchmark Test Functions

Benchmark functions are a set of functions with different known characteristics (separability, modality and dimensionality) and often used to evaluate the performance of optimization algorithms. In the present paper, we measure the performance of our proposed variant AWOA through two benchmark suites.

- Benchmark Suite 1: In this suite, 23 conventional benchmark functions are considered, out of which 7 are unimodal and rest are multimodal and fixed dimension functions. The details of benchmark functions, such as mathematical definition, minima, dimensions and range are incorporated in Table 1. For further details, one can refer to [46–48]. The shapes of the used benchmark functions are given in Figure 4.
- Benchmark Suite 2: For further benchmarking our proposed variant, we also choose a set of 29 functions of diverse nature from CEC 2017. Table 2 showcases the minor de-

tails of these functions. For other details, such as optima and mathematical definitions, we can follow [49].

Table 1. Details of Benchmark Functions Suite 1.

Function	Dim	Range	Minima
Unimodal Benchmark Function			
$G_1(x) = \sum_{i=1}^{n} x_i^2$ (BF1)	30	$[-100, 100]$	0
$G_2(x) = \sum_{i=1}^{n} \lvert x_i \rvert + \prod_{i=1}^{n} \lvert x_i \rvert$ (BF2)	30	$[-10, 10]$	0
$G_3(x) = \sum_{i=1}^{n} \left(\sum_{j-1}^{i} x_j \right)^2$ (BF3)	30	$[-100, 100]$	0
$G_4(x) = \max_i\{\lvert x_i \rvert \quad 1 \le i \le n$ (BF4)	30	$[-100, 100]$	0
$G_5(x) = \sum_{i=1}^{n-1} [100(x_{i+1} - x_i^2)^2 + (x_i - 1)^2]$ (BF5)	30	$[-30, 30]$	0
$G_6(x) = \sum_{i=1}^{n-1} ([x_i + 0.5])^2$ (BF6)	30	$[-100, 100]$	0
$G_7(x) = \sum_{i=1}^{n-1} i x_i^4 + random[0, 1]$ (BF7)	30	$[-1.28, 1.28]$	0
Multimodal Benchmark Function			
$G_8(x) = \sum_{i=1}^{n} -x_i \sin\left(\sqrt{\lvert z_i \rvert}\right)$ (BF8)	30	$[-500, 500]$	-418.9829×5
$G_9(x) = \sum_{i=1}^{n} [x_i{}^2 - 10 \cos(2\pi x_i) + 10]$ (BF9)	30	$[-5.12, 5.12]$	0
$G_{10}(x) = -20 \exp\left(-0.2 \sqrt{\frac{1}{n} \sum_{i=1}^{n} x_i{}^2}\right) - \exp\left(\frac{1}{n} \sum_{i=1}^{n} \cos(2\pi x_i)\right) + 20 + e$ (BF10)	30	$[-32, 32]$	0
$G_{11}(x) = \frac{1}{4000} \sum_{i=1}^{n} x_i{}^2 - \prod_{i=1}^{n} \cos\left(\frac{x_i}{\sqrt{i}}\right) + 1$ (BF11)	30	$[-600, 600]$	0
$G_{12}(x) = \frac{\pi}{n}\left\{10 \sin(\pi y_1) + \sum_{i=1}^{n-1} (y_i - 1)^2 [1 + 10\sin^2(\pi y_{i+1})] + (y_n - 1)^2\right\} + \sum_{i=1}^{n} u(x_i, 10, 100, 4)$ (BF12) $y_i = 1 + \frac{x_{i+1}}{4}$ $u(x_i, a, k, m) = \begin{cases} k(x_i - a)^m & x_i > a \\ 0 & -a < x_i < a \\ k(-x_i - a)^m & x_i < -a \end{cases}$	30	$[-50, 50]$	0
$G_{13}(x) = 0.1\{sin^2(3\pi x_1) + \sum_{i=1}^{n} (x_i - 1)^2 [1 + \sin^2(3\pi x_i + 1)] + (x_n - 1)^2 [1 + \sin^2(2\pi x_n)]\} + \sum_{i=1}^{n} u(x_i, 5, 100, 4)$ (BF13)	30	$[-50, 50]$	0
Fixed-Dimension Multimodal Benchmark Function			
$G_{14}(x) = \left(\frac{1}{500} + \sum_{j=1}^{25} \frac{1}{j + \sum_{i=1}^{2} (x_i - a_{ij})^6} \right)^{-1}$ (BF14)	2	$[-65, 65]$	1
$G_{15}(x) = \sum_{j=1}^{11} \left[a_i - \frac{x_1(b_i^2 + b_i x_2)}{b_i^2 + b_i x_3 + x_4} \right]^2$ (BF15)	4	$[-5, 5]$	0.00030
$G_{16}(x) = 4x_1^2 - 2.1x_1^4 + \frac{1}{3}x_1^6 + x_1 x_2 - 4x_2^2 + 4x_2^4$ (BF16)	2	$[-5, 5]$	-1.0316
$G_{17}(x) = \left(x_2 - \frac{5.1}{4\pi^2} x_1^2 + \frac{5}{\pi} x_1 - 6\right)^2 + 10\left(1 - \frac{1}{8\pi}\right) \cos x_1 + 10$ (BF17)	2	$[-5, 5]$	0.398
$G_{18}(x) = A(z) \times B(x)$ $A(x) = 1 + (x_1 + x_2 + 1)^2 (19 - 14x_1 + 3x_1^2 - 14x_2 + 6x_1 x_2 + 3x_2^2)$ $B(x) = 30 + (2x_1 - 3x_2)^2 \times (18 - 32x_1 + 12x_1^2 + 48x_2 - 36x_1 x_2 + 27x_2^2)$ (BF18)	2	$[-2, 2]$	3
$G_{19}(x) = -\sum_{i=1}^{4} c_i \exp\left(-\sum_{j=1}^{3} a_{ij}(x_j - p_{ij})^2\right)$ (BF19)	3	$[1, 3]$	-3.86
$G_{20}(x) = -\sum_{i=1}^{4} c_i \exp\left(-\sum_{j=1}^{6} a_{ij}(x_j - p_{ij})^2\right)$ (BF20)	6	$[0, 1]$	-3.32
$G_{21}(x) = -\sum_{i=1}^{5} \left[(X - a_i)(X - a_i)^T + c_i\right]^{-1}$ (BF21)	4	$[0, 10]$	-10.1532
$G_{22}(x) = -\sum_{i=1}^{7} \left[(X - a_i)(X - a_i)^T + c_i\right]^{-1}$ (BF22)	4	$[0, 10]$	-10.4028
$G_{23}(x) = -\sum_{i=1}^{10} \left[(X - a_i)(X - a_i)^T + c_i\right]^{-1}$ (BF23)	4	$[0, 10]$	-10.5363

Table 2. Details of CEC-2017 (Benchmark Suite 2).

Function Name	Optima
Unimodal Functions	
Shifted and Rotated Bent Cigar Function (CEC-G_1) (F1)	100
Shifted and Rotated Zakharov Function (CEC-G_3) (F3)	300
Simple Multimodal Functions	
Shifted and Rotated Rosenbrock's Function (CEC-G_4) (F4)	400
Shifted and Rotated Rastrigin's Function (CEC-G_5) (F5)	500
Shifted and Rotated Expanded Scaffer's Function (CEC-G_6) (F6)	600
Shifted and Rotated Lunacek Bi Rastrigin Function (CEC-G_7) (F7)	700
Shifted and Rotated Non-continuous Rastrigin Function (CEC-G_8) (F8)	800
Shifted and Rotated Levy Function (CEC-G_9) (F9)	900
Shifted and Rotated Schwefel's Function (CEC-G_{10}) (F10)	1000
Hybrid Functions	
Hybrid Function 1 (N = 3) (CEC-G_{11}) (F11)	1100
Hybrid Function 2 (N = 3) (CEC-G_{12}) (F12)	1200
Hybrid Function 3 (N = 3) (CEC-G_{13}) (F13)	1300
Hybrid Function 4 (N = 4) (CEC-G_{14}) (F14)	1400
Hybrid Function 5 (N = 4) (CEC-G_{15}) (F15)	1500
Hybrid Function 6 (N = 4) (CEC-G_{16}) (F16)	1600
Hybrid Function 7 (N = 5) (CEC-G_{17}) (F17)	1700
Hybrid Function 8 (N = 5) (CEC-G_{18}) (F18)	1800
Hybrid Function 9 (N = 5) (CEC-G_{19}) (F19)	1900
Hybrid Function 10 (N = 6) (CEC-G_{20}) (F20)	2000
Composite Functions	
Composition Function 1 (N = 3) (CEC-G_{21}) (F21)	2100
Composition Function 2 (N = 3) (CEC-G_{22}) (F22)	2200
Composition Function 3 (N = 4) (CEC-G_{23}) (F23)	2300
Composition Function 4 (N = 4) (CEC-G_{24}) (F24)	2400
Composition Function 5 (N = 5) (CEC-G_{25}) (F25)	2500
Composition Function 6 (N = 5) (CEC-G_{26}) (F26)	2600
Composition Function 7 (N = 6) (CEC-G_{27}) (F27)	2700
Composition Function 8 (N = 6) (CEC-G_{28}) (F28)	2800
Composition Function 9 (N = 3) (CEC-G_{29}) (F29)	2900
Composition Function 10 (N = 3) (CEC-G_{30}) (F30)	3000

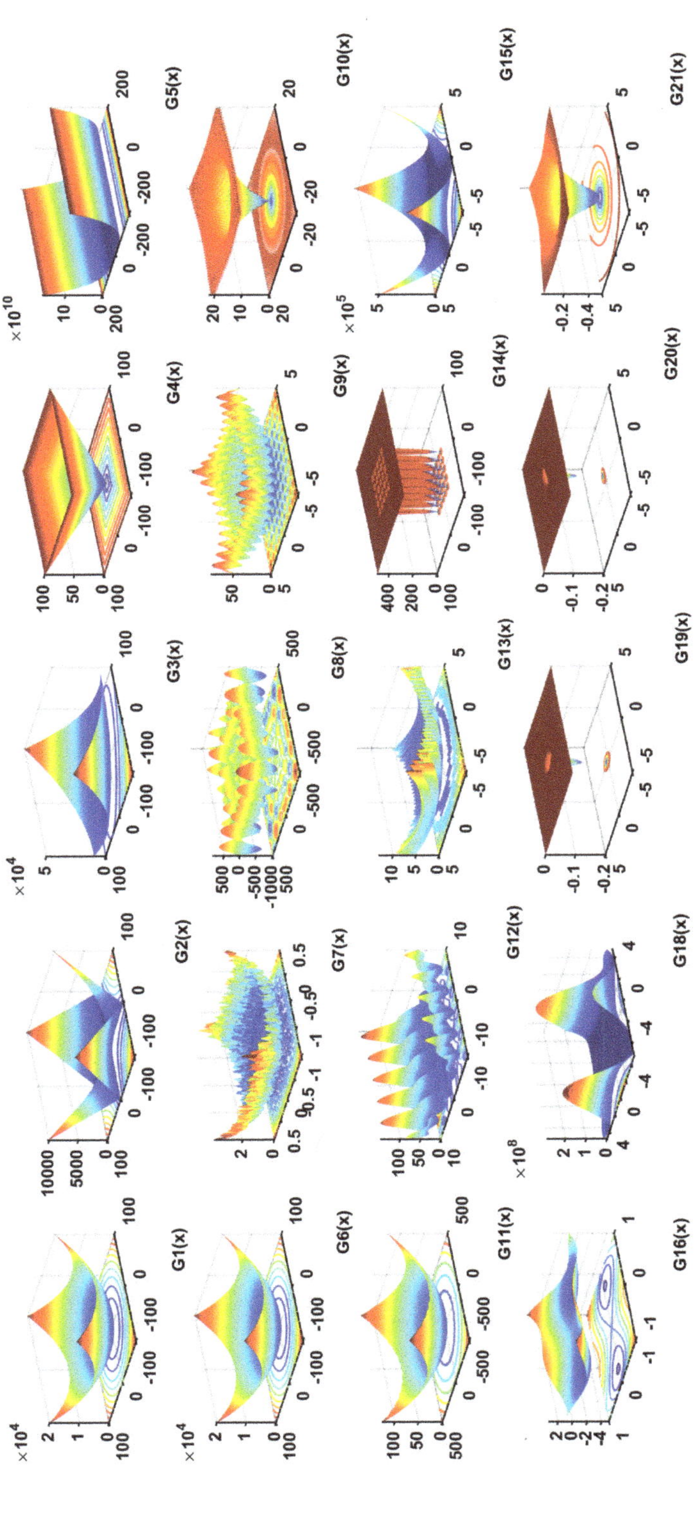

Figure 4. Benchmark Suite 1.

5. Result Analysis

In this section, various analyses that can check the efficacy of the proposed modifications are exhibited. For judging the optimization performance of the proposed AWOA, we have chosen some recently developed variants of WOA for comparison purpose. These variants are:

- Lévy flight trajectory-based whale optimization algorithm (LWOA) [50].
- Improved version of the whale optimization algorithm that uses the opposition-based learning, termed OWOA [41].
- Chaotic Whale Optimization Algorithm (CWOA) [51].

5.1. Benchmark Suite 1

Table 3 shows the optimization results of AWOA on Benchmark Suite 1 along with the leading. The table shows entries of mean and standard deviation (SD) of function values of 30 independent runs. Maximum function evaluations are set to 15,000. The first four functions in the table are unimodal functions. Benchmarking of any algorithm on unimodal functions gives us the information of the exploration capabilities of the algorithm. Inspecting the results of proposed AWOA on unimodal functions, it can be easily observed that the mean values are very competitive for the proposed AWOA as compared with other variants of WOA.

For rest of the functions, indicated mean values are competitive and the best results are indicated in bold face. From this statistical analysis, we can easily derive a conclusion that proposed modifications in AWOA are meaningful and yield positive implications on optimization performance of the AWOA specially on unimodal functions. Similarly, for multimodal functions BF-7 and BF-9 to 11, BF-15 to 19 and BF-22 have optimal values of mean parameter. We observed that the values of mean are competitive for rest of the functions and performance of proposed AWOA has not deteriorated.

5.1.1. Convergence Property Analysis

Similarly, the convergence plots for functions BF1 to BF4 have also been plotted in Figure 5 for the sake of clarity. From these convergence curves, it is observed that the proposed variant shows better convergence characteristics and the proposed modifications are fruitful to enhance the convergence and exploration properties of WOA. As it can be seen that convergence properties of AWOA is very swift as compared to other competitors. It is to be noted here that BF1–BF4 are unimodal functions and performance of AWOA on unimodal functions indicates enhanced exploitation properties. Furthermore, for showcasing the optimization capabilities of AWOA on multimodal functions the plots of convergence are exhibited in Figure 6. These are plotted for BF9 to BF12. From these results of proposed AWOA, it can easily be concluded that the results are also competitive.

5.1.2. Wilcoxon Rank Sum Test

A rank sum test analysis has been conducted and the p-values of the test are indicated in Table 4. We have shown the values of Wilcoxon rank sum test by considering a 5% level of significance [52]. Values that are indicated in boldface are less than 0.05, which indicates that there is a significance difference between the AWOA results and other opponents.

5.1.3. Boxplot Analysis

To present a fair comparison between these two opponents, we have plotted boxplots and convergence of some selected functions. Figure 7 shows the boxplots of function (BF1–BF12). From the boxplots, it is observed that the width of the boxplots of AWOA are optimal in these cases; hence, it can be concluded that the optimization performance of AWOA is competitive with other variants of WOA. The mean values shown in the boxplots are also optimal for these functions. The performance of AWOA on the remaining functions of this suite has been depicted through boxplots shown in Figure 8. From these, it can be concluded that the performance of proposed AWOA is competitive, as mean values depicted in the plots are optimal for most of the functions.

Table 3. Results of Benchmark Suite-1.

Function	Parameter	AWOA	CWOA	LWOA	OWOA	WOA
BF1	Mean	**0.00**	1.33×10^{-97}	2.04×10^{-8}	2.37×10^{-172}	1.24×10^{-172}
	SD	**0.00**	4.06×10^{-97}	2.30×10^{-8}	0.00	0.00
BF2	Mean	**2.71×10^{-297}**	1.96×10^{-59}	2.77×10^{-4}	4.15×10^{-117}	3.96×10^{-120}
	SD	**0.00**	4.93×10^{-59}	1.35×10^{-4}	1.01×10^{-116}	1.51×10^{-119}
BF3	Mean	**0.00**	9.27×10^{3}	8.11×10^{2}	6.04×10^{3}	7.02×10^{3}
	SD	**0.00**	9.34×10^{3}	5.41×10^{2}	4.82×10^{3}	6.55×10^{3}
BF4	Mean	**3.6×10^{-313}**	1.39×10^{-2}	5.88×10^{-1}	8.02×10	4.74
	SD	**0.00**	5.71×10^{-2}	3.38×10^{-1}	1.98×10	1.33×10
BF5	Mean	2.84×10	2.78×10	2.77×10	**2.71×10**	2.74×10
	SD	6.08×10^{-1}	6.12×10^{-1}	**2.32×10^{-1}**	8.95×10^{-1}	9.66×10^{-1}
BF6	Mean	4.49×10^{-1}	1.36×10^{-97}	**2.73×10^{-3}**	5.46×10^{-1}	5.02×10^{-1}
	SD	2.01×10^{-1}	4.81×10^{-1}	**1.09×10^{-3}**	2.46×10^{-1}	3.71×10^{-1}
BF7	Mean	**1.55×10^{-4}**	4.94×10^{-4}	7.58×10^{-3}	1.53×10^{-3}	1.75×10^{-3}
	SD	**1.87×10^{-4}**	4.88×10^{-4}	6.70×10^{-3}	1.96×10^{-3}	1.93×10^{3}
BF8	Mean	-7.80×10^{3}	-6.93×10^{3}	-9.50×10^{3}	-1.03×10^{4}	**-9.02×10^{3}**
	SD	1.70×10^{3}	**1.51×10^{3}**	1.59×10^{3}	2.13×10^{3}	2.02×10^{3}
BF9	Mean	**0.00**	0.00	1.88	0.00	2.84×10^{-15}
	SD	**0.00**	0.00	4.94	0.00	1.27×10^{-14}
BF10	Mean	**8.88×10^{-16}**	4.80×10^{-15}	8.75×10^{-5}	4.09×10^{-15}	4.09×10^{-15}
	SD	**0.00**	2.28×10^{-15}	3.34×10^{-5}	1.59×10^{-15}	2.55×10^{-15}
BF11	Mean	**0.00**	5.58×10^{-3}	2.09×10^{-3}	0.00	0.00
	SD	**0.00**	2.50×10^{-2}	6.61×10^{-3}	0.00	0.00
BF12	Mean	2.03×10^{-2}	7.91×10^{-2}	**2.28×10^{-4}**	3.44×10^{-2}	3.64×10^{-2}
	SD	9.28×10^{-3}	3.22×10^{-2}	**7.37×10^{-5}**	2.11×10^{-2}	2.35×10^{-2}
BF13	Mean	5.69×10^{-1}	1.23	**8.76×10^{-3}**	9.87×10^{-1}	1.01
	SD	1.97×10^{-1}	3.56×10^{-1}	**6.05×10^{-3}**	2.51×10^{-1}	3.37×10^{-1}
BF14	Mean	2.14	1.89	**1.05**	3.16	2.77
	SD	9.80×10^{-1}	1.01	**2.22×10^{3}**	3.41	2.88
BF15	Mean	**4.00×10^{-4}**	4.00×10^{-4}	5.30×10^{-4}	5.21×10^{-4}	1.51×10^{-3}
	SD	3.77×10^{-4}	2.82×10^{-4}	2.70×10^{-4}	**2.39×10^{-4}**	4.05×10^{-3}
BF16	Mean	**−1.03**	−1.03	−1.03	−1.03	−1.03
	SD	1.57×10^{-8}	1.12×10^{-8}	2.32×10^{-8}	**6.20×10^{-11}**	7.34×10^{-11}
BF17	Mean	**3.98×10^{-1}**	3.98×10^{-1}	3.98×10^{-1}	3.98×10^{-1}	3.98×10^{-1}
	SD	1.73×10^{-8}	**8.73×10^{-9}**	4.40×10^{-6}	1.39×10^{-7}	1.23×10^{-6}
BF18	Mean	**3.00**	3.00	3.00	3.00	3.00
	SD	1.12×10^{-4}	1.30×10^{-4}	**9.86×10^{-7}**	3.88×10^{-5}	4.88×10^{-5}
BF19	Mean	**−3.86**	−3.86	−3.86	−3.86	−3.86
	SD	3.81×10^{-3}	3.61×10^{-3}	**4.01×10^{-5}**	3.09×10^{-3}	1.75×10^{-3}
BF20	Mean	−3.22	−3.24	**−3.27**	**−3.27**	−3.23
	SD	1.30×10^{-1}	8.36×10^{-1}	**6.38×10^{-2}**	7.17×10^{-2}	1.23×10^{-1}
BF21	Mean	−6.56	−7.74	−7.51	−8.27	**−8.50**
	SD	**2.35**	2.70	3.41	3.34	2.64
BF22	Mean	**−8.71**	−6.58	−8.62	−6.38	−8.03
	SD	3.04	2.97	**2.83**	3.48	3.42
BF23	Mean	−5.85	−7.20	**−7.83**	−7.79	−7.47
	SD	2.87	3.15	**2.77**	3.20	3.22

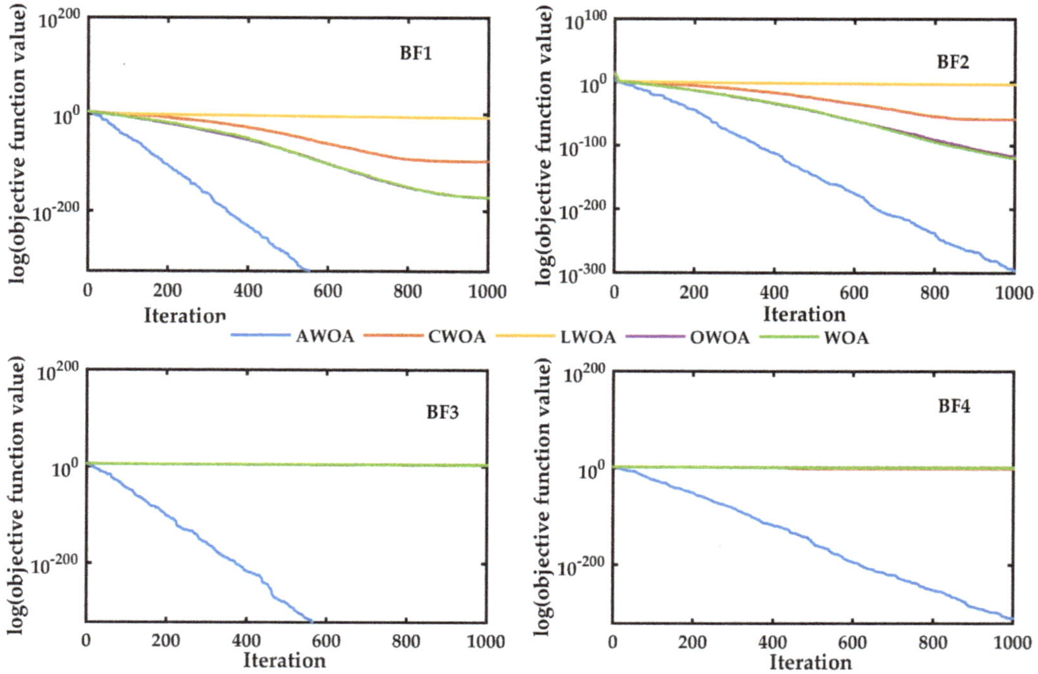

Figure 5. Convergence property analysis of unimodal functions.

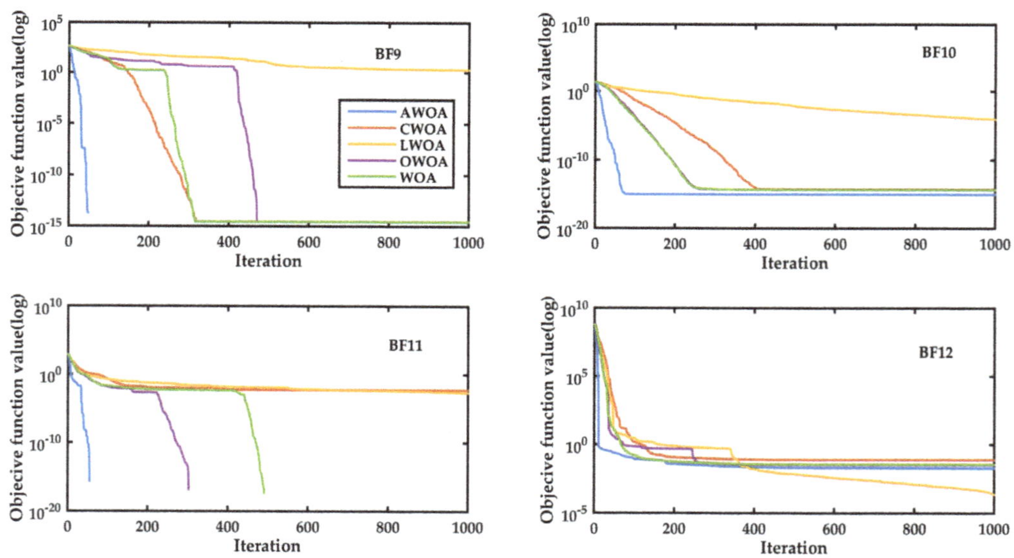

Figure 6. Convergence property analysis of multimodal functions.

Table 4. Results of Wilcoxon rank sum test of AWOA.

Function	CWOA	LWOA	OWOA	WOA
BF1	**8.01×10^{-9}**	8.01×10^{-9}	8.01×10^{-9}	8.01×10^{-9}
BF2	**5.73×10^{-8}**	**5.73×10^{-8}**	**5.73×10^{-8}**	**5.73×10^{-8}**
BF3	**8.01×10^{-9}**	**8.01×10^{-9}**	**8.01×10^{-9}**	**8.01×10^{-9}**
BF4	**1.96×10^{-8}**	**1.96×10^{-8}**	**1.96×10^{-8}**	**1.96×10^{-8}**
BF5	2.14×10^{-3}	2.22×10^{-4}	**4.68×10^{-5}**	3.38×10^{-4}
BF6	2.22×10^{-7}	**6.80×10^{-8}**	1.99×10	9.46×10^{-1}
BF7	**8.36×10^{-4}**	**7.90×10^{-8}**	**2.92×10^{-5}**	**6.01×10^{-7}**
BF8	1.20×10^{-1}	**6.04×10^{-3}**	**7.58×10^{-4}**	1.02×10^{-1}
BF9		**8.01×10^{-9}**		3.42×10^{-1}
BF10	**2.14×10^{-7}**	**8.01×10^{-9}**	**1.11×10^{-7}**	**7.43×10^{-6}**
BF11	3.42×10^{-1}	**8.01×10^{-9}**		
BF12	**1.23×10^{-7}**	**6.80×10^{-8}**	**1.33×10^{-2}**	**3.15×10^{-2}**
BF13	**1.58×10^{-6}**	**6.80×10^{-8}**	**1.81×10^{-5}**	**4.68×10^{-5}**
BF14	1.33×10^{-1}	1.56×10^{-1}	5.25×10^{-1}	4.73×10^{-1}
BF15	1.72×10^{-1}	**8.35×10^{-3}**	**1.67×10^{-2}**	**6.22×10^{-4}**
BF16	9.89×10^{-1}	**3.06×10^{-3}**	**3.99×10^{-6}**	**8.60×10^{-6}**
BF17	9.03×10^{-1}	**1.66×10^{-7}**	2.23×10^{-2}	**7.71×10^{-3}**
BF18	1.20×10^{-1}	**4.70×10^{-3}**	9.25×10^{-1}	6.55×10^{-1}
BF19	4.41×10^{-1}	**2.00×10^{-4}**	3.79×10^{-1}	1.99×10^{-1}
BF20	6.55×10^{-1}	**6.56×10^{-3}**	**2.75×10^{-2}**	1.40×10^{-1}
BF21	2.18×10^{-1}	**2.75×10^{-2}**	**7.71×10^{-3}**	**2.22×10^{-4}**
BF22	6.17×10^{-1}	**1.35×10^{-3}**	9.25×10^{-1}	**1.93×10^{-2}**
BF23	1.40×10^{-1}	**9.28×10^{-5}**	**1.12×10^{-3}**	**3.97×10^{-3}**

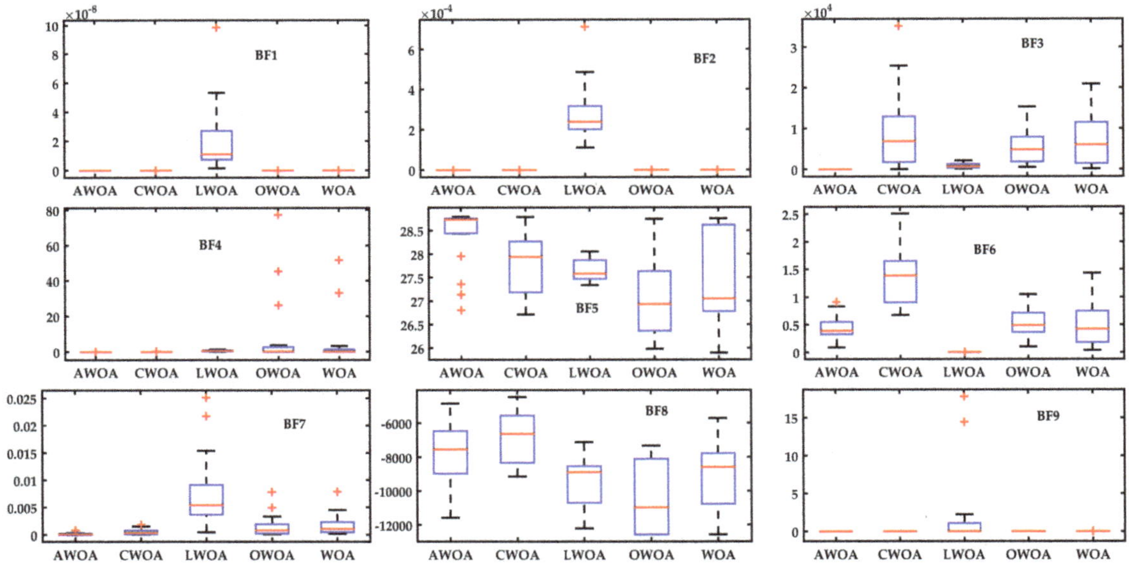

Figure 7. Boxplot analysis of Benchmark Suite 1.

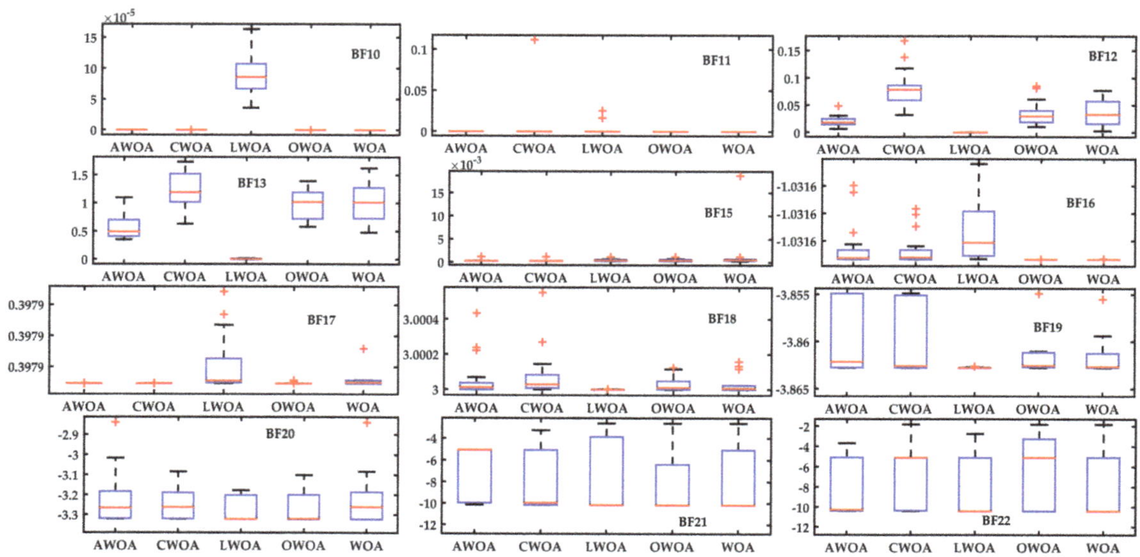

Figure 8. Boxplot analysis of the remaining functions of Benchmark Suite 1.

5.2. Benchmark Suite 2

In this section, we report the results of the proposed variant on CEC17 functions. The details of CEC 17 functions have been exhibited in Table 2. To check the applicability of the proposed variant on higher as well as lower dimension functions, 10- and 30-dimension problems are chosen deliberately. While performing the simulations we have obeyed the criterion of CEC17; for example, the number of function evaluations have been kept $10^4 \times D$ for AWOA and other competitors. The results are averaged over 51 independent runs, as indicated by CEC guidelines. The results of the optimization are expressed as mean and standard deviation of the objective function values obtained from the independent runs. Tables 5 and 6 show these analyses and the bold face entries in the tables show the best performer. Tables 7 and 8 also report the statistical comparison results of objective function values obtained from independent runs through Wilcoxon rank sum test with 5% level of significance. These results are p-values indicated in the each column of the observation table when the opponent is compared with the proposed AWOA. These values are indicator of the statistical significance.

5.3. Results of the Analysis of 10D Problems

For 10D problems, the depiction of results are in terms of the mean values and standard deviation values obtained from 51 different independent runs that are indicated for each opponent of AWOA. Furthermore, the following are the noteworthy observations from this study:

- From the table, it is observed that the values obtained from optimization process and their statistical calculation indicate that the substantial enhancement is evident in terms of mean and standard deviation values. These values are shown in bold face. We observe that out of 29 functions, the proposed variant provides optimal mean values for 23 functions. In addition to that, we have observed that the value of the mean parameter is optimal for 23 functions for AWOA. Except CECF16, 17, 18, 23, 24, 26 and CECF29, the mean values of the optimization runs are optimal for AWOA. This supports the fact that the proposed modifications are helpful for enhancing the optimization performance of the original WOA. Inspecting other statistical parameters, namely standard deviation values, also gives a clear insight into the enhanced performance.

- We observe that for unimodal functions, these values are optimal as compared to different versions of WOA as compared to AWOA; hence, it can be said that for unimodal functions, AWOA outperforms. Unimodal functions are useful to test the exploration capability of any optimizer.
- Inspecting the performance of the proposed version of WOA on multimodal functions that are from CECF4-F10 gives a clear insight on the fact that the proposed modifications are meaningful in terms of enhanced exploitation capabilities. Naturally, in multimodal functions, more than one minimum exist, and to converge the optimization process to global minima can be a troublesome task.
- The results of optimization runs indicated in bold face depict the performance of AWOA.

Table 5. Results of Benchmark Suite-2 (10D).

Function	Parameter	WOA	OWOA	AWOA	LWOA	CWOA
F1	Mean	6.85×10^4	7.03×10^6	$\mathbf{9.50 \times 10^3}$	1.48×10^7	1.08×10^7
	SD	1.43×10^5	4.97×10^7	$\mathbf{5.84 \times 10^3}$	5.32×10^7	3.97×10^7
F3	Mean	6.81×10^2	8.53×10^2	$\mathbf{3.00 \times 10^2}$	9.30×10^2	6.17×10^2
	SD	7.92×10^2	1.15×10^3	$\mathbf{2.43 \times 10^2}$	1.15×10^3	5.82×10^2
F4	Mean	4.20×10^2	4.23×10^2	$\mathbf{4.05 \times 10^2}$	4.31×10^2	4.29×10^2
	SD	2.83×10	3.16×10	$\mathbf{1.33 \times 10}$	4.11×10	3.56×10
F5	Mean	5.40×10^2	5.36×10^2	$\mathbf{5.28 \times 10^2}$	5.34×10^2	5.33×10^2
	SD	1.68×10	1.57×10	**9.68**	1.04×10	1.55×10^2
F6	Mean	6.14×10^2	6.16×10^2	$\mathbf{6.03 \times 10^2}$	6.12×10^2	6.11×10^2
	SD	7.96	7.89	**5.00**	6.04	5.65
F7	Mean	7.59×10^2	7.61×10^2	$\mathbf{7.45 \times 10^2}$	7.63×10^2	7.51×10^2
	SD	1.64×10	1.88×10	$\mathbf{1.22 \times 10}$	1.50×10	1.54×10
F8	Mean	8.32×10^2	8.31×10^2	$\mathbf{8.27 \times 10^2}$	8.29×10^2	8.29×10^2
	SD	1.08×10	1.13×10	$\mathbf{1.11 \times 10}$	1.03×10	1.10×10
F9	Mean	1.03×10^3	1.04×10^3	$\mathbf{9.15 \times 10^2}$	9.99×10^2	9.88×10^2
	SD	1.11×10^2	1.71×10^2	$\mathbf{3.97 \times 10}$	9.15×10	1.05×10^2
F10	Mean	1.99×10^3	1.94×10^3	$\mathbf{1.81 \times 10^3}$	1.94×10^3	1.84×10^3
	SD	2.87×10^2	3.38×10^2	$\mathbf{3.12 \times 10^2}$	3.41×10^2	2.72×10^2
F11	Mean	1.16×10^3	1.16×10^3	$\mathbf{1.13 \times 10^3}$	1.17×10^3	1.17×10^3
	SD	6.27×10	5.89×10	$\mathbf{1.14 \times 10}$	4.84×10	6.47×10
F12	Mean	1.96×10^6	1.03×10^6	$\mathbf{5.29 \times 10^4}$	2.59×10^6	2.19×10^6
	SD	2.41×10^6	1.82×10^6	$\mathbf{5.19 \times 10^4}$	2.90×10^6	2.25×10^6
F13	Mean	1.66×10^4	1.21×10^4	$\mathbf{1.02 \times 10^4}$	1.91×10^4	1.54×10^4
	SD	1.31×10^4	9.71×10^3	$\mathbf{8.32 \times 10^3}$	1.38×10^4	1.21×10^4
F14	Mean	1.71×10^3	1.71×10^3	$\mathbf{1.47 \times 10^3}$	1.64×10^3	1.70×10^3
	SD	8.69×10^2	8.71×10^2	$\mathbf{3.13 \times 10}$	6.95×10^2	7.96×10^2
F15	Mean	2.41×10^3	2.81×10^3	$\mathbf{1.58 \times 10^3}$	2.64×10^3	2.58×10^3
	SD	1.17×10^3	1.41×10^3	$\mathbf{4.47 \times 10}$	1.30×10^3	1.22×10^3
F16	Mean	1.76×10^3	1.78×10^3	1.76×10^3	1.78×10^3	$\mathbf{1.73 \times 10^3}$
	SD	1.22×10^2	1.25×10^2	1.37×10^2	1.01×10^2	$\mathbf{9.82 \times 10}$
F17	Mean	1.77×10^3	1.77×10^3	1.77×10^3	$\mathbf{1.76 \times 10^3}$	1.77×10^3
	SD	3.23×10	3.60×10	3.16×10	$\mathbf{2.46 \times 10}$	3.08×10
F18	Mean	1.70×10^4	1.71×10^4	1.72×10^4	$\mathbf{1.62 \times 10^4}$	1.62×10^4
	SD	1.24×10^4	1.14×10^4	1.02×10^4	$\mathbf{1.20 \times 10^4}$	1.07×10^4
F19	Mean	8.18×10^3	1.69×10^4	$\mathbf{2.32 \times 10^3}$	4.93×10^3	5.40×10^3
	SD	6.91×10^3	5.21×10^4	$\mathbf{6.54 \times 10^2}$	5.01×10^3	5.25×10^3

Table 5. *Cont.*

Function	Parameter	WOA	OWOA	AWOA	LWOA	CWOA
F20	Mean	2.09×10^3	2.10×10^3	$\mathbf{2.05 \times 10^3}$	2.11×10^3	2.11×10^3
	SD	5.62×10	5.21×10	$\mathbf{4.18 \times 10}$	5.48×10	5.48×10
F21	Mean	2.31×10^3	2.31×10^3	2.30×10^3	$\mathbf{2.27 \times 10^3}$	2.29×10^3
	SD	5.97×10	5.40×10	6.20×10	$\mathbf{6.29 \times 10}$	5.86×10
F22	Mean	2.33×10^3	2.31×10^3	$\mathbf{2.30 \times 10^3}$	2.31×10^3	2.31×10^3
	SD	1.63×10^2	9.37	$\mathbf{1.63 \times 10}$	2.19×10	7.34
F23	Mean	2.64×10^3	2.64×10^3	2.64×10^3	$\mathbf{2.63 \times 10^3}$	2.64×10^3
	SD	1.80×10	1.46×10	1.44×10	$\mathbf{1.11 \times 10}$	1.41×10
F24	Mean	2.75×10^3	2.76×10^3	2.75×10^3	2.75×10^3	$\mathbf{2.74 \times 10^3}$
	SD	8.30×10	5.41×10	7.43×10	5.89×10	$\mathbf{7.11 \times 10}$
F25	Mean	2.94×10^3	2.93×10^3	$\mathbf{2.92 \times 10^3}$	2.94×10^3	2.93×10^3
	SD	4.61×10	4.91×10	$\mathbf{5.31 \times 10}$	2.03×10	4.42×10
F26	Mean	3.22×10^3	3.13×10^3	3.04×10^3	$\mathbf{3.03 \times 10^3}$	3.03×10^3
	SD	3.78×10^2	2.83×10^2	2.54×10^2	$\mathbf{1.75 \times 10^2}$	1.87×10^2
F27	Mean	3.12×10^3	3.11×10^3	$\mathbf{3.11 \times 10^3}$	3.11×10^3	3.11×10^3
	SD	2.86×10	2.62×10	$\mathbf{2.61 \times 10}$	2.79×10	2.21×10
F28	Mean	3.33×10^3	3.31×10^3	$\mathbf{3.30 \times 10^3}$	3.33×10^3	3.33×10^3
	SD	1.51×10^2	1.47×10^2	$\mathbf{1.48 \times 10^2}$	1.11×10^2	1.36×10^2
F29	Mean	3.27×10^3	3.27×10^3	3.24×10^3	$\mathbf{3.23 \times 10^2}$	3.25×10^3
	SD	6.70×10	6.43×10	5.72×10	$\mathbf{5.74 \times 10}$	6.53×10
F30	Mean	2.19×10^5	3.56×10^5	$\mathbf{9.26 \times 10^4}$	1.37×10^5	2.36×10^5
	SD	3.74×10^5	5.50×10^5	$\mathbf{2.82 \times 10^5}$	3.16×10^5	4.30×10^5

5.3.1. Statistical Significance Test by the Wilcoxon Rank Sum Test

The results of the rank sum test are depicted in Table 7. It is always important to judge the statistical significance of the optimization run in terms of calculated *p*-values. For this reason, the proposed AWOA has been compared with all opponents and results in terms of the *p*-values that are depicted. Bold face entries show that there is a significance difference between optimization runs obtained in AWOA and other opponents. This fact demonstrates the superior performance of AWOA.

Table 6. Results of Benchmark Suite-2 (30D).

Function	Parameter	WOA	OWOA	AWOA	LWOA	CWOA
F1	Mean	1.35×10^9	1.61×10^9	$\mathbf{4.53 \times 10^5}$	2.36×10^9	2.65×10^9
	SD	1.23×10^9	2.06×10^9	$\mathbf{1.71 \times 10^5}$	1.64×10^9	1.50×10^9
F3	Mean	4.85×10^4	4.78×10^4	$\mathbf{3.24 \times 10^2}$	4.83×10^4	4.57×10^4
	SD	1.53×10^4	1.34×10^4	**6.57**	7.64×10^3	1.14×10^4
F4	Mean	5.93×10^2	6.05×10^2	$\mathbf{4.95 \times 10^2}$	7.73×10^2	7.48×10^2
	SD	6.03×10	7.17×10	$\mathbf{2.29 \times 10}$	1.81×10^2	1.40×10^2
F5	Mean	7.60×10^2	7.67×10^2	$\mathbf{7.13 \times 10^2}$	7.68×10^2	7.52×10^2
	SD	5.98×10	5.95×10	$\mathbf{5.24 \times 10}$	4.44×10	4.98×10
F6	Mean	6.66×10^2	6.65×10^2	$\mathbf{6.51 \times 10^2}$	6.58×10^2	6.58×10^2
	SD	1.21×10	1.06×10	**9.99**	1.00×10	9.64
F7	Mean	1.18×10^3	1.16×10^3	$\mathbf{1.09 \times 10^3}$	1.15×10^3	1.14×10^3
	SD	1.09×10^2	8.42×10	$\mathbf{9.02 \times 10}$	8.04×10	6.47×10
F8	Mean	1.01×10^3	1.01×10^3	$\mathbf{9.80 \times 10^2}$	1.01×10^3	1.00×10^3
	SD	4.78×10	4.62×10	$\mathbf{4.87 \times 10}$	2.94×10	4.26×10

Table 6. *Cont.*

Function	Parameter	WOA	OWOA	AWOA	LWOA	CWOA
F9	Mean	7.31×10^3	7.61×10^3	$\mathbf{6.48 \times 10^3}$	6.58×10^3	6.74×10^3
	SD	2.91×10^3	2.61×10^3	$\mathbf{2.08 \times 10^3}$	1.64×10^3	2.04×10^3
F10	Mean	5.93×10^3	6.06×10^3	$\mathbf{4.98 \times 10^3}$	6.81×10^3	6.42×10^3
	SD	7.21×10^2	6.72×10^2	$\mathbf{6.81 \times 10^2}$	7.10×10^2	8.61×10^2
F11	Mean	2.09×10^3	1.80×10^3	$\mathbf{1.27 \times 10^3}$	1.94×10^3	2.08×10^3
	SD	9.83×10^2	7.53×10^2	$\mathbf{5.97 \times 10}$	5.86×10^2	6.85×10^2
F12	Mean	5.19×10^7	5.45×10^7	$\mathbf{4.36 \times 10^6}$	2.38×10^8	1.76×10^8
	SD	5.05×10^7	4.00×10^7	$\mathbf{2.82 \times 10^6}$	2.39×10^8	1.25×10^8
F13	Mean	2.60×10^5	1.58×10^5	$\mathbf{1.46 \times 10^5}$	7.88×10^6	2.13×10^6
	SD	7.92×10^5	1.75×10^5	$\mathbf{1.05 \times 10^5}$	2.55×10^5	1.10×10^7
F14	Mean	4.41×10^5	3.52×10^5	$\mathbf{2.46 \times 10^4}$	4.22×10^5	4.79×10^5
	SD	7.29×10^2	4.31×10^5	$\mathbf{1.56 \times 10^4}$	4.92×10^5	5.11×10^5
F15	Mean	2.78×10^5	2.51×10^6	$\mathbf{7.96 \times 10^4}$	1.67×10^6	4.31×10^6
	SD	5.75×10^5	9.42×10^6	$\mathbf{4.71 \times 10^4}$	2.63×10^6	9.62×10^6
F16	Mean	3.22×10^3	3.25×10^3	$\mathbf{2.87 \times 10^3}$	3.42×10^3	3.43×10^3
	SD	3.71×10^2	4.08×10^2	$\mathbf{3.13 \times 10^2}$	3.97×10^2	3.65×10^2
F17	Mean	2.42×10^3	2.42×10^3	$\mathbf{2.37 \times 10^3}$	2.41×10^3	2.42×10^3
	SD	2.33×10^2	2.43×10^2	$\mathbf{2.62 \times 10^2}$	1.97×10^2	1.81×10^2
F18	Mean	1.74×10^6	2.30×10^6	$\mathbf{2.29 \times 10^5}$	4.18×10^6	2.74×10^6
	SD	1.77×10^6	2.52×10^6	$\mathbf{1.89 \times 10^5}$	3.89×10^6	2.57×10^6
F19	Mean	1.78×10^6	2.25×10^6	$\mathbf{1.22 \times 10^5}$	7.62×10^6	6.83×10^6
	SD	1.64×10^6	2.01×10^6	$\mathbf{7.15 \times 10^4}$	5.58×10^6	1.12×10^7
F20	Mean	2.69×10^3	2.67×10^3	$\mathbf{2.60 \times 10^3}$	2.67×10^3	2.67×10^3
	SD	1.99×10^2	1.81×10^2	$\mathbf{2.11 \times 10^2}$	1.70×10^2	2.02×10^2
F21	Mean	2.54×10^3	2.53×10^3	$\mathbf{2.51 \times 10^3}$	2.53×10^3	2.53×10^3
	SD	5.43×10	5.18×10	$\mathbf{4.98 \times 10^3}$	4.82×10	4.72×10
F22	Mean	6.51×10^3	6.39×10^3	$\mathbf{5.69 \times 10^3}$	6.19×10^3	7.42×10^3
	SD	2.08×10^3	1.93×10^3	$\mathbf{1.90 \times 10^3}$	2.46×10^3	1.59×10^3
F23	Mean	2.97×10^3	2.97×10^3	$\mathbf{2.93 \times 10^3}$	2.94×10^3	2.94×10^3
	SD	8.35×10	7.33×10	$\mathbf{8.35 \times 10}$	6.26×10	5.59×10
F24	Mean	3.12×10^3	3.10×10^3	3.15×10^3	3.09×10^3	$\mathbf{3.08 \times 10^3}$
	SD	7.23×10	7.51×10	8.51×10	5.79×10	$\mathbf{4.63 \times 10}$
F25	Mean	3.01×10^3	3.00×10^3	$\mathbf{2.89 \times 10^3}$	3.07×10^3	3.05×10^3
	SD	5.54×10	5.79×10	$\mathbf{1.62 \times 10}$	4.41×10	4.56×10
F26	Mean	6.63×10^3	6.94×10^3	$\mathbf{6.12 \times 10^3}$	6.60×10^3	6.56×10^3
	SD	9.57×10^2	8.47×10^2	$\mathbf{1.12 \times 10^3}$	8.13×10^2	8.41×10^2
F27	Mean	3.32×10^3	3.32×10^3	$\mathbf{3.27 \times 10^3}$	3.37×10^3	3.35×10^3
	SD	4.56×10	5.12×10	$\mathbf{4.04 \times 10}$	6.38×10	6.36×10
F28	Mean	3.40×10^3	3.42×10^3	$\mathbf{3.22 \times 10^3}$	3.50×10^3	3.50×10^3
	SD	7.82×10	8.98×10	$\mathbf{2.20 \times 10}$	1.13×10^2	9.80×10
F29	Mean	4.63×10^3	4.58×10^3	$\mathbf{4.06 \times 10^3}$	4.67×10^3	4.57×10^3
	SD	3.07×10^2	3.11×10^2	$\mathbf{2.77 \times 10^2}$	3.56×10^2	3.82×10^2
F30	Mean	8.90×10^6	9.96×10^6	$\mathbf{4.28 \times 10^5}$	2.54×10^7	2.38×10^7
	SD	5.90×10^6	6.80×10^6	$\mathbf{1.92 \times 10^5}$	2.30×10^7	1.83×10^7

5.3.2. Boxplot Analysis

Boxplot analysis for 10D functions are performed for 20 independent runs of objective function values. This analysis is depicted in Figures 9 and 10. From these boxplots, it is easily to state that the results obtained from the optimization process acquire an optimal Inter Quartile Range and low mean values. For showcasing the efficacy of the proposed AWOA, all the optimal entries of mean values are depicted with an oval shape in boxplots.

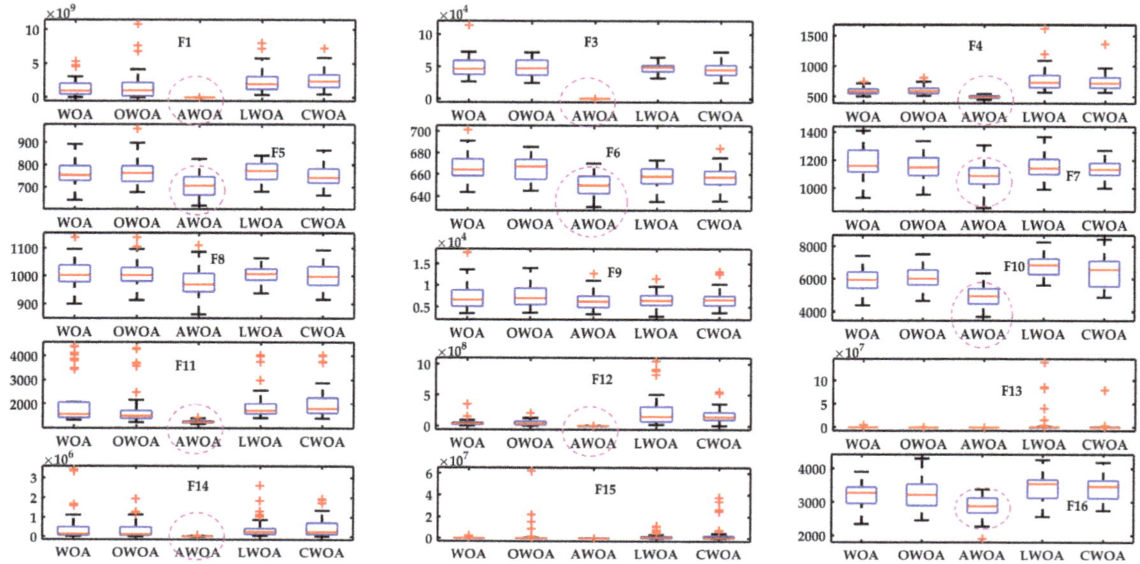

Figure 9. Boxplot analysis of the 10D functions of Benchmark Suite 2.

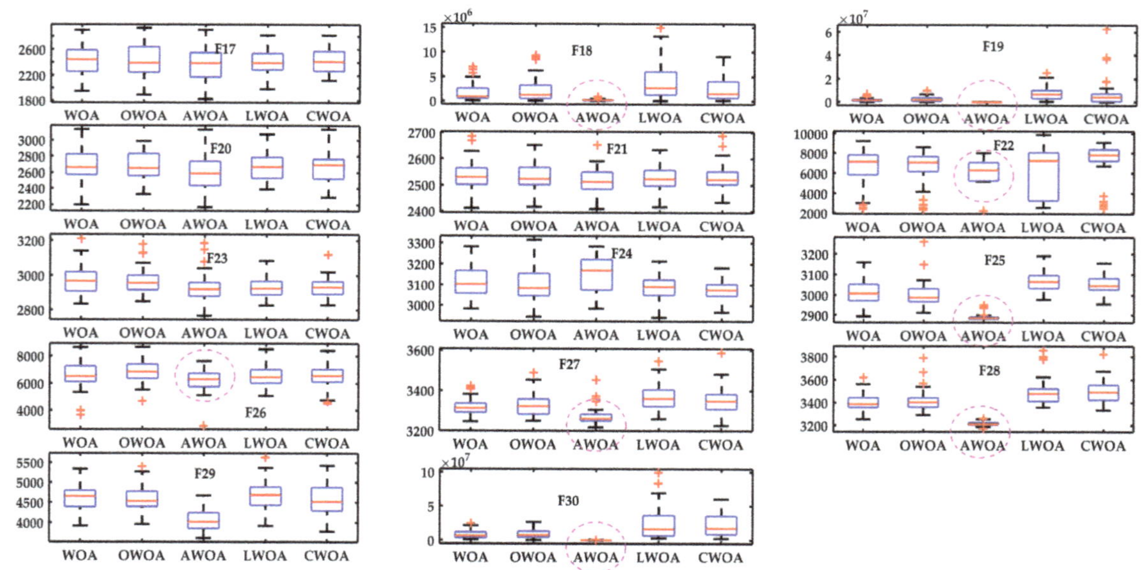

Figure 10. Boxplot analysis of the remaining 10D functions of Benchmark Suite 2.

5.4. Results of the Analysis of 30D Problems

The results of the proposed AWOA, along with other variants of WOA, are depicted in terms of statistical attributes of independent 51 runs in Table 6. From the results, it is clearly evident that except for F24, the proposed AWOA provides optimal results as compared to other opponents. Mean values of objective functions and standard deviation of the objective functions obtained from independent runs are shown in bold face.

Table 7. Results of the rank sum test on Benchmark Suite-2 (10D).

Function	WOA	OWOA	LWOA	CWOA
F1	2.58×10^{-1}	3.99×10^{-1}	3.30×10^{-18}	3.30×10^{-18}
F3	**3.30×10^{-18}**	**3.30×10^{-18}**	**3.30×10^{-18}**	**3.30×10^{-18}**
F4	**4.20×10^{-9}**	**2.99×10^{-13}**	**3.00×10^{-15}**	**4.73×10^{-16}**
F5	**1.40×10^{-4}**	**1.08×10^{-2}**	**3.92×10^{-3}**	**9.97×10^{-2}**
F6	**1.56×10^{-13}**	**5.13×10^{-15}**	**6.26×10^{-13}**	**9.11×10^{-12}**
F7	8.04×10^{-6}	1.73×10^{-5}	1.23×10^{-8}	3.99×10^{-2}
F8	3.22×10^{-2}	1.29×10^{-1}	3.15×10^{-1}	4.45×10^{-1}
F9	2.57×10^{-13}	4.90×10^{-13}	8.00×10^{-13}	4.51×10^{-12}
F10	5.59×10^{-3}	5.15×10^{-2}	5.73×10^{-2}	4.70×10^{-1}
F11	1.35×10^{-3}	1.56×10^{-4}	4.44×10^{-10}	1.32×10^{-10}
F12	**1.47×10^{-14}**	**2.33×10^{-10}**	**2.33×10^{-13}**	**1.74×10^{-12}**
F13	**4.94×10^{-3}**	2.90×10^{-1}	**9.03×10^{-5}**	**1.06×10^{-2}**
F14	**4.09×10^{-3}**	**1.02×10^{-3}**	**4.20×10^{-4}**	2.34×10^{-1}
F15	**9.26×10^{-13}**	**5.40×10^{-13}**	**3.17×10^{-15}**	**1.66×10^{-15}**
F16	6.02×10^{-1}	1.72×10^{-1}	8.30×10^{-2}	6.06×10^{-1}
F17	5.38×10^{-1}	2.18×10^{-1}	7.89×10^{-1}	4.66×10^{-1}
F18	5.83×10^{-1}	8.30×10^{-1}	3.73×10^{-1}	5.47×10^{-1}
F19	2.47×10^{-8}	5.71×10^{-8}	2.61×10^{-1}	6.57×10^{-2}
F20	1.20×10^{-5}	1.14×10^{-6}	2.47×10^{-7}	4.22×10^{-8}
F21	7.39×10^{-2}	2.55×10^{-1}	2.21×10^{-1}	2.50×10^{-1}
F22	**1.60×10^{-6}**	**6.88×10^{-6}**	**6.60×10^{-7}**	**9.26×10^{-11}**
F23	**5.37×10^{-3}**	5.73×10^{-2}	8.36×10^{-1}	1.29×10^{-1}
F24	6.83×10^{-1}	2.87×10^{-1}	1.08×10^{-1}	1.54×10^{-2}
F25	**2.01×10^{-5}**	**3.43×10^{-4}**	**1.32×10^{-3}**	**1.02×10^{-2}**
F26	**1.17×10^{-3}**	**2.60×10^{-3}**	1.43×10^{-1}	3.00×10^{-1}
F27	**2.58×10^{-2}**	**3.17×10^{-2}**	1.30×10^{-1}	9.83×10^{-2}
F28	6.06×10^{-1}	3.32×10^{-1}	**1.29×10^{-3}**	**2.54×10^{-3}**
F29	**4.68×10^{-2}**	**3.22×10^{-2}**	2.47×10^{-1}	9.25×10^{-1}
F30	**4.70×10^{-6}**	**1.49×10^{-5}**	**2.23×10^{-6}**	**1.65×10^{-6}**

The results of the rank sum test are depicted in Table 8. It is always important to judge the statistical significance of the optimization run in terms of calculated p-values. For this reason, the proposed AWOA was compared with all opponents and the results in terms of p-values are depicted. Bold face entries show that there is a significance difference between optimization runs obtained in AWOA and other opponent, as the obtained p-values are less than 0.05. We observe that for the majority of the functions, calculated p-values are less than 0.05. Along with the optimal mean and standard deviation values, p-values indicated that the proposed AWOA outperforms. In addition to these analyses, a boxplot analysis was performed of the proposed AWOA with other opponents, as depicted in Figures 11 and 12. From these figures, it is easy to learn that the IQR and mean values are very competitive and optimal in almost all cases for 30-dimension problems. Inspecting the convergence curves for some of the functions, such as unimodal functions F1 and F3 and for some other multimodal and hybrid functions, as depicted in Figure 13.

Table 8. Results of the rank sum test on Benchmark Suite-2 (30D).

Function	WOA	OWOA	LWOA	CWOA
F1	**3.30×10^{-18}**	**3.30×10^{-18}**	**3.30×10^{-18}**	**3.30×10^{-18}**
F3	**3.30×10^{-18}**	**3.30×10^{-18}**	**3.30×10^{-18}**	**3.30×10^{-18}**
F4	**1.05×10^{-16}**	**1.39×10^{-16}**	**3.30×10^{-18}**	**3.30×10^{-18}**
F5	**1.13×10^{-4}**	**1.06×10^{-5}**	**7.07×10^{-7}**	**3.17×10^{-4}**
F6	**6.03×10^{-9}**	**5.14×10^{-9}**	**7.08×10^{-4}**	**1.17×10^{-3}**
F7	**3.74×10^{-5}**	**3.01×10^{-4}**	**8.80×10^{-4}**	**3.23×10^{-3}**
F8	**2.96×10^{-3}**	**3.68×10^{-3}**	**3.99×10^{-4}**	1.28×10^{-2}
F9	2.34×10^{-1}	**3.17×10^{-2}**	4.66×10^{-1}	4.34×10^{-1}
F10	**1.09×10^{-8}**	**1.79×10^{-10}**	**2.43×10^{-16}**	**3.08×10^{-12}**
F11	**3.78×10^{-17}**	**9.65×10^{-16}**	**3.72×10^{-18}**	**3.72×10^{-18}**
F12	**1.42×10^{-17}**	**1.27×10^{-17}**	**3.30×10^{-18}**	**4.70×10^{-18}**
F13	5.83×10^{-1}	7.53×10^{-1}	**1.63×10^{-14}**	**2.84×10^{-13}**
F14	**2.56×10^{-15}**	**1.41×10^{-15}**	**8.44×10^{-18}**	**5.41×10^{-15}**
F15	7.39×10^{-2}	**8.19×10^{-4}**	**7.30×10^{-14}**	**1.34×10^{-13}**
F16	**2.30×10^{-6}**	**6.88×10^{-6}**	**1.64×10^{-9}**	1.26×10^{-10}
F17	3.29×10^{-1}	4.58×10^{-1}	4.22×10^{-1}	3.00×10^{-1}
F18	**4.30×10^{-12}**	**1.07×10^{-12}**	**3.72×10^{-15}**	**4.15×10^{-14}**
F19	**1.95×10^{-16}**	**1.34×10^{-15}**	**3.72×10^{-18}**	**1.72×10^{-14}**
F20	**3.80×10^{-2}**	9.17×10^{-2}	1.10×10^{-1}	1.30×10^{-1}
F21	**3.44×10^{-2}**	1.13×10^{-1}	1.99×10^{-1}	1.45×10^{-1}
F22	**5.82×10^{-4}**	**1.07×10^{-3}**	**5.71×10^{-3}**	**5.50×10^{-10}**
F23	**8.53×10^{-3}**	**9.23×10^{-3}**	4.14×10^{-1}	2.44×10^{-1}
F24	**3.86×10^{-2}**	**3.30×10^{-3}**	**2.26×10^{-4}**	**1.58×10^{-5}**
F25	**1.27×10^{-17}**	**8.44×10^{-18}**	**3.30×10^{-18}**	**3.30×10^{-18}**
F26	**2.67×10^{-2}**	**1.56×10^{-4}**	7.72×10^{-2}	**4.26×10^{-2}**
F27	**1.14×10^{-8}**	**6.53×10^{-9}**	**4.60×10^{-14}**	**3.56×10^{-12}**
F28	**5.61×10^{-18}**	**3.30×10^{-18}**	**3.30×10^{-18}**	**3.30×10^{-18}**
F29	**3.64×10^{-13}**	**5.98×10^{-12}**	**9.26×10^{-13}**	**5.74×10^{-10}**
F30	**3.30×10^{-18}**	**1.27×10^{-17}**	**3.30×10^{-18}**	**3.30×10^{-18}**

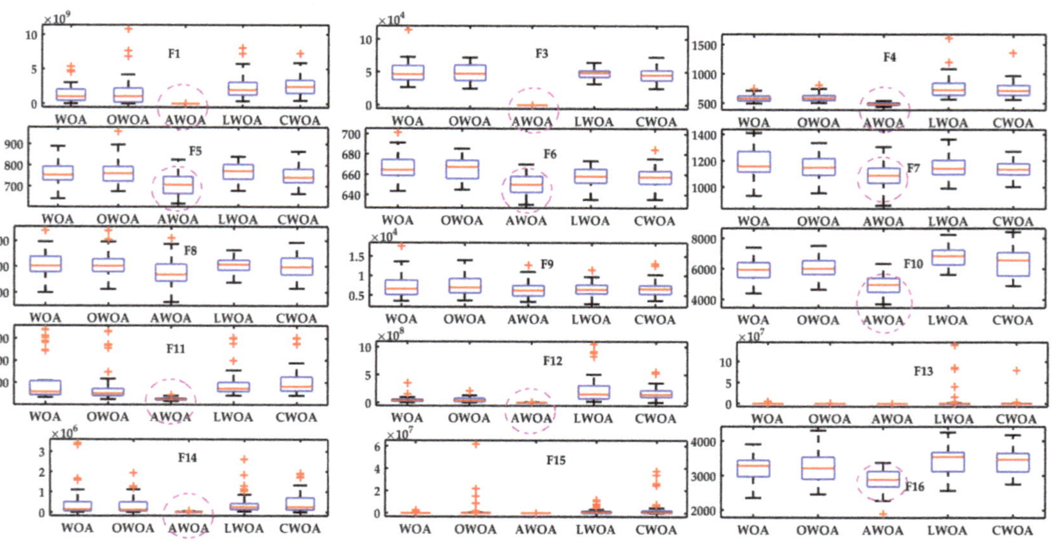

Figure 11. Boxplot analysis of the 30D functions of Benchmark Suite 2.

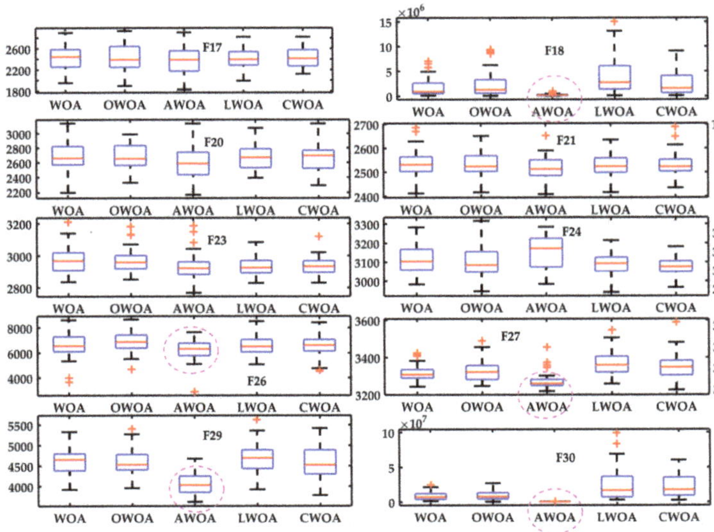

Figure 12. Boxplot analysis of the remaining 30D functions of Benchmark Suite 2.

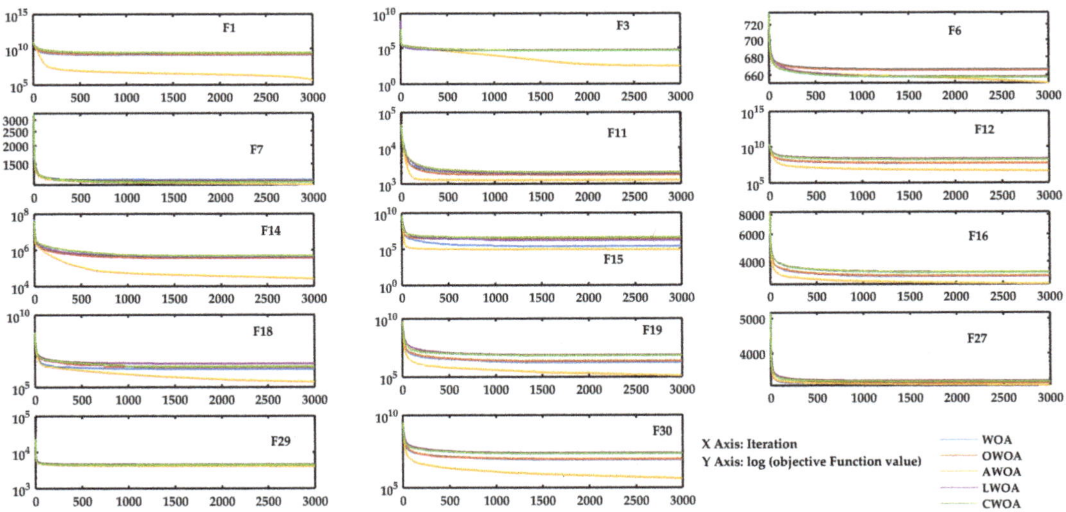

Figure 13. Convergence property analysis of some 30D functions of Benchmark Suite 2.

5.5. Comparison with Other Algorithms

To validate the efficacy of the proposed variant, a fair comparison on CEC 2017 criteria is executed. The optimization results of the proposed variant along with some contemporary and classical optimizers are reported in Table 9. The competitive algorithms are Moth flame optimization (MFO) [15], Sine cosine algorithm [53], PSO [54] and Flower pollination Algorithm [55]. It can be easily observed that the results of our proposed variant are competitive for almost all the functions.

Table 9. Comparison of AWOA with other algorithms for 30D.

	Algorithm				
Function	**SCA**	**PSO**	**MFO**	**FPA**	**AWOA**
F1	1.27×10^{10}	5.56×10^{9}	1.31×10^{10}	1.07×10^{8}	4.53×10^{5}
F3	3.67×10^{4}	1.33×10^{5}	9.48×10^{4}	1.10×10^{5}	3.24×10^{2}
F4	9.90×10^{2}	5.09×10^{2}	9.70×10^{2}	5.79×10^{2}	4.95×10^{2}
F5	2.75×10^{2}	3.04×10^{2}	2.20×10^{2}	8.06×10^{2}	7.13×10^{2}
F6	5.00×10^{1}	5.60×10^{1}	4.00×10^{1}	6.69×10^{2}	6.51×10^{2}
F7	4.30×10^{2}	4.30×10^{2}	4.60×10^{2}	1.33×10^{3}	1.09×10^{3}
F8	2.50×10^{2}	2.90×10^{2}	2.20×10^{2}	1.07×10^{3}	9.80×10^{2}
F9	4.74×10^{3}	5.70×10^{3}	6.57×10^{3}	1.31×10^{4}	6.48×10^{3}
F10	7.13×10^{3}	8.29×10^{3}	4.34×10^{3}	6.20×10^{3}	4.98×10^{3}
F11	9.70×10^{2}	2.54×10^{3}	5.30×10^{3}	1.54×10^{3}	1.27×10^{3}
F12	1.18×10^{9}	6.47×10^{8}	3.81×10^{8}	4.84×10^{7}	4.36×10^{6}
F13	3.96×10^{8}	1.93×10^{8}	9.52×10^{7}	2.61×10^{6}	1.46×10^{5}
F14	1.53×10^{5}	1.11×10^{6}	2.32×10^{5}	1.66×10^{5}	2.46×10^{4}
F15	1.62×10^{7}	3.91×10^{7}	5.21×10^{4}	4.22×10^{5}	7.96×10^{4}
F16	2.04×10^{3}	2.35×10^{3}	1.55×10^{3}	3.46×10^{3}	2.87×10^{3}
F17	7.00×10^{2}	9.60×10^{2}	8.80×10^{2}	2.71×10^{3}	2.37×10^{3}
F18	3.16×10^{6}	7.90×10^{6}	3.19×10^{6}	3.17×10^{6}	2.29×10^{5}
F19	2.37×10^{7}	5.17×10^{7}	2.42×10^{7}	2.30×10^{6}	1.22×10^{5}
F20	6.10×10^{2}	1.02×10^{3}	6.80×10^{2}	2.64×10^{3}	2.60×10^{3}
F21	4.60×10^{2}	5.00×10^{2}	4.10×10^{2}	2.57×10^{3}	2.51×10^{3}
F22	5.78×10^{3}	4.64×10^{3}	4.27×10^{3}	6.11×10^{3}	5.69×10^{3}
F23	6.90×10^{3}	7.80×10^{2}	5.30×10^{2}	3.00×10^{3}	2.93×10^{3}
F24	7.60×10^{2}	8.10×10^{2}	5.90×10^{2}	3.13×10^{3}	3.15×10^{3}
F25	7.10×10^{2}	7.10×10^{2}	8.30×10^{2}	2.97×10^{3}	2.89×10^{3}
F26	4.34×10^{3}	4.05×10^{3}	3.26×10^{3}	7.63×10^{3}	6.12×10^{3}
F27	7.00×10^{2}	6.60×10^{2}	5.60×10^{2}	3.34×10^{3}	3.27×10^{3}
F28	1.00×10^{3}	8.40×10^{2}	1.76×10^{3}	3.35×10^{3}	3.22×10^{3}
F29	1.73×10^{3}	2.02×10^{3}	1.25×10^{3}	4.64×10^{3}	4.06×10^{3}
F30	6.69×10^{7}	4.85×10^{7}	1.02×10^{6}	6.79×10^{6}	4.28×10^{5}

6. Applications of AWOA in Engineering Test Problems

6.1. Model Order Reduction

In control system engineering, most of the linear time invariant systems are of a higher order, and thus, difficult to analyze. This problem has been solved using the reduced model order technique, which is easy to use and less complex in comparison to earlier control paradigm techniques. Nature-inspired optimization algorithms have proved to be an efficient tool in this field, as they help to minimize the integral square of lower-order systems. This approach was first introduced in [56] followed by [39,57,58] and many more. These works advocate the efficacy of optimization algorithm in solving the reduced model order technique, as these reduce the complexity, computation time and cost of the reducing process. For testing the applicability of AWOA on some real-world problems, we have considered the Model Order Reduction problem in this section. In MOR, large complex systems with known transfer functions are converted with the help of an optimization application to the reduced order system. The following are the steps of the conversion:

1. Consider a large complex system with a higher order and obtain the step response of the system. Stack the response in the form of a numerical array.
2. Construct a second-order system with the help of some unknown variables that are depicted in the following equation. Furthermore, obtain the step response of the system and stack those numbers in a numerical array.
3. Construct a transfer function that minimizes the error function, preferably the Integral Square Error (ISE) criterion.

6.1.1. Problem Formulation

In this technique, a transfer function given by $X(t) : u \rightarrow v$ of a higher order is reduced, in function $X(t) : u \rightarrow \tilde{v}$ of a lower order, without affecting the input $u(x)$; the output is $\tilde{v}(x) \approx v(x)$. The integral error defined by the following equation is minimized in the process using the optimization algorithm:

$$\mathrm{IE} = \int_{0}^{\infty} [v(x) - \tilde{v}(x)]^2 dx \tag{17}$$

where $X(t)$ is a transfer function of any Single Input and Single Output system defined by:

$$X(s) = \frac{a_0 + a_1 t + a_2 t^2 + \ldots + a_m t^m}{b_0 + b_1 t + b_2 t^2 + \ldots + b_n t^n} \tag{18}$$

For a reduced order system, $X(s)'$ can be given by:

$$X(t)' = \frac{a'_0 + a'_1 t + a'_2 t^2 + \ldots + a'_{m_r} t^{m_r}}{b'_0 + b'_1 t + b'_2 t^2 + \ldots + b'_{n_r} t^{n_r}} \tag{19}$$

where $(n_r \geq m_r, m_r, n_r \in I)$. In this study, we calculate the value of coefficients of the numerator and denominator of a reduced order system defined in Equation (21) while minimizing the error. To establish the efficiency of our proposed variant, we have reported two numerical examples.

6.1.2. Numerical Examples and Discussions

- Function 1

$$X(s) = \frac{(s^3 + 7s^2 + 24s + 24)}{(s^4 + 10s^3 + 35s^2 + 50s + 24)} \tag{20}$$

- Function 2

$$X(s) = \frac{(s + 4)}{(s^4 + 19s^3 + 113s^2 + 245s + 150)} \tag{21}$$

The results of the optimization process by depicting the values of time domain specifications, namely rise time and settling time for both functions, are exhibited in Table 10. Furthermore, the convergence proofs of the algorithm on both functions are depicted in Figures 14 and 15. Errors in the time domain specifications as compared to the original system are depicted in Table 11.

Table 10. Simulated models for different WOA variants and time domain specifications.

Function	Function 1		Function 2	
Parameters	Rise Time	Settling Time	Rise Time	Settling Time
Original	2.1398	4.8603	2.2985	4.9724
AWOA	2.1471	4.8388	2.2649	4.3923
WOA	2.0838	4.6762	3.1631	6.6672
OWOA	2.4744	5.4009	3.1783	6.689
LWOA	2.1002	4.7188	2.4078	5.1828
CWOA	2.45	4.965	3.1755	6.68

Table 11. Error analysis of MOR results on both functions.

Parameter	% Error Function 1		% Error Function 2	
Time	Rise Time	Settling Time	Rise Time	Settling Time
AWOA	**0.341**	**0.442**	**1.462**	11.666
WOA	2.617	3.788	37.616	34.084
OWOA	15.637	11.123	38.277	34.523
LWOA	1.851	2.911	4.755	4.231
CWOA	14.497	2.154	38.155	34.342

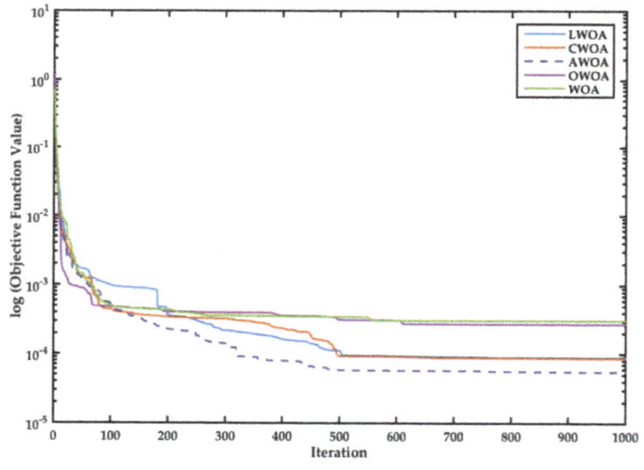

Figure 14. Results of MOR for function 1.

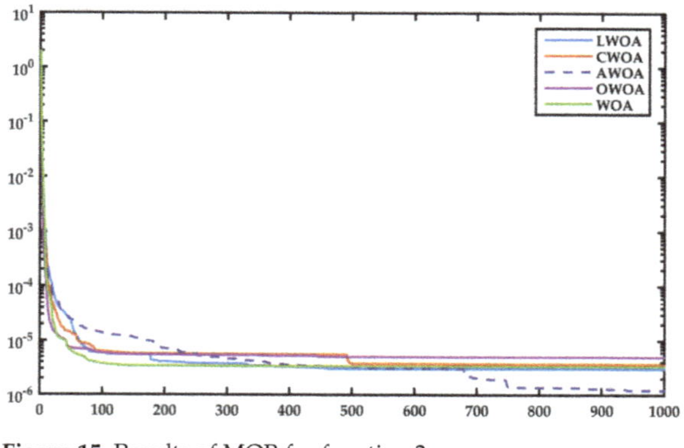

Figure 15. Results of MOR for function 2.

From these analyses, it is quite evident that MOR performed by AWOA leads to a configuration of the system that follows the time domain specifications of the original system quite closely. In addition to that, the error in objective function values are also optimal in the case of AWOA.

6.2. Frequency-Modulated Sound Wave Parameter Estimation Problem

This problem has been taken in many approaches to benchmark the applicability of different optimizers. This problem was included in the 2011 Congress on Evolutionary computation competition for testing different evolutionary optimization algorithms on real problems [59]. This problem is a six-dimensional problem, where the parameters of a sound wave are estimated in such a manner that it should be matched with the target wave.

The mathematical representation of this problem can be given as:

$$K = (\alpha_1, \delta_1, \alpha_2, \delta_2, \alpha_3, \delta_3) \tag{22}$$

The equations of the predicted sound wave and target sound wave are as follows:

$$J(t) = \alpha_1.\sin(\delta_1.t.\theta + \alpha_2.\sin(\delta_2.t.\theta + \alpha_3.\sin(\delta_3.t.\theta))) \tag{23}$$

$$J_0(t) = (1.0).\sin((5.0).t.\theta - (1.5).\sin((4.8).t.\theta + (2.0).\sin((4.9)t.\theta))) \tag{24}$$

$$Min\ f(\overrightarrow{K}) = \sum_{t=0}^{100} (J(t) - J_0(t))^2 \tag{25}$$

The results of this design problem are shown in terms of different analyses that include the boxplot and convergence property, which are obtained from 20 independent runs. The Figure 16 shows this analysis. A comparison of the performance on the basis of error in the objective function values is depicted in Figure 17. Here, boxplot axis entry 1, 2, 3, 4 and 5 show LWOA, CWOA, proposed AWOA, OWOA and WOA, respectively.

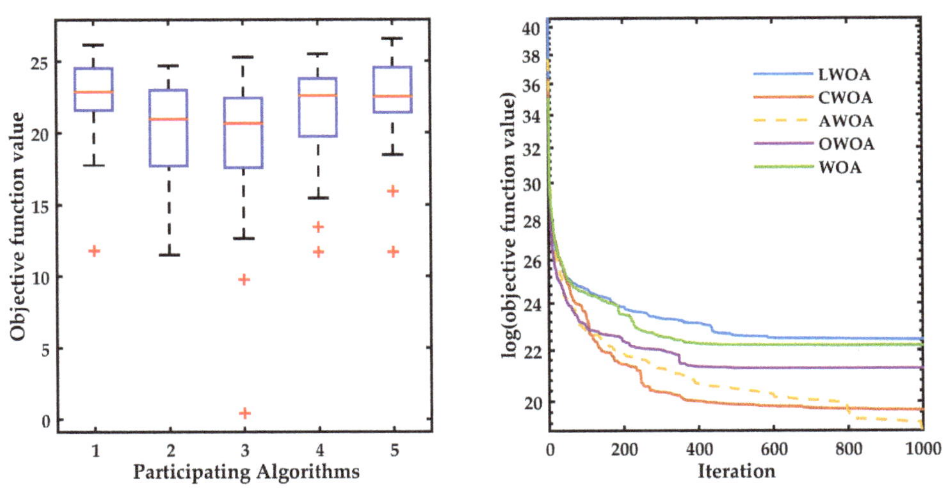

Figure 16. Boxplot and Convergence Property analysis for the FM problem.

6.3. PID Control of DC Motors

In today's machinery era, DC motors are used in various fields such as the textile industry, rolling mills, electric vehicles and robotics. Among the various controllers available for DC motors, the Proportional Integral Derivative (PID) is the most widely used and proved its efficiency as an accurate result provider without disturbing the steady state error and overshoot phenomena [60]. With this controller, we also needed an efficient tuning method to control the speed and other parameters of DC motors. In recent years, some researchers have explored the meta-heuristic algorithm in tuning of different types of PID controllers. In [61], the authors presented a comparative study between simulated annealing, particle swarm optimization and genetic algorithm. Stochastic fractal search has been applied to the DC motor problem in [62]. The sine cosine algorithm is also used in the determination of optimal parameters of the PID controller of DC motors in [20]. In [63], the authors proposed the chaotic atom search optimization for optimal tuning of the PID controller of DC motors with a fractional order. A hybridized version of foraging optimization and simulated annealing to solve the same problem was reported in [64].

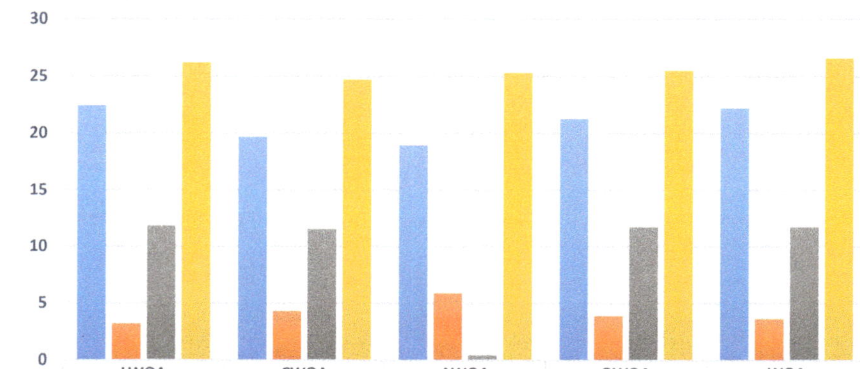

	LWOA	CWOA	AWOA	OWOA	WOA
Mean	22.44294433	19.67957724	18.94163348	21.27588287	22.19529618
SD	3.166458724	4.289888794	5.855781317	3.896087392	3.624564023
Min	11.76954173	11.49001778	0.424191058	11.68272924	11.6882669
Max	26.16739527	24.69547923	25.28085635	25.49910482	26.57275953

Figure 17. Comparative results of different statistical measures of independent runs.

6.3.1. Mathematical Model of DC Motors

The DC motor problem used here is a specific type of DC motor which controlled its speed through input voltage or change in current. In DC motors, the applied voltage $f_b(t)$ is directly proportional to the angular speed $\beta(t) = \frac{d\alpha(t)}{dt}$, while the flux is constant, i.e.:

$$f_b(t) = H_b \frac{d\alpha(t)}{dt} = H_b \beta(t) \tag{26}$$

The initial voltage of armature $f_a(t)$ satisfies the following differential equation:

$$f_b(t) = P_a \frac{dr_a(t)}{dt} + K_a r_a(t) + f_a(t) \tag{27}$$

The motor torque (due to various friction) developed in the process (neglecting the disturbance torque) is given by:

$$\tau(t) = L \frac{d\beta(t)}{dt} + T\beta(t) = H_m r_a(t) \tag{28}$$

Taking the Laplace transform of these equations and assuming all the initial condition to zero, we get:

$$F_b(s) = H_b X(s) \tag{29}$$

$$F_a(s) = (P_a s + K_a) R_a(s) + F_b(s) \tag{30}$$

$$\Omega(s) = (Ls + T) X(s) = H_m R_a(s) \tag{31}$$

On simplifying these equations, open loop transfer function of DC motor can be given as:

$$\frac{X(s)}{F_a(s)} = \frac{H_m}{(P_a s + K_a)(Ls + T) + H_b H_m} \tag{32}$$

6.3.2. Results and Discussion

All the parameters and constant values considered in this experiment are given in Table 12. The simulation results for tuning the PID controller for plant DC motors are depicted in Table 13. First column entries show the plant and controller combined realization as a closed system and the other two entries show specification of time domain simulation conducted when the system is subjected to step input.

After a careful observation, it is concluded that the closed loop system realized with the proposed AWOA possesses optimal settling and rise time that itself depicts a fast transient response of the system. Although the comparative analysis of other algorithms also depicts very competitive values of these times, the response and convergence process of AWOA are swift as compared to other opponents. The boxplot analysis and convergence property analysis are shown in Figure 18. The boxplot shows the comparison of the optimization results when the optimization is run 20 independent times. The X axis shows the AWOA, CWOA, LWOA, OWOA and WOA algorithms. The optimal entries of settling time and rise time are in bold face to showcase the efficacy of the AWOA. The step response of these controllers has been shown in Figure 19.

Table 12. Various parameters of DC motors.

Motor Parameter	Symbol	Value
Resistance	K_a	0.4 ω
Inductance	P_a	2.7 H
Initial torque of motor	L	0.0004 kg m^2
constant of friction in motor	T	0.0022 Nm s/rad^2
Motor torque	H_m	0.015 Nm/A
Emf constant	H_b	0.05 V s/rad

Table 13. Comparison of AWOA with other algorithms for the DC motor controller design problem.

Algorithm	DC Motor Closed Loop Transfer Function	Settling Time	Rise Time
OWOA	$\frac{0.03684s^2+0.2999s+0.1358}{0.00108s^3+0.04438s^2+0.3095s+0.1358}$	0.0994	0.0603
WOA	$\frac{0.03623s^2+0.3s+0.106}{0.00108s^3+0.04377s^2+0.3095s+0.106}$	0.0997	0.0609
CWOA	$\frac{0.03703s^2+0.3s+0.1447}{0.00108s^3+0.04457s^2+0.3095s+0.1447}$	0.0993	0.0602
LWOA	$\frac{0.03664s^2+0.3s+0.1255}{0.00108s^3+0.04418s^2+0.3095s+0.1255}$	0.0995	0.0605
AWOA	$\frac{0.03703s^2+0.3s+0.1447}{0.00108s^3+0.04457s^2+0.3095s+0.1447}$	**0.0991**	**0.0598**

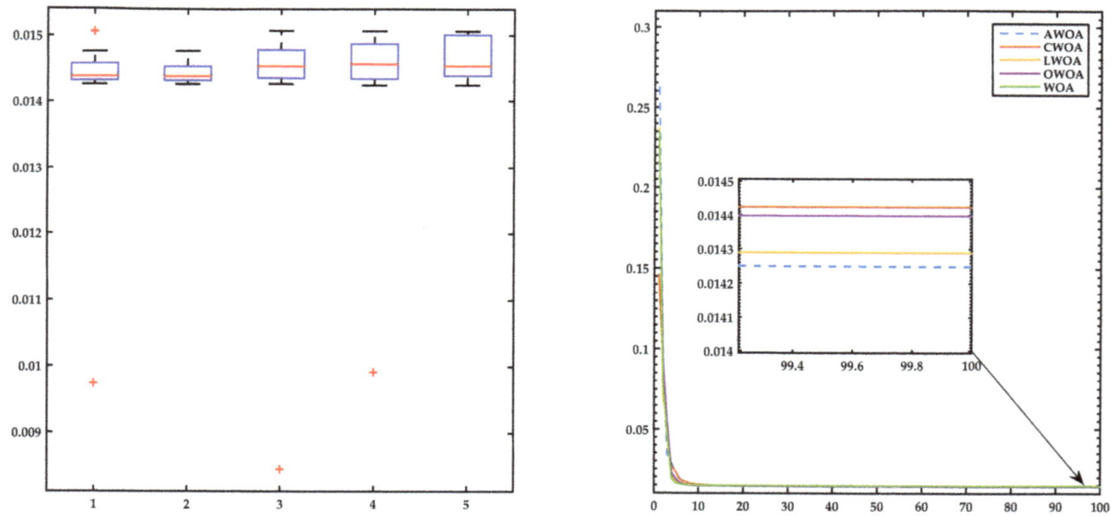

Figure 18. Comparative results of different controllers for DC motors.

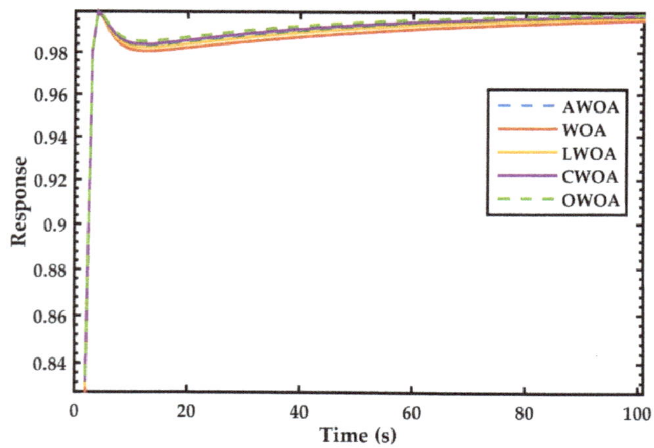

Figure 19. Step Response Analysis of Different Controllers.

7. Conclusions

This paper is a proposal of a new variant of WOA. The singing behavior of whales is mimicked with the help of opposition-based learning in the initialization phase and Cauchy mutation in the position update phase. The following are the major conclusions drawn from this study:

- The proposed AWOA was validated on two benchmark suits (conventional and CEC 2017 functions). These benchmark suits comprise mathematical functions of distinct nature (unimodal, multimodal, hybrid and composite). We have observed that for the majority of the functions, AWOA shows promising results. It is also observed that the performance of AWOA is competitive with other algorithms.
- The statistical significance of the obtained results is verified with the help of a boxplot analysis and Wilcoxon rank sum test. It is observed that boxplots are narrow for the proposed AWOA and the p-values are less than 0.05. These results show that the proposed variant exhibits better exploration and exploitation capabilities, and with these results, one can easily see the positive implications of the proposed modifications.

- The proposed variant is also tested for challenging engineering design problems. The first problem is the model order reduction of a complex control system into subsequent reduced order realizations. For this problem, AWOA shows promising results as compared to WOA. As a second problem, the frequency-modulated sound wave parameter estimation problem was addressed. The performance of the proposed AWOA is competitive with contemporary variants of WOA. In addition to that, the application of AWOA was reported for tuning the PID controller of the DC motor control system. All these applications indicate that the modifications suggested for AWOA are quite meaningful and help the algorithm find global optima in an effective way.

The proposed AWOA can be applied to various other engineering design problem, such as network reconfiguration, solar cell parameter extraction and regulator design. These problems will be the focus of future research.

Author Contributions: Formal analysis, K.A.A.; Funding acquisition, K.A.A.; Investigation, K.A.A.; Methodology, S.S. and A.S.; Project administration, A.W.M.; Software, K.M.S.; Supervision, A.S. and A.W.M.; Validation, K.M.S.; Visualization, K.M.S.; Writing—original draft, S.S. and A.S.; Writing—review & editing, S.S. and A.S. All authors have read and agreed to the published version of the manuscript.

Funding: The research is funded by Researchers Supporting Program at King Saud University, (RSP-2021/305).

Acknowledgments: The authors present their appreciation to King Saud University for funding the publication of this research through Researchers Supporting Program (RSP-2021/305), King Saud University, Riyadh, Saudi Arabia.

Conflicts of Interest: The authors declare no conflict of interest.

References

1. Yang, X.S. *Nature-Inspired Metaheuristic Algorithms*; Luniver Press: Beckington, UK, 2010.
2. Glover, F. Future paths for integer programming and links to artificial intelligence. *Comput. Oper. Res.* **1986**, *13*, 533–549. [CrossRef]
3. Holland, J.H. Genetic algorithms. *Sci. Am.* **1992**, *267*, 66–73. [CrossRef]
4. Rechenberg, I. Evolution strategy: Nature's way of optimization. In *Optimization: Methods and Applications, Possibilities and Limitations*; Springer: Berlin/Heidelberg, Germany, 1989; pp. 106–126.
5. Dorigo, M.; Di Caro, G. Ant colony optimization: A new meta-heuristic. In Proceedings of the 1999 Congress on Evolutionary Computation-CEC99 (Cat. No. 99TH8406), IEEE, Washington, DC, USA, 6–9 July 1999; Volume 2, pp. 1470–1477.
6. Basturk, B. An artificial bee colony (ABC) algorithm for numeric function optimization. In Proceedings of the IEEE Swarm Intelligence Symposium, Indianapolis, IN, USA, 12–14 May 2006.
7. Yang, X.S. A new metaheuristic bat-inspired algorithm. In *Nature Inspired Cooperative Strategies for Optimization (NICSO 2010)*; Springer: Berlin/Heidelberg, Germany, 2010; pp. 65–74.
8. Yang, X.S.; Deb, S. Cuckoo search via Lévy flights. In Proceedings of the 2009 World Congress on Nature & Biologically Inspired Computing (NaBIC), Coimbatore, India, 9–11 December 2009; pp. 210–214.
9. Gandomi, A.H.; Alavi, A.H. Krill herd: A new bio-inspired optimization algorithm. *Commun. Nonlinear Sci. Numer. Simul.* **2012**, *17*, 4831–4845. [CrossRef]
10. Yang, X.S. Firefly algorithm, stochastic test functions and design optimisation. *Int. J. Bio-Inspir. Comput.* **2010**, *2*, 78–84. [CrossRef]
11. Mirjalili, S.; Mirjalili, S.M.; Lewis, A. Grey wolf optimizer. *Adv. Eng. Softw.* **2014**, *69*, 46–61. [CrossRef]
12. Das, S.; Biswas, A.; Dasgupta, S.; Abraham, A. Bacterial foraging optimization algorithm: Theoretical foundations, analysis, and applications. In *Foundations of Computational Intelligence*; Springer: Berlin/Heidelberg, Germany, 2009; Volume 3, pp. 23–55.
13. James, J.; Li, V.O. A social spider algorithm for global optimization. *Appl. Soft Comput.* **2015**, *30*, 614–627.
14. Chu, S.C.; Tsai, P.W.; Pan, J.S. Cat swarm optimization. In *Pacific Rim International Conference on Artificial Intelligence*; Springer: Berlin/Heidelberg, Germany, 2006; pp. 854–858.
15. Mirjalili, S. Moth-flame optimization algorithm: A novel nature-inspired heuristic paradigm. *Knowl.-Based Syst.* **2015**, *89*, 228–249. [CrossRef]
16. Mirjalili, S. The ant lion optimizer. *Adv. Eng. Softw.* **2015**, *83*, 80–98. [CrossRef]
17. Askarzadeh, A. A novel metaheuristic method for solving constrained engineering optimization problems: Crow search algorithm. *Comput. Struct.* **2016**, *169*, 1–12. [CrossRef]

18. Saremi, S.; Mirjalili, S.; Lewis, A. Grasshopper optimisation algorithm: Theory and application. *Adv. Eng. Softw.* **2017**, *105*, 30–47. [CrossRef]
19. Mohamed, A.W.; Hadi, A.A.; Mohamed, A.K. Gaining-sharing knowledge based algorithm for solving optimization problems: A novel nature-inspired algorithm. *Int. J. Mach. Learn. Cybern.* **2020**, *11*, 1501–1529. [CrossRef]
20. Agarwal, J.; Parmar, G.; Gupta, R. Application of sine cosine algorithm in optimal control of DC motor and robustness analysis. *Wulfenia J.* **2017**, *24*, 77–95.
21. Agrawal, P.; Ganesh, T.; Mohamed, A.W. Chaotic gaining sharing knowledge-based optimization algorithm: An improved metaheuristic algorithm for feature selection. *Soft Comput.* **2021**, *25*, 9505–9528. [CrossRef]
22. Agrawal, P.; Ganesh, T.; Mohamed, A.W. A novel binary gaining–sharing knowledge-based optimization algorithm for feature selection. *Neural Comput. Appl.* **2021**, *33*, 5989–6008. [CrossRef]
23. Agrawal, P.; Ganesh, T.; Oliva, D.; Mohamed, A.W. S-shaped and v-shaped gaining-sharing knowledge-based algorithm for feature selection. *Appl. Intell.* **2022**, *52*, 81–112. [CrossRef]
24. Erol, O.K.; Eksin, I. A new optimization method: Big bang–big crunch. *Adv. Eng. Softw.* **2006**, *37*, 106–111. [CrossRef]
25. Hatamlou, A. Black hole: A new heuristic optimization approach for data clustering. *Inf. Sci.* **2013**, *222*, 175–184. [CrossRef]
26. Rashedi, E.; Nezamabadi-Pour, H.; Saryazdi, S. GSA: A gravitational search algorithm. *Inf. Sci.* **2009**, *179*, 2232–2248. [CrossRef]
27. Formato, R.A. Central force optimization. *Prog. Electromagn. Res.* **2007**, *77*, 425–491. [CrossRef]
28. Kaveh, A.; Talatahari, S. A novel heuristic optimization method: Charged system search. *Acta Mech.* **2010**, *213*, 267–289. [CrossRef]
29. Azadeh, A.; Asadzadeh, S.M.; Jalali, R.; Hemmati, S. A greedy randomised adaptive search procedure–genetic algorithm for electricity consumption estimation and optimisation in agriculture sector with random variation. *Int. J. Ind. Syst. Eng.* **2014**, *17*, 285–301. [CrossRef]
30. Blum, C.; Pinacho, P.; López-Ibáñez, M.; Lozano, J.A. Construct, merge, solve & adapt a new general algorithm for combinatorial optimization. *Comput. Oper. Res.* **2016**, *68*, 75–88.
31. Thiruvady, D.; Blum, C.; Ernst, A.T. Solution merging in matheuristics for resource constrained job scheduling. *Algorithms* **2020**, *13*, 256. [CrossRef]
32. Wolpert, D.H.; Macready, W.G. *No Free Lunch Theorems for Search*; Technical Report; Technical Report SFI-TR-95-02-010; Santa Fe Institute: Santa Fe, NM, USA, 1995.
33. Lones, M.A. Mitigating metaphors: A comprehensible guide to recent nature-inspired algorithms. *SN Comput. Sci.* **2020**, *1*, 1–12. [CrossRef]
34. Mirjalili, S.; Lewis, A. The whale optimization algorithm. *Adv. Eng. Softw.* **2016**, *95*, 51–67. [CrossRef]
35. Kaveh, A.; Ghazaan, M.I. Enhanced whale optimization algorithm for sizing optimization of skeletal structures. *Mech. Based Des. Struct. Mach.* **2017**, *45*, 345–362. [CrossRef]
36. Touma, H.J. Study of the economic dispatch problem on IEEE 30-bus system using whale optimization algorithm. *Int. J. Eng. Technol. Sci. (IJETS)* **2016**, *5*, 11–18. [CrossRef]
37. Ladumor, D.P.; Trivedi, I.N.; Jangir, P.; Kumar, A. A whale optimization algorithm approach for unit commitment problem solution. National Conference on Advancements in Electrical and Power Electronics Engineering (AEPEE-2016), Morbi, Indea, 28–29 June 2016; pp. 4–17.
38. Cui, D. Application of whale optimization algorithm in reservoir optimal operation. *Adv. Sci. Technol. Water Resour.* **2017**, *37*, 72–79.
39. Saxena, A. A comprehensive study of chaos embedded bridging mechanisms and crossover operators for grasshopper optimisation algorithm. *Expert Syst. Appl.* **2019**, *132*, 166–188. [CrossRef]
40. Ibrahim, R.A.; Elaziz, M.A.; Lu, S. Chaotic opposition-based grey-wolf optimization algorithm based on differential evolution and disruption operator for global optimization. *Expert Syst. Appl.* **2018**, *108*, 1–27. [CrossRef]
41. Elaziz, M.A.; Oliva, D. Parameter estimation of solar cells diode models by an improved opposition-based whale optimization algorithm. *Energy Convers. Manag.* **2018**, *171*, 1843–1859. [CrossRef]
42. Xu, Q.; Wang, L.; Wang, N.; Hei, X.; Zhao, L. A review of opposition-based learning from 2005 to 2012. *Eng. Appl. Artif. Intell.* **2014**, *29*, 1–12. [CrossRef]
43. Mahdavi, S.; Rahnamayan, S.; Deb, K. Opposition based learning: A literature review. *Swarm Evol. Comput.* **2018**, *39*, 1–23. [CrossRef]
44. Gupta, S.; Deep, K. Cauchy Grey Wolf Optimiser for continuous optimisation problems. *J. Exp. Theor. Artif. Intell.* **2018**, *30*, 1051–1075. [CrossRef]
45. Wang, G.G.; Zhao, X.; Deb, S. A novel monarch butterfly optimization with greedy strategy and self-adaptive. In Proceedings of the Soft Computing and Machine Intelligence (ISCMI), 2015 Second International Conference on IEEE, Hong Kong, China, 23–24 November 2015; pp. 45–50.
46. Digalakis, J.G.; Margaritis, K.G. On benchmarking functions for genetic algorithms. *Int. J. Comput. Math.* **2001**, *77*, 481–506. [CrossRef]
47. Molga, M.; Smutnicki, C. Test functions for optimization needs. *Test Funct. Optim. Needs* **2005**, *101*, 48.
48. Yang, X.S. Test problems in optimization. *arXiv* **2010**, arXiv:1008.0549.

49. Awad, N.; Ali, M.; Liang, J.; Qu, B.; Suganthan, P. *Problem Definitions and Evaluation Criteria for the CEC 2017 Special Session and Competition on Single Objective Bound Constrained Real-Parameter Numerical Optimization*; Technical Report; Nanyang Technological University Singapore: Singapore, 2016.
50. Ling, Y.; Zhou, Y.; Luo, Q. Lévy flight trajectory-based whale optimization algorithm for global optimization. *IEEE Access* **2017**, *5*, 6168–6186. [CrossRef]
51. Oliva, D.; Abd El Aziz, M.; Hassanien, A.E. Parameter estimation of photovoltaic cells using an improved chaotic whale optimization algorithm. *Appl. Energy* **2017**, *200*, 141–154. [CrossRef]
52. Wilcoxon, F. Individual comparisons by ranking methods. *Biom. Bull.* **1945**, *1*, 80–83. [CrossRef]
53. Mirjalili, S. SCA: A sine cosine algorithm for solving optimization problems. *Knowl.-Based Syst.* **2016**, *96*, 120–133. [CrossRef]
54. Kennedy, J.; Eberhart, R. Particle swarm optimization. In Proceedings of the IEEE International Conference on Neural Networks IV, Perth, WA, Australia, 27 November–1 December 1995; Volume 1000.
55. Yang, X.S. Flower pollination algorithm for global optimization. In *International Conference on Unconventional Computing and Natural Computation*; Springer: Berlin/Heidelberg, Germany, 2012; pp. 240–249.
56. Biradar, S.; Hote, Y.V.; Saxena, S. Reduced-order modeling of linear time invariant systems using big bang big crunch optimization and time moment matching method. *Appl. Math. Model.* **2016**, *40*, 7225–7244. [CrossRef]
57. Dinkar, S.K.; Deep, K. Accelerated opposition-based antlion optimizer with application to order reduction of linear time-invariant systems. *Arab. J. Sci. Eng.* **2019**, *44*, 2213–2241. [CrossRef]
58. Shekhawat, S.; Saxena, A. Development and applications of an intelligent crow search algorithm based on opposition based learning. *ISA Trans.* **2020**, *99*, 210–230. [CrossRef]
59. Das, S.; Suganthan, P.N. *Problem Definitions and Evaluation Criteria for CEC 2011 Competition on Testing Evolutionary Algorithms on Real World Optimization Problems*; Jadavpur University: Kolkata, India; Nanyang Technological University: Singapore, 2010.
60. Shah, P.; Agashe, S. Review of fractional PID controller. *Mechatronics* **2016**, *38*, 29–41. [CrossRef]
61. Hsu, D.Z.; Chen, Y.W.; Chu, P.Y.; Periasamy, S.; Liu, M.Y. Protective effect of 3, 4-methylenedioxyphenol (sesamol) on stress-related mucosal disease in rats. *BioMed Res. Int.* **2013**, *2013*, 481827. [CrossRef]
62. Bhatt, R.; Parmar, G.; Gupta, R.; Sikander, A. Application of stochastic fractal search in approximation and control of LTI systems. *Microsyst. Technol.* **2019**, *25*, 105–114. [CrossRef]
63. Hekimoğlu, B. Optimal tuning of fractional order PID controller for DC motor speed control via chaotic atom search optimization algorithm. *IEEE Access* **2019**, *7*, 38100–38114. [CrossRef]
64. Ekinci, S.; Izci, D.; Hekimoğlu, B. Optimal FOPID Speed Control of DC Motor via Opposition-Based Hybrid Manta Ray Foraging Optimization and Simulated Annealing Algorithm. *Arab. J. Sci. Eng.* **2021**, *46*, 1395–1409. [CrossRef]

mathematics

Article

A Novel Approach Based on Honey Badger Algorithm for Optimal Allocation of Multiple DG and Capacitor in Radial Distribution Networks Considering Power Loss Sensitivity

Mohamed A. Elseify [1], Salah Kamel [2,*], Hussein Abdel-Mawgoud [2] and Ehab E. Elattar [3]

1 Department of Electrical Engineering, Faculty of Engineering, Al-Azhar University, Qena 83513, Egypt; mohamed_1988@azhar.edu.eg
2 Department of Electrical Engineering, Faculty of Engineering, Aswan University, Aswan 81542, Egypt; hussein.abdelmawgoud@yahoo.com
3 Department of Electrical Engineering, College of Engineering, Taif University, P.O. Box 11099, Taif 21944, Saudi Arabia; e.elattar@tu.edu.sa
* Correspondence: skamel@aswu.edu.eg

Abstract: Recently, the integration of distributed generators (DGs) in radial distribution systems (RDS) has been widely evolving due to its sustainability and lack of pollution. This study presents an efficient optimization technique named the honey badger algorithm (HBA) for specifying the optimum size and location of capacitors and different types of DGs to minimize the total active power loss of the network. The Combined Power Loss Sensitivity (CPLS) factor is deployed with the HBA to accelerate the estimation process by specifying the candidate buses for optimal placement of DGs and capacitors in RDS. The performance of the optimization algorithm is demonstrated through the application to the IEEE 69-bus standard RDS with different scenarios: DG Type-I, DG Type-III, and capacitor banks (CBs). Furthermore, the effects of simultaneously integrating single and multiple DG Type-I with DG Type-III are illustrated. The results obtained revealed the effectiveness of the HBA for optimizing the size and location of single and multiple DGs and CBs with a considerable decline in the system's real power losses. Additionally, the results have been compared with those obtained by other known algorithms.

Keywords: HBA; radial distribution systems; power loss; sensitivity analysis; optimization; DG optimal allocation; voltage deviation; capacitor banks

MSC: 35B05; 35F99; 37N40

Citation: Elseify, M.A.; Kamel, S.; Abdel-Mawgoud, H.; Elattar, E.E. A Novel Approach Based on Honey Badger Algorithm for Optimal Allocation of Multiple DG and Capacitor in Radial Distribution Networks Considering Power Loss Sensitivity. *Mathematics* **2022**, *10*, 2081. https://doi.org/10.3390/math10122081

Academic Editor: Jian Dong

Received: 13 April 2022
Accepted: 13 June 2022
Published: 15 June 2022

1. Introduction

1.1. Background

In recent decades, energy demand has undergone rapid growth due to the intricate life cycle of humans and limitations on fossil fuel sources. Therefore, voltage dips and power losses have increased in distribution systems, leading to the significance of the incorporation of distributed generators (DGs), particularly renewable energy resources in radial distribution systems (RDS) [1,2]. Electric power utilities have been initially designed based on unidirectional power flow. As a result, the DGs integrated into the distribution system may change the direction and magnitude of the power flow. The integration of DGs has some positive effects on the operation of the distribution networks, which is represented in system voltage support, reliability improvement, and reduction in power losses and operation costs. Several aspects must be addressed when placing DG units in a distribution system, including the technology with which they are designed, the quantity and capacity of the DG units, the optimal allocation, and the kind of grid connection. The integration of DGs has an influence on several factors, including total system losses, bus voltage level, reliability, and stability, decreased kVA demand from the distribution system, energy-saving possibility, and postponed capacity of distribution transformers. The optimal installation of DGs in the distribution system is critical for maximizing the benefits of DGs in terms of economy and operation. The random installation of distributed generators units in the network may make the losses of the system larger and impair the voltage profile and other characteristics, all of which might contribute to higher costs. Thus, DGs should be installed optimally to maximize network efficiency. The decentralized generators are an electric power source that is directly linked to the radial distribution network and can be divided into four categories as follows [3]:

- Type-I: inserts real power only to the network at power factor unity, such as photovoltaic cells (PVs).
- Type-II: inserts only reactive power at zero leading power factor, such as synchronous compensators.
- Type-III: inserts both reactive and real power into the network, such as doubly fed induction generators of the wind turbine.
- Type-IV: consumes reactive power and inserts real power into the network, such as squirrel cage induction generators of the wind turbine.

Additionally, the best size and sites of capacitor banks (CBs) in the RDS require static or switchable capacitors for power factor improvement at strategically recognized places in RDS to handle the power quality performance problems. This also delivers several technical and economic benefits, such as decreased power loss, increased load bus voltage, enhanced power factor, and lower reactive power consumption from the sending end side [4–6]. To deal with the ever-increasing energy demand as well as technical and economic problems in distribution systems, efficient and effective reactive power compensation planning is required [4,6].

1.2. Literature Survey

Optimization techniques are continuously developed to gain the highest benefits of distributed generators. There are several classifications for optimization algorithms. Metaheuristic optimization techniques are among the best algorithms and are utilized for many optimization problems in a wide range of different disciplines while using less execution time than other optimization techniques. Numerous studies have been conducted to decrease system losses by optimizing the capacity and location of DGs using various methodologies and techniques. The loss sensitivity factor (LSF) was utilized to identify the nominee bus and reduce the search space before applying an algorithm to choose the optimum size and location of the DG [7–13]. Therefore, most researchers have calculated the active power loss as a single objective function [11–16], whether in single or multiple DG placement problems. The new hybrid algorithm based on moth flame optimization (MFO) and sine cosine algorithm (SCA) [11] was employed to provide the best placement and sizing of the DG and capacitor bank in different test cases. Abdel-Mawgoud et al. [12] determined the optimal sites and sizing of DG Type-I and DG Type-III in RDS using the chaotic moth flame optimization technique (CMFO). The proposed technique was applied in IEEE 33-bus RDS, and the results have been compared with other techniques. The BAT optimization algorithm has been utilized to minimize total line losses and obtain the optimal placement and sizing of DG in IEEE 33-bus RDS [13,14]. A comparison study between FPA, GSA, ICA, and BAT novel heuristic techniques used for minimizing active losses in RDS incorporated with renewable DG sources was discussed in [15]. Hybrid GMSA was suggested to minimize the active power loss by optimally determining the best site and size of the synchronous condenser and DG in IEEE 33-bus RDS [16].

In addition, the whale optimization algorithm (WOA) was utilized to provide the optimal integration of one unit from different types of DG in distribution systems [17]. The objective function considered in this work is the minimization of active power losses. The manta ray foraging optimization algorithm (MRFO) was proposed [18] to reduce active power loss by the optimal installation of DG Type-I into RDS. An optimal installation of the

DG in RDS using the hybrid gray wolf optimization (HGWO) algorithm [19] was developed to minimize the system power loss. This technique was simulated with different types of DGs through the application to IEEE 33-, IEEE 69-, and Indian 85-bus distribution networks, and the results obtained are the global optimum. The simultaneous integration of shunt capacitors and renewable DGs was addressed in [20] using the Gbest-guided artificial bee colony (GABC) optimization technique for minimizing active power losses. This algorithm was applied to IEEE 33-bus and IEEE 85-bus RDS, and the numerical solutions obtained validated the effectiveness for optimal allocation of DGs and CBs. A recent multileader particle swarm optimization (MLPSO) algorithm was proposed [21] for specifying the best size and location of DGs with the objective of minimizing real power losses. However, it has slow convergence characteristics with the increasing number of state variables of the problem.

On the other hand, several techniques were utilized to provide the optimal incorporation of DGs and CBs in radial distribution networks using multi-objective functions [22–28] regardless of the algorithms utilized for solving these objective functions. An efficient cuckoo search algorithm was proposed [22] to provide the optimal size and location of capacitors in RDS. The objective function was expressed to minimize the total active loss and improve the voltage profile of the distribution network. In [9], the authors developed an ant lion optimization (ALO) algorithm for optimal placement and sizing of single and multiple renewable DGs in RDS. The weighted objective function utilized in this method minimized power loss and enhanced the voltage stability index and the voltage level of the distribution system. The gray wolf optimizer (GWO) was suggested [23] for multiple allocations of the DG in the distribution system. The multi-objective function was converted into a single objective function using the weighted sum method for minimizing the reactive system losses and voltage deviation index. The slap swarm algorithm (SSA) was introduced [24] for simultaneous allocation of distributed generators and capacitor banks in RDS to accomplish environmental, technical, and economic benefits. An intersect mutation differential evolution (IMDE) algorithm for simultaneous installment and sizing of the capacitor banks and DGs in IEEE 33-bus and IEEE 69-bus RDS was proposed [25]. In this technique, the loss expense and power loss were utilized as a minimized objective function. The authors in [26] developed an improved decomposition-based evolutionary algorithm (I-DBEA) for the selection of optimum number, size, and location of DG Type-I and DG Type-III with specified power factor to increase the voltage stability index and reduce active power losses and voltage dips in RDS. The obtained numerical solutions proved the robustness of the I-DBEA algorithm for the optimal installation of DGs in RDS. Further, a two-stage robust optimum allocation model of the DG was also suggested [27], taking into account the capacity curve and real-time price-based demand response. The objective taken in this technique was the system income, investment cost of equipment, and operation cost of the system. The problem was solved using the column and constraint generation algorithm, and the results proved that the suggested model was effective in enhancing the total annual profit and the usage of renewable sources. The optimal allocation of DGs and CBs based on the hybrid ALO and PSO with the fuzzy logic controller was proposed [28] to minimize the active losses, voltage deviation index, and operation cost and improve the voltage stability index. The proposed hybrid technique was tested on IEEE 33-bus RDS, and the numerical solutions demonstrated its effectiveness for the optimal allocation of the DG in RDS. However, it may take more computational time because the hybrid technique is executed for each objective function obtained using the fuzzy logic controller.

In the above literature review, very few researchers addressed the simultaneous integration of single and multiple DG Type-I and DG Type-III, which is outlined in the present study using a new metaheuristic optimization named the honey badger algorithm (HBA). The HBA was proposed by Hashim et al. [29] in 2022, and it is based on the honey badger's intelligent foraging behavior to establish a mathematically efficient search technique for addressing the different optimization problems. In the HBA, the honey badger's dynamic search behavior with digging and honey finding tactics is structured into exploration and exploitation stages. In addition, most metaheuristic algorithms have an effective exploration rate to explore the promising area in the search space and have low exploitation rate to obtain the local solutions in the promising area. The HBA includes high exploration rate and maintains sufficient population variety even during the exploitation phase because of controlled randomized mechanisms to obtain the best global solutions and avoid the local solutions in the promising area. The comparative study proved that the HBA is better than other efficient algorithms at determining the preferable allocation of DGs and capacitors in RDS.

1.3. Paper Contribution and Organization

This paper proposes a novel honey badger optimization technique for optimal allocation of single and multiple different types of DGs and capacitors on RDS. Three different types of DGs were successfully employed with four scenarios through the application to the IEEE 69-bus RDS. For single and multiple integrations of DGs and capacitors in the IEEE 69-bus radial distribution network, the total active power loss was utilized as a single objective function in the present work. The proposed HBA optimization algorithm was simulated with four different scenarios as follows:

Scenario 1: the DG is generating real power only (DG Type-I).
Scenario 2: the Capacitor Bank is generating only reactive power (CBs).
Scenario 3: the DG is producing both reactive and active power (DG Type-III).
Scenario 4: simultaneous installation of DG Type-I with DG Type-III.

Additionally, combined power loss sensitivity (CLPS) was utilized to assess the bus system's sensitivity and identify the best vulnerable nodes for incorporating the single and multiple DGs and capacitors in RDS. Further, CPLS lowers both the search agents of the proposed algorithm and the total computational burden of the simulation process. The effectiveness of the HBA was validated by comparing the acquired results to those of other well-known hybrid techniques such as the hybrid algorithm based on the analytical algorithm with the PSO technique [30].

The remainder of this article is organized as follows: The next section explains the mathematical model of the system and its constraints. Section 3 depicts the combined power loss sensitivity. The proposed HBA is presented in Section 4. The obtained simulation results and discussion are represented in Section 5. The last section concludes the work and recommends potential directions for further research studies.

2. Problem Formulation

2.1. Principles of Forward–Backward Power Flow Algorithm

RDS include some specific characteristics, for instance, unbalanced loads, radial construction, and a high ratio of R/X. Due to the mentioned properties above, the Newton–Raphson (NR), fast decoupled (FD), and Gauss–Seidel (GS) techniques are inadequate in RDS analysis. Consequently, a forward–backward load flow algorithm [31] was utilized in this study to solve the load flow problem of RDS, which can be partitioned into two phases: forward sweep and backward sweep. In the backward sweep, the power flow is determined from the receiving end to the sending end, whereas the voltage is calculated from the sending end to the receiving end in the forward sweep. Figure 1 displays a portion of two buses in RDS; the active and reactive power flow from bus m to bus n is evaluated using backward sweep by the following expressions.

$$P_m = P_n + P_{L_n} + R_{m,n}\left(\frac{(P_n + P_{L_n})^2 + (Q_n + Q_{L_n})^2}{|V_n|^2}\right), \tag{1}$$

$$Q_m = Q_n + Q_{L_n} + X_{m,n}\left(\frac{(P_n + P_{L_n})^2 + (Q_n + Q_{L_n})^2}{|V_n|^2}\right), \tag{2}$$

and the voltage and phase angle of each bus can be evaluated in the forward sweep as given in (3) and (4), respectively.

$$V_n = \left(V_m^2 - 2(R_{m,n}P_m + X_{m,n}Q_m) + \left({R_{m,n}}^2 + {X_{m,n}}^2\right)\left(\frac{P_m^2 + Q_m^2}{|V_m|^2}\right)\right)^{1/2}, \tag{3}$$

$$\theta_n = \theta_m + \tan^{-1}\left(\frac{Q_m R_{m,n} - P_m X_{m,n}}{V_m^2 - (P_m R_{m,n} + Q_m X_{m,n})}\right), \tag{4}$$

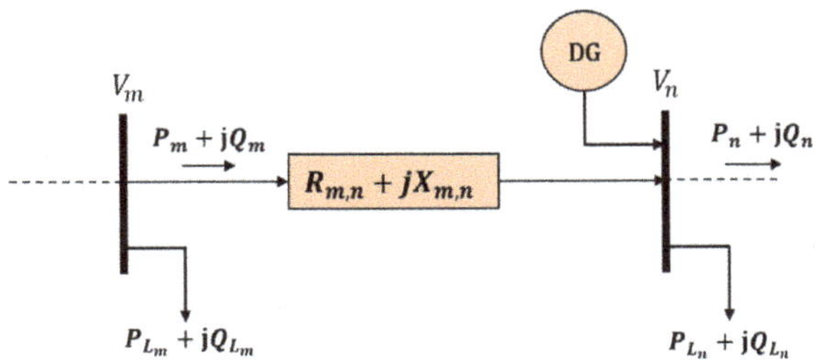

Figure 1. Portion of two nodes in radial distribution system.

The line between busses m and n has a reactance and resistance $X_{m,n}$ and $R_{m,n}$. The active and reactive power delivered across the line between bus m and bus n is denoted by P_m and Q_m, respectively. The voltages of buses m and n are V_m and V_n, respectively.

Installation of photovoltaic systems (PVs), capacitor banks (CBs), and DFIG-based wind turbines (WTs) changes the line power flow. Therefore, the active and reactive line flow between buses m and n after installation of DG at bus n in RDS is modified as follows:

- **DG Type-I**

$$P_m = P_n + P_{L_n} + R_{m,n}\left(\frac{(P_n + P_{L_n})^2 + (Q_n + Q_{L_n})^2}{|V_n|^2}\right) - P_{DG_n}, \tag{5}$$

- **Capacitor Bank**

$$Q_m = Q_n + Q_{L_n} + X_{m,n}\left(\frac{(P_n + P_{L_n})^2 + (Q_n + Q_{L_n})^2}{|V_n|^2}\right) - Q_{CB_n}, \tag{6}$$

- **DG Type-III**

$$P_m = P_n + P_{L_n} + R_{m,n}\left(\frac{(P_n + P_{L_n})^2 + (Q_n + Q_{L_n})^2}{|V_n|^2}\right) - P_{DG_n}, \tag{7}$$

$$Q_m = Q_n + Q_{L_n} + X_{m,n}\left(\frac{(P_n + P_{L_n})^2 + (Q_n + Q_{L_n})^2}{|V_n|^2}\right) - Q_{DG_n}, \tag{8}$$

Thus, the active $P_{loss(m,n)}$ and reactive $Q_{loss(m,n)}$ power losses in the line between buses n and m are evaluated by (9) and (10), respectively.

$$P_{loss(m,n)} = R_{m,n}\left(\frac{(P_m^2 + Q_m^2)}{|V_n|^2}\right), \tag{9}$$

$$Q_{loss(m,n)} = X_{m,n}\left(\frac{(P_m^2 + Q_m^2)}{|V_n|^2}\right), \tag{10}$$

2.2. Objective Function and Operation Constraints

Generally, including DGs in RDS minimizes the system power losses by decreasing the amount of current flowing through the branches; it can also increase the network efficiency by enhancing the voltage profile. Therefore, in this study, the total active power loss was chosen as the optimization structure's objective function, and it may be calculated as follows:

$$F_{obj} = P_{total\text{-}loss} = \sum_{t=1}^{n_{br}} P_{loss(m,n)_t}, \tag{11}$$

where n_{br} and $P_{total\text{-}loss}$ denote the active power loss of the n_{br} th branch and the number of lines in the network, respectively. The objective function expressed in (11) is minimized and subjected to the following equality and inequality constraints.

2.2.1. Equality Constraints

The equality constraints are the balanced reactive and active power flow in RDS, and they are given as follows:

$$P_{slack} + \sum_{i=1}^{n_{DG}} P_{DG}(i) = \sum_{k=1}^{n_{br}} P_{loss}(k) + \sum_{l=1}^{n} P_L(l), \tag{12}$$

$$Q_{slack} + \sum_{i=1}^{n_{DG}} Q_{DG}(i) = \sum_{k=1}^{n_{br}} Q_{loss}(k) + \sum_{l=1}^{n} Q_L(l), \tag{13}$$

where Q_{slack} and P_{slack} are the generated reactive and active power from the swing bus in RDS, respectively. $Q_L(l)$ and $P_L(l)$ denote the reactive and active load demand at bus l, while the active and reactive power losses in branch (k) are represented, respectively, by $P_{loss}(k)$ and $Q_{loss}(k)$. $Q_{DG}(i)$ and $P_{DG}(i)$ illustrate the injected reactive and real power from DGs to RDS at bus i. n_{DG}, n_{br}, and n denote the number of DGs, the number of branches, and the number of buses in RDS, respectively.

2.2.2. Inequality Constraints

The upper and lower bounds of the estimated state variables of the RDS can be represented as follows:

- Bus voltage constraints

Each bus of the RDS must have a voltage between the minimum voltage (V_{min}) and maximum voltage (V_{max}).

$$V_{min} \leq V_i \leq V_{max}, \tag{14}$$

- DG capacity limits

The total active power (P_{DG}) generated by DGs should be greater than $(P_{DG_{min}})$ and less than $(P_{DG_{max}})$. Further, the operating power factor (PF_{DG}) of DGs should be lie in the interval $[PF_{DG_{min}}, PF_{DG_{max}}]$. These constraints are given by (15)–(17).

$$\sum_{i=1}^{n_{DG}} P_{DG}(i) \leq 0.75\left(\sum_{k=1}^{n_{br}} P_{loss}(k) + \sum_{l=1}^{n} P_L(l)\right), \tag{15}$$

$$P_{DG_{min}} \leq P_{DG} \leq P_{DG_{max}} \tag{16}$$

$$PF_{DG_{min}} \leq PF_{DG} \leq PF_{DG_{max}} \tag{17}$$

- Thermal capacity constraints

In this paper, the line current (I_d) of the simulated IEEE 69-bus RDS must satisfy the following constraint [32]:

$$I_d \leq I_{max,d} \text{ for } d = 1, 2, 3, \ldots, n_{br}, \tag{18}$$

where $I_{max,d}$ depicts the highest allowable value of the d-th line current.

2.3. Loss Sensitivity Factor

Combined power loss sensitivity factors (CPLSF) were used in this study to specify the best placement for renewable DG and capacitors in RDS. They are able to indicate which bus has the highest loss reduction when a DG is installed. Consequently, these vulnerable buses might be considered candidates for DG incorporation in RDS. Therefore, the optimization algorithm's search space and simulation time are reduced, as only a few buses can be candidate buses for compensation. CPLSF mainly depend on the variation of apparent power losses to apparent power injection from the DG [33], as given in (19).

$$CPLS = \frac{\partial P_{loss(m,n)}}{\partial P_n} + j\frac{\partial Q_{loss(m,n)}}{\partial Q_n} = R_{m,n}\left(\frac{2P_n}{|V_n|^2}\right) + X_{m,n}\left(\frac{2Q_n}{|V_n|^2}\right), \tag{19}$$

It can be observed from Figure 2 that the buses which have high CPLS values can be defined as candidate buses for DG installation. These candidate buses which comprise up to 50% of the system buses are 57, 58, 7, 6, 61, 60, 10, 59, 55, 56, 12, 13, 14, 54, 15, 53, 8, 64, 49, 11, 9, 17, 65, 16, 5, 48, 21, 19, 41, 63, 68, 34, 20, and 62.

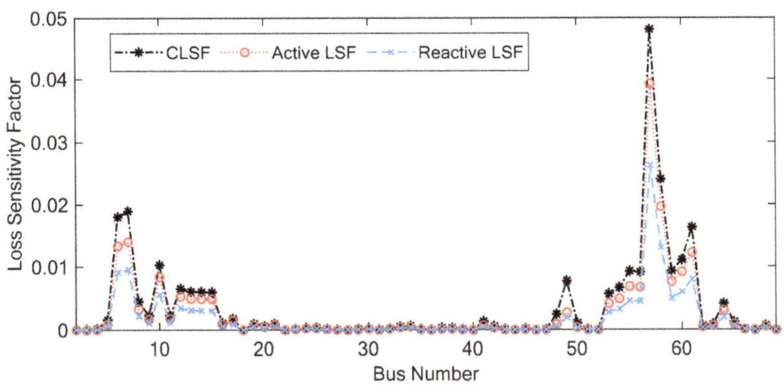

Figure 2. The value of CPLS factors for IEEE 69-bus RDS.

3. Optimization Algorithm

3.1. Honey Badger Optimization Algorithm

Honey badgers are mammals with white and black fluffy fur that are usually located in semi-arid and African rainforests, the Asian Southwest, and the Indian subcontinent. They are approximately 7 to 13 kg in bodyweight and 60 to 77 cm in body length, and it is a bold forager which preys on 60 different species including deadly snakes. They are clever mammals that can utilize tools and enjoys honey. They live alone in self-dug tunnels and only interact with other badgers for mating. Honey badgers are divided into 12 subspecies. Honey badgers do not have a set mating season because cubs are born all year. They are strong animals due to their courageous nature, and they never hesitate to attack even much larger predators when they cannot flee. Further, these mammals can efficiently climb trees to access food sources such as bird nests and beehives [34,35]. The following sections discuss the mathematical model of the HBA and its inspiration, which resembles honey badger (HB) behavior in nature.

3.1.1. Inspiration

The honey badger algorithm mimics the honey badger's foraging behavior. The HB either smells and digs for food sources or tracks the honeyguide bird. The first situation is referred to as the digging mode, while the other is referred to as the honey mode. In the previous phase, it utilizes its sniffing skills to estimate the position of the prey; once there, it wanders around it to find the best spot for digging and grabbing it. In the last mode, the honey badger uses the honeyguide bird as a guide to locate the beehive directly.

3.1.2. Mathematical Model

The mathematical models of the HBA are explained in these subsections. The HBA is a global optimization method in theory since it includes both exploration and exploitation stages. Mathematically, the population of candidate solutions (X) in the HBA is expressed as:

$$X = \begin{bmatrix} x_{11} & x_{12} & x_{13} & \cdots & x_{1d} \\ x_{21} & x_{22} & x_{23} & \cdots & x_{2d} \\ \cdots & \cdots & \cdots & \ddots & \cdots \\ x_{n1} & x_{n2} & x_{n3} & \cdots & x_{nd} \end{bmatrix}, \tag{20}$$

$$\text{j-th honey badger position } x_j = \left[x_j^1\ x_j^2\ \ldots\ x_j^d\right], \tag{21}$$

Step 1: Initialization phase: The respective positions of honey badgers with n population can be initialized using the following expression:

$$x_j = LB_i + r_1(UB_i - LB_i),\ r_1 \in [0,1], \tag{22}$$

where UB_i, and LB_i represent the upper and lower bounds of the search space, respectively, while x_j is the j-th honey badger position and refers to a nominee solution in a population with size n.

Step 2: Intensity Definition: Intensity (I) depends mainly on the prey concentration strength and the distance between it and the j-th honey badger. I_j is the scent intensity of the prey; if the scent is low, the motion becomes slow and vice versa. It is provided by inverse square law (ISL) [36], as represented in Figure 3 and described by (23) as:

$$I_j = \frac{r_2 S}{4\pi d_j^2},\ r_2 \in [0,1], \tag{23}$$

$$S = \left(x_j - x_{j+1}\right)^2 \tag{24}$$

$$d_j = x_{prey} - x_j \tag{25}$$

where S represents the source intensity or concentration intensity (prey position, as depicted in Figure 3). d_j is the distance between the j-th badger and prey.

Step 3: Density factor update: To guarantee a seamless transition from exploration to exploitation, the density factor (α) governs time-varying randomness. Using (26), the updated decreasing factor (α) is decreased with iterations to reduce randomization over time:

$$\alpha = C \times \exp\left(\frac{\text{-iter}}{max_{iter}}\right), \tag{26}$$

where (C) is a constant number more than 1 (the default value is 2), and max_{iter} denotes the maximum number of iterations.

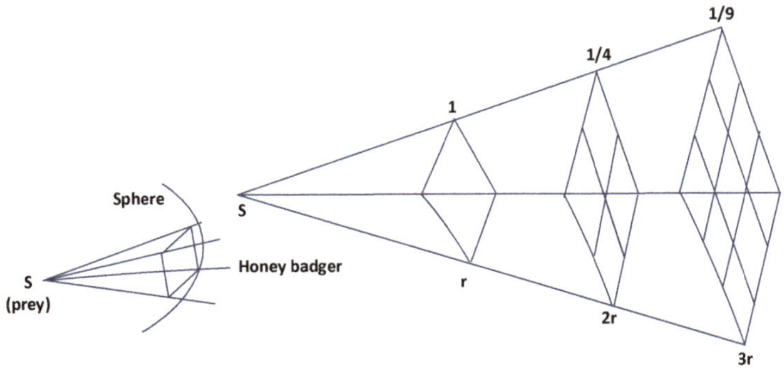

Figure 3. ISL. I is smell intensity, S is prey position, and r ∈ [0, 1] [29].

Step 4: Fleeing from local solution: The current step and the two next ones are applied in the HBA to flee from the local solution area. In this scenario, the HBA optimization algorithm makes use of a flag (F) that changes the search direction, giving agents more chances to scan the search area precisely.

Step 5: Updating the locations of the agents: As previously stated, the HBA position update process (x_{new}) is split into two phases: "digging phase" and "honey phase". The following is a more detailed description:

- **Digging phase.** A honey badger digs in a cardioid shape [37] during the digging phase, as seen in Figure 4. Equation (27) simulates the approximate cardioid motion as:

$$x_{new} = x_{prey} + F\beta I x_{prey} + F r_3 \alpha d_j |\cos(2\pi r_4)[1 - \cos(2\pi r_5)]|, \tag{27}$$

where x_{prey} denotes the best position of the prey obtained so far, in other words the global optimum. $\beta \geq 1$ represents the ability of the honey badger to find food (default = 6). r_3, r_4, and r_5 are three different generated random numbers within the interval [0,1]. F is a flag that changes the search direction, and it is determined by (28):

$$F = \begin{cases} 1 & \text{if } r_6 \leq 1/2 \\ -1 & \text{otherwise} \end{cases} \quad r_6 \in [0, 1], \tag{28}$$

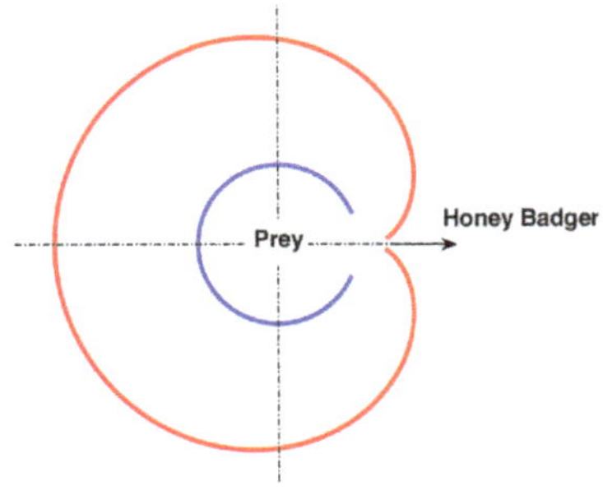

Figure 4. Digging phase: the red outline indicates the strength of the smell, while the blue circular line indicates the position of the prey [29].

In the digging phase, a honey badger is highly influenced by three different factors: the scent intensity (I) of the prey (x_{prey}), the distance between honey badger and prey (d_j), and the decreasing operator (α). Furthermore, a badger may sense any disruption (F) while digging, allowing it to detect even the best prey position (see Figure 4).

- **Honey phase.** Equation (29) simulates the case when the HB tracks the honeyguide bird to a beehive.

$$x_{new} = x_{prey} + \alpha d_j r_7 F,\ r_7 \in [0, 1], \tag{29}$$

Equations (26) and (28) determine the value of (α) and (F), respectively, whereas x_{new}, and x_{prey} show the HB's new position and prey location, respectively. It can be observed from (29) that the HB proceeds to search near the optimized prey position x_{prey}, depending on the distance information (d_j). At this point, search behavior that changes over time (α) influences the search. A honey badger may also face a perturbation (F).

Because of the exploration and exploitation stages, the HBA is considered a global optimization method in theory. The number of operators that must be modified is kept to a minimum to make the HBA simple to implement and comprehend. In general, the HBA mainly depends on three parameters, i.e., the number of state variables (d), the maximum number of iterations (max_{iter}), and the number of populations (n) or the number of solutions. The HBA optimization technique guarantees strong local search ability via honey attraction and guides the individuals in the population to approach the optimal individuals. Furthermore, the density factor achieves the algorithm's global search capabilities and preserves the divergent population to guarantee that the local optimal solutions are avoided. The pseudocode of the HBA optimization algorithm is represented in Algorithm 1. Figure 5 shows the complete flowchart of the HBA optimization algorithm implemented for specifying the optimal sizing and placement of DGs and CBs in distribution systems.

Algorithm 1: Pseudocode of HBA

```
Set parameters:
    n: population size.
    d: no. of state variables.
    max_iter: maximum number of iterations.
    β, and C: constant numbers with initial values 6, and 2 respectively.
    LB, and UB : state variable lower and upper limits.
Using Equation (22) for random initialization of initial population positions.
Compute the fitness of every honey badger position x_j using F_obj and assign to
F_j, j ∈ [1, 2,..., n].
Select initial best position x_prey and related best fitness f_prey.
Set iter = 1
while iter ≤ max_iter do
    Modernize the decreasing operator ∝ by (26).
    Evaluate the intensity (I) using (23) for each position.
    Set j = 1
    while j ≤ n do
        while i ≤ d do
            Determine the distance given in (23).
            if rand < 0.5 (Digging Phase)
                Update each element x_new(j, i) in each position using (27)
            else (Honey Phase)
                Update each element x_new(j, i) in each position using (29)
            end if
        end while
        Determine the fitness f_new of the current position x_new (j)
        if f_new ≤ f_j
            Update the x_j = x_new (j) and f_j = f_new
        end if
    end while
    if f_new ≤ f_prey
        Set f_prey = f_new and x_prey = x_new
    end if
end while (main loop)
Print the best solution: f_prey and x_prey
```

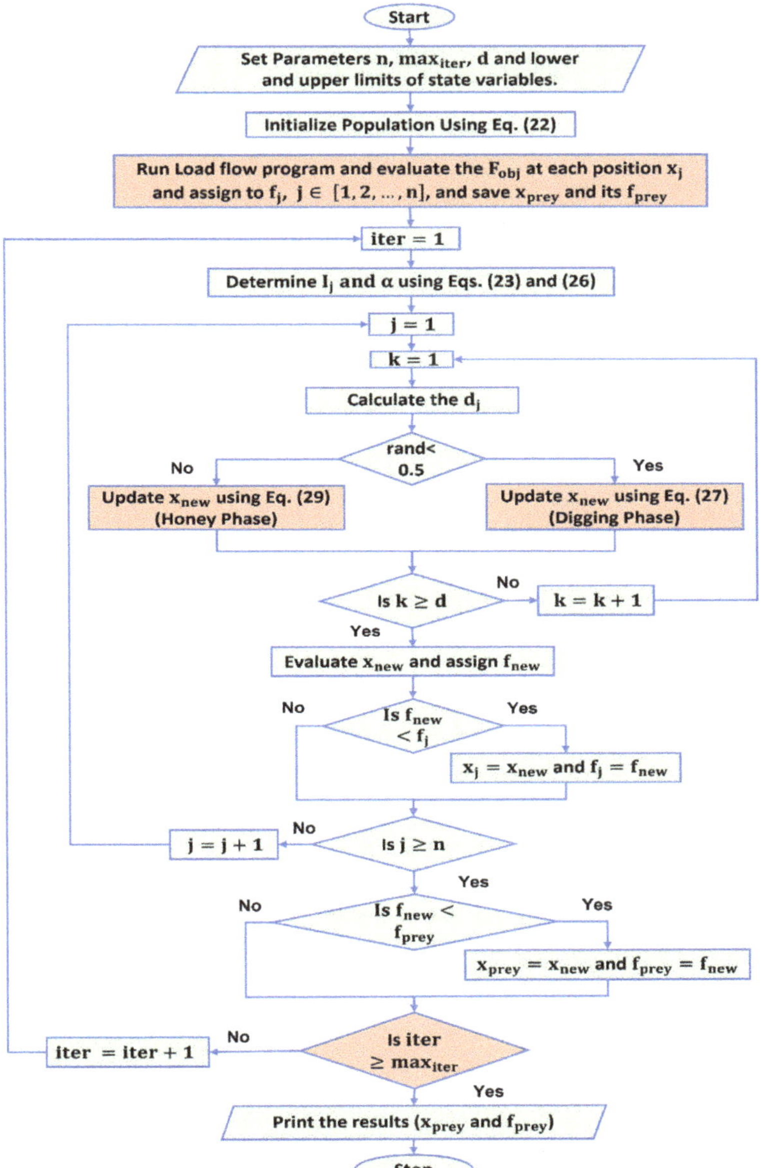

Figure 5. Implementation process of HBA optimization algorithm.

4. Simulation Results

As previously stated, the HBA was simulated on IEEE 69-bus standard test systems to find the best sizing and location of the capacitor and renewable DG in such systems while minimizing power loss using the forward–backward sweep load flow algorithm. The CPLS factor was utilized to limit the search space of the optimization algorithm by identifying the best candidate buses for installing single and multiple DGs and CBs in distribution systems. The proposed method was implemented using MATLAB 2020a M-file on a system with a 64-bit Core i5 CPU and 8GB RAM. This work studied the optimal allocation of single or multi-units of DG Type-I, CBs, DG Type-III, and simultaneous integration of DG Type-I and

DG Type-III. Further, the effectiveness of the HBA optimization algorithm was validated by comparing the acquired solutions to those of other well-known hybrid techniques reported in the literature. Eventually, the optimal allocation of three PVs considering uncertainty was used as a difficult optimization problem to measure the performance of the HBA. The modeling of PV and system load are given in [38]. Table 1 depicts the constraints of the system state variables in p.u. and the tuning parameters for the optimization algorithm.

Table 1. Operating limits and tuning parameters of the presented technique.

Parameters	Used Value
max_{iter}	100
Population size n	50
$[V_{min}, V_{max}]$	[0.9, 1.05]
$[P_{DG_{min}}, P_{DG_{max}}]$	[0 .3, 3]
$[Q_{CB_{min}}, Q_{CB_{max}}]$	[0.15, 1.5]
$[PF_{DG_{min}}, PF_{DG_{max}}]$	[0 .7, 1]

The bus system voltage, which is a security metric that exhibits power quality, was utilized to measure the performance of the HBA optimization technique. In other words, any change in voltage profile affects the performance of the power system. It is computed by the summation of voltage deviation (SVD) as given in (30) where V_k, and V_{slack} represent the k-th bus voltage magnitude and the reference bus voltage equal to 1 p.u.

$$SVD = \sum_{k=1}^{n_b} (|V_k - V_{slack}|), \tag{30}$$

Further, for measuring the performance of the HBA, the voltage stability index (VSI) was employed to identify the distribution system's sensitivity level. Equation (31) is used to provide the sensitivity of each bus to voltage collapse [39]. The bus becomes more stable, and the chances of voltage collapse are low if it has a high value of VSI. VSI for every bus in the distribution system is increased by the appropriate arrangement of DGs in RDS. The overall value of VSI for all buses in RDS is the voltage stability index summation (TVSI) as expressed in (32).

$$VSI_n = |V_m|^4 - 4((P_n + P_{L_n})X_{m,n} - (Q_n + Q_{L_n})R_{m,n})^2 - 4((P_n + P_{L_n})X_{m,n} + (P_n + P_{L_n})R_{m,n})|V_m|^2 \tag{31}$$

$$TVSI = \sum_{i}^{n_b} VSI_i \tag{32}$$

where VSI_n, and V_m denote the VSI at the bus n and voltage at bus n, respectively, while $X_{m,n}$ and $R_{m,n}$ indicate, respectively, the reactance and resistance of branch between buses m, and n, as illustrated in Section 2. n_b represents the total number of nodes.

Figure 6 shows the IEEE 69-bus radial distribution system, which comprises 69 buses and 68 lines with load demands of 2694.6 KVAR and 3801.49 KW. Moreover, the testing system also uses a 12.66 KV standard base voltage and a 10 MVA standard base power. Without installing DGs, the system's real power loss is 224.999 KW; bus 65 has the lowest voltage, i.e., 0.90919, and the maximum deviation 0.0908; the summation of VSI is 61.2181; the minimum VSI is 0.6833; and the voltage deviation summation is 1.8374 p.u. The suggested hybrid technique is studied with the following different scenarios:

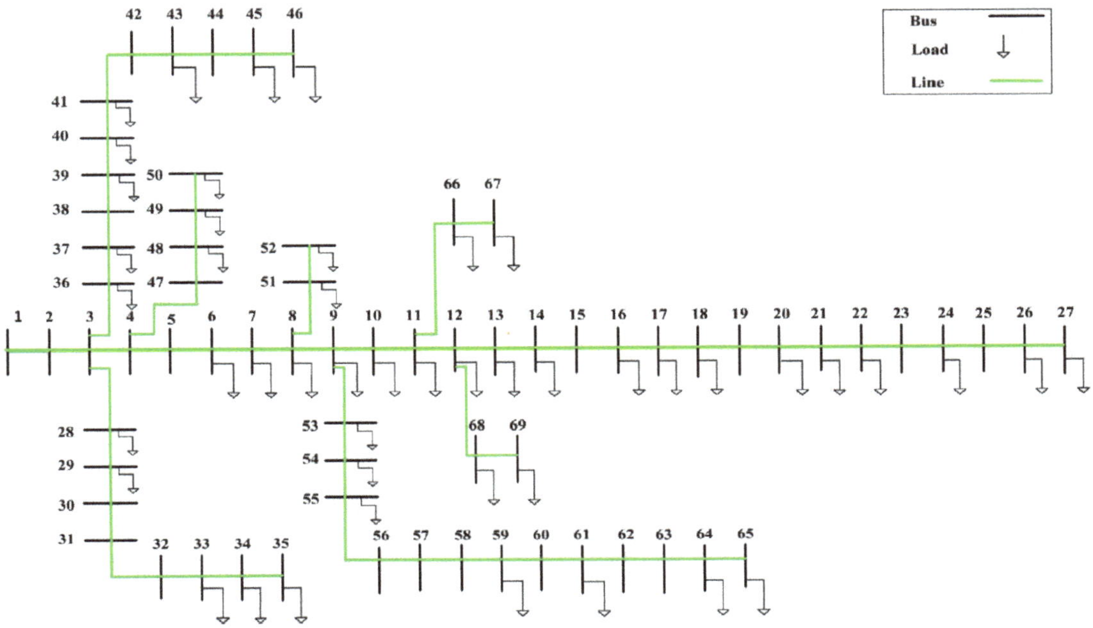

Figure 6. IEEE 69-bus RDS single line diagram [32].

4.1. Scenario 1: DG Type-I Installation on RDS

This form of DG has recently become very popular for injecting real power only into RDS such as solar systems (PVs). Figures 7–9 represent the voltage profile, voltage stability index, and voltage deviation for the IEEE 69-bus distribution system using the HBA with one, two, and three PV-based DGs installed. By single unit, the overall active power loss is reduced from the base case to 83.2224 KW with a 63.01 percent reduction in power loss, as depicted in Table 2. It is depicted in Figures 7 and 8 that bus 27 has a minimum voltage of 0.9683 p.u., with a minimal voltage stability index of typically 0.8791 p.u. It has a maximum voltage deviation of approximately 0.0317 p.u., as shown in Figure 9. On the other hand, combining numerous DGs produces more efficient outcomes than using one DG. By installing two and three PV-based DGs in the present test system, the minimum voltage profile found at bus 65 is improved to 0.97893 and 0.9790 p.u., respectively, compared to the base case. Furthermore, it enhances the minimum VSI found at bus 65 (approximately 0.9183 and 0.9185) and decreases the maximum voltage deviation at the same bus to 0.0211 and 0.0210, respectively. Table 2 represents the optimal locations and sizing of the PV-based DG by the proposed method for IEEE 69-bus RDS. It can be observed from Table 2 that the HBA provides the optimal allocation of single and multiple DG Type-I on RDS compared with other techniques. The HBA was compared with the modified MRFO algorithm by installing three PVs in RDS considering uncertainty as shown in Table 3. Figure 10 illustrates the output power for three PVs for 24 h considering uncertainty, which demonstrates the robustness of the HBA while considering uncertainty.

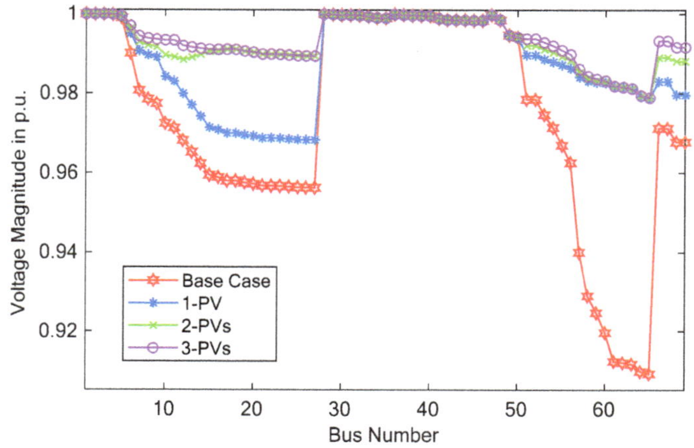

Figure 7. Bus voltage magnitude comparison with and without DG Type-I for IEEE 69-bus RDS for scenario 1.

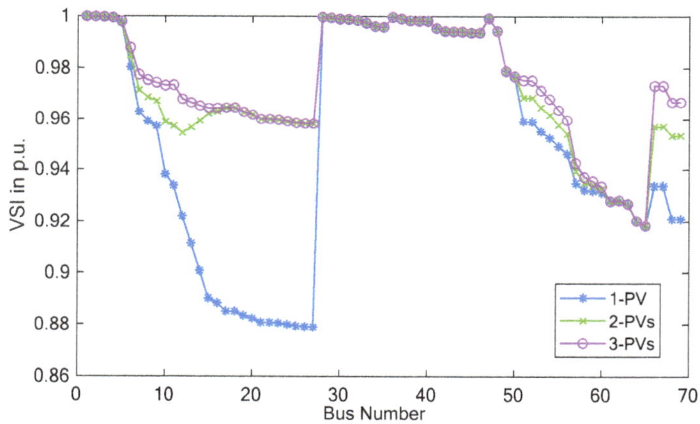

Figure 8. Bus voltage stability index after compensation on IEEE 69-bus RDS for scenario 1.

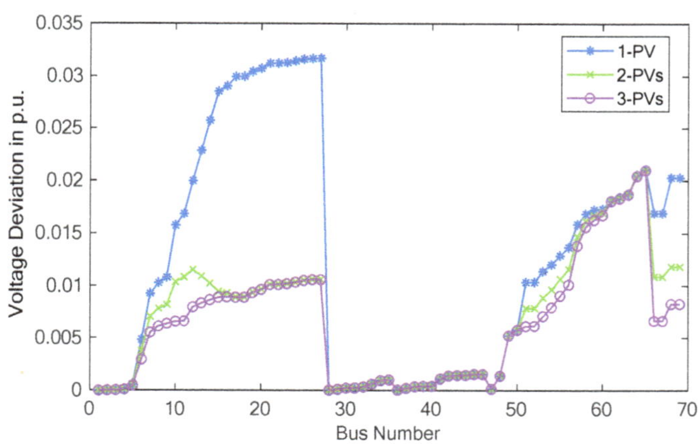

Figure 9. Bus voltage deviation after compensation on IEEE 69-bus RDS for scenario 1.

Table 2. Optimal results of single and multiple DG Type-I on an IEEE 69-bus using HBA compared with other algorithms for scenario 1.

No. of DGs	Technique	Total Loss (KW)	Reduction (%)	Location	DG Size (KW) Unit Capacity	DG Size (KW) Total Capacity	Min. VSI (p.u.)	Min. Voltage (p.u.)
Without DG		224.975	-	-	-	-	0.6833	0.90919
One PV	Proposed	83.2224	63.01	61	1872.71	1872.71	0.8791	0.9683
	Hybrid [30]	83.37	62.95	61	1800	1800	-	-
	EA [40]	83.23	63.00	61	1878	1878	-	-
	Hybrid [41]	83.37	62.95	61	1810	1810	-	0.9679
Two PVs	Proposed	71.6745	68.14	17 61	531.48 1781.47	2312.98	0.9183	0.9789
	Hybrid [30]	71.80	68.09	17 61	520 1720	2240	-	-
	EA [40]	71.68	68.14	17 61	534 1795	2329	-	-
	Hybrid [41]	71.804	68.09	17 61	518 1724	2242	-	0.9769
Three PVs	Proposed	69.4266	69.14	11 17 61	526.70 380.49 1718.97	2626.16	0.9185	0.9790
	Hybrid [30]	69.54	69.09	11 17 61	510 380 1670	2560	-	-
	EA [40]	69.62	69.05	11 18 61	467 380 1795	2642	-	-
	Hybrid [41]	69.5456	69.09	11 18 61	499 377 1668	2544	-	0.9770

Table 3. Results for installing three-DG Type-I in RDS considering uncertainty.

No. of DGs	Technique	Bus (Size (KW))	Total Loss (KW)
-	Without DG	-	2173.8506
Three PVs	Modified MRFO [38]	61 (1991.45) 17 (439.53) 11 (599.51)	1021.694
Three PVs	Proposed	61 (1991.5) 18 (439.4) 11 (599.7)	1021.694

4.2. Scenario 2: Capacitor Bank Installation on RDS

Figures 11–13 show the voltage profile, voltage stability index, and voltage deviation for the IEEE 69-bus distribution system using the HBA with single and multiple CBs installed. It can be demonstrated from these figures that increasing the number of capacitor units and their total installed KVAR improves the voltage profile of the RDS, increase the stability index at all buses, and decreases the estimated voltage deviation. The optimal sizing and location of one, two, and three capacitors reduce the total real losses to 152.0348,

146.435, and 45.109KVAR, respectively, with percent loss reductions of 32.422, 34.91, and 35.5, as depicted in Table 4 which reveals that the CB does not considerably minimize the active losses as compared to DG Type-I. However, the proposed algorithm provides the optimal placement of CBs compared with other approaches for scenario 2 for IEEE 69-bus RDS.

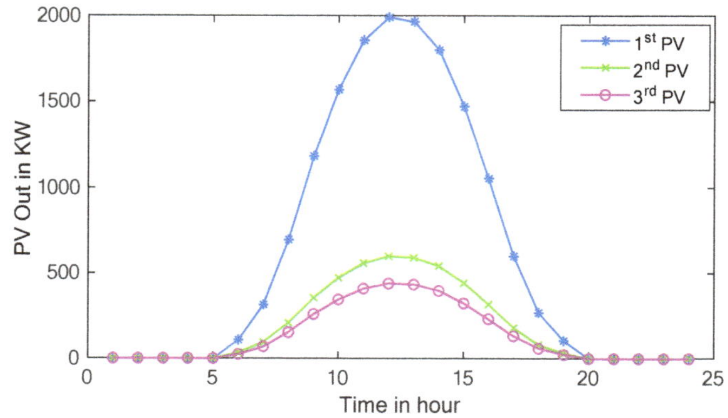

Figure 10. Output of three-DG Type-I on IEEE 69-bus RDS considering uncertainty.

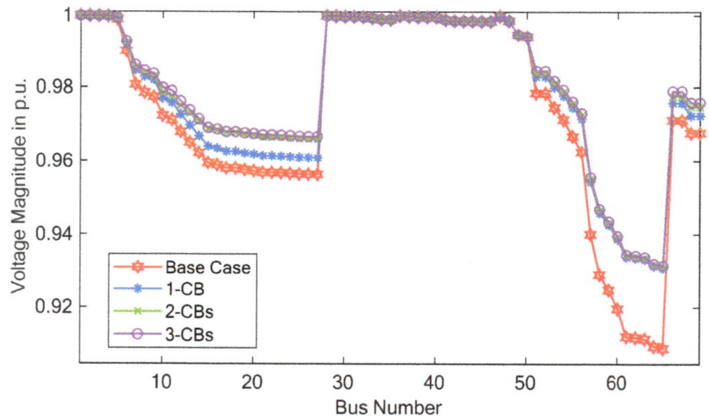

Figure 11. Bus voltage magnitude comparison with and without CBs for IEEE 69-bus RDS for scenario 2.

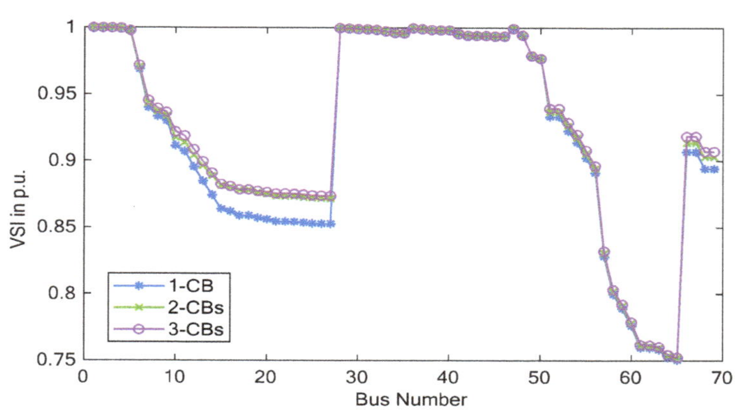

Figure 12. Bus voltage stability index after compensation on IEEE 69-bus RDS for scenario 2.

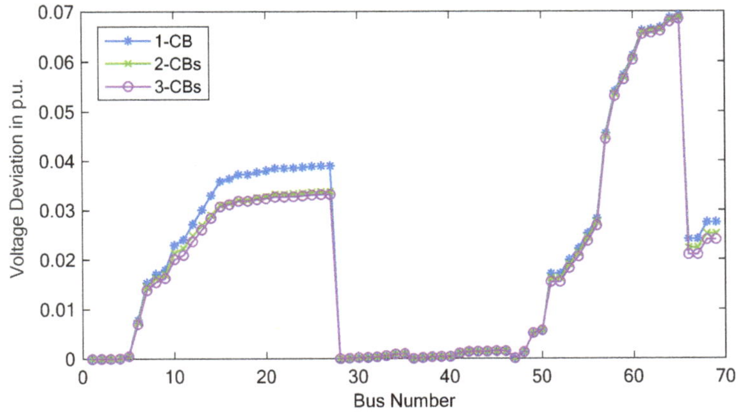

Figure 13. Bus voltage deviation after compensation on IEEE 69-bus RDS for scenario 2.

Table 4. Optimal results of single and multiple CBs on an IEEE 69-bus using HBA compared with other algorithms for scenario 2.

No. of DGs	Technique	Total Loss (KW)	Reduction (%)	Location	DG Size (KVAR)		Min. VSI (p.u.)	Min. Voltage (p.u.)
					Unit Capacity	Total Capacity		
Without DG	-	224.975	-	-	-	-	0.6833	0.90919
One CB	Proposed	152.0348	32.422	61	1330.01	1330.01	0.750418	0.930729
	Hybrid [30]	152.10	32.40	61	1290	1290	-	-
Two CBs	Proposed	146.4346	34.9107	17 61	361.081 1275.06	1636.14	0.751709	0.931129
	Hybrid [30]	146.52	34.88	18 61	350 1240	1590	-	-
	SCA [42]	147.762	34.33	18 61	250 1150	1400	-	0.9290
Three CBs	Proposed	145.10916	35.4999	11 21 61	413.139 230.698 232.406	8762.43	0.752669	0.931426
	Hybrid [30]	145.24	35.45	11 18 61	330 250 1190	1770	-	-
	GSA [43]	145.9	35.15	26 13 15	150 150 1050	1350	-	-

4.3. Scenario 3: DG Type-III Installation on RDS

Similarly, as demonstrated in Figures 14–16, the DG Type-III has better results than DG Type-I because it supplies apparent power to the RDS. The best location and sizing of one-, two-, and three-DG Type-III decreases the total real losses to 23.1688, 7.2013, and 4.2664 KW, respectively, with percent loss reductions of 89.7, 96.8, and 98.1. This mode of DG integration also enhances the minimum VSI (Figure 14) to 0.8943, 0.9772, and 0.9773, respectively, compared to the base case (0.6833 at bus 64). Regarding the minimum bus voltage profile (Figure 15), a single DG Type-III improves it to 0.97247 found at bus 27, while the two and three units improve the 50th bus voltage profile to 0.99426 and 0.99427 p.u., respectively. When employing a single DG Type-III, the maximum voltage deviation

(Figure 16) is improved to 0.0275 (0.0908 at bus 65 for the base case). Nonetheless, the maximum VD at bus 50 is approximately 0.0057 p.u. for both two and three units of DGs Type-III. Consequently, the suggested HBA method gives the best allocation of single and multiple DGs Type-III on RDS compared with other algorithms, as shown in Table 5.

Table 5. Optimal results of single and multiple DG Type-III on an IEEE 69-bus using HBA compared with other algorithms for scenario 3.

No. of DGs	Technique	Total Loss (KW)	Reduction (%)	Location	DG Size (KW)		Min. VSI (p.u.)	Min. Voltage (p.u.)
					Unit Capacity	Optimal P.F		
Without DG	-	224.975	-	-	-	-	0.6833	0.90919
One WT	Proposed	23.1688	89.702	61	1828.47	0.8149	0.8943	0.9725
	Hybrid [30]	23.19	89.69	61	2240	0.81	-	-
	TLBO-GWO [44]	58.80	73.86	61	1000	0.81	-	0.9598
	EA-OPF [40]	23.17	89.7	61	1828	0.82	-	-
Two WTs	Proposed	7.2013	96.8	17 61	522.03 1734.78	0.828 0.814	0.9772	0.9943
	Hybrid [30]	7.21	96.7	17 61	630 2120	0.82 0.81	-	-
	TLBO-GWO [44]	23.28	89.65	61 62	1000 820	0.81 0.83	-	0.9724
	EA-OPF [40]	7.20	96.8	61 17	1735 522	0.81 0.83	-	-
Three WTs	Proposed	4.2664	98.10	11 17 61	493.15 378.92 1675.08	0.8120 0.8332 0.8140	0.9773	0.9943
	Hybrid [30]	4.30	98.01	18 61 66	480 2060 530	0.77 0.83 0.82	-	-
	TLBO-GWO [44]	7.27	96.77	18 61 62	523 1000 723	0.83 0.82 0.8	-	0.9942
	EA-OPF [40]	4.48	97.12	11 18 61	495 379 1674	0.81 0.83 0.81	-	-

4.4. Scenario 4: Simultaneous Installation of DG Type-I with DG Type-III on RDS

The hybridization of renewable energy sources is a prominent concern. PV and WT are the most common types of renewable distributed generators in RDS. In this scenario, the simultaneous combining of DG Type-I and Type-III on the present test system yielded superior results to the two last scenarios. It can be seen from Table 6 that the optimized simultaneous distribution of one PV with one WT, two PVs with two WTs, and three PVs with three WTs on the distribution network decrease the summation of the line's power losses to 12.1068, 4.4567, and 3.6741 KW, respectively. This type of DG integration increases the voltage stability index at all buses, as shown in Figure 17, and decreases the bus voltage deviation as depicted in Figure 18. From Figure 19, it also improves the voltage profile, where the minimum voltage is found at bus 69 (i.e., 0.9921 p.u.) for one PV with one WT, and bus 50 and 65 (0.9950 p.u., and 0.9968 p.u., respectively) for two PVs with two WTs and three PVs with three WTs, respectively. As a result, compared to the EA-OPF algorithm, the HBA method provides the optimal simultaneous distribution of the DG based on Type-I with Type-III on RDS, as depicted in Table 6.

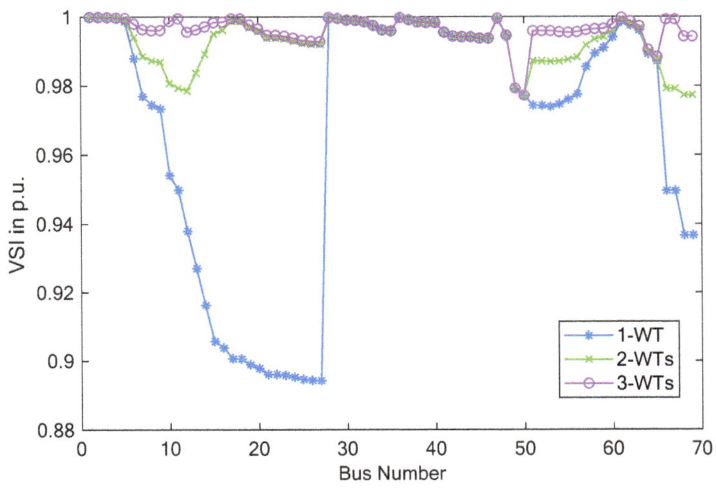

Figure 14. Bus voltage stability index after compensation on IEEE 69-bus RDS for scenario 3.

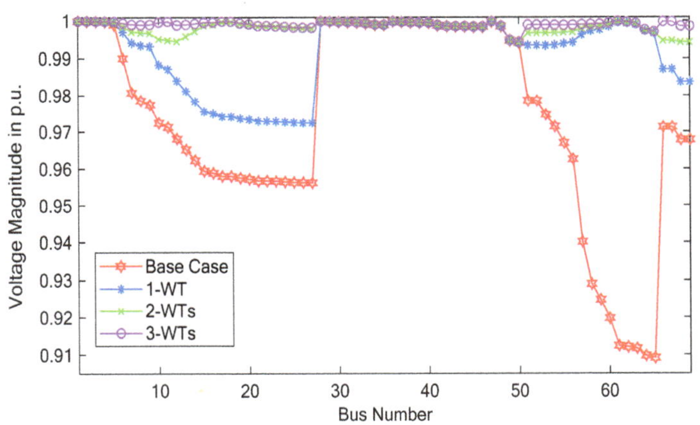

Figure 15. Bus voltage magnitude comparison with and without DG Type-III for IEEE 69-bus RDS for scenario 3.

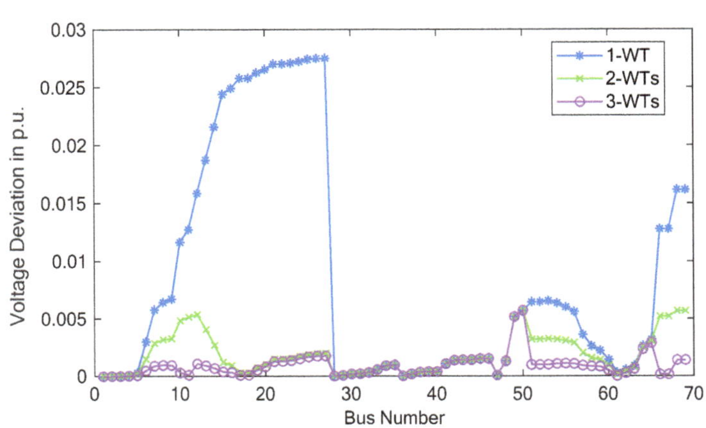

Figure 16. Bus voltage deviation after compensation on IEEE 69-bus RDS for scenario 3.

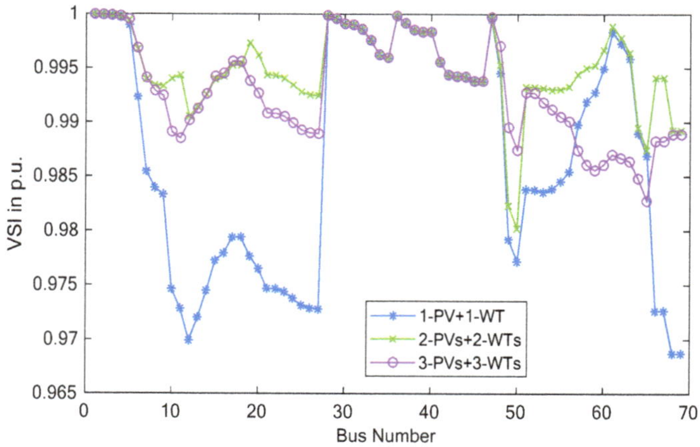

Figure 17. Bus voltage stability index after compensation on IEEE 69-bus RDS for scenario 4.

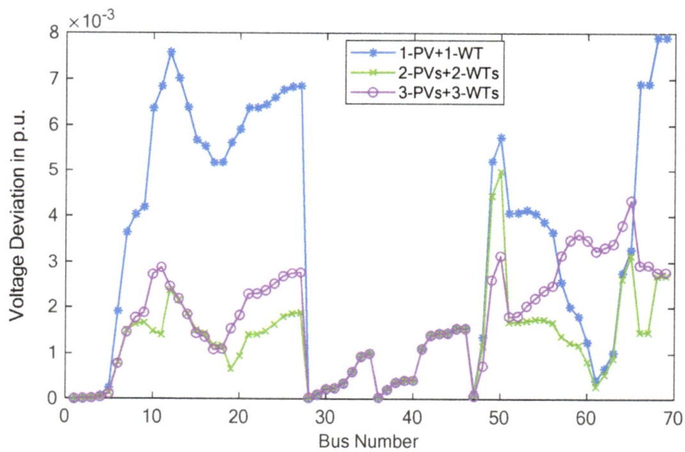

Figure 18. Bus voltage deviation after compensation on IEEE 69-bus RDS for scenario 4.

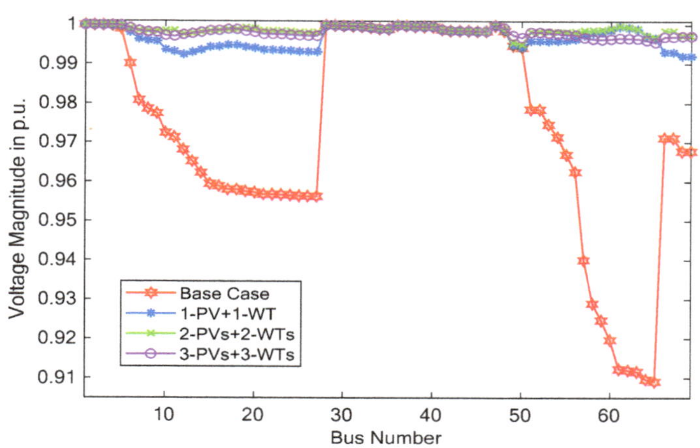

Figure 19. Bus voltage magnitude comparison with and without DG Type-I and DG Type-III for IEEE 69-bus RDS for scenario 4.

Table 6. Optimal results of single and multiple DG Type-I and Type-III on IEEE 69-bus using HBA compared with other algorithms for scenario 4.

No. of DGs	Technique	Total Loss (KW)	Reduction (%)	Location	DG Size (KW)		Min. VSI (p.u.)	Min. Voltage (p.u.)
					Unit Capacity	Optimal P.F		
Without DG	-	224.975	-	-	-	-	0.6833	0.90919
One PV with One WT	Proposed	12.1068	94.62	17 61	523.66 1736.19	1.00 0.80	0.9688	0.9921
	EA-OPF [40]	12.35	94.51	17 61	531 225 (KVA)	1.00 -	-	-
Two PVs with two WTs	Proposed	4.4567	98.02	10 49 17 61	493.342 301.04 389.148 1670.522	1.00 1.00 0.74 0.804	0.9801	0.9950
three PVs with three WTs	Proposed	3.6741	98.37	12 64 58 49 61 19	300 300 300 300 1194.4 377.18	1.00 1.00 1.00 0.70 0.70 0.74	0.9872	0.9968

5. Discussion

As discussed in the previous section, the HBA provides the optimal allocation of single and multiple DGs and capacitors on IEEE 69-bus RDS. Figure 20 illustrates the total active power loss obtained using the suggested HBA for the four test scenarios. It can be seen from this figure that the HBA gives the best solution in all test cases. Regarding the summation of voltage deviation (SVD) (shown in Figure 21), the three units of DG Type-III give the minimum SVD, while the maximum SVD is obtained using one capacitor. Figure 22 shows the total voltage stability index for the HBA on IEEE 69-bus RDS in different scenarios. This figure proves that the proposed algorithm increases the TVSI for the studied cases.

On the other hand, the convergence characteristics of the HBA for scenario one are represented in Figure 23, which illustrates that the suggested algorithm gives the optimum solution in fewer iterations. Figures 24 and 25 illustrate the high conversion rate obtained by the proposed algorithm for scenarios two and three, respectively. Additionally, Figure 26 illustrates the high convergence characteristics of the HBA for specifying the best sizing and location on the IEEE 69-bus standard test system in scenario 4.

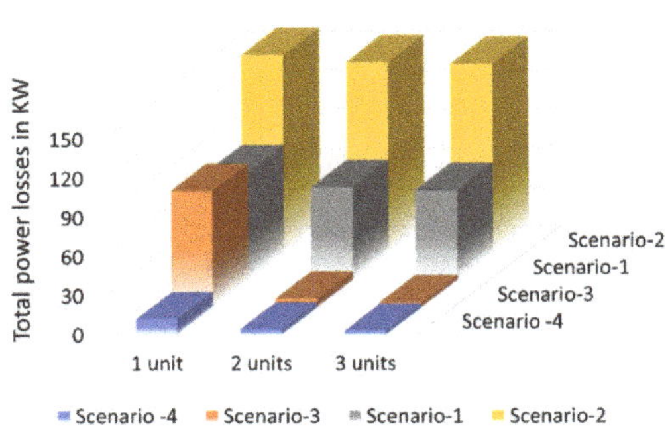

Figure 20. Summary of total active power losses after compensation for IEEE 69-bus RDS.

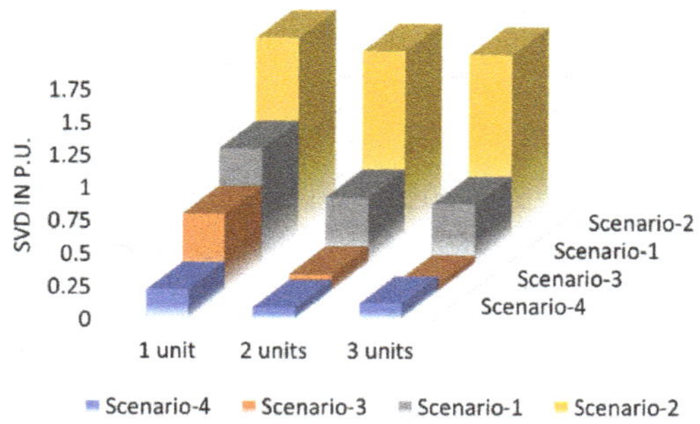

Figure 21. Summary of voltage deviation summation after compensation for IEEE 69-bus RDS.

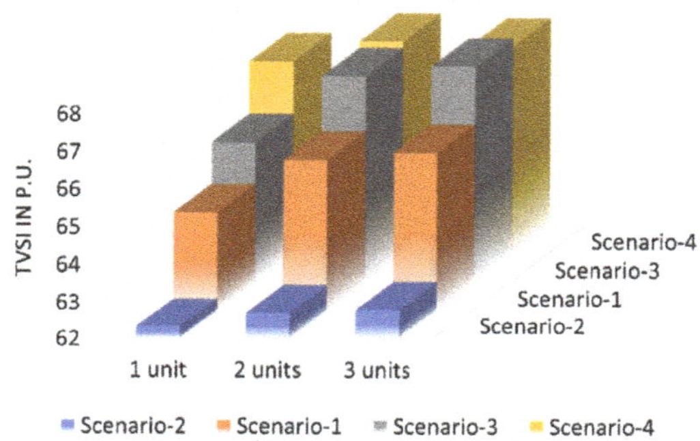

Figure 22. Summary of TVSI after compensation for IEEE 69-bus RDS.

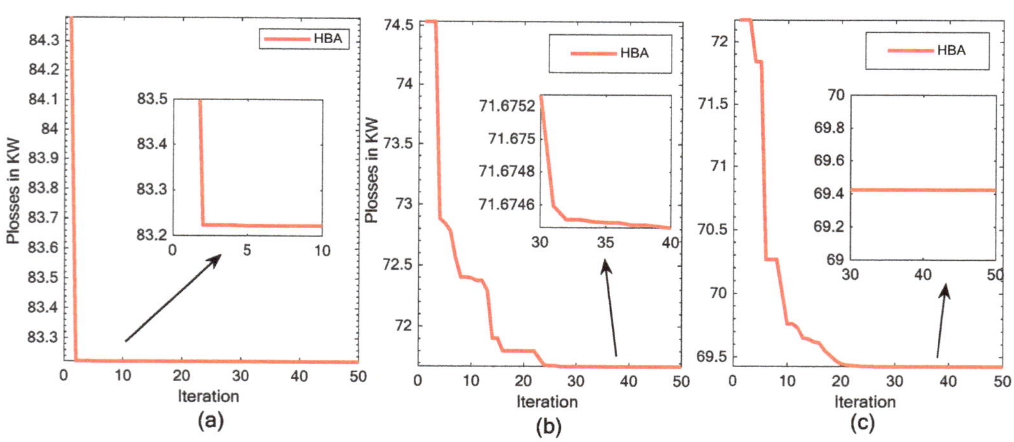

Figure 23. Convergence curves for scenario 1 in IEEE 69-bus RDS. (**a**) One unit, (**b**) two units, and (**c**) three units.

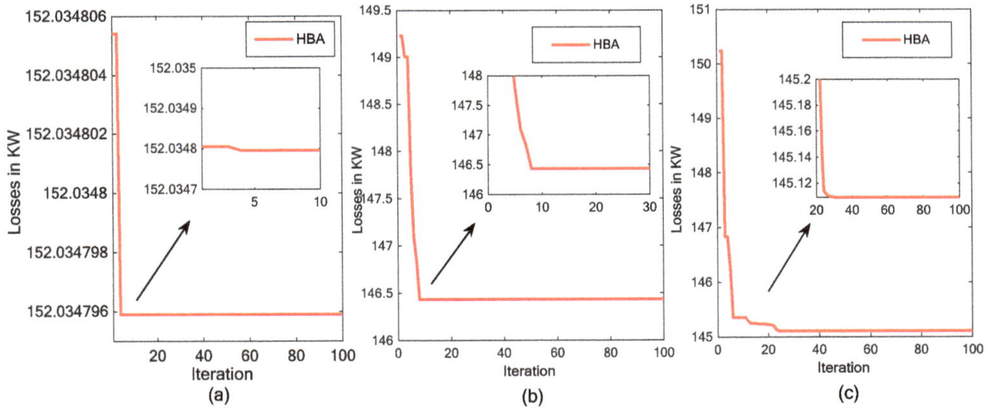

Figure 24. Convergence curves for scenario 2 in IEEE 69-bus RDS. (**a**) One unit, (**b**) two units, and (**c**) three units.

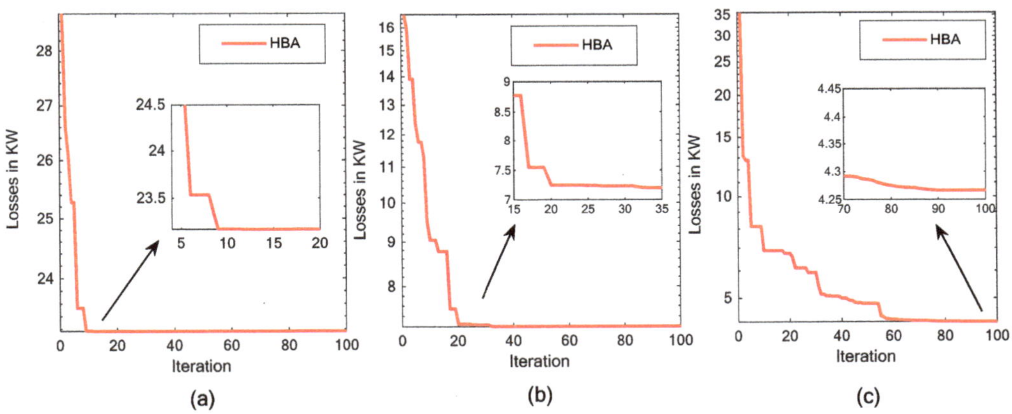

Figure 25. Convergence curves for scenario 3 in IEEE 69-bus RDS. (**a**) One unit, (**b**) two units, and (**c**) three units.

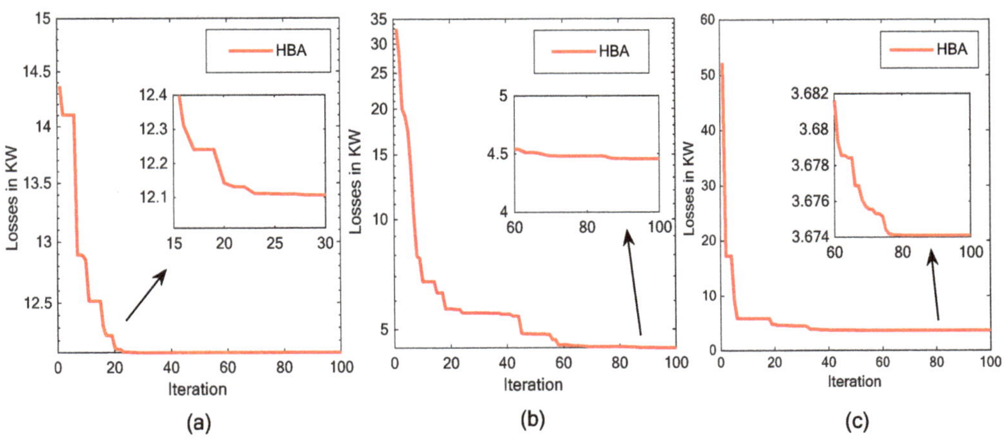

Figure 26. Convergence curves for scenario 4 in IEEE 69-bus RDS. (**a**) One unit, (**b**) two units, and (**c**) three units.

6. Conclusions

In this paper, a new efficient HBA optimization algorithm is applied for the first time to specify the optimal size and location of different types of DGs and capacitors in RDS. To prove the effectiveness of the suggested algorithm, the simulation results were compared with those of other recent optimization techniques. The convergence characteristics of the HBA were introduced for all studied test cases, which show high performance, even increasing the number of state variables. Additionally, the voltage profile, voltage stability index, and voltage deviation of the IEEE 69-bus are discussed and given in figures. From simulation results, the integration of multiple DGs or capacitors is found to be superior to the integration of a single DG or capacitor alone. Investigating the four test scenarios, integration of CBs seems to be the worst scenario in reducing the total active power loss at roughly 145.10916 KVAR. However, simultaneous integration of DG Type-I and DG Type-III provides the lowest total active power losses, approximately 3.6741 KW, and improves both the voltage profile and voltage stability index in the IEEE 69-bus distribution system. The high accuracy obtained from the proposed algorithm will motivate future researchers to utilize this algorithm in large-scale optimization problems.

Author Contributions: Conceptualization, M.A.E.; Investigation, S.K.; Methodology, H.A.-M.; Validation, E.E.E. All authors have read and agreed to the published version of the manuscript.

Funding: This work was supported by Taif University Researchers Supporting Project number (TURSP-2020/86): Taif University, Taif, Saudi Arabia.

Institutional Review Board Statement: Not applicable.

Informed Consent Statement: Not applicable.

Data Availability Statement: Not applicable.

Conflicts of Interest: The authors declare no conflict of interest.

References

1. Qian, K.; Zhou, C.; Allan, M.; Yuan, Y. Effect of load models on assessment of energy losses in distributed generation planning. *Int. J. Electr. Power Energy Syst.* **2011**, *33*, 1243–1250. [CrossRef]
2. El-Samahy, I.; El-Saadany, E. The effect of DG on power quality in a deregulated environment. In Proceedings of the IEEE Power Engineering Society General Meeting, San Francisco, CA, USA, 12–16 June 2005. [CrossRef]
3. Singh, B.; Mukherjee, V.; Tiwari, P. A survey on impact assessment of DG and FACTS controllers in power systems. *Renew. Sustain. Energy Rev.* **2015**, *42*, 846–882. [CrossRef]
4. Saddique, M.W.; Haroon, S.S.; Amin, S.; Bhatti, A.R.; Sajjad, I.A.; Liaqat, R. Optimal placement and sizing of shunt capacitors in radial distribution system using polar bear optimization algorithm. *Arab. J. Sci. Eng.* **2021**, *46*, 873–899. [CrossRef]
5. Bayat, A.; Bagheri, A. Optimal active and reactive power allocation in distribution networks using a novel heuristic approach. *Appl. Energy* **2019**, *233–234*, 71–85. [CrossRef]
6. Taha, I.B.M.; Elattar, E.E. Optimal reactive power resources sizing for power system operations enhancement based on improved grey wolf optimiser. *IET Gener. Transm. Distrib.* **2018**, *12*, 3421–3434. [CrossRef]
7. Ali, E.S.; Abd Elazim, S.M.; Abdelaziz, A.Y. Ant Lion optimization algorithm for optimal location and sizing of renewable distributed generations. *Renew. Energy* **2017**, *101*, 1311–1324. [CrossRef]
8. Mahmoud, I.; Kamel, S.; Abdel-Mawgoud, H.; Nasrat, L.; Jurado, F. Integration of DG and Capacitor in Radial Distribution Networks Using an Efficient Hybrid Optimization Method. *Electr. Power Compon. Syst.* **2020**, *48*, 1102–1110. [CrossRef]
9. Ali, E.S.; Abd Elazim, S.M.; Abdelaziz, A.Y. Optimal allocation and sizing of renewable distributed generation using ant lion optimization algorithm. *Electr. Eng.* **2018**, *100*, 99–109. [CrossRef]
10. Li, Y.; Feng, B.; Li, G.; Qi, J.; Zhao, D.; Mu, Y. Optimal distributed generation planning in active distribution networks considering integration of energy storage. *Appl. Energy* **2018**, *210*, 1073–1081. [CrossRef]
11. Abdel-Mawgoud, H.; Kamel, S.; El-Ela, A.A.A.; Jurado, F. Optimal Allocation of DG and Capacitor in Distribution Networks Using a Novel Hybrid MFO-SCA Method. *Electr. Power Compon. Syst.* **2021**, *49*, 259–275. [CrossRef]
12. Abdel-mawgoud, H.; Kamel, S.; Tostado, M.; Yu, J.; Jurado, F. Optimal installation of multiple DG using chaotic moth-flame algorithm and real power loss sensitivity factor in distribution system. In Proceedings of the International Conference on Smart Energy Systems and Technologies (SEST 2018), Seville, Spain, 10–12 September 2018; pp. 1–5. [CrossRef]
13. Devabalaji, K.R.; Imran, A.M.; Yuvaraj, T.; Ravi, K.J.E.P. Power loss minimization in radial distribution system. *Energy Procedia* **2015**, *79*, 917–923. [CrossRef]

14. Yuvaraj, T.; Devabalaji, K.R.; Ravi, K. Optimal allocation of DG in the radial distribution network using bat optimization algorithm. In Proceedings of the Advances in Power Systems and Energy Management, Singapore, 28 November 2017; pp. 563–569. [CrossRef]
15. Ibrahim, A.M.; Swief, R.A. Comparison of modern heuristic algorithms for loss reduction in power distribution network equipped with renewable energy resources. *Ain Shams Eng. J.* **2018**, *9*, 3347–3358. [CrossRef]
16. Mohamed, E.A.; Mohamed, A.A.A.; Mitani, Y. Hybrid GMSA for optimal placement and sizing of distributed generation and shunt capacitors. *J. Eng. Sci. Technol. Rev.* **2018**, *11*, 55–65. [CrossRef]
17. Reddy, P.; Reddy, V.C.; Manohar, T.G. Whale optimization algorithm for optimal sizing of renewable resources for loss reduction in distribution systems. *Renewables* **2017**, *4*, 3. [CrossRef]
18. Hemeida, M.G.; Ibrahim, A.A.; Mohamed, A.A.A.; Alkhalaf, S.; El-Dine, A.M.B. Optimal allocation of distributed generators DG based Manta Ray Foraging Optimization algorithm (MRFO). *Ain Shams Eng. J.* **2021**, *12*, 609–619. [CrossRef]
19. Sanjay, R.; Jayabarathi, T.; Raghunathan, T.; Ramesh, V.; Mithulananthan, N. Optimal allocation of distributed generation using hybrid grey wolf optimizer. *IEEE Access* **2017**, *5*, 14807–14818. [CrossRef]
20. Dixit, M.; Kundu, P.; Jariwala, H.R. Incorporation of distributed generation and shunt capacitor in radial distribution system for techno-economic benefits. *Eng. Sci. Technol. Int. J.* **2017**, *20*, 482–493. [CrossRef]
21. Karunarathne, E.; Pasupuleti, J.; Ekanayake, J.; Almeida, D. Optimal placement and sizing of DGs in distribution networks using MLPSO algorithm. *Energies* **2020**, *13*, 6185. [CrossRef]
22. Devabalaji, K.R.; Yuvaraj, T.; Ravi, K. An efficient method for solving the optimal sitting and sizing problem of capacitor banks based on cuckoo search algorithm. *Ain Shams Eng. J.* **2018**, *9*, 589–597. [CrossRef]
23. Sultana, U.; Khairuddin, A.B.; Mokhtar, A.S.; Zareen, N.; Sultana, B. Grey wolf optimizer-based placement and sizing of multiple distributed generation in the distribution system. *Energy* **2016**, *111*, 525–536. [CrossRef]
24. Sambaiah, K.S.; Jayabarathi, T. Optimal allocation of renewable distributed generation and capacitor banks in distribution systems using salp swarm algorithm. *Int. J. Renew. Energy Res.* **2019**, *9*, 96–107. [CrossRef]
25. Khodabakhshian, A.; Andishgar, M.H. Simultaneous Placement and Sizing of DGs and Shunt Capacitors in Distribution Systems by Using IMDE algorithm. *Electr. Power Energy Syst.* **2016**, *82*, 599–607. [CrossRef]
26. Ali, A.; Keerio, M.U.; Laghari, J.A. Optimal site and size of distributed generation allocation in radial distribution network using multi-objective optimization. *J. Mod. Power Syst. Clean Energy* **2020**, *9*, 404–415. [CrossRef]
27. Shuaijia, H.; Hongjun, G.; Hao, T.; Lingfeng, W.; Youbo, L.; Junyong, L. A Two-stage Robust Optimal Allocation Model of Distributed Generation Considering Capacity Curve and Real-time Price Based Demand Response. *J. Mod. Power Syst. Clean Energy* **2021**, *9*, 114–127. [CrossRef]
28. Samala, R.K.; Kotapuri, M.R. Optimal allocation of distributed generations using hybrid technique with fuzzy logic controller radial distribution system. *SN Appl. Sci.* **2020**, *2*, 191. [CrossRef]
29. Hashim, F.A.; Houssein, E.H.; Hussain, K.; Mabrouk, M.S.; Al-Atabany, W. Honey Badger Algorithm: New metaheuristic algorithm for solving optimization problems. *Math. Comput. Simul.* **2022**, *192*, 84–110. [CrossRef]
30. Kansal, S.; Kumar, V.; Tyagi, B. Hybrid approach for optimal placement of multiple DGs of multiple types in distribution networks. *Int. J. Electr. Power Energy Syst.* **2016**, *75*, 226–235. [CrossRef]
31. Eminoglu, U.; Hocaoglu, M.H. Distribution systems forward/backward sweep-based power flow algorithms: A review and comparison study. *Electr. Power Compon. Syst.* **2008**, *37*, 91–110. [CrossRef]
32. Aman, M.M.; Jasmon, G.B.; Bakar, A.H.A.; Mokhlis, H. A new approach for optimum simultaneous multi-DG distributed generation Units placement and sizing based on maximization of system loadability using HPSO (hybrid particle swarm optimization) algorithm. *Energy* **2014**, *66*, 202–215. [CrossRef]
33. Kumar, A.; Vijay Babu, P.; Murty, V.V.S.N. Distributed generators allocation in radial distribution systems with load growth using loss sensitivity approach. *J. Inst. Eng.* **2017**, *98*, 275–287. [CrossRef]
34. Begg, C.M.; Begg, K.S.; Du Toit, J.T.; Mills, M.G.L. Scent-marking behaviour of the honey badger, mellivora capensis (mustelidae), in the southern Kalahari. *Anim. Behav.* **2003**, *66*, 917–929. [CrossRef]
35. Begg, C.M.; Begg, K.S.; Du Toit, J.T.; Mills, M.G.L. Life-history variables of an atypical mustelid, the honey badger mellivora capensis. *J. Zool.* **2005**, *265*, 17–22. [CrossRef]
36. Kapner, D.J.; Cook, T.S.; Adelberger, E.G.; Gundlach, J.H.; Heckel, B.R.; Hoyle, C.D.; Swanson, H.E. Tests of the gravitational inverse-square law below the dark-energy length scale. *Phys. Rev. Lett.* **2007**, *98*, 021101. [CrossRef]
37. Akopyan, A.V. Geometry of the cardioid. *Amer. Math. Mon.* **2015**, *122*, 144–150. [CrossRef]
38. Abdel-Mawgoud, H.; Ali, A.; Kamel, S.; Rahmann, C.; Abdel-Moamen, M.A. A Modified Manta Ray Foraging Optimizer for Planning Inverter-Based Photovoltaic with Battery Energy Storage System and Wind Turbine in Distribution Networks. *IEEE Access* **2021**, *9*, 91062–91079. [CrossRef]
39. Ali, E.S.; Abd Elazim, S.M.; Abdelaziz, A.Y. Ant lion optimization algorithm for renewable distributed generations. *Energy* **2016**, *116*, 445–458. [CrossRef]
40. Mahmoud, K.; Yorino, N.; Ahmed, A. Optimal distributed generation allocation in distribution systems for loss minimization. *IEEE Trans. Power Syst.* **2016**, *31*, 960–969. [CrossRef]

41. Mohamed, A.A.; Kamel, S.; Selim, A.; Khurshaid, T.; Rhee, S.B. Developing a Hybrid Approach Based on Analytical and Metaheuristic Optimization Algorithms for the Optimization of Renewable DG Allocation Considering Various Types of Loads. *Sustainability* **2021**, *13*, 4447. [CrossRef]
42. Biswal, S.R.; Shankar, G. Optimal sizing and allocation of capacitors in radial distribution system using sine cosine algorithm. In Proceedings of the IEEE International Conference on Power Electronics, Drives and Energy Systems (PEDES 2018), Chennai, India, 18–21 December 2018; pp. 1–4. [CrossRef]
43. Shuaib, Y.M.; Kalavathi, M.S.; Rajan, C.C.A. Optimal capacitor placement in radial distribution system using gravitational search algorithm. *Int. J. Electr. Power Energy Syst.* **2015**, *64*, 384–397. [CrossRef]
44. Nowdeh, S.A.; Davoudkhani, I.F.; Moghaddam, M.H.; Najmi, E.S.; Abdelaziz, A.Y.; Ahmadi, A.; Razavi, S.E.; Gandoman, F.H. Fuzzy multi-objective placement of renewable energy sources in distribution system with objective of loss reduction and reliability improvement using a novel hybrid method. *Appl. Soft Comput.* **2019**, *77*, 761–779. [CrossRef]

mathematics

Article

Harris Hawk Optimization-Based Deep Neural Networks Architecture for Optimal Bidding in the Electricity Market

Kavita Jain [1], Muhammed Basheer Jasser [2], Muzaffar Hamzah [3,*], Akash Saxena [1] and Ali Wagdy Mohamed [4,5]

1 Department of Electrical Engineering, Swami Keshvanand Institute of Technology, Management and Gramothan, Jaipur 302017, Rajasthan, India; kjkavitajain.21@gmail.com (K.J.); akash@skit.ac.in (A.S.)
2 Department of Computing and Information Systems, School of Engineering and Technology, Sunway University, Petaling Jaya 47500, Selangor, Malaysia; basheerj@sunway.edu.my
3 Faculty of Computing and Informatics, Universiti Malaysia Sabah, Kota Kinabalu 88450, Sabah, Malaysia
4 Operations Research Department, Faculty of Graduate Studies for Statistical Research, Cairo University, Giza 12613, Egypt; aliwagdy@gmail.com
5 Department of Mathematics and Actuarial Science, School of Sciences Engineering, The American University in Cairo, New Cairo 11835, Egypt
* Correspondence: muzaffar@ums.edu.my

Abstract: In the power sector, competitive strategic bidding optimization has become a major challenge. Digital plate-form provides a superior technical base as well as backing for the optimization's execution. The state-of-the-art frameworks used for simulating strategic bidding decisions in deregulated electricity markets (EM's) in this article are bi-level optimization and neural networks. In this research, we provide HHO-NN (Harris Hawk Optimization-Neural network), a novel algorithm based on Harris Hawk Optimization (HHO) that is capable of fast convergence when compared to previous evolutionary algorithms for automatically searching for meaningful multilayered perceptron neural networks (MPNNs) topologies for optimal bidding. This technique usually demands a considerable amount of time and computer resources. This method sets up the problem in multi-dimensional continuous state-action spaces, allowing market players to get precise information on the effect of their bidding judgments on the market clearing results, as well as implement more valuable bidding decisions by utilizing a whole action domain and accounting for non-convex operating principles. Due to the use of the MPNN, case studies show that the suggested methodology delivers a much larger profit than other state-of-the-art methods and has a better computational performance than the benchmark HHO technique.

Keywords: electricity market; optimal bidding; Harris Hawk Optimization; multi layered neural network; bi-level optimization; strategic bidding

MSC: 68T01; 68T05; 68T07; 68T09; 68T20; 68T30

Citation: Jain, K.; Jasser, M.B.; Hamzah, M.; Saxena, A.; Mohamed, A.W. Harris Hawk Optimization-Based Deep Neural Networks Architecture for Optimal Bidding in the Electricity Market. *Mathematics* **2022**, *10*, 2094. https://doi.org/10.3390/math10122094

Academic Editor: Jian Dong

Received: 16 May 2022
Accepted: 10 June 2022
Published: 16 June 2022

1. Introduction

Many economic systems used in the power sector's research are centralized, optimize the objective of the system (e.g., maximizing social welfare) and assume that market participants behave in a perfectly competitive (price-taking) manner. However, increasing attempts to deregulate the power industry have resulted in increased competition among several self-interested (profit-driven) market competitors, particularly in the production and supplier domains. Due to the fact that self-interested market player's nature is not always allied with global targets, existing centralized frameworks are no longer able to give accurate perspectives. Consequently, emerging market methods that are useful are capable of tracking the strategic (price-making) behavior of self-interested market players as well as recognizing the market outcomes that result from their interactions [1].

Power production and transmission have evolved from vertically integrated operations to market-driven operations in the world's main economies. The liberalization of the power sector has resulted in increased effectiveness through rivalry among market players. In the energy sector, generators are the ideal candidates for iteration in rivalry to enhance the effectiveness and competitiveness in allocation of resources, as well as to compete for the cheapest cost with the superior products. Real-time balancing and day ahead are the two kinds of energy markets. In a real market, rivals purchase energy during the business days, and energy prices are established daily or hourly based on requirement and production. A study of spikes in electricity price has been conducted in reference [2]. In a day ahead market, participants purchase wholesale energy in the day-ahead power sector a day before the operating days, and the discrepancy among planned and real needs on the operating day is compensated in the real time marketplace [3].

An energy pool in the day ahead marketplace is one of the key services in the wholesale competitive liberated energy sector in the reformation of the electrical energy industry across the world [4]. The Independent System Operator (ISO) finalized generators bids for every hour of the next day in the day ahead marketplace. So each generator provides bids to the ISO for each hour of the following day. The proposed price must be greater than zero but less than the industry restriction. The ISO examines bids to establish the hourly MCP and the amount of power to be delivered by each generator's framework of the proposed cost and MCP [5]. The EM mechanism that is explained above is shown in Figure 1.

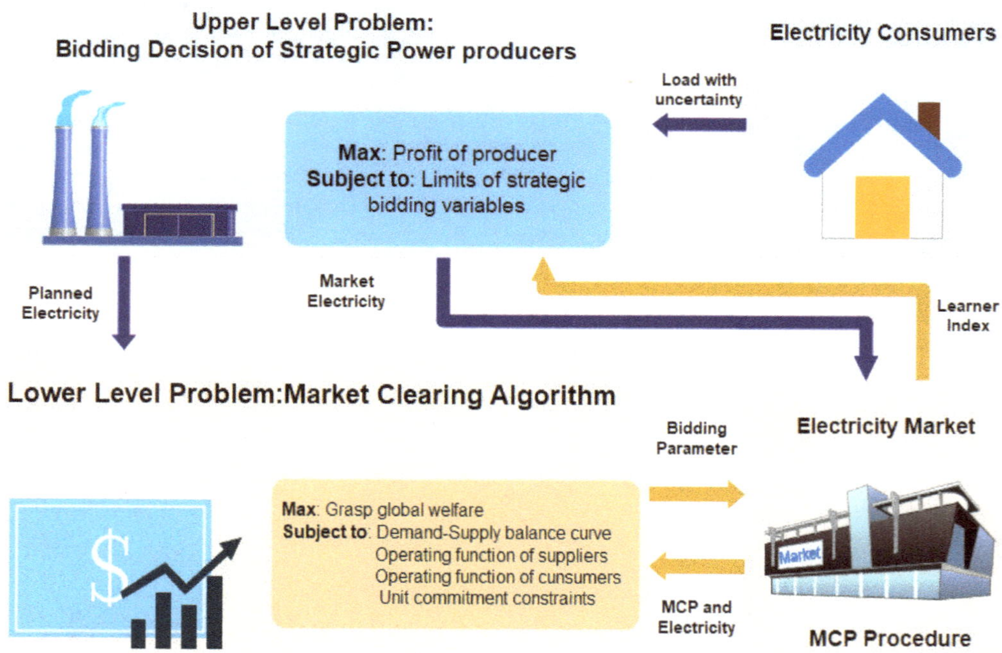

Figure 1. Electricity Market Mechanism.

A two-auction system exists: (a) uniform price, which provides just at agreed level (with such a price available at a cheaper clearance cost) based on hourly MCP, and (b) pay-as-bid auction, which pays at the accepted level of each generator based on its applicable rate [6]. In every marketplace, the price-forecasting process is linked to: (a) size of the market (the amount of prospective producers and consumers); (b) market structure and process (including such payment methods or accessibility) [7]; (c) degree of access to market and player's information; and (d) risk analysis options [8]. Even so, there really are discrepancies among energy and other commodity markets, such as:

a Energy cannot be conveniently collected and should be used instantaneously produced because the physiological delivery method works much quicker than any industry [9];
b Energy transportation needs to carry massive losses and expenses, as well as special distribution facilities;
c Power systems are the most destructive especially in comparison to other traded commodities, and all of these factors conspire to create energy as the most turbulent commodity.
d Although production and consumption should be coordinated at all times, electricity supply must be demanded precisely at any given time from across the system.
e At the annual, weekly, and daily levels, the MCP demonstrates considerable periodicity [10].
f The electrical consumer has no control over which generator creates the load, and the generator has no control over which customers receive electricity [10].

Optimization approaches influenced by nature: swarm intelligence is a popular branch of artificial intelligence in which algorithms are created by emulating the intelligent behaviour of various animals such as wolves, whales, ants, lions, crows, and bees. HHO [11] is a swarm intelligence-based method that was recently discovered to solve real-world optimization problems. Ali Asghar Heidari et al. found it in 2019 [11] after being inspired by Harris 'hawks' cooperative behaviour and chasing style in a setting known as amazement jump. A few hawks agreeably jump a victim from varied angles in order to astonish it. Harris hawks can find a variety of pursuing examples based on the rabbit's distinct concept of situations and getting away from instances. To nurture an optimization method, this research endeavour numerically simulates such powerful examples and behaviours. Regardless of the fact that there are various nature-inspired optimization methods based on stochastic behaviour available in the literature, the HHO algorithm was chosen in this study due to its acceptable search space exploration strength when compared to other meta-heuristic algorithms. A multi-strategy search was inspired by the prey hunting behaviour of Harris's hawk. The least squares support vector machine (LSSVM) was utilised to represent the reactive power output of the synchronous condenser, and the developed Harris Hawks optimization algorithm was employed to optimise it.

Times series system [12], GARCH system [13], a mixture of wavelet transform and ARIMA [14], fuzzy auto regression framework [15], game theory [16], Bayesian optimization [17], neural network [18], and a combination of a machine learning algorithm and bat [19] have all been presented in the literature as methodologies for predicting electricity prices. Game theory, time series models, and simulation models make up the MCP prediction method; time series architectures are classified into three categories: stochastic models, machine intelligence models, and casual models [20].

1.1. Related Work

ANN has been identified to be the most appropriate model for predicting MCP from the above described models. They can evaluate the complicated relationship among next day MCP and past information of demand and other factors such as type of day, load, temperature, settling point, period, and so on. Among the most extensively utilized techniques for forecasting MCP judging by past data are NN architectures [21]. Authors used an NN to estimate MCP for the Australian power industry for many hours. Because the synthetic data and the Euclidean distance norm with normalized considerations were used to pick comparable days, the study revealed a significant exponential relationship with a rise in the hourly price prediction from 9.75% for one-hour-ahead forecasts to 20.03% for six-hour-ahead forecasts [22].

A Combinatorial Neural Network (CNN) was presented by Abedinia et al. to predict MCP in the Pennsylvania-New Jersey-Maryland (PJM) and mainland Spain markets. The parameters of the NN in CNN are optimized using the Chemical Reaction Optimization (CRO) technique in this system, and the mean WME is equivalent to 4.04% [5]. Authors created a novel hybrid method for predicting MCP in the Spanish and Pennsylvania-New Jersey-Maryland energy markets by merging the bat optimization with an NN; numerical results reveal that the average MAPE value is less than 1% [19]. Anbazhagan and Kumarappan suggested a model to predict MCP in the Spanish and New York electrical markets, with improvements in the average MPCE of 0.7 percent and 0.9 percent above the NN method, correspondingly [23].

The above-mentioned NN methods can be subdivided as: a heuristic technique whihc was used to measure the periodicity pattern of MCP in group 1, and another which was used to improve NN performance in group 2. Each of these qualities has indeed been addressed in this article. It is difficult to enhance MCP forecast accuracy because of its inherent stochastic and nonlinear tendencies. As a result, we report a novel hybrid model architecture that combines NN, PSO, and GA algorithms. Rather than using the classic back propagation method, PSO is used to enhance the learning power of a conventional neural network and optimize the weights of the NN, resulting in a local optimal configuration [19]. The GA is used to optimize the number of hidden layers on the NN [19] because networks are important to a number of neurons in their hidden layers. Since MCP has a periodicity tendency, the K-means method was used to analyse the NN's training dataset and identify MCP's periodicity trend [24]. This study proposes a machine learning-driven portfolio optimization methodology for virtual bidding in electricity markets that takes both risk and price sensitivity into account. To maximise profit, an algorithmic trading strategy is built from the standpoint of a proprietary trading firm [25]. The goal of this article is to maximise power market transactions and clearing price using metaheuristic algorithms. To achieve feasible results in a short amount of time, the exhaustive search algorithm is implemented using a parallel computer architecture. The global optimal outcome is used as a metric to compare the effectiveness of various metaheuristic algorithms. The results, discussion, comparison, and recommendations for the suggested set of algorithms and performance tests are presented in this work [26]. This article gives a case study of Pakistan's electricity system, with information on electricity generated, connected load, frequency deviation, and load shedding during the course of a 24-h period. The data were evaluated using two methods: a traditional artificial neural network (ANN) with a feed forward back propagation model and a Bootstrap aggregating or bagging approach.

1.2. Major Contributions and Paper Structure

As previously stated, the following is a summary of our suggested method's contribution:

a The article presents a novel fusion architecture for optimal bidding in the power industry that fuses neural networks, and HHO.

b In order to select the best records from past data to acquire NN, hourly data have been clustered based on the demands and bidding data of market participants;

c To check the efficacy of HHO-NN, the results are compared against some recently developed, strong algorithms.

The arrangement of this manuscript is systematized as follows in Figure 2.

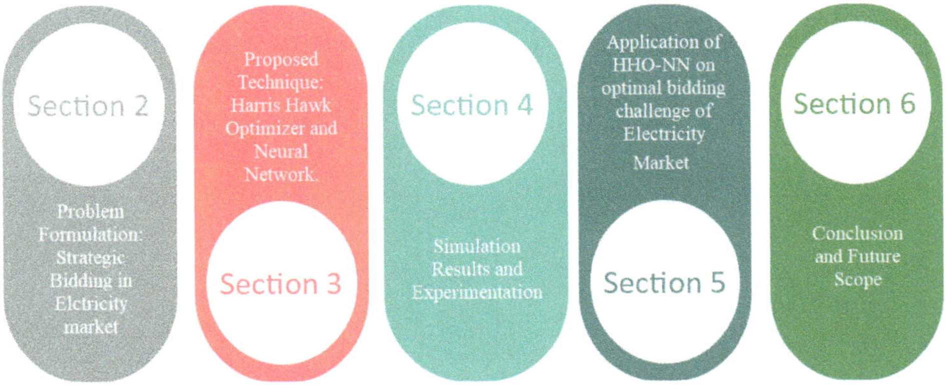

Figure 2. Systematized format of manuscript.

2. Problem Formulation

The following section presents a brief overview of the Gen-Co bidding strategy approach as well as the issue's algebraic formulation. The sub-sections that follow cover everything that was previously mentioned.

2.1. Bidding Strategy

A generating company has run at a high degree of efficiency to flourish in a fierce competition. However, in the electricity sector, good execution may not be enough since, in order to generate the most profit, it must sell its products at a competitive price. Different factors affect a producing company's profit, including its own bids, bids submitted by competitors, overall energy demands, and so on. Despite the fact that a generating company has no control over its competitors' bids or the energy demand, it can create its own strategy for putting in a bid that maximizes profit while minimizing risk, as shown in Figure 3.

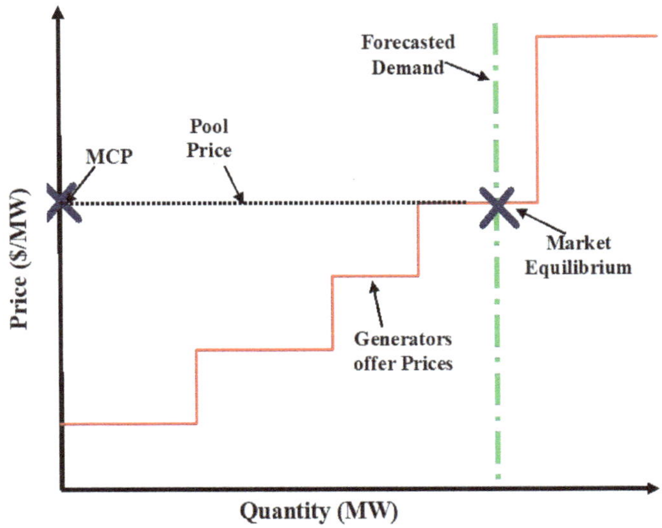

Figure 3. Supplier side's bidding strategy.

2.2. Mathematical Formulation

The market operator plots an upward production possibilities curve and a vertical line for consumer expectations following accepting offers from the Gen-Co's. The point where the two curves intersect is the equilibrium point, and the straight line drawn from the equilibrium point on the y-axis determines the system's MCP.

2.2.1. Objective Function

The profit of Gen-Co is calculated using the given (1).

$$Gen - Co_{k,profit} = Revenue - Gen - Co_{k,cost} \tag{1}$$

here,

$$Revenue = MCP \times Q_k \tag{2}$$

$$Gen - Co_{k,cost} = a_k Q_k + b_k Q_k^2 \tag{3}$$

where, Q_k is the amount of quantity of kth Gen-Co trade in the market. a_k and b_k are the cost coefficients.

2.2.2. Operating Constraints

i Generation Limits

$$Q_{min} U_{k(t)} \leq Q_{k(t)} \leq Q_{max} U_{k(t)}\ ,\ \forall t \in T \tag{4}$$

ii Inter-temporal constraints

$$(1 - U_{k(t+1)}) M_k^{ut} \leq h_{k(t)}^{on},\ if\ U_{k(t)} = 1. \tag{5}$$

$$U_{k(t+1)} M_k^{dt} \leq h_{k(t)}^{off},\qquad if\ U_{k(t)} = 0. \tag{6}$$

iii Limits on bid price

$$C_{min} \leq Gen - Co_{k,cost} \leq \overline{C} \tag{7}$$

3. Proposed Technique

3.1. Harris Hawks Optimization Algorithm: A Framework

Ali Asghar Heidari et al. [11] presented the Harris Hawks Optimization (HHO) meta-heuristic algorithm in the year 2019. Harris hawks exhibit superb social behavior with respect to hunting and attacking the bunny. Searching for a bunny, hitting it in various ways, and executing a rapid jump are all part of the exploitative aspects of the technique. Harris hawks spread to various locations in search of rabbits, and they use two distinct investigating tactics. Aspirants are perhaps the intended prey or very close to it, with the targeted prey or really close to it being the ideal. Harris hawks perch in a spot similar to those of other families, as well as the bunny in the very first encounter (prey). The hawks in the second step look for tall trees randomly. The HHO then progresses an optimization process by mathematically faking such beneficial approaches and behaviors.

3.1.1. Initialization Step

At this step, the search space and objective function are defined. Furthermore, the first population-based chaotic maps are being developed. In addition, all of the attribute values have been specified.

3.1.2. The Step of Exploration

During this step, all Harris hawks are viable candidate responses. In each cycle, the fitness value is computed for each of these viable alternatives based on the desired prey. Two approaches have been introduced to replicate the exploring capabilities of Harris hawks in the search area, as specified in Equation (8).

$$z(i+1) = \begin{cases} z_r(i) - g_1 |z_r(i) - 2g_2 z(i)| & q \geq 0.5 \\ (z_{rabbit}(i) - z_a(i)) - g_3(lb + g_4(ub - lb)) & q < 0.5, \end{cases} \tag{8}$$

The hawks' positions within (ub-lb) borders are based upon two precepts: (1) create the responses using a hawk from the current population as well as other hawks randomly and (2) build outcomes based on the prey's position, the average hawk's location, and random weighted elements. Despite the fact that g3 is a scale parameter, if the value of r4 reaches one, it will help to boost the unpredictability of the algorithm. This law adds an arbitrarily scaled drive length to lb.

Additional dynamic capabilities to investigate other sections of the feature space are explored with a random scaled component. The average hawk posture (solutions) is stated as follows in Equation (9):

$$z_a(i) = \frac{1}{n}\sum_{l=1}^{n} z_l(i) \tag{9}$$

Once the hawk uses the random hawks' information to catch the rabbit, rule 1 is usually applied in Equation (8). Rule 2 is executed once all hawks have accepted the finest hawk and the optimal option have been picked.

3.1.3. From Exploration to Exploitation Transition

This step depicts how HHO progresses from exploration to exploitation based on the bunny's level of energy (E). The strength of the bunny is gradually depleted as a result of the bunny's escaping behaviors, as according HHO. The energy needed decline is modeled in Figure 4.

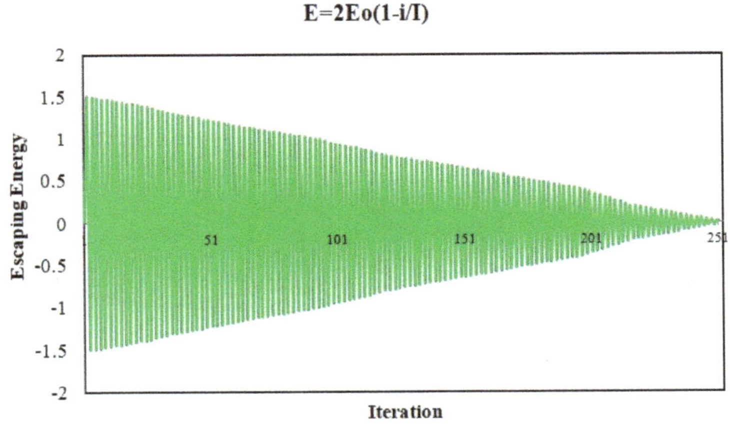

Figure 4. For 250 iteration, E's behavior changes with time.

E_0 is the expected power decline, as shown in Equation (10).

$$E = 2E_0\left(1 - \frac{i}{I}\right), \quad E_0 \in [-1,\ 1] \tag{10}$$

3.1.4. Step of Exploitation

In this step, the exploitation step is accomplished by employing four distinct factors. The position that was discovered during the exploration stage determines these strategies. Despite the hawks' best efforts to track it down and catch it, the prey frequently sought to flee. To emulate the hawks' offensive style, HHO exploitation employs four basic strategies. The four strategies are soft besiege, soft besiege with progressive speedy dives, hard besiege, and hard besiege with progressive speedy dives. These approaches are contingent on two variables, r and $|E|$, which label the technique to be cast-off. Where, $|E|$ is the prey's escaping energy and r is the probability of escaping, with $r < 0.5$ indicating a better likelihood of the prey escaping effectively and $r \geq 0.5$ representing an unsuccessful escape.

The following is an overview of these approaches:

- Soft besiege approach
  The rabbit has some energy to escape in the soft besiege method, where $r \geq 0.5$ and $|E| \geq 0.5$, while the hawks are softly encircling the prey suddenly lost additional energy before completing the unexpected pounce. In Equations (11)–(13), soft besiege is described mathematically.

$$z(i+1) = \Delta z(i) - E|jz_{rabbit} - z(i)| \tag{11}$$

$$\Delta z(i) = z_{rabbit} - z(i) \tag{12}$$

$$j - 2(1 - r_5), g_5 \in [0, 1] \tag{13}$$

- Hard besiege approach
  The prey is so tired when $r \geq 0.5$ and $|E| < 0.5$ and at this time the escaping energy is very low. In addition, the Harris hawks scarcely encircle the planned prey to at long last play out the unexpected pounce. The present positions are updated in this condition by using Equation (14).

$$z(i+1) = z_{rabbit}(i) - E|\Delta z(i)| \tag{14}$$

An easy instance of this step with one hawk is represented in Figure 5.

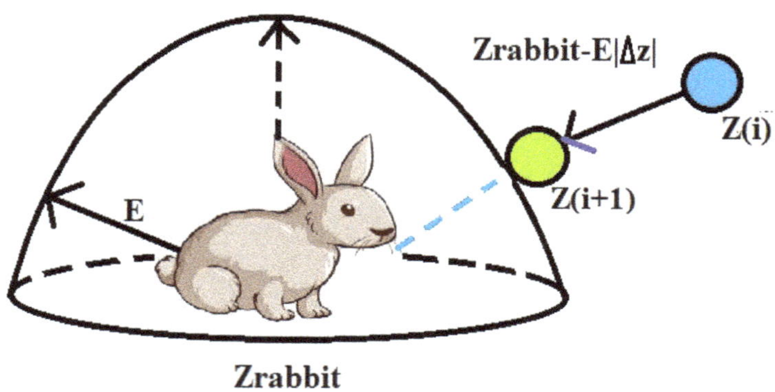

Figure 5. In the scenario of a hard besiege, a sample of overall vectors.

- Soft besiege approach with progressive speedy dives
  In this circumstance $r < 0.5$ and $|E| \geq 0.5$, the rabbit has enough energy to flee. The hawks move astutely around the prey and calmly plunges before the amazed jump. The harris hawk's position is refreshed in two stages throughout this action, which is referred to as adaptive soft besiege. In the initial stage, the harris hawks advance near the rabbit by assessing the following move of the rabbit as shown by Equation (15).

$$y = z_{rabbit}(i) - E|jz_{rabbit}(i) - z(i)| \tag{15}$$

In the subsequent stage, the harris hawks concluded to jump, in view of the examination between the past jump and the conceivable outcome. In case it is not, the harris hawk delivers an unpredictable jump, based on the Levy Flight (LF) idea, as detailed in Equation (16).

$$x = y + rv \times lf(Dim) \tag{16}$$

In Equation (16), the *Dim* represents the dimension of the solutions, *rv* is random vector of size 1 × *Dim*. *lf* is for the levy fight function and it is calculated using Equation (17).

$$lf(z) = 0.001 \times \frac{u \times \sigma}{|v|^{\frac{1}{\beta}}}, \sigma = \left(\frac{\Gamma(1+\beta) \times sin(\frac{\Pi\beta}{2})}{\Gamma(\frac{1+\beta}{2}) \times \beta \times 2(\frac{\beta-1}{2})}\right)^{\frac{1}{\beta}} \tag{17}$$

where u, v are random values inside (0.1) and β is a default constant and it is 1.5. In the soft besiege stage, Equation (11) can update the positions of hawks in the final strategy.

$$x = \begin{cases} yiff(y) < f(z(i)) \\ xiff(x) < f(z(i)) \end{cases} \tag{18}$$

An example of this process for one hawk is shown in Figure 6. Sometimes during iterations, the position background of LF-based leapfrog trends is also documented and shown in this illustration. There is an LF-based trend in one trial, and the colored dots are the location footprints. It will only be possible to pick the best position Y or Z in every step. It is the same for all of the search agents.

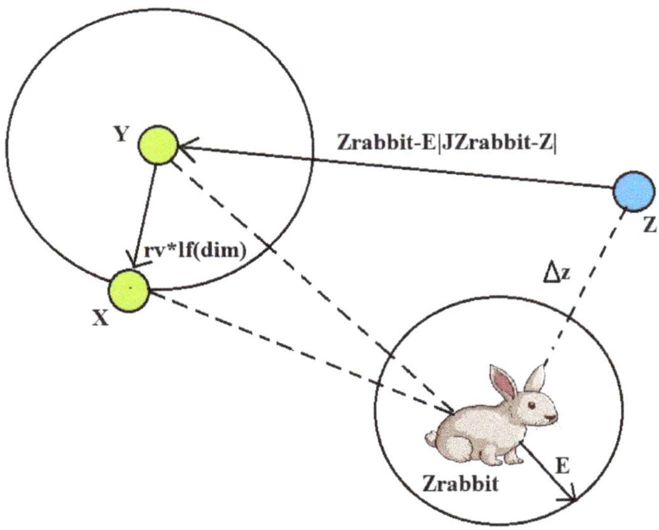

Figure 6. In the scenario of a soft besiege with progressive speedy dives, a sample of overall vectors.

- Hard besiege with progressive speedy dives
  The rabbit has not so much energy to escape at $r < 0.5$ and $|E| < 0.5$ and before the surprise pounce to capture and kill the prey, a hard besiege is constructed is shown in Figure 7.
  There are similarities between this step and the soft besiege, and yet this time, the hawks try to reduce one's average distance from the escaping prey. This is why it is necessary to follow all aspects when under hard besiege:

$$x = \begin{cases} yiff(y) < f(z(i)) \\ xiff(x) < f(z(i)) \end{cases} \tag{19}$$

where, y and x are calculated using Equations (20) and (21).

$$y = z_{rabbit}(i) - E|jz_{rabbit}(i) - z_a(i)| \tag{20}$$

$$x = y + rv \times lf(Dim) \tag{21}$$

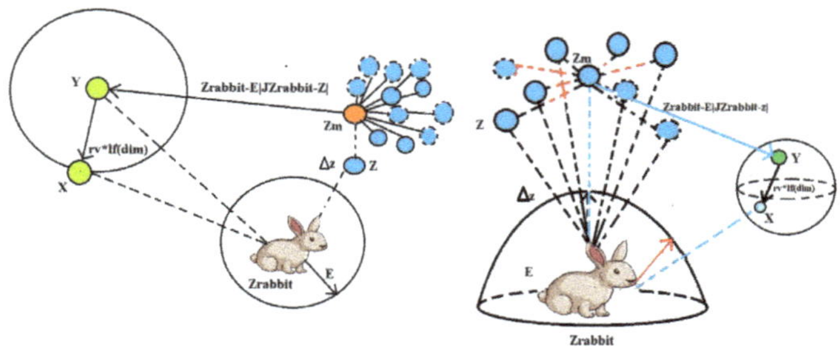

(**a**) 2D (**b**) 3D

Figure 7. In the circumstance of a hard besiege with progressive speedy dives in 2D and 3D dimension, an example of overall vectors.

The procedure of the HHO algorithm is presented in Figure 8.

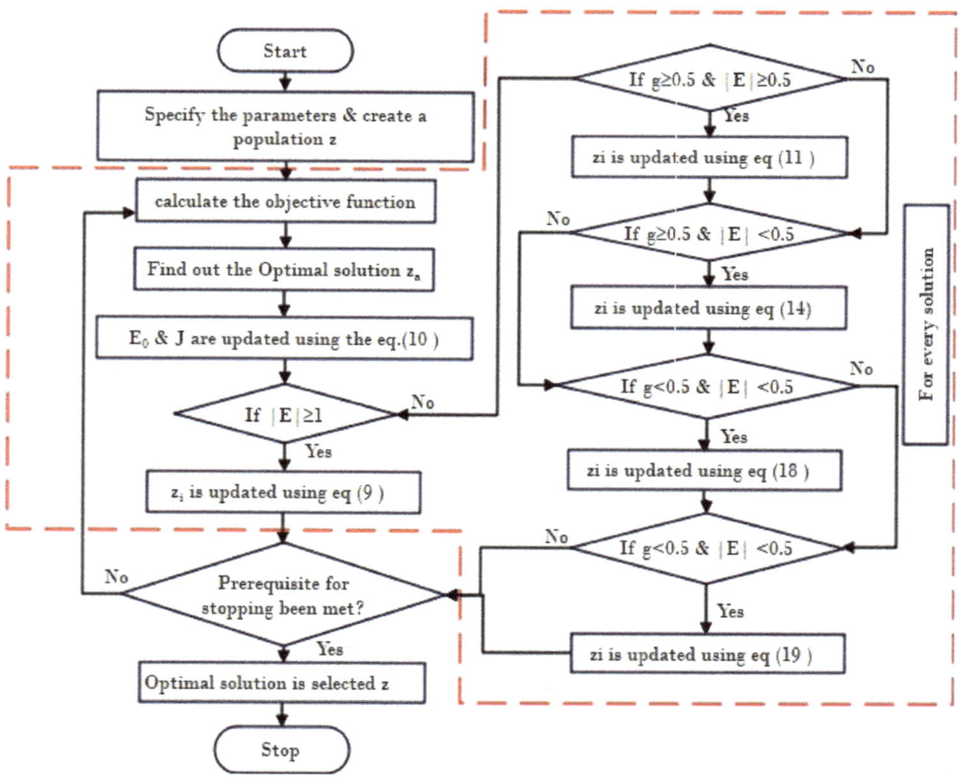

Figure 8. The Procedure of HHO.

4. Deep Neural Network

Deep neural network is a machine learning discipline that focuses on understanding several levels of representations by creating a structure of features in which the top levels are described by the lower tiers, and the same lower tier features can be used to construct many top level features [27]. The relation between artificial intelligence, machine learning and deep learning is presented in Figure 9.

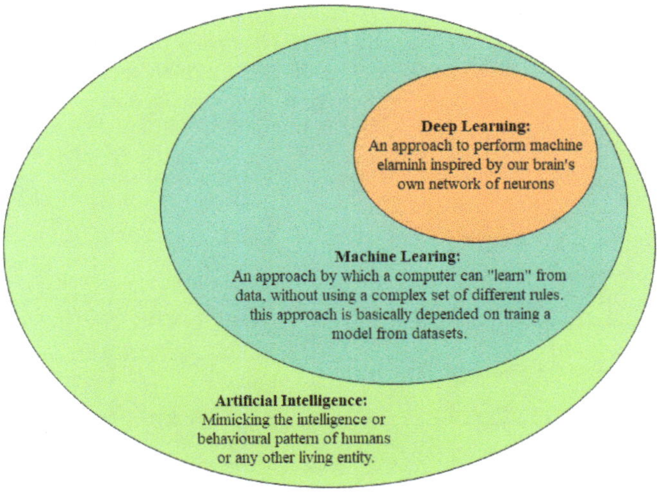

Figure 9. Relation between Artificial Intelligence, Machine Learning and Deep Learning.

To describe more complicated and nonlinear relationships, the DL (Deep Learning) structure extends classic neural networks (NN) by adding more hidden layers to the network design between the input and output layers. This approach has piqued the interest of academics in recent years due to its superior performance in a variety of EM applications [28–30]. Convolutional-Neural Networks (C-NN) have become a popular DL design in recent years because they can perform sophisticated functions using convolution filters. Another DL design that is commonly used for classification or regression with success in many areas is the Deep Neural Network (DNN). It is a common feed forward network in which the input passes from the input layer to the output layer via a number of hidden layers that exceed two [30]. The usual design for DNNs is shown in Figure 10, where Ni is the input layer, which contains neurons for input features, No is the output layer, which contains neurons for output classes, and Nh,l are the hidden layers.

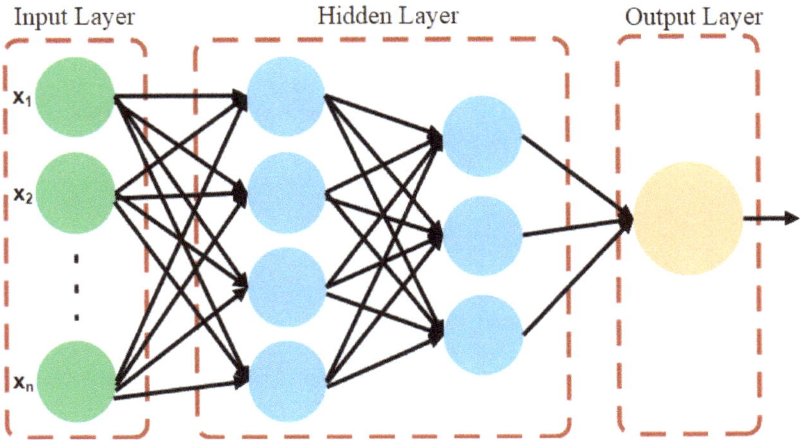

Figure 10. Three Layered Neural Network.

5. Harris Hawk Optimization of Deep Neural Networks Architecture

Figure 11 shows the general framework of the suggested model for estimating the optimal bids in EM. The suggested model's main goal is to improve the performance of the

NN by applying the HHO algorithm to discover the ideal NN weights, hence the name HHO-NN. The suggested HHO-NN begins by determining the beginning value for a group of N individuals X. Each of these individuals represents the NN weights, thus we have a collection of N networks from which to choose the best. As a result, the data set is randomly divided into training and testing sets of 70% and 30% respectively.

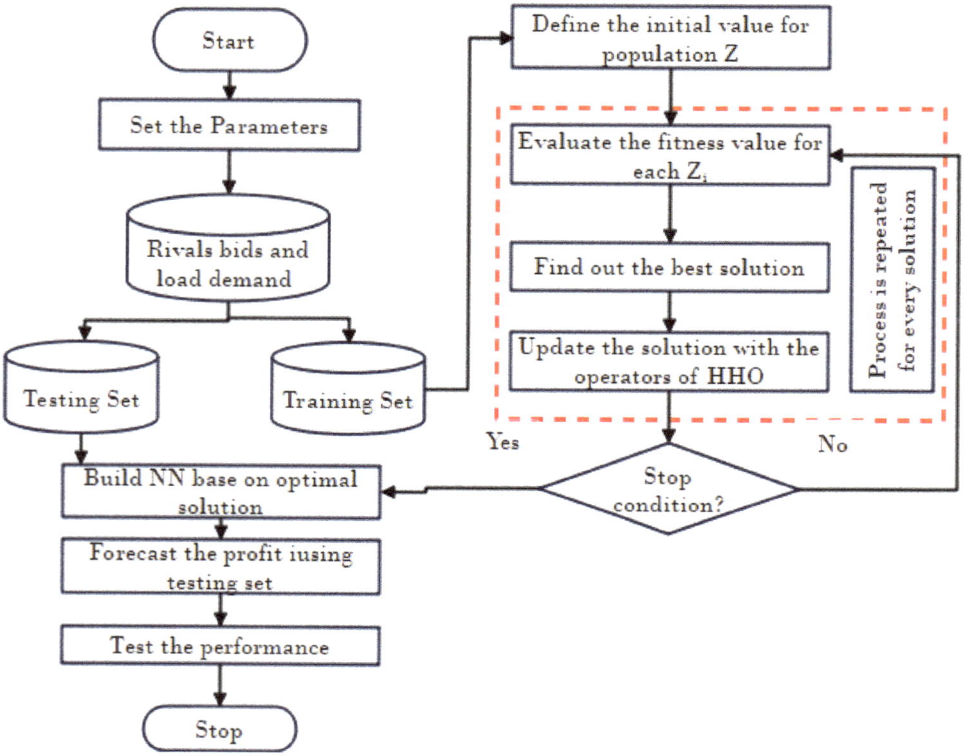

Figure 11. The proposed HHO-NN method.

The training data set is used to analyse the existing network's (solution) effectiveness by determining the corresponding objective function, which is dependent on the original value *yi* and the forecast value *y*.

$$fit=\sqrt{\frac{\sum_{l=1}^{ns} y_l-\hat{y}_l}{ns}} \tag{22}$$

The next phase is to locate the network, Yb, with the lowest fitness value. Then, using the optimal solution and the HHO's operation, the other solutions will be modified. When the stopping circumstances are achieved, the process of updating solutions and determining the best option will be completed. The test set is used to determine the quality of the output to evaluate the performance of the best network developed during the training phase.

6. Simulation Results and Experimentation

The variation is written in MATLAB 2019 and operates on a 4.00 GHz i5 processor with 8 GB of RAM. The number of iterations and population size for all algorithms are kept constant in order to draw an evaluation of optimization routines (i.e., maximum number of iterations = 500 and number of search agents = 50).

To test the forecasting potential of the ANN version, extraordinary criteria are used. This potential can be checked after the MCP is calculated. The four types of errors are checked in this, which are the root mean of squared error (RMSE), the mean absolute error (MAE), the mean absolute percentage error (MAPE) and the coefficient of co-relation (CC).The performance result of these tests is shown in Table 1 Regression verification of the proposed algorithm was also undertaken to check the validation of the same.

- Mean Absolute Error (MAE)
  The MAE is the average of the absolute values of the forecasting error and s calculated with Equation (23).

$$MAE = \frac{1}{1000}\sum_{i=1}^{1000}\left|f_i - \hat{f}_i\right| \tag{23}$$

- Mean Absolute Percentage Error (MAPE)
  The mean absolute percentage error is usually taken as a loss function for solving the problem of regression and in evaluation of model because of its very instinctive clarification in terms of relative error, as shown in Equation (24).

$$MAPE = \frac{1}{1000}\sum_{i=1}^{1000}\left|\frac{f_i - \hat{f}_i}{f_i}\right| \times 100 \tag{24}$$

- Root Mean Square Error (RMSE)
  The RMSE is defined as the square root of the second sample moment of the differences between predicted and actual data. RMSE is shown in Equation (25).

$$RMSE = \sqrt{\frac{1}{1000}\sum_{i=1}^{1000}(f_i - \hat{f}_i)^2} \tag{25}$$

- Coefficient of Co-relation (CC)
  To determine the strength of a relationship between data, correlation coefficient formulas are utilized as shown in Equation (26). The formulas return a number between −1 and 1, with the following values:
  - A strong positive association is indicated by a value of one.
  - A negative association is indicated by a value of −1.
  - A zero means that there is no connection at all.

$$CC = \frac{\sum_{i=1}^{1000}(\hat{f}_i - \overline{\hat{f}}_i)(f_i - \overline{f}_i)}{\sqrt{\sum_{i=1}^{1000}(\hat{f}_i - \overline{\hat{f}}_i)^2 \sum_{i=1}^{1000}(f_i - \overline{f}_i)^2}} \tag{26}$$

- Regression Verification Regression verification is the practice of ensuring that no significant errors have been created in the algorithm after the adjustments have been made by testing the altered sections of the code as well as the parts that may be affected by the modifications shown in Figure 12.
- A fair comparison has been made between different optimization algorithm tuned neural networks such as GWO-NN, ALO-NN, SCA-NN, WOA-NN and HHO-NN on the basis of error indices calculations, here we have reported MSE, RMSE and MAE values of the prediction it has been observed that proposed architecture yields the least errors in training and testing mode.

Table 1. Performance Test Results.

Model	Performance Test Result			
	MAE (m)	MAPE (%)	RMSE (m)	CC
Training Period				
ALO-NN	0.286	49.369	0.3054	0.9154
GWO-NN	0.21	45.658	0.2721	0.9514
SCA-NN	0.268	48.246	0.3012	0.9264
WOA-NN	0.254	46.565	0.2748	0.9421
HHO-NN	0.179	42.124	0.2541	0.9668
Testing Period				
ALO-NN	0.281	35.61	0.2967	0.8755
GWO-NN	0.204	31.74	0.2682	0.8977
SCA-NN	0.258	35.87	0.2964	0.8869
WOA-NN	0.249	32.54	0.2699	0.8013
HHO-NN	0.177	28.87	0.252	0.821

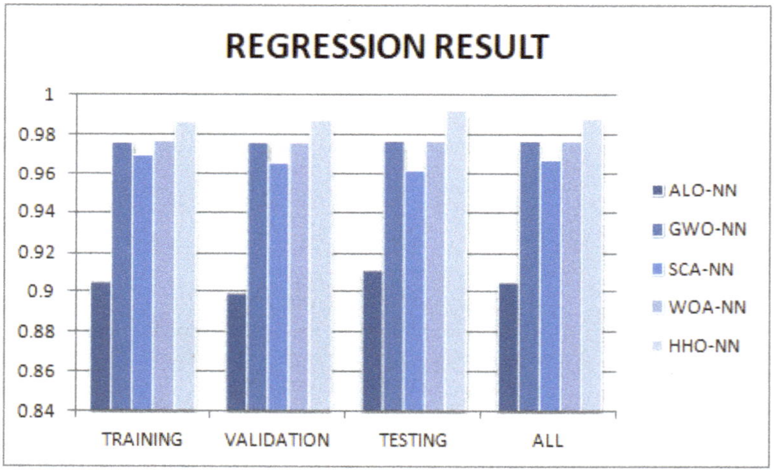

Figure 12. Regression Verification.

7. Application of HHO-NN on Optimal Bidding Challenge of Electricity Market

IEEE-14 bus test system is taken, where, three competing generating companies compete with Gen-Co-G. The competition is for selling power in EM, the bidding strategy is designed for optimum output. Table 2 shows the bid data of competitor prices and Table 3 shows the power-blocks data of Gen-Co-G [30].

For constructing the neural network, we have generated 1000 samples for preparing the HHO-NN, out of these data, 70% has been used for training and the remaining 15% has been kept for validation purposes. We report the results of some unknown samples in this analysis. A toal fo ten unknown samples were taken and the analysis of these samples is depicted through Figures 13 and 14 are the input and target data to train the NN. The input data to train the NN for the strategic bidding problem in EM are competitors' bidding data and the target data are profit of Gen-Co-G for the same inputs.

Table 2. Rival's Bidding Data for IEEE-14 Bus System [30].

Blocks	Q/Std. Dev./Mean	R1	R2	R3
Block I	Q (MW)	200	150	150
	Std. Dev. ($/MWh)	2	3	2
	Mean ($/MWh)	9	11	10
Block II	Q (MW)	120	120	140
	Std. Dev. ($/MWh)	3	2	3
	Mean ($/MWh)	15	17	18
Block III	Q (MW)	100	120	100
	Std. Dev. ($/MWh)	2	3	3
	Mean ($/MWh)	19	18	17
Block IV	Q (MW)	120	130	120
	Std. Dev. ($/MWh)	2	3	2
	Mean ($/MWh)	21	25	26
Block V	Q (MW)	50	45	40
	Std. Dev. ($/MWh)	2	3	3
	Mean ($/MWh)	27	32	25

Table 3. Power Blocks data of Gen-Co-G for IEEE-14 Bus System [30].

Block	c_0 ($/MW^{2}H)	c_I ($/MWH)	c_{II} ($/H)	P_{max}	P_{min}	MUT	MDT	C_{hs}	C_{cs}	t_c	c_n^{sd}
Block I	0.00375	2	0	250	10	1	1	70	176	1	50
Block II	0.0175	1.75	0	140	20	2	1	74	187	1	60
Block III	0.0625	1	0	100	15	1	1	50	113	1	30
Block IV	0.00834	3.25	0	120	10	1	2	110	267	1	85
Block V	0.025	3	0	45	10	1	1	72	180	4	52

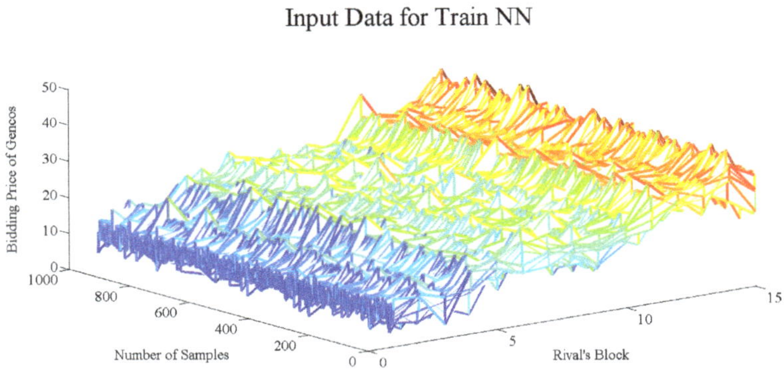

Figure 13. Input data for training the Neural Network.

Figure 15 represents the input data for testing the trained NN for the specific problem of attaining the optimal bids and optimal profit of the Gen-Co-G in the EM.

Figure 16 represents the profit curve obtained by the selected algorithms. From the figure, it can be observed that the proposed supervised net yields maximum profit as compared to other Monte Carlo-based optimization approaches. The cumulative profit calculated by this architecture is ($153,275). However, the profit calculated by HHO is ($138,758.75) , ALO-NN is ($128,543.42), GWO-NN is ($117,641), MFO-NN is ($121,051), ALO is ($80,176.20458), GWO is ($126,070.0738), SSA is ($86,375.01205) and WOA is ($119,826.25). This is due to the better anticipating capability of market conditions by the HHO tuned neural network.

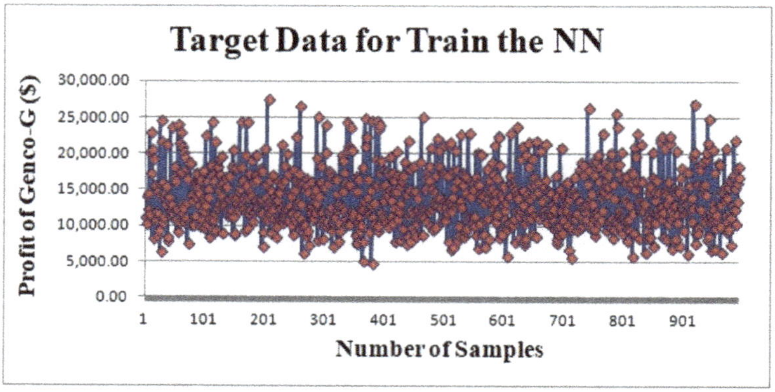

Figure 14. Target data for training the Neural Network.

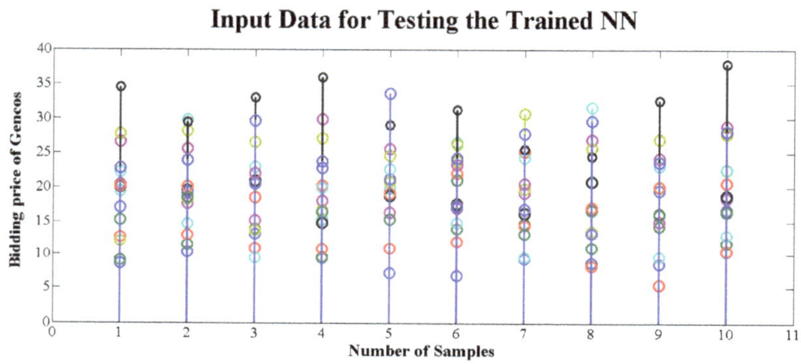

Figure 15. Input data for testing the Trained Neural Network.

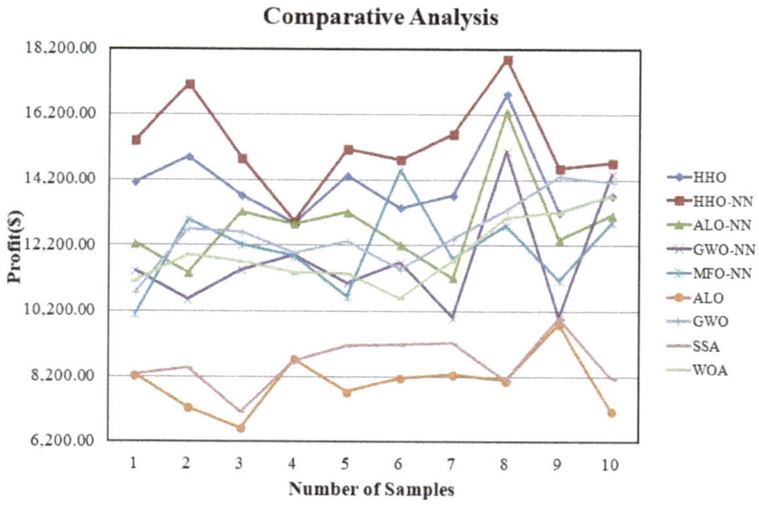

Figure 16. Comparative Analysis Cumulative Profit.

8. Conclusions and Future Scope

The proposed Harris Hawk Optimization-based Deep Neural Networks Architecture is used to investigate the optimum bidding strategy problem in the power market. Using the expected load and competitors' bidding data, the planned architecture determines the best bidding technique for maximising the profit. For various power demand values, provider end income, customer end profit, and MCP values, the proposed methodology is examined. IEEE 14 is used to dissect the viability of the suggested technique in the MATLAB/Simulink platform. The proposed approach displays excellent productivity by combining the relative examination with alternate techniques such as ALO-NN, GWO-NN, MFO-NN, ALO, GWO, SSA, WOA and standard HHO.

The proposed calculations have the advantages of reduced computational complexity and good accuracy in extrapolating subjective data. Furthermore, the proposed work's statistical measurements such as mean and standard deviation, as well as performance metrics such as best, worst, average, and computational time, were validated. It was demonstrated that the proposed methodology outperformed other strategies in terms of statistical measures when compared to methodologies for comparing results.

Furthermore, the investigations on the bigger network with multiple players and more constraints pertaining to generation, transmission limits, transmission congestion and consumer side bidding, will be addressed in our future publications.

Author Contributions: Conceptualization, K.J., A.S. and M.B.J. writing—original draft preparation: K.J. and A.S.; Data curation, K.J. and A.S.; Funding acquisition, M.H.; Investigation, K.J., A.S., M.B.J., M.H. and A.W.M.; Methodology, A.S.; Project administration, Resources, Supervision, A.S., M.B.J., M.H. and A.W.M.; Writing—review & editing, K.J., A.S., M.B.J. and A.W.M. All authors have read and agreed to the published version of the manuscript.

Funding: This research is funded by the UMS publication grant scheme.

Institutional Review Board Statement: Not applicable.

Informed Consent Statement: Not applicable.

Data Availability Statement: Not applicable.

Conflicts of Interest: The authors declare no conflict of interest.

Abbreviations

Acronym	
HHO	Harris Hawk Optimization
ANN	Artificial Neural Network
MPNN	Multilayered Perceptron Neural Networks
C-NN	Convolutional-Neural Networks
PJM	Pennsylvania-New Jersey-Maryland
EM	Electricity Market
ISO	Independent System Operator
MCP	Market Clearing Price
PSO	Particle Swarm Optimization
WOA	Whale Optimization Algorithm
SSA	Salp Swarm Algorithm
ALO	Ant Lion Optimizer
MAE	Mean Absolute Error
RMSE	Root Mean Square Error
MAPE	Mean Absolute Percentage Error
MSE	Mean of Squared Error
CC	Coefficient of Co-relation
DNN	Deep Neural Network
Gen-co	Generating Company

GARCH	Generalized Auto Regressive Conditional Heteroskedasticity
ARIMA	Auto Regressive Integrated Moving Average
CRO	Chemical Reaction Optimization
DL	Deep Learning
Nomenclature	
Q_{min}	Minimum limit of kth block of Gen-Co [MW].
Q_{max}	Maximum limit of kth block of Gen-Co-C [MW].
$U_{k(t)}$	Binary variable, which is equal to 1, if the kth block is committed at hour t; otherwise, 0.
M_k^{ut}	Minimum up time of kth block of Gen-Co [Hour].
M_k^{dt}	Minimum down time of kth block of Gen-Co [Hour].
$h_{k(t)}^{off}$	At the end of hour t [hr], the number of hours the kth block of Gen-Co has been continually OFF
$h_{k(t)}^{on}$	At the end of hour t [hr], the number of hours the kth block of Gen-Co has been continually ON.
$\underline{C}_{min}$	Gen-Co's operating expenses for the kth block.
$\overline{C}$	Cap on bid price
$z(i+1)$	s the position of Hawks in 2nd iteration i
z_{rabbit} (i)	the position of prey
z_r	the random solutions in the current population
$z(i)$	Hawks' position vector in the current iteration i
g_1, g_2, g_3, g_4 and q	Within [0, 1], a random scaled factor
lb and ub	lower bound and upper bound of variables
z_a	the number of solutions that are on average.
z_a (i)	In the current iteration, the average number of solutions.
n	all viable options
z_l (i)	In iteration i, the location of each solution
t	the maximum number of iterations
i	current iteration
$\Delta z(i)$	the difference between the position vector of the prey and the present location in iteration i
j	the prey's jump power
g_5	the random variable
Dim	the dimension of the solution
rv	random vector of size 1*dim
lf	the function of levy flight

References

1. Zaman, F.; Elsayed, S.M.; Ray, T.; Sarker, R.A. Co-evolutionary approach for strategic bidding incompetitive electricity markets. *Appl. Soft Comput.* **2017**, *51*, 1–22. [CrossRef]
2. Sandhu, H.S.; Fang, L.; Guan, L. Forecasting day-ahead price spikes for the Ontario electricity market. *Electr. Power Syst. Res.* **2016**, *141*, 450–459. [CrossRef]
3. Girish, G.P. Spot electricity price forecasting in Indian electricity market using autoregressive-Garch models. *Energy Strategy Rev.* **2016**, *11–12*, 52–57. [CrossRef]
4. Abedinia, O.; Amjadi, N.; Shafie-Khah, M.; Catalao, J.P.S. Electricity price forecast using combinatorial neural network trained by a new stochastic search method. *Energy Convers. Manag.* **2015**, *105*, 642–654. [CrossRef]
5. Grilli, L. *Deregulated Electricity Market and Auctions: The Italian Case*; Scientic Research an Academic Publisher: Wuhan, China, 2010; Volume 2, pp. 238–242.
6. Bunn, D.W. Forecasting loads and prices in competitive power markets. *IEEE Xplore* **2000**, *88*, 163–169. [CrossRef]
7. Girish, G.P.; Rath, B.N.; Akram, V. Spot electricity price discovery in Indian electricity market. *Renew. Sustain. Energy Rev.* **2018**, *82*, 73–79. [CrossRef]
8. Khosravi, A.; Nahav, I.S.; Creighton, D. A neural network-GARCH-based method for construction of prediction intervals. *Electr. Power Syst. Res.* **2013**, *96*, 185–193. [CrossRef]
9. Janczura, J.; Truck, S.; Weron, R.; Wol, R.C. Identifying spikes and seasonal components in electricity spot price data: A guide to robust modeling. *Energy Econ.* **2013**, *38*, 96–110. [CrossRef]
10. Heidari, A.A.; Mirjalili, S.; Faris, H.; Aljarah, I.; Mafarja, M.; Chen, H. Harris hawks optimization: Algorithm and applications. *Future Gener. Comput. Syst.* **2019**, *97*, 849–872. [CrossRef]

11. Tharani, S.; Yamini, C. Classification using convolutional neural network for heart and diabetics data-sets. *Int. J. Adv. Res. Comput. Commun. Eng.* **2016**, *5*, 417–422.
12. Jiao, S.; Wang, C.; Gao, R.; Li, Y.; Zhang, Q. Harris Hawks Optimization with Multi-Strategy Search and Application. *Symmetry* **2021**, *13*, 2364. [CrossRef]
13. Nogales, F.J.; Contreras, J.; Conejo, A.J.; Espinola, R. Forecasting next-day electricity prices by time series models. *IEEE Trans. Power Syst.* **2002**, *17*, 342–348. [CrossRef]
14. Zhang, J.; Tan, Z.; Yang, S. Day-ahead electricity price forecasting by a new hybrid method. *Comput. Ind. Eng.* **2012**, *63*, 695–701. [CrossRef]
15. Yang, Z.; Ce, L.; Lian, L. Electricity price forecasting by a hybrid model, combining wavelet transform. ARMA and kernel-based extreme learning machine methods. *Appl. Energy* **2017**, *190*, 291–305. [CrossRef]
16. Khashei, M.; Rafeiei, M.F.; Bijari, M. Hybrid fuzzy auto-regressive integrated moving average (FARIMAH) model for forecasting the foreign exchange markets. *Int. J. Comput. Intell. Syst.* **2013**, *6*, 954–968. [CrossRef]
17. Qi, Y.; Liu, Y.; Wu, Q. Non-cooperative regulation coordination based on game theory for wind farm clusters during ramping events. *Energy* **2017**, *132*, 136–146. [CrossRef]
18. Lago, J.; De Ridder, F.; Vrancx, P.; de Schutter, B. Forecasting day-ahead electricity prices in Europe: The importance of considering market integration. *Appl. Energy* **2018**, *211*, 890–903. [CrossRef]
19. Gholipour Khajeh, M.; Maleki, A.; Rosen, M.A.; Ahmadi, M.H. Electricity price forecasting using neural networks with an improved iterative training algorithm. *Int. J. Ambient. Energy* **2018**, *39*, 147–158. [CrossRef]
20. Bento, P.M.R.; Pombo, J.A.N.; Calado, M.R.A.; Mariano, S.J.P.S. A bat optimized neural network and wavelet transform approach for short-term price forecasting. *Appl. Energy* **2018**, *210*, 88–97. [CrossRef]
21. Aggarwal, S.K.; Saini, L.M.; Kumar, A. Electricity price forecasting in deregulated markets: A review and evaluation. *Int. J. Electr. Power Energy Syst.* **2009**, *31*, 13–22. [CrossRef]
22. Singhal, D.; Swarup, K.S. Electricity price forecasting using artificial neural networks. *Int. J. Electr. Power Energy Syst.* **2011**, *33*, 550–555. [CrossRef]
23. Mandal, P.; Senjyu, T.; Funabashi, T. Neural networks approach to forecast several hour ahead electricity prices and loads in deregulated market. *Energy Convers. Manag.* **2006**, *47*, 2128–2142. [CrossRef]
24. Pao, H.-T. Forecasting electricity market pricing using artificial neural networks. *Energy Convers. Manag.* **2007**, *48*, 907–912. [CrossRef]
25. Ostadi, B.; Sedeh, O.M.; Kashan, A.H. Risk-based optimal bidding patterns in the deregulated power market using extended Markowitz model. *Energy* **2020**, *191*, 116516. [CrossRef]
26. Kavita, J.; Saxena, A. Evolutionary Neural Network based hybrid architecture for strategic bidding in electricity market. In Proceedings of the 2021 IEEE 2nd International Conference on Smart Technologies for Power, Energy and Control (STPEC), Bilaspur, India, 19–22 December 2021.
27. Anbazhagan, S.; Kumarappan, N. Day-ahead deregulated electricity market price classification using neural network input featured by DCT. *Int. J. Electr. Power Energy Syst.* **2012**, *37*, 103–109. [CrossRef]
28. Li, Y.; Yu, N.; Wang, W. Machine learning-driven virtual bidding with electricity market efficiency analysis. *IEEE Trans. Power Syst.* **2021**, *37*, 354–364. [CrossRef]
29. Angulo, A.; Rodríguez, D.; Garzón, W.; Gómez, D.F.; Al Sumaiti, A.; Rivera, S. Algorithms for Bidding Strategies in Local Energy Markets: Exhaustive Search through Parallel Computing and Metaheuristic Optimization. *Algorithms* **2021**, *14*, 269. [CrossRef]
30. Tahir, M.F.; Saqib, M.A. Optimal scheduling of electrical power in energy-deficient scenarios using artificial neural network and Bootstrap aggregating. *Int. J. Electr. Power Energy Syst.* **2016**, *83*, 49–57. [CrossRef]

Σ mathematics

MDPI

Article

DL-Aided Underground Cavity Morphology Recognition Based on 3D GPR Data

Feifei Hou, Xu Liu, Xinyu Fan and Ying Guo *

School of Automation, Central South University, Changsha 410083, China
* Correspondence: yingguo@csu.edu.cn

Abstract: Cavity under urban roads has increasingly become a huge threat to traffic safety. This paper aims to study cavity morphology characteristics and proposes a deep learning (DL)-based morphology classification method using the 3D ground-penetrating radar (GPR) data. Fine-tuning technology in DL can be used in some cases with relatively few samples, but in the case of only one or very few samples, there will still be overfitting problems. To address this issue, a simple and general framework, few-shot learning (FSL), is first employed for the cavity classification tasks, based on which a classifier learns to identify new classes given only very few examples. We adopt a relation network (RelationNet) as the FSL framework, which consists of an embedding module and a relation module. Furthermore, the proposed method is simpler and faster because it does not require pre-training or fine-tuning. The experimental results are validated using the 3D GPR road modeling data obtained from the gprMax3D system. The proposed method is compared with other FSL networks such as ProtoNet, R2D2, and BaseLine relative to different benchmarks. The experimental results demonstrate that this method outperforms other prior approaches, and its average accuracy reaches 97.328% in a *four-way five-shot* problem using few support samples.

Keywords: ground-penetrating radar (GPR); cavity morphology recognition; few-shot learning (FSL); deep learning (DL); relation network (RelationNet)

MSC: 86-08

Citation: Hou, F.; Liu, X.; Fan, X.; Guo, Y. DL-Aided Underground Cavity Morphology Recognition Based on 3D GPR Data. *Mathematics* **2022**, *10*, 2806. https://doi.org/10.3390/math10152806

Academic Editor: Andrej Brodnik

Received: 27 June 2022
Accepted: 1 August 2022
Published: 8 August 2022

1. Introduction

Urban areas around the world continue to experience a series of sudden sinkhole collapses that cause severe traffic disruptions and significant economic losses. Underground cavities are the main reason for the formation of sinkholes. Complex conditions such as changes in drainage patterns, excessive pavement loads, and disturbances in infrastructure construction often lead to various cavities [1]. Therefore, the cavities may vary in morphology, for example, cavities with different shapes or combinations of several basic shapes, or they may be filled with different media or have different positions and sizes. Due to the unpredictability and morphological complexity of cavities, there is a growing need for their early recognition.

Ground-penetrating radar (GPR) has gradually been applied to the detection and perception of underground cavities [2], owing to its nondestructive inspection, strong penetrating ability, and high-precision characteristics. GPR transmitters emit electromagnetic (EM) waves into the surface at multiple spatial positions, and then the reflected signal can be measured by the GPR receiver to establish a two-dimensional (2D) GPR image. Three-dimensional (3D) GPR images can be obtained immediately when multichannel GPR transmitters and receivers exist parallel to the scanning direction at the same time [3,4]. The morphological scale of a cavity can reflect the evolution speed of the cavity and the severity of future road collapse, and it can also accurately reflect the 3D space state of the cavity. Therefore, the accurate detection of morphology has scientific value for studying the mechanism of cavity formation and summarizing the corresponding prevention and repair methods. However, as the quantity of the 3D GPR data increases, the manual analysis of the GPR data becomes time-consuming and difficult to meet the requirements of the efficient and fine detection of cavity morphology.

Three challenges in automating this task cannot be ignored. The first challenge is the selection and extraction of morphological features. Environmental complexities, such as the interference of surrounding pipelines and groundwater leakage, may impose difficulties in describing cavity morphological features. It is impossible to comprehensively describe the reflection properties with one or a few features. Additionally, the acquired morphological attributes still need to be inferred and identified by experienced professionals, making it difficult to obtain a general description feature. The second challenge is the fine classification of cavity morphology in the GPR data. Due to the variety of types, varying sizes, distinct directions and extensions, and irregular shapes, cavity morphology analysis faces difficulties in identification and fine classification. The third challenge is to address the issue of insufficiently labeled GPR data. Compared with objects such as buried rebars and pipes, the scale and diameter distribution of a cavity with collapse threat is relatively large. It is very laborious to make such a large target in the lab, and the targets are generally in regular forms, not universal and representative. To obtain reliable results, the lack of sample data must be considered and addressed.

Therefore, in this study, a novel deep learning (DL)-aided framework was proposed to extract the morphological features of cavities and classify them in facing a small number of 3D GPR data. Figure 1 shows the details of the proposed framework. The contribution of this work is twofold:

(i) First, a joint characterization algorithm was developed for cavity morphology that generates 2D morphological images and fully exploits 3D GPR spatial information;

(ii) Second, we implemented a novel few-shot learning (FSL) network for cavity morphology classification and embedded a relation network (RelationNet) into the FSL model to adapt to different few-sample cavity scenarios.

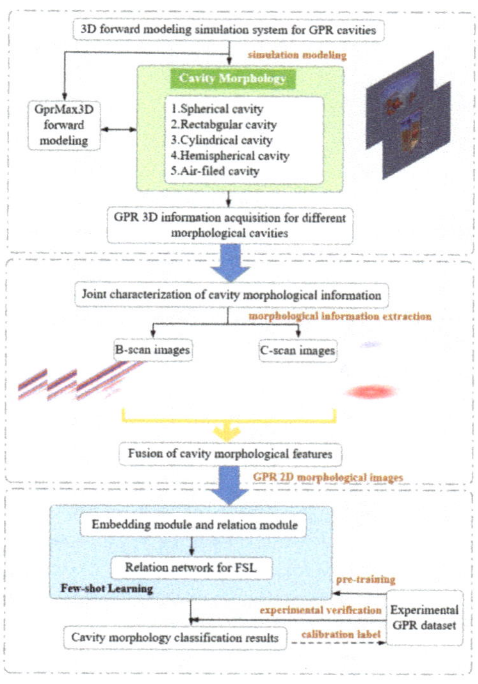

Figure 1. GPR cavity morphology recognition framework.

The rest of this paper is organized as follows: Section 2 introduces the literature review of the GPR cavity detection. In Section 3, the imaging scheme of the 3D GPR data is proposed. Section 4 introduces the details of the FSL network and RelationNet structure for morphological classification. In Section 5, the experimental results are compared and analyzed, and finally, in Section 6, conclusions are drawn.

2. Literature Review

Previous studies have focused on the automated GPR cavity detection process. Qin et al. [5] proposed a pattern recognition method based on the support vector machine (SVM) classifier to identify cavities in GPR images. Park et al. [6] combined instantaneous phase analysis with the GPR technique to identify hidden cavities. Hong et al. [7] developed a new time-domain-reflectometry-based penetrometer system to accurately estimate the relative permittivity at different depths and estimate the state of a cavity. Yang et al. [8] constructed a horizontal filter to identify cavity disease and eliminate the interference of rebar echo. Based on the data collected by multisensors such as unmanned aerial vehicles (UAVs) and GPR, the authors of [9,10] detected and analyzed cavity diseases in disaster-stricken areas to rescue potential victims trapped in cavities. In 2022, Rasol et al. [11] reviewed state-of-the-art processing techniques such as machine learning and intelligent data analysis methods, as well as their applications and challenges in GPR road pavement diagnosis. To better localize pavement cracks and solve the interference of various factors in the on-site scene, Liu et al. [12] integrated a ResNet50vd-deformable convolution backbone into YOLOv3, along with a hyperparameter optimization method. To detect subsurface road voids, Yamaguchi et al. [13] constructed a 3D CNN to extract hyperbolic reflection characteristics from GPR images.

Previous results were based on the processing of only B-scans; however, once faced with specific subsurface objects, it was difficult to classify them using B-scans alone. In particular, the characteristics of various cavities in GPR B-scan images tended to be similar. Therefore, to improve the classification performance, both the GPR B-scan and C-scan images were considered in the classification process using the DL network [14–17]. Compared with the 2D GPR data, 3D data can provide rich spatial information and greatly improve the process in terms of data volume, imaging methods, and disease detection accuracy. Luo et al. [18] established a cavity pattern database including C-scans and B-scans, where the C-scan provides location information of objects, and B-scan information assists in verifying object types. Kim et al. [19] proposed a triplanar convolutional neural network (CNN) for processing the 3D GPR data, enabling automated underground object classification. Kang et al. [20] designed the UcNet framework to reduce the misclassification of cavities, and the next year, Kang et al. [21] developed a transfer-enhanced CNN to improve the classification accuracy. Khudoyarov et al. [22] proposed a 3D CNN architecture to process the 3D GPR data. The authors of another study [23] visualized and distinguished underground hidden cavities from other objects (such as buried pipes, and manholes). In 2021, Kim et al. [24] used the AlexNet network with the transfer learning technology to achieve underground object classification, further improving detection accuracy and speed. Abhinaya et al. [25] detected cavities around sewers using in-pipe GPR equipment and confirmed that YOLOv3 [26] was suitable for cavity recognition tasks. Liu et al. [27] combined the YOLO model and the information embedded in 3D GPR images to address the recognition issue of road defects. The above research demonstrated that, compared with using only B-scan images, the developed CNNs using both the B-scans and C-scans improved the classification performance. However, it was found that the cavity morphology is still indistinguishable due to the difficulty of cavity data acquisition and the lack of a GPR database.

Faced with such a problem, FSL [28,29], as a novel DL technique, was developed to generalize the network with very few or fewer training samples for each class. This changes the situation where traditional DL models must require large quantities of labeled data. FSL can be divided into three categories: model-based, optimization-based, and metric-based learning methods [30]. The model-based learning method first designs the model structure and then uses the designed model to quickly update parameters on a small number of samples, and finally directly establishes the mapping function of the input and prediction values. Santoro et al. [31] proposed the use of memory augmentation to solve this task and a memory-based neural network approach to adjust bias through weight updates. Munkhdalai et al. [32] proposed a meta-learning network, and its fast generalization ability is derived from the "fast weight" mechanism, where the gradients generated during training are used for fast weight generation. The optimization-based learning method completes the task of small sample classification by adjusting the optimization method instead of the conventional gradient descent method. Based on the fact that gradient-based optimization algorithm does not work well with a small quantity of data, Ravi et al. [33] studied an updated function or rule for model parameters. The method proposed by Finn et al. [34] can deal with situations with a small number of samples and can obtain better model generalization performance with only a small number of training times. The main advantages of this method are that it does not depend on the model form, nor does it need to add new parameters to the meta-learning network. The metric-based learning method is developed to measure the distance/similarity between the training set and the support set and completes the classification with the help of the nearest neighbor method. Vinyals et al. [35] proposed a new matching network, which aims to build different encoders for the support set and the batch set, respectively. Sung et al. [36] proposed a RelationNet network to model the measurement method, which learns the distance measurement method by training a CNN network.

3. Imaging Scheme of 3D GPR Data

3.1. The 3D GPR Data Format

The GPR data comes in three forms: A-, B-, and C-scan. The transmitter radiates EM waves to the underground, and the receiver collects signals reflected by underground objects or stratum interfaces, so as to obtain underground information. The original data format of the reflected signal is a one-dimensional (1D) waveform, which can also be called a GPR A-scan waveform. By scanning a region of interest with the single-channel GPR system, a 2D radargram can be obtained, called a GPR B-scan image. A single C-scan image is formed by imaging data points at the same depth in multiple B-scan images.

As shown in Figure 2, the x-axis is the same as the scanning direction, the y-axis denotes the width direction of the radar antenna device, and the z-axis indicates the depth direction of the measured object. The 3D GPR data can be represented as two kinds of orthogonal planes: B-scan and C-scan. B-scan and C-scan are arbitrary sections perpendicular to y- and z-axes. This is conducive to identifying the cavity morphology from multiple different perspectives, which can effectively avoid the misjudgment of a single angle in the 2D image. Therefore, 3D GPR can guarantee the accuracy of the detection type and reduce the number of core sampling verifications.

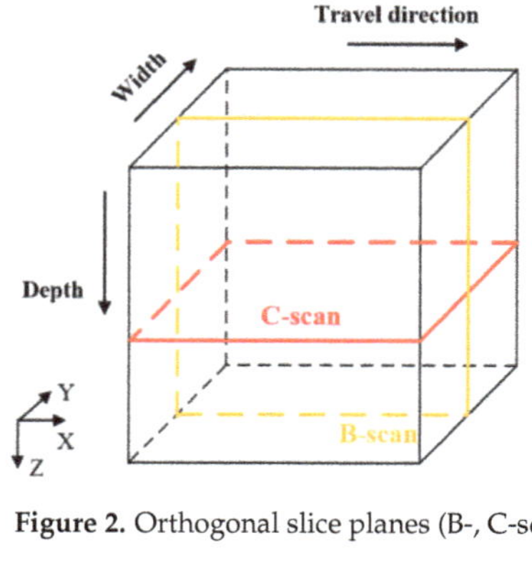

Figure 2. Orthogonal slice planes (B-, C-scan) of 3D GPR data.

3.2. GPR Morphological Data Extraction

The hyperbolic signature in B-scan images is a kind of typical characteristic that is often used in the detection of underground objects. The C-scan image can reflect the detailed shape information of the subsurface cavity. The B-scan and C-scan images contain morphological information in length–depth and length–width directions, respectively. The color on scan images reflects the field strength (V/m) of subsurface media. In this study, we propose an automatic algorithm for cavity morphology classification using GPR B-scan and C-scan images simultaneously.

The two forms are extracted from the 3D GPR data S. Take the irregular cavity as an example: (1) B-scan images are sequentially extracted parallel to the XOZ plane, and their stacked display is shown in Figure 3a. It can be expressed as $S_1 = \{B_1, B_2, B_3, \cdots, B_n\}$, $n = l_y / \triangle y$, where B_n represents each slice image, S_1 is a collection of n B-scan slices, l_y, and $\triangle y$ are the model space length and space step size in the y-axis direction. (2) C-scan images are sequentially extracted parallel to the XOY plane. The horizontal slices are extracted at equal intervals, and their stacked display is shown in Figure 3b. The slices can be expressed as $S_2 = \{C_1, C_2, C_3, \cdots, C_m\}$, $m = l_z / \triangle z$, where C_m represents each C-scan image, S_2 is the set of m C-scan slices, l_z and $\triangle z$ are the model space length and space step size in the z-axis direction.

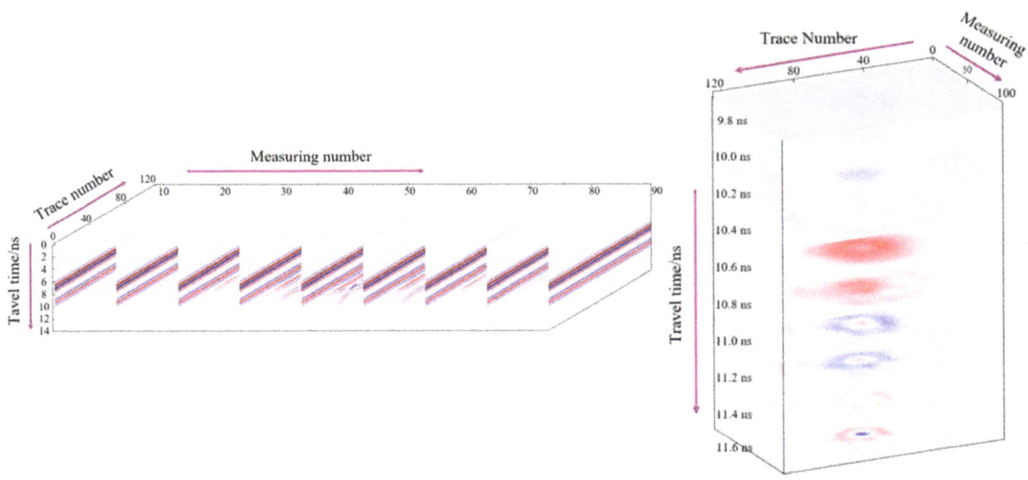

Figure 3. Sacked morphological images extracted from an irregular cavity: (**a**) stacked B-scan images; (**b**) stacked C-scan images.

The typical GPR B-scan and the corresponding C-scan images of an irregular cavity are shown in Figures 4 and 5. The C-scan images (right) are intersectional layers of red lines on the B-scan images (left). In the B-scan image, the horizontal x-axis and the vertical t-axis indicate the GPR scanning trajectory (m) and the two-way travel time of EM wave (ns), respectively. In the C-scan image, the x- and y-axes indicate the GPR scanning trajectory (m) and the width of GPR equipment (m), respectively. As shown in Figure 4, the irregular cavity shows a hyperbolic pattern on the B-scan image and elliptical signatures on the C-scan image. As shown in Figure 5, the rectangular cavity shows a double hyperbolic signature on the B-scan image and quadrilateral signatures (Figure 5b) on the C-scan images. Therefore, different morphologies of cavities can be well-recognized using B-scan and C-scan images.

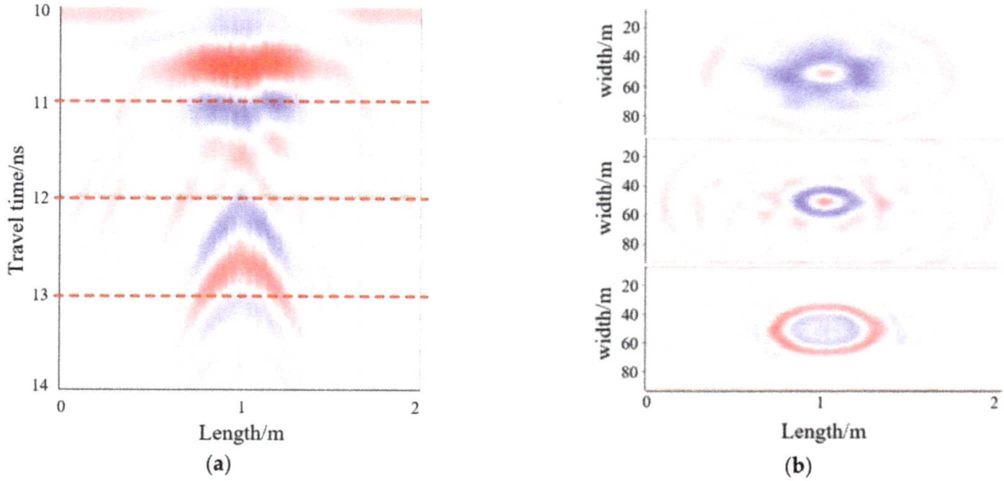

Figure 4. Typical GPR images of an irregular cavity: (**a**) B-scan image; (**b**) C-scan images.

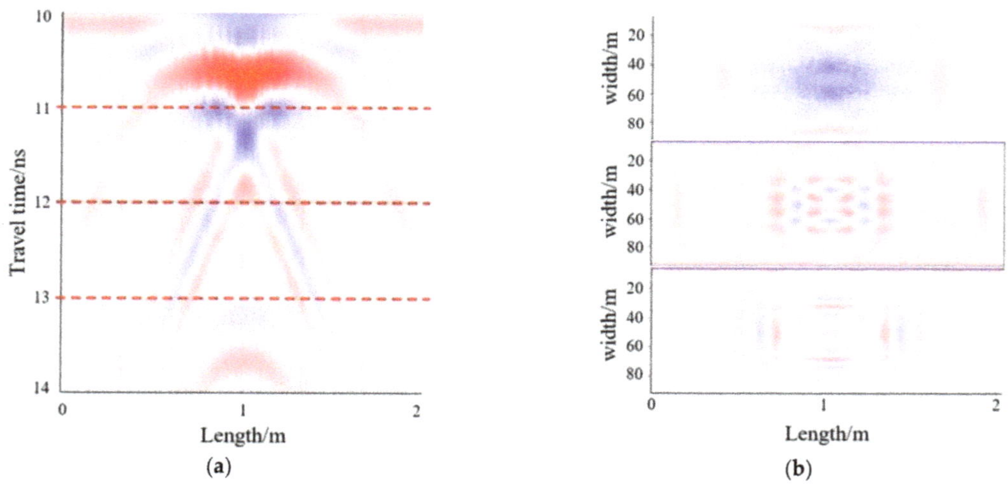

Figure 5. Typical GPR images of a rectangular cavity: (**a**) B-scan image; (**b**) C-scan images.

3.3. The 2D Morphological Image Generation

Multiple B-scan and C-scan images are integrated into a 2D morphological map, where the B-scan and C-scan images are assigned to the upper and lower parts of the morphological map, respectively. Each cavity model corresponds to a 2D morphological image $I = \{S_1, S_2\}$, which consists of 8 B-scan images $S_1 = \{B_1, B_2, B_3, B_4, B_5, B_6, B_7, B_8\}$, and 12 C-scan images $S_2 = \{C_1, C_2, C_3, C_4, C_5, C_6, C_7, C_8, C_9, C_{10}, C_{11}, C_{12}\}$. The morphological image I consists of S_1 and S_2, which is formed into a new 5×4 matrix and can also be expressed as Equation (1). Examples of the morphological images for each model are presented in Figure 6. The 2D morphological image is then used as the input of the following deep network.

$$I = \begin{Bmatrix} B_1 & B_2 & B_3 & B_4 \\ B_5 & B_6 & B_7 & B_8 \\ C_1 & C_2 & C_3 & C_4 \\ C_5 & C_6 & C_7 & C_8 \\ C_9 & C_{10} & C_{11} & C_{12} \end{Bmatrix} \quad (1)$$

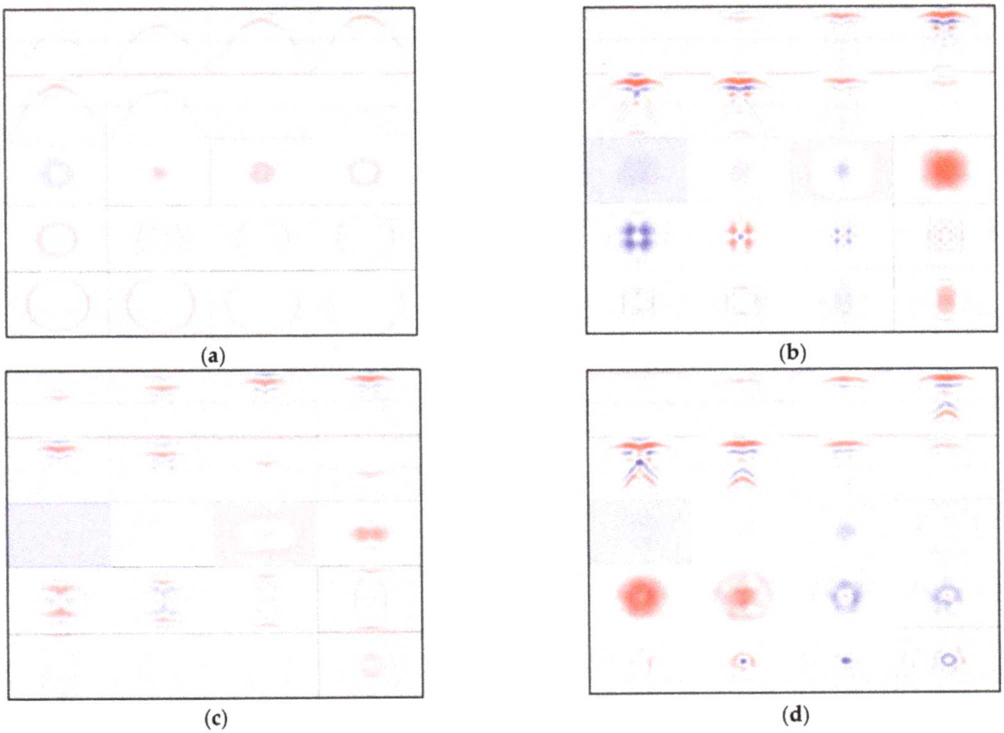

Figure 6. The 2D GPR morphological images of (a) a spherical cavity, (b) a rectangular cavity, (c) a cylindrical cavity, and (d) an irregular cavity.

4. Few-Shot Learning Designed for Morphology Classification

4.1. FSL Definition

FSL is able to quickly identify new classes on very few samples. It is generally divided into three kinds of datasets: training set, support set, and testing set. The training set can be further divided into a sample set and a query set. If the support set contains K labeled examples for each of C unique classes, the target few-shot problem is called *C-way K-shot*. Figure 7 shows the FSL architecture for a *four-way one-shot* problem.

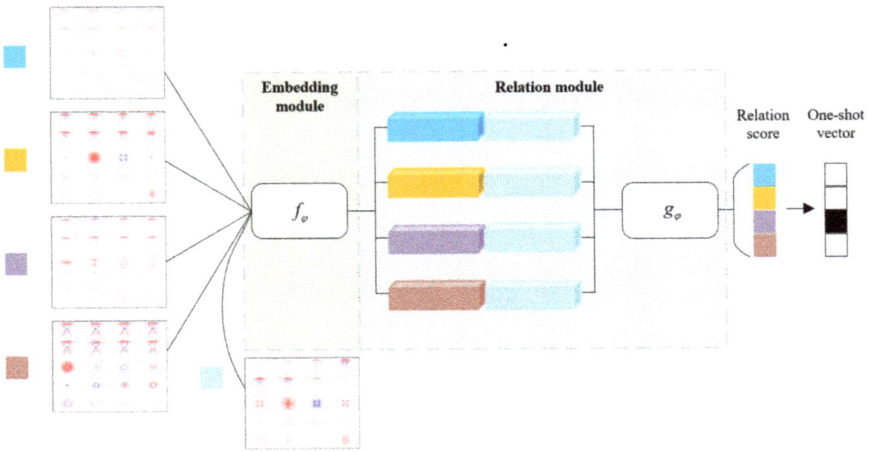

Figure 7. FSL architecture for a *four-way one-shot* problem with one query example.

The parameters θ are optimized by the training set, hyperparameters are tuned using the support set, and finally, the performance of function $f(x,\theta)$ is evaluated on the test set. Each sample $\hat{x}$ is assigned a class label $\hat{y}$. The data structure in the training phase is constructed to be similar to that in the testing phase; that is, the sample set S and query set Q during the training simulate the support set and testing set at the testing time. The sample set $S = \{(x_1, y_1), (x_2, y_2), \ldots, (x_m, y_m)\}$ is built by randomly picking C classes from the training set with K labeled samples, and the rest of these samples are used in the query set $Q = \{(x_1, y_1), (x_2, y_2), \ldots, (x_n, y_n)\}$.

4.2. Relation Network Architecture and Relation Score Computation

The relation network (RelationNet) is a typical metric-learning-based FSL method. In essence, metric-learning-based methods [36–41] compare the similarities between query images and support classes through a feed-forward pass through an episodic training mechanism [35]. The core of RelationNet is to learn a nonlinear metric through deep CNN, rather than selecting a fixed metric function. RelationNet is a two-branch architecture that includes an embedding module and a relation module. The embedding module is used to extract image features. The relation module obtains the correlation score between query images and sample images; that is, it measures their similarity, so as to realize the recognition task of a small number of samples.

Figure 8 represents the RelationNet architecture settings for FSL. The embedding module utilizes four convolutional blocks, and each convolutional block consists of a 64-filter 3×3 convolution, a batch normalization, and a ReLU nonlinearity layer. In addition to the above, the first two convolutional blocks also include a 2×2 max-pooling layer, and the latter two convolutional blocks do not contain the pooling layer. The output feature maps are then obtained for the following convolutional layers in the relation module. The relation module consists of two convolutional blocks and two fully connected layers. Each convolutional block is a 3×3 convolution containing 64 filters, followed by batch normalization, ReLU nonlinearity, and 2×2 max-pooling. For the network architectures, in order to generate relation scores within a reasonable range, in all fully connected layers, ReLU functions are employed, except for the output layer, in which Sigmoid is used.

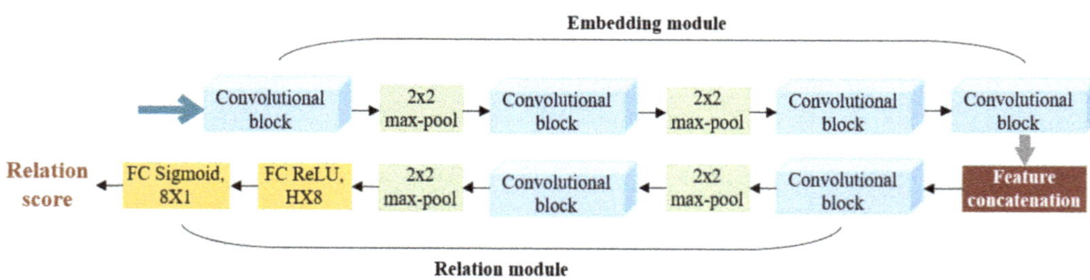

Figure 8. RelationNet architecture settings.

The prior few-shot works use fixed pre-specified distance metrics, such as the Euclidean or cosine distances, to perform classification [35,42]. Compared with the previously used fixed metrics, RelationNet can be viewed as a metric capable of learning deep embeddings and deep nonlinearities. By learning the similarity using a flexible function approximator, RelationNet can better identify matching/mismatching pairs. Sample x_j in the query set Q and sample x_i in the sample set S are fed through the embedding module f_φ to produce feature maps $f_\varphi(x_i)$ and $f_\varphi(x_j)$, respectively. Then, these two feature maps $f_\varphi(x_i)$ and $f_\varphi(x_j)$ are combined using the operator $\mathbb{C}(f_\varphi(x_i), f_\varphi(x_j))$. After that, the combined feature map is fed into the relation module g_φ, which finally produces a scalar in the range of 0–1 to represent the similarity between x_i and x_j, also called the relation score. Thus, the relation score $r_{i,j}$ is generated as shown in Equation (2):

$$r_{i,j} = g_\phi(\mathbb{C}(f_\varphi(x_i), f_\varphi(x_j))),\ \mathrm{i} = 1, 2, \ldots, \mathrm{C} \quad (2)$$

Here, the mean square error loss is computed to train the model, as shown in Equation (3), regressing the relation score $r_{i,j}$ to the ground truth: the similarity of matched pairs is 1, and the similarity of unmatched pairs is 0.

$$\varphi, \phi \leftarrow \underset{\varphi,\phi}{\operatorname{argmin}} \sum_{i=1}^{m} \sum_{j=1}^{n} \left(r_{i,j} - 1\left(y_i == y_j\right)\right)^2 \tag{3}$$

4.3. RelationNet-Based Cavity Morphology Classification Scheme

Based on the data and structural characteristics of the GPR cavity morphological recognition system, we divide the complex processing process into two main parts: a training phase and a testing phase, as shown in Figure 9. The cavity morphologies are discussed here, e.g., cylindrical, rectangular, spherical, and irregular hemispherical. First, a training set is inputted to learn classification rules inside the network in the training phase. Then, in the testing phase, a small number of support samples (labeled) and test samples (unlabeled) are inputted into the trained network model, and the unlabeled test samples are predicted and classified, thereby outputting the final morphological classification results.

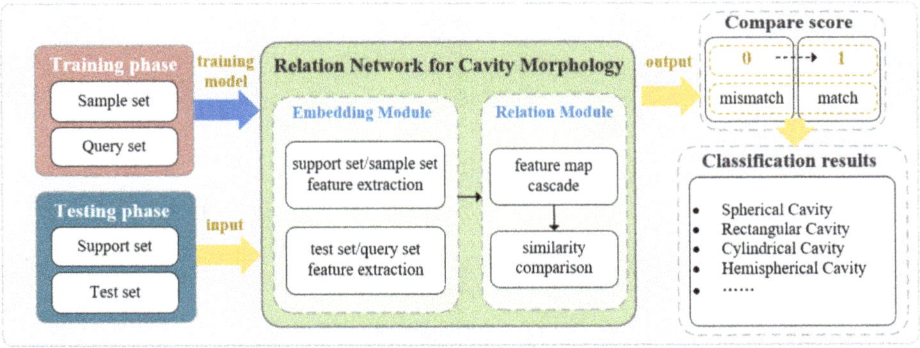

Figure 9. RelationNet-based GPR cavity morphology classification scheme.

Based on the above principle, the RelationNet-based GPR cavity morphology classification system first obtains the trained model on the training set and then recognizes the new category of cavity images. The embedding model is used to extract the feature information of each inputted GPR image and then concatenates the image features between the test sample and support sample. Then, the integrated features are inputted into the relation model for comparison. According to the comparison results, it is judged to which category the test sample belongs, so as to achieve the classification of cavity morphologies.

5. Experiments and Results

5.1. Experimental Settings

The classification category should be labeled for each morphological image since the DL-based classification algorithm is essentially a supervised learning algorithm. The choice of category is related to the morphology of the cavity. There are four types of cavities involved, namely cylindrical cavity, rectangular cavity, spherical cavity, and irregular cavity. To train CNN, the 2D morphological images with each image size of $498 \times 395 \times 3$ pixels were fed to the input layer, and then the convolutional layers were used to extract multilevel image features by convolution kernels. A total of 68 GPR morphological images were obtained, each consisting of 8 B-scans and 12 C-scans. Among them, there were 17 spherical cavity images, 17 cylindrical cavity images, 17 rectangular cavity images, and 17 irregular cavity images.

We used the PyTorch 1.5 implementations of the LibFewShot package [43], which is a comprehensive FSL library and integrates the most advanced FSL methods. The code was implemented using NVIDIA RTX 3080Ti GPU and Intel i9-12900K CPU. In the training phase, in the FSL in all experiments, we used the Adam optimizer [44] with an initial learning rate of 10−3 and step decay. The backbone adopted Conv64F. The batch size was set to 128. In the testing phase, the test epoch was set to 10, and the test episode was 17, the *four-way one-shot* contained 16 query images, and the *four-way five-shot* had 12 query images for each of the 4 classes in each training episode.

We compared the results against those of various networks for few-shot recognition, including ProtoNet [42], R2D2 [45], and BaseLine [46]. Embedding backbones, such as Conv64F, ResNet12, and ResNet18, were also compared to identify and select the main backbone with a better performance. The main experiments were conducted on two benchmark datasets: miniImageNet [35] and tieredImageNet [47]. The miniImageNet dataset [35] consists of 60,000 color images with 100 classes, and the input images are resized to 84 × 84. The tieredImageNet dataset [47] consists of 779,165 color images with 608 classes, each of size 84 × 84.

5.2. The 3D GPR Cavity Data Acquisition

The GPR data are difficult to collect and label. To address the issue, a 3D GPR forward modeling tool, GprMax3D [48,49], is often used for the 3D modeling and simulation of underground structures. Based on the finite-difference time-domain (FDTD) method, the technique increases the volume of training data by creating synthetic GPR images. Maxwell's equations govern the propagation of EM waves used by the GPR. Figure 10 shows the flowchart of the GprMax3D forward simulation technique. GprMax3D was used to generate synthetic GPR images [50]. To further imitate the real situation, we set up cavity objects with uneven surfaces and random media to approximate real objects. An example of the GPR system's parameter setting is shown in Table 1.

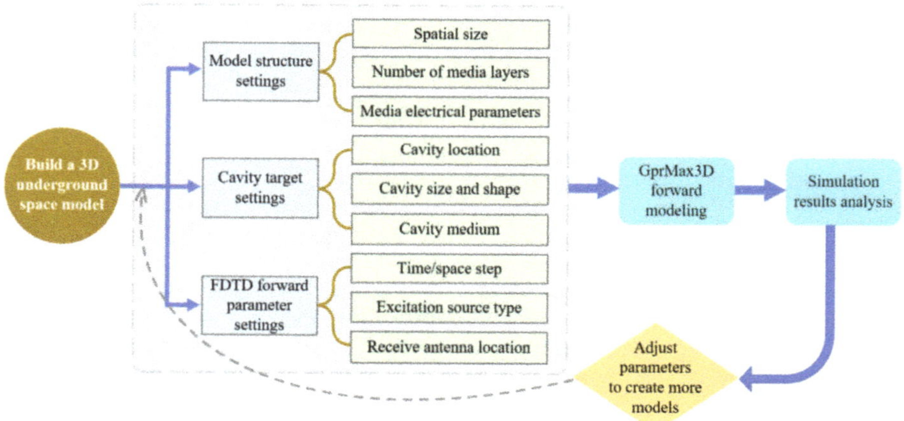

Figure 10. GprMax3D simulation flowchart.

Table 1. GPR system parameters in road structure scene.

System Parameters	Value
Spatial resolution/m	0.01
Time window/ns	14
Initial coordinate of transmit antenna/m	(0.45, 1.0, 0.0)
Initial coordinate of receive antenna/m	(0.35, 1.0, 0.0)
Antenna step distance/m	(0.01, 0, 0)
Measuring point number	100
Excitation signal type	Ricker
Excitation signal frequency/MHz	800

Road cavity is generally distributed in the underground range of 0.3–1 m, which is also the junction of the pavement structure and the subgrade. The subgrade is generally a soil structure, while the pavement structure is generally a flexible, semi-rigid, or rigid structure, generally made of cement or asphalt concrete; in particular, its bottom layer is generally made of hard materials such as gravel. Due to the high probability of soil erosion, cavities are most likely to appear at the junction of soft and hard layers. Figure 11 shows a simulation model example of a road structure with the first layer of asphalt, the second layer of concrete, and the third layer of sandstone. Their attribute parameter settings are shown in Table 2. In addition, the subgrade is generally dominated by soil, and a more realistic soil model was established by simulating random media. A number of soil dispersion materials were defined as follows: soil with 50% sand, 50% clay, sand density of 2.66 g/cm^3, clay bulk density of 2 g/cm^3, and volumetric water content ranging from 0.001 to 0.25. These materials were distributed over a model with a volume of $2 \times 1.2 \times 1$ m^3 (in which the soil layers were randomly distributed).

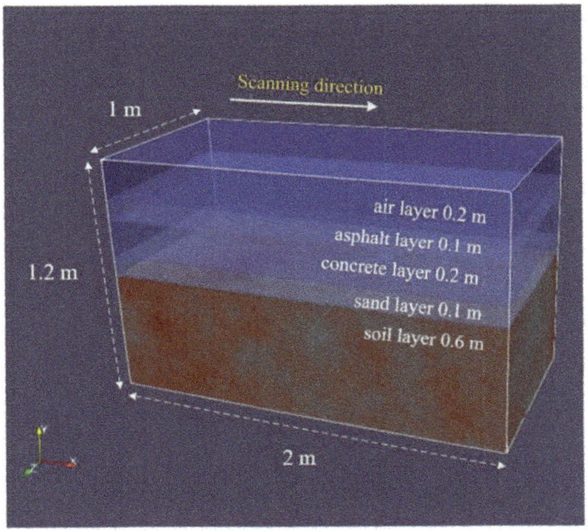

Figure 11. Road structural simulation model.

Table 2. Dielectric properties of road structure.

System Parameters	Relative Permittivity	Conductivity (S/m)
Air	1	0
Asphalt	6	0.005
Concrete (dry)	9	0.05
Gravel	12	0.1

Figure 12 presents the simulated models of four representative cavity morphologies: spherical, rectangular, cylindrical, and irregular hemispherical cavities. The first three cavities have smooth surfaces, and the last one shows an uneven surface. Figure 13 shows the representative 2D GPR morphological images of cavities. Figure 13a shows the case of spherical cavities with parabolic and circular features, which can be observed on the B-scan and C-scan images, respectively. As shown in Figure 13b, rectangular cavities generally have distinguishable features, namely a double parabola shape in B-scans. Similar features are also revealed in the cylindrical case of Figure 13c. However, Figure 13b,c can be distinguished by C-scans because they, respectively, show quadrilateral signatures and double circular intersection features in C-scans. Compared with Figure 13a, it can be observed in Figure 13d that the C-scan images of the irregular cavity show unsmoothed circular features with considerable noise randomly distributed inside the circle. Due to these distinguishable and representative characteristics, the cavity morphology can be classified well with the FSL frameworks.

Category	Model Internal Structure Display	Partial Random Media Presentation
(**a**) Spherical cavity	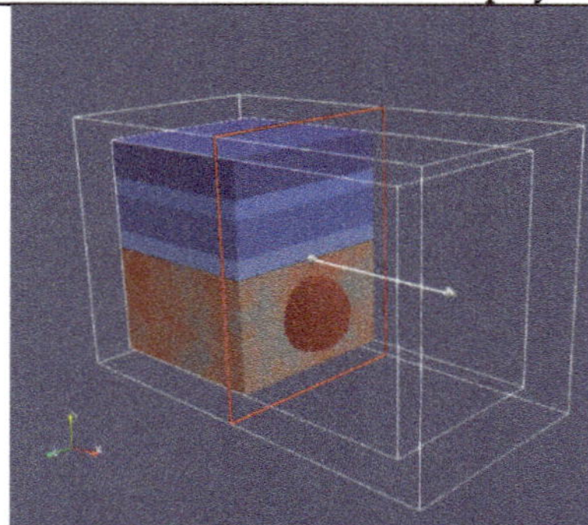	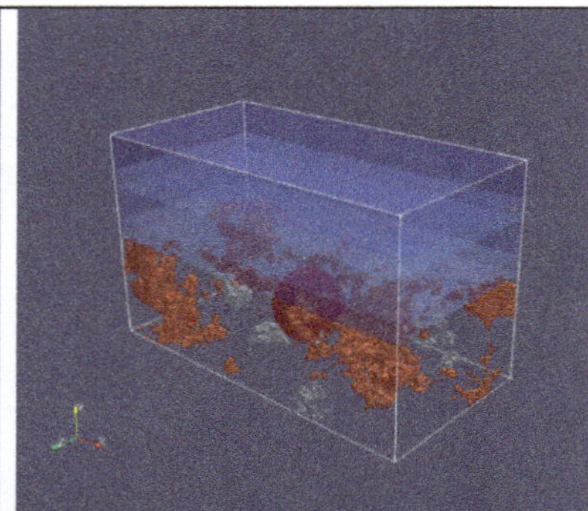
(**b**) Rectangular cavity	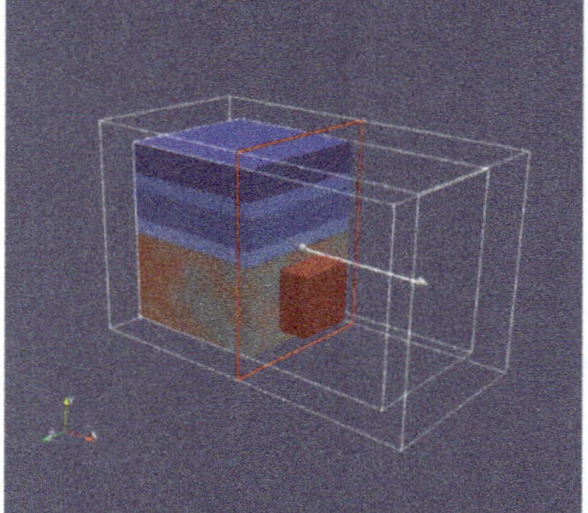	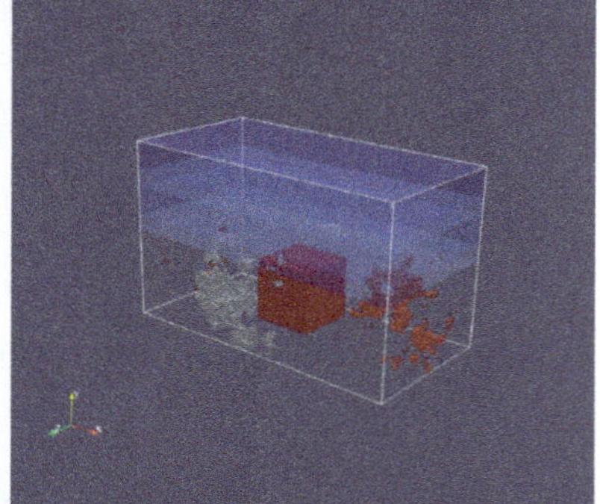
(**c**) Cylindrical cavity	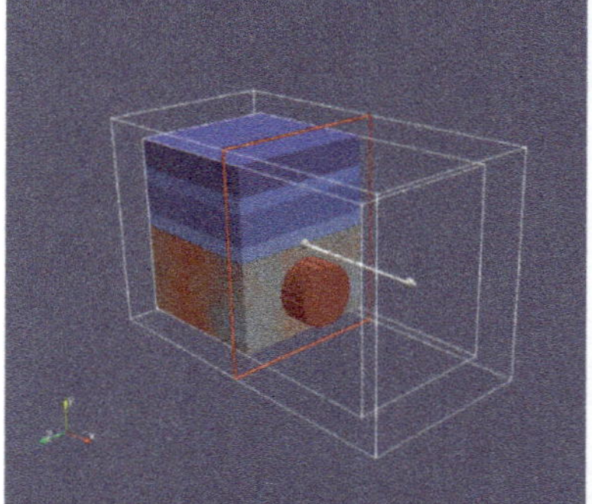	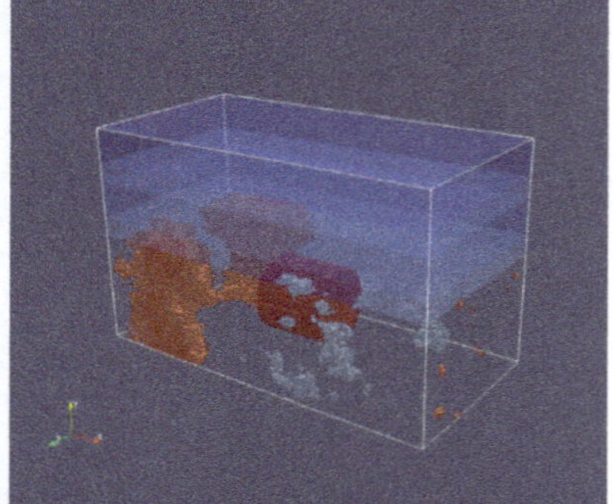
(**d**) Irregular hemispherical cavity	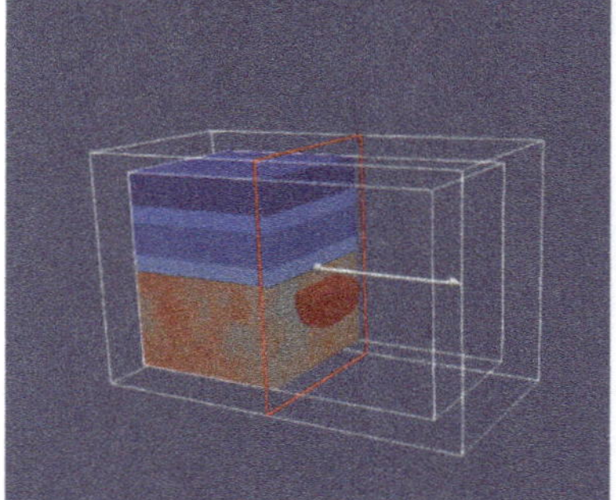	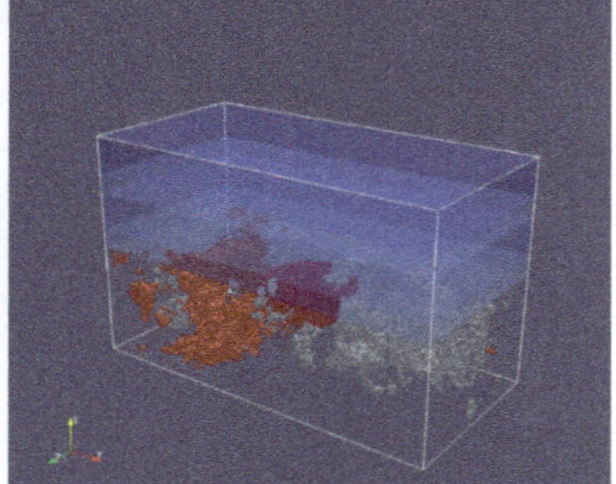

Figure 12. Display of simulation model from different perspectives (cavity in red).

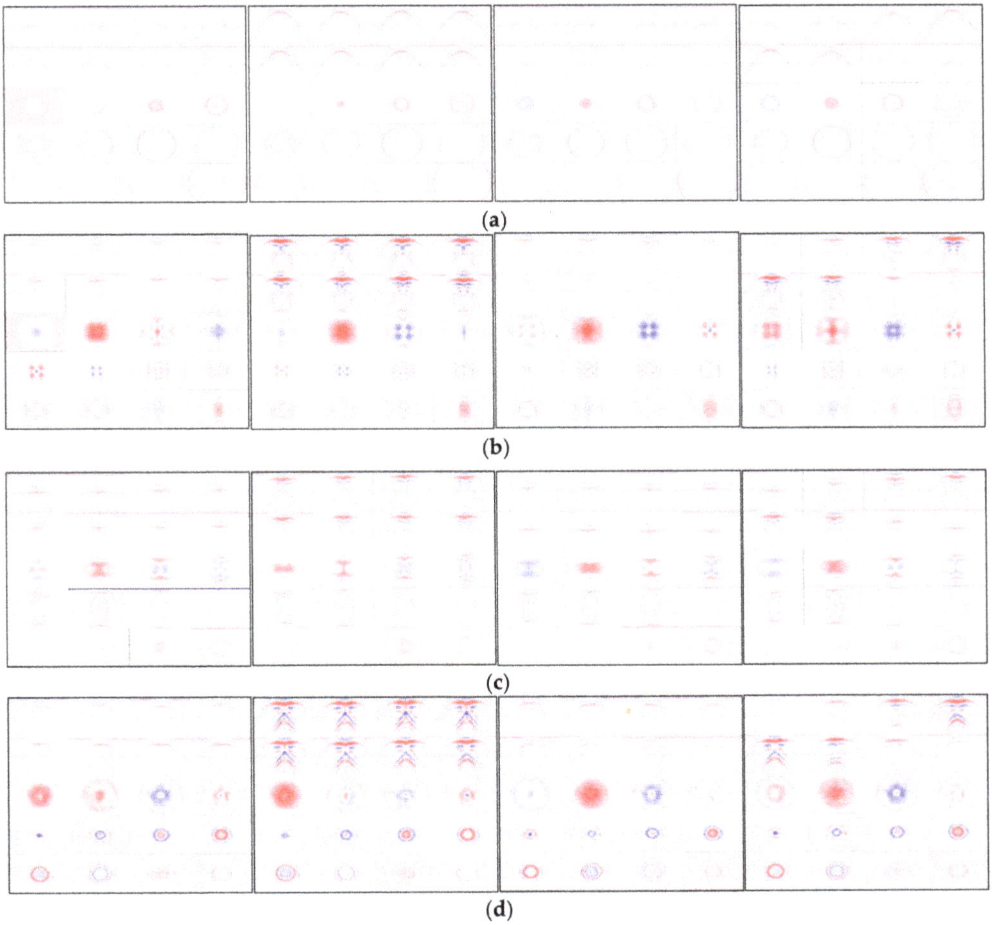

Figure 13. Representative 2D GPR images of cavities: (**a**) spherical, (**b**) rectangular, (**c**) cylindrical, and (**d**) irregular hemispherical.

5.3. Classification Results and Analysis

Figure 14 shows the RelationNet-based underground cavity morphology classification results. These results were obtained based on the network settings of the backbone Conv64F, the benchmark dataset tieredImageNet, and in a *four-way five-shot* problem. As expected, compared with the ground truth, the irregular hemispherical cavity with significant characteristics in the GPR morphological image was correctly classified. Moreover, the classification accuracy rates of spherical, rectangular, and cylindrical cavities were 97.5%, 98.33%, and 98.33%, respectively. However, 0.83% and 1.67% of spherical were misclassified as cylindrical and hemispherical due to their similar morphological features. In addition, 1.67% of rectangular were misclassified as hemispherical due to their double parabola shapes in B-scans, while 0.83% and 0.83% of cylindrical were, respectively, misclassified as spherical and hemispherical, due to their similar features in B- or C-scans. The classification performance of RelationNet was evaluated based on the indices (*precision*, *recall*, and *F-score*) using the following Equations (4)–(6):

$$precision = \frac{true\ positive}{true\ positive + false\ positive} \tag{4}$$

$$recall = \frac{true\ positive}{true\ positive + false\ negative} \quad (5)$$

$$F - score = \frac{2 \cdot precision \cdot recall}{precision + recall} \quad (6)$$

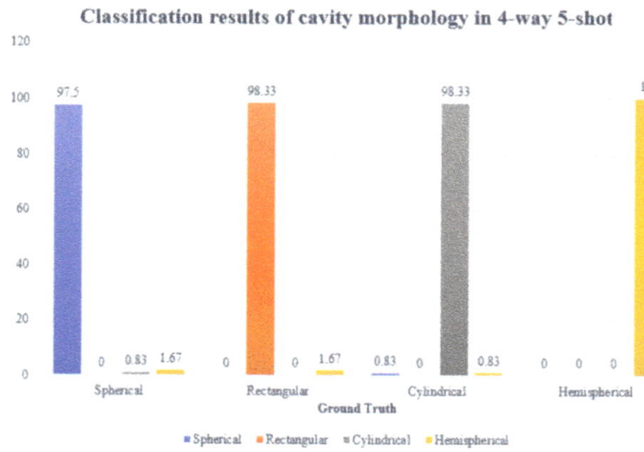

Figure 14. The results of RelationNet-based cavity morphological classification.

Table 3 shows the statistical results obtained from the RelationNet results, namely the *precision*, *recall*, and *F-score* values. For the rectangular cases, 99.15% *precision* and 97.5% *recall* indicated that false-positive (FP) and false-negative (FN) results occurred, and the number of FN results was greater than those of FP. Similarly, the 99.16% *precision* and 98.33% *recall* values of the cylindrical case meant the FP and FN alarms because RelationNet sometimes recognized a cylindrical cavity as a spherical or hemispherical. For rectangular cases, 100% *precision* and the relatively low *recall* value indicated that FN occurred due to the misclassification between rectangular and hemispherical. On the contrary, 96% *precision* and 100% *recall* values meant that the hemispherical samples were properly classified using RelationNet, but multiple samples in other categories were misclassified as hemispherical at the same time. According to the *F-scores*, it can be concluded that the performance of RelationNet was acceptable.

Table 3. Statistical results obtained from RelationNet (%).

System Parameters	*Precision*	*Recall*	*F-Score*
Spherical	99.15	97.5	98.32
Rectangular	100	98.33	99.16
Cylindrical	99.16	98.33	98.74
Hemispherical	96	100	97.96

5.4. Comparison Experiments

5.4.1. RelationNet Evaluation on Different Embedding Backbones

The performance of RelationNet relies on the quality of the embedding backbone. To select a suitable main embedding backbone, we compared three different embedding backbones: Conv64F, ResNet12, and ResNet18. The above experiments were run for 10 epochs on the miniImageNet dataset. Other settings remained the same. Conv64F consisted of four convolutional blocks, and each block was composed of a convolutional layer, a batch-normalization layer, a ReLU layer, and a max-pooling layer. ResNet12 consisted of four residual blocks, each of which contained three convolutional blocks along with a skip connection layer. ResNet18 had the same architecture as used in [50]. Table 4 shows the comparison results among different backbones. It can be observed that RelationNet equipped with Conv64F backbone achieved the best performance in either a *four-way one-shot* or *four-way five-shot* problem.

Table 4. Comparison results on different embedding backbones (%) (the best results in bold).

Embedding Backbones	*Four-Way One-Shot*	*Four-Way Five-Shot*
Conv64F	**78.097**	**88.934**
ResNet12	69.467	72.500
ResNet18	69.926	79.865

5.4.2. RelationNet Evaluation on Different Benchmark Datasets

Table 5 compares the performance of RelationNet on miniImageNet and tieredImageNet datasets by controlling the most implementation details. For this comparison, RelationNet adopted Conv64F as the main backbone. As can be seen from Table 5, in the *four-way one-shot* problem, the accuracy achieved on the miniImageNet dataset was slightly higher than that on the tieredImageNet dataset. In the *four-way five-shot* problem, competitive accuracy could be achieved using the tieredImageNet dataset compared with using the miniImageNet dataset, improving the accuracy by 8.394%. Therefore, the accuracy results indicated that RelationNet performed well when trained on the tieredImageNet dataset.

Table 5. Comparison results on different benchmark datasets: miniImageNet vs. tieredImageNet (%) (the best results in bold).

Embedding Backbones	*Four-Way One-Shot*	*Four-Way Five-Shot*
miniImageNet	**78.097**	88.934
tieredImageNet	77.086	**97.328**

5.4.3. Performance Comparison of Different FSL Networks

To validate the effectiveness of RelationNet, the four experimental validation results of ProtoNet, R2D2, BaseLine, and RelationNet were compared. We used the exact same embedding backbone Conv64F and benchmark dataset miniImageNet. It can be observed from Table 6 that RelationNet achieved the best results in the *four-way one-shot* problem, even improving the accuracy by 11.994% over the BaseLine. With the increase in the number of sample images, these four frameworks achieved substantial improvements in facing the *four-way five-shot* problem, and RelationNet still achieved the highest accuracy over the other three frameworks.

Table 6. Statistical results obtained from RelationNet (%) (the best results in bold).

FSL Networks	*Four-Way One-Shot*	*Four-Way Five-Shot*
ProtoNet	70.965	85.221
R2D2	76.562	88.659
BaseLine	66.103	83.505
RelationNet	**78.097**	**88.934**

6. Conclusions

In this paper, we first applied the FSL technique to classify and identify cavity morphology characteristics based on the 3D GPR data. RelationNet was adopted as the FSL framework and trained end-to-end from scratch. Based on the advantages of learning a deep distance metric, RelationNet addressed the issue of insufficient cavity data and obtained the classification results using only a few samples. The experiment results demonstrated the effectiveness of using RelationNet in morphology classification performance. The RelationNet model achieved an average classification accuracy value of 97.328% in the *four-way five-shot* and 78.097% in the *four-way one-shot* problem.

There is a limitation that could be addressed in future research. In the experiments, all the models were trained on the source domain (e.g., miniImageNet and tieredImageNet) and directly tested on the target domain (e.g., cavity radar dataset). However, the performance hardly improved or significantly dropped when there was a large domain shift.

In this paper, based on the fact that there was no intersection between the source set and our cavity radar dataset, there was a large domain offset between the source and target domains. Future efforts need to be made to integrate prior knowledge into FSL or explore *one-shot* or *zero-shot* classification methods.

For on-site applications, there are two limitations that could be addressed in future research. First, the real cavity data are difficult to collect for training the proposed method. Additionally, the publicly available GPR cavity datasets are limited. Efforts need to be made in the future to collect and prepare GPR datasets to facilitate the implementation of this method. Second, the proposed method was only tested for cavity morphology classification using the GprMax3D data. The scalability of the method in other challenging environments and applications needs further investigation. Future studies could test this method for collecting cavity data and classifying their morphologies in on-site city roads.

Author Contributions: F.H.: Conceptualization, Methodology, Writing—Original Draft Preparation, Software. X.L.: Data Curation, Writing, Validation. X.F.: Visualization, Investigation. Y.G.: Supervision, Writing—Reviewing and Editing. All authors have read and agreed to the published version of the manuscript.

Funding: This work was funded by the National Natural Science Foundation of China (no. 61871407).

Institutional Review Board Statement: Not applicable.

Conflicts of Interest: The authors declare no conflict of interest.

References

1. Gutiérrez, F.; Parise, M.; Waele, J.; Jourde, H. A review on natural and human-induced geohazards and impacts in karst. *Earth Sci. Rev.* **2014**, *138*, 61–88.
2. Garcia-Garcia, F.; Valls-Ayuso, A.; Benlloch-Marco, J.; Valcuende-Paya, M. An optimization of the work disruption by 3D cavity mapping using GPR: A new sewerage project in Torrente (Valencia, Spain). *Constr. Build. Mater.* **2017**, *154*, 1226–1233. [CrossRef]
3. Jol, H.M. *Ground Penetrating Radar Theory and Applications*; Elseviere: Amsterdam, The Netherlands, 2008.
4. Meyers, R.; Smith, D.; Jol, H.; Peterson, C. Evidence for eight great earthquake-subsidence events detected with ground-penetrating radar, Willapa barrier, Washington. *Geology* **1996**, *24*, 99–102. [CrossRef]
5. Qin, Y.; Huang, C. Identifying underground voids using a GPR circular-end bow-tie antenna system based on a support vector machine. *Int..J. Remote Sens.* **2016**, *37*, 876–888. [CrossRef]
6. Park, B.; Kim, J.; Lee, J.; Kang, M.-S.; An, Y.-K. Underground object classification for urban roads using instantaneous phase analysis of Ground-Penetrating Radar (GPR) Data. *Remote Sens.* **2018**, *10*, 1417. [CrossRef]
7. Hong, W.-T.; Lee, J.-S. Estimation of ground cavity configurations using ground penetrating radar and time domain reflectometry. *Nat. Hazards* **2018**, *92*, 1789–1807. [CrossRef]
8. Yang, Y.; Zhao, W. Curvelet transform-based identification of void diseases in ballastless track by ground-penetrating radar. *Struct. Control Health Monit.* **2019**, *26*, e2322–e2339. [CrossRef]
9. Chen, J.; Li, S.; Liu, D.; Li, X. AiRobSim: Simulating a Multisensor Aerial Robot for Urban Search and Rescue Operation and Training. *Sensors* **2020**, *20*, 5223–5242. [CrossRef] [PubMed]
10. Hu, D.; Li, S.; Chen, J.; Kamat, V.R. Detecting, locating, and characterizing voids in disaster rubble for search and rescue. *Adv. Eng. Inform.* **2019**, *42*, 100974–100982. [CrossRef]
11. Rasol, M.; Pais, J.; Pérez-Gracia, V.; Solla, M.; Fernandes, F.; Fontul, S.; Ayala-Cabrera, D.; Schmidt, F.; Assadollahi, H. GPR monitoring for road transport infrastructure: A systematic review and machine learning insights. *Constr. Build. Mate.* **2022**, *324*, 126686. [CrossRef]
12. Liu, Z.; Gu, X.; Yang, H.; Wang, L.; Chen, Y.; Wang, D. Novel YOLOv3 Model With Structure and Hyperparameter Optimization for Detection of Pavement Concealed Cracks in GPR Images. *IEEE T Intell. Transp. Syst.* **2022**, *1*, 1–11. [CrossRef]
13. Yamaguchi, T.; Mizutani, T.; Meguro, K.; Hirano, T. Detecting Subsurface Voids From GPR Images by 3-D Convolutional Neural Network Using 2-D Finite Difference Time Domain Method. *IEEE J. Sel. Top. Appl. Earth Obs. Remote Sens.* **2022**, *15*, 3061–3073. [CrossRef]
14. Yamashita, Y.; Kamoshita, T.; Akiyama, Y.; Hattori, H.; Kakishita, Y.; Sadaki, T.; Okazaki, H. Improving efficiency of cavity detection under paved road from GPR data using deep learning method. In Proceedings of the 13th SEGJ International Symposium, Tokyo, Japan, 12–14 November 2018; Society of Exploration Geophysicists and Society of Exploration Geophysicists of Japan: Tykyo, Japan, 2019; pp. 526–529.
15. Ni, Z.-K.; Zhao, D.; Ye, S.B.; Fang, G. City road cavity detection using YOLOv3 for ground-penetrating radar. In Proceedings of the18th International Conference on Ground Penetrating Radar, Golden, CO, USA, 14–19 June 2020; Society of Exploration Geophysicists: Houston, TX, USA, 2020; pp. 2159–6832.

16. Liu, H.; Shi, Z.; Li, J.; Liu, C.; Meng, X.; Du, Y.; Chen, J. Detection of road cavities in urban cities by 3D ground-penetrating radar. *Geophysics* **2021**, *86*, WA25–WA33. [CrossRef]
17. Feng, J.; Yang, L.; Hoxha, E.; Xiao, J. Improving 3D Metric GPR Imaging Using Automated Data Collection and Learning-based Processing. *IEEE Sens. J.* **2022**, 1–13. [CrossRef]
18. Luo, T.; Lai, W. GPR pattern recognition of shallow subsurface air voids. *Tunn. Undergr. Sp. Tech.* **2020**, *99*, 103355–103366. [CrossRef]
19. Kim, N.; Kim, S.; An, Y.-K.; Lee, J.-J. Triplanar imaging of 3-D GPR data for deep-learning-based underground object detection. *IEEE J. Sel. Top. Appl. Earth Obs. Remote Sens.* **2019**, *12*, 4446–4456. [CrossRef]
20. Kang, M.-S.; Kim, N.; Im, S.B.; Lee, J.-J.; An, Y.-K. 3D GPR image-based UcNet for enhancing underground cavity detectability. *Remote Sens.* **2019**, *11*, 2545–2562. [CrossRef]
21. Kang, M.-S.; Kim, N.; Lee, J.-J.; An, Y.-K. Deep learning-based automated underground cavity detection using three-dimensional ground penetrating radar. *Struct. Health Monit.* **2020**, *19*, 173–185. [CrossRef]
22. Khudoyarov, S.; Kim, N.; Lee, J.-J. Three-dimensional convolutional neural network–based underground object classification using three-dimensional ground penetrating radar data. *Struct. Health Monit.* **2020**, *19*, 1884–1893. [CrossRef]
23. Kim, N.; Kim, K.; An, Y.-K.; Lee, H.-J.; Lee, J.-J. Deep learning-based underground object detection for urban road pavement. *Int. J. Pavement Eng.* **2020**, *21*, 1638–1650. [CrossRef]
24. Kim, N.; Kim, S.; An, Y.-K.; Lee, J.-J. A novel 3D GPR image arrangement for deep learning-based underground object classification. *Int. J. Pavement Eng.* **2021**, *22*, 740–751. [CrossRef]
25. Abhinaya, A. Using Machine Learning to Detect Voids in an Underground Pipeline Using in-Pipe Ground Penetrating Radar. Master's Thesis, University of Twente, Enschede, Holland, 2021.
26. Redmon, J.; Farhadi, A. Yolov3: An incremental improvement. *arXiv* **2018**, arXiv:1804.02767.
27. Liu, Z.; Wu, W.; Gu, X.; Li, S.; Wang, L.; Zhang, T. Application of combining YOLO models and 3D GPR images in road detection and maintenance. *Remote Sens.* **2021**, *13*, 1081–1099. [CrossRef]
28. Lu, J.; Gong, P.; Ye, J.; Zhang, C. Learning from very few samples: A survey. *arXiv* **2020**, arXiv:2009.02653.
29. Yang, S.; Liu, L.; Xu, M. Free lunch for few-shot learning: Distribution calibration. *arXiv* **2021**, arXiv:2101.06395.
30. Wang, Y.; Yao, Q.; Kwok, J.; Ni, L. Generalizing from a few examples: A survey on few-shot learning. *ACM Comput. Surv.* **2020**, *53*, 1–34. [CrossRef]
31. Santoro, A.; Bartunov, S.; Botvinick, M.; Wierstra, D.; Lillicrap, T. One-shot learning with memory-augmented neural networks. *arXiv* **2016**, arXiv:1605.06065.
32. Munkhdalai, T.; Yu, H. Meta networks. In Proceedings of the International Conference on Machine Learning, Sydney, Australia, 6–17 August 2017.
33. Ravi, S.; Larochelle, H. Optimization as a model for few-shot learning. In Proceedings of the International Conference on Learning Representations (ICLR), Toulon, France, 24–26 April 2017.
34. Finn, C.; Abbeel, P.; Levine, S. Model-agnostic meta-learning for fast adaptation of deep networks. In Proceedings of the International Conference on Machine Learning, Sydney, Australia, 6–17 August 2017.
35. Vinyals, O.; Blundell, C.; Lillicrap, T.; Kavukcuoglu, K.; Wierstra, D. Matching networks for one shot learning. *Adv. Neural Inf. Process. Syst.* **2016**, *29*, 3630–3638.
36. Sung, F.; Yang, Y.; Zhang, L.; Xiang, T.; Torr, P.; Hospedales, T. Learning to compare: Relation network for few-shot learning. In Proceedings of the IEEE conference on computer vision and pattern recognition, Salt Lake City, UT, USA, 18–22 June 2018; pp. 1199–1208.
37. Koch, G.; Zemel, R.; Salakhutdinov, R. Siamese neural networks for one-shot image recognition. *ICML Deep. Learn. Workshop* **2015**, *2*, 2015.
38. Li, W.; Wang, L.; Xu, J.; Huo, J.; Gao, Y.; Luo, J. Revisiting local descriptor based image-to-class measure for few-shot learning. In Proceedings of the IEEE/CVF Conference on Computer Vision and Pattern Recognition, California, CA, USA, 16–20 June 2019; pp. 7260–7268.
39. Wertheimer, D.; Tang, L.; Hariharan, B. Few-shot classification with feature map reconstruction networks. In Proceedings of the IEEE/CVF Conference on Computer Vision and Pattern Recognition, Nashville, TN, USA, 19–25 June 2021; pp. 8012–8021.
40. Kang, D.; Kwon, H.; Min, J.; Cho, M. Relational Embedding for Few-Shot Classification. In Proceedings of the IEEE/CVF International Conference on Computer Vision, Montreal, QC, Canada, 11–17 October 2021; pp. 8822–8833.
41. Zhang, C.; Cai, Y.; Lin, G.; Shen, C. Deepemd: Few-shot image classification with differentiable earth mover's distance and structured classifiers. In Proceedings of the IEEE/CVF conference on computer vision and pattern recognition, Seattle, WA, USA, 13–19 June 2020; pp. 12203–12213.
42. Snell, J.; Swersky, K.; Zemel, R. Prototypical networks for few-shot learning. *Adv. Neural Inf. Process. Syst.* **2017**, *30*, 1–11.
43. Li, W.; Dong, C.; Tian, P.; Qin, T.; Yang, X.; Wang, Z.; Huo, J.; Shi, Y.; Wang, L.; Gao, Y.; et al. LibFewShot: A Comprehensive Library for Few-shot Learning. *arXiv* **2021**, arXiv:2109.04898.
44. Kingma, D.; Ba, J. Adam: A method for stochastic optimization. *arXiv* **2014**, arXiv:1412.6980.
45. Bertinetto, L.; Henriques, J.; Torr, P.; Vedaldi, A. Meta-learning with differentiable closed-form solvers. *arXiv* **2018**, arXiv:1805.08136.
46. Chen, W.-Y.; Liu, Y.-C.; Kira, Z.; Wang, Y.-C.; Huang, J.-B. A closer look at few-shot classification. *arXiv* **2019**, arXiv:1904.04232.

47. Ren, M.; Triantafillou, E.; Ravi, S.; Snell, J.; Swersky, K.; Tenenbaum, J.; Larochelle, H.; Zemel, R. Meta-learning for semi-supervised few-shot classification. *arXiv* **2018**, arXiv:1803.00676, 2018.
48. Warren, C.; Giannopoulos, A.; Giannakis, I. gprMax: Open source software to simulate electromagnetic wave propagation for ground penetrating radar. *Comput. Phys. Commun.* **2016**, *209*, 163–170. [CrossRef]
49. Giannakis, I.; Giannopoulos, A.; Warren, C. A realistic FDTD numerical modeling framework of ground penetrating radar for landmine detection. *IEEE J. Sel. Top. Appl. Earth Obs. Remote Sens.* **2016**, *9*, 37–51. [CrossRef]
50. He, K.; Zhang, X.; Ren, S.; Sun, J. Deep residual learning for image recognition. In Proceedings of the IEEE conference on computer vision and pattern recognition, Las Vegas, NV, USA, 27–30 June 2016; pp. 770–778.

mathematics

Article

IN-ME Position Error Compensation Algorithm for the Near-Field Beamforming of UAVs

Yinan Zhang, Guangxue Wang, Yi Leng *, Guowen Yu and Shirui Peng *

Department of Information Countermeasure, Air Force Early Warning Academy, Wuhan 430010, China
* Correspondence: lengyi200209@163.com (Y.L.); psr99@21.cn (S.P.)

Abstract: The target of an unmanned aerial vehicle swarm will present near-field characteristics when it is integrated as an array, and the existence of the unmanned aerial vehicle swarm motion error will greatly deteriorate the beam pattern formed by the array. To solve these problems, a near-field array beamforming model with array element position error is constructed, and the Taylor expansion of the phase difference function is used to approximately simplify the model. The improved Newton maximum entropy algorithm is proposed to estimate and compensate for the phase errors. The maximum entropy objective function is established, and the Newton iterative algorithm is used to estimate the phase error iteratively. To select the proper Newton iteration initial value, based on a single reference source signal, the initial value of the phase error is estimated through the phase gradient information of the received array signal. Beamforming is carried out after phase error compensation regarding the array. In order to assess the mismatch of the phase error compensation function based on the proposed method, when the beam is scanning, the effectively compensated spatial area of the array beamforming is divided, which lays a foundation for subsequent spatial region division and unmanned aerial vehicle swarm path planning. The simulation results show that the beam formed by the method proposed in this paper has a lower sidelobe level, and as the signal-to-noise ratio changes, the robustness of the proposed method is better validated. The proposed algorithm can effectively suppress the adverse influence of array element position error on array beamforming, and when the beam is scanning, the effectively compensated area of the phase error compensation function is divided, based on the proposed method.

Keywords: unmanned aerial vehicle swarm; antenna array; near-field beamforming; array element position error compensation; spatial area division

MSC: 94-08

Citation: Zhang, Y.; Wang, G.; Leng, Y.; Yu, G.; Peng, S. IN-ME Position Error Compensation Algorithm for the Near-Field Beamforming of UAVs. *Mathematics* **2022**, *10*, 3256. https://doi.org/10.3390/math10183256

Academic Editor: Paolo Crippa

Received: 19 July 2022
Accepted: 30 August 2022
Published: 7 September 2022

1. Introduction

With the development of beamforming technology and unmanned aerial vehicle swarm (UAVs) technology, the antenna array elements equipping the UAVs are combined into a distributed beamforming system through collaboration among the swarm to achieve directional high gain signal transmission. Therefore, using beamforming technology to improve the combat capability of UAVs in a fierce confrontation environment is a growing trend [1]. It is obvious that taking UAVs as an array has many advantages, such as using low-cost UAVs to achieve high gain signal transmission, which is also known as the beam pattern, but the targets of the array are often located in the near-field, and the motion error [2–5] of a single UAV as an array element will deteriorate the beam pattern formed by the array. At present, the array position error calibration is mainly founded on the calibration method of three or more known radiant sources, based on far-field signals, or the rotating array calibration method, based on a single known as a radiant source [6–8], but the latter is, in essence, also a multi-radiant source calibration method exchanging time for space. Reference [2] proposes using three simultaneously existing auxiliary sources to calibrate the position error of the array, but this method can only use the Taylor first-order expansion of the array steering vector with error when the position error has a very small disturbance, which means the position error cannot be corrected by this method when it is too large. In array beamforming, the beam cannot be formed when an array element position error exists, but as long as the phase error caused by the position error is compensated for, the beam can be formed effectively. It is easier to solve a one-dimensional phase error than to solve two- or three- dimensional position errors, and the phase error can be obtained by using a single known radiant source as a reference source [9–12]. As for the solution to phase error, based on the information of the reference source, the phase error can be estimated using the phase gradient (PG) value of the received signal between the array elements [13–17], but this method requires a high signal-to-noise ratio (SNR), and under the condition of low SNR, the deviation of the phase error estimation value from the real value is large. Phase error can also be solved by iteration. The authors of [18–21] take the entropy of the image as the objective function and estimate the phase error by using the Newton iterative method, but this method presents problems, such as the selection of the initial value affecting the algorithm time, causing the algorithm to fall into local optimization. When the expected main-lobe direction of beamforming is the same as the reference source direction, the phase error in main-lobe direction can be compensated for by the estimated phase error compensation function, but when it is not the same as the reference source direction, the mismatch of the phase error compensation function occurs, which will affect the beamforming pattern. Therefore, it is necessary to study the influence of phase error compensation function mismatch, which is the same as the division of the area effectively compensated by the estimated phase error compensation function. The authors of [22] propose that when the near-field radial compensation filter is used to filter out interference sources, the beamforming pattern will deteriorate when the sources are far away from the array, but the study does not specifically analyze the pattern deterioration level. The work in [23] proposes a method to form a multi-focus antenna array in the near-field, with specified amplitude and phase conditions for the multi-focus problem of the near-field array, but this study does not involve the analysis of the mismatch of the single-focus filter.

Based on the above analysis, firstly, a near-field array beamforming model with UAV position error is constructed in Section 2, and the model is approximately simplified by the Taylor expansion of the phase difference function of the near-field signal. Secondly, the improved Newton maximum entropy (IN-ME) algorithm is used to estimate and correct the phase error in Section 3. Under the condition of low SNR, taking the single known radiant source as a reference source, the initial value of the phase error is estimated through the PG information of the received array signal, and then, taking the maximum entropy function of the array synthetic power at the reference source as the objective function, the Newton iterative solution to the phase error is carried out. After the phase error is compensated, beamforming is carried out. Thirdly, when phase error estimation based on proposed IN-ME algorithm is used to compensate for beamforming, if the array forms beam scanning, the phase compensation function will be mismatched. Based on the phase error compensation function of the IN-ME algorithm, the effectively compensated area which can be compensated for to effectively form the beam pattern is further divided in Section 4, laying a foundation for the subsequent spatial region division and UAV path planning. The simulation results in Section 5 show the effectiveness of the algorithm, and the conclusions are given in Section 6. The adverse influence of UAV position errors on near-field array beamforming is effectively suppressed, and the effectively compensated area, with phase compensation function mismatch, is divided.

2. Near-Field Beamforming Model

2.1. Array Signal Model

Under the condition of targets being in the near-field, the assumption that the electromagnetic wave is the plane wave is not tenable, and it should be modeled as a spherical wave. As shown in Figure 1, it is assumed that the near-field antenna array of N UAVs which can be seen as N elements is linearly distributed along the axis x at equal intervals, the total length of the array is L, the coordinate of the nth element is $(x_n, 0)$, where, $n = 1, 2, \cdots, N$, and $-\frac{L}{2} \leq x_n \leq \frac{L}{2}$, r_n refers to the distance from the nth antenna array element to the source P, R refers to the distance from the source P to the array center O, θ is the included angle between OP and the axis y, and when the direction of OP projection on the x axis is the same as positive direction of the x axis, θ is positive, and vice versa. The coordinate of source P is $P(x_P, y_P)$.

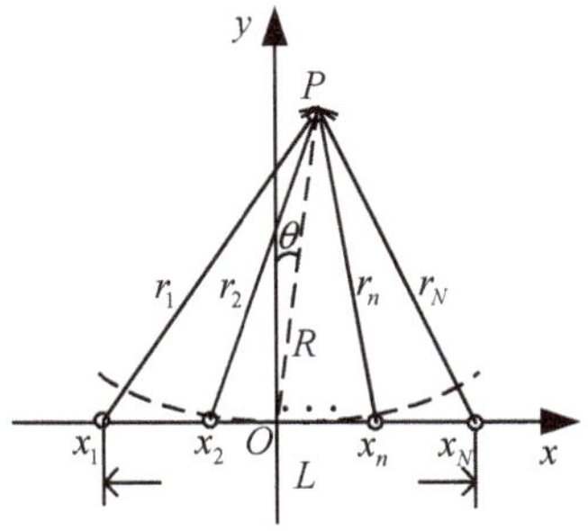

Figure 1. Near-field array model.

For any radiant source P in the near-field, according to the spherical wave theory, the radiant signal received by the array element can be expressed as

$$s(x_n) = \frac{A}{r_n}\exp\left[\mathrm{j}\left(2\pi ft - 2\pi\frac{\Delta r_n}{\lambda}\right)\right] = \frac{\widetilde{A}}{r_n}\exp(-\mathrm{j}k\Delta r_n) \tag{1}$$

where, $\widetilde{A} = A\exp(j2\pi ft)$ is the radiant signal of the source P, j is the imaginary unit, f is the radiant signal frequency, λ is the wavelength, $k = \frac{2\pi}{\lambda}$ is the wavenumber, and Δr_n is the wave path difference from the source P to the nth antenna array element, with the array center O as the reference point.

Theorem 1. ([24]) *Suppose that $r(x)$ is a differentiable function for which $r\prime(a), \cdots, r^{(n)}(a)$ all exist, and there is neighborhood $U(a)$ of a, in which the function value of $r(x)$ at $x = \mathrm{a}$ can be written as $r(x) = r(a) + r\prime(a)(x-a) + \frac{r''(a)(x-a)^2}{2!} + o\left((x-a)^2\right)$.*

Theorem 1 is also known as Taylor's theorem. For the antenna array composed of UAVs, although the targets of interest in wireless communication, electronic reconnaissance, and jamming are generally located in the near-field of the array, the distances from the targets of interest to the antenna center are usually much greater than the aperture of the antenna. Therefore, it can be assumed that $R \gg L \geq 2|x_n|$. Then, the Taylor series expansion of Δr_n can be obtained by

$$\Delta r_n = r_n - R = \sqrt{(x_n - x_P)^2 + (y_P)^2} - R \approx -\sin\theta \cdot x_n + \frac{\cos^2\theta}{2R}x_n^2 \tag{2}$$

Through Equation (2), the phase difference between the received signal of the nth array element and the received signal at the array center O is

$$\Delta\varphi_n = -\frac{2\pi}{\lambda}\Delta r_n \approx -k\left(-\sin\theta \cdot x_n + \frac{\cos^2\theta}{2R}x_n^2\right) \tag{3}$$

By substituting Equation (3) into Equation (1) and ignoring the influence of distance on signal amplitude, the received signal model of the nth array element in the near-field can be approximately written as

$$s(x_n) \approx \widetilde{A}\exp\left(-jk\left(-\sin\theta \cdot x_n + \frac{\cos^2\theta}{2R}x_n^2\right)\right) \tag{4}$$

For M radiant sources in the near-field, the radiant signal amplitude of the mth radiant source is A_m, the frequency is f_m, the polar coordinate is (θ_m, R_m), and the distance from the nth array element to the mth radiant source is r_{nm}, where, $m = 1, \cdots, M$. Then, the received signal of the array is

$$\boldsymbol{X} = \sum_{m=1}^{M} s_m(x_n) + \boldsymbol{V} = \widetilde{A}\boldsymbol{A}(\theta, R) + \boldsymbol{V} \tag{5}$$

where, $s_m(x_n) = \widetilde{A}_m\exp\left(-jk\left(-\sin\theta_m \cdot x_n + \frac{\cos^2\theta_m}{2R_m}x_n^2\right)\right), \widetilde{A}_m = A_m\exp(j2\pi f_m t)$, $X = [x_1\ x_2\ \cdots\ x_N]^T$ is a $N \times 1$ dimensional receiving data vector, $\boldsymbol{A}(\theta, R)$ is a $N \times M$ dimensional array steering vector, $\boldsymbol{S}$ is a $M \times 1$ dimensional signal vector, and $\boldsymbol{V}$ is a $N \times 1$ dimensional noise vector. There is

$$\boldsymbol{A}(\theta, R) = \begin{bmatrix}\boldsymbol{a}(\theta_1, R_1) & \boldsymbol{a}(\theta_2, R_2) & \cdots & \boldsymbol{a}(\theta_M, R_M)\end{bmatrix} \tag{6}$$

$$\begin{aligned}\boldsymbol{a}(\theta_m, R_m) &= \begin{bmatrix} a_1(\theta_m, R_m) & a_2(\theta_m, R_m) & \cdots & a_N(\theta_m, R_m) \end{bmatrix}^{\mathrm{T}} \\ &= \begin{bmatrix} e^{\left(-jk\left(-\sin\theta_m \cdot x_1 + \frac{\cos^2\theta_m}{2R_m}x_1^2\right)\right)} & e^{\left(-jk\left(-\sin\theta_m \cdot x_2 + \frac{\cos^2\theta_m}{2R_m}x_2^2\right)\right)} & \ldots & e^{\left(-jk\left(-\sin\theta_m \cdot x_N + \frac{\cos^2\theta_m}{2R_m}x_N^2\right)\right)} \end{bmatrix}^{\mathrm{T}}\end{aligned} \tag{7}$$

$$\boldsymbol{V} = \begin{bmatrix} v_1 & v_2 & \cdots & v_N \end{bmatrix}^{\mathrm{T}} \tag{8}$$

where, $[\cdot]^{\mathrm{T}}$ represents matrix transpose, and the $N \times 1$ dimensional vector $a(\theta_m, R_m)$ is the steering vector of the array under the mth radiant source.

The received signals of each array element are weighted and summed to obtain the array output as, which is beamforming

$$Y = \boldsymbol{W}^{\mathrm{H}}\boldsymbol{X} = \boldsymbol{W}^{\mathrm{H}}\left(\widetilde{A}\boldsymbol{A}(\theta, R) + \boldsymbol{V}\right) \tag{9}$$

where, $[\cdot]^{\mathrm{H}}$ represents the conjugate transpose of the matrix, and $\boldsymbol{W} = \begin{bmatrix} w_1 & w_2 & \cdots & w_N \end{bmatrix}^{\mathrm{T}}$ is the $N \times 1$ dimensional weighted vector of the array. When the polar coordinate of the expected signal is (θ_P, R_P), and the distance from the nth array element is r_{nP}, there is $w_n = \exp(-jk\Delta r_{nP})$, where, $\Delta r_{nP} = -\sin\theta_P \cdot x_n + \frac{\cos^2\theta_P}{2R_P}x_n^2$.

2.2. Actual Near-Field Beamforming

When there are errors in the positions of the array elements, the actual coordinate of the nth array element is $(\hat{x}_n, \hat{y}_n)$, where, $\hat{x}_n = x_n + \Delta x_n$, and $\hat{y}_n = y_n + \Delta y_n$. Under the model of this paper, $y_n = 0$. Similar to 2.1., the modified actual wave path difference $\Delta\hat{r}_n$ in the Taylor series expansion is

$$\begin{aligned}\Delta\hat{r}_n \approx &-\sin\theta\hat{x}_n - \cos\theta\hat{y}_n + \frac{\cos^2\theta}{2R}\hat{x}_n{}^2 \\ &+ \frac{\sin^2\theta}{2R}\hat{y}_n^2 + \frac{(\cos\theta + \sin\theta)}{2R^2}\hat{x}_n\hat{y}_n\end{aligned} \tag{10}$$

By using Equation (10) to approximately simplify $s(\hat{x}_n)$, the actual nth array signal model can be expressed as

$$s(\hat{x}_n) \approx \widetilde{A}\exp\left(-jk\left(\begin{array}{c} -\sin\theta\hat{x}_n - \cos\theta\hat{y}_n + \dfrac{\cos^2\theta}{2R}\hat{x}_n{}^2 \\ +\dfrac{\sin^2\theta}{2R}\hat{y}_n^2 + \dfrac{(\cos\theta+\sin\theta)}{2R^2}\hat{x}_n\hat{y}_n \end{array}\right)\right) \tag{11}$$

Then the actual received signal of the array is

$$\hat{\mathbf{X}} = \sum_{m=1}^{M} s_m(\hat{x}_n) + \mathbf{V} = \widetilde{A}\hat{\mathbf{A}}(\theta, R) + \mathbf{V} \tag{12}$$

where, $\hat{\mathbf{X}} = \begin{bmatrix}\hat{X}_1 & \hat{X}_2 & \cdots & \hat{X}_N\end{bmatrix}^T$ is an actual $N \times 1$ dimensional received data vector, $s_m(\hat{x}_n)$ is the actual mth, $m = 1, \cdots, M$ is the received radiant source signal, $\hat{\mathbf{A}}(\theta, R)$ is an actual $N \times M$ dimensional array steering vector, and

$$s_m(\hat{x}_n) = s_m(x_n)\cdot w_{en} = s_m(x_n)\cdot\exp\left(-jk\left(\begin{array}{c} -\sin\theta_m\cdot\Delta x_n - \cos\theta_m\cdot\Delta y_n + \dfrac{\cos^2\theta_m}{R_m}x_n\Delta x_n + \dfrac{\cos^2\theta_m}{2R_m}\Delta x_n{}^2 \\ +\dfrac{\sin^2\theta_m}{2R_m}\Delta y_n^2 + \dfrac{(\cos\theta_m+\sin\theta_m)}{2R_m^2}(x_n+\Delta x_n)\Delta y_n \end{array}\right)\right) \tag{13}$$

$$\hat{\mathbf{A}}(\theta, R) = \begin{bmatrix}\hat{\mathbf{a}}(\theta_1, R_1) & \hat{\mathbf{a}}(\theta_2, R_2) & \ldots & \hat{\mathbf{a}}(\theta_M, R_M)\end{bmatrix} \tag{14}$$

$$\begin{aligned} &\hat{\mathbf{a}}(\theta_m, R_m) = [\hat{a}_1(\theta_m, R_m)\ \hat{a}_2(\theta_m, R_m)\ \cdots\ \hat{a}_N(\theta_m, R_m)]^{\mathrm{T}} \\ &= \left[\exp\left(-jk\left(\begin{array}{c} -\sin\theta_m\hat{x}_1 - \cos\theta_m\hat{y}_1 + \dfrac{\cos^2\theta_m}{2R_m}\hat{x}_1^2 \\ +\dfrac{\sin^2\theta_m}{2R_m}\hat{y}_1^2 \dfrac{(\cos\theta_m\sin\theta_m)}{2R_m^2}\hat{x}_1\hat{y}_1 \end{array}\right)\right) \cdots \exp\left(-jk\left(\begin{array}{c} -\sin\theta_m\hat{x}_N - \cos\theta_m\hat{y}_N\dfrac{\cos^2\theta_m}{2R_m}\hat{x}_N^2 \\ \dfrac{\sin^2\theta_m}{2R_m}\hat{y}_N^2 \dfrac{(\cos\theta_m\sin\theta_m)}{2R_m^2}\hat{x}_N\hat{y}_N \end{array}\right)\right)\right]^{\mathrm{T}} \end{aligned} \tag{15}$$

where, w_{en} is the error value of the nth array element. When $M = 1$, the actual beamforming formula can be written as

$$\hat{Y} = \mathbf{W}^{\mathrm{H}}\hat{\mathbf{X}} = \sum_{n=1}^{N} w_n^* \cdot (w_{en}s(x_n) + v_n) \tag{16}$$

where, w_n^* is the conjugate complex of w_n.

Obviously, due to the presence of array position errors and noises, it is impossible to effectively carry out near-field beamforming by using the signal weight that can be obtained when the array is at the nominal value to compensate for the actual signal.

3. IN-ME Phase Error Compensation Algorithm Based on Reference Source

Only by compensating for phase error can the array effectively form a beam pattern. We propose the IN-ME algorithm, which, compared to Newton maximum entropy (N-ME) algorithm, can obtain higher convergent value within a shorter period, as well as form a lower sidelobe-level beam pattern with a higher SNR.

3.1. Phase Error Estimation Based on Newton Maximum Entropy Algorithm

Entropy is a measurement of information uncertainty. The maximum entropy principle is a criterion of probabilistic model learning, and when the probability distribution of random variables obeys uniform distribution, the entropy reaches its highest level. As for beamforming, we expect that after phase error compensation, the synthetic powers in the main-lobe direction of the array's received signals in all snapshots increase, which becomes a multi-objective optimization problem. If we regard the ratio of synthetic power in the main-lobe direction of the array's received signals in one snapshot to the sum of the synthetic powers in all snapshots as the probability distribution, compared to the maximum entropy principle, it can be seen as that when this ratio obeys uniform distribution, the synthetic power in every snapshot can increase, which means that the phase error compensation is effective for the signals in every snapshot. Therefore, the objective function should be the maximum entropy of that ratio.

Assuming that there is a reference source in the target scene, if the array beamforming is expected to form a main-lobe at the source, the weighted value of the array can be obtained as $\mathbf{W} = \begin{bmatrix} w_1 & w_2 & \cdots & w_N \end{bmatrix}^{\mathrm{T}}$. When the snapshots are certain, Q_g, representing the total ideal synthetic power of all snapshots at the reference point, is a constant, and can be obtained by

$$Q_g = \sum_{ss=1}^{SS} |G(ss)|^2 \tag{17}$$

where, SS is the total number of snapshots, and $G(ss)$ is the synthesized signal at the reference source after ideally weighting and summing the received signals in the ssth snapshot. The synthetic power in the main-lobe direction of the array's received signals in one snapshot can be obtained by

$$g(ss) = \sum_{n=1}^{N} w_n^* \cdot (s(\hat{x}_n) + v_n)_{ss} \cdot e^{\mathrm{j}\varphi_n} \tag{18}$$

where, $(s(\hat{x}_n) + v_n)_{ss}$ is the received signal in the ssth snapshot of the array element, and φ_n is the phase error of the nth array element to be estimated. Because Q_g is a constant, the entropy objective function of $g(ss)$ can be written as

$$E_g = -\frac{1}{Q_g} \sum_{ss=1}^{SS} |g(ss)|^2 \ln \frac{|g(ss)|^2}{Q_g} \tag{19}$$

The entropy objective function E_g is the function of the phase φ_n to be estimated. Thus, the phase estimation based on the maximum entropy can be expressed as

$$\hat{\varphi}_n = \underset{\varphi_n}{\operatorname{argmax}} E_g(\varphi_n) \tag{20}$$

Theorem 2. ([25]) *Suppose that* $E''(x)$, *which is the* second derivation of E, *is continuous in an open neighborhood of* a , *and that* $E\prime(\mathrm{a}) = 0$ *and* $E''(x)$ *is negative definite. Then* a *is a strict local maximizer of* $E(x)$.

Proof. Because $E''(x)$, which is also known as the Hessian, is a continuous and negative definite at a, we can choose a radius $r > 0$ so that $E''(x)$ remains negative definite for all x in the open ball $D = \{z | \|z - \mathrm{a}\| < r\}$. Taking any nonzero vector p with $\|p\| \le r$, we have $\mathrm{a} + p \in D$, and so $E(\mathrm{a} + p) = E(\mathrm{a}) + p^{\mathrm{T}} E'(\mathrm{a}) + \frac{1}{2} p^{\mathrm{T}} E''(z) p = E(\mathrm{a}) + \frac{1}{2} p^{\mathrm{T}} E''(z) p$, where, $z = \mathrm{a} + tp$ for some $t \in (0, 1)$. Since $z \in D$, we have $p^{\mathrm{T}} E''(z) p < 0$, and therefore $E(\mathrm{a} + p) < E(\mathrm{a})$, giving the results. □

By combining Theorem 1 and Theorem 2, we can use the Newton method for Formula (20). There is an iterative solution of φ_n as

$$\varphi_n^{(l+1)} = \varphi_n^{(l)} - \left(\frac{\partial^2 E_g}{\partial \varphi_n^2} \right)^{-1} \frac{\partial E_g}{\partial \varphi_n} \Bigg|_{\varphi_n = \varphi_n^{(l)}} \tag{21}$$

where, superscript (l) indicates the lth iteration. To solve Equation (21), the first and second derivation of E_g against φ_n need to be calculated. The first derivative expression can be expressed as

$$\frac{\partial E_g}{\partial \varphi_n} = -\frac{1}{Q_g}\sum_{ss=1}^{SS}\left(1+\ln\frac{|g(ss)|^2}{Q_g}\right)\cdot\frac{\partial |g(ss)|^2}{\partial \varphi_n} \tag{22}$$

The second derivative expression can be expressed as

$$\frac{\partial^2 E_g}{\partial \varphi_n^2} = -\frac{1}{Q_g}\sum_{ss=1}^{SS}\left(\frac{1}{|g(ss)|^2}\cdot\left(\frac{\partial |g(ss)|^2}{\partial \varphi_n}\right)^2 + \left(1+\ln\frac{|g(ss)|^2}{Q_g}\right)\cdot\frac{\partial^2 |g(ss)|^2}{\partial \varphi_n^2}\right) \tag{23}$$

where,

$$\begin{aligned}\frac{\partial |g(ss)|^2}{\partial \varphi_n} &= g(ss)\frac{\partial g^*(ss)}{\partial \varphi_n} + g^*(ss)\frac{\partial g(ss)}{\partial \varphi_n}\\ &= 2\mathrm{Re}\left(g^*(ss)\frac{\partial g(ss)}{\partial \varphi_n}\right)\end{aligned} \tag{24}$$

$$\frac{\partial g(ss)}{\partial \varphi_n} = jw_n^*\cdot(w_{en}s(x_n)+v_n)_{ss}\cdot e^{j\varphi_n} \tag{25}$$

$$\begin{aligned}\left(\frac{\partial |g(ss)|^2}{\partial \varphi_n}\right)^2 &= \left(g(ss)\frac{\partial g^*(ss)}{\partial \varphi_n} + g^*(ss)\frac{\partial g(ss)}{\partial \varphi_n}\right)^2\\ &= 2\mathrm{Re}\left(\left(g^*(ss)\frac{\partial g(ss)}{\partial \varphi_n}\right)^2\right) + 2|g(ss)|^2\left|\frac{\partial g(ss)}{\partial \varphi_n}\right|^2\end{aligned} \tag{26}$$

$$\frac{\partial^2 |g(ss)|^2}{\partial \varphi_n^2} = 2\left|\frac{\partial g(ss)}{\partial \varphi_n}\right|^2 + 2\mathrm{Re}\left(g^*(ss)\frac{\partial^2 g(ss)}{\partial \varphi_n^2}\right) \tag{27}$$

$$\frac{\partial^2 g(ss)}{\partial \varphi_n^2} = -w_n^*\cdot(w_{en}s(x_n)+v_n)_{ss}\cdot e^{j\varphi_n} \tag{28}$$

where, $\mathrm{Re}(\cdot)$ represents the real part operation.

In practical cases, the phase errors in signals received by different array elements are relatively independent from each other [26]. Therefore, the phase error of each array element is searched separately, and in Formula (23), only the diagonal elements of the Hessian, which is also the second derivative $\frac{\partial^2 E_g}{\partial \varphi_n^2}$, of the entropy with respect to phase error are derived, while the off-diagonal elements $\frac{\partial^2 E_g}{\partial \varphi_n \partial \varphi_m}, n \neq m$ are ignored.

By taking Equations (24) and (25) into Equation (22), the analytical formula of the first derivative is obtained

$$\frac{\partial E_g}{\partial \varphi_n} = -\frac{2}{Q_g}\sum_{ss=1}^{SS}\left(1+\ln\frac{|g(ss)|^2}{Q_g}\right)\cdot\mathrm{Re}\left(j\cdot g^*(ss)\cdot w_n^*\cdot(w_{en}s(x_n)+v_n)_{ss}\cdot e^{j\varphi_n}\right) \tag{29}$$

By taking Equation (24) to Equation (28) into Equation (23), the analytical formula of the first derivative is obtained

$$\frac{\partial^2 E_g}{\partial \varphi_n^2} = -\frac{2}{Q_g}\sum_{ss=1}^{SS}\left(\begin{array}{l}\frac{1}{|g(ss)|^2}\cdot\left(\mathrm{Re}\left(\left(jg^*(ss)w_n^*(w_{en}s(x_n)+v_n)_{ss}e^{j\varphi_n}\right)^2\right)+|g(ss)|^2\left|jw_n^*(w_{en}s(x_n)+v_n)_{ss}e^{j\varphi_n}\right|^2\right)\\ +\left(1+\ln\frac{|g(ss)|^2}{Q_g}\right)\cdot\left(\left|jw_n^*(w_{en}s(x_n)+v_n)_{ss}e^{j\varphi_n}\right|^2-\mathrm{Re}\left(g^*(ss)w_n^*(w_{en}s(x_n)+v_n)_{ss}e^{j\varphi_n}\right)\right)\end{array}\right) \tag{30}$$

After performing phase error calibration for Equation (16), the beamforming with error calibration is

$$\widetilde{Y} = \mathbf{W}_c^{\mathrm{H}} \odot \mathbf{W}^{\mathrm{H}}\hat{\mathbf{X}} = \sum_{n=1}^{N} w_{cn}^*\cdot w_n^*\cdot(w_{en}s(x_n)+v_n) \tag{31}$$

where, $\odot$ represents the Hadamard product of the matrix, and $\boldsymbol{W}_c = \begin{bmatrix} w_{c1} & w_{c2} & \dots & w_{cN} \end{bmatrix}^{\mathrm{T}}$ $= \begin{bmatrix} e^{-j\hat{\varphi}_1} & e^{-j\hat{\varphi}_2} & \dots & e^{-j\hat{\varphi}_N} \end{bmatrix}^{\mathrm{T}}$.

3.2. Initial Value Estimation of Phase Error Based on PG

According to the principle of Newton's maximum entropy algorithm, the selection of the initial value of the phase error will directly affect the iteration efficiency. If the initial value of the phase error is randomly selected, such as directly setting the initial value of phase error to zero, which is the N-ME algorithm, it may not only greatly slow down the convergence speed of the algorithm, but also make the algorithm fall into the local optimal solution. Therefore, a method based on a reference source to select the initial value of the phase error is proposed to improve the N-ME algorithm.

When there are noises and array position errors, after weighting the received signals, the initial received signals of the array without phase error calibration can be written as

$$\begin{aligned} \boldsymbol{S} &= \boldsymbol{W}^* \odot \hat{\boldsymbol{X}} = \begin{bmatrix} S_1 & S_2 & \dots & S_N \end{bmatrix}^{\mathrm{T}} \\ &= \begin{bmatrix} \tilde{A} w_1^* e^{\left(-jk\left(-\sin\theta \cdot x_1 + \frac{\cos^2\theta}{2R} x_1^2\right)\right)} \cdot e^{j\varphi_1^{(0)}} & \tilde{A} w_2^* e^{\left(-jk\left(-\sin\theta \cdot x_2 + \frac{\cos^2\theta}{2R} x_2^2\right)\right)} \cdot e^{j\varphi_2^{(0)}} & \cdots & \tilde{A} w_N^* e^{\left(-jk\left(-\sin\theta \cdot x_N + \frac{\cos^2\theta}{2R} x_N^2\right)\right)} \cdot e^{j\varphi_N^{(0)}} \end{bmatrix}^{\mathrm{T}} \end{aligned} \quad (32)$$

where, $[\cdot]^*$ represents conjugation, $S_n, n = 1, \cdots, N$ represents the initial output signal of the nth array element, and $\varphi_n^{(0)}, n = 1, \cdots, N$ represents the initial phase error of the nth array element caused by noise and array position error.

Ideally, after weighting the received signals, the phase error caused by different distances is fully compensated, and the PG between the output signals of the array elements is constant. For discrete sequences, the phase difference between the output signals of adjacent array elements is the PG. We define the correlation sequence of the array as

$$\boldsymbol{\rho} = \begin{bmatrix} \rho_1 & \rho_2 & \cdots & \rho_{N-1} \end{bmatrix}^{\mathrm{T}} = \begin{bmatrix} S_1 \cdot S_2 & S_2 \cdot S_3 & \cdots & S_{N-1} \cdot S_N \end{bmatrix}^{\mathrm{T}} \quad (33)$$

The PG between adjacent elements is estimated as

$$\Delta\boldsymbol{\varphi}^{(0)} = \begin{bmatrix} \Delta\varphi_1^{(0)} & \Delta\varphi_2^{(0)} & \cdots & \Delta\varphi_{N-1}^{(0)} \end{bmatrix}^{\mathrm{T}} = \arg(\boldsymbol{\rho}) \quad (34)$$

By taking the phase of the first array element as a reference, the initial value of phase error to be compensated for each array element is estimated by calculating the cumulative sum between adjacent array elements. There is

$$\boldsymbol{\varphi}^{(0)} = \begin{bmatrix} \varphi_1^{(0)} & \varphi_2^{(0)} & \cdots & \varphi_N^{(0)} \end{bmatrix}^{\mathrm{T}} = \begin{bmatrix} 0 & \mathrm{cusum}\left(\Delta\boldsymbol{\varphi}^{(0)}\right) \end{bmatrix}^{\mathrm{T}} \quad (35)$$

where, cusum$(\cdot)$ represents the cumulative sum.

The IN-ME phase error compensation algorithm, based on the reference source, is shown in Algorithm 1.

Algorithm 1 The IN-ME phase error compensation algorithm based on reference source.

Input: received signals of array $\hat{X}$, reference source $P(x_P, y_P)$
Output: beamform after phase error calibration $\widetilde{Y}$

Step 1: Calculate weighted signal, weights $W = \begin{bmatrix} w_1 & w_2 & \cdots & w_N \end{bmatrix}^{\mathrm{T}}$, and weighted signal $S = W^* \odot \hat{X}$;

Step 2: Calculate the correlation sequence of the array, $\rho = \begin{bmatrix} S_1 \cdot S_2 & S_2 \cdot S_3 & \cdots & S_{N-1} \cdot S_N \end{bmatrix}^{\mathrm{T}}$;

Step 3: Estimate initial value of phase error based on PG:

1. Estimate the PG between adjacent elements,
$\Delta\varphi^{(0)} = \begin{bmatrix} \Delta\varphi_1^{(0)} & \Delta\varphi_2^{(0)} & \cdots & \Delta\varphi_{N-1}^{(0)} \end{bmatrix}^{\mathrm{T}} = \arg(\rho)$;

2. Estimate initial value of phase error,
$\varphi^{(0)} = \begin{bmatrix} \varphi_1^{(0)} & \varphi_2^{(0)} & \cdots & \varphi_N^{(0)} \end{bmatrix}^{\mathrm{T}} = \begin{bmatrix} 0 & \mathrm{cusum}\left(\Delta\varphi^{(0)}\right) \end{bmatrix}^{\mathrm{T}}$;

Step 4: Improved Newton Maximum Entropy Algorithm:

1. Calculate the array's synthetic signal at the reference source,
$g(ss) = \sum_{n=1}^{N} w_n^* \cdot (s(\hat{x}_n) + v_n)_{ss} \cdot e^{j\varphi_n}$;

2. Form the entropy objective function, $E_g = -\frac{1}{Q_g} \sum_{ss=1}^{SS} |g(ss)|^2 \ln \frac{|g(ss)|^2}{Q_g}$;

3. Calculate the first and second derivatives of E_g to φ_n,

$$\frac{\partial E_g}{\partial \varphi_n} = -\frac{2}{Q_g} \sum_{ss=1}^{SS} \left(1 + \ln \frac{|g(ss)|^2}{Q_g}\right) \cdot \mathrm{Re}\left(j \cdot g^*(ss) \cdot w_n^* \cdot (w_{en} s(x_n) + v_n)_{ss} \cdot e^{j\varphi_n}\right),$$

$$\frac{\partial^2 E_g}{\partial \varphi_n^2} = -\frac{2}{Q_g} \sum_{ss=1}^{SS} \left(\begin{array}{c} \frac{1}{|g(ss)|^2} \cdot \left(\begin{array}{c} \mathrm{Re}\left(\left(j g^*(ss) w_n^* (w_{en} s(x_n) + v_n)_{ss} e^{j\varphi_n} \right)^2 \right) + \\ |g(ss)|^2 \left| j w_n^* (w_{en} s(x_n) + v_n)_{ss} e^{j\varphi_n} \right|^2 \end{array} \right) \\ + \left(1 + \ln \frac{|g(ss)|^2}{Q_g}\right) \cdot \left(\begin{array}{c} \left| j w_n^* (w_{en} s(x_n) + v_n)_{ss} e^{j\varphi_n} \right|^2 - \\ \mathrm{Re}\left(g^*(ss) w_n^* (w_{en} s(x_n) + v_n)_{ss} e^{j\varphi_n} \right) \end{array} \right) \end{array} \right);$$

4. Use Newton iterative method for optimization, $\varphi_n^{(l+1)} = \varphi_n^{(l)} - \left(\frac{\partial^2 E_g}{\partial \varphi_n^2}\right)^{-1} \frac{\partial E_g}{\partial \varphi_n}\Big|_{\varphi_n = \varphi_n^{(l)}}$;

Step 5: Beamform after error calibration, $\widetilde{Y} = \mathrm{W}_c^{\mathrm{H}} \odot \mathrm{W}^{\mathrm{H}} \hat{X} = \sum_{n=1}^{N} w_{cn}^* \cdot w_n^* \cdot (w_{en} s(x_n) + v_n)$.

4. Effectively Compensated Area

The phase error compensation based on phase error compensation function of the IN-ME algorithm is aimed at the situation in which the expected main-lobe of beamforming is just at the reference source $P(x_P, y_P)$. When the expected main-lobe of beamforming is not at the reference source, there is a mismatch between the phase error compensation function and the actual phase error. Thus, it is necessary to discuss the effectively compensated area based on the phase error compensation function of the IN-ME algorithm.

Assuming that the position errors of the array elements are independent of each other and meet the normal distribution with the mean value of 0 and the variance of σ^2, which is, for the nth UAV element, $\Delta x_n \sim N(0, \sigma^2)$ and $\Delta y_n \sim N(0, \sigma^2)$, and the two-dimensional joint distribution of the two also meets the normal distribution, according to the "3σ rule", the elements can be regarded approximately as that they are located in a circle with the radius centered on the ideal array element position, as shown in Figure 2. When the expected main-lobe of beamforming is at the source $B(x_B, y_B)$, but the reference source of the IN-ME algorithm is $P(x_P, y_P)$, the effectively compensated area based on the phase error compensation function of the IN-ME algorithm can be approximately solved by geometric methods.

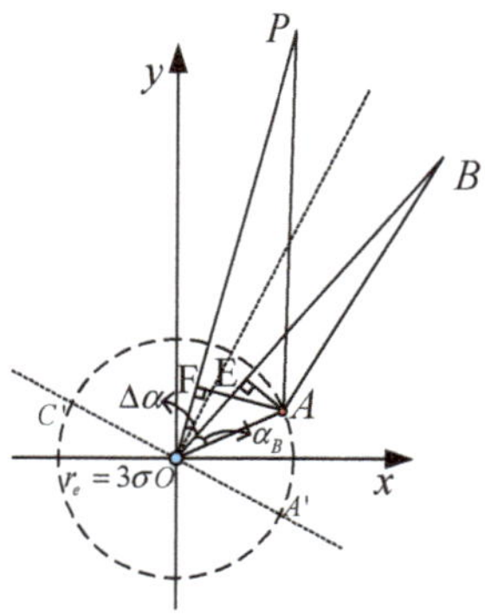

Figure 2. Geometric relation between the array elements, with position error and radiant source.

Obviously, when the actual position of the array element is on the circle, the phase error is larger than when it is in the circle. Point A is set as a moving point on the circle to represent the actual position of the nth array element. When the two sources, $P(x_P, y_P)$ and $B(x_B, y_B)$, have relative phase errors $|\Delta\varphi_{BP}| \leq \frac{\pi}{4}$, it is considered that the compensation is effective [27,28]. There is

$$\begin{cases} \max fit = |(PA - PO) - (BA - BO)| \leq \frac{\lambda}{8} \\ s.t. \\ x_A^2 + y_A^2 = r_e^2 \end{cases} \tag{36}$$

where, x_A and y_A are respectively the x axis and y axis coordinates of point A.

As shown in Figure 2, crossing point A, the plumb line AF, which is perpendicular to PO, is made, and the point of intersection is point F. The plumb line AE, which is perpendicular to BO, is made, and the point of intersection is point E. We let $\angle AOB = \alpha_B$, $\angle AOP = \alpha_P$, and $\angle BOP = \Delta\alpha$. When $PO \gg r_e$ and $BO \gg r_e$, the electromagnetic wave from $P(x_P, y_P)$ or $B(x_B, y_B)$ to any point on the circle can be approximately simplified to the plane wave, and we have $|PA - PO| \approx FO$ and $|BA - BO| \approx EO$. Then Equation (36) is approximately simplified as

$$\begin{cases} \max fit = |r_e \cos(\alpha_P) - r_e \cos(\alpha_B)| \leq \frac{\lambda}{8} \\ s.t. \\ PO \gg r_e \\ BO \gg r_e \\ \alpha_P = \alpha_B + \Delta\alpha \end{cases} \tag{37}$$

By using sum-to-product addition formulas, there is $fit = 2r_e \sin\left(\frac{\Delta\alpha}{2}\right) \cdot \left|\sin\left(\alpha_B + \frac{\Delta\alpha}{2}\right)\right|$. Then there is

$$\max(fit) = 2r_e \sin\left(\frac{\Delta\alpha}{2}\right), \text{ when } \alpha_B + \tfrac{\Delta\alpha}{2} = \tfrac{\pi}{2} + i\pi,\ i = \pm 1, \pm 2, \ldots \tag{38}$$

As shown in Figure 2, the perpendicular line of the $\Delta\alpha$ angular bisector which is made through the center O of the circle intersects with the circle at A′ and C′ . Equation (38) shows that the expected point A which can get max(*fit*) approximately locates at A′ or C′ , according to

$$\max(fit) = 2r_e \sin\left(\frac{\Delta\alpha}{2}\right) \leq \frac{\lambda}{8} \tag{39}$$

The area of $B(x_B, y_B)$ that can be compensated based on $P(x_P, y_P)$ for the nth array element can be obtained by

$$\Delta\alpha_{\max} = 2\arcsin(\lambda/(16r_e)) \tag{40}$$

After finding out the upper and lower bounds of the area of $B(x_B, y_B)$ the phase error for each array element can be effectively compensated, and the area can be divided by finding the intersection of the area of all array elements. As shown in Figure 3, the connecting line from the nth array element to $P(x_P, y_P)$ is marked as line $a_n, n = 1, 2, 3, \ldots, N$, which is the angular bisector of $2\Delta\alpha$, and the line towards the negative angle direction is line b_n, while the line towards the positive angle direction is line c_n. The intersection point of line c_1 and line b_N is marked as point D. The intersection point of line c_1 and line c_2 is marked as point G. The line g parallel to line c_N is started from point G, and the connecting line between G and D is marked as line e. The intersection point of b_{N-1} and b_N is marked as point H, and line f parallel to b_1 is started from H. The connecting line between H and D is marked as line d. Then the effectively compensated area of the array for $B(x_B, y_B)$ based on $P(x_P, y_P)$ is within the area encircled by four sides of g, e, d, and f.

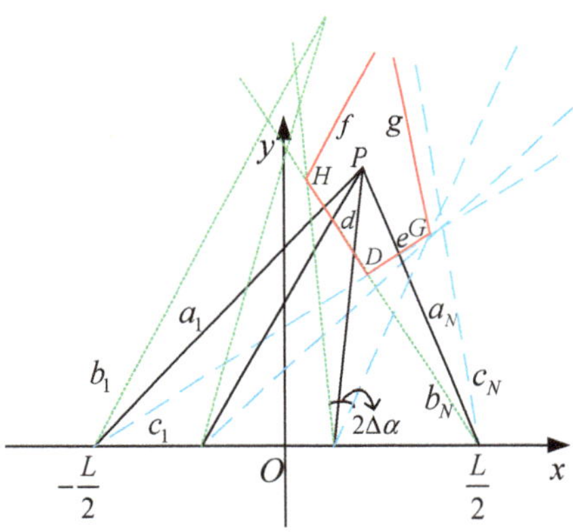

Figure 3. The effectively compensated area of emitter $B(x_B, y_B)$.

As shown in Figure 3, the problem of finding the effectively compensated area is transformed into the problem of finding the intersection point of the lines, and the equations of the black line cluster $a_n, n = 1, 2, 3, \ldots, N$ can be expressed as

$$y = \frac{y_P}{x_P - x_n}(x - x_n) \tag{41}$$

The equation of the green line cluster $b_n, n = 1, 2, 3, \ldots, N$ can be expressed as

$$y = \tan\left(\arctan\left(\frac{y_P}{x_P - x_n}\right) + \Delta\alpha\right)(x - x_n) \tag{42}$$

The equation of the blue line cluster $c_n, n = 1, 2, 3, \ldots, N$ can be expressed as

$$y = \tan\left(\arctan\left(\frac{y_P}{x_P - x_n}\right) - \Delta\alpha\right)(x - x_n) \tag{43}$$

Let $k_{an} = \frac{y_P}{x_P - x_n}$, $k_{bn} = \tan\left(\arctan\left(\frac{y_P}{x_P - x_n}\right) + \Delta\alpha\right)$, and $k_{cn} = \tan\left(\arctan\left(\frac{y_P}{x_P - x_n}\right) - \Delta\alpha\right)$, and coordinates of H, D and G can be obtained by

$$\begin{cases} x_H = \dfrac{k_{b(N-1)}x_{(N-1)} - k_{bN}x_N}{k_{b(N-1)} - k_{bN}}, y_H = k_{b(N-1)}k_{bN}\dfrac{x_{(N-1)} - x_N}{k_{b(N-1)} - k_{bN}} \\ x_D = \dfrac{k_{c1}x_1 - k_{bN}x_N}{k_{c1} - k_{bN}}, y_D = k_{c1}k_{bN}\dfrac{x_1 - x_N}{k_{c1} - k_{bN}} \\ x_G = \dfrac{k_{c1}x_1 - k_{c2}x_2}{k_{c1} - k_{c2}}, y_G = k_{c1}k_{c2}\dfrac{x_1 - x_2}{k_{c1} - k_{c2}} \end{cases} \tag{44}$$

The analytic expressions of the red four sides g, e, d, and f are

$$\begin{cases} f : y = k_{b1}(x - x_H) + y_H \\ d : y = k_{bN}(x - x_D) + y_D \\ e : y = k_{c1}(x - x_D) + y_D \\ g : y = k_{cN}(x - x_G) + y_G \end{cases} \tag{45}$$

The area encircled by the four edges shown in Equation (45) is the effectively compensated area of $B(x_B, y_B)$ that can be compensated based on IN-ME algorithm.

By estimating and compensating the phase errors, the phase errors of the received signals caused by the position of the array elements in the array are calibrated so that the antenna array of UAVs can effectively carry out beamforming. The analysis of the effectively compensated area based on the reference source can provide a reference for the target area division and path planning of UAVs.

5. Simulation Analysis

5.1. IN-ME Phase Error Compensation Algorithm Based on Reference Source

We suppose that the signal frequency $f_0 = 300$ MHz, wavelength ˇ = 1 m, number of array elements $N = 26$, array aperture $L = 500$ˇ, main-lobe of beam is at known radiant source $P(x_P, y_P)$, whose polar coordinates are $\theta_P = 0^\circ$ or $\theta_P = 6^\circ$ and $R_P = 30$ km, the number of signal snapshots $SS = 100$, array element position error Δx_n and Δy_n are independent of each other, and they both meet the normal distribution with a mean value of 0 and a standard deviation of 3ˇ, and the low SNR is −3 dB. We use the N-ME algorithm, IN-ME algorithm, adaptive differential evolution algorithm (ADE) [29], and genetic algorithm (GA), respectively, to estimate the phase error; the changes in the maximum entropy of the array signal synthetic power, along with the number of iterations of the algorithms, are shown in Figure 4. The reason why we adopt ADE and GA is because they are both artificial intelligence algorithms, which are different from our algorithm and are widely used in solving multi-objective search problems and beamforming [29–33]. The objective function of both ADE and GA is the entropy objective function, as shown in Formula (19). The parameters of ADE are that the population number of the genetic algorithm is 100, the mutation rate is 0.5, and the crossover probability is 0.9. The parameters of GA are that the hybridization rate is 0.7, the mutation rate is 0.05, and the "roulette wheel" selection is used. The elitist retention strategy is adopted. It is worth noting that all of our simulation tests are respectively based on the average of 1000 Monte Carlo tests.

As shown in Figure 4, the convergence rates of ADE and GA are slower than those of N-ME and IN-ME, and within 50 iterations, the entropy value of ADE and GA cannot reach the same high rate as those reached by N-ME or IN-ME, which shows that ADE and GA are inferior to N-ME and IN-ME, and this is because the search direction of ADE and GA is aimless, while N-ME and IN-ME search along the gradient descent direction. Compared with IN-ME, the N-ME algorithm will require more iterations and a longer period to converge, and will easily fall into local optimization, eventually reaching a smaller entropy value. Compared with the N-ME algorithm, the IN-ME algorithm proposed in this paper makes the entropy objective function of the algorithm converge faster and reach a larger entropy value, which verifies the effectiveness of IN-ME. Because of the adverse performance of ADE and GA, N-ME and IN-ME are used to form beams and make comparisons. After phase error compensation, when $\theta_P = 0^\circ$, beamforming is shown in Figure 5a. When the beam is scanning and $\theta_P = 6^\circ$, the compensation effect is shown in Figure 5b.

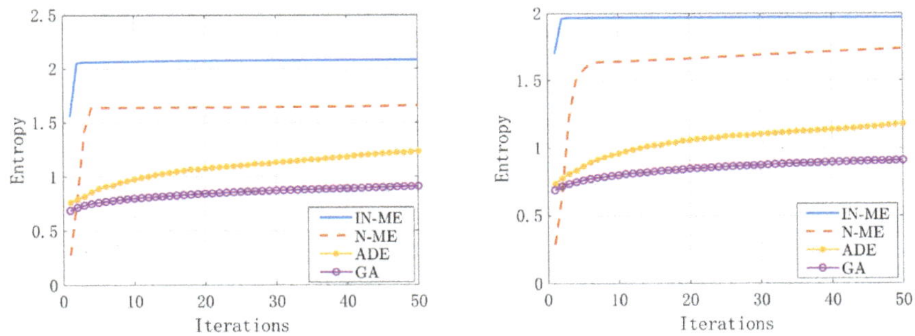

(**a**) (**b**)

Figure 4. Comparison of different algorithms. (**a**) $\theta_P = 0^\circ$; (**b**) $\theta_P = 6^\circ$.

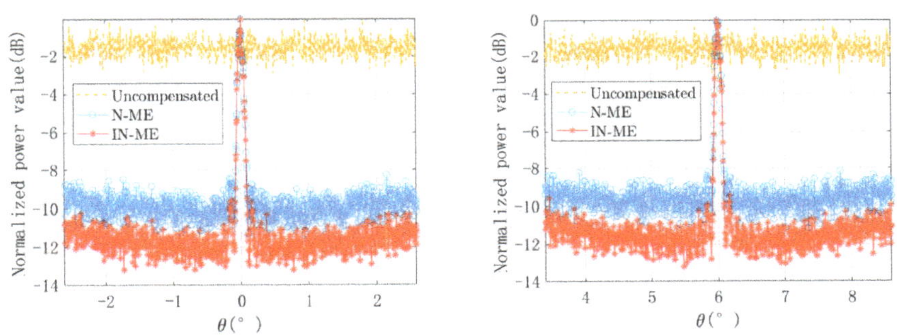

(**a**) (**b**)

Figure 5. Comparison of the beam forming effect after phase compensation. (**a**) $\theta_P = 0^\circ$; (**b**) $\theta_P = 6^\circ$.

As shown in Figure 5, whether beam scans or not, beams cannot be formed because of the uncompensated phase error; the sidelobe level of the N-ME algorithm is approximately −9.5 dB, and the sidelobe level of IN-ME algorithm is approximately −12 dB, which means that the beamforming algorithm proposed in this paper can better compensate for the phase error of array elements and obtain a lower sidelobe level.

In order to compare the ideal beamforming (IB) with noise, phase gradient beamforming (PGB), the N-ME beamforming algorithm, and the IN-ME beamforming algorithm in different SNR backgrounds, by taking beamforming without scanning as an example, scenarios in which SNR changes from −12 dB to 9 dB are simulated, and the beamforming results are shown in Figure 6.

As shown in Figure 6, with the SNR changing from −12 dB to 9 dB, both the N-ME and IN-ME algorithms can effectively form a beam pattern. When the SNR is low, using the phase error estimated by PG information to compensate the array cannot effectively form a beam pattern, but with increasing SNR, the beam formed by PG gradually improves, compared to the beam formed by the N-ME. The IN-ME beamforming algorithm proposed in this paper can continuously remain nearly the same as ideal beamforming with noise; when the SNR is low, it performs better than PGB, and when SNR is high, it performs better than the N-ME beamforming algorithm, which shows the advantages of the IN-ME algorithm.

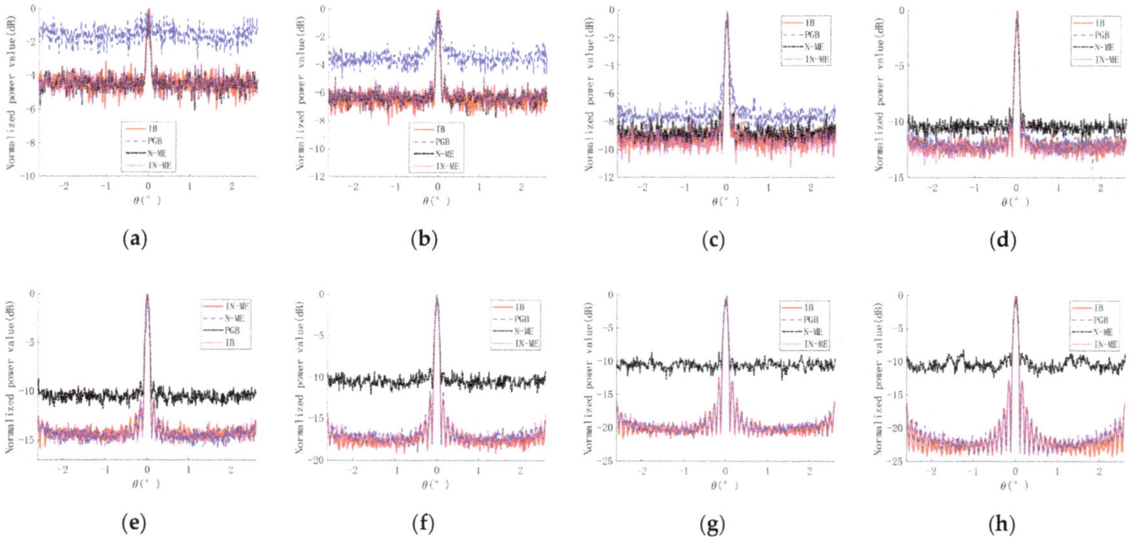

Figure 6. Beamforming contrast of two algorithms when SNR changes. (**a**) SNR = −12 dB; (**b**) SNR = −9 dB; (**c**) SNR = −6 dB; (**d**) SNR = −3 dB; (**e**) SNR = 0 dB; (**f**) SNR = 3 dB; (**g**) SNR = 6 dB; (**h**) SNR = 9 dB.

5.2. Effectively Compensated Area

We assume that the position errors corresponding to the phase errors Δx_r and Δy_r are independent of each other and meet the normal distribution of 0 mean value and $\sigma_r = \frac{\lambda}{2}$, which is $\Delta x_r \sim N\left(0, \left(\frac{\lambda}{2}\right)^2\right)$ and $\Delta y_r \sim N\left(0, \left(\frac{\lambda}{2}\right)^2\right)$. According to the "$3\sigma$ rule", we can get $r_e = 1.5\lambda$, and $\Delta\alpha \approx 4.77^{\circ}$ from Equation (40). The area that can be effectively compensated by each array element is within the area whose angular bisector is the line from the known radiant source $P(x_P, y_P)$ shown as red * to the ideal position of the array element, and the angular area is between $2\Delta\alpha = 9.55^{\circ}$, as shown in Figure 3. As shown in Figure 2, we set $\theta_P = 0^{\circ}$ or $\theta_P = 6^{\circ}$, $OP \equiv 30$ km, and $\angle POB \equiv \Delta\alpha = 4.77^{\circ}$ or $\angle POB \equiv -\Delta\alpha = -4.77^{\circ}$. According to Equation (36) through Equation (45), the effectively compensated area and the corresponding dividing points D, H, and G are shown as red * in Figure 7.

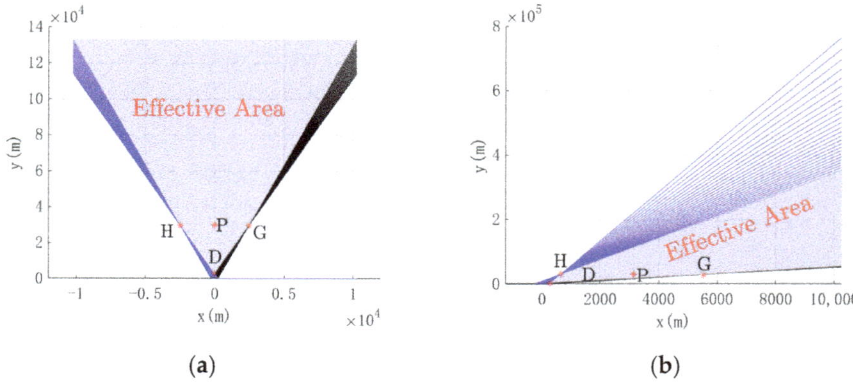

Figure 7. Effectively compensated area. (**a**) $\theta_P = 0^{\circ}$; (**b**) $\theta_P = 6^{\circ}$.

According to Figure 7, we see that when the radiant source is located on the vertical line in the array, the effectively compensated area is greater than when it is located at a certain angle relative to the vertical line of the array. In order to verify the effectively compensated area shown in Figure 7, taking Figure 7a as an example, let the radiant source M be a moving source, whose coordinates are $y_M \equiv y_H$ and $x_M = -5$ km : 0.01 km : 5 km, the main-lobe is expected to point to the direction of the radiant source M, and the phase calibration function based on the IN-ME algorithm is used to compensate the beamforming. The movement track of the radiant source M is shown by the thick solid green line in Figure 8a. The power value change in the direction of the radiant source M is calculated, which is in the direction of the main-lobe, and the boundary points H, G, and x_P of $P(x_P, y_P)$ are marked, as shown in Figure 8b.

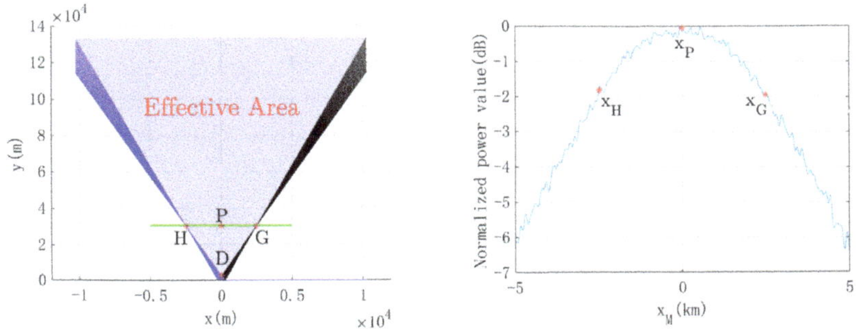

(a) **(b)**

Figure 8. Change of main-lobe power within the effectively compensated area; (**a**) moving radiant source M trajectory; (**b**) variation of main-lobe power value with x_M.

As shown in Figure 8, due to the influence of noise, when $y_M \equiv y_H$, the power value in the main-lobe direction, where the radiant source M is located, fluctuates, but changes regularly as a whole with the change of x_M. When $x_M \leq x_H \cup x_M \geq x_G$, the radiant source M is outside the effectively compensated area, and the power value in the main-lobe direction decreases by more than 3 dB, which shows that the compensation is invalid. When $x_H \leq x_M \leq x_G$, the radiant source M is within the effectively compensated area, and the power value in the main-lobe direction drops within 3 dB, which shows that the compensation is effective. The closer x_M is to x_P, the greater the power value is in the main-lobe direction, which means the better the compensation is.

Similarly, the main-lobe power change within the effectively compensated area during beam scanning is simulated in Figure 9.

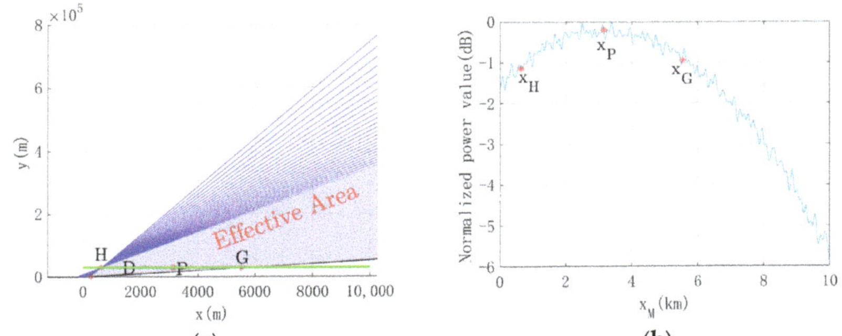

(a) **(b)**

Figure 9. Change of main-lobe power within the effectively compensated area using beam scanning; (**a**) moving radiant source M trajectory; (**b**) variation of main-lobe power value with x_M.

A conclusion similar to that in Figure 8 is obtained from Figure 9. When the radiant source M is outside the effectively compensated area, the power value in the main-lobe direction decreases by more than 1 dB, which is considered that the compensation is noneffective. When the radiant source M is within the effectively compensated area and the power value in the main-lobe direction drops within 1.5 dB, which is considered that the compensation is effective. The closer x_M is to x_P, the greater the power value is in the main-lobe direction, which means the better the compensation is.

All in all, as can be seen from Figures 8b and 9b, the method proposed in this paper divides the area into a subset of the area with the power value in the main-lobe direction decreasing by 3 dB as a boundary value, ensuring the effectiveness of the division area for compensation. This effectively compensated area is related to the selection of the effective standard for phase compensation in Equation (36).

6. Conclusions

In order to solve the problems of UAV near-field beamforming, UAV position error compensation, and the effectively compensated area of compensation, this paper firstly constructs a near-field array beamforming model based on element position error, and approximately simplifies the model using the Taylor expansion of the near-field signal phase difference function. Moreover, an IN-ME algorithm is proposed to estimate and compensate for the phase error. Based on the known reference source signal, the initial value of the phase error is estimated through the PG information of the array's received signal, and then the array signal entropy objective function is established to iteratively optimize the phase error value using the Newton iteration method, and the beam pattern is formed after the phase error compensation. Thirdly, when the beam scanning leads to the phase compensation function mismatch, based on the phase error compensation function of the IN-ME algorithm, the effectively compensated area is further divided, which lays a foundation for the subsequent area region division and UAV path planning. Finally, the validity of the conclusion is verified by simulation. By using the IN-ME algorithm proposed in this paper, the influence of a single UAV's position error on array beamforming is effectively suppressed, and the effectively compensated area is divided because of phase compensation function mismatch, which provides a theoretical basis for the UAV beamforming application in wireless communication, electronic reconnaissance, and jamming. As the signal wavelength becomes shorter, the adverse influence of the UAV's position error increases, and the beam pattern will deteriorate sharply, which is worthy of further research.

Author Contributions: Conceptualization, S.P., G.W., Y.Z., G.Y. and Y.L.; data curation, Y.Z. and G.W.; formal analysis, Y.Z. and G.W.; funding support, Y.L.; writing—original draft, Y.Z.; writing—review and editing, S.P., G.W., G.Y. and Y.L. All authors have read and agreed to the published version of the manuscript.

Funding: This research was funded by the Military Scientific and Technological Commission, and the Airforce of the People's Liberation Army, Government of China, under grant number 21KJ3C1-0090R and PGGC-2021-003.

Institutional Review Board Statement: Not applicable.

Informed Consent Statement: Not applicable.

Data Availability Statement: Not applicable.

Conflicts of Interest: The authors declare no conflict of interest. The funders had no role in the design of the study; in the collection, analyses, or interpretation of data; in the writing of the manuscript; or in the decision to publish the results.

References

1. Silvus to Develop DARPA Distributed Beamforming Technology. Available online: https://www.unmannedsystemstechnology.com/2021/03/silvus-to-develop-distributed-beamforming-technology-for-darpa/ (accessed on 19 March 2021).
2. Wang, Y.L.; Chen, H.; Peng, Y.; Wan, Q. *Spatial Spectrum Estimation Theory and Algorithm*; Tsinghua University Press: Beijing, China, 2004; pp. 416–417.
3. Shu, R.; Xu, Z. *Lidar Imaging Principle and Motion Error Compensation Method*; Science Press: Beijing, China, 2014; pp. 28–32.
4. Feng, F.Y.P.; Rihan, M.; Huang, L. Positional Perturbations Analysis for Micro-UAV Array With Relative Position-Based Formation. *IEEE Commun. Lett.* **2021**, *25*, 2918–2922. [CrossRef]
5. Umeyama, A.Y.; Salazar-Cerreno, J.L.; Fulton, C.J. UAV-Based Far-Field Antenna Pattern Measurement Method for Polarimetric Weather Radars: Simulation and Error Analysis. *IEEE Access* **2020**, *8*, 191124–191137. [CrossRef]
6. Wang, D.; Zhang, P.; Yang, Z.; Wei, F.; Wang, C. A Novel Estimator for TDOA and FDOA Positioning of Multiple Disjoint Sources in the Presence of Calibration Emitters. *IEEE Access* **2020**, *8*, 1613–1643. [CrossRef]
7. Ni, M.; Chen, H.; Cheng, Y.; Ni, L.; Wang, X. Sensor Position Errors Calibration Algorithm of Near-field Source Based on Fourth-order Cumulant. In Proceedings of the IEEE International Conference on Signal, Information and Data Processing, Chongqing, China, 11–13 December 2019; pp. 1–5. [CrossRef]
8. Sippel, E.; Lipka, M.; Geiß, J.; Hehn, M.; Vossiek, M. In-Situ Calibration of Antenna Arrays Within Wireless Locating Systems. *IEEE Trans. Antennas Propag.* **2020**, *68*, 2832–2841. [CrossRef]
9. Ahmed, M.M.; Ho, D.K.C.; Wang, G. Localization of a Moving Source by Frequency Measurements. *IEEE Trans. Signal Process.* **2020**, *68*, 4839–4854. [CrossRef]
10. Shi, S.; Li, C.; Hu, J.; Zhang, X.; Fang, G. Study of Phase Error Reconstruction and Motion Compensation for Terahertz SAR With Sparsity-Promoting Parameter Estimation. *IEEE Trans. Terahertz Sci. Technol.* **2021**, *11*, 122–134. [CrossRef]
11. Yang, C.; Zheng, Z.; Wang, W.-Q. Calibrating Nonuniform Linear Arrays With Model Errors Using a Source at Unknown Location. *IEEE Commun. Lett.* **2020**, *24*, 2917–2921. [CrossRef]
12. Wei, T.; Liao, B.; Huang, H.; Quan, Z. Online Mutual Coupling Calibration Using a Signal Source at Unknown Location. In Proceedings of the IEEE the 10th Sensor Array and Multichannel Signal Processing Workshop, Sheffield, UK, 8–11 July 2018; pp. 189–193.
13. Zhou, L.; Yu, H.; Lan, Y. Deep Convolutional Neural Network-Based Robust PG Estimation for Two-Dimensional Phase Unwrapping Using SAR Interferograms. *IEEE Trans. Geosci. Remote Sens.* **2020**, *58*, 4653–4665. [CrossRef]
14. Li, Y.; O'Young, S. Kalman Filter Disciplined PG Autofocus for Stripmap SAR. *IEEE Trans. Geosci. Remote Sens.* **2020**, *58*, 6298–6308. [CrossRef]
15. Li, Q.; Liu, W.; Huang, L.; Sun, W.; Zhang, P. An Undersampled Phase Retrieval Algorithm via Gradient Iteration. In Proceedings of the IEEE the 10th Sensor Array and Multichannel Signal Processing Workshop, Sheffield, UK, 8–11 July 2018; pp. 228–231.
16. Zou, H.; Zhong, L.; Li, J.; Sun, Z.; Liu, Y.; Ning, Q.; Lu, X. Phase Extraction Algorithm Based on the Spatial Carrier-Frequency Phase-Shifting Gradient. *IEEE Photonics J.* **2019**, *11*, 1–7. [CrossRef]
17. Kumar, B.; Kumar, A.; Bahl, R. Performance Analysis of Phase and Amplitude Gradient Method for DoA Estimation using Underwater Acoustic Vector Sensor. In Proceedings of the 2019 IEEE Underwater Technology, Kaohsiung, Taiwan, 16–19 April 2019; IEEE: Taiwan, China, 2019; pp. 1–4.
18. Shi, S.; Li, C.; Fang, G.; Zhang, X. A THz SAR Autofocus Algorithm Based on Minimum-Entropy Criterion. In Proceedings of the 44th International Conference on Infrared, Millimeter, and Terahertz Waves, Paris, France, 1–6 September 2019; pp. 1–2. [CrossRef]
19. Li, G.; Fang, S.; Han, B.; Zhang, Z.; Hong, W.; Wu, Y. Compensation of Phase Errors for Spotlight SAR With Discrete Azimuth Beam Steering Based on Entropy Minimization. *IEEE Geosci. Remote Sens. Lett.* **2021**, *18*, 841–845. [CrossRef]
20. Li, J.; Ye, Q.; Guo, J.; Min, R.; Li, Y. Motion Compensation Algorithm Based on Entropy-Minimization for Terahertz SAR. In Proceedings of the 14th UK-Europe-China Workshop on Millimetre-Waves and Terahertz Technologies, Lancaster, UK, 13–15 September 2021; pp. 1–3.
21. Zhang, S.; Liu, Y.; Li, X.; Bi, G. Joint Sparse Aperture ISAR Autofocusing and Scaling via Modified Newton Method-Based Variational Bayesian Inference. *IEEE Trans. Geosci. Remote Sens.* **2019**, *57*, 4857–4869. [CrossRef]
22. Fisher, E.; Rafaely, B. Near-Field Spherical Microphone Array Processing With Radial Filtering. *IEEE Trans. Audio Speech Lang. Process.* **2011**, *19*, 256–265. [CrossRef]
23. Liu, R.; Wu, K. Antenna Array for Amplitude and Phase Specified Near-Field Multifocus. *IEEE Trans. Antennas Propag.* **2019**, *67*, 3140–3150. [CrossRef]
24. Spivak, M. *Calculus*, 3rd ed.; Perish Inc.: Houston, TX, USA, 1967; pp. 405–411.
25. Nocedal, J.; Wright, S.J. *Numerical Optimization*; Springer: New York, NY, USA, 1999; pp. 15–18.
26. Zhang, S.; Liu, Y.; Li, X. Fast Entropy Minimization Based Autofocusing Technique for ISAR Imaging. *IEEE Trans. Signal Process.* **2015**, *63*, 3425–3434. [CrossRef]
27. Van Tree, H.L. *Optimum Array Processing*; John Wiley & Sons, Inc.: New York, NY, USA, 2002; pp. 120–126.
28. Johnson, D.H.; Dudgon, D.E. *Array Signal Processing: Concepts and Techniques*; PTR Prentice Hall: Upper Saddle River, NJ, USA, 1993; pp. 124–182.

29. Zhang, Y.N.; Yu, G.W.; Peng, S.R.; Leng, Y.; Wang, G.X. Antenna Beam Optimization for Near-field Super-sparse Array Based on UAVs. In Proceedings of the 5th International Conference on Electronic Information Technology and Computer Engineering (EITCE), Xiamen, China, 22–24 October 2021; pp. 1541–1548.
30. Jiang, Z.J.; Zhao, S.; Chen, Y.; Cui, T.J. Beamforming Optimization for Time-Modulated Circular-Aperture Grid Array With DE Algorithm. *IEEE Antennas Wirel. Propag. Lett.* **2018**, *17*, 2434–2438. [CrossRef]
31. Pradhan, D.; Wang, S.; Ali, S.; Yue, T.; Liaaen, M. CBGA-ES+: A Cluster-Based Genetic Algorithm with Non-Dominated Elitist Selection for Supporting Multi-Objective Test Optimization. *IEEE Trans. Softw. Eng.* **2021**, *47*, 86–107. [CrossRef]
32. Dadallage, S.; Yi, C.; Cai, J. Joint Beamforming, Power, and Channel Allocation in Multiuser and Multichannel Underlay MISO Cognitive Radio Networks. *IEEE Trans. Veh. Technol.* **2016**, *65*, 3349–3359. [CrossRef]
33. Souto, V.D.P.; Souza, R.D.; Uchôa-Filho, B.F.; Li, Y. A Novel Efficient Initial Access Method for 5G Millimeter Wave Communications Using Genetic Algorithm. *IEEE Trans. Veh. Technol.* **2019**, *68*, 9908–9919. [CrossRef]

mathematics

MDPI

Article

Oppositional Pigeon-Inspired Optimizer for Solving the Non-Convex Economic Load Dispatch Problem in Power Systems

Rajakumar Ramalingam [1], Dinesh Karunanidy [1], Sultan S. Alshamrani [2], Mamoon Rashid [3,*], Swamidoss Mathumohan [4] and Ankur Dumka [5,6]

1 Department of Computer Science and Technology, Madanapalle Institute of Technology & Science, Madanapalle 517325, Andhra Pradesh, India
2 Department of Information Technology, College of Computers and Information Technology, Taif University, P.O. Box 11099, Taif 21944, Saudi Arabia
3 Department of Computer Engineering, Faculty of Science and Technology, Vishwakarma University, Pune 411048, Maharashtra, India
4 Department of CSE, Unnamalai Institute of Technology, Kovilpatti 628502, Tamil Nadu, India
5 Department of Computer Science and Engineering, Women Institute of Technology, Dehradun 248007, Uttarakhand, India
6 Department of Computer Science and Engineering, Graphic Era Deemed to be University, Dehradun 248007, Uttarakhand, India
* Correspondence: mamoon.rashid@vupune.ac.in; Tel.: +91-7814346505

Abstract: Economic Load Dispatch (ELD) belongs to a non-convex optimization problem that aims to reduce total power generation cost by satisfying demand constraints. However, solving the ELD problem is a challenging task, because of its parity and disparity constraints. The Pigeon-Inspired Optimizer (PIO) is a recently proposed optimization algorithm, which belongs to the family of swarm intelligence algorithms. The PIO algorithm has the benefit of conceptual simplicity, and provides better outcomes for various real-world problems. However, this algorithm has the drawback of premature convergence and local stagnation. Therefore, we propose an Oppositional Pigeon-Inspired Optimizer (OPIO) algorithm—to overcome these deficiencies. The proposed algorithm employs Oppositional-Based Learning (OBL) to enhance the quality of the individual, by exploring the global search space. The proposed algorithm would be used to determine the load demand of a power system, by sustaining the various equality and inequality constraints, to diminish the overall generation cost. In this work, the OPIO algorithm was applied to solve the ELD problem of small- (13-unit, 40-unit), medium- (140-unit, 160-unit) and large-scale (320-unit, 640-unit) test systems. The experimental results of the proposed OPIO algorithm demonstrate its efficiency over the conventional PIO algorithm, and other state-of-the-art approaches in the literature. The comparative results demonstrate that the proposed algorithm provides better results—in terms of improved accuracy, higher convergence rate, less computation time, and reduced fuel cost—than the other approaches.

Keywords: economic load dispatch; pigeon-inspired optimizer; oppositional-based learning; swarm intelligence algorithm; oppositional-based pigeon-inspired optimizer

MSC: 68W50; 60G05; 60G51; 90C27

Citation: Ramalingam, R.; Karunanidy, D.; Alshamrani, S.S.; Rashid, M.; Mathumohan, S.; Dumka, A. Oppositional Pigeon-Inspired Optimizer for Solving the Non-Convex Economic Load Dispatch Problem in Power Systems. *Mathematics* **2022**, *10*, 3315. https://doi.org/10.3390/math10183315

Academic Editor: Jian Dong

Received: 29 July 2022
Accepted: 9 September 2022
Published: 13 September 2022

Publisher's Note: MDPI stays neutral with regard to jurisdictional claims in published maps and institutional affiliations.

1. Introduction

With the rapid growth in technologies, ELD is considered one of the foremost challenging optimization problems in power systems. The main motive for addressing the ELD problem is to reduce the cost of power generation, by sustaining the different constraints involved in the generation units [1]. Several researchers have applied mathematical models, knowledge discovery and optimization techniques to resolve the ELD problem. The standard techniques, like lambda-generation techniques, and base-point techniques from [2], provide optimal solutions, by incorporating the incremental cost curves of linear functions. However, these methods have failed to solve highly non-linear functions, and provide unsatisfactory solutions which result in huge losses in power generation costs. The non-smooth functionalities of generating units contain various features, like prohibited zones, different fuel options, value-point effects, ramp-rate limits and a start-up cost function which converts linear into non-linear characteristics [3]. Owing to the large-scale generating units, conventional methods have provided unreliable solutions, and have taken a lot of computational time to solve ELD problems. In later studies, dynamic programming techniques [4] have been used for ELD problems, but these have required high computational efforts to solve large-scale generating units.

In recent studies, many researchers have utilized various optimization algorithms to solve non-convex ELD problems with only value-point effects, viz., Particle Swarm Optimization with Sequential Quadratic Programming (PSO-SQP) [5], Genetic Algorithm (GA) [6], Evolutionary Programming (EP) [7], Improved Group Search Optimization (IGSO) [8], Incremental Artificial Bee Colony with Local Search (IABC-LS) [9], Hybrid Grey Wolf Optimizer (HGWO) [10], Self-Organizing Hierarchical Particle Swarm Optimization (SOH-PSO) [11], Genetic Algorithm with Pattern Search and SQP (GA-PS-SQP) [12], Modified Shuffled Frog-Leaping Algorithm (MSFLA) [13], Firefly Optimization (FA) [14], Chaotic Self-Adaptive Particle Swarm Optimization Algorithm (CSAPSO) [15], Combined Social Engineering Particle Swarm Optimization (SEPSO) [16], Starling Murmuration Optimizer (SMO) [17], Improved Moth-Flame optimization (IMFO) [18] and Diversity-Maintained Differential Evolution (DMDE) [19]. Among these search techniques, GA is considered to be the least efficient technique, because its optimal individuals are generally trapped in intensification rather than diversification, and it also suffers from the determination of control parameters, which results in excessive simulation time. Several new techniques, like IGSO, MSFLA, FA, HGWO, SOH-PSO, GA-PS-SQP and CSAPSO, have virtuoso competence in finding optimal solutions for non-convex generating units; however, the simulation time of the system is quite long; specifically, for CSAPSO, several iterations are carried out to specify the control parameter values; this limitation results in the technique having excessive execution time, and a large number of runs.

In addition, some sets of optimization algorithms are considered to solve non-convex ELD problems with only multi-fuel possibilities. These algorithms include Integer Coded Differential Evolution-Dynamic Programming (ICDEDP) [20], Chaotic Ant Swarm Optimization (CASO) [21], Bacteria Foraging Optimization (BFO) [22], Ant Colony Optimization (ACO) [23], Biogeography-Based Optimization (BBO) [24] and Krill Herd (KH) [25]. Among these techniques, ACO is the technique initially utilized for solving optimization problems in the engineering domain, specifically in path-identifying and parameter-tuning in electrical engineering. Although ACO and CASO have the cap potential of leading complicated constraints and non-convex goal features, in addition to their simplicity of simulation for optimization problems, they nevertheless suffer from numerous negative aspects, together with low-quality optimization individual and lengthy simulation time. The modified DE method, namely the ICDEDP technique, can be considered a more efficient technique than the other techniques, because it can obtain a good-quality solution within a short span of simulation; this DE technique has been globally utilized in power system optimization problems. In addition, other techniques—such as BBO, KH and BFO—have good capability in determining the optimal solutions for non-convex problems; however, the simulation times of these techniques are longer, due to the vast number of control parameters.

In contrast to the aforementioned sets, the techniques in the set of neural networks including the Adaptive Hopfield Neural Network (AHNN) [26], the Enhanced Augmented Lagrange Hopfield Network (EALHN) [27] and the Augmented Lagrange Hopfield Network (ALHN) [28] can impact on large-scale problems, but fail to deal with the ELD problem with a non-convex objective function. In EALHN and ALHN, the Lagrange function is merged with the Hopfield network to enhance efficacy. This process will help the techniques to converge towards the optimal more smoothly, and to obtain a good-quality solution. However, in real-time power systems, both value points and fuel points need to be considered, for accurate and practical ELD solutions.

In some studies, both the constraints of value points and different fuel possibilities are considered for realistic ELD solutions comprising the Improved Particle Swarm Optimization (IPSO) [29], the Crisscross Optimization Algorithm (COA) [30], Differential Evolution and Particle Swarm Optimization (DEPSO) [31], the Oppositional Grey Wolf Optimization algorithm (OGWO) [32], Estimation of Distribution and Differential Evolution Cooperation (ED-DE) [33], the Real-Coded Chemical Reaction Algorithm (RCCRO) [34], Synergic Predator–Prey Optimization (SPPO) [35], the One Rank Cuckoo Search Algorithm (ORCSA) [36], the Real-Coded Genetic Algorithm (RCGA) [37] and the Improved Genetic Algorithm [38]. By utilizing the pros of each search technique, these improved novel techniques have adequate capability in finding good-quality solutions with better simulation time. However, the improved technique can lead to more complications with vast control parameters, and it can suffer from inappropriate selection of these parameters; in addition, its performance is degraded when applied to large-scale power systems entailing n number of generating units with various fuel possibilities and value-point effects.

A large portion of the above studies have focused on the adjustments of stochastic search techniques. Nonetheless, they have, once in a while, given consideration to the method of handling constraints. In reality, dealing with the constraints of ELD problems is significant when working with stochastic search techniques, for enhancing the optimization results. Our study aimed to fill the research gap, by contributing more towards addressing the constraints of ELD problems. Our contributions were twofold: initially, an enhanced PIO algorithm was introduced, to enrich the performance of the standard PIO algorithm; subsequently, a constraint-handling technique was utilized, to appropriately handle the equality constraints.

The Pigeon-Inspired Optimizer algorithm was inspired by the homing bias of pigeons, and was proposed by Duan and Qiao in 2014. This optimization algorithm was used because of its optimum performance at high merging speeds [39]. However, the PIO algorithm suffers in regard to global exploration and premature convergence. In addition, its performance is degraded when applied to high-dimensional problems. This problem can be overcome by using the Opposition-Based Learning technique. The OBL technique is widely used by researchers to boost convergence speed, by exploring the search space. In this work, a new metaheuristic algorithm—namely, the Oppositional Pigeon-Inspired Optimizer technique (OPIO)—was utilized, to solve non-convex ELD problems with various fuel possibilities and value-point effects.

The major contribution of this work is illustrated as follows:

(1) The proposed OPIO algorithm solves the non-convex ELD problem with multi-fuel possibilities and value-point effects, through two operators: namely, map and compass operator, and landmark operator. These operators enhance the local search ability by adopting the search boundary limits. Later, the Opposition-Based Learning strategy helps to explore the search space, as well as to enhance the exploration ability for target search agents. This process improves the search capability, and eradicates premature convergence, though the large-scale test system holds both multiple fuel possibilities and value-point effects.

(2) The proposed OPIO algorithm has a unique adjustable parameter: jump rate J_r. Parameter J_r helps to determine the global optimal solution, by influencing the adjustable value, within the range of 0 to 0.4. This parameter promotes the OPIO algorithm, to be robust and adaptable in solving ELD problems with different constraints.

(3) To validate the efficiency of the proposed OPIO algorithm, we used several test cases, which varied according to three scales: small-scale (i.e., 13, 40); medium-scale (i.e., 140, 160); and large-scale (i.e., 320, 640) generation units. The results of the various test cases confirmed that the proposed technique is a better potential solution than the state-of-the-art metaheuristic algorithms in the literature. The OPIO algorithm provided better performance in the 320- and 640-unit generation systems. This shows that the

formulated technique is a superior and reliable solution for large-scale ELD problems over multiple trials.

The rest of this work is categorized as follows: Section 2 delivers the mathematical formulation of the ELD problem, with objective functions and multiple constraints. The proposed Oppositional Pigeon-Inspired Optimizer algorithm is presented in detail in Section 3. In Section 4, the implementation of the OPIO algorithm, in solving the ELD problem, is presented. Section 5 provides proposed OPIO algorithm experimentation details, from six different test cases that varied from small-scale to large-scale systems, and the outcomes are compared with state-of-the-art metaheuristics algorithms. The conclusion of this work is presented in Section 6.

2. ELD Problem Formulation

The main motive of ELD is to reduce the overall power generation cost, by solving different disparity and parity constraints, to provide optimal generation among power producing units [32]. The objective function and the different constraints of the ELD problem are presented in this section.

2.1. Fitness Function

The fitness function of the ELD problem is to reduce the total power production cost by solving various constraints, and to gratify the load demand over some reasonable stage. A quadratic function is formulated, to approximate the fuel cost of the power-producing unit. The mathematical formulation of the power-generating unit is formulated as below:

$$\min \sum_{j=1}^{n} F_c(\Psi_j) \quad (1)$$

Here F_c denotes the fuel cost of the generator (in \$/h); Ψ_j denotes the output power of generator j (in MW); n stands for the overall power-generating unit in the power system.

In view of the value-point effects, ELD cost functions will have non-smooth points which provide inefficient results in practical generators. To process the practical generators, sinusoidal functions are included in the quadratic functions. The cost function, with value points of unit j, is represented as follows:

$$F_c = k_j\Psi_j^2 + l_j\Psi_j + m_j + \left|a_j \times \sin\left(b_j \times \left(\Psi_j^{low} - \Psi_j\right)\right)\right| \quad (2)$$

Here, k_j, l_j and m_j stand for the fuel cost coefficients of generator j; a_j and b_j stand for the value-point loading coefficients of generator j; Ψ_j^{low} is the low-level range power production of generator j.

The overall fuel cost function of n generator in real-time ELD is mathematically formulated as follows:

$$\min \sum_{j=1}^{n} \hat{F}_c(\Psi_j) = \sum_{j=1}^{n} \left[k_j\Psi_j^2 + l_j\Psi_j + m_j + \left|a_j \times \sin\left(b_j \times \left(\Psi_j^{low} - \Psi_j\right)\right)\right|\right] \quad (3)$$

where $\hat{F}_c$ stands for the real-time fuel cost of the generator.

To attain an accurate and more appropriate solution for the ELD problem, both various fuel possibilities and value-point effects are added with the cost functions. Most thermal generating units utilize multiple fuel possibilities, using the load and suitability of the power generation units. The cost function of generating unit j, with various fuel possibilities (q) and value-point effects, is mathematically formulated and presented as follows:

$$F_c(\Psi_j) = \begin{cases} k_{j1}(\Psi_j)^2 + l_{j1}(\Psi_j) + m_{j1} + \left|a_{j1} \times \sin\left(b_{j1} \times \left(\Psi_j^{low} - \Psi_j\right)\right)\right| if \Psi_j^{low} \le \Psi_j \le \Psi_{j1} \\ k_{j2}(\Psi_j)^2 + l_{j2}(\Psi_j) + m_{j2} + \left|a_{j2} \times \sin(b_{j2} \times (\Psi_{j2} - \Psi_j))\right| if \Psi_{j1} \le \Psi_j \le \Psi_{j2} \\ k_{jq}(\Psi_j)^2 + l_{jq}(\Psi_j) + m_{jq} + \left|a_{jq} \times \sin\left(b_{jq} \times \left(\Psi_{jq} - \Psi_j^{low}\right)\right)\right| if \Psi_{jq} \le \Psi_j \le \Psi_j^{upper} \end{cases} \quad (4)$$

2.2. Constraints of the ELD Problem

The fitness function in Section 2.1 is formulated with a set of constraints, which are given below.

2.2.1. Operating Unit Limit

The power-generating unit must relay within the lower and upper boundary limits:

$$\Psi_j^{low} \leq \Psi_j \leq \Psi_j^{upper} j = 1, 2, \ldots, n \tag{5}$$

where Ψ_j^{upper} and Ψ_j^{low} denote the upper and lower boundary, respectively, of the output power of the generator j.

2.2.2. Power-Stabilizing Constraints

The overall generated power should be the same as the overall losses and overall load request of the units. This constraint is mathematically formulated as follows:

$$\sum\nolimits_{j=1}^{n} \Psi_j - \Psi_{Demand} - \Psi_{Loss} = 0 \tag{6}$$

where Ψ_{Loss} and Ψ_{Demand} represent the overall power loss and power demand of the units. Based on Kron's loss technique, the transmission loss is given as follows:

$$\Psi_{Loss} = \sum\nolimits_{j=1}^{n} \sum\nolimits_{i=1}^{n} \Psi_j \beta_{ji} \Psi_i + \sum\nolimits_{j=1}^{n} \beta_{0j} \Psi_j + \beta_{00} \tag{7}$$

where β_{ji} represents the loss coefficient element j and i of the symmetric matrix β; β_{0j} denotes the loss coefficient vector of j symmetric matrix β; and β_{00} represents a fixed loss coefficient concerning standard operating situations.

2.2.3. Restricted Operating Regions (RORs)

Due to oscillation or steam value process in the shaft bearing, the restricted operating region is considered. To avoid these issues, choosing the best operating region will drastically increase the optimum economy of the generating units. The boundary constraints of the standard operating section of generator j are formulated as follows:

$$\Psi_j \in \begin{cases} \Psi_j^{low} \leq \Psi_j \leq \Psi_{j,1}^{l} \\ \Psi_{j,i-1}^{l} \leq \Psi_j \leq \Psi_{j,i}^{l} \\ \Psi_{j,n_i}^{l} \leq \Psi_j \leq \Psi_j^{upper} \end{cases} \quad i = 2,\ 3,\ \ldots,\ n_j,\ \mathrm{j} = 1, 2, \ldots, \mathrm{n} \tag{8}$$

where l, u denotes the lower and upper limits of specific power generating units, and n_j determines the number of restricted regions of generating unit j.

2.2.4. Ramp-Rate (RR) Constraint

In view of the lower and upper power production of the generator, the ramp-rate limit is considered. Each generating unit is controlled by the ramp-rate limit, which instructs the generator to function continually for the two nearest operating regions. This ramp-rate constraint is represented as follows:

$$max\left(\Psi_j^{low},\ \Psi_j^0 - LSL_j\right) \leq \Psi_j \leq min\left(\Psi_j^{upper},\ \Psi_j^0 + USL_j\right) \tag{9}$$

where LSL_j and USL_j represent the lower and upper slope (or ramp) limit of the generating unit j, and Ψ_j^0 denotes the current power generating unit j.

3. Preliminaries

In this section, we present three major mechanisms; firstly, the generic working process of the Pigeon-Inspired Optimizer is presented, secondly, the core concept of the Opposition-Based Learning technique is discussed; and, finally, the proposed methodology, with its working process, is presented.

3.1. *Overview of Pigeon-Inspired Optimizer*

The Pigeon-Inspired Optimizer (PIO) belongs to the family of swarm intelligence algorithms that were proposed by Haibin Duan and Peixin Qiao (2014) [39]. The PIO algorithm mimics the homing behaviors of pigeons. Most researchers apply SI algorithms to solve their domain-related NP-hard problems, in which search space is vast. SI algorithms are inspired by the social behavior of the swarm, with intellectual learning to determine high-quality solutions using mathematical formulations. The mathematical formulation of the swarm includes the position and velocity of the swarm iteration by iterations.

Pigeons have the ability to explore for food over the course of long intervals. In addition, pigeons exhibit intellectual homing behavior: for example, they carried messages during the First and Second World Wars. The PIO algorithm works on the basis of two unique operators, viz., map and landmark operators. This algorithm provides good optimum performance and higher merge speed than the other state-of-the-art metaheuristic algorithms like Ant Colony Optimization, Particle Swarm Optimization, Artificial Bee Colony Optimization and Differential Evolution algorithms.

3.1.1. Map and Compass Operator

Pigeons have a natural ability to perceive the orbital meadow, with the aid of a magnetic function that enables them to map. They utilize the altitude of the sun as a compass to fine-tune their current directions. Generally, pigeons depend less on the sun and on magnetic particles as they near their destinations. The map and compass operator can be mathematically formulated as follows:

$$V_j^{t+1} = V_j^t \times e^{-\rho t} + rand \times \left(X_g - X_j^t\right) \tag{10}$$

$$X_j^{t+1} = X_j^t + V_j^{t+1} \tag{11}$$

where V_j^t and X_j^t represent the velocity and position of the j individuals in the t iterations; ρ denotes the map and compass factor; $rand$ determines the uniform random variable within [0, 1]; X_g denotes the global best individual; and X_j^{t+1} and V_j^{t+1} represent the new position and velocity of the j individual in the next t iteration.

3.1.2. Landmark Operator

A pigeon relies on natural landmarks once it has reached its destination. However, if the pigeon is far away from its destination, then it relies on the adjacent pigeons to adjust its position. In this algorithm, half of the pigeon population is allowed to adjust position, with the aid of the centered pigeons, while the pigeons comprising the other half of the population adjust their position in accordance with the desirable destination position. Most pigeons will not be familiar with their landmark in this view, so they will follow the top-ranked pigeons to determine their desired destination. The half-number of pigeons adjust their position with the following mathematical formulations:

$$N_P^{t+1} = \frac{N_p^t}{2} \tag{12}$$

$$X_c^{t+1} = \frac{\sum X_j^{t+1} \times Fit\left(X_j^{t+1}\right)}{N_p \sum Fit\left(X_j^{t+1}\right)} \tag{13}$$

where N_p^t represents the number of pigeons or population size in the current iteration t; and $Fit\left(X_c^{t+1}\right)$ denotes the fitness of the centered pigeons in the $t+1$ iteration. The new pigeon position is represented as:

$$X_j^{t+1} = X_j^t + rand \times \left(X_c^{t+1} - X_j^t\right) \tag{14}$$

The generic flow of the PIO algorithm is represented in Algorithm 1. In this algorithm, the map and compass operator is given in the initial while loop, and another loop is used to access their route and its correction in position.

Algorithm 1: Standard Pigeon-Inspired Optimizer (PIO)

Input: Number of Population N_p problem space D, Map and compass factor ρ, Number of generations ng_1, ng_2 where $ng_1 > ng_2$.
Output: X_g–Global best solution
Randomly generate the solution X_j
Compute the fitness of solutions $(X_1, X_2, \ldots, X_{N_p})$
Determine the minimal fitness solution as X_g.
while ($ng \geq 1$) do.
    Determine the velocity and position for each solution by Equations (10) and (11).
    Compute fitness values of solutions $(X_1, X_2, \ldots, X_{N_p})$
Update global best solution X_g.
end while
while ($N_p \geq 1$) do
    Sort solutions by their fitness.
    $N_p = N_p/2$
    Compute the desired destination by Equation (13).
    Update the position of the solution by Equation (14).
    Update global best solution X_g
end while

3.2. Opposition-Based Learning Technique

The Opposition-Based Learning technique (OBL) was introduced by Tizhoosh [40] to enhance the convergence speed of traditional metaheuristic algorithms. This method utilizes the valuation of a current population against its opposite population, to determine the better solution for a specific problem. The OBL method has been utilized in different metaheuristic algorithms, to boost convergence speed [41,42]. The mathematical formulation of the OBL is defined as follows:

Let $\mu(\mu \in [p, q])$ be an actual integer. The contradictory integer μ^0 is formulated as:

$$\mu^0 = p + q - \mu^0 \tag{15}$$

For d–dimensional search space, the contradictory integer μ^0 is defined as:

$$\mu_j^0 = p_j + q_j - \mu_j \tag{16}$$

where $\mu_1, \mu_2, \ldots, \mu_d$ is a point in d-dimensional search space, i.e., $\mu_i \in \left[p_j, q_j\right]$; $j = \{1, 2, 3, \ldots, d\}$, and d represents the number of decision variables.

The Oppositional-Based Learning technique is generally used in two stages: firstly, in the initialization procedure; and secondly, in generating an opposite solution, using the jumping rate J_r. The proposed OBL algorithm is given in Algorithm 2.

Algorithm 2: Oppositional-Based Learning Algorithm

1: Initially the solutions are randomly initialized within the upper and lower boundary regions.
2: Determine the opposite solutions:
  2.1: *for i = 1:N_p*
  2.2: *for j = 1:d*
  2.3: *μ_(i,j)^0 = p_j + q_j − μ_(i,j)*
  2.4: *end for*
  2.5: *end for*
3: Sort the current solutions and opposite solutions in ascending order.
4: Choose the N_p the number of best candidate solutions.
5: Update the control parameters.
6: Generate the opposite solutions from current solutions using jumping rate J_r:
  6.1: *for j = 1:N_p*
  6.2: *for I = 1:d*
  6.3: *if J_r > rand*
  6.4: *opp(j,i) = min(i) + max(i) − P(j,i);*
  6.5: *else*
  6.6: *opp(j,i) = P(j,i);*
  6.7: *end*
  6.8: *end for*
  6.9: *end for*
7: Repeat steps 3 to 6 until the termination criterion is met.

4. Oppositional Pigeon-Inspired Optimizer Algorithm (Proposed)

The proposed Oppositional Pigeon-Inspired Optimizer algorithm is discussed in this section. The common search strategy of the proposed OPIO algorithm is like the PIO. However, the proposed OPIO algorithm utilizes a unique methodology to explore the search space of the pigeon, to discover the position of its hiding location. Moreover, the modified method provides better convergence in the pigeon population, which helps to achieve the optimal solution. As part of enhancement by the proposed method, in every iteration, the best pigeon is selected as the target. The selected pigeon position will be updated with the Oppositional-Based Learning, to enhance the convergence rate. However, selecting an arbitrary pigeon, from among the population, may result in a bad-quality landmark solution, with a large value for the fitness function (in the minimization problem), which leads to an unsuitable end point to move. In addition, selecting a random pigeon for the exploration phase will tend towards a bad destination, which minimizes the convergence rate. To select the best solution among the population at each iteration is a challenging task.

In this work, a priority-based election mechanism was introduced. This mechanism could be utilized for the minimization problem at each iteration for the pigeon i, so that ψ of the best pigeons in the solution set were elected. The benefit of this election mechanism was to elect the target pigeon among the list of the best pigeons in the stack. By this process, the pigeons could perform better in improvising their positions, by following the better target pigeons, and this resulted in a better convergence rate for the algorithm. Nevertheless, electing the value of ψ was significant: electing a very trivial value of ψ among the pigeons i could lead to being stuck in the local optima. In addition, selecting a large value for ψ could cause the bad target pigeon to be tricked. To eradicate these issues, in the initial iterations ψ started from a large value, for better diversification, and its number was reduced according to Equation (17); over the course of the iterations, its tendency towards the local optimum resulted in the ψ having a small value:

$$\psi^t = round\left(\psi_{max} - \frac{\psi_{max} - \psi_{min}}{N_g} \times t\right) \tag{17}$$

where, ψ^t stood for the value for selecting the best pigeon in iteration t, and ψ_{max} and ψ_{min} stood for the maximum and minimum values of ψ.

4.1. Constraint-Handling Technique

The ELD problem is complicated to solve, when considering the constraints. In past decades, various techniques have been adopted, to handle the constraints. The penalty function is considered to one of the most common constraint-handling techniques: it deals with the constraint problem by including some additional value to the objective function in (4). This function has been broadly utilized by various researchers, because of its simplicity and efficiency. The objective function is the minimization of the following representation:

$$F_{CN} = F_c + \varphi\left|\sum_{j=1}^{n} \Psi_j - \Psi_{Demand} - \Psi_{Loss}\right| \quad (18)$$

where F_{CN} stands for constraint-based objective function, and φ stands for the penalty coefficient of a real integer. If constraint (6) is other than zero, then the value of the second part in Equation (17) will be other than zero too, multiplied by the penalty value φ, and, finally, will be added to the fuel cost F_c. In other words, if Equation (6) does not meet the constraint, then this implies that the solution has a large objective function, and is likely to be rejected. On the other hand, if the solution meets the constraint (6), this implies that the solution holds a small objective function value, and is likely to be accepted. If the φ value is fixed with a large value, then the performance of the algorithm will be reduced, and this will lead to premature convergence. In addition, fixing the small value for φ fails to meet the inequality constraints.

4.2. Implementation of the OPIO Algorithm for the ELD Problem

In this section, the strategies for applying the OPIO algorithm, to solve the ELD problem, are examined. The main objective of the ELD optimization problem is to reduce the overall power generation cost. In the ELD problem, the total power generating unit (n) is proportional to the total decision variable of the optimization problem (d). Each position of the pigeon is represented as each anticipated power output of the generating units. In general, the ELD problem consists of some impartiality and disparity constraints, as discussed in Section 2.2. Each solution in the population should satisfy the constraints. For the smooth process of constraint handling, the value of φ is fixed as 100 in Equation (17) for the entire simulation, which attains an adequate performance with the power equality constraint.

The overall computational procedures of the proposed OPIO algorithm are described in detail as follows. In addition, the flowchart of the proposed OPIO algorithm is represented in Figure 1, and the proposed OPIO algorithm for solving the ELD problem is represented in Algorithm 3.

Step 1: Define the initial parameters with the characteristics of the generation units: φ; number of pigeons; maximum generations (n_g); other data, such as J_r, ρ.

Step 2: Initially, the arbitrary values for all generating units within the lower and upper operating boundary are generated using (5), except for the last generating unit. The computation of the last unit of power generation is calculated using (6), and it is validated, to ensure whether it satisfies the inequality constraints (5) or not. If the solution satisfies the constraints, then the solution is sustained; otherwise, it is abandoned. The pigeon position X, concerning the generating units, is initialized as follows:

$$X = \begin{bmatrix} X_1 \\ \vdots \\ X_i \\ \vdots \\ X_G \end{bmatrix} = \begin{bmatrix} X_{1,1} & \cdots & X_{1,b} & \cdots & X_{1,d} \\ \vdots & \ddots & \vdots & \ddots & \vdots \\ X_{i,1} & \cdots & X_{i,b} & \cdots & X_{i,d} \\ \vdots & \ddots & \vdots & \ddots & \vdots \\ X_{N_p,1} & \cdots & X_{N_p,b} & \cdots & X_{N_p,d} \end{bmatrix} i = 2, \ldots N_p; b = 1, 2, \ldots, d \quad (19)$$

where the component $X_{i,d}$ is the power outcome of the bth unit in individual X_i. For the OPIO algorithm, there is only one adjustable parameter: the jumping rate J_r, which is fixed within the range of 0 to 0.4 for all test cases used in the experimentation.

Step 3: For each pigeon in the population, the power generating unit must satisfy the ramp-rate boundary, and not relay in the restricted operating zones. If the solution does not meet the constraints, then power outputs should be altered near to the boundary of the feasible solution. After processing the initialization, the main procedure of the OPIO algorithm process is as follows:

Step 4: Determine the velocity of the pigeon, using Equation (10), and update the position of the pigeon, using Equation (14). If the updated position of the pigeon does not satisfy the constraints, then alter the pigeon's position, as shown in Step 3.

Step 5: Compute the ψ factor, as in Equation (17).

Step 6: Choose the ψ of the best solutions from the population, and update the position for the selected pigeon, using the OBL technique (Algorithm 2).

Step 7: Check this step for the pigeon i:

a. The output power of the generating units must not reside in the RORs (see (8)) or contravene the operating unit limit (see (5)).

b. The lower and upper boundary rates of each of the generating units, from the preliminary state, should be in the satisfactory ranges, as given in (9). If the preliminary output power of the generating units is not specified, then the preliminary power of all power generating units should be within the satisfactory ranges.

c. If the RORs and ramp-rate limits are contravened, adjust the power outputs near to the feasible solution.

Step 8: Compute the overall power loss of the transmission lines for the pigeon i, as in (6).

Step 9: Compute the quality of the pigeon i, by interleaving its power outputs in the fitness function, as in (17).

Step 10: Repeat steps 4–9, until the stop criterion is met.

Step 11: The ELD solution is the best solution in the last iteration.

Algorithm 3: Proposed OPIO algorithm for solving ELD

```
Generate the initial population.
Determine the preliminary parameters.
Arbitrarily initialize the position of the pigeon in the search boundary space.
Check the RR and RORs constraints.
While (ng ≥ 1) do
    Determine the velocity and position of the pigeon.
    Determine the φ factor.
    Select φ of the best pigeons from the population.
    Apply OBL technique, using Algorithm 2.
    If (fit (Opp) < fit (X_(i,t))) then
        Replace the Opp solution
    Else
        do nothing
    End if
    Check the feasibility of the new position of the pigeons.
    Calculate the transmission loss.
    Evaluate the fitness of the new position of the pigeons.
    Update the global best solution.
End while
Output: Visualize the global best solution.
```

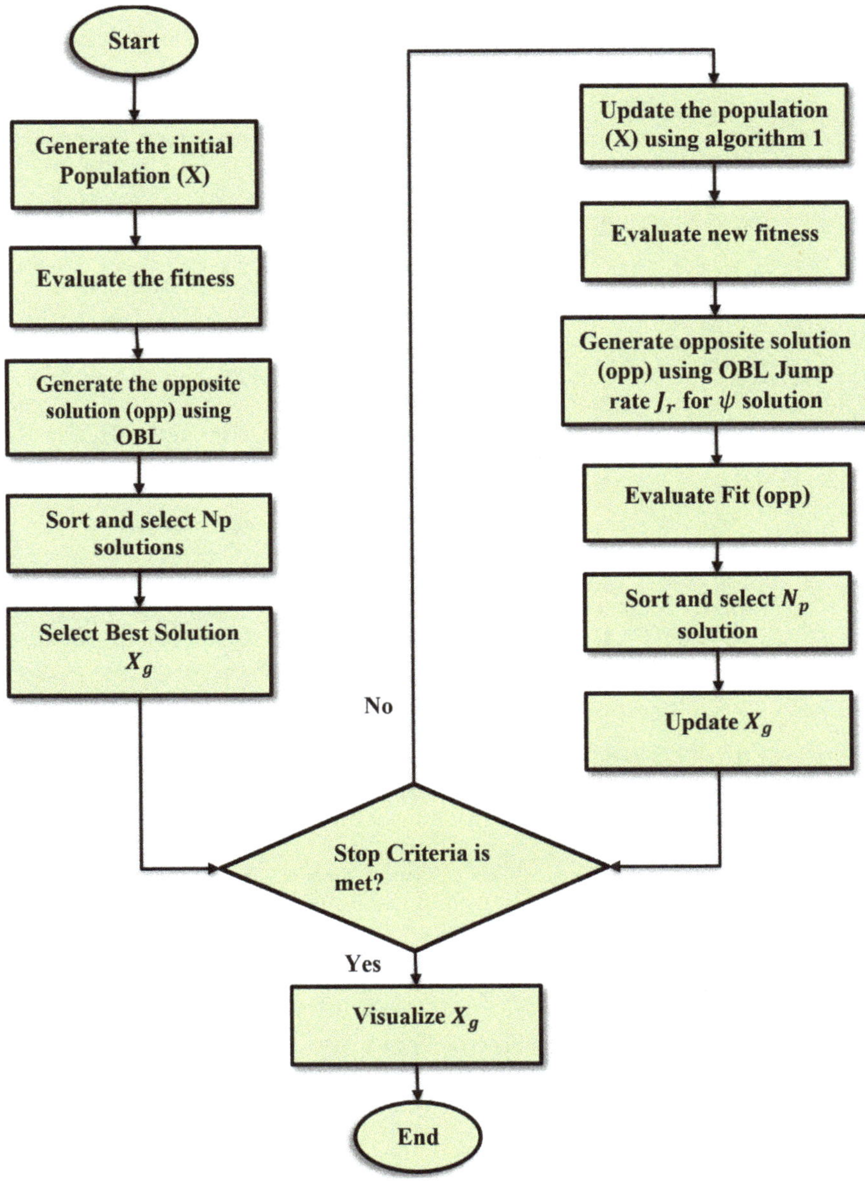

Figure 1. Flowchart of Proposed OPIO algorithm.

5. Results and Discussion

The proposed OPIO algorithm was applied to solve ELD issues. Three various test systems with three different fuel possibilities and non-linearities, such as ramp-rate ranges, value-point consequences and interdicted working region, were studied, to assess the execution of the formulated OPIO method. The formulated OPIO technique was written in MATLAB R2016a, implemented on a 2.6 GHz Intel I5 PC. The execution of the formulated OPIO algorithm was justified by utilizing three different test systems: small- (13-unit, 40-unit), medium- (140-unit, 160-unit) and large-scale (320-unit and 640-unit). The acquired outcomes from the formulated OPIO technique were differentiated to various state-of-the-art metaheuristic techniques reported in the literature. The different test systems, with the number of generating units and their constraints, are outlined below:

(i) *Test Case 1: Small-Scale Test Systems (13-Unit and 40-unit)*

a. 13-unit test case: in this test case, a 13-unit generator system, with constraints such as different fuel costs and value-point effects, was considered. The power load demand (P_D) of the system was fixed at P_D = 2520 MW [7,43];

b. 40-unit test case: this test case held a 40-unit generator system, with value-point effects considered, and the power load demand of the system was fixed at P_D = 10,500 MW [7,43].

(ii) *Test Case 2: Medium-Scale Test Systems (140-unit and 160-unit)*

a. 140-unit test case: in this test case, a 140-unit generator system, with constraints such as value-point effects, ramp-rate limits, and prohibited accomplishment unit, was considered. The power load demand (P_D) of the system was fixed at P_D = 49,342 MW [44];

b. 160-unit test case: this test case held a 160-unit generator system, with value-point effects considered. The power load demand of the system was fixed at P_D = 43,200 MW [45].

(iii) *Test Case 3: Large-Scale Test Systems (320-unit and 640-unit)*

a. 320-unit test case: a large-scale system with a 320-unit generator system, with different fuel options and value-point loading effects, was considered here. The power load demand of the system was fixed at P_D = 86,400 MW. The input data of the 10-unit system were duplicated 32 times in this system [46].

b. 640-unit test case: a test case with a 640-unit generator system, with multiple fuel options and value-point load effects, was considered here. The load demand of the system was increased by up to P_D = 1,72,800 MW. The input data of the 10-unit system were replicated 64 times in this system [30].

The convergence of metaheuristic algorithms mainly relies on the possibility of a proper value. The proposed technique may deliver a different solution when the choice of insert value is not appropriate. To select the proper input parameters, repeated simulation is required. For the OPIO algorithm, after a repeated number of runs, the lower and upper jumping rates were fixed within the range of 0 to 0.4. For effective simulation, we considered a population size of 50, and 100 was selected as the maximum number of iterations for the test systems.

5.1. Test Case 1a: 13-Unit

In this instance, the formulated OPIO technique was tested on a small-scale 13-unit system, which held uneven fuel cost and value-point effects. The dataset of the fuel cost and the limit utility of numerous vigorous energy providers were taken from [43], and the load order was fixed as 2520 MW. To examine the execution of the proposed OPIO technique and the conventional PIO algorithm, the assumed outcomes were differentiated from the various metaheuristic algorithms, viz., Oppositional Grey Wolf Optimization (OGWO) [32], Improved Particle Swarm Optimization (IPSO) [29], One Rank Cuckoo Search Algorithm (ORCSA) [36], Crisscross Optimization Algorithm (COA) [30], Real-Coded Genetic Algorithm (RCGA) [37], Improved Genetic Algorithm (IGA) [38] and Pigeon-Inspired Optimization (PIO) [39].

Table 1 provides the comparative results of the OPIO and PIO algorithms for active power generators along with other techniques. As shown in Table 1, the solution provided by the OPIO algorithm reached a fuel cost of 24512.45$/hr, which was less than all the compared algorithms; the outcomes of the formulated techniques conveyed that it was superior in finding the best or near-best solution. To ensure the efficacy and effectiveness of the technique, the simulation was carried out over 100 runs, on both the proposed OPIO algorithm and the conventional PIO algorithm, and its result is given in Table 2. As shown in Table 2, the OPIO produced a better solution for 97 runs, which was far better than all compared algorithms. The statistical outcomes conveyed that the formulated OPIO algorithm delivered better results compared with various algorithms. The convergence of the minimization fuel-cost function over the iteration cycles of the proposed OPIO algorithm and the standard PIO algorithm were noted, and are displayed in Figure 2. Figure 2 shows that the proposed algorithm converged faster towards the optimal solution that did not have further changes, which validated the active constancy of the formulated technique.

Table 1. Test outcomes of various algorithms for a 13-unit system with PD = 2520 MW.

Unit	OGWO	IPSO	COA	ORCSA	PIO	OPIO (Proposed)
1	628.2948	628.1678	628.3451	628.4524	628.3124	628.5647
2	299.0451	298.8798	298.5478	298.3575	298.3567	298.9856
3	296.4501	297.6984	297.6874	297.3457	297.4254	297.6245
4	159.6421	159.2387	159.3564	159.2349	159.6548	159.7542
5	159.7154	159.1254	159.8957	159.5796	159.5347	159.6589
6	159.5484	159.3567	159.3567	159.2134	159.8975	159.3521
7	159.6879	159.8954	159.6542	159.6875	159.7543	159.1256
8	159.6877	159.6872	159.6513	159.3579	159.5421	159.2564
9	159.6542	159.9877	159.3542	159.7765	158.8578	159.3658
10	76.4854	77.6513	77.6854	77.5587	77.3567	77.6574
11	114.8742	113.3685	114.2314	114.2254	113.3687	114.8975
12	91.5874	92.6975	92.8674	92.6478	92.6898	92.8785
13	92.5412	92.3515	92.4578	92.3542	92.3277	92.8547
Fuel Cost ($/h)	24,513.4847	24,514.6875	24,512.8754	24,513.5464	24,514.5467	**24,512.4578**
Power loss (MW)	40.2975	40.3051	40.3645	40.3897	40.5781	**40.1584**

Table 2. Comparison outcomes of different algorithms for a 13-unit system.

Algorithms	Best ($/H)	Mean ($/H)	Worst ($/H)	Standard Deviation	Successful Runs (%)	Test time (S)
OGWO	24,512.72	24,512.86	24,514.65	0.1031	92	5.89
IPSO	24,517.68	24,517.96	24,518.21	0.3154	84	5.98
IGA	24,516.42	24,517.76	24,519.78	NA	82	6.21
RCGA	24,514.54	24,515.87	24,517.89	0.1578	88	6.89
COA	24,512.87	24,513.65	24,515.68	0.1047	93	5.47
ORCSA	24,513.54	24,513.54	24,516.67	NA	87	8.65
PIO	24520.54	24521.75	24532.95	0.2645	79	11.00
OPIO (Proposed)	24512.45	**24512.67**	24513.54	0.0875	97	5.14

5.2. Test Case 1b: 40-Unit

To access the feasibility of the proposed OPIO algorithm, another small-scale test case, of a 40-unit power generation system along with value-point belongings, was used. The benchmark value of the 40-unit power system was approached from [43], and its load demand was fixed as 10,500 MW. The outputs of the power generation and fuel cost of various algorithms like OGWO, IPSO, IGA, RCGA, COA, ORCSA, PIO and OPIO are shown in Table 3: the best cost of the PIO and OPIO algorithms reached 136,588.57 $/h and 136,447.87$/h, respectively; it is also notable that the OPIO algorithm provided the best solution among the compared techniques, by achieving the load demand and other constraints.

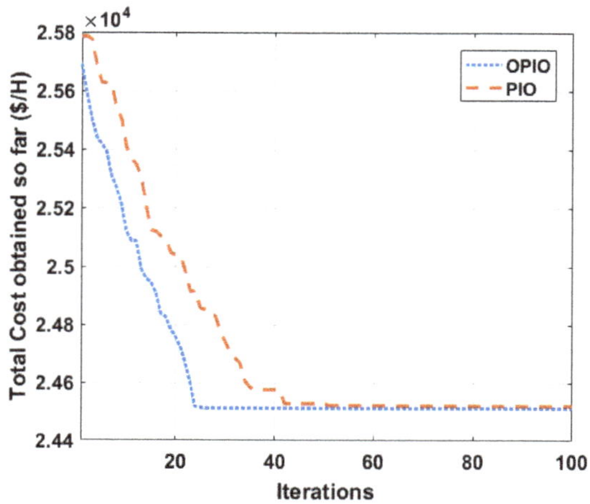

Figure 2. Convergence results of the OPIO and PIO algorithms for a 13-unit system.

Table 3. Simulation outcomes of different algorithms for a 40-unit system with PD = 10,500 MW.

Unit	OGWO	IPSO	COA	ORCSA	PIO	OPIO (Proposed)
1	114.2743	114.2876	113.8502	110.12	111.52	114.24
2	114.4501	114.4621	114.1203	112.28	112.34	114.12
3	120.3567	120.4212	119.7458	120.23	119.28	120.31
4	183.3685	181.5412	182.4127	188.54	182.45	190.54
5	87.1256	87.3542	88.5864	85.37	87.34	97.56
6	140.3645	140.3747	140.3289	140.24	139.52	140.25
7	300.1254	300.2346	299.6517	250.28	198.24	300.54
8	300.2349	300.3277	292.3428	290.74	186.38	300.26
9	300.4501	300.4578	299.6433	300.52	193.12	300.49
10	279.0451	279.3874	279.5423	282.31	179.41	205.49
11	243.3277	243.6752	168.2597	180.25	162.27	226.47
12	94.5874	94.3259	94.2355	168.52	94.39	204.56
13	484.3051	484.4578	484.2511	469.78	486.22	346.52
14	484.1584	484.3277	484.6425	484.26	487.33	434.58
15	484.2314	484.3542	484.3266	487.39	483.26	431.29
16	484.5412	484.1564	484.6501	482.62	484.25	440.21
17	489.5781	489.6475	489.4523	499.16	494.61	500.34
18	489.4578	489.5423	489.6244	411.19	489.76	500.33
19	511.8785	511.6432	511.1289	510.27	512.34	550.27
20	511.8754	511.5428	511.6451	542.37	513.21	550.96
21	523.3228	523.5746	549.3347	544.29	543.18	550.14
22	546.3738	547.7433	549.6455	550.29	548.38	550.54
23	523.1035	523.4728	523.4589	550.37	521.56	550.32
24	523.0678	523.1532	523.4313	528.18	525.23	550.46
25	523.5181	523.4421	523.1204	524.67	529.67	550.28
26	523.4767	523.4775	523.4217	539.28	540.31	550.39
27	10.3344	10.1067	10.1265	10.34	12.46	11.27
28	10.8011	10.7836	10.1024	10.24	10.96	11.34
29	10.6445	10.4521	10.2301	10.22	10.34	11.16
30	87.302	87.9827	87.6658	96.42	89.45	97.16
31	190.5847	190.2498	190.1322	185.24	189.04	190.34
32	190.8664	190.3277	189.4582	189.26	189.47	190.28
33	190.9983	190.4562	190.4251	189.37	187.43	190.64
34	200.5471	200.2841	199.2217	199.16	198.27	200.34
35	200.5847	200.6128	200.7541	196.54	199.69	200.41
36	164.9983	164.9833	164.3242	185.28	165.34	200.67
37	110.2147	110.2348	110.2323	109.58	109.54	110.24
38	110.3341	110.4355	109.2344	110.76	109.31	110.11
39	110.4616	110.5436	110.3333	95.17	109.44	110.37
40	511.9904	511.2239	550.4219	532.59	548.23	550.16
Fuel Cost ($/h)	136,441.8527	136,446.7842	136,442.689	136,549.8756	136,588.5746	136,441.876
Power loss (MW)	964.75	963.2045	945.2143	958.39	979.85	940.12

The comparative outcomes of the overall fuel cost, success rate, standard deviation and execution time acquired by the OPIO algorithm, along with the various techniques, are given in Table 4. Based on Table 4, the OPIO algorithm achieved the best solution 96 times out of 100 trials. In addition, the mean costs of the OPIO and IPSO algorithms were equal to 136,441.87$/h and 136,542.87$/h, respectively. This clearly shows that the statistical outcomes of the OPIO algorithm were more stable than those of the OGWO, IPSO, COA, RCGA, ORCSA and PIO algorithms. In addition, the time required to achieve the minimal fuel cost for the proposed algorithm was 10.14/sec, which was minimal in relation to other algorithms. The convergence graph of the total fuel cost of the proposed OPIO algorithm and the conventional PIO algorithm is given in Figure 3. Based on Figure 3, it can be seen that the formulated OPIO procedure provides the best active rate compared to the PIO algorithm.

Table 4. Comparison results of various algorithms for a 40-unit system.

Algorithms	Best ($/H)	Mean ($/H)	Worst ($/H)	Standard Deviation	Successful Runs (%)	Test Time (S)
OGWO	136,441.85	136,445.87	136,447.54	0.1365	94	11.52
IPSO	136,446.78	136,542.87	136,588.55	0.2345	89	12.65
IGA	136,454.56	NA	NA	NA	NA	NA
RCGA	136,587.21	136,687.52	136,742.65	0.3874	84	13.41
COA	136,442.68	136,448.54	136,468.54	0.1865	92	12.87
ORCSA	136,549.87	NA	NA	NA	NA	NA
PIO	136,588.57	136,698.32	136,721.54	NA	NA	NA
OPIO (Proposed)	136,441.87	**136,441.95**	136,443.81	0.1021	96	10.14

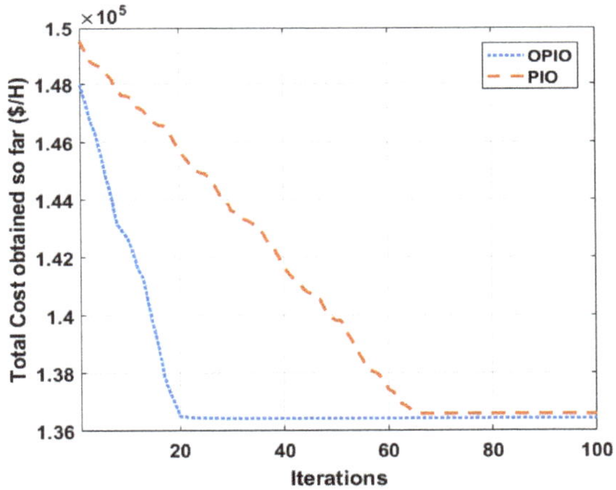

Figure 3. Convergence results of the OPIO and PIO algorithms for a 40-unit system.

5.3. Test Case 2a: 140-Unit

In this instance, the formulated PIO algorithm was tested on the medium-scale of a 140-unit power generation system, and the load order was taken as 49,342 MW [46]. In this test case, non-smooth constraints, such as value-point consequence, interdicted executing section and ramp-limits were included. The execution was repeated for 100 trials, to confirm the dominance of the proposed methods with the obtained results of the OGWO, IPSO, COA, RCGA, ORCSA and PIO algorithms, which are presented in Table 5. As shown in Table 5, the OPIO reached 1,559,498.78$/h, which was the minimum, compared to the other algorithms. In other words, the obtained outcomes clearly showed that the OPIO algorithm achieved a low fuel-cost value, compared to other methods.

Table 5. Test outcomes of various algorithms for a 140-unit system with PD = 49,342 MW.

Unit	PIO	OPIO (Proposed)	Unit	PIO	OPIO (Proposed)	Unit	PIO	OPIO (Proposed)
1	114.3542	119.1244	48	250.2564	250.4159	95	978.1244	978.2456
2	189.2341	189.2344	49	250.3577	250.3648	96	682.3277	682.1247
3	190.2134	190.2333	50	250.4525	250.3014	97	720.2441	720.1689
4	190.2625	190.2455	51	165.2134	165.4258	98	718.2355	718.2245
5	168.7569	168.6479	52	165.3426	165.2486	99	720.2466	720.3144
6	190.2345	190.3247	53	165.5412	165.4857	100	964.2344	964.2188
7	490.2625	490.2655	54	165.5122	165.5574	101	958.3477	958.2177
8	490.3438	490.3677	55	180.3211	180.2675	102	1007.1255	1007.5248
9	496.5255	496.5829	56	180.2144	180.5974	103	1006.3425	1006.7413
10	496.5648	496.5574	57	103.2644	103.4428	104	1013.6487	1013.6944
11	496.6522	496.6548	58	198.4522	198.5674	105	1020.6666	1020.1024
12	496.7566	496.7742	59	312.3248	312.4295	106	954.2377	954.2188
13	506.2256	506.2389	60	280.9517	282.5479	107	952.1244	952.1277
14	509.3364	509.4861	61	163.3211	163.4287	108	106.3244	1006.2384
15	506.2355	506.2479	62	95.2347	95.2261	109	1013.2311	1013.5244
16	505.2144	505.2498	63	160.2358	160.4521	110	1021.6322	1021.5644
17	506.3422	506.3451	64	160.3459	160.2349	111	1015.2344	1015.2988
18	506.9548	506.4692	65	490.2378	490.2587	112	94.2155	94.2577
19	505.2344	505.6498	66	196.4356	196.5477	113	94.3157	94.2188
20	505.3214	505.4582	67	490.5612	490.6287	114	94.4233	94.1024
21	505.4255	505.2398	68	490.6458	489.3017	115	244.5612	244.1657
22	505.5412	505.2179	69	130.2648	130.2688	116	244.6124	244.1287
23	505.5378	505.2489	70	234.8465	234.5144	117	244.8477	244.5218
24	505.6522	505.9548	71	137.2659	137.2955	118	95.3244	95.2476
25	537.4612	537.2144	72	325.5641	325.4872	119	95.6245	95.2348
26	537.2344	537.3499	73	195.2347	195.3488	120	116.2377	116.2478
27	549.6254	549.2674	74	175.4529	175.6247	121	175.4298	175.3489
28	549.3244	549.3014	75	175.2349	175.4277	122	2.2144	2.1758
29	501.2333	501.2648	76	175.8945	175.6648	123	4.3322	4.1689
30	501.4622	501.3478	77	175.5217	175.2486	124	15.4625	15.4873
31	506.2477	506.2018	78	330.2175	330.2487	125	9.2344	9.2481
32	506.2344	506.3014	79	531.2648	531.1248	126	12.9588	12.6475
33	506.2237	506.4251	80	531.2647	531.2476	127	10.2647	10.6598
34	506.8546	506.6517	81	398.4275	436.2186	128	112.6599	112.4581
35	500.2649	500.2689	82	56.1975	56.2874	129	4.2689	43275
36	500.2014	500.2478	83	115.2348	115.3495	130	5.2644	5.1694
37	241.3645	241.2349	84	115.4756	115.6248	131	5.6544	5.4572
38	241.6477	241.2847	85	115.2679	115.7749	132	50.2688	50.6489
39	774.2655	774.5842	86	207.6548	207.4568	133	5.2177	5.1483
40	769.8542	769.4158	87	207.1673	207.1168	134	42.6588	42.5976
41	3.9655	3.2685	88	175.9485	175.4906	135	42.7588	42.6577
42	3.8522	3.1749	89	175.2648	175.2681	136	41.2355	41.6572
43	250.3466	250.3489	90	175.3348	175.6489	137	17.6588	17.2954
44	246.5147	249.5681	91	175.2247	175.2213	138	17.4955	17.3597
45	250.3416	250.3189	92	580.2234	580.6477	139	7.2655	7.2265
46	250.3429	250.6475	93	645.1958	645.2188	140	26.5884	26.4621
47	240.3168	249.6257	94	984.2655	984.2377	Fuel Cost ($/H)	1,560,412.55	1,559,498.78

Moreover, the statistical outcomes of the formulated OPIO algorithm, and various conventional procedures, are given in Table 6. Based on Table 6, the formulated OPIO algorithm provided the best outcomes, in terms of best, worst and mean cost, and less execution time compared to the various procedures. However, the best and mean costs of the OPIO and COA algorithms were equal to 1,559,498.78 $/h, 1,559,499.21 $/h, 1,559,521.36 $/h and 1,559,521.88 $/h, respectively. Even though the COA algorithm competed with the OPIO algorithm, the OPIO algorithm was quite efficient in achieving the best outcome in minimal iterations, compared to the various procedures. The convergence of the formulated OPIO algorithm and the conventional PIO methods with iteration cycles is displayed in fig 4. From Figure 4, it can be seen that the OPIO technique attained the best solution within 20 iterations; this confirms that the OPIO algorithm had better convergence, because of its magnificent diversification and intensification abilities.

Table 6. Statistical comparison results of test case 2a (140-unit system with PD = 49,342 MW).

Algorithms	Best ($/H)	Mean ($/H)	Worst ($/H)	Standard Deviation	Successful Runs (%)	Test Time (S)
OGWO	1,559,710.65	1,559,715.64	1,559,751.21	0.1512	95	43.98
IPSO	1,560,453.89	NA	NA	NA	NA	NA
IGA	1,561,254.85	NA	NA	NA	NA	NA
RCGA	1,559,957.62	1,560,521.35	1,561,542.96	0.5641	84	49.54
COA	1,559,499.21	1,559,521.88	1,559,645.21	0.1234	92	44.66
ORCSA	1,559,987.42	1,560,387.36	1,561,662.54	NA	NA	NA
PIO	1,560,412.55	1,561,542.13	1,562,874.62	NA	NA	NA
OPIO (Proposed)	1,559,498.78	**1,559,521.36**	1,559,587.62	0.1123	96	40.21

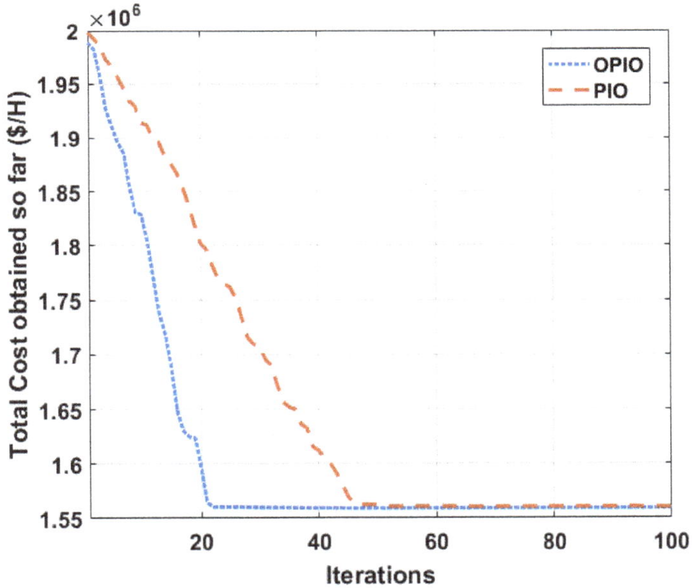

Figure 4. Convergence results of the OPIO and PIO algorithms for a 140-unit system.

5.4. *Test Case 2b: 160-Unit*

To access the feasibility of the formulated OPIO technique, another medium-scale test case of a 160-unit test system, along with non-convex value-point properties, was used. As to validation, the viability and efficacy of the formulated technique transmission loss was unnoticeable. For this medium-scale unit, a replicated 10 different fuel-option values were taken from [41], the power load was increased by 16, and the power load was fixed as 43,200 MW. Table 7 provides the attained better cost of the proposed OPIO algorithm, with other algorithms, by satisfying the constraints. Based on Table 7, the OPIO achieved 9625.15 $/h, which was the best result, compared to the other algorithms. This confirms that the least total fuel cost was for the 160-unit generation system.

Table 7. Test outcomes of various algorithms for 160-unit system with PD = 43,200 MW.

Unit	PIO	OPIO (Proposed)	Unit	PIO	OPIO (Proposed)	Unit	PIO	OPIO (Proposed)
1	211.1057	224.3218	55	207.3485	265.4215	109	402.5278	430.2109
2	208.4572	200.6548	56	254.6289	257.1026	110	272.9458	260.5614
3	335.6534	355.2671	57	294.3275	277.3041	111	199.2658	217.4259
4	243.9547	228.4601	58	245.2964	235.4216	112	204.7594	199.6504
5	266.1958	305.4286	59	420.3581	394.5027	113	251.4298	357.2169
6	237.4295	249.5013	60	270.1485	278.1659	114	249.5048	251.4209
7	282.1473	309.4681	61	198.3475	240.3415	115	266.4175	267.2044
8	239.6475	218.4627	62	212.3458	213.1452	116	240.5219	252.3011
9	408.6427	335.2485	63	348.2571	241.6521	117	290.3584	290.4255
10	265.4581	270.4195	64	259.2543	248.6574	118	242.1507	233.4452
11	225.1049	187.2589	65	292.8594	232.2485	119	412.6259	329.5622
12	217.4685	195.4271	66	221.6579	245.6574	120	242.4957	300.4586
13	336.4216	353.2049	67	286.5419	310.2415	121	211.1048	237.5248
14	232.4582	241.6204	68	242.3859	232.5218	122	210.6247	207.6648
15	259.3248	273.4209	69	348.5796	353.2016	123	245.6284	237.5601
16	237.4581	228.1064	70	288.6473	281.4025	124	227.2094	210.6598
17	265.3482	277.4295	71	227.4961	219.4259	125	273.4587	241.2045
18	236.5219	224.1058	72	215.3333	220.4015	126	250.6418	246.5129
19	414.2188	404.6257	73	339.4857	343.2016	127	258.6458	293.3277
20	272.3158	314.2045	74	244.6589	250.4012	128	243.4109	245.2011
21	222.2507	205.4952	75	280.4276	273.5248	129	382.4692	431.2655
22	204.3258	200.4672	76	231.5942	217.5486	130	296.4108	248.5555
23	333.2429	374.1526	77	286.4957	305.4295	131	200.1472	199.7468
24	237.3854	234.1059	78	225.3489	243.4582	132	214.2845	217.4511
25	304.5521	284.1057	79	282.6472	253.6241	133	334.2074	242.6589
26	245.2965	221.4695	80	265.3485	271.9648	134	234.6248	229.3544
27	265.5421	253.1284	81	223.4685	223.4258	135	286.3049	250.3014
28	237.4951	223.6244	82	200.1479	191.3045	136	247.1658	236.1045
29	381.2659	241.5019	83	334.6517	349.5261	137	290.6547	305.1588
30	267.3204	280.6642	84	246.5923	234.5201	138	229.3104	230.4266
31	223.1584	175.4269	85	274.2986	275.2496	139	391.6248	430.2984
32	214.6549	203.6248	86	249.1634	208.4257	140	270.6248	257.1659
33	334.5671	348.2015	87	297.5842	282.5967	141	212.4286	228.4358
34	247.9547	219.5202	88	240.6713	255.3048	142	226.1958	184.2384
35	250.4682	283.4029	89	340.2986	409.4672	143	335.2648	370.5691
36	229.4572	244.1527	90	291.4726	269.3541	144	245.1382	219.4581
37	265.4953	313.2658	91	212.4589	192.3547	145	261.2017	263.1594
38	243.1572	236.1259	92	210.4976	201.1064	146	244.6218	235.4275
39	413.2685	340.2015	93	337.4682	350.2496	147	294.3581	300.6598
40	277.5878	333.3541	94	236.4196	258.6412	148	235.2481	242.1574
41	202.1574	230.5298	95	261.77165	290.3485	149	390.2571	387.4598
42	228.6257	209.9654	96	235.6279	226.4153	150	253.4192	267.4125
43	352.1469	341.4027	97	278.9648	299.4035	151	193.2488	184.5298
44	227.4583	233.6248	98	237.5944	223.4257	152	222.5027	212.4158
45	272.4159	299.1047	99	420.6519	366.6591	153	355.9418	376.1548
46	241.6051	263.5218	100	268.1695	288.4251	154	242.3158	248.5476
47	266.5384	243.6201	101	224.3186	227.2045	155	277.6428	278.1549
48	230.4572	212.3048	102	209.6581	210.5499	156	246.7128	223.2435
49	423.6514	362.4295	103	337.9547	363.2011	157	318.5472	264.6248
50	254.9571	303.2048	104	230.9528	222.3495	158	241.6014	234.5278
51	280.9654	181.4269	105	269.4681	234.1058	159	341.6547	390.4855
52	211.4582	211.5274	106	235.6428	232.4259	160	261.2485	286.4597
53	337.4692	364.6542	107	274.9648	282.3045	Fuel Cost ($/H)	9738.4526	9625.1573
54	238.4729	234.9512	108	244.3018	236.4159			

The statistical results from over 100 trials of the proposed algorithm, compared to the OGWO, IPSO, IGA, RCGA, COA, ORCSA and PIO algorithms, are shown in Table 8: as can be seen, the OPIO algorithm performance—for example, best (9625.44 $/h), mean (9647.62 $/h) and worst (9649.62 $/h)—was relatively acceptable, whereas the other algorithms deteriorated, due to an increase in the number of generators and traps in the locally optimal solutions. As per the acquired outcomes, we observed that the formulated OPIO technique was more vigorous and systematically structured, compared to the conventional and various algorithms. The active loop of formulated technique and conventional algorithm with iteration cycle is displayed in Figure 5. Figure 5 shows that the formulated procedure provided feasible convergence within 25 iterations, though there was an increase in the number of generation units compared to the standard PIO algorithm.

Table 8. Statistical comparison results for test case 2b (160-unit with PD = 43,200 MW).

Algorithms	Best ($/H)	Mean ($/H)	Worst ($/H)	Standard Deviation	Successful Runs (%)	Test time (S)
OGWO	9768.62	9772.21	9774.62	0.1421	94	18.52
IPSO	10,008.65	10,009.65	10,010.56	0.3654	85	36.95
IGA	10,009.82	10,010.98	10,011.26	NA	NA	NA
RCGA	9954.23	10,002.62	10,004.63	0.4521	90	27.62
COA	9664.32	9702.36	9776.85	0.1262	94	16.85
ORCSA	9845.45	9898.12	9902.42	NA	NA	NA
PIO	9738.45	9812.64	9836.95	0.3641	88	44.34
OPIO (Proposed)	9625.15	**9647.62**	9649.62	0.1145	96	16.21

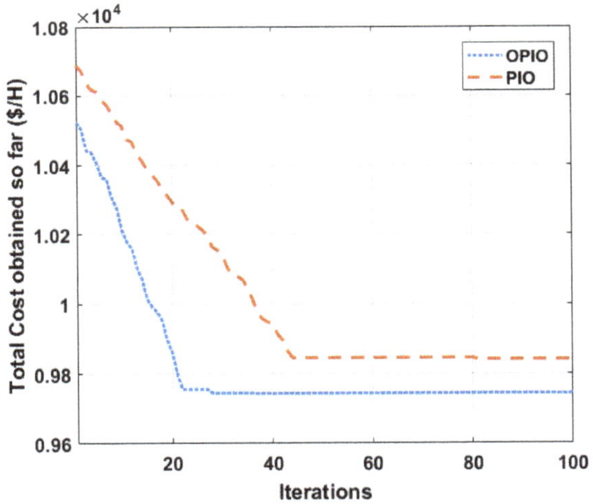

Figure 5. Convergence results of the OPIO and PIO algorithms for a 160-unit system.

5.5. Test Case 3a: 320-Unit

In this instance, a wide scale 320-unit generation system, that included a value-point effect and three various fuel possibilities, was used to evaluate the execution of the formulated OPIO technique. For this 320-unit system, 32 times replicated, 10 different fuel options were taken from [41], and the power load was considered as 86,400 MW. Simulation results were carried out for 1000 iterations, for the 320-unit generation system, and its comparative results are illustrated in Table 9. Table 9 shows that the OPIO algorithm provided 19,968.95$/h, which was the minimal production cost compared to different state-of-the-art algorithms. On the other hand, the test times of the COA and OPIO algorithms were nearly equal, at 412.95/sec and 410.65/sec, respectively. However, the OPIO algorithm showed a unique performance, in attaining the best fuel cost for 96 runs out of 100 trials. This proves that the formulated OPIO algorithm was vigorous, and deliberately well-organized, compared to the PIO algorithm and the different approaches presented in this study. To ensure the efficacy of the formulated OPIO technique, the convergence over different iterations is shown in Figure 6. From Figure 6, it can be seen that the execution of the OPIO technique provided the best convergence over the standard PIO algorithm.

Table 9. Statistical comparison results of test case 3a (320-unit system with PD = 86,400 MW).

Algorithms	Best ($/H)	Mean ($/H)	Worst ($/H)	Standard Deviation	Successful Runs (%)	Test Time (S)
OGWO	19,985.62	19,989.41	19,992.34	0.5465	86	489.35
COA	19,971.43	19,986.37	19,990.75	0.7248	92	412.95
ORCSA	20,045.29	NA	NA	NA	NA	NA
PIO	20,254.42	20,267.95	20,312.61	NA	NA	527.24
OPIO (Proposed)	19,968.95	**19,972.16**	19,978.91	0.4087	96	410.65

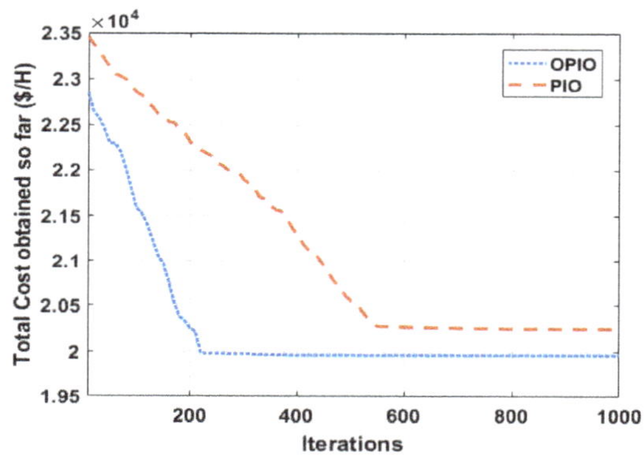

Figure 6. Convergence results of the OPIO and PIO algorithms for a 320-unit system.

5.6. Test Case 3b: 640-Unit

To ensure the efficacy of the formulated OPIO method, we tested it on another large-scale generation system, a 640-unit system with value-point properties and three various fuel possibilities. This 640-unit system included the data of 10 multiple-fuel systems from [41], which were duplicated 64 times, and the load demand was fixed at 172,800 MW. The simulation results of the 640-unit system were iterated over 1000 iterations, and its comparative results are shown in Table 10, where it can be seen that the OPIO algorithm achieved minimum fuel cost related to the various state-of-the-art techniques. The statistical results achieved, by performing 100 trials of the different algorithms and their comparative outcomes, are illustrated in Table 10, which shows that the OPIO algorithm reached 39,963.78 $/h by balancing the local search and global search, as well as converging faster towards the optimal solution. Moreover, the OPIO algorithm achieved the best solution for almost 96 runs out of 100 trials, which clearly demonstrates that the proposed algorithm can sustain the best position for various runs. The convergence results of the proposed OPIO algorithm and the PIO algorithm are displayed in Figure 7. In Figure 7, the formulated OPIO technique provided better convergence, which demonstrates its superiority over the standard PIO algorithm and other state-of-the-art techniques. The overall experimentation outcomes convey that the proposed OPIO algorithm achieved better efficiency, along with a trade-off between exploration and exploitation.

Table 10. Comparison results of various algorithms on a 640-unit system.

Algorithms	Best ($/H)	Mean ($/H)	Worst ($/H)	Standard Deviation	Successful Runs (%)	Test time (S)
OGWO	40,123.65	40,132.85	40,152.18	0.8542	90	704.85
COA	39,968.81	39,970.52	39,974.32	0.3419	94	682.54
ORCSA	40,189.62	NA	NA	NA	NA	NA
PIO	41,072.28	NA	NA	NA	NA	NA
OPIO (Proposed)	39,963.78	39,964.75	39,967.82	0.2451	96	677.27

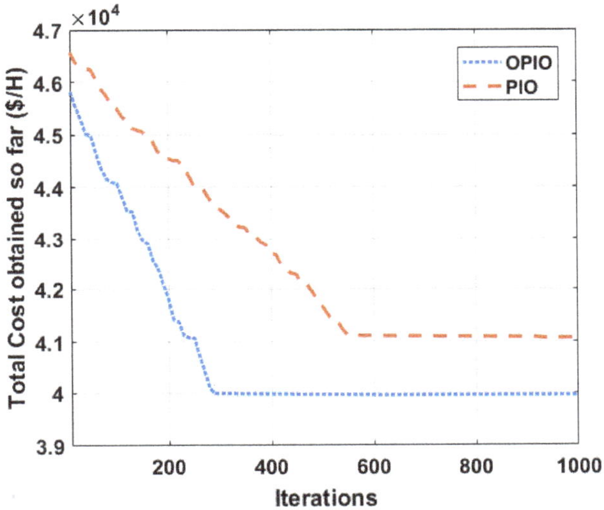

Figure 7. Convergence results of the OPIO and PIO algorithms for a 640-unit system.

5.7. The Result Analysis of Wilcoxon Signed-Rank Test

In this work, a non-parametric test—namely, the Wilcoxon signed-rank test—was utilized, to perform the statistical comparison of the proposed algorithm with the compared algorithms. The best solutions were attained by each technique for the corresponding test cases during 30 independent runs. In this study, the Wilcoxon signed-rank test was performed with a significance level $\alpha = 0.05$. The results, analyzed by the Wilcoxon signed-rank test, are presented in Table 11 for test cases of 13, 40, 140, 160, 320 and 640-generating units. In Table 11, the significance differences of the proposed algorithm and compared algorithms are marked with the value of H (i.e., H with a value of 1 specifies that there was a significance difference; otherwise, the H value is 0, if there was no significance difference). In addition, the symbol S with "+", "=" and "_" denotes that the proposed technique was superior, equal or inferior, respectively, to the compared algorithms. Furthermore, we used four compared algorithms generically, to determine the significance difference with the proposed algorithm. It is clear from Table 11 that the proposed OPIO algorithm provided results superior to those of the COA, ORCSA and PIO algorithms, and equal to the OGWO algorithm for the test case 13-unit system. For the test case 40-unit system, the OPIO algorithm provided results superior to those of the COA, ORCSA and PIO algorithms, but not to the OGWO algorithm. Finally, w/t/l specified the win/tie/loss count by Wilcoxon signed-rank test for the six test case generating unit systems. Thus, from the above discussion, it is clear that the proposed OPIO algorithm attained better solutions, and had better exploring capability, compared to the existing algorithms.

Table 11. Wilcoxon signed-rank test between OPIO and four compared algorithms for test case 13, 40, 140, 160, 320 and 640-unit systems.

Test Case	OPIO vs											
	OGWO			COA			ORCSA			PIO		
	p-Value	H	S	p-Value	H	S	p-Value	H	S	p-Value	H	S
13-unit	1.00×10^{0}	0	=	1.88×10^{-6}	1	+	1.51×10^{-6}	1	+	1.98×10^{-6}	1	+
40-unit	3.85×10^{-1}	0	–	1.00×10^{0}	0	=	1.88×10^{-6}	1	+	1.75×10^{-6}	1	+
140-unit	1.87×10^{-6}	1	+	1.70×10^{-6}	1	+	1.46×10^{-6}	1	+	1.65×10^{-6}	1	+
160-unit	1.55×10^{-6}	1	+	1.00×10^{0}	0	=	1.65×10^{-6}	1	+	1.75×10^{-6}	1	+
320-unit	1.73×10^{-6}	1	+	1.75×10^{-6}	1	+	1.75×10^{-6}	1	+	1.79×10^{-6}	1	+
640-unit	1.55×10^{-6}	1	+	1.11×10^{-6}	1	+	1.73×10^{-6}	1	+	1.75×10^{-6}	1	+
w/t/l	4/1/1			4/2/0			6/0/0			6/0/0		

6. Conclusions and Future Work

In this article, we have provided a novel metaheuristic algorithm named the Oppositional Pigeon-Inspired Optimizer (OPIO), which is formulated to deal with the ELD problem, with value-point consequences and numerous fuel possibilities. From the literature, it can be seen that the standard PIO algorithm is considered a promising optimization technique, which attracts the researcher by its superiority in addressing various optimization problems. However, it suffers in regard to global search ability and premature convergence when it is applied to large-scale optimization problems. Because of these issues, we merged Opposition-Based Learning into a standard PIO algorithm, which helped to eradicate early convergence, aided knowledge discovery and enhanced comprehensive searchability. The formulated OPIO algorithm was applied to non-convex ELD problems with different constraints, such as multiple fuel possibilities, value-point consequence, interdicted zones and ramp-rate. The experimentation was carried out on three different ELD test cases, viz., small-scale (13-unit and 40-unit), medium-scale (140-unit and 160-unit) and large-scale (320-unit and 640-unit) test cases. The exploratory outcomes showed the superiority of the formulated OPIO technique—in relation to higher potential solutions, better convergence rate, robustness and better computational efficiency—over the PIO algorithm and other state-of-the-art metaheuristic algorithms. In future, this work could be used in other fields of optimization, owing to the technique's high potential for dealing with the problematic optimization issues of many practical power systems. In addition, the outcome of the results can be compared with potential algorithms such as SEPSO [16], SA-QSFS [42] and QANA [47].

Author Contributions: Conceptualization, R.R.; methodology, R.R. and D.K.; validation, S.S.A. and M.R.; formal analysis, A.D.; writing—original draft preparation, R.R.; writing—review and editing, M.R. and S.M.; supervision, R.R. and D.K; funding acquisition, S.S.A. All authors have read and agreed to the published version of the manuscript.

Funding: This study was funded by the Deanship of Scientific Research, Taif University Researchers Supporting Project number (TURSP-2020/215), Taif University, Taif, Saudi Arabia.

Institutional Review Board Statement: Not applicable.

Informed Consent Statement: Not applicable.

Data Availability Statement: Data in this research paper will be shared upon request to the corresponding author.

Conflicts of Interest: The authors declare no conflict of interest.

References

1. Balamurugan, R. Application of Shuffled Frog Leaping Algorithm for Economic Dispatch with Multiple Fuel Options. In Proceedings of the 2012 International Conference on Emerging Trends in Electrical Engineering and Energy Management (ICETEEEM), Chennai, India, 13–15 December 2012; pp. 191–197. [CrossRef]
2. Aravindhababu, P.; Nayar, K.R. Economic dispatch based on optimal lambda using radial basis function network. *Int. J. Electr. Power Energy Syst.* **2002**, *24*, 551–556. [CrossRef]
3. Wood, A.J.; Wollenberg, B.F.; Sheblé, G.B. *Power Generation, Operation, and Control*; John Wiley & Sons: Hoboken, NJ, USA, 2013.
4. Liang, Z.X.; Glover, J.D. A zoom feature for a dynamic programming solution to economic dispatch including transmission losses. *IEEE Trans. Power Syst.* **1992**, *7*, 544–550. [CrossRef]
5. Victoire, T.A.A.; Jeyakumar, A.E. Hybrid PSO-SQP for economic dispatch with valve-point effect. *Electr. Power Syst. Res.* **2004**, *71*, 51–59. [CrossRef]
6. Chiang, C.L. Genetic-based algorithm for power economic load dispatch. *IEE Proc. Gener. Trans. Distrib.* **2007**, *1*, 261–269. [CrossRef]
7. Sinha, N.; Chakrabarti, R.; Chattopadhyay, P.K. Evolutionary programming techniques for economic load dispatch. *IEEE Evol. Comput.* **2003**, *7*, 83–94. [CrossRef]
8. Tan, Y.; Li, C.; Cao, Y.; Lee, K.Y.; Li, L.; Tang, S.; Zhou, L. Improved group search optimization method for optimal power flow problem considering valve-point loading effects. *Neurocomputing* **2015**, *148*, 229–239. [CrossRef]
9. Aydin, D.; Ozyon, S. Solution to non-convex economic dispatch problem with valve point effects by incremental artificial bee colony with local search. *Appl. Soft Comput.* **2013**, *13*, 2456–2466. [CrossRef]
10. Jayabarathi, T.; Raghunathan, T.; Adarsh, B.R. Ponnuthurai Nagaratnam Suganthan. Economic dispatch using hybrid grey wolf optimizer. *Energy* **2016**, *111*, 630–641. [CrossRef]
11. Chaturvedi, K.T.; Pandit, M.; Srivastava, L. Self-organizing hierarchical particle swarm optimization for nonconvex economic dispatch. *IEEE Trans. Power Syst.* **2008**, *23*, 1079–1087. [CrossRef]
12. Alsumait, J.S.; Sykulski, J.K.; Al-Othman, A.K. A hybrid GA-PS-SQP method to solve power system valve-point economic dispatch problems. *Appl. Energy* **2010**, *87*, 1773–1781. [CrossRef]
13. Roy, P.; Roy, P.; Chakrabarti, A. Modified shuffled frog leaping algorithm with genetic algorithm crossover for solving economic load dispatch problem with valve-point effect. *Appl. Soft Comput.* **2013**, *13*, 4244–4252. [CrossRef]
14. Yang, X.; Hosseini, S.S.S.; Gandomi, A.H. Firefly Algorithm for solving non-convex economic dispatch problems with valve loading effect. *Appl. Soft Comput.* **2012**, *12*, 1180–1186. [CrossRef]
15. Wang, Y.; Zhou, J.; Lu, Y.; Qin, H.; Wang, Y. Chaotic self-adaptive particle swarm optimization algorithm for dynamic economic dispatch problem with valvepoint effects. *Expert Syst. Appl.* **2011**, *38*, 14231–14237.
16. Faisal, A.N.; Cao, M.; Shen, L.; Fu, R.; Šumarac, D. The combined social engineering particle swarm optimization for real-world engineering problems: A case study of model-based structural health monitoring. *Appl. Soft Comput.* **2022**, *123*, 108919.
17. Zamani, H.; Nadimi-Shahraki, M.H.; Gandomi, A.H. Starling murmuration optimizer: A novel bio-inspired algorithm for global and engineering optimization. *Comput. Methods Appl. Mech. Eng.* **2022**, *392*, 114616. [CrossRef]
18. Nadimi-Shahraki, M.; Ali Fatahi, H.Z.; Abualigah, L. An improved moth-flame optimization algorithm with adaptation mechanism to solve numerical and mechanical engineering problems. *Entropy* **2021**, *23*, 1637. [CrossRef]
19. Nadimi-Shahraki, M.; Zamani, H. DMDE: Diversity-maintained multi-trial vector differential evolution algorithm for non-decomposition large-scale global optimization. *Expert Syst. Appl.* **2022**, *198*, 116895. [CrossRef]
20. Balamurugan, R.; Subramanian, S. Hybrid integer coded differential evolution dynamic programming approach for economic load dispatch with multiple fuel options. *Energy Convers. Manag.* **2008**, *49*, 608–614. [CrossRef]
21. Cai, J.; Mab, X.; Li, Q.; Li, L.; Peng, H. A multi-objective chaotic ant swarm optimization for environmental/economic dispatch. *Int. J. Electr. Power Energy Syst.* **2010**, *32*, 337–344. [CrossRef]
22. Ghoshal, S.P.; Chatterjee, A.; Mukherjee, V. Bio-inspired fuzzy logic based tuning of power system stabilizer. *Expert Syst. Appl.* **2009**, *36*, 9281–9292. [CrossRef]
23. Pothiya, S.; Ngamroo, I.; Kongprawechnon, W. Ant colony optimisation for economic dispatch problem with non-smooth cost functions. *Int. J. Electr. Power Energy Syst.* **2010**, *32*, 478–487. [CrossRef]
24. Roy, P.K.; Ghoshal, S.P.; Thakur, S.S. Biogeography-based optimization for economic load dispatch problems. *Elect. Power Compon. Syst.* **2010**, *38*, 166–181. [CrossRef]
25. Mandal, B.; Roy, P.K.; Mandal, S. Economic load dispatch using krill herd algorithm. *Int. J. Electr. Power Energy Syst.* **2014**, *57*, 1–10. [CrossRef]
26. Lee, K.Y.; Sode-Yome, A.; Park, J.H. Adaptive Hopfield neural networks for economic load dispatch. *IEEE Trans. Power Syst.* **1998**, *13*, 519–525. [CrossRef]
27. Vo, D.N.; Ongsakul, W. Economic dispatch with multiple fuel types by enhanced augmented Lagrange Hopfield network. *Appl. Energy* **2012**, *91*, 281–289. [CrossRef]
28. Vo, N.D.; Ongsakul, W.; Polprasert, J. The augmented Lagrange Hopfield network for economic dispatch with multiple fuel options. *Math. Comput. Model.* **2013**, *57*, 30–39.
29. Barisal, A.K. Dynamic search space squeezing strategy based intelligent algorithm solutions to economic dispatch with multiple fuels. *Int. J. Electr. Power Energy Syst.* **2013**, *45*, 50–59. [CrossRef]

30. Meng, A.; Li, J.; Yin, H. An efficient crisscross optimization solution to large-scale non-convex economic load dispatch with multiple fuel types and valve-point effects. *Energy* **2016**, *113*, 1147–1161. [CrossRef]
31. Sayah, S.; Hamouda, A. A hybrid differential evolution algorithm based on particle swarm optimization for nonconvex economic dispatch problems. *Appl. Soft Comput.* **2013**, *13*, 1608–1619. [CrossRef]
32. Pradhan, M.; Roy, P.K.; Pal, T. Oppositional based grey wolf optimization algorithm for economic dispatch problem of power system. *Ain Shams Eng. J.* **2017**, *9*, 2015–2025. [CrossRef]
33. Wang, Y.; Li, B.; Weise, T. Estimation of distribution and differential evolution cooperation for large scale economic load dispatch optimization of power systems. *Inf. Sci.* **2010**, *180*, 2405–2420. [CrossRef]
34. Bhattacharjee, K.; Bhattacharya, A.; Dey, S.H.N. Chemical reaction optimization for different economic dispatch problems. *IET Gener. Transm. Dis.* **2014**, *8*, 530–541. [CrossRef]
35. Singh, N.J.; Dhillon, J.S.; Kothari, D.P. Synergic predator-prey optimization for economic thermal power dispatch problem. *Appl. Soft Comput.* **2016**, *43*, 298–311. [CrossRef]
36. Thang, T.N.; Dieu, N.V. The application of one rank cuckoo search algorithm for solving economic load dispatch problems. *Appl. Soft Comput.* **2015**, *37*, 763–773.
37. Amjady, N.; Nasiri-Rad, H. Nonconvex economic dispatch with AC constraints by a new real coded genetic algorithm. *IEEE Trans. Power Syst.* **2009**, *24*, 1489–1502. [CrossRef]
38. Chiang, C.-L. Improved Genetic Algorithm for Power Economic Dispatch of Units with Valve-Point Effects and Multiple Fuels. *IEEE Trans. Power Syst.* **2005**, *20*, 4. [CrossRef]
39. Duan, H.; Qiao, P. Pigeon-inspired optimization: A new swarm intelligence optimizer for air robot path planning. *Int. J. Intell. Comput. Cybern.* **2014**, *7*, 24–37. [CrossRef]
40. Tizhoosh, H.R. Opposition-Based Learning: A New Scheme for Machine Intelligence. In Proceedings of the International Conference on Computational Intelligence for Modeling, Control and Automation, Vienna, Austria, 28–30 November 2005; pp. 695–701.
41. Roy, P.K.; Paul, C.; Sultana, S. Oppositional teaching learning-based optimization approach for combined heat and power dispatch. *Int. J. Elect. Power Energy Syst.* **2014**, *57*, 392–403. [CrossRef]
42. Alkayem, N.F.; Shen, L.; Asteris, P.G.; Sokol, M.; Xin, Z.; Cao, M. A new self-adaptive quasi-oppositional stochastic fractal search for the inverse problem of structural damage assessment. *Alex. Eng. J.* **2022**, *61*, 1922–1936. [CrossRef]
43. Coelho, L.D.S.; Mariani, V.C. Combining of chaotic differential evolution and quadratic programming for economic dispatch optimization with valve point effect. *IEEE Trans. Power Syst.* **2006**, *21*, 989–996.
44. Zou, D.; Li, S.; Wang, G.G.; Li, Z.; Ouyang, H. An improved differential evolution algorithm for the economic load dispatch problems with or without valve-point effects. *Appl. Energy* **2016**, *181*, 375–390. [CrossRef]
45. Srinivasa Reddy, A.; Vaisakh, K. Shuffled differential evolution for large scale economic dispatch. *Electr. Power Syst. Res.* **2013**, *96*, 237–245. [CrossRef]
46. Sahoo, S.; Mahesh Dash, K.; Prusty, R.C.; Barisal, A.K. Comparative analysis of optimal load dispatch through evolutionary algorithms. *Ain Shams Eng. J.* **2015**, *6*, 107–120. [CrossRef]
47. Mohammad, Z.H.; Nadimi-Shahraki, H.; Amir, H.G. QANA: Quantum-based avian navigation optimizer algorithm. *Eng. Appl. Artif. Intell.* **2021**, *104*, 104314.

mathematics

MDPI

Article

CLTSA: A Novel Tunicate Swarm Algorithm Based on Chaotic-Lévy Flight Strategy for Solving Optimization Problems

Yi Cui, Ronghua Shi and Jian Dong *

School of Computer Science and Engineering, Central South University, Changsha 410083, China
* Correspondence: dongjian@csu.edu.cn

Abstract: In this paper, we proposed a tunicate swarm algorithm based on Tent-Lévy flight (TLTSA) to avoid converging prematurely or failing to escape from a local optimal solution. First, we combined nine chaotic maps with the Lévy flight strategy to obtain nine different TSAs based on a Chaotic-Lévy flight strategy (CLTSA). Experimental results demonstrated that a TSA based on Tent-Lévy flight (TLTSA) performed the best among nine CLTSAs. Afterwards, the TLTSA was selected for comparative research with other well-known meta-heuristic algorithms. The 16 unimodal benchmark functions, 14 multimodal benchmark functions, 6 fixed-dimension functions, and 3 constrained practical problems in engineering were selected to verify the performance of TLTSA. The results of the test functions suggested that the TLTSA was better than the TSA and other algorithms in searching for global optimal solutions because of its excellent exploration and exploitation capabilities. Finally, the engineering experiments also demonstrated that a TLTSA solved constrained practical engineering problems more effectively.

Keywords: tunicate swarm algorithm; chaotic mapping; Lévy flight strategy; benchmark test functions; engineering design problems; meta-heuristic

MSC: 68W50

Citation: Cui, Y.; Shi, R.; Dong, J. CLTSA: A Novel Tunicate Swarm Algorithm Based on Chaotic-Lévy Flight Strategy for Solving Optimization Problems. *Mathematics* **2022**, *10*, 3405. https://doi.org/10.3390/math10183405

Academic Editor: José Antonio Sanz

Received: 2 August 2022
Accepted: 15 September 2022
Published: 19 September 2022

1. Introduction

Because of the rapid pace of scientific development and innovation, more and more engineering design problems need urgent optimization. The problem is to avoid local solutions yet maintain the optimization trend, and that is the focus of this research [1]. Many of these issues involve complicated nonlinear constraints and high dimensions [2,3]. However, traditional gradient-based optimization methods rely excessively on a large amount of gradient information. When the target engineering problem has more constraints or more extreme values, the gradient search becomes inefficient, that is, the optimal solution obtained may not be the global optimal solution. Therefore, traditional optimization methods are no longer suitable for solving complex engineering design problems.

In recent years, researchers have applied meta-heuristic algorithms because of their high efficiency, wide applicability, and expandability. Most have been proposed after watching and studying natural phenomena or the behavior of creatures. According to different inspiration sources, these algorithms can be divided into four categories: swarm intelligence (SI) algorithms, evolutionary algorithms (EAs), physics-based algorithms, and human-based algorithms. The evolutionary algorithms, inspired by the theory of evolution by natural selection, simulate the crossover, mutation, selection, and other evolutionary behaviors in the process of biological evolution, such as genetic algorithms (GAs) proposed by Holland [4]. Physics-based algorithms are inspired by physical phenomena in nature, such as simulated annealing (SA) algorithm [5], black hole (BH) algorithm [6], central force optimization (CFO) [7], water cycle algorithm (WCA) [8], and lightning attachment procedure optimization (LAPO) [9]. Human-based algorithms are mainly inspired by human behaviors, such as human teaching behaviors, social behaviors, learning behaviors, emotional behaviors, and management behaviors. For example, teaching-learning-based-optimization (TLBO) simulates teaching and learning behaviors [10]. Political optimizer (PO) builds a model based on the multistage process of politics [11,12].

The particle swarm algorithm (PSO) proposed by Kennedy and Eberhart is one of the most widespread and successful [13,14]. By studying the cooperative predation behavior of birds, PSO uses information sharing among individuals in the population to find the global optimal solution, which may enable the algorithm to jump from the local optimal solution. As PSO is paid more attention, more and more swarm intelligence algorithms like PSO are proposed, such as ant colony optimization (ACO) [15], artificial bee colony (ABC) algorithm [16], glowworm swam optimization (GSO) [17], cow search algorithm (CSA) [18], sailfish optimizer (SFO) [19], Harris hawks optimization (HHO) [20,21], manta ray foraging optimization (MRFO) [22], and mayfly algorithm (MA) [23]. In general, swarm intelligence algorithms are superior to evolutionary algorithms in some respects, for example, each individual can improve their fitness by updating position, which enhances the search efficiency of the population. While in evolutionary algorithms, only the current best individuals and descendants produced similar to them in terms of features are allowed to enter the subsequent iterations, individuals with poor fitness are discarded. In addition, swarm intelligence algorithms are easier to use because of fewer operators [24,25].

Although different algorithms have their advantages, their whole optimization processes can be regarded as the combination of the exploration phase and exploitation phase. In the exploration phase, the algorithm produces a population as random as possible to explore a potential promising area in the search space. In the exploitation phase, it attempts to develop the promising region found in the previous phase to search for the optimal solution.

Chaos, randomness generated by a deterministic system, is an important concept in nonlinear dynamics [26,27]. Chaotic mapping, because of its traversal behavior and randomness, has wide application in the search to optimize meta-heuristic algorithms [28]. At present, improved meta-heuristic algorithms based on chaotic maps include chaotic artificial bee colony (CABC) algorithm [29], chaotic grey wolf optimization (CGWO) algorithm [30], chaotic butterfly optimization algorithm (CBOA) [31], chaotic firefly algorithm (CFA) [32], and so on.

Although algorithms based on chaotic mapping can escape the local optimal solution, they have weak exploration. To enhance it while maintaining a balance with exploitation, the introduction of the Lévy flight strategy is an effective method. Lévy flight is a random walk strategy with step size that satisfies the Lévy distribution; the research has found that many animals' behavior obeys it [33]. For example, animals move around an existing food source, but they occasionally travel long distances in search of a new food source [34,35]. The small sizes of Lévy flight allow the algorithm to exploit regions near the current solution. In addition, a long-distance movement sporadically generated by Lévy flight enables the algorithm to jump out of the local optimal solution. When combined with chaotic mapping, it produces a step size with greater randomness. From this perspective, it is feasible to apply the chaotic mapping mechanism to Lévy flight.

In this study, an improved tunicate swarm optimization algorithm based on a Chaotic-Lévy flight strategy (CLTSA) is proposed to solve the shortcomings of the original TSA. The strategy is introduced when the search agents move toward the current solution so that they can update their positions according to the randomly generated step sizes. The next sections of this paper are displayed as follows: In Section 2, the inspiration, principle, and mathematical model of the TSA are introduced. Next, several common chaotic maps, Lévy flight strategy, and application of the two optimization methods to improve the TSA are described. In the fourth and fifth sections, the TLTSA, as the best performer among CLTSAs, is selected to evaluate the capability of optimizing benchmark functions by comparing them with other well-known meta-heuristic algorithms to measure the capability of TLTSA to solve practical engineering problems. The article concludes in Section 6.

2. Related Work

Various works recently investigated the use of Lévy flight in swarm intelligence algorithms. Lévy flight refers to a random walk in which the probability distribution of the step size is heavy tailed. There is a relatively high probability of large strides in the random walk, which is widely used to improve swarm intelligence optimization algorithms. Yang et al. proposed a cuckoo search algorithm (CS) [36] based on Lévy flight, in which search logic simulates the breeding behavior of cuckoos. The algorithm first generates n initial positions called nests. Then, a new nest is generated using the Lévy flight mechanism and compared to the solution of the random nest: If the fitness value of the new position is better than the previous one, the new solution is used to replace the previous one. In each iteration, some of the worst solutions are replaced to obtain a better set of nest positions, such that the process is executed until the optimal solution is found. Another optimization algorithm based on Lévy flight is the Lévy flight whale optimization algorithm (LWOA) [37]. The whale's predation strategy mainly includes three behaviors: encircling prey, bubble-net attacking, and find prey. Most of the development of search agents take place in bubble-net attacking. Due to the trajectories of humpback whales during prey being spiral, the search agent moving towards the food will be replaced by a new random position on spiral curve. In LWOA, the performance of the algorithm is improved by replacing the spiral walk with the Lévy flight strategy. The Lévy flight strategy is also introduced in flower pollination algorithm (FPA) [38]. According to the FPA, each pollen particle represents a solution that walks in the search space under two different search rules: local pollination and global pollination. For each step, one of the update rules is selected stochastically: If the local pollination is selected, the pollen particle walks in a limited around area, and the step-size is multiplied by a random number generated by the uniform distribution $U(0,1)$; if the selected movement is global pollination, the pollen particle walks toward the global optimal solution, and the step-size is multiplied by a random number generated by the Lévy flight. Amirsadri et al. introduced LF-based grey wolf optimization algorithm blended with back propagation (LF-BP-GWO) [39] to train neural networks. First of all, the Lévy flight is applied to improve the exploration ability of GWO. Then, the back propagation which enhances the exploitation ability in combination with improved GWO was used to train neural network. Each individual in the proposed LF-BP-GWO is considered as the weights and the biases set in the neural network. As a random walk strategy, Lévy flight generates a large step size that keeps a small number of search agents away from the current optimal solution, which enhances the algorithm's exploration ability; the generated small step size allows most search agents to continue at the current optimal solution development near the solution, thus balancing the exploration and development of the algorithm.

Chaotic mapping is used to generate chaotic sequences, which are sequences of randomness produced by simple deterministic systems. In the field of optimization, chaotic mapping can be used as an alternative to pseudo-random number generators, generating chaotic numbers between 0 and 1, often with better results than pseudo-random numbers. Chaotic mapping is also widely used in swarm intelligence algorithms. Bilal Alatas proposed three chaotic artificial bee colony algorithms (CABC) [29]: CABC1, CABC2, and CABC3. According to CABC1, the use of the chaos mapping is mainly reflected in the population initialization period. Through chaotic mapping, a set of initial populations with better diversity are generated. In CABC2, if a solution called food is not enhanced by a defined number of trials, the hired bee will give up the position and the scout bee of this hired bee will perform chaotic search for a better food source. CABC3 is a combination of the above two improved algorithms. It not only uses the selected chaotic map to generate a diverse initial population, but also performs chaotic search. Mohammad Tubishat et al. proposed an improved Sine cosine algorithm (ISCA) for Hadith classification [40]. The first modification includes replacing a random number with a chaotic sequence generated by a singer map. This modification allows ISCA to control the switching between sine and cosine equations, which are applied to update the position of search agents. The second modification is improving development ability by combining with simulated annealing.

At the end of each iteration, the best solution obtained by SCA will be considered as the initial solution of simulated annealing. If simulated annealing finds a better solution, it will replace the current optimal solution with new one. Talatahari et al. improved the traditional algorithm and proposed a chaotic imperialist competitive algorithm (CICA) [41]. Through the comparative research and evaluation of different chaos maps, the experimental results proved the superiority of logistic and sinusoidal maps. In order to enhance the global exploration ability, the firefly algorithm (FA) [32] also introduces chaotic mapping to set light and other absorption parameters. The results show that the Gaussian map has the best effect as the absorption coefficient. The chaotic mapping is also applied to improve KH algorithm [42]. According to CKH, many types of movements of krill are proposed using different chaotic maps, among which the singer map performs best.

The TSA has received a lot of attention because of its simplicity and optimal. E. H. Houssein et al. introduced the local escape operator into TSA (TSA-LEO) to enhance its optimization effect [43]. In the TSA-LEO, several solutions such as the best position, two randomly generated individual, two randomly selected individual, and a new randomly generated individual were used to obtain the alternative solutions with excellent performance of the algorithm. Specifically, the TSA-LEO enhances the quality of solutions by updating their positions under some criteria. The TSA–LEO was further tested on a real-world problem, namely, segmentation based on the objective functions of Otsu and Kapur, and solved multilevel threshold problems while seeking the optimal thresholds for image separation. F. S. Gharehchopogh proposed an improved TSA with best-random mutation strategy (QLGCTSA) [44]. According to the QLGCTSA, the Quantum Rotation Gate mechanism, Lévy Mutation, Cauchy Mutation, and Gaussian Mutation were used to enhance the TSAs' performance. These methods have different functions, increasing the QLGCTSA's performance at a given stage in the optimization operation. The quantum rotation gate was proposed to increase the population diversity; Lévy flight enabled each individual to find better position and increase the ability to search deeper; Cauchy mutation was used to modify the capability to search in search agents or add neighbors of each generation; and Gaussian mutation helped the algorithm execute the global exploration. Table 1 is the comparison of improved algorithms.

Table 1. Comparison of algorithms involved in related work.

Year	Algorithm	Method Used	Application Area(s)	Shortcoming
2013	CS [36]	Lévy flight	Global optimization	poor global exploration ability
2018	LWOA [37]	Lévy flight	Global optimization	
2012	FPA [38]	Lévy flight	Nonlinear design benchmark and global optimization	
2017	LF-BP-GWO [39]	Lévy flight Back propagation	Neural network	poor global exploration ability and running slow
2010	CABC [29]	Chaotic mapping	Global numerical optimization	poor solution accuracy
2022	ISCA [40]	Singer chaotic map simulated annealing	Feature selection problem for Hadith classification	
2012	CICA [41]	Chaotic mapping	Truss structures design problem	
2014	CKH [42]	Chaotic mapping	Global optimization	
2021	TSA-LEO [43]	Local escape operator	Global optimization and Image segmentation	
2022	QLGCTSA [44]	Quantum Rotation Gate Lévy flight Cauchy Mutation Gaussian Mutation	Numerical optimization CEC2017 and engineering design problem	unbalanced exploration and development and high computational complexity

3. The Proposed CLTSA

3.1. TSA

The TSA was proposed by Kaur et al. after observing the social behavior of a tunicate searching for prey [45]. In the process of hunting, this marine invertebrate uses water jets and swarm intelligence to search for prey. Each tunicate can quickly discharge previously inhaled seawater through the siphons of the atrium, generating a kind of jet propulsion, which propels it rapidly. Moreover, tunicates display swarm intelligence when they share search information about the location of food. To establish the mathematical model of its jet propulsion mechanism, the tunicate is required to meet the following three important constraints:

- Avoiding clashes between each search agent.
- Each agent is guaranteed to move in the direction of the optimal individual.
- Make the search agents converge to the region near the optimal individual.

3.1.1. Avoiding Clashes between Each Search Agent

To prevent search agents from generating unnecessary clashes, the following formulas are used to calculate the new location of the agent:

$$\vec{A} = \frac{\vec{G}}{\vec{M}} \tag{1}$$

$$\vec{G} = c_2 + c_3 - \vec{F} \tag{2}$$

$$\vec{F} = 2 \cdot c_1 \tag{3}$$

where $\vec{A}$ is a vector used to find the new position of each agent; $\vec{G}$ is gravity; $\vec{F}$ is the water flow in the deep sea; and c_1, c_2, and c_3 are three random numbers in the interval 0 to 1 inclusive. $\vec{M}$ is a vector the value of which is expressed as the social strength between the search agents and is defined as:

$$\vec{M} = P_{\min} + c_1 \cdot (P_{\max} - P_{\min}) \tag{4}$$

where P_{min} and P_{max} indicate the incipient and secondary speeds that enable search agents to build social interaction. In this paper, P_{min} and P_{max} are set to 1 and 4 respectively.

3.1.2. Move in the Direction of the Optimal Individual

After resolving clashes between adjacent search agents, each one should move toward the neighboring individual having the highest fitness value. The mathematical model of moving towards the best search agent is established as:

$$\vec{PD} = \left| \vec{X_{best}} - r_{rand} \cdot \vec{X(t)} \right| \tag{5}$$

where $\vec{PD}$ is a vector that represents the spatial distance between the target food and the tunicate; $\vec{X_{best}}$ stands for food that is at the position of the current optimal individual; r_{rand} is a random number in the interval [0, 1]; and $\vec{X(t)}$ stores the location information of the current search agent in the t-th iteration.

3.1.3. Make the Search Agents Converge to the Optimal Individual

To make the search agents carry out sufficient local exploration near the optimal individual to find the optimal solution of the current iteration, their locations are calculated by Equation (6):

$$X(t) = \begin{cases} X_{best} - \vec{A} \cdot \vec{PD}, & if\ r_{rand} < 0.5 \\ X_{best} + \vec{A} \cdot \vec{PD}, & if\ r_{rand} \geq 0.5 \end{cases} \tag{6}$$

At iteration t, each search agent explores the region near the optimal individual X_{best} and assigns the result to $X(t)$ to update its position.

3.1.4. Swarm Behavior

The swarm behavior of the tunicate transmits location information between the search agents. This mechanism is driven by the position of the current search agent in the next iteration and is obtained according to the position updated by the current search agent. This is done through the optimal individual and the position updated by the previous individual through swarm behavior. The mathematical model is defined as:

$$\vec{X_i}(t+1) = \begin{cases} \frac{\vec{X_i}(t) + \vec{X_{i-1}}(t+1)}{2+c_1} & if\ i > 1 \\ \vec{X_i}(t) & if\ i = 1 \end{cases} \tag{7}$$

where $i = 1, \ldots, N$, N is the size of the tunicate population, $\vec{X_i}(t+1)$ is the position of the current search agent in the next iteration, $\vec{X_{i-1}}(t+1)$ is the position of the previous search agent in the next iteration, and $\vec{X_i}(t)$ is computed by Equation (6).

To illustrate the detailed process of the TSA, the main steps to update the positions of search agents are listed below:

Step 1: Initialize the original population of search agents $\vec{X}$.

Step 2: Assign values to the max-iterations and other initial parameters.

Step 3: Compute the fitness value of each tunicate and select the individual with the best fitness value as the optimal search agent.

Step 4: Update the location of each search agent by Equation (7).

Step 5: Keep each search agent in the search space.

Step 6: Calculate the fitness value of each updated search agent; if there is a better individual than the previous optimal search agent in the population, update $\vec{X_{best}}$.

Step 7: If the maximum iteration is reached, then the procedures stop. Otherwise, continue with steps 4–7.

Step 8: Print the best individual (X_{best}) so far.

3.2. Lévy Flight

Lévy flight is a random walk strategy whose step size satisfies the Lévy distribution [46]. Having stable distribution with infinite mean value and divergent variance, it enables the search agents to generate a long jump distance during exploration. Another important advantage of the Lévy flight strategy is its combination of global exploration and exploitation. When search agents walk randomly, there are usually more small step sizes and a handful of large step sizes; therefore, the Lévy flight strategy not only helps the search agents to carry out a local search by jumping in small step sizes near the optimal solution but also enable the search agents to fully explore the unknown area of the search space by jumping in large step sizes. Above all, the small step sizes random walk ensures that the search agents carefully explore the area around the best individual and improve the possibility of the population's position in the search space. In addition, exploration capability and mutation reflect the advantage in the global exploration. The Lévy flight strategy is mathematically defined as [47]:

$$L(s,\gamma,\mu) = \begin{cases} \sqrt{\frac{\gamma}{2\pi}} \cdot exp\left[-\frac{\gamma}{2(s-\mu)}\right] \frac{1}{(s-\mu)^{\frac{3}{2}}} & , 0 < \mu < s < \infty \\ 0 & , otherwise \end{cases} \tag{8}$$

where s is the samples; γ is a transmission parameter; and μ is the minimum step size. When $s \to \infty$, the above formula can be simplified as:

$$L(s,\gamma,\mu) \approx \sqrt{\frac{\gamma}{2\pi}} \cdot \frac{1}{s^{\frac{3}{2}}} \tag{9}$$

The Equation (9) is transformed into a Fourier transform:

$$F(k) = exp\left[-\alpha|k|^{\beta}\right], 0 < \beta \leq 2 \tag{10}$$

where α is a transmission parameter. In general, the analytical form of Equation (10) is described as follows:

$$L(s) = \frac{1}{\pi} \int_0^{\infty} exp\left[-\alpha|q|^{\beta}\right] \cos(qs)dq \tag{11}$$

$$L(s) \to \frac{\alpha\beta\Gamma(\beta)\sin\left(\frac{\pi\beta}{2}\right)}{\pi|s|^{1+\beta}}, s \to \infty \tag{12}$$

where $\Gamma(\beta)$ is the Gamma Function. In most cases, the most direct and effective method of symmetric, stable Lévy distribution is to use the Mantegna algorithm, which generates a random step size that satisfies the Lévy distribution. The random step size is calculated as follows [48,49]:

$$S = \frac{u}{|v|^{\frac{1}{\beta}}} \tag{13}$$

where u and v satisfy the following normal distribution [47]:

$$u \sim \left(0, {\sigma_u}^2\right), \qquad v \sim \left(0, {\sigma_v}^2\right) \tag{14}$$

$$\sigma_u = \left[\frac{\Gamma(1+\beta) \cdot \sin\left(\frac{\pi\beta}{2}\right)}{\Gamma\left[\frac{1+\beta}{2}\right]\beta \cdot 2^{\beta-\frac{1}{2}}}\right]^{\frac{1}{\beta}} \tag{15}$$

$$\sigma_v = 1 \tag{16}$$

where $0 < \beta < 2$ is a parameter that controls the shape of the distribution. In general, β directly affects the balance between development capability and exploration capability.

Figure 1 displays the Lévy flight trajectory of continuous moving 500 times with different β in a two-dimensional space. The study found that the range of step sizes is registered with maximal values in the range of $10^2 \times [-14, 2]$ for the x and $10^2 \times [-2, 12]$ for the y dimension when β = 1; the smallest in the range of $10^{-15} \times [-2, 10]$ for the x and $10^{-15} \times [-6, 2]$ for y dimension when β = 2; and kept a balance when β = 1.5 with range $[-100, 0]$ for the x and $[-10, 80]$ for the y dimension. Hence, β was set to 1.5 in this research. The factor S depended on the dimension of the problem to be solved; otherwise, the Lévy flight strategy showed high aggressiveness and generated solutions beyond the scope of the problem. It is obvious that the Lévy Flight strategy generates both small-step random walks and large-step random jumps in the search space, simultaneously taking into account development and exploration.

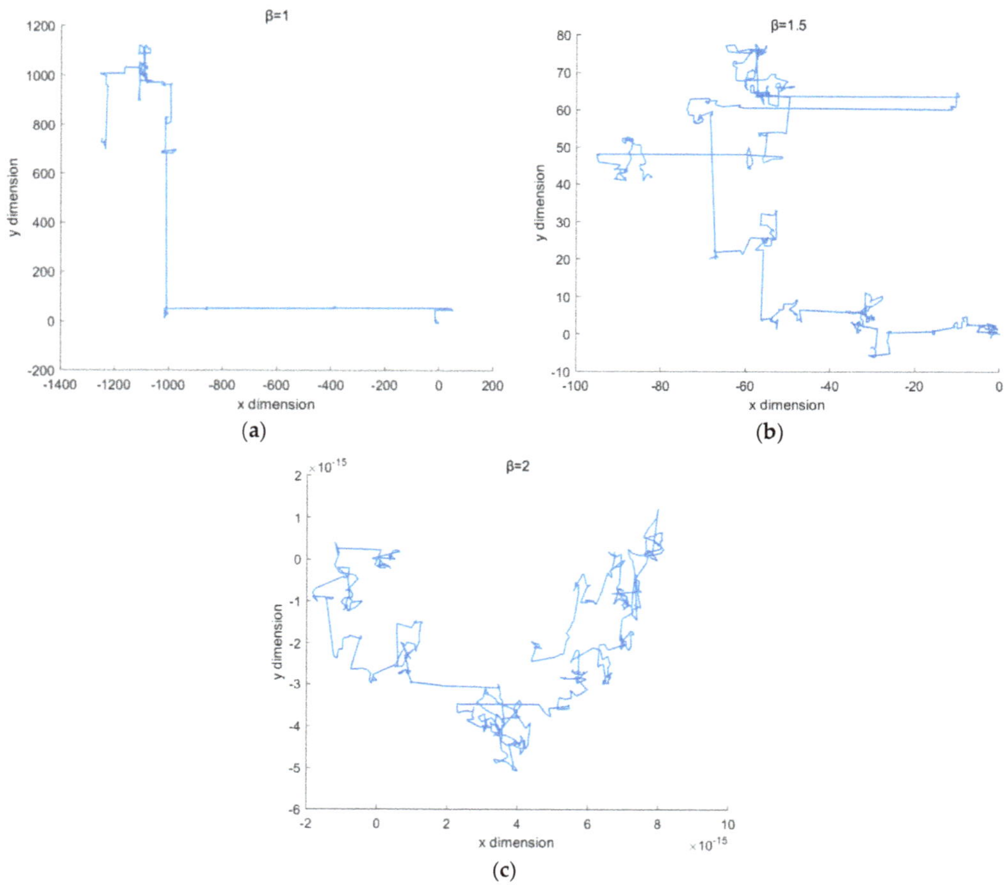

Figure 1. Lévy flight track in a two-dimensional search space with different β. (**a**) β = 1; (**b**) β = 1.5; (**c**) β = 2.

3.3. Chaotic Maps

Chaotic mapping is a mechanism used to generate random chaotic sequences generated by a simple deterministic system. These sequences have the characteristics of nonlinearity, ergodicity, non-repeatability, and randomness [50]. Therefore, chaotic sequences help search agents explore a search space more fully, make the algorithm escape from the local optimal solution, and increase the diversity of the population. In the field of optimization algorithms, chaotic maps are often more advantageous than pseudo-random number generators for generate chaotic numbers between 0 and 1 [51]. The common mapping functions are listed below, and their distribution graphs are shown in Figure 2:

- Chebyshev map

  The mapping function of the Chebyshev map is defined as follows [52]:

$$x_{k+1} = \cos\left(\alpha \cos^{-1} x_k\right) \tag{17}$$

where α is a control parameter of the Chebyshev map.

- Circle map

The Circle map could be denoted by Equation (18) [53]:

$$x_{k+1} = x_k + \beta - \left(\frac{\alpha}{2\pi}\sin(2\pi x_k)\right) mod(1) \tag{18}$$

when α is set to 0.5 and β is set to 0.2, the circle map could generate stochastic numbers between 0 and 1.

- Gauss map

  The Gauss chaotic numbers are calculated by the following equation [54]:

$$x_{k+1} = \begin{cases} 0, & if\ x_k = 0 \\ \frac{1}{x_k} mod(1) & if\ x_k \neq 0 \end{cases} \tag{19}$$

- Iterative chaotic map with infinite collapses (ICMIC)

  The mapping function of the iterative map is listed below [55]:

$$x_{k+1} = \text{abs}\left(\sin\left(\frac{\alpha}{x_k}\right)\right) \tag{20}$$

where α is a parameter for controlling the chaotic map, and the iterative map could gain superior performance when α = 0.7.

- Logistic map

  The Logistic map is a one-dimensional nonlinear chaotic map and one of the most commonly used chaotic maps, and it is represented as follows [56]:

$$x_{k+1} = \alpha x_k(1 - x_k) \tag{21}$$

where α is a control parameter whose value is between 3.5 and 4 to make the Logistic map produce chaotic sequences. Generally, α is set to 4.

- Sine map

  The Sine map is a unimodal map, it is given in Equation (22) [32]:

$$x_{k+1} = \frac{\alpha}{4}\sin(\pi x_k) \tag{22}$$

where α. is a control parameter with a value range in $(0,\ 4]$.

- Singer map

  The mapping function of the Singer map is defined as follows [57]:

$$x_{k+1} = \alpha\left(7.86x_k - 23.31x_k^2 + 28.75x_k^3 - 13.203875x_k^4\right) \tag{23}$$

when the value of control parameter α is in (0.9,1.08), the Singer map could produce chaotic sequences.

- Sinusoidal map

  The chaotic numbers of the Sinusoidal map are computed as [56]:

$$x_{k+1} = \alpha x_k^2 \sin(\pi x_k) \tag{24}$$

where α is set to 2.3 to generate chaotic numbers.

- Tent map

The Tent map is shown by Equation (25) [58]:

$$x_{k+1} = \begin{cases} \dfrac{x_k}{\alpha} & x_k \leq \alpha \\ \dfrac{(1-x_k)}{1-\alpha} & \alpha < x_k \leq 1 \end{cases} \tag{25}$$

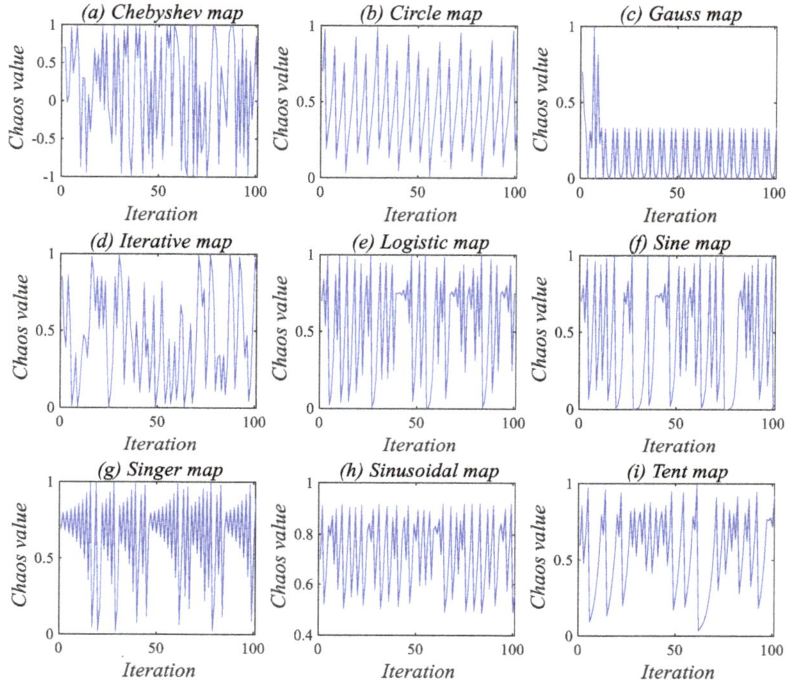

Figure 2. Distribution graphs of nine common chaotic maps.

3.4. Chaotic-Lévy Flight TSA

The current research shows that it is feasible to optimize the meta-heuristic algorithm by combining chaotic mapping and Lévy flight [59,60]. To solve the shortcomings of the TSA, such as falling easily into local optimal solutions and insufficient exploration [43], this section introduces an improved TSA from using the Chaotic-Lévy flight strategy (CLTSA). It allows search agents to find a suitable location in the area near the optimal solution, fully explore the search space, and avoid the emergence of a local optimal solution.

In this paper, the modification to the TSA is mainly reflected in Equation (6). In short, the aim was to improve its performance in the stage of convergence towards the candidate agent. Due to the randomness of chaotic mapping, the Chaotic-Lévy flight generates a more diverse population that jumps out of the local optimal solution. The convergence stage formula after introducing the Chaotic-Lévy flight strategy is shown as:

$$X(t) = \begin{cases} chaos(t) * levy. * \left(X_{best} - \vec{A} \cdot \vec{PD} \right), & if\ r_{rand} < 0.5 \\ chaos(t) * levy. * \left(X_{best} + \vec{A} \cdot \vec{PD} \right), & if\ r_{rand} \geq 0.5 \end{cases} \tag{26}$$

where t indicates that the current iteration number belongs to the t-th generation; $chaos(t)$ represents the chaotic value generated by the chaotic map in the t-th generation; $levy$ is the step size calculated by Lévy flight strategy; and the meanings of unexplained parameters are the same as those in Equation (6). Because the TSA search agents have difficulty searching randomly in the search space and have not explored the optimal solution, the algorithm easily falls into a local optimal solution. However, the small step sizes of the Chaotic-Lévy flight strategy make it possible for the search agents to move to a random position near the candidate solution, thus greatly improving the probability that the best solution will be chosen. In addition, the large step sizes of Chaotic-Lévy flight produce mutability, which occasionally enables search agents to appear elsewhere in the search space to explore other promising areas and avoid premature convergence. Moreover, the value between (0, 1) generated by a chaotic map can also prevent search agents from leaving the search space because of long-distance movement. Due to the randomness and non-repeatability of chaotic mapping, the Chaotic-Lévy flight strategy can generate steps at random, which enhances population diversity. Because of the diversity of chaotic maps, choosing a suitable one to combine with Lévy flight will be studied in the next section. The main process of the improved TSA can be summarized in the pseudo-code displayed in Algorithm 1, and the CLTSA process is illustrated in the flow chart in Figure 3, which describes the important steps of the algorithm.

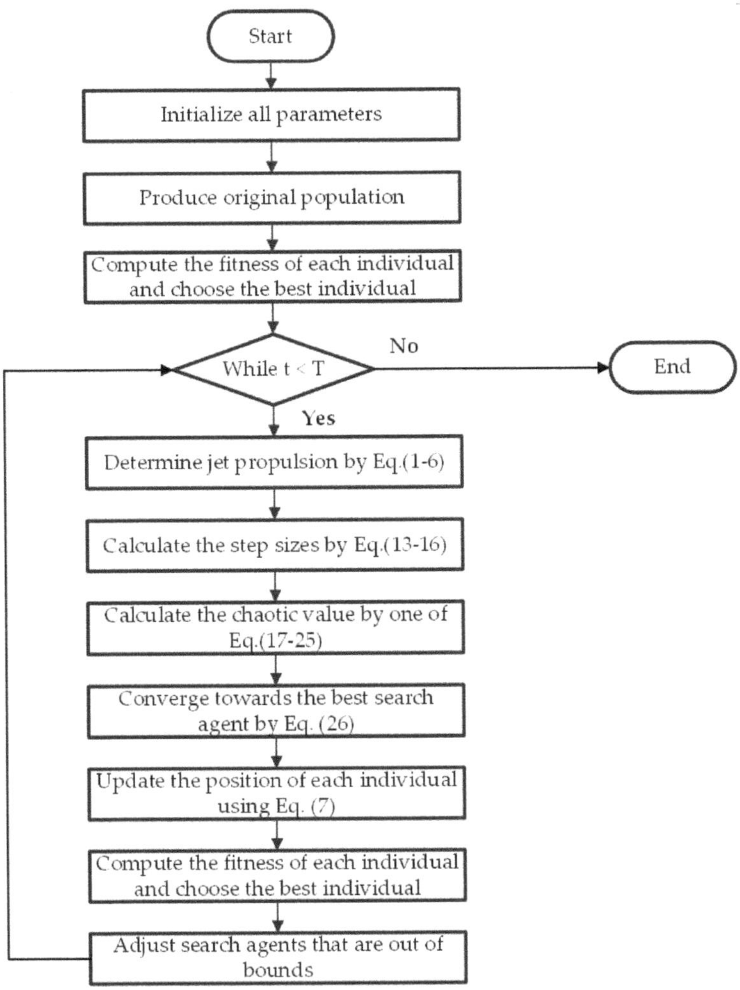

Figure 3. The flowchart of CLTSA.

Algorithm 1: Algorithm CLTSA

procedure CLTSA
Initialize the original population X and the $chaos(0)$ randomly
Initialize the parameters $\vec{A}$, $\vec{G}$, $\vec{F}$, $\vec{M}$, and maximum number of iterations T
set $P_{min} \leftarrow 1, P_{max} \leftarrow 4$
Calculate fitness of each individual, and choose the best candidate solution as X_{best}
  while $(t < T)$ **do**
    for $i \leftarrow 1$ *to* N **do**
/* **Jet propulsion behavior** */
      $c_1, c_2, c_3, r_{rand} \leftarrow Rand()$
      $\vec{M} \leftarrow \lfloor P_{min} + c_1 \cdot (P_{max} - P_{min}) \rfloor$ Equation (4)
      $\vec{F} \leftarrow 2 \cdot c_1$ Equation (3)
      $\vec{G} \leftarrow c_2 + c_3 - \vec{F}$ Equation (2)
      $\vec{A} \leftarrow \frac{\vec{G}}{\vec{M}}$ Equation (1)
      $\vec{PD} \leftarrow abs\left(\vec{X_{best}} - r_{rand} \cdot \vec{X(t)}\right)$ Equation (5)
      $chaos(t) \leftarrow F_{Tent\ map}(chaos(t-1))$ Equation (17)–(25)
      $levy \leftarrow F_{levy\ flight}(D)$ Equation (13)–(16)
/* **Swarm behavior** */
      if $i = 1$
        if $r_{rand} < 0.5$
          $X_i(t+1) \leftarrow X_{best} - \vec{A} \cdot \vec{PD}$ Equation (6)
        else
          $X_i(t+1) \leftarrow X_{best} + \vec{A} \cdot \vec{PD}$
        end if
      else
        if $r_{rand} < 0.5$
          $X_i(t) \leftarrow chaos(t) * levy. * \left(X_{best} - \vec{A} \cdot \vec{PD}\right)$ Equation (26)
        else
          $X_i(t) \leftarrow chaos(t) * levy. * \left(X_{best} + \vec{A} \cdot \vec{PD}\right)$
        end if
        $X_i(t+1) \leftarrow \frac{(X_i(t) + X_{i-1}(t+1))}{(2+c_1)}$ Equation (7)
    end for
    Calculate fitness of each individual, and choose the best solution as X_{best}
    $t \leftarrow t + 1$
  end while
return X_{best}
end procedure

3.5. *Complexity Analysis of CLTSA*

Complexity is an important indicator for evaluating the performance of an algorithm: time complexity estimates running time, and space complexity represents the amount of solution space required. This subsection evaluates the time and space complexity of the CLTSA.

3.5.1. Time Complexity

In the initialization phase, the algorithm generates the original population containing N search agents for a problem with dimension D, so the time complexity of the initialization is $O(N \times D)$. Moreover, CLTSA requires $O(T \times N \times D)$ time to compute the fitness of each individual, where T indicates the maximum number of iterations. Finally, $O(M)$ time is used to execute the main steps, where M denotes the number of jet propulsion and swarm behaviors. Therefore, the overall time complexity of CLTSA is $O(T \times N \times M \times D)$.

3.5.2. Space Complexity

The number of solution spaces required by CLTSA is N search agents generated for D-dimensional problems in the initialization phase. Hence, the space complexity is estimated to be $O(N \times D)$.

4. Experimental Results and Analysis

In the field of meta-heuristic algorithms, using benchmark functions with different characteristics is the most common method for measuring algorithmic performance. These functions can reflect the convergence speed and value of algorithms to evaluate its exploration and development capabilities. To control the accuracy of the experimental results, each algorithm runs independently 30 times on the same software and computer. The software for coding the proposed algorithm is MATLAB 2020a, and the algorithm was run on a computer with AMD Ryzen 7 4800H processor and 16 GB RAM.

4.1. Benchmark Test Functions

The main characteristics of benchmark function are modality, dimensionality, separability, differentiability, and continuity. According to the above characteristics, benchmark functions can be classified to evaluate the performance of algorithms from different perspectives. To comprehensively assess the property of CLTSA, a set of benchmark functions containing all the above features is used [11]. The test set is divided into two groups based on the number of minimums of benchmark functions in a given interval:

1. Unimodal benchmark functions: The detailed information of the unimodal functions test set is listed in Table 2, and their mathematical expressions are shown in Table A1 in Appendix A [11].
2. Multimodal benchmark functions: The detailed information of the test set which is composed of 14 multimodal benchmark functions is listed in Table 3, and their mathematical expressions are shown in Table A2 in Appendix A [11].

Table 2. Unimodal benchmark functions.

Function	Range	Dim	F_{min}
F1-Sphere	[−100, 100]	50	0
F2-Quartic Noise	[−1.28, 1.28]	20	0
F3-Powell Sum	[−1, 1]	50	0
F4-Schwefel's 2.20	[−100, 100]	50	0
F5-Schwefel's 2.21	[−100, 100]	50	0
F6-Schwefel's 1.20	[−100, 100]	50	0
F7-Schwefel's 2.22	[−100, 100]	50	0
F8-Schwefel's 2.23	[−10, 10]	50	0
F9-RosenBrock	[−30, 30]	50	0
F10-Brown	[−1, 4]	50	0
F11-Dixon and Price	[−10, 10]	50	0
F12-Powell Singular	[−4, 5]	50	0
F13-Zakharow	[−5, 10]	50	0
F14-Three-Hump Camel	[−5, 5]	2	0
F15-Matyas	[−10, 10]	2	0
F16-WayBurn Seader 3	[−500, 500]	2	21.35

4.2. Comparison of Chaotic Maps

The logistic map is used by most optimization algorithms based on the chaos mechanism in current research [58], but its chaotic values are generally distributed in the intervals [0, 0.1] and [0.9, 1]. This uneven traversal affects the optimization efficiency of the algorithm [43]. To select the most suitable chaotic map, the above nine common chaotic maps are combined with the Lévy flight strategy to optimize the TSA. Then, the 30 well-known unimodal test functions and multi-modal test functions (see the Appendix A) are used to evaluate the algorithm's performance. The run results are shown in Tables 4 and 5.

Table 3. Multimodal benchmark functions.

Function	Range	Dim	F_{min}
F17-Rastrigin	[5.12, 5.12]	50	0
F18-Periodic	[−10, 10]	50	0
F19-Alpine N. 1	[−10, 10]	50	0
F20-Xin-She Yang	[−5, 5]	50	0
F21-Ackley	[−32, 32]	50	0
F22-Trignometric 2	[−500, 500]	50	1
F23-Salomon	[−100, 100]	50	0
F24-Griewank	[−100, 100]	50	0
F25-Gen. Penalized	[−50, 50]	50	0
F26-Penalized	[−50, 50]	50	0
F27-Egg Crate	[−5, 5]	2	0
F28-Bird	[-2π, 2π]	2	−106.7645
F29-Goldstein Price	[−2, 2]	2	3
F30-Bartels Conn	[−500, 500]	2	1

Table 4. Results of 9 chaotic maps combined with Lévy flight on unimodal benchmark functions.

Fn	Criteria	Chebyshev	Circle	Gauss	Iterative	Logistic	Sine	Singer	Sinusoidal	Tent
F1	Mean	**0.00E+00**	**0.00E+00**	**0.00E+00**	**0.00E+00**	**0.00E+00**	**0.00E+00**	**0.00E+00**	**0.00E+00**	**0.00E+00**
	Best	**0.00E+00**	**0.00E+00**	**0.00E+00**	**0.00E+00**	**0.00E+00**	**0.00E+00**	**0.00E+00**	**0.00E+00**	**0.00E+00**
	Std	**0.00E+00**	**0.00E+00**	**0.00E+00**	**0.00E+00**	**0.00E+00**	**0.00E+00**	**0.00E+00**	**0.00E+00**	**0.00E+00**
F2	Mean	4.45E−05	1.59E−04	2.16E−05	2.09E−05	8.52E−05	4.65E−05	1.04E−04	6.45E−05	**2.04E−05**
	Best	2.51E−07	5.10E−06	1.57E−06	8.60E−07	8.85E−06	1.34E−05	1.17E−06	1.07E−06	**5.05E−07**
	Std	5.32E−05	9.45E−05	2.18E−05	1.42E−04	4.02E−05	3.50E−05	3.57E−05	3.14E−05	**1.48E−05**
F3	Mean	**0.00E+00**	**0.00E+00**	**0.00E+00**	**0.00E+00**	**0.00E+00**	**0.00E+00**	**0.00E+00**	**0.00E+00**	**0.00E+00**
	Best	**0.00E+00**	**0.00E+00**	**0.00E+00**	**0.00E+00**	**0.00E+00**	**0.00E+00**	**0.00E+00**	**0.00E+00**	**0.00E+00**
	Std	**0.00E+00**	**0.00E+00**	**0.00E+00**	**0.00E+00**	**0.00E+00**	**0.00E+00**	**0.00E+00**	**0.00E+00**	**0.00E+00**
F4	Mean	4.17E−228	1.97E−205	**0.00E+00**	1.26E−179	**0.00E+00**	**0.00E+00**	**0.00E+00**	**0.00E+00**	**0.00E+00**
	Best	1.48E−231	3.23E−217	**0.00E+00**	1.91E−180	**0.00E+00**	**0.00E+00**	**0.00E+00**	**0.00E+00**	**0.00E+00**
	Std	0.00E+00	0.00E+00	**0.00E+00**	0.00E+00	**0.00E+00**	**0.00E+00**	**0.00E+00**	**0.00E+00**	**0.00E+00**
F5	Mean	1.28E−210	8.66E−187	**0.00E+00**	3.67E−157	**0.00E+00**	**0.00E+00**	**0.00E+00**	**0.00E+00**	**0.00E+00**
	Best	3.79E−216	2.01E−192	**0.00E+00**	3.38E−161	**0.00E+00**	**0.00E+00**	**0.00E+00**	**0.00E+00**	**0.00E+00**
	Std	0.00E+00	0.00E+00	**0.00E+00**	3.66E−152	**0.00E+00**	**0.00E+00**	**0.00E+00**	**0.00E+00**	**0.00E+00**
F6	Mean	**0.00E+00**	**0.00E+00**	**0.00E+00**	6.08E−306	**0.00E+00**	**0.00E+00**	**0.00E+00**	**0.00E+00**	**0.00E+00**
	Best	**0.00E+00**	**0.00E+00**	**0.00E+00**	6.08E−306	**0.00E+00**	**0.00E+00**	**0.00E+00**	**0.00E+00**	**0.00E+00**
	Std	**0.00E+00**	**0.00E+00**	**0.00E+00**	0.00E+00	**0.00E+00**	**0.00E+00**	**0.00E+00**	**0.00E+00**	**0.00E+00**
F7	Mean	7.33E−233	3.48E−210	**0.00E+00**	3.06E−178	**0.00E+00**	**0.00E+00**	**0.00E+00**	**0.00E+00**	**0.00E+00**
	Best	2.58E−233	6.75E−214	**0.00E+00**	4.83E−180	**0.00E+00**	**0.00E+00**	**0.00E+00**	**0.00E+00**	**0.00E+00**
	Std	0.00E+00	0.00E+00	**0.00E+00**	0.00E+00	**0.00E+00**	**0.00E+00**	**0.00E+00**	**0.00E+00**	**0.00E+00**
F8	Mean	**0.00E+00**	**0.00E+00**	**0.00E+00**	**0.00E+00**	**0.00E+00**	**0.00E+00**	**0.00E+00**	**0.00E+00**	**0.00E+00**
	Best	**0.00E+00**	**0.00E+00**	**0.00E+00**	**0.00E+00**	**0.00E+00**	**0.00E+00**	**0.00E+00**	**0.00E+00**	**0.00E+00**
	Std	**0.00E+00**	**0.00E+00**	**0.00E+00**	**0.00E+00**	**0.00E+00**	**0.00E+00**	**0.00E+00**	**0.00E+00**	**0.00E+00**
F9	Mean	4.87E+01	4.88E+01	4.89E+01	4.89E+01	4.89E+01	4.89E+01	4.90E+01	4.89E+01	**4.72E+01**
	Best	4.81E+01	4.81E+01	4.87E+01	4.81E+01	4.81E+01	4.87E+01	4.81E+01	4.88E+01	**4.72E+01**
	Std	2.44E−01	2.50E−01	7.79E−02	2.54E−01	2.66E−01	9.36E−02	2.51E−01	6.45E−02	**5.32E−03**
F10	Mean	**0.00E+00**	**0.00E+00**	**0.00E+00**	**0.00E+00**	**0.00E+00**	**0.00E+00**	**0.00E+00**	**0.00E+00**	**0.00E+00**
	Best	**0.00E+00**	**0.00E+00**	**0.00E+00**	**0.00E+00**	**0.00E+00**	**0.00E+00**	**0.00E+00**	**0.00E+00**	**0.00E+00**
	Std	**0.00E+00**	**0.00E+00**	**0.00E+00**	**0.00E+00**	**0.00E+00**	**0.00E+00**	**0.00E+00**	**0.00E+00**	**0.00E+00**
F11	Mean	6.67E−01	6.67E−01	6.67E−01	6.67E−01	6.67E−01	6.67E−01	6.67E−01	6.67E−01	**6.67E−01**
	Best	6.67E−01	6.67E−01	6.67E−01	6.67E−01	6.67E−01	6.67E−01	6.67E−01	6.67E−01	**6.67E−01**
	Std	2.78E−08	9.92E−06	2.93E−08	4.24E−08	2.68E−05	2.08E−05	1.91E−08	1.92E−08	**1.69E−08**
F12	Mean	**0.00E+00**	**0.00E+00**	**0.00E+00**	**0.00E+00**	**0.00E+00**	**0.00E+00**	**0.00E+00**	**0.00E+00**	**0.00E+00**
	Best	**0.00E+00**	**0.00E+00**	**0.00E+00**	**0.00E+00**	**0.00E+00**	**0.00E+00**	**0.00E+00**	**0.00E+00**	**0.00E+00**
	Std	**0.00E+00**	**0.00E+00**	**0.00E+00**	**0.00E+00**	**0.00E+00**	**0.00E+00**	**0.00E+00**	**0.00E+00**	**0.00E+00**
F13	Mean	**0.00E+00**	3.10E−165	**0.00E+00**	3.77E−260	**0.00E+00**	**0.00E+00**	**0.00E+00**	**0.00E+00**	**0.00E+00**
	Best	**0.00E+00**	3.69E−215	**0.00E+00**	8.92E−273	**0.00E+00**	**0.00E+00**	**0.00E+00**	**0.00E+00**	**0.00E+00**
	Std	**0.00E+00**	0.00E+00	**0.00E+00**	0.00E+00	**0.00E+00**	**0.00E+00**	**0.00E+00**	**0.00E+00**	**0.00E+00**

Table 4. *Cont.*

Fn	Criteria	Chebyshev	Circle	Gauss	Iterative	Logistic	Sine	Singer	Sinusoidal	Tent
F14	Mean	**0.00E+00**	**0.00E+00**	**0.00E+00**	**0.00E+00**	**0.00E+00**	**0.00E+00**	**0.00E+00**	**0.00E+00**	**0.00E+00**
	Best	**0.00E+00**	**0.00E+00**	**0.00E+00**	**0.00E+00**	**0.00E+00**	**0.00E+00**	**0.00E+00**	**0.00E+00**	**0.00E+00**
	Std	**0.00E+00**	**0.00E+00**	**0.00E+00**	**0.00E+00**	**0.00E+00**	**0.00E+00**	**0.00E+00**	**0.00E+00**	**0.00E+00**
F15	Mean	**0.00E+00**	**0.00E+00**	**0.00E+00**	**0.00E+00**	**0.00E+00**	**0.00E+00**	**0.00E+00**	**0.00E+00**	**0.00E+00**
	Best	**0.00E+00**	**0.00E+00**	**0.00E+00**	**0.00E+00**	**0.00E+00**	**0.00E+00**	**0.00E+00**	**0.00E+00**	**0.00E+00**
	Std	**0.00E+00**	**0.00E+00**	**0.00E+00**	**0.00E+00**	**0.00E+00**	**0.00E+00**	**0.00E+00**	**0.00E+00**	**0.00E+00**
F16	Mean	1.91E+01	1.91E+01	1.91E+01	1.92E+01	1.49E+02	1.91E+01	1.91E+01	1.49E+02	**1.91E+01**
	Best	1.91E+01	1.91E+01	1.91E+01	1.91E+01	1.91E+01	1.91E+01	1.91E+01	1.91E+01	**1.91E+01**
	Std	1.54E−02	1.63E−02	1.82E−02	1.56E−02	9.88E+01	1.76E+02	2.17E−02	2.37E+01	**1.30E−02**

Table 5. Results of 9 chaotic maps combined with Lévy flight on multimodal benchmark functions.

Fn	Criteria	Chebyshev	Circle	Gauss	Iterative	Logistic	Sine	Singer	Sinusoidal	Tent
F17	Mean	**0.00E+00**	**0.00E+00**	**0.00E+00**	**0.00E+00**	**0.00E+00**	**0.00E+00**	**0.00E+00**	**0.00E+00**	**0.00E+00**
	Best	**0.00E+00**	**0.00E+00**	**0.00E+00**	**0.00E+00**	**0.00E+00**	**0.00E+00**	**0.00E+00**	**0.00E+00**	**0.00E+00**
	Std	**0.00E+00**	**0.00E+00**	**0.00E+00**	**0.00E+00**	**0.00E+00**	**0.00E+00**	**0.00E+00**	**0.00E+00**	**0.00E+00**
F18	Mean	9.00E−01	1.26E+01	**9.00E−01**	9.00E−01	9.00E−01	9.00E−01	9.00E−01	9.00E−01	9.00E−01
	Best	9.00E−01	1.13E+01	**9.00E−01**	9.00E−01	9.00E−01	9.00E−01	9.00E−01	9.00E−01	9.00E−01
	Std	8.46E−16	5.64E−01	**3.64E−16**	8.49E−16	4.92E−16	3.77E−16	7.31E−16	6.97E−16	4.52E−16
F19	Mean	1.91E−231	2.58E−211	**0.00E+00**	5.57E−182	**0.00E+00**	**0.00E+00**	**0.00E+00**	**0.00E+00**	**0.00E+00**
	Best	7.41E−234	1.89E−218	**0.00E+00**	3.14E−182	**0.00E+00**	**0.00E+00**	**0.00E+00**	**0.00E+00**	**0.00E+00**
	Std	0.00E+00	0.00E+00	**0.00E+00**	0.00E+00	**0.00E+00**	**0.00E+00**	**0.00E+00**	**0.00E+00**	**0.00E+00**
F20	Mean	**0.00E+00**	1.93E−218	**0.00E+00**	**0.00E+00**	**0.00E+00**	**0.00E+00**	**0.00E+00**	**0.00E+00**	**0.00E+00**
	Best	**0.00E+00**	3.76E−260	**0.00E+00**	**0.00E+00**	**0.00E+00**	**0.00E+00**	**0.00E+00**	**0.00E+00**	**0.00E+00**
	Std	**0.00E+00**	1.11E−57	**0.00E+00**	**0.00E+00**	**0.00E+00**	**0.00E+00**	**0.00E+00**	**0.00E+00**	**0.00E+00**
F21	Mean	**−8.88E−16**	**−8.88E−16**	**−8.88E−16**	**−8.88E−16**	**−8.88E−16**	**−8.88E−16**	**−8.88E−16**	**−8.88E−16**	**−8.88E−16**
	Best	**−8.88E−16**	**−8.88E−16**	**−8.88E−16**	**−8.88E−16**	**−8.88E−16**	**−8.88E−16**	**−8.88E−16**	**−8.88E−16**	**−8.88E−16**
	Std	**0.00E+00**	**0.00E+00**	**0.00E+00**	**0.00E+00**	**0.00E+00**	**0.00E+00**	**0.00E+00**	**0.00E+00**	**0.00E+00**
F22	Mean	1.49E+02	1.48E+02	1.61E+02	1.54E+02	1.63E+02	1.48E+02	1.61E+02	**1.46E+02**	1.53E+02
	Best	1.42E+02	1.38E+02	1.38E+02	1.28E+02	1.23E+02	1.29E+02	1.37E+02	**1.36E+02**	1.30E+02
	Std	4.81E+01	6.50E+00	7.57E+00	6.99E+00	4.81E+01	4.95E+01	7.94E+00	**7.82E+00**	9.19E+00
F23	Mean	0.00E+00	1.79E−145	**0.00E+00**	3.98E−153	**0.00E+00**	**0.00E+00**	0.00E+00	**0.00E+00**	**0.00E+00**
	Best	0.00E+00	0.00E+00	**0.00E+00**	0.00E+00	**0.00E+00**	**0.00E+00**	0.00E+00	**0.00E+00**	**0.00E+00**
	Std	1.82E−02	5.07E−02	**0.00E+00**	3.79E−02	**0.00E+00**	**0.00E+00**	1.82E−02	**0.00E+00**	**0.00E+00**
F24	Mean	**0.00E+00**	**0.00E+00**	**0.00E+00**	**0.00E+00**	**0.00E+00**	**0.00E+00**	**0.00E+00**	**0.00E+00**	**0.00E+00**
	Best	**0.00E+00**	**0.00E+00**	**0.00E+00**	**0.00E+00**	**0.00E+00**	**0.00E+00**	**0.00E+00**	**0.00E+00**	**0.00E+00**
	Std	**0.00E+00**	**0.00E+00**	**0.00E+00**	**0.00E+00**	**0.00E+00**	**0.00E+00**	**0.00E+00**	**0.00E+00**	**0.00E+00**
F25	Mean	4.90E+00	**4.73E+00**	4.90E+00	4.80E+00	4.99E+00	4.99E+00	4.90E+00	4.90E+00	4.88E+00
	Best	4.51E+00	**4.35E+00**	4.80E+00	4.53E+00	4.84E+00	4.98E+00	4.80E+00	4.80E+00	4.70E+00
	Std	9.90E−02	**9.85E−02**	4.02E−02	8.54E−02	3.79E−02	4.82E−03	4.13E−02	3.29E−02	4.34E−02
F26	Mean	9.11E−01	7.47E−01	9.93E−01	**5.76E−01**	1.29E+00	1.05E+00	7.85E−01	1.06E+00	9.19E−01
	Best	6.94E−01	6.08E−01	5.60E−01	**5.48E−01**	4.82E−01	4.23E−01	6.39E−01	6.59E−01	5.23E−01
	Std	1.11E−01	1.68E−01	1.54E−01	**1.56E−01**	2.80E−01	2.09E−01	1.30E−01	2.04E−01	1.89E−01
F27	Mean	**0.00E+00**	**0.00E+00**	**0.00E+00**	**0.00E+00**	**0.00E+00**	**0.00E+00**	**0.00E+00**	**0.00E+00**	**0.00E+00**
	Best	**0.00E+00**	**0.00E+00**	**0.00E+00**	**0.00E+00**	**0.00E+00**	**0.00E+00**	**0.00E+00**	**0.00E+00**	**0.00E+00**
	Std	**0.00E+00**	**0.00E+00**	**0.00E+00**	**0.00E+00**	**0.00E+00**	**0.00E+00**	**0.00E+00**	**0.00E+00**	**0.00E+00**
F28	Mean	−106.722	−106.727	−106.73	−106.74	−87.3035	−106.619	−106.688	−106.716	**−106.748**
	Best	−106.764	−106.763	−106.764	−106.764	−106.764	−106.761	−106.763	−106.764	**−106.763**
	Std	4.04E−02	5.28E−02	2.12E−02	4.33E−02	8.37E+00	6.71E+00	7.75E−02	3.42E−02	**2.57E−02**
F29	Mean	3.00E+00	3.00E+00	3.00E+00	3.00E+00	3.00E+00	3.01E+00	3.00E+00	3.00E+00	**3.00E+00**
	Best	3.00E+00	3.00E+00	3.00E+00	3.00E+00	3.00E+00	3.00E+00	3.00E+00	3.00E+00	**3.00E+00**
	Std	2.23E−05	3.53E−04	5.85E−05	1.13E−05	6.85E+00	1.60E+01	3.69E−04	1.78E−04	**9.53E−16**
F30	Mean	8.23E−02	1.19E−01	7.87E−02	9.06E−02	5.93E+01	8.97E−01	6.00E+01	**6.45E−03**	8.59E+00
	Best	3.17E−02	2.30E−02	3.83E−02	2.30E−02	1.56E−02	1.85E−02	5.16E−03	**2.76E−03**	8.49E−03
	Std	1.50E+01	1.46E+00	4.24E+01	9.77E−01	4.80E+01	5.73E+01	1.81E+01	**1.50E+01**	2.03E+01

To ensure the fairness and validity of the experimental results, each Chaotic-Lévy TSA was run 30 times independently, and the maximum number of iterations, population size, and problem dimension were set to 500, 50, and 50 respectively. The mean was the mean value of the 30 optimal solutions. Best was the optimal value among the experimental results obtained by running an algorithm 30 times; std was standard deviation. In this paper, the ranking rule of algorithm performance was mean, best, and std in that order. The algorithm with the best results for each benchmark function is emphasized in bold.

From the experimental results, the Tent-Lévy flight TSA (TLTSA) had far better optimization compared to the Chaotic-Lévy TSAs (CLTSAs). Among the 30 benchmark functions, the TLTSA had 25 optimal solutions more than the CLTSAs and ranked first. In the following research, it was used for comparative experiments and to optimize solutions to engineering problems.

4.3. Parameter Settings of TLTSA and Other Algorithms

The TSA relies on two main parameters to build social interactions, P_{min} and P_{max}. P_{min} was taken as 1, 2, 3, 4 for the experiment and other parameter settings were kept unchanged. The study found that the TSA achieved the best performances when the value of P_{min} was set to 1. In the same way, P_{max} was taken as 1, 2, 3, 4 for the experiment and the other parameter settings were kept unchanged. The TSA achieved the best performances when the value of P_{max} was set to 4 [45]. The proposed TLTSA was compared with TSA and other metaheuristic algorithms, including grey wolf optimizer (GWO) [61], sine cosine algorithm (SCA) [62], sparrow search algorithm (SSA) [63], water circle algorithm (WCA) [8], whale optimization algorithm (WOA) [24], marine predators algorithm (MPA) [64], lighting search algorithm (LSA) [28], and hybrid glowworm swarm optimization (HGSO) [65]. The parameter settings of all algorithms are listed in Table 6, and all parameter values were derived from the literature.

Table 6. The main parameter settings of the algorithms that need to be compared and analyzed.

Algorithm	Parameter Setting
Common Settings	Population size: N = 50 maximum number of iterations: T = 500 Dimensions of problem: Dim = 50 Number of independent runs: $Repetition$ = 30
GWO	$\vec{a}$ decays from 2 to 0 $\vec{A}, \vec{C}$ are calculated by corresponding formulas
SCA	$a = 2$, $r_{1,2,3,4}$ are calculated by corresponding formulas
SSA	Q is a random number and $Q \sim N(\mu, \sigma^2)$ is a random number and $\beta \sim N(0, 1)$
WCA	C = 2 and μ = 0.1
WOA	$\vec{\alpha}$ decays from 2 to 0 b = 1
MPA	p = 0.5, $FADs$ = 0.2 CF is calculated by corresponding formulas
LSA	Channel time: ch_{time} = 10
HGSO	ρ = 0.4, γ = 0.6, β = 0.08, s = 0.03, CR = 0.9, λ = 0.9415
TSA	P_{min}= 1 and P_{max} = 4
TLTSA	P_{min}= 1 and P_{max} = 4 *lévy* and *chaos(t)* are calculated by corresponding formulas

4.4. Results and Analysis

4.4.1. Experimental Data Analysis

Since a fixed-dimensional function is closer to a real-world optimization problem, six were selected to verify TLTSA convergence speed and accuracy. These functions are listed in Table 7, and the mathematical expressions are detailed in Table A3 in the Appendix A.

Table 7. Fixed-dimension benchmark functions.

Function	Range	Dim	F_{min}
F1-Shekel's Foxholes	$[-65, 65]$	2	1
F2-Kowalik	$[-5, 5]$	4	0.0003075
F3-Hartman 3	$[0, 1]$	4	−3.86
F4-Shekel 1	$[0, 10]$	4	−10.1532
F5-Shekel 2	$[0, 10]$	4	−10.4029
F6-Shekel 3	$[0, 10]$	4	−10.5364

Because unimodal benchmark functions have only one global minimum, it is not only suitable for assessing development capability, but also for examining the algorithm convergence speed. According to the experimental data in Table 8, the TLTSA was more competitive in the unimodal benchmark functions compared to other algorithms. For F1, F3, F4, F5, F6, and F7, only the TLTSA quickly and accurately found the standard optimal value 0. In addition, the std was also zero, which showed that running TLTSA 30 times produced the best global solution and fully reflected its stability. For the other algorithms, it was difficult for them to find the global optimal solution with an order of magnitude less than −100, especially the SCA, SSA, and LSA. These three converged prematurely because they could not escape the local optimal solution. For F10, F12, F13, F14, and F15, although some of the other comparison algorithms also had good performance, there was still a large gap with the TLTSA, which quickly found the exact global optimal solution. For these unimodal benchmark functions, the order of magnitude of the mean value of the HGSO reached −100 even −200, and the std reached 0. However, the mean, best, and std of the TLTSA were all zero, which meant that the TLTSA had strong optimization capability and stability. From the comparison of these three criteria, it more carefully developed the vicinity of the optimal solution than did the HGSO, thereby enhancing the selectivity of the optimal solution. For F2, F9, and F11, although the best result of TLTSA is not optimal solution 0, it has the best mean value, optimal solution, and std among the algorithms selected for comparison. It was proven that the proposed TLTSA was indeed focused on exploration and exploitation to improve performance. For F8, although both the TLTSA and HGSO had the best calculation accuracy, the convergence curve indicates that the convergence speed of TLTSA was significantly better, showing that it has more exploration and exploitation advantages. For F16, TLTSA obtains the same global optimal solution as the other algorithms, but was slightly unstable. In addition, compared with the original TSA algorithm, the TLTSA had a greatly improved mean value and standard deviation as well as a high-er search accuracy. Overall, in the test of 16 unimodal benchmark functions, the TLTSA took first place 15 times and eighth once among 10 algorithms.

It was clearly better suited to solving precise engineering problems, and its higher sensitivity to unimodal benchmark functions proved a strong exploitation capability. The Tent-Lévy flight strategy generated a number of small step sizes with greater randomness, which made search agents explore the search space fully when converging towards the candidate solution, and improve the possibility of the optimal solution being selected. Tent-Lévy flight as a random-walk strategy efficiently enhanced the algorithm's exploration and exploitation abilities.

Table 8. Comparison of TLTSA with other optimization algorithms for unimodal benchmark functions.

Fn	Criteria	GWO	SCA	SSA	WCA	WOA	MPA	LSA	HGSO	LFPSO [47]	chTLBO [66]	TSA	TLTSA
F1	Mean	8.11E−24	5.78E+02	2.35E−03	9.98E−10	4.43E−83	5.10E−21	1.13E−04	4.52E−114	1.06E−04	7.32E−05	9.65E−18	**0.00E+00**
	Best	5.29E−25	2.13E+00	6.05E−05	6.97E−14	9.90E−93	6.88E−23	7.36E−08	6.97E−150		1.45E−06	7.93E−20	**0.00E+00**
	Std	1.10E−23	7.67E+02	2.17E−03	2.33E−09	2.19E−82	7.53E−21	3.07E−04	2.48E−113	1.58E−04		1.40E−17	**0.00E+00**
F2	Mean	2.12E−03	2.16E+00	3.41E−01	3.78E−02	2.55E−03	1.32E−03	7.88E−02	2.47E−04	4.34E−02	1.63E−01	1.14E−02	**4.03E−05**
	Best	8.10E−04	1.54E−01	1.67E−01	2.12E−02	1.34E−05	2.63E−04	5.21E−02	1.69E−05		7.61E−02	2.55E−03	**7.99E−07**
	Std	9.10E−04	2.55E+00	8.43E−02	1.26E−02	3.17E−03	6.51E−04	1.44E−02	2.46E−04	1.11E−02		4.85E−03	**4.00E−05**
F3	Mean	3.54E−107	6.52E−03	7.77E−07	2.23E−22	7.09E−124	8.98E−62	8.36E−32	5.16E−207			1.14E−75	**0.00E+00**
	Best	1.13E−118	1.56E−04	4.63E−08	6.84E−29	3.47E−153	5.70E−72	1.21E−39	1.45E−234	—	—	6.46E−92	**0.00E+00**
	Std	1.53E−106	1.15E−02	8.57E−07	7.45E−22	3.88E−123	3.66E−61	4.52E−31	0.00E+00			3.67E−75	**0.00E+00**
F4	Mean	1.10E−13	2.52E+00	4.22E+01	1.29E−04	8.52E−53	2.70E−11	7.13E−01	5.68E−71			1.25E−10	**0.00E+00**
	Best	7.13E−14	7.05E−02	1.27E+01	1.42E−05	3.87E−58	3.05E−12	3.24E−03	2.94E−75	—	—	4.08E−11	**0.00E+00**
	Std	3.95E−14	2.33E+00	2.47E+01	2.51E−04	2.54E−52	1.78E−11	8.78E−01	8.55E−71			8.80E−11	**0.00E+00**
F5	Mean	5.80E−05	6.33E+01	1.58E+01	2.98E+00	8.14E+01	2.93E−08	1.64E+01	3.03E−66	1.21E+01	2.10E−03	4.62E+00	**0.00E+00**
	Best	5.88E−06	4.21E+01	1.39E+01	8.40E−01	6.45E+01	1.52E−08	9.02E+00	2.73E−73		2.10E−03	6.55E−01	**0.00E+00**
	Std	6.34E−05	1.01E+01	1.61E+00	9.16E−01	9.43E+00	1.01E−08	4.59E+00	7.42E−66	6.22E+00		2.84E+00	**0.00E+00**
F6	Mean	5.43E−03	3.91E+04	4.64E+03	7.44E+00	1.52E+05	1.86E−02	2.84E+03	4.34E−126	1.18E+03	1.84E−02	2.11E+00	**0.00E+00**
	Best	3.01E−06	1.42E+04	1.46E+03	2.36E+00	7.99E+04	2.79E−04	1.25E+03	4.94E−144		1.30E−03	8.37E−03	**0.00E+00**
	Std	1.14E−02	1.50E+04	3.18E+03	4.92E+00	3.20E+04	2.74E−02	6.87E+02	2.31E−125	5.66E+02		3.51E+00	**0.00E+00**
F7	Mean	2.02E−13	3.64E+00	6.49E+28	1.74E+25	6.01E−53	2.79E−11	1.21E+02	1.19E−66	1.73E−03	1.00E−02	1.99E−10	**0.00E+00**
	Best	7.59E−14	1.44E−01	6.69E+08	7.88E−07	6.42E−59	5.29E−13	2.30E−01	1.58E−75		1.61E−01	2.70E−12	**0.00E+00**
	Std	9.92E−14	4.69E+00	3.35E+29	9.54E+25	2.97E−52	4.13E−11	1.47E+02	6.34E−66	4.53E−03		1.89E−10	**0.00E+00**
F8	Mean	6.74E−77	1.13E+08	1.13E−03	2.14E−25	9.77E−226	4.43E−94	1.68E−18	**0.00E+00**			3.87E−42	**0.00E+00**
	Best	2.32E−85	4.09E+06	8.06E−08	1.51E−34	3.93E−293	2.50E−101	6.12E−24	**0.00E+00**	—	—	3.46E−59	**0.00E+00**
	Std	2.48E−76	1.50E+08	3.16E−03	1.13E−24	0.00E+00	1.52E−93	4.90E−18	**0.00E+00**			1.84E−41	**0.00E+00**
F9	Mean	4.66E+01	5.12E+06	4.55E+02	9.41E+01	4.76E+01	4.88E+01	1.45E+02	4.88E+01	9.78E+01	**1.99E+01**	4.87E+01	4.54E+01
	Best	4.58E+01	2.00E+05	8.01E+01	4.32E+01	4.68E+01	4.81E+01	2.98E+01	4.87E+01		**1.86E+01**	4.85E+01	4.48E+01
	Std	5.25E−01	6.33E+06	7.95E+02	3.62E+01	5.00E−01	2.57E−01	5.99E+01	1.02E−01	6.53E+01		1.17E−01	4.92E−01
F10	Mean	2.30E−26	2.11E−01	6.37E−05	1.33E−13	1.46E−87	8.85E−24	2.62E−05	7.86E−136			5.73E−20	**0.00E+00**
	Best	1.26E−27	2.93E−03	4.30E−07	7.28E−17	5.40E−96	8.02E−25	2.01E−09	6.09E−160	—	—	3.01E−22	**0.00E+00**
	Std	3.23E−26	3.43E−01	2.04E−04	2.72E−13	4.77E−87	7.70E−24	6.42E−05	3.82E−135			1.16E−19	**0.00E+00**
F11	Mean	6.67E−01	2.26E+04	1.30E+01	6.67E−01	6.67E−01	6.67E−01	6.05E+00	6.67E−01			7.56E−01	**6.67E−01**
	Best	6.67E−01	1.77E+02	1.80E+00	6.67E−01	6.67E−01	6.67E−01	1.03E+00	6.67E−01	—	—	6.67E−01	**6.67E−01**
	Std	1.41E−05	3.49E+04	1.38E+01	3.83E−04	1.87E−04	8.56E−08	3.35E+00	2.87E−06			1.50E−01	**4.32E−08**
F12	Mean	1.63E−05	2.24E+02	9.05E+00	1.10E−03	9.15E−13	2.08E−15	4.20E−01	8.34E−116			5.15E−04	**0.00E+00**
	Best	2.27E−06	2.64E+00	1.08E+00	3.03E−04	5.82E−95	5.71E−23	5.57E−02	1.93E−150	—	—	8.95E−05	**0.00E+00**
	Std	1.09E−05	2.32E+02	6.07E+00	4.65E−04	4.84E−12	1.13E−14	5.10E−01	4.57E−115			4.46E−04	**0.00E+00**
F13	Mean	8.68E−05	1.28E+02	2.60E+02	1.75E+02	8.52E+02	1.70E−01	1.09E+02	1.85E−119			1.27E−06	**0.00E+00**
	Best	4.11E−07	5.14E+01	1.55E+02	2.86E+01	5.96E+02	4.60E−02	6.30E+01	1.81E−138	—	—	1.67E−08	**0.00E+00**
	Std	1.03E−04	4.94E+01	6.69E+01	7.29E+01	1.09E+02	9.01E−02	2.18E+01	9.73E−119			2.30E−06	**0.00E+00**
F14	Mean	1.89E−240	8.74E−78	3.49E−15	1.45E−39	1.21E−95	7.53E−80	5.67E−253	9.51E−183			2.99E−02	**0.00E+00**
	Best	1.39E−307	5.19E−87	2.81E−18	9.77E−45	9.31E−119	1.42E−119	1.88E−263	4.51E−220	—	—	4.96E−150	**0.00E+00**
	Std	0.00E+00	3.35E−77	4.60E−15	4.31E−39	6.62E−95	4.12E−79	0.00E+00	0.00E+00			9.11E−02	**0.00E+00**
F15	Mean	2.45E−140	5.74E−61	8.63E−16	1.91E−40	2.15E−213	1.04E−70	1.60E−149	1.39E−181			1.25E−86	**0.00E+00**
	Best	1.23E−165	2.56E−79	4.10E−18	3.89E−46	1.09E−270	1.25E−90	5.17E−171	5.05E−213	—	—	3.25E−101	**0.00E+00**
	Std	1.29E−139	3.14E−60	1.05E−15	4.12E−40	0.00E+00	5.68E−70	8.64E−149	0.00E+00			5.64E−86	**0.00E+00**
F16	Mean	1.91E+01	1.91E+01	1.91E+01	1.91E+01	1.91E+01	**1.91E+01**	1.91E+01	1.93E+01			6.80E+01	1.91E+01
	Best	1.91E+01	1.91E+01	1.91E+01	1.91E+01	1.91E+01	**1.91E+01**	1.91E+01	1.91E+01	—	—	1.91E+01	1.91E+01
	Std	1.03E−05	2.15E−02	2.86E−10	9.49E−15	3.61E−03	**5.15E−15**	1.35E−14	1.85E−01			1.24E+02	3.71E−02

Table 9 is the experimental data of multimodal benchmark functions. A significant characteristic of the multimodal benchmark functions is that they may have multiple local minimum values in a given interval, so the multimodal benchmark functions are important tools to evaluate the global search capability of optimization algorithms. For F18, F19, F20, F23, F27, and F29, the three statistics of TLTSA are all better than other comparison algorithms, which means that TLTSA can always easily jump out of the local optimal value and concentrate on finding the global optimal solution. It can be seen that TLTSA ranks first in each group. For F17, F21, and F24, the optimization effect of mean, best, and std of TLTSA is obvious. The proposed TLTSA enhances the global exploration capability on the basis of TSA and solves the premature convergence problem, tied for first place with some algorithms in each group. For F22 and F25, the mean of TLTSA is better than SCA, SSA, HGSO, and TSA, which demonstrates that TLTSA makes progress on exploring in search space. For F26, F28, and F30, the performance of TLTSA is greatly ameliorated compared with TSA, which makes TLTSA more competitive. Through the above experimental results analysis, it is shown that TLTSA has enough global exploration capability to escape from the local optimal solution. The ergodicity and randomness of the Tent map promote the search agents to distribute in search space randomly, which improves the diversity of the population. In addition, when the Tent-Lévy flight strategy executes random walk, the large step sizes are generated with a certain probability, which enables TLTSA to effectively search for possible areas in the space.

Table 9. Comparison of TLTSA with other optimization algorithms for multimodal benchmark functions.

Fn	Criteria	GWO	SCA	SSA	WCA	WOA	MPA	LSA	HGSO	LFPSO [47]	chTLBO [66]	TSA	TLTSA
F17	Mean	3.27E+00	1.05E+02	7.11E+01	8.48E+01	**0.00E+00**	**0.00E+00**	1.22E+02	**0.00E+00**	2.96E+01	3.58E+02	3.72E+02	**0.00E+00**
	Best	5.68E−14	1.35E+01	3.28E+01	5.57E+01	**0.00E+00**	**0.00E+00**	7.36E+01	**0.00E+00**		3.48E+02	2.32E+02	**0.00E+00**
	Std	3.98E+00	6.25E+01	1.89E+01	2.74E+01	**0.00E+00**	**0.00E+00**	2.33E+01	**0.00E+00**	4.29E+00		7.09E+01	**0.00E+00**
F18	Mean	1.67E+00	1.25E+01	1.00E+00	1.00E+00	1.24E+00	1.08E+00	1.00E+00	9.03E−01			8.73E+00	**9.00E−01**
	Best	1.17E+00	9.76E+00	1.00E+00	1.00E+00	9.00E−01	1.00E+00	1.00E+00	9.00E−01	—	—	6.64E+00	**9.00E−01**
	Std	3.77E−01	1.13E+00	7.12E−05	1.60E−11	8.27E−01	6.78E−02	1.67E−03	1.75E−02			1.13E+00	**4.52E−16**
F19	Mean	7.42E−04	6.62E+00	5.63E+00	2.06E−04	5.67E−55	5.95E−13	3.78E−01	7.13E−71			5.87E+01	**0.00E+00**
	Best	9.42E−14	6.05E−02	1.38E+00	5.13E−09	2.22E−60	2.22E−14	3.98E−03	1.58E−79	—	—	3.07E+01	**0.00E+00**
	Std	8.85E−04	5.37E+00	2.14E+00	7.50E−04	2.18E−54	5.64E−13	4.70E−01	1.80E−70			1.10E+01	**0.00E+00**
F20	Mean	1.38E−20	1.04E+09	2.58E+01	9.62E−05	5.06E−03	5.91E−16	2.44E−08	4.94E−73			4.74E−01	**0.00E+00**
	Best	1.14E−45	8.95E−01	7.61E−02	1.38E−09	2.96E−36	1.06E−27	2.13E−13	1.14E−113	—	—	3.30E−03	**0.00E+00**
	Std	7.57E−20	3.40E+09	6.00E+01	5.15E−04	2.72E−02	3.18E−15	6.38E−08	2.70E−72			1.13E+00	**0.00E+00**
F21	Mean	5.35E−13	1.87E+01	3.33E+00	4.23E−01	2.43E−15	1.03E−11	3.56E+00	**−8.88E−16**	2.99E−02	5.62E−02	1.66E+00	**−8.88E−16**
	Best	2.51E−13	3.34E+00	2.01E+00	7.13E−07	−8.88E−16	5.71E−13	2.20E+00	**−8.88E−16**		5.12E−02	1.75E−10	**−8.88E−16**
	Std	1.80E−13	4.88E+00	6.61E−01	8.73E−01	2.79E−15	5.17E−12	1.66E+00	**0.00E+00**	1.18E−01		1.59E+00	**0.00E+00**
F22	Mean	5.66E+01	1.31E+04	5.14E+02	7.11E+01	1.23E+02	**4.76E+01**	1.50E+02	1.58E+02			2.23E+02	1.56E+02
	Best	3.83E+01	8.29E+02	3.22E+02	9.02E+00	6.58E+01	**3.49E+01**	5.80E+01	1.51E+02	—	—	1.49E+02	1.35E+02
	Std	9.32E+00	1.88E+04	1.36E+02	5.04E+01	3.22E+01	**7.42E+00**	5.00E+01	3.13E+00			3.77E+01	1.11E+01
F23	Mean	2.07E−01	3.29E+00	3.27E+00	9.57E−01	1.23E−01	1.80E−01	1.00E+00	1.91E−18			4.80E−01	**0.00E+00**
	Best	9.99E−02	1.30E+00	2.20E+00	7.00E−01	5.97E−44	9.99E−02	6.00E−01	4.03E−69	—	—	3.00E−01	**0.00E+00**
	Std	3.65E−02	1.25E+00	5.31E−01	1.30E−01	6.26E−02	4.07E−02	2.57E−01	1.04E−17			7.61E−02	**0.00E+00**
F24	Mean	1.04E−03	1.17E+00	3.54E−02	6.97E−03	**0.00E+00**	**0.00E+00**	1.20E−02	**0.00E+00**	1.13E−02	8.21E−07	4.91E−03	**0.00E+00**
	Best	0.00E+00	4.15E−01	1.24E−02	7.18E−13	**0.00E+00**	**0.00E+00**	2.37E−10	**0.00E+00**		1.39E−08	0.00E+00	**0.00E+00**
	Std	4.02E−03	3.85E−01	1.79E−02	1.45E−02	**0.00E+00**	**0.00E+00**	1.74E−02	**0.00E+00**	1.61E−02		8.38E−03	**0.00E+00**
F25	Mean	1.59E+00	2.01E+07	5.71E+01	3.66E−04	4.65E−01	6.81E−02	1.14E−01	4.88E+00	1.33E−02	**5.42E−06**	5.37E+00	4.85E+00
	Best	9.77E−01	4.33E+04	2.72E+01	4.96E−14	1.43E−01	6.01E−03	5.57E−07	4.79E+00		**3.73E−07**	4.24E+00	4.73E+00
	Std	3.51E−01	2.24E+07	1.65E+01	2.01E−03	1.81E−01	6.24E−02	2.40E−01	3.94E−02	2.59E−02		7.47E−01	3.87E−02
F26	Mean	6.58E−02	1.05E+07	9.15E+00	**4.31E−08**	2.32E−02	9.92E−04	3.08E−01	9.28E−01	2.91E−01	7.91E−08	9.94E+00	9.14E−01
	Best	2.33E−02	7.18E+00	3.70E+00	**1.07E−13**	3.22E−03	4.44E−05	1.28E−06	8.34E−01		1.61E−09	2.96E+00	6.08E−01
	Std	2.21E−02	1.42E+07	4.52E+00	**1.38E−07**	7.11E−02	1.30E−03	4.67E−01	4.81E−02	6.59E−01		4.39E+00	1.88E−01
F27	Mean	3.14E−261	3.05E−76	7.12E−14	1.40E−38	8.54E−141	9.38E−93	2.03E−258	8.73E−183			6.42E−121	**0.00E+00**
	Best	1.03E−305	1.25E−86	2.24E−15	2.09E−45	2.89E−168	3.46E−128	3.47E−266	3.57E−203	—	—	9.57E−162	**0.00E+00**
	Std	0.00E+00	1.49E−75	6.91E−14	4.05E−38	4.54E−140	5.14E−92	0.00E+00	0.00E+00			3.44E−120	**0.00E+00**
F28	Mean	−105.468	−106.721	−106.765	−106.765	−106.765	−106.765	**−106.765**	−106.371			−104.17	−106.723
	Best	−106.765	−106.763	−106.765	−106.765	−106.765	−106.765	**−106.765**	−106.757	—	—	−106.765	−106.764
	Std	4.94E+00	4.72E−02	1.05E−12	3.75E−14	6.76E−06	6.92E−14	**3.73E−14**	3.95E−01			6.73E+00	5.47E−02
F29	Mean	3.00E+00	3.00E+00	3.00E+00	3.00E+00	3.00E+00	3.00E+00	3.00E+00	3.00E+00			9.30E+00	**3.00E+00**
	Best	3.00E+00	3.00E+00	3.00E+00	3.00E+00	3.00E+00	3.00E+00	3.00E+00	3.00E+00	—	—	3.00E+00	**3.00E+00**
	Std	2.21E−05	7.52E−05	2.69E−13	1.16E−15	1.11E−05	1.81E−15	1.59E−04	2.29E−03			1.69E+01	**8.45E−16**
F30	Mean	3.16E+01	3.10E−01	1.97E+00	**1.27E−05**	7.90E+00	1.27E−05	5.92E+00	2.99E+00			4.64E+01	6.52E+00
	Best	3.00E−05	1.54E−02	1.27E−05	**1.27E−05**	1.28E−05	1.27E−05	1.27E−05	3.69E−03	—	—	9.80E−04	1.51E−02
	Std	3.00E+01	2.96E−01	1.08E+01	**0.00E+00**	2.05E+01	4.66E−14	1.81E+01	3.09E+00			4.90E+01	1.80E+01

Table 10 depicts the experimental results of the fixed-dimension functions. For F33, the TLTSA always found the optimal solution and kept the std to a minimum. For other functions, it greatly improved solution accuracy compared with the original algorithms and was significantly better than most optimization algorithms, showing that it had sufficient ability to jump out of the local optimal solution. Because fixed-dimensional functions are closer to real-life optimization problems and the TLTSA is competitive at solving them, it showed that it could solve constrained engineering problems.

Table 10. Comparison of TLTSA with other optimization algorithms for fixed-dimension functions.

Fn	Criteria	GWO	SCA	SSA	WCA	WOA	MPA	LSA	HGSO	LFPSO [47]	chTLBO [66]	TSA	TLTSA
F31	Mean	2.81E+00	1.66E+00	1.16E+00	9.98E−01	2.21E+00	9.98E−01	6.89E+00	1.41E+00	9.98E−01	1.02E+01	8.41E+00	1.06E+00
	Best	9.98E−01	9.98E−01	9.98E−01	9.98E−01	9.98E−01	9.98E−01	9.98E−01	9.98E−01		9.99E+00	1.99E+00	9.98E−01
	Std	2.35E+00	9.51E−01	5.87E−01	8.25E−17	2.47E+00	1.62E−16	4.79E+00	5.21E−01	9.21E−17		4.96E+00	2.52E−01
F32	Mean	4.20E−03	1.07E−03	2.12E−03	4.30E−04	7.26E−04	**3.07E−04**	5.93E−04	4.82E−04	1.18E−03	3.61E−02	5.87E−03	5.08E−04
	Best	3.07E−04	3.83E−04	3.08E−04	3.07E−04	3.15E−04	**3.07E−04**	3.07E−04	3.41E−04		9.10E−03	3.08E−04	3.35E−04
	Std	1.16E−02	3.85E−04	4.97E−03	3.17E−04	4.65E−04	**2.76E−15**	4.59E−04	7.56E−05	3.63E−03		8.99E−03	1.29E−04
F33	Mean	−3.86E+00	−3.85E+00	−3.86E+00	−3.86E+00	−3.86E+00	−3.86E+00	−3.86E+00	−3.85E+00	−3.86E+00	−3.60E+00	−3.86E+00	**−3.86E+00**
	Best	−3.86E+00	−3.86E+00	−3.86E+00	−3.86E+00	−3.86E+00	−3.86E+00	−3.86E+00	−3.86E+00		−3.69E+00	−3.86E+00	**−3.86E+00**
	Std	2.37E−03	2.39E−03	2.94E−13	2.61E−15	5.39E−03	2.71E−15	3.49E−03	5.98E−03	2.66E−15		2.55E−03	**2.32E−15**
F34	Mean	**−9.31E+00**	−3.23E+00	−8.30E+00	−3.60E+00	−8.12E+00	−1.02E+01	−7.38E+00	−3.86E+00	−8.28E+00	−6.05E+00	−6.93E+00	−8.80E+00
	Best	**−1.02E+01**	−7.89E+00	−1.02E+01	−5.04E+00	−1.02E+01	−1.02E+01	−1.02E+01	−6.98E+00		−6.85E+00	−1.01E+01	−1.02E+01
	Std	**1.92E+00**	1.92E+00	2.73E+00	1.96E+00	2.77E+00	3.00E−11	2.91E+00	9.06E−01	2.74E+00		3.04E+00	2.28E+00
F35	Mean	−1.04E+01	−3.33E+00	−8.97E+00	−3.88E+00	−7.49E+00	−1.04E+01	−6.75E+00	−3.84E+00	−9.97E+00	**−1.04E+01**	−5.50E+00	−1.00E+01
	Best	−1.04E+01	−5.62E+00	−1.04E+01	−5.08E+00	−1.04E+01	−1.04E+01	−1.04E+01	−5.22E+00		**−1.19E+01**	−1.04E+01	−1.04E+01
	Std	8.68E−04	1.69E+00	2.70E+00	1.87E+00	3.44E+00	3.34E−11	3.34E+00	5.28E−01	1.66E+00		3.01E+00	1.35E+00
F36	Mean	−1.01E+01	−4.49E+00	−4.98E+00	−9.24E+00	−7.60E+00	**−1.05E+01**	−8.68E+00	−3.98E+00	−1.01E+01	−9.23E+00	−5.75E+00	−8.88E+00
	Best	−1.05E+01	−8.60E+00	−9.31E+00	−1.05E+01	−1.05E+01	**−1.05E+01**	−1.05E+01	−7.55E+00		−1.05E+01	−1.05E+01	−1.05E+01
	Std	1.75E+00	1.76E+00	1.84E+00	2.41E+00	3.46E+00	**3.64E−11**	3.16E+00	8.86E−01	1.67E+00		3.63E+00	3.10E+00

To evaluate the fairness and accuracy of TLTSA, the LFPSO [47], chTLBO [66], TSA-LEO [43], and QLGCTSA [44] were selected for comparison. The experimental data of them came from the original literature. Tables 8–10 show that the TLTSA was superior to LFPSO and chTLBO just using chaotic mapping or Lévy flight. From Table 11, it can be seen that the optimization performance of TLTSA and QLGCTSA was significantly better than that of TSA-LEO because local escape operator was difficult to help search agents explore potential areas. Compared with QLGCTSA, the proposed TLTSA performed better in unimodal functions and was similar in multimodal functions, thus demonstrating that chaotic mapping combined with Lévy flight had a stronger global exploration and development ability. In the proposed TLTSA, a number of search agents executing small-step random walks improved the development ability, and several large-step random walks and chaotic mapping enhanced the global exploration. This method overcame the QLGCTSA's disadvantage that used too many operators to improve the global exploration ability, resulting in unbalanced exploration and development. Hence, the proposed Tent-Lévy flight strategy is more suitable for algorithms like the TSA, which converged prematurely from a lack of exploration and exploitation ability.

Table 11. Comparison of TLTSA with other improved TSAs for benchmark functions.

Fn		F1	F2	F5	F6	F7	F9	F13	F17	F21
QLGCTSA [44]	Mean	**0.00E+00**	9.06E−05	6.34E−209	**0.00E+00**	1.15E−213	**3.54E−05**		**0.00E+00**	8.88E−16
	Best	**0.00E+00**	7.77E−06	3.67E−251	**0.00E+00**	7.16E−240	**9.23E−06**	——	**0.00E+00**	8.88E−16
	Std	**0.00E+00**	1.09E−04	0.00E+00	**0.00E+00**	0.00E+00	**1.81E−05**		**0.00E+00**	0.00E+00
TSA-LEO [43]	Mean						5.80E+02	6.44E+04	7.07E+02	3.31E+04
	Best	——	——	——	——	——				
	Std						7.25E+01	8.79E+03	3.71E+01	2.69E+04
TLTSA	Mean	**0.00E+00**	**4.03E−05**	**0.00E+00**	**0.00E+00**	**0.00E+00**	4.54E+01	**0.00E+00**	**0.00E+00**	**−8.88E−16**
	Best	**0.00E+00**	**7.99E−07**	**0.00E+00**	**0.00E+00**	**0.00E+00**	4.48E+01	**0.00E+00**	**0.00E+00**	**−8.88E−16**
	Std	**0.00E+00**	**4.00E−05**	**0.00E+00**	**0.00E+00**	**0.00E+00**	4.92E−01	**0.00E+00**	**0.00E+00**	**0.00E+00**
Fn		**F24**	**F26**	**F31**	**F32**	**F33**	**F34**	**F35**	**F36**	
QLGCTSA [44]	Mean	**0.00E+00**	**3.11E−09**	1.33E+00	**3.72E−04**	−3.86E+00	**−1.02E+01**	**−1.04E+01**	**−1.05E+01**	
	Best	**0.00E+00**	**7.05E−10**	9.98E−01	**3.07E−04**	−3.86E+00	**−1.02E+01**	**−1.04E+01**	**−1.05E+01**	
	Std	**0.00E+00**	**1.53E−09**	7.78E−01	**2.36E−04**	6.83E−14	**1.36E−12**	**1.23E−12**	**6.51E−13**	
TSA-LEO [43]	Mean	5.05E+03								
	Best		——	——	——	——	——	——	——	
	Std	6.32E+03								
TLTSA	Mean	**0.00E+00**	9.14E−01	**1.06E+00**	5.08E−04	**−3.86E+00**	−8.80E+00	−1.00E+01	−8.88E+00	
	Best	**0.00E+00**	6.08E−01	**9.98E−01**	3.35E−04	**−3.86E+00**	−1.02E+01	−1.04E+01	−1.05E+01	
	Std	**0.00E+00**	1.88E−01	**2.52E−01**	1.29E−04	**2.32E−15**	2.28E+00	1.35E+00	3.10E+00	

4.4.2. Convergence Curve and Boxplot Analysis

The convergence curve intuitively reflects the convergence speed and calculation precision. The boxplot is frequently used in the analysis of variance (ANOVA) test, which is useful for observing outliers and comparing algorithm stability. Figure 4 shows the convergence curves and boxplot of some benchmark functions. For F1, F3, F4, F7, F8, F10, F12-F15, F17, F19, F20, F23, F27, and F29, the TLTSA generally converged to 0 after 150–300 iterations. Its convergence curves show that it found global optimal solutions with fewer iterations. For F11, the TLTSA greatly improved convergence speed without changing the TSA calculation precision, which put its convergence speed at the forefront of all algorithms. For F2, F18, F21, and F28, where the Tent-Lévy flight strategy was introduced, the exploration and exploitation capabilities of the TLTSA were boosted greatly. For F30, some of the other algorithms had an ad-vantage in global optimization ability, but the TLTSA overcame the problem of local optimal solutions, avoided search stagnation, and improved both calculation precision and convergence speed allowing it to escape the local optimal solution. In addition, the boxplots also reflected its superior stability. It was obvious that the TLTSA box-plots had fewer or no outliers compared to the original TSA.

In conclusion, the proposed TLTSA combined the merits of the Lévy flight strategy and Tent map and solved the original algorithm's lack of global exploration and exploitation ability. The Tent map made step sizes of the Lévy flight strategy mutate randomly, which led to each search agent having a chance to be selected. The large step sizes of the Tent-Lévy flight strategy boosted the global exploration ability, and the small step-sized random walk improved exploitation ability such that the TLTSA maintained a dynamic equilibrium between exploration and exploitation, which not only widened the search scope to avoid the search stagnation but also enhanced the search diversity near the candidate solution. Synthesizing the above analytical results and experimental data, the calculation precision and convergence speed of the TLTSA were evidently the best. Moreover, the boxplots also attested to its strong stability and robustness. Hence, it is feasible to introduce the Tent-Lévy flight strategy into the TSA to solve the function optimization problem.

4.4.3. Statistical Test

The statistical test is an important criterion for evaluating the fairness and accuracy of the proposed algorithm. A Wilcoxon nonparametric test was performed at a significance level of 0.05 to verify that the experimental results of the TLTSA were significantly different from those of other algorithms. A *p*-value lower than 0.05, would be sufficient proof of the null hypothesis. The test in 50 dimensions is shown in Table 10, and $p > 0.05$ is displayed in bold. NaN suggested that the result generated by the sum-of-values test was not a number. The last row shows all counts in (+/≈/−) format, where "+" means that the proposed TLTSA was superior at the 95% significance level ($\alpha = 0.05$); "−" means that the TLTSA optimization was less effective; and "≈" means that there was no significant statistical difference between the TLTSA and other algorithms. Table 12 shows the Wilcoxon test results and it is easy to see that the vast majority of *p*-values were less than 0.05 compared to the other algorithms. It also shows that the TLTSA had a statistically significant advantage on optimizing problems compared to other algorithms.

F1

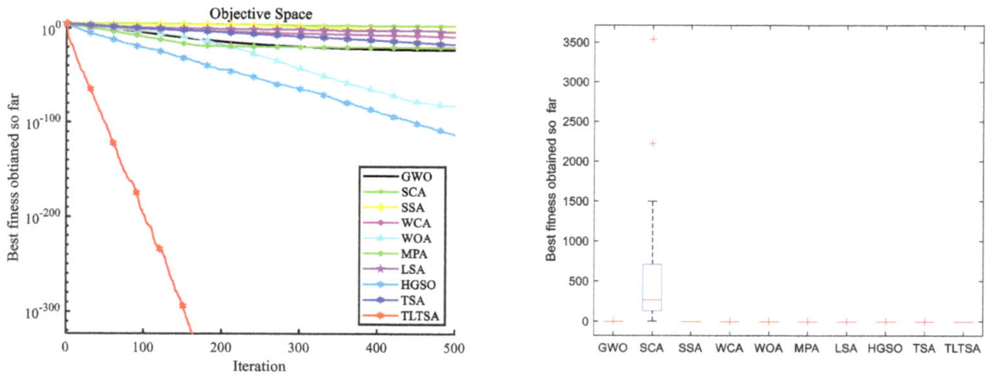

F2

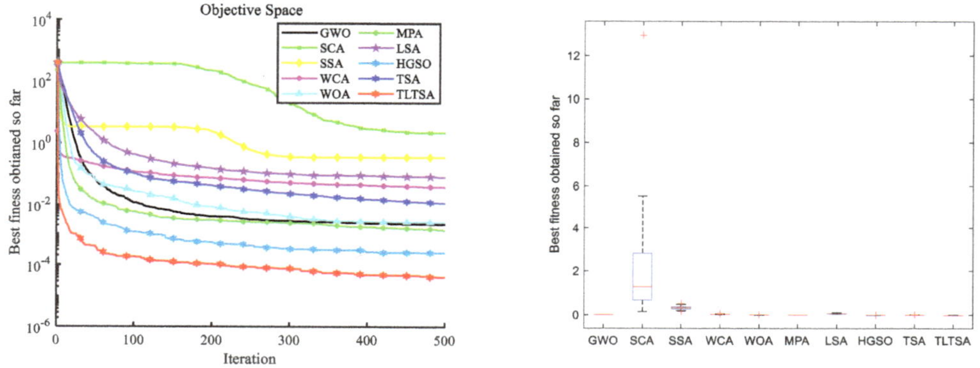

F3

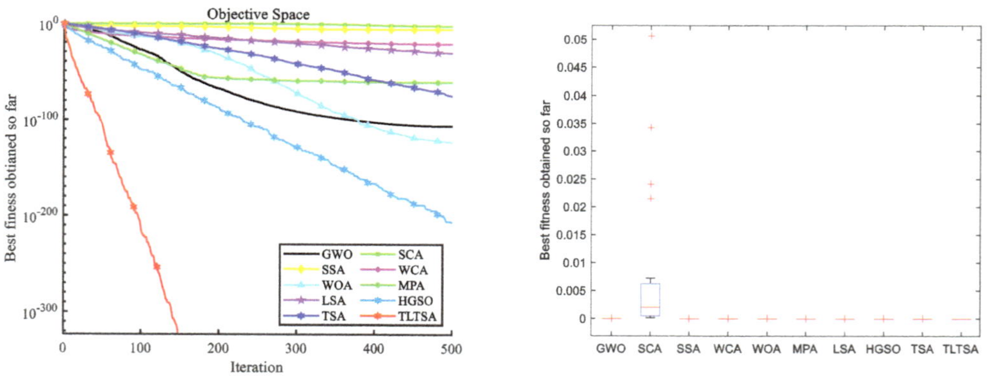

Figure 4. *Cont.*

F4

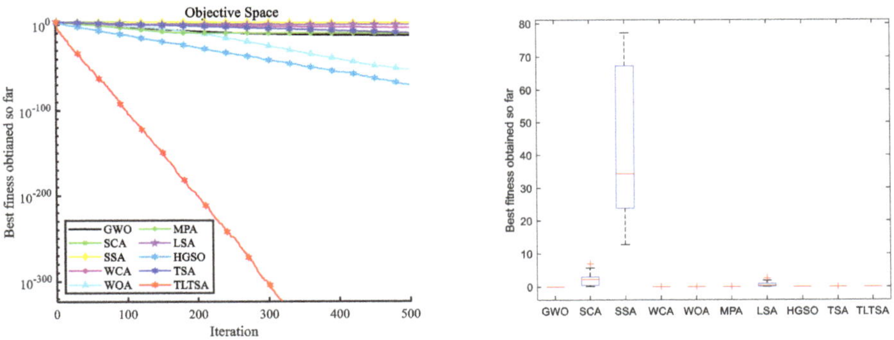

F7

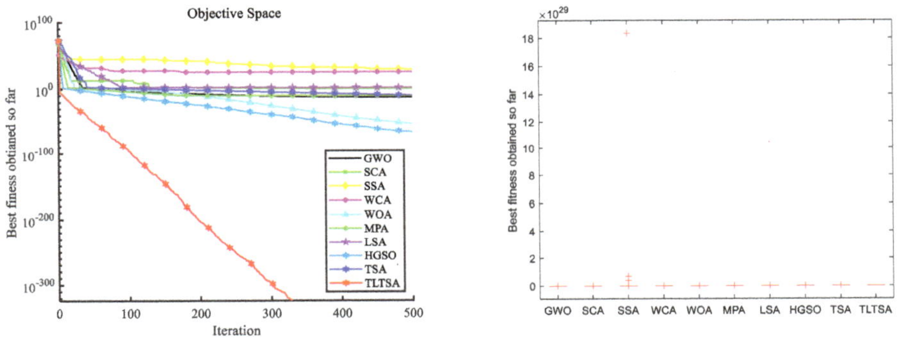

F8

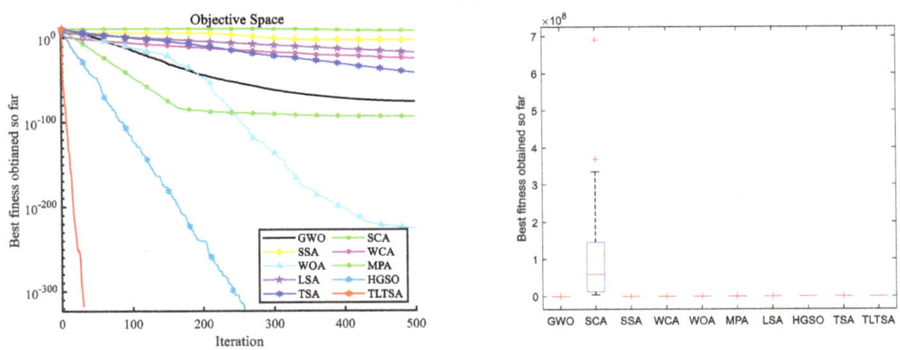

F10

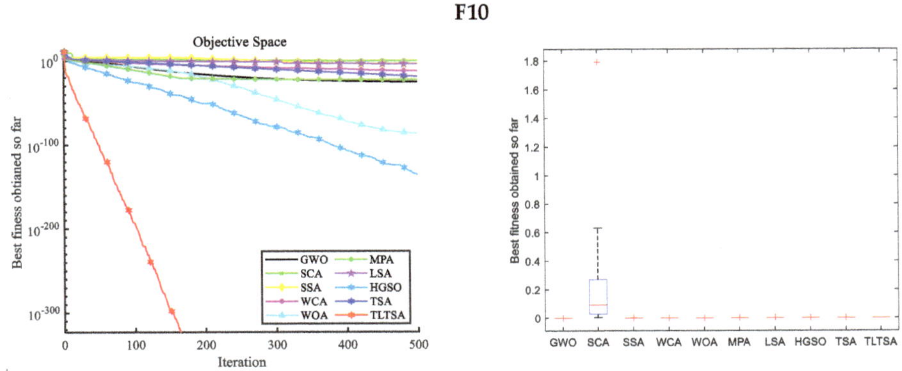

Figure 4. *Cont.*

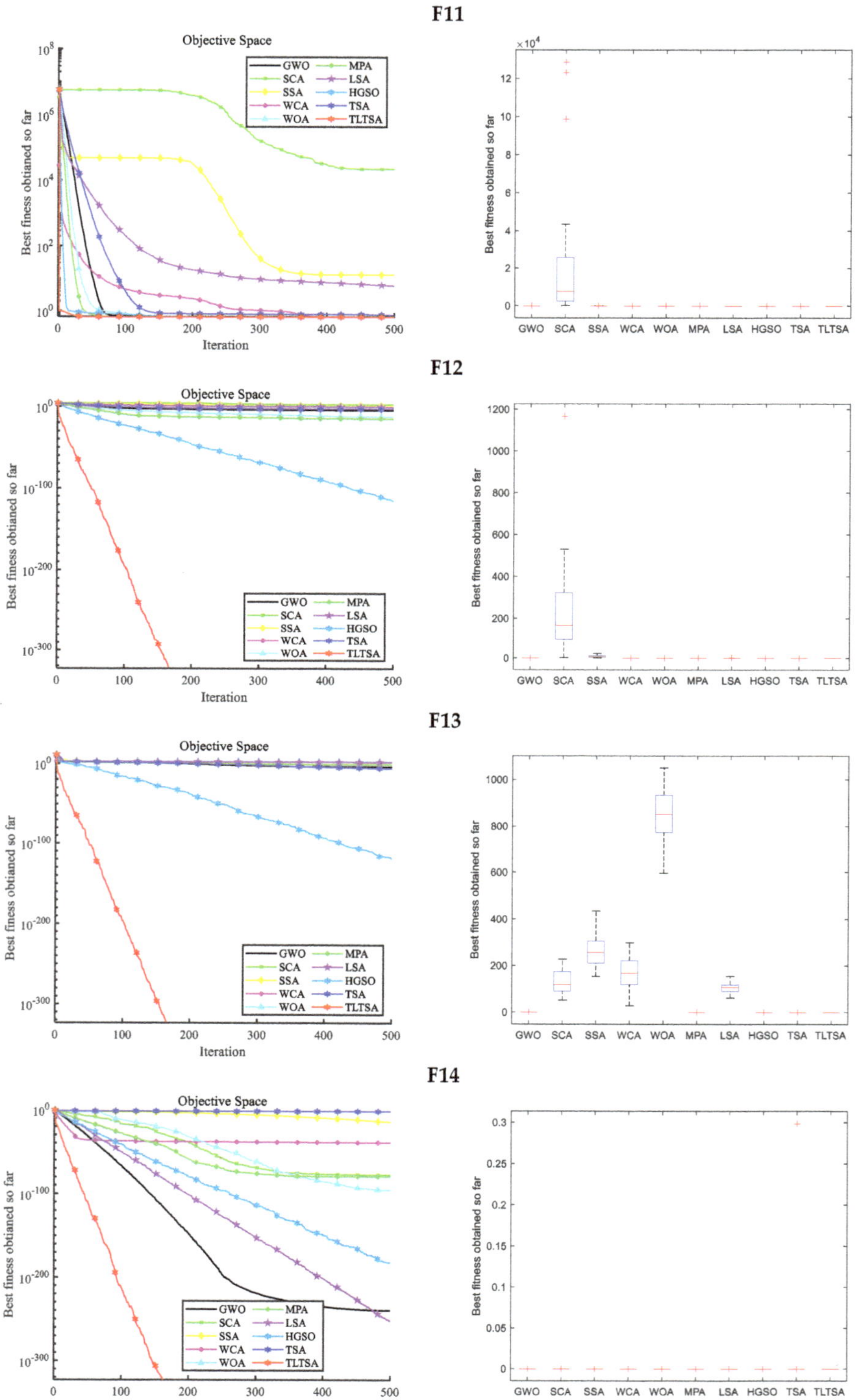

Figure 4. *Cont.*

F15

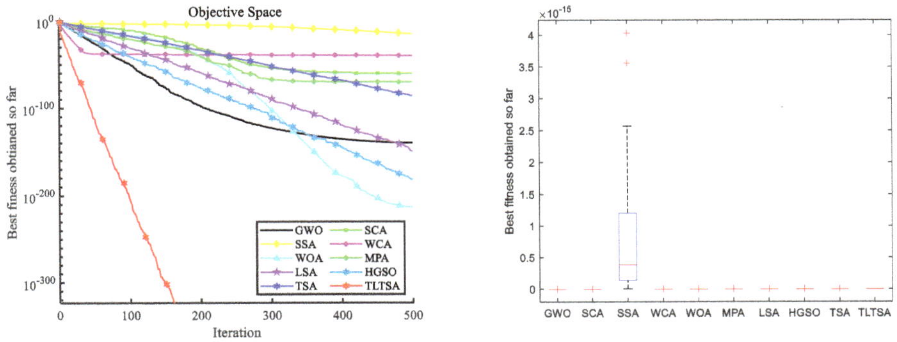

F17

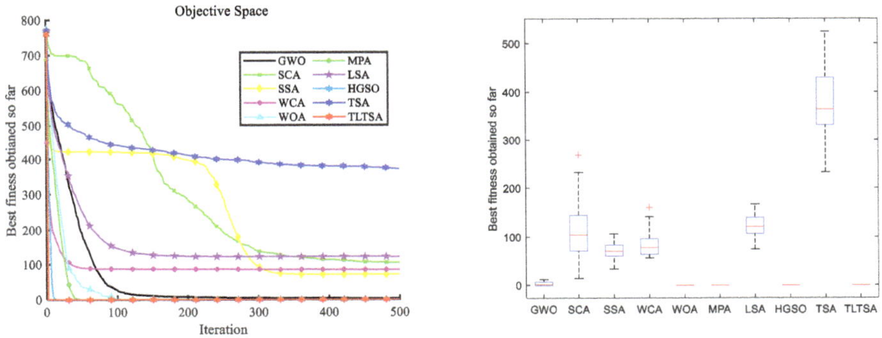

F18

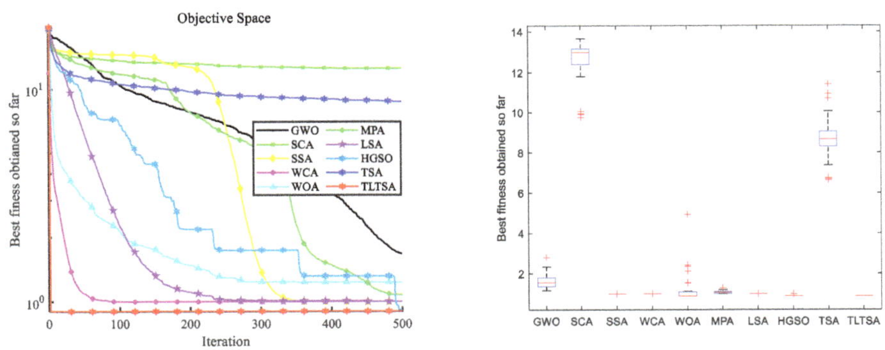

F19

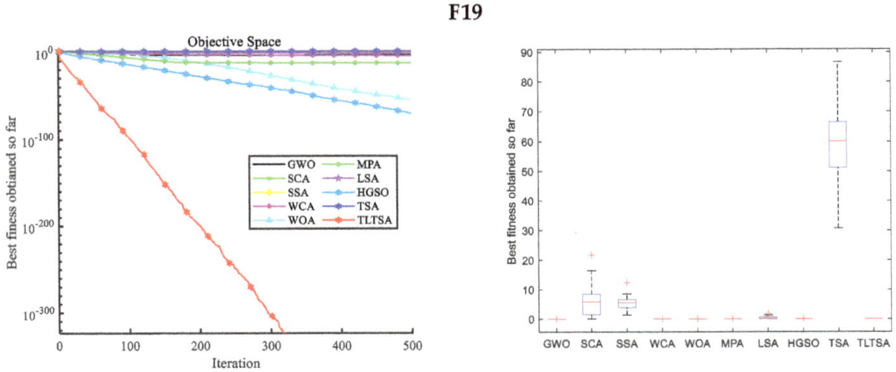

Figure 4. *Cont.*

F20

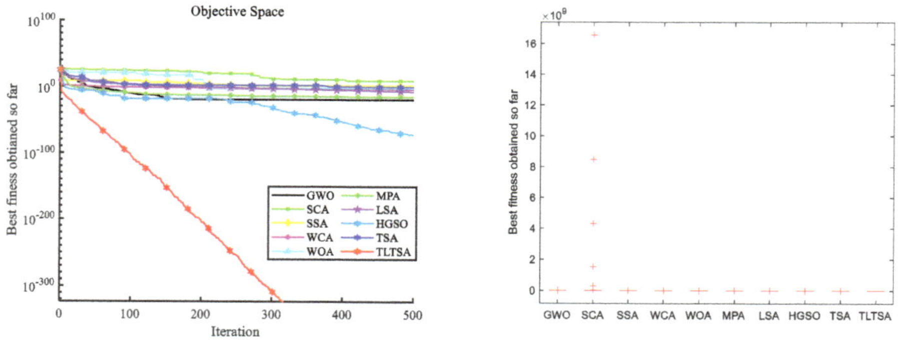

F21

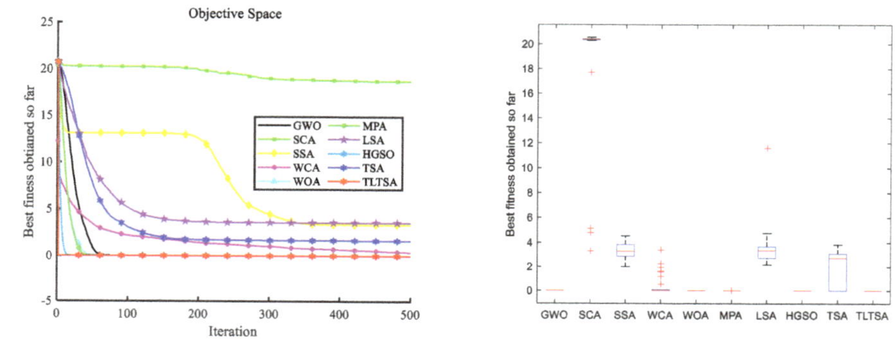

F23

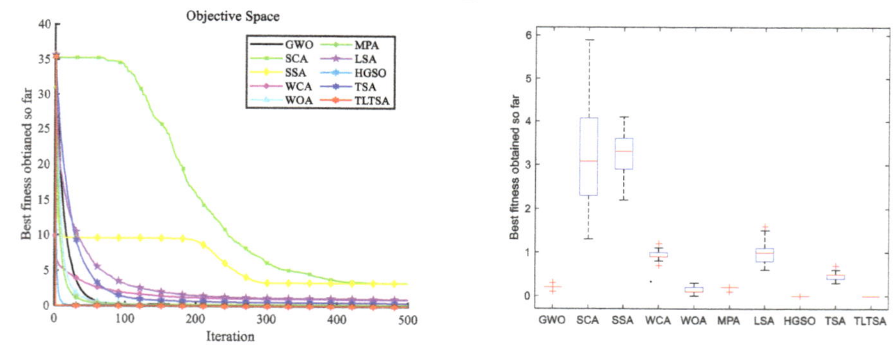

F27

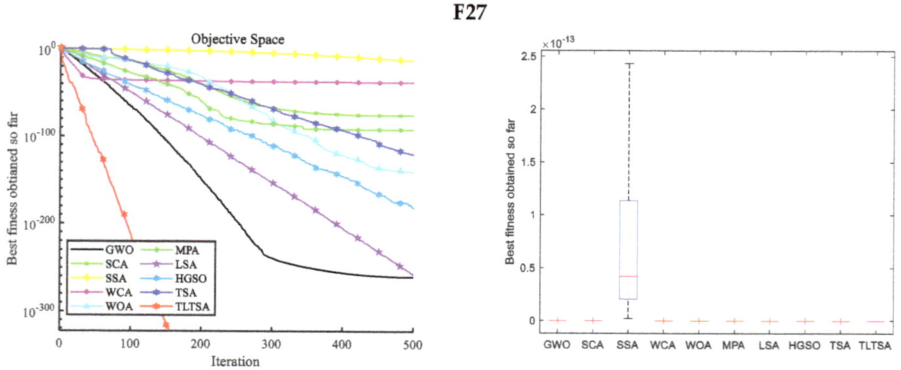

Figure 4. *Cont.*

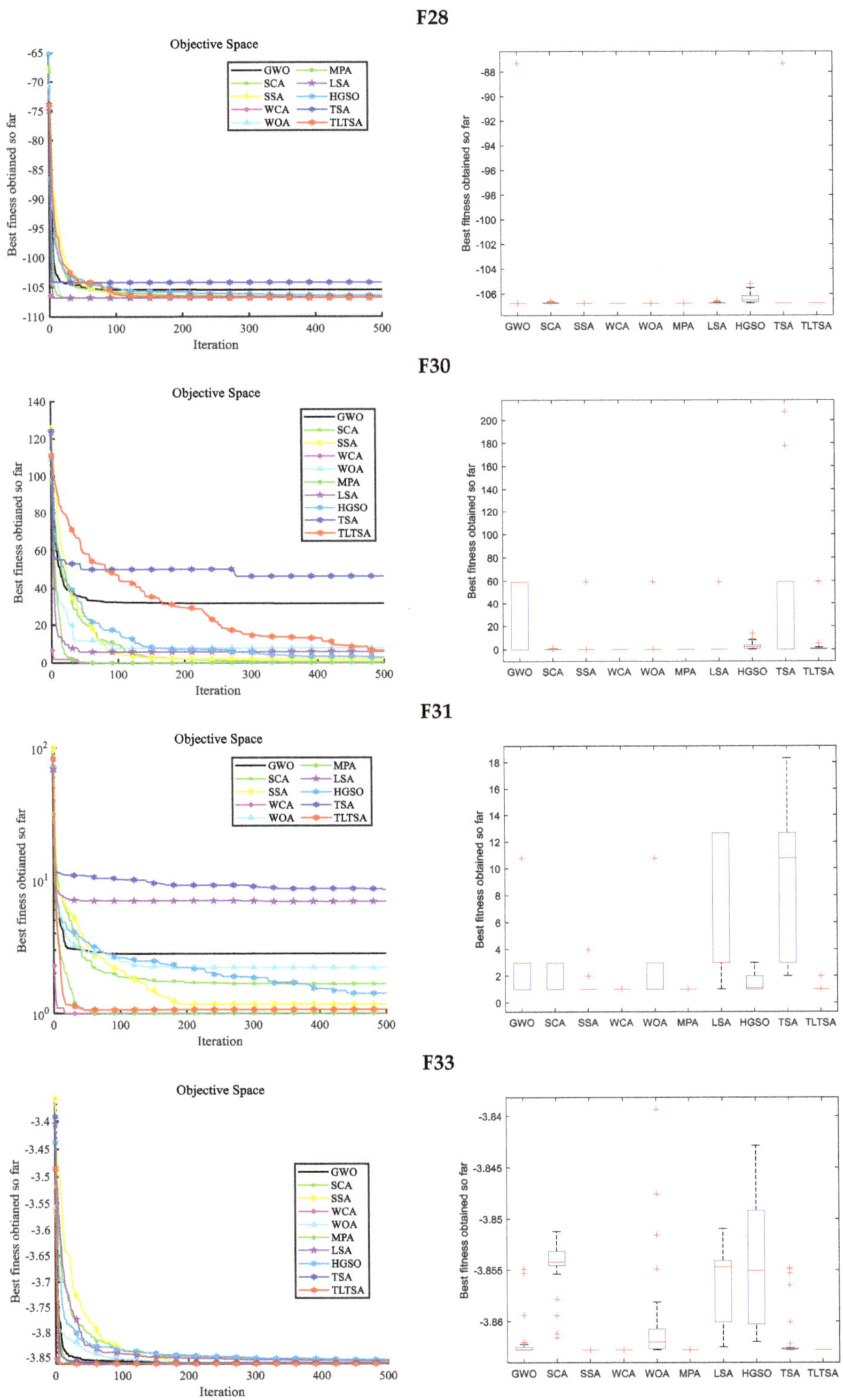

Figure 4. *Cont.*

F34

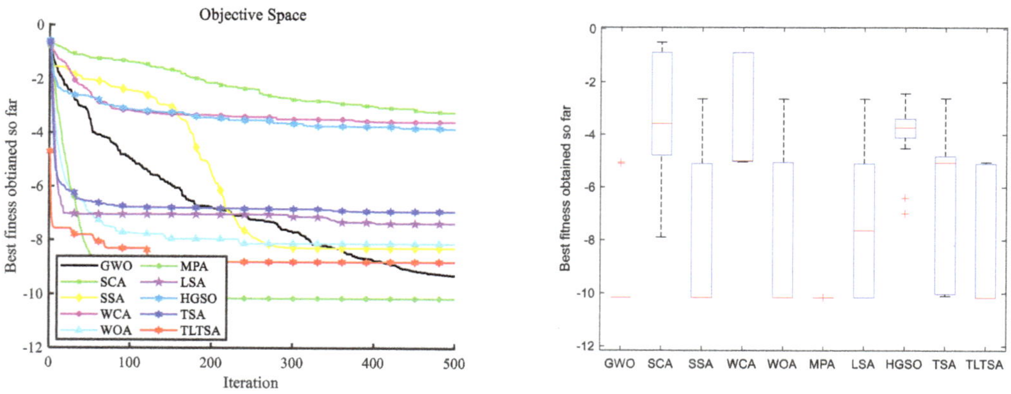

F35

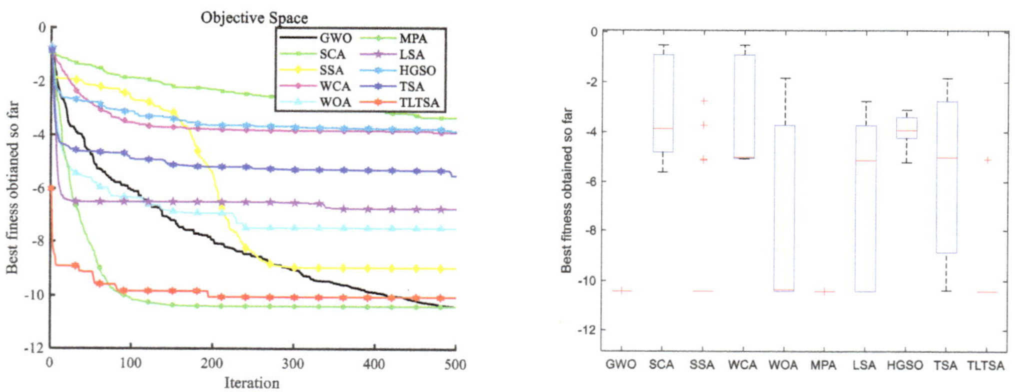

F36

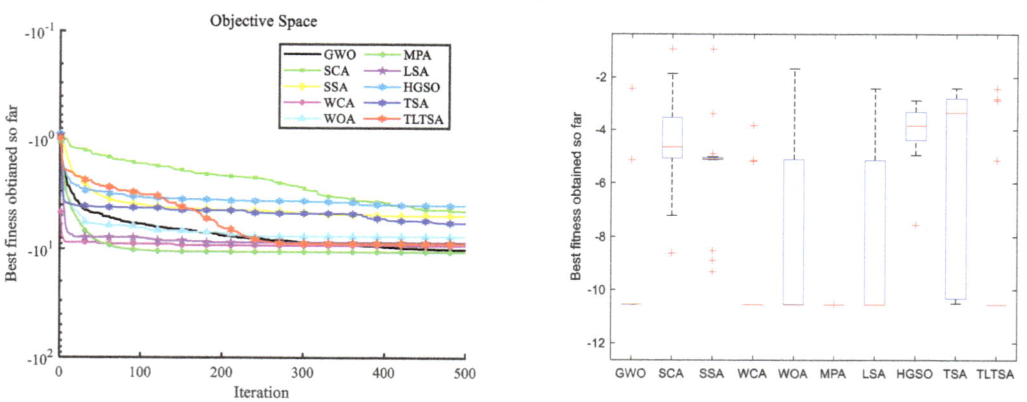

Figure 4. The convergence curve and boxplot of 36 benchmark function.

Table 12. Statistical results of the Wilcoxon rank-sum test.

Fn	GWO	SCA	SSA	WCA	WOA	MPA	LSA	HGSO	TSA
F1	4.11E−12	4.11E−12	4.11E−12	4.11E−12	4.11E−12	4.11E−12	4.11E−12	4.11E−12	4.11E−12
F2	7.39E−11	3.02E−11	3.02E−11	3.02E−11	1.96E−10	2.37E−10	3.02E−11	9.83E−08	3.02E−11
F3	1.21E−12	1.21E−12	1.21E−12	1.21E−12	1.21E−12	1.21E−12	1.21E−12	1.21E−12	1.21E−12
F4	3.02E−11	3.02E−11	3.02E−11	3.02E−11	3.02E−11	3.02E−11	3.02E−11	3.02E−11	3.02E−11
F5	3.02E−11	3.02E−11	3.02E−11	3.02E−11	3.02E−11	3.02E−11	3.02E−11	3.02E−11	3.02E−11
F6	3.02E−11	3.02E−11	3.02E−11	3.02E−11	3.02E−11	3.02E−11	3.02E−11	3.02E−11	3.02E−11
F7	3.02E−11	3.02E−11	3.02E−11	3.02E−11	3.02E−11	3.02E−11	3.02E−11	3.02E−11	3.02E−11
F8	1.21E−12	1.21E−12	1.21E−12	1.21E−12	1.21E−12	1.21E−12	1.21E−12	NaN	1.21E−12
F9	4.50E−11	3.02E−11	3.02E−11	**0.589451**	3.02E−11	3.02E−11	5.57E−10	3.02E−11	4.50E−11
F10	1.21E−12	1.21E−12	1.21E−12	1.21E−12	1.21E−12	1.21E−12	1.21E−12	1.21E−12	1.21E−12
F11	3.02E−11	3.02E−11	3.02E−11	**0.0962628**	3.02E−11	3.08E−08	3.02E−11	7.09E−08	7.37E−10
F12	1.10E−11	1.10E−11	1.10E−11	1.10E−11	1.10E−11	1.10E−11	1.10E−11	1.10E−11	1.10E−11
F13	3.02E−11	3.02E−11	3.02E−11	3.02E−11	3.02E−11	3.02E−11	3.02E−11	3.02E−11	3.02E−11
F14	1.21E−12	1.21E−12	1.21E−12	1.21E−12	1.21E−12	1.21E−12	1.21E−12	1.21E−12	1.21E−12
F15	1.21E−12	1.21E−12	1.21E−12	1.21E−12	1.21E−12	1.21E−12	1.21E−12	1.21E−12	1.21E−12
F16	3.02E−11	3.02E−11	1.85E−03	1.48E−11	2.00E−06	1.83E−11	1.99E−11	2.20E−07	6.52E−09
F17	4.50E−12	1.21E−12	1.21E−12	1.21E−12	**0.333711**	NaN	1.21E−12	NaN	1.21E−12
F18	1.21E−12	1.21E−12	1.21E−12	1.21E−12	1.26E−05	1.21E−12	1.21E−12	**0.333711**	1.21E−12
F19	3.02E−11	3.02E−11	3.02E−11	3.02E−11	3.02E−11	3.02E−11	3.02E−11	3.02E−11	3.02E−11
F20	1.27E−11	1.27E−11	1.27E−11	1.27E−11	1.27E−11	1.27E−11	1.27E−11	1.27E−11	1.27E−11
F21	8.85E−12	8.85E−12	8.85E−12	8.85E−12	3.53E−06	8.85E−12	8.85E−12	2.70E−03	8.85E−12
F22	3.02E−11	3.02E−11	3.02E−11	8.15E−11	4.64E−05	3.02E−11	**0.118817**	2.57E−07	3.34E−11
F23	3.02E−11	3.02E−11	3.02E−11	2.46E−11	2.35E−10	4.11E−11	3.02E−11	1.68E−04	3.02E−11
F24	2.79E−03	1.21E−12	1.21E−12	1.21E−12	**0.160802**	NaN	1.21E−12	NaN	6.61E−05
F25	3.02E−11	3.02E−11	3.02E−11	3.02E−11	3.02E−11	3.02E−11	3.02E−11	8.99E−11	3.56E−04
F26	3.02E−11	3.02E−11	3.02E−11	3.02E−11	3.02E−11	3.02E−11	1.29E−06	5.26E−04	3.02E−11
F27	1.21E−12	1.21E−12	1.21E−12	1.21E−12	1.21E−12	1.21E−12	1.21E−12	1.21E−12	1.21E−12
F28	5.57E−10	3.01E−11	4.43E−03	1.29E−11	3.02E−11	2.83E−11	1.46E−11	3.20E−09	2.50E−03
F29	3.03E−03	3.02E−11	**0.0594279**	1.69E−11	**0.311188**	2.33E−11	1.88E−11	3.02E−11	2.05E−03
F30	6.77E−05	8.46E−09	**0.56922**	1.21E−12	6.77E−05	2.10E−11	2.47E−08	1.25E−05	1.95E−03
F31	2.68E−10	1.78E−07	4.84E−10	**0.198282**	3.27E−10	2.18E−07	8.02E−12	8.67E−10	1.69E−11
F32	1.77E−03	7.04E−07	2.39E−08	5.43E−10	2.71E−02	3.02E−11	2.15E−02	**0.0701266**	**0.0750587**
F33	8.10E−10	3.02E−11	**0.0656713**	4.08E−12	**0.0678689**	7.57E−12	1.72E−12	**0.17145**	3.02E−11
F34	9.70E−04	7.21E−05	1.30E−10	1.30E−10	3.04E−04	7.51E−03	**0.228715**	5.36E−11	3.49E−06
F35	5.35E−07	1.07E−07	2.36E−10	3.21E−11	9.76E−09	7.30E−07	**0.202628**	1.41E−11	4.77E−09
F36	3.50E−03	9.79E−05	4.22E−04	1.67E−06	4.46E−04	4.71E−04	1.22E−02	6.77E−05	4.35E−05
+/≈/−	36/0/0	36/0/0	33/0/3	33/0/3	32/0/4	34/2/0	33/0/3	30/3/3	35/0/1

5. TLTSA for Complex Problems in the Engineering Field

An improved optimization algorithm was proposed to settle practical problems in engineering more efficiently. The benchmark functions were different because engineering problems are often constrained. In addition, the optimal solutions to most engineering problems are not clear. Therefore, a practical, constrained engineering problem is an important criterion for measuring the performance of optimization algorithms. In this section, three constrained engineering problems were selected to verify the ability of the TLTSA to solve them: Three-bar truss design problem, welded beam design problem, and optimal design of an industrial refrigeration system. The best results of each experiment are highlighted in bold.

5.1. Three-Bar Truss Design Problem

The three-bar truss design problem is a classic in the engineering structure field. The optimization goal is to design a truss with the smallest weight while satisfying three constraints on stress, deflection, and buckling. The structural model and parameters are displayed in Figure 5. The mathematical expression is defined as follows [67]:

Deem:

$$\vec{x} = [x_1, x_2] = [A_1, A_2] \quad (27)$$

Objective function:

$$f(\vec{x}) = \left(2\sqrt{2}x_1 + x_2\right) \times L \quad (28)$$

Constraint functions:

$$\begin{aligned} g_1(\vec{x}) &= \frac{\sqrt{2}x_1 + x_2}{\sqrt{2}x_1^2 + 2x_1x_2} P - \sigma \le 0 \\ g_2(\vec{x}) &= \frac{x_2}{\sqrt{2}x_1^2 + 2x_1x_2} P - \sigma \le 0 \\ g_3(\vec{x}) &= \frac{1}{\sqrt{2}x_2 + x_1} P - \sigma \le 0 \end{aligned} \quad (29)$$

Variable range:

$$0 \le x_1, x_2 \le 1$$

where $L = 100$ cm, $P = 2\frac{\text{KN}}{\text{cm}^2}$, $\sigma = 2\frac{\text{KN}}{\text{cm}^2}$.

Table 13 shows the experimental results of the TLTSA and other algorithms. According to the experimental results and convergence curve in Figure 6, the results for the TLTSA were the same as those for the MPA, WCA, and SSA; its optimal cost was the smallest. This demonstrated that the proposed TLTSA is feasible for settling the three-bar truss design problem.

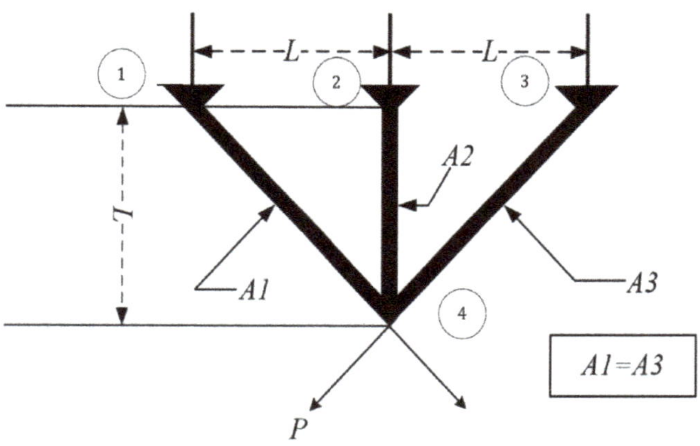

Figure 5. Three-bar truss design problem.

Table 13. Comparison of TLTSA with other optimization algorithms for three-bar truss design problem.

Algorithm	Optimal Variable A_1	Optimal Variable A_2	Optimal Cost
GWO	0.78693	0.28779	186.3860
SCA	0.77940	0.30414	186.4062
SSA	0.78685	0.28801	186.3859
WCA	0.78685	0.28801	186.3859
WOA	0.83937	0.19509	186.7164
MPA	0.78685	0.28801	186.3859
LSA	0.79784	0.26626	186.4503
HGSO	0.78921	0.28358	186.4424
TSA	0.78698	0.28764	186.3864
TLTSA	**0.78685**	**0.28801**	**186.3859**

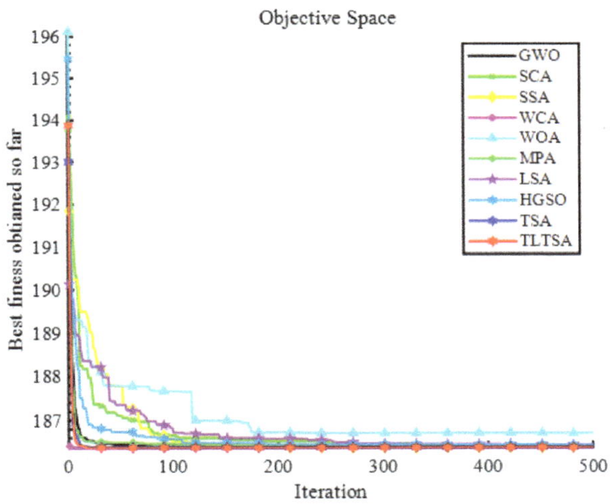

Figure 6. Convergence curve for three-bar truss design problem.

5.2. Welded Beam Design Problem

The welded beam design problem is also well-known. The optimization objective was found to be the most suitable value for each variable in calculating the minimum cost of a welded beam subject to shear stress (τ), beam-bending stress (σ), bar buckling load (P_c) and beam end deflection (δ). This design problem is influenced by four variables: weld thickness (h), clamped-bar length (l), bar height (t), and bar thickness (b). The structural model and the meaning of the parameters are shown in Figure 7. The mathematical expression is listed below [68]:

Deem:

$$\vec{z} = [z_1, z_2, z_3, z_4] = [h, l, t, b] \tag{30}$$

Objective function:

$$f\left(\vec{z}\right) = 1.10471 z_1^2 z_2 + 0.04811 z_3 z_4 (14 + z_2) \tag{31}$$

Constraint functions:

$$\begin{gathered}
g_1\left(\vec{z}\right) = \tau\left(\vec{z}\right) - 13600 \le 0 \\
g_2\left(\vec{z}\right) = \sigma\left(\vec{z}\right) - 30000 \le 0 \\
g_3\left(\vec{z}\right) = \delta\left(\vec{z}\right) - 0.25 \le 0 \\
g_4\left(\vec{z}\right) = z_1 - z_4 \le 0 \\
g_5\left(\vec{z}\right) = 6000 - P_c\left(\vec{z}\right) \le 0 \\
g_6\left(\vec{z}\right) = 0.125 - z_1 \le 0 \\
g_7\left(\vec{z}\right) = 1.10471 z_1^2 z_2 + 0.04811 z_3 z_4 (14 + z_2) - 5 \le 0
\end{gathered} \tag{32}$$

Variable range:

$$0.1 \le z_1, z_2 \le 2,\ 0.1 \le z_2, z_3 \le 10$$

Other parameters:

$$\begin{aligned}
\tau\left(\vec{z}\right) &= \sqrt{(\tau')^2 + (z_2\tau'\tau'')/\sqrt{\frac{\left(z_2^2 + (z_1+z_3)^2\right)}{4}} + (\tau'')^2} \\
\tau' &= \frac{6000}{\sqrt{2}z_1z_2},\ \sigma\left(\vec{z}\right) = \frac{504{,}000}{z_3^2z_4},\ \delta\left(\vec{z}\right) = \frac{65{,}856{,}000}{(30\times10^6)z_1z_3^3} \\
\tau'' &= \frac{6000(14+0.5z_2)\sqrt{0.25\left(z_2^2+(z_1+z_3)^2\right)}}{2\left[0.707z_1z_2\left(\frac{1}{12z_2^2}+0.25(z_1+z_3)^2\right)\right]}
\end{aligned} \tag{33}$$

Table 14 shows the comparison between the proposed TLTSA and the other algorithms in optimal variables and optimal costs. The Figure 8 displays the convergence curves. It can be seen that the proposed TLTSA is the most competitive. TLTSA gains the optimal cost $f(z_{1-4}) = 1.6952$ at the most suitable position $(z_1, z_2, z_3, z_4) = (0.20573, 3.2530, 9.0336, 0.20573)$, and ranked first. The experimental results showed that it had strong global exploration and exploitation ability to optimize the welded beam design problem to reduce engineering costs.

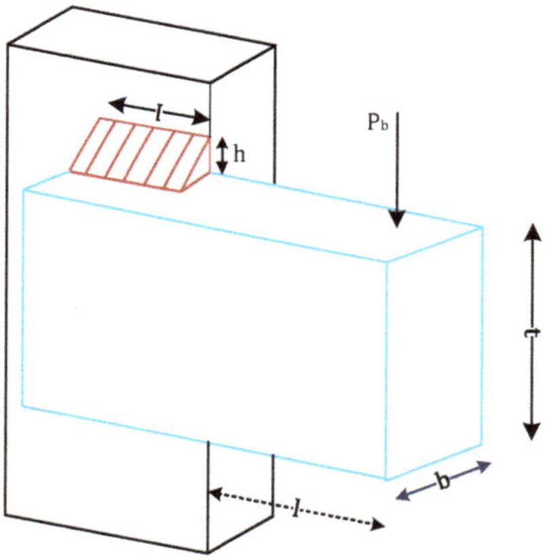

Figure 7. Welded beam design problem.

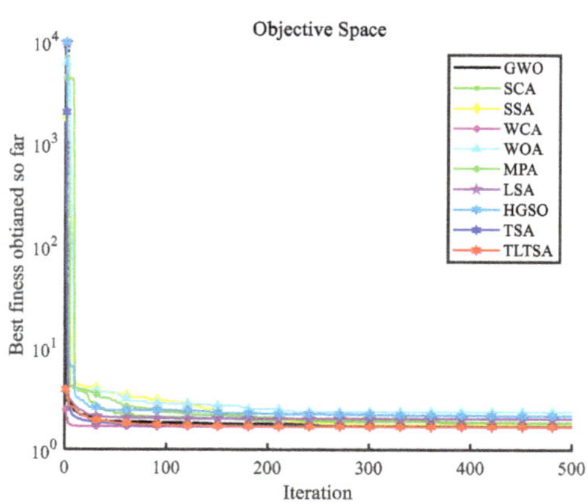

Figure 8. Convergence curve for welded design problem.

Table 14. Comparison of TLTSA with other optimization algorithms for welded beam design problem.

Algorithm	Optimal Variable				Optimal Cost
	h	l	t	b	
GWO	0.20095	3.3454	9.0465	0.20569	1.7000
SCA	0.20044	3.8852	9.4553	0.20645	1.8402
SSA	0.20648	3.2282	9.0796	0.20645	1.7686
WOA	0.21850	4.1900	5.6288	0.53853	2.3655
MPA	0.16971	3.9050	10	0.20207	1.8539
LSA	0.20573	3.2530	9.0366	0.20573	2.0274
HGSO	0.14780	4.8333	8.9045	0.21856	2.1737
TSA	0.20054	3.4016	9.0598	0.20624	1.7142
TLTSA	**0.20573**	**3.2530**	**9.0366**	**0.20573**	**1.6952**

5.3. Optimal Design Problem of Industrial Refrigeration System

As a nonlinear inequality-constrained optimization design problem, because it contains a lot of constraints, the optimal design problem of the industrial refrigeration system is suitable for evaluating the ability of the algorithm to solve an actual engineering problem. The optimal objective is to reduce the design costs as much as possible. The mathematical model is [69]:

Objective function:

$$\begin{aligned} f\left(\vec{x}\right) &= 63098.88x_2x_4x_{12} + 5441.5x_2^2x_{12} + 115055.5x_2^{1.664}x_6 + 6172.27x_2^2x_6 \\ &+63098.88x_1x_3x_{11} + 5441.5x_1^2x_{11} + 115055.5x_1^{1.664}x_5 + 6172.27x_1^2x_5 \\ &+140.53x_1x_{11} + 281.29x_3x_{11} + 70.26x_1^2 + 281.29x_1x_3 \\ &+281.29x_3^2 + 14437x_8^{1.8812}x_{12}^{0.3424}x_{10}x_{14}^{-1}x_1^2x_7x_9^{-1} \\ &+20470.2x_7^{2.893}x_{11}^{0.316}x_1^2 \end{aligned} \tag{34}$$

Constraint functions:

$$\begin{aligned} g_1\left(\vec{x}\right) &= 1.524x_7^{-1} \leq 1 \\ g_2\left(\vec{x}\right) &= 1.524x_8^{-1} \leq 1 \\ g_3\left(\vec{x}\right) &= 0.07789x_1 - 2x_7^{-1}x_9 - 1 \leq 0 \\ g_4\left(\vec{x}\right) &= 7.05305x_9^{-1}x_1^2x_{10}x_8^{-1}x_2^{-1}x_{14}^{-1} - 1 \leq 0 \\ g_5\left(\vec{x}\right) &= 0.0833x_{13}^{-1}x_{14} - 1 \leq 0 \\ g_6\left(\vec{x}\right) &= 47.136x_2^{0.333}x_{10}^{-1}x_{12} - 1.333x_8x_{13}^{2.1195} + 62.08x_{13}^{2.1195}x_{12}^{-1}x_8^{0.2}x_{10}^{-1} - 1 \leq 0 \\ g_7\left(\vec{x}\right) &= 0.04771x_{10}x_8^{1.8812}x_{12}^{0.3424} - 1 \leq 0 \\ g_8\left(\vec{x}\right) &= 0.0488x_9x_7^{1.893}x_{11}^{0.316} - 1 \leq 0 \\ g_9\left(\vec{x}\right) &= 0.099x_1x_3^{-1} - 1 \leq 0 \\ g_{10}\left(\vec{x}\right) &= 0.0193x_2x_4^{-1} - 1 \leq 0 \\ g_{11}\left(\vec{x}\right) &= 0.0298x_1x_5^{-1} - 1 \leq 0 \\ g_{12}\left(\vec{x}\right) &= 0.056x_2x_6^{-1} - 1 \leq 0 \\ g_{13}\left(\vec{x}\right) &= 2x_9^{-1} - 1 \leq 0 \\ g_{14}\left(\vec{x}\right) &= 2x_{10}^{-1} - 1 \leq 0 \\ g_{15}\left(\vec{x}\right) &= x_{12}x_{11}^{-1} - 1 \leq 0 \end{aligned} \tag{35}$$

Variable range:

$$0.001 \leq x_i \leq 5, i = 1, \ldots, 14$$

Six well-known meta-heuristic optimization algorithms—-GWO, SSA, WCA, WOA, and HGSO, and the original TSA—-were selected for comparison with TLTSA. The experimental results of optimal costs and variables are given in Table 15. The TLTSA obtained optimal costs $f(x_{1-14}) = 0.19637$, which were significantly lower. In addition, the convergence curves in Figure 9 also indicate the proposed TLTSA is superior.

Table 15. Comparison of TLTSA with other algorithms for optimal design problem of industrial refrigeration system.

Optimal Value	GWO	SSA	WCA	WOA	HGSO	TSA	TLTSA
Optimal variable x_1	0.001	0.001	0.001	0.001	0.0010561	0.001	**0.001**
Optimal variable x_2	0.0010912	0.001	0.001	0.001	0.0029744	0.0010534	**0.0010461**
Optimal variable x_3	0.0010052	0.0010118	0.001	0.015982	0.0028955	0.0010950	**0.0010241**
Optimal variable x_4	0.0013333	4.8584	0.001	0.001	0.0032518	0.0076186	**0.10488**
Optimal variable x_5	0.0010012	2.7978	0.001	0.001	0.1921	0.0048673	**0.074202**
Optimal variable x_6	0.0011156	1.2464	0.001	0.011293	0.0045721	0.0040403	**0.01525**
Optimal variable x_7	1.5252	3.5466	1.5240	1.5787	2.1326	1.5383	**1.7251**
Optimal variable x_8	1.5249	3.9266	1.5240	1.5235	4.4739	1.5280	**1.5473**
Optimal variable x_9	5	3.7794	5	2.8120	2.1012	4.8173	**4.5901**
Optimal variable x_{10}	2.5139	2.0191	2	3.7725	2.0096	2.1429	**2.3255**
Optimal variable x_{11}	0.019292	0.001	0.001	0.023963	0.0016401	0.0089912	**0.001**
Optimal variable x_{12}	0.019167	0.001	0.001	0.001	0.0015673	0.0083106	**0.001**
Optimal variable x_{13}	0.032051	0.0057349	0.0072934	0.0074685	0.0020327	0.020283	**0.0057234**
Optimal variable x_{14}	0.38109	0.065408	0.087557	0.061517	0.001172	0.24036	**0.049644**
Optimal cost	286.4233	357.3893	93.9437	1.6727	59.7011	211.5825	**0.19637**

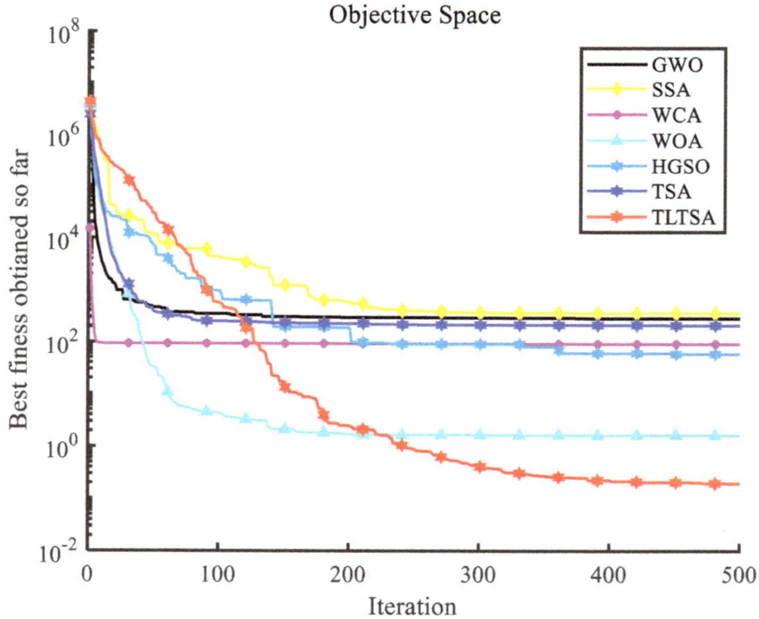

Figure 9. Convergence curve for optimal design problem of industrial refrigeration system.

6. Conclusions and Future Work

In this paper, an improved TSA based on Chaotic-Lévy flight strategy (CLTSA) was proposed to overcome defects of the original algorithm, such as premature convergence and poor solution accuracy. As a random walk strategy, Chaotic-Lévy flight made the search agents produce a mass of small step-sized moves and a small number of large ones when converging towards the candidate solution. The small-step random walks enabled search agents to exploit the vicinity of the candidate solution fully, which improves its exploitation ability. The mutability generated by the large-step random walks gave the search agent a chance to appear at any position in the solution space, thereby boosting the global exploration capability of the CLTSA and increasing tunicate population diversity. However, it was crucial to combine a suitable chaotic map with Lévy flight, and from a comparison of chaotic maps, the tent map was the most appropriate. Because the chaotic values generated by the tent map were more evenly distributed in (0, 1), the combination with the step sizes generated by the Lévy flight strategy had a high degree of randomness, so it was easier for TLTSA to strengthen the richness of the population and avoid becoming trapped in local minimization. In addition, the values in (0,1) generated by the tent map ensured that the search agents moved within the search range as much as possible. The Tent-Lévy flight strategy not only helped the search agents find potential areas, but also strengthened exploration around the current solution, which made the algorithm maintain an exploration–exploitation equilibrium that enhanced the TLTSA optimization efficiency.

To verify the feasibility of the TLTSA in finding the optimal solution and solving the practical problem, 36 benchmark functions and 3 practical constrained engineering problems were selected for contrast experiments. The data indicates that the proposed TLTSA was a great improvement over the original algorithm in performing test functions. TLTSA not only overcame the shortcomings of the original algorithm, such as search stagnation and premature convergence, but also had greater calculation accuracy. Another advantage was that it had a smaller standard deviation, which meant greater stability. In addition, the convergence curves also attested to a more competitive convergence speed. In addition, the design costs optimized by the TLTSA for three engineering design problems were clearly lower than those of other algorithms. Therefore, TLTSA, the best algorithm among the CLTSAs, provides new possibilities for solving real-world engineering problems.

Even though our proposed TLTSA is a great improvement over the original TSA, it still had research value. Our research is limited to combining one-dimensional chaotic mapping with Lévy flight. In the following research, we will consider applying two-dimensional chaotic mapping to algorithm optimization. Furthermore, because of the characteristic antenna design problems, the proposed TLTSA can only optimize the antenna with continuous parameters (the antenna structure needs to be specified), and we will propose the binary and multi-objective versions of the TSA algorithm to improve the TLTSA's optimization efficiency to solve complex antenna and frequency-selective surface design problems.

Author Contributions: Conceptualization, Y.C. and J.D.; methodology, Y.C. and J.D.; software, Y.C.; validation, Y.C., R.S. and J.D.; formal analysis, R.S.; investigation, Y.C. and J.D.; resources, J.D.; data curation, R.S.; writing—original draft preparation, Y.C.; writing—review and editing, R.S and J.D.; visualization, R.S.; supervision, J.D.; project administration, Y.C., R.S. and J.D.; funding acquisition, J.D. and R.S. All authors have read and agreed to the published version of the manuscript.

Funding: This research was funded in part by the National Natural Science Foundation of China under grant numbers 61801521 and 61971450, in part by the Natural Science Foundation of Hunan Province under grant number 2018JJ2533 and 2022JJ30052, and in part by the Fundamental Research Funds for the Central Universities under grant number 2018gczd014 and 20190038020050.

Institutional Review Board Statement: Not applicable.

Informed Consent Statement: Not applicable.

Data Availability Statement: Not applicable.

Conflicts of Interest: The authors declare no conflict of interest.

Appendix A

Table A1. Mathematical expressions of unimodal benchmark functions.

Function Expressions
$F1 = \sum_{i=1}^{n} x_i^2$
$F2 = \sum_{i=1}^{n} ix_i^4 + random[0,1]$
$F3 = \sum_{i=1}^{D} \lvert x_i \rvert^{i+1}$
$F4 = \sum_{i=1}^{n} \lvert x_i \rvert$
$F5 = max(\lvert x_i \rvert, 1 \le i \le n)$
$F6 = \sum_{i=1}^{n} \left(\sum_{j=1}^{i} x_j \right)^2$
$F7 = \sum_{i=1}^{n} \lvert x_i \rvert + \prod_{i=1}^{n} \lvert x_i \rvert$
$F8 = \sum_{i=1}^{n} x_i^{10}$
$F9 = \sum_{i=1}^{n-1} \left[100 (x_{i+1} - x_i^2)^2 + (x_i - 1)^2 \right]$
$F10 = \sum_{i=1}^{n-1} (x_i^2)^{(x_{i+1}{}^2+1)} + \left(x_{i+1}^2 \right)^{(x^2+1)}$
$F11 = (x_1 - 1)^2 + \sum_{i=2}^{D} i (2x_i^2 - x_{i-1})^2$
$F12 = \sum_{i=1}^{\frac{D}{4}} (x_{4i-3} + 10x_{4i-2})^2 + 5(x_{4i-1} - 10x_{4i})^2 + (x_{4i-2} - x_{4i-1})^2 + 10(x_{4i-3} - x_{4i})^2$
$F13 = \sum_{i=1}^{n} x_i^2 + \left(\sum_{i=1}^{n} 0.5ix_i \right)^2 + \left(\sum_{i=1}^{n} 0.5ix_i \right)^4$
$F14 = 2x_1^2 - 1.05x_1^4 + \frac{x_1^6}{6} + x_1 x_2 + x_2^2$
$F15 = 0.26(x_1^2 + x_2^2) - 0.48x_1 x_2$
$F16 = 100(x_2 - x_1^2)^2 + (1 - x_1)^2 f$

Table A2. Mathematical expressions of multimodal benchmark functions.

Function Expressions
$F17 = \sum_{i=1}^{n} \left[x_i^2 - 10\cos(2\pi x_i) + 10 \right]$
$F18 = 1 + \sum_{i=1}^{n} \sin^2(x_i) - 0.1e^{(\sum_{i=1}^{n} x_i^2)}$
$F19 = \sum_{i=1}^{n} \lvert x_i \sin(x_i) + 0.1x_i \rvert$
$F20 = \sum_{i=1}^{n} \epsilon_i \lvert x_i \rvert^i$
$F21 = -20\exp\left(-0.2\sqrt{\frac{1}{n} \times \sum_{i=1}^{n} x_i^2} \right) - \exp\left(\frac{1}{n} \times \sum_{i=1}^{n} \cos(2\pi x_i) \right) + 20 + e$
$F22 = \sum_{i=1}^{n} 8\sin^2\left[7(x_i - 0.9)^2 \right] + 6\sin^2\left[14(x_1 - 0.9)^2 \right] + (x_i - 0.9)^2$
$F23 = 1 - \cos\left(2\pi \sqrt{\sum_{i=1}^{n} x_i^2} \right) + 0.1\sqrt{\sum_{i=1}^{n} x_i^2}$
$F24 = \frac{1}{4000} \sum_{i=1}^{n} x_i^2 - \prod_{i=1}^{n} \cos\left(\frac{x_i}{\sqrt{i}} \right) + 1$
$F25 = 0.1\left\{ \sin^2(3\pi x_1) + \sum_{i=1}^{n} (x_i - 1)^2 [1 + \sin^2(3\pi x_i + 1)] + (x_n - 1)^2 [1 + \sin^2(2\pi x_n)] \right\} + \sum_{i=1}^{n} u(x_i, 5, 100, 4)$
$F26 = \frac{\pi}{n} \left\{ 10\sin(\pi y_i) + \sum_{i=1}^{n-1} (y_i - 1)^2 [1 + 10\sin^2(\pi y_{i+1})] + (y_n - 1)^2 \right\} + \sum_{i=1}^{n} u(x_i, 10, 100, 4)$
$F27 = x^2 + y^2 + 25\left[\sin^2(x) + \sin^2(y) \right]$
$F28 = \sin(x) e^{(1-\cos(y))^2} + \cos(y) e^{(1-\sin(x))^2} + (x - y)^2$
$F29 = \left[1 + (x_1 + x_2 + 1)^2 (19 - 14x_1 + 3x_1^2 - 14x_2 + 6x_1 x_2 + 3x_2^2) \right]$ $\times \left[30 + (2x_1 - 3x_2)^2 (18 - 32x_1 + 12x_1^2 + 48x_2 - 36x_1 x_2 + 27x_2^2) \right]$
$F30 = \lvert x^2 + y^2 + xy \rvert + \lvert \sin(x) \rvert + \lvert \cos(y) \rvert$

Table A3. Mathematical expressions of fixed-dimension functions.

Function Expressions
$F31 = \left(\frac{1}{500} + \sum_{j=1}^{25} \frac{1}{j+\sum_{i=1}^{2}(x_i - a_{ij})^6} \right)^{-1}$
$F32 = \sum_{i=1}^{11} \left[a_i - \frac{x_1(b_i^2 + b_i x_2)}{b_i^2 + b_i x_3 + x_4} \right]^2$
$F33 = -\sum_{i=1}^{4} c_i exp\left[-\sum_{j=1}^{4} a_{ij}\left(x_j - p_{ij}\right)\right]$
$F34 = -\sum_{i=1}^{5} \left[(x - a_i)(x - a_i)^T + c_i \right]^{-1}$
$F35 = -\sum_{i=1}^{7} \left[(x - a_i)(x - a_i)^T + c_i \right]^{-1}$
$F36 = -\sum_{i=1}^{10} \left[(x - a_i)(x - a_i)^T + c_i \right]^{-1}$

References

1. Qu, B.Y.; Liang, J.J.; Suganthan, P.N. Niching particle swarm optimization with local search for multi-modal optimization. *Inf. Sci.* **2012**, *197*, 131–143. [CrossRef]
2. Mohapatra, P.; Das, K.N.; Roy, S. A modified competitive swarm optimizer for large scale optimization problems. *Appl. Soft Comput.* **2017**, *59*, 340–362. [CrossRef]
3. Wang, L.Y.; Zhao, W.G.; Tian, Y.L.; Pan, G.Z. A bare bones bacterial foraging optimization algorithm. *Cogn. Syst. Res.* **2018**, *52*, 301–311. [CrossRef]
4. Holland, J.H. Genetic algorithms. *Sci. Am.* **1992**, *267*, 66–72. [CrossRef]
5. Kirkpatrick, S.; Gelatt, C.D., Jr.; Vecchi, M.P. Optimization by simulated annealing. *Science* **1983**, *220*, 671–680. [CrossRef]
6. Hatamlou, A. Black hole: A new heuristic optimization approach for data clustering. *Inf. Sci.* **2013**, *222*, 175–184. [CrossRef]
7. Formato, R.A. Central force optimization: A new metaheuristic with applications in applied electromagnetics. *Prog. Electromagn. Res.* **2007**, *77*, 425–491. [CrossRef]
8. Eskandar, H.; Sadollah, A.; Bahreininejad, A.; Hamdi, M. Water cycle algorithm—A novel metaheuristic optimization method for solving constrained engineering optimization problems. *Comput. Struct.* **2012**, *110*, 151–166. [CrossRef]
9. Nematollahi, A.F.; Rahiminejad, A.; Vahidi, B. A novel physical based meta-heuristic optimization method known as Lightning Attachment Procedure Optimization. *Appl. Soft Comput.* **2017**, *59*, 596–621. [CrossRef]
10. Rao, R.V.; Savsani, V.J.; Vakharia, D.P. Teaching-learning-based optimization: A novel method for constrained mechanical design optimization problems. *Comput. Aided Design* **2011**, *43*, 303–315. [CrossRef]
11. Askari, Q.; Younas, I.; Saeed, M. Political Optimizer: A novel socio-inspired meta-heuristic for global optimization. *Knowl.-Based Syst.* **2020**, *195*, 105709. [CrossRef]
12. Dong, J.; Zou, H.; Li, W.; Wang, M. A hybrid greedy political optimizer with fireworks algorithm for numerical and engineering optimization problems. *Sci. Rep.* **2022**, *12*, 13243. [CrossRef]
13. Kennedy, J.; Eberhart, R. Particle swarm optimization. In Proceedings of the ICNN'95—International Conference on Neural Networks, Perth, WA, Australia, 27 November–1 December 1995; Volume 1944, pp. 1942–1948.
14. Dong, J.; Li, Q.; Deng, L. Design of fragment-type antenna structure using an improved BPSO. *IEEE Trans. Antennas Propag.* **2017**, *66*, 564–571. [CrossRef]
15. Dorigo, M.; Birattari, M.; Stutzle, T. Ant colony optimization. *IEEE Comput. Intell. Mag.* **2006**, *1*, 28–39. [CrossRef]
16. Basturk, B.; Karaboga, D. An artificial bee colony (ABC) algorithm for numeric function optimization. In Proceedings of the IEEE Swarm Intelligence Symposium, Indianapolis, IN, USA, 12–14 May 2006.
17. Krishnanand, K.N.; Ghose, D. Glowworm Swarm Optimisation: A New Method for Optimising Multi-Modal Functions. *Int. J. Comput. Intell. Stud.* **2009**, *1*, 93. [CrossRef]
18. Askarzadeh, A. A novel metaheuristic method for solving constrained engineering optimization problems: Crow search algorithm. *Comput. Struct.* **2016**, *169*, 1–12. [CrossRef]
19. Shadravan, S.; Naji, H.R.; Bardsiri, V.K. The Sailfish Optimizer: A novel nature-inspired metaheuristic algorithm for solving constrained engineering optimization problems. *Eng. Appl. Artif. Intell.* **2019**, *80*, 20–34. [CrossRef]
20. Heidari, A.A.; Mirjalili, S.; Faris, H.; Aljarah, I.; Mafarja, M.; Chen, H.L. Harris hawks optimization: Algorithm and applications. *Future Gener. Comput. Syst.* **2019**, *97*, 849–872. [CrossRef]
21. Li, W.; Shi, R.; Dong, J. Harris hawks optimizer based on the novice protection tournament for numerical and engineering optimization problems. *Appl. Intell.* **2022**, 1–26. [CrossRef]
22. Zhao, W.G.; Zhang, Z.X.; Wang, L.Y. Manta ray foraging optimization: An effective bio-inspired optimizer for engineering applications. *Eng. Appl. Artif. Intell.* **2020**, *87*, 103300. [CrossRef]

23. Zervoudakis, K.; Tsafarakis, S. A mayfly optimization algorithm. *Comput. Ind. Eng.* **2020**, *145*, 106559. [CrossRef]
24. Mirjalili, S.; Lewis, A. The Whale Optimization Algorithm. *Adv. Eng. Softw.* **2016**, *95*, 51–67. [CrossRef]
25. Alsattar, H.A.; Zaidan, A.A.; Zaidan, B.B. Novel meta-heuristic bald eagle search optimisation algorithm. *Artif. Intell. Rev.* **2020**, *53*, 2237–2264. [CrossRef]
26. Pecora, L.M.; Carroll, T.L. Synchronization in chaotic systems. *Phys. Rev. Lett.* **1990**, *64*, 821–824. [CrossRef]
27. Feng, J.H.; Zhang, J.; Zhu, X.S.; Lian, W.W. A novel chaos optimization algorithm. *Multimed. Tools Appl.* **2017**, *76*, 17405–17436. [CrossRef]
28. Ouertani, M.W.; Manita, G.; Korbaa, O. Chaotic lightning search algorithm. *Soft Comput.* **2021**, *25*, 2039–2055. [CrossRef]
29. Alatas, B. Chaotic bee colony algorithms for global numerical optimization. *Expert Syst. Appl.* **2010**, *37*, 5682–5687. [CrossRef]
30. Kohli, M.; Arora, S. Chaotic grey wolf optimization algorithm for constrained optimization problems. *J. Comput. Des. Eng.* **2018**, *5*, 458–472. [CrossRef]
31. Arora, S.; Singh, S. An improved butterfly optimization algorithm with chaos. *J. Intell. Fuzzy Syst.* **2017**, *32*, 1079–1088. [CrossRef]
32. Gandomi, A.H.; Yang, X.S.; Talatahari, S.; Alavi, A.H. Firefly algorithm with chaos. *Commun. Nonlinear Sci.* **2013**, *18*, 89–98. [CrossRef]
33. Reynolds, A.M.; Frye, M.A. Free-Flight Odor Tracking in Drosophila Is Consistent with an Optimal Intermittent Scale-Free Search. *PLoS ONE* **2007**, *2*, e354. [CrossRef] [PubMed]
34. Viswanathan, G.M.; Afanasyev, V.; Buldyrev, S.V.; Murphy, E.J.; Prince, P.A.; Stanley, H.E. Lévy flight search patterns of wandering albatrosses. *Nature* **1996**, *381*, 413–415. [CrossRef]
35. Viswanathan, G.M. Fish in Lévy-flight foraging. *Nature* **2010**, *465*, 1018–1019. [CrossRef] [PubMed]
36. Gandomi, A.H.; Yang, X.-S.; Alavi, A.H. Cuckoo search algorithm: A metaheuristic approach to solve structural optimization problems. *Eng. Comput.* **2013**, *29*, 17–35. [CrossRef]
37. Emary, E.; Zawbaa, H.M.; Sharawi, M. Impact of Lèvy flight on modern meta-heuristic optimizers. *Appl. Soft Comput.* **2019**, *75*, 775–789. [CrossRef]
38. Yang, X.-S. Flower pollination algorithm for global optimization. In Proceedings of the International Conference on Unconventional Computing and Natural Computation, Orléans, France, 3–7 September 2012; pp. 240–249.
39. Amirsadri, S.; Mousavirad, S.J.; Ebrahimpour-Komleh, H. A Levy flight-based grey wolf optimizer combined with back-propagation algorithm for neural network training. *Neural Comput. Appl.* **2018**, *30*, 3707–3720. [CrossRef]
40. Tubishat, M.; Ja'afar, S.; Idris, N.; Al-Betar, M.A.; Alswaitti, M.; Jarrah, H.; Ismail, M.A.; Omar, M.S. Improved sine cosine algorithm with simulated annealing and singer chaotic map for Hadith classification. *Neural Comput. Appl.* **2022**, *34*, 1385–1406. [CrossRef]
41. Talatahari, S.; Kaveh, A.; Sheikholeslami, R. Chaotic imperialist competitive algorithm for optimum design of truss structures. *Struct. Multidiscip. Optim.* **2012**, *46*, 355–367. [CrossRef]
42. Wang, G.-G.; Guo, L.; Gandomi, A.H.; Hao, G.-S.; Wang, H. Chaotic Krill Herd algorithm. *Inf. Sci.* **2014**, *274*, 17–34. [CrossRef]
43. Houssein, E.H.; Helmy, B.E.D.; Elngar, A.A.; Abdelminaam, D.S.; Shaban, H. An Improved Tunicate Swarm Algorithm for Global Optimization and Image Segmentation. *IEEE Access* **2021**, *9*, 56066–56092. [CrossRef]
44. Gharehchopogh, F.S. An Improved Tunicate Swarm Algorithm with Best-random Mutation Strategy for Global Optimization Problems. *J. Bionic Eng.* **2022**, *19*, 1177–1202. [CrossRef]
45. Kaur, S.; Awasthi, L.K.; Sangal, A.L.; Dhiman, G. Tunicate Swarm Algorithm: A new bio-inspired based metaheuristic paradigm for global optimization. *Eng. Appl. Artif. Intell.* **2020**, *90*, 103541. [CrossRef]
46. Chawla, M.; Duhan, M. Levy Flights in Metaheuristics Optimization Algorithms—A Review. *Appl. Artif. Intell.* **2018**, *32*, 802–821. [CrossRef]
47. Chegini, S.N.; Bagheri, A.; Najafi, F. PSOSCALF: A new hybrid PSO based on Sine Cosine Algorithm and Levy flight for solving optimization problems. *Appl. Soft Comput.* **2018**, *73*, 697–726. [CrossRef]
48. Hakli, H.; Uguz, H. A novel particle swarm optimization algorithm with Levy flight. *Appl. Soft Comput.* **2014**, *23*, 333–345. [CrossRef]
49. Yan, B.L.; Zhao, Z.; Zhou, Y.C.; Yuan, W.Y.; Li, J.; Wu, J.; Cheng, D.J. A particle swarm optimization algorithm with random learning mechanism and Levy flight for optimization of atomic clusters. *Comput. Phys. Commun.* **2017**, *219*, 79–86. [CrossRef]
50. Emary, E.; Zawbaa, H.M. Impact of Chaos Functions on Modern Swarm Optimizers. *PLoS ONE* **2016**, *11*, e158738. [CrossRef]
51. Caponetto, R.; Fortuna, L.; Fazzino, S.; Xibilia, M.G. Chaotic sequences to improve the performance of evolutionary algorithms. *IEEE Trans. Evolut. Comput.* **2003**, *7*, 289–304. [CrossRef]
52. Jordehi, A.R. Chaotic bat swarm optimisation (CBSO). *Appl. Soft Comput.* **2015**, *26*, 523–530. [CrossRef]
53. Zheng, W.-M. Kneading plane of the circle map. *Chaos Solitons Fractals* **1994**, *4*, 1221–1233. [CrossRef]
54. Bucolo, M.; Caponetto, R.; Fortuna, L.; Frasca, M.; Rizzo, A. Does chaos work better than noise? *IEEE Circuits Syst. Mag.* **2002**, *2*, 4–19. [CrossRef]
55. He, D.; He, C.; Jiang, L.G.; Zhu, H.W.; Hu, G.R. Chaotic characteristics of a one-dimensional iterative map with infinite collapses. *IEEE Trans. Circuits Syst. I* **2001**, *48*, 900–906. [CrossRef]
56. May, R.M. Simple mathematical models with very complicated dynamics. *Nature* **1976**, *261*, 459–467. [CrossRef]
57. Peitgen, H.O.; Jürgens, H.; Saupe, D. *Chaos and Fractals: New Frontiers of Science*; Springer: Berlin/Heidelberg, Germany, 2004.

58. Tavazoei, M.S.; Haeri, M. Comparison of different one-dimensional maps as chaotic search pattern in chaos optimization algorithms. *Appl. Math. Comput.* **2007**, *187*, 1076–1085. [CrossRef]
59. Igiri, C.P.; Singh, Y.; Bhargava, D. An improved African Buffalo Optimization Algorithm Using Chaotic Map and Chaotic-Levy Flight. *Int. J. Eng. Technol.* **2018**, *7*, 4570–4576.
60. Lin, J.H.; Chou, C.W.; Yang, C.H.; Tsai, H.L. A Chaotic Levy Flight Bat Algorithm for Parameter Estimation in Nonlinear Dynamic Biological Systems. *Comput. Inf. Technol.* **2012**, *2*, 56–63.
61. Mirjalili, S.; Mirjalili, S.M.; Lewis, A. Grey Wolf Optimizer. *Adv. Eng. Softw.* **2014**, *69*, 46–61. [CrossRef]
62. Mirjalili, S. SCA: A Sine Cosine Algorithm for solving optimization problems. *Knowl.-Based Syst.* **2016**, *96*, 120–133. [CrossRef]
63. Xue, J.K.; Shen, B. A novel swarm intelligence optimization approach: Sparrow search algorithm. *Syst. Sci. Control Eng.* **2020**, *8*, 22–34. [CrossRef]
64. Faramarzi, A.; Heidarinejad, M.; Mirjalili, S.; Gandomi, A.H. Marine Predators Algorithm: A nature-inspired metaheuristic. *Expert Syst. Appl.* **2020**, *152*, 113377. [CrossRef]
65. Zhou, Y.Q.; Zhou, G.; Zhang, J.L. A hybrid glowworm swarm optimization algorithm to solve constrained multimodal functions optimization. *Optimization* **2015**, *64*, 1057–1080. [CrossRef]
66. Shukla, A. Chaos teaching learning based algorithm for large-scale global optimization problem and its application. *Concurr. Comput. Pract. Exp.* **2021**, *34*, e6514. [CrossRef]
67. Mirjalili, S.; Mirjalili, S.M.; Hatamlou, A. Multi-Verse Optimizer: A nature-inspired algorithm for global optimization. *Neural Comput. Appl.* **2016**, *27*, 495–513. [CrossRef]
68. Coello, C.A.C. Use of a self-adaptive penalty approach for engineering optimization problems. *Comput. Ind.* **2000**, *41*, 113–127. [CrossRef]
69. Kumar, A.; Wu, G.H.; Ali, M.Z.; Mallipeddi, R.; Suganthan, P.N.; Das, S. A test-suite of non-convex constrained optimization problems from the real-world and some baseline results. *Swarm. Evol. Comput.* **2020**, *56*, 100693. [CrossRef]

mathematics

MDPI

Article

A Multi-Population Mean-Field Game Approach for Large-Scale Agents Cooperative Attack-Defense Evolution in High-Dimensional Environments †

Guofang Wang [1,2,3], Ziming Li [1,2], Wang Yao [2,3,4,*] and Sikai Xia [1,2]

1 School of Mathematical Sciences, Beihang University, Beijing 100191, China; wangguofang@buaa.edu.cn (G.W.); zimingli@buaa.edu.cn (Z.L.); xiasikai_buaa@buaa.edu.cn (S.X.)
2 Key Laboratory of Mathematics, Informatics and Behavioral Semantics, Ministry of Education, Beijing Advanced Innovation Center for Big Data and Brain Computing, Beijing Advanced Innovation Center for Future Blockchain and Privacy Computing, Beihang University, Beijing 100191, China
3 Peng Cheng Laboratory , Shenzhen 518055, China
4 Institute of Artificial Intelligence, Beihang University, Beijing 100191, China
* Correspondence: yaowang@buaa.edu.cn

† This paper is an extended version of our paper published in Proceedings of the Genetic and Evolutionary Computation Conference Companion (GECCO'22), Association for Computing Machinery, New York, NY, USA, 9–13 July 2022.

Abstract: As one of the important issues of multi-agent collaboration, the large-scale agents' cooperative attack–defense evolution requires a large number of agents to make stress-effective strategies to achieve their goals in complex environments. Multi-agent attack and defense in high-dimensional environments (3D obstacle scenarios) present the challenge of being able to accurately control high-dimensional state quantities. Moreover, the large scale makes the dynamic interactions in the attack and defense problems increase dramatically, which, using traditional optimal control techniques, can cause a dimensional explosion. How to model and solve the cooperative attack–defense evolution problem of large-scale agents in high-dimensional environments have become a challenge. We jointly considered energy consumption, inter-group attack and defense, intra-group collision avoidance, and obstacle avoidance in their cost functions. Meanwhile, the high-dimensional state dynamics were used to describe the motion of agents under environmental interference. Then, we formulated the cooperative attack–defense evolution of large-scale agents in high-dimensional environments as a multi-population high-dimensional stochastic mean-field game (MPHD-MFG), which significantly reduced the communication frequency and computational complexity. We tractably solved the MPHD-MFG with a generative-adversarial-network (GAN)-based method using the MFGs' underlying variational primal–dual structure. Based on our approach, we carried out an integrative experiment in which we analytically showed the fast convergence of our cooperative attack–defense evolution algorithm by the convergence of the Hamilton–Jacobi–Bellman equation's residual errors. The experiment also showed that a large number of drones can avoid obstacles and smoothly evolve their attack and defense behaviors while minimizing their energy consumption. In addition, the comparison with the baseline methods showed that our approach is advanced.

Keywords: large-scale agents; attack and defense; multi-population mean-field game; high-dimensional solution space; neural networks

MSC: 91A16; 93-10; 49N80

Citation: Wang, G.; Li, Z.; Yao, W.; Xia, S. A Multi-Population Mean-Field Game Approach for Large-Scale Agents Cooperative Attack-Defense Evolution in High-Dimensional Environments. *Mathematics* **2022**, *10*, 4075. https://doi.org/10.3390/math10214075

Academic Editor: Ioannis G. Tsoulos

Received: 28 September 2022
Accepted: 31 October 2022
Published: 2 November 2022

1. Introduction

Cooperative control among multiple agent has always been an important research topic in swarm intelligence [1]. Game theory, as a branch of modern mathematics, studies optimal decision-making problems under conflicting adversarial conditions and can provide a theoretical basis for multi-agent cooperative decision-making problems. This paper is oriented toward the large-scale agents' cooperative attack–defense evolution, one of the important issues of multi-agent collaboration, which requires a large number of agents to make stress-effective strategies to achieve their goals in complex environments [2]. The multi-player continuous attack–defense game, as the mainstream research method for multi-agent attack–defense evolution, is a differential game between two adversarial teams of cooperative players playing in an area with targets. The attacker attempts to reach the set destination. The goal of the defender is to delay or stop the attacker by catching it [3]. The attack–defense game problem can be described as an optimal decision-making problem under complex multi-constraint conditions [4].

The classic attack–defense games have long been studied in multi-agent cooperative control. The multiple-pursuer-one-evader problem has been well documented. In [5], the Voronoi diagram construct was used for the capture of an evader within a bounded domain. Based on differential game theory and optimal control theory, differential game models have been established to solve optimal strategies by setting some rules and assumptions. In [6], based on the geometric relationship between two pursuers and an evader, a differential game model was established through coordinate transformation to solve the optimal cooperative strategy. Paper [7] studied the optimal guidance law of two missiles intercepting a single target based on the hypothesis of the missile hit sequence. Reference [8] proposed an online decision-making technique based on deep reinforcement learning (DRL) for solving the environmental sensing and decision-making problems in the chase and escape games. For the case of N-pursuers and M-evaders, more complex interactions need to be analyzed. Paper [9] studied a multiplayer border-defense problem and extended classical differential game theory to simultaneously address weapon assignments and multiplayer pursuit–evasion scenarios. Papers [10,11] proposed some methods based on linear programming, and applied deep reinforcement learning methods to deal with a simplified version of the RoboFlag competition [4]. An approach to the task allocation of many agents was proposed in [12], where Bakolas and Tsiotras used the Voronoi diagram construct to control the system. To solve general attack–defense games, the Hamilton–Jacobi–Isaacs (HJI) approach is ideal when the game is low-dimensional. However, because its complexity increases exponentially with the number of agents, the HJI approach is only tractable for the two-player game [13]. However, the above methods cannot be directly applied to the large-scale attack–defense game we are concerned with, because these traditional optimization and control technologies deal with the dynamic interactions between individuals separately. Moreover, to conduct more accurate real-time control for agents, the state variables used to characterize their kinematics are usually high-dimensional. Thus, with the increase in the agents' number, the modeling process of cooperative attack–defense problems tends to be complex, and the difficulty of solving the optimal strategy will increase significantly.

To solve the communication and calculation difficulties caused by agents' interactions on a large scale, mean-field games (MFGs) were proposed by Lasry and Lions [14–16] and Huang, Malhame, and Caines [17–19] independently. MFGs have been widely used in industrial engineering [20–22], crowd motion [23–26], swarm robotics [27,28], epidemic modeling [29,30], and data science [31–33]. In the MFG, each agent can obtain the evolution of the global or macroscopic information (mean-field) by solving the Fokker–Planck–Kolmogorov (FPK) equation. The optimal strategy of each agent is found by solving the Hamilton–Jacobi–Bellman (HJB) equation [34]. Recently, a machine-learning-based method, named APAC-net, has been proposed to solve high-dimensional stochastic MFGs [35]. Intuitively, the large-scale attack–defense problems are more consistent with the multi-population model. The multi-population mean-field game is a critical subclass of mean-field games (MFGs). It is a theoretically feasible multi-agent model for simulating and analyzing the game between multiple heterogeneous populations of interacting massive agents. We proposed a numerical solution method (CA-Net) for multi-population high-dimensional stochastic MFGs in [36], and studied the large-scale attack–defense problem in a 3D blank scenario based on CA-Net in [37]. In this paper, we focus on a 3D obstacle scene. The presence of multiple obstacles in the 3D space brings qualitative changes to the attack and defense decisions of large-scale agents, i.e., a "diversion" phenomenon. How to model and solve the cooperative attack–defense evolution problem of large-scale agents in 3D obstacle scenarios has become a challenge.

Inspired by the above-mentioned cutting-edge works, in this paper, we jointly considered energy consumption, inter-group attack and defense, intra-group collision avoidance, and obstacle avoidance in their cost functions. Meanwhile, the high-dimensional state dynamics were used to describe the motion of agents under environmental interference. Then, we made the following main contributions:

- We formulated the cooperative attack–defense evolution of large-scale agents in high-dimensional environments as a multi-population high-dimensional stochastic mean-field game (MPHD-MFG), which significantly reduced the communication frequency and computational complexity.
- We propose ECA-Net, an extended nonlinear coupled alternating neural network composed of multiple generators and multiple discriminators. We tractably solved the MPHD-MFG with the ECA-Net algorithm using MFGs' underlying variational primal–dual structure.
- We carried out an integrative experiment in which we analytically showed the fast convergence of our cooperative attack–defense evolution algorithm by the convergence of the Hamilton–Jacobi–Bellman equation's residual errors. The experiment also showed that a large number of drones can avoid obstacles and smoothly evolve their attack and defense behaviors while minimizing their energy consumption. The comparison with the baseline methods showed that our approach is advanced.

Our approach accomplishes a breakthrough from few-to-few to mass-to-mass in terms of attack–defense game theory in 3D obstacle scenarios.

In Section 2, we model the cooperative attack–defense evolution of large-scale agents in a 3D obstacle scene and formulate it as an MPHD-MFG. In Section 3, we propose ECA-Net to tractably solve the MPHD-MFG. Section 4 shows the performance of our algorithm with numerical results, and in Section 5, we draw our conclusions.

2. Modeling and Formulating

The system model consists of the objective function and the kinematics equation, which describe how large-scale agents evolve paths through attack–defense relationships. We considered a 3D obstacle attack–defense scenario with N agents, as shown in Figure 1. The blue side $\mathbb{N}_1$ as the attacker with N_1 agents hopes to break through the red side's interception and successfully reach the destination; the red side $\mathbb{N}_2$ as the defender with N_2 agents hopes to complete the interception against the blue side in the given area to prevent the blue side from penetrating. The state of agent i is denoted by $\mathbf{x}_i^p(t) \in \mathbb{R}^n$; $p = 1$ represents the blue side; $p = 2$ represents the red side, $i \in \mathbb{N}_1$ or $\mathbb{N}_2$, and $N_1 + N_2 = N$.

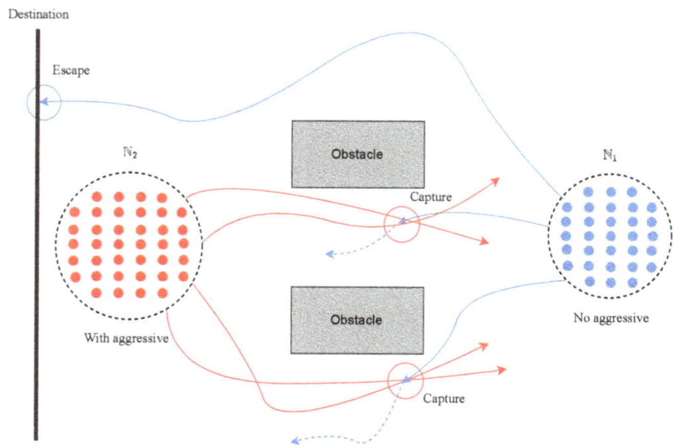

Figure 1. Vertical view of large-scale agents attacking and defending in 3D obstacle scene.

2.1. Kinematics Equation

Each agent $i \in \mathbb{N} = \mathbb{N}_1 \cup \mathbb{N}_2$ belongs to a population $p(i) \in \mathbb{Q} = \{1,2\}$ and is characterized by a state $\mathbf{x}_i^p(t) \in \mathbb{R}^n$ at time $t \in [0,T]$. We considered that the continuous-time state $\mathbf{x}_i^p(t)$ of player i of population p has the dynamic–kinematic equation of the following form

$$\mathrm{d}\mathbf{x}_i^p = \mathbf{h}_i^p(\mathbf{x}_i^p, \mathbf{x}_i^{p^-}, \mathbf{x}_i^{-p^-}, \mathbf{u}_i^p)\mathrm{d}t, \tag{1}$$

where $\mathbf{u}_i^p : [0,T] \to \mathcal{U}_p \subseteq \mathbb{R}^m$ is the control input (strategy) implemented by agent i in view of the state $\mathbf{x}_i^p$ at time t, $\mathbf{x}_i^{p^-} : \mathbb{R}^n \times [0,T] \to \mathcal{P}_2(\mathbb{R}^n)$ is the states of all other intra-group agents, $\mathbf{x}_i^{-p^-}$ describes the states of all other inter-group agents, and $\mathbf{h}_i^p : \mathbb{R}^n \times \mathcal{P}_2(\mathbb{R}^n)^2 \times \mathcal{U}_p \to \mathbb{R}^n$ is the nonlinear evolution function, $p = 1,2$.

2.2. Objective Function

For player i of population p, $p = 1,2$, we considered the cost function of the following form:

$$\begin{aligned} J_i^p(\mathbf{x}_i^p, \mathbf{x}_i^{p^-}, \mathbf{x}_i^{-p^-}, \mathbf{u}_i^p) = \int_0^T & L_i^p(\mathbf{x}_i^p(t), \mathbf{u}_i^p(t)) + F_i^p(\mathbf{x}_i^p(t), \mathbf{x}_i^{p^-}(\mathbf{x}_i^p(t),t), \mathbf{x}_i^{-p^-}(\mathbf{x}_i^{-p}(t),t))\mathrm{d}t \\ & + G_i^p(\mathbf{x}_i^p(T), \mathbf{x}_i^{p^-}(\mathbf{x}_i^p(T),T), \mathbf{x}_i^{-p^-}(\mathbf{x}_i^{-p}(T),T)), \end{aligned} \tag{2}$$

where $L_i^p : \mathbb{R}^n \times \mathcal{U}_p \to \mathbb{R}$ is the running cost incurred by agent i based solely on its actions, $F_i^p : \mathbb{R}^n \times \mathcal{P}_2(\mathbb{R}^n)^2 \to \mathbb{R}$ is the running cost incurred by agent i based on its interactions with the rest of the same population and the other population, and $G_i^p : \mathbb{R}^n \times \mathcal{P}_2(\mathbb{R}^n)^2 \to \mathbb{R}$ is a terminal cost incurred by agent i based on its final state and the final states of the whole of the related populations.

2.2.1. Blue-Side Control Problem

In the 3D obstacle space, the blue side's agents traveling from a common source hope to break through the red side's interception while avoiding obstacles and successfully reach the destination, where a straight line segment in the area above the red side's initial distribution is set as the destination. At time $t \geq 0$, the i-th agent controls its strategy $\mathbf{u}_i^1$ to minimize its: (1) motion energy, (2) red side capture, (3) blue side inter-agent collision,

(4) collision of the blue side with the obstacles, and (5) travel time during the remaining travel to the destination. The running cost L_i^1 is given by

$$L_i^1 = \underbrace{c_1\|\mathbf{u}_i^1(t)\|^2}_{\text{(1) motion energy minimization}}, \tag{3}$$

where c_1 is a constant. The running cost L_i^1 denotes the control effort implemented by agent i. The interaction cost F_i^1 is given by

$$\begin{aligned} F_i^1 = & \underbrace{c_2\left(-\frac{1}{N_2}\sum_{k=1}^{N_2}\left\|\mathbf{p}_i^1(t) - (\mathbf{p}_k^2(t) + e_r\mathbf{e})\right\|\right)}_{\text{(2) red side capture minimization}} + \underbrace{c_3\left(\frac{1}{N_1}\sum_{j\neq i}^{N_1}\mathbf{1}_{\|\mathbf{p}_i^1(t)-\mathbf{p}_j^1(t)\|\leq e_0}\right)}_{\text{(3) blue side inter-agent collision avoidance}} \\ & \underbrace{+ c_4\left(\frac{1}{N_1}\sum_{i=1}^{N_1}\begin{cases}\sum_{a=1}^{A}\gamma_{obs,a}\frac{1}{Q_a(\mathbf{p}_i,t)} & \text{if } \mathbf{p}_i \in \Omega_{obs,trn} \\ 0 & \text{otherwise}\end{cases}\right)}_{\text{(4) blue side obstacle collision avoidance}}, \end{aligned} \tag{4}$$

$$\Omega_{obs,trn} = \bigcup_{a=1}^{A}\Omega_{obs,trn,a} \tag{5}$$

$$\Omega_{obs,trn,a}: \quad Q_a(x,y,z) = \frac{1}{3v_{1,a}^2}(x-x_{0,a})^2 + \frac{1}{3v_{2,a}^2}(y-y_{0,a})^2 + \frac{1}{3v_{3,a}^2}(z-z_{0,a})^2 \leq 1.1, \quad a = 1,\ldots,A, \tag{6}$$

$$\Omega_{obs,a} = \{(x,y,z)||x-x_{0,a}| \leq v_{1,a}, |y-y_{0,a}| \leq v_{2,a}, |z-z_{0,a}| \leq v_{3,a}\}, \quad a = 1,\ldots,A. \tag{7}$$

where $\mathbf{p} = (x,y,z)$ is the agent's usual Euclidean spatial coordinate position, $\mathbf{e}$ is the unit vector of the spherical coordinate system, e_r is the capture radius of the red side agent, e_0 is the safe distance between agents, c_2, c_3, c_4 are constants, $\gamma_{obs,a}$, $a = 1,\ldots,A$, is the repulsive force gain coefficient between the agent i and other obstacles, $(x_{0,a}, y_{0,a}, z_{0,a})$ is the center of the corresponding obstacle, and $(\pm v_{1,a}, \pm v_{2,a}, \pm v_{3,a})$ are its vertices, which are parallel with the x, y, z axes, respectively. The interaction cost F_i^1 denotes the sum of the trajectory collision loss of the intra-group, inter-group, and with obstacles about agent i.

Remark 1. *In our 3D obstacle scene, obstacles were rectangular solids Ω_{obs}. For training, the cuboid obstacle repulsion is formulated as a differentiable unit ellipsoid repulsion function $\frac{1}{Q}$ [38]. To better reduce the collision between agents and obstacles, the radius of $\Omega_{obs,trn}$ is 10% larger than that of the unit circumscribed ellipsoid of Ω_{obs}. Our algorithm was trained by using ellipsoidal repulsion, which can produce gradient information smoothly in obstacles, stimulating the model to learn trajectories to avoid obstacles [39].*

The terminal cost G_i^1 is given by

$$G_i^1 = \underbrace{c_5\|\mathbf{x}_i^1(T) - \mathbf{x}_0\|_2}_{\text{(5) travel time minimization}}, \tag{8}$$

where c_5 is a constant, $\mathbf{x}_i^1(T)$ is the final state of agent i, and $\mathbf{x}_0$ is the target state in which we want the agents to reach the objective. The terminal cost G_i^1 denotes the distance between agent i's terminal state and the desired state.

In summary, by defining the cost function as (2), the optimal control problem faced by agent i of the blue side is given by

$$\begin{aligned} \inf_{\mathbf{u}_i^1 \in \mathcal{U}_1} \quad & J_i^1(\mathbf{x}_i^1, \mathbf{x}_i^{1^-}, \mathbf{x}_i^{2^-}, \mathbf{u}_i^1) \\ \text{s.t.} \quad & \mathrm{d}\mathbf{x}_i^1 = \mathbf{h}_i^1(\mathbf{x}_i^1, \mathbf{x}_i^{1^-}, \mathbf{x}_i^{2^-}, \mathbf{u}_i^1)\mathrm{d}t. \end{aligned} \tag{9}$$

2.2.2. Red Side Control Problem

The red side's agents traveling from a common source avoid obstacles and hope to complete the interception against the blue side to prevent the blue side from penetrating. At time $t \geq 0$, the i-th agent controls its strategy $\mathbf{u}_i^2$, to minimize its: (1) motion energy, (2) distance to the blue side, (3) red side inter-agent collision, and (4) the collision of the red side with the obstacles during the remaining travel time. The running cost L_i^2 is given by

$$L_i^2 = \underbrace{l_1 \|\mathbf{u}_i^2(t)\|^2}_{\text{(1) motion energy minimization}}, \tag{10}$$

where l_1 is a constant. The running cost L_i^2 denotes the control effort implemented by agent i. The interaction cost F_i^2 is given by

$$\begin{aligned} F_i^2 = & \underbrace{l_2 \left(\frac{1}{N_1} \sum_{k=1}^{N_1} \left\| \mathbf{p}_i^2(t) - \mathbf{p}_k^1(t) \right\| \right)}_{\text{(2) distance to blue side minimization}} + \underbrace{l_3 \left(\frac{1}{N_2} \sum_{j \neq i}^{N_2} \mathbf{1}_{\|\mathbf{p}_i^2(t) - \mathbf{p}_j^2(t)\| \leq e_0} \right)}_{\text{(3) red side inter-agent collision avoidance}} \\ & \underbrace{+ l_4 \left(\frac{1}{N_2} \sum_{i=1}^{N_2} \begin{cases} \sum_{a=1}^{A} \gamma_{obs,a} \frac{1}{Q_a(\mathbf{p}_i, t)} & \text{if } \mathbf{p}_i \in \Omega_{obs,trn} \\ 0 & \text{otherwise} \end{cases} \right)}_{\text{(4) red side obstacle collision avoidance}}, \end{aligned} \tag{11}$$

where l_2, l_3, l_4 are constants. The interaction cost F_i^2 denotes the sum of the trajectory collision loss of the intra-group, inter-group, and with obstacles about agent i.

In summary, by defining the cost function as (2), the optimal control problem faced by agent i of the red side is given by

$$\begin{aligned} &\inf_{u_i^2 \in \mathcal{U}_2} \quad J_i^2(\mathbf{x}_i^2, \mathbf{x}_i^{2^-}, \mathbf{x}_i^{1^-}, \mathbf{u}_i^2) \\ &\text{s.t.} \quad \mathrm{d}\mathbf{x}_i^2 = \mathbf{h}_i^2(\mathbf{x}_i^2, \mathbf{x}_i^{2^-}, \mathbf{x}_i^{1^-}, \mathbf{u}_i^2)\mathrm{d}t. \end{aligned} \tag{12}$$

To this end, the cooperative attack–defense evolution for large-scale agents in the 3D obstacle scene is formulated as a non-cooperative differential game. Thus, an N-player non-cooperative game is formed. Its obvious solution is the Nash equilibrium, that is no agent can unilaterally reduce its cost under this control decision [16].

2.3. *Multi-Population High-Dimensional Mean-Field Game*

With the increase of the number N of game participants, the complexity of solving differential games will increase significantly. For the current agent in the cooperative attack–defense problem (16), the neighborhood interactions of intra-group collision avoidance, the inter-group interactions of attack and defense, and the ecological interactions of obstacle avoidance will lead to the need for a large amount of communication and computing resources. Traditional optimization and control methods usually deal with the increasing interactions separately, leading to the dimension explosion problem. The mean-field game is able to overcome the communication and computational difficulties associated with a large scale, and its core technology is to inscribe a large number of interacting swarm intelligence problems as coupled sets of partial differential equations (PDEs). Therefore, we propose the multi-population high-dimensional stochastic MFG (MPHD-MFG) reformulation of the cooperative attack–defense problem (16). Under the framework of the MPHD-MFG, a generic player only reacts to the collective behaviors (mean field) of all players instead of the behavior of each player, which greatly reduces the amount of communication and computation. Here, "mean-field" means the states' probability distribution. Now, we can drop the index i since players are indistinguishable within each population of the MPHD-MFG. Let $\rho^p(\mathbf{x}^p, t) : \mathbb{R}^n \times [0, T] \to \mathcal{P}_2(\mathbb{R}^n)$ denote the probability density function of state $\mathbf{x}^p$ at time t, then the cost function (2) is transformed into

$$
\begin{aligned}
&J^p(\mathbf{x}^p,\rho^p,\rho^{-p},\mathbf{u}^p) = \\
&\mathbb{E}\Big[\int_0^T L^p(\mathbf{x}^p(t),\mathbf{u}^p(t)) + F^p(\mathbf{x}^p(t),\rho^p(\mathbf{x}^p(t),t),\rho^{-p}(\mathbf{x}^{-p}(t),t))\mathrm{d}t + G^p(\mathbf{x}^p(T),\rho^p(\mathbf{x}^p(T),T),\rho^{-p}(\mathbf{x}^{-p}(T),T))\Big] \\
&= \int_0^T\Big\{\int_\Omega L^p(\mathbf{x}^p(t),\mathbf{u}^p(t))\rho^p(\mathbf{x}^p,t)\mathrm{d}\mathbf{x}\Big\}\mathrm{d}t + \int_0^T\Big\{\int_\Omega F^p(\mathbf{x}^p(t),\rho^p(\mathbf{x}^p(t),t),\rho^{-p}(\mathbf{x}^{-p}(t),t))\rho^p(\mathbf{x}^p,t)\mathrm{d}\mathbf{x}\Big\}\mathrm{d}t \\
&\qquad + \int_\Omega G^p(\mathbf{x}^p(T),\rho^p(\mathbf{x}^p(T),T),\rho^{-p}(\mathbf{x}^{-p}(T),T))\rho^p(\mathbf{x}^p,t)\mathrm{d}\mathbf{x} \\
&= \int_0^T\Big\{\int_\Omega L^p(\mathbf{x}^p(t),\mathbf{u}^p(t))\rho^p(\mathbf{x}^p,t)\mathrm{d}\mathbf{x}\Big\}\mathrm{d}t + \int_0^T \mathcal{F}^p(\mathbf{x}^p(t),\rho^p(\mathbf{x}^p(t),t),\rho^{-p}(\mathbf{x}^{-p}(t),t))\mathrm{d}t \\
&\qquad + \mathcal{G}^p(\mathbf{x}^p(T),\rho^p(\mathbf{x}^p(T),T),\rho^{-p}(\mathbf{x}^{-p}(T),T)),
\end{aligned} \tag{13}
$$

where $\Omega \in \mathbb{R}^n$ is the state space containing all possible states of the generic agent and variational derivatives of functionals $\mathcal{F},\mathcal{G}$ for ρ are the interaction and terminal costs F and G, respectively. Meanwhile, the state dynamic–kinematic equation in (1) is transformed into

$$
\mathrm{d}\mathbf{x}^p = \mathbf{h}^p(\mathbf{x}^p,\rho^p,\rho^{-p},\mathbf{u}^p)\mathrm{d}t + \sigma^p\mathrm{d}\mathbf{W}_t^p, \tag{14}
$$

where $\sigma^p \in \mathbb{R}^{n\times m}$ denotes a fixed coefficient matrix of a population-dependent volatility term and $\mathbf{W}^p$ means an m-dimensional Wiener process springs from the environment, in which each component $\mathbf{W}_k^p$ is independent of $\mathbf{W}_l^p$ for all $k \neq l$, $p = 1,2$. According to Ito's lemma [40], (14) can be expressed in terms of the mean field $\rho^p(\mathbf{x}^p,t)$ and then will be equivalent to the Fokker–Planck (FPK) equation given by

$$
\partial_t\rho^p - \frac{\sigma^{p2}}{2}\Delta\rho^p + \nabla\cdot(\rho^p\mathbf{h}^p) = 0. \tag{15}
$$

With cost function (13) and FPK Equation (15), the multi-population high-dimensional MFG, which describes the cooperative attack–defense evolution of a large number of agents, is now summarized as

$$
\begin{aligned}
&\inf_{\rho^p,\mathbf{u}^p} J^p(\mathbf{x}^p,\rho^p,\rho^{-p},\mathbf{u}^p) \\
\text{s.t. } &\partial_t\rho^p - \frac{\sigma^{p2}}{2}\Delta\rho^p + \nabla\cdot(\rho^p\mathbf{h}^p) = 0, \quad \rho^p(\mathbf{x}^p,0) = \rho_0^p(\mathbf{x}^p) \\
&\partial_t\rho^{-p} - \frac{\sigma^{-p2}}{2}\Delta\rho^{-p} + \nabla\cdot(\rho^{-p}\mathbf{h}^{-p}) = 0, \quad \rho^{-p}(\mathbf{x}^{-p},0) = \rho_0^{-p}(\mathbf{x}^{-p}) \\
&p = 1,2,
\end{aligned} \tag{16}
$$

where ρ_0^p is the initial probability distribution of population p's agents. To this end, the cooperative attack–defense evolution for large-scale agents in the 3D obstacle scene is formulated as a multi-population high-dimensional MFG. For every population $p = 1,2$, each agent i of population $p(i)$ forecasts a distribution $\{\rho^p(\cdot,t)\}_{t=0}^T$ and aims at minimizing its cost, which eventually reaches the Nash equilibrium, where no agent can decrease its individual cost by changing its control strategy unilaterally. The formulaic representation, for every $\mathbf{x}^p \in \mathbb{R}^n$:

$$
J^p(\mathbf{x}^p,\rho^p,\rho^{-p},\hat{\mathbf{u}}^p) \leq J^p(\mathbf{x}^p,\rho^p,\rho^{-p},\mathbf{u}^p), \quad \forall\mathbf{u}^p : [0,T] \to \mathcal{U}_p, \tag{17}
$$

where $\hat{\mathbf{u}}^p$ is the agent's equilibrium strategy at state $\mathbf{x}^p$. Here, we assumed that the agent is small, and its unilateral actions will not change the density ρ^p. Reference [41] provides a sufficient condition for the solution to the multi-population MFG PDEs, and Reference [42] provides the necessary one.

Remark 2. *Under appropriate assumptions, the MFG's solution will offer an approximate Nash equilibrium (ϵ-NE) for the corresponding game with a large, but finite number of agents [41].*

3. GAN-Based Approach for MPHD-MFG

In this section, we put forward a generative-adversarial-network (GAN)-based method for solving the multi-population high-dimensional MFG in (16). Inspired by Wasserstein GANs [43], APAC-Net [35], and CA-Net [36,37], we formulated (16) as a convex-concave saddle-point problem using MFG's variational primal–dual structure. Then, we propose an extended coupled alternating neural network (ECA-Net) algorithm to solve the MPHD-MFG in (16).

3.1. Variational Primal–Dual Structure of MPHD-MFG

We reveal the underlying primal–dual structure of the MPHD-MFG, then deduce the convex–concave saddle-point problem equivalent to (16). Denote $\Phi_p : \Phi_p(\mathbf{x}^p, t) = \inf_{\mathbf{u}^p} J^p(\mathbf{x}^p, \rho^p, \rho^{-p}, \mathbf{u}^p)$ as the Lagrange multiplier; we can add the differential constraint (15) (FPK equation) into the cost function (13) to obtain the extended cost function:

$$
\begin{aligned}
\sup_{\Phi_p} \inf_{\rho^p, \mathbf{u}^p} \Big\{ & \int_0^T \int_\Omega L^p(\mathbf{x}^p(t), \mathbf{u}^p(t)) \rho^p(\mathbf{x}^p, t) \mathrm{d}\mathbf{x} \mathrm{d}t + \int_0^T \mathcal{F}^p(\mathbf{x}^p(t), \rho^p(\mathbf{x}^p(t), t), \rho^{-p}(\mathbf{x}^{-p}(t), t)) \mathrm{d}t \\
& + \mathcal{G}^p(\mathbf{x}^p(T), \rho^p(\mathbf{x}^p(T), T), \rho^{-p}(\mathbf{x}^{-p}(T), T)) \\
& - \int_0^T \int_\Omega \Phi_p(\mathbf{x}^p, t)(\partial_t \rho^p - \frac{\sigma^{p2}}{2} \Delta \rho^p + \nabla \cdot (\rho^p(\mathbf{x}^p, t) \mathbf{h}^p(\mathbf{x}^p, \rho^p, \rho^{-p}, \mathbf{u}^p))) \mathrm{d}\mathbf{x}^p \mathrm{d}t \\
& - \int_0^T \int_\Omega \Phi_{-p}(\mathbf{x}^{-p}, t)(\partial_t \rho^{-p} - \frac{\sigma^{-p2}}{2} \Delta \rho^{-p} + \nabla \cdot (\rho^{-p}(\mathbf{x}^{-p}, t) \mathbf{h}^{-p}(\mathbf{x}^{-p}, \rho^{-p}, \rho^p, \mathbf{u}^{-p}))) \mathrm{d}\mathbf{x}^{-p} \mathrm{d}t \Big\}.
\end{aligned} \tag{18}
$$

The Hamiltonian $H_p : \mathbb{R}^n \times \mathcal{P}_2(\mathbb{R}^n)^2 \times \mathbb{R}^n \to \mathbb{R}$, $p = 1, 2$ is defined as

$$
H_p(\mathbf{x}^p, \rho^p, \rho^{-p}, z^p) = \sup_{\mathbf{u}^p} \{ -L_p(\mathbf{x}^p, \mathbf{u}^p) - z^{p\top} \mathbf{h}^p(\mathbf{x}^p, \rho^p, \rho^{-p}, \mathbf{u}^p) \}. \tag{19}
$$

Utilizing (19) and integrating by parts, we can rewrite (18) as

$$
\begin{aligned}
\inf_{\rho^p} \sup_{\Phi_p} \Big\{ & \int_0^T \int_\Omega (\partial_t \Phi_p + \frac{\sigma^{p2}}{2} \Delta \Phi_p - H_p(\mathbf{x}^p, \nabla \Phi_p)) \rho^p(\mathbf{x}^p, t) \mathrm{d}\mathbf{x}^p \mathrm{d}t + \int_0^T \mathcal{F}^p(\mathbf{x}^p(t), \rho^p(\mathbf{x}^p(t), t), \rho^{-p}(\mathbf{x}^{-p}(t), t)) \mathrm{d}t \\
& + \mathcal{G}^p(\mathbf{x}^p(T), \rho^p(\mathbf{x}^p(T), T), \rho^{-p}(\mathbf{x}^{-p}(T), T)) + \int_\Omega \Phi_p(\mathbf{x}^p, 0) \rho_0^p(\mathbf{x}^p) \mathrm{d}\mathbf{x}^p - \int_\Omega \Phi_p(\mathbf{x}^p, T) \rho^p(\mathbf{x}^p, T) \mathrm{d}\mathbf{x}^p \\
& + \int_0^T \int_\Omega (\partial_t \Phi_{-p} + \frac{\sigma^{-p2}}{2} \Delta \Phi_{-p} + \nabla \Phi_{-p} \cdot \mathbf{h}^{-p}) \rho^{-p}(\mathbf{x}^{-p}, t) \mathrm{d}\mathbf{x}^{-p} \mathrm{d}t + \int_\Omega \Phi_{-p}(\mathbf{x}^{-p}, 0) \rho_0^{-p}(\mathbf{x}^{-p}) \mathrm{d}\mathbf{x}^{-p} \\
& - \int_\Omega \Phi_{-p}(\mathbf{x}^{-p}, T) \rho^{-p}(\mathbf{x}^{-p}, T) \mathrm{d}\mathbf{x}^{-p} \Big\}.
\end{aligned} \tag{20}
$$

Here, our derivation path follows that of [44–46]. The formulation (20) is the cornerstone of our approach.

3.2. ECA-Net for Cooperative Attack–Defense Evolution

We solved (20) by training a GAN-based neural network. The solving network of the multi-population MFG in the 3D obstacle scene is an extended nonlinear coupled alternating neural network formed by multiple generators and multiple discriminators, named ECA-Net. We coupled the obstacle avoidance loss term in the design of the loss function of the ECA-Net algorithm. The structure and training process of ECA-Net are shown in Figure 2.

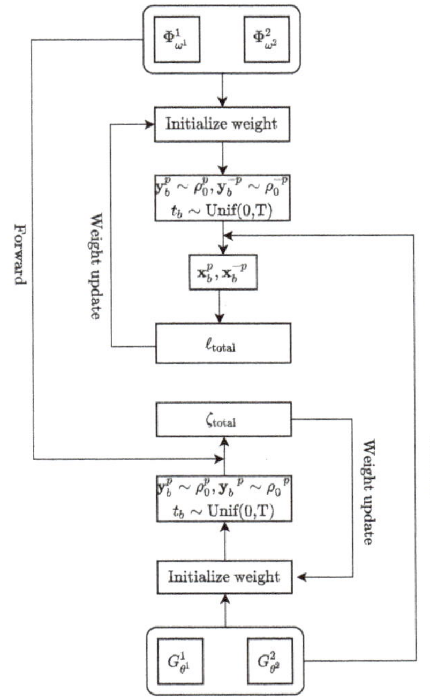

Figure 2. Visualization of the structure and training process of ECA-Net. Its training process is divided into two pairs of coupled alternating training parts—generators and discriminators.

First, we initialized two pairs of neural networks $N^p_{\omega^p}(\mathbf{x}^p, t)$ and $N^p_{\theta^p}(\mathbf{y}^p, t)$, $p = 1, 2$. Let

$$\Phi^p_{\omega^p}(\mathbf{x}^p, t) = (1-t)N^p_{\omega^p}(\mathbf{x}^p, t) + tG^p(\mathbf{x}^p), \quad \mathcal{G}^p_{\theta^p}(\mathbf{y}^p, t) = (1-t)\mathbf{y}^p + tN^p_{\theta^p}(\mathbf{y}^p, t), \tag{21}$$

where $\mathbf{y}^p \sim \rho_0^p$ is a sample drawn from the initial distribution. The formulation of $\Phi^p_{\omega^p}$ (the value function for the generic agent of population p) and $\mathcal{G}^p_{\theta^p}$ (the density distribution of population p) in (21) automatically encodes the terminal condition $G^p(\cdot, T)$ and initial distribution $\rho_0^p(\cdot)$, respectively. Moreover, ECA-Net encodes the underlying structure of the MPHD-MFG by (20) and (21), exempting the neural network from learning the entire game solution from scratch.

Our approach for training this neural network includes parallel–alternate training of two pairs of $\mathcal{G}^p_{\theta^p}$ and $\Phi^p_{\omega^p}$, $p = 1, 2$. Intuitively, to gain the equilibrium of the MPHD-MFG of the cooperative attack–defense problem, we trained an extended coupled alternating neural network (ECA-Net) about multi-group distributions and agent controls. Specifically, we trained $\Phi^p_{\omega^p}$ by first sampling a batch $\{\mathbf{y}_b^p\}_{b=1}^B$ from given initial distribution ρ_0^p, another batch $\{\mathbf{y}_b^{-p}\}_{b=1}^B$ from given initial density ρ_0^{-p}, and $\{t_b\}_{b=1}^B$ uniformly from $[0, T]$. Then, we computed the push-forward states $\mathbf{x}_b^p = \mathcal{G}^p_{\theta^p}(\mathbf{y}_b^p, t_b)$, $\mathbf{x}_b^{-p} = \mathcal{G}^{-p}_{\theta^{-p}}(\mathbf{y}_b^{-p}, t_b)$ for $b = 1, \ldots, B$. The main loss term for training the discriminator $\Phi^p_{\omega^p}$ is given by

$$\text{loss}_{\Phi^p} = \frac{1}{B}\sum_{b=1}^{B} \Phi^p_{\omega^p}(\mathbf{x}_b^p, 0) + \frac{1}{B}\sum_{b=1}^{B}\left\{\partial_t \Phi^p_{\omega^p}(\mathbf{x}_b^p, t_b) + \frac{\sigma^{p2}}{2}\Delta\Phi^p_{\omega^p}(\mathbf{x}_b^p, t_b) - H_p(\nabla_{\mathbf{x}^p}\Phi^p_{\omega^p}(\mathbf{x}_b^p, t_b))\right\}. \tag{22}$$

We need to consider adding a dual term for the distribution of the neighboring population:

$$\text{penalty}_{\text{neighbors}} = \eta\left\{\frac{1}{B}\sum_{b=1}^{B}\left[\partial_t \Phi^{-p}_{\omega^{-p}}(\mathbf{x}_b^{-p}, t_b) + \frac{\sigma^{-p2}}{2}\Delta\Phi^{-p}_{\omega^{-p}}(\mathbf{x}_b^{-p}, t_b) + \nabla_{\mathbf{x}^{-p}}\Phi^{-p}_{\omega^{-p}}(\mathbf{x}_b^{-p}, t_b)\cdot \mathbf{h}^{-p}(\mathbf{x}_b^{-p}, \mathbf{x}_b^p, t_b)\right]\right\} \tag{23}$$

to correct for the density update of the other population (which tends to obey the FPK equation) [36]. We can optionally add a regularization term:

$$\text{penalty}_{\text{HJB}} = \lambda\left\{\frac{1}{B}\sum_{b=1}^{B}\|\partial_t\Phi^p_{\omega^p}(\mathbf{x}^p_b,t_b)+\frac{\sigma^{p2}}{2}\Delta\Phi^p_{\omega^p}(\mathbf{x}^p_b,t_b)-H_p(\nabla_{\mathbf{x}^p}\Phi^p_{\omega^p}(\mathbf{x}^p_b,t_b))+F^p(\mathbf{x}^p_b,\mathbf{x}^{-p}_b,t_b)\|\right\} \tag{24}$$

to penalize deviations from the HJB equations. Finally, we backpropagated the total loss ℓ_{total} to update the weights of the discriminator $\Phi^p_{\omega^p}$.

To train the generator, we again sampled $\{\mathbf{y}^p_b\}^B_{b=1}$, $\{\mathbf{y}^{-p}_b\}^B_{b=1}$ and $\{t_b\}^B_{b=1}$, $p=1,2$ as before and computed

$$\text{loss}_{\mathcal{G}^p} = \frac{1}{B}\sum_{b=1}^{B}\left\{\partial_t\Phi^p_{\omega^p}(\mathcal{G}^p_{\theta^p}(\mathbf{y}^p_b),t_b)+\frac{\sigma^{p2}}{2}\Delta\Phi^p_{\omega^p}(\mathcal{G}^p_{\theta^p}(\mathbf{y}^p_b),t_b)-H_p(\nabla_{\mathbf{x}^p}\Phi^p_{\omega^p}(\mathcal{G}^p_{\theta^p}(\mathbf{y}^p_b),t_b))+F^p(\mathcal{G}^p_{\theta^p}(\mathbf{y}^p_b),\mathcal{G}^{-p}_{\theta^{-p}}(\mathbf{y}^{-p}_b),t_b)\right\}. \tag{25}$$

Finally, we backpropagated the total loss ζ_{total} to update the weights of the generator $\mathcal{G}^p_{\theta^p}$.

In conclusion, in each time slot $t\in[0,T]$, the ECA-Net will be trained. The generator $\mathcal{G}^p_{\theta^p}$ will generate the state distribution of population p at time t, and the discriminator $\Phi^p_{\omega^p}$ will obtain the result of the value function of population p at time t, $p=1,2$. Please refer to Algorithm 1 for the detailed operation flow.

Algorithm 1 ECA-Net for cooperative attack–defense evolution.

Require: σ^p diffusion parameter, G^p terminal cost, H_p Hamiltonian, F^p interaction term, $p=1,2$.
Require: Initialize neural networks $N^p_{\omega^p}$ and $N^p_{\theta^p}$, batch size B.
Require: Set $\Phi^p_{\omega^p}$ and $\mathcal{G}^p_{\theta^p}$ as in (21).
While not converged, **do**
    train $\Phi^p_{\omega^p}$:
Sample batch $\{(\mathbf{y}^p_b,t_b)\}^B_{b=1}$, $\{(\mathbf{y}^{-p}_b,t_b)\}^B_{b=1}$, where $\mathbf{y}^p_b\sim\rho^p_0$, $\mathbf{y}^{-p}_b\sim\rho^{-p}_0$ and $t_b\sim\text{Unif}(0,T)$.
$\mathbf{x}^p_b\leftarrow\mathcal{G}^p_{\theta^p}(\mathbf{y}^p_b,t_b)$, $\mathbf{x}^{-p}_b\leftarrow\mathcal{G}^{-p}_{\theta^{-p}}(\mathbf{y}^{-p}_b,t_b)$ for $b=1,\ldots,B$.
$\ell^p_0\leftarrow\frac{1}{B}\sum^B_{b=1}\Phi^p_{\omega^p}(\mathbf{x}^p_b,0)$
$\ell^p_t\leftarrow\frac{1}{B}\sum^B_{b=1}\left\{\partial_t\Phi^p_{\omega^p}(\mathbf{x}^p_b,t_b)+\frac{\sigma^{p2}}{2}\Delta\Phi^p_{\omega^p}(\mathbf{x}^p_b,t_b)-H_p(\nabla_{\mathbf{x}^p}\Phi^p_{\omega^p}(\mathbf{x}^p_b,t_b))\right\}$
$\ell^p_n\leftarrow\eta\left\{\frac{1}{B}\sum^B_{b=1}\left[\partial_t\Phi^{-p}_{\omega^{-p}}(\mathbf{x}^{-p}_b,t_b)+\frac{\sigma^{-p2}}{2}\Delta\Phi^{-p}_{\omega^{-p}}(\mathbf{x}^{-p}_b,t_b)+\nabla_{\mathbf{x}^{-p}}\Phi^{-p}_{\omega^{-p}}(\mathbf{x}^{-p}_b,t_b)\cdot\mathbf{h}^{-p}(\mathbf{x}^{-p}_b,\mathbf{x}^p_b,t_b)\right]\right\}$
$\ell^p_{\text{HJB}}\leftarrow\lambda\left\{\frac{1}{B}\sum^B_{b=1}\|\partial_t\Phi^p_{\omega^p}(\mathbf{x}^p_b,t_b)+\frac{\sigma^{p2}}{2}\Delta\Phi^p_{\omega^p}(\mathbf{x}^p_b,t_b)-H_p(\nabla_{\mathbf{x}^p}\Phi^p_{\omega^p}(\mathbf{x}^p_b,t_b))+F^p(\mathbf{x}^p_b,\mathbf{x}^{-p}_b,t_b)\|\right\}$
$\ell^p_{\text{total}}\leftarrow\ell^p_0+\ell^p_t+\ell^p_n+\ell^p_{\text{HJB}}$
Backpropagate total loss $\ell_{\text{total}}=\sum_p\ell^p_{\text{total}}$ to $\omega=(\omega^p)_{p=1,2}$ weights.

    train $\mathcal{G}^p_{\theta^p}$:
Sample batch $\{(\mathbf{y}^p_b,t_b)\}^B_{b=1}$, $\{(\mathbf{y}^{-p}_b,t_b)\}^B_{b=1}$, where $\mathbf{y}^p_b\sim\rho^p_0$, $\mathbf{y}^{-p}_b\sim\rho^{-p}_0$ and $t_b\sim\text{Unif}(0,T)$.
$\zeta^p_t\leftarrow\frac{1}{B}\sum^B_{b=1}\left\{\partial_t\Phi^p_{\omega^p}(\mathcal{G}^p_{\theta^p}(\mathbf{y}^p_b),t_b)+\frac{\sigma^{p2}}{2}\Delta\Phi^p_{\omega^p}(\mathcal{G}^p_{\theta^p}(\mathbf{y}^p_b),t_b)-H_p(\nabla_{\mathbf{x}^p}\Phi^p_{\omega^p}(\mathcal{G}^p_{\theta^p}(\mathbf{y}^p_b),t_b))\right.$
$\left.+F^p(\mathcal{G}^p_{\theta^p}(\mathbf{y}^p_b),\mathcal{G}^{-p}_{\theta^{-p}}(\mathbf{y}^{-p}_b),t_b)\right\}$
Backpropagate total loss $\zeta_{\text{total}}=\sum_p\zeta^p_t$ to $\theta=(\theta^p)_{p=1,2}$ weights.
end while

---

4. Simulation Results

In this section, we carry out an integrative experiment based on Algorithm 1 and demonstrate the feasibility and effectiveness of our approach via the following numerical simulation results. To prove the advanced nature of our approach, we finally compare its performance with that of baseline methods.

4.1. Experimental Setup

For the attack–defense obstacle scenario in Figure 3, the initial density of the two populations is discrete uniform distributions $\rho_0^p, p = 1, 2$. The initial spatial coordinates (x, y, z) of the blue and red sides are located in the cuboid areas $((-5,5),(-9,-7),(-9,-7))$ and $((-5,5),(7,9),(-9,-7))$, respectively. Note that we set all other initial coordinates to zero—initial angular position, initial velocity, and initial angular velocity were all set to zero. The coordinates of the terminal line were set to $(\cdot, 8, 8)$. Two obstacles were placed between the attacking and defending groups. The obstacles were represented by cuboids, specified by the coordinates of their vertices. The first obstacle was placed at $((-3,-1),(-2,2),(-10,10))$, and the second obstacle was placed at $((1,3),(-2,2),(-10,10))$.

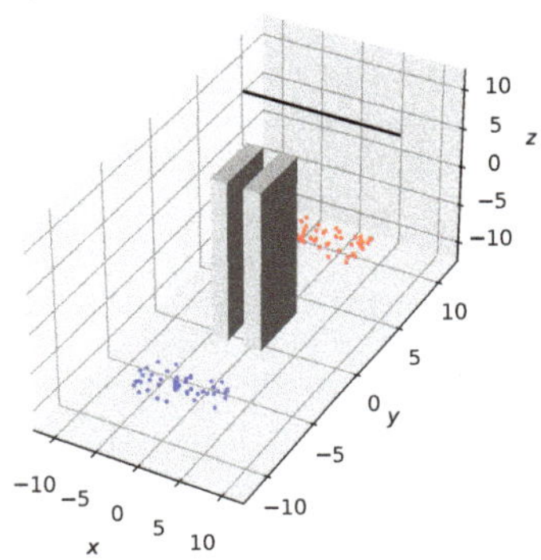

Figure 3. The 3D attack and defense experimental scenario.

We examined with this high-dimensional scene where the dynamics was that of quadrotor crafts. The dynamic–kinematic equation of the generic quadrotor craft i of population p, $p = 1, 2$, is given by

$$\begin{cases} \dot{x}_p = v_{x_p} \\ \dot{y}_p = v_{y_p} \\ \dot{z}_p = v_{z_p} \\ \dot{\psi}_p = v_{\psi_p} \\ \dot{\theta}_p = v_{\theta_p} \\ \dot{\phi}_p = v_{\phi_p} \\ \dot{v}_{x_p} = \frac{u_p}{m_p}(\sin(\phi_p)\sin(\psi_p) + \cos(\phi_p)\cos(\psi_p)\sin(\theta_p)) \\ \dot{v}_{y_p} = \frac{u_p}{m_p}(-\cos(\psi_p)\sin(\phi_p) + \cos(\phi_p)\sin(\theta_p)\sin(\psi_p)) \\ \dot{v}_{z_p} = \frac{u_p}{m_p}(\cos(\theta_p)\cos(\phi_p)) - g \\ \dot{v}_{\psi_p} = \tilde{\tau}_{\psi_p} \\ \dot{v}_{\theta_p} = \tilde{\tau}_{\theta_p} \\ \dot{v}_{\phi_p} = \tilde{\tau}_{\phi_p} \end{cases}, \tag{26}$$

which we compactly denote as $\dot{\mathbf{x}^p} = \mathbf{h}^p(\mathbf{x}^p, \mathbf{u}^p)$, where $\mathbf{h}^p$ is a 12-dimensional vector function in the right-hand side of (26), $\mathbf{x}^p = [x_p, y_p, z_p, \psi_p, \theta_p, \phi_p, v_{x_p}, v_{y_p}, v_{z_p}, v_{\psi_p}, v_{\theta_p}, v_{\phi_p}]^\top \in \mathbb{R}^{12}$ is the state with velocities $\mathbf{v}^p = [v_{x_p}, v_{y_p}, v_{z_p}, v_{\psi_p}, v_{\theta_p}, v_{\phi_p}]^\top \in \mathbb{R}^6$, and $\mathbf{u}^p = [u_p, \tilde{\tau}_{\psi_p}, \tilde{\tau}_{\theta_p}, \tilde{\tau}_{\phi_p}]^\top \in \mathbb{R}^4$ is the control. In the stochastic case, we added a noise term to the dynamics: $\mathrm{d}\mathbf{x}^p = \mathbf{h}^p(\mathbf{x}^p, \mathbf{u}^p)\mathrm{d}t + \sigma^p \mathrm{d}\mathbf{W}_t^p$, where $\mathbf{W}$ means a standard Brownian motion, meaning the quadcopter suffers from noisy measurements. The cost functions of the blue side and red side are given in Section 2.2.

For the model hyperparameters, we set $c_1 = 0.5$ (in (3)), $c_2 = 1, c_3 = 20, c_4 = 5$ (in (4)), $c_5 = 5$ (in (8)), $l_1 = 0.5$ (in (10)), and $l_2 = 1, l_3 = 20, l_4 = 5$ (in (11)). For ECA-Net, both networks have three linear hidden layers with 100 hidden units in each layer. Residual neural networks (ResNets) were used for both networks, with a skip connection weight of 0.5. The tanh activation function was used in $\Phi^p_{\omega^p}$, while the ReLU activation function was used in $\mathcal{G}^p_{\theta^p}$. For training, we used ADAM with $\beta = (0.5, 0.9)$, learning rate $2e-4$ for $\Phi^p_{\omega^p}$, learning rate $5e-5$ for $\mathcal{G}^p_{\theta^p}$, weight decay of $1e-4$ for both networks, batch size 50, $\lambda = 2$ (the HJB penalty coefficient), and $\eta = 2.5e-3$ (the neighbors' penalty coefficient) in Algorithm 1. As in standard machine learning methods, all the plots in Section 4.3 and Appendices A.1 and A.2 were generated using validation data (data not used in training), to ensure the general adaptability of ECA-Net.

4.2. Convergence Analysis

The convergence of the MPHD-MFG method and the ECA-Net algorithm can be observed by checking the convergence of the HJB residual errors, along with the convergence of the total loss. In Figure 4a, we plot the HJB residual errors of the red and blue sides, i.e., ℓ^p_{HJB} in Algorithm 1, which measures the deviation from the objective function (13) and shows the convergence of the theoretical model, the MPHD-MFG. Without an efficient strategy control, the HJB residuals under different stochasticity parameters ($\nu = \frac{\sigma^2}{2} = 0$, 0.04, 0.08) were relatively high. The HJB residuals dropped fast after we applied a series of controls. After around 2×10^5 iterations, the error curves tended to be bounded and stable when we obtained the optimal control for the drones. In Figure 4b, we plot the total loss of the red and blue sides, i.e., ℓ^p_{total} in Algorithm 1. After around 2×10^5 iterations, the total loss value curves under different stochasticity parameters ($\nu = \frac{\sigma^2}{2} = 0, 0.04, 0.08$) tended to be bounded and stable, which means that the weight update of the neural network was completed, proving the good convergence of the solution algorithm, ECA-Net.

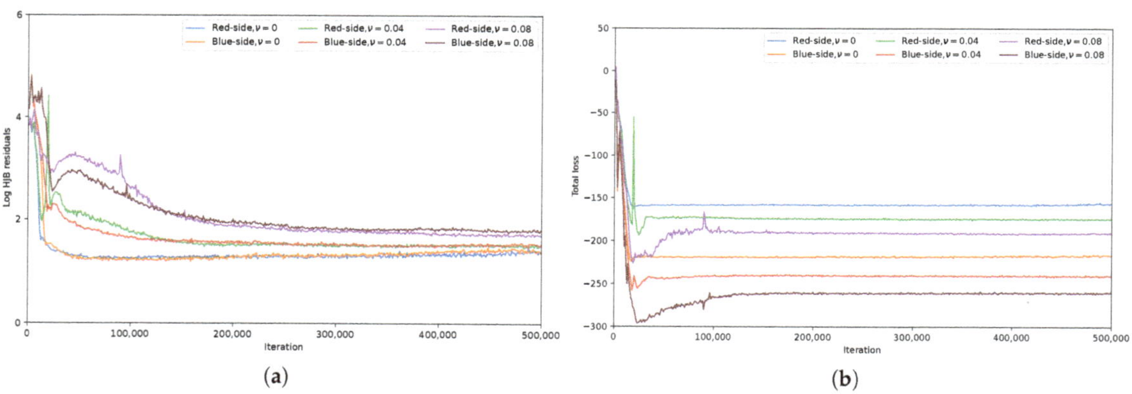

Figure 4. Convergence analysis. (**a**) Convergence of HJB residual; (**b**) Convergence of total loss.

4.3. Performance Analysis

We set the same number for the blue side and red side, $N_1 = N_2 = 100$. Now, we obtained the model from the above training and predicted the trajectories of the red and blue sides. Assuming that the blue side is not aggressive and the red side is aggressive, if the blue UAV is surrounded by two or more red UAVs within e_r, the blue individual will be captured. We give the evolutionary trajectories of the red and blue sides under different stochasticity parameters ($\nu = \frac{\sigma^2}{2} = 0, 0.04, 0.08$) and different capture radii ($e_r = 0.7, 0.9$, 1.1), as shown in Figure 5. When stochasticity parameter ν was fixed, observing Figure 5a–c over time t, respectively, the UAVs successfully avoided obstacles while minimizing their energy consumption; the smaller the capture radius of the red side, the higher the survival rate of the blue side is. At the same capture radius e_r and at the same moment t, the larger the stochasticity parameter, the more scattered the distribution of the UAVs is, which increases the difficulty for the red side to completely capture the blue side. For example, in the case of $e_r = 1.1$, comparing the first line of Figure 5a–c, the larger ν is, the higher the survival rate of the blue side. In particular, Figure 5c shows the diversion phenomenon. At $\nu = 0.08$, the third moment, the UAVs are flying through the obstacles. In order to avoid collision with the obstacles, the UAVs choose three different paths, i.e., a diversion occurs, which demonstrates the adaptive nature of the UAV. In addition, the corresponding 3D run diagram of Figure 5 is placed in Appendix A.1. Appendix A.2 shows and analyzes the offensive and defensive effects of the UAV swarms in the asymmetric case.

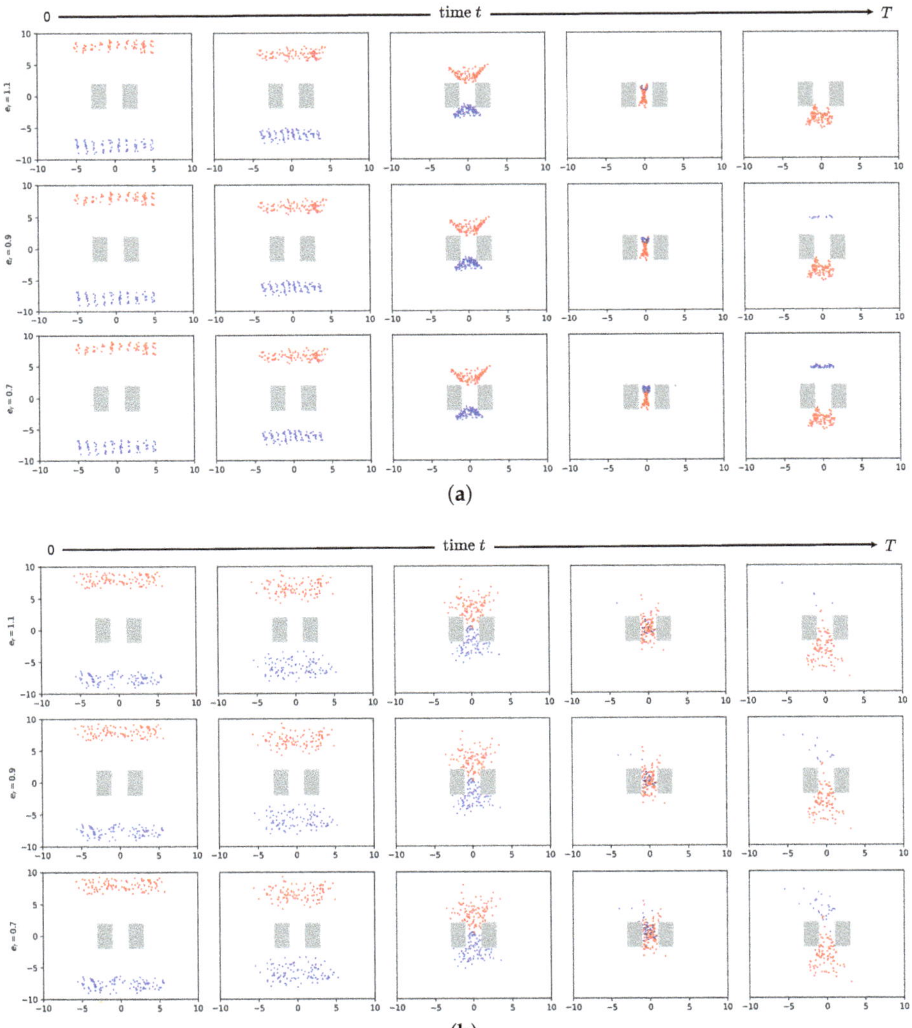

Figure 5. *Cont.*

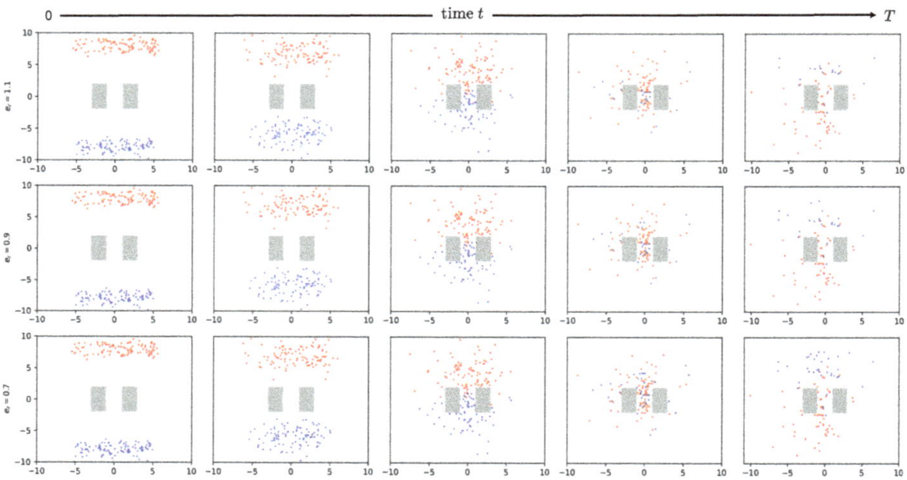

(c)

Figure 5. Vertical view of the large-scale UAV attack and defense behaviors under different stochasticity parameters and different capture radii. (**a**) Snapshots of the distributions of the UAVs' locations under different capture radii when $\nu = 0$; (**b**) Snapshots of the distributions of the UAVs' locations under different capture radii when $\nu = 0.04$; (**c**) Snapshots of the distributions of the UAVs' locations under different capture radii when $\nu = 0.08$.

4.4. Comparison with Baselines

We verified the progressiveness of our approach by comparing its performance with that of some typical baseline methods for attack–defense games in Table 1. From Table 1, it can be seen that our approach handled the most complex application scene and simplified the large-scale communication. For more details about the following baseline methods, please refer to the related References [7–9,37], etc.

Table 1. Comparison with baseline methods for attack–defense games.

Method	Scene	Scale of UAVs	Scene Complexity	Communication
[7]	3D blank scene	Small	0.67 [1]	$\mathcal{O}(N)$ [2]
[8]	2D obstacle scene	Small	0.67	$\mathcal{O}(N)$
[9]	2D blank scene	Large	0.67	$\mathcal{O}(N)$
[37]	3D blank scene	Large	0.83	$\mathcal{O}(1)$
Ours	3D obstacle scene	Large	1	$\mathcal{O}(1)$

[1] The measurement method of scene complexity is as follows: here, it is a scoring system, [2D, 3D] = [$1'$, $2'$]; [blank scene, obstacle scene] = [$1'$, $2'$]; [small, large] = [$1'$, $2'$]. We accumulated the scores for each literature experiment scene according to each item and finally normalized them. [2] $\mathcal{O}()$ is infinitesimal of the same order.

5. Conclusions

In this paper, we formulated the cooperative attack–defense evolution of large-scale agents in high-dimensional environments as a multi-population high-dimensional stochastic mean-field game (MPHD-MFG), which significantly reduced the communication frequency and computational complexity of the swarm intelligence system. Then, we tractably solved the MPHD-MFG with a generative-adversarial-network (GAN)-based method using the MFGs' underlying variational primal–dual structure. Based on our approach, we conducted a comprehensive experiment. The good convergence of the MPHD-MFG method and the ECA-Net algorithm was corroborated by checking the bounded stable convergence of the HJB residual error and the total loss. Through simulations, we saw that a large number of UAVs can avoid obstacles (even showing diversions) and smoothly evolve their attack and defense behaviors while minimizing their energy consumption.The comparison with the baseline methods showed that our approach is advanced. In the future, we will consider in-depth research in the asymmetric case of 3D obstacle scenarios, for example the evolution of a cooperative attack and defense between multiple (greater than or equal to three) large-scale swarms and the evolution of a cooperative attack and defense under the existence of individual performance (speed, acceleration, turning range) differences between attackers and defenders.

Author Contributions: Conceptualization, G.W. and Z.L.; Formal analysis, G.W.; Investigation, Z.L.; Methodology, G.W. and W.Y.; Software, G.W.; Supervision, W.Y. and S.X.; Validation, W.Y. and S.X.; Visualization, G.W.; Writing—original draft, G.W. and Z.L.; Writing—review and editing, W.Y. and S.X. All authors have read and agreed to the published version of the manuscript.

Funding: This work was supported by the Science and Technology Innovation 2030-Key Project under Grant 2020AAA0108200.

Institutional Review Board Statement: Not applicable.

Informed Consent Statement: Not applicable.

Data Availability Statement: Not applicable.

Acknowledgments: We thank Zhiming Zheng for his fruitful discussions, valuable opinions, and guidance.

Conflicts of Interest: The authors declare no conflict of interest.

Abbreviations

The following abbreviations are used in this manuscript:

MFG	Mean-field game
3D	Three-dimensional
UAV	Unmanned aerial vehicle
GANs	Generative adversarial neural networks
ECA-Net	Extended coupled alternating neural network
HJB	Hamilton–Jacobi–Bellman (partial differential equation)
FPK	Fokker–Planck (equation)

Appendix A. The 3D Renderings of Numerical Results and More Experiments

Appendix A.1. The 3D Run Diagram Figure A1 about Figure 5

Here, we give the 3D experimental run diagram Figure A1 about its vertical view Figure 5 for reference. In the following diagrams, time is represented by color. Specifically, purple represents the starting time, red represents the final time, and the intermediate colors represent intermediate times.

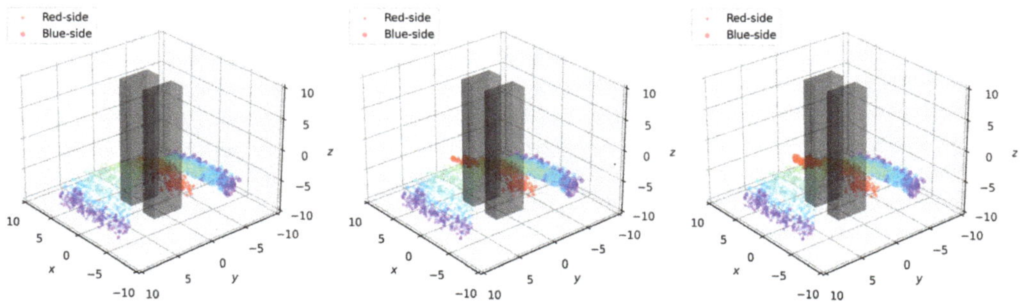

(a) $v = 0, e_r = 1.1$ **(b)** $v = 0, e_r = 0.9$ **(c)** $v = 0, e_r = 0.7$

Figure A1. *Cont.*

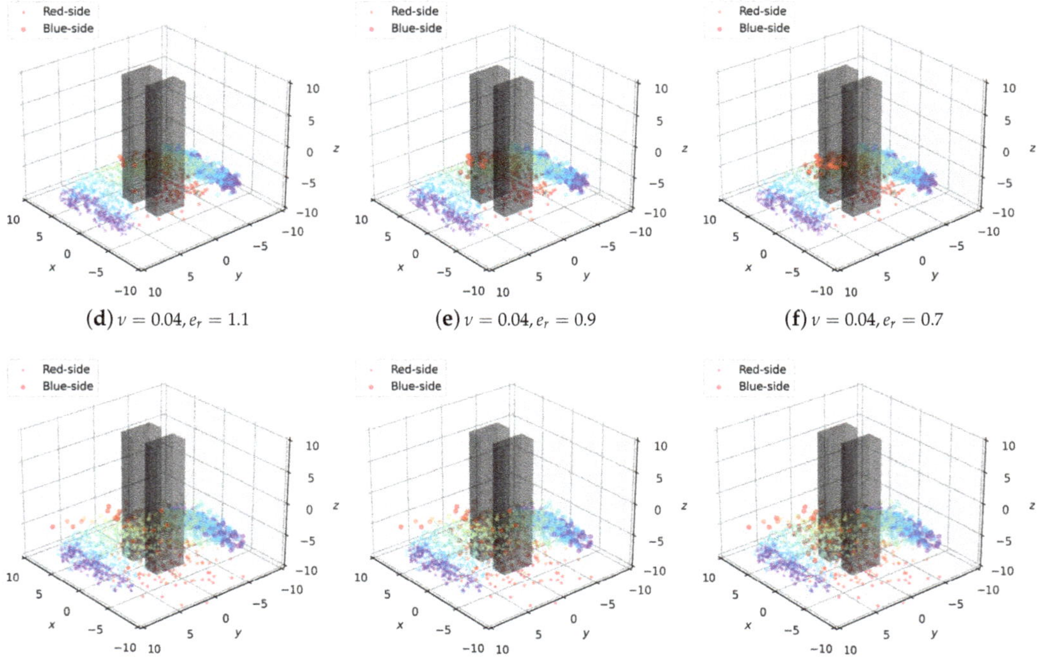

(d) $\nu = 0.04, e_r = 1.1$ **(e)** $\nu = 0.04, e_r = 0.9$ **(f)** $\nu = 0.04, e_r = 0.7$

(g) $\nu = 0.08, e_r = 1.1$ **(h)** $\nu = 0.08, e_r = 0.9$ **(i)** $\nu = 0.08, e_r = 0.7$

Figure A1. The 3D run diagram of large-scale UAV attack and defense behaviors under different stochasticity parameters and different capture radii.

Appendix A.2. Asymmetric Case Study

Here, we set different numbers of the blue side and red side, $N_1 = 100, N_2 = 60$ or $N_1 = 60, N_2 = 100$. Let $\nu = 0.08, e_r = 1.1$ and the capture conditions be consistent with Section 4.3. Now, we can predict its trajectory, as shown in Figures A2 and A3. Taking the given parameters as an example, with the fixed stochasticity parameter and capture radius, this section shows the deduction of the diversion obstacle avoidance and attack–defense behaviors of the red and blue sides with asymmetric numbers.

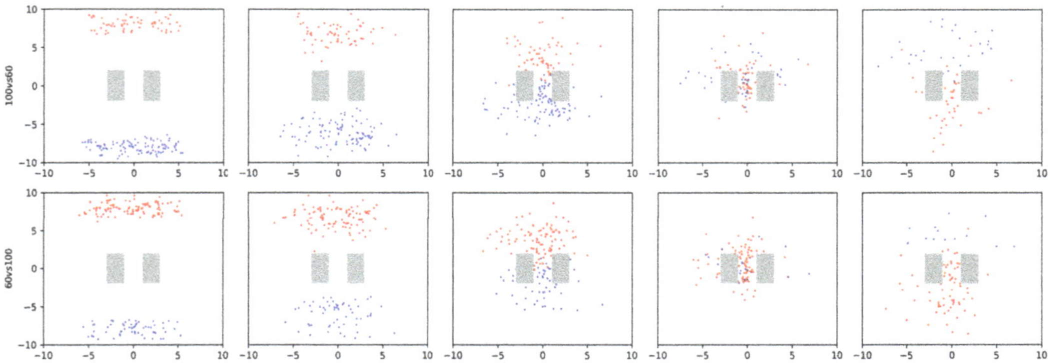

Figure A2. Vertical view of the asymmetric case about large-scale UAV attack and defense behaviors under $\nu = 0.08, e_r = 1.1$.

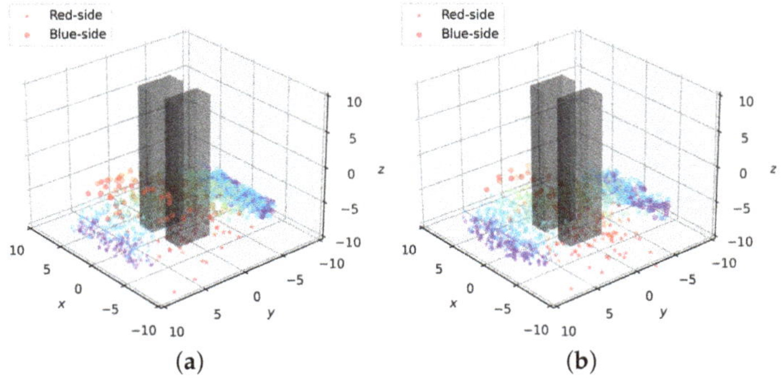

Figure A3. The 3D run diagram of the asymmetric case about large-scale UAV attack and defense behaviors under $v = 0.08, e_r = 1.1$. (**a**) Blue side vs. red side: 100 vs. 60; (**b**) Blue side vs. red side: 60 vs. 100.

References

1. Yu, C.; Zhang, M.; Ren, F.; Tan, G. Multiagent Learning of Coordination in Loosely Coupled Multiagent Systems. *IEEE Trans. Cybern.* **2015**, *45*, 2853–2867. [CrossRef]
2. Yang, Y.; Luo, R.; Li, M.; Zhou, M.; Zhang, W.; Wang, J. Mean Field Multi-Agent Reinforcement Learning. In Proceedings of the 35th International Conference on Machine Learning, Stockholm, Sweden, 10–15 July 2018; Volume 80, pp. 5571–5580.
3. Chen, C.; Mo, L.; Zheng, D. Cooperative attack–defense game of multiple UAVs with asymmetric maneuverability. *Acta Aeronaut. Astronaut. Sin.* **2020**, *41*, 324152. [CrossRef]
4. Huang, L.; Fu, M.; Qu, H.; Wang, S.; Hu, S. A deep reinforcement learning-based method applied for solving multi-agent defense and attack problems. *Expert Syst. Appl.* **2021**, *176*, 114896. [CrossRef]
5. Huang, H.; Zhang, W.; Ding, J.; Stipanovic, D.M.; Tomlin, C.J. Guaranteed decentralized pursuit-evasion in the plane with multiple pursuers. In Proceedings of the IEEE Conference on Decision and Control and European Control Conference, Orlando, FL, USA, 12–15 December 2011. [CrossRef]
6. Zha, W.; Chen, J.; Peng, Z.; Gu, D. Construction of Barrier in a Fishing Game With Point Capture. *IEEE Trans. Cybern.* **2017**, *47*, 1409–1422. [CrossRef] [PubMed]
7. Liu, Y.; Qi, N.; Tang, Z. Linear Quadratic Differential Game Strategies with Two-pursuit Versus Single-evader. *Chin. J. Aeronaut.* **2012**, *25*, 896–905. [CrossRef]
8. Wan, K.; Wu, D.; Zhai, Y.; Li, B.; Gao, X.; Hu, Z. An Improved Approach towards Multi-Agent Pursuit–Evasion Game Decision-Making Using Deep Reinforcement Learning. *Entropy* **2021**, *23*, 1433. [CrossRef]
9. Garcia, E.; Casbeer, D.W.; Moll, A.V.; Pachter, M. Multiple Pursuer Multiple Evader Differential Games. *IEEE Trans. Autom. Control* **2021**, *66*, 2345–2350. [CrossRef]
10. Earl, M.; D'Andrea, R. Modeling and control of a multi-agent system using mixed integer linear programming. In Proceedings of the 41st IEEE Conference on Decision and Control, Las Vegas, NV, USA, 10–13 December 2002. [CrossRef]
11. Earl, M.; D'Andrea, R. A study in cooperative control: The RoboFlag drill. In Proceedings of the Proceedings of the 2002 American Control Conference (IEEE Cat. No.CH37301), Anchorage, AK, USA, 8–10 May 2002. [CrossRef]
12. Bakolas, E.; Tsiotras, P. Optimal pursuit of moving targets using dynamic Voronoi diagrams. In Proceedings of the 49th IEEE Conference on Decision and Control (CDC), Atlanta, GA, USA, 15–17 December 2010. [CrossRef]
13. Isaacs, R. *Differential Games*; Wiley: Hoboken, NJ, USA, 1967.
14. Lasry, J.M.; Lions, P.L. Jeux à champ moyen. I–Le cas stationnaire. *Comptes Rendus Math.* **2006**, *343*, 619–625. [CrossRef]
15. Lasry, J.M.; Lions, P.L. Jeux à champ moyen. II–Horizon fini et contrôle optimal. *Comptes Rendus Math.* **2006**, *343*, 679–684. [CrossRef]
16. Lasry, J.M.; Lions, P.L. Mean field games. *Jpn. J. Math.* **2007**, *2*, 229–260. [CrossRef]
17. Huang, M.; Caines, P.; Malhame, R. Individual and mass behaviour in large population stochastic wireless power control problems: Centralized and nash equilibrium solutions. In Proceedings of the 42nd IEEE International Conference on Decision and Control (IEEE Cat. No.03CH37475), Maui, HI, USA, 9–12 December 2003. [CrossRef]
18. Caines, P.E.; Huang, M.; Malhamé, R.P. Large population stochastic dynamic games: Closed-loop McKean-Vlasov systems and the Nash certainty equivalence principle. *Commun. Inf. Syst.* **2006**, *6*, 221–252. [CrossRef]
19. Huang, M.; Caines, P.E.; Malhame, R.P. Large-Population Cost-Coupled LQG Problems With Nonuniform Agents: Individual-Mass Behavior and Decentralized ε-Nash Equilibria. *IEEE Trans. Autom. Control* **2007**, *52*, 1560–1571. [CrossRef]
20. Gomes, D.; Saúde, J. A mean-field game approach to price formation in electricity markets. *arXiv* **2018**, arXiv:1807.07088.
21. Kizilkale, A.C.; Salhab, R.; Malhamé, R.P. An integral control formulation of mean field game based large scale coordination of loads in smart grids. *Automatica* **2019**, *100*, 312–322. [CrossRef]

22. Paola, A.D.; Trovato, V.; Angeli, D.; Strbac, G. A Mean Field Game Approach for Distributed Control of Thermostatic Loads Acting in Simultaneous Energy-Frequency Response Markets. *IEEE Trans. Smart Grid* **2019**, *10*, 5987–5999. [CrossRef]
23. Lachapelle, A.; Wolfram, M.T. On a mean field game approach modeling congestion and aversion in pedestrian crowds. *Transp. Res. Part B Methodol.* **2011**, *45*, 1572–1589. [CrossRef]
24. Burger, M.; Francesco, M.D.; Markowich, P.A.; Wolfram, M.T. Mean field games with nonlinear mobilities in pedestrian dynamics. *Discret. Contin. Dyn. Syst.-B* **2014**, *19*, 1311–1333. [CrossRef]
25. Aurell, A.; Djehiche, B. Mean-Field Type Modeling of Nonlocal Crowd Aversion in Pedestrian Crowd Dynamics. *SIAM J. Control Optim.* **2018**, *56*, 434–455. [CrossRef]
26. Achdou, Y.; Lasry, J.M. Mean Field Games for Modeling Crowd Motion. In *Computational Methods in Applied Sciences*; Springer International Publishing: Cham, Switzerland, 2018; pp. 17–42. [CrossRef]
27. Liu, Z.; Wu, B.; Lin, H. A Mean Field Game Approach to Swarming Robots Control. In Proceedings of the IEEE 2018 Annual American Control Conference (ACC), Milwaukee, WI, USA, 27–29 June 2018. [CrossRef]
28. Elamvazhuthi, K.; Berman, S. Mean-field models in swarm robotics: A survey. *Bioinspir. Biomimet.* **2019**, *15*, 015001. [CrossRef]
29. Lee, W.; Liu, S.; Tembine, H.; Li, W.; Osher, S. Controlling Propagation of Epidemics via Mean-Field Control. *SIAM J. Appl. Math.* **2021**, *81*, 190–207. [CrossRef]
30. Chang, S.L.; Piraveenan, M.; Pattison, P.; Prokopenko, M. Game theoretic modelling of infectious disease dynamics and intervention methods: A review. *J. Biol. Dyn.* **2020**, *14*, 57–89. [CrossRef] [PubMed]
31. E, W.; Han, J.; Li, Q. A mean-field optimal control formulation of deep learning. *Res. Math. Sci.* **2018**, *6*, 10. [CrossRef]
32. Guo, X.; Hu, A.; Xu, R.; Zhang, J. Learning Mean-Field Games. In *Advances in Neural Information Processing Systems*; Wallach, H., Larochelle, H., Beygelzimer, A., d'Alché-Buc, F., Fox, E., Garnett, R., Eds.; Curran Associates, Inc.: Red Hook, NY, USA, 2019; Volume 32.
33. Carmona, R.; Laurière, M.; Tan, Z. Linear-Quadratic Mean-Field Reinforcement Learning: Convergence of Policy Gradient Methods. *arXiv* **2019**, arXiv:1910.04295.
34. Guéant, O.; Lasry, J.M.; Lions, P.L. Mean Field Games and Applications. In *Paris-Princeton Lectures on Mathematical Finance 2010*; Springer: Berlin/Heidelberg, Germany, 2011; pp. 205–266. [CrossRef]
35. Lin, A.T.; Fung, S.W.; Li, W.; Nurbekyan, L.; Osher, S.J. Alternating the population and control neural networks to solve high-dimensional stochastic mean-field games. *Proc. Natl. Acad. Sci. USA* **2021**, *118*, e2024713118. [CrossRef] [PubMed]
36. Wang, G.; Yao, W.; Zhang, X.; Niu, Z. Coupled Alternating Neural Networks for Solving Multi-Population High-Dimensional Mean-Field Games with Stochasticity. *TechRxiv Preprint* **2022**. [CrossRef]
37. Wang, G.; Zhang, X.; Yao, W.; Ren, L. Cooperative attack–defense evolution of large-scale agents. In Proceedings of the ACM Genetic and Evolutionary Computation Conference Companion, Boston, MA, USA, 9–13 July 2022. [CrossRef]
38. Chang, K.; Xia, Y.; Huang, K. UAV formation control design with obstacle avoidance in dynamic three-dimensional environment. *SpringerPlus* **2016**, *5*, 1124. [CrossRef] [PubMed]
39. Onken, D.; Nurbekyan, L.; Li, X.; Fung, S.W.; Osher, S.; Ruthotto, L. A Neural Network Approach for High-Dimensional Optimal Control Applied to Multiagent Path Finding. *IEEE Trans. Control. Syst. Technol.* **2022**, 1–17. [CrossRef]
40. Schulte, J.M. Adjoint Methods for Hamilton–Jacobi–Bellman Equations. Ph.D. Thesis, University of Munster, Münster, Germany, 2010.
41. Fujii, M. Probabilistic Approach to Mean Field Games and Mean Field Type Control Problems with Multiple Populations. *SSRN Electron. J.* **2019**. [CrossRef]
42. Bensoussan, A.; Huang, T.; Laurière, M. Mean Field Control and Mean Field Game Models with Several Populations. *arXiv* **2018**, arXiv:1810.00783.
43. Arjovsky, M.; Chintala, S.; Bottou, L. Wasserstein Generative Adversarial Networks. In Proceedings of the 34th International Conference on Machine Learning—Volume 70 (ICML'17), Sydney, Australia, 6–11 August 2017; pp. 214–223.
44. Benamou, J.D.; Carlier, G.; Santambrogio, F. Variational Mean Field Games. In *Active Particles*; Modeling and Simulation in Science, Engineering & Technology; Springer International Publishing: Cham, Switzerland, 2017; Volume 1, pp. 141–171.
45. Cardaliaguet, P.; Graber, P.J. Mean field games systems of first order. *ESAIM Control. Optim. Calc. Var.* **2015**, *21*, 690–722. [CrossRef]
46. Cardaliaguet, P.; Graber, P.J.; Porretta, A.; Tonon, D. Second order mean field games with degenerate diffusion and local coupling. *Nonlinear Differ. Equ. Appl. NoDEA* **2015**, *22*, 1287–1317. [CrossRef]

mathematics

Article

Throughput Optimization for NOMA Cognitive Relay Network with RF Energy Harvesting Based on Improved Bat Algorithm

Yi Luo [1], Chenyang Wu [1], Yi Leng [2,*], Nüshan Huang [1], Lingxi Mao [1] and Junhao Tang [1]

1 Hunan Provincial Key Laboratory of Intelligent Computing and Language Information Processing, Hunan Normal University, Changsha 410081, China
2 Department of Information Countermeasure, Air Force Early Warning Academy, Wuhan 430019, China
* Correspondence: lengyi200209@163.com

Abstract: Due to the shortcomings of the standard bat algorithm (BA) for multi-parameter optimization, an improved bat algorithm is proposed. The benchmark function test shows that the proposed algorithm has better realization of high-dimensional function optimization by introducing multiple flight modes, adopting adaptive strategy based on group trend, and employing loudness mutation flight selection strategy based on Brownian motion. Aiming at the characteristics of complex networks structure and multiple design variables of energy harvesting non-orthogonal multiple access cognitive relay networks (EH-NOMA-CRNs), we utilize the proposed hybrid strategy improved bat algorithm (HSIBA) to optimize the performance of EH-NOMA-CRNs. At first, we construct a novel two-hop underlay power beacon assisted EH-NOMA-CRN, and derive the closed-form expressions of secondary network's outage probability and throughput. Then, the secondary network performance optimization is formulated as the throughput maximation problem with regard to EH ratio and power allocation factors. Subsequently, the HSIBA is employed to optimize the above parameters. Numerical results show that the proposed HSIBA can achieve optimization to the constructed EH-NOMA-CRN with faster convergence speed and higher stability.

Keywords: bat algorithm; hybrid strategy; energy harvesting; NOMA; cognitive relay network

MSC: 94A05

Citation: Luo, Y.; Wu, C.; Leng, Y.; Huang, N.; Mao, L.; Tang, J. Throughput Optimization for NOMA Cognitive Relay Network with RF Energy Harvesting Based on Improved Bat Algorithm. *Mathematics* **2022**, *10*, 4357. https://doi.org/10.3390/math10224357

Academic Editor: Oliviu Matei

Received: 22 August 2022
Accepted: 11 November 2022
Published: 19 November 2022

1. Introduction

Non-orthogonal multiple access (NOMA) is an effective method to increase frequency efficiency. It has drawn great attention for its promising applications in the fields of 5G, 6G and Internet of things (IoT) networks [1–3]. Especially in the military scenarios of unmanned aerial vehicles (UAVs) battlefield situation awareness [4], covert military operations and tactical area communications [5], UAV-NOMA relaying communications [6], and hybrid satellite-UAV networks [7], the NOMA technology has been widely used. The core concept of NOMA is that when the non-orthogonal transmission is adopted at the transmitter, the interference signals are actively introduced, and the correct demodulation is achieved at the receiver by applying serial interference cancellation (SIC) technique. It can be seen that reliable interference cancellation techniques and strategies [8,9] are the basis for realizing NOMA. Although the use of SIC technique will increase the complexity of the receiver, it can improve the spectrum efficiency.

In order to further improve the utilization efficiency of the authorized spectrum and the expand the coverage of networks, many scholars have combined NOMA technique with cognitive relay network (CRN) to build and optimize some novel NOMA-CRN models. In [10], the authors achieved in-band full-duplex and two-way cognitive relaying transmission in a cooperative NOMA system, and applied the successive inner approximation technique to maximize the energy efficiency. In [11], the error rate performance of an underlay NOMA-CRN with partial relay selection (PRS) scheme was studied, and the optimum power coefficients were optimized to minimize the average bit error rate union bound by using numerical methods. In [12], the physical-layer security of NOMA-CRN with relay cooperation was investigated, and the particle swarm optimization (PSO) algorithm was adopted to optimize the power allocation to maximize the secrecy sum-rate. In [13], the authors utilized the NOMA-CRN for device to device (D2D) transmission, and proposed a deep neural networks framework for optimizing resource allocation to maximize the sum rate. In [14], the NOMA-CRN with a single primary transmitter/receiver (PT/PR) and PRS scheme was constructed, and the PSO algorithm was employed for determining the jointly optimal power allocation factors to realize the maximization of throughput.

In addition to extend the lifetime and improve the energy efficiency of energy-constrained relay networks using NOMA technique, the radio frequency energy harvesting (RF-EH) technique has been introduced into NOMA relay network to construct the new energy harvesting NOMA relay networks (EH-NOMA-RNs). Ref. [15] considered a cooperative EH-NOMA-RN, and adopted a one-dimensional search algorithm for optimizing power allocation coefficient to attain the maximization of weighted sum rate. Ref. [16] used the EH-NOMA-RN with interfering signal for IoT systems, and adopted the Golden section search method to maximize the sum-throughput. Ref. [17] applied EH-NOMA-RN system to layered video multicast transmission, and used the initial feasible point search algorithm to minimize the base station's average transmission power. Ref. [18] constructed a full-duplex EH-NOMA-RN with cooperative relaying, and made use of the alternating optimization technique to achieve the outage probability (OP) minimization and throughput maximization of the system. Similar to [16], ref. [19] also applied Golden section search algorithm for optimization of a power beacon (PB)-assisted EH-NOMA-RN IoT-based system to minimize OP and maximize sum-throughput of the system.

Recently, based on the research of NOMA-CRNs and EH-NOMA-RNs, integrating RF-EH technique into NOMA-CRN to form the brand-new energy harvesting NOMA cognitive relay networks (EH-NOMA-CRNs) and solving the corresponding networks' performance optimization problems have gradually become a novel research direction. In [20], the authors employed a two-loop procedure using one-dimensional search to solve the minimum transmission power problem of a multiple-input single-output EH-NOMA-CRN with non-linear EH model and robust beamforming. In [21], two-level bisection search algorithms were developed to realize the maximal secondary throughput of EH-NOMA-CRN by optimizing resource allocation coefficients. In [22], a joint optimization algorithm based on one-dimensional search was proposed to maximize the energy efficiency of EH-NOMA-CRN with a discrete EH scheme. In [23], the physical layer security of EH-NOMA-CRN with multi-input multi-output two-way relaying was investigated, and a joint path-following-based optimization algorithm was put to use for maximizing the sum achievable secrecy rate. Later, ref. [24] designed two iterative optimization algorithms based on a deep neural network frame for the ergodic capacity prediction of IoT PB assisted EH-NOMA-CRN to minimize OP users and maximizing system throughput.

According to the existing researches, it is known as follows:

(1). optimizing the power allocation factors or resource allocation coefficient has obvious effect on improving the performance of NOMA-CRNs, EH-NOMA-RNs, and EH-NOMA-CRNs, such as decreasing OP [18], increasing energy efficiency [10], secrecy sum-rate [12], and throughput [21]. So how to design a low-complexity and high-efficiency optimization algorithm is worth investigating.

(2). At present, the following methods are mainly used to optimize the network system: (i) when the objective function is convex, iterative numerical method or one-dimensional search is directly adopted for system optimization [11,16,22]. Although the complexity of numerical methods is lower, it needs more time to carry out multi-parameter and multi-objective optimization. (ii) when the objective function is non-convex, the non-convex function is equivalently transformed into convex by using methods such as successive inner approximation technique [10], the difference of convex programming [17], semi-definite relaxation [20], and path-following-based algorithm [23], et. al, and then convex optimization is performed. However, the transformation process is more complicated. (iii) Algorithms based on deep learning [13,24] are introduced into system performance optimization. Nevertheless, the deep neural networks framework requires stronger computing power, which is not very suitable for energy-constrained EH-NOMA-CRNs' nodes with lower storage and computing capacity. (iv) The meta-heuristic algorithm based on PSO is initially used to solve the system optimization problem [12,14]. Although the PSO algorithm is simple, its performance is poor. It is worth studying to design a new high-performance meta-heuristic algorithm suitable for performance optimization of EH-NOMA-CRN.

(3). According to different sources of energy, RF-EH mainly exists in the following two ways: simultaneous wireless information and power transfer (SWIPT) [16,23], and wireless power transmission (WPT) such as PB-assisted EH [19,24]. The latter has higher wireless power transmission efficiency than the former, so our paper adopts the latter.

(4). There are two models of RF-EH: linear EH [18,22] and non-linear EH [20]. When the network model is complex, in order to simplify the analysis and derive the closed-form results, the linear EH model is usually made use of. Therefore, our paper also employs the linear EH model.

To the best of our knowledge, there is no existing paper studying meta-heuristic algorithms other than PSO algorithm for system performance optimization of EH-NOMA-CRNs, which motivates us to write this treatise. Compared with other existing swarm intelligence algorithms, Bat algorithm (BA) has many advantages, such as implementation simplicity, less control parameters and excellent global ability. Since the BA was proposed, its improvement has been carried out continuously. Especially in the last two years, some novel improved BA algorithms have been proposed successively, such as the enhanced Levy flight bat algorithm (ELBA) [25], and the improved BA with extremal optimization algorithm (IBA-EO) [26]. Therefore, how to further enhance the global search ability and convergence rate of improved BA for coping with different engineering application scenarios is still a problem worth studying. Like other meta-heuristic algorithms, BA has some inherent deficiencies. Due to a single flight mode that has limited ability to search the solution space, the accuracy of the algorithm is insufficient, and it is easy to fall into the local optimal solution in high-dimensional search space. In this paper, a novel improved BA has been proposed.

Explicitly, the major contributions of our paper are summarized as follows:

- First, based on the standard BA, we propose a novel hybrid strategy improved bat algorithm (HSIBA) with adaptive strategy and several different flight modes, which can obviously improve the accuracy and astringency of the proposed improved BA.
- Second, we proposed a novel underlay two-hop PB-assisted EH-NOMA-CRN with multiple PRs. The closed-form expressions of secondary network (SN) OP and delay-limited throughput are derived.
- Third, because of the derived throughput expression's complexity, we employ the HSIBA to jointly optimize the EH ratio and power allocation factors of SN nodes for achieving throughput maximization. The simulation results show that the HSIBA is perfect for optimizing performance of the proposed EH-NOMA-CRN.

The remainder of our paper is organized as follows. Section 2 introduces the standard BA and HSIBA, and verifies the performance of HSIBA. Section 3 describes the EH-NOMA-CRN model, and derives the closed-form solutions of SN's OP and throughput. In Section 4, the HSIBA is adopted to optimize the throughput of SN, and simulation results are shown. Then, the conclusions are presented in Section 5.

2. Hybrid Strategy Improved Bat Algorithm

2.1. Standard Bat Algorithm

The bat algorithm (BA) proposed by Xin-She Yang is a novel metaheuristic algorithm [27], which adopts the echolocation of microbats. The standard BA is based on the following three idealized rules:

(1). All bats use echolocation to sense distance and judge the difference between food/prey and obstacles;
(2). The i-th bat at position x_i fly randomly with a fixed frequency f_{min} and velocity v_i, $i \in \{1, 2, \cdots, I\}$, varying frequency f_i and loudness A_0 to search the food/prey. It can spontaneously adjust the frequency f_i of its emitted pulse and accommodate the rate of pulse emission $r_i \in [0, 1]$, depending on the proximity of its target;
(3). Although the loudness can alter in various ways, it is assumed that the loudness changes from a large constant (positive) A_0 to a minimum value A_{min}.

Originally, the i-th bat is randomly given a frequency obeying uniform distribution from f_{min} to f_{max}. In the t-th iteration, the new position x_i^t and velocity v_i^t of the i-th bat can be respectively calculated as

$$f_i = f_{min} + (f_{max} - f_{min})\beta \quad (1)$$

$$v_i^t = v_i^{t-1} + \left(x_i^{t-1} - x^*\right) f_i \quad (2)$$

$$x_i^t = x_i^{t-1} + v_i^t \quad (3)$$

where $\beta \in [0, 1]$ is a random vector obeying uniform distribution, and x^* is the current global best location (solution) determined after comparing the locations of all n bats.

During the local search process, once a solution is chosen from the current best solutions, a new solution for each bat can be generated by

$$x_{\text{new}} = x_{\text{old}} + \varepsilon A^t \quad (4)$$

where $\varepsilon \in [-1, 1]$ is a random scaling factor, and A^t is the mean loudness of all n bats during the t-th iteration.

Furthermore, in the (t+1)-th iteration, the i-th bat's loudness A_i^{t+1} and rate of pulse emission r_i^{t+1} can be respectively updated as

$$A_i^{t+1} = \theta A_i^t \quad (5)$$

$$r_i^{t+1} = r_i^0 \left(1 - \mathrm{e}^{-\varphi t}\right) \quad (6)$$

where θ and φ are constants. For simplicity, θ and φ are respectively set as 0.8 and 0.9 in our paper. In order to clearly describe the optimization process of standard BA, the pseudocode of standard BA is given in Algorithm 1.

2.2. Algorithm Improvement Based on Hybrid Strategy

The standard BA has a fast convergence speed, which can adjust and balance the local search and global search in the optimization process by gradually increasing the pulse transmission frequency r_i and reducing the pulse loudness A_i. However, the accuracy of the algorithm is insufficient due to a single flight mode that has limited ability to search the solution space. In our paper, we adopt adaptive strategy based on group trend, add several different flight modes, and introduce loudness mutation factor to select between the proposed modes as the bat flight mode during different search stages. This method can greatly improve the accuracy and astringency of the hybrid strategy improved bat algorithm.

Algorithm 1 Pseudocode of standard BA

Input: The objective function $fit(x)$ and design variables
Output: Optimal solution of objective function
Initialize the bat population x_i and velocity $v_i (i = 1, 2, \ldots, I)$
Initialize the bat pulse rates r_i and the loudness A_i
while (stopping condition is not met) **do**
  Calculate the fitness values of bat
  Set x^* as the position of best bat
  for (each bat (x_i)) **do**
    Update speed of bat using Equation (2)
    Update the position of bat using Equation (3)
    if $(rand > r_i)$ **then**
      Select a new solution among the best solutions using Equation (4)
    end if
    if $(rand < A_i \& fit(x_i) < fit(x^*))$ **then**
      Accept the new solutions, and update r_i using Equation (6), and update A_i using Equation (5)
    end if
  end for
end while
Return x^*

2.2.1. Adaptive Strategy Based on Group Trend

For the standard BA, bat individuals fly freely in a wide area independently of each other in the process of solving. Due to the lack of group awareness to adapt to the current situation, it is difficult to balance the distance of each flight in the iterative process, and it is easy to miss the optimal solution, which is not conducive to local optimization. For example, it is assumed that the i-th bat is selected for local optimization at the global optimization in the t-th iteration. For the (t+1)-th iteration, if its position update is still carried out according to a large step size, it is easy to make it out of the optimal position, which is not conducive to local optimization. Therefore, HSIBA introduces an adaptive strategy based on group trend to change flight weight ω which can update the bat's flight weight ω according to the current search situation. To describe the group trend, B_i^t and O^t are respectively defined as

$$B_i^t = \begin{cases} 1 & if\left(fit(x_i^{t-1}) < fit(x_i^t)\right) \\ 0 & others \end{cases} \tag{7}$$

where $fit(\cdot)$ denotes fitness operation.

$$O^t = \frac{\sum_{i=1}^{I} B_i^{t-1}}{I} \tag{8}$$

When there are more bat individuals flying in the better direction in the population, the value of O^t is larger. The adaptive flight weight ω can be calculated as

$$\omega = \omega_{min} + (\omega_{max} - \omega_{min})O^t \tag{9}$$

When there are more individuals flying in the favorable direction in the population, the value of ω is larger, so that bats can adopt a larger velocity weight to expand the search range and prevent the algorithm from falling into the local optimal solution; when most individuals in the population are difficult to find a better solution, the value of ω is smaller to avoid missing the optimal solution, which will effectively speed up the convergence speed of the algorithm.

2.2.2. Introducing Multiple Flight Modes

To change the single flight mode such as Equation (3) adopted in the standard BA, four flight modes are introduced in HSIBA. The four flight modes are adjusted by adaptive velocity weights ω, and selected by loudness mutation factor β_i (see Section 2.2.3) and random number *rand* with uniform distribution of 0∼1.

(1). Adaptive weight bit flight mode
The position update Equation (3) in the standard BA is changed to Equation (10), and the bat's flying speed is adjusted by adaptive flight weight.

$$x_i^{t+1} = x_i^t + \omega \cdot v_i^{t+1} \tag{10}$$

When $|\beta_i| < 0.1$ and *rand* < 0.4, the bats adopt the adaptive weight bit flight mode and update their positions by using Equation (10).

(2). Position exchange variant flight mode
In the standard BA, all bats only take the optimal individual of the current population as the flight direction, and there is no information exchange between bat individuals. Therefore, in the HSIBA, position exchange variant flight is innovatively introduced to enhance information exchange among bat individuals and obtain more information about the feasible solution space. In position-exchange variant flight mode, the bats' positions are updated as follows

$$x_i^{t+1} = \omega \times \left|2 \times rand \times x^* - x_I^t\right| \times \left(\beta_i^t + rand\right), \quad i = 1, \tag{11}$$

$$x_i^{t+1} = \omega \times \left|\, 2 \times rand \times x^* - x_{i-1}^{t+1} \,\right| \times \left(\beta_i^t + rand\right), \quad i \geq 2 \tag{12}$$

The first bat performs a variant flight based on the *I*-th bat's position of the *t*-th iteration, and obtains the position of the (*t*+1)-th iteration through Equation (11), and the *i*-th bat performs a variant flight based on the (*i*-1)-th bat's position of the (*t*+1)-th iteration, and obtains the position of the (*t*+1)-th iteration through Equation (12).
When $|\beta_i| \geq 0.1$ and *rand* < 0.6, the bats apply the position exchange variant flight mode and update their positions by using Equations (11) and (2).

(3). Rotary flight mode
In [28], the African vulture's rotating flight foraging model was proposed and simulated. Inspired by this model, the rotary flight mode is introduced to our HSIBA, which makes the bats rotate around the optimal individual of the population to expand the search range and improve the ability of jumping out the local optimal solution. The rotation flight vectors are respectively expressed as

$$\phi_1 = x^* \times \left(\frac{rand \times x_i^t}{2\pi}\right) \times \cos\left(x_i^t\right) \tag{13}$$

$$\phi_2 = x^* \times \left(\frac{rand \times x_i^t}{2\pi}\right) \times \sin\left(x_i^t\right) \tag{14}$$

and the *i*-th bats' position is updated as

$$x_i^{t+1} = x^* - \omega \cdot (\phi_1 + \phi_2) \tag{15}$$

When $|\beta_i| \geq 0.1$ and $rand \geq 0.6$, the bats employ the rotary flight mode and update their positions by using Equation (15).

(4). Levy flight mode
In order to ensure that every bat can catch food in the process of predation, it is sure that each bat does not fly alone. If there is no companion around the *i*-th bat, it adopts

the random walk scheme to update the step. The i-th bat can apply Levy flight [29] mode, its position can be updated as

$$x_i^{t+1} = x^* - \left|x^* - x_i^t\right| \times \omega \times Levy(d) \tag{16}$$

where d is the dimension of the i-th bat's position vector, and Levy function can be calculated as

$$Levy(x) = 0.01 \times \frac{\mu_1 \times \varepsilon}{|\mu_2|^{\frac{1}{\psi}}} \tag{17}$$

where μ_1 and μ_2 are random numbers on the interval of 0~1, ψ is a constant, and ε can be computed as

$$\varepsilon = \left(\frac{\Gamma(1+\psi) \times \sin\left(\frac{\pi\beta}{2}\right)}{\Gamma\left(\frac{1+\psi}{2}\right) \times \psi \times 2^{\frac{\psi-1}{2}}} \right)^{\frac{1}{\psi}} \tag{18}$$

where $\Gamma(x) = (x-1)!$

When $|\beta_i| < 0.1$ and $rand \geq 0.4$, the bats use Levy flight mode and update their positions by applying Equation (16).

2.2.3. Loudness Mutation Flight Selection Strategy Based on Brownian Motion

This strategy is inspired by the physical phenomenon that the random motion of particles decreases with the temperature reduction in Brownian motion. In the HSIBA, the decreasing loudness A is understood as the decreasing temperature, and the loudness mutation factor β is the intensity of random motion that decreases with the decrease of temperature. During the t-th iteration, the loudness mutation factor of the i-th bat can be expressed as

$$\beta_i^t = A_i^t \times (randn - 1) \tag{19}$$

where $randn$ is a random number that obeys a normal distribution with a mean of 0 and a variance of 1. In the search process, the pulse loudness A_i gradually decreases, and the loudness mutation factor β_i dynamically converges to zero.

In the HSIBA, the flight mode employed by the i-th bat is decided by β_i. When $|\beta_i| \geq 0.1$, the algorithm is in the early stage of the search. The bat tends to fly with more intense motion, and update its position by Equations (11), (12) and (15), which can achieve faster convergence speed; When $|\beta_i| < 0.1$, the algorithm is at the end of the search. The bat tends to fly in a flight mode with small intensity and higher degree of randomness, and update its position through Equations (10) and (16), which can improve the ability of jumping out of the local optimal solution.

The improved bat algorithm fully takes into account the adjustment of the flight mode of bats in different search stages, which effectively improves the shortage of single flight mode used by standard BA in the optimization process. In order to conveniently understand the advantages of the HSIBA, its pseudocode and optimization flow chart are respectively shown in Algorithm 2 and Figure 1.

2.3. *Algorithm Performance Verification*

In order to verify the performance of HSIBA, sixteen frequently-used benchmark functions are selected as test functions. The test functions are shown in Table 1, including single-peak and multi-peak functions. At the same time, advanced African vulture optimization algorithm (AVOA) [28], the wild horse optimizer (WHO) algorithm [30], the arithmetic optimization algorithm (AOA) [31], hunter-prey optimization (HPO) algorithm [32], enhanced Lévy flight bat algorithm (ELBA) [26] and standard BA are selected for comparative analysis. The parameter settings of above algorithms and HSIBA are shown in Table 2. The number of all algorithm populations tested is 30, the maximum number of iterations is 100, and each test function runs 30 times independently, the test results are shown in Tables 3 and 4, and the iteration diagram and total time for each algorithm are shown in Figures 2 and 3 . (The algorithms have been tested and executed using the Matlab 9.0 (R2016a) on a laptop computer, which runs Windows 10 Enterprise 64-bit with an AMD Ryzen 7 4800H, Radeon Graphics 2.90 GHz processor, and 16.00 GB RAM).

Algorithm 2 Pseudocode of HSIBA

Input: The objective function $fit(x)$ and design variables
Output: Optimal solution of objective function

Initialize the bat population x_i and velocity $v_i(i = 1, 2, ..., I)$
while (stopping condition is not met) **do**
    Calculate the fitness values of bat
    Set x^* as the position of best bat
    for (each bat (x_i)) **do**
        Update the β_i and ω using Equations (19) and (9)
        Update speed of bat using Equation (2)
        if ($(|\beta_i| \geq 0.1)$) **then**
            if ($rand < 0.6$) **then**
                Update the bat's position using Equations (11) and (12)
            else
                Update the bat's position using Equation (15)
            end if
        else
            if ($rand < 0.4$) **then**
                Update the bat's position using Equation (10)
            else
                Update the bat's position using Equation (16)
            end if
        end if
        if ($rand > r_i$) **then**
            Select a new solution among the best solutions using Equation (4)
        end if
        if ($rand < A_i \& fit(x_i) < fit(x^*)$) **then**
            Accept the new solutions and update $r_i$andA_i by using Equations (6) and (5)
        end if
    end for
end while
Return x^*

As shown in Tables 3 and 4, the test results and the performance rank of seven algorithms under 16 test functions are given. By comparing the test results in Tables 3 and 4, it can be seen that the optimization performance of HSIBA is far better than standard BA on single-peak and multi-peak test functions, and the HSIBA also has higher accuracy and stability than other advanced optimization algorithms. Moreover, by comparing the test results of all algorithms in 30 and 100 dimensions, the HSIBA has superior performance in solving high-dimensional optimization problems. Therefore, HSIBA is highly capable of maintaining balance in exploration and exploitation against large-scale issues.

In order to further compare the performance of different optimization algorithms, as shown in Figure 2 the iterative curves of the five optimization algorithms under 8 test functions are given. By the comparison of the five algorithm iterations curves, it can be seen that the HSIBA achieves better results with a minimum number of iterations in all test functions. Consequently, when solving the same problem, HSIBA can find a better solution quickly, so as to save computing time and power. Meanwhile, it can be seen that the fitness calculated by HSIBA decreases steadily with the increase of the number of iterations, which can effectively avoid the abrupt change of the convergence speed and falling into the local optimal value.

Figure 3 illustrates the computing time of seven algorithms. The results show that HSIBA does not significantly increase the complexity of the operation, but can improve the convergence speed and accuracy. The main reason is that the HSIBA adopts advanced search strategies and a variety of flight modes for selection.

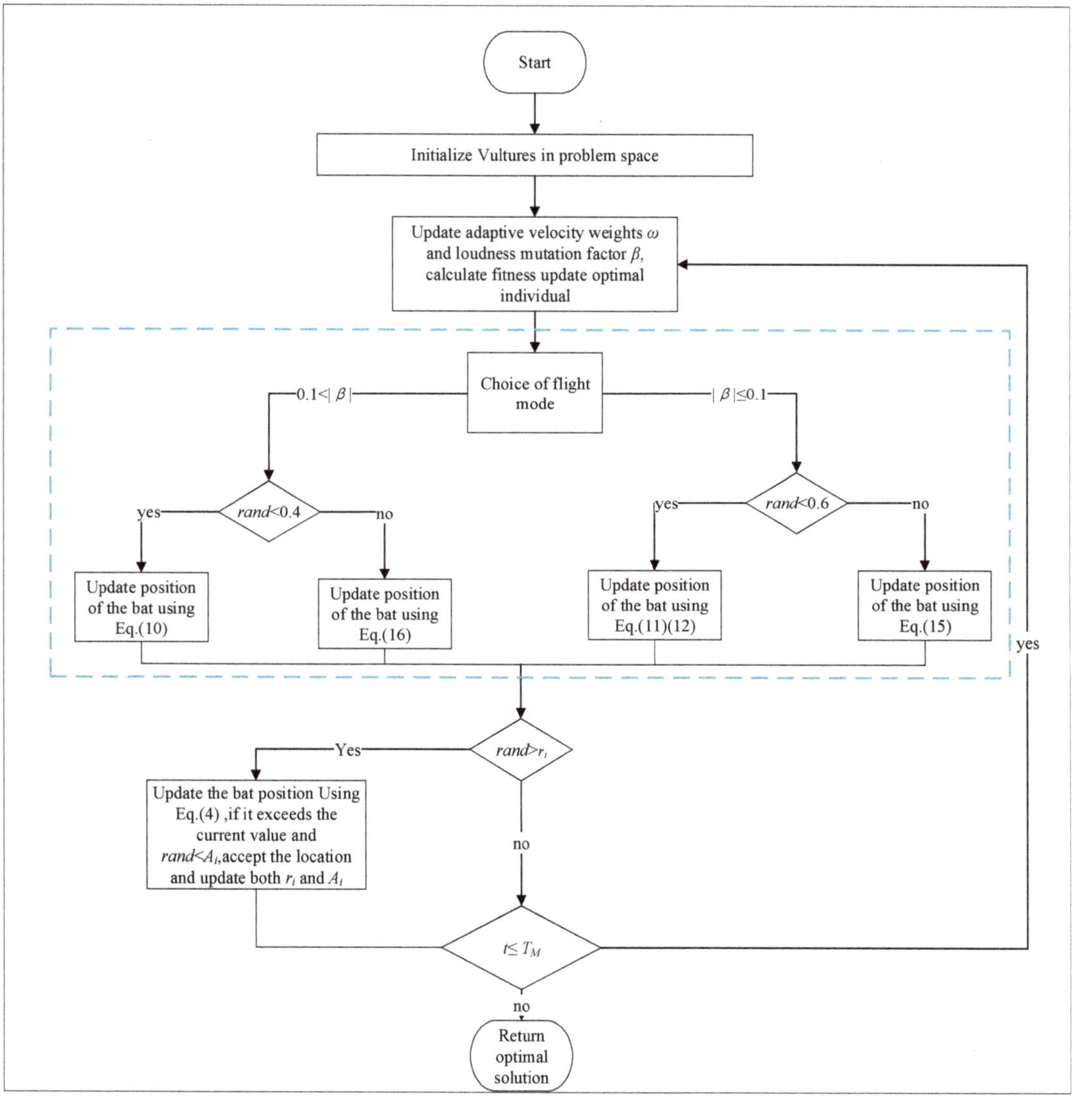

Figure 1. Optimization flow chart of HSIBA.

Table 1. Test functions.

Test Function	Range	F_{min}
$F1(x) = x_1^2 + 10^6 \sum_{i=2}^{d} x_i^2$	$[-10, 10]$	0
$F2(x) = \sum_{i=1}^{d} \lvert x_i \rvert^{i+1}$	$[-100, 100]$	0
$F3(x) = \sum_{i=1}^{d} x_i^2 + \left(\sum_{i=1}^{d} 0.5x_i\right)^2 + \left(\sum_{i=1}^{d} 0.5x_i\right)^4$	$[-5, 100]$	0
$F4(x) = \sum_{i=1}^{d} \left(x_i^2 - 10\cos(2\pi x_i) + 10\right)$	$[-5.12, 5.12]$	0
$F5(x) = \sum_{i=1}^{d} \frac{x_i^2}{4000} - \prod_{i=1}^{d} \cos\left(\frac{x_i}{\sqrt{i}}\right) + 1$	$[-600, 600]$	0
$F6(x) = \sin^2(\pi\omega_1) + \sum_{i=1}^{d-1} (\omega_i - 1)^2 \left[1 + 10\sin^2(\pi\omega_i + 1)\right]$ $+(\omega_d - 1)^2\left[1 + \sin^2(2\pi\omega_d)\right]$ $\omega_1 = 1 + \frac{x_i - 1}{4}, \forall i = 1, \ldots, d$	$[-10, 10]$	0
$F7(x) = \sum_{i=1}^{d} x_i^2$	$[-100, 100]$	0
$F8(x) = \sum_{i=1}^{d} \lvert x_i \rvert + \prod_{i=1}^{d} \lvert x_i \rvert$	$[-10, 10]$	0
$F9(x) = \sum_{i=1}^{d} \left(\sum_{j=1}^{i} x_j\right)^2$	$[-100, 100]$	0
$F10(x) = max_i\{\lvert x_i \rvert, 1 \le i \le d\}$	$[-100, 100]$	0
$F11(x) = \sum_{i=1}^{d-1} \left[100\left(x_{i+1} - x_i^2\right)^2 + (x_i - 1)^2\right]$	$[-30, 30]$	0
$F12(x) = \sum_{i=1}^{d} (\lvert x_i + 0.5 \rvert)^2$	$[-100, 100]$	0
$F13(x) = \sum_{i=1}^{d} i x_i^4 + random[0, 1)$	$[-128, 128]$	0
$F14(x) = -20\exp\left(-0.2\sqrt{\frac{1}{d}\sum_{i=1}^{d} x_i^2}\right)$ $-\exp\left(\frac{1}{d}\sum_{i=1}^{d} \cos 2\pi x_i\right) + 20 + e$	$[-32, 32]$	0
$F15(x) = \frac{\pi}{d}\left\{10\sin(\pi y_1) + (y_d - 1)^2\right\}$ $+\frac{\pi}{d}\sum_{i=1}^{d-1} (y_1 - 1)^2\left[1 + 10\sin^2(\pi y_{i+1})\right] + \sum_{i=1}^{d} U(x_i, 10, 100, 4) y_i$ $= 1 + \frac{x_i + 1}{4} U(x_i, a, k, m) = \begin{cases} k(x_i - a)^m x_i > a \\ 0 - a < x_i < a \\ k(-x_i - a)^m x_i < -a \end{cases}$	$[-50, 50]$	0
$F16(x) = 0.1\sin^2(3\pi x_1) + 0.1\sum_{i=1}^{d} (x_i - 1)^2\left[1 + \sin^2(3\pi x_i + 1)\right]$ $+0.1(x_d - 1)^2\left[1 + \sin^2(2\pi x_d)\right] + \sum_{i=1}^{d} U(x_i, 5, 100, 4)$	$[-50, 50]$	0

Table 2. Parameter settings of optimization algorithms for comparison and evaluation of the HSIBA.

Algorithm	Parameter	Value
ELBA [26]	Initial value of loudness	1
	Final value of loudness	0
	Initial value of pulse rate	0
	Final value of pulse rate	1
	Initial value of frequency	0
	Final value of frequency	5
	flight exponent (beta)	1.7
AVOA [28]	L_1	0.8
	L_2	0.8
	W	2.5
	P_1	0.6
	P_2	0.4
	P_3	0.6
AOA [31]	α	5
	μ	0.5
HPO [32]	C	$\in [1, 0.02]$
	β	0.1
WHO [30]	Crossover percentage	$PC = 0.13$
	Stallions percentage (number of groups)	$PS = 0.2$
	Crossover	Mean
BA [27]	A_0	0.7
	α	0.8
	r_0	0
	γ	0.9
	f_{min}	−2
	f_{max}	2
HSIBA	Fixed frequency	$f_{min} = -2, f_{max} = 2$
	Fixed flight weight	$\omega_{min} = 0.2, \omega_{max} = 0.8$
	Initial pulse frequency	$r_i^0 = 0, i \in \{1, 2, \cdots, I\}$
	Initial pulse loudness	$A_i^0 = 2, i \in \{1, 2, \cdots, I\}$

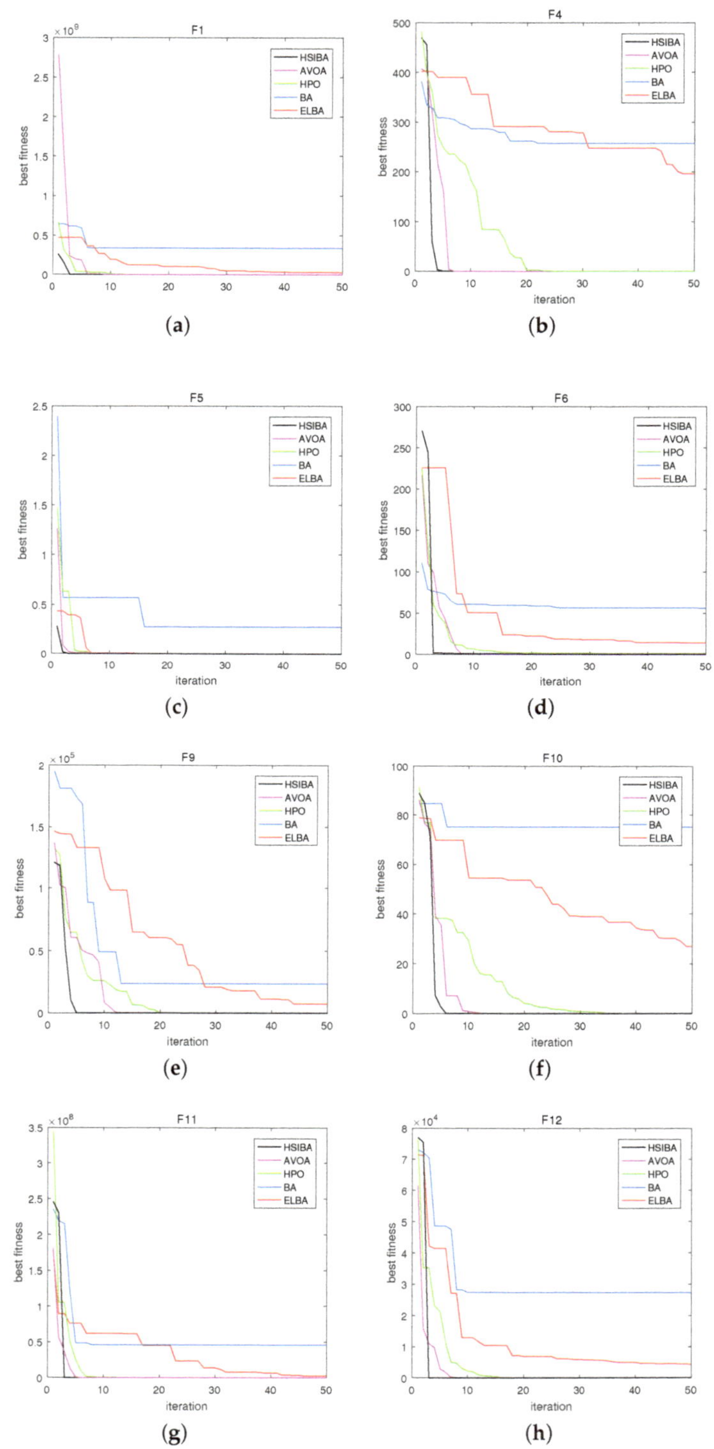

Figure 2. Iteration diagram of different optimization algorithms. (**a**) F1. (**b**) F4. (**c**) F5. (**d**) F6. (**e**) F9. (**f**) F10. (**g**) F11. (**h**) F12.

Table 3. Test results (d = 30).

Function		AVOA	AOA	WHO	BA	HPO	ELBA	HSIBA	Rank
F1	Mean	3.094×10^{-44}	5.546×10^{-104}	2.829×10^{-1}	1.469×10^{7}	2.621×10^{-26}	2.023×10^{7}	**0**	1
	Variance	1.274×10^{-86}	9.229×10^{-206}	9.759×10^{-1}	1.539×10^{14}	8.292×10^{-51}	5.532×10^{13}	**0**	
F2	Mean	4.896×10^{-124}	**0**	6.570×10^{-56}	2.312×10^{-6}	4.389×10^{-60}	3.665×10^{-25}	**0**	1
	Variance	7.191×10^{-246}	**0**	1.279×10^{-109}	1.380×10^{-11}	5.447×10^{-118}	2.039×10^{-48}	**0**	
F3	Mean	1.157×10^{-16}	4.465×10^{2}	4.727×10^{0}	4.884×10^{2}	4.864×10^{-18}	2.713×10^{2}	**0**	1
	Variance	3.996×10^{-31}	5.162×10^{3}	6.121×10^{2}	4.800×10^{4}	4.537×10^{-34}	1.289×10^{4}	**0**	
F4	Mean	**0**	**0**	1.253×10^{0}	1.840×10^{2}	**0**	1.584×10^{2}	**0**	1
	Variance	**0**	**0**	1.276×10^{1}	2.235×10^{0}	**0**	6.889×10^{2}	**0**	
F5	Mean	**0**	**0**	**0**	1.068×10^{-4}	**0**	2.009×10^{-15}	**0**	1
	Variance	**0**	**0**	**0**	2.204×10^{-8}	**0**	7.976×10^{-29}	**0**	
F6	Mean	$\mathbf{3.200 \times 10^{-3}}$	2.556×10^{0}	4.255×10^{0}	4.276×10^{1}	1.065×10^{0}	1.070×10^{1}	7.836×10^{-1}	2
	Variance	2.669×10^{-4}	$\mathbf{1.994 \times 10^{-4}}$	1.872×10^{1}	2.316×10^{2}	7.030×10^{-2}	2.577×10^{1}	1.292×10^{-1}	
F7	Mean	2.986×10^{-47}	4.810×10^{-5}	2.070×10^{-5}	3.483×10^{4}	2.486×10^{-31}	2.307×10^{3}	**0**	1
	Variance	2.670×10^{-92}	6.248×10^{-8}	2.810×10^{-9}	7.286×10^{7}	9.799×10^{-61}	4.206×10^{35}	**0**	
F8	Mean	1.883×10^{-22}	6.529×10^{-73}	2.000×10^{-3}	4.204×10^{10}	1.108×10^{-17}	2.268×10^{1}	$\mathbf{2.005 \times 10^{-171}}$	1
	Variance	1.049×10^{-42}	1.278×10^{-143}	5.591×10^{-5}	2.069×10^{22}	3.326×10^{-34}	2.993×10^{1}	**0**	
F9	Mean	3.720×10^{-29}	2.900×10^{-2}	1.571×10^{-1}	8.840×10^{4}	3.332×10^{-24}	3.214×10^{3}	$\mathbf{1.397 \times 10^{-307}}$	1
	Variance	1.534×10^{-56}	1.600×10^{-3}	1.688×10^{-1}	1.193×10^{9}	2.478×10^{-46}	1.438×10^{6}	**0**	
F10	Mean	1.526×10^{-24}	3.420×10^{-2}	2.180×10^{-2}	7.245×10^{1}	9.123×10^{-15}	1.660×10^{1}	$\mathbf{2.279 \times 10^{-163}}$	1
	Variance	4.126×10^{-47}	3.059×10^{-4}	5.750×10^{-4}	5.554×10^{1}	2.892×10^{-28}	6.801×10^{0}	**0**	
F11	Mean	$\mathbf{9.498 \times 10^{-1}}$	2.870×10^{1}	1.513×10^{2}	7.802×10^{7}	2.687×10^{1}	3.491×10^{5}	2.867×10^{1}	3
	Variance	2.631×10^{1}	5.270×10^{-2}	2.747×10^{5}	6.637×10^{14}	5.869×10^{-1}	5.022×10^{10}	$\mathbf{7.900 \times 10^{-3}}$	
F12	Mean	$\mathbf{4.150 \times 10^{-2}}$	4.280×10^{0}	4.792×10^{0}	3.580×10^{4}	6.929×10^{-1}	2.257×10^{3}	2.147×10^{-1}	2
	Variance	$\mathbf{7.500 \times 10^{-3}}$	5.710×10^{-2}	1.925×10^{1}	1.243×10^{8}	9.330×10^{-2}	26.778×10^{5}	1.470×10^{-2}	
F13	Mean	8.072×10^{-4}	$\mathbf{2.637 \times 10^{-4}}$	1.200×10^{-2}	4.074×10^{1}	2.200×10^{-3}	3.343×10^{-1}	4.149×10^{-4}	2
	Variance	4.622×10^{-7}	$\mathbf{3.746 \times 10^{-8}}$	7.709×10^{-5}	4.146×10^{2}	1.197×10^{-5}	3.324×10^{-2}	8.395×10^{-8}	
F14	Mean	$\mathbf{8.881 \times 10^{-16}}$	1.006×10^{-15}	7.587×10^{-4}	1.936×10^{1}	1.125×10^{-15}	1.045×10^{1}	$\mathbf{8.881 \times 10^{-16}}$	1
	Variance	**0**	4.207×10^{-31}	1.346×10^{-6}	4.988×10^{-1}	8.124×10^{-31}	1.131×10^{0}	**0**	
F15	Mean	$\mathbf{1.700 \times 10^{-3}}$	7.790×10^{-1}	6.705×10^{-1}	1.333×10^{8}	1.730×10^{-2}	2.145×10^{1}	1.020×10^{-2}	2
	Variance	$\mathbf{1.3894 \times 10^{-5}}$	3.100×10^{-3}	4.802×10^{-1}	7.988×10^{15}	1.114×10^{-4}	2.754×10^{2}	4.685×10^{-5}	
F16	Mean	$\mathbf{3.000 \times 10^{-3}}$	2.899×10^{0}	1.744×10^{0}	3.050×10^{8}	1.039×10^{0}	5.332×10^{4}	2.730×10^{-1}	2
	Variance	$\mathbf{4.917 \times 10^{-5}}$	7.200×10^{-3}	3.261×10^{-1}	2.202×10^{16}	1.484×10^{-1}	6.837×10^{9}	3.080×10^{-2}	

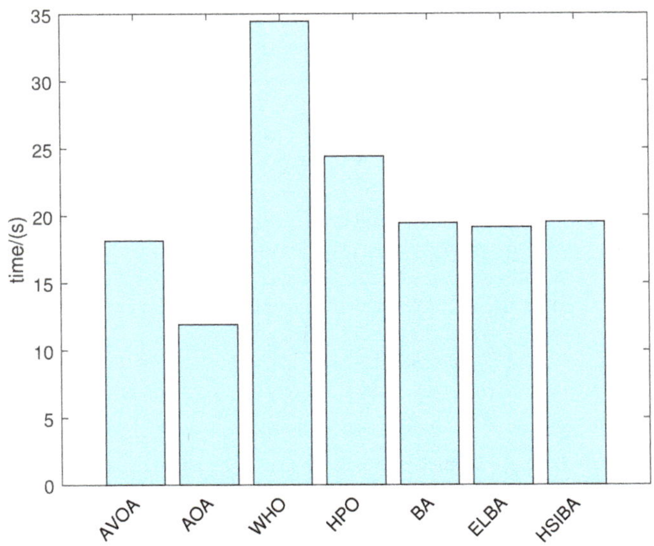

Figure 3. Computing time of different algorithms.

Table 4. Test results (d = 100).

Function		AVOA	AOA	WHO	BA	HPO	ELBA	HSIBA	Rank
F1	Mean	6.165×10^{-41}	5.200×10^{-3}	5.610×10^{1}	1.494×10^{9}	5.112×10^{-24}	1.270×10^{8}	**0**	1
	Variance	1.130×10^{-79}	7.958×10^{-4}	2.828×10^{4}	1.165×10^{17}	7.688×10^{-46}	2.551×10^{14}	**0**	
F2	Mean	4.361×10^{-117}	**0**	3.140×10^{-58}	3.857×10^{-1}	1.086×10^{-57}	3.660×10^{-26}	**0**	1
	Variance	5.707×10^{-232}	**0**	3.396×10^{-114}	3.771×10^{-1}	3.457×10^{-113}	8.986×10^{-51}	**0**	
F3	Mean	6.732×10^{2}	2.536×10^{3}	8.348×10^{2}	3.803×10^{3}	2.400×10^{-3}	5.001×10^{3}	**0**	1
	Variance	5.815×10^{5}	9.138×10^{4}	1.945×10^{5}	3.877×10^{5}	1.001×10^{-4}	5.391×10^{6}	**0**	
F4	Mean	**0**	6.276×10^{-15}	4.129×10^{0}	1.025×10^{3}	**0**	7.706×10^{2}	**0**	1
	Variance	**0**	8.229×10^{-28}	4.756×10^{2}	3.352×10^{4}	**0**	2.110×10^{3}	**0**	
F5	Mean	**0**	**0**	**0**	4.256×10^{-5}	**0**	1.032×10^{-15}	**0**	1
	Variance	**0**	**0**	**0**	4.949×10^{-9}	**0**	2.520×10^{-29}	**0**	
F6	Mean	**1.820×10^{-2}**	8.923×10^{0}	5.580×10^{1}	2.068×10^{2}	6.795×10^{0}	7.165×10^{1}	3.759×10^{0}	2
	Variance	4.000×10^{-3}	**7.433×10^{-5}**	1.570×10^{3}	5.246×10^{3}	2.441×10^{-1}	2.543×10^{2}	5.136×10^{-1}	
F7	Mean	2.405×10^{-41}	4.720×10^{-2}	3.900×10^{-3}	1.493×10^{5}	1.572×10^{-29}	1.259×10^{4}	**0**	1
	Variance	1.735×10^{-80}	2.061×10^{-4}	4.630×10^{-5}	1.108×10^{9}	2.915×10^{-57}	3.178×10^{6}	**0**	
F8	Mean	4.881×10^{-26}	5.178×10^{-8}	4.995×10^{1}	2.953×10^{45}	1.525×10^{-15}	9.613×10^{1}	**2.084×10^{-174}**	1
	Variance	5.429×10^{-50}	8.042×10^{-14}	1.034×10^{4}	2.612×10^{92}	4.483×10^{-29}	7.017×10^{1}	**0**	
F9	Mean	1.706×10^{-18}	1.053×10^{0}	4.046×10^{1}	9.128×10^{5}	3.201×10^{-22}	4.354×10^{4}	**5.542×10^{-294}**	1
	Variance	7.407×10^{-35}	2.796×10^{-1}	3.198×10^{3}	1.457×10^{11}	$2.250 \times 10^{6-42}$	1.310×10^{8}	**0**	
F10	Mean	1.534×10^{-25}	1.040×10^{-1}	1.554×10^{-1}	8.490×10^{1}	1.326×10^{-13}	2.615×10^{1}	**8.600×10^{-168}**	1
	Variance	6.484×10^{-49}	1.993×10^{-4}	3.410×10^{-2}	4.554×10^{1}	6.859×10^{-26}	8.110×10^{0}	**0**	
F11	Mean	**2.301×10^{1}**	9.893×10^{1}	4.541×10^{2}	4.162×10^{8}	9.830×10^{1}	3.315×10^{6}	9.811×10^{1}	2
	Variance	1.773×10^{3}	**3.100×10^{-3}**	3.781×10^{6}	3.482×10^{16}	2.603×10^{-1}	8.023×10^{11}	3.200×10^{-3}	
F12	Mean	**7.231×10^{-1}**	1.995×10^{1}	2.409×10^{1}	1.496×10^{5}	1.246×10^{1}	1.357×10^{4}	9.716×10^{-1}	2
	Variance	2.355×10^{0}	3.027×10^{-1}	2.334×10^{1}	1.401×10^{9}	9.962×10^{-1}	4.223×10^{6}	**1.600×10^{-1}**	
F13	Mean	8.402×10^{-4}	**3.776×10^{-4}**	1.500×10^{-2}	6.539×10^{2}	1.700×10^{-3}	5.745×10^{0}	7.208×10^{-4}	2
	Variance	1.105×10^{-6}	**1.392×10^{-7}**	1.116×10^{-4}	8.228×10^{4}	3.663×10^{-6}	2.760×10^{0}	6.438×10^{-7}	
F14	Mean	**8.881×10^{-16}**	1.990×10^{-3}	4.900×10^{-3}	1.989×10^{1}	2.190×10^{-15}	1.205×10^{1}	**8.881×10^{-16}**	1
	Variance	**0**	2.567×10^{-6}	5.982×10^{-5}	1.994×10^{-1}	8.254×10^{-30}	4.395×10^{-1}	**0**	
F15	Mean	**1.600×10^{-3}**	1.039×10^{0}	1.152×10^{0}	7.267×10^{8}	3.030×10^{-1}	2.159×10^{4}	8.800×10^{-3}	2
	Variance	**2.876×10^{-5}**	8.413×10^{-4}	2.842×10^{-1}	1.913×10^{17}	4.400×10^{-3}	1.165×10^{9}	3.646×10^{-5}	
F16	Mean	**4.600×10^{-2}**	9.998×10^{0}	1.295×10^{1}	1.700×10^{9}	9.254×10^{0}	1.731×10^{6}	7.374×10^{-1}	2
	Variance	3.250×10^{-2}	**1.000×10^{-3}**	1.098×10^{1}	5.370×10^{17}	1.749×10^{-1}	1.743×10^{12}	3.240×10^{-1}	

3. Throughput Optimization for EH-NOMA-CRN

3.1. System Model

As shown in Figure 4, we consider an underlay PB-assisted EH-NOMA-CRN, where primary network (PN) includes a set of N PR nodes, Q_n, $n \in \{1, 2, \cdots, N\}$, and SN consists of a secondary source node S that employs the power domain NOMA technique to communicate with two secondary destination nodes D_1 and D_2 with the help of a secondary decode-and-forward (DF) relay node R. Similar to [11,12,24], It is assumed that the interference from PN to SN is neglected. It is also assumed that all nodes except the PB node W in our system model are equipped with a single antenna, and all SN nodes working in half-duplex mode only use the energy harvested from RF signals of W installed M antennas. All wireless channels are assumed to undergo quasi-static independent Rayleigh flat fading where each channel coefficient keeps constant during a frame but varies independently between different frames.

Let $h_{j,k}$ denote the fading channel coefficient corresponding to the link from node j to k, where $j \in \{\mathrm{S}, \mathrm{R}, \mathrm{W}\}$, $k \in \{\mathrm{Q}_n, \mathrm{R}, \mathrm{D}_1, \mathrm{D}_2\}$, and $j \neq k$. Accordingly, The channel power gain $\left|h_{j,k}\right|^2$ is exponentially distributed with expectation value $\frac{1}{\lambda_{j,k}}$; for example, $\lambda_{j,k} = d_{j,k}^{\xi}$, where $d_{j,k}$ is the distance between node j and k, and ξ is the path loss factor. Moreover, it is assumed that all D_n are closely located in one center point. Therefore, $\left|h_{\mathrm{S},\mathrm{Q}_n}\right|^2$ and $\left|h_{\mathrm{R},\mathrm{Q}_n}\right|^2$ are independent identically distributed random variables, respectively, i.e., $\lambda_{\mathrm{S},\mathrm{Q}_n} = \lambda_{\mathrm{S},\mathrm{Q}}$, and $\lambda_{\mathrm{R},\mathrm{Q}_n} = \lambda_{\mathrm{R},\mathrm{Q}}$.

Similar to [33], the three-phase time division broadcasting protocol with precise synchronization is adopted in our system model. Node l, $l \in \{\mathrm{S}, \mathrm{R}\}$ simultaneously harvest energy from RF signals of W for a duration of αT at the beginning of every frame, where

T is the period of one frame, and $0 < \alpha < 1$ is EH ratio. During the EH phase, the energy harvested by node l can be written as

$$E_l = \sum_{m=1}^{M} \eta\left(P_t |h_{m,l}|^2\right)\alpha T \quad (20)$$

where $0 < \eta < 1$ is the energy conversion efficiency, P_t is the transmit power of single W's antenna, and $|h_{m,l}|^2$ is the channel power gain of link from the W's m-th antenna to node l, $m \in \{1, 2, \cdots, M\}$, $\lambda_{m,l} = \lambda_{W,l}$, respectively. Subsequently, the phase $(1-\alpha)T$ is equally divided into two time slots for the two-hop data transmission of SN. During the phase of data transmission, the RF-EH circuit of node l is turned off, and the transceivers of R, D_1 and D_2 are turned on. We assume that regardless of energy harvested by node l in each frame, they can be stored in its configured storage device (e.g., a supercapacitor) and can be immediately applied for subsequent data transmission. Furthermore, the storage device of node l lacks energy management function and has obvious leakage of electricity, which causes the node l's residual energy at the end of each frame to be completely leaked [24,33].

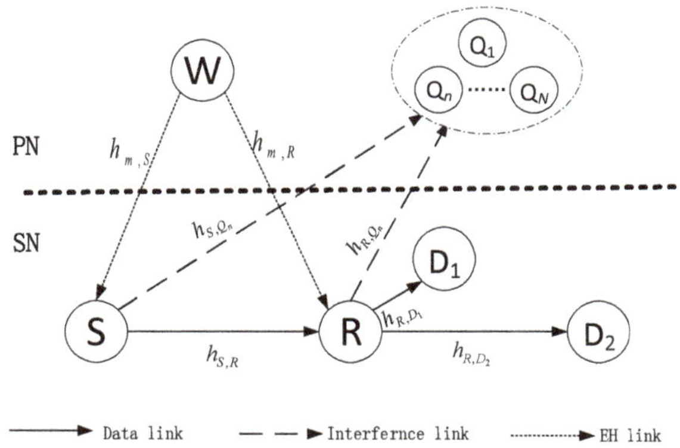

Figure 4. Network system model.

In underlay paradigm, the instantaneous transmit power of node l must be strictly constrained such that the interference induced by node l remains below the threshold P_I, i.e., the peak interference power that Q_n can tolerate. It is also assumed that the circuit energy consumption of node l is ignored, i.e., the energy harvested by node l is only used for data transmission. Consequently, the transmit power of node i can be set as

$$P_l = \min\left(\frac{2E_l}{(1-\alpha)T}, \frac{P_I}{Y_l}\right) = \min\left(\rho P_t Z_l, \frac{P_I}{Y_l}\right) \quad (21)$$

where $\rho = \frac{2\eta\alpha}{1-\alpha}, Z_l = \sum_{m=1}^{M} |h_{m,l}|^2$, and $Y_l = \max_{n=1,2,\cdots,N}\left\{|h_{l,n}|^2\right\}$

Let $S_1(t)$ and $S_2(t)$ respectively denote the data signals transmitted to D_1 and D_2 by S at time t. S produces the NOMA signal $S_s(t)$ by allocating distinct power coefficients a_1 and a_2 for D_1 and D_2 respectively, i.e., the power $P_S a_1$ and $P_S a_2$ are respectively allocated to D_1 and D_2 at S. Moreover, it is assumed that D_1 is near node and D_2 is far node. Due to the principle that lower power is allocated to near node D_1 at S, $a_2 > a_1$ and $a_1 + a_2 = 1$. During the first time slot of every frame, R receives the signal $S(t)$ transmitted by S. Since the far node D_2's data $S_2(t)$ with large power are firstly decoded and the near node D_1 's data $S_1(t)$ are secondly decoded using successfully perfect SIC [22] by R, the corresponding signal-to-noise ratio (SNR) to $S_2(t)$ and $S_1(t)$ at R can be respectively given by

$$\gamma_{R,S_2} = \frac{a_2 P_S X_1}{a_1 P_S X_1 + \sigma^2} \quad (22)$$

and

$$\gamma_{R,S_1} = \frac{a_1 P_S X_1}{\sigma^2} \tag{23}$$

where σ^2 is the variance of additive complex white Gaussian noise, and $X_1 = |h_{S,R}|^2$.

During the second time slot of every frame, R adopts superposition coding to make the new NOMA signal $S_R(t)$ and send it to D_1 and D_2. Let b_1 and b_2 be the power allocation coefficients at R for D_1 and D_2, respectively. Since D_1 is closer to R than D_2, higher power is allocated to D_2's data in $S_R(t)$ at R as well, i.e., $b_2 > b_1$ and $b_1 + b_2 = 1$. Now the far node D_2 decodes its data $S_2(t)$ from the signals forwarded by R, and the corresponding SNR for $S_2(t)$ at D_2 can be expressed as

$$\gamma_{D_2,S_2} = \frac{b_2 P_R X_2}{b_1 P_R X_2 + \sigma^2} \tag{24}$$

where $X_2 = \left|h_{R,D_2}\right|^2$

At the near node D_1, the far node D_2's data $S_2(t)$ with larger power are first decoded and later D_1's data $S_1(t)$ are decoded by achieving successfully perfect SIC [22]. Hence, the corresponding SINRs for $S_2(t)$ and $S_1(t)$ at D_1 can be respectively given as

$$\gamma_{D_1,S_2} = \frac{b_2 P_R X_3}{b_1 P_R X_3 + \sigma^2} \tag{25}$$

and

$$\gamma_{D_1,S_1} = \frac{b_1 P_R X_3}{\sigma^2} \tag{26}$$

where $X_3 = \left|h_{R,D_1}\right|^2$

3.2. *Outage Probability Analysis of SN*

In this section, the outage probability experienced by D_1 and D_2 will be studied. Let R_1 and R_2 respectively denote the target rates for D_1 and D_2. Since two consecutive time slots are needed to realize the communication from S to D_1 and D_2 in every frame, the achieved rates are halved. Hence, the target SINRs for successful decoding of $S_1(t)$ and $S_2(t)$ are respectively expressed as $\gamma_1 = 2^{\frac{2R_1}{1-\alpha}} - 1$ and $\gamma_2 = 2^{\frac{2R_2}{1-\alpha}} - 1$.

3.2.1. OP for D_1

To achieve the reliable transmission of $S_1(t)$ from S to D_1, both $S_1(t)$ and $S_2(t)$ should be successfully decoded by R and D_1. Accordingly, the OP for D_1 is defined as

$$P_{\text{out},1} = 1 - \Pr\{\gamma_{R,S_2} \geq \gamma_2, \gamma_{R,S_1} \geq \gamma_1, \gamma_{D_1,S_2} \geq \gamma_2, \gamma_{D_1,S_1} \geq \gamma_1\} \tag{27}$$

Proposition 1. *Assuming* $0 < a_1 < \frac{1}{1+\gamma_2}$ *and* $0 < b_1 < \frac{1}{1+\gamma_2}$, *OP expression for* D_1 *is calculated as*

$$\begin{aligned} P_{out,1} = 1 - &\left(\sum_{n=0}^{N} \binom{N}{n} (-1)^n \frac{2\lambda_{S,R}}{\Gamma(M)} C_1^{\frac{M}{2}} C_2^{\frac{M}{2}-1} K_M\left(2\sqrt{C_1 C_2}\right)\right) \\ \times &\left(\sum_{n=0}^{N} \binom{N}{n} (-1)^n \frac{2\lambda_{R,D_1}}{\Gamma(M)} C_3^{\frac{M}{2}} C_4^{\frac{M}{2}-1} K_M\left(2\sqrt{C_3 C_4}\right)\right) \end{aligned} \tag{28}$$

where $\Gamma(\cdot)$ *and* $K_\vartheta(\cdot)$ *are respectively gamma function and the modified Bessel function of second kind with order* ϑ, *and* C_1, C_2, C_3, *and* C_4 *are defined in Appendix A.*

Proof. See Appendix A. □

3.2.2. OP for D_2

For completing successful transmission of $S_2(t)$ from S to D_2, at first both $S_1(t)$ and $S_2(t)$ need to be reliably decoded by R; subsequently, $S_2(t)$ in $S_R(t)$ transmitted by R should be successfully decoded at D_2. Accordingly, OP for D_2 is determined by

$$P_{\text{out},2} = 1 - \Pr\{\gamma_{\text{R},S_2} \geq \gamma_2, \gamma_{\text{R},S_1} \geq \gamma_1, \gamma_{D_2,S_2} \geq \gamma_2\} \tag{29}$$

Proposition 2. *Assuming* $0 < a_1 < \frac{1}{1+\gamma_2}$ *and* $0 < b_1 < \frac{1}{1+\gamma_2}$, *OP expression for* D_2 *is given by*

$$\begin{aligned} P_{out,2} = 1 - &\left(\sum_{n=0}^{N} \binom{N}{n} (-1)^n \frac{2\lambda_{S,R}}{\Gamma(M)} C_1^{\frac{M}{2}} C_2^{\frac{M}{2}-1} K_M\left(2\sqrt{C_1 C_2}\right) \right) \\ \times &\left(\sum_{n=0}^{N} \binom{N}{n} (-1)^n \frac{2\lambda_{R,D_2}}{\Gamma(M)} C_5^{\frac{M}{2}} C_6^{\frac{M}{2}-1} K_M\left(2\sqrt{C_5 C_6}\right) \right) \end{aligned} \tag{30}$$

where C_5 *and* C_6 *are defined in Appendix B.*

Proof. See Appendix B. □

3.3. Analysis and Optimization of SN's Throughput

In this section, to achieve the maximization of SN's throughput, the jointly optimal EH ratio (α^*) and power allocation factors at S (a_1^*, a_2^*) and R (b_1^*, b_2^*) have to be determined. Considering delay-limited transmission mode, where the fixed target rates at D_1 and D_2 are respectively R_1 and R_2, the throughput of SN is expressed as [14]

$$\tau = R_1(1 - P_{out,1}) + R_2(1 - P_{out,2}) \tag{31}$$

where Pout_1 is the outage probability of SN_1 and Pout_2 is the outage probability of SN_2.

For the purpose of maximize the throughput of SN, the resource allocation problem with respect to EH ratio α and power allocation factors a_1,a_2,b_1 and b_2 can be formulated as

$$\left.\begin{array}{l} \max\limits_{(\alpha,a_1,a_2,b_1,b_2)=(\alpha^*,a_1^*,a_2^*,b_1^*,b_2^*)} \quad \tau \\ \text{s.t.} a_1 + a_2 = 1, b_1 + b_2 = 1 \\ 0 < \alpha < 1, a_1 < a_2, b_1 < b_2 \end{array}\right\} \tag{32}$$

To our best knowledge, the convexity of the objective function is hard to be estimated due to the complex expression of SN's throughput. Consequently, the throughput optimization problem is difficult to be settled in general methods, such as convex optimization. For resolving the SN's throughput optimization problem, a meta-heuristic algorithm based on HSIBA is applied in our paper.

4. Optimization Results and Performance Analysis

In this section, to maximize the throughput of SN, we apply the HSIBA to optimize the EH ratio and power allocation factors of the EH-NOMA-CRN. Without any loss of generality, the network system environment follows by the system model described in Section 3. The nodes S, R, W, D_1, D_2 and Q_n are located at $(-1, 0)$, $(0, 0)$, $(0, -1)$, $(0.5, 0.5)$, $(1, 0)$ and $(1, 1)$, respectively. Unless otherwise stated, the key simulation parameters are listed in Table 5.

In Figures 5 and 6, we plot unoptimized SN's throughput and the optimized SN's throughput by the proposed HSIBA as a function of $P_t(P_I)$ with different $N(R_1$ and $R_2)$, respectively. Moreover, we also compare the HSIBA with the exhaustive searching algorithm. The results show that: (1) the throughput increases with the increase of $P_t(P_I)$ and tends to be saturated gradually. That is because SN nodes' transmission power increases with the increase of $P_t(P_I)$, which leads to the throughput raise. Nevertheless, due to the limitation of $P_I(P_t)$, SN nodes' transmission power, OP and throughput of the SN all tend to saturation; and (2) In Figure 5, for given P_t, the probability that interference channel obtains higher power gain increases with increase of N, which leads to throughput increasing; and (3) In Figure 6, for given P_I, different values of R_1 and R_2 correspond to different SN's throughput; and (4) From Figures 5 and 6, it is distinctly observed that the optimized throughput values are significantly higher than those unoptimized values either for given P_t or P_I; and (5) It also can be clearly observed that the optimal throughput curves by proposed HSIBA extremely approximate the optimal curves by the greedy search algorithm. However, the latter has to search the optimal solution in a three-dimensional continuous space generated by α, a_1 and b_1, which results in a much higher computational complexity than the former.

Table 5. Simulation parameters and values.

Description	Value
Number of node Q_n	$N = 5$
Number of node W's antennas	$M = 3$
Peak interference power at node Q_n	$P_I = 10$ dB
Single antenna's transmission power of node W	$P_t = 40$ dB
Noise power	$\sigma^2 = 1$
Energy conversion efficiency	$\eta = 0.8$
Path loss factor	$\xi = 2.5$
Energy harvesting ratio	$\alpha = 0.5$
Power allocation factors of node S	$a_1 = 0.17, a_2 = 0.83$
Power allocation factors of node R	$b_1 = 0.23, b_2 = 0.77$
The target rate of D_1	$R_1 = 0.3$ bit/s/Hz
The target rate of D_2	$R_2 = 0.5$ bit/s/Hz
Maximum number of iterations	$T_M = 100$
Bat population	$I = 30$
Algorithmic dimension	$d = 3$

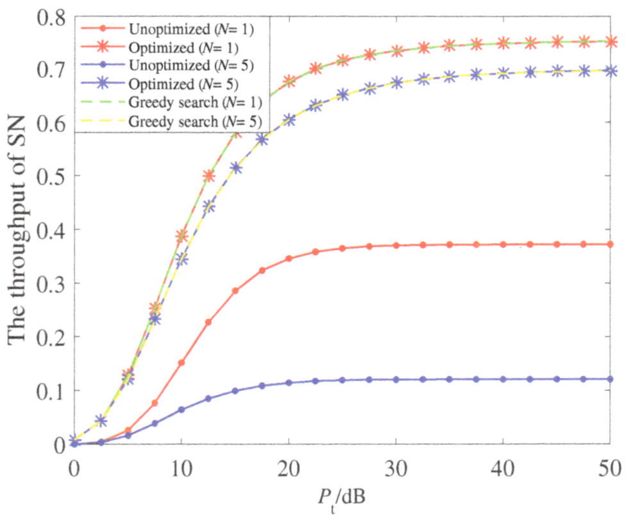

Figure 5. Throughput versus P_t for various N.

Figure 7 shows the relationship between optimal SN's throughput value search of five different optimization algorithms and the number of iteration t. It can be observed that: (1) The four kinds of optimization algorithms except AOA can all effectively optimize the proposed EH-NOMA-CRN and successively search the optimal SN's throughput value; (2) For HSIBA, HPO, AOVA, ELBA and standard BA, they need 8, 21, 31, 33 and 42 iterations to converge, respectively. Thus it can be seen that the HSIBA has better convergence speed and higher stability.

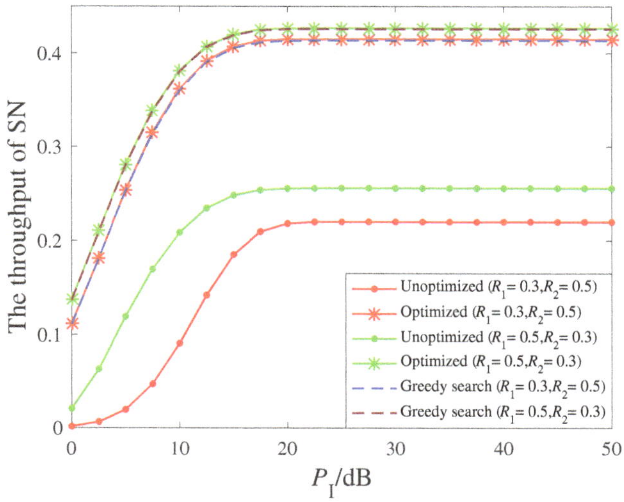

Figure 6. Throughput versus P_I for various R_1 and R_2.

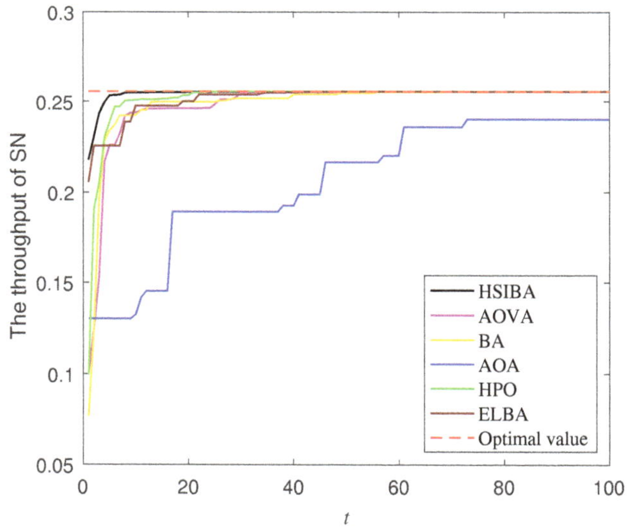

Figure 7. Optimal throughput search versus t.

5. Conclusions

In this paper, we propose a novel HSIBA with adaptive strategy and multiple flight modes selection, and respectively derive the closed-form solutions of SN's OP and throughput. On the base of the throughput analysis, we further formulate the throughput maximation problem with regard to EH ratio and power allocation factors. In addition, due to the complexity of throughput solution, we employ the HSIBA to jointly optimize EH ratio and power allocation factors to maximize the SN's throughput. Through comparing with other advanced meta-heuristic algorithms, we confirm the correctness and effectiveness of proposed HSIBA by a large number of benchmark functions' test and numerical results. Based on the network parameters setting and grasp of channel state information, the proposed

HSIBA can achieve joint optimization to EH-NOMA-CRN based on three parameters with faster convergence speed and higher stability.

Author Contributions: Conceptualization: Y.L. (Yi Luo) and C.W.; experimentation and data analysis: N.H. and L.M.; writing—original draft preparation: Y.L. (Yi Luo), N.H. and C.W.; writing—review and editing: C.W., Y.L. (Yi Leng), N.H. and J.T.; funding acquisition: Y.L. (Yi Leng), C.W. and N.H. All authors have read and agreed to the published version of the manuscript.

Funding: This work was supported in part by Airforce of People's Liberation Army, Government of China under grant No. PGGC-2021-003, the Hunan Provincial Science and Technology Project Foundation under Grant 2018TP1018, and Hunan Normal University Undergraduates Innovative Experiment Project and Entrepreneurship Program (Grant No. 2022180 and No. 2022183).

Institutional Review Board Statement: Not applicable.

Informed Consent Statement: Not applicable.

Data Availability Statement: Not applicable.

Conflicts of Interest: The authors declare no conflict of interest.

Appendix A

In this Appendix A, we offer a proof of Proposition 1. To simplify the derivation process, we firstly provide the probability density function (PDF) and cumulative distribution function (CDF) of Y_l, Z_l, and $U_l = P_l/\sigma^2$.

Note that Y_l is the maximum of N independent exponential random variables (RVs) with the same expectation value $1/\lambda_{\mathrm{W},l}$, and Z_l is the sum of M independent exponential RVs with the same expectation value $1/\lambda_{l,\mathrm{Q}}$. Therefore, the CDF and PDF of Y_l and Z_l can be respectively computed as

$$F_{Y_l}(y_l) = \left(1 - \mathrm{e}^{-\lambda_{l,\mathrm{Q}} y_l}\right)^N = \sum_{n=0}^{N} \binom{N}{n} (-1)^n \mathrm{e}^{-n\lambda_{l,\mathrm{Q}} y_l} \tag{A1}$$

$$f_{Y_l}(y_l) = N\lambda_{l,\mathrm{Q}} \sum_{n=0}^{N-1} \binom{N-1}{n} (-1)^n \mathrm{e}^{-(n+1)\lambda_{l,\mathrm{Q}} y_l} \tag{A2}$$

$$F_{Z_l}(z_l) = 1 - \frac{\Gamma(M, z_l \lambda_{\mathrm{W},l})}{\Gamma(M)} \tag{A3}$$

and

$$f_{Z_l}(z_l) = \frac{\lambda_{\mathrm{W},l}^M z_l^{M-1} \mathrm{e}^{-\lambda_{\mathrm{W},l} z_l}}{\Gamma(M)} \tag{A4}$$

where $\Gamma(.)$ is the upper incomplete gamma function.

Subsequently, we can calculate the CDF of U_l as follows

$$\begin{aligned} F_{U_l}(u_l) &= 1 - \Pr\left\{Z_l > \tfrac{u_l \sigma^2}{\rho P_t}\right\} \Pr\left\{Y_l < \tfrac{P_\mathrm{I}}{u_l \sigma^2}\right\} \\ &= 1 - \sum_{n=0}^{N} \binom{N}{n} (-1)^n \frac{\Gamma\left(M, \frac{\lambda_{\mathrm{W},l} u_l \sigma^2}{\rho P_t}\right)}{\Gamma(M)} \mathrm{e}^{-\frac{n\lambda_{l,\mathrm{Q}} P_\mathrm{I}}{u_l \sigma^2}} \end{aligned} \tag{A5}$$

Then, Equation (27) can be reformulated as

$$P_{\mathrm{out},1} = 1 - \underbrace{\Pr\left\{\frac{a_2 U_S X_1}{a_1 U_S X_1 + 1} \geq \gamma_2, a_1 U_S X_1 \geq \gamma_1\right\}}_{A_{00}} \underbrace{\Pr\left\{\frac{b_2 U_R X_3}{b_1 U_R X_3 + 1} \geq \gamma_2, b_1 U_R X_3 \geq \gamma_1\right\}}_{A_{01}} \tag{A6}$$

By conditioning A_{00} in Equation (A6) on X_1 and taking the expected value of the results over the distribution of X_1, we can obtain

$$A_{00} = \Pr\{U_S X_1 \geq H \mid X_1 = x_1\} = 1 - \int_0^\infty F_{U_S}\left(\frac{H}{x_1}\right)\lambda_{S,R} e^{-\lambda_{S,R}x_1} dx_1 \tag{A7}$$

where $H = \max\left(\frac{\gamma_2}{a_2 - a_1\gamma_2}, \frac{\gamma_1}{a_1}\right)$

Applying Equation (6.453) in [34], A_{00} can be expressed as

$$A_{00} = \sum_{n=0}^{N} \binom{N}{n} (-1)^n \frac{2\lambda_{S,R}}{\Gamma(M)} C_1^{\frac{M}{2}} C_2^{\frac{M}{2}-1} K_M\left(2\sqrt{C_1 C_2}\right) \tag{A8}$$

where $C_1 = \frac{\lambda_{W,S} H \sigma^2}{\rho P_t}$ and $C_2 = \frac{n\lambda_{S,Q} P_I}{H\sigma^2} + \lambda_{S,R}$.

In the same manner, the term A_{01} in Equation (A10) can be obtained as

$$A_{01} = \sum_{n=0}^{N} \binom{N}{n} (-1)^n \frac{2\lambda_{R,D_1}}{\Gamma(M)} C_3^{\frac{M}{2}} C_4^{\frac{M}{2}-1} K_M\left(2\sqrt{C_3 C_4}\right) \tag{A9}$$

where $C_3 = \frac{\lambda_{W,R} G \sigma^2}{\rho P_t}$, $C_4 = \frac{n\lambda_{R,Q} P_I}{G\sigma^2} + \lambda_{R,D_1}$, and $G = \max\left(\frac{\gamma_2}{b_2 - b_1\gamma_2}, \frac{\gamma_1}{b_1}\right)$

The OP for D_1 can be calculated by applying the results obtained from Equations (A8) and (A9).

Appendix B

In this Appendix B, we provide a proof of Proposition 2. Equation (29) can be rewritten as follows

$$P_{out,2} = 1 - \underbrace{\Pr\{\gamma_{R,S_2} \geq \gamma_2, \gamma_{R,S_1} \geq \gamma_1\}}_{A_{00}} \underbrace{\Pr\{\gamma_{D_2,S_2} \geq \gamma_2\}}_{B_{00}} \tag{A10}$$

The term A_{00} of Equation (A10) has been calculated in Appendix A, and the term B_{00} of Equation (A10) can be computed as

$$B_{00} = 1 - \int_0^\infty F_{U_R}\left(\frac{V}{X_2}\right)\lambda_{R,D_2} e^{-\lambda_{R,D_2}x_2} dx_2 \tag{A11}$$

where $V = \frac{\gamma_2}{b_2 - b_1\gamma_2}$. Applying Equation (6.453) in [34], B_{00} can be presented as

$$B_{00} = \sum_{n=0}^{N} \binom{N}{n} (-1)^n \frac{2\lambda_{R,D_2}}{\Gamma(M)} C_5^{\frac{M}{2}} C_6^{\frac{M}{2}-1} K_M\left(2\sqrt{C_5 C_6}\right) \tag{A12}$$

where $C_5 = \frac{\lambda_{W,R} V \sigma^2}{\rho P_t}$ and $C_6 = \frac{n\lambda_{R,Q} P_I}{V\sigma^2} + \lambda_{R,D_2}$.

The OP for D_2 can be calculated by applying the results obtained from Equations (A8) and (A12).

References

1. Ding, Z.; Lei, X.; Karagiannidis, G.; Schober, R.; Yuan, J.; Bhargava, V. A survey on non-orthogonal multiple access for 5G networks: Research challenges and future trends. *IEEE J. Sel. Areas Commun.* **2017**, *35*, 2181–2197. [CrossRef]
2. Liu, Y.; Zhang, S.; Mu, X.; Ding, Z.; Schober, R.; Al-Dhahir, N.; Hossain, K.; Shen, X. Evolution of NOMA toward next generation multiple access (NGMA) for 6G. *IEEE J. Sel. Areas Commun.* **2022**, *40*, 1037–1071. [CrossRef]
3. Shahab, M.B.; Abbas, R.; Shirvanimoghaddam, M.; Johnson, S.J. Grant-free non-orthogonal multiple access for IoT: A survey. *IEEE Commun. Surv. Tut.* **2020**, *22*, 1805–1838. [CrossRef]
4. Pogaku, A.C.; Do, D.-T.; Lee, B.M.; Nguyen, N.D. UAV-assisted RIS for future wireless communications: A survey on optimization and performance analysis. *IEEE Access* **2022**, *10*, 16320–16336. [CrossRef]

5. Cotton, S.L.; Scanlon, W.G.; Madahar, B.K. Millimeter-wave soldier-to-soldier communications for covert battlefield operations. *IEEE Commun. Mag.* **2009**, *47*, 72–81. [CrossRef]
6. Do, D.-T.; Le, A.-T.; Liu, Y.; Jamalipour, A. User Grouping and Energy Harvesting in UAV-NOMA System With AF/DF Relaying. *IEEE Trans. Veh. Technol.* **2021**, *70*, 11855–11868. [CrossRef]
7. Mirbolouk, S.; Valizadeh, M.; Amirani, M.C.; Ali, S. Relay Selection and Power Allocation for Energy Efficiency Maximization in Hybrid Satellite-UAV Networks with CoMP-NOMA Transmission. *IEEE Trans. Veh. Technol.* **2022**, *71*, 5087–5100. [CrossRef]
8. Song, J.; Lu, Z.; Xiao, Z.; Li, B.; Sun, G. Optimal order of time-domain adaptive filter for anti-jamming navigation receiver. *Remote Sens.* **2022**, *14*, 48. [CrossRef]
9. Kilzi, A.; Farah, J.; Nour C.A.; Douillard, C. Mutual successive interference cancellation strategies in NOMA for enhancing the spectral efficiency of CoMP systems. *IEEE Trans. Commun.* **2020**, *68*, 1213–1226. [CrossRef]
10. Tang, R.; Cheng, J.; Cao, Z. Energy-efficient power allocation for cooperative NOMA systems with IBFD-enabled two-way cognitive transmission. *IEEE Commun. Lett.* **2019**, *23*, 1101–1104. [CrossRef]
11. Bariah, L.; Muhaidat, S.; Al-Dweik A. Error performance of NOMA-based cognitive radio networks with partial relay selection and interference power constraints. *IEEE Trans. Commun.* **2020**, *68*, 765–777. [CrossRef]
12. Garcia, C.E.; Camana, M.R.; Koo, I. Relay selection and power allocation for secrecy sum rate maximization in underlying cognitive radio with cooperative relaying NOMA. *Neurocomputing* **2021**, *452*, 756–767. [CrossRef]
13. Ali, Z.; Sidhu, G.A.S.; Gao, F.; Jiang, J.; Wang, X. Deep learning based power optimizing for NOMA based relay aided D2D transmissions. *IEEE Trans. Cogn. Commun. Netw.* **2021**, *7*, 917–928. [CrossRef]
14. Aswathi, V.; Babu, A.V. Performance analysis of NOMA-based underlay cognitive radio networks with partial relay selection. *IEEE Trans. Veh. Technol.* **2021**, *70*, 4615–4630.
15. Nguyen, B. V.; Vu Q.-D.; Kim, K. Analysis and optimization for weighted sum rate in energy harvesting cooperative NOMA systems. *IEEE Trans. Veh. Technol.* **2018**, *67*, 12379–12383. [CrossRef]
16. Rauniyar, A.; Engelstad, P.E.; sterb, O.N. Performance analysis of RF energy harvesting and information transmission based on NOMA with interfering signal for IoT relay. *IEEE Sens. J.* **2019**, *19*, 7668–7682. [CrossRef]
17. Li, T.; Zhang, H.; Zhou, X; Yuan, D. NOMA-enabled layered video multicast in wireless-powered relay systems. *IEEE Commun. Lett.* **2019**, *23*, 2118–2121. [CrossRef]
18. Aswathi, V.; Babu, A.V. Outage and throughput analysis of full-duplex cooperative NOMA system with energy harvesting. *IEEE Trans. Veh. Technol.* **2021**, *70*, 11648–11664. [CrossRef]
19. Vu, T.-H.; Kim, S. Performance evaluation of power-beacon-assisted wire-powered NOMA IoT-based systems. *IEEE Internet Things J.* **2021**, *8*, 11655–11665. [CrossRef]
20. un, H.; Zhou F.; Hu R.Q.; Hanzo, L. Robust beamforming design in a NOMA cognitive radio network relaying on SWIPT. *IEEE J. Sel. Areas Commun.* **2019**, *37*, 142–155.
21. Li, F.; Jiang, H.; Fan R.; Tan, P. Cognitive non-orthogonal multiple access with energy harvesting: An optimal resource allocation approach. *IEEE Trans. Veh. Technol.* **2019**, *68*, 7080–7095. [CrossRef]
22. Wang, H.; Shi, R.; Tang, K.; Dong, J.; Liao S. Performance analysis and optimization of a cooperative transmission protocol in NOMA-assisted cognitive radio networks with discrete energy harvesting. *Entropy* **2021**, *23*, 785. [CrossRef] [PubMed]
23. Hu, C.; Li, Q.; Zhang, Q.; Qin, J. Security optimization for an AF MIMO two-way relay-assisted cognitive radio nonorthogonal multiple access networks with SWIPT. *IEEE Trans. Foren. Sec.* **2022**, *17*, 1481–1496. [CrossRef]
24. Vu, T.-H.; Nguyen, T.-V.; Kim, S. Wireless powered cognitive NOMA-based IoT relay networks: Performance analysis and deep learning evaluation. *IEEE Internet Things J.* **2022**, *9*, 3913–3929. [CrossRef]
25. Chen, M.; Huang, Y.; Zeng, G.; Lu, K.; Yang, L. An improved bat algorithm hybridized with extremal optimization and Boltzmann selection. *Expert Syst. Appl.* **2021**, *175*, 114812. [CrossRef]
26. Deotti, L.M.P.; Pereira, J.L.R.; da Silva, I.C., Jr. Parameter extraction of photovoltaic models using an enhanced Lévy flight bat algorithm. *Energy Convers. Manag.* **2020**, *221*, 113114. [CrossRef]
27. Gandomi, A.H.; Yang X.-S. Chaotic bat algorithm. *J. Comput. Sci-Neth.* **2014**, *5*, 224–232. [CrossRef]
28. Abdollahzadeh, B.; Gharehchopogh, F.S.; Mirjalili, S. African vultures optimization algorithm: A new nature-inspired metaheuristic algorithm for global optimization problems. *Comput. Ind. Eng.* **2021**, *158*, 107408. [CrossRef]
29. Pavlyukevich, I. Levy flights, non-local search and simulated annealing. *Mathematics* **2007**, *226*, 1830–1844. [CrossRef]
30. Naruei, I.; Keynia, F. Wild horse optimizer: A new meta-heuristic algorithm for solving engineering optimization problems. *Eng. Comput.* **2021**, *2021*, 1–32. [CrossRef]
31. Abualigah, L.; Diabat, A.; Mirjalili, S.; Elaziz, M.A; Gandomi, A.H. The arithmetic optimization algorithm. *Comput. Methods Appl. Mech. Engrg.* **2021**, *376*, 113609. [CrossRef]
32. Naruei, I.; Keynia, F.; Sabbagh M.A. Hunter–prey optimization: Algorithm and applications. *Soft Comput.* **2022**, *26*, 1279–1314. [CrossRef]
33. Liu, Y.; Mousavifa, S.A.; Deng, Y.; Leung, C.; Elkashlan, M. Wireless energy harvesting in a cognitive relay network. *IEEE Trans. Wirel. Commun.* **2016**, *15*, 2498–2508. [CrossRef]
34. Gradshteyn, I.S.; Ryzhik, I.M. *Table of Integrals, Series and Products*, 7th ed.; Academic Press: San Diego, CA, USA, 2007.

mathematics

MDPI

Article

A Partition-Based Random Search Method for Multimodal Optimization

Ziwei Lin [1], Andrea Matta [1], Sichang Du [2] and Evren Sahin [3,*]

1 Politecnico di Milano, Department of Mechanical Engineering, 20133 Milan, Italy
2 Department of Industrial Engineering and Management, School of Mechanical Engineering, Shanghai Jiao Tong University, Shanghai 200240, China
3 Laboratoire Genie Industriel, CentraleSupelec, Paris Saclay University, 3 Rue Joliot-Curie, 91192 Gif-sur-Yvette, France
* Correspondence: evren.sahin@centralesupelec.fr

Abstract: Practical optimization problems are often too complex to be formulated exactly. Knowing multiple good alternatives can help decision-makers easily switch solutions when needed, such as when faced with unforeseen constraints. A multimodal optimization task aims to find multiple global optima as well as high-quality local optima of an optimization problem. Evolutionary algorithms with niching techniques are commonly used for such problems, where a rough estimate of the optima number is required to determine the population size. In this paper, a partition-based random search method is proposed, in which the entire feasible domain is partitioned into smaller and smaller subregions iteratively. Promising regions are partitioned faster than unpromising regions, thus, promising areas will be exploited earlier than unpromising areas. All promising areas are exploited in parallel, which allows multiple good solutions to be found in a single run. The proposed method does not require prior knowledge about the optima number and it is not sensitive to the distance parameter. By cooperating with local search to refine the obtained solutions, the proposed method demonstrates good performance in many benchmark functions with multiple global optima. In addition, in problems with numerous local optima, high-quality local optima are captured earlier than low-quality local optima.

Keywords: multimodal optimization; multiple optima; partition-based random search; niching

MSC: 90B40; 90-08

Citation: Lin, Z.; Matta, A.; Du, S.; Sahin, E. A Partition-Based Random Search Method for Multimodal Optimization. *Mathematics* **2023**, *11*, 17. https://doi.org/10.3390/math11010017

Academic Editor: Ioannis G. Tsoulos

Received: 3 November 2022
Revised: 7 December 2022
Accepted: 9 December 2022
Published: 21 December 2022

1. Introduction

Most optimization algorithms can only provide one of the optimal solutions when it is applied, even if more than one optimal solution may exist. Nevertheless, in some situations, finding multiple optimal solutions is desired, for example the following:

- The global optimal solution is not always implementable in real-world problems, due to some unforeseen physical, financial, or political constraints, such as the availability of some critical resources in the future and the dynamic environment in path-planning problems. Knowing multiple good alternatives is helpful for decision-makers to switch the solutions quickly when needed. For instance, if a machine fails during production and its repair is time-consuming, the decision-maker can quickly change the production plans without using the machine during that time.
- It is common in practice that some issues are difficult to formulate into the objective function or to evaluate exactly, such as the sensitivity of the selected machine parameters, the maintenance policy, and the preferences of decision-makers. In this situation, having a set of different and good alternatives in advance is often desired for further analysis.

- In some cases, it is critical to determine all highly valued areas (or all possibilities), such as the contaminant source identification in the water distribution network [1].
- In surrogate-based optimization methods [2,3], the promising solution pointed out by optimizing the constructed surrogate model is simulated iteratively. Finding multiple promising solutions in one iteration allows the methods to take advantage of parallel computing to run several time-consuming simulations simultaneously.
- Finding different locations of the peaks of the objective function in the search space can indicate some structural knowledge of the optimized function and provide some helpful insights into the properties of the studied system.

Multimodal optimization problem is concerned with locating multiple optima in one single run [4]. The aim of this paper is to deal with multimodal optimization problems, seeking multiple global optimal solutions and high-quality local optimal solutions (local optimal solutions with good objective function values) of the given problem. The benefits of applying multimodal optimization have been studied in many fields [5], such as seismological problems [6], metabolic network modeling [7], job-shop scheduling [8], virtual camera configuration problems [9], and feature selection [10].

In order to handle multimodal optimization tasks, classic optimization methods can be applied in multiple runs hoping to find different optima. Nevertheless, the same optimal solution may be obtained in different runs. If all m optimal solutions have the same probability to be found, the expectation of the number of optimization runs required to locate all optima is $m^{(m-1)}/(m-1)!$. This value is usually much larger in practice since one of the optima may have higher probability to be discovered than others. To avoid converging to the same solution, a common approach is that if one optimal solution is determined, the fitness (i.e., the objective function values) in the observed region is depressed in subsequent runs so that different optimal solutions can be found sequentially, e.g., [11,12]. Still, at least the same number of optimization runs as the number of the optimal solutions are required. In addition, if the fitness derating function and the distance parameter that defines the neighbor range are not carefully selected, it may result in elimination of other optima that have not been found, or spurious optima caused by the modified objective function, although the occurrence of spurious optima can be reduced by incorporating a local search method based on the original objective function, e.g., sequential niching memetic algorithm (SNMA) [13]. Approaches without the determination of the neighbor radius can also be found in the literature, but a lot of effort is spent in an additional sampling of interior points, e.g., [14,15].

Evolutionary algorithms (EAs), e.g., genetic algorithm (GA) [16], particle swarm optimization (PSO) [17], and differential evolution (DE) [18], have the ability to preserve multiple solutions during the optimization process. With the help of niching techniques, they are capable of capturing multiple optima in a single run. Niching techniques were originally developed to preserve the population diversity and reduce the impact of the genetic shift. They are also used in multiobjective optimization problems to search for the Pareto-optimal set, e.g., nondominated sorting GA II (NSGA-II) [19]. In multimodal optimization problems, the use of niching techniques promotes population diversity, allowing multiple optima to be found and maintained. Among the niching techniques in the literature, the clearing procedure [20] eliminates neighbors before the selection until only a few dominating individuals remain in the clearing radius. Singh and Deb [21] reallocate the cleared individuals outside the clearing radius, hoping to find other areas of interest. Fitness sharing methods [22–24] depress the fitness of densely located individuals according to the population density within the sharing radius. Clustering algorithms, e.g., k-means method [25], can be used in fitness sharing methods for the formation of niches to reduce the computational cost and avoid the determination of sharing radius, e.g., [26]. In crowding approaches [27,28], the new generated individual replaces the most similar individual to maintain the initial diversity, if better fitness is observed. In restricted tournament selection [29], the new generated individuals compete with the nearest individuals in a subpopulation randomly sampled from the population. In species conservation [30,31], the species seeds dominating other individuals in the same species are conserved into the next generation and updated iteratively. Li [32] designed a ring topology [33] on the particle swarm and used the *lbest* PSO to create small niches without niching parameters. A detailed survey on some basic niching techniques in multimodal optimization can be found in [34]. In addition, several niching mutation operator strategies for DE have been proposed for multimodal optimization problems recently. For example, local-binary-pattern-based adaptive DE (LBPADE) [35] uses the local binary pattern operator to identify multiple regions of interests; distributed individuals DE (DIDE) [36] constructs a virtual population for each individual so that each individual can search for its own optima; automatic niching DE (ANDE) [37] locates multiple peaks based on the affinity propagation clustering.

In the aforementioned niching techniques, the entire population evolves together and genetic operators are designed to preserve the population diversity. In contrast, some niching algorithms divide the entire population into parallel subpopulations, including forking GA [38], multinational GA [39], multipopulation GA [40], NichePSO [41], speciation-based PSO (SPSO) [42], swarms [43,44], culture algorithm with fuzzing cluster [45], LAM-ACO [46], and dual-strategy DE (DSDE) [47]. Each subpopulation evolves independently, searching for its own optimum. Different from classic EAs with multiple runs, subpopulations will be merged, split, interchanged, or reformed during the search process according to the positions of the individuals in the entire population. As a consequence, repeated convergence and inefficiency search are avoided.

Most existing niching techniques are sensitive to the selected parameters, which are usually application-dependent and may be heterogeneous in the search space, such as the radius parameters in clearing and fitness sharing, the species distance in species conservation, the window size in restricted tournament selection, and the number of seeds in clustering algorithms. Adaptive methods are studied to make the algorithms more robust to the distance parameters or to let the parameters vary in the search space, e.g., [48–50]. Some approaches are developed to detect whether two individuals belong to the same peak without the use of distance parameters, such as the hill–valley function [39] and the recursive middling [51]. Nevertheless, a great amount of additional fitness evaluations are required, significantly reducing the efficiency of the algorithm. The formation of the niches is still a challenge in the multimodal optimization community.

Recently, some researchers solved the multimodal optimization problem by converting it into a multiobjective optimization problem, named *multiobjectivization* [52]. For instance, biobjective multipopulation genetic algorithm (BMPGA) [53,54] uses the average absolute value of the gradient as another ranking criterion, in addition to the original objective function, for elitism and selection in the GA framework, thus providing a chance for survival for local optima. Deb and Saha [55,56] created a second objective function (e.g., the norm of the gradient or the number of better neighboring solutions) so that all optima are located in the weak Pareto-optimal set. Then, the modified NSGA-II algorithm [19], developed for multiobjective optimization problems, was applied to find all the optima in a single run. Diversity indicators, such as the distance from other individuals and the density of niches, are also considered as the second objective function to maintain the population diversity (similar to the niching techniques), e.g., [57,58]. Conflicting objective functions were also designed to increase the efficiency of the applied multiobjective optimization algorithm, e.g., multiobjective optimization for multimodal optimization (MOMMOP) [59] and triobjective differential evolution for multimodal optimization (TriDEMO) [60].

All the multimodal optimization methods mentioned above are developed under the framework of EAs, in which the population size should be determined based on the number of desired optima. However, the number of optima is usually unknown before executing the algorithm, although in some cases it can be estimated from prior knowledge about the system. Saving the obtained optima in an archive and reinitializing the individuals can extend the optimal solution set, but it may cause the population to converge to the previous found solutions.

Moreover, when dealing with the local optima, the existing multimodal optimization methods may fall into the following situations:

- Can only find multiple global optimal solutions (e.g., MOMMOP [59] and TriDEMO [60]), i.e., the local optimal solutions cannot be found.
- Assume that the global optimal solutions and local optimal solutions with different objective function values have the same importance (e.g., [55,56]).
- Prefer local optimal solutions in sparse areas to local optimal solutions with good objective function values (e.g., EAs with niching).
- Prior knowledge to determine the threshold (or tolerance) of the objective function value to decide whether to save a solution or not.

Therefore, when the computational time is limited, these methods cannot meet the demand of searching only the global optimal solutions and high-quality local optimal solutions (i.e., local optimal solutions with good objective function values) without prior knowledge.

A completely different approach, which requires no prior knowledge about number of optima in the studied problem, is proposed in this paper. In the proposed method, the feasible domain is partitioned into smaller and smaller subregions iteratively. At each iteration, solutions from different subregions are sampled and evaluated. Based on the observed information, different regions are partitioned at different rates. By controlling the partition rates of different regions, promising areas are exploited and reach the smallest size (e.g., singleton regions in discrete cases or regions with acceptable precision in continuous cases) earlier than nonpromising areas. Multiple promising areas can be partitioned in parallel, allowing multiple optimal solutions to be found in a single run. If the available budget size (the budget size indicates the number of evaluations of the objective function) is unlimited, all areas of the feasible domain will eventually be partitioned into subregions of the smallest size, i.e., all optima (both global and local) will be discovered eventually.

Partition-based random search methods, such as nested partition (NP) [61], COMPASS [62] and adaptive hyperbox algorithm [63], are efficient in optimization problems with large search space, i.e., the feasible range of the decision variable is large compared to its desired precision. The entire domain is partitioned into subregions, based on previous observations, trying to guide the search towards a promising region. However, in most partition-based methods, only the most promising region can be identified and stored; thus, only one optimal solution can be found. The probabilistic branch and bound (PBnB) [64,65] is developed to locate a subset of feasible solutions whose objective function values reach the given quantile level. Different from our approach, the partition rates are homogeneous in the search space in the PBnB. All regions are partitioned at the same rate until they are pruned (statistically, no solutions in this region belong to the subset of interest) or maintained (statistically, all solutions in this region belong to the desired subset). The PBnB method may also be extended to find multiple global optimal solutions by setting an extremely small quantile level. However, this will result in a large budget spent on estimating quantiles.

The classification of related works and the difference compared to the proposed algorithm are summarized in Table 1. A previous version of the proposed algorithm was presented in a conference paper [66], which mainly focused on searching for the global optimal solution under the interference of a large number of local optimal solutions. The algorithm is extended in this paper to find and store multiple global optimal solutions as well as high-quality local optimal solutions, including a scheme to extract the optimal solutions and a local search to refine the extracted optimal solutions during the optimization process. The research contributions of this paper are summarized below:

- Estimating the number of optima is not needed before performing the proposed method (which is required in all EA-based multimodal optimization methods). All optimal solutions (both global optimal solutions and local optimal solutions) will be discovered subsequently as the algorithm proceeds.

- Given a computational time, global optimal solutions and high-quality local optimal solutions are captured with higher probabilities than low-quality local optimal solutions, and no prior knowledge about the objective function is needed. Current multimodal optimization methods either cannot find local optimal solutions or treat all optimal solutions as equally important.
- The proposed method can also handle the cases in which the optimal solutions are regions rather than single points, i.e., there exists a region in the feasible domain where all solutions are optimal. The density of the solutions in the region depends on the user-defined precision level. This is new compared to all multimodal optimization methods.

The proposed method is tested in benchmark functions. The numerical results show that the proposed method works as expected and demonstrates good performance compared to other state-of-the-art multimodal optimization methods in the literature.

Table 1. Classification of selected related works.

Related Works	Algorithm Framework	Multimodal Optimization	Single Run
[12]	Sequential runs with tricks	✓	
[14]	Sequential runs with tricks	✓	
[15]	Sequential runs with tricks	✓	
LBPADE [35]	EA with niching	✓	✓
DIDE [36]	EA with niching	✓	✓
ANDE [37]	EA with niching	✓	✓
SPSO [42]	EA with subpopulations	✓	✓
LAM-ACO [46]	EA with subpopulations	✓	✓
DSDE [47]	EA with subpopulations	✓	✓
[55,56]	Multiobjectivization (EA)	✓	✓
BMPGA [53,54]	Multiobjectivization (EA)	✓	✓
MOMMOP [59]	Multiobjectivization (EA)	✓	✓
NP [61]	Partition-based random search		✓
PBnB [65]	Partition-based random search		✓
The proposed method	Partition-based random search	✓	✓

This paper is organized as follows. Section 2 describes the proposed method in detail. Section 3 combines the proposed method with a local search method to improve the efficiency of the algorithm. Numerical results on benchmark functions are discussed in Section 4. An engineering case showing the application of the proposed method is presented in Section 5. Finally, conclusions and future developments are presented in Section 6.

2. Proposed Method

Without loss of generality, a minimization problem is considered: $\min_x f(x)$. The objective function is deterministic and the feasible domain is denoted as $\mathcal{D}$, where $\mathcal{D} \subset \mathbb{R}^d$.

In the proposed method, the entire feasible domain $\mathcal{D}$ is iteratively partitioned into subregions $\mathcal{D}_k$ such that $\cup_k \mathcal{D}_k = \mathcal{D}$ and $\cap_k \mathcal{D}_k = \emptyset$. Each subregion contains a set of feasible solutions. In most partition-based optimization methods, the extreme value, the mean, or the quantile of the sampled values, i.e., the objective function values of sampled solutions, are commonly used to rank the regions. Compared to the extreme value, the quantile contains more global information about the region so that the influence of outliers can be mitigated. Compared to the mean, the quantile focuses more on the good part of solutions in this region, rather than the overall region. Therefore, the quantile is adopted as the ranking criterion in this paper. The lower the estimated α-quantile, where $\alpha < 0.5$, the more promising the region. A promising region is further partitioned into smaller subregions so that this region can be further exploited. Multiple promising regions can be partitioned in parallel in order to obtain a set of optimal solutions. More specifically, different partition rates are adopted for different regions, and promising regions would be partitioned faster (exploited earlier) than nonpromising regions.

In this paper, we define the partition rate of a region as the reciprocal of the number of iterations required for this region to be further partitioned. The idea of controlling the partition rates for different regions is realized with the help of a budget allocation strategy [67], which is introduced for the sake of completeness in Section 2.1. The computational complexity of the proposed method is analyzed in Section 2.3. Section 2.2 describes the proposed method in detail and a simple example is introduced in Section 2.4 to give the reader a better understanding of the proposed method.

2.1. Budget Allocation for Quantile Minimization (BAQM)

The BAQM method [67] is proposed to allocate a budget of size N to K groups, i.e., sample N values from K groups, aiming to minimize the α-quantile of all the sampled values. The budget is allocated to each group dynamically, based on the previous observations, trying to let the sample size in group k be approximately proportional to its posterior probability of being the best group, i.e., the group having the lowest α-quantile. This budget allocation method is developed on the assumption that the values sampled from a group are independently, identically, and normally distributed. Nevertheless, the numerical results show that it also has good performance, even if the normality assumption is not satisfied.

Assume that for any group k, $n_{1,k}$ values have been observed and the group sample mean $\hat{\mu}_k$ and the group sample variance $\hat{\sigma}_k^2$ are calculated based on the $n_{1,k}$ observations. According to [67], at each sampling stage, a new budget of size Δ should be allocated using the following equations:

$$\frac{n_k}{n_{\hat{b}}} = \frac{F(C_{k,\hat{b}}; n_{1,k}-1, n_{1,\hat{b}}-1)}{F(C_{\hat{b},k}; n_{1,\hat{b}}-1, n_{1,k}-1)}, \forall k \neq \hat{b}, \tag{1}$$

$$n_{\hat{b}} = \left(\Delta + \sum_{\forall k} n_{1,k}\right) / \left(\sum_{\forall k} \frac{F(C_{k,\hat{b}}; n_{1,k}-1, n_{1,\hat{b}}-1)}{F(C_{\hat{b},k}; n_{1,\hat{b}}-1, n_{1,k}-1)}\right), \tag{2}$$

where n_k denotes the total budget size allocated to group k, $\hat{b}$ is the current best group defined as $\hat{b} = \arg\min_k\{\hat{\mu}_k + z_\alpha\hat{\sigma}_k\}$, z_α is the α-quantile of the standard normal distribution, $\hat{\tau} = \min_k\{\hat{\mu}_k + z_\alpha\hat{\sigma}_k\}$, $F(\cdot; v_1, v_2)$ is the cumulative distribution function of the F-distribution with degrees of freedom v_1 and v_2,

$$C_{i,j} = \frac{1 + \frac{1}{\hat{c}_j^2} - \frac{1}{n_{1,j}}}{1 + \frac{1}{\hat{c}_i^2} - \frac{1}{n_{1,i}}}, \forall i, j \tag{3}$$

and $\hat{c}_k = \frac{\hat{\sigma}_k}{\hat{\mu}_k - \hat{\tau}}, \forall k$. Then, additional $\max(0, [n_k] - n_{1,k})$ values should be sampled from group k at this sampling stage, where $[\cdot]$ indicates that the value is rounded to the nearest integer.

The BAQM method is easy to implement and it links the sample size to the ranking of groups defined by quantiles. Therefore, it is selected as the budget allocation strategy in the proposed method.

2.2. Partition-Based Random Search for Multimodal Optimization

Denote by $\mathbb{D}^s = \{\mathcal{D}_i^s\}$ the set of stored regions in iteration s. By regarding a region $\mathcal{D}_i^s$ as a group, the BAQM method can be applied to sample solutions from different regions dynamically. Gradually, the sample sizes in different regions, denoted by $n_i^s, \forall i$, will be approximately proportional to their posterior probability of being the best region, i.e., the region having the minimal α-quantile, based on the previous observations. If we set a threshold $n_{\max}$, the sample sizes in promising regions will achieve this threshold faster than that in nonpromising regions because more samples are allocated. Therefore, we further partition a region when its sample size reaches the threshold. This makes the promising regions have a higher partition rate than the nonpromising regions.

In the proposed method, the data observed in previous iterations are reused. This allows the deviations caused by the sampling noise to be transmitted to subsequent iterations. To mitigate the influence of the sampling noise, the BAQM formulas are modified. Denote by l_i^s the partition depth of a region $\mathcal{D}_i^s$. In this paper, the partition depth of a region refers to the minimum number of partition actions required to obtain this region, which is often related to the size of the region. The smaller the region size, the larger the partition depth. The adjusted sample size n_i^{adj} is calculated based on the partition depth as follows:

$$n_i^{\text{adj}} = \max\left(2, \left[\frac{l_i^s}{\max_j\{l_j^s\}} n_i^s\right]\right), \forall i, \tag{4}$$

where n_i^s is the number of observations in region $\mathcal{D}_i^s$ and $[\cdot]$ indicates that the value is rounded to the nearest integer. This modification aims at forcing the method to also sample from nonpromising but broad regions. As all regions shrink, i.e., all l_i^s increase, and the influence of Equation (4) will decrease. Then, according to the BAQM formulas, the weight assigned to region $\mathcal{D}_i^s$ is calculated as follows:

$$w_i = \frac{F(C_{i,\hat{b}}; n_i^{\text{adj}} - 1, n_{\hat{b}}^{\text{adj}} - 1)}{F(C_{\hat{b},i}; n_{\hat{b}}^{\text{adj}} - 1, n_i^{\text{adj}} - 1)} = \frac{1}{1 - F(C_{i,\hat{b}}; n_i^{\text{adj}} - 1, n_{\hat{b}}^{\text{adj}} - 1)} - 1, \forall i, \tag{5}$$

where

$$C_{i,\hat{b}} = \frac{1 + z_\alpha^2 - 1/n_{\hat{b}}^{\text{adj}}}{1 + \left(\frac{\hat{\mu}_i - \hat{\tau}}{\hat{\sigma}_i}\right)^2 - 1/n_i^{\text{adj}}}, \forall i, \tag{6}$$

$\hat{b}$ is the current best region defined as $\hat{b} = \arg\min_k\{\hat{\mu}_k + z_\alpha \hat{\sigma}_k\}$, z_α is the α-quantile of the standard normal distribution, and $\hat{\mu}_i$ and $\hat{\sigma}_i^2$ are the sample mean and sample variance of the objective function values of solutions sampled from region $\mathcal{D}_i^s$, respectively. $\hat{\tau} = \hat{\mu}_{\hat{b}} + z_\alpha \hat{\sigma}_{\hat{b}}$, $F(\cdot; v_1, v_2)$ is the cumulative distribution function of the F-distribution with degrees of freedom v_1 and v_2. Given the new budget size Δ, the theoretical total budget sizes in each region n_i can be calculated as follows:

$$n_i = \left(\Delta + \sum_i n_i^{\text{adj}}\right) \cdot \frac{w_i}{\sum_i w_i} \tag{7}$$

The proposed method is very straightforward and easy to implement. The flow chart is as shown in Figure 1 and the main framework is presented in Algorithm 1. Four algorithm parameters are required:

- α — The quantile level in the definition of the best region, $0 < \alpha < 0.5$;
- n_0 — The base sample size, $n_0 \geq 2$;
- $n_{\max}$ — The sample size threshold to further partition a region, $n_{\max} > n_0$;
- Δ — The new budget size at each iteration.

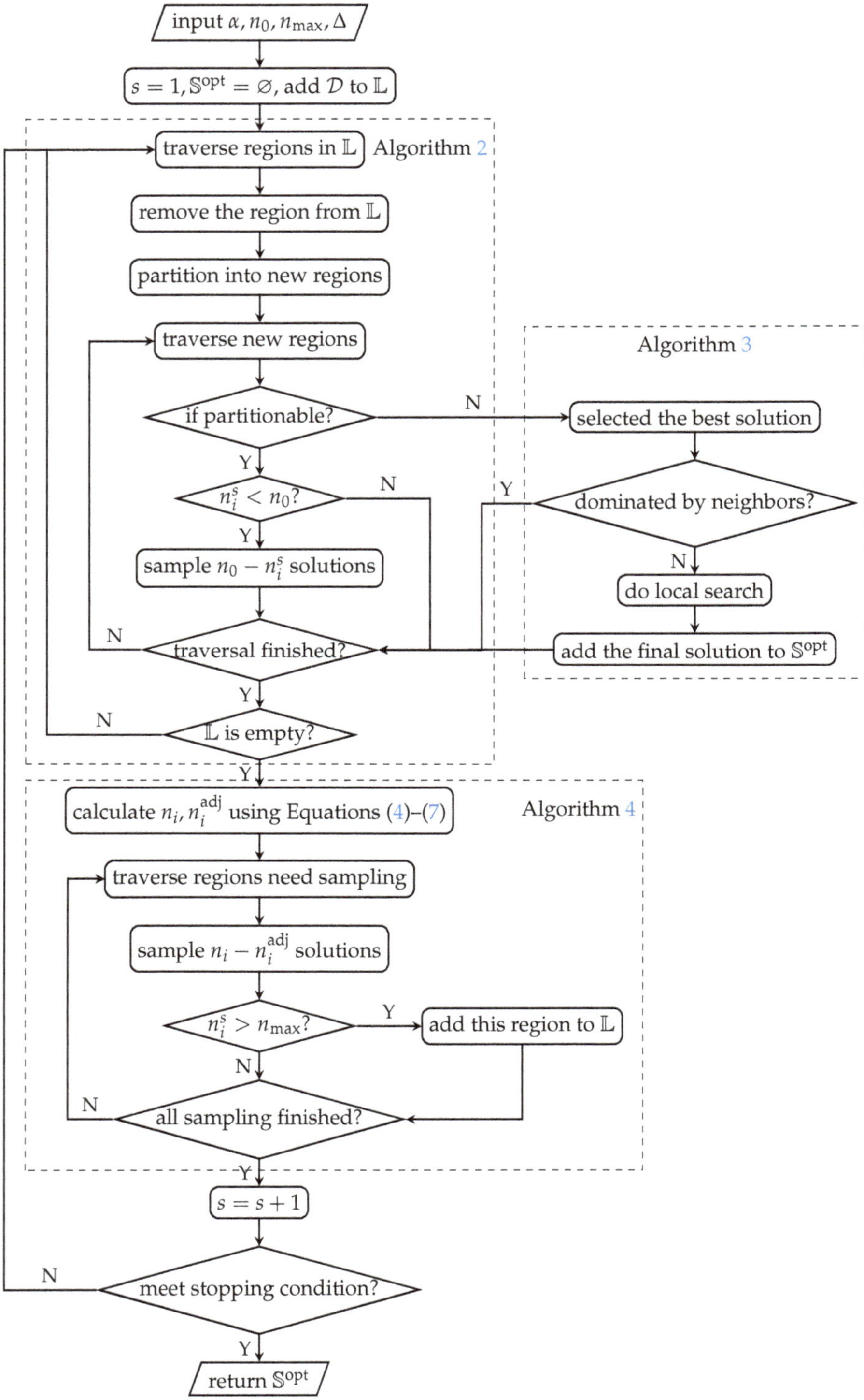

Figure 1. The flow chart of the proposed algorithm (Algorithm 1).

Algorithm 1 PAR- MMO.

Input: $\alpha, n_0, n_{\max}, \Delta, \mathcal{P}(\cdot), \mathcal{S}(\cdot,\cdot), U(\cdot), C^{\text{stop}}$
Output: $\mathbb{X}, \mathbb{S}^{\text{opt}}$

$s \leftarrow 1$
$\mathbb{D}^s \leftarrow \{\mathcal{D}_1^s = \mathcal{D}\}, n_1^s \leftarrow 0$
$\mathbb{L} \leftarrow \{1\}$
while $\neg C^{\text{stop}}$ **do**
  Partitioning (Algorithm 2)
  if $I^{\text{new}} = 1$ **then**
    Updating $\mathbb{S}^{\text{opt}}$ (Algorithm 3)
    $I^{\text{new}} \leftarrow 0$
  end if
  Budget Allocation (Algorithm 4)
  $s \leftarrow s + 1$
end while

Algorithm 2 Partitioning.

for $i \in \mathbb{L}$ **do**
  $\mathbb{D}^{\text{new}} \leftarrow \mathcal{P}(\mathcal{D}_i^s)$
  $\mathbb{D}^s \leftarrow \mathbb{D}^s \setminus \{\mathcal{D}_i^s\} \cup \mathbb{D}^{\text{new}}$
  for $j : \mathcal{D}_j^s \in \mathbb{D}^{\text{new}}$ **do**
    update n_j^s, l_j^s
    if $n_j^s \geq n_{\max}$ & $\neg I_{\mathbb{D}^*}(\mathcal{D}_j^s)$ **then**
      $\mathbb{L} \leftarrow \mathbb{L} \cup \{j\}$
    else
      if $n_j^s < n_0$ **then**
        $\mathbb{X} \leftarrow \mathbb{X} \cup \mathcal{S}(n_0 - n_j^s, \mathcal{D}_j^s)$
      end if
      update $\hat{\mu}_j, \hat{\sigma}_j^2$
      if $\neg I_{\mathbb{D}^*}(\mathcal{D}_j^s)$ **then**
        $n_j^{\text{adj}} \leftarrow$ Equation (4)
        $w_j \leftarrow$ Equation (5)
      else
        $n_j^{\text{adj}} \leftarrow 0$
        $w_j \leftarrow 0$
        $\mathbb{X}^{\text{opt}} \leftarrow \mathbb{X}^{\text{opt}} \cup \{\boldsymbol{x}_k : \boldsymbol{x}_k \in \mathcal{D}_j^s\}$
        $I_k^{\text{new}} \leftarrow 1$
      end if
    end if
  end for
end for
$\mathbb{L} \leftarrow \emptyset$

Algorithm 3 Extracting.

$i \leftarrow \min\{j : I_j^{\text{opt}} = 1\}$
while $i \neq \emptyset$ **do**
  $I_j^{\text{opt}} \leftarrow 0, \forall j \in \{k : \boldsymbol{x}_k \in U(\boldsymbol{x}_i) \cap \mathbb{X}^{\text{opt}}; f(\boldsymbol{x}_k) > f(\boldsymbol{x}_i)\}$
  if $f(\boldsymbol{x}_i) > \min_{j \in \{k : \boldsymbol{x}_k \in U(\boldsymbol{x}_i) \cap \mathbb{X}^{\text{opt}}\}} f(\boldsymbol{x}_j)$ **then**
    $I_i^{\text{opt}} \leftarrow 0$
  end if
  $i \leftarrow \min\{j : j > i; I_j^{\text{opt}} = 1\}$
end while
$\mathbb{S}^{\text{opt}} \leftarrow \{\boldsymbol{x}_i : I_i^{\text{opt}} = 1\}$

Algorithm 4 Budget allocation.

$N^{\text{adj}} \leftarrow \Delta + \sum_i n_i^{\text{adj}}$
$w = \sum_i w_i$
$n_i \leftarrow N^{\text{adj}} \cdot w_i / w, \forall i$
for $i : [n_i - n_i^{\text{adj}}] > 0$ **do**
  $\mathbb{X} \leftarrow \mathbb{X} \cup \mathcal{S}([n_i - n_i^{\text{adj}}], \mathcal{D}_i^s)$
  update n_i^s
  if $n_i^s \geq n_{\max}$ **then**
    $\mathbb{L} \leftarrow \mathbb{L} \cup \{i\}$
  else
    update $\hat{\mu}_i, \hat{\sigma}_i^2$
    $n_i^{\text{adj}} \leftarrow$ Equation (4)
    $w_i \leftarrow$ Equation (5)
  end if
end for

$\mathcal{P}(\text{region})$, $\mathcal{S}(\text{sample size, region})$, $U(\text{solution})$, and C^{stop} are the user-defined partition strategy, sampling strategy, neighborhood of the selected solution, and stopping criteria, respectively. The output $\mathbb{X}$ is the set of all sampled solutions and $\mathbb{S}^{\text{opt}}$ is the set of obtained optimal solutions. At the beginning of the algorithm, the set of the current regions $\mathbb{D}^s$ and the partition list $\mathbb{L}$ is set as the entire feasible domain $\mathcal{D}$. In the subsequent iterations, partitioning all regions in the partition list using Algorithm 2 and allocating budget to each region using Algorithm 4 are performed alternatively until the stopping criterion is met, such as the available budget is exhausted, the desired number of optimal solutions are obtained, or the number of obtained optimal solutions are not changed in several iterations. After the partitioning phase, if new potential optimal solutions are generated, i.e., $I^{\text{new}} = 1$, the set of optimal solutions $\mathbb{S}^{\text{opt}}$ are updated using Algorithm 3. This step can also be executed only at the end of the whole algorithm to save the computational effort, if $\mathbb{S}^{\text{opt}}$ is not related to the stopping criterion.

Algorithm 2 describes in detail the partitioning phase in Algorithm 1. $\mathbb{D}^*$ denotes the set of nonpartitionable regions and $I_{\mathbb{D}^*}(\cdot)$ is the indicator function. Every region in the partition list $\mathbb{L}$ is partitioned into several new subregions. The new subregions are added to the partition list if they are partitionable and their sample size n_j^s is still larger than or equal to the threshold $n_{\max}$. Otherwise, new solutions are sampled so that the sample size in this new subregion is not less than the base sample size n_0. Then, the group sample mean $\hat{\mu}_j$ and the group sample variance $\hat{\sigma}_j^2$ are updated. The adjusted sample size n_j^{adj} is calculated using Equation (4) and the weight for the budget allocation w_j is calculated using Equation (5). After traversing the entire partition list $\mathbb{L}$, $\mathbb{L}$ is set to an empty set.

Once a new nonpartitionable region is generated, the weight w_j and the adjusted sample size n_j^{adj} are set to zero, since the solutions within this region are considered not different; thus, it is not necessary to keep sampling from this region. If the current best region $\mathbb{D}_{\hat{b}}^s$ is nonpartitionable, $n_{\hat{b}}^{\text{adj}}$ is saved for the calculation of Equation (5). All the samples in the new generated nonpartitionable region are considered as potential optimal solutions; thus, they are added into the set of optima candidates $\mathbb{X}^{\text{opt}}$, and I^{new} is set to one to send the signal to run Algorithm 3.

Remark 1. *In Algorithm 2, if the maximal partition depth, i.e.,* $\max_i\{l_i^s\}$*, in Equation (4) is changed, the adjusted sample size* n_i^{adj} *of all regions should be recalculated. Thus, all weights* w_i *also need to be recalculated.*

Remark 2. *In Algorithm 2, if the current optimal region, i.e.,* $\hat{b}$*, in Equation (5) is changed, all weights* w_i *should be recalculated.*

Algorithm 3 presents the detailed procedure to extract the set of the optimal solutions $\mathbb{S}^{\text{opt}}$ from the set of potential optima $\mathbb{X}^{\text{opt}}$. In the algorithm, $I_i^{\text{opt}} = 1$ indicates that solution $\boldsymbol{x}_i$ is not dominated by the neighboring solutions. The I_i^{opt} values are set to one for all solutions newly added into $\mathbb{X}^{\text{opt}}$. Starting from the first solution with $I_i^{\text{opt}} = 1$, the I_j^{opt} values are set to zero for all the solutions $\boldsymbol{x}_j$ in the neighborhood whose objective function value is worse than the objective function value of the selected solution $\boldsymbol{x}_i$. If there exists a better solution in the neighborhood, the I_i^{opt} value of the selected solution is also set to zero. In optimization problems with continuous variables, a commonly used neighborhood function is $U(\boldsymbol{x}_i) = \{\boldsymbol{x} : ||\boldsymbol{x} - \boldsymbol{x}_i||_2 \leq r\} \cap \mathcal{D}$, where $||\boldsymbol{x} - \boldsymbol{x}_i||_2$ is the Euclidean distance between $\boldsymbol{x}$ and $\boldsymbol{x}_i$. In this case, Algorithm 3 is not sensitive to the selection of r.

Algorithm 4 describes in detail how to allocate a new budget of size Δ at each iteration. The adjusted total budget size N^{adj} is calculated by summing the adjusted region sample size n_i^{adj} and Δ. The theoretical total budget size at each region n_i is calculated using the weight w_i. Then, $\max(0, [n_i - n_i^{\text{adj}}])$ new solutions are sampled from region $\mathcal{D}_i^s$, where $[\cdot]$ indicates that the value is rounded into the nearest integer. Once the sample size in a region reaches the threshold $n_{\max}$, this region is added to the partition list $\mathbb{L}$.

2.3. Computational Complexity

As the total budget size increases, the number of existing regions grows as well, which will results in raised computational time in later iterations. The computational complexity of the proposed method is investigated in this section to understand the extent to which the total budget size affects the computational effort.

In Algorithm 2, the maximal length of the partition list is Δ in each iteration; thus, the time complexity of Algorithm 2 is $O(\Delta)$ in each iteration. The number of total iterations is less than N/Δ, where N is the total budget size allocated. Thus, the time complexity of Algorithm 2 is $O(N)$ in the entire optimization process.

Similar to Algorithm 2, the time complexity of lines 5–13 in Algorithm 4 is $O(\Delta)$ in each iteration and $O(N)$ in the entire optimization process, respectively. As for lines 1–4 in Algorithm 4, the n_i value should be calculated and compared to n_i^{adj} for all existing regions in each iteration. Thus, the time complexity is $O(|\mathbb{D}^s|)$ in iteration s. The number of existing regions $|\mathbb{D}^s|$ is less than $(h-1)\Delta s$, where h indicates the maximal number of subregions that will be generated after a partition action. Therefore, the time complexity of lines 1–4 becomes $O(\Delta s)$ in iteration s. In the entire optimization process, the time complexity is $O(\Delta \sum_{s=1}^{N/\Delta} s) = O(N + N^2/\Delta)$, i.e., it is increasing quadratically with respect to the total budget size N.

Algorithm 3 is only executed when new potential optimal solutions appear. Since the distance between every two solutions in the set of the potential optimal solutions $\mathbb{X}^{\text{opt}}$ should be calculated to determine the neighboring solutions, the time complexity of Algorithm 3 is $O(|\mathbb{X}^{\text{opt}}|^2)$ in the entire optimization process. Usually, the number of potential optima is much less than the total budget size.

Therefore, the overall time complexity of the proposed method with respect to the total budget size is $O(N^2/\Delta)$ due to line 3 and line 4 in Algorithm 4.

2.4. An Illustrative Example

Minimizing the Himmelblau's function is considered in this section as an illustrative example for the reader to better understand the proposed method. This problem has four global optimal solutions, and the objective function value varies from 0 to 2186 (the detailed information can be found in the selected benchmark function F2 in Appendix A Figure A1). The goal of this problem is to find and store all these four global optimal solutions.

The proposed method is applied with $n_0 = 4, \alpha = 0.3, n_{\max} = 10$, and $\Delta = 3$. The regions are evenly partitioned into half from the horizontal and vertical directions iteratively until all edges of all regions are smaller than 0.05, which are considered as nonpartitionable regions. Figure 2 presents the partition states on the entire feasible domain as the budget size N increases. The sampled solutions are shown by dots, where their colors represent their objective function values. The darker the color, the lower the objective function value.

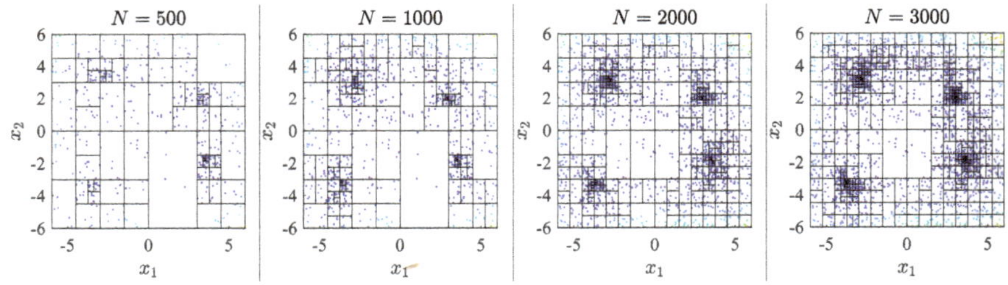

Figure 2. The partition states and the sampled solutions as the budget size N increases in the Himmelblau function minimization problem.

It can be seen that as the budget size increases, regions containing good solutions are partitioned at higher rates than other regions. The areas around the four global optimal solutions are exploited in parallel and reach the smallest size earlier than other areas. The sampling of solutions is guided by the proposed method. At the beginning of the algorithm, solutions are sampled evenly among the entire domain. As the budget size increases, the sampling probability of good solutions increases as well.

After about 3000 solutions are evaluated, Algorithm 3 is performed with $U(x_i) = \{x : ||x - x_i||_2 \leq r\} \cap \mathcal{D}$, where $r = 0.0938$, i.e., twice the length of the shortest edge of a nonpartitionable region. Four solutions are contained in $\mathbb{S}^{\text{opt}}$ and their objective function values are all less than 6×10^{-3}. The distances from the four solutions to their corresponding real optimal solutions are all less than 0.014. The same results can be obtained with r varying from 0.042 to 3.9, which shows that Algorithm 3 is not sensitive to the selection of the distance parameter r.

3. Cooperating with Local Search

The proposed partition-based random search method behaves conservatively. It can maintain a global perspective, thereby reducing the probability of losing some optimal solutions. It can be found in Section 2.4 that the proposed method detects the four promising areas fast, but it takes a lot of effort to obtain a precise optimal solution in the detected promising area. The search is always guided by the thought that there may be multiple local optima in a region. Thus, it cannot focus on exploitation to improve the accuracy of the obtained optimum in a detected promising area (also called detected peaks in maximization problems), especially when the promising area is relatively flat, i.e., the difference between the regions in the promising area is small.

In contrast, the local search method is efficient in locating the precise local optimal solution if the starting point is located nearby. The main issue of adopting local search in a multimodal optimization problem is the number and the locations of the starting points. If the starting points are not located carefully, it may result in loss of optima or waste of budget caused by multiple starting points within the same promising area, whereas the set $\mathbb{S}^{\text{opt}}$ extracted from Algorithm 3 contains different good solutions from different promising areas, which provides multiple good locations for the local search to start from. Therefore, the proposed partition-based random search can be used to detect promising areas, from which a local search is utilized to refine the solution in the set of obtained optimal solutions $\mathbb{S}^{\text{opt}}$ to obtain more precise optimal solutions. A similar idea appears in EMO-MMO [68], in which an algorithm is developed to detect peaks from solutions sampled by multiobjectivization methods and a swarm-based method is used within each peak.

Any new solution that appears in $\mathbb{S}^{\text{opt}}$ after executing Algorithm 3 is used as the starting point in a local search method to obtain a more precise optimal solution with higher accuracy. Algorithm 5 introduces a simple local search method for problems with continuous domain. The current solution iteratively moves to the best neighboring solution with one step difference in one dimension. In the algorithm, e_j is a d-dimensional vector whose j-th element is one and the rest of the elements are all zero. The initial step δ is set as the distance parameter r in Algorithm 3 and it is shrinking as the search proceeds. The local search is repeated until the stopping criteria is met, such as when the step δ is smaller than a threshold δ^*, the desired objective function value is obtained, or the budget is exhausted. All the new sampled solutions are added into the set of optima candidates $\mathbb{X}^{\text{opt}}$ with $I_i^{\text{opt}} = 0$, except the local optima whose I_i^{opt} is assigned to one. Algorithm 5 is an example of how the accuracy of the obtained optima can be improved. Other optimization algorithms with strong local search capacity can also be applied according to the features of the studied problem.

Algorithm 5 Local search.

Input: $\boldsymbol{x}_i \in \mathbb{S}^{\text{opt}}, \delta^*$
Output: $\boldsymbol{x}_i^*$

$\boldsymbol{x}_i^* \leftarrow \boldsymbol{x}_i$
$\delta \leftarrow r$
$C_2^{\text{stop}} \leftarrow 0$
while $C_2^{\text{stop}} = 0$ **do**
  $\boldsymbol{x}' \leftarrow \boldsymbol{x}_i^*$
  for $j = 1, \cdots, d$ **do**
    $\boldsymbol{x}_i^* \leftarrow \arg\min_{\{\boldsymbol{x}_i^* - \delta e_j, \boldsymbol{x}_i^*, \boldsymbol{x}_i^* + \delta e_j\}} f(\boldsymbol{x})$
  end for
  if $\boldsymbol{x}' = \boldsymbol{x}_i^*$ **then**
    if $\delta < \delta^*$ **then**
      $C_2^{\text{stop}} \leftarrow 1$
    end if
    $\delta \leftarrow \delta/2$
  end if
end while
$\mathbb{S}^{\text{opt}} \leftarrow \mathbb{S}^{\text{opt}} \setminus \{\boldsymbol{x}_i\} \cup \{\boldsymbol{x}_i^*\}$

4. Numerical Results

The proposed method is applied to minimization problems constructed by several benchmark functions with different properties extracted from the well-known test problems of the CEC'2013 competition for multimodal optimization [34,69]. Table 2 shows the selected objective function, the dimension of the decision variable, the number of global optima and local optima, the feasible domain, the objective function value range, and the maximum budget size `Max_Fes` in different test problems. F1–F3 are simple examples with multiple global optima. F4 is a volatile function with numerous local optima. The optimal solutions in F5 are located in different topographies in the feasible domain. F6 contains multiple global optimal solutions distributed in a grid. F7 is composited by different basic functions such that the properties of different functions are mixed. F1–F7 contain multiple global optima, while F8 and F9 have only one global optimum and multiple local optima of different qualities. In F10, there are several regions in which all points are local optimal solutions. The detailed information and the surface plots of the benchmark functions can be found in Appendix A.

Table 2. The parameters of the tested problems.

Func	Dim	No.g	No.l	Domain	Value Range	Radius	Max_Fes
F1	1	5	0	$[0,1]$	$[0,1]$	0.015	5×10^4
F2	2	4	0	$[-6,6]^2$	$[0,2185.8]$	0.1	5×10^4
F3	2	2	4	$[-1.9,1.9],[-1.1,1.1]$	$[-4.1265,23.4]$	0.1	5×10^4
F4(2D)	2	18	>700	$[-10,10]^2$	$[-186.7309,210.5]$	0.01	2×10^5
F4(3D)	3	81	>2000	$[-10,10]^3$	$[-2709.0935,3053.7]$	0.01	4×10^5
F5(2D)	2	36	0	$[0.25,10]^2$	$[0,2]$	0.03	2×10^5
F5(3D)	3	216	0	$[0.25,10]^3$	$[0,2]$	0.03	4×10^5
$F6_{(3,4)}$	2	12	0	$[0,1]^2$	$[2,38]$	0.01	2×10^5
$F6_{(3,3,3)}$	3	27	0	$[0,1]^3$	$[3,57]$	0.01	4×10^5
$F6_{(2,\cdots,2)}$	5	32	0	$[0,1]^5$	$[5,95]$	0.02	4×10^5
F7(1-2D)	2	6	>500	$[-5,5]^2$	$[0,2204.2]$	0.01	2×10^5
F7(2-2D)	2	8	>600	$[-5,5]^2$	$[0,2050.2]$	0.01	2×10^5
F7(3-2D)	2	6	>2000	$[-5,5]^2$	$[0,3701.5]$	0.01	2×10^5
F7(3-3D)	3	6	>2000	$[-5,5]^3$	$[0,4126.1]$	0.01	4×10^5
F8	1	1	4	$[0.02,1]$	$[0,1]$	0.01	5×10^5
F9(2D)	2	1	120	$[-5.12,5.12]^2$	$[0,80.7]$	0.1	3×10^4
F9(3D)	3	1	1330	$[-5.12,5.12]^3$	$[0,121.1]$	0.1	1×10^5
F10	2	1	4 [a]	$[-10,10]^2$	$[0.0097,0.9975]$	-	-

[a] The local optima are not single points.

In the following experiments, if the deviation from the objective function value of an obtained optimal solution to the objective function value of a real optimal solution is below ε (level of accuracy) and the distance between these two solutions is less than the radius in Table 2 (level of precision), this real optimal solution is considered as being found. For the proposed method, a solution is considered as an obtained optimal solution only when it is stored in $\mathbb{S}^{\text{opt}}$ (]the datasets generated during and/or analyzed during the current study are available from the corresponding author on reasonable request).

For the sake of simplicity, the proposed method, denoted as "PAR-MMO", is applied with $\alpha = 0.3, n_0 = 4, n_{\max} = 10$, and $\Delta = 3$ for all the following experiments, unless specifically stated. If a budget is allocated to a region, new solutions are sampled from this region uniformly (the sampling strategy). If the partitioning condition is met, the region is partitioned evenly into two subregions from the dimension with the largest range (the partition strategy). The accuracy level of the obtained optima is controlled by the acceptable precision of the obtained solution, i.e., the size of the nonpartitionable region. Once a region reaches the smallest size, i.e., it is nonpartitionable, the proposed method will stop sampling from this region and the accuracy of the obtained optima in this region will not be further improved. The smaller the region that is considered nonpartitionable, the more precise the solution obtained, and the larger the budget required. In the following experiments, the size of a nonpartitionable region is defined specific to the problem in order to met the required accuracy level ε (as shown in Appendix B). In practice, the size of the nonpartitionable region can be defined according to the acceptable precision of the solution obtained. The neighborhood function in Algorithm 3 for extracting optimal solutions from the sample set is selected as $U(\boldsymbol{x}_i) = \{\boldsymbol{x} : ||\boldsymbol{x} - \boldsymbol{x}_i||_2 \leq r\} \cap \mathcal{D}$, where r is twice the length of the shortest edge of a nonpartitionable region.

In the case that local search is adopted, denoted as "PARL-MMO", the size of the nonpartitionable region can be much larger (as shown in Appendix B), since both the accuracy level of the obtained optima and the precision of the obtained solution can be improved through the local search. In the following experiments, the step threshold δ^* in Algorithm 5 for local search is selected as the half length of the edge of the nonpartitionable region defined when the PAR-MMO method is used without local search.

Section 4.1 presents how the selected parameters affect the proposed method. In Section 4.2, the proposed method is applied to some problems with multiple global optima and compared with other approaches in the literature. Section 4.3 shows how the proposed method performs in the problems with multiple local optima of different qualities. Section 4.4 deals with problems that exist an region in which all solutions are optimal. The computational time of the proposed method is analyzed in Section 4.5.

4.1. *Effect of Algorithm Parameters*

This section investigates how the algorithm parameters, i.e., the quantile level α, the base sample size n_0, the partition sample size threshold $n_{\max}$, and the new budget size Δ, affect the proposed method. In this section, "PARL-MMO" is applied and the accuracy level ε is set as]1E-4. The base sample size n_0 is set to avoid the situation where too few samples remain in a subregion after a partition action. Thus, the n_0 is set as $\lceil n_{\max}/3 \rceil$, where $\lceil \cdot \rceil$ means that the value is rounded up to the nearest integer.

4.1.1. Main Effect Plot

Figure 3 shows the main effect plot and the table of analysis of variance (ANOVA) after running a full factorial design in Problem $F6_{(3,3,3)}$ with three factors: $\alpha = \{0.1, 0.2, 0.3, 0.4\}$, $n_{\max} = \{6, 10, 15, 20\}, and \Delta = \{3, 5, 10, 20\}$. A total of 500 independent replications are executed and they are divided into 10 batches. The response is the average total budget size, which is required to obtain all global optima, in a batch. The ANOVA is implemented after the Box–Cox transformation so that the standardized residuals do not violate the normality assumption (the p-value equals 0.376 in the Anderson–Darling test) and the equal variance assumption (the p-value equals 0.983 in the Levene test). All the parameters and interactions have significant effect on the proposed method with significant level 5%. The influences of the $n_{\max}$ value and the Δ value are much larger than that of the α value and the interactions based on the F-values. Similar conclusions can be drawn in other problems (see Appendix C), except for Problem F5, where the optima are located in different topographies in the feasible domain, and Problem F7(2-2D). According to the Tukey pairwise comparison with confidence level 95%, the optimal combinations of parameters for Problem $F6_{(3,3,3)}$ are $\alpha = \{0.2, 0.3, 0.4\}, n_{\max} = 10$, and $\Delta = 3$.

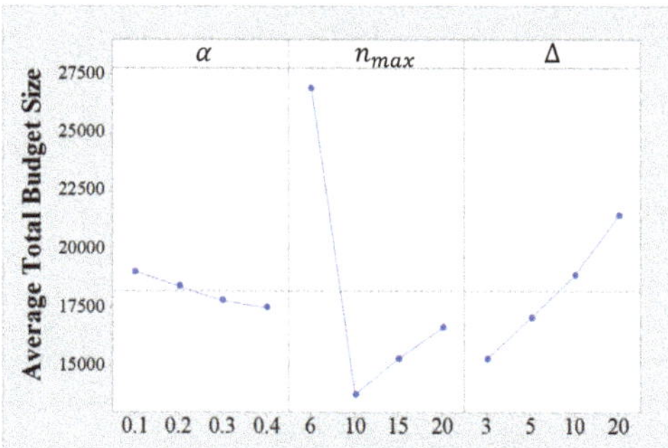

Source	DF	F-Value	P-Value
α	3	66.37	0.000
n_{max}	3	5999.95	0.000
Δ	3	1674.54	0.000
$\alpha * n_{max}$	9	8.10	0.000
$\alpha * \Delta$	9	7.90	0.000
$n_{max} * \Delta$	9	30.38	0.000
$\alpha * n_{max} * \Delta$	27	2.08	0.002
Error	576		
Total	639		

Figure 3. The main effect plot and the ANOVA table. A total of 500 replications are executed and divided into 10 batches. The Box–Cox transformation is performed, and $R^2_{adj} = 98.67\%$.

Figure 4 shows the main effect plot and the ANOVA table for Problem F5(2D). Although the normality hypothesis and the equal variance hypothesis are not met with confidence level 95%, the F-test is robust since the experiments with all combinations are performed with the same number of replications. Different from Problem $F6_{(3,3,3)}$, the parameter α has the highest effect on the algorithm performance. According to the Tukey pairwise comparison with confidence level 95%, the optimal combinations of the algorithm parameters for Problem F5(2D) are $\alpha = 0.3, n_{\max} = 10$, and $\Delta = 3$.

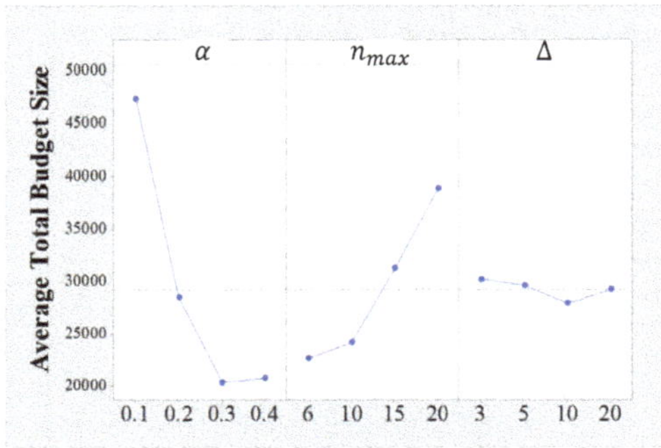

Source	DF	F-Value	P-Value
α	3	11598.64	0.000
n_{max}	3	3677.19	0.000
Δ	3	47.75	0.000
$\alpha * n_{max}$	9	1719.85	0.000
$\alpha * \Delta$	9	605.19	0.000
$n_{max} * \Delta$	9	136.74	0.000
$\alpha * n_{max} * \Delta$	27	32.26	0.000
Error	576		
Total	639		

Figure 4. The main effect plot and the ANOVA table for Problem F5(2D). A total of 500 replications are executed and divided into 10 batches. The Box–Cox transformation is performed, and $R^2_{adj} = 99.08\%$.

4.1.2. Effect of the Partition Sample Size Threshold $N_{\max}$

As the $n_{\max}$ value increases, the average total budget size required to obtain all optima declines first and then rises. This is because when the $n_{\max}$ value is too small, the partition action is executed based on biased information due to the small sample size. When the $n_{\max}$ value is too large, the budget that could be used to exploit subregions with good performance is wasted on exploring the current region. A similar phenomenon can be observed in different problems, as shown in Figure 5, in which the budget size in the figure is scaled according to the maximal average budget size in different problems, i.e., the values in the legend.

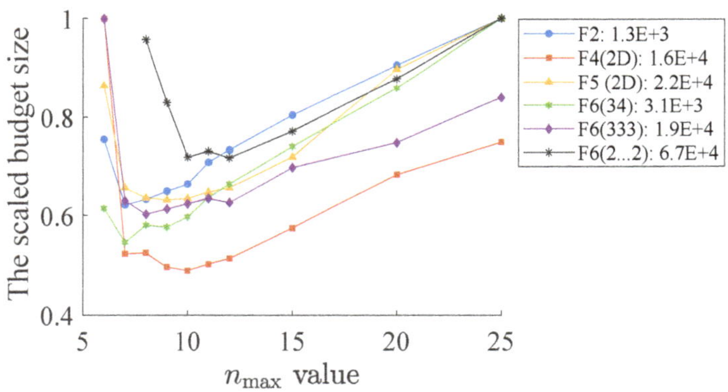

Figure 5. The scaled average budget size required to obtain all global optima in different problems with varying $n_{\max}$ value. A total of 100 replications are executed.

4.1.3. Effect of the New Budget Size Δ

The results of the ANOVA in Figure 3 show that a small Δ value is preferred in Problem $F6_{(3,3,3)}$ in terms of the total budget size, because it allows more budgets to be allocated after obtaining more information and generating more precise regions. Nevertheless, according to the discussion in Section 2.3, a small Δ value may increase the computational time of the proposed method. In Figure 6, the average total budget sizes and the corresponding computational times required to obtain all optima in Problem $F6_{(3,3,3)}$ with different Δ values are presented. The confidence intervals with confidence level 95% are also plotted. The experiments are executed in Matlab R2020a on a computer (Intel(R) Core(TM) i7-7700U CPU @ 3.6 GHz and 16 GB of RAM).

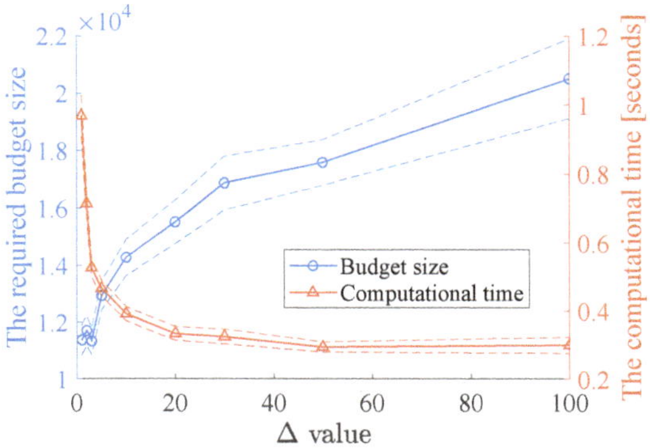

Figure 6. The average total budget size and the average computational time required to obtain all optima in Problem $F6_{(3,3,3)}$. A total of 100 replications are executed.

In this problem, it is very fast to calculate the objective function. Thus, the computational time is mainly affected by the computational complexity of the algorithm, i.e., $O(N^2/\Delta)$, where N is the total budget size. This is why the total computational time in Figure 6 decreases as the Δ value increases. In practice, if the calculation of the objective function is time-consuming, a small Δ value can be used to save the expensive budget, whereas if the calculation of the objective function is not critical, a relatively large Δ value can be used to reduce the computational time.

4.1.4. Effect of the Quantile Level α

The definition of promising regions is affected by the selected α value. A low α value prefers regions with high variability; thus, the proposed method will focus more on exploration to avoid the loss of some promising areas, whereas a high α value prefers regions with a low sample mean, so that the detected promising area will be firstly exploited. Although the effect of the α value is less significant than the other two parameters in Problem $F6_{(3,3,3)}$, it has a great influence in Problem F5(2D), where some optimal solutions are located in flat areas and others are located in steep areas. A low α value will make promising regions in flat areas struggle to reach the smallest size due to their small variability; thus, the samples in these regions are not considered as potential optimal solutions.

Figure 7 presents another influence of the α value in Problem F5(2D). In 100 replications, the frequencies of the optimal solutions in different locations being captured within a budget of size 8000 is represented by different colors and shapes. In the studied case, the size of nonpartitionable regions are the same among the whole domain. A promising region in flat areas (i.e., large x_1 and x_2 values) has a small sample mean, while a promising region of the same size in steep areas (i.e., small x_1 and x_2 values) has a large sample variance. When the α value is high ($\alpha = 0.3$), promising regions in flat areas will be partitioned earlier, and the global optimal solutions located in these areas can be found with a higher frequency (larger than 0.8). When the α value is reduced to a lower value (e.g., 0.1 or 0.2), the influence of the sample variance rises. Therefore, the frequency of finding the optimal solutions in flat areas decreases, whereas the frequency of finding the optimal solutions in steep areas increases.

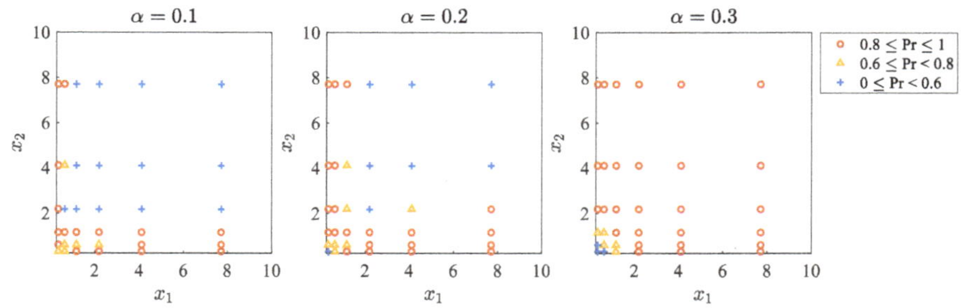

Figure 7. The frequencies of capturing different optimal solutions among 100 replications with varying α in Problem F5(2D). The budget size is 8000. As the α value increases, the frequency of finding optima in steep areas is reduced while the frequency of finding optima in flat areas is increased.

4.2. Comparison with Other Methods on Multiple Global Optima

The functions F1–F7, which have multiple global optima, are considered in this section. The proposed method is compared with other multimodal optimization methods developed from different mechanisms: multiobjectivization, subpopulations, differential evolution with niching mutation operator, and two-phase method. In addition, they all have good performance in the selected benchmark functions.

MOMMOP [59] transfers the multimodal optimization problem to a multiobjective optimization problem with $2d$ conflicting objective functions so that all optima are located in the Pareto front. Then, differential evolution combined with modified nondominated sorting [19] is used to solve the multiobjective optimization problem. The MOMMOP method belongs to the category of multiobjectivization and it is superior to ten state-of-the-art multimodal optimization algorithms in 20 benchmark functions.

LAMS-ACO [46] divides the entire population into subpopulations that evolve separately through a modified ant colony optimization algorithm ACO_R [70]. Random cluster size is adopted. A local search scheme is applied to refine the obtained solution at each iteration. The LAMS-ACO method belongs to the category of population-based niching using subpopulations and demonstrates good performance with respect to the required total number of evaluations compared to the other twelve multimodal optimization algorithms.

DIDE [36] constructs a virtual population for each individual so that each individual can track its own peak. The DIDE method belongs to the category of population-based method using niching mutation operator, and it has good performance compared to the other 13 methods in the benchmark functions.

EMO-MMO [68] develops an algorithm to detect the peaks from solutions sampled by a multiobjectivization method. Then, the competitive swarm optimizer (CSO) [71] is applied within each peak to refine the obtained optima. The idea of the EMO-MMO method is very similar to the proposed method; thus, it is also applied for comparison purposes.

These methods are applied with parameters suggested by the authors.

Three criteria are adopted for the assessment of the applied algorithms [69]. The first one is the peak ratio (PR), which measures the average percentage of the found global optima. The second one is the success rate (SR), which is the percentage of runs that find all the global optima. The third one is the convergence speed (CS), which is the average budget size, i.e., the average number of evaluations of the objective function, required to find all the global optima. If not all global optima are found when the budget is exhausted, the maximum budget size `Max_Fes` is used in the calculation.

The results of the applied algorithms are presented in Table 3 with the accuracy level ε varying from 1×10^{-1} to 1×10^{-4}. The winners are highlighted in bold and marked with dark background color (determined through the Wilcoxon rank sum test with p-value smaller than 0.0125 for the PR and p-value smaller than 0.0167 for the CS). All the experiments are repeated 100 times independently. It should be noticed that the EMO-MMO method uses all the available budget; thus, the CS column is not presented.

Table 3. Comparisons (from top to bottom: $\varepsilon = 1 \times 10^{-1}$, 1×10^{-2}, 1×10^{-3}, and 1×10^{-4}).

	PAR-MMO			PARL-MMO			MOMMOP			LAMS-ACO			DIDE [1]		EMO-MMO	
Func	PR	SR	CS	PR	SR	CS	PR	SR	CS	PR	SR	CS	PR	SR	PR	SR
F1	1.00	1.00	1.6×10^2	1.00	1.00	**1.3×10^2**	1.00	1.00	**1.4×10^2**	1.00	1.00	**1.4×10^2**	-	-	1.00	1.00
	1.00	1.00	2.8×10^2	1.00	1.00	**1.4×10^2**	1.00	1.00	4.2×10^2	1.00	1.00	2.9×10^2	-	-	1.00	1.00
	1.00	1.00	3.7×10^2	1.00	1.00	**1.6×10^2**	1.00	1.00	1.2×10^3	1.00	1.00	4.8×10^2	1.00	1.00	1.00	1.00
	1.00	1.00	5.5×10^2	1.00	1.00	**1.9×10^2**	1.00	1.00	3.3×10^3	1.00	1.00	7.6×10^2	1.00	1.00	1.00	1.00
F2	1.00	1.00	2.4×10^3	1.00	1.00	**7.0×10^2**	1.00	1.00	2.1×10^2	1.00	1.00	1.2×10^3	-	-	1.00	1.00
	1.00	1.00	3.7×10^3	1.00	1.00	**7.6×10^2**	1.00	1.00	3.2×10^2	1.00	1.00	2.0×10^3	-	-	1.00	1.00
	1.00	1.00	7.1×10^3	1.00	1.00	**8.0×10^2**	1.00	0.99	3.5×10^2	1.00	1.00	2.9×10^3	1.00	1.00	1.00	1.00
	1.00	1.00	1.2×10^2	1.00	1.00	**8.5×10^2**	0.99	0.97	3.7×10^2	1.00	1.00	4.0×10^3	1.00	1.00	1.00	1.00
F3	1.00	1.00	3.4×10^2	1.00	1.00	**2.0×10^2**	1.00	1.00	1.2×10^3	1.00	1.00	3.6×10^2	-	-	1.00	1.00
	1.00	1.00	7.5×10^2	1.00	1.00	**2.4×10^2**	1.00	1.00	9.8×10^3	1.00	1.00	7.7×10^2	-	-	1.00	1.00
	1.00	1.00	1.2×10^3	1.00	1.00	**2.5×10^2**	1.00	1.00	1.5×10^2	1.00	1.00	1.4×10^3	1.00	1.00	1.00	1.00
	1.00	1.00	2.1×10^3	1.00	1.00	**2.9×10^2**	1.00	1.00	1.8×10^2	1.00	1.00	1.9×10^3	1.00	1.00	1.00	1.00
F4(2D)	1.00	1.00	2.4×10^2	1.00	1.00	**6.6×10^3**	1.00	0.99	5.1×10^2	0.99	0.74	1.0×10^5	-	-	1.00	1.00
	1.00	1.00	3.4×10^2	1.00	1.00	**7.1×10^3**	0.97	0.95	5.9×10^2	0.98	0.67	1.3×10^5	-	-	1.00	1.00
	1.00	1.00	5.5×10^2	1.00	1.00	**7.6×10^3**	0.96	0.95	6.2×10^2	0.98	0.71	1.3×10^5	1.00	1.00	1.00	1.00
	1.00	0.97	9.2×10^2	1.00	1.00	**8.1×10^3**	0.97	0.94	6.5×10^2	0.98	0.65	1.4×10^5	1.00	1.00	1.00	1.00
F4(3D)	0.55	0.00	4.0×10^5	**1.00**	0.98	2.1×10^5	**0.98**	0.94	2.3×10^5	0.77	0.00	4.0×10^5	-	-	**1.00**	**1.00**
	0.42	0.00	4.0×10^5	**1.00**	0.94	2.4×10^5	**0.99**	0.97	2.5×10^5	0.75	0.00	4.0×10^5	-	-	**1.00**	**1.00**
	0.26	0.00	4.0×10^5	**1.00**	0.97	2.2×10^5	**0.98**	0.95	2.8×10^5	0.73	0.00	4.0×10^5	0.69	0.00	**1.00**	**1.00**
	0.17	0.00	4.0×10^5	**1.00**	0.96	2.4×10^5	**0.98**	0.95	3.1×10^5	0.71	0.00	4.0×10^5	0.69	0.00	**1.00**	**0.99**
F5(2D)	1.00	0.97	3.7×10^2	1.00	1.00	**1.3×10^2**	1.00	1.00	4.7×10^2	0.79	0.00	2.0×10^5	-	-	1.00	0.98
	1.00	1.00	4.9×10^2	1.00	1.00	**1.3×10^2**	1.00	1.00	5.5×10^2	0.76	0.00	2.0×10^5	-	-	1.00	0.98
	1.00	0.89	1.1×10^5	1.00	1.00	**1.4×10^2**	1.00	1.00	6.4×10^2	0.69	0.00	2.0×10^5	0.92	0.04	1.00	0.97
	1.00	0.87	1.4×10^5	1.00	1.00	**1.4×10^2**	1.00	1.00	7.7×10^2	0.64	0.00	2.0×10^5	0.92	0.04	1.00	0.96
F5(3D)	0.61	0.00	4.0×10^5	0.98	0.03	4.0×10^5	1.00	1.00	**2.3×10^5**	0.31	0.00	4.0×10^5	-	-	0.88	0.00
	0.46	0.00	4.0×10^5	0.98	0.01	4.0×10^5	1.00	1.00	**2.4×10^5**	0.31	0.00	4.0×10^5	-	-	0.87	0.00
	0.21	0.00	4.0×10^5	0.97	0.01	4.0×10^5	1.00	1.00	**3.0×10^5**	0.28	0.00	4.0×10^5	0.58	0.00	0.88	0.00
	0.07	0.00	4.0×10^5	0.97	0.00	4.0×10^5	**1.00**	**0.86**	3.7×10^5	0.23	0.00	4.0×10^5	0.57	0.00	0.88	0.00
$F6_{(3,4)}$	1.00	1.00	3.1×10^3	1.00	1.00	**1.5×10^3**	1.00	1.00	2.5×10^2	1.00	0.99	5.4×10^3	-	-	1.00	1.00
	1.00	1.00	6.0×10^3	1.00	1.00	**1.6×10^3**	1.00	1.00	3.9×10^2	1.00	0.98	1.0×10^2	-	-	1.00	1.00
	1.00	1.00	1.1×10^2	1.00	1.00	**1.8×10^3**	1.00	1.00	4.3×10^2	1.00	0.96	2.2×10^2	1.00	1.00	1.00	1.00
	1.00	1.00	1.4×10^2	1.00	1.00	**1.9×10^3**	1.00	1.00	4.4×10^2	0.99	0.90	4.4×10^2	1.00	1.00	1.00	1.00
$F6_{(3,3,3)}$	1.00	1.00	4.5×10^2	1.00	1.00	**1.1×10^2**	1.00	1.00	9.1×10^2	0.96	0.27	3.3×10^5	-	-	1.00	1.00
	1.00	0.99	1.5×10^5	1.00	1.00	**1.1×10^2**	1.00	1.00	1.1×10^5	0.92	0.06	3.9×10^5	-	-	1.00	1.00
	0.99	0.83	2.9×10^5	1.00	1.00	**1.1×10^2**	1.00	1.00	1.1×10^5	0.85	0.00	4.0×10^5	-	-	1.00	1.00
	0.96	0.37	3.8×10^5	1.00	1.00	**1.2×10^2**	1.00	1.00	1.1×10^5	0.78	0.00	4.0×10^5	-	-	1.00	1.00
$F6_{(2,\cdots,2)}$	0.48	0.00	4.0×10^5	1.00	1.00	**4.5×10^2**	1.00	1.00	1.3×10^5	0.92	0.05	3.9×10^5	-	-	1.00	1.00
	0.03	0.00	4.0×10^5	1.00	1.00	**4.5×10^2**	1.00	1.00	1.6×10^5	0.83	0.00	4.0×10^5	-	-	1.00	1.00
	0.02	0.00	4.0×10^5	1.00	1.00	**4.7×10^2**	1.00	1.00	1.6×10^5	0.71	0.00	4.0×10^5	-	-	1.00	1.00
	0.02	0.00	4.0×10^5	1.00	1.00	**4.8×10^2**	1.00	1.00	1.7×10^5	0.65	0.00	4.0×10^5	-	-	1.00	1.00
F7(1-2D)	0.57	0.00	2.0×10^5	1.00	1.00	**2.8×10^3**	1.00	0.98	1.0×10^5	0.99	0.94	9.1×10^2	-	-	1.00	1.00
	0.42	0.00	2.0×10^5	1.00	1.00	**2.9×10^3**	0.99	0.91	1.2×10^5	0.98	0.85	1.3×10^5	-	-	1.00	1.00
	0.33	0.00	2.0×10^5	1.00	1.00	**3.0×10^3**	0.94	0.69	1.7×10^5	0.95	0.67	1.6×10^5	1.00	1.00	1.00	1.00
	0.32	0.00	2.0×10^5	1.00	1.00	**3.0×10^3**	0.72	0.03	2.0×10^5	0.92	0.53	1.7×10^5	1.00	1.00	1.00	1.00
F7(2-2D)	0.60	0.00	2.0×10^5	1.00	1.00	**1.4×10^2**	0.98	0.86	1.3×10^5	0.97	0.77	9.1×10^2	-	-	1.00	1.00
	0.31	0.00	2.0×10^5	1.00	1.00	**1.6×10^2**	0.98	0.84	1.5×10^5	0.95	0.56	1.3×10^5	-	-	1.00	1.00
	0.25	0.00	2.0×10^5	1.00	1.00	**1.7×10^2**	0.96	0.66	1.7×10^5	0.96	0.70	1.2×10^5	1.00	1.00	1.00	1.00
	0.20	0.00	2.0×10^5	1.00	1.00	**1.9×10^2**	0.93	0.52	1.9×10^5	0.96	0.67	1.3×10^5	1.00	1.00	1.00	1.00
F7(3-2D)	0.44	0.00	2.0×10^5	0.96	0.77	1.4×10^2	0.96	0.73	1.4×10^5	0.71	0.00	2.0×10^5	-	-	**0.99**	**0.95**
	0.25	0.00	2.0×10^5	0.94	0.65	1.6×10^2	0.91	0.47	1.8×10^5	0.69	0.00	2.0×10^5	-	-	**1.00**	**0.97**
	0.21	0.00	2.0×10^5	0.92	0.56	1.7×10^2	0.65	0.00	2.0×10^5	0.67	0.00	2.0×10^5	0.99	0.92	**0.99**	**0.95**
	0.20	0.00	2.0×10^5	0.92	0.57	1.9×10^2	0.65	0.00	2.0×10^5	0.67	0.00	2.0×10^5	0.99	0.92	**0.99**	**0.94**
F7(3-3D)	0.27	0.00	4.0×10^5	0.68	0.01	4.0×10^5	**0.80**	0.00	4.0×10^5	0.67	0.00	4.0×10^5	-	-	0.75	0.03
	0.26	0.00	4.0×10^5	0.68	0.00	4.0×10^5	**0.73**	0.00	4.0×10^5	0.67	0.00	4.0×10^5	-	-	**0.73**	0.03
	0.30	0.00	4.0×10^5	0.67	0.00	4.0×10^5	0.67	0.00	4.0×10^5	0.67	0.00	4.0×10^5	0.78	0.04	**0.74**	0.02
	0.28	0.00	4.0×10^5	0.68	0.00	4.0×10^5	0.67	0.00	4.0×10^5	0.67	0.00	4.0×10^5	0.77	0.02	**0.74**	0.03

[1] The data of DIDE are from [36]. "-" means these data are not presented in the paper.

As discussed in Section 3, if the PAR-MMO method is used alone, as the ε value decreases, the average number of evaluations required to find all the optima increases a lot, or the percentage of global optima found reduces rapidly. However, if the PAR-MMO method is applied to detect the promising areas and local search is applied to improve the accuracy level of the obtained optima, i.e., the PARL-MMO method, the evaluation budget can be saved significantly, especially when the ε value is small. When the PARL-MMO method is applied, the number of evaluations used in the PAR-MMO method is not much different, regardless of the ε value, because the definition of the nonpartitionable region is the same. The required total budget size differs depending on the budget required in the local search stage, which is less affected by the ε value compared to the PAR-MMO method.

In most cases, the PARL-MMO method behaves better than the three state-of-the-art methods, except for problems F4(3D), F5(3D), F7(3-2D), and F7(3-3D). In Problem F5(3D), the MOMMOP method has the best performance. Although the PARL-MMO method does not have good performance in this problem according to the criterion SR, the PR is still high (not less than 0.97 for all ε values). For the LAMS-ACO method, a large ant size is required to generate sufficient subpopulations, especially when the number of optima is high. For example, poor performance is observed for Problem F5(3D), because an ant size of 300 is too small for 216 optima. However, a too-large ant size may result in waste of budget. Prior knowledge about the number of optima is important for methods that divide the whole population into subpopulations, whereas this knowledge is not needed in the proposed method.

In Problem F4(3D), the criterion SR of the PARL-MMO method is not as good as that of the EMO-MMO method, but almost all the global optima are discovered (the PR values are all close to one). In addition, a lot of local optima are also contained in the $\mathbb{S}^{opt}$ in the PARL-MMO method. In problems F7(3-2D) and F7(3-3D), there are numerous local optima that are very close to one of the global optima. For example, in Problem F7(3-2D), the distance between a global optimum and one of the local optima with objective function value 0.5761 is 3×10^{-6}. In this case, if the size of the nonpartitionable region is not small enough to separate these optimal solutions, Algorithm 5 may be stuck in one of the local optima, i.e., the results of PARL-MMO. However, if the size of the nonpartitionable region is small enough, the maximum budget size is not sufficient to reach the corresponding nonpartitionable region, i.e., the results of PAR-MMO. In the EMO-MMO method, the CSO method, which has the ability to escape the local optima, is applied to locally search the promising areas. Therefore, good performance is observed for the EMO-MMO method in problems F7(3-2D) and F7(3-3D).

As for the composition functions with more than five dimensions in the CEC'2013 functions, the proposed method does not have good performance, although all multimodal optimization methods hardly find all global optima in these functions within the given budget. The proposed method has difficulty handling functions with large jumps everywhere. In this case, an intelligent partitioning strategy developed from the system knowledge would be required to make the function smoother.

In summary, the PARL-MMO method has good performance in most of the benchmark functions for capturing multiple global optimal solutions.

4.3. Effect of Local Optima

The PARL-MMO method is applied to functions F8 (one-dimensional increasing optima) and F9 (Rastrigin function), which have only one global optimum and multiple local optima with different qualities, i.e., different objective function values. In this section, the accuracy level ε is set as 1×10^{-4} and 500 replications are executed. Figure 8 shows the frequencies of different optima being found as the total budget size grows. In the Rastrigin function, similar performance is observed for optimal solutions having the same objective function values due to the symmetry property. Thus, to make the figure clear, they are combined as a single line. In the legend, the number in bold shows the number of optimal solutions having this objective function value. Many other local optimal solutions of the Rastrigin function with worse objective function values are not all found due to the budget limitation. Thus, they are not plotted in Figure 8.

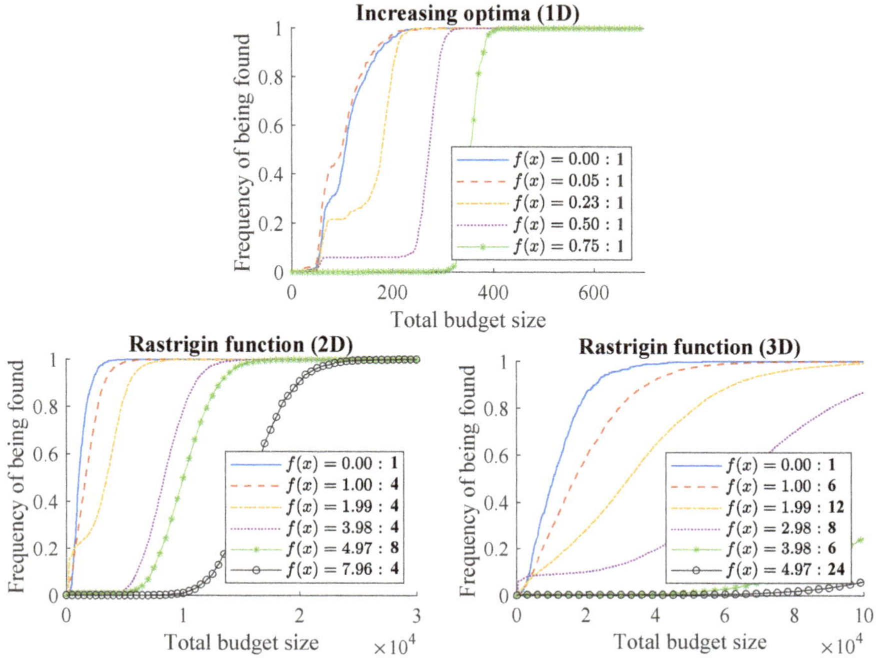

Figure 8. The frequencies of local optima of different qualities being found as the total budget size increases. The number in bold shows the number of optima having this objective function value. A total of 500 replications are executed.

It can be found from Figure 8 that, in the studied cases, the global optimum and the high-quality local optima have higher frequencies to be found than low-quality local optima when the available budget size is small. As the total budget size increases, the rest of the local optima will be found subsequently according to their objective function values. This is one of the features of the proposed method. Other multimodal optimization methods either cannot store local optima, e.g., MOMMOP [59], LAM-ACO [46], and EMO-MMO [68], or optima with different qualities are considered equally important, e.g., [55].

4.4. Schaffer's Function

In this section, the PARL-MMO method is applied to Problem F10, in which the local optimal solution is not a single point. There is only one global optima $f(\mathbf{0}) = 0$ and there are several regions in which all solutions are local optimal solutions with slightly worse objective function values. The optimal solutions located in the same circle have the same objective function values, which are 0.0097, 0.0372, 0.0782, and 0.1270 from inner circle to outer circle, respectively.

Figure 9 shows the partition states and the obtained optima, i.e., the solutions in $\mathbb{S}^{\text{opt}}$, as the total budget size N increases. Unlike EA-based methods, the number of optimal solutions contained in the optimal solution set provided by the proposed method can grow without limit. Multiple local optimal solutions can be captured and the density of the solutions is affected by the size of the nonpartitionable regions and the distance parameter r in Algorithm 3. As discussed in the previous section, the inner circles are found earlier than outer circles.

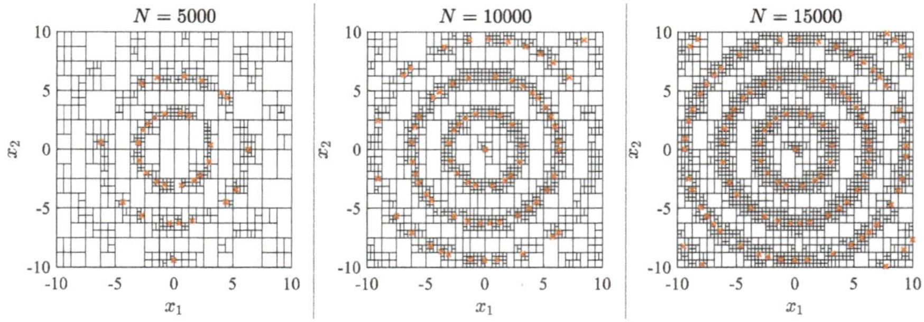

Figure 9. The partition states (a square indicates a region) and the obtained optima (the red crosses) as the total budget size N increases for the Schaffer's function minimization problem.

It should be noticed that if the optimal area is flat in all the dimensions, the variances of all regions (broad and partitionable) within this area will be zero. These regions will not reach the smallest size, since zero weights are assigned according to Equation (5). Thus, the solutions within these regions are not considered as potential optimal solutions in the algorithm. In this situation, an archive can be created to store all the partitionable regions with a good mean and a very low variance.

4.5. Computational Time

In this section, the PAR-MMO method, in which local search is not included, is applied to Problem $F4_{(2,\cdots,2)}$ (five dimensions) with $\varepsilon = 1 \times 10^{-4}$. A total of 20 independent replications are executed in Matlab R2020a on a computer (Intel(R) Core(TM) i7-7700U CPU @ 3.6 GHz and 16 GB of RAM). Figure 10 shows how the average computational time changes as the total budget size increases. It can be found that the computational time increases quadratically as discussed in Section 2.3 ($R^2 = 100.0\%$ for the quadratic regression). Although the proposed method will become time-consuming when the total budget size is very large, it is still efficient in the studied case (on average, 121 s for a budget of size 1×10^6) and the computational time climbs slowly before the total budget size reaches one million.

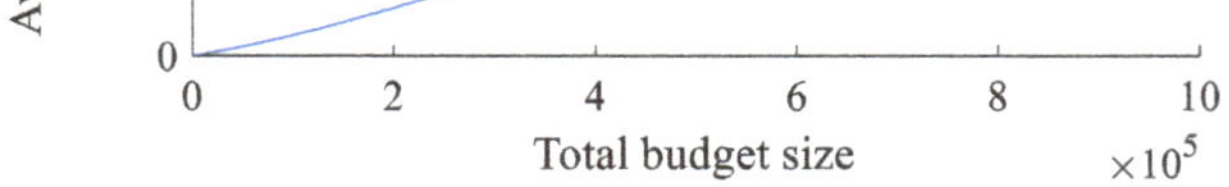

Figure 10. The average computational time required for the proposed method in Problem $F4_{(2,\cdots,2)}$ as the total budget increases. A total of 20 replications are executed.

5. Application

The optimal control problem of a nonlinear stirred tank reactor [72] is considered in this section. The chemical process can be modeled by the following differential equations:

$$\dot{x}_1 = -(2+u)(x_1+0.25) + (x_2+0.5)\exp\left(\frac{25x_1}{x_1+2}\right), \tag{8}$$

$$\dot{x_2} = 0.5 - x_2 - (x_2 + 0.5)\exp\left(\frac{25x_1}{x_1 + 2}\right), \tag{9}$$

$$\dot{x_3} = x_1^2 + x_2^2 + 0.1u^2. \tag{10}$$

where $u(t), u(t) \in [0.0, 5.0]$ is the flow rate of the cooling fluid, $x_1(t)$ is the dimensionless steady temperature, $x_2(t)$ is the deviation from dimensionless steady concentration, and the interval of integration is $0 \leq t \leq 0.78$. The performance index to minimize is $f = x_3(0.78)$, which can be evaluated using *ode45* in Matlab, and the initial condition is $x_1(0) = 0.09, x_2(0) = 0.09, x_3(0) = 0$. The problem has a global optimum $x_3(0.78) = 0.13309$ and a local optimum $x_3(0.78) = 0.24442$. These two values are directly associated with two different control trajectories [72].

To solve the problem, the time interval is discretized into 13 time slots in order to obtain a reasonably good integration accuracy, and constant control is used within a time slot. Then, $u(t)$ becomes 13 decision variables $[u(1), u(2), \cdots, u(13)]^T$. The PARLMMO method is applied with $\alpha = 0.3, n_0 = 3, n_{\max} = 8, \Delta = 3$. The edge threshold that is considered as nonpartitionable is set to 0.8 and the stop threshold of the local search is set as 0.01. The maximum budget size is 1×10^5.

Twenty replications are carried out. The optimum is regarded as found only when the algorithm recognizes that the point is an optimum and saves it in $\mathbb{S}^{\text{opt}}$. Table 4 shows the number of the replications that find each optimum, the average budget to find each optimum, and the average absolute percentage gap of the objective function value compared to the real optimum (0.13309 and 0.24442). It should be noticed that the gap could be caused by the precision of the captured solution, the calculation of the integration, and the discretization of $u(t)$.

Table 4. The results of the nonlinear stirred tank reactor control problem (20 replications).

PARL-MMO	Successful Replications	Average Budget	Average Absolute Percentage Gap
Global optimum	20	34,156	1.8%
Local optimum	3	771	0.5%
MOMMOP	**Successful Replications**	**Average Budget**	**Average Absolute Percentage Gap**
Global optimum	20	-	1.4%
Local optimum	0	-	-

For comparison purpose, the MOMMOP method [59], which outperforms other methods in the benchmark functions, is also applied with population size 30, mutation factor 0.5, crossover index 0.7, crowded radius 0.01, and maximum budget size 1×10^5. The optimal solution is considered as captured if it is contained in the Pareto set.

The first comment is that the global optimum is captured in all replications. In addition, no points other than these two optimal solutions appear in the final optimization set. This means that the algorithm will not mislead the users with fake optima.

However, the local optimum is captured only in three replications. This is because the local optimum is 84% worse than the global optimum. Thus, the area around the local optimum is not considered as promising by the algorithm, unless other areas with better objective function values have not been discovered or have been exploited. In this case, according to the budget size required to find each optimum, the area around the local optimum is only searched before the area around the global optimum is discovered. This result is consistent with the feature of the algorithm that focuses on the global optima and the high-quality local optima. When only good solutions are of interest, the algorithm would not waste budget to search for optima with poor objective functions. However, this may become a disadvantage when all optima (no matter if good or poor) are required.

The MOMMOP method is proposed for seeking multiple global optimal solutions. Thus, all points in the Pareto set are points around the global optimum, and the local optimum is not identified in any replication. The best solution in the Pareto set is used to calculate the average absolute percentage gap. This gap is less than the PARL-MMO. A possible reason for this is that the function around the global optimum is not smooth due to the discretization of the integration. Therefore, the local search may be trapped when refining the found solution in the PARL-MMO method. This may be improved by using different algorithms, such as EA, in the refining phase.

6. Conclusions

A partition-based random search method is proposed, in which by controlling the partition rates of different regions, promising areas are exploited probabilistically earlier than nonpromising areas. Multiple optimal solutions (both global and local) can be found and stored. It does not require prior knowledge about the number of optima in the studied problem and it is not sensitive to the distance parameter.

Numerical results show that, by cooperating with local search, the proposed method has good performance in finding multiple global optimal solutions in 14 benchmark functions compared to four state-of-the-art methods. In problems containing local optima of different qualities, i.e., different objective function values, high-quality local optima will be found earlier than low-quality optima. Therefore, it will focus on exploiting global optima and high-quality local optima when the budget is not quite sufficient. In addition, the proposed method can also deal with optimization problems that exist in regions where all solutions are optimal solutions.

One of the limitations of the proposed method is that a large amount of calculation memory is needed because all existing regions and all sampled solutions are stored. The increased number of regions also makes the computational time increase quadratically as the total budget size increases, although it is still efficient when the total budget size is not extremely large. Therefore, the pruning of the stored regions is one of the directions of further work. The other limitation is introduced by the property of the partition-based random search framework. Partition-based methods are efficient for problems in which each decision variable has a large search space. However, it could be inefficient for high-dimensional problems if the partition strategy is simply partitioning each dimension into several ranges. In this case, intelligent partition strategies should be developed based on the features of the studied problem to improve the efficiency of the algorithm. The efficiency of the proposed method could be highly affected by selection of the partition strategy.

The future development includes several directions. The first one is the development of an algorithm for the deletion of less interesting regions to solve the problem of quadratically increased computational time. The second one is adopting an adaptive α value in the proposed method. As discussed in the paper, a low α value focuses more on exploration, whereas a high α value focuses more on exploitation. Therefore, an increasing α value may improve the efficiency of the proposed method. The third one is to deal with the optimization problems with constraints. Although the constraints can be handled by manipulating the sampling strategy to avoid the sampling of infeasible solutions, this action may be difficult for some applications. Penalty function is another common way to deal with constraints, but the regions containing the boundary may have biased performance estimates, which may affect the proposed method. Therefore, an adaptive penalty function to deal with the constraints in the proposed method will be an interesting research direction. The last one is extending the method to optimization problems with stochastic objective function or constraints.

Author Contributions: All the authors contributed to the conceptualization of this research. Z.L. also contributed to the development of the methodology, software coding, draft writing, and validation of results. A.M. also contributed to the supervision of the research, development of the methodology and validation of results. S.D. also ncontributed to the validation of results, funding acquisition and administration. E.S. also contributed to the validation of results and editing. All authors have read and agreed to the published version of the manuscript.

Funding: This work was supported by the National Natural Science Foundation of China (Grant No. 52275499) and the National key R&D plan of China (No. 2022YFF0605700).

Conflicts of Interest: The authors declare no conflict of interest.

Appendix A. Selected Benchmark Functions

The functions considered for numerical experiments are here summarized and show in Figure A1.

F1: One-dimensional equal optima

$f(x) = 1 - \sin^6(5\pi x), x \in [0,1]$.

Property: Five global optima evenly distributed: $x_i^* = 0.2i - 0.1$ that $f(x_i^*) = 0$.

F2: Himmelblau's function

$f(\boldsymbol{x}) = (x_1^2 + x_2 - 11)^2 + (x_1 + x_2^2 - 7)^2, x_i \in [-6,6], i = 1,2$.

Property: Four global optima with two closer to each other: $\boldsymbol{x}_1^* = (3.0, 2.0)$, $\boldsymbol{x}_2^* = (-2.805118, 3.131312)$, $\boldsymbol{x}_3^* = (-3.779310, -3.283186)$ and $\boldsymbol{x}_4^* = (3.584428, -1.848126)$ that $f(\boldsymbol{x}_i^*) = 0$.

F3: Six-hump camel back

$f(\boldsymbol{x}) = 4((4 - 2.1x_1^2 + x_1^4/3)x_1^2 + x_1x_2 + (4x_2^2 - 4)x_2^2), x_1 \in [-1.9, 1.9], x_2 \in [-1.1, 1.1]$.

Property: Two global optima: $\boldsymbol{x}_1^* = (0.0898, -0.7126)$ and $\boldsymbol{x}_2^* = (-0.0898, 0.7126)$ that $f(\boldsymbol{x}_i^*) = -4.1265$. Four local optima: $\boldsymbol{x}_3^* = (1.7035, -0.7961)$ and $\boldsymbol{x}_4^* = (-1.7035, 0.7961)$ that $f(\boldsymbol{x}_i^*) = -0.8619$ and $\boldsymbol{x}_5^* = (-1.6071, -0.5687)$ and $\boldsymbol{x}_6^* = (1.6071, 0.5687)$ that $f(\boldsymbol{x}_i^*) = 8.4170$.

F4: Shubert function

$f(\boldsymbol{x}) = \prod_{i=1}^d \sum_{j=1}^5 j\cos((j+1)x_i + j), x_i \in [-10, 10], \forall i$.

Property: $d \cdot 3^d$ global optima in 3^d groups with d optima in each group and many poor local optima. The global optima are $f(\boldsymbol{x}_i^*) = -186.7309$ for two dimensions and $f(\boldsymbol{x}_i^*) = -2709.0935$ for three dimensions.

F5: Vincent function

$f(\boldsymbol{x}) = 1 - \frac{1}{d}\sum_{i=1}^d \sin(10\log(x_i)), x_i \in [0.25, 10], \forall i$.

Property: 6^d global optima unevenly distributed: $\boldsymbol{x}_{i_1,\cdots,i_d}^* = \left(\exp\left(\frac{(4i_1-11)\pi}{20}\right), \cdots, \exp\left(\frac{(4i_d-11)\pi}{20}\right)\right)$ that $f(\boldsymbol{x}_i^*) = 0$.

F6: Modified Rastrigin function $(k_1, \cdots, k_d)$

$f(\boldsymbol{x}) = \sum_{i=1}^d (10 + 9\cos(2\pi k_i x_i)), x_i \in [0,1], \forall i$.

Property: $\prod_{i=1}^d k_i$ global optima evenly distributed: $\boldsymbol{x}_{i_1,\cdots,i_d}^* = \left(\frac{2i_1-1}{2k_1}, \cdots, \frac{2i_d-1}{2k_d}\right)$ that $f\left(\boldsymbol{x}_{i_1,\cdots,i_d}^*\right) = d$.

F7: Composition function

Property: A multimodal function composed of several basic functions; thus, different functions' properties are mixed together. More details can be found in [69]. The label "F7(*a*-*d*D)" in the paper indicates the composition function *a* with *d* dimension.

F8: One-dimensional increasing optima

$f(x) = 1 - \exp\left(-2\log(2)\left(\frac{x-0.08}{0.854}\right)^2\right)\sin^6(5\pi(x^{3/4} - 0.05)), x \in [0.02, 1]$.

Property: One global optimum and four increasing local optima.

F9: Rastrigin function

$f(\boldsymbol{x}) = \sum_{i=1}^d (x_i^2 - 10\cos(2\pi x_i) + 10), x_i \in [-5.12, 5.12], \forall i$.

Property: One global optimum: $f(\mathbf{0}) = 0$, and $11^d - 1$ local optima with different qualities.

F10: Schaffer's function

$$f(\boldsymbol{x}) = 0.5 + \frac{\sin^2\left(\sqrt{\sum_{i=1}^{d} x_i^2}\right) - 0.5}{(1+0.001(\sum_{i=1}^{d} x_i^2))^2}, x_i \in [-10, 10], \forall i.$$

Property: One global optimum $f(\mathbf{0}) = 0$ and seven regions where all solutions are local optimal.

Appendix B. Algorithm Parameter

The regions are considered as nonpartitionable regions when all edges are smaller than values in Table A1 of Appendix B.

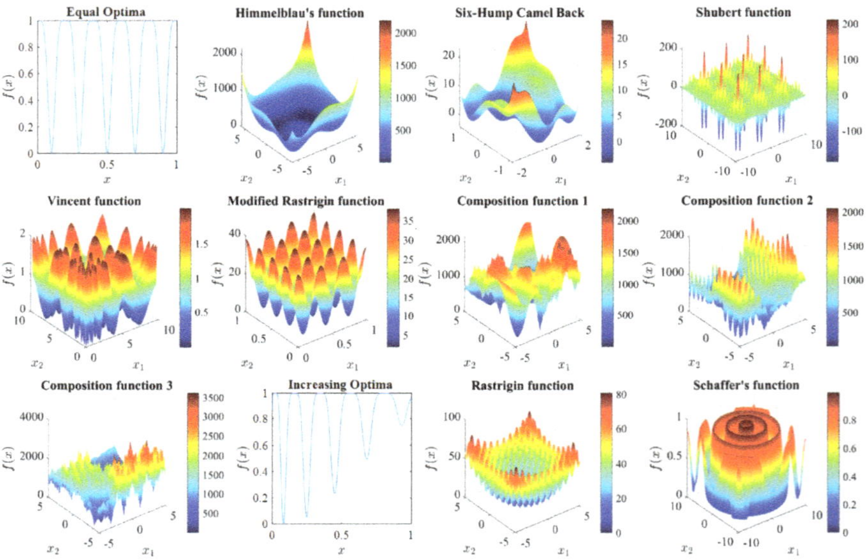

Figure A1. The surface plots of the selected benchmark functions. f_4, f_5, f_6, f_7, f_9 only show 2D cases.

Table A1. The edge threshold of nonpartitionable regions.

Func \ ε	0.1	0.01	0.001	0.0001	Local Search
F1	2.3×10^{-2}	7.5×10^{-3}	2.3×10^{-3}	7.5×10^{-4}	4.0×10^{-2}
F2	7.4×10^{-2}	2.4×10^{-2}	7.4×10^{-3}	2.4×10^{-3}	4.0×10^{-1}
F3	8.5×10^{-2}	2.8×10^{-2}	8.5×10^{-3}	2.8×10^{-3}	1.5×10^{-1}
F4(2D)	9.6×10^{-3}	3.0×10^{-3}	9.6×10^{-4}	3.0×10^{-4}	1.6×10^{-1}
F4(3D)	2.0×10^{-3}	6.4×10^{-4}	2.0×10^{-4}	6.4×10^{-5}	1.6×10^{-1}
F5(2D)	3.0×10^{-2}	9.6×10^{-3}	3.0×10^{-3}	9.6×10^{-4}	8.0×10^{-2}
F5(3D)	3.0×10^{-2}	9.6×10^{-3}	3.0×10^{-3}	9.6×10^{-4}	8.0×10^{-2}
$F6_{(3,4)}$	9.6×10^{-3}	3.0×10^{-3}	9.6×10^{-4}	3.0×10^{-4}	4.0×10^{-2}
$F6_{(3,3,3)}$	9.0×10^{-3}	3.0×10^{-3}	9.0×10^{-4}	3.0×10^{-4}	4.0×10^{-2}
$F6_{(2,\cdots,2)}$	1.1×10^{-2}	3.4×10^{-3}	1.1×10^{-3}	3.4×10^{-4}	7.0×10^{-2}
F7(1-2D)	5.0×10^{-7}	1.6×10^{-8}	1.1×10^{-9}	3.2×10^{-1}	1.6×10^{-1}
F7(2-2D)	1.6×10^{-6}	5.6×10^{-8}	1.8×10^{-9}	5.5×10^{-1}	1.6×10^{-1}
F7(3-2D)	9.5×10^{-8}	2.0×10^{-9}	1.5×10^{-1}	4.3×10^{-1}	2.0×10^{-2}
F7(3-3D)	9.0×10^{-8}	2.5×10^{-9}	1.4×10^{-1}	3.8×10^{-1}	2.0×10^{-2}
F8	1.7×10^{-2}	5.2×10^{-3}	1.7×10^{-3}	5.2×10^{-4}	2.0×10^{-2}
F9(2D)	3.0×10^{-2}	1.0×10^{-2}	3.0×10^{-3}	1.0×10^{-3}	1.0×10^{-1}
F9(3D)	2.6×10^{-2}	8.0×10^{-3}	2.6×10^{-3}	8.0×10^{-4}	1.0×10^{-1}
F10	4.0×10^{-1}	4.0×10^{-1}	2.0×10^{-1}	8.0×10^{-2}	4.0×10^{-1}

Appendix C. ANOVA

In this Appendix C the main effect plots and the ANOVA tables on functions, where all the global optima could be found within the maximum budget, are presented (as shown in Figure A2). The experimental settings are the same as in Section 4.1. A total of 500 replications are executed and divided into ten batches, except for Problem $F6_{(2,\cdots,2)}$, where 20 replications are executed. Similar to Problem $F6_{(3,3,3)}$, almost all factors have significant effects on the algorithm, except some interactions. The effects of parameter $n_{\max}$ and parameter Δ are larger than the effect of parameter α based on the F-values (except for Problem F7(2-2D)), although the influence of parameter α is comparable to that of parameter Δ on Problem F2. For Problem F7(2-2D), the influences of the three parameters are comparable.

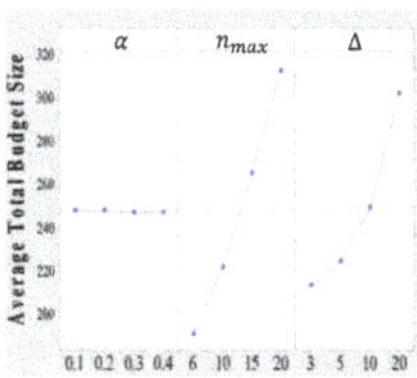

Source	DF	F-Value	P-Value
α	3	3.56	0.014
n_{max}	3	43557.37	0.000
Δ	3	22662.70	0.000
$\alpha * n_{max}$	9	0.72	0.694
$\alpha * \Delta$	9	0.80	0.618
$n_{max} * \Delta$	9	130.40	0.000
$\alpha * n_{max} * \Delta$	27	0.86	0.676
Error	576		
Total	639		

(a)

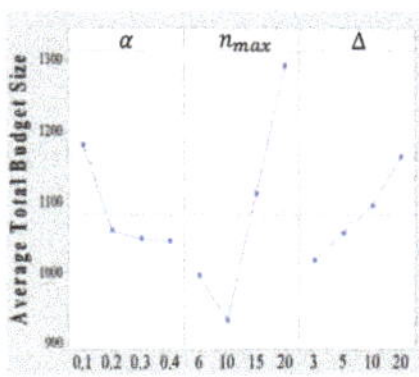

Source	DF	F-Value	P-Value
α	3	410.13	0.000
n_{max}	3	2407.77	0.000
Δ	3	373.21	0.000
$\alpha * n_{max}$	9	24.86	0.000
$\alpha * \Delta$	9	10.83	0.000
$n_{max} * \Delta$	9	35.46	0.000
$\alpha * n_{max} * \Delta$	27	1.58	0.032
Error	576		
Total	639		

(b)

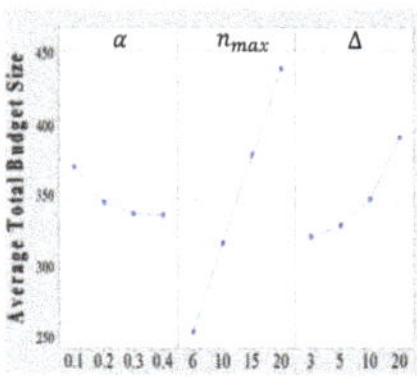

Source	DF	F-Value	P-Value
α	3	310.97	0.000
n_{max}	3	8620.25	0.000
Δ	3	1254.66	0.000
$\alpha * n_{max}$	9	33.30	0.000
$\alpha * \Delta$	9	13.75	0.000
$n_{max} * \Delta$	9	20.19	0.000
$\alpha * n_{max} * \Delta$	27	2.16	0.001
Error	576		
Total	639		

(c)

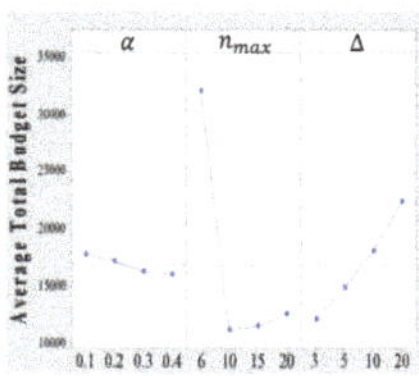

Source	DF	F-Value	P-Value
α	3	132.21	0.000
n_{max}	3	14929.26	0.000
Δ	3	4267.01	0.000
$\alpha * n_{max}$	9	4.69	0.000
$\alpha * \Delta$	9	11.32	0.000
$n_{max} * \Delta$	9	179.84	0.000
$\alpha * n_{max} * \Delta$	27	2.89	0.000
Error	576		
Total	639		

(d)

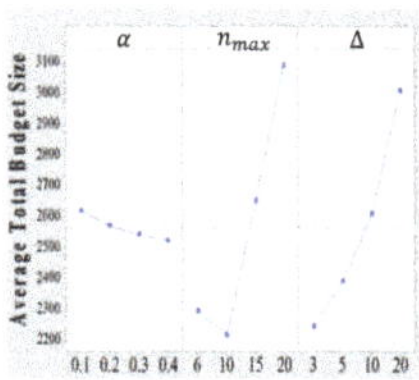

Source	DF	F-Value	P-Value
α	3	62.05	0.000
n_{max}	3	5539.98	0.000
Δ	3	3849.75	0.000
$\alpha * n_{max}$	9	3.87	0.000
$\alpha * \Delta$	9	1.21	0.283
$n_{max} * \Delta$	9	54.92	0.000
$\alpha * n_{max} * \Delta$	27	0.95	0.540
Error	576		
Total	639		

(e)

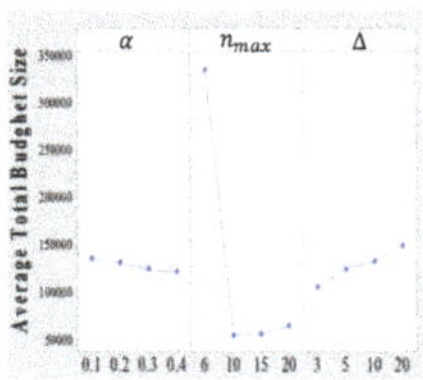

Source	DF	F-Value	P-Value
α	3	3.49	0.015
n_{max}	3	2358.98	0.000
Δ	3	57.98	0.000
$\alpha * n_{max}$	9	1.09	0.365
$\alpha * \Delta$	9	1.24	0.269
$n_{max} * \Delta$	9	1.89	0.051
$\alpha * n_{max} * \Delta$	27	0.80	0.754
Error	576		
Total	639		

(f)

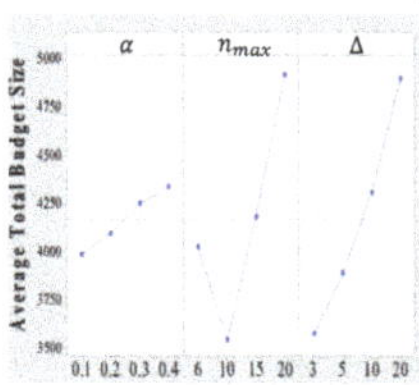

Source	DF	F-Value	P-Value
α	3	91.80	0.000
n_{max}	3	1260.12	0.000
Δ	3	1269.78	0.000
$\alpha * n_{max}$	9	11.20	0.000
$\alpha * \Delta$	9	1.81	0.063
$n_{max} * \Delta$	9	49.63	0.000
$\alpha * n_{max} * \Delta$	27	1.53	0.044
Error	576		
Total	639		

(g)

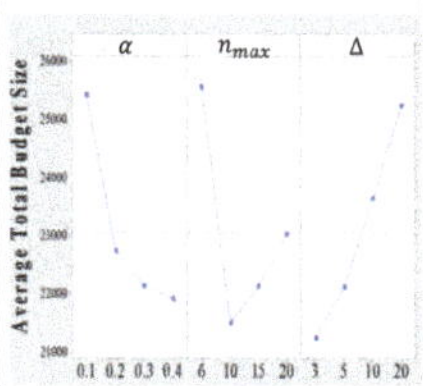

Source	DF	F-Value	P-Value
α	3	310.88	0.000
n_{max}	3	355.72	0.000
Δ	3	380.86	0.000
$\alpha * n_{max}$	9	2.68	0.005
$\alpha * \Delta$	9	8.14	0.000
$n_{max} * \Delta$	9	7.11	0.000
$\alpha * n_{max} * \Delta$	27	1.31	0.138
Error	576		
Total	639		

(h)

Figure A2. The main effect plots and the ANOVA tables on different multimodal optimization benchmark functions. (**a**) F1: One-dimensional equal optima. (**b**) F2: Himmelblau's function. (**c**) F3: Six-hump camel back. (**d**) F4(2D): Shubert function. (**e**) $F6_{(3,4)}$: Modified Rastrigin function. (**f**) $F6_{(2,\cdots,2)}$: Modified Rastrigin function. (**g**) F7(1-2D): Composition function 1. (**h**) F7(2-2D): Composition function 2.

References

1. Hu, C.; Zhao, J.; Yan, X.; Zeng, D.; Guo, S. A MapReduce based Parallel Niche Genetic Algorithm for contaminant source identification in water distribution network. *Ad Hoc Netw.* **2015**, *35*, 116–126. [CrossRef]
2. Forrester, A.I.; Keane, A.J. Recent advances in surrogate-based optimization. *Prog. Aerosp. Sci.* **2009**, *45*, 50–79. [CrossRef]

3. Shahriari, B.; Swersky, K.; Wang, Z.; Adams, R.P.; De Freitas, N. Taking the human out of the loop: A review of bayesian optimization. *Proc. IEEE* **2016**, *104*, 148–175. [CrossRef]
4. Qu, B.Y.; Liang, J.J.; Wang, Z.; Chen, Q.; Suganthan, P.N. Novel benchmark functions for continuous multimodal optimization with comparative results. *Swarm Evol. Comput.* **2016**, *26*, 23–34. [CrossRef]
5. Li, X.; Epitropakis, M.G.; Deb, K.; Engelbrecht, A. Seeking multiple solutions: An updated survey on niching methods and their applications. *IEEE Trans. Evol. Comput.* **2017**, *21*, 518–538. [CrossRef]
6. Koper, K.D.; Wysession, M.E.; Wiens, D.A. Multimodal function optimization with a niching genetic algorithm: A seismological example. *Bull. Seismol. Soc. Am.* **1999**, *89*, 978–988. [CrossRef]
7. Kronfeld, M.; Dräger, A.; Aschoff, M.; Zell, A. On the benefits of multimodal optimization for metabolic network modeling. In Proceedings of the German Conference on Bioinformatics 2009. Gesellschaft für Informatik eV, Halle (Saale), Germany, 28–30 September 2009.
8. Pérez, E.; Posada, M.; Herrera, F. Analysis of new niching genetic algorithms for finding multiple solutions in the job shop scheduling. *J. Intell. Manuf.* **2012**, *23*, 341–356. [CrossRef]
9. Preuss, M.; Burelli, P.; Yannakakis, G.N. Diversified virtual camera composition. In Proceedings of the European Conference on the Applications of Evolutionary Computation, Malaga, Spain, 11–13 April 2012; Springer: Berlin/Heidelberg, Germany, 2012, pp. 265–274.
10. Kamyab, S.; Eftekhari, M. Feature selection using multimodal optimization techniques. *Neurocomputing* **2016**, *171*, 586–597. [CrossRef]
11. Beasley, D.; Bull, D.R.; Martin, R.R. A sequential niche technique for multimodal function optimization. *Evol. Comput.* **1993**, *1*, 101–125. [CrossRef]
12. Parsopoulos, K.E.; Vrahatis, M.N. On the computation of all global minimizers through particle swarm optimization. *IEEE Trans. Evol. Comput.* **2004**, *8*, 211–224. [CrossRef]
13. Vitela, J.E.; Castaños, O. A sequential niching memetic algorithm for continuous multimodal function optimization. *Appl. Math. Comput.* **2012**, *218*, 8242–8259. [CrossRef]
14. Zhang, J.; Huang, D.S.; Lok, T.M.; Lyu, M.R. A novel adaptive sequential niche technique for multimodal function optimization. *Neurocomputing* **2006**, *69*, 2396–2401. [CrossRef]
15. Li, L.; Hong-Qi, L.; Shao-Long, X. Particle swarm multi_optimizer for locating all local solutions. In Proceedings of the 2008 IEEE Congress on Evolutionary Computation (IEEE World Congress on Computational Intelligence), Hong Kong, China, 1–6 June 2008, pp. 1040–1046.
16. Srinivas, M.; Patnaik, L.M. Genetic algorithms: A survey. *Computer* **1994**, *27*, 17–26. [CrossRef]
17. Kennedy, J.; Eberhart, R. Particle swarm optimization. In Proceedings of the IEEE International Conference on Neural Networks, Perth, WA, Australia, 27 November–1 December 1995; Volume 4, pp. 1942–1948.
18. Storn, R.; Price, K. Differential evolution—A simple and efficient heuristic for global optimization over continuous spaces. *J. Glob. Optim.* **1997**, *11*, 341–359. [CrossRef]
19. Deb, K.; Pratap, A.; Agarwal, S.; Meyarivan, T. A fast and elitist multiobjective genetic algorithm: NSGA-II. *IEEE Trans. Evol. Comput.* **2002**, *6*, 182–197. [CrossRef]
20. Pétrowski, A. A clearing procedure as a niching method for genetic algorithms. In Proceedings of the 3rd IEEE International Conference on Evolutionary Computation (ICEC'96), Nayoya University, Nayoya, Japan, 20–22 May 1996; pp. 798–803.
21. Singh, G.; Deb, K. Comparison of multi-modal optimization algorithms based on evolutionary algorithms. In Proceedings of the 8th Annual Conference on Genetic and eVolutionary Computation, Seattle, WA, USA, 8–12 July 2006; pp. 1305–1312.
22. Goldberg, D.E.; Richardson, J. Genetic algorithms with sharing for multimodal function optimization. In Proceedings of the Second International Conference on Genetic algorithms and Their Applications, Hillsdale, NJ, USA, 28–31 July 1987; pp. 41–49.
23. Deb, K.; Goldberg, D.E. An investigation of niche and species formation in genetic function optimization. In Proceedings of the Third International Conference on Genetic Algorithms, San Francisco, CA, USA, 4–7 June 1989; pp. 42–50.
24. Goldberg, D.E.; Wang, L. Adaptive niching via coevolutionary sharing. *Genet. Algorithms Evol. Strategy Eng. Comput. Sci.* **1997**, *97007*, 21–38.
25. MacQueen, J. Some methods for classification and analysis of multivariate observations. In Proceedings of the Fifth Berkeley Symposium on Mathematical Statistics and Probability, University of California, Berkeley, CA, USA, 21 June–18 July 1965; Volume 1, pp. 281–297.
26. Yin, X.; Germay, N. A fast genetic algorithm with sharing scheme using cluster analysis methods in multimodal function optimization. In Proceedings of the Artificial Neural Nets and Genetic Algorithms, Innsbruck, Austria, 14–16 April 1993; pp. 450–457.
27. Mahfoud, S.W. Crowding and preselection revisited. In Proceedings of the PPSN, Amsterdam, The Netherlands, April 1992; Volume 2, pp. 27–36.
28. Mengshoel, O.J.; Goldberg, D.E. Probabilistic crowding: Deterministic crowding with probabilistic replacement. In Proceedings of the Genetic and Evolutionary Computation Conference (GECCO1999), Orlando, FL, USA, 13–17 July 1999; Volume 1, pp. 409–416.
29. Harik, G.R. Finding Multimodal Solutions Using Restricted Tournament Selection. In Proceedings of the ICGA, Pittsburgh, PA, USA, 15–19 July 1995; pp. 24–31.

30. Li, J.P.; Balazs, M.E.; Parks, G.T.; Clarkson, P.J. A species conserving genetic algorithm for multimodal function optimization. *Evol. Comput.* **2002**, *10*, 207–234. [CrossRef]
31. Li, J.P.; Wood, A. Random search with species conservation for multimodal functions. In Proceedings of the 2009 IEEE Congress on Evolutionary Computation, Trondheim, Norway, 18–21 May 2009; pp. 3164–3171.
32. Li, X. Niching without niching parameters: Particle swarm optimization using a ring topology. *IEEE Trans. Evol. Comput.* **2010**, *14*, 150–169. [CrossRef]
33. Eberhart, R.; Kennedy, J. A new optimizer using particle swarm theory. In Proceedings of the Sixth International, Symposium on Micro Machine and Human Science, Nagoya, Japan, 4–6 October 1995; pp. 39–43.
34. Das, S.; Maity, S.; Qu, B.Y.; Suganthan, P.N. Real-parameter evolutionary multimodal optimization—A survey of the state-of-the-art. *Swarm Evol. Comput.* **2011**, *1*, 71–88. [CrossRef]
35. Zhao, H.; Zhan, Z.H.; Lin, Y.; Chen, X.; Luo, X.N.; Zhang, J.; Kwong, S.; Zhang, J. Local binary pattern-based adaptive differential evolution for multimodal optimization problems. *IEEE Trans. Cybern.* **2019**, *50*, 3343–3357. [CrossRef]
36. Chen, Z.G.; Zhan, Z.H.; Wang, H.; Zhang, J. Distributed individuals for multiple peaks: A novel differential evolution for multimodal optimization problems. *IEEE Trans. Evol. Comput.* **2019**, *24*, 708–719. [CrossRef]
37. Wang, Z.J.; Zhan, Z.H.; Lin, Y.; Yu, W.J.; Wang, H.; Kwong, S.; Zhang, J. Automatic niching differential evolution with contour prediction approach for multimodal optimization problems. *IEEE Trans. Evol. Comput.* **2020**, *24*, 114–128. [CrossRef]
38. Tsutsui, S.; Fujimoto, Y.; Ghosh, A. Forking genetic algorithms: GAs with search space division schemes. *Evol. Comput.* **1997**, *5*, 61–80. [CrossRef] [PubMed]
39. Ursem, R.K. Multinational evolutionary algorithms. In Proceedings of the 1999 Congress on Evolutionary Computation-CEC99 (Cat. No. 99TH8406), Washington, DC, USA, 6–9 July 1999; Volume 3, pp. 1633–1640.
40. Siarry, P.; Pétrowski, A.; Bessaou, M. A multipopulation genetic algorithm aimed at multimodal optimization. *Adv. Eng. Softw.* **2002**, *33*, 207–213. [CrossRef]
41. Brits, R.; Engelbrecht, A.P.; Bergh, F.V.D. A niching particle swarm optimizer. In Proceedings of the 4th Asia-Pacific Conference on Simulated Evolution And Learning, Singapore, 18–22 November 2002; Volume 2.
42. Parrott, D.; Li, X. Locating and tracking multiple dynamic optima by a particle swarm model using speciation. *IEEE Trans. Evol. Comput.* **2006**, *10*, 440–458. [CrossRef]
43. Wang, J.; Xie, Y.; Xie, S.; Chen, X. Cooperative particle swarm optimizer with depth first search strategy for global optimization of multimodal functions. *Appl. Intell.* **2022**, *52*, 10161–10180. [CrossRef]
44. Lin, X.; Luo, W.; Xu, P.; Qiao, Y.; Yang, S. PopDMMO: A general framework of population-based stochastic search algorithms for dynamic multimodal optimization. *Swarm Evol. Comput.* **2022**, *68*, 101011. . [CrossRef]
45. Alami, J.; El Imrani, A.; Bouroumi, A. A multipopulation cultural algorithm using fuzzy clustering. *Appl. Soft Comput.* **2007**, *7*, 506–519. [CrossRef]
46. Yang, Q.; Chen, W.N.; Yu, Z.; Gu, T.; Li, Y.; Zhang, H.; Zhang, J. Adaptive multimodal continuous ant colony optimization. *IEEE Trans. Evol. Comput.* **2017**, *21*, 191–205. [CrossRef]
47. Wang, Z.J.; Zhan, Z.H.; Lin, Y.; Yu, W.J.; Zhang, J. Dual-strategy differential evolution with affinity propagation clustering for multimodal optimization problems. *IEEE Trans. Evol. Comput.* **2018**, *22*, 894–908. [CrossRef]
48. Bird, S.; Li, X. Adaptively choosing niching parameters in a PSO. In Proceedings of the 8th Annual Conference on Genetic and Evolutionary Computation, Seattle, WA, USA, 8–12 July 2006; pp. 3–10.
49. Shir, O.M.; Bäck, T. Niche radius adaptation in the cma-es niching algorithm. In *Parallel Problem Solving from Nature-PPSN IX*; Springer: Berlin/Heidelberg, Germany, 2006; pp. 142–151.
50. Nayak, S.; Kar, S.K.; Dash, S.S.; Vishnuram, P.; Thanikanti, S.B.; Nastasi, B. Enhanced Salp Swarm Algorithm for Multimodal Optimization and Fuzzy Based Grid Frequency Controller Design. *Energies* **2022**, *15*, 3210. . [CrossRef]
51. Yao, J.; Kharma, N.; Zhu, Y.Q. On clustering in evolutionary computation. In Proceedings of the 2006 IEEE International Conference on Evolutionary Computation, Vancouver, BC, Canada, 16–21 July 2006; pp. 1752–1759.
52. Wessing, S.; Preuss, M.; Rudolph, G. Niching by multiobjectivization with neighbor information: Trade-offs and benefits. In Proceedings of the 2013 IEEE Congress on Evolutionary Computation (CEC), Cancun, Mexico, 20–23 June 2013; pp. 103–110.
53. Yao, J.; Kharma, N.; Grogono, P. BMPGA: A bi-objective multi-population genetic algorithm for multi-modal function optimization. In Proceedings of the IEEE Congress on Evolutionary Computation, Edinburgh, UK, 2–4 September 2005; Volume 1, pp. 816–823.
54. Yao, J.; Kharma, N.; Grogono, P. Bi-objective multipopulation genetic algorithm for multimodal function optimization. *IEEE Trans. Evol. Comput.* **2010**, *14*, 80–102.
55. Deb, K.; Saha, A. Finding multiple solutions for multimodal optimization problems using a multi-objective evolutionary approach. In Proceedings of the 12th Annual Conference on Genetic and Evolutionary Computation, Portland, OR, USA, 7–11 July 2010; pp. 447–454.
56. Deb, K.; Saha, A. Multimodal optimization using a bi-objective evolutionary algorithm. *Evol. Comput.* **2012**, *20*, 27–62. [CrossRef] [PubMed]
57. Basak, A.; Das, S.; Tan, K.C. Multimodal optimization using a biobjective differential evolution algorithm enhanced with mean distance-based selection. *IEEE Trans. Evol. Comput.* **2013**, *17*, 666–685. [CrossRef]
58. Bandaru, S.; Deb, K. A parameterless-niching-assisted bi-objective approach to multimodal optimization. In Proceedings of the 2013 IEEE Congress on Evolutionary Computation (CEC), Cancun, Mexico, 20–23 June 2013; pp. 95–102.

59. Wang, Y.; Li, H.X.; Yen, G.G.; Song, W. MOMMOP: Multiobjective optimization for locating multiple optimal solutions of multimodal optimization problems. *IEEE Trans. Cybern.* **2015**, *45*, 830–843. [CrossRef] [PubMed]
60. Yu, W.J.; Ji, J.Y.; Gong, Y.J.; Yang, Q.; Zhang, J. A tri-objective differential evolution approach for multimodal optimization. *Inf. Sci.* **2018**, *423*, 1–23. [CrossRef]
61. Shi, L.; Olafsson, S. *Nested Partitions Method, Theory and Applications*; Springer: Berlin/Heidelberg, Germany, 2009.
62. Hong, L.J.; Nelson, B.L. Discrete optimization via simulation using COMPASS. *Oper. Res.* **2006**, *54*, 115–129. [CrossRef]
63. Xu, J.; Nelson, B.L.; Hong, L.J. An adaptive hyperbox algorithm for high-dimensional discrete optimization via simulation problems. *INFORMS J. Comput.* **2013**, *25*, 133–146. [CrossRef]
64. Zabinsky, Z.B.; Wang, W.; Prasetio, Y.; Ghate, A.; Yen, J.W. Adaptive probabilistic branch and bound for level set approximation. In Proceedings of the 2011 Winter Simulation Conference (WSC), Phoenix, AZ, USA, 11–14 December 2011; pp. 4146–4157.
65. Zabinsky, Z.B.; Huang, H. A partition-based optimization approach for level set approximation: Probabilistic branch and bound. In *Women in Industrial and Systems Engineering*; Springer: Berlin/Heidelberg, Germany, 2020; pp. 113–155.
66. Lin, Z.; Matta, A.; Du, S. A new partition-based random search method for deterministic optimization problems. In Proceedings of the 2019 Winter Simulation Conference (WSC), National Harbor, MD, USA, 8–11 December 2019; pp. 3504–3515.
67. Lin, Z.; Matta, A.; Du, S. A budget allocation strategy minimizing the sample set quantile for initial experimental design. *IISE Trans.* **2020**, *53*, 39–57. [CrossRef]
68. Cheng, R.; Li, M.; Li, K.; Yao, X. Evolutionary multiobjective optimization-based multimodal optimization: Fitness landscape approximation and peak detection. *IEEE Trans. Evol. Comput.* **2018**, *22*, 692–706. [CrossRef]
69. Li, X.; Engelbrecht, A.; Epitropakis, M.G. *Benchmark Functions for CEC'2013 Special Session and Competition on Niching Methods for Multimodal Function Optimization*; Technical Report; RMIT University, Evolutionary Computation and Machine Learning Group: Melbourne, Australia, 2013.
70. Socha, K.; Dorigo, M. Ant Colony Optimization For Continuous Domains. *Eur. J. Oper. Res.* **2008**, *185*, 1155–1173. [CrossRef]
71. Cheng, R.; Jin, Y. A competitive swarm optimizer for large scale optimization. *IEEE Trans. Cybern.* **2015**, *45*, 191–204. [CrossRef] [PubMed]
72. Ali, M.M.; Storey, C.; Torn, A. Application of stochastic global optimization algorithms to practical problems. *J. Optim. Theory Appl.* **1997**, *95*, 545–563. [CrossRef]

mathematics

MDPI

Article

MFO-SFR: An Enhanced Moth-Flame Optimization Algorithm Using an Effective Stagnation Finding and Replacing Strategy

Mohammad H. Nadimi-Shahraki [1,2,*], Hoda Zamani [1,2], Ali Fatahi [1,2] and Seyedali Mirjalili [3,4,*]

1 Faculty of Computer Engineering, Najafabad Branch, Islamic Azad University, Najafabad 8514143131, Iran
2 Big Data Research Center, Najafabad Branch, Islamic Azad University, Najafabad 8514143131, Iran
3 Centre for Artificial Intelligence Research and Optimisation, Torrens University Australia, Brisbane 4006, Australia
4 Yonsei Frontier Lab, Yonsei University, Seoul 03722, Republic of Korea
* Correspondence: nadimi@iaun.ac.ir (M.H.N.-S.); ali.mirjalili@torrens.edu.au (S.M.)

Abstract: Moth-flame optimization (MFO) is a prominent problem solver with a simple structure that is widely used to solve different optimization problems. However, MFO and its variants inherently suffer from poor population diversity, leading to premature convergence to local optima and losses in the quality of its solutions. To overcome these limitations, an enhanced moth-flame optimization algorithm named MFO-SFR was developed to solve global optimization problems. The MFO-SFR algorithm introduces an effective stagnation finding and replacing (SFR) strategy to effectively maintain population diversity throughout the optimization process. The SFR strategy can find stagnant solutions using a distance-based technique and replaces them with a selected solution from the archive constructed from the previous solutions. The effectiveness of the proposed MFO-SFR algorithm was extensively assessed in 30 and 50 dimensions using the CEC 2018 benchmark functions, which simulated unimodal, multimodal, hybrid, and composition problems. Then, the obtained results were compared with two sets of competitors. In the first comparative set, the MFO algorithm and its well-known variants, specifically LMFO, WCMFO, CMFO, ODSFMFO, SMFO, and WMFO, were considered. Five state-of-the-art metaheuristic algorithms, including PSO, KH, GWO, CSA, and HOA, were considered in the second comparative set. The results were then statistically analyzed through the Friedman test. Ultimately, the capacity of the proposed algorithm to solve mechanical engineering problems was evaluated with two problems from the latest CEC 2020 test-suite. The experimental results and statistical analysis confirmed that the proposed MFO-SFR algorithm was superior to the MFO variants and state-of-the-art metaheuristic algorithms for solving complex global optimization problems, with 91.38% effectiveness.

Keywords: global optimization problems; metaheuristic algorithms; moth-flame optimization; premature convergence; population diversity

MSC: 68T20

Citation: Nadimi-Shahraki, M.H.; Zamani, H.; Fatahi, A.; Mirjalili, S. MFO-SFR: An Enhanced Moth-Flame Optimization Algorithm Using an Effective Stagnation Finding and Replacing Strategy. *Mathematics* **2023**, *11*, 862. https://doi.org/10.3390/math11040862

Academic Editor: Jian Dong

Received: 2 December 2022
Revised: 22 January 2023
Accepted: 3 February 2023
Published: 8 February 2023

1. Introduction

Global optimization problems are complex and characterized by various properties, for instance, they can be non-linear, non-separable, symmetric, asymmetrical, smooth with narrow ridges, unimodal, and multimodal, and can involve non-differentiable functions and high dimensionality [1,2]. These properties create challenges for existing optimization algorithms, and finding the global optimum is one of the long-standing goals in this area of study. To overcome such challenges, a series of metaheuristic algorithms have been introduced using various innovative approaches. Metaheuristic algorithms have exhibited impressive performance in exploring the problem space and approximating the promising regions in reasonable timeframes. They have been widely improved upon and adapted to solve optimization problems in diverse fields such as computer science [3,4], engineering [5,6], and medicine [7–9]. Metaheuristic algorithms can be classified into two groups: single-solution-based and population-based algorithms [10,11]. Single-solution-based metaheuristic algorithms are more oriented towards exploitation searches and they manipulate a single solution during the optimization process, which increases its potential to easily become stuck in local optima [12]. To solve this challenge, population-based metaheuristic algorithms were developed to be more exploration-oriented and to share the information in order to promote significant diversification in the search space [13,14]. Based on the source of inspiration, these algorithms can be classified as evolutionary-based, physics-based, human-based, and swarm intelligence-based algorithms [15,16].

Evolutionary-based algorithms involve a heuristic approach inspired by the biological evolution of species, such as animals, insects, and plants in nature [17,18]. Some prominent optimizers in this group are genetic algorithms [19], differential evolution [20], and the evolution strategy [21]. Physics-based algorithms are defined based on the main concepts of mathematics and physics, such as quantum physics [22–24], gravity [25,26], and optics [27], with the aim of performing a meaningful search in the problem space. Human-based algorithms simulate various human activities in order to generate innovative solutions in solving optimization problems. The imperialist competitive algorithm [28], the harmony search algorithm [29], teaching learning-based optimization [30], brain storm optimization (BSO) [31], the soccer league competition algorithm [32], the volleyball premier league algorithm [33], poor and rich optimization (PRO) [34], and past present future (PPF) [35] are some of the state-of-the-art optimizers in this group. Swarm intelligence-based optimization algorithms originated from the collective and self-organized behavior of unsophisticated agents such as insects, terrestrial, fish, and birds [36,37]. Ant colony optimization [38] and particle swarm optimization [39] were the most successful swarm intelligence-based optimization algorithms proposed in the 1990s. From the 21st century onwards, some new algorithms have been put forward in this group, such as artificial bee colony (ABC) [40], cuckoo search (CS) [41], the whale optimization algorithm (WOA) [42], elephant herding optimization (EHO) [43], moth-flame optimization (MFO) [44], the horse herd optimization algorithm (HOA) [45], the quantum-based avian navigation optimizer algorithm (QANA) [46], the African vultures optimization algorithm [47], farmland fertility [48], dwarf mongoose optimization (DMO) [49], the starling murmuration optimizer (SMO) [50], and the artificial gorilla troops optimizer [51].

Most population-based metaheuristic algorithms lack mechanisms that can maintain population diversity and the imbalance between search strategies and premature convergence problems. Hence, many effective mechanisms have been proposed to alleviate the weaknesses of these algorithms [52,53]. The artificial bee colony algorithm (ABC) is a prominent population-based metaheuristic algorithm that suffers from poor local search performance. Hence, Zhu et al. [54] proposed the Gbest-guided ABC (GABC) algorithm to incorporate information on the global best solution into the search strategy in order to improve the ability to exploit the algorithm. Other algorithms that have achieved significant performance improvements in terms of their local search ability are the quick artificial bee colony (qABC), best-so-far ABC [55], and grey artificial bee colony (GABC) algorithms [56]. Nadimi-Shahraki et al. [57] introduced a diversity-maintained multi-trial vector-differential evolution algorithm to increase population diversity and suspend the risk of premature convergence during the evolutionary process.

The moth-flame optimization (MFO) algorithm was inspired by the navigation behavior of moths toward a light source in nature and is used to solve global optimization problems. The MFO algorithm benefits from having a straightforward structure and a small number of control parameters, which increases its versatility. However, the MFO algorithm suffers from problems related to low population diversity [58], which leads it to become stuck in unpromising regions and to achieve low-quality solutions. Many MFO variants have been developed by introducing and hybridizing different search strategies and operators to overcome such challenges. Kaur et al. [59] proposed an enhanced moth flame optimization (E-MFO) method to solve global optimization problems. The E-MFO algorithm applied a Cauchy distribution function and the influence of the best flame parameter to enhance its exploration and exploitation capabilities, respectively. Moreover, an adaptive step size and division of iterations were proposed to balance search strategies. Li et al. [60] presented the Lévy-flight moth-flame optimization (LMFO) algorithm to prevent premature convergence into local optima and enable a trade-off between the algorithm's exploration and exploitation abilities during the search process. Khalilpourazari et al. [61] introduced the WCMFO algorithm, which is a hybridized form of two algorithms, the water cycle and moth-flame optimization algorithms, to increase the exploitation ability of MFO and the exploration ability of the water cycle algorithm. To cope with the weaknesses of MFO, Hongwei et al. [62] proposed chaos-enhanced moth-flame optimization (CMFO) using ten chaotic maps. The chaotic maps are applied in population initialization, boundary handling, and the tuning of the distance parameter. Other variants of MFO are sine-cosine moth-flame optimization (SMFO) [63], combining MFO with Gaussian, Cauchy, and Lévy mutations (LGCMFO) [64], the enhancement of the local search mechanism based on shuffled frog leaping and a death mechanism with MFO (ODSFMFO) [65], and the chaotic local search and Gaussian mutation-enhanced MFO (CLSGMFO) approach [66].

Although the mentioned MFO variants have attained effective modifications in performance, they may still suffer from poor population diversity, which leads to premature convergence to local optima and a decrease in the quality of the algorithms' solutions when tackling complex optimization problems. Moreover, due to the approximate nature of metaheuristic algorithms, there is always an opportunity for improvement in their search strategies. Therefore, this study was devoted to proposing an enhanced moth-flame optimization algorithm named MFO-SFR with the aim of solving global optimization problems. The proposed MFO-SFR algorithm is equipped with an effective stagnation finding and replacing (SFR) strategy to establish diversity throughout the search process and overcome the drawbacks of previous MFO approaches. Moreover, the boundary handling of the MFO algorithm is rectified by generating new random solutions in the range of the problem space. Overall, the main contributions of this study can be summarized as follows.

- We propose the MFO-SFR algorithm, boosting the performance and enriching the diversity of the canonical MFO;
- We introduce an effective stagnation finding and replacing (SFR) strategy to boost the performance of the search process; and
- We introduce an archive to incorporate the representative and the global best flames throughout the search process in order to enrich the diversity.

The performance of the proposed MFO-SFR algorithm was assessed with the CEC 2018 test functions [67] in 30 and 50 dimensions. Then, the MFO-SFR algorithm was compared with two sets of MFO variants and well-known optimizers. In the first set of contender algorithms, the canonical MFO [44] and its variants— Lévy-flight moth-flame optimization LMFO [60], an efficient hybrid algorithm based on the water cycle and moth-flame algorithms (WCMFO) [61], chaos-enhanced moth-flame optimization (CMFO) [62], death mechanism-based moth–flame optimization (ODSFMFO) [65], the synthesis of the moth-flame optimizer with sine cosine mechanisms (SMFO) [63], and the hybrid of whale and moth-flame optimization (WMFO) [68]—were selected. In the second set, the particle swarm optimization (PSO) [39], krill herd (KH) [69], grey wolf optimization (GWO) [70], the crow search algorithm (CSA) [71], and the horse herd optimization algorithm (HOA) [45] were considered. Furthermore, the results obtained using the proposed and contender algorithms were statistically analyzed using the Friedman test. Ultimately, two well-known mechanical engineering problems from the CEC 2020 test suite [72] were considered to assess the applicability of MFO-SFR in solving real-world optimization problems. The experimental results indicated that the proposed MFO-SFR algorithm boosted the performance of the canonical MFO by using an effective stagnation finding and replacing (SFR) strategy and an archive construction mechanism. Moreover, the statistical analysis revealed that the performance of the proposed MFO-SFR algorithm was superior to that of the contender algorithms.

The structure of the paper is as follows. Section 2 contains a review of related literature. Section 3 presents the MFO algorithm. In Section 4, the proposed MFO-SFR algorithm is explained in detail. Section 5 thoroughly evaluates the MFO-SFR's performance in addressing CEC 2018 benchmark test functions. Section 6 evaluates the applicability of the proposed MFO-SFR using two real-world mechanical engineering problems from the latest CEC 2020 test suite. Finally, Section 6 summarizes the results and outlines possible future directions of research.

2. Related Works

MFO variants used to solve different optimization problems are reviewed in this section.

Li et al. [60] boosted the performance of the canonical MFO by using the Lévy-flight strategy. Nadimi-Shahraki et al. [73] proved that the canonical MFO suffers from premature convergence, low population diversity, and an imbalance between search strategies in solving global optimization problems. Therefore, they proposed an improved moth-flame optimization (I-MFO) algorithm to cope with the abovementioned deficiencies. The I-MFO algorithm is equipped with the adapted wandering-around search strategy to maintain population diversity and escape from local optima. The chaos-enhanced MFO (CMFO) [62] algorithm was proposed to improve the performance of the MFO algorithm by incorporating chaos maps into population initialization, boundary handling, and parameter tuning. Pelusi et al. [74] proposed the improved moth-flame optimization (IMFO) algorithm using a hybrid phase, a dynamic crossover mechanism, and a fitness-dependent weight factor. The hybrid phase achieved a good trade-off between the exploration and exploitation phases, the dynamic crossover mechanism enhanced the population diversity, and the fitness-dependent weight factor improved the exploitation phase.

Xu et al. [64] proposed a series of MFO variants by combining the standard MFO algorithm with Gaussian mutation, Cauchy mutation, and Lévy mutation. Gaussian mutation was employed to improve its neighborhood-informed capability, Cauchy mutation was used to enhance its global exploration ability, and the Lévy mutation was employed to increase the randomness in the search process. Li et al. [65] proposed the ODSFMFO algorithm, which consists of an improved flame generation mechanism based on opposition-based learning and the differential evolution algorithm, an enhanced local search mechanism based on the shuffled frog leaping algorithm and a death mechanism. This algorithm maintained the quality of the population through opposition-based learning, population diversity using the differential evolution algorithm, the global search ability through the use of the shuffled frog leaping algorithm, and provided an escape from local optima via the use of the death mechanism. Nadimi-Shahraki et al. [75] proposed a migration-based moth–flame optimization (M-MFO) algorithm with a random migration operator, a guided migration operator, and a guiding archive to alleviate the low population diversity and poor exploration ability of MFO.

Ma et al. [76] developed an improved moth-flame optimization algorithm to prevent premature convergence to local minima. This algorithm uses the inertia weight of diversity feedback control to strike a balance between search strategies and maintain population diversity. Moreover, the mutation probability was added to improve the optimization performance. To enhance the diversity in the position of flames and the search strategy used for moths, Zhao et al. [77] developed an improved MFO (IMFO) algorithm. In this algorithm, the flames are generated through orthogonal opposition-based learning, and their positions are updated using a linear search and a mutation operator. Sapre et al. [78] introduced an opposition-based moth flame optimization method with Cauchy mutation and evolutionary boundary constraint handling (OMFO) to bypass the local optima and accelerate the convergence speed towards promising areas. Sahoo et al. [79] proposed a modified dynamic-opposite-learning-based MFO algorithm named m-MFO, using a modified dynamic-opposite learning strategy to enrich the performance of MFO in solving optimization problems. Other MFO variants include the double-evolutionary learning MFO algorithm (DELMFO) [80], the improved moth-flame optimization algorithm (IMFO) [81], the hybrid MFO and hill climbing (MFOHC) method [82], an enhanced MFO algorithm integrated with orthogonal learning and the Broyden–Fletcher–Goldfarb–Shanno (BFGSOLMFO) method [83], and quantum-behaved simulated annealing algorithm-based moth-flame optimization (QSMFO) [84].

Due to the simple structure of MFO and its low number of control parameters, it has great potential to solve real-world applications. However, the canonical MFO critically suffers from local optimum trapping and premature convergence during the optimization process, which results in low-quality solutions [85–87]. Therefore, many improved and hybrid variants have been developed to overcome these challenges. Sayed et al. [88] presented the SA-MFO algorithm, a hybrid of the MFO approach and the simulated annealing (SA) algorithm, to escape from local optima using SA and accelerate the search process using MFO. Many researchers have applied the MFO algorithm to solve the optimal power flow (OPF) problem [89–91]. An effective hybridization of the whale optimization algorithm and a modified moth-flame optimization algorithm named WMFO [68] was proposed to solve diverse scales of the OPF problem. Sahoo et al. [92] proposed a hybrid MFO and butterfly optimization algorithm (h-MFOBOA) to overcome shortcomings such as a slow convergence speed and poor exploitation ability in both optimizers. Sattar Khan et al. [93] adapted the MFO algorithm for an integrated power plant system containing stochastic wind. MFO has been applied to the solution of problems related to fuel cells in a renewable active distribution network [94], the identification of parameters for photovoltaic modules [95], and fuel consumption in variable-cycle engines [96], with promising results.

3. Moth-Flame Optimization (MFO) Algorithm

Nocturnal moths use celestial light sources to navigate over long distances accurately. They fly in a straight line with a constant angle toward the Moon or stars, and this behavior is called transverse orientation. However, when a moth flies toward a nearby artificial light, it thinks it is a star or the Moon. Therefore, the moth continually changes its flight angle to keep going in a straight line toward the light, resulting in a spiral motion around the artificial light. In 2015, this behavior was mathematically modeled in the moth-flame optimization algorithm [44] developed by Mirjalili to solve the global optimization problem, described in detail as follows.

In this approach to solving the optimization problem, the positions of moths evolve during predefined iterations. In the first iteration, moths are randomly distributed in the problem space using Equation (1), where X_{id} denotes the dth dimension of the ith moth position and the parameters Ub_d and Lb_d are the upper and lower boundaries for the dth dimension, respectively.

$$X_{id} = rand_{i,d} \times (Ub_d - Lb_d) + Lb_d, \qquad 1 \leq d \leq D \tag{1}$$

For the rest of the iterations, their new positions are updated based on the position of the flame. Therefore, the flame number (R) is computed using Equation (2), where the parameters N and $MaxIterations$ denote the number of moths and the maximum number of iterations, respectively. Then, the positions of the flames are determined based on the stepwise procedure denoted in Table 1.

$$R = round\left(N - t \times \frac{N-1}{MaxIterations}\right) \tag{2}$$

Ultimately, for the flame number (R), each moth can update its position using the two different trials denoted in Equation (3), where $X_i\ (t+1)$ is the new position of the ith moth, $D_i'(t)$ is computed using Equation (4), b is the constant value, k is calculated using Equations (5) and (6), and F_i (t) denotes the ith flame.

$$RX_i(t+1) = \begin{cases} D_i'(t) \times e^{bk} \times cos(2\pi k) + F_i(t) & i \leq R \\ D_i''(t) \times e^{bk} \times cos(2\pi k) + F_R(t) & i > R \end{cases} \tag{3}$$

$$D_i'(t) = |F_i(t) - X_i(t)| \tag{4}$$

$$k = (a-1) \times rand(0,1) + 1 \tag{5}$$

$$a = -1 + t \times \left(\frac{-1}{MaxIterations} \right) \tag{6}$$

In the second trial (when $i > R$), the parameter $D_i''(t)$ is computed using Equation (7), and F_R (t) is the current position of the Rth flame.

$$D_i'(t) = |F_R(t) - X_i(t)| \tag{7}$$

Table 1. Flame construction procedure.

Input: X: the positions of moths, Fit: the fitness values of moths, F: the position of the flame, and OF: the fitness values of flames.
Flame construction in the first iteration when $t = 1$. 1. Sort the vector Fit in ascending order and extract the sorted index in $\{j_1, j_2, \ldots, j_N\}$. 2. Construct the flame matrix $F(t) = \{F_1 \leftarrow X_{j1}, F_2 \leftarrow X_{j2}, \ldots, F_N \leftarrow X_{jN}\}$. Flame construction for the rest iteration when $t > 1$. 1. Construct matrix $dual_{Pop}$ by combining matrices $F(t)$ and $X(t-1)$. 2. Construct vector $dual_{Fit}$ by combining vectors $OF(t)$ and $Fit(t-1)$. 3. Sort the vector $dual_{Fit}$ in ascending order and extract the sorted index in $\{j_1, j_2, \ldots, j_{2N}\}$. 4. Construct the flame matrix $F(t) = \{F_1 \leftarrow X_{j1}, F_2 \leftarrow X_{j2}, \ldots, F_N \leftarrow X_{jN}\}$.

4. The Proposed MFO-SFR Algorithm

According to the literature, the canonical MFO lacks an efficient operator to maintain population diversity. The search process may be biased by the best solutions obtained in each iteration [97]. This deficiency leads to premature convergence into unpromising regions, local optimum stagnation, and a decrease in the solution quality when solving complex problems. Hence, in this study, we were motivated to propose an enhanced moth-flame optimization algorithm named MFO-SFR to effectively maintain population diversity and mitigate the deficiencies mentioned above by introducing an effective stagnation finding and replacing (SFR) strategy.

Stagnation finding and replacing (SFR) strategy: Suppose that the matrix $X(t) = \{X_{1D}(t), \ldots, X_{iD}(t), \ldots, X_{ND}(t)\}$ denotes a moth population in the current iteration t in a D-dimensional search space. Each vector $X_{iD}(t)$ denotes the position of the ith moth in the problem space. The matrix $X(t)$ is initialized for the first iteration using a uniform random distribution. For the rest of the iterations (when $t \geq 2$), the new positions of the moths are determined using Equation (8), where $D_i^{\alpha}(t)$ and $D_i^{\beta}(t)$ are the main elements of the SFR strategy, which is computed using Equations (9) and (10), respectively. A constant b expresses the shape of the logarithmic spiral, and τ is a random number between the intervals -1 and 1. $F_j(t)$ and $F_R(t)$ are the positions of the jth flame and the Rth flame such that the parameter R is computed using Equation (2). In Equation (9), vector $M_i(t)$ is determined using Definition 1. To find the stagnant solutions, the mean of the distance or φ_i is calculated using Equation (11), where X_{iq} is the qth dimension of the ith moth. F_{jq} is the qth dimension of the jth flame in which the index j is determined by Equation (12), which sorts the results obtained from Equation (11) in descending order to obtain the indexes, then applies them as flame indexes in Equation (10).

$$X_i(t+1) = \begin{cases} D_i^{\alpha}(t) \times e^{b\tau} \times cos(2\pi t) + F_j(t) & if\ i \leq R(t) \\ D_i^{\beta}(t) \times e^{b\tau} \times cos(2\pi t) + F_R(t) & else \end{cases} \quad (8)$$

$$D_i^{\alpha}(t) = |F_j(t) - M_i(t)| \quad (9)$$

$$D_i^{\beta}(t) = \begin{cases} |F_j(t) - X_i(t)| & \varphi_i > 0 \\ Selecting\ a\ random\ position\ from\ the\ Arc & \varphi_i = 0 \end{cases} \quad (10)$$

$$\{\varphi_1, \ldots, \varphi_i, \ldots, \varphi_N\} \leftarrow \varphi_i = \frac{1}{D} \times \sum_{q=1}^{D} |F_{jq}(t) - X_{iq}(t)| \quad (11)$$

$$\{\varphi_1, \ldots, \varphi_j, \ldots, \varphi_N\} \leftarrow \text{Sort}(\varphi_1, \ldots, \varphi_i, \ldots, \varphi_N) \quad (12)$$

Definition 1. (*Archive construction*): *The main idea behind archive construction is to enrich the population diversity by preserving the generated representative flame and boost the convergence of solutions toward promising areas by preserving the best solutions in each iteration. To construct the archive Arc, consider the matrix* $M = \{M_1, \ldots, M_i, \ldots, M_\kappa\}$ *as the memory of the Arc with predefined* κ. *Each* $M_i = [m_{i1}, m_{i2}, \ldots, m_{iD}]$ *denotes this memory's vector position, which is generated using Algorithm 1. First,* $dual_{Pop}$ *and* $dual_{Fit}$ *are created based on the flame construction process described in* Table 1. *Then, the representative flame (RF) with the average of flames' positions is computed using Equation (13), where C is the total number of considered moths and* F_{id} *denotes the dth dimension of the ith flame. Finally, the global best flame and RF position are archived as two new entries in the memory M. In regard to inserting these new entries; they are randomly replaced with two existing entries if the memory is full.*

$$RF_d(t) = \frac{1}{C} \sum_{i=1}^{C} F_{id}(t) \quad (13)$$

In addition, MFO-SFR checks the feasibility of the position of the new moths to return those that have violated the problem space boundaries by generating random positions in the range of the problem space.

Algorithm 1. The pseudocode of the archive construction process.

Input: C: Number of considered flames, and κ: the maximum size of the archive *Arc*.
Output: Returns the archive *Arc*.
begin
$dual_{Pop}$ and $dual_{Fit}$ are created based on flame construction defined in Table 1.
Fit_{Best} = Ascending order of the vector $dual_{Fit}$ and selecting the best N values.
Pop_{Best} = The corresponding positions of vector Fit_{Best}.
Computing *RF* using Equation (13) for C number of considered flames.
If the current memory size < $\kappa-1$.
    Inserting *RF* and the global best flame into the Arc.
else
    Replacing *RF* and the global best flame with two existing memory entries.
end if
end

Complexity Analysis

Regarding the pseudocode of MFO-SFR shown in Algorithm 2, the MFO-SFR algorithm consists of six distinct phases: initialization, flame construction, archive construction, movement, correcting the violated positions, and updating the positions. In the initialization phase, N moths are randomly distributed in a D-dimensional search space with an O(ND) computational complexity. In the flame construction phase, flames are constructed differently with the computational complexity of O(N^2), considering the worst case for the quicksort algorithm. The computational complexity of the archive construction phase using Algorithm 1 is O(N^2 + ND), because lines 2−4 have the complexity of O(N^2) with respect to the original paper's definition of MFO, and Equation (13) has O(ND) in the worst case. The cost of the movement phase is O(ND), using either Equations (8) and (9) when $i \leq R$ or using Equations (8) and (10) when $i > R$. Then, the feasibility of the new positions is checked to correct the violated positions with the computational complexity of O(ND). Finally, the updating phase is performed with O(ND) computational complexity. Therefore, considering T iterations, the computational complexity of MFO-SFR is O(ND + N^2 + T($2N^2$ + $4ND$) or O(TN^2 + TND). In the same fashion, the space complexity is O(N + ND + κ), considering that the memory is reusable and the size of the memory is κ. Thus, the space complexity of MFO-SFR is O(ND + $D^2 log$ N).

Algorithm 2. The pseudocode of the proposed MFO-SFR algorithm.

```
Input: N: Number of moths, MaxIterations: Maximum iterations, and D: Dimension size.
Output: Returns the position of the global best flame and its fitness value.
Begin
Initiating matrix X (t) using a uniform random distribution in the D-dimensional search space.
Computing the fitness value of X (t) and storing them in vector OX (t).
Constructing the flame fitness value OF by ascending order of the vector OM (t).
Constructing the flame positions F based on their obtained vector OF.
While t ≤ MaxIterations
  Updating F and OF by the best N moths from F and current X.
  Computing the flame number R using Equation (2).
  Archiving using Algorithm 1.
  For i = 1: N
    If i ≤ R
      Computing the distance between flame F_i (t) and M_i (t) using Equation (9).
      Updating the position of X_i (t) using Equation (8).
    else
      Computing the distance using Equation (10).
      Updating the position of X_i (t) using Equation (8).
    End if
    Checking the feasibility and correcting the new position.
    Computing the fitness value of the new position.
  End for
  Updating the global best flame.
End while
```

5. Evaluation of the Proposed MFO-SFR Algorithm

In this section we present our evaluation of the performance of the proposed MFO-SFR algorithm in solving global optimization problems from the CEC 2018 benchmark test suite [67]. This test suite is suitable for evaluating the proposed algorithm in terms of its local optimum avoidance ability and the diversity of solutions as it consists of 29 test functions with different characteristics, such as unimodal, multimodal, and hybrid functions, as well as compositions with various dimensions (D), specifically, 30 and 50 dimensions. Moreover, in this section, we also present two separate sets of experiments conducted to extensively assess and compare the performance of the proposed MFO-SFR algorithm with several well-known optimization methods. The proposed algorithm was compared to the original MFO and its variants in the first set, and then, in the second experimental set, it was compared to other prominent and recent optimizers. In both experiment sets, all comparative algorithms' control parameter values were adjusted to match those in their original articles, as depicted in Table 2. All of the algorithms were executed 20 times on a laptop with an Intel Core i7-10750H CPU (2.60 GHz), 24 GB of memory, and MATLAB R2022a with a maximum of $(D \times 10^4)/N$ iterations, where D represents the dimension size of the problem and N is the population size, which was set to 100 in this study.

Table 2. Parameter values for the optimization algorithms.

Alg.	Parameter Settings
MFO	$b = 1$, a decreased linearly from -1 to -2.
LMFO	$\beta = 1.5$, μ and v are normal distributions, Γ is the gamma function.
WCMFO	The number of rivers and seas = 4.
CMFO	$b = 1$, a decreased linearly from -1 to -2, chaotic map = Singer.
ODSFMFO	$m = 6, pc = 0.5, \gamma = 5, \alpha = 1, l = 10, b = 1, \beta = 1.5$.
SMFO	r_4 = random number between the interval (0, 1).
WMFO	α decreased linearly from 2 to 0, $b = 1$.
PSO	$c_1 = c_2 = 2, vmax = 6, w = 0.9$.
KH	$V_f = 0.02, D_{max} = 0.005, N_{max} = 0.01, Sr = 0$.
GWO	The parameter a decreased linearly from 2 to 0.
CSA	$AP = 0.1, fl = 2$.
HOA	$w = 1, \delta_D = 0.02, \delta_I = 0.02, g_\delta = 1.5, h_\beta = 0.9, h_\gamma = 0.5, s_\beta = 0.2, s_\gamma = 0.1, i_\gamma = 0.3,$ $d_\alpha = 0.5, d_\beta = 0.2, d_\gamma = 0.1, r_\delta = 0.1, r_\gamma = 0.05$
MFO-SFR	$b = 1$, a decreased linearly from -1 to -2, κ = round $(D^2 \times (log\ N))$, $C = N/5$.

To investigate the impact of the archive introduced in Equation (10), a numerical pretest was performed on the canonical MFO algorithm using the CEC 2018 benchmark test suite on dimension 30. In this pre-test percentage of situations when the parameter φ_i was equal to zero is computed and reported in Table A1 of Appendix A. The results reported in Table A1 in Appendix A showed that for some test functions, especially hybrid and composition ones, the percentage of stagnant solutions was high enough to affect the quality of the generated solutions.

5.1. Comparing the Proposed MFO-SFR Algorithm with MFO Variants

In this set of experiments, we compared the proposed MFO-SFR algorithm with moth-flame optimization (MFO) [44] and its variants, including LMFO [60], WCMFO [61], CMFO [62], ODSFMFO [65], SMFO [63], and WMFO [68]. Table 3 compares the results of the proposed MFO-SFR algorithm with those of MFO and its variants in solving the CEC 2018 test functions with 30 dimensions. The results acquired from the unimodal test functions F_1 and F_3 demonstrated that MFO-SFR had an acceptable exploitation potential compared to the other algorithms. The results from multimodal test functions F_4–F_{10} indicated that the proposed algorithm was able to efficiently search the problem space and find the unvisited areas by maintaining its population diversity throughout the optimization process. The overall results of the hybrid and composition functions F_{11}–F_{30} confirmed that MFO-SFR avoided local optimum solutions by striking a balance between exploration and exploitation abilities. Moreover, the final rows of Tables 3 and 4 reveal that according to the Friedman test [98], the proposed MFO-SFR algorithm ranked first among the algorithms, including MFO and the other investigated variants.

Table 3. Comparison of MFO-SFR with MFO variants for CEC 2018 test functions with D = 30.

F.	Metrics	MFO	LMFO	WCMFO	CMFO	ODSFMFO	SMFO	WMFO	MFO-SFR
F_1	Avg	6.278×10^9	2.544×10^7	1.317×10^4	1.078×10^8	6.016×10^6	3.119×10^{10}	3.822×10^3	1.791×10^3
	Min	1.027×10^9	1.899×10^7	1.924×10^3	3.760×10^6	9.949×10^5	1.734×10^{10}	1.013×10^2	1.017×10^2
F_3	Avg	9.453×10^4	3.473×10^3	1.541×10^3	5.059×10^4	3.050×10^4	8.300×10^4	3.909×10^2	1.312×10^4
	Min	1.203×10^4	1.499×10^3	3.111×10^2	2.945×10^4	1.631×10^4	7.186×10^4	3.007×10^2	7.513×10^3
F_4	Avg	8.558×10^2	4.919×10^2	4.846×10^2	6.960×10^2	5.356×10^2	5.612×10^3	4.810×10^2	4.914×10^2
	Min	4.991×10^2	4.742×10^2	4.009×10^2	5.139×10^2	4.985×10^2	2.322×10^3	4.249×10^2	4.700×10^2

Table 3. *Cont.*

F.	Metrics	MFO	LMFO	WCMFO	CMFO	ODSFMFO	SMFO	WMFO	MFO-SFR
F_5	Avg	6.740×10^2	6.300×10^2	6.721×10^2	6.073×10^2	5.506×10^2	8.725×10^2	6.739×10^2	5.227×10^2
	Min	6.114×10^2	5.816×10^2	6.126×10^2	5.736×10^2	5.270×10^2	8.105×10^2	6.234×10^2	5.109×10^2
F_6	Avg	6.260×10^2	6.030×10^2	6.236×10^2	6.189×10^2	6.037×10^2	6.814×10^2	6.366×10^2	6.000×10^2
	Min	6.113×10^2	6.018×10^2	6.137×10^2	6.086×10^2	6.010×10^2	6.571×10^2	6.143×10^2	6.000×10^2
F_7	Avg	1.007×10^3	8.716×10^2	9.050×10^2	9.430×10^2	8.099×10^2	1.359×10^3	1.056×10^3	7.669×10^2
	Min	8.538×10^2	8.311×10^2	8.045×10^2	8.684×10^2	7.824×10^2	1.198×10^3	9.248×10^2	7.460×10^2
F_8	Avg	9.895×10^2	9.375×10^2	9.839×10^2	9.097×10^2	8.528×10^2	1.093×10^3	9.539×10^2	8.209×10^2
	Min	9.126×10^2	8.978×10^2	9.344×10^2	8.645×10^2	8.343×10^2	1.052×10^3	8.547×10^2	8.090×10^2
F_9	Avg	6.219×10^3	9.256×10^2	8.623×10^3	2.331×10^3	1.118×10^3	9.431×10^3	4.543×10^3	9.038×10^2
	Min	3.323×10^3	9.074×10^2	5.118×10^3	1.476×10^3	9.647×10^2	7.359×10^3	1.675×10^3	9.005×10^2
F_{10}	Avg	5.259×10^3	4.240×10^3	4.848×10^3	5.005×10^3	4.332×10^3	8.272×10^3	5.192×10^3	4.062×10^3
	Min	4.231×10^3	3.205×10^3	4.003×10^3	4.204×10^3	3.570×10^3	7.449×10^3	3.759×10^3	2.461×10^3
F_{11}	Avg	3.967×10^3	1.314×10^3	1.363×10^3	1.985×10^3	1.284×10^3	5.799×10^3	1.248×10^3	1.143×10^3
	Min	1.370×10^3	1.180×10^3	1.252×10^3	1.206×10^3	1.204×10^3	2.547×10^3	1.170×10^3	1.107×10^3
F_{12}	Avg	9.043×10^7	5.251×10^6	1.416×10^6	2.113×10^7	2.157×10^6	4.342×10^9	1.014×10^5	1.508×10^5
	Min	7.305×10^4	1.578×10^6	3.718×10^4	7.171×10^5	2.328×10^5	2.607×10^9	6.932×10^3	2.035×10^4
F_{13}	Avg	4.593×10^6	4.072×10^5	9.457×10^4	9.006×10^3	1.184×10^4	7.405×10^8	6.660×10^3	6.405×10^3
	Min	1.003×10^4	1.634×10^5	1.150×10^4	2.446×10^3	1.596×10^3	1.145×10^8	1.400×10^3	1.690×10^3
F_{14}	Avg	6.942×10^4	2.500×10^4	1.872×10^4	3.941×10^4	5.651×10^4	1.715×10^6	1.406×10^4	8.200×10^3
	Min	5.450×10^3	2.821×10^3	4.075×10^3	6.379×10^3	4.686×10^3	7.879×10^4	3.027×10^3	2.021×10^3
F_{15}	Avg	3.090×10^4	8.218×10^4	3.207×10^4	5.756×10^3	5.070×10^3	4.161×10^7	1.157×10^4	5.614×10^3
	Min	5.117×10^3	4.614×10^4	2.547×10^3	1.707×10^3	1.703×10^3	1.868×10^6	1.609×10^3	1.515×10^3
F_{16}	Avg	2.956×10^3	2.564×10^3	2.867×10^3	2.709×10^3	2.366×10^3	4.223×10^3	2.662×10^3	1.855×10^3
	Min	2.398×10^3	2.101×10^3	2.267×10^3	2.241×10^3	1.965×10^3	3.565×10^3	2.068×10^3	1.617×10^3
F_{17}	Avg	2.349×10^3	2.192×10^3	2.315×10^3	2.056×10^3	1.985×10^3	2.788×10^3	2.234×10^3	1.745×10^3
	Min	1.975×10^3	1.925×10^3	1.942×10^3	1.818×10^3	1.764×10^3	2.359×10^3	1.958×10^3	1.727×10^3
F_{18}	Avg	2.830×10^6	2.674×10^5	1.804×10^5	7.780×10^5	8.975×10^5	5.330×10^7	8.188×10^4	1.493×10^5
	Min	7.725×10^4	3.452×10^4	4.774×10^4	7.998×10^4	9.364×10^4	2.825×10^6	6.883×10^3	4.305×10^4
F_{19}	Avg	4.261×10^6	7.040×10^4	3.083×10^4	2.505×10^4	7.822×10^3	7.588×10^7	1.560×10^4	6.534×10^3
	Min	1.293×10^4	3.487×10^4	2.168×10^3	3.280×10^3	1.968×10^3	5.192×10^6	2.310×10^3	1.910×10^3
F_{20}	Avg	2.537×10^3	2.398×10^3	2.528×10^3	2.402×10^3	2.287×10^3	2.837×10^3	2.690×10^3	2.091×10^3
	Min	2.215×10^3	2.117×10^3	2.103×10^3	2.185×10^3	2.053×10^3	2.454×10^3	2.294×10^3	2.004×10^3
F_{21}	Avg	2.472×10^3	2.439×10^3	2.485×10^3	2.384×10^3	2.351×10^3	2.630×10^3	2.462×10^3	2.321×10^3
	Min	2.420×10^3	2.378×10^3	2.430×10^3	2.338×10^3	2.331×10^3	2.363×10^3	2.389×10^3	2.312×10^3
F_{22}	Avg	6.353×10^3	4.878×10^3	6.611×10^3	2.380×10^3	2.319×10^3	8.681×10^3	5.292×10^3	2.300×10^3
	Min	3.223×10^3	2.325×10^3	5.330×10^3	2.319×10^3	2.305×10^3	5.677×10^3	2.300×10^3	2.300×10^3
F_{23}	Avg	2.811×10^3	2.754×10^3	2.796×10^3	2.797×10^3	2.722×10^3	3.273×10^3	2.861×10^3	2.671×10^3
	Min	2.740×10^3	2.724×10^3	2.749×10^3	2.734×10^3	2.697×10^3	3.027×10^3	2.763×10^3	2.654×10^3
F_{24}	Avg	2.979×10^3	2.924×10^3	2.972×10^3	2.948×10^3	2.872×10^3	3.482×10^3	3.003×10^3	2.844×10^3
	Min	2.926×10^3	2.888×10^3	2.927×10^3	2.887×10^3	2.848×10^3	3.217×10^3	2.912×10^3	2.828×10^3
F_{25}	Avg	3.181×10^3	2.888×10^3	2.894×10^3	3.011×10^3	2.925×10^3	3.972×10^3	2.900×10^3	2.887×10^3
	Min	2.895×10^3	2.885×10^3	2.884×10^3	2.935×10^3	2.890×10^3	3.467×10^3	2.884×10^3	2.887×10^3
F_{26}	Avg	5.650×10^3	4.854×10^3	5.538×10^3	4.465×10^3	4.415×10^3	9.093×10^3	5.841×10^3	3.903×10^3
	Min	4.921×10^3	4.504×10^3	5.074×10^3	3.113×10^3	2.876×10^3	5.057×10^3	4.741×10^3	3.739×10^3
F_{27}	Avg	3.233×10^3	3.223×10^3	3.229×10^3	3.285×10^3	3.244×10^3	3.754×10^3	3.276×10^3	3.219×10^3
	Min	3.206×10^3	3.194×10^3	3.204×10^3	3.238×10^3	3.218×10^3	3.538×10^3	3.220×10^3	3.208×10^3
F_{28}	Avg	3.756×10^3	3.270×10^3	3.192×10^3	3.376×10^3	3.294×10^3	5.462×10^3	3.199×10^3	3.216×10^3
	Min	3.263×10^3	3.211×10^3	3.100×10^3	3.265×10^3	3.271×10^3	4.419×10^3	3.122×10^3	3.196×10^3

Table 3. *Cont.*

F.	Metrics	MFO	LMFO	WCMFO	CMFO	ODSFMFO	SMFO	WMFO	MFO-SFR
F_{29}	Avg	4.014×10^3	3.764×10^3	3.949×10^3	4.040×10^3	3.691×10^3	5.639×10^3	4.068×10^3	3.414×10^3
	Min	3.499×10^3	3.410×10^3	3.574×10^3	3.629×10^3	3.475×10^3	4.728×10^3	3.545×10^3	3.323×10^3
F_{30}	Avg	2.524×10^5	1.426×10^5	3.318×10^4	7.742×10^5	1.803×10^4	2.326×10^8	1.079×10^4	7.835×10^3
	Min	7.219×10^3	6.606×10^4	1.642×10^4	5.609×10^4	7.769×10^3	2.468×10^7	5.674×10^3	6.362×10^3
Average rank		6.06	3.95	4.51	4.57	3.28	7.91	4.18	1.55
Total rank		7	3	5	6	2	8	4	1

Table 4. Comparison of MFO-SFR with MFO variants for CEC 2018 test functions with D = 50.

F.	Metrics	MFO	LMFO	WCMFO	CMFO	ODSFMFO	SMFO	WMFO	MFO-SFR
F_1	Avg	3.036×10^{10}	1.091×10^8	6.099×10^4	1.323×10^9	2.624×10^8	7.209×10^{10}	4.264×10^3	3.463×10^4
	Min	7.064×10^3	8.074×10^7	8.054×10^2	1.287×10^8	3.470×10^7	5.140×10^{10}	1.054×10^2	9.385×3
F_3	Avg	1.540×10^5	3.139×10^4	1.413×10^4	1.004×10^5	9.325×10^4	1.770×10^5	9.948×10^2	5.495×10^4
	Min	1.176×10^4	1.960×10^4	2.418×10^3	7.381×10^4	6.538×10^4	1.457×10^5	3.217×10^2	4.223×10^4
F_4	Avg	4.178×10^3	5.786×10^2	5.431×10^2	1.182×10^3	7.401×10^2	1.835×10^4	5.385×10^2	5.867×10^2
	Min	1.187×10^3	5.296×10^2	4.286×10^2	5.419×10^2	6.608×10^2	1.005×10^4	4.961×10^2	5.196×10^2
F_5	Avg	9.086×10^2	8.080×10^2	9.240×10^2	8.065×10^2	6.269×10^2	1.125×10^3	8.608×10^2	5.624×10^2
	Min	7.996×10^2	7.226×10^2	7.743×10^2	6.742×10^2	5.862×10^2	1.032×10^3	7.209×10^2	5.318×10^2
F_6	Avg	6.455×10^2	6.078×10^2	6.395×10^2	6.356×10^2	6.075×10^2	6.888×10^2	6.513×10^2	6.001×10^2
	Min	6.270×10^2	6.035×10^2	6.165×10^2	6.239×10^2	6.041×10^2	6.780×10^2	6.291×10^2	6.000×10^2
F_7	Avg	1.728×10^3	1.081×10^3	1.139×10^3	1.207×10^3	9.855×10^2	1.937×10^3	1.461×10^3	8.682×10^2
	Min	1.119×10^3	1.011×10^3	1.023×10^3	1.031×10^3	8.795×10^2	1.769×10^3	1.204×10^3	8.099×10^2
F_8	Avg	1.217×10^3	1.107×10^3	1.213×10^3	1.055×10^3	9.213×10^2	1.406×10^3	1.131×10^3	8.610×10^2
	Min	1.050×10^3	1.021×10^3	1.096×10^3	9.983×10^2	8.625×10^2	1.315×10^3	1.021×10^3	8.318×10^2
F_9	Avg	1.651×10^4	1.737×10^3	2.097×10^4	6.212×10^3	1.717×10^3	3.051×10^4	1.190×10^4	9.243×10^2
	Min	8.748×10^3	9.529×10^2	1.190×10^4	3.607×10^3	1.299×10^3	1.925×10^4	5.498×10^3	9.066×10^2
F_{10}	Avg	8.426×10^3	7.527×10^3	7.974×10^3	7.980×10^3	7.490×10^3	1.387×10^4	7.755×10^3	6.534×10^3
	Min	6.288×10^3	6.340×10^3	6.303×10^3	6.040×10^3	5.766×10^3	1.198×10^4	6.397×10^3	5.135×10^3
F_{11}	Avg	5.571×10^3	1.594×10^3	1.469×10^3	2.114×10^3	1.865×10^3	1.495×10^4	1.299×10^3	1.259×10^3
	Min	1.574×10^3	1.439×10^3	1.291×10^3	1.417×10^3	1.394×10^3	8.985×10^3	1.200×10^3	1.146×10^3
F_{12}	Avg	2.581×10^9	4.574×10^7	6.833×10^6	1.705×10^8	1.999×10^7	3.109×10^{10}	5.722×10^5	1.873×10^6
	Min	6.409×10^7	2.731×10^7	1.384×10^6	1.878×10^6	7.129×10^6	1.600×10^{10}	1.341×10^5	1.078×10^6
F_{13}	Avg	2.561×10^8	2.672×10^6	9.255×10^4	1.340×10^5	1.729×10^4	1.251×10^{10}	8.898×10^3	5.362×10^3
	Min	1.454×10^5	1.614×10^6	3.011×10^4	5.781×10^3	9.648×10^3	1.435×10^9	2.611×10^3	1.749×10^3
F_{14}	Avg	9.567×10^5	1.375×10^5	6.855×10^4	1.073×10^5	4.132×10^5	2.622×10^7	3.670×10^4	4.016×10^4
	Min	1.246×10^4	3.771×10^4	2.161×10^4	9.772×10^3	7.234×10^4	8.185×10^5	1.148×10^4	1.202×10^4
F_{15}	Avg	1.078×10^7	5.308×10^5	6.616×10^4	8.967×10^3	6.016×10^3	1.341×10^9	7.075×10^3	2.964×10^3
	Min	4.298×10^4	3.335×10^5	1.422×10^4	1.884×10^3	2.543×10^3	1.237×10^8	1.943×10^3	1.534×10^3
F_{16}	Avg	4.104×10^3	3.570×10^3	3.769×10^3	3.335×10^3	2.915×10^3	6.808×10^3	3.575×10^3	2.614×10^3
	Min	3.133×10^3	2.836×10^3	2.788×10^3	2.616×10^3	2.404×10^3	5.302×10^3	2.509×10^3	2.148×10^3
F_{17}	Avg	3.846×10^3	3.218×10^3	3.787×10^3	3.151×10^3	2.690×10^3	4.919×10^3	3.478×10^3	2.474×10^3
	Min	3.034×10^3	2.568×10^3	3.044×10^3	2.615×10^3	2.084×10^3	3.399×10^3	2.827×10^3	2.018×10^3
F_{18}	Avg	4.168×10^6	1.053×10^6	3.688×10^5	2.670×10^6	1.816×10^6	5.905×10^7	1.937×10^5	1.247×10^6
	Min	1.543×10^5	2.843×10^5	1.381×10^5	2.302×10^5	1.304×10^5	5.306×10^6	3.375×10^4	1.067×10^5
F_{19}	Avg	2.346×10^6	2.754×10^5	2.368×10^4	6.213×10^4	1.682×10^4	9.590×10^8	1.541×10^4	1.276×10^4
	Min	5.030×10^3	1.841×10^5	2.700×10^3	5.247×10^3	2.057×10^3	2.437×10^7	2.172×10^3	2.447×10^3
F_{20}	Avg	3.529×10^3	2.999×10^3	3.311×10^3	3.108×10^3	2.830×10^3	3.923×10^3	3.317×10^3	2.485×10^3
	Min	3.116×10^3	2.429×10^3	2.655×10^3	2.572×10^3	2.495×10^3	3.475×10^3	2.534×10^3	2.081×10^3

Table 4. *Cont.*

F.	Metrics	MFO	LMFO	WCMFO	CMFO	ODSFMFO	SMFO	WMFO	MFO-SFR
F_{21}	Avg	2.682×10^3	2.604×10^3	2.720×10^3	2.503×10^3	2.408×10^3	3.071×10^3	2.635×10^3	2.360×10^3
	Min	2.575×10^3	2.528×10^3	2.590×10^3	2.445×10^3	2.379×10^3	2.938×10^3	2.518×10^3	2.335×10^3
F_{22}	Avg	1.028×10^4	9.106×10^3	9.780×10^3	7.972×10^3	5.227×10^3	1.605×10^4	9.538×10^3	8.339×10^3
	Min	8.688×10^3	7.734×10^3	8.346×10^3	2.497×10^3	2.436×10^3	1.474×10^4	8.203×10^3	6.317×10^3
F_{23}	Avg	3.133×10^3	3.009×10^3	3.095×10^3	3.137×10^3	2.888×10^3	3.969×10^3	3.183×10^3	2.793×10^3
	Min	3.013×10^3	2.945×10^3	2.974×10^3	2.979×10^3	2.822×10^3	3.594×10^3	3.056×10^3	2.761×10^3
F_{24}	Avg	3.197×10^3	3.135×10^3	3.224×10^3	3.217×10^3	3.030×10^3	4.292×10^3	3.274×10^3	2.970×10^3
	Min	3.098×10^3	3.071×10^3	3.101×10^3	3.098×10^3	2.978×10^3	3.875×10^3	3.095×10^3	2.931×10^3
F_{25}	Avg	5.123×10^3	3.062×10^3	3.048×10^3	3.889×10^3	3.242×10^3	1.069×10^4	3.061×10^3	3.070×10^3
	Min	3.031×10^3	2.994×10^3	2.964×10^3	3.242×10^3	3.176×10^3	7.290×10^3	3.021×10^3	2.985×10^3
F_{26}	Avg	8.137×10^3	6.855×10^3	8.205×10^3	8.456×10^3	5.513×10^3	1.577×10^4	8.342×10^3	4.406×10^3
	Min	6.910×10^3	6.234×10^3	7.239×10^3	5.759×10^3	4.905×10^3	1.445×10^4	2.900×10^3	4.051×10^3
F_{27}	Avg	3.538×10^3	3.403×10^3	3.489×10^3	4.237×10^3	3.525×10^3	5.612×10^3	3.759×10^3	3.307×10^3
	Min	3.407×10^3	3.297×10^3	3.361×10^3	3.897×10^3	3.448×10^3	4.453×10^3	3.460×10^3	3.266×10^3
F_{28}	Avg	7.554×10^3	3.555×10^3	3.296×10^3	4.481×10^3	3.749×10^3	9.637×10^3	3.300×10^3	3.378×10^3
	Min	4.720×10^3	3.268×10^3	3.259×10^3	3.882×10^3	3.472×10^3	8.008×10^3	3.259×10^3	3.310×10^3
F_{29}	Avg	5.133×10^3	4.380×10^3	4.681×10^3	5.199×10^3	4.191×10^3	1.608×10^4	4.870×10^3	3.545×10^3
	Min	4.271×10^3	3.944×10^3	3.587×10^3	4.366×10^3	3.748×10^3	8.290×10^3	4.292×10^3	3.289×10^3
F_{30}	Avg	2.924×10^7	5.428×10^6	2.810×10^6	2.564×10^7	1.768×10^6	2.271×10^9	1.204×10^6	1.144×10^6
	Min	2.389×10^6	3.442×10^6	1.262×10^6	8.984×10^6	9.999×10^5	2.782×10^8	6.441×10^5	9.567×10^5
Average rank		6.29	3.82	4.25	4.78	3.34	7.93	3.79	1.79
Total rank		7	3	5	6	2	8	4	1

Table 4 presents the average and minimum fitness values obtained from the proposed MFO-SFR algorithms, MFO, and its six variants in solving the CEC 2018 benchmark test functions with 50 dimensions. Overall, the results showed that the proposed MFO-SFR algorithm provided competitive results for most test functions, and it ranked first according to the Friedman test results, which are reported in the final row of the table. Additionally, an exploratory data analysis is depicted in Figure 1 to show the ranking of algorithms for each function. Overall, it can be seen that the proposed MFO-SFR algorithm surrounds the center of the radar chart for most test functions in 30 and 50 dimensions. For instance, for F_1, the proposed MFO-SFR algorithm was ranked first in 30 dimensions and third in 50 dimensions, whereas WMFO and the canonical MFO algorithms were ranked second and seventh for 30 and 50 dimensions, respectively. For F_{12}, it can be seen that MFO-SFR was ranked second, MFO was ranked seventh, and WMFO was ranked first for 30 dimensions, and these three algorithms were ranked second, seventh, and first, respectively, for 50 dimensions. For F_{27}, MFO-SFR and WMFO were ranked first and sixth in both 30 and 50 dimensions, whereas the canonical MFO algorithm was ranked fourth in 30 dimensions and fifth in 50 dimensions.

The convergence comparison of the proposed MFO-SFR algorithm and the other studied algorithms is shown in Figure 2. For F_1 in 30 dimensions, it can be seen that although MFO-SFR exhibited prolonged convergence, it provided the best solution compared to the other algorithms. In 50 dimensions, however, it ranked second after WMFO. For multimodal functions F_5 and F_7, the convergence trend of MFO-SFR continued up to the final iterations, whereas most of the competitors were flattened in local optimum zones. As evidence of the adequate balance between exploration and exploitation, for hybrid functions F_{10} and F_{16}, MFO-SFR exhibited sharp movements in the first half of the iterations and relatively modest fluctuations in the second half. Ultimately, for composition test functions F_{21}, F_{26}, and F_{30}, MFO-SFR exhibited a gradual trend toward the optimum solutions after beginning its convergence with a sharply descending slope. This behavior indicates the capacity of MFO-SFR to bypass the local optimum and avoid premature convergence.

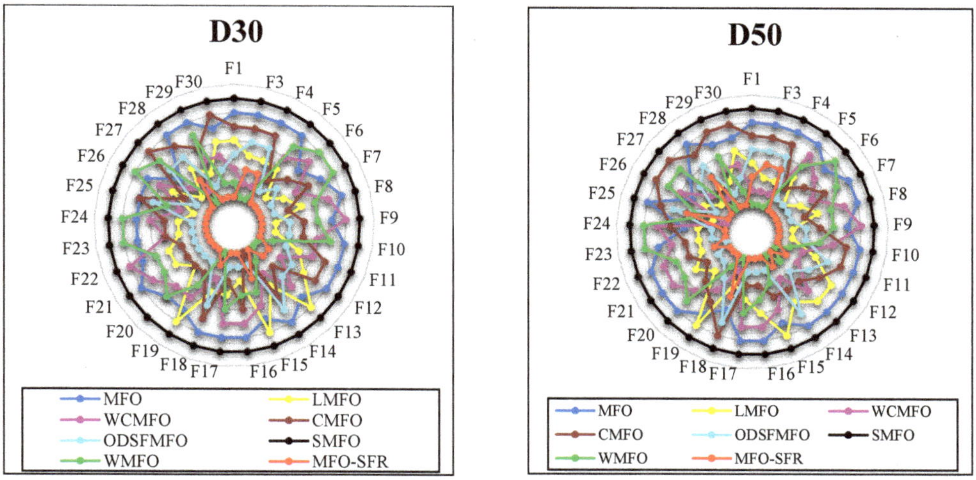

Figure 1. Exploratory data analysis of MFO-SFR, MFO, and its variants on CEC 2018 with 30 and 50 dimensions.

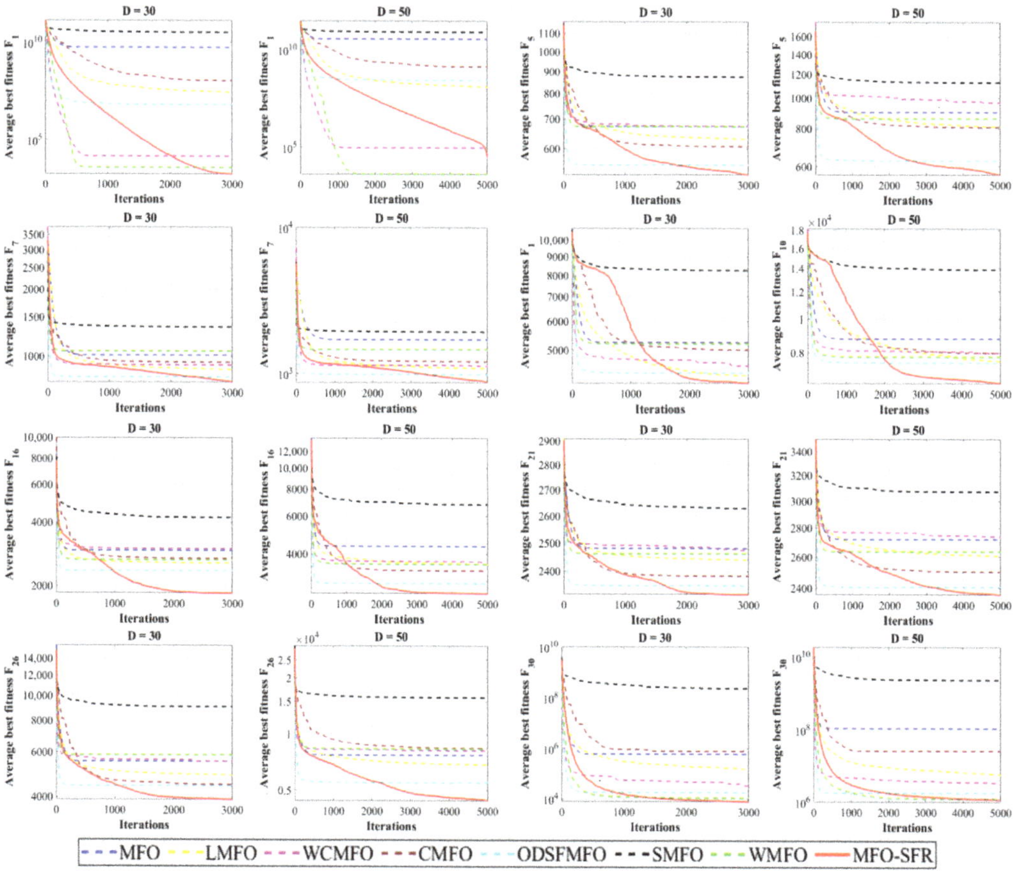

Figure 2. Convergence comparison of MFO-SFR, MFO, and its variants on CEC 2018 with D = 30 and 50.

5.2. Comparing the Proposed MFO-SFR Algorithm with Other Well-Known Optimization Algorithms

The second set of experiments, we compared the performance of the proposed MFO-SFR algorithm with the well-known representative metaheuristic algorithms presented in the literature, including particle swarm optimization (PSO) [39], krill herd (KH) [69], grey wolf optimization (GWO) [70], the crow search algorithm (CSA) [71], and the horse herd optimization algorithm (HOA) [45]. The algorithms' source codes were gathered from publicly available resources, and their parameter values were the same ones considered in the original papers, as reported in Table 2. Tables 5 and 6 compare the average and minimum fitness values produced by the proposed MFO-SFR algorithm and the other algorithms for 30 and 50 dimensions. The results of the test functions F_1 and F_3–F_{10} for both numbers of dimensions demonstrated that MFO-SFR exhibited impressive exploitation and exploration capabilities and generated better solutions while dealing with unimodal and multimodal tests. The results of test functions F_{11}–F_{30} demonstrated that the MFO-SFR avoided local optimum trapping and balanced the trade-off between exploration and exploitation abilities. Furthermore, the final two rows present the results of the Friedman test for each algorithm, in which MFO-SFR ranked first among the comparative algorithms for both 30 and 50 dimensions.

Table 5. Comparison of MFO-SFR with well-known algorithms for CEC 2018 test functions with D = 30.

F.	Metrics	PSO	KH	GWO	CSA	HOA	MFO-SFR
F_1	Avg	5.907×10^{10}	1.963×10^{4}	1.145×10^{9}	3.246×10^{10}	3.003×10^{9}	1.791×10^{3}
	Min	3.270×10^{10}	7.354×10^{3}	1.583×10^{8}	2.130×10^{10}	2.203×10^{9}	1.017×10^{2}
F_3	Avg	1.308×10^{5}	4.403×10^{4}	2.987×10^{4}	9.600×10^{4}	3.075×10^{4}	1.312×10^{4}
	Min	1.039×10^{5}	2.051×10^{4}	1.476×10^{4}	5.473×10^{4}	2.032×10^{4}	7.513×10^{3}
F_4	Avg	1.183×10^{4}	4.965×10^{2}	5.369×10^{2}	5.726×10^{3}	1.047×10^{3}	4.914×10^{2}
	Min	7.302×10^{3}	4.041×10^{2}	4.933×10^{2}	3.185×10^{3}	8.889×10^{2}	4.700×10^{2}
F_5	Avg	9.635×10^{2}	6.454×10^{2}	5.950×10^{2}	8.509×10^{2}	7.938×10^{2}	5.227×10^{2}
	Min	8.845×10^{2}	6.115×10^{2}	5.511×10^{2}	8.017×10^{2}	7.612×10^{2}	5.109×10^{2}
F_6	Avg	6.921×10^{2}	6.418×10^{2}	6.047×10^{2}	6.683×10^{2}	6.605×10^{2}	6.000×10^{2}
	Min	6.828×10^{2}	6.303×10^{2}	6.009×10^{2}	6.554×10^{2}	6.496×10^{2}	6.000×10^{2}
F_7	Avg	2.511×10^{3}	8.400×10^{2}	8.512×10^{2}	1.730×10^{3}	1.029×10^{3}	7.669×10^{2}
	Min	2.201×10^{3}	7.960×10^{2}	7.932×10^{2}	1.552×10^{3}	9.979×10^{2}	7.460×10^{2}
F_8	Avg	1.220×10^{3}	9.054×10^{2}	8.709×10^{2}	1.134×10^{3}	1.061×10^{3}	8.209×10^{2}
	Min	1.163×10^{3}	8.647×10^{2}	8.450×10^{2}	1.105×10^{3}	1.041×10^{3}	8.090×10^{2}
F_9	Avg	1.735×10^{4}	3.138×10^{3}	1.360×10^{3}	1.040×10^{4}	4.292×10^{3}	9.038×10^{2}
	Min	1.271×10^{4}	2.368×10^{3}	9.830×10^{2}	7.223×10^{3}	2.668×10^{3}	9.005×10^{2}
F_{10}	Avg	8.218×10^{3}	4.797×10^{3}	3.874×10^{3}	8.279×10^{3}	8.340×10^{3}	4.062×10^{3}
	Min	7.661×10^{3}	3.165×10^{3}	3.030×10^{3}	7.738×10^{3}	7.745×10^{3}	2.461×10^{3}
F_{11}	Avg	1.018×10^{4}	1.711×10^{3}	1.408×10^{3}	4.700×10^{3}	1.797×10^{3}	1.143×10^{3}
	Min	7.488×10^{3}	1.304×10^{3}	1.236×10^{3}	3.395×10^{3}	1.699×10^{3}	1.107×10^{3}
F_{12}	Avg	6.824×10^{9}	2.220×10^{6}	3.441×10^{7}	2.979×10^{9}	3.763×10^{8}	1.508×10^{5}
	Min	3.870×10^{9}	7.468×10^{5}	2.122×10^{6}	1.516×10^{9}	2.821×10^{8}	2.035×10^{4}
F_{13}	Avg	3.156×10^{9}	3.457×10^{4}	1.505×10^{6}	9.478×10^{8}	1.051×10^{8}	6.405×10^{3}
	Min	5.760×10^{8}	1.430×10^{4}	4.674×10^{4}	5.211×10^{8}	3.296×10^{7}	1.690×10^{3}
F_{14}	Avg	7.227×10^{5}	2.910×10^{5}	1.926×10^{5}	4.342×10^{5}	1.340×10^{5}	8.200×10^{3}
	Min	1.041×10^{5}	1.873×10^{4}	2.446×10^{4}	1.482×10^{5}	5.216×10^{4}	2.021×10^{3}
F_{15}	Avg	2.025×10^{8}	1.788×10^{4}	1.956×10^{5}	7.286×10^{7}	3.143×10^{7}	5.614×10^{3}
	Min	1.064×10^{7}	9.433×10^{3}	1.435×10^{4}	2.378×10^{7}	8.141×10^{6}	1.515×10^{3}

Table 5. *Cont.*

F.	Metrics	PSO	KH	GWO	CSA	HOA	MFO-SFR
F_{16}	Avg	4.452×10^3	2.884×10^3	2.385×10^3	3.989×10^3	3.786×10^3	1.855×10^3
	Min	3.827×10^3	2.377×10^3	1.949×10^3	3.147×10^3	3.419×10^3	1.617×10^3
F_{17}	Avg	3.298×10^3	2.277×10^3	1.943×10^3	2.628×10^3	2.361×10^3	1.745×10^3
	Min	2.755×10^3	1.804×10^3	1.778×10^3	2.256×10^3	2.102×10^3	1.727×10^3
F_{18}	Avg	6.473×10^6	4.258×10^5	8.049×10^5	7.890×10^6	1.212×10^6	1.493×10^5
	Min	6.593×10^5	4.192×10^4	6.880×10^4	2.022×10^6	4.281×10^5	4.305×10^4
F_{19}	Avg	2.509×10^8	9.593×10^4	7.374×10^5	1.358×10^8	4.426×10^7	6.534×10^3
	Min	3.341×10^7	1.081×10^4	3.279×10^3	6.263×10^7	1.774×10^7	1.910×10^3
F_{20}	Avg	2.847×10^3	2.624×10^3	2.362×10^3	2.759×10^3	2.681×10^3	2.091×10^3
	Min	2.574×10^3	2.303×10^3	2.146×10^3	2.476×10^3	2.487×10^3	2.004×10^3
F_{21}	Avg	2.707×10^3	2.416×10^3	2.379×10^3	2.625×10^3	2.575×10^3	2.321×10^3
	Min	2.615×10^3	2.359×10^3	2.351×10^3	2.587×10^3	2.539×10^3	2.312×10^3
F_{22}	Avg	8.759×10^3	3.018×10^3	4.411×10^3	6.831×10^3	4.513×10^3	2.300×10^3
	Min	6.900×10^3	2.300×10^3	2.406×10^3	5.558×10^3	2.705×10^3	2.300×10^3
F_{23}	Avg	3.239×10^3	2.880×10^3	2.729×10^3	3.143×10^3	3.133×10^3	2.671×10^3
	Min	3.101×10^3	2.807×10^3	2.678×10^3	3.061×10^3	3.059×10^3	2.654×10^3
F_{24}	Avg	3.539×10^3	3.107×10^3	2.890×10^3	3.319×10^3	3.188×10^3	2.844×10^3
	Min	3.253×10^3	2.994×10^3	2.849×10^3	3.206×10^3	3.122×10^3	2.828×10^3
F_{25}	Avg	7.655×10^3	2.911×10^3	2.958×10^3	4.890×10^3	3.137×10^3	2.887×10^3
	Min	5.843×10^3	2.887×10^3	2.916×10^3	4.344×10^3	3.069×10^3	2.887×10^3
F_{26}	Avg	8.709×10^3	5.651×10^3	4.483×10^3	8.661×10^3	4.738×10^3	3.903×10^3
	Min	6.500×10^3	2.800×10^3	3.473×10^3	7.772×10^3	3.736×10^3	3.739×10^3
F_{27}	Avg	3.827×10^3	3.400×10^3	3.230×10^3	3.690×10^3	3.720×10^3	3.219×10^3
	Min	3.591×10^3	3.283×10^3	3.212×10^3	3.537×10^3	3.616×10^3	3.208×10^3
F_{28}	Avg	6.851×10^3	3.228×10^3	3.356×10^3	5.474×10^3	3.519×10^3	3.216×10^3
	Min	5.611×10^3	3.198×10^3	3.283×10^3	4.541×10^3	3.468×10^3	3.196×10^3
F_{29}	Avg	5.426×10^3	4.194×10^3	3.642×10^3	5.253×10^3	4.726×10^3	3.414×10^3
	Min	4.907×10^3	3.858×10^3	3.439×10^3	4.952×10^3	4.454×10^3	3.323×10^3
F_{30}	Avg	2.946×10^8	1.043×10^6	2.842×10^6	1.084×10^8	2.610×10^7	7.835×10^3
	Min	8.913×10^7	8.260×10^4	5.249×10^5	4.274×10^7	1.221×10^7	6.362×10^3
Average rank		5.84	2.68	2.45	5.00	3.93	1.09
Total rank		6	3	2	5	4	1

Table 6. Comparison of MFO-SFR with well-known algorithms for CEC 2018 test functions with D = 50.

F.	Metrics	PSO	KH	GWO	CSA	HOA	MFO-SFR
F_1	Avg	1.526×10^{11}	1.703×10^5	4.506×10^9	9.609×10^{10}	1.149×10^{10}	3.463×10^4
	Min	8.451×10^{10}	1.932×10^4	7.183×10^8	8.123×10^{10}	8.346×10^9	9.385×10^3
F_3	Avg	2.549×10^5	1.192×10^5	7.730×10^4	2.070×10^5	8.230×10^4	5.495×10^4
	Min	1.957×10^5	7.643×10^4	4.662×10^4	1.774×10^5	6.990×10^4	4.223×10^4
F_4	Avg	3.307×10^4	5.428×10^2	8.017×10^2	1.712×10^4	2.589×10^3	5.867×10^2
	Min	1.811×10^4	4.765×10^2	6.224×10^2	1.286×10^4	2.058×10^3	5.196×10^2
F_5	Avg	1.367×10^3	7.662×10^2	6.775×10^2	1.211×10^3	1.047×10^3	5.624×10^2
	Min	1.256×10^3	7.090×10^2	6.316×10^2	1.145×10^3	1.011×10^3	5.318×10^2

Table 6. *Cont.*

F.	Metrics	PSO	KH	GWO	CSA	HOA	MFO-SFR
F_6	Avg	7.114×10^2	6.499×10^2	6.112×10^2	6.862×10^2	6.745×10^2	6.001×10^2
	Min	6.991×10^2	6.393×10^2	6.075×10^2	6.776×10^2	6.645×10^2	6.000×10^2
F_7	Avg	4.585×10^3	1.052×10^3	9.899×10^2	3.206×10^3	1.338×10^3	8.682×10^2
	Min	4.142×10^3	9.353×10^2	9.057×10^2	2.735×10^3	1.289×10^3	8.099×10^2
F_8	Avg	1.687×10^3	1.059×10^3	9.862×10^2	1.499×10^3	1.354×10^3	8.610×10^2
	Min	1.575×10^3	1.033×10^3	9.423×10^2	1.423×10^3	1.283×10^3	8.318×10^2
F_9	Avg	5.170×10^4	9.873×10^3	4.844×10^3	3.622×10^4	2.153×10^4	9.243×10^2
	Min	3.909×10^4	7.955×10^3	2.552×10^3	3.021×10^4	1.416×10^4	9.066×10^2
F_{10}	Avg	1.441×10^4	7.948×10^3	5.919×10^3	1.429×10^4	1.412×10^4	6.534×10^3
	Min	1.356×10^4	6.701×10^3	4.473×10^3	1.342×10^4	1.324×10^4	5.135×10^3
F_{11}	Avg	2.610×10^4	4.813×10^3	2.766×10^3	1.573×10^4	3.782×10^3	1.259×10^3
	Min	1.947×10^4	3.034×10^3	1.652×10^3	1.157×10^4	3.239×10^3	1.146×10^3
F_{12}	Avg	4.300×10^{10}	1.287×10^7	3.406×10^8	2.210×10^{10}	2.417×10^9	1.873×10^6
	Min	2.464×10^{10}	4.289×10^6	3.715×10^7	1.421×10^{10}	1.705×10^9	1.078×10^6
F_{13}	Avg	1.683×10^{10}	5.864×10^4	1.026×10^8	6.132×10^9	5.696×10^8	5.362×10^3
	Min	5.672×10^9	2.099×10^4	8.150×10^4	3.709×10^9	4.310×10^8	1.749×10^3
F_{14}	Avg	6.142×10^6	5.701×10^5	3.453×10^5	4.140×10^6	8.316×10^5	4.016×10^4
	Min	1.659×10^6	1.615×10^5	2.928×10^4	1.829×10^6	2.222×10^5	1.202×10^4
F_{15}	Avg	5.029×10^9	1.956×10^4	4.078×10^6	1.190×10^9	2.294×10^8	2.964×10^3
	Min	2.307×10^9	9.499×10^3	2.722×10^4	4.163×10^8	9.908×10^7	1.534×10^3
F_{16}	Avg	7.306×10^3	3.250×10^3	2.896×10^3	6.252×10^3	5.184×10^3	2.614×10^3
	Min	6.699×10^3	2.463×10^3	2.326×10^3	5.731×10^3	4.749×10^3	2.148×10^3
F_{17}	Avg	1.334×10^4	3.359×10^3	2.661×10^3	5.190×10^3	3.888×10^3	2.474×10^3
	Min	5.938×10^3	2.849×10^3	2.264×10^3	4.547×10^3	3.183×10^3	2.018×10^3
F_{18}	Avg	3.800×10^7	2.330×10^6	3.051×10^6	3.471×10^7	8.478×10^6	1.247×10^6
	Min	1.430×10^7	1.131×10^6	3.848×10^5	1.224×10^7	4.500×10^6	1.067×10^5
F_{19}	Avg	2.060×10^9	1.719×10^5	1.231×10^6	5.231×10^8	7.924×10^7	1.276×10^4
	Min	6.897×10^8	2.586×10^4	9.261×10^3	2.060×10^8	2.979×10^7	2.447×10^3
F_{20}	Avg	4.010×10^3	3.276×10^3	2.743×10^3	3.903×10^3	3.675×10^3	2.485×10^3
	Min	3.712×10^3	2.764×10^3	2.380×10^3	3.680×10^3	3.261×10^3	2.081×10^3
F_{21}	Avg	3.164×10^3	2.556×10^3	2.473×10^3	2.994×10^3	2.850×10^3	2.360×10^3
	Min	3.046×10^3	2.455×10^3	2.422×10^3	2.896×10^3	2.767×10^3	2.335×10^3
F_{22}	Avg	1.609×10^4	1.049×10^4	8.211×10^3	1.603×10^4	1.527×10^4	8.339×10^3
	Min	1.492×10^4	9.115×10^3	6.990×10^3	1.493×10^4	4.474×10^3	6.317×10^3
F_{23}	Avg	4.077×10^3	3.379×10^3	2.916×10^3	3.777×10^3	3.749×10^3	2.793×10^3
	Min	3.763×10^3	3.052×10^3	2.826×10^3	3.595×10^3	3.533×10^3	2.761×10^3
F_{24}	Avg	4.174×10^3	3.643×10^3	3.109×10^3	3.983×10^3	3.744×10^3	2.970×10^3
	Min	3.943×10^3	3.406×10^3	2.991×10^3	3.738×10^3	3.597×10^3	2.931×10^3
F_{25}	Avg	2.556×10^4	3.092×10^3	3.355×10^3	1.580×10^4	4.331×10^3	3.070×10^3
	Min	1.693×10^4	3.052×10^3	3.146×10^3	1.384×10^4	3.997×10^3	2.985×10^3
F_{26}	Avg	1.697×10^4	9.335×10^3	5.804×10^3	1.506×10^4	5.800×10^3	4.406×10^3
	Min	1.280×10^4	3.159×10^3	4.993×10^3	1.326×10^4	5.170×10^3	4.051×10^3
F_{27}	Avg	5.456×10^3	4.354×10^3	3.516×10^3	5.185×10^3	5.049×10^3	3.307×10^3
	Min	4.582×10^3	3.985×10^3	3.402×10^3	4.636×10^3	4.657×10^3	3.266×10^3
F_{28}	Avg	1.242×10^4	3.346×10^3	3.927×10^3	1.039×10^4	4.740×10^3	3.378×10^3
	Min	9.606×10^3	3.311×10^3	3.545×10^3	8.991×10^3	4.469×10^3	3.310×10^3

Table 6. *Cont.*

F.	Metrics	PSO	KH	GWO	CSA	HOA	MFO-SFR
F_{29}	Avg	1.018×10^4	5.360×10^3	4.202×10^3	8.981×10^3	6.514×10^3	3.545×10^3
	Min	8.653×10^3	4.196×10^3	3.826×10^3	7.451×10^3	6.113×10^3	3.289×10^3
F_{30}	Avg	2.508×10^9	4.241×10^7	7.032×10^7	1.287×10^9	3.337×10^8	1.144×10^6
	Min	1.281×10^9	1.429×10^7	3.629×10^7	6.453×10^8	2.374×10^8	9.567×10^5
Average rank		5.93	2.70	2.29	4.98	3.92	1.18
Total rank		6	3	2	5	4	1

The exploratory data analysis shown in Figure 3 was conducted to investigate the ranking of algorithms for each test function. Overall, it can be noted that the proposed MFO-SFR algorithm was ranked first among the other compared algorithms for all test functions, except for F_{10} in 30 dimensions. For 50 dimensions, it is notable that MFO-SFR was ranked first for all test functions except for F_4, F_{10}, F_{22}, and F_{28}.

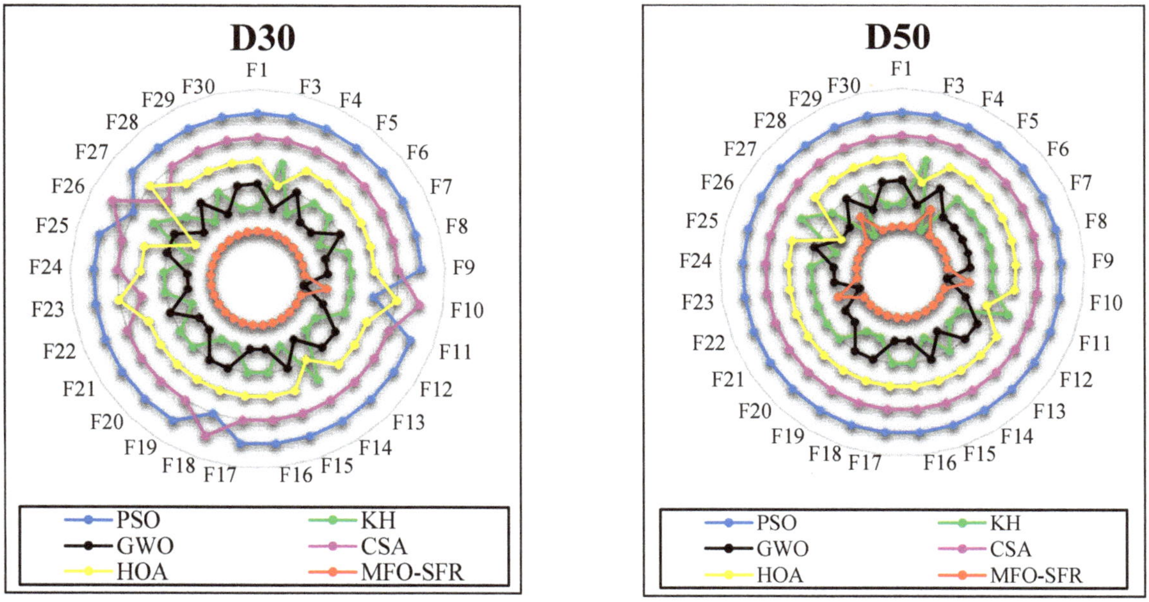

Figure 3. Exploratory data analysis of MFO-SFR and other well-known MFO algorithms on CEC 2018 with 30 and 50 dimensions.

As shown in Figure 4, we analyzed MFO-SFR's convergence behavior and compared it with that of the other algorithms. Overall, it can be seen that the proposed MFO-SFR algorithm was able to converge toward more accurate solutions by avoiding local optimum solutions and striking a balance between its search abilities. It is also notable that the proposed MFO-SFR algorithm maintained its solution accuracy by enhancing the number of dimensions, which demonstrates the scalability of the proposed algorithm.

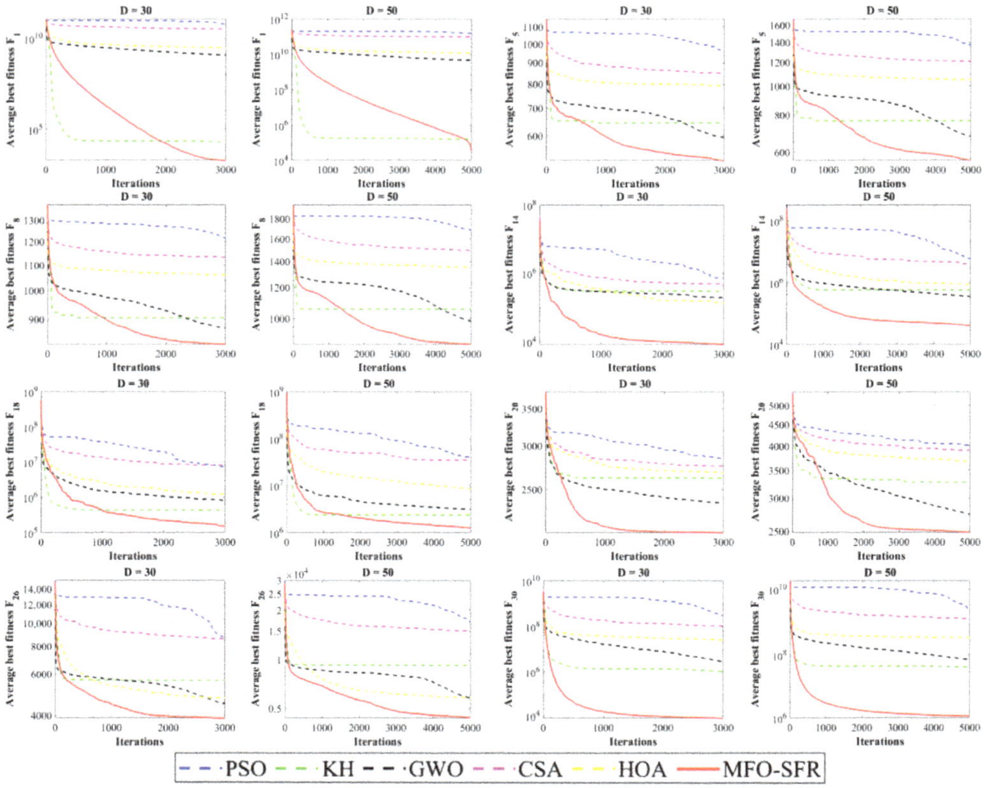

Figure 4. Comparison of the convergence behavior of MFO-SFR and well-known algorithms for CEC 2018 test functions with 30 and 50 dimensions.

5.3. Population Diversity Analysis

Maintaining population diversity is essential in metaheuristic algorithms since low diversity among search agents may cause the algorithm to become stuck at local optimum areas. In this experiment, the population diversity of MFO-SFR and five representatives of comparative algorithms was investigated on several CEC 2018 benchmark test suites with 30 and 50 dimensions. The population diversity curves presented in Figure 5 were calculated by measuring the moment of inertia (I_c) [99], where I_c denotes the spreading of each individual from their centroid, which was determined by Equation (14), and the centroid c_j for j = 1, 2, ... D was calculated using Equation (15). Comparing the population diversity curves with the convergence curves plotted in Figures 2 and 4, it can be noted that the proposed MFO-SFR algorithm effectively maintained diversification among solutions until the near-optimal solution was met. This behavior occurred mainly because of the introduced SFR strategy, which identified stagnant solutions using a distance-based technique and replaced them with a solution selected from the archive constructed from the previous solutions. The introduced archive was able to maintain not only the diversification of solutions by preserving the generated representative flame but also the convergence of solutions toward promising areas by preserving the best solutions in each iteration.

$$I_c = \sum_{i=1}^{D} \sum_{j=1}^{N} \left(M_{ij} - c_i\right)^2 \tag{14}$$

$$c_i = \frac{1}{N} \sum_{j=1}^{N} M_{ij} \tag{15}$$

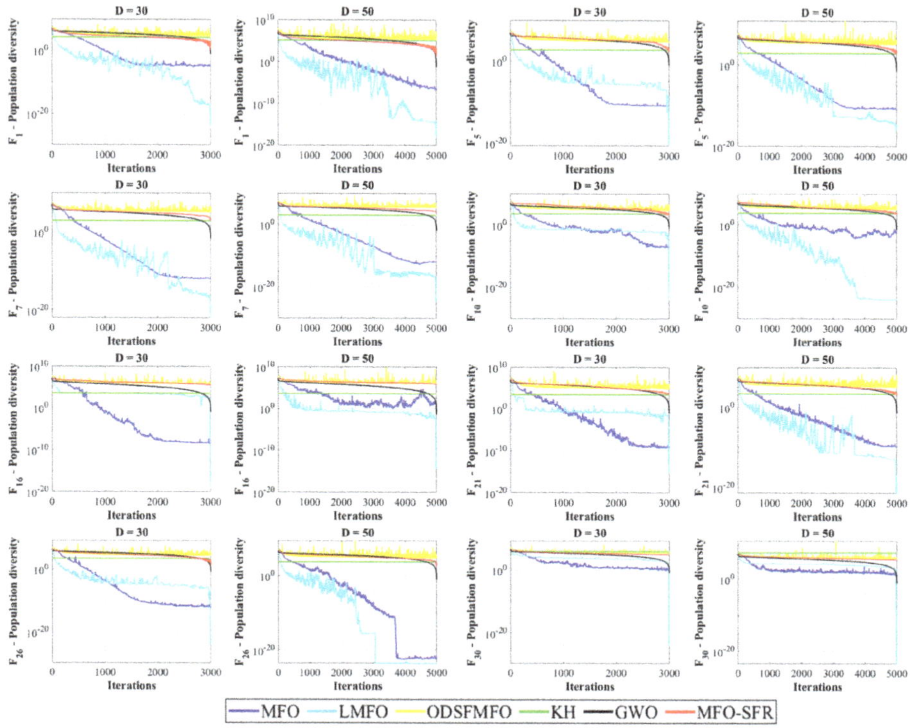

Figure 5. Population diversity of MFO-SFR and comparative algorithms on CEC 2018 test functions.

5.4. The Overall Effectiveness of MFO-SFR

The overall effectiveness (OE) achieved by the proposed MFO-SFR algorithm in solving test functions with 30 and 50 dimensions was computed using Equation (16) and the results are reported in Tables 7 and 8. OE_i indicates the overall effectiveness of the i-th algorithm, L_i is the total number of test functions that the i-th algorithm lost, and TF is the total number of test functions. Table 7 compares the OE achieved by the proposed MFO-SFR with the other MFO variants, showing that MFO-SFR attained the highest OE value, equal to 74.14%. Moreover, Table 8 shows that MFO-SFR achieved a higher OE value of 91.38% compared to other well-known optimization algorithms.

$$OE_i(\%) = \frac{TF - L_i}{TF} \tag{16}$$

Table 7. The overall effectiveness of MFO-SFR and MFO variants.

Algorithms	30 (W|T|L)	50 (W|T|L)	Total (W|T|L)	OE
MFO	0|0|29	0|0|29	0|0|58	0%
LMFO	0|0|29	0|0|29	0|0|58	0%
WCMFO	1|0|28	2|0|27	3|0|55	5.17%
CMFO	0|0|29	0|0|29	0|0|58	0%
ODSFMFO	1|0|28	1|0|28	2|0|56	3.45%
SMFO	0|0|29	0|0|29	0|0|58	0%
WMFO	4|0|25	6|0|23	10|0|48	17.24%
MFO-SFR	23|0|6	20|0|9	43|0|15	74.14%

Table 8. The overall effectiveness of MFO-SFR and contender algorithms.

Algorithms	30 (W|T|L)	50 (W|T|L)	Total (W|T|L)	OE
PSO	0|0|29	0|0|29	0|0|58	0%
KH	0|0|29	2|0|27	2|0|56	3.45%
GWO	1|0|28	2|0|27	3|0|55	5.17%
CSA	0|0|29	0|0|29	0|0|58	0%
HOA	0|0|29	0|0|29	0|0|58	0%
MFO-SFR	28|0|1	25|0|4	53|0|5	91.38%

6. Applicability of MFO-SFR to Solving Mechanical Engineering Problems

There is a growing interest in using optimization algorithms in mechanical and engineering systems to improve performance, cost, and product lifespan [50,100]. Therefore, in this section we assessed the applicability of MFO-SFR using two challenging real-world optimization issues from the most recent CEC 2020 test suite [72]. The constraints of the problems were handled using a death penalty function. The maximum number of iterations for MFO-SFR and the variants of MFO was $(D \times 10^4)/N$, where D is the number of decision variables and N is the number of search agents, which was set to 20.

6.1. Welded Beam Design (WBD) Problem

The WBD [101], stated in Equation (17), is a well-known optimization issue in constrained engineering problems. The primary goal of this task, as indicated in Figure 6, is to minimize the total fabrication cost of a welded beam by determining the best design parameters for the clamped bar length (l), weld thickness (h), bar thickness (b), and bar height (t). The results tabulated in Table 9 indicate that the proposed MFO-SFR exhibited superior performance compared with the other algorithms.

$$
\begin{aligned}
&\text{Consider} && \vec{x} = [x_1, x_2, x_3, x_4] = [h, l, t, b], \qquad (17)\\
&\text{Min} && f(\vec{x}) = 1.10471x_1^2x_2 + 0.04811x_3x_4(14.0 + x_2),\\
&\text{Subject to} && g_1(\vec{x}) = \tau(\vec{x}) - \tau_{max} \le 0,\\
& && g_2(\vec{x}) = \sigma(\vec{x}) - \sigma_{max} \le 0,\\
& && g_3(\vec{x}) = x_1 - x_4 \le 0,\\
& && g_4(\vec{x}) = 1.10471x_1^2 + 0.04811x_3x_4(14.0 + x_2) - 5.0 \le 0,\\
& && g_5(\vec{x}) = 0.125 - x_1 \le 0,\\
& && g_6(\vec{x}) = \delta(\vec{x}) - \delta_{max} \le 0,\\
& && g_7(\vec{x}) = P - P_c \le 0,\\
&\text{Variable range} && 0.1 \le x_i \le 2, i = 1,4,\\
& && 0.1 \le x_i \le 10, i = 2,3.\\
&\text{where} && \tau(\vec{x}) = \sqrt{(\tau')^2 + 2\tau'\tau''\tfrac{x_2}{2R} + (\tau'')^2}, \tau' = \tfrac{P}{\sqrt{2}x_1x_2}, \tau'' = \tfrac{MR}{J}, M = P\left(L + \tfrac{x_2}{2}\right),\\
& && R = \sqrt{\tfrac{x_2^2}{4} + \left(\tfrac{x_1+x_3}{2}\right)^2}, \quad J = 2\left\{\sqrt{2}x_1x_2\left[\tfrac{x_2^2}{12} + \left(\tfrac{x_1+x_3}{2}\right)^2\right]\right\}, \sigma(\vec{x}) = \tfrac{6PL}{x_4x_3^2},\\
& && \delta(\vec{x}) = \tfrac{6PL^3}{Ex_3^2x_4}, P_c(\vec{x}) = \frac{4.013E\sqrt{\frac{x_3^2x_4^6}{36}}}{Ex_3^2x_4}\left(1 - \tfrac{x_3}{2L}\sqrt{\tfrac{E}{4G}}\right), P = 6000lb, L = 14in.,\\
& && E = 30 \times 10^6 psi, G = 12 \times 10^6 psi, \tau_{max} = 13{,}600psi, \sigma_{max} = 30{,}000psi,\\
& && \delta_{max} = 0.25\ in.
\end{aligned}
$$

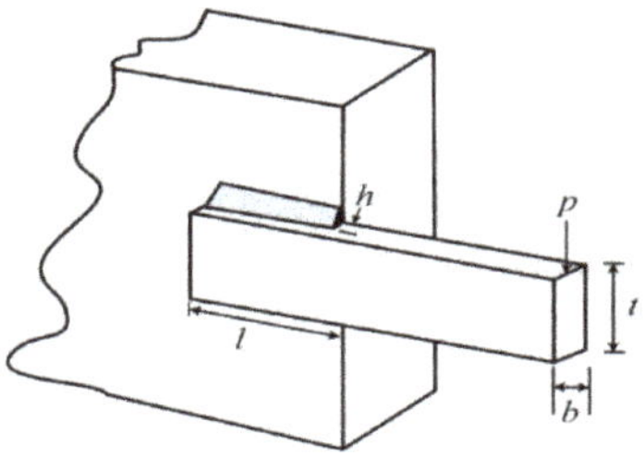

Figure 6. Schematic of the welded beam design problem [101].

Table 9. Comparison of the results obtained for the welded beam design problem.

Algorithms	**Optimal Values for Variables**				**Optimum Cost**
	h	l	t	b	
MFO	0.20576	3.47017	9.03582	0.20577	1.72499
LMFO	0.20739	3.43588	9.25131	0.20807	1.77799
WCMFO	0.20573	3.47035	9.03670	0.20573	1.72489
CMFO	0.18276	4.49027	8.98308	0.20819	1.82934
ODSFMFO	0.20569	3.47128	9.03662	0.20573	1.72490
SMFO	0.20836	3.46324	8.99144	0.20853	1.74135
WMFO	0.20722	3.45341	8.99834	0.20748	1.73151
MFO-SFR	0.20573	3.47056	9.03662	0.20573	1.72486

6.2. The Four-Stage Gearbox Problem

The design of a four-stage gearbox [102] was the second engineering design optimization problem examined in this study. To reduce the weight of the gearbox, the mathematical model specified in Equation (18) was used, together with 86 non-linear constraints and 22 discrete decision variables. According to the results reported in Table 10, the MFO-SFR algorithm outperformed the other algorithms in terms of the quality of its solution.

$$\text{Minimize}: \ F\left(\bar{x}\right) = \left(\frac{\pi}{1000}\right)\sum_{i=1}^{4} \frac{b_i c_i^2\left(N_{pi}^2 + N_{gi}^2\right)}{\left(N_{pi} + N_{gi}\right)^2}, \ i = (1, 2, 3, 4) \tag{18}$$

Table 10. Comparison of the results obtained for the four-stage gearbox problem.

Variables	**MFO**	**LMFO**	**WCMFO**	**CMFO**	**ODSFMFO**	**SMFO**	**WMFO**	**MFO-SFR**
x_1	21.9311	26.0390	13.2709	14.4470	19.9522	7.4896	11.6081	19.7537
x_2	56.2686	59.6014	38.0428	35.9087	42.7879	36.8603	36.5289	51.3053
x_3	6.5100	23.4280	47.0038	13.7051	16.7363	9.6905	32.5497	17.3633
x_4	21.2349	62.1487	64.7345	27.4891	34.3685	35.0066	48.2554	35.7343
x_5	17.8415	41.7704	6.9925	19.5000	15.1662	15.4976	18.6551	17.4063
x_6	37.9201	50.8023	16.3730	32.6744	27.1178	36.7195	35.1674	30.5308
x_7	23.1300	18.5328	16.3790	13.5190	22.4386	37.1973	15.6177	21.5071
x_8	27.5979	49.6525	33.9110	31.5029	56.4417	15.5455	38.4569	44.0394
x_9	0.5100	0.9809	0.7443	1.3021	0.9727	2.0702	1.4277	0.8917
x_{10}	3.3914	0.5964	0.8894	2.4919	0.8552	0.7589	1.3920	1.2137
x_{11}	0.5100	0.7173	4.2285	1.4999	1.2069	0.8063	0.9781	0.6197
x_{12}	0.5100	0.5100	1.2452	1.4996	0.9356	1.3444	1.0893	1.1821
x_{13}	7.8792	5.4735	6.3799	3.4649	2.3679	0.9250	1.6757	4.1070
x_{14}	5.9533	4.8956	5.5138	6.4560	5.1076	4.7899	5.7668	6.8698
x_{15}	5.3993	4.9521	5.8834	5.1835	5.0748	0.5867	5.6259	2.6797
x_{16}	6.9070	4.8722	2.7391	5.1577	4.1023	4.6470	5.0989	2.2119
x_{17}	6.7122	4.6078	5.4174	6.4936	5.1441	4.0477	4.6631	4.2234
x_{18}	7.5214	7.5663	8.3727	6.4751	5.1403	3.3638	3.5762	1.5645
x_{19}	4.7338	3.7869	3.5741	4.4972	3.9364	3.6366	3.7593	3.7526
x_{20}	5.3254	4.3966	3.3184	3.4597	4.8508	4.6303	3.5222	5.4510
x_{21}	4.8923	3.3528	5.7764	4.4278	2.8171	2.9203	2.6439	4.0416
x_{22}	5.6086	4.0724	4.8985	4.4763	2.7781	3.9267	5.6805	5.2131
Optimum Weight	7.2632×10^1	6.6228×10^1	2.1631×10^{12}	5.2157×10^1	3.6565×10^1	3.4380×10^{17}	2.6870×10^{14}	3.6555×10^1

Subject to:

$$g_1\left(\bar{x}\right) = \left(\frac{366000}{\pi\omega_1} + \frac{2c_1N_{p1}}{N_{pi}+N_{g1}}\right)\left(\frac{\left(N_{p1}+N_{g1}\right)^2}{4b_1c_1^2N_{p1}}\right) - \frac{\sigma_N J_R}{0.0167WK_0K_m} \leq 0$$
$$g_2\left(\bar{x}\right) = \left(\frac{366000N_{g1}}{\pi\omega_1 N_{p1}} + \frac{2c_2N_{p2}}{N_{p2}+N_{g2}}\right)\left(\frac{\left(N_{p2}+N_{g2}\right)^2}{4b_2c_2^2N_{p2}}\right) - \frac{\sigma_N J_R}{0.0167WK_0K_m} \leq 0$$
$$g_3\left(\bar{x}\right) = \left(\frac{366000N_{g1}N_{g2}}{\pi\omega_1 N_{p1}N_{p2}} + \frac{2c_3N_{p3}}{N_{p3}+N_{g3}}\right)\left(\frac{\left(N_{p3}+N_{g3}\right)^2}{4b_3c_3^2N_{p3}}\right) - \frac{\sigma_N J_R}{0.0167WK_0K_m} \leq 0$$
$$g_4\left(\bar{x}\right) = \left(\frac{366000N_{g1}N_{g2}N_{g3}}{\pi\omega_1 N_{p1}N_{p2}N_{p3}} + \frac{2c_4N_{p4}}{N_{p4}+N_{g4}}\right)\left(\frac{\left(N_{p4}+N_{g4}\right)^2}{4b_4c_4^2N_{p4}}\right) - \frac{\sigma_N J_R}{0.0167WK_0K_m} \leq 0$$
$$g_5\left(\bar{x}\right) = \left(\frac{366000}{\pi\omega_1} + \frac{2c_1N_{p1}}{N_{p1}+N_{g1}}\right)\left(\frac{\left(N_{p1}+N_{g1}\right)^3}{4b_1c_1^2N_{g1}N_{p1}^2}\right) - \left(\frac{\sigma_H}{C_p}\right)^2\left(\frac{sin(\varnothing)cos(\varnothing)}{0.0334WK_0K_m}\right) \leq 0$$
$$g_6\left(\bar{x}\right) = \left(\frac{366000N_{g1}}{\pi\omega_1 N_{p1}} + \frac{2c_2N_{p2}}{N_{p2}+N_{g2}}\right)\left(\frac{\left(N_{p2}+N_{g2}\right)^3}{4b_2c_2^2N_{g2}N_{p2}^2}\right) - \left(\frac{\sigma_H}{C_p}\right)^2\left(\frac{sin(\varnothing)cos(\varnothing)}{0.0334WK_0K_m}\right) \leq 0$$
$$g_7\left(\bar{x}\right) = \left(\frac{366000N_{g1}N_{g2}}{\pi\omega_1 N_{p1}N_{p2}} + \frac{2c_3N_{p3}}{N_{p3}+N_{g3}}\right)\left(\frac{\left(N_{p3}+N_{g3}\right)^3}{4b_3c_3^2N_{g3}N_{p3}^2}\right) - \left(\frac{\sigma_H}{C_p}\right)^2\left(\frac{sin(\varnothing)cos(\varnothing)}{0.0334WK_0K_m}\right) \leq 0$$
$$g_8\left(\bar{x}\right) = \left(\frac{366000N_{g1}N_{g2}N_{g3}}{\pi\omega_1 N_{p1}N_{p2}N_{p3}} + \frac{2c_4N_{p4}}{N_{p4}+N_{g4}}\right)\left(\frac{\left(N_{p4}+N_{g4}\right)^2}{4b_4c_4^2N_{g4}N_{p4}^2}\right) - \left(\frac{\sigma_H}{C_p}\right)^2\left(\frac{sin(\varnothing)cos(\varnothing)}{0.0334WK_0K_m}\right) \leq 0$$
$$g_{9\text{–}12}\left(\bar{x}\right) = -N_{pi}\sqrt{\frac{\sin^2(\varnothing)}{4} - \frac{1}{N_{pi}} + \left(\frac{1}{N_{pi}}\right)^2} + N_{gi}\sqrt{\frac{sin^2(\varnothing)}{4} - \frac{1}{N_{gi}} + \left(\frac{1}{N_{gi}}\right)^2} + \frac{sin(\varnothing)\left(N_{pi}+N_{gi}\right)}{2} + CR_{min}\pi\cos(\varnothing) \leq 0$$
$$g_{13\text{–}16}\left(\bar{x}\right) = d_{min} - \frac{2c_iN_{pi}}{N_{pi}+N_{gi}} \leq 0$$
$$g_{17\text{–}20}\left(\bar{x}\right) = d_{min} - \frac{2c_iN_{gi}}{N_{pi}+N_{gi}} \leq 0$$
$$g_{21}\left(\bar{x}\right) = x_{p1} + \left(\frac{\left(N_{p1}+2\right)c_1}{N_{p1}+N_{g1}}\right) - L_{max} \leq 0$$
$$g_{22\text{–}24}\left(\bar{x}\right) = -L_{max} + \left(\frac{\left(N_{pi}+2\right)c_i}{N_{pi}+N_{gi}}\right)_{i=2,3,4} + x_{g(i-1)} \leq 0$$
$$g_{25}\left(\bar{x}\right) = -x_{p1} + \left(\frac{\left(N_{p1}+2\right)c_1}{N_{p1}+N_{g1}}\right) \leq 0$$
$$g_{26\text{–}28}\left(\bar{x}\right) = \left(\frac{\left(N_{pi}+2\right)c_i}{N_{pi}+N_{gi}} - x_{g(i-1)}\right)_{i=2,3,4} \leq 0$$
$$g_{29}\left(\bar{x}\right) = y_{p1} + \frac{\left(N_{p1}+2\right)c_1}{N_{p1}+N_{g1}} - L_{max} \leq 0$$
$$g_{30\text{–}32}\left(\bar{x}\right) = -L_{max} + \left(\frac{c_i\left(2+N_{pi}\right)}{N_{pi}+N_{gi}} - y_{g(i-1)}\right)_{i=2,3,4} \leq 0$$
$$g_{33}\left(\bar{x}\right) = \frac{\left(2+N_{p1}\right)c_1}{N_{p1}+N_{g1}} - y_{p1} \leq 0$$
$$g_{34\text{–}36}\left(\bar{x}\right) = \left(\frac{c_i\left(2+N_{pi}\right)}{N_{pi}+N_{gi}} - y_{g(i-1)}\right)_{i=2,3,4} \leq 0$$
$$g_{37\text{–}40}\left(\bar{x}\right) = -L_{max} + \frac{\left(2+N_{gi}\right)c_1}{N_{pi}+N_{gi}} + x_{gi} \leq 0$$
$$g_{41\text{–}44}\left(\bar{x}\right) = -x_{gi} + \left(\frac{\left(N_{gi}+2\right)c_i}{N_{pi}+N_{gi}}\right) + x_{gi} \leq 0$$
$$g_{45\text{–}48}\left(\bar{x}\right) = -y_{gi} + \left(\frac{\left(N_{gi}+2\right)c_i}{N_{pi}+N_{gi}}\right) - L_{max} \leq 0$$
$$g_{49\text{–}52}\left(\bar{x}\right) = -y_{gi} + \left(\frac{\left(N_{gi}+2\right)c_i}{N_{pi}+N_{gi}}\right) \leq 0$$
$$g_{53\text{–}56}\left(\bar{x}\right) = (b_i - 8.255)(b_i - 5.715)(b_i - 12.70)(-N_{pi} + 0.945c_i - N_{gi})(-1) \leq 0$$
$$g_{57\text{–}60}\left(\bar{x}\right) = (b_i - 8.255)(b_i - 3.175)(b_i - 12.70)(-N_{pi} + 0.646c_i - N_{gi}) \leq 0$$
$$g_{61\text{–}64}\left(\bar{x}\right) = (b_i - 5.715)(b_i - 3.175)(b_i - 12.70)(-N_{pi} + 0.504c_i - N_{gi}) \leq 0$$
$$g_{65\text{–}68}\left(\bar{x}\right) = (b_i - 5.715)(b_i - 3.175)(b_i - 8.255)(0c_i - N_{gi} - N_{pi}) \leq 0$$

$$
\begin{aligned}
&g_{69\text{–}72}\left(\bar{x}\right) = (b_i - 8.255)(b_i - 5.715)(b_i - 12.70)(N_{gi} + N_{pi} - 1.812c_i) \le 0 \\
&g_{73\text{–}76}\left(\bar{x}\right) = (b_i - 8.255)(b_i - 3.175)(b_i - 12.70)(-0.945c_i + N_{pi} + N_{gi}) \le 0 \\
&g_{77\text{–}80}\left(\bar{x}\right) = (b_i - 5.715)(b_i - 3.175)(b_i - 12.70)(-0.646c_i + N_{pi} + N_{gi})(-1) \le 0 \\
&g_{81\text{–}84}\left(\bar{x}\right) = (b_i - 5.715)(b_i - 3.175)(b_i - 8.255)(N_{pi} + N_{gi} - 0.504c_i) \le 0 \\
&g_{85}\left(\bar{x}\right) = \omega_{min} + \frac{\omega_1 (N_{p1}N_{p2}N_{p3}N_{p4})}{(N_{g1}N_{g2}N_{g3}N_{g4})} \le 0 \\
&g_{86}\left(\bar{x}\right) = \frac{\omega_1 (N_{p1}N_{p2}N_{p3}N_{p4})}{(N_{g1}N_{g2}N_{g3}N_{g4})} - \omega_{min} \le 0
\end{aligned}
\tag{1}
$$

where

$$
\begin{aligned}
&\bar{x} = \{N_{p1}, N_{g1}, N_{p2}, N_{g2} \ldots b_1, b_2 \ldots x_{p1}, x_{g1}, x_{g2} \ldots y_{p1}, y_{g1}, y_{g2} \ldots y_{g4}\} \\
&c_i = \sqrt{(y_{gi} - y_{pi})^2 + (x_{gi} - x_{pi})^2}, K_0 = 1.5, d_{min} = 25, J_R = 0.2, \varnothing = 120^\circ, W = 55.9, \\
&K_M = 1.6, CR_{min} = 1.4, \\
&L_{max} = 127, C_p = 464, \sigma_H = 3290, \omega_{max} = 255, \omega_1 = 5000, \sigma_N = 2090, \omega_{min} = 245.
\end{aligned}
$$

with bounds:

$$
\begin{aligned}
&b_1 \in \{3.175, 12.7, 8.255, 5.715\} \\
&y_{p1}, x_{p1}, y_{gi}, x_{gi} \in \{12.7, 38.1, 25.4, 50.8, 76.2, 63.5, 88.9, 114.3, 101.6\} \\
&7 \le N_{gi}, N_{pi} \le 76 \in integer.
\end{aligned}
$$

7. Conclusions and Future Works

MFO is a prominent metaheuristic algorithm, inspired by the nighttime convergent behavior of moths in relation to a light source. A large part of MFO's popularity in recent years has been attributed to its straightforward construction. However, due to its rapid loss of population diversity and inadequate exploration ability, the MFO algorithm often encounters local optimum entrapment and premature convergence. In this study, an enhanced moth-flame optimization (MFO-SFR) algorithm was proposed to tackle these weaknesses. MFO-SFR introduces an effective stagnation finding and replacing (SFR) strategy to effectively maintain population diversity by finding stagnant solutions using a distance-based technique and replacing them with a solution selected from the archive constructed on the basis of previous solutions.

The performance of the proposed MFO-SFR algorithm was evaluated on global optimization problems using the CEC 2018 benchmark test suite in two different sets of experiments. In the first set of experiments, the performance of MFO-SFR was benchmarked by conducting the CEC 2018 benchmark functions with 30 and 50 dimensions. The obtained results were compared to those obtained using MFO and its six recent variants, including Lévy-flight moth-flame optimization (LMFO), an efficient hybrid algorithm based on the water cycle and moth-flame (WCMFO), chaos-enhanced moth-flame optimization (CMFO), death mechanism-based moth-flame optimization (ODSFMFO), the synthesis of the moth-flame optimizer with sine cosine mechanisms (SMFO), and the hybrid of whale and moth-flame optimization (WMFO). In the second set of experiments, the results obtained using MFO-SFR were compared with the results of five well-known swarm intelligence algorithms, including particle swarm optimization (PSO), krill herd (KH), the grey wolf optimizer (GWO), the crow search algorithm (CSA), and the horse herd optimization algorithm (HOA) in 30 and 50 dimensions. Furthermore, the results of the two sets of experiments were statistically analyzed and ranked based on their average fitness values. To further analyze the performance of the proposed algorithms, convergence and population diversity results were plotted and compared with those of the other studied algorithms. The plotted curves showed that MFO-SFR could avoid premature convergence and local optimum solutions by maintaining its population diversity throughout the optimization process. To verify the viability of MFO-SFR in solving real-world optimization problems, two well-known mechanical engineering problems from the CEC 2020 dataset were considered. For future studies, solving the problem of improving the exploitation ability of MFO-SFR without degrading its exploration ability is a worthwhile direction of research. Furthermore, the SFR strategy could be considered as a reference in solving the issue of low population diversity for those metaheuristic algorithms that suffer from this problem. Moreover, alternative methods to construct an archive, such as history-based methods, as used in SHADE [103], can be investigated in future studies.

Author Contributions: Conceptualization, M.H.N.-S., A.F. and H.Z.; methodology, M.H.N.-S., A.F. and H.Z.; software, M.H.N.-S., A.F. and H.Z.; validation, M.H.N.-S., H.Z. and S.M.; formal analysis, M.H.N.-S., H.Z., A.F. and S.M.; investigation, M.H.N.-S., A.F. and H.Z.; resources, M.H.N.-S., H.Z. and S.M.; data curation, M.H.N.-S., A.F. and H.Z.; writing, M.H.N.-S., H.Z. and A.F.; original draft preparation, M.H.N.-S., A.F. and H.Z.; writing—review and editing, M.H.N.-S., H.Z., A.F. and S.M.; visualization, M.H.N.-S., A.F. and H.Z.; supervision, M.H.N.-S., H.Z. and S.M.; project administration, M.H.N.-S. and S.M. All authors have read and agreed to the published version of the manuscript.

Funding: This research received no external funding.

Institutional Review Board Statement: Not applicable.

Informed Consent Statement: Not applicable.

Data Availability Statement: The data and code used in the research may be obtained from the corresponding author upon request.

Conflicts of Interest: The authors declare no conflict of interest.

Appendix A

Table A1 provides the results of the pretest conducted on the canonical MFO in 30 dimensions to investigate the average and maximum percentages of situations when φ_i was equal to 0.

Table A1. The analysis of situations where φ_i was equal to zero with D = 30.

#F	Max Percentage	Average Percentage	#F	Max Percentage	Average Percentage	#F	Max Percentage	Average Percentage
F_1	2.03	0.40	F_{12}	26.05	3.32	F_{22}	22.13	3.51
F_3	0.00	0.00	F_{13}	1.16	0.16	F_{23}	0.12	0.01
F_4	0.90	0.13	F_{14}	6.85	0.34	F_{24}	3.41	0.42
F_5	0.60	0.16	F_{15}	2.12	0.21	F_{25}	0.27	0.03
F_6	0.00	0.00	F_{16}	0.10	0.01	F_{26}	2.53	0.65
F_7	4.25	0.34	F_{17}	0.02	0.00	F_{27}	3.40	0.28
F_8	14.97	0.84	F_{18}	0.37	0.02	F_{28}	11.15	0.64
F_9	0.01	0.00	F_{19}	2.00	0.13	F_{29}	28.22	1.46
F_{10}	12.05	1.22	F_{20}	5.24	0.81	F_{30}	9.30	0.47
F_{11}	1.25	0.31	F_{21}	0.01	0.00			

References

1. Zabinsky, Z.B. Stochastic methods for practical global optimization. *J. Glob. Optim.* **1998**, *13*, 433–444. [CrossRef]
2. Pardalos, P.M.; Romeijn, H.E.; Tuy, H. Recent developments and trends in global optimization. *J. Comput. Appl. Math.* **2000**, *124*, 209–228. [CrossRef]
3. Hosseinzadeh, M.; Masdari, M.; Rahmani, A.M.; Mohammadi, M.; Aldalwie, A.H.M.; Majeed, M.K.; Karim, S.H.T. Improved butterfly optimization algorithm for data placement and scheduling in edge computing environments. *J. Grid Comput.* **2021**, *19*, 1–27. [CrossRef]
4. Hassan, B.A.; Rashid, T.A.; Mirjalili, S. Formal context reduction in deriving concept hierarchies from corpora using adaptive evolutionary clustering algorithm star. *Complex Intell. Syst.* **2021**, *7*, 2383–2398. [CrossRef]

5. Hassan, B.A. CSCF: A chaotic sine cosine firefly algorithm for practical application problems. *Neural Comput. Appl.* **2021**, *33*, 7011–7030. [CrossRef]
6. Yi, H.; Duan, Q.; Liao, T.W. Three improved hybrid metaheuristic algorithms for engineering design optimization. *Appl. Soft Comput.* **2013**, *13*, 2433–2444. [CrossRef]
7. Nadimi-Shahraki, M.H.; Asghari Varzaneh, Z.; Zamani, H.; Mirjalili, S. Binary Starling Murmuration Optimizer Algorithm to Select Effective Features from Medical Data. *Appl. Sci.* **2022**, *13*, 564. [CrossRef]
8. Piri, J.; Mohapatra, P.; Acharya, B.; Gharehchopogh, F.S.; Gerogiannis, V.C.; Kanavos, A.; Manika, S. Feature Selection Using Artificial Gorilla Troop Optimization for Biomedical Data: A Case Analysis with COVID-19 Data. *Mathematics* **2022**, *10*, 2742. [CrossRef]
9. Nadimi-Shahraki, M.H.; Fatahi, A.; Zamani, H.; Mirjalili, S. Binary Approaches of Quantum-Based Avian Navigation Optimizer to Select Effective Features from High-Dimensional Medical Data. *Mathematics* **2022**, *10*, 2770. [CrossRef]
10. Talbi, E.-G. *Metaheuristics: From Design to Implementation*; John Wiley & Sons: Hoboken, NJ, USA, 2009.
11. Siddiqi, U.F.; Shiraishi, Y.; Dahb, M.; Sait, S.M. A memory efficient stochastic evolution based algorithm for the multi-objective shortest path problem. *Appl. Soft Comput.* **2014**, *14*, 653–662. [CrossRef]
12. Kavoosi, M.; Dulebenets, M.A.; Abioye, O.; Pasha, J.; Theophilus, O.; Wang, H.; Kampmann, R.; Mikijeljević, M. Berth scheduling at marine container terminals: A universal island-based metaheuristic approach. *Marit. Bus. Rev.* **2019**, *5*, 30–66. [CrossRef]
13. Dokeroglu, T.; Sevinc, E.; Kucukyilmaz, T.; Cosar, A. A survey on new generation metaheuristic algorithms. *Comput. Ind. Eng.* **2019**, *137*, 106040. [CrossRef]
14. Agushaka, J.O.; Ezugwu, A.E. Initialisation Approaches for Population-Based Metaheuristic Algorithms: A Comprehensive Review. *Appl. Sci.* **2022**, *12*, 896. [CrossRef]
15. Singh, A.; Kumar, A. Applications of nature-inspired meta-heuristic algorithms: A survey. *Int. J. Adv. Intell. Paradig.* **2021**, *20*, 388–417. [CrossRef]
16. Fister Jr, I.; Yang, X.-S.; Fister, I.; Brest, J.; Fister, D. A brief review of nature-inspired algorithms for optimization. *arXiv* **2013**, arXiv:1307.4186.
17. Dehghani, M.; Mardaneh, M.; Malik, O.P.; NouraeiPour, S.M. DTO: Donkey theorem optimization. In Proceedings of the 2019 27th Iranian Conference on Electrical Engineering (ICEE), Yazd, Iran, 30 April–2 May 2019; pp. 1855–1859.
18. Fard, E.S.; Monfaredi, K.; Nadimi, M.H. An Area-Optimized Chip of Ant Colony Algorithm Design in Hardware Platform Using the Address-Based Method. *Int. J. Electr. Comput. Eng.* **2014**, *4*, 989–998. [CrossRef]
19. Holland, J.H. Genetic algorithms. *Sci. Am.* **1992**, *267*, 66–73. [CrossRef]
20. Storn, R.; Price, K. Differential evolution–a simple and efficient heuristic for global optimization over continuous spaces. *J. Glob. Optim.* **1997**, *11*, 341–359. [CrossRef]
21. Beyer, H.-G.; Schwefel, H.-P. Evolution strategies–a comprehensive introduction. *Nat. Comput.* **2002**, *1*, 3–52. [CrossRef]
22. Jiao, L.; Li, Y.; Gong, M.; Zhang, X. Quantum-inspired immune clonal algorithm for global optimization. *IEEE Trans. Syst. Man Cybern. Part B* **2008**, *38*, 1234–1253. [CrossRef]
23. Lu, T.-C.; Juang, J.-C. Quantum-inspired space search algorithm (QSSA) for global numerical optimization. *Appl. Math. Comput.* **2011**, *218*, 2516–2532. [CrossRef]
24. Arpaia, P.; Maisto, D.; Manna, C. A Quantum-inspired Evolutionary Algorithm with a competitive variation operator for Multiple-Fault Diagnosis. *Appl. Soft Comput.* **2011**, *11*, 4655–4666. [CrossRef]
25. Rashedi, E.; Nezamabadi-Pour, H.; Saryazdi, S. GSA: A gravitational search algorithm. *Inf. Sci.* **2009**, *179*, 2232–2248. [CrossRef]
26. Hatamlou, A. Black hole: A new heuristic optimization approach for data clustering. *Inf. Sci.* **2013**, *222*, 175–184. [CrossRef]
27. Kashan, A.H. A new metaheuristic for optimization: Optics inspired optimization (OIO). *Comput. Oper. Res.* **2015**, *55*, 99–125. [CrossRef]
28. Atashpaz-Gargari, E.; Lucas, C. Imperialist competitive algorithm: An algorithm for optimization inspired by imperialistic competition. In Proceedings of the 2007 IEEE Congress on Evolutionary Computation, Singapore, 25–28 September 2007; pp. 4661–4667.
29. Geem, Z.W.; Kim, J.H.; Loganathan, G.V. A new heuristic optimization algorithm: Harmony search. *Simulation* **2001**, *76*, 60–68. [CrossRef]
30. Rao, R.V.; Savsani, V.J.; Vakharia, D. Teaching–learning-based optimization: A novel method for constrained mechanical design optimization problems. *Comput. -Aided Des.* **2011**, *43*, 303–315. [CrossRef]
31. Shi, Y. Brain storm optimization algorithm. In Proceedings of the International Conference in Swarm Intelligence, Chongqing, China, 12–15 June 2011; pp. 303–309.
32. Moosavian, N.; Roodsari, B.K. Soccer league competition algorithm: A novel meta-heuristic algorithm for optimal design of water distribution networks. *Swarm Evol. Comput.* **2014**, *17*, 14–24. [CrossRef]
33. Moghdani, R.; Salimifard, K. Volleyball premier league algorithm. *Appl. Soft Comput.* **2018**, *64*, 161–185. [CrossRef]
34. Moosavi, S.H.S.; Bardsiri, V.K. Poor and rich optimization algorithm: A new human-based and multi populations algorithm. *Eng. Appl. Artif. Intell.* **2019**, *86*, 165–181. [CrossRef]
35. Naik, A.; Satapathy, S.C. Past present future: A new human-based algorithm for stochastic optimization. *Soft Comput.* **2021**, *25*, 12915–12976. [CrossRef]
36. Chakraborty, A.; Kar, A.K. Swarm intelligence: A review of algorithms. *Nat. -Inspired Comput. Optim.* **2017**, *10*, 475–494.

37. Zamani, H.; Nadimi-Shahraki, M.H.; Gandomi, A.H. CCSA: Conscious neighborhood-based crow search algorithm for solving global optimization problems. *Appl. Soft Comput.* **2019**, *85*, 105583. [CrossRef]
38. Dorigo, M.; Birattari, M.; Stutzle, T. Ant colony optimization. *IEEE Comput. Intell. Mag.* **2006**, *1*, 28–39. [CrossRef]
39. Kennedy, J.; Eberhart, R. Particle swarm optimization. In Proceedings of the ICNN'95-International Conference on Neural Networks, Perth, WA, Australia, 27 November–1 December 1995; pp. 1942–1948.
40. Karaboga, D.; Basturk, B. A powerful and efficient algorithm for numerical function optimization: Artificial bee colony (ABC) algorithm. *J. Glob. Optim.* **2007**, *39*, 459–471. [CrossRef]
41. Gandomi, A.H.; Yang, X.-S.; Alavi, A.H. Cuckoo search algorithm: A metaheuristic approach to solve structural optimization problems. *Eng. Comput.* **2013**, *29*, 17–35. [CrossRef]
42. Mirjalili, S.; Lewis, A. The whale optimization algorithm. *Adv. Eng. Softw.* **2016**, *95*, 51–67. [CrossRef]
43. Wang, G.-G.; Deb, S.; Coelho, L.d.S. Elephant herding optimization. In Proceedings of the 2015 3rd International Symposium on Computational and Business Intelligence (ISCBI), Bali, Indonesia, 7–9 December 2015; pp. 1–5.
44. Mirjalili, S. Moth-flame optimization algorithm: A novel nature-inspired heuristic paradigm. *Knowl. -Based Syst.* **2015**, *89*, 228–249. [CrossRef]
45. MiarNaeimi, F.; Azizyan, G.; Rashki, M. Horse herd optimization algorithm: A nature-inspired algorithm for high-dimensional optimization problems. *Knowl. -Based Syst.* **2021**, *213*, 106711. [CrossRef]
46. Zamani, H.; Nadimi-Shahraki, M.H.; Gandomi, A.H. QANA: Quantum-based avian navigation optimizer algorithm. *Eng. Appl. Artif. Intel.* **2021**, *104*, 104314. [CrossRef]
47. Abdollahzadeh, B.; Gharehchopogh, F.S.; Mirjalili, S. African vultures optimization algorithm: A new nature-inspired metaheuristic algorithm for global optimization problems. *Comput. Ind. Eng.* **2021**, *158*, 107408. [CrossRef]
48. Shayanfar, H.; Gharehchopogh, F.S. Farmland fertility: A new metaheuristic algorithm for solving continuous optimization problems. *Appl. Soft Comput.* **2018**, *71*, 728–746. [CrossRef]
49. Agushaka, J.O.; Ezugwu, A.E.; Abualigah, L. Dwarf mongoose optimization algorithm. *Comput. Method Appl. M* **2022**, *391*, 114570. [CrossRef]
50. Zamani, H.; Nadimi-Shahraki, M.H.; Gandomi, A.H. Starling murmuration optimizer: A novel bio-inspired algorithm for global and engineering optimization. *Comput. Methods Appl. Mech. Eng.* **2022**, *392*, 114616. [CrossRef]
51. Abdollahzadeh, B.; Soleimanian Gharehchopogh, F.; Mirjalili, S. Artificial gorilla troops optimizer: A new nature-inspired metaheuristic algorithm for global optimization problems. *Int. J. Intell. Syst.* **2021**, *36*, 5887–5958. [CrossRef]
52. Pandey, H.M.; Chaudhary, A.; Mehrotra, D. A comparative review of approaches to prevent premature convergence in GA. *Appl. Soft Comput.* **2014**, *24*, 1047–1077. [CrossRef]
53. Chaitanya, K.; Somayajulu, D.; Krishna, P.R. Memory-based approaches for eliminating premature convergence in particle swarm optimization. *Appl. Intell.* **2021**, *51*, 4575–4608. [CrossRef]
54. Zhu, G.; Kwong, S. Gbest-guided artificial bee colony algorithm for numerical function optimization. *Appl. Math. Comput.* **2010**, *217*, 3166–3173. [CrossRef]
55. Banharnsakun, A.; Achalakul, T.; Sirinaovakul, B. The best-so-far selection in artificial bee colony algorithm. *Appl. Soft Comput.* **2011**, *11*, 2888–2901. [CrossRef]
56. Xiang, W.-L.; Li, Y.-Z.; Meng, X.-L.; Zhang, C.-M.; An, M.-Q. A grey artificial bee colony algorithm. *Appl. Soft Comput.* **2017**, *60*, 1–17. [CrossRef]
57. Nadimi-Shahraki, M.H.; Zamani, H. DMDE: Diversity-maintained multi-trial vector differential evolution algorithm for non-decomposition large-scale global optimization. *Expert Syst. Appl.* **2022**, *198*, 116895. [CrossRef]
58. Wang, F.; Liao, X.; Fang, N.; Jiang, Z. Optimal Scheduling of Regional Combined Heat and Power System Based on Improved MFO Algorithm. *Energies* **2022**, *15*, 3410. [CrossRef]
59. Kaur, K.; Singh, U.; Salgotra, R. An enhanced moth flame optimization. *Neural Comput. Appl.* **2020**, *32*, 2315–2349. [CrossRef]
60. Li, Z.; Zhou, Y.; Zhang, S.; Song, J. Lévy-flight moth-flame algorithm for function optimization and engineering design problems. *Math. Probl. Eng.* **2016**, *2016*, 1–22. [CrossRef]
61. Khalilpourazari, S.; Khalilpourazary, S. An efficient hybrid algorithm based on Water Cycle and Moth-Flame Optimization algorithms for solving numerical and constrained engineering optimization problems. *Soft Comput.* **2019**, *23*, 1699–1722. [CrossRef]
62. Hongwei, L.; Jianyong, L.; Liang, C.; Jingbo, B.; Yangyang, S.; Kai, L. Chaos-enhanced moth-flame optimization algorithm for global optimization. *J. Syst. Eng. Electron.* **2019**, *30*, 1144–1159.
63. Chen, C.; Wang, X.; Yu, H.; Wang, M.; Chen, H. Dealing with multi-modality using synthesis of Moth-flame optimizer with sine cosine mechanisms. *Math. Comput. Simul.* **2021**, *188*, 291–318. [CrossRef]
64. Xu, Y.; Chen, H.; Luo, J.; Zhang, Q.; Jiao, S.; Zhang, X. Enhanced Moth-flame optimizer with mutation strategy for global optimization. *Inf. Sci.* **2019**, *492*, 181–203. [CrossRef]
65. Li, Z.; Zeng, J.; Chen, Y.; Ma, G.; Liu, G. Death mechanism-based moth–flame optimization with improved flame generation mechanism for global optimization tasks. *Expert Syst. Appl.* **2021**, *183*, 115436. [CrossRef]
66. Xu, Y.; Chen, H.; Heidari, A.A.; Luo, J.; Zhang, Q.; Zhao, X.; Li, C. An efficient chaotic mutative moth-flame-inspired optimizer for global optimization tasks. *Expert Syst. Appl.* **2019**, *129*, 135–155. [CrossRef]

67. Awad, N.; Ali, M.; Liang, J.; Qu, B.; Suganthan, P. *Problem Definitions and Evaluation Criteria for the CEC 2017 Special Session and Competition on Single Objective Bound Constrained Real-Parameter Numerical Optimization*; Technical Report; Nanyang Technological University: Singapore, 2016.
68. Nadimi-Shahraki, M.H.; Fatahi, A.; Zamani, H.; Mirjalili, S.; Oliva, D. Hybridizing of Whale and Moth-Flame Optimization Algorithms to Solve Diverse Scales of Optimal Power Flow Problem. *Electronics* **2022**, *11*, 831. [CrossRef]
69. Gandomi, A.H.; Alavi, A.H. Krill herd: A new bio-inspired optimization algorithm. *Commun. Non-Linear Sci. Numer. Simul.* **2012**, *17*, 4831–4845. [CrossRef]
70. Mirjalili, S.; Mirjalili, S.M.; Lewis, A. Grey wolf optimizer. *Adv. Eng. Softw.* **2014**, *69*, 46–61. [CrossRef]
71. Askarzadeh, A. A novel metaheuristic method for solving constrained engineering optimization problems: Crow search algorithm. *Comput. Struct.* **2016**, *169*, 1–12. [CrossRef]
72. Kumar, A.; Wu, G.; Ali, M.Z.; Mallipeddi, R.; Suganthan, P.N.; Das, S. A test-suite of non-convex constrained optimization problems from the real-world and some baseline results. *Swarm Evol. Comput.* **2020**, *56*, 100693. [CrossRef]
73. Nadimi-Shahraki, M.H.; Fatahi, A.; Zamani, H.; Mirjalili, S.; Abualigah, L. An improved moth-flame optimization algorithm with adaptation mechanism to solve numerical and mechanical engineering problems. *Entropy* **2021**, *23*, 1637. [CrossRef] [PubMed]
74. Pelusi, D.; Mascella, R.; Tallini, L.; Nayak, J.; Naik, B.; Deng, Y. An Improved Moth-Flame Optimization algorithm with hybrid search phase. *Knowl. -Based Syst.* **2020**, *191*, 105277. [CrossRef]
75. Nadimi-Shahraki, M.H.; Fatahi, A.; Zamani, H.; Mirjalili, S.; Abualigah, L.; Abd Elaziz, M. Migration-based moth-flame optimization algorithm. *Processes* **2021**, *9*, 2276. [CrossRef]
76. Ma, L.; Wang, C.; Xie, N.-g.; Shi, M.; Ye, Y.; Wang, L. Moth-flame optimization algorithm based on diversity and mutation strategy. *Appl. Intell.* **2021**, *51*, 5836–5872. [CrossRef]
77. Zhao, X.; Fang, Y.; Liu, L.; Li, J.; Xu, M. An improved moth-flame optimization algorithm with orthogonal opposition-based learning and modified position updating mechanism of moths for global optimization problems. *Appl. Intell.* **2020**, *50*, 4434–4458. [CrossRef]
78. Sapre, S.; Mini, S. Opposition-based moth flame optimization with Cauchy mutation and evolutionary boundary constraint handling for global optimization. *Soft Comput.* **2019**, *23*, 6023–6041. [CrossRef]
79. Sahoo, S.K.; Saha, A.K.; Nama, S.; Masdari, M. An improved moth flame optimization algorithm based on modified dynamic opposite learning strategy. *Artif. Intell. Rev.* **2022**, 1–59. [CrossRef]
80. Li, C.; Niu, Z.; Song, Z.; Li, B.; Fan, J.; Liu, P.X. A double evolutionary learning moth-flame optimization for real-parameter global optimization problems. *IEEE Access* **2018**, *6*, 76700–76727. [CrossRef]
81. Li, Y.; Zhu, X.; Liu, J. An improved moth-flame optimization algorithm for engineering problems. *Symmetry* **2020**, *12*, 1234. [CrossRef]
82. Shehab, M.; Alshawabkah, H.; Abualigah, L.; AL-Madi, N. Enhanced a hybrid moth-flame optimization algorithm using new selection schemes. *Eng. Comput.* **2021**, *37*, 2931–2956. [CrossRef]
83. Zhang, H.; Li, R.; Cai, Z.; Gu, Z.; Heidari, A.A.; Wang, M.; Chen, H.; Chen, M. Advanced orthogonal moth flame optimization with Broyden–Fletcher–Goldfarb–Shanno algorithm: Framework and real-world problems. *Expert Syst. Appl.* **2020**, *159*, 113617. [CrossRef]
84. Yu, C.; Heidari, A.A.; Chen, H. A quantum-behaved simulated annealing algorithm-based moth-flame optimization method. *Appl. Math. Model.* **2020**, *87*, 1–19. [CrossRef]
85. Alzaqebah, M.; Alrefai, N.; Ahmed, E.A.; Jawarneh, S.; Alsmadi, M.K. Neighborhood search methods with moth optimization algorithm as a wrapper method for feature selection problems. *Int. J. Electr. Comput. Eng.* **2020**, *10*, 3672. [CrossRef]
86. Xu, L.; Li, Y.; Li, K.; Beng, G.H.; Jiang, Z.; Wang, C.; Liu, N. Enhanced moth-flame optimization based on cultural learning and Gaussian mutation. *J. Bionic Eng.* **2018**, *15*, 751–763. [CrossRef]
87. Helmi, A.; Alenany, A. An enhanced Moth-flame optimization algorithm for permutation-based problems. *Evol. Intell.* **2020**, *13*, 741–764. [CrossRef]
88. Sayed, G.I.; Hassanien, A.E. A hybrid SA-MFO algorithm for function optimization and engineering design problems. *Complex Intell. Syst.* **2018**, *4*, 195–212. [CrossRef]
89. Buch, H.; Trivedi, I.N.; Jangir, P. Moth flame optimization to solve optimal power flow with non-parametric statistical evaluation validation. *Cogent Eng.* **2017**, *4*, 1286731. [CrossRef]
90. Trivedi, I.N.; Jangir, P.; Parmar, S.A.; Jangir, N. Optimal power flow with voltage stability improvement and loss reduction in power system using Moth-Flame Optimizer. *Neural Comput. Appl.* **2018**, *30*, 1889–1904. [CrossRef]
91. Jangir, P.; Jangir, N. Optimal power flow using a hybrid particle Swarm optimizer with moth flame optimizer. *Glob. J. Res. Eng.* **2017**, *17*, 15–32.
92. Sahoo, S.K.; Saha, A.K. A hybrid moth flame optimization algorithm for global optimization. *J. Bionic Eng.* **2022**, *19*, 1522–1543. [CrossRef]
93. Khan, B.S.; Raja, M.A.Z.; Qamar, A.; Chaudhary, N.I. Design of moth flame optimization heuristics for integrated power plant system containing stochastic wind. *Appl. Soft Comput.* **2021**, *104*, 107193. [CrossRef]
94. Singh, P.; Bishnoi, S. Modified moth-Flame optimization for strategic integration of fuel cell in renewable active distribution network. *Electr. Power Syst. Res.* **2021**, *197*, 107323. [CrossRef]

95. Zhang, H.; Heidari, A.A.; Wang, M.; Zhang, L.; Chen, H.; Li, C. Orthogonal Nelder-Mead moth flame method for parameters identification of photovoltaic modules. *Energy Convers. Manag.* **2020**, *211*, 112764. [CrossRef]
96. Cui, Z.; Li, C.; Huang, J.; Wu, Y.; Zhang, L. An improved moth flame optimization algorithm for minimizing specific fuel consumption of variable cycle engine. *IEEE Access* **2020**, *8*, 142725–142735. [CrossRef]
97. Khurma, R.A.; Aljarah, I.; Sharieh, A. A simultaneous moth flame optimizer feature selection approach based on levy flight and selection operators for medical diagnosis. *Arab. J. Sci. Eng.* **2021**, *46*, 8415–8440. [CrossRef]
98. Derrac, J.; García, S.; Molina, D.; Herrera, F. A practical tutorial on the use of nonparametric statistical tests as a methodology for comparing evolutionary and swarm intelligence algorithms. *Swarm Evol. Comput.* **2011**, *1*, 3–18. [CrossRef]
99. Morrison, R.W. *Designing Evolutionary Algorithms for Dynamic Environments*; Springer: Berlin/Heidelberg, Germany, 2004; Volume 178.
100. Altabeeb, A.M.; Mohsen, A.M.; Abualigah, L.; Ghallab, A. Solving capacitated vehicle routing problem using cooperative firefly algorithm. *Appl. Soft Comput.* **2021**, *108*, 107403. [CrossRef]
101. Ragsdell, K.; Phillips, D. Optimal design of a class of welded structures using geometric programming. *Eng. Ind.* **1976**, *98*, 1021–1025. [CrossRef]
102. Yokota, T.; Taguchi, T.; Gen, M. A solution method for optimal weight design problem of the gear using genetic algorithms. *Comput. Ind. Eng.* **1998**, *35*, 523–526. [CrossRef]
103. Tanabe, R.; Fukunaga, A. Success-history based parameter adaptation for differential evolution. In Proceedings of the 2013 IEEE Congress on Evolutionary Computation, Cancun, Mexico, 20–23 June 2013; pp. 71–78.

mathematics

MDPI

Article

A Compact and High-Performance Acoustic Echo Canceller Neural Processor Using Grey Wolf Optimizer along with Least Mean Square Algorithms

Eduardo Pichardo *, Esteban Anides *, Angel Vazquez, Luis Garcia, Juan G. Avalos, Giovanny Sánchez, Héctor M. Pérez and Juan C. Sánchez

Instituto Politécnico Nacional, ESIME Culhuacan, Av. Santa Ana No. 1000, Ciudad de México 04260, Mexico
* Correspondence: edua_95pim@hotmail.es (E.P.); eanidesc1800@alumno.ipn.mx (E.A.); Tel.: +52-55-2101-9551 (E.P. & E.A.)

Abstract: Recently, the use of acoustic echo canceller (AEC) systems in portable devices has significantly increased. Therefore, the need for superior audio quality in resource-constrained devices opens new horizons in the creation of high-convergence speed adaptive algorithms and optimal digital designs. Nowadays, AEC systems mainly use the least mean square (LMS) algorithm, since its implementation in digital hardware architectures demands low area consumption. However, its performance in acoustic echo cancellation is limited. In addition, this algorithm presents local convergence optimization problems. Recently, new approaches, based on stochastic optimization algorithms, have emerged to increase the probability of encountering the global minimum. However, the simulation of these algorithms requires high-performance computational systems. As a consequence, these algorithms have only been conceived as theoretical approaches. Therefore, the creation of a low-complexity algorithm potentially allows the development of compact AEC hardware architectures. In this paper, we propose a new convex combination, based on grey wolf optimization and LMS algorithms, to save area and achieve high convergence speed by exploiting to the maximum the best features of each algorithm. In addition, the proposed convex combination algorithm shows superior tracking capabilities when compared with existing approaches. Furthermore, we present a new neuromorphic hardware architecture to simulate the proposed convex combination. Specifically, we present a customized time-multiplexing control scheme to dynamically vary the number of search agents. To demonstrate the high computational capabilities of this architecture, we performed exhaustive testing. In this way, we proved that it can be used in real-world acoustic echo cancellation scenarios.

Keywords: grey wolf optimization; swarm intelligence; real world application; spiking neural P system; AEC system; LMS; neuromorphic architecture; FPGA

MSC: 68W10; 68Q06; 68Q45; 68W99; 94A12

Citation: Pichardo, E.; Anides, E.; Vazquez, A.; Garcia, L.; Avalos, J.G.; Sánchez, G.; Pérez, H.M.; Sánchez, J.C. A Compact and High-Performance Acoustic Echo Canceller Neural Processor Using Grey Wolf Optimizer along with Least Mean Square Algorithms. *Mathematics* **2023**, *11*, 1421. https://doi.org/10.3390/math11061421

Academic Editor: Gaige Wang

Received: 1 February 2023
Revised: 28 February 2023
Accepted: 13 March 2023
Published: 15 March 2023

1. Introduction

Nowadays, acoustic echo canceller (AEC) systems mainly use the least mean square (LMS) adaptive filter algorithm, since it exhibits low computational complexity [1]. Therefore, this algorithm is easy to implement in low-area devices. However, its use can cause instability in the system, since it has an uni-model error surface. Hence, this algorithm is limited when a multimodal error surface is considered, since this algorithm must be initialized in the valley of the global optimum to converge to the global optimum [2]. Another aspect is linked to its convergence speed, because this depends on the eigen-value spread of the correlation Matrix (R) [3]. To overcome these problems, bio-inspired evolutionary [4,5] and swarm intelligence (SI) techniques [6–8], have emerged as potential solutions for the parameter optimization. Recently, the grey wolf optimization (GWO) algorithm [6], which is considered to be one of the most recent metaheuristic SI methods, has proven to be very successful in multiple fields, such as image processing [9,10], health care/bioinformatics [11,12], control systems [13], electromagnetics [14,15], environmental applications [16,17], and adaptive filtering [18,19], among others [20,21], since this algorithm offers impressive characteristics in contrast with other swarm intelligence methods.

In general terms, the GWO algorithm shows a good balance between the exploration and exploitation processes during the search. As a consequence, this allows high accuracy. From the engineering point of view, this algorithm can be seen as a potential solution in practical applications, since it involves fewer parameters and less memory compared with the most advanced metaheuristic SI methods. Therefore, this algorithm requires few controlling parameters. As a consequence, its practicality is increased significantly [21]. Based on these features, new variants of the GWO algorithm can be developed to be applied in practical and real-time acoustic echo canceller (AEC) systems.

In general, bio-inspired algorithms are capable of globally optimizing any class of adaptive filter structures. Therefore, the use of these algorithms opens new opportunities in the development of advanced adaptive filters and enables their implementation in embedded devices [22]. Specifically, recent studies have proven that the particle swarm optimization (PSO) algorithm can be used in the development of AEC systems. For example [23] proposed a PSO-based AEC system to guarantee a high degree of accuracy in terms of echo return loss enhancement (ERLE). Specifically, the authors used the PSO to perform the error minimization in the frequency domain. Ref. [24] presented a PSO-based AEC system, in which the PSO algorithm provides a very fast convergence rate by performing the error minimization in the time domain. Another PSO-based AEC system was developed by [25]. This approach was applied to multichannel systems to improve stability.

After analysing all the works mentioned above, we found that the PSO algorithm may suffer some limitations, especially when a heavy constraint optimization is required. Under this situation, one may get trapped in local minima. To avoid this, the GWO algorithm can be seen as a potential solution, since it offers a high convergence rate at the cost of exhibiting high computational complexity and low tracking capabilities [26–28]. In particular, good performance can be obtained, especially when a large population is used, i.e., population-based meta-heuristics generally have greater exploration when compared to a single solution-based algorithm [6]. However, its implementation in current embedded devices becomes infeasible. Hence, the development of new variants of GWO algorithms, to decrease their computational cost whilst maintaining performance, is still a great challenge. Recently, some authors have proposed convex combinations of adaptive filters, in which two adaptive algorithms with complementary capabilities are used to improve the steady-state MSE and the tracking performance [29,30]. With respect to the latter, the tracking performance determines the capabilities of the system to track variations in the statistics of the signals of interest [31]. Therefore, in practical AEC systems, the improvement of this factor is highly required [32].

Here, we propose a new variant of the convex adaptive filter, based on the GWO and LMS algorithms. In addition, we include the block-processing scheme in both algorithms to easily implement them in parallel hardware architectures. As a consequence, these algorithms were applied to real-time and practical AEC applications. Specifically, we used the GWO algorithm to guarantee a high convergence rate and high tracking capabilities. With respect to the latter, we added new exploration capabilities by dynamically adjusting the search space, especially in the context of abrupt changes occurring in the acoustic environment, which cannot be achieved when using the conventional GWO algorithm. A significant improvement in terms of computational cost was achieved by dynamically decreasing the population of the GWO algorithm over the filtering process. In addition, the use of the LMS allowed us to improve the steady-state MSE.

From an engineering perspective, the development of low computational complexity metaheuristic SI methods makes their implementation in current resource-constrained devices feasible. In addition, the development of advanced and novel implementation techniques also opens new opportunities in the creation of compact and high-performance devices. Specifically, the simulation of the proposed convex GWO/LMS adaptive filter requires an enormous number of large precision multipliers. Therefore, the development of low area, low latency and large precision adders and multipliers is still a challenging task. Inspired by the neural phenomena, Ionescu presented, for the first time, a class of distributing and parallel computing models, denominated as spiking neural P systems [33]. This new area of membrane computing intends to exploit, to the maximum, the intrinsic parallel capabilities of the soma of the neurons to create novel processing systems. In recent years, several authors focused their efforts to create advanced arithmetic circuits, such as adders and multipliers.

- *Parallel neural adder.*
  Recently, Ref. [34] developed a neural adder circuit to compute two large integer numbers in parallel. In spite of this achievement, this adder demands an enormous number of synapses and neurons to process large integer numbers. As a result, its use for simulation purposes becomes impractical, since metaheuristic SI methods demand high precision numerical accuracy.
- *Parallel neural multiplier.*
  In [35], the authors intended to significantly reduce the number of synapses to create an ultra-compact parallel multiplier. Despite decreasing the area consumption, the processing speed was still high.

Analyzing previous works, we noted that these circuits were proposed to process large integer numbers in parallel at the cost of increasing their processing speed. Therefore, any of these circuits can be used in the simulation of real-time AEC systems. In addition, arithmetic circuits with more precision exhibit a clear trade-off between area consumption and processing speed. From an engineering perspective, several authors still continue to make tremendous efforts to design advanced neural arithmetic circuits with high-precision to be used in real-time AEC systems. Specifically, these developments face two large challenges:

- Design of high-speed and high-precision neural adders and neural multipliers.
- Design of high-processing speed hardware architectures to efficiently simulate the proposed convex GWO/LMS adaptive filter in embedded devices.

Regarding the latter, we developed three potential proposals:

1. *Design of a high-precision floating-point parallel adder circuit.* Here, we present, for the first time, a neural adder, which computes the numbers in a customized floating-point model. We employ new variants of the SN P systems, called coloured-spikes [36], rules on the synapses [37], target indications, extended channel rules [38] and extended rules [39] to process numbers under this format in the proposed arithmetic circuit.
2. *Design of a high-precision floating-point parallel multiplier.* Here, we present, for the first time, the development of a neural multiplier to compute floating-point numbers at high processing speeds.
3. *Design of a new FPGA-based GWO/LMS neuromorphic architecture.* We design the proposed neuromorphic architecture employing basic digital components, such as shift registers, adders and multiplexors, to guarantee a low area consumption. Since the proposed convex GWO/LMS adaptive filter dynamically varies the number of search agents, we propose, for the first time, a time-multiplexing control scheme to adequately support this behavior.

Our results showed that the proposal of new variants of the GWO algorithm, along with new implementation techniques, generates a compact neuromorphic architecture to be used in practical and real-time AEC applications.

The paper is structured as follows. Section 2 introduces the fundamentals of GWO and LMS algorithms. Additionally, we introduce the proposed Convex GWO/LMS algorithm, which involves the use of a new set of equations to improve its tracking capabilities and computational complexity. Section 3 presents software simulation tests, including the justification of the selection of some tuning parameters and display comparisons between existing approaches and the proposed algorithm. In Section 4, we present a new parallel neural adder circuit and a new parallel neural multiplier circuit, which are highly demanded in the computation of the proposed algorithm. In addition, this section introduces experimental results of the implementation of the proposed Convex GWO/LMS algorithm in the Stratix IV GX EP4SGX530 FPGA. Finally, in Section 5 we provide the conclusions.

2. The Proposed Block Convex GWO/LMS Algorithm

2.1. GWO Algorithm

In general terms, the GWO is considered a population-based optimization technique inspired by the behavior of the Canis lupus [6]. This algorithm intends to mimic the hunting and hierarchical behavior of grey wolves. Regarding the latter, this algorithm involves four hierarchical levels; alpha (α) represents the fittest solution in the population, while beta (β) and delta (δ) denote the second and third best solutions, respectively. Finally, omega (ω) are the search agents. To simulate the GWO algorithm, the following equations are used:

$$\vec{W}(n+1) = \vec{W}_p(n) - \vec{A} \cdot |\vec{C} \times \vec{W}_p(n) - \vec{W}(n)| \tag{1}$$

where n denotes the current iteration, $\vec{W}_p$ is the position vector of the prey, $\vec{W}$ represents the position of a grey wolf, $\vec{A} = 2\vec{a} \cdot \vec{r}_1 - \vec{a}$ and $\vec{C} = 2\vec{r}_2$ denote coefficient vectors, where $\vec{r}_1$ and $\vec{r}_2$ represent random vectors in $[0,1]$, respectively, and $\vec{a}$ is linearly decreased from 2 to 0 using the following equation

$$\vec{a}(t) = 2 - \frac{2t}{MaxIter} \tag{2}$$

where $MaxIter$ is the total number of iterations.

To update the position of the search agents, the following equations must be used

$$\vec{W}_1(n) = \vec{W}_\alpha(n) - \vec{A}_1 \cdot |\vec{C}_1 \cdot \vec{W}_\alpha(n) - \vec{W}(n)| \tag{3}$$

$$\vec{W}_2(n) = \vec{W}_\beta(n) - \vec{A}_2 \cdot |\vec{C}_2 \cdot \vec{W}_\beta(n) - \vec{W}(n)| \tag{4}$$

$$\vec{W}_3(n) = \vec{W}_\delta(n) - \vec{A}_3 \cdot |\vec{C}_3 \cdot \vec{W}_\delta(n) - \vec{W}(n)| \tag{5}$$

$$\vec{W}_p(n+1) = \frac{\vec{W}_1(n) + \vec{W}_2(n) + \vec{W}_3(n)}{3} \tag{6}$$

where $\vec{W}_\alpha(n)$, $\vec{W}_\beta(n)$, $\vec{W}_\delta(n)$ are the best three wolves at each iteration and $\vec{W}_p(n+1)$ is the new position of the prey.

2.2. LMS Algorithm

The LMS algorithm is a practical method to obtain estimates of a filter's weights, $\mathbf{w}(n)$, in real time [1]. The equation for updating the weights of the LMS algorithm in a sample by sample fashion is given by:

$$\mathbf{w}(n+1) = \mathbf{w}(n) + \mu e(n)\mathbf{x}(n) \tag{7}$$

where $\mathbf{x}(n)$ is the current input vector, μ is a fixed step-size [0, 1], $e(n)$ is the error signal and is calculated using:

$$e(n) = d(n) - \mathbf{w}^T(n)\mathbf{x}(n) \tag{8}$$

and $d(n)$ is the desired signal.

2.3. Convex GWO/LMS

As discussed above, the GWO algorithm is widely used to solve a variety of problems since it exhibits significant properties. However, it has a number of limitations and suffers from inevitable drawbacks. The main limitation comes from the no-free-lunch (NFL) theorem, which states that no optimization algorithm is able to solve all optimization problems [40]. This means that GWO might require modification when solving some real-world problems. In particular, we proposed some modifications to the conventional GWO to be used in the development of AEC systems. Specifically, we present a new combination between the GWO and the LMS algorithms to improve tracking-capabilities and the steady-state error of the filter, respectively, since it has been proven that the use of convex combination approaches significantly improve the performance of adaptive schemes by using two adaptive algorithms [41].

As can be observed in Figure 1, the proposed system computes the coefficients of the filters, $\mathbf{w}_1$ and $\mathbf{w}_2$, as follows:

- *The calculation of the filter coefficients by employing the LMS algorithm.* Here, we use the block LMS algorithm to calculate the $\mathbf{w}_1$ weights. This has allowed us to create efficient implementations by using commercially available embedded devices [42,43]. The adaptive filter coefficients $\mathbf{w}_1$ are defined as:

$$\mathbf{w}_1(n+1) = \mathbf{w}_1(n) + \mu\mathbf{X}(n)\mathbf{e}_{LMS}(n) \tag{9}$$

where $\mathbf{w}_1(n)$ is the weight-vector $\mathbf{w}_1(n) = \begin{bmatrix} w(0), & w(1), & \cdots & w(N-1) \end{bmatrix}^T$, μ is the step-size, and $\mathbf{e}_{LMS}(n)$ is the error vector. The error vector is composed as:

$$\mathbf{e}_{LMS}(n) = \begin{bmatrix} e(nL), & e(nL-1), & \cdots & e(L(n+1)+1) \end{bmatrix}^T \tag{10}$$

and $\mathbf{X}(n)$ is derived from the current input block

$$\mathbf{x}(n) = \begin{bmatrix} x(nL), & x(nL-1), & \cdots & x(nL-N+1) \end{bmatrix} \tag{11}$$

where L depicts the length of the block and N is the size of the filter. Additionally, $\mathbf{X}(n)$ is calculated as follows:

$$\mathbf{X}(n) = \begin{bmatrix} x(nL), & x(nL-1), & \cdots & x(nL-N+1) \\ x(nL-1) & x(nL-2) & \cdots & x(nL-N) \\ \vdots & \vdots & \ddots & \vdots \\ x(nL-L+1) & x(nL-L) & \cdots & x(nL-L-N+2) \end{bmatrix}^T \tag{12}$$

The error vector is obtained as follows:

$$\mathbf{e}_{LMS}(n) = \mathbf{d}(n) - \mathbf{y}_{LMS}(n) \tag{13}$$

where the desired response vector $\mathbf{d}(n)$ is given by L

$$\mathbf{d}(n) = \begin{bmatrix} d(nL), & d(nL-1), & \cdots & d(nL-N+1) \end{bmatrix}^T \tag{14}$$

The filter output $\mathbf{y}_{LMS}(n)$ of each block is given by the following matrix vector product:

$$\mathbf{y}_{LMS}(n) = \mathbf{X}(n) \cdot \mathbf{w}_1(n) \tag{15}$$

- *The calculation of the filter coefficients by employing the GWO algorithm.* Here, the use of the block-processing scheme in SI algorithms allowed us to process the signal in real-time applications. As a consequence, this potentially allows full exploitation of the performance capabilities of the parallel hardware architectures by simulating the intrinsic parallel computational capabilities of the SI algorithms. In this work, we introduce, for the first time, the block-based GWO algorithm to be applied in practical and real-time AEC applications, as shown in Figure 2.

The encircling behavior of the grey wolves is mathematically described as follows:

$$\overrightarrow{W}(n+1) = \overrightarrow{W}_p(n) - \overrightarrow{A} \cdot |\overrightarrow{C} \cdot \overrightarrow{W}_p(n) - \overrightarrow{W}(n)| \tag{16}$$

where $\overrightarrow{A} = 2\phi(n) \cdot \overrightarrow{r}_1 - \phi(n)$ denotes a coefficient vector, and $\phi(n)$ is in function of the value of instantaneous error. In addition, this value is in a range of 0 and 2. This can be described by:

$$\phi(n) = \frac{4}{1 + e^{-\lfloor e_{GWO}(n) \rceil}} - 2 \tag{17}$$

To obtain the best solution, a fitness function, which is defined in terms of the mean square error (MSE), is used to evaluate each search agent. Hence, the fitness value f_k of the position $\overrightarrow{W}$ is expressed as:

$$f_k(n) = \frac{1}{L} \sum_{i=1}^{L} e_k^2(i) \tag{18}$$

where $k = 1, 2, \ldots, P(n)$. Here, we propose a mechanism to dynamically adjust the number of search agents over the filtering process, i.e., $P(n)$ denotes the current number of search agents. Specifically, this adjustment is a function of the power of the instantaneous error, and is obtained as follows:

$$P(n) = \lfloor \frac{2 \cdot (P_{max} - P_{min})}{(1 + e^{-\lfloor e_{GWO}(n) \rceil})} - (P_{max} - P_{min}) \rfloor + P_{min} \tag{19}$$

where P_{max} and P_{min} defines the maximum and the minimum number of search agents, respectively. In addition, we use Equations (3)–(6) to update the position of the search agents and the prey. On the other hand, the error signal, $e_{GWO}(n)$, and filter output, $y_{GWO}(n)$, are described as follows:

$$\mathbf{e}_{GWO}(n) = \mathbf{d}(n) - \mathbf{y}_{GWO}(n) \tag{20}$$

$$\mathbf{y}_{GWO}(n) = \mathbf{X}(n) \cdot \mathbf{w}_2(n) \tag{21}$$

where $\mathbf{w}_2(n) = \overrightarrow{W}_\alpha$.
Considering the output of both filters, $\mathbf{y}_{GWO}(n)$ and $\mathbf{y}_{LMS}(n)$ at time n, we obtain the output of the parallel filter as:

$$\mathbf{y}(n) = \lambda(n) \cdot \mathbf{y}_{GWO}(n) - [1 - \lambda(n)] \cdot \mathbf{y}_{LMS}(n) \tag{22}$$

where $\lambda(n)$ is a mixing parameter, which is in the range [0, 1]. This parameter is used to control the combination of the two filters at each iteration, and is defined by:

$$\lambda(n) = \frac{1}{e^{-a(n)}} \tag{23}$$

where $a(n)$ is an auxiliary parameter used to minimize the instantaneous square error of the filters, and is obtained as follows:

$$a(n+1) = a(n) + \mu_a \cdot e(1) \cdot \{e_{GWO}(1) - e_{LMS}(1)\} \cdot \lambda(n) \cdot [1 - \lambda(n)] \tag{24}$$

Finally, the performance of the combined filter can be further improved by transferring a portion of $\mathbf{w}_1$ to $\overrightarrow{W}_\alpha$, $\overrightarrow{W}_\beta$ and $\overrightarrow{W}_\delta$. This can be formulated as follows:

$$\overrightarrow{W}_\alpha(n) = \lambda(n) \cdot \overrightarrow{W}_\alpha(n) - [1 - \lambda(n)] \cdot \mathbf{w}_1(n) \tag{25}$$

$$\overrightarrow{W}_\beta(n) = \lambda(n) \cdot \overrightarrow{W}_\beta(n) - [1 - \lambda(n)] \cdot \mathbf{w}_1(n) \tag{26}$$

$$\overrightarrow{W}_{\delta}(n) = \lambda(n) \cdot \overrightarrow{W}_{\delta}(n) - [1 - \lambda(n)] \cdot \mathbf{w}_1(n) \tag{27}$$

In this way, the GWO filter can reach a lower steady-state MSE and continues to keep a high convergence rate.

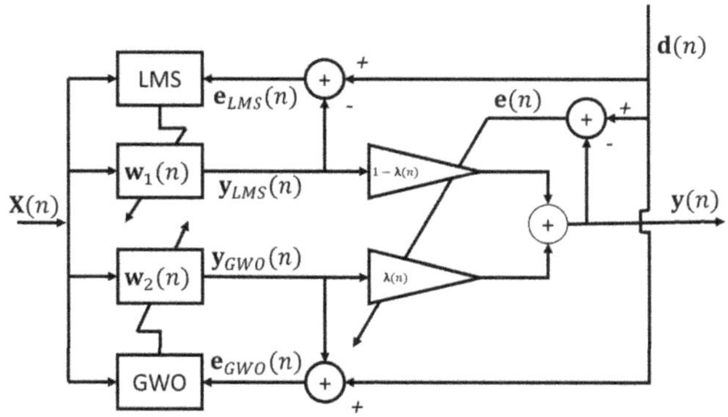

Figure 1. Proposed convex structure.

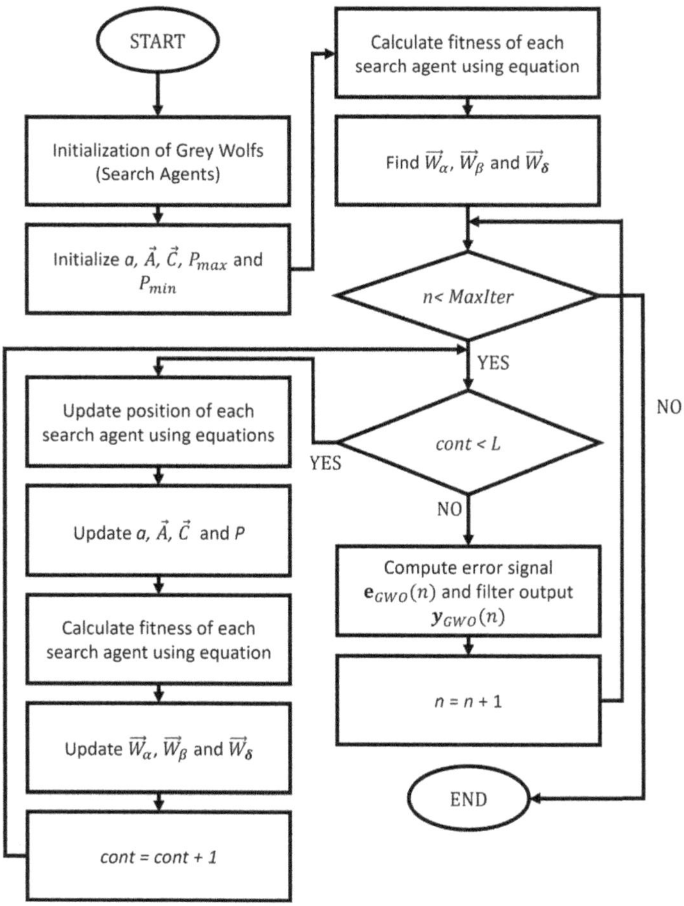

Figure 2. The flowchart of the block GWO algorithm.

3. Pure Software Simulation

Before implementing the proposed convex GWO/LMS adaptive filter in parallel hardware architectures, we simulated it in Matlab software for testing and comparison purposes. Specifically, we simulated the conventional LMS, GWO and our proposal to compare their performances. In addition, we used AEC structure, in which the existing approaches and the proposed convex GWO/LMS adaptive filter were used, as shown in Figure 3. As can be observed, $x(n)$ is the far-end input signal, $e(n)$ denotes the residual echo signal, $d(n)$ represents the sum of the echo signal, $y(n)$ and the background noise, $e_0(n)$.

To simulate the proposed convex GWO/LMS adaptive filter and existing approaches, we considered the following conditions:

1. We used an impulse response as the echo path, obtained from the ITU-T G168 recommendation [44]. This echo path was modeled using 500 coefficients, as shown in Figure 4.
2. The echo signal was mixed with white Gaussian noise (SNR = 20 dB).
3. We used an AR(1) process as input signal.
4. The filter and the block had the same length as the echo path. As is well known, the efficiency of the block processing scheme is guaranteed when the length of the blocks is greater than, or equal to, the order of the filter [45,46].
5. In the proposed algorithm, the swarm size was defined in the range of 15–30 search agents.
6. To test the tracking capabilities of the proposed algorithm, we induced an abrupt change in the impulse response of the acoustic echo path in the middle of the adaptive filtering process by multiplying the acoustic paths by −1.
7. The maximum number of iterations was set to 2,000,000.

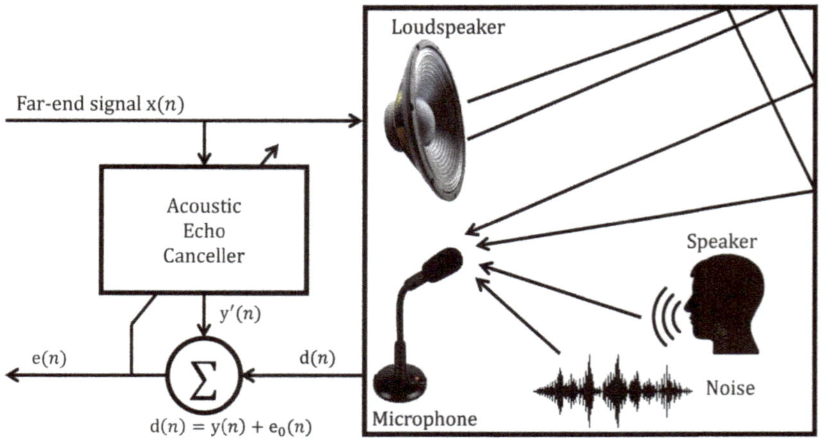

Figure 3. Structure of the acoustic echo canceller.

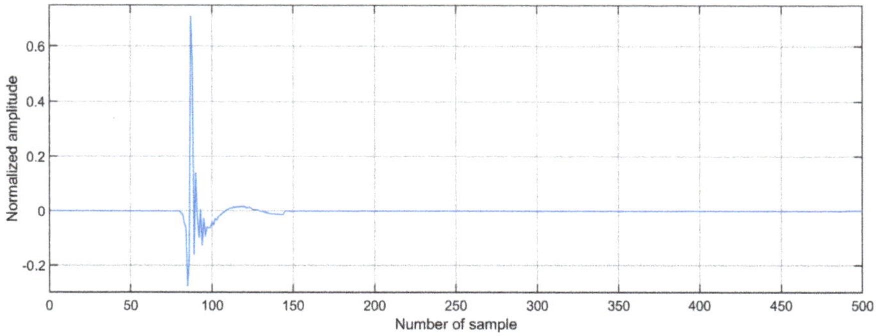

Figure 4. Acoustic echo path used for the simulation of the existing and the proposed algorithms.

Considering a single-talk scenario, we performed three experiments to verify the performance of the proposed convex GWO/LMS adaptive filter in terms of echo return loss enhancement, ($ERLE = 10log_{10}(\frac{d(n)^2}{e(n)^2})$).

- *Effect of changing the order of the adaptive filter.*
  Figure 5 shows the evaluation of the ERLE level of the proposed algorithm. In this evaluation, we used a population size of 30 search agents and varied the number of coefficients of the adaptive filter from 150 to 500. The aim of this experiment was to observe how the ERLE level was affected by using different numbers of coefficients. Here, the proposed convex GWO/LMS adaptive filter guaranteed the same ERLE level regardless of the number of coefficients, as shown in Figure 5. Therefore, we used the minimum number of coefficients, since this factor is relevant, especially when it is implemented in resource-constrained devices.

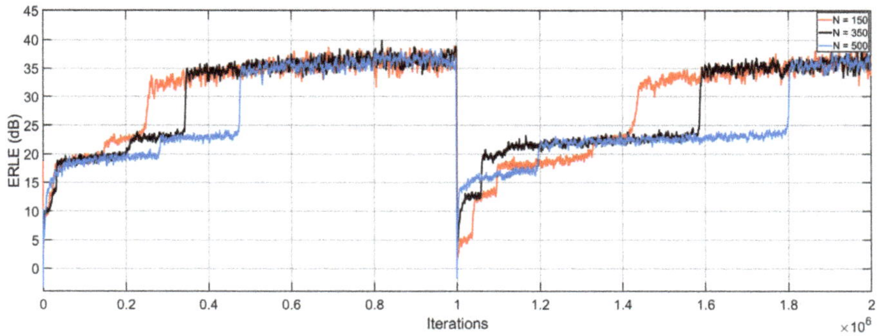

Figure 5. ERLE level for different number of coefficients N.

- *Effect of varying the number of search agents of the proposed convex GWO/LMS adaptive filter*. In this experiment, we varied the number of search agents from 30 to 200 to evaluate the performance of the proposed algorithm in terms of ERLE level. Since the minimum number of adaptive filter coefficients (150) guaranteed a good ERLE level, we used this number for the experiment. As can be observed from Figure 6, we obtained the same performance by using different numbers of search agents. In this way, we confirmed that, when employing the minimum number of search agents, the proposed method reached a good ERLE level. From an engineering perspective, this has a great impact on the performance of resource-constrained devices, since the proposed algorithm intends to reduce its computational cost by decreasing the number of search agents over the adaptive process.

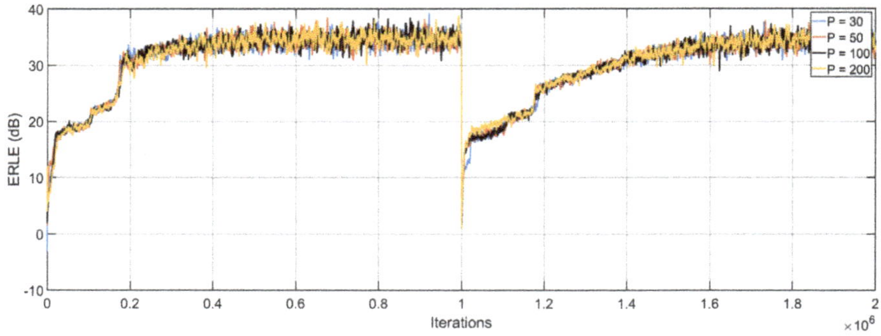

Figure 6. ERLE for different numbers of search agents P.

- *Performance comparison between the proposed convex GWO/LMS and existing approaches.* We performed two experiments to make a coherent comparison between the proposed convex GWO/LMS and the following existing approaches: LMS algorithm [1], conventional GWO [6], PSO [23], differential evolution (DE) algorithm [47], artificial bee colony optimization (ABC) [48], hybrid PSO–LMS [49] and modified ABC (MABC) [50]. In the first experiment, we shifted the acoustic path, and in the second experiment, we multiplied the acoustic path by -1 at the middle of the adaptive process. In addition, the tuning parameters of all the algorithms were selected to guarantee the best performance. Such tuning parameters are displayed in the following list:

1. **LMS**
   - Convergence factor $= 9 \times 10^{-7}$
2. **GWO**
   - a decreases linearly from 2 to 0
   - lower bound $= -1$
   - Upper bound $= 1$
   - Population size $= 50$
3. **PSO**
   - Acceleration coefficient, $c_1 = 1.6$
   - Acceleration coefficient, $c_2 = 1$
   - Inertia weight $= 0.8$
   - Lower bound $= -1$
   - Upper bound $= 1$
   - Population size $= 100$
4. **DE**
   - Crossover rate $= 0.35$
   - Scaling factor $= 0.8$
   - Combination factor $= 0.25$
   - Lower bound $= -1$
   - Upper bound $= 1$
   - Population size $= 50$
5. **ABC**
   - Evaporation parameter $= 0.1$
   - Pheromone $= 0.6$
   - Lower bound $= -1$
   - Upper bound $= 1$
   - Population size $= 50$

6. **PSO-LMS**
   - Acceleration coefficient, $c_1 = 0.00005$
   - Acceleration coefficient, $c_2 = 1.2$
   - Inertia weight $= 1$
   - Lower bound $= -1$
   - Upper bound $= 1$
   - Convergence factor $= 1 \times 10^{-9}$
   - Population size $= 60$
7. **MABC**
   - Evaporation parameter $= 0.1$
   - Pheromone $= 0.6$
   - Lower bound $= -1$
   - Upper bound $= 1$
   - Population size $= 50$
   - Convergence factor $= 3 \times 10^{-5}$

As can be observed from Figure 7, the proposed convex GWO/LMS adaptive filter showed the best performance, in terms of ERLE level and convergence speed, by expending a large number of additions and multiplications, as shown in Table 1. In contrast, the LMS algorithm expended fewer additions and multiplications compared with the proposed algorithm at the cost of exhibiting a slow convergence speed. In general, the excessive number of additions and multiplications makes the implementation of the GWO adaptive filter in current embedded devices, such as DSP and FPGA devices, impractical since they have a limited number of these circuits. Here, our proposal intended to dynamically decrease the number of search agents, as shown in Figure 8. As a consequence, the number of multiplications and additions also reduced (Equation (19)). In this way, the implementation of our proposal in embedded devices can be feasible.

Table 1. Comparison between the proposed convex GWO/LMS system and existing approaches in terms of the number of additions and multiplications.

Algorithm	Multiplications	Additions
LMS [1]	6,000,118,333	6,000,118,333
GWO [6]	1,349,996,758,333	2,249,994,508,333
PSO [23]	1,500,036,249,900	1,500,036,249,900
DE [47]	149,999,625,000	299,999,250,000
ABC [48]	600,058,499,850	749,938,125,150
PSO-LMS [49]	903,077,742,300	906,037,734,900
MABC [50]	1,799,955,500,100	1,620,075,949,800
Convex GWO/LMS	73,599,043,327	46,560,966,659

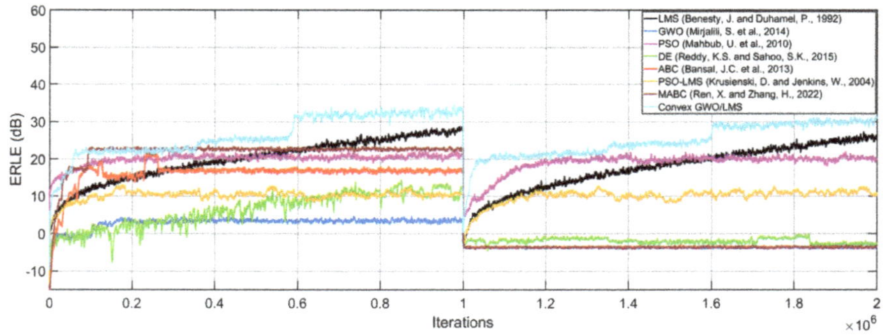

(a)

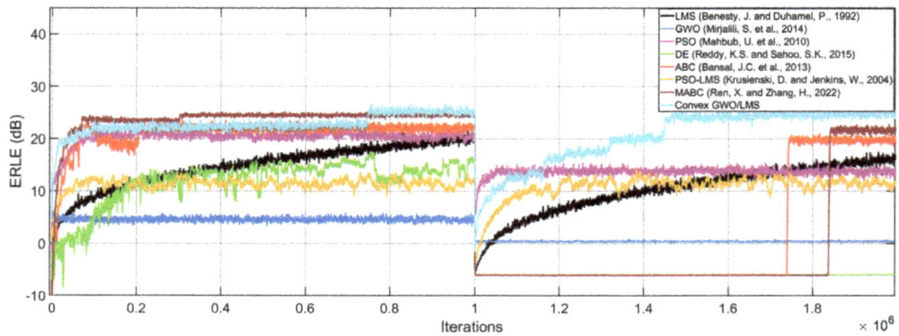

(b)

Figure 7. ERLE learning curves obtained by simulating existing approaches and the proposed algorithm; (**a**) by shifting the acoustic path at the middle of iterations and (**b**) by multiplying the acoustic path by −1 at the middle of iterations [1,15,23,48–51].

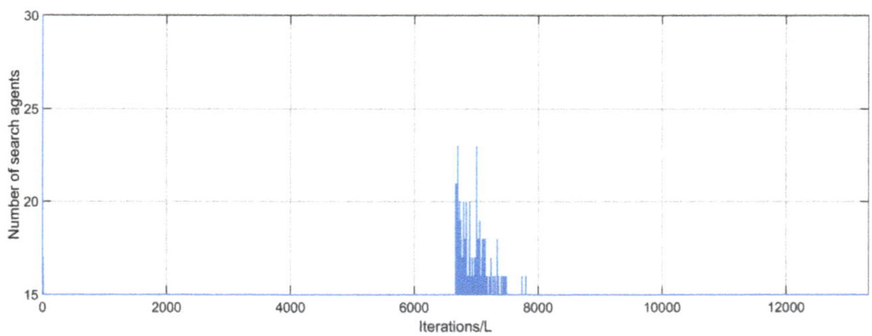

Figure 8. The number of search agents used during the adaptation process.

- *Statistical comparison between the proposed convex GWO/LMS and existing approaches* Statistical results were obtained with two different evaluations: average value of ERLE in dB and its corresponding standard deviation. The maximum number of iterations was set to 2,000,000 and each algorithm ran 10 times. The results are reported in Table 2.

Table 2. Comparison between the proposed convex GWO/LMS system and existing approaches in terms of average value of ERLE and standard deviation in dB.

Algorithm	Average Value	Standard Deviation
LMS [1]	14.7202	4.1761
GWO [6]	4.5653	0.3892
PSO [23]	20.2452	1.5622
DE [47]	11.7972	4.4434
ABC [48]	21.0656	3.4164
PSO-LMS [49]	11.2859	1.1497
MABC [50]	23.6927	3.0326
Convex GWO/LMS	22.7590	2.0259

As can be observed from Table 2, the proposed convex GWO/LMS achieved a good average ERLE level, in comparison with other existing algorithms. It should be noted that the MABC algorithm possessed the highest average value. Nonetheless, this algorithm presented a lower convergence speed, especially when abrupt changes occurred, as shown in Figure 7b. On the other hand, the GWO, PSO and PSO-LMS algorithms presented lower standard deviations in comparison with the proposed Convex GWO/LMS algorithm. Nonetheless, the proposed method achieved a higher average value.

4. Pure Hardware Simulation

To adequately simulate the proposed convex GWO/LMS system, we made extraordinary efforts to develop compact, high-processing and high-precision neural arithmetic circuits, such as adder and multiplier, since these two circuits are highly demanded in the computation of the proposed algorithm, as shown in Table 1. Specifically, we developed, for the first time, a customized floating-point representation to perform additions and multiplications with high precision.

To compute the numbers in floating-point format, we established the format criteria of the input numbers u and v to be either added or multiplier, as follows:

1. In general terms, the numbers u and v are separated in integer and fractional digits. Specifically, the number of integer digits and the number of fractional digits can be chosen over a range $(u_{g_0} \cdots u_{g_1} \cdots u_{g_m}, v_{g_0} \cdots v_{g_1} \cdots v_{g_m})$, as shown in Figure 9. Here, we painted the digits with a specific color by using a variant of the SN P systems called coloured spikes to easily distinguish the units, tens, hundreds, etc., of the integer part and tenths, hundredths, thousandths, etc., of the fractional part. This strategy was also used to represent the digits of the results of the addition and multiplication operations.

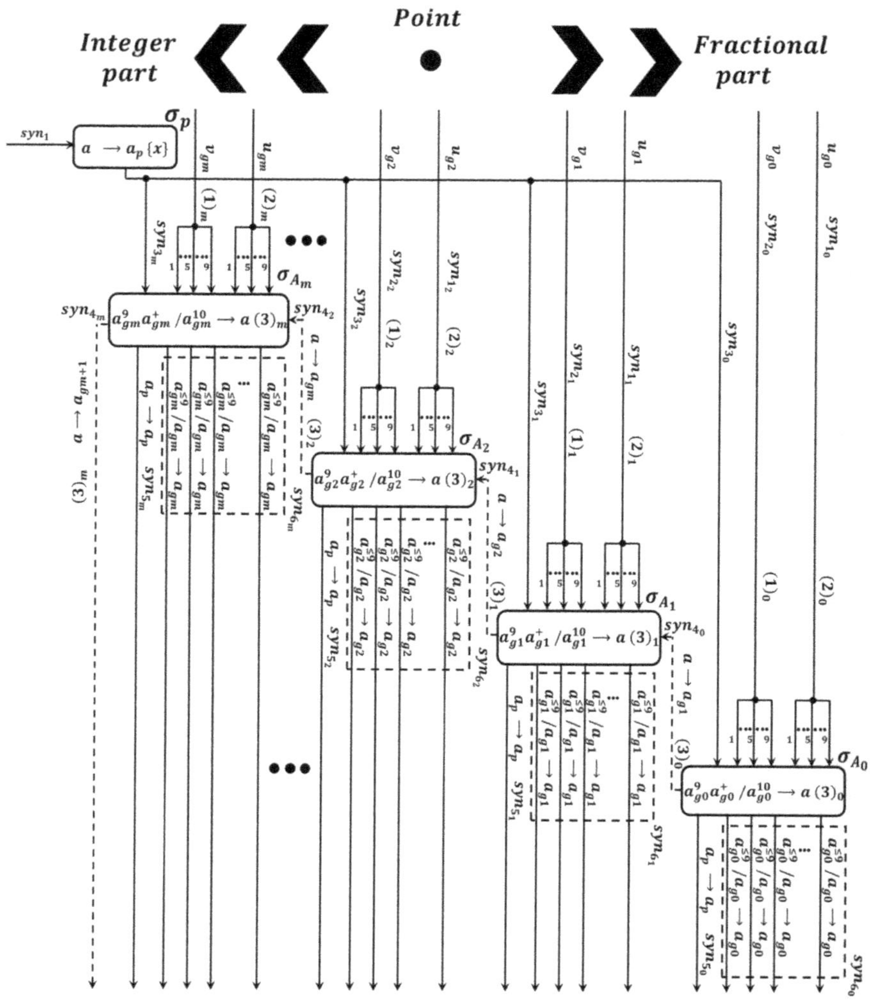

Figure 9. General structure of the proposed floating-point neural adder.

2. Here, each synaptic channel (1) and synaptic channel (2) has a set of dendritic branches. To perform customized floating-point addition, the integer and fractional digits of u and v were represented as the number of active dendritic branches, labeled as $1, \cdots, 9$. In the case of calculating a customized floating-point multiplication, the integer and fractional digits of u are represented as the number of spikes denoted in the extended rule $(a^p_u)^+/a^p_u \rightarrow a^p_u$. On the other hand, the integer and fractional digits of v activate the number of branches according to their value.

- *Parallel neural adder circuit* $\prod_{add}$.
The proposed neural adder circuit $\prod_{add}$ has a set of neurons, $\sigma_{A_0}, \cdots, \sigma_{A_m}, \cdots$, and a neuron, σ_p. The set of neurons σ_A is in charge of computing the addition of two numbers, where each number is composed of an integer part and a fractional part, and neuron, σ_p, determines the position of the point to segment the number into an integer part and a fractional part, as shown in Figure 9.
The proposed neural adder circuit $\prod_{add}$ computes the addition as follows:
In the initial state, the neurons, σ_A, are empty. At this time, the dendritic branches of synaptic channels, (1) and (2), are activated according to the value of the digits, u and

v, respectively. For example, if the value of a digit, v or u, is equal to five, then five dendritic branches are activated. Therefore, these dendritic branches allow the flow of five spikes towards a specific neuron, σ_A. Simultaneously, the neuron, σ_p, places the point to segment the number into integer digits and the fractional digits by setting the firing rule, $a \rightarrow a_p\{X\}$. This spiking rule implies that, if neuron σ_p receives a spike at any time, it fires and sends a spike to a specific neuron, σ_{A_x}. To do this, we used a variant of the SN P systems called target indications. In this way, the point was allocated according to the desired precision. Therefore, the point, which was represented as a spike, was stored in a specific neuron, σ_{A_x}. Once the neural circuit was configured, the partial additions of the spikes started.

Here, the addition of the numbers was performed in a single simulation step, since all neurons, σ_A, processed their respective input spikes simultaneously. Additionally, the carry spike was obtained when any neuron, σ_A, accumulated ten spikes. At this moment, the spiking rule, $a^9a^+/a^{10} \rightarrow a(3)$, was set. After one simulation step, the result, represented by the remaining spikes in the soma of each neuron, is placed at the output synapses. In addition, neuron σ_{A_x} sends the spike point to the environment by enabling its spiking rule, $a_p \rightarrow a_p$.

In this work, we proved that the use of several variants of the SN P systems, such as coloured-spikes [36], rules on the synapses [37], target indications [51], extended channel rules [38], extended rules [39] and dendritic trunks [52] creates an ultra-compact and high performance circuit, instead of only using the soma as conventional SN P systems do. In particular, the proposed neural circuit required fewer simulation steps, neurons and synapses compared with the existing approach [34], as shown in Table 3.

Table 3. Comparison between the existing neural adder [34] and this work in terms of synapses/neurons and simulation steps. Here, n represents the number of digits of v and u. Adapted from [53].

Approach	[34]	This Work
Synapses	$41\,n$	$14\,n$
Neurons	$12\,n$	n
Simulation steps	$28 + (n/2 - 1)$	1

- *Parallel neural multiplier circuit* $\prod_{mul}$.

  Since the multiplier is one of the most demanding in terms of processing and area consumption, a large number of techniques have been developed to minimize these factors. Recently, several authors have used SN P systems to create an efficient parallel multiplier circuit. However, the improvement of processing speed is still an issue since most of the studies improved the area consumption. The improvement of this factor potentially allows the development of high performance systems to support AEC systems in real-time. In addition, the development of a high-precision neural multiplier is still a challenging task, since this factor is especially relevant when metaheuristic algorithms are simulated. Here, we developed a neural multiplier that shows higher processing speeds, in comparison with existing approaches, by keeping the area consumption low. To achieve this, we reduced the processing time by using cutting-edge variants of the SN P systems, such as coloured-spikes [36], rules on the synapses [37], target indications [51], extended rules [39] and dendritic trunks [52]. Specifically, we used these variants to significantly improve the time expended in the computation of the partial products of the multiplication, in comparison with the most recent approach [35].

  The proposed neural multiplier circuit $\prod_{mul}$ is composed of a set of neurons (σ_{A_0}, $\dots, \sigma_{A_{n-j}}, \dots, \sigma_{A_{n-1}}, \dots, \sigma_{A_{2(n-j)}}, \dots, \sigma_{A_{2n-1}}$), and neuron, σ_{in}, as shown in Figure 10. In general terms, neurons, σ_A, perform the addition of the partial products, where each partial product is computed by using dendritic branches. In particular, each neuron σ_A computes the partial product between a single digit of u and a digit of v, where the digits of u are represented as p spikes, which are generated by neuron σ_{in} when its spiking rule, $(a_u^p)^+/a_u^p \rightarrow a_u^p$, is applied, and the value of each digit of v activates an equal number of dendritic branches.

The proposed neural multiplier circuit $\prod_{mul}$ performs the multiplication, as follows: At the initial simulation step, neurons, σ_A, are empty. At this time, neuron, σ_{in}, places the spike point by receiving a spike. Therefore, it fires and sends the spike point to a specific neuron, σ_{A_x}, using the target indications [51]. In this way, the digits of u or v are segmented into integer and fractional parts. Once the multiplier is configured, $m \cdot n$ partial products are executed in parallel. To perform any partial product, neuron, σ_{in}, fires p spikes which are sent to its corresponding neuron, σ_A. The soma of this neuron receives many copies of the spikes, p, in function of the number of active dendritic branches. For example, if neuron multiplies 3×3, this implies that neuron, σ_{A_x}, receives three copies of three spikes by means of three dendritic branches. In this way, the neuron, σ_A, increases its potential of the soma by performing three additions. Therefore, the synaptic weights are not required since many approaches use them to perform partial products. Hence, the number of branched connections can be variable. In this way, the neuron σ_A enables the optimal number of synaptic connections. From an engineering perspective, we proposed the use of a variable number of forked connections, since the implementation of a very-large number of synaptic connections in advanced FPGAs creates critical routing problems. Once the result is obtained, neuron, σ_{in}, places the spike point according to the addition of the number of fractional digits, as in conventional multiplication. Therefore, σ_A, which received the spike point at the initial simulation, fired the point spike by applying it firing rule $(a_p \rightarrow a_p)$.

As can be observed from Table 4, we achieved a significant improvement in terms of simulation steps, since only one simulation step was required to perform a multiplication of two numbers with any length. This aspect is relevant, especially when real-time AEC system simulations are required. Additionally, we reduced the number of synapses in comparison with the existing work.

Table 4. Comparison between the proposed neural multiplier and the existing neural multiplier [35] in terms of simulation steps, synapses and neurons. Where n denotes the number of digits of v and u. Adapted from [53].

Existing Neural Multiplier	[35]	This Work
Synapses	$9 \cdot n \cdot m$	$n \cdot m$
Neurons	n	n
Simulation steps	10	1

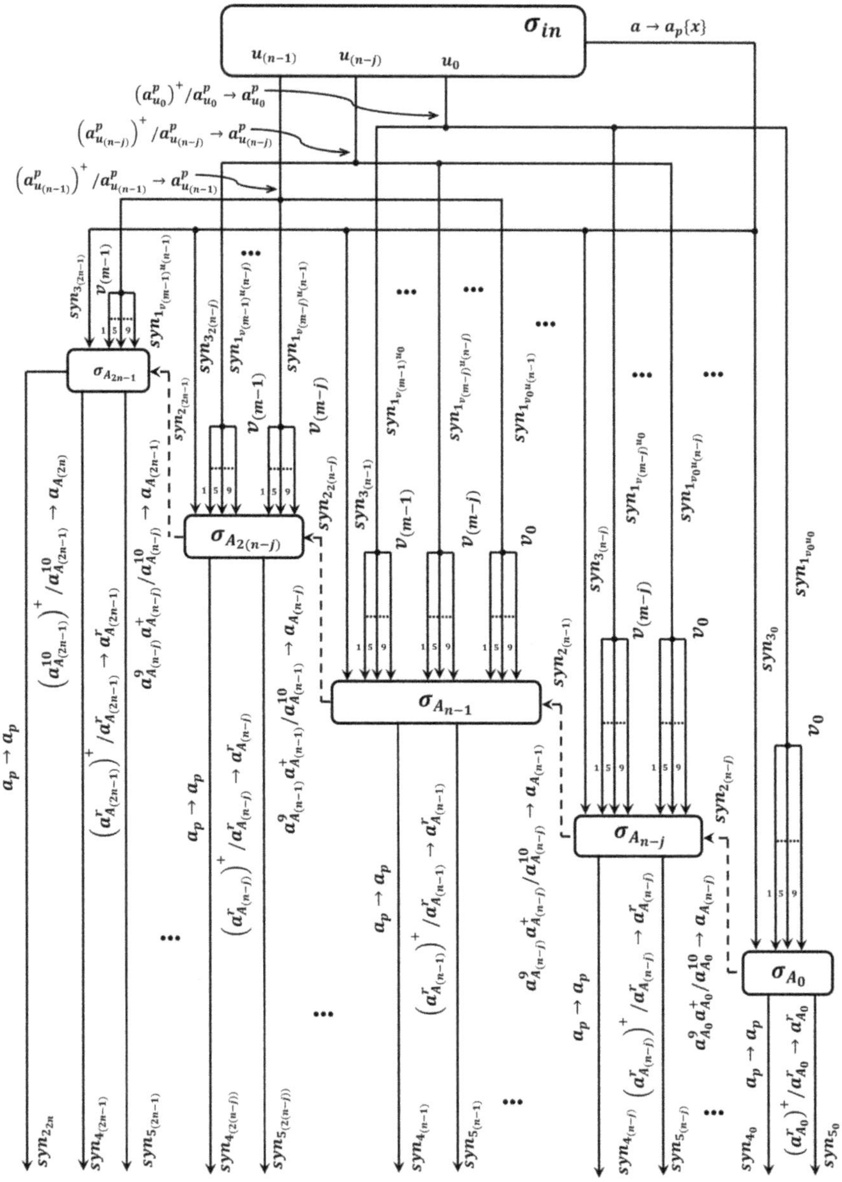

Figure 10. Structure of the neural multiplier.

4.1. Experimental Results

To demonstrate the computational capabilities of the proposed convex GWO/LMS adaptive filter, we considered an arbitrary single-talk scenario, as shown in Figure 11.

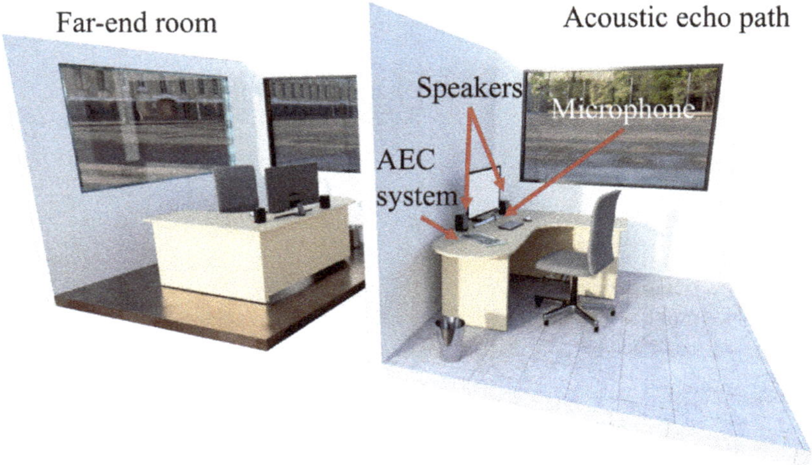

Figure 11. Scheme of the AEC prototype.

Under this configuration, we used the proposed AEC system to perform the simulation of the proposed algorithm by using the experimental setup of Figure 11. Specifically, the proposed system has an AEC neural processor as its main core to cancel the echo signal and the background noise by simulating the proposed convex GWO/LMS adaptive filter. As can be observed from Figure 12, the AEC neural processor is composed of a control unit, CU, a set of processing cores, α, β, δ, ω, LMS, convex, and BRAMs. Figure 13 shows a sequence diagram to specify how each processing core computes specific parts of the proposed convex GWO/LMS adaptive filter. Here, we used the BRAMs to store L and N samples of the signals, x, and d, where $L = N$. In this way, we implemented the block processing scheme. Once these values are stored in their respective BRAMs, the computation of the proposed convex GWO/LMS adaptive filter starts. In this way, the AEC neural processor computes the new variant of the GWO algorithm and the LMS algorithm simultaneously. Specifically, we propose a new time-multiplexing control scheme to automatically update the number of search agents of the GWO algorithm over the processing time. Under this scheme, the number of search agents, ω, which are divided into three parts, is enabled or disabled either by the processor, α, or β, or δ. It is important to keep in mind that processing cores, α, β, δ evaluate the response of their respective processors, ω, simultaneously. According to this, the proposed time-multiplexing control scheme uses the signals, en_w_α, en_w_β, and en_w_δ, to enable or disable the number of search agents according to the simulation needs, as shown in Figure 12. Here, the use of the time-multiplexing control scheme allowed us to significantly decrease the number of buses to transfer the coefficients between the processing cores, ω, and the processing cores, α, or β, or δ. This saving allowed us to implement a full connection between the processing cores, α, β and δ. As a consequence, the evaluation of the searching point of each agent was performed by processing cores, α, β and δ simultaneously.

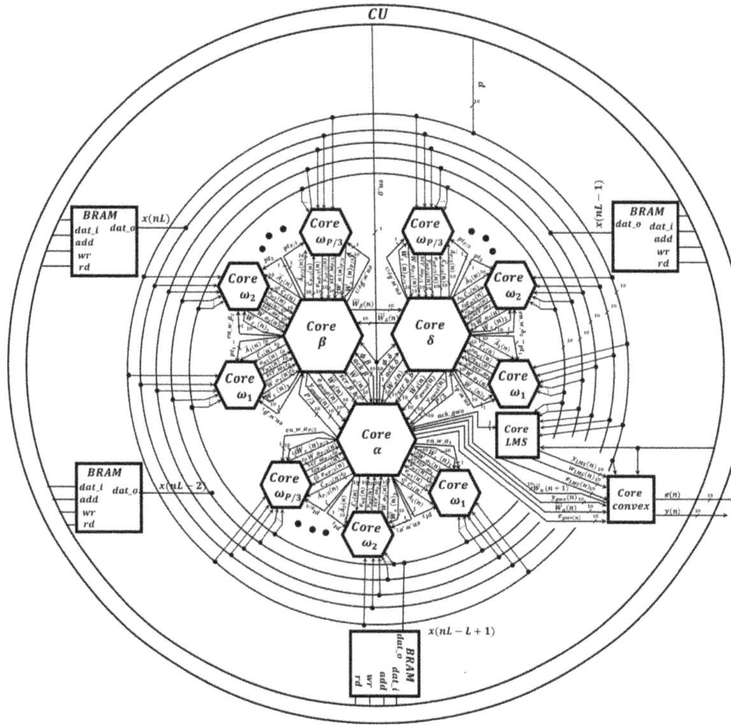

Figure 12. Scheme of the proposed AEC neural processor.

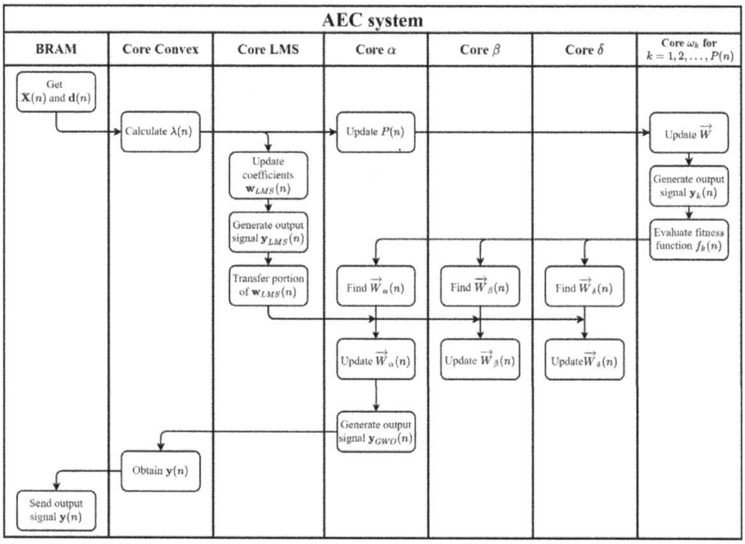

Figure 13. The sequential diagram to describe how the proposed convex GWO/LMS adaptive filter is executed by means of the processing cores.

In this work, we used the proposed AEC neural processor to simulate the single-talk and double-talk scenarios by considering the following conditions:

- We employed 1024 adaptive filter coefficients and varied the search agents from 70 to 15.

- The filter and the block had the same length as the echo path.
- As input signals, we used an AR(1) process and speech sequence signals.
- The step-size of the LMS algorithm was set to $\mu = 0.000001$ and the step-size of the convex algorithm was selected to be $\mu_a = 15$
- The search agents were initialized using normally distributed random numbers and their positions were bounded between $[-1, 1]$ over the filtering process.

4.2. Single-Talk Scenario

In this section, we demonstrate the computational capabilities of the proposed algorithm under a single-talk scenario. As can be observed from Figures 14 and 15, the proposed AEC neural processor, which simulated the proposed convex GWO/LMS algorithm, reached a good ERLE level by processing two different signals. To carry this out, we configured the AEC neural processor to support one α, one β, one δ, and 70 ω processing cores. Here, the most demanding core, in terms of area and processing speed, was the ω processing core, since each one required 1000 neural multipliers and 1000 neural adders. Therefore, we physically implemented six ω processing cores to simulate virtually 70 ω processing cores. In this way, we saved a large area consumption. In general terms, the implementation of these components required 420,380 LEs, which represented 79% of the total area of an Stratix IV GX EP4SGX530 FPGA. Furthermore, the AEC neural processor required 114.56 µs, which was obtained by multiplying 14,320 clock cycles by the system clock period (8 ns) to simulate the proposed convex GWO/LMS algorithm. This time was calculated when all the search agents were used, i.e., by considering the worse case. However, the number of search agents decreased over the processing time. In the case of employing fifteen search agents, which represented the minimum number, only 1300 clock cycles were expended. Therefore, the processing time reduced from 114.56 µs to 10.4 µs. Therefore, the simulation of real-time AEC systems was guaranteed since the maximum latency was 125 µs.

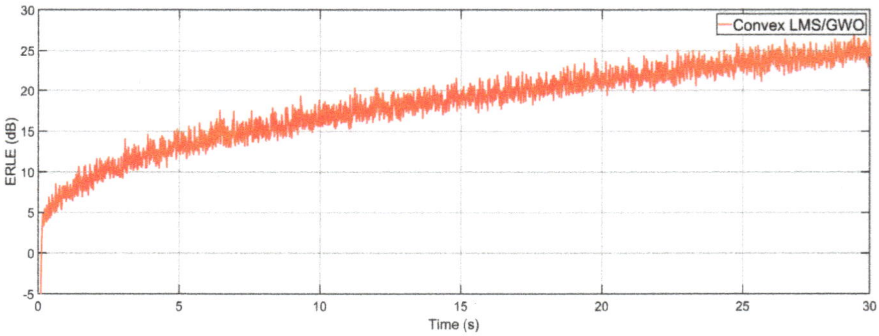

Figure 14. ERLE learning curve of the proposed convex GWO/LMS considering an AR(1) process as input signal.

4.3. Double-Talk Scenario

To perform the experiments under this configuration, we employed a double-talk detector circuit to avoid adaptation during periods of simultaneous far and near-end speech. It should be noted that the area consumption in the implementation of this circuit was negligible. Therefore, this implementation expended around 79% of the total area of an Stratix IV GX EP4SGX530 FPGA, as in the previous case. Figures 16 and 17 show the ERLE of the proposed Convex GWO/LMS algorithm by considering an AR(1) process and a speech sequence signal, respectively. As can be observed from the above figures, the proposed algorithm showed good tracking capabilities and achieved a good ERLE level. This aspect is relevant since these levels are required in the development of practical and real-world AEC applications.

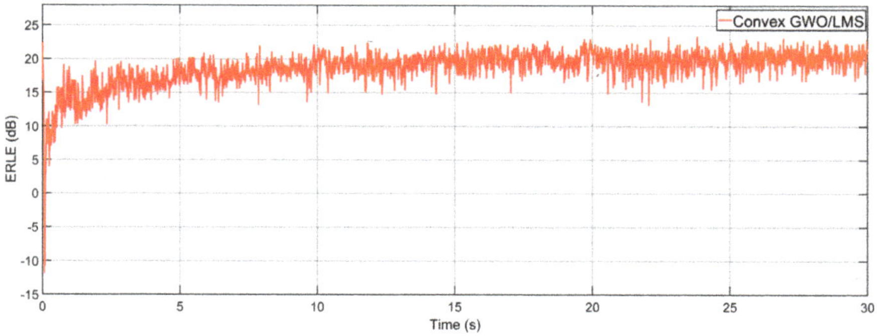

Figure 15. ERLE learning curve of the proposed convex GWO/LMS considering a speech sequence signal as input signal.

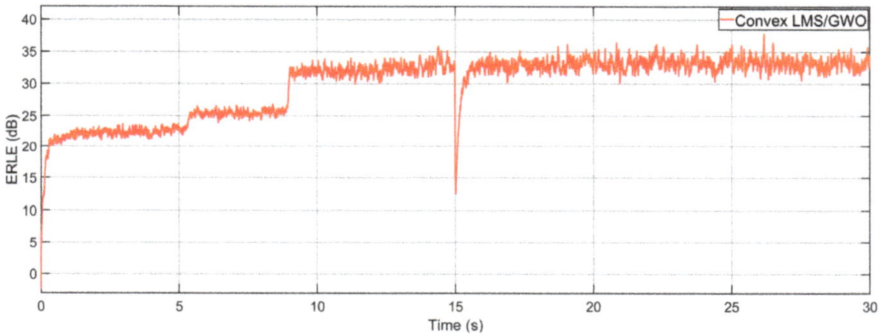

Figure 16. ERLE learning curve of the proposed convex GWO/LMS considering an AR(1) process as input signal and a double-talk scenario.

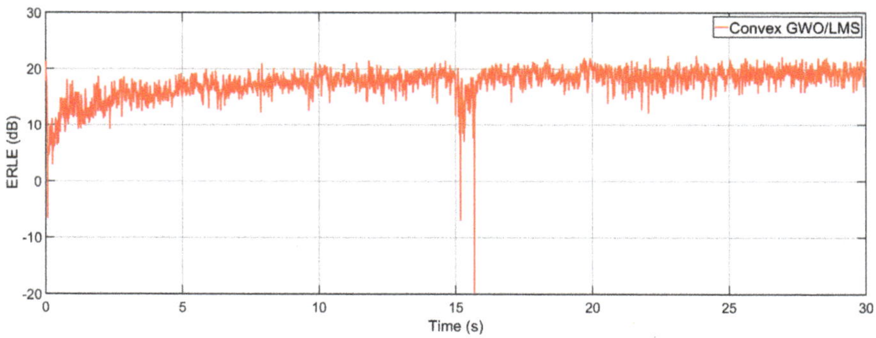

Figure 17. ERLE learning curve of the proposed convex GWO/LMS considering a speech sequence signal as input signal considering a double-talk scenario.

5. Conclusions

In this work, we present, for the first time, the development of a high-speed and compact FPGA-based AEC neural processor to efficiently simulate a new convex GWO/LMS algorithm. Here, we grouped our contributions as follows:

- *From the AEC model point of view.*
  Here, we made intensive efforts to reduce the computational cost of the AEC systems to be implemented in resource-constrained devices. In addition, we significantly increased the convergence properties of these systems by using a cutting-edge metaheuristic swarm intelligence method, in combination with a gradient descent algorithm to be used in practical acoustic environments. Specifically, we present a new

variant of GWO algorithm along with the LMS algorithm. The use of this combination allowed us to guarantee a higher convergence rate and lower MSE level, in comparison to when gradient descent algorithms or metaheuristic SI methods were used separately. To improve the tracking capabilities of the conventional GWO algorithm, the proposed variant has new exploration capabilities, since the search space is dynamically adjusted. To make the implementation of the proposed variant of the GWO algorithm in embedded devices feasible, we used the block-processing scheme. In this way, the proposed convex GWO/LMS algorithm can be easily implemented in parallel hardware architectures. As a consequence, it can be simulated at high processing speeds. In addition, we significantly reduced the computational cost of the proposed convex GWO/LMS algorithm. To achieve this aim, we propose a method to dynamically decrease the population of a variant of the GWO algorithm over the filtering process.

- *From the SN P systems point of view.*
  Here, we present, for the first time, a compact and high-processing speed floating-point neural adder and multiplier circuit. We used cutting-edge variants of the SN P systems, coloured-spikes, rules on the synapses, target indications, extended channel rules, extended rules and dendritic trunks to create a customized floating-point neural adder and multiplier. Specifically, the proposed neural adder and multiplier exhibits higher processing speed, compared with existing SN P adders and multipliers, since both expend only one simulation step, which is the best improvement achieved until now.
- *From the digital point of view.*
  In this work, we present, for the first time, the development of a parallel hardware architecture to simulate a variable number of search agents by using the proposed time-multiplexing control scheme. In this way, we implemented the proposed GWO method properly, in which the number of search agents increase or decrease according to the simulation needs. In addition, the use of this scheme allowed us to exploit, to the maximum, the flexibility and scalability features of the GWO algorithm.

Finally, we carried out several experiments to prove that the proposed convex GWO/LMS algorithm, along with the new techniques inspired by biological neural processes, potentially allow the creation of practical and real-time AEC processing tools. Part of the future work is to develop new convex combinations, in which other meta-heuristic algorithms can be used in other adaptive filtering applications, such as active noise control, channel equalization and noise cancellers. In addition, new digital techniques will be explored to mimic bio-inspired behavior with high accuracy.

Author Contributions: Conceptualization, E.P.; Data curation, L.G. and H.M.P.; Formal analysis, G.S.; Funding acquisition, J.G.A. and J.C.S.; Investigation, A.V. and J.G.A.; Methodology, J.G.A. and G.S.; Resources, E.P., E.A. and A.V.; Software, E.P., E.A. and A.V.; Supervision, G.S. and J.C.S.; Validation, E.P. and E.A.; Writing—original draft, L.G. and H.M.P.; Writing—review & editing, H.M.P. All authors have read and agreed to the published version of the manuscript.

Funding: The authors would like to thank the Instituto Politécnico Nacional for the financial support.

Institutional Review Board Statement: Not applicable.

Informed Consent Statement: Not applicable.

Data Availability Statement: No new data were created or analyzed in this study. Data sharing is not applicable to this article.

Acknowledgments: The authors would like to thank the Consejo Nacional de Ciencia y Tecnologia (CONACYT) and the IPN for the financial support to make this work.

Conflicts of Interest: The authors declare no conflict of interest.

References

1. Benesty, J.; Duhamel, P. A fast exact least mean square adaptive algorithm. *IEEE Trans. Signal Process.* **1992**, *40*, 2904–2920. [CrossRef] [PubMed]
2. Eberhart, R.; Kennedy, J. A new optimizer using particle swarm theory. In Proceedings of the MHS'95, Sixth International Symposium on Micro Machine and Human Science, Nagoya, Japan, 4–6 October 1995; pp. 39–43.
3. Ling, Q.; Ikbal, M.A.; Kumar, P. Optimized LMS algorithm for system identification and noise cancellation. *J. Intell. Syst.* **2021**, *30*, 487–498. [CrossRef]
4. Botzheim, J.; Cabrita, C.; Kóczy, L.T.; Ruano, A. Fuzzy rule extraction by bacterial memetic algorithms. *Int. J. Intell. Syst.* **2009**, *24*, 312–339. [CrossRef]
5. Ariyarit, A.; Kanazaki, M. Multi-modal distribution crossover method based on two crossing segments bounded by selected parents applied to multi-objective design optimization. *J. Mech. Sci. Technol.* **2015**, *29*, 1443–1448. [CrossRef]
6. Mirjalili, S.; Mirjalili, S.M.; Lewis, A. Grey wolf optimizer. *Adv. Eng. Softw.* **2014**, *69*, 46–61. [CrossRef]
7. Mirjalili, S.; Lewis, A. The whale optimization algorithm. *Adv. Eng. Softw.* **2016**, *95*, 51–67. [CrossRef]
8. Kennedy, J.; Eberhart, R. Particle swarm optimization. In Proceedings of the ICNN'95-International Conference on Neural Networks, Perth, WA, Australia, 27 November–1 December 1995; Volume 4, pp. 1942–1948.
9. Khehra, B.S.; Singh, A.; Kaur, L.M. Masi Entropy-and Grey Wolf Optimizer-Based Multilevel Thresholding Approach for Image Segmentation. *J. Inst. Eng. Ser. B* **2022**, *103*, 1619–1642. [CrossRef]
10. Vashishtha, G.; Kumar, R. An amended grey wolf optimization with mutation strategy to diagnose bucket defects in Pelton wheel. *Measurement* **2022**, *187*, 110272. [CrossRef]
11. Rajammal, R.R.; Mirjalili, S.; Ekambaram, G.; Palanisamy, N. Binary Grey Wolf Optimizer with Mutation and Adaptive K-nearest Neighbour for Feature Selection in Parkinson's Disease Diagnosis. *Knowl.-Based Syst.* **2022**, *246*, 108701. [CrossRef]
12. Reddy, V.P.C.; Gurrala, K.K. Joint DR-DME classification using deep learning-CNN based modified grey-wolf optimizer with variable weights. *Biomed. Signal Process. Control* **2022**, *73*, 103439. [CrossRef]
13. Dey, S.; Banerjee, S.; Dey, J. Implementation of Optimized PID Controllers in Real Time for Magnetic Levitation System. In *Computational Intelligence in Machine Learning*; Springer: Berlin/Heidelberg, Germany, 2022; pp. 249–256.
14. Zhang, X.; Li, D.; Li, J.; Liu, B.; Jiang, Q.; Wang, J. Signal-Noise Identification for Wide Field Electromagnetic Method Data Using Multi-Domain Features and IGWO-SVM. *Fractal Fract.* **2022**, *6*, 80. [CrossRef]
15. Premkumar, M.; Jangir, P.; Kumar, B.S.; Alqudah, M.A.; Nisar, K.S. Multi-objective grey wolf optimization algorithm for solving real-world BLDC motor design problem. *Comput. Mater. Contin.* **2022**, *70*, 2435–2452. [CrossRef]
16. Nagadurga, T.; Narasimham, P.; Vakula, V.; Devarapalli, R. Gray wolf optimization-based optimal grid connected solar photovoltaic system with enhanced power quality features. *Concurr. Comput. Pract. Exp.* **2022**, *34*, e6696. [CrossRef]
17. Musharavati, F.; Khoshnevisan, A.; Alirahmi, S.M.; Ahmadi, P.; Khanmohammadi, S. Multi-objective optimization of a biomass gasification to generate electricity and desalinated water using Grey Wolf Optimizer and artificial neural network. *Chemosphere* **2022**, *287*, 131980. [CrossRef]
18. Meidani, K.; Hemmasian, A.; Mirjalili, S.; Barati Farimani, A. Adaptive grey wolf optimizer. *Neural Comput. Appl.* **2022**, *34*, 7711–7731. [CrossRef]
19. Zhang, L.; Yu, C.; Tan, Y. A method for pulse signal denoising based on VMD parameter optimization and Grey Wolf optimizer. Journal of Physics: Conference Series. In Proceedings of the 2021 2nd International Conference on Electrical, Electronic Information and Communication Engineering (EEICE 2021), Tianjin, China, 16–18 April 2021; Volume 1920, p. 012100.
20. Negi, G.; Kumar, A.; Pant, S.; Ram, M. GWO: A review and applications. *Int. J. Syst. Assur. Eng. Manag.* **2021**, *12*, 1–8. [CrossRef]
21. Faris, H.; Aljarah, I.; Al-Betar, M.A.; Mirjalili, S. Grey wolf optimizer: A review of recent variants and applications. *Neural Comput. Appl.* **2018**, *30*, 413–435. [CrossRef]
22. Salinas, G.; Pichardo, E.; Vázquez, Á.A.; Avalos, J.G.; Sánchez, G. Grey wolf optimization algorithm for embedded adaptive filtering applications. *IEEE Embed. Syst. Lett.* **2022**, 1. [CrossRef]
23. Mahbub, U.; Acharjee, P.P.; Fattah, S.A. A time domain approach of acoustic echo cancellation based on particle swarm optimization. In Proceedings of the International Conference on Electrical & Computer Engineering (ICECE 2010), Dhaka, Bangladesh, 18–20 December 2010; pp. 518–521.
24. Mahbub, U.; Acharjee, P.P.; Fattah, S.A. An acoustic echo cancellation scheme based on particle swarm optimization algorithm. In Proceedings of the TENCON 2010—2010 IEEE Region 10 Conference, Fukuoka, Japan, 21–24 November 2010; pp. 759–762.
25. Kimoto, M.; Asami, T. Multichannel Acoustic Echo Canceler Based on Particle Swarm Optimization. *Electron. Commun. Jpn.* **2016**, *99*, 31–40. [CrossRef]
26. Mishra, A.K.; Das, S.R.; Ray, P.K.; Mallick, R.K.; Mohanty, A.; Mishra, D.K. PSO-GWO optimized fractional order PID based hybrid shunt active power filter for power quality improvements. *IEEE Access* **2020**, *8*, 74497–74512. [CrossRef]
27. Suman, S.; Chatterjee, D.; Mohanty, R. Comparison of PSO and GWO Techniques for SHEPWM Inverters. In Proceedings of the 2020 International Conference on Computer, Electrical & Communication Engineering (ICCECE), Kolkata, India, 17–18 January 2020; pp. 1–7.
28. Şenel, F.A.; Gökçe, F.; Yüksel, A.S.; Yiğit, T. A novel hybrid PSO–GWO algorithm for optimization problems. *Eng. Comput.* **2019**, *35*, 1359–1373. [CrossRef]

29. Wang, W.; Wang, J. Convex combination of two geometric-algebra least mean square algorithms and its performance analysis. *Signal Process.* **2022**, *192*, 108333. [CrossRef]
30. Bakri, K.J.; Kuhn, E.V.; Matsuo, M.V.; Seara, R. On the behavior of a combination of adaptive filters operating with the NLMS algorithm in a nonstationary environment. *Signal Process.* **2022**, *196*, 108465. [CrossRef]
31. Jeong, J.J.; Kim, S. Robust adaptive filter algorithms against impulsive noise. *Circuits Syst. Signal Process.* **2019**, *38*, 5651–5664. [CrossRef]
32. Silva, M.T.; Nascimento, V.H. Improving the tracking capability of adaptive filters via convex combination. *IEEE Trans. Signal Process.* **2008**, *56*, 3137–3149. [CrossRef]
33. Ionescu, M.; Păun, G.; Yokomori, T. Spiking neural P systems. *Fundam. Inform.* **2006**, *71*, 279–308.
34. Frias, T.; Sanchez, G.; Garcia, L.; Abarca, M.; Diaz, C.; Sanchez, G.; Perez, H. A new scalable parallel adder based on spiking neural P systems, dendritic behavior, rules on the synapses and astrocyte-like control to compute multiple signed numbers. *Neurocomputing* **2018**, *319*, 176–187. [CrossRef]
35. Avalos, J.G.; Sanchez, G.; Trejo, C.; Garcia, L.; Pichardo, E.; Vazquez, A.; Anides, E.; Sanchez, J.C.; Perez, H. High-performance and ultra-compact spike-based architecture for real-time acoustic echo cancellation. *Appl. Soft Comput.* **2021**, *113*, 108037. [CrossRef]
36. Song, T.; Rodríguez-Patón, A.; Zheng, P.; Zeng, X. Spiking neural P systems with colored spikes. *IEEE Trans. Cogn. Dev. Syst.* **2017**, *10*, 1106–1115. [CrossRef]
37. Peng, H.; Chen, R.; Wang, J.; Song, X.; Wang, T.; Yang, F.; Sun, Z. Competitive spiking neural P systems with rules on synapses. *IEEE Trans. NanoBiosci.* **2017**, *16*, 888–895. [CrossRef]
38. Lv, Z.; Bao, T.; Zhou, N.; Peng, H.; Huang, X.; Riscos-Núñez, A.; Pérez-Jiménez, M.J. Spiking neural p systems with extended channel rules. *Int. J. Neural Syst.* **2021**, *31*, 2050049. [CrossRef] [PubMed]
39. Chen, H.; Ionescu, M.; Ishdorj, T.O.; Păun, A.; Păun, G.; Pérez-Jiménez, M.J. Spiking neural P systems with extended rules: Universality and languages. *Nat. Comput.* **2008**, *7*, 147–166. [CrossRef]
40. Adam, S.P.; Alexandropoulos, S.A.N.; Pardalos, P.M.; Vrahatis, M.N. No free lunch theorem: A review. In *Approximation and Optimization*; Springer: Berlin/Heidelberg, Germany, 2019; pp. 57–82.
41. Scarpiniti, M.; Comminiello, D.; Uncini, A. Convex combination of spline adaptive filters. In Proceedings of the 2019 27th European Signal Processing Conference (EUSIPCO), A Coruna, Spain, 2–6 September 2019; pp. 1–5.
42. Khan, M.T.; Kumar, J.; Ahamed, S.R.; Faridi, J. Partial-LUT designs for low-complexity realization of DA-based BLMS adaptive filter. *IEEE Trans. Circuits Syst. II Express Briefs* **2020**, *68*, 1188–1192. [CrossRef]
43. Khan, M.T.; Shaik, R.A. Analysis and implementation of block least mean square adaptive filter using offset binary coding. In Proceedings of the 2018 IEEE International Symposium on Circuits and Systems (ISCAS), Florence, Italy, 27–30 May 2018; pp. 1–5.
44. International Telecommunication Union ITU-T. *Digital Network Echo Cancellers*; Standardization Sector of ITU: Geneva, Switzerland, 2002.
45. Clark, G.; Mitra, S.; Parker, S. Block implementation of adaptive digital filters. *IEEE Trans. Acoust. Speech Signal Process.* **1981**, *29*, 744–752. [CrossRef]
46. Burrus, C. Block implementation of digital filters. *IEEE Trans. Circuit Theory* **1971**, *18*, 697–701. [CrossRef]
47. Reddy, K.S.; Sahoo, S.K. An approach for FIR filter coefficient optimization using differential evolution algorithm. *AEU-Int. J. Electron. Commun.* **2015**, *69*, 101–108. [CrossRef]
48. Bansal, J.C.; Sharma, H.; Jadon, S.S. Artificial bee colony algorithm: A survey. *Int. J. Adv. Intell. Paradig.* **2013**, *5*, 123–159. [CrossRef]
49. Krusienski, D.; Jenkins, W. A particle swarm optimization-least mean squares algorithm for adaptive filtering. In Proceedings of the Conference Record of the Thirty-Eighth Asilomar Conference on Signals, Systems and Computers, Pacific Grove, CA, USA, 7–10 November 2004; Volume 1, pp. 241–245.
50. Ren, X.; Zhang, H. An Improved Artificial Bee Colony Algorithm for Model-Free Active Noise Control: Algorithm and Implementation. *IEEE Trans. Instrum. Meas.* **2022**, *71*, 1–11. [CrossRef]
51. Wu, T.; Zhang, L.; Pan, L. Spiking neural P systems with target indications. *Theor. Comput. Sci.* **2021**, *862*, 250–261. [CrossRef]
52. Garcia, L.; Sanchez, G.; Vazquez, E.; Avalos, G.; Anides, E.; Nakano, M.; Sanchez, G.; Perez, H. Small universal spiking neural P systems with dendritic/axonal delays and dendritic trunk/feedback. *Neural Netw.* **2021**, *138*, 126–139. [CrossRef]
53. Maya, X.; Garcia, L.; Vazquez, A.; Pichardo, E.; Sanchez, J.C.; Perez, H.; Avalos, J.G.; Sanchez, G. A high-precision distributed neural processor for efficient computation of a new distributed FxSMAP-L algorithm applied to real-time active noise control systems. *Neurocomputing* **2023**, *518*, 545–561. [CrossRef]

Σ mathematics

MDPI

Article

Improved Multi-Strategy Harris Hawks Optimization and Its Application in Engineering Problems

Fulin Tian *, Jiayang Wang and Fei Chu

School of Computer Science and Engineering, Central South University, Changsha 410083, China
* Correspondence: fulintian@csu.edu.cn

Abstract: In order to compensate for the low convergence accuracy, slow rate of convergence, and easily falling into the trap of local optima for the original Harris hawks optimization (HHO) algorithm, an improved multi-strategy Harris hawks optimization (MSHHO) algorithm is proposed. First, the population is initialized by Sobol sequences to increase the diversity of the population. Second, the elite opposition-based learning strategy is incorporated to improve the versatility and quality of the solution sets. Furthermore, the energy updating strategy of the original algorithm is optimized to enhance the exploration and exploitation capability of the algorithm in a nonlinear update manner. Finally, the Gaussian walk learning strategy is introduced to avoid the algorithm being trapped in a stagnant state and slipping into a local optimum. We perform experiments on 33 benchmark functions and 2 engineering application problems to verify the performance of the proposed algorithm. The experimental results show that the improved algorithm has good performance in terms of optimization seeking accuracy, the speed of convergence, and stability, which effectively remedies the defects of the original algorithm.

Keywords: swarm intelligence; Harris hawks optimization; elite opposition-based learning; Sobol sequence; nonlinear weight; Gaussian walk learning

MSC: 68T20

Citation: Tian, F.; Wang, J.; Chu, F. Improved Multi-Strategy Harris Hawks Optimization and Its Application in Engineering Problems. *Mathematics* **2023**, *11*, 1525. https://doi.org/10.3390/math11061525

Academic Editor: Gaige Wang

Received: 19 February 2023
Revised: 13 March 2023
Accepted: 18 March 2023
Published: 21 March 2023

1. Introduction

The swarm intelligence algorithm is a common approach in computational intelligence and an emerging evolutionary computing technique whose basic theory is to emulate the behavior of groups of ants, birds, bees, wolves, bacteria, and other organisms in nature and to use the mechanism of interaction to form group intelligence to solve complex problems through the exchange of information and cooperation between groups. Numerous researchers have carried out much work on such intelligent algorithms and proposed many novel algorithms, such as the grey wolf optimizer (GWO) [1], lightning search algorithm (LSA) [2], marine predators algorithm (MPA) [3], sine cosine algorithm (SCA) [4], salp swarm algorithm (SSA) [5], water cycle algorithm (WCA) [6], whale optimization algorithm (WOA) [7], cuckoo serach (CS) [8], artificial bee colony (ABC) [9], and moth flame optimization (MFO) [10].

The Harris hawks optimization (HHO) algorithm is a novel swarm intelligence algorithm proposed by Herdari et al. [11], who were inspired by observing the chase and escape action between Harris hawks and their prey. The algorithm is simple in principle, with few parameters while having a powerful global search capability, so it has received widespread attention and has been adopted in many engineering fields since its introduction. However, similar to other intelligent optimization algorithms, the basic Harris hawks algorithm is susceptible to such defects as low precision of convergence and the trend of falling into the local optimum during the search process when solving complex optimization problems. Numerous scholars have proposed different improvement schemes to address these shortcomings. Qu et al. [12] introduced a method of information exchange to increase the diversity of populations, and a nonlinear energy escape factor was proposed and perturbed by chaotic interference to balance the local exploitation and global exploration of the algorithm. Xiaolong Liu et al. [13] optimized the method by setting up a square neighborhood topology with multiple subgroups to lead individuals in each subgroup to explore randomly in both directions. Andi Tang et al. [14] introduced the elite hierarchy strategy to make full use of the dominant population for enhancing the population diversity and improving the convergence of the algorithm in terms of speed and accuracy. Kaveh et al. [15] combined HHO and the imperialist competitive algorithm (ICA) [16] named imperialist competitive Harris hawks optimization (ICHHO), and it had good performance in structure optimization problems. Elgamal et al. [17] presented application of the chaotic maps at the initialization phase of the HHO, and the current best solution was analyzed using the simulated annealing (SA) [18] algorithm to improve the utilization of the HHO. Wenyu Li [19] invented a form of HHO by incorporating the novice protection tournament (NpTHHO), which was developed by adding a novice protection mechanism to better reallocate resources and introducing a variation mechanism in the exploration phase to further enhance the global search efficiency of the HHO algorithm. Essam H. et al. [20] combined HHO with a support vector machine (SVM) for the selection of chemical descriptors as well as the activity of compounds and drug design and discovery. Wunnava et al. [21] introduced an adaptive improvement algorithm performed by differencing to address the problem of the exploration ability of the algorithm being limited if the escape energy of the HHO is equal to zero, resulting in invalid random behavior at that stage, and they applied the algorithm to image segmentation.

In summary, the main improvement of the HHO algorithm is to improve the optimization ability of local exploitation and global exploration through various optimization strategies and then improve the the accuracy of convergence and performance of the algorithm before applying it in practical engineering. Among the existing improved versions of HHO, some are achieved by incorporating other algorithms, such as those in [15,17], while others are achieved by improving one or several stages of the underlying algorithm to achieve optimization. Compared with the improved algorithms that have been proposed, the improved strategies proposed in this paper include a more comprehensive scope, including the population initialization phase, the population update phase, the energy escape factor optimization, and the variation strategy. To overcome the weaknesses of the basic Harris hawks algorithm, such as low accuracy, slow speed of convergence, and easily being trapped in the local optimum, this paper presents improved multi-strategy Harris hawks optimization (MSHHO). The main contributions of this research are as follows:

- We propose an improved multi-strategy Harris hawks optimization algorithm. To compensate for the shortcomings of the algorithm, four strategies are adopted in this work to improve the basic HHO algorithm. First, the population is initialized using Sobol sequences to increase the variety of the population. Second, we incorporate elite opposition-based learning to improve the population diversity and quality. Furthermore, the energy update strategy of the basic HHO algorithm is optimized to enhance the exploration and exploitation capability of the algorithm in a nonlinear update manner. Finally, Gaussian walk learning is introduced to avoid the algorithm being trapped in a stagnant state and falling into a local optimum.
- The presentation of the proposed algorithm in working out 33 global optimization benchmark functions in multiple dimensions is investigated by comparing it with other novel swarm intelligence algorithm experiments. The results suggest that MSHHO had a positive performance. The Wilcoxon signed-rank test was passed to validate the effectiveness of the scheme. The advantages of this algorithm are demonstrated by comparing it with other HHO improvement algorithms. The original HHO algorithm is selected for comparison tests on each benchmark function in 100 dimensions versus 500 dimensions to inspect the utility of the algorithm in high-dimensional problems.

- We apply it to two engineering application problems to inspect the practicality of the introduced algorithm. A new scheme is provided for the swarm intelligence algorithm in practical engineering applications.

This paper is organized as follows. Section 1 describes the current state of development of swarm intelligence algorithms and some existing strategies for improving the Harris hawks algorithm. Section 2 describes the basic principles of the basic Harris hawks algorithm. Section 3 details the improvement strategy introduced in this paper and gives the time complexity of the algorithm. Section 4 shows the experimental results conducted to demonstrate the effectiveness of the proposed algorithm. Section 5 shows the application of the algorithm presented in this paper to engineering optimization problems. Section 6 concludes the paper and provides an outlook for future work.

2. Harris Hawks Optimization (HHO)

The HHO algorithm models the Harris hawk's strategy for capturing prey under different mechanisms in a mathematical formulation, where individual Harris hawks form candidate solutions and the optimal solution produced by every iteration is considered the prey. The algorithm comprises two main phases, namely exploration and exploitation, and transitions between the two phases are performed by the magnitude of the prey's escape energy. The original Harris hawks optimization algorithm is described below.

2.1. Exploration Phase

The global search phase is majorly dictated by the location information of the Harris hawk population, and its update strategy is as follows:

$$X(t+1) = \begin{cases} X_{rand}(t) - r_1|X_{rand}(t) - 2r_2X(t)| & q \geq 0.5 \\ (X_{prey}(t) - X_m(t)) - r_3(LB + r_4(UB - LB)) & q < 0.5 \end{cases} \tag{1}$$

where $X(t+1)$ represents the location of the hawks in the iteration $t+1$, $X_{prey}(t)$ represents the location of the prey, $X(t)$ represents the position of the hawks in the current generation t, r_1–r_4 and q are randomly generated between (0,1), being renewed in each iteration, UB and LB are the upper and lower bounds of the population, respectively, $X_{rand}(t)$ represents a hawk chosen randomly from the current population, and $X_m(t)$ represents the average of the positions of individuals in the current population, which is obtained from Equation (2):

$$X_m(t) = \frac{1}{n}\sum_{k=1}^{n} X_k(t) \tag{2}$$

where $X_k(t)$ denotes the position of hawk k in the iteration t and n denotes the number of hawks.

2.2. Transition from Exploration to Exploitation

The energy equation controlling the escape of prey is as follows:

$$E = 2E_0(1 - t/T) \tag{3}$$

where t is the current number of iterations, T denotes the maximum number of iterations, and the value of E_0 is a random number within (−1,1) that indicates the initial state of the energy. When the escape energy $|E| \geq 1$, the Harris hawks search different areas to further explore for the location of the prey, which corresponds to the global exploration phase, and when $|E| < 1$, the Harris hawks explore the adjacent solutions locally, thus corresponding to the local exploitation phase.

2.3. Exploitation Phase

In this phase, the Harris hawk will besiege the target prey after finding it, based on the exploration results of the previous phases, while the prey will try to escape from the pursuit. On the basis of the behavior of Harris's hawk and prey, four possible strategies are proposed to be used for this phase of the simulation. The hard beseige and soft besiege by Harris's hawk are simulated by E. The parameter r is specified to indicate whether the prey successfully escapes or not.

2.3.1. Soft Besiege

When $|E| \geq 0.5$ and $r \geq 0.5$, the prey tries to escape from the pursuit by jumping, and the Harris hawk will use a soft besiege to gradually consume the prey's energy. The behavior is modeled as follows:

$$X(t+1) = \Delta X(t) - E\left|JX_{prey}(t) - X(t)\right| \tag{4}$$

$$\Delta X(t) = X_{prey}(t) - X(t) \tag{5}$$

where r_5 represents a randomly generated number within (0,1) and J is introduced to simulate the nature of prey movement, with its value randomly varied in each iteration.

2.3.2. Hard Besiege

When $|E| < 0.5$ and $r \geq 0.5$, the prey does not have enough energy to escape, and so the Harris hawk attacks in a hard besiege manner, using Equation (6) to update the current position:

$$X(t+1) = X_{prey}(t) - E|\Delta X(t)| \tag{6}$$

2.3.3. Soft Besiege with Progressive Rapid Dives

When $|E| \geq 0.5$ and $r < 0.5$, at this time, the prey has enough energy to escape from the pursuit. Harris hawks will update their positions according to the rule in Equation (7):

$$Y = X_{prey}(t) - E\left|JX_{prey}(t) - X(t)\right| \tag{7}$$

$$Z = Y + S \times LF(D) \tag{8}$$

where D is the dimension of the problem, S is a random vector of a size $1 \times D$, and LF is the levy flight function, which can be described as in Equation (9):

$$\begin{cases} LF(x) = 0.01 \times \frac{u \times \sigma}{|v|^{\frac{1}{\beta}}} \\ \sigma = \left(\frac{\Gamma(1+\beta) \times \sin(\frac{\pi\beta}{2})}{\Gamma(\frac{1+\beta}{2}) \times \beta \times 2^{(\frac{\beta-1}{2})}} \right)^{\frac{1}{\beta}} \end{cases} \tag{9}$$

where u and v are random values within (0,1) and β is the default constant, set to 1.5.

Hence, the final strategy for updating the hawks' positions during the soft siege phase can be executed by Equation (10):

$$X(t+1) = \begin{cases} Y, \text{if} F(Y) < F(X(t)) \\ Z, \text{if} F(Z) < F(X(t)) \end{cases} \tag{10}$$

where Y and Z are obtained using Equations (7) and (8), respectively.

2.3.4. Hard Besiege with Progressive Rapid Dives

When $|E| < 0.5$ and $r < 0.5$, the prey does not have enough energy to make an escape, and the following strategy is defined to be executed under these conditions:

$$X(t+1) = \begin{cases} Y, \text{if} F(Y) < F(X(t)) \\ Z, \text{if} F(Z) < F(X(t)) \end{cases} \tag{11}$$

$$Y = X_{prey}(t) - E\left|JX_{prey}(t) - X_m(t)\right| \tag{12}$$

$$Z = Y + S \times LF(D) \tag{13}$$

where $X_m(t)$ is obtained using Equation (2).

2.4. *The Main Steps of HHO*

The main steps of the overall HHO algorithm are as shown in Algorithm 1.

Algorithm 1 Main steps of HHO algorithm

Input: Population size N and the maximum number of iterations T
Initialize the population
while $t < T$ **do**
    Calculate the fitness of each solution and get the optimal individual
    for i=1:N **do**
        According to Equation (3) update the escape energy E
        if $|E| \geq 1$ **then**
            According to Equation (1) update the location
        else if then$|E| < 1$
            if $|E| \geq 0.5$ and $r \geq 0.5$ **then**
                According to Equation (4) update the location
            else if then$|E| < 0.5$ and $r \geq 0.5$
                According to Equation (6) update the location
            else if then$|E| \geq 0.5$ and $r < 0.5$
                According to Equation (10) update the location
            else if then$|E| < 0.5$ and $r < 0.5$
                According to Equation (11) update the location
            end if
        end if
    end for
    $t = t + 1$
end while
return X_{prey}

3. Improved Multi-Strategy Harris Hawks Optimization (MSHHO)

The HHO algorithm has multiple development modes, and the algorithm shifts between the different modes, making it good for local development, but it is also prone to the problem of falling into the local optimum. To remedy this deficiency, we introduce four improvement strategies to improve the original algorithm in this chapter, which are described in detail in the following subsections.

3.1. *Sobol Sequence Initialization Populations*

The distribution of the primitive solution in the solution space largely affects the convergence speed and the convergence precision of the intelligent algorithm. In the basic HHO algorithm, the initialized population is generated by randomization. However, the individuals generated in this way are not homogeneously distributed throughout the exploration space, which in turn affects the speed of convergence and precision of the algorithm. The Sobol sequence [22] is a deterministic low-difference sequence that has the feature of distributing the points in the space as uniformly as possible compared to the random sequence. The expression for the original population generated by the Sobol sequence can be represented by

$$X_i = Lb + S_n \times (Ub - Lb) \tag{14}$$

where Lb and Ub are the lower and upper bounds of the exploration space, respectively, and S_n is the random number generated by the Sobol sequence, where $S_n \in [0, 1]$.

Assuming that the search space is two-dimensional, the population size is 100, and the upper and lower bounds are 1 and 0, respectively, the distribution of the original population space comparing the random initialization and the Sobol sequence initialization population space is shown in Figure 1.

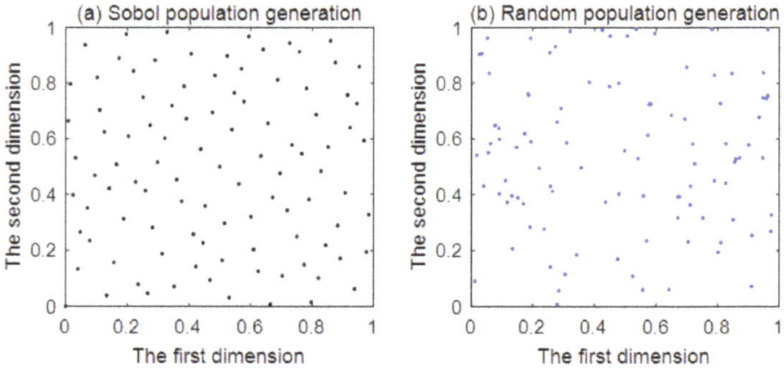

Figure 1. Comparison of Sobol population generation and random population generation.

As shown in Figure 1, the original population generated by the Sobol sequence is more uniformly distributed, thus enabling the optimization algorithm to perform a better global exploration in the exploration space, increasing the diversity of the population and enhancing the convergence speed of the algorithm.

3.2. Elite Opposition-Based Learning

Opposition-based learning (OBL) [23] is an effective method of intelligent computing which was proposed by Tizhoosh in 2005. In recent years, this strategy has been employed for the improvement of various algorithms and has achieved outstanding optimization results [24,25]. Assuming that a feasible solution in a d-dimensional search space is $\mathbf{X}= (x_1, x_2, \cdots, x_d)(x_j \in [a_j, b_j])$, then its opposition-based solution is defined as $\overline{\mathbf{X}}= (\overline{x_1}, \overline{x_2}, \cdots, \overline{x_d})$, where $\overline{x_j} = r(a_j + b_j) - x_j$, r is the coefficient of uniform distribution inside $[0, 1]$.

The inverse solution generated by the opposition-based learning strategy is not necessarily searching for the global optimal solution more easily than the current exploration space. To address this problem, elite opposition-based learning (EOBL) is proposed. Assuming that the extreme point of the current population in the search space is the elite individual $\mathbf{X}_e = (x_1^e, x_2^e, \cdots, x_d^e)$, then its inverse solution $\overline{\mathbf{X}_e} = (\overline{x_1^e}, \overline{x_2^e}, \cdots, \overline{x_d^e})$ can be specified as follows:

$$\overline{x_j^e} = k \cdot (a_j + b_j) - x_j^e \tag{15}$$

where $x_j^e \in [a_j, b_j]$, k is a random value inside $[0, 1]$, b_j and a_j are the upper and lower bounds of the dynamic boundary, respectively, and $a_j = \min(x_j^e)$, $b_j = \max(x_j^e)$. Replacing the fixed boundary with a dynamic boundary is beneficial for making the generated inverse solution gradually reduce the search space and speed up the convergence of the algorithm. Since the elite inverse solution may jump out of the boundary and lose its feasibility, the following approach is taken to reset the value:

$$\overline{x_i^e} = rand(a_j, b_j) \tag{16}$$

3.3. Escape Energy Update Optimization

In the basic HHO, a Harris hawk relies on the energy factor E to manage the transition of the algorithm from the global search phase to the local search phase. However, as shown in Equation (3), its energy factor E is reduced from 2 to 1 using a linear update, which tends to trap it in a local optimum in the second half of the iteration. To overcome the deficiency of only local searching when the algorithm proceeds to the later phase, a new updated version of the energy factor is used:

$$E = \begin{cases} \cos(\pi \times (t/T + 1/2) + 2), t \leq T/2 \\ \cos(\pi \times (t/T - 1/2)^{1/3}), t > T/2 \end{cases} \tag{17}$$

$$E_1 = E \times (2 \times rand - 1) \tag{18}$$

where t is the current number of iterations, T is the maximum number of iterations, and r is the random number inside $[0, 1]$.

From Figure 2, we can see that early in the iteration, the deceleration rate is fast to control the global search capability of the algorithm. In the middle of the iteration, the decreasing rate slows down to balance the capability of local exploitation and global exploration. In the later part of the iteration, the local search speeds up, and its value becomes smaller rapidly. From Figure 3, it can be seen that E_1 has fluctuating energy parameters throughout the iterative process and is capable of both global and local searching throughout the iterative process, with global exploration being undertaken mainly in the early stage and more local exploitation while still retaining the possibility of global exploration in the later stage.

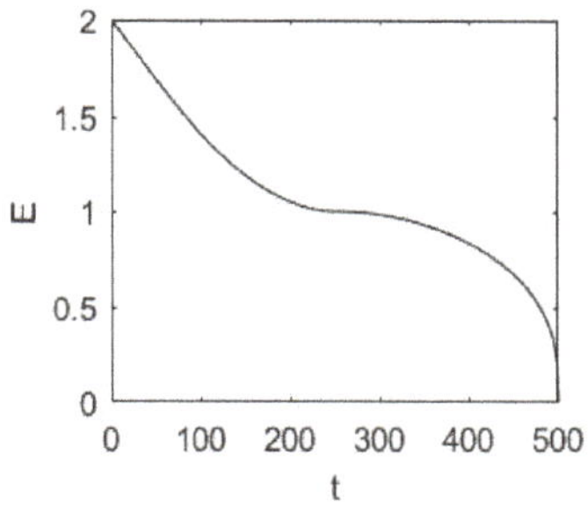

Figure 2. Iterative change graph of E.

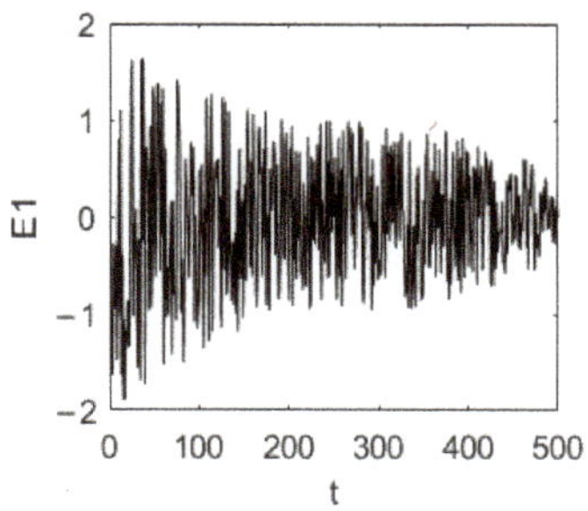

Figure 3. Iterative change graph of E_1.

3.4. Gaussian Walk Learning

Gaussian walk learning (GWL) is a classical stochastic walk strategy with strong exploitation capability [26–28]. Thus, this paper uses this strategy to mutate the population individuals to improve the diversity of the population while helping it leap out of the local optimum trap. The Gaussian walk learning model is shown in Equation (19):

$$X(t+1) = Gauss(X(t), \tau) \tag{19}$$

$$\tau = \cos(\pi/2 \times (t/T)^2) \times (X(t) - X_r(t)) \tag{20}$$

where $X(t)$ indicates the individual in the generation population t, $Gauss(X(t), \tau)$ is the Gaussian distribution with $X(t)$ as the expectation and τ as the standard deviation, and $X(t)$ is the location of the random individual in the generation population t. The step size of Gaussian walk learning is adjusted by the function $\cos(\pi/2 \times (t/T)^2)$. An image of this is shown in Figure 4. To balance the search ability of the algorithm, the perturbation applied in the early iterations is larger and rapidly decreases in the later stages to increase the algorithm's development ability.

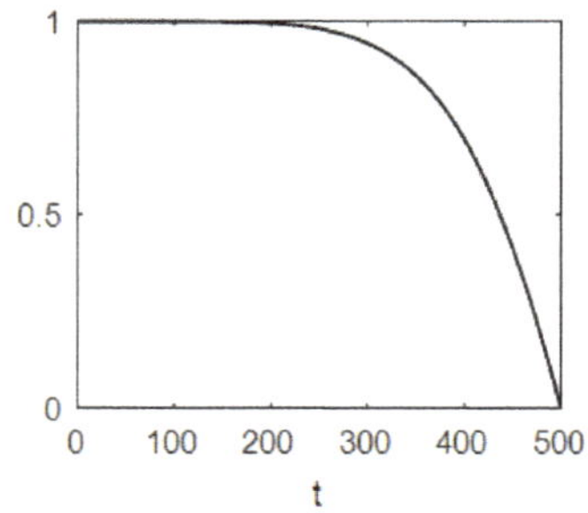

Figure 4. Graph of wandering step length change control.

3.5. *Flow of the MSHHO Algorithm*

In summary, the main steps of the the improved multi-strategy Harris hawks optimization (MSHHO) algorithm is shown in Algothrim 2, and the flow chart of MSHHO is shown in Figure 5.

Algorithm 2 Main steps of MSHHO algorithm

Input: Population size N and the maximum number of iterations T

According to Equation (14) initialize the population
while $t < T$ **do**
    Generate the reverse population using the elite opposition-based learning mechanism and calculate the fitness of the original population and its reverse population individuals
    if the algorithm is stagnant **then**
        According to Equation (19) update the location
    else
        for i=1:N **do**
            According to Equation (18) update the escape energy E
            if $|E| \geq 1$ **then**
                According to Equation (1) update the location
            else if then$|E| < 1$
                if $|E| \geq 0.5$ and $r \geq 0.5$ **then**
                    According to Equation (4) update the location
                else if then$|E| < 0.5$ and $r \geq 0.5$
                    According to Equation (6) update the location
                else if then$|E| \geq 0.5$ and $r < 0.5$
                    According to Equation (10) update the location
                else if then$|E| < 0.5$ and $r < 0.5$
                    According to Equation (11) update the location
                end if
            end if
        end for
    end if
    $t = t + 1$
end while
return X_{prey}

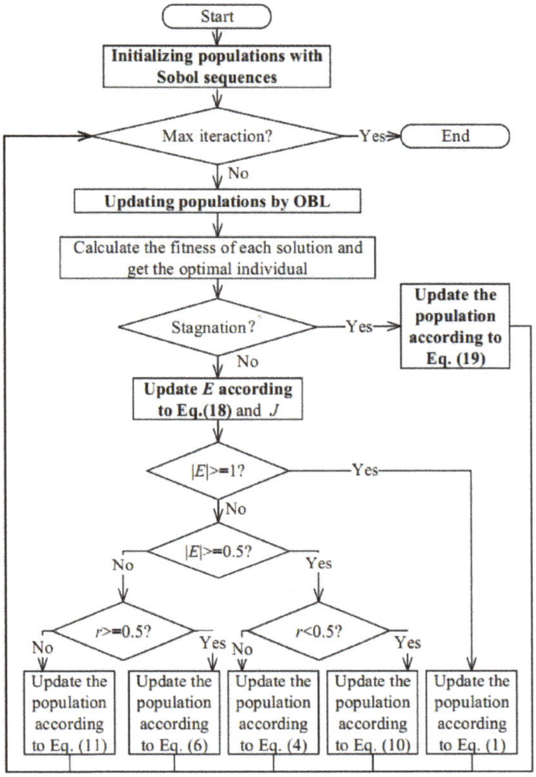

Figure 5. The flow chart of MSHHO.

3.6. Time Complexity Analysis of the Algorithm

The time complexity of the basic HHO algorithm depends mainly on three stages: the initialization phase, the fitness calculation process, and the location update operation of the population. Assuming that the size of the Harris hawk population is N, the problem dimension is D, and the maximum number of iterations is T, the time complexity of the initialization phase is $O(N)$, and the time complexity of finding the prey's location and updating the population's location vector is $O(N * T) + O(N * D * T)$, so the time complexity of the basic HHO algorithm is $O(N * (1 + T + D * T))$. For the improved algorithm proposed in this paper, the time complexity of the Sobol sequence initialization population is $O(N * D)$, the time complexity of the elite reverse learning strategy to optimize the population is $O(N * D * T)$, and the average time complexity of the Gaussian random wandering strategy is $O(N/2 * D * T)$. Thus, the time complexity of MSHHO is $O(N * (3/2 * D * T + D + 1))$.

4. Experiment and Results

To verify the performance of the proposed MSHHO algorithm, the GWO [1], SCA [4], SSA [5], and WOA [7] approaches were selected for running a comparison with the original HHO [11] algorithm. The same experimental environment, platform, and parameters were selected for the experiments. Table 1 shows the parameter settings of the comparison algorithms. The environment of the simulation test for the experiment was the 64 bit Windows 10 operating system, the CPU was an Intel(R) Core(TM) i7-7700HQ at 2.80 GHz, and the simulation software was MATLAB R2016b.

Table 1. Parameter sets of the algorithms.

Algorithm	Parameters
GWO	A variable decreases linearly from 2 to 0 r1, r2 (random numbers) $\in [0, 1]$
SSA	C2, C3 (random numbers) $\in [0, 1]$
SCA	A (constant) = 2
WOA	A variable decreases linearly from 2 to 0 a2 variable decreases linearly from 2 to 0

4.1. Benchmark Functions and Numerical Experiment

Twenty-three functions were selected from the CEC2005 benchmark [29,30], where F_1–F_7 are unimodal functions, F_8–F_{13} are multimodal functions, and F_{14}–F_{23} are fixed-dimension functions. The specific information of the benchmark function is shown in Tables A1–A3. For this experiment, the selected dimension of the test functions F_1–F_{13} was 30, while the other functions had different dimensions lower than 30. For each algorithm, the population size was set to 30, and the maximum number of iterations was 500. Each algorithm was run 30 times independently on each test function to prevent chance from bringing bias to the experimental results, and the mean, best value, and standard deviation of each algorithm run are shown in Tables 2 and 3.

The CEC2017 benchmark functions are characterized by a large problem size and more complex optimization searching, which can effectively distinguish the direct differences in the searching ability of different algorithms. There are 30 single-objective benchmark functions in CEC2017, including unimodal functions (F_1–F_3), simple multimodal functions (F_4–F_{10}), hybrid functions (F_{11}–F_{20}), and composition functions (F_{21}–F_{30}). In order to further verify the improvement effect of the MSHHO algorithm, 10 benchmark functions (F_1, F_3, F_5, F_7, F_{14}, F_{15}, F_{18}, F_{21}, F_{24}, and F_{30}) with different characteristics were selected for testing in the experiment, and their characteristics are shown in Table 4. Each algorithm was also run 30 times in the experiment, with a maximum number of iterations of 1000 and a population size of 100. The experimental results are shown in Table 5.

4.2. Results Analysis

In the experiment with CEC2005 as the test function, the unimodal functions F_1–F_7 selected for this experiment were used to test the development capability of the algorithm.

From the experimental results, it can be seen that for the test functions F_1–F_4, MSHHO could directly find the best value of zero, and HHO has the second-best performance, while the SCA, SSA and WOA performed poorly to varying degrees. For F_5 and F_6, MSHHO performed best in terms of both average and best results and with much higher accuracy than the other algorithms. For F_7, MSHHO performed similarly to HHO, but numerically, MSHHO had a slightly better mean, optimal value, and stability and performed significantly better than the other comparison algorithms. Overall, among all unimodal test functions, MSHHO had the best performance, stable results, and significantly better optimization than the comparison algorithms.

F_8–F_{23} are multimodal functions to evaluate the exploration capability of the algorithm. The experimental results show that in functions F_8–F_{23}, compared with the other algorithms, MSHHO could achieve the optimal optimization effect in most functions, and many functions could find the best value, such as F_9, F_{11}, F_{14},F_{16}, F_{17}, F_{18}, and F_{19}. In F_{17} and F_{19}, the stability performance of MSHHO was slightly inferior to that of the SSA. Overall, the combined performance of MSHHO in the multimodal test function was still the best result.

In the experiments with CEC2017 as the test function, it can be seen that MSHHO performed well in the hybrid functions and composition functions, both of which could obtain the best optimal and mean values with good stability. In unimodal functions and simple multimodal functions, although the performance was not the best, it had a great improvement effect compared with the original HHO.

To visualize the convergence performance of MSHHO, the iterative convergence curves of the test functions were experimentally plotted, and the convergence plots of some of the test functions are shown in Figures 6–9. As can be seen from the figures, both in terms of the speed of convergence and the accuracy of convergence, MSHHO outperformed the other comparison algorithms. It showed good performance not only in the unimodal test functions but also the multimodal functions. The box graph shows that MSHHO also performed better in terms of stability compared with the other algorithms.

Table 2. Results of CEC2005 benchmark functions.

Fun	Item	MSHHO	HHO	GWO	SCA	SSA	WOA
F1	Ave	**0.00E+00**	1.86E−99	1.12E−27	1.84E+01	2.01E−07	1.64E−73
	Best	**0.00E+00**	1.36E−116	3.16E−29	4.46E−02	2.50E−08	7.96E−91
	Std	**0.00E+00**	5.80E−99	1.91E−27	4.25E+01	2.80E−07	6.89E−73
F2	Ave	**0.00E+00**	4.53E−49	9.67E−17	4.13E−02	2.30E+00	9.59E−50
	Best	**0.00E+00**	3.91E−58	1.51E−17	4.04E−05	8.17E−02	1.41E−58
	Std	**0.00E+00**	2.44E−48	6.31E−17	1.17E−01	1.56E+00	2.94E−49
F3	Ave	**0.00E+00**	1.00E−69	1.68E−05	8.64E+03	1.80E+03	4.34E+04
	Best	**0.00E+00**	1.32E−95	1.89E−08	5.50E+02	3.28E+02	1.69E+04
	Std	**0.00E+00**	5.50E−69	4.68E−05	4.43E+03	1.27E+03	1.45E+04
F4	Ave	**0.00E+00**	2.18E−47	5.89E−07	3.42E+01	1.14E+01	4.05E+01
	Best	**0.00E+00**	7.44E−57	3.16E−08	1.59E+01	4.69E+00	1.93E−03
	Std	**0.00E+00**	1.19E−46	3.23E−07	9.96E+00	4.13E+00	2.68E+01
F5	Ave	**2.73E−06**	1.22E−02	2.70E+01	3.57E+04	2.65E+02	2.80E+01
	Best	**4.98E−09**	6.77E−06	2.61E+01	3.36E+01	2.73E+01	2.75E+01
	Std	**4.55E−06**	1.76E−02	6.27E−01	6.43E+04	3.70E+02	3.98E−01
F6	Ave	**9.27E−09**	2.00E−04	7.53E−01	1.51E+01	3.40E−07	4.92E−01
	Best	**6.52E−12**	1.58E−07	8.51E−05	4.37E+00	2.77E−08	5.80E−02
	Std	**1.55E−08**	2.75E−04	4.13E−01	1.37E+01	8.01E−07	3.22E−01
F7	Ave	**6.17E−05**	1.28E−04	1.88E−03	8.26E−02	1.72E−01	2.97E−03
	Best	**2.04E−06**	1.13E−06	8.16E−04	7.69E−03	5.79E−02	6.12E−05
	Std	**4.51E−05**	1.73E−04	9.00E−04	8.56E−02	6.42E−02	3.80E−03
F8	Ave	**−12,537.7**	−12,493.4	−5872.01	−3826.45	−7321.88	−10,872.7
	Best	**−12,569.5**	−12,569.5	−7039.92	−4714.89	−8719.91	−12,563.3
	Std	**1.74E+02**	3.74E+02	7.59E+02	3.14E+02	8.06E+02	1.64E+03
F9	Ave	**0.00E+00**	0.00E+00	3.21E+00	3.15E+01	5.65E+01	1.89E−15
	Best	**0.00E+00**	0.00E+00	0.00E+00	3.53E−01	1.79E+01	0.00E+00
	Std	**0.00E+00**	0.00E+00	4.32E+00	3.42E+01	2.41E+01	1.04E−14
F10	Ave	**8.88E−16**	8.88E−16	9.65E−14	9.77E+00	2.69E+00	4.44E−15
	Best	**8.88E−16**	8.88E−16	7.55E−14	2.32E−02	1.65E+00	8.88E−16
	Std	**0.00E+00**	0.00E+00	1.85E−14	9.50E+00	6.90E−01	2.64E−15
F11	Ave	**0.00E+00**	0.00E+00	8.17E−03	9.35E−01	1.80E−02	1.18E−02
	Best	**0.00E+00**	0.00E+00	0.00E+00	1.17E−01	5.11E−04	0.00E+00
	Std	**0.00E+00**	0.00E+00	1.23E−02	2.69E−01	1.35E−02	4.53E−02
F12	Ave	**2.58E−09**	7.55E−06	5.32E−02	4.12E+04	7.10E+00	2.26E−02
	Best	**3.05E−11**	2.78E−08	1.32E−02	7.84E−01	2.63E+00	7.38E−03
	Std	**4.14E−09**	1.35E−05	2.45E−02	2.18E+05	4.09E+00	1.71E−02

Table 3. Results of CEC2005 benchmark functions.

Fun	Item	MSHHO	HHO	GWO	SCA	SSA	WOA
F13	Ave	**2.86E−08**	9.53E−05	6.28E−01	4.14E+04	1.24E+01	5.56E−01
	Best	**3.40E−10**	4.10E−09	3.62E−01	7.40E+00	6.43E−02	1.02E−01
	Std	**4.29E−08**	1.23E−04	2.06E−01	7.62E+04	1.26E+01	2.87E−01
F14	Ave	**0.998004**	1.22863	5.85033	2.11766	1.03114	2.96061
	Best	**0.998004**	0.998004	0.998004	0.998004	0.998004	0.998004
	Std	**2.92E−16**	9.23E−01	4.84E+00	1.90E+00	1.81E−01	3.31E+00
F15	Ave	**0.0003106**	0.0003540	0.0051331	0.0010104	0.0022031	0.0007264
	Best	**0.0003075**	0.0003093	0.0003075	0.0003330	0.0005801	0.0003134
	Std	**1.42E−05**	4.40E−05	8.55E−03	3.73E−04	4.94E−03	4.69E−04
F16	Ave	**−1.03163**	−1.03163	−1.03163	−1.03156	−1.03163	−1.03163
	Best	**−1.03163**	−1.03163	−1.03163	−1.03163	−1.03163	−1.03163
	Std	1.23E−13	1.34E−09	2.28E−08	7.53E−05	**1.98E−14**	9.76E−10
F17	Ave	**0.397887**	0.397895	0.397888	0.399336	0.397887	0.397903
	Best	**0.397887**	0.397887	0.397887	0.3979	0.397887	0.397887
	Std	1.09E−11	1.37E−05	9.13E−07	0.00123355	**1.20E−14**	4.34E−05
F18	Ave	**3**	3	3.00004	3.00014	3	3.00018
	Best	**3**	3	3	3	3	3
	Std	**5.99E−13**	3.38E−07	5.20E−05	2.98E−04	1.74E−12	3.37E−04
F19	Ave	**−3.86278**	−3.86063	−3.86161	−3.85458	−3.86278	−3.85393
	Best	**−3.86278**	−3.86278	−3.86278	−3.86093	−3.86278	−3.86278
	Std	1.69E−07	4.26E−03	2.31E−03	2.45E−03	**5.41E−10**	1.82E−02
F20	Ave	**−3.32199**	−3.05318	−3.27542	−2.89641	−3.2164	−3.22982
	Best	**−3.32199**	−3.24908	−3.32199	−3.12557	−3.322	−3.32197
	Std	**7.06E−06**	9.88E−02	6.34E−02	3.92E−01	5.50E−02	1.03E−01
F21	Ave	−5.90486	−5.21017	**−9.56373**	−3.03801	−7.48769	−10.1446
	Best	**−10.1532**	−9.80978	**−10.1532**	−7.11165	**−10.1532**	−10.1531
	Std	1.76E+00	**8.69E−01**	1.83E+00	1.96E+00	3.59E+00	2.91E+00
F22	Ave	−6.3279	−5.24959	−10.0479	−3.06053	−8.91931	**−10.3984**
	Best	**−10.4029**	−10.1296	−10.4026	−6.68804	**−10.4029**	−10.4013
	Std	2.29E+00	**9.22E−01**	1.34E+00	1.68E+00	2.78E+00	2.96E+00
F23	Ave	−7.29165	−5.46617	**−10.535**	−3.35072	−8.67822	−10.535
	Best	**−10.5364**	−10.4401	−10.536	−6.52536	**−10.5364**	−10.535
	Std	2.69E+00	1.30E+00	**6.93E−04**	1.72E+00	3.20E+00	3.46E+00

Table 4. The CEC2017 benchmark functions selected for the experiment.

Type	Function	Dim	Range	*fmin*
Unimodal Functions	Shifted and Rotated Bent Cigar Function (CEC2017-01)	10	[−100,100]	100
	Shifted and Rotated Zakharov Function (CEC2017-03)	10	[−100,100]	300
Simple Multimodal Functions	Shifted and Rotated Rastrigin's Function (CEC2017-05)	10	[−100,100]	500
	Shifted and Rotated Lunacek Bi_Rastrigin Function (CEC2017-07)	10	[−100,100]	700
Hybrid Functions	Hybrid Function 4 (N = 4) (CEC2017-14)	10	[−100,100]	1400
	Hybrid Function 5 (N = 4) (CEC2017-15)	10	[−100,100]	1500
	Hybrid Function 6 (N = 5) (CEC2017-18)	10	[−100,100]	1800
Composition Functions	Composition Function 1 (N = 3) (CEC2017-21)	10	[−100,100]	2100
	Composition Function 4 (N = 4) (CEC2017-24)	10	[−100,100]	2400
	Composition Function 10 (N = 3) (CEC2017-30)	10	[−100,100]	3000

Table 5. Results of CEC2017 benchmark functions.

Fun	Item	MSHHO	HHO	GWO	SCA	SSA	WOA
CEC2017-01	Ave	49,440.6	181,877	2.48E+06	5.99E+08	**3183.02**	338,954
	Best	3140.59	63,447.7	3764.24	1.40E+08	**100.984**	23,441.5
	Std	108,718	117,594	8.64E+06	2.35E+08	**3397.61**	755,780
CEC2017-03	Ave	300.329	300.732	625.499	975.373	**300**	573.145
	Best	300.037	300.165	336.522	495.131	**300**	308.754
	Std	0.272803	0.270405	496.478	371.953	**4.94E−10**	289.931
CEC2017-05	Ave	519.841	538.494	**511.584**	542.678	524.008	551.057
	Best	**502.985**	511.036	505.978	527.153	508.955	526.905
	Std	10.1552	10.6904	**3.68135**	7.29722	11.1746	15.8918
CEC2017-07	Ave	733.654	772.701	**725.715**	767.856	735.3	781.678
	Best	718.843	734.95	**709.702**	753.853	718.987	730.015
	Std	**6.70906**	17.7422	9.62029	7.82372	10.7958	27.0508
CEC2017-14	Ave	**1478.58**	1510.07	2341.04	1555.82	1484.17	1527.32
	Best	**1433.7**	1471.91	1433.95	1462.98	1442.56	1439.08
	Std	**24.7266**	25.6782	1573.34	51.9076	28.7598	45.6609
CEC2017-15	Ave	**1664.99**	1934.25	2292.48	1867.08	1940.31	3336.1
	Best	**1522.89**	1558.06	1535.8	1556.09	1590.51	1644.25
	Std	**98.0525**	510.481	1068.21	234.834	434.466	1660.81
CEC2017-18	Ave	**14,985.7**	16,253.9	25882.7	75,409.4	16,880.7	17,233.1
	Best	**2206.4**	2398.88	3143.44	23,592.5	2254.64	2129.58
	Std	12612.1	**10,061.8**	17,274.9	39,931.8	11,704.2	13,153.9
CEC2017-21	Ave	**2204.27**	2315.2	2303.95	2219.69	2257.21	2299.47
	Best	**2201.18**	2202.1	2201.51	2204.12	2202.02	2203.47
	Std	**1.79373**	58.7998	35.5829	32.6286	60.6996	61.1923
CEC2017-24	Ave	**2503.62**	2756.83	2743.72	2760.06	2738.66	2767.97
	Best	**2500.03**	2500.86	2729.3	2535.92	2501.05	2503.79
	Std	19.301	106.455	**9.339**	64.0151	45.6911	52.9464
CEC2017-30	Ave	**102,074**	953,406	528643	591,396	198,622	523,855
	Best	**5427.23**	6507.98	5859.89	91465.3	6371.17	5601.07
	Std	**238,447**	1.37E+06	679,480	463,886	377,547	590,372

4.3. Nonparametric Statistical Analysis

In order to analyze the test results of each experiment more precisely and avoid the influence of chance on the validation of the experimental results, the results of 30 instances of the 6 algorithms solving 33 test functions were passed through the Wilcoxon rank sum test at a significance level of 0.05 to identify significant discrepancies between the results of the comparison algorithms and MSHHO. If the p-value of the rank sum test was greater than 0.05, then this meant that there was no significant difference between the two results; otherwise, it meant that the results of the two algorithms were significantly different in the whole. The results of the rank sum test are shown in Table 6, and NaN indicates that the two groups of samples were the same. For the CEC2005 benchmark functions, the results in the table show that MSHHO was significantly different from GWO and the SCA and SSA in all 23 functions, from HHO in 22 functions, and from WOA in 19 functions. Among the 10 benchmark functions in CEC2017, MSHHO was significantly different from the SCA in all functions, from HHO and the WOA in 9 functions, from GWO in 8 functions, and from the SSA in 5 functions. Therefore, it can be concluded that there was a statistically significant difference in the optimization performance of MSHHO compared with the other algorithms, and the MSHHO algorithm performed significantly better.

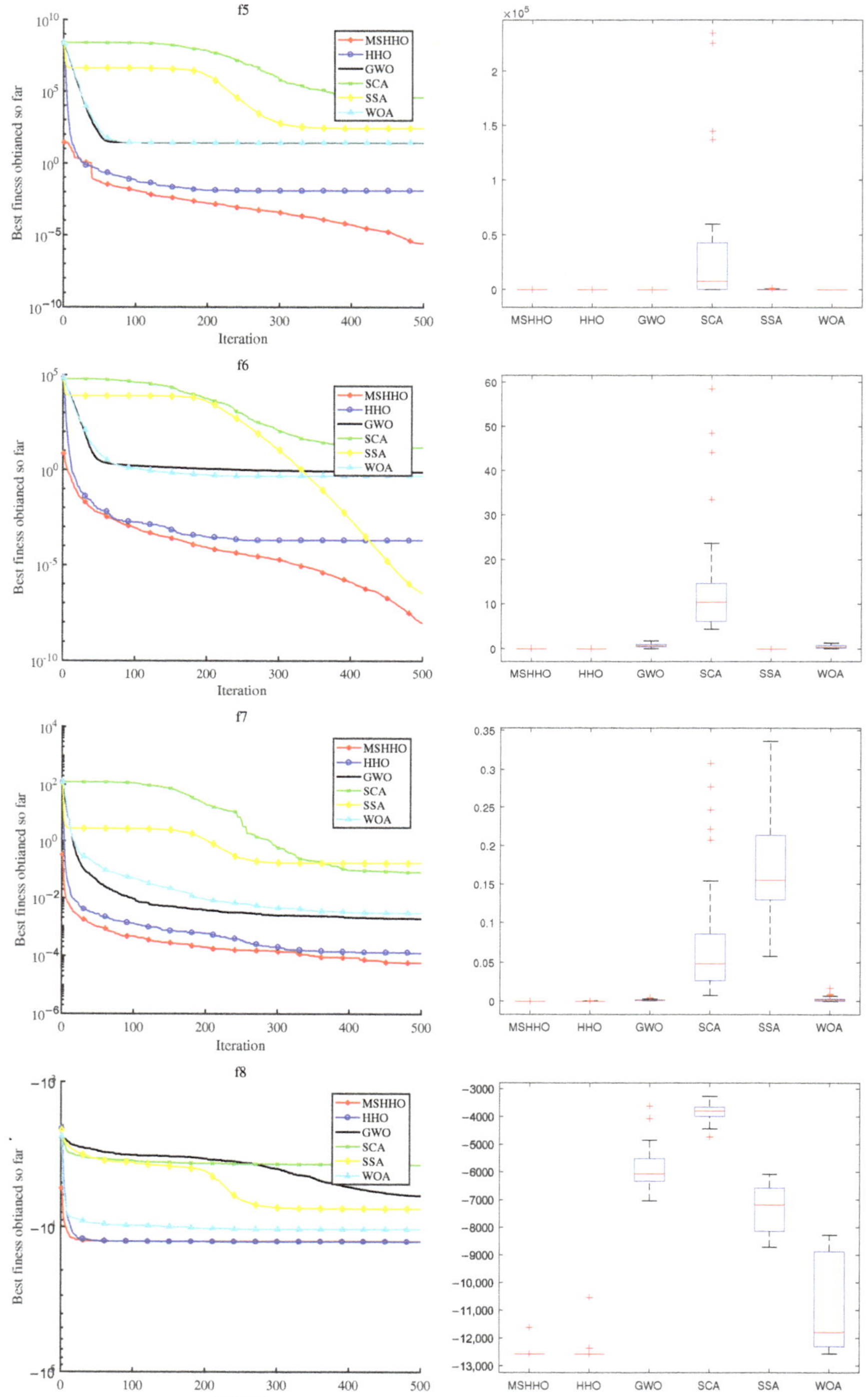

Figure 6. Qualitative results of F5, F6, F7, and F8 (CEC2005).

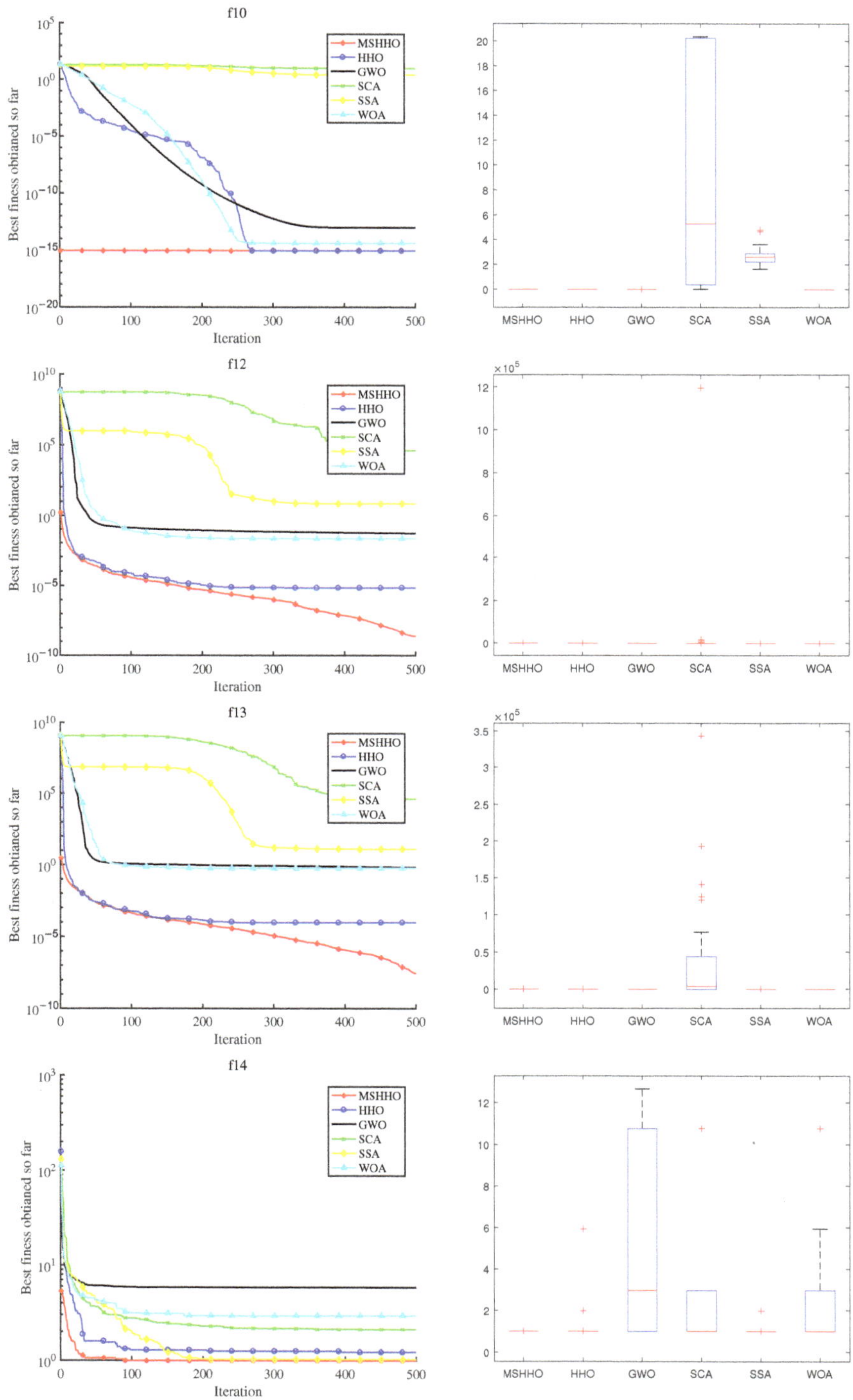

Figure 7. Qualitative results of F10, F12, F13, and F14 (CEC2005).

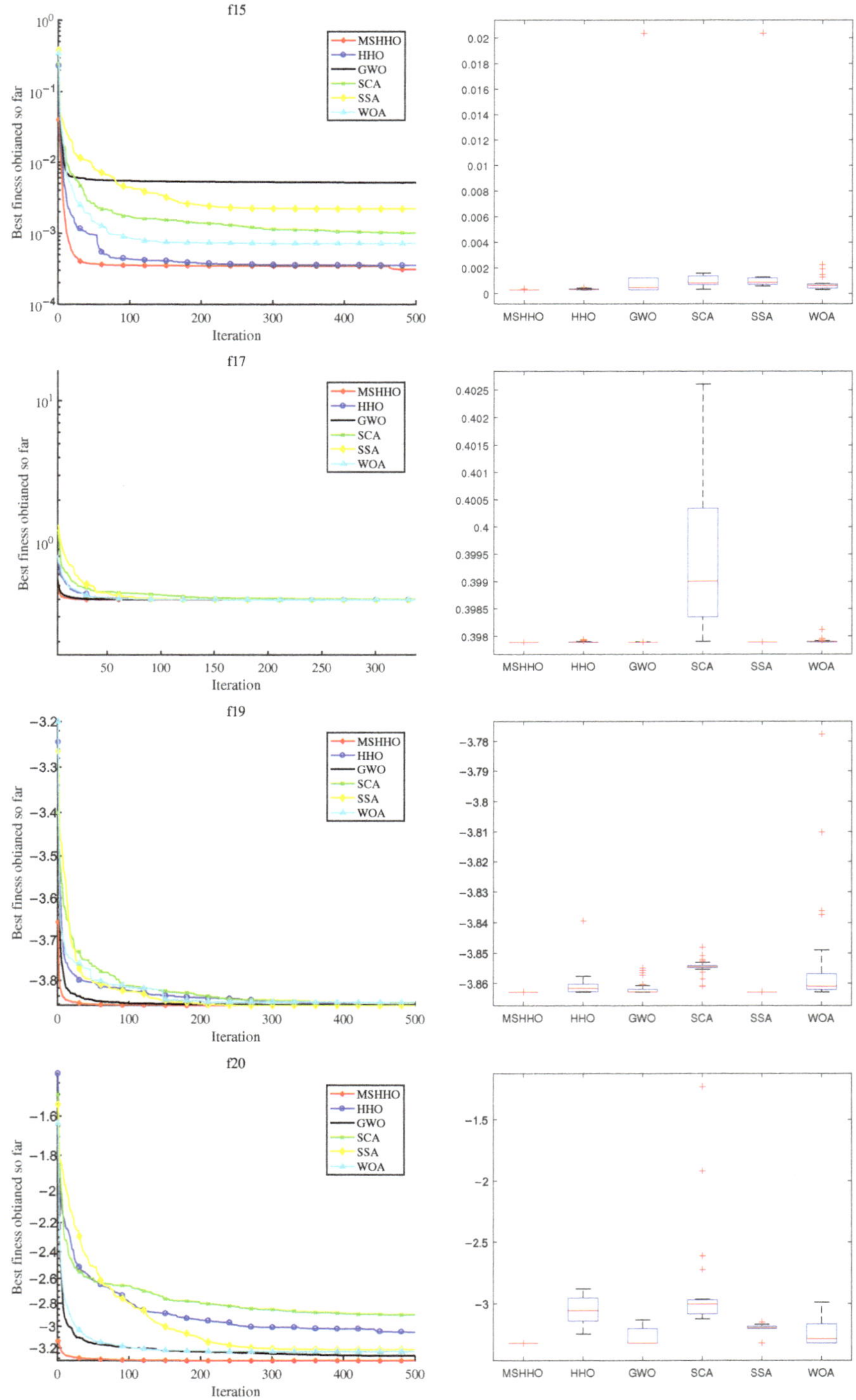

Figure 8. Qualitative results of F15, F17, F19, and F20 (CEC2005).

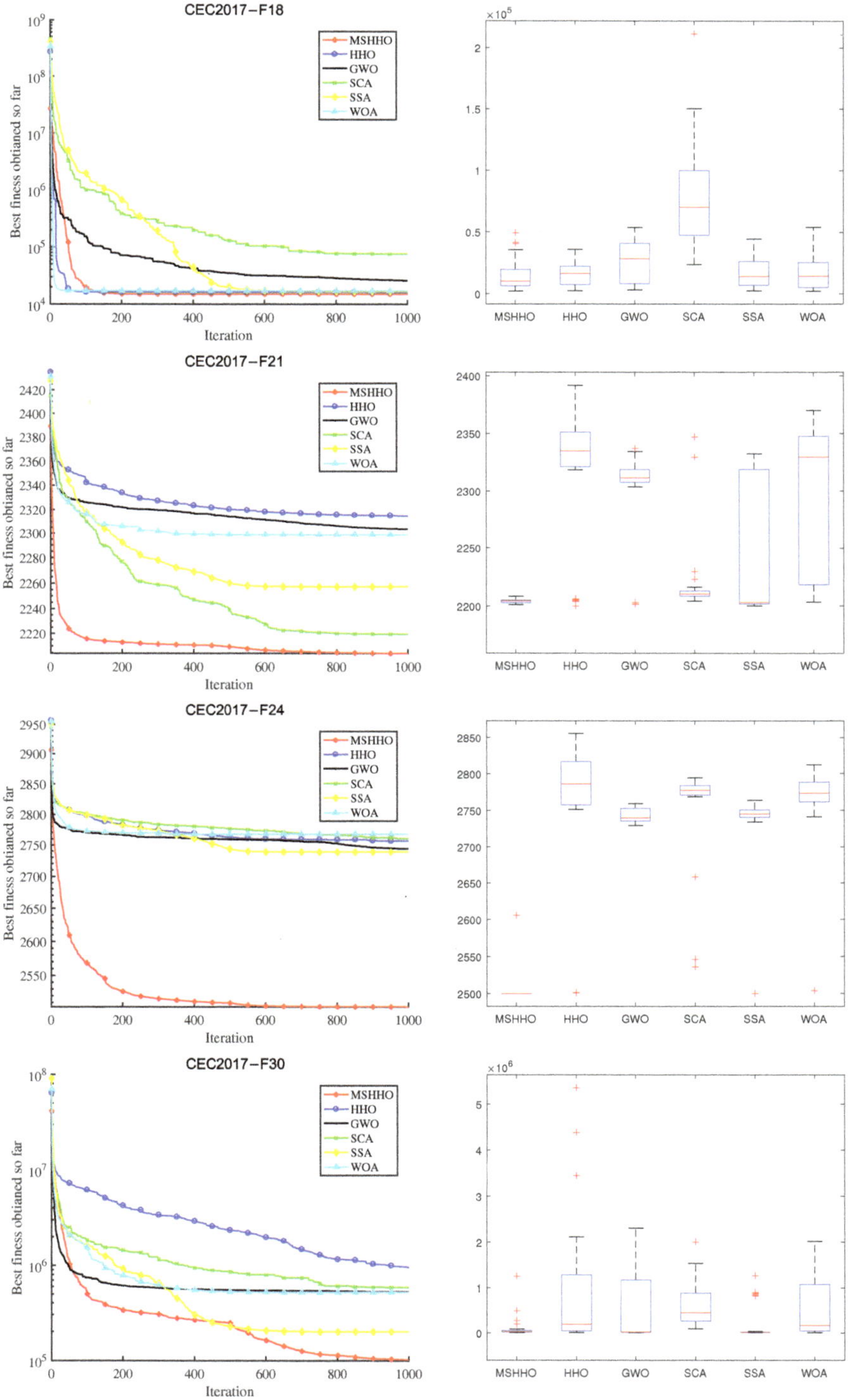

Figure 9. Qualitative results of F18, F21, F24, and F30 (CEC2017).

Table 6. Results of Wilcoxon rank sum test for different algorithms.

Fun	HHO	GWO	SCA	SSA	WOA
CEC2005-F1	1.21E−12	1.21E−12	1.21E−12	1.21E−12	1.21E−12
CEC2005-F2	1.21E−12	1.21E−12	1.21E−12	1.21E−12	1.21E−12
CEC2005-F3	1.21E−12	1.21E−12	1.21E−12	1.21E−12	1.21E−12
CEC2005-F4	1.21E−12	1.21E−12	1.21E−12	1.21E−12	1.21E−12
CEC2005-F5	4.50E−11	3.02E−11	3.02E−11	3.02E−11	3.02E−11
CEC2005-F6	3.02E−11	3.02E−11	2.61E−10	3.02E−11	3.02E−11
CEC2005-F7	**0.093341**	3.02E−11	3.02E−11	3.02E−11	1.33E−10
CEC2005-F8	1.85E−09	3.00E−11	3.00E−11	3.00E−11	1.46E−10
CEC2005-F9	NaN	4.53E−12	1.21E−12	1.21E−12	**0.333711**
CEC2005-F10	NaN	1.13E−12	1.21E−12	1.21E−12	1.22E−08
CEC2005-F11	NaN	6.61E−05	1.21E−12	1.21E−12	**0.160802**
CEC2005-F12	3.02E−11	3.02E−11	3.02E−11	3.02E−11	3.02E−11
CEC2005-F13	2.37E−10	3.02E−11	3.02E−11	3.02E−11	3.02E−11
CEC2005-F14	2.16E−11	2.15E−11	1.79E−05	2.16E−11	2.16E−11
CEC2005-F15	3.47E−10	8.84E−07	3.02E−11	3.34E−11	5.49E−11
CEC2005-F16	1.14E−09	2.92E−11	2.19E−03	2.92E−11	2.92E−11
CEC2005-F17	1.63E−05	3.01E−11	5.42E−07	3.01E−11	1.09E−10
CEC2005-F18	1.20E−08	3.01E−11	6.00E−08	3.01E−11	3.01E−11
CEC2005-F19	3.02E−11	3.69E−11	9.92E−11	3.02E−11	6.07E−11
CEC2005-F20	3.02E−11	2.20E−07	6.77E−05	3.02E−11	3.34E−11
CEC2005-F21	3.82E−10	4.08E−05	0.0281287	3.82E−10	**0.304177**
CEC2005-F22	3.02E−11	2.84E−04	9.53E−07	2.92E−09	**0.53951**
CEC2005-F23	2.03E−09	1.95E−03	1.11E−04	9.06E−08	1.56E−02
CEC2017-F1	3.69E−11	**0.28378**	3.02E−11	5.57E−10	3.50E−09
CEC2017-F3	2.38E−07	3.02E−11	3.02E−11	3.02E−11	3.02E−11
CEC2017-F5	1.36E−07	2.53E−04	6.12E−10	**0.52978**	3.65E−08
CEC2017-F7	2.37E−10	2.26E−03	1.46E−10	**0.8418**	1.78E−10
CEC2017-F14	2.13E−05	1.18E−04	5.97E−09	**0.37108**	2.49E−06
CEC2017-F15	3.03E−04	1.02E−04	5.27E−05	1.34E−05	2.61E−10
CEC2017-F18	**0.36322**	0.024157	2.87E−10	**0.40354**	**0.53951**
CEC2017-F21	4.68E−08	4.31E−08	4.62E−10	**0.72827**	1.96E−10
CEC2017-F24	4.50E−11	3.02E−11	3.69E−11	5.57E−10	3.34E−11
CEC2017-F30	9.03E−04	**0.70617**	7.11E−09	0.00824	0.00111

4.4. Comparison with Other Improved Strategies of the HHO Algorithm

To better illustrate the improvement of the algorithm in terms of optimization performance, the experimental results of the chaotic elite Harris hawks optimization (CEHHO) algorithm in [14] were selected for comparison with the MSHHO algorithm proposed in this paper, with the same parameters as those set in [14], setting the number of populations to 50 and the maximum number of iterations to 300, with 17 common test functions selected for the experiments, and the comparison results are shown in Table 7.

Table 7. Comparison of the results of different improved algorithms.

Fun	CEHHO		MSHHO	
	Ave	Std	Ave	Std
CEC2005-F1	3.11E−82	9.82E−82	**0.00E+00**	0.00E+00
CEC2005-F2	4.57E−40	2.50E−39	**0.00E+00**	0.00E+00
CEC2005-F3	1.59E−59	8.70E−59	**0.00E+00**	0.00E+00
CEC2005-F4	3.03E−44	1.04E−43	**0.00E+00**	0.00E+00
CEC2005-F5	6.62E−04	8.52E−04	**7.31E−06**	2.73E−05
CEC2005-F6	6.04E−06	7.14E−06	**1.73E−18**	9.41E−18
CEC2005-F7	1.32E−04	1.18E−04	**7.48E−05**	9.25E−05
CEC2005-F9	0.00E+00	0.00E+00	**0.00E+00**	0.00E+00
CEC2005-F10	8.88E−16	0.00E+00	**8.88E−16**	0.00E+00
CEC2005-F11	0.00E+00	0.00E+00	**0.00E+00**	0.00E+00
CEC2005-F12	5.41E−07	6.13E−07	**4.43E−12**	2.00E−11
CEC2005-F14	1.16E+00	3.77E−01	**9.98E−01**	9.06E−14
CEC2005-F15	3.28E−04	1.49E−05	**3.08E−04**	1.39E−06
CEC2005-F16	−1.03E+00	2.88E−10	**−1.03E+00**	6.86E−12
CEC2005-F17	3.00E+00	3.59E−08	**3.00E+00**	1.37E−12
CEC2005-F18	−3.86E+00	3.16E−04	**−3.86E+00**	7.00E−07
CEC2005-F20	−3.20E+00	8.75E−02	**−3.32E+00**	7.60E−06

From the results in the table, it is apparent that for functions F_9, F_{10}, and F_{11}, both optimization algorithms could reach the optimal results with a standard deviation of zero, while for F_{16}, F_{17}, and F_{18}, both algorithms found the optimal values as well. The standard deviation of MSHHO was smaller, and the algorithm was more stable in comparison. For the other functions, MSHHO had better performance in terms of both mean and standard deviation.

4.5. Experimental Analysis of Solving High-Dimensional Functions

Based on the experimental results above, we verified the optimization effectiveness of the improved MSHHO algorithm in low-dimensional functions. However, most algorithms would be much less effective or even fail when solving complex problems in high-dimensional functions.

In order to verify the practicality of MSHHO in high-dimensional problems, the original HHO algorithm and the improved MSHHO algorithm were selected for comparison experiments on 100-dimensional and 500-dimensional F_1–F_{13} functions, respectively, and the experimental results are shown in Table 8.

From the results in Table 8, it can be seen that the improved MSHHO algorithm still had better result values than the original HHO algorithm for each test function in 100 and 500 dimensions with good stability, and the MSHHO algorithm still found the optimal results in functions F_1–F_4.

Table 8. Experimental analysis of solving high-dimensional functions.

Fun	Dim	HHO		MSHHO	
		Ave	Std	Ave	Std
CEC2005-F1	100	2.40E−94	8.30E−94	**0.00E+00**	0.00E+00
	500	4.64E−94	2.53E−93	**0.00E+00**	0.00E+00
CEC2005-F2	100	3.08E−50	1.21E−49	**0.00E+00**	0.00E+00
	500	4.11E−49	1.22E−48	**0.00E+00**	0.00E+00
CEC2005-F3	100	2.23E−54	9.48E−54	**0.00E+00**	0.00E+00
	500	1.46E−30	7.38E−30	**0.00E+00**	0.00E+00
CEC2005-F4	100	4.93E−47	2.68E−46	**0.00E+00**	0.00E+00
	500	3.30E−48	1.48E−47	**0.00E+00**	0.00E+00
CEC2005-F5	100	5.06E−02	6.33E−02	**1.75E−04**	4.20E−04
	500	2.42E−01	2.62E−01	**2.56E−02**	3.82E−02
CEC2005-F6	100	4.59E−04	6.12E−04	**7.23E−05**	7.42E−05
	500	1.82E−03	1.84E−03	**2.70E−03**	5.80E−03
CEC2005-F7	100	1.55E−04	1.69E−04	**8.85E−05**	1.15E−04
	500	1.91E−04	1.89E−04	**1.91E−04**	1.89E−04
CEC2005-F8	100	−4.19E+04	1.47E+00	**−4.19E+04**	1.33E−03
	500	−2.09E+05	2.65E+01	**−2.09E+05**	6.97E−06
CEC2005-F9	100	0.00E+00	0.00E+00	**0.00E+00**	0.00E+00
	500	0.00E+00	0.00E+00	**0.00E+00**	0.00E+00
CEC2005-F10	100	8.88E−16	0.00E+00	**8.88E−16**	0.00E+00
	500	8.88E−16	0.00E+00	**8.88E−16**	0.00E+00
CEC2005-F11	100	0.00E+00	0.00E+00	**0.00E+00**	0.00E+00
	500	0.00E+00	0.00E+00	**0.00E+00**	0.00E+00
CEC2005-F12	100	5.74E−06	7.54E−06	**9.23E−07**	1.12E−06
	500	3.43E−06	3.78E−06	**2.72E−06**	2.30E−06
CEC2005-F13	100	1.77E−04	1.63E−04	**4.65E−05**	3.73E−05
	500	7.29E−04	7.97E−04	**3.95E−04**	3.58E−04

5. Engineering Optimization Problems

5.1. Pressure Vessel Design Problem

The pressure vessel is an essential and important piece of equipment in industrial production, the main function of which is to store liquids or gases under a certain pressure. The design problem of the pressure vessel is a nonlinear programming problem that belongs to the category of existence of multiple constraints. The objective of the problem is to minimize the cost of making the pressure vessel. The design of the pressure vessel is shown in Figure 10.

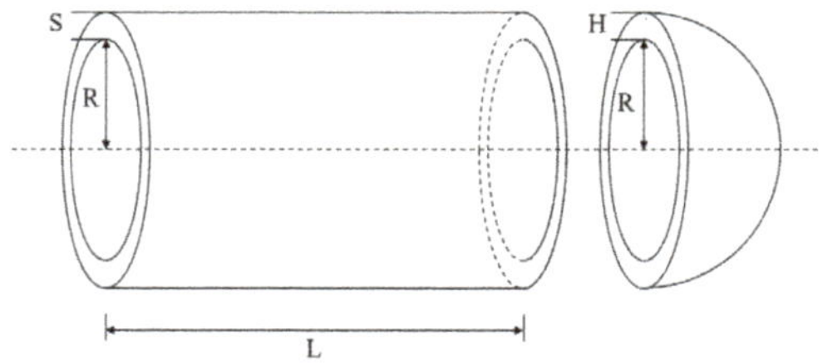

Figure 10. Pressure vessel design problem.

The pressure vessel was composed of a cylindrical vessel part and a hemispherical capping part at the head end and a tail end. L is the length of the cylindrical section, R is the radius of the inner wall of the vessel section, S is the wall thickness of the vessel section, and H is the wall thickness of the hemispherical cap, where, L, R, S, and H were the four variables to be optimized for the pressure vessel design problem. The objective function and constraints of the problem can be expressed as follows:

$$\begin{aligned} &x = [x_1, x_2, x_3, x_4] = [S, H, R, L] \\ &Min f(x) = 0.6224x_1x_3x_4 + 1.7781x_2x_3^2 + 3.1661x_1^2x_4 + 19.84x_1^2x_3 \end{aligned}$$

subject to

$$\begin{aligned} &g_1(x) = -x_1 + 0.0193x_3 \leq 0 \\ &g_2(x) = -x_2 + 0.00954x_3 \leq 0 \\ &g_3(x) = -\pi x_3^2 - \tfrac{4}{3}\pi x_3^3 + 1296000 \leq 0 \\ &g_4(x) = x_4 - 240 \leq 0 \\ &0 \leq x_i \leq 100, i = 1,2 \\ &10 \leq x_i \leq 200, i = 3,4 \end{aligned}$$

The problem was solved by the MSHHO and HHO algorithms [11] as well as the SCA [4], SSA [5], and WOA [7] with the same relevant parameter settings for the algorithms, and the results are shown in Table 9. It can be seen that MSHHO demonstrated the best results in solving this problem.

Table 9. Results of pressure vessel design problem for different algorithms.

Algorithm	S	H	R	L	Ave	Best	Std
MSHHO	1.08995	4.04e−10	65.13547	10.3871	**2530.8**	**2302.55**	384.066
HHO	0.48292	0	41.29134	186.901	3033.73	**2302.55**	427.569
SCA	0	0	40.39128	200	5199.8	2310.76	1590.27
SSA	0.55132	0	43.5991	158.888	3495.34	**2302.55**	**379.247**
WOA	1.15242	0	65.22523	10	4074.13	2302.56	2367.06

The convergence curve and box plot of the problem are shown in Figure 11. It can be visually seen that the MSHHO performed well in terms of accuracy and stability.

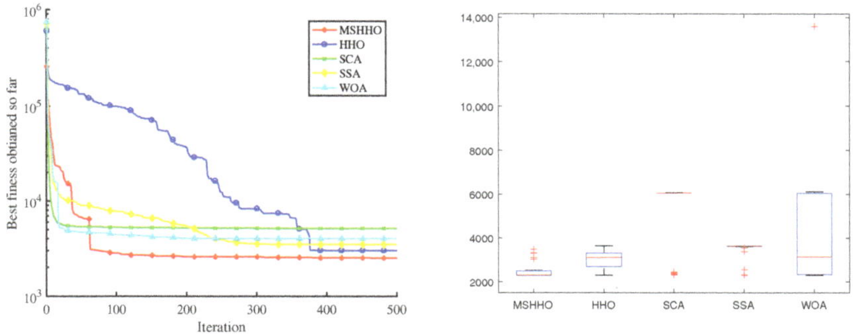

Figure 11. Qualitative results of pressure vessel design problem.

5.2. Compression Spring Design Problem

The optimal design of the spring must achieve the minimum value of its mass within the constraints of the shear stress, surge frequency, fluke curvature, and other relevant index criteria. The design is shown in Figure 12 and includes three design variables, namely the spring wire diameter d, the average spring coil diameter D, and the number of effective spring coils N. The objective function and constraints are described as follows:

$$x = [x_1, x_2, x_3] = [d, D, N]$$
$$Min f(x) = (x_3 + 2)x_1^2 x_2$$

subject to

$$g_1(x) = 1 - \frac{x_2^3 x_3}{71785 x_1^4} \le 0$$
$$g_2(x) = \frac{x_2^2 - x_1 x_2}{12566(x_1^3 x_2 - x_1^4)} + \frac{1}{5108 x_1^2} \le 0$$
$$g_3(x) = 1 - \frac{140.45 x_1}{x_2^2 x_3} \le 0$$
$$g_4(x) = \frac{x_1 + x_2}{1.5} \le 0$$
$$0.05 \le x_1 \le 2.00$$
$$0.25 \le x_2 \le 1.3$$
$$2.00 \le x_3 \le 15.0$$

The problem was solved by the MSHHO and HHO algorithms [11], as well as the SCA [4], SSA [5], and WOA [7] with the same relevant parameter settings for the algorithms, and the results are shown in Table 10, while the convergence curve and box plot of the spring design problem are shown in Figure 13. It can be seen that MSHHO demonstrated the best results in solving this problem.

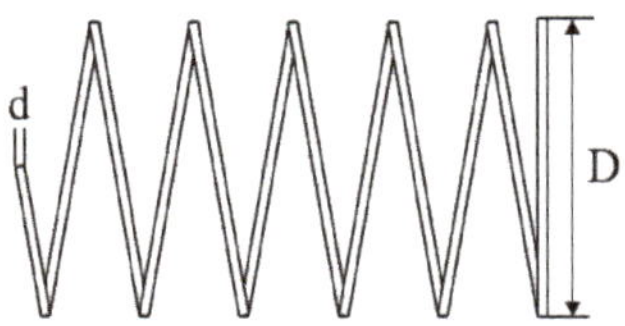

Figure 12. Sping design problem.

Table 10. Results of spring design problem for different algorithms.

Algorithm	d	D	N	Ave	Best	Std
MSHHO	0.13904	1.29578	11.9715	**3.67349**	**3.66189**	**0.022855**
HHO	0.13865	1.28423	12.1601	3.69087	**3.66189**	0.029172
SCA	0.13531	1.19215	13.9361	3.7371	3.66788	0.058998
SSA	0.13505	1.18479	13.9285	3.71434	3.66192	0.123823
WOA	0.13622	1.21712	13.3052	3.70061	**3.66189**	0.028036

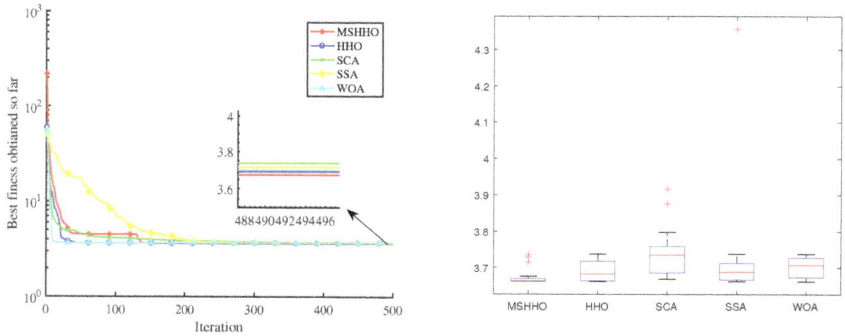

Figure 13. Qualitative results of spring design problem.

6. Conclusions

In this paper, a multi-strategy improvement method was presented to improve the original Harris hawks optimization algorithm by removing the weaknesses, such as low accuracy, slow speed of convergence, and easy being trapped in the local optimality. The improvement algorithm first uses a Sobol sequence to initialize the population and improve the population diversity. In the process of population update iteration, elite opposition-based learning is used to increase the population diversity and population quality. The energy update strategy in the original algorithm is improved to balance the exploration and exploitation capability of the algorithm in a nonlinear update way. The Gaussian walk learning strategy is incorporated to avoid the algorithm from stagnating and falling into the local optimum.

To validate the performance of MSHHO, 23 benchmark functions with unimodal, multimodal, and fixed dimensions in CEC2005 and 10 benchmark functions with unimodal functions, simple multimodal functions, hybrid functions, and composition functions in CEC2017 were selected for comparison experiments with other algorithms, including and HHO GWO as well as the SCA, SSA, and WOA. Subsequently, comparisons with the basic HHO algorithm were made at 100 and 500 dimensions to verify the practicality of the high-dimensional problem. The results show that the improved algorithm had good performance in terms of search accuracy, convergence speed, and stability, which effectively compensated for the defects of the original algorithm. In addition, the MSHHO algorithm was applied to solve two engineering application problems in this paper. The experimental results show that MSHHO could achieve the best results compared with the other algorithms.

In future work, the next step in research focuses on applying the MSHHO algorithm to solving large-scale, complex multi-objective optimization and practical engineering applications, such as microgrid scheduling optimization problems.

Author Contributions: Conceptualization, F.T. and J.W.; methodology, F.T.; software, F.T. and F.C.; validation, F.T., J.W., and F.C.; formal analysis, F.T.; investigation, F.T.; resources, J.W.; data curation, F.T.; writing—original draft preparation, F.T.; writing—review and editing, F.T.; visualization, F.T.; supervision, J.W.; project administration, J.W.; funding acquisition, J.W. All authors have read and agreed to the published version of the manuscript.

Funding: This research was funded by the National Natural Science Foundation of China under grant number 61772031 and the Natural Science Foundation of Hunan Province under grant number 2020JJ4753.

Institutional Review Board Statement: Not applicable.

Informed Consent Statement: Not applicable.

Data Availability Statement: Not applicable.

Conflicts of Interest: The authors declare no conflict of interest.

Appendix A

Appendix A.1

Tables A1–A3 provide specific information on the benchmark function.

Table A1. Information on unimodal benchmark functions.

Function	Dimension	Range	$fmin$
$F_1(x) = \sum_{1}^{n} x_i^2$	30	[−100,100]	0
$F_2(x) = \sum_{i=1}^{n} \lvert x_i \rvert + \prod_{i=1}^{n} \lvert x_i \rvert$	30	[−10,10]	0
$F_3(x) = \sum_{i=1}^{n} \left(\sum_{j=1}^{i} \lvert x_j \rvert \right)^2$	30	[−100,100]	0
$F_4(x) = \max_i \{ \lvert x_i \rvert, 1 \leq i \leq n \}$	30	[−100,100]	0
$F_5(x) = \sum_{i=1}^{n} \left[100(x_i^2 - x_{i+1})^2 + (x_i - 1)^2 \right]$	30	[−30,30]	0
$F_6(x) = \sum_{i=1}^{n} ([x_i + 0.5])^2$	30	[−100,100]	0
$F_7(x) = \sum_{i=1}^{n} i x_i^4 + random[0,1)$	30	[−1.28,1.28]	0

Table A2. Information on multimodal benchmark functions.

Function	Dimension	Range	$fmin$
$F_8(x) = \sum_{i=1}^{n} -x_i \sin(\sqrt{\lvert x_i \rvert})$	30	[−500,500]	$-418.9829 * n$
$F_9(x) = \sum_{i=1}^{n} [x_i^2 - 10\cos(2\pi x_i) + 10]$	30	[−5.12,5.12]	0
$F_{10}(x) = -20\exp\left(-0.2\sqrt{\frac{1}{n}\sum_{i=1}^{n} x_i^2}\right) - \exp\left(\frac{1}{n}\sum_{i=1}^{n}\cos(2\pi x_i)\right) + 20 + e$	30	[−32,32]	0
$F_{11}(x) = \frac{1}{4000}\sum_{i=1}^{n} x_i^2 - \prod_{i=1}^{n}\cos\left(\frac{x_i}{\sqrt{i}}\right) + 1$	30	[−600,600]	0
$F_{12}(x) = \frac{\pi}{n}\left\{10\sin(\pi y_1) + \sum_{i=1}^{n-1}(y_i - 1)^2[1 + 10\sin^2(\pi y_{i+1})] + (y_n - 1)^2\right\} + \sum_{i=1}^{n} u(x_i, 10, 100, 4)$ $y_i = 1 + \frac{x_i+1}{4}, u(x_i, a, k, m) = \begin{cases} k(x_i - a)^m, x_i > a \\ 0, -a < x_i < a \\ k(-x_i - a)^m, x_i < -a \end{cases}$	30	[−50,50]	0
$F_{13}(x) = 0.1\left\{\sin^2(3\pi x_i) + \sum_{i=1}^{n}(x_i - 1)^2[1 + \sin^2(3\pi x_i + 1)] + (x_i - 1)^2[1 + \sin^2(2\pi x_i)]\right\} + \sum_{i=1}^{n} u(x_i, 5, 100, 4)$	30	[−50,50]	0

Table A3. Information on fixed-dimension benchmark functions.

Function	Dimension	Range	$fmin$
$F_{14}(x) = \left(\frac{1}{500} + \sum_{j=1}^{25} \frac{1}{j+\sum_{i=1}^{2}(x_i-a_{ij})^6}\right)^{-1}$	2	[−65,65]	1
$F_{15}(x) = \sum_{i=1}^{11}\left[a_i - \frac{x_1(b_i^2+b_ix_2)}{b_i^2+b_ix_3+x_4}\right]^2$	4	[−5,5]	0.00030
$F_{16}(x) = 4x_1^2 - 2.1x_1^4 + \frac{1}{3}x_1^6 + x_1x_2 - 4x_2^2 + 4x_2^4$	2	[−5,5]	−1.0316
$F_{17}(x) = \left(x_2 - \frac{5.1}{4\pi^2}x_1^2 + \frac{5}{\pi}x_1 - 6\right)^2 + 10(1-\frac{1}{8\pi})\cos x_1 + 10$	2	[−5,5]	0.398
$F_{18}(x) = [1+(x_1+x_2+1)^2(19-14x_1+3x_1^2-14x_2+6x_1x_2+3x_2^2)]$ $\times[30+(2x_1-3x_2)^2\times(18-32x_1+12x_1^2+48x_2-36x_1x_2+27x_2^2)]$	2	[−2,2]	3
$F_{19}(x) = -\sum_{i=1}^{4} c_i \exp\left(-\sum_{j=1}^{3} a_{ij}(x_j-p_{ij})^2\right)$	3	[0,1]	−3.86
$F_{20}(x) = -\sum_{i=1}^{4} c_i \exp\left(-\sum_{j=1}^{6} a_{ij}(x_j-p_{ij})^2\right)$	6	[0,1]	−3.32
$F_{21}(x) = -\sum_{i=1}^{5}\left[(X-a_i)(X-a_i)^T + c_i\right]^{-1}$	4	[0,10]	−10.1532
$F_{22}(x) = -\sum_{i=1}^{7}\left[(X-a_i)(X-a_i)^T + c_i\right]^{-1}$	4	[0,10]	−10.4028
$F_{23}(x) = -\sum_{i=1}^{10}\left[(X-a_i)(X-a_i)^T + c_i\right]^{-1}$	4	[0,10]	−10.5363

References

1. Mirjalili, S.; Mirjalili, S.M.; Lewis, A. Grey wolf optimizer. *Adv. Eng. Softw.* **2014**, *69*, 46–61. [CrossRef]
2. Shareef, H.; Ibrahim, A.A.; Mutlag, A.H. Lightning search algorithm. *Appl. Soft Comput.* **2015**, *36*, 315–333. [CrossRef]
3. Faramarzi, A.; Heidarinejad, M.; Mirjalili, S.; Gandomi, A.H. Marine Predators Algorithm: A nature-inspired metaheuristic. *Expert Syst. Appl.* **2020**, *152*, 113377. [CrossRef]
4. Mirjalili, S. SCA: A sine cosine algorithm for solving optimization problems. *Knowl.-Based Syst.* **2016**, *96*, 120–133. [CrossRef]
5. Mirjalili, S.; Gandomi, A.H.; Mirjalili, S.Z.; Saremi, S.; Faris, H.; Mirjalili, S.M. Salp Swarm Algorithm: A bio-inspired optimizer for engineering design problems. *Adv. Eng. Softw.* **2017**, *114*, 163–191. [CrossRef]
6. Eskandar, H.; Sadollah, A.; Bahreininejad, A.; Hamdi, M. Water cycle algorithm–A novel metaheuristic optimization method for solving constrained engineering optimization problems. *Comput. Struct.* **2012**, *110*, 151–166. [CrossRef]
7. Mirjalili, S.; Lewis, A. The whale optimization algorithm. *Adv. Eng. Softw.* **2016**, *95*, 51–67. [CrossRef]
8. Yang, X.S.; Deb, S. Cuckoo search via Lévy flights. In Proceedings of the 2009 World Congress on Nature & Biologically Inspired Computing (NaBIC), Coimbatore, India, 9–11 December 2009; pp. 210–214.
9. Karaboga, D.; Basturk, B. A powerful and efficient algorithm for numerical function optimization: artificial bee colony (ABC) algorithm. *J. Glob. Optim.* **2007**, *39*, 459–471. [CrossRef]
10. Mirjalili, S. Moth-flame optimization algorithm: A novel nature-inspired heuristic paradigm. *Knowl.-Based Syst.* **2015**, *89*, 228–249. [CrossRef]
11. Heidari, A.A.; Mirjalili, S.; Faris, H.; Aljarah, I.; Mafarja, M.; Chen, H. Harris hawks optimization: Algorithm and applications. *Future Gener. Comput. Syst.* **2019**, *97*, 849–872. [CrossRef]
12. Qu, C.; He, W.; Peng, X.; Peng, X. Harris hawks optimization with information exchange. *Appl. Math. Model.* **2020**, *84*, 52–75. [CrossRef]
13. Liu, X.; Liang, T. Harris hawk optimization algorithm based on square neighborhood and random array. *Control. Decis.* **2021**, *37*, 2467–2476.
14. TANG, A.; HAN, T.; XU, D. Chaotic elite Harris hawks optimization algorithm. *J. Comput. Appl.* **2021**, *41*, 2265.
15. Kaveh, A.; Rahmani, P.; Eslamlou, A.D. An efficient hybrid approach based on Harris Hawks optimization and imperialist competitive algorithm for structural optimization. *Eng. Comput.* **2021**, *38*, 1555–1583. [CrossRef]
16. Atashpaz-Gargari, E.; Lucas, C. Imperialist competitive algorithm: an algorithm for optimization inspired by imperialistic competition. In Proceedings of the 2007 IEEE Congress on Evolutionary Computation, Singapore, 25–28 September 2007; pp. 4661–4667.
17. Elgamal, Z.M.; Yasin, N.B.M.; Tubishat, M.; Alswaitti, M.; Mirjalili, S. An improved harris hawks optimization algorithm with simulated annealing for feature selection in the medical field. *IEEE Access* **2020**, *8*, 186638–186652. [CrossRef]

18. Kirkpatrick, S.; Gelatt Jr, C.D.; Vecchi, M.P. Optimization by simulated annealing. *Science* **1983**, *220*, 671–680. [CrossRef]
19. Li, W.; Shi, R.; Dong, J. Harris hawks optimizer based on the novice protection tournament for numerical and engineering optimization problems. *Appl. Intell.* **2023**, *53*, 6133–6158. [CrossRef]
20. Houssein, E.H.; Hosney, M.E.; Oliva, D.; Mohamed, W.M.; Hassaballah, M. A novel hybrid Harris hawks optimization and support vector machines for drug design and discovery. *Comput. Chem. Eng.* **2020**, *133*, 106656. [CrossRef]
21. Wunnava, A.; Naik, M.K.; Panda, R.; Jena, B.; Abraham, A. A differential evolutionary adaptive Harris hawks optimization for two dimensional practical Masi entropy-based multilevel image thresholding. *J. King Saud-Univ.-Comput. Inf. Sci.* **2022**, *34*, 3011–3024. [CrossRef]
22. Bratley, P.; Fox, B. Implementing sobols quasirandom sequence generator (algorithm 659). *ACM Trans. Math. Softw.* **2003**, *29*, 49–57.
23. Tizhoosh, H.R. Opposition-based learning: A new scheme for machine intelligence. In Proceedings of the International Conference on Computational Intelligence for Modelling, Control and Automation and International Conference on Intelligent Agents, Web Technologies and Internet Commerce (CIMCA-IAWTIC'06), Washington, DC, USA, 28–30 November 2005; Volume 1, pp. 695–701.
24. Tubishat, M.; Idris, N.; Shuib, L.; Abushariah, M.A.; Mirjalili, S. Improved Salp Swarm Algorithm based on opposition based learning and novel local search algorithm for feature selection. *Expert Syst. Appl.* **2020**, *145*, 113122. [CrossRef]
25. Ewees, A.A.; Abd Elaziz, M.; Houssein, E.H. Improved grasshopper optimization algorithm using opposition-based learning. *Expert Syst. Appl.* **2018**, *112*, 156–172. [CrossRef]
26. Peng, H.; Zeng, Z.; Deng, C.; Wu, Z. Multi-strategy serial cuckoo search algorithm for global optimization. *Knowl.-Based Syst.* **2021**, *214*, 106729. [CrossRef]
27. Zhu, X.; Ghahramani, Z.; Lafferty, J.D. Semi-supervised learning using gaussian fields and harmonic functions. In Proceedings of the 20th International Conference on Machine Learning (ICML-03), Washington, DC, USA, 21–24 August 2003; pp. 912–919.
28. Farahani, S.M.; Abshouri, A.A.; Nasiri, B.; Meybodi, M. A Gaussian firefly algorithm. *Int. J. Mach. Learn. Comput.* **2011**, *1*, 448. [CrossRef]
29. Suganthan, P.N.; Hansen, N.; Liang, J.J.; Deb, K.; Chen, Y.P.; Auger, A.; Tiwari, S. Problem definitions and evaluation criteria for the CEC 2005 special session on real-parameter optimization. *KanGAL Rep.* **2005**, *2005005*, 2005.
30. García, S.; Molina, D.; Lozano, M.; Herrera, F. A study on the use of non-parametric tests for analyzing the evolutionary algorithms' behaviour: a case study on the CEC'2005 special session on real parameter optimization. *J. Heuristics* **2009**, *15*, 617–644. [CrossRef]

mathematics

MDPI

Article

Further Optimization of Maxwell-Type Dynamic Vibration Absorber with Inerter and Negative Stiffness Spring Using Particle Swarm Algorithm

Yuying Chen [1], Jing Li [1,*], Shaotao Zhu [1,2,*] and Hongzhen Zhao [1]

[1] Interdisciplinary Research Institute, Faculty of Science, Beijing University of Technology, Beijing 100124, China
[2] Faculty of Information Technology, Beijing University of Technology, Beijing 100124, China
* Correspondence: leejing@bjut.edu.cn (J.L.); zhushaotao@bjut.edu.cn (S.Z.)

Abstract: Dynamic vibration absorbers (DVAs) are widely used in engineering practice because of their good vibration control performance. Structural design or parameter optimization could improve its control efficiency. In this paper, the viscoelastic Maxwell-type DVA model with an inerter and multiple stiffness springs is investigated with the combination of the traditional theory and an intelligent algorithm. Firstly, the expressions and approximate optimal values of the system parameters are obtained using the fixed-point theory to deal with the H_∞ optimization problem, which can provide help with the range of parameters in the algorithm. Secondly, we innovatively introduce the particle swarm optimization (PSO) algorithm to prove that the algorithm could adjust the value of the approximate solution to minimize the maximum amplitude by analyzing and optimizing the single variable and four variables. Furthermore, the validity of the parameters is further verified by simulation between the numerical solution and the analytical solution using the fourth-order Runge–Kutta method. Finally, the DVA demonstrated in this paper is compared with typical DVAs under random excitation. The timing sequence and variances, as well as the decreased ratios of the displacements, show that the presented DVA has a more satisfactory control performance. The inerter and negative stiffness spring can indeed bring beneficial effects to the vibration absorber. Remarkably, the intelligent algorithm can make the resonance peaks equal in the parameter optimization of the vibration absorber, which is quite difficult to achieve with theoretical methods at present. The results may provide a theoretical and computational basis for the optimization design of DVA.

Keywords: particle swarm optimization algorithm; dynamic vibration absorber; Maxwell-type; inerter; negative stiffness

MSC: 37N99; 68W99

Citation: Chen, Y.; Li, J.; Zhu, S.; Zhao, H. Further Optimization of Maxwell-Type Dynamic Vibration Absorber with Inerter and Negative Stiffness Spring Using Particle Swarm Algorithm. *Mathematics* **2023**, *11*, 1904. https://doi.org/10.3390/math11081904

Academic Editor: Jian Dong

Received: 6 March 2023
Revised: 7 April 2023
Accepted: 14 April 2023
Published: 17 April 2023

1. Introduction

Dynamic vibration absorbers (DVAs), known as tuned mass dampers (TMDs), are widely utilized in mechanical equipment and building structures owing to their favorable vibration control performance. The fundamental principle is to reduce the vibration state when an exciting force response occurs in the frequency domain by choosing the forms and parameters of the DVA as well as the coupling relationship with the primary system. In 1909, Frahm first proposed the concept of DVA as a passive vibration control device. In 1928, Ormondroyd and Den Hartog [1] introduced the damping effect to obtain the classical Voigt-type DVA and set minimizing the maximum amplitude response as the optimization goal. Hahnkamm [2] and Brock [3] successively derived the optimum tuning ratio and optimum damping ratio of this model, the method of which is now called the fixed-point theory through the textbook written by Den Hartog [4]. Subsequently, the design of three-element type DVA was further improved by Asami and Nishihara [5] based on the superb properties of viscoelastic devices. In 2001, Ren [6] developed a grounded damped DVA that significantly enhances the vibration control. Under identical parameter conditions, the optimized Asami model and Ren model perform with superior control performance to the Voigt-type DVA. These three traditional models provide an irreplaceable reference value for future scholars to improve and optimize DVA structures.

Before introducing Maxwell model, we first trace the air damper that has a history of more than 80-year. This kind of damper is proposed due to its benefits such as temperature independent, less maintenance, low cost, and no long-term change. Asami and Sekiguchi [7,8] further put forward the piston-cylinder type air damper that could be represented by the Voigt model. This means that the elements of spring and damping were set in parallel. However, this equivalent structure made both the spring and damping parameters change with the frequency and affect each other. Taking into account the connection between the damping and restoring force in the actual damper, Asami and Nishihara [5] optimized the prior model and designed Maxwell structure, in which the spring and damping were connected in series. Moreover, the addition of a second spring element positioned parallel to the air damper could drive the piston to recover, and together they constitute the three-element type DVA. For viscoelastic materials with both damping and stiffness properties, the mechanical model with the Maxwell structure exhibits better results under the same mass ratio, one that has the value of further research in this paper.

Numerous experts also consider how to select and adapt parameters to achieve the best reduction in structural vibration in DVA while designing the ideal structure. The H_∞ optimization, the H_2 optimization, and the stability maximization criterion [9,10] are three common optimization criteria. The H_∞ optimization used in this study is more intuitive and convenient in practical application. The principle is to minimize the maximum amplitude when harmonic excitation acts on the primary system. Once we determined the optimization objective, the fixed-point theory can be applied as an approximate way to solve the parameter problem of the system. In addition, a new method was also developed by Asami et al. [11,12] to address the precise solution of H_∞ optimization. Both approaches aid in further improving the vibration reduction capacity of DVA. The conclusion shows that the approximate optimal solution is quite close to the precise solution, which verifies the usefulness of the fixed-point theory in an engineering context. Considering the simple and convenient reasons, this paper chooses the fixed-point theory to deal with H_∞ optimization and adjusts the value of the approximate solution with an intelligent algorithm to achieve minimizing the maximum amplitude more efficiently.

In the structural design of the vibration absorber, we can achieve the effect of vibration reduction by adding components. Negative stiffness usually means that the displacement of the object is opposite to the direction of the external force. It is a characteristic that is different from the negative Poisson ratio. Springs with negative stiffness are less stable. However, the study discovered that better vibration control performance will play out, and the natural frequency will decrease if the system has both positive and negative stiffness springs. This combination not only plays a role in high flexibility and high deformability but also maintains optimal stability under certain parameter conditions [13–15]. A negative stiffness characteristic has been applied to the design of composite materials and seismic retrofitting [16]. To lower the amplitude of the primary system, Shen and Wang et al. [17,18] inserted negative stiffness into the vibration absorbers (Ren model, three-element model) and confirmed the effective control performance. In addition to the negative stiffness elements discussed above, there is another element that is receiving increasing attention. Smith [19] proposed the idea of an inerter and solved the problem of synthesis on mechanical networks in 2002. As a new type of structural control device with two independent and free endpoints, the inerter has been found to achieve good results in vibration reduction or isolation and applied to suspension support design and simulation quality [20,21]. Based on the classical theory, Barredo et al. [22,23] and Wang et al. [24,25] optimized the DVA with an inerter, proving that it could maximize the applicable frequency range in vibration control. Furthermore, adding an amplifying mechanism [26] or distributed arrangement [27,28] also makes the structure of the vibration absorber able to be further optimized, which is worth discussing in future work.

The optimization of DVA/TMD parameters has been investigated in depth in different various research backgrounds. Zhang and Xu [29] developed the optimization approach of TMD parameters, blending nonlinear aeroelastic effects for speeding control. Wang et al. [30] proposed a quasi-zero-stiffness energy harvesting DVA and optimized the parameters with the perturbation method to suppress vibration. In this paper, a swarm intelligence algorithm is innovatively introduced to find the global optimal value by following the currently searched optimal value and then determining the actual optimal value of each parameter [31,32]. In 1995, Kennedy and Eberhart proposed particle swarm optimization (PSO) when studying the predation behavior of birds. The algorithm transforms the entire group from disorder to order in the solution space by utilizing the sharing of information among group individuals. Moreover, the two extreme values of individual optimal value and group optimal value are tracked and updated by calculating the fitness of each particle. The particle swarm can identify the best position in accordance with the iteration termination condition and output the optimal parameter values when the maximum number of iterations is set. The theoretical optimal value obtained by the fixed-point theory to deal with the H_∞ optimization problem directly determines the range of parameters. With the support of the particle swarm optimization algorithm, the effect of the equal resonance peak is further realized, and the maximum amplitude of the primary system is minimized. This cannot be directly achieved by only using the theoretical method for parameter optimization. Using the algorithm to further optimize on the basis of the fixed-point theory can fully demonstrate its advantages in data processing. In the existing research on a Maxwell-type DVA/TMD with an inerter and negative stiffness spring, the combination of intelligent algorithm and theoretical analysis to automatically adjust the parameter strategy is our motivation and novelty.

The organization of this paper is as follows. The basic DVA model is given and the expressions of the system parameters are obtained in Section 2. The PSO algorithm is introduced in detail, and the numerical simulation is carried out according to different situations in Section 3. The DVA studied in this paper is compared with typical DVAs in Section 4. Finally, conclusion and prospect are drawn in Section 5.

2. Dynamic Vibration Absorber Model and Basic Parameter Optimization

2.1. The Basic Model and the Amplitude Response

This paper investigates the viscoelastic Maxwell-type DVA with an inerter and multiple stiffness springs, as displayed in Figure 1. The DVA is connected to a primary system with a single degree of freedom. m_1, m_2, k_1, and k_2 are the masses and linear stiffness coefficients of the primary system and DVA severally. k_3 and c describe the stiffness and damping coefficient of Maxwell structure. b is the inerter. k_4 is the stiffness coefficient of the grounded negative stiffness spring. F_0 and ω denote the amplitude and frequency of the exciting force. x_1, x_2, and x_3 express the displacement of the primary system, DVA, and the division point about spring and damping in Maxwell structure.

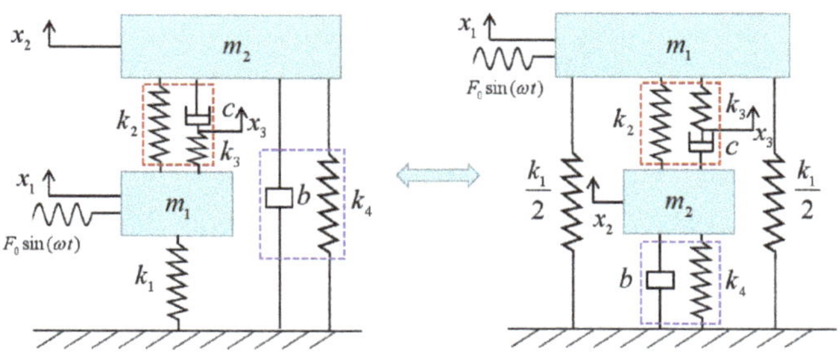

Figure 1. The viscoelastic Maxwell-type DVA with an inerter and multiple stiffness springs.

The dynamic equation of the system is established and obtained in accordance with Newton's second law

$$\begin{cases} m_1\ddot{x}_1 + k_1x_1 + k_2(x_1 - x_2) + k_3(x_1 - x_3) = F_0 \sin(\omega t) \\ m_2\ddot{x}_2 + b\ddot{x}_2 + c(\dot{x}_2 - \dot{x}_3) + k_2(x_2 - x_1) + k_4x_2 = 0 \\ c(\dot{x}_3 - \dot{x}_2) + k_3(x_3 - x_1) = 0 \end{cases} \tag{1}$$

By using the following parametric transformations

$$\omega_1 = \sqrt{\frac{k_1}{m_1}}, \omega_2 = \sqrt{\frac{k_2}{m_2}}, \xi = \frac{c}{2m_2\omega_2}, \mu = \frac{m_2}{m_1}, \alpha_1 = \frac{k_3}{k_1}, \alpha_2 = \frac{k_4}{k_1}, \beta = \frac{b}{m_1}, f = \frac{F_0}{m_1}$$

Equation (1) can be expressed as

$$\begin{cases} \ddot{x}_1 + \omega_1^2x_1 + \mu\omega_2^2(x_1 - x_2) + \alpha_1\omega_1^2(x_1 - x_3) = f \sin(\omega t) \\ \ddot{x}_2 + \frac{\beta}{\mu}\ddot{x}_2 + 2\omega_2\xi(\dot{x}_2 - \dot{x}_3) + \omega_2^2(x_2 - x_1) + \frac{\alpha_2\omega_1^2}{\mu}x_2 = 0 \\ 2\mu\omega_2\xi(\dot{x}_3 - \dot{x}_2) + \alpha_1\omega_1^2(x_3 - x_1) = 0 \end{cases} \tag{2}$$

It should be noted that the representations of parameters $\alpha_1, \alpha_2, \beta$ are different from the existing literature [25]. Using this expressive method makes the process of theoretical derivation easier to implement in software. On the basis of Laplace transform, Equation (2) becomes

$$\begin{cases} (s^2 + \omega_1^2 + \mu\omega_2^2 + \alpha_1\omega_1^2)X_1(s) - \mu\omega_2^2X_2(s) - \alpha_1\omega_1^2X_3(s) = fe^{j\omega t} \\ -\omega_2^2X_1(s) + \left(s^2 + \frac{\beta}{\mu}s^2 + 2\omega_2\xi s + \omega_2^2 + \frac{\alpha_2\omega_1^2}{\mu}\right)X_2(s) - 2\omega_2\xi sX_3(s) = 0 \\ -\alpha_1\omega_1^2X_1(s) - 2\mu\omega_2\xi sX_2(s) + (2\mu\omega_2\xi s + \alpha_1\omega_1^2)X_3(s) = 0 \end{cases} \tag{3}$$

Supposing $X_1(s) = H_1(j\omega)e^{j\omega t}$, $X_2(s) = H_2(j\omega)e^{j\omega t}$, $X_3(s) = H_3(j\omega)e^{j\omega t}$ and letting $s = j\omega, j = \sqrt{-1}$, one could obtain by substituting them into Equation (3)

$$H_1(j\omega) = \frac{f(A_1 + B_1j)}{C_1 + D_1j}$$

The other parameters are presented as

$$\begin{aligned} A_1 =& \alpha_1\omega_1^2\left[\alpha_2\omega_1^2 + \mu\omega_2^2 - (\mu + \beta)\omega^2\right] \\ B_1 =& 2\mu\omega\omega_2\xi\left[(\alpha_1 + \alpha_2)\omega_1^2 + \mu\omega_2^2 - (\mu + \beta)\omega^2\right] \\ C_1 =& \alpha_1\omega_1^2\{(\mu + \beta)\omega^4 - \left[(\alpha_2 + \mu + \beta)\omega_1^2 + \mu(1 + \mu + \beta)\omega_2^2\right]\omega^2 \\ &+ \mu(1 + \alpha_2)\omega_1^2\omega_2^2 + \alpha_2\omega_1^4\} \\ D_1 =& 2\mu\omega\omega_2\xi\{(\mu + \beta)\omega^4 + \mu(1 + \alpha_2)\omega_1^2\omega_2^2 + (\alpha_1 + \alpha_2 + \alpha_1\alpha_2)\omega_1^4 \\ &- \{[\alpha_1 + \alpha_2 + (\mu + \beta)(1 + \alpha_1)]\omega_1^2 + \mu(1 + \mu + \beta)\omega_2^2\}\omega^2\} \end{aligned}$$

Introducing the parameters

$$\nu = \frac{\omega_2}{\omega_1}, \lambda = \frac{\omega}{\omega_1}, X_{st} = \frac{F_0}{k_1}$$

where X_{st} is the static deformation of the primary system under sinusoidal excitation. The amplitude amplification factor should be

$$A^2 = \left|\frac{H_1}{X_{st}}\right|^2 = \frac{A_2^2 + \xi^2B_2^2}{C_2^2 + \xi^2D_2^2} \tag{4}$$

where

$$\begin{aligned} A_2 =& \alpha_1 \left[\alpha_2 + \mu v^2 - (\mu + \beta) \lambda^2 \right] \\ B_2 =& 2\mu\lambda v \left[\alpha_1 + \alpha_2 + \mu v^2 - (\mu + \beta) \lambda^2 \right] \\ C_2 =& \alpha_1 \{ (\mu + \beta) \lambda^4 - \left[\alpha_2 + \mu + \beta + \mu(1 + \mu + \beta) v^2 \right] \lambda^2 \\ & + \mu(1 + \alpha_2) v^2 + \alpha_2 \} \\ D_2 =& 2\mu\lambda v \{ (\mu + \beta) \lambda^4 + \mu(1 + \alpha_2) v^2 + \alpha_1 + \alpha_2 + \alpha_1 \alpha_2 \\ & - \left[\alpha_1 + \alpha_2 + (\mu + \beta)(1 + \alpha_1) + \mu(1 + \mu + \beta) v^2 \right] \lambda^2 \} \end{aligned}$$

2.2. *The Optimum Frequency Ratio v_{opt} and the Optimum Stiffness Ratio α_{1opt}*

It can be demonstrated after simple derivation of Equation (4) that the normalized amplitude–frequency curves pass through three fixed points of DVA, which are independent of the damping ratio ξ. Figure 2a provides the curves under different damping ratios of 0.3, 0.5, and 0.9. Three fixed points are represented here as P, Q, and R. Other parameters are fixed as $\mu = 0.1$, $\beta = 0.3$, $v = 1.4$, $\alpha_1 = 0.3$, and $\alpha_2 = -0.1$. Since the fixed points are independent of the damping ratio, it is necessary to make the response values of $\xi \to 0$ and $\xi \to \infty$ equal to solve its analytical expression, which satisfies the following equation

$$\left| \frac{A_2}{C_2} \right|_{\xi \to 0} = \left| \frac{B_2}{D_2} \right|_{\xi \to \infty} \tag{5}$$

One can obtain from simplification

$$g(\lambda) = a_1 \lambda^6 + a_2 \lambda^4 + a_3 \lambda^2 + a_4 = 0 \tag{6}$$

where

$$\begin{aligned} a_1 =& -2(\mu + \beta)^2 \\ a_2 =& 2v^2\mu^3 + \left[2 + \alpha_1 + 4(1 + \beta) v^2 \right] \mu^2 + [2(\alpha_1 + 2\alpha_2) + \beta(2 + \alpha_1)]\beta \\ & + 2\left[\alpha_1(1 + \beta) + 2(\alpha_2 + \beta) + \beta(2 + \beta) v^2 \right] \mu \\ a_3 =& -\{ 2\mu^3 v^4 + 2\left[2 + \alpha_1 + 2\alpha_2 + (1 + \beta) v^2 \right] \mu^2 v^2 \\ & + 2\{ [\alpha_1(1 + \beta) + 2\alpha_2 + 2\beta(1 + \alpha_2)] v^2 + \alpha_1(1 + \alpha_2) + 2\alpha_2 \} \mu \\ & + 2\beta[\alpha_1(1 + \alpha_2) + 2\alpha_2] + 2\alpha_2(\alpha_1 + \alpha_2) \} \\ a_4 =& 2(1 + \alpha_2)\mu^2 v^4 + 2\mu[\alpha_1(1 + \alpha_2) + \alpha_2(2 + \alpha_2)] v^2 + \alpha_1\alpha_2(2 + \alpha_2) + 2\alpha_2^2 \end{aligned}$$

When $\xi \to 0$, one has

$$|A| = \left| \frac{H_1}{X_{st}} \right| = \left| \frac{A_3}{C_3} \right| \tag{7}$$

When $\xi \to \infty$, one has

$$|A| = \left| \frac{H_1}{X_{st}} \right| = \left| \frac{B_3}{D_3} \right| \tag{8}$$

where

$$A_3 = \frac{A_2}{\alpha_1}, B_3 = \frac{B_2}{2\mu\lambda v}, C_3 = \frac{C_2}{\alpha_1}, D_3 = \frac{D_2}{2\mu\lambda v}$$

Equations (7) and (8) are combined to determine the coordinates of three points:

$$|A| = \left| \frac{H_1}{X_{st}} \right| = \left| \frac{\alpha_1 + 2\alpha_2 + 2\mu v^2 - 2(\mu + \beta)\lambda^2}{\alpha_1[1 + \alpha_2 - (1 + \mu + \beta)\lambda^2]} \right| \tag{9}$$

Let λ_P^2, λ_Q^2, and λ_R^2 be the three roots of Equation (9). As long as the values of λ_P, λ_Q, and λ_R are determined, the coordinates of the three points can be written. The optimum frequency ratio, the optimum stiffness ratio, and the optimum damping ratio can be obtained when the vertical ordinates are adjusted to the same height, thereby solving the problem of minimizing the maximum amplitude. By drawing the normalized amplitude–frequency curves of $\xi \to 0$ and $\xi \to \infty$ as shown in Figure 2b, it is found that there is a fixed phase difference between two points P, R, and point Q. Therefore, there is a positive and negative sign difference when the absolute value is removed in Equation (9).

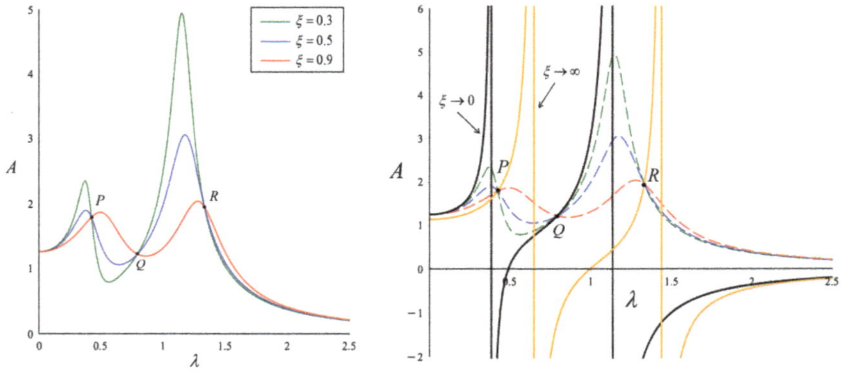

(**a**) (**b**)

Figure 2. The normalized amplitude–frequency curves under different damping ratios: (**a**) $\xi = 0.3$, $\xi = 0.5$, and $\xi = 0.9$; (**b**) $\xi \to 0$ and $\xi \to \infty$.

The first step is adjusting the ordinates of point P and point R to the equal height

$$\left|\frac{H_1}{X_{st}}\right|_P = \left|\frac{A_4 + B_4\lambda_P^2}{C_4 + D_4\lambda_P^2}\right|, \left|\frac{H_1}{X_{st}}\right|_R = \left|\frac{A_4 + B_4\lambda_R^2}{C_4 + D_4\lambda_R^2}\right| \tag{10}$$

where

$$A_4 = \alpha_1 + 2\alpha_2 + 2\mu\nu^2,\ B_4 = -2(\mu + \beta)$$
$$C_4 = \alpha_1(1 + \alpha_2),\ D_4 = -\alpha_1(1 + \mu + \beta)$$

When the parameter α_1 satisfies $A_4D_4 = B_4C_4$, the ordinates of two fixed points P and R are independent of λ^2. One could gain

$$\alpha_1 = \frac{2\left[\mu + \beta - \alpha_2 - \mu(1 + \mu + \beta)\nu^2\right]}{1 + \mu + \beta} \tag{11}$$

Substituting α_1 into Equation (6), we can obtain

$$\begin{aligned}\frac{2}{1 + \mu + \beta}\left[(1 + \mu + \beta)\lambda^2 - (1 + \alpha_2)\right]\{(\mu + \beta)^2\lambda^4 - 2(\mu + \beta)^2\lambda^2 \\ - (1 + \mu + \beta)\mu^2\nu^4 + 2(\mu + \beta - \alpha_2)\mu\nu^2 + \alpha_2[2(\mu + \beta) - \alpha_2]\} = 0\end{aligned} \tag{12}$$

The values of λ_P^2, λ_Q^2 and λ_R^2 are obtained from Equation (12)

$$\lambda_P^2 = \frac{\mu + \beta - \sqrt{(1 + \mu + \beta)\mu^2\nu^4 - 2(\mu + \beta - \alpha_2)\mu\nu^2 + (\mu + \beta - \alpha_2)^2}}{\mu + \beta} \tag{13a}$$

$$\lambda_Q^2 = \frac{1 + \alpha_2}{1 + \mu + \beta} \tag{13b}$$

$$\lambda_R^2 = \frac{\mu+\beta+\sqrt{(1+\mu+\beta)\mu^2\nu^4 - 2(\mu+\beta-\alpha_2)\mu\nu^2 + (\mu+\beta-\alpha_2)^2}}{\mu+\beta} \tag{13c}$$

Then, Equation (9) becomes

$$\left|\frac{H_1}{X_{st}}\right|_{P,R} = \frac{\mu+\beta}{\mu+\beta-\alpha_2-\mu(1+\mu+\beta)\nu^2} \tag{14a}$$

$$\left|\frac{H_1}{X_{st}}\right|_{Q} = \frac{(1+\mu+\beta)\left[\mu+\beta-\alpha_2-\mu(1+\mu+\beta)\nu^2\right]}{(\mu+\beta-\alpha_2)^2} \tag{14b}$$

The second step is adjusting the ordinates of point P (or R) and point Q to the same height. The optimum frequency ratio could be

$$\nu_{opt} = \sqrt{\frac{(1+\mu+\beta)(\mu+\beta-\alpha_2)-\sqrt{(\mu+\beta)(\mu+\beta-\alpha_2)^2(1+\mu+\beta)}}{\mu(1+\mu+\beta)^2}} \tag{15}$$

Then, we can substitute Equation (15) into Equation (11) to obtain

$$\alpha_{1opt} = \frac{2\sqrt{(\mu+\beta)(\mu+\beta-\alpha_2)^2(1+\mu+\beta)}}{(1+\mu+\beta)^2} \tag{16}$$

and

$$\left|\frac{H_1}{X_{st}}\right|_{P,Q,R} = \sqrt{\frac{(\mu+\beta)(1+\mu+\beta)}{(\mu+\beta-\alpha_2)^2}} \tag{17}$$

2.3. The Optimum Stiffness Ratio α_{2opt} and the Optimum Damping Ratio ξ_{opt}

Because the inappropriate stiffness value will make the system unstable, it is discovered that the system will be in a stable state when the displacement caused by the pre-load is equivalent to the response value at the fixed point.

$$\left|\frac{H_1}{X_{st}}\right|_{\lambda=0} = \left|\frac{H_1}{X_{st}}\right|_{P,Q,R} \tag{18}$$

that is,

$$\left|\frac{H_1}{X_{st}}\right|_{\lambda=0} = \frac{(1+\mu+\beta)(\mu+\beta)(1+\alpha_2)-M_1}{\alpha_2(1+\mu+\beta)^2+(1+\alpha_2)\{(1+\mu+\beta)(\mu+\beta-\alpha_2)-M_1\}} \tag{19}$$

where

$$M_1 = \sqrt{(\mu+\beta)(\mu+\beta-\alpha_2)^2(1+\mu+\beta)}$$

Based on Equations (17) and (19), the stiffness ratio α_2 of system is shown as the following five possible forms

$$\alpha_{2a,2b} = \frac{\mu+\beta+2(1+\mu+\beta)\left[\mu+\beta\pm\sqrt{(\mu+\beta)(1+\mu+\beta)}\right]}{3(1+\mu+\beta)+1} \tag{20a}$$

$$\alpha_{2c,2d} = \frac{\mu+\beta+(1+\mu+\beta)\left[\mu+\beta\pm\sqrt{(\mu+\beta)(2+\mu+\beta)}\right]}{2+\mu+\beta} \tag{20b}$$

$$\alpha_{2e} = -1 \tag{20c}$$

The frequency of force excitation is obtained according to Equation (4)

$$\omega_{(1,2)}^2 = \frac{(\mu+\beta+\alpha_2)\omega_1^2 + \mu(1+\mu+\beta)\omega_2^2 \pm \sqrt{\Delta}}{2(\mu+\beta)} \tag{21}$$

where

$$\Delta = \left[(\mu+\beta+\alpha_2)\omega_1^2 + \mu(1+\mu+\beta)\omega_2^2\right]^2 - 4(\mu+\beta)\left[\mu(1+\alpha_2)\omega_1^2\omega_2^2 + \alpha_2\omega_1^4\right]$$

When

$$\alpha_2 > -\frac{\mu\omega_2^2}{\omega_1^2+\mu\omega_2^2} = \alpha_2 > -\frac{1}{1+\frac{1}{\mu v^2}} > -1$$

the frequency of force excitation is nonnegative. From this condition, it can be determined that the value of α_2 should first exclude $\alpha_{2e} = -1$, and the other value relationship is shown in Figure 3. Furthermore, we substitute α_{2a}–α_{2d} into v and find that α_{2a} or α_{2c} makes v purely imaginary. This loses the significance of variables optimizing the system, so α_{2b} and α_{2d} are the best values for now. In other words, the inerter-to-mass ratio can keep the system stable and reduce the vibration within the corresponding range when $\alpha_{opt} = \alpha_{2b}$ and $\alpha_{opt} = \alpha_{2d}$. We discuss the selection of the optimal parameters in the following two situations. The relationship between $(\mu, \beta, v(\alpha_2))$ and $(\mu, \beta, \alpha_1(\alpha_2))$ can be seen from Figures 4 and 5.

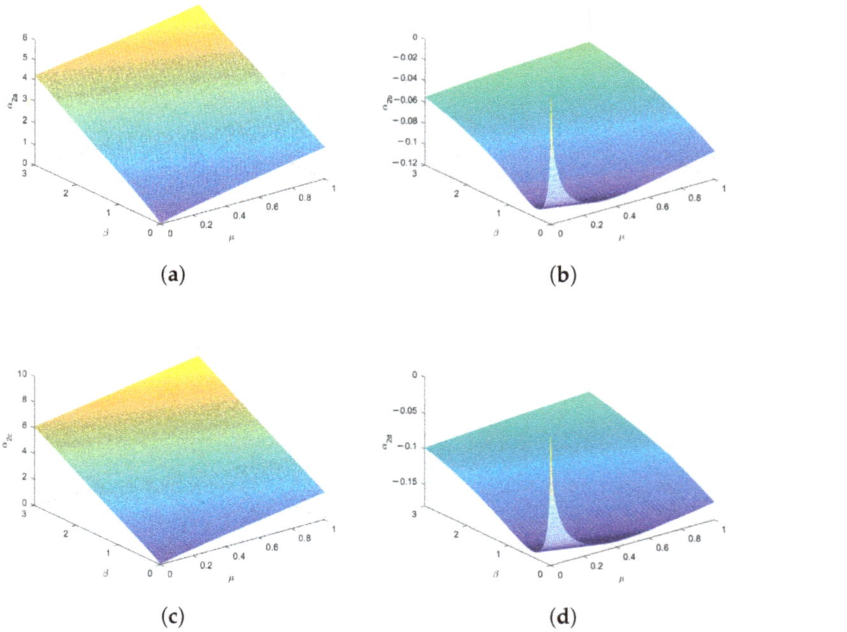

Figure 3. The relationship of (μ, β, α_2): (**a**) $(\mu, \beta, \alpha_{2a})$ space; (**b**) $(\mu, \beta, \alpha_{2b})$ space; (**c**) $(\mu, \beta, \alpha_{2c})$ space; (**d**) $(\mu, \beta, \alpha_{2d})$ space.

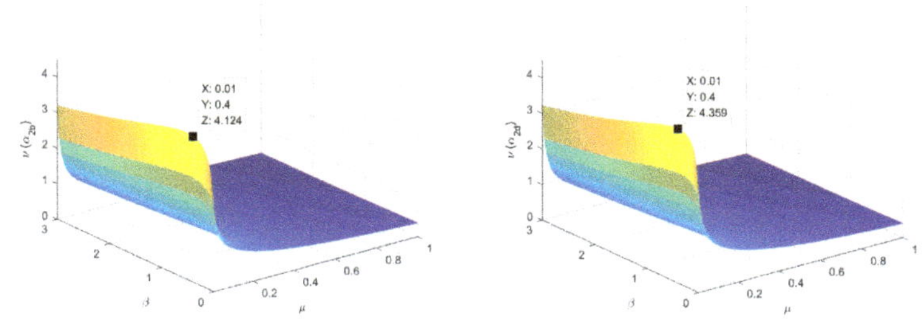

(**a**) (**b**)

Figure 4. The relationship of $(\mu, \beta, \nu(\alpha_2))$: (**a**) $(\mu, \beta, \nu(\alpha_{2b}))$ space; (**b**) $(\mu, \beta, \nu(\alpha_{2d}))$ space.

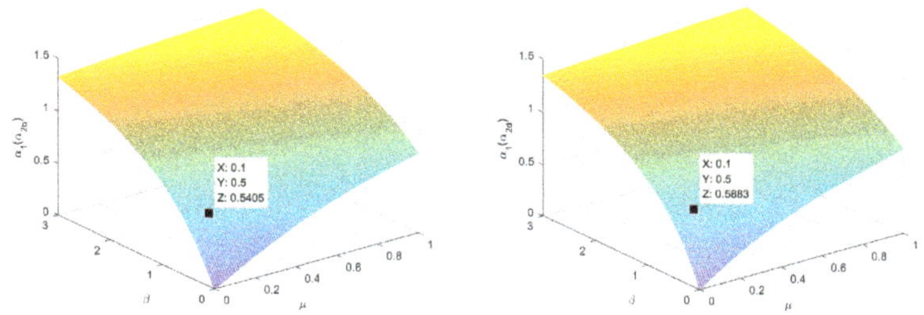

(**a**) (**b**)

Figure 5. The relationship of $(\mu, \beta, \alpha_1(\alpha_2))$: (**a**) $(\mu, \beta, \alpha_1(\alpha_{2b}))$ space; (**b**) $(\mu, \beta, \alpha_1(\alpha_{2d}))$ space.

According to the fixed-point theory, any damping ratio change will go through three fixed points. When the three fixed points are adjusted to the same height, the two resonance peaks can be also maintained to be equal as possible by changing the damping ratio ξ. In order to obtain the optimum damping ratio, it is necessary to know the horizontal coordinates of two resonance peaks, namely λ_1 and λ_2. It can be observed that when the two resonance peaks are almost at the same height, the vicinity of point Q is in the region where the slope of the amplitude-frequency curve is zero. According to the previous calculation results, the abscissa of point Q has been solved. The explicit expression can obtain the approximate optimum damping ratio based on the abscissa of point Q.

$$(1)\ \alpha_{2opt} = \alpha_{2b} \Rightarrow \begin{cases} \frac{\partial A^2}{\partial \lambda_Q^2} = 0 \\ \alpha_{1opt} = \frac{2\sqrt{(\mu+\beta)(\mu+\beta-\alpha_{2b})^2(1+\mu+\beta)}}{(1+\mu+\beta)^2} \\ \nu_{opt} = \sqrt{\frac{(1+\mu+\beta)(\mu+\beta-\alpha_{2b})-\sqrt{(\mu+\beta)(\mu+\beta-\alpha_{2b})^2(1+\mu+\beta)}}{\mu(1+\mu+\beta)^2}} \\ \alpha_{2b} = \frac{\mu+\beta+2(1+\mu+\beta)\left[\mu+\beta-\sqrt{(\mu+\beta)(1+\mu+\beta)}\right]}{3(1+\mu+\beta)+1} \\ \lambda_Q^2 = \frac{1+\alpha_{2b}}{1+\mu+\beta} \end{cases}$$

$$(2)\ \alpha_{2opt} = \alpha_{2d} \Rightarrow \begin{cases} \frac{\partial A^2}{\partial \lambda_Q^2} = 0 \\ \alpha_{1opt} = \frac{2\sqrt{(\mu+\beta)(\mu+\beta-\alpha_{2d})^2(1+\mu+\beta)}}{(1+\mu+\beta)^2} \\ v_{opt} = \sqrt{\frac{(1+\mu+\beta)(\mu+\beta-\alpha_{2d})-\sqrt{(\mu+\beta)(\mu+\beta-\alpha_{2d})^2(1+\mu+\beta)}}{\mu(1+\mu+\beta)^2}} \\ \alpha_{2d} = \frac{\mu+\beta+(1+\mu+\beta)\left[\mu+\beta-\sqrt{(\mu+\beta)(2+\mu+\beta)}\right]}{2+\mu+\beta} \\ \lambda_Q^2 = \frac{1+\alpha_{2d}}{1+\mu+\beta} \end{cases}$$

$$\begin{aligned} p_1 = (A_2^2)' &= 2\alpha_1^2(\mu+\beta)\left[(\mu+\beta)\lambda^2 - \alpha_2 - \mu v^2\right] \\ p_2 = (B_2^2)' &= 4\mu^2 v^2\left[3(\mu+\beta)^2\lambda^4 - 4(\mu+\beta)M_2\lambda^2 + M_2^2\right] \\ q_1 = (C_2^2)' &= 2\alpha_1^2\{2(\mu+\beta)^2\lambda^6 - 3(\mu+\beta)M_3\lambda^4 + \left[M_3^2 + 2(\mu+\beta)M_4\right]\lambda^2 - M_3M_4\} \\ q_2 = (D_2^2)' &= 4\mu^2 v^2\{5(\mu+\beta)^2\lambda^8 - 8(\mu+\beta)M_5\lambda^6 + 3\left[M_5^2 + 2(\mu+\beta)M_6\right]\lambda^4 \\ &\quad - 4M_5M_6\lambda^2 + M_6^2\} \end{aligned}$$

where

$$\begin{aligned} M_2 &= \alpha_1 + \alpha_2 + \mu v^2 \\ M_3 &= \alpha_2 + \mu + \beta + \mu(1+\mu+\beta)v^2 \\ M_4 &= \alpha_2 + \mu(1+\alpha_2)v^2 \\ M_5 &= \alpha_1 + \alpha_2 + (\mu+\beta)(1+\alpha_1) + \mu(1+\mu+\beta)v^2 \\ M_6 &= \alpha_1 + \alpha_2 + \alpha_1\alpha_2 + \mu(1+\alpha_2)v^2 \end{aligned}$$

Let $p = A_2^2 + \xi^2 B_2^2$ and $q = C_2^2 + \xi^2 D_2^2$

$$\frac{\partial A^2}{\partial \lambda_Q^2} = \left(\frac{p}{q}\right)' = \frac{p'q - pq'}{q^2} = 0 \Leftrightarrow \left(p_1 + \xi^2 p_2\right)' q - (q_1 + \xi^2 q_2)' p = 0 \Leftrightarrow solve\ \xi$$

In the previous analysis and calculation, we obtained the optimal-value expressions of some parameters related to μ and β. For the mass ratio μ related to the primary system and DVA, the final control results are ideal when μ is limited between 0.05 and 0.5. This is because the range of m_2 is not arbitrarily determined in the actual design of DVA, and it is usually necessary to consider the installation space, manufacturing cost, installation difficulty, and other factors. If m_2 is very small, the natural frequency will be too close to reduce the vibration control. If m_2 is too large, the practicability of the whole device will be greatly affected. Therefore, it is found in the literature that experts and scholars usually take the range of μ to optimize the design, so as to determine the optimal value.

We take $\alpha_{2opt} = \alpha_{2b}$ as an example to compare the numerical and analytical solutions for different mass ratios μ and different inerter-to-mass ratios β in order to confirm the accuracy of the solution procedure. According to the optimization results derived from the previous formulas, the basic optimal parameter values are provided in Table 1. The numerical solution of the harmonic excitation with excitation amplitude F=1000N is obtained by using the fourth-order Runge–Kutta method when the calculation time is 2000 s. After the transient response is ignored, the greatest value of the steady-state solution is chosen as the excitation response amplitude and normalized. The normalized amplitude–frequency curves of the numerical and analytical solutions to the system are shown in Figure 6. The circle represents the numerical solution and the solid line represents the analytical solution. Various colors signify the selection of certain parameters. It can be seen intuitively from the figures that two kinds of solutions are completely consistent under the same case, which proves the correctness of each parameter expression solved in this paper.

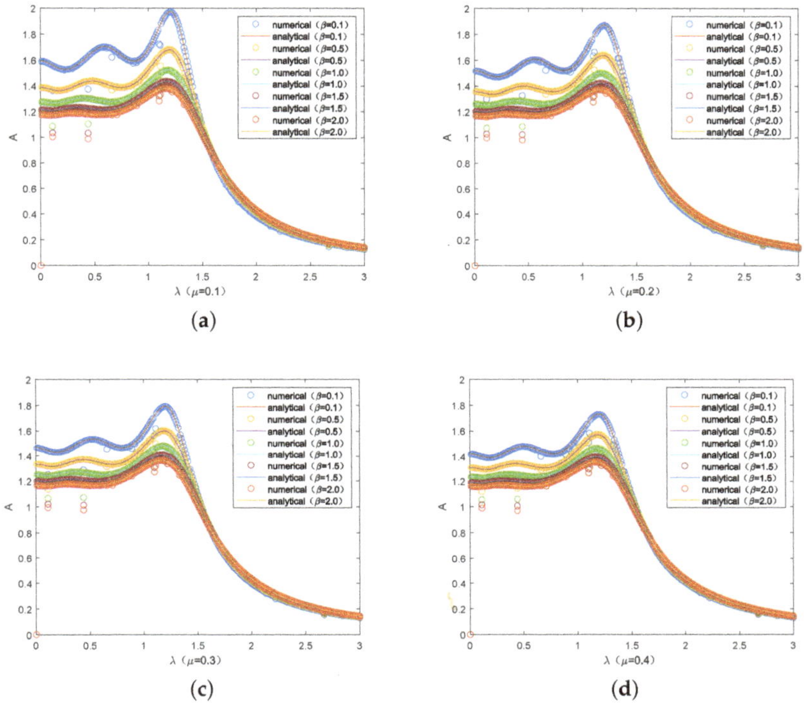

Figure 6. Comparison between the numerical solution and analytical solution in initial optimization ($\alpha_{2opt} = \alpha_{2b}$): (**a**) $\mu = 0.1$; (**b**) $\mu = 0.2$; (**c**) $\mu = 0.3$; (**d**) $\mu = 0.4$.

From the macroscopic perspective, the normalized amplitude amplification factor A of the primary system can be reduced by increasing the value of the inerter-to-mass ratio β under the same parameter μ. Meanwhile, the distance between the transverse coordinates corresponding to the peaks becomes larger. In a word, the larger the inerter-to-mass ratio is, the smaller the amplitude of the system is and the wider the frequency band is. By simply drawing the amplitude–frequency curves and obtaining the parameters, two different situations of parameter α_2 have different effects. It can be found that the distance between the vertical coordinates of the two formants in case $\alpha_{2opt} = \alpha_{2d}$ is closer than that in case $\alpha_{2opt} = \alpha_{2b}$. However, for the details, the fitting effect of the graph in $\alpha_{2opt} = \alpha_{2b}$ is better than $\alpha_{2opt} = \alpha_{2d}$. The main reason is that only when $\alpha_{2d} > -0.1150$, the ordinate of the initial position will gradually become lower than two resonance peaks, and the other results are not particularly ideal. Therefore, we consider the case of $\alpha_{2opt} = \alpha_{2b}$ in further optimization analysis. However, it is worth noting that there are some deviations in the solution process of this parameter. In the following part of the paper, we will introduce the PSO algorithm to further optimize the parameters, so as to make the two formants reach the horizontal height under certain parameter conditions.

Table 1. The specific parameters of the system with different inerter-to-mass ratios in initial optimization ($\alpha_{2opt} = \alpha_{2b}$).

Case 1: $\mu = 0.1$, $\alpha_{2opt} = \alpha_{2b}$	
$\beta = 0.1$	$\alpha_1 = 0.2094$, $\alpha_2 = -0.1078$, $\nu = 1.2320$, $\xi = 0.6389$
$\beta = 0.5$	$\alpha_1 = 0.5405$, $\alpha_2 = -0.1061$, $\nu = 1.3079$, $\xi = 1.3554$
$\beta = 1.0$	$\alpha_1 = 0.8209$, $\alpha_2 = -0.0909$, $\nu = 1.2516$, $\xi = 1.9951$
$\beta = 1.5$	$\alpha_1 = 1.0125$, $\alpha_2 = -0.0780$, $\nu = 1.1794$, $\xi = 2.5051$
$\beta = 2.0$	$\alpha_1 = 1.1511$, $\alpha_2 = -0.0679$, $\nu = 1.1124$, $\xi = 2.9397$
Case 2: $\mu = 0.2$, $\alpha_{2opt} = \alpha_{2b}$	
$\beta = 0.1$	$\alpha_1 = 0.3037$, $\alpha_2 = -0.1110$, $\nu = 0.9063$, $\xi = 0.6002$
$\beta = 0.5$	$\alpha_1 = 0.6063$, $\alpha_2 = -0.1031$, $\nu = 0.9200$, $\xi = 1.0597$
$\beta = 1.0$	$\alpha_1 = 0.8648$, $\alpha_2 = -0.0880$, $\nu = 0.8749$, $\xi = 1.4885$
$\beta = 1.5$	$\alpha_1 = 1.0437$, $\alpha_2 = -0.0757$, $\nu = 0.8241$, $\xi = 1.8364$
$\beta = 2.0$	$\alpha_1 = 1.1744$, $\alpha_2 = -0.0661$, $\nu = 0.7778$, $\xi = 2.1355$
Case 3: $\mu = 0.3$, $\alpha_{2opt} = \alpha_{2b}$	
$\beta = 0.1$	$\alpha_1 = 0.3899$, $\alpha_2 = -0.1106$, $\nu = 0.7523$, $\xi = 0.5969$
$\beta = 0.5$	$\alpha_1 = 0.6667$, $\alpha_2 = -0.1000$, $\nu = 0.7454$, $\xi = 0.9428$
$\beta = 1.0$	$\alpha_1 = 0.9057$, $\alpha_2 = -0.0853$, $\nu = 0.7059$, $\xi = 1.2763$
$\beta = 1.5$	$\alpha_1 = 1.0730$, $\alpha_2 = -0.0736$, $\nu = 0.6649$, $\xi = 1.5509$
$\beta = 2.0$	$\alpha_1 = 1.1964$, $\alpha_2 = -0.0645$, $\nu = 0.6281$, $\xi = 1.7889$
Case 4: $\mu = 0.4$, $\alpha_{2opt} = \alpha_{2b}$	
$\beta = 0.1$	$\alpha_1 = 0.4686$, $\alpha_2 = -0.1087$, $\nu = 0.6548$, $\xi = 0.6007$
$\beta = 0.5$	$\alpha_1 = 0.7222$, $\alpha_2 = -0.0969$, $\nu = 0.6395$, $\xi = 0.8799$
$\beta = 1.0$	$\alpha_1 = 0.9437$, $\alpha_2 = -0.0827$, $\nu = 0.6040$, $\xi = 1.1561$
$\beta = 1.5$	$\alpha_1 = 1.1006$, $\alpha_2 = -0.0716$, $\nu = 0.5691$, $\xi = 1.3865$
$\beta = 2.0$	$\alpha_1 = 1.2172$, $\alpha_2 = -0.0629$, $\nu = 0.5380$, $\xi = 1.5876$

3. Further Optimization Analysis of Particle Swarm Optimization Algorithm

This section studies the further parameter optimization problem of Maxwell-type DVA involving inerters and negative stiffness elements when the external excitation is harmonic excitation. In the previous part, we followed the H_∞ optimization criterion and obtained the approximate optimal solution of the model parameters using the fixed-point theory. Considering the practical engineering applications, the slight difference in parameter values may cause different effects. The numerical simulation using the Runge–Kutta method shows that the approximate optimal solution does not make the resonance peak at the same level, which indicates that the parameters of the model are worth further optimizing. It should be emphasized that the approximate optimal solution obtained by theoretical analysis plays a crucial part in introducing the PSO algorithm in this section, because only when a range is roughly determined can the process of algorithm iteration be infinitely close to the optimal value.

3.1. Optimizing the Single Variable

There are many parameters that can be adjusted in the model. We first check to see if adjusting the single variable can minimize the maximum amplitude of the primary system. Here, the amplitude of the primary system is selected as the objective function, and the PSO algorithm is employed to optimize it. The condition of the algorithm is that the dimension of the selected particle is 1; that is, the parameter ξ to be determined. The values of parameters other than ξ are the same as those in Table 1 according to the settings of μ and β. In order to obtain more accurate vibration absorption parameters, we set the following: (1) there are 40 particles in total; (2) the maximum number of iterations is 1000; (3) the learning factors c_1 and c_2 are both 2; (4) the maximum and minimum values of inertia weight are 0.6 and 0.4; (5) the random number sequence in the population is added; (6) the position and velocity of particles have a definite proportional connection.

The initial state of the algorithm is a group of random particles with two attributes, velocity and position. The particles update their velocity vector and position vector by continuously tracking the individual optimal value and global optimal value. Specifically, the particle will store the magnitude and direction of the preceding velocity in memory and self-recognize the current point with its own best point while completing group cognition with the best point in the population. In this way, each particle achieves collaboration and optimal solution information sharing between populations. When the maximum number of iterations is set, the particle swarm can seek the best position according to the termination condition of iterations and output the ideal parameter values. By analyzing the rule of the amplitude curves, the system will produce two wave peaks depending on the parameter values, and the two peaks will reach equal height when the parameters are optimal. When designing the PSO algorithm, the maximum values of the amplitude curve of the i-th iteration are obtained first, and then the damping ratio that minimizes the maximum amplitude in all iterations is the optimal damping ratio under the single variable optimization we are looking for.

As shown in Table 2, we obtained more comprehensive values than in Table 1 according to the PSO algorithm after optimizing the single parameter ξ, including the maximum amplitude under the optimal parameter values, the abscissas λ (λ_{peak1}, λ_{peak2}) corresponding to the two peaks and the difference between them. From this information, we can see the following: (1) Under the same mass ratio μ, the value of the optimal damping ratio is larger than the approximate damping ratio obtained in the previous section with the increase in the inerter-to-mass ratio β, and the amplitude becomes smaller. The λ_{peak1} corresponding to the left peak gradually moves to the left. The λ_{peak2} corresponding to the right peak gradually moves to the right. The larger difference means that the resonance frequency band is getting wider, and the resonance effect is becoming better and more stable. (2) Under the same coefficient β, the system amplitude decreases slowly with the increase in μ and the abscissas λ (λ_{peak1}, λ_{peak2}) become wider. This is consistent with the results of other scholars, who found that mass ratio can effectively suppress the amplitude of the system when studying vibration absorbers.

It can be clearly observed in Figures 6 and 7 that the amplitude of the system after optimization is significantly reduced, showing better stability. Moreover, the number of iterations largely determines the accuracy of the optimal value. The amplitude of the primary system finally tends to a straight line after 1000 iterations using PSO from Figure 8. At the initial iteration, a specific downward trend in the amplitude change can be seen from the enlarged color section. It should be noted here that the minimum number of iterations at which the amplitude flattens out is not the optimal number of iterations. Different iterations make the amplitude have different forms of decline. According to the final stationary state in the figure, the mass ratio can suppress the amplitude under the same inerter parameters. The range of parameter given during the iteration is critical, which determines whether the identified optimal value is reliable. We also calculate the mean square response of the primary system before and after optimizing the single parameter ξ. Taking $\mu = 0.1$ as an example, the optimized mean square response outperforms the value before optimization with the same parameter β. With the increase in β, the response before and after optimization is gradually reduced. The mean square response reflects the dispersion degree of individuals in the data set and can be used as a result to measure the degree of system distribution. For example, two data with the same mean may not have the same mean square response. If the overall mean square response value is low, it can be judged that its stability is also good.

Table 2. The specific parameters of the system in different cases of the inerter-to-mass ratio when optimizing the single variable ξ ($\alpha_{2opt} = \alpha_{2b}$).

Case 1:	$\mu = 0.1$							
β	ξ_{ori}	$\sigma^2_{ori}(\frac{\pi S_0}{\omega_1^3})$	ξ_{opt}	$\sigma^2_{opt}(\frac{\pi S_0}{\omega_1^3})$	A_{max}	λ_{peak1}	λ_{peak2}	$\lvert\lambda_{peak1} - \lambda_{peak2}\rvert$
0.1	0.6389	2.7821	0.7063	2.7370	1.8288	0.625	1.234	0.609
0.5	1.3554	2.2072	1.5275	2.1358	1.5391	0.517	1.243	0.726
1.0	1.9951	1.9117	2.2771	1.8269	1.3865	0.437	1.249	0.812
1.5	2.5051	1.7570	2.8845	1.6649	1.3046	0.383	1.253	0.870
2.0	2.9397	1.6612	3.4085	1.5641	1.2529	0.344	1.257	0.913
Case 2:	$\mu = 0.2$							
β	ξ_{ori}	$\sigma^2_{ori}(\frac{\pi S_0}{\omega_1^3})$	ξ_{opt}	$\sigma^2_{opt}(\frac{\pi S_0}{\omega_1^3})$	A_{max}	λ_{peak1}	λ_{peak2}	$\lvert\lambda_{peak1} - \lambda_{peak2}\rvert$
0.1	0.6002	2.5747	0.6679	2.5200	1.7248	0.591	1.237	0.646
0.5	1.0597	2.1280	1.1979	2.0531	1.4986	0.498	1.244	0.746
1.0	1.4885	1.8735	1.7022	1.7870	1.3664	0.425	1.250	0.825
1.5	1.8364	1.7344	2.1177	1.6411	1.2925	0.375	1.254	0.879
2.0	2.1355	1.6463	2.4791	1.5483	1.2447	0.337	1.258	0.921
Case 3:	$\mu = 0.3$							
β	ξ_{ori}	$\sigma^2_{ori}(\frac{\pi S_0}{\omega_1^3})$	ξ_{opt}	$\sigma^2_{opt}(\frac{\pi S_0}{\omega_1^3})$	A_{max}	λ_{peak1}	λ_{peak2}	$\lvert\lambda_{peak1} - \lambda_{peak2}\rvert$
0.1	0.5969	2.4220	0.6677	2.3602	1.6480	0.563	1.239	0.676
0.5	0.9428	2.0613	1.0687	1.9834	1.4642	0.481	1.245	0.764
1.0	1.2763	1.8396	1.4623	1.7515	1.3485	0.413	1.251	0.838
1.5	1.5509	1.7138	1.7910	1.6195	1.2814	0.366	1.255	0.889
2.0	1.7889	1.6324	2.0792	1.5336	1.2371	0.331	1.259	0.928
Case 4:	$\mu = 0.4$							
β	ξ_{ori}	$\sigma^2_{ori}(\frac{\pi S_0}{\omega_1^3})$	ξ_{opt}	$\sigma^2_{opt}(\frac{\pi S_0}{\omega_1^3})$	A_{max}	λ_{peak1}	λ_{peak2}	$\lvert\lambda_{peak1} - \lambda_{peak2}\rvert$
0.1	0.6007	2.3031	0.6746	2.2359	1.5878	0.539	1.241	0.702
0.5	0.8799	2.0043	0.9999	1.9237	1.4347	0.465	1.247	0.782
1.0	1.1561	1.8092	1.3269	1.7196	1.3324	0.403	1.252	0.849
1.5	1.3865	1.6948	1.6034	1.5995	1.2711	0.359	1.256	0.897
2.0	1.5876	1.6194	1.8474	1.5199	1.2300	0.325	1.260	0.935

In addition to optimizing the single variable ξ, the parameters ν, α_1, and α_2 can also be considered as the case of optimizing the single variable. The following Table 3 shows the system's optimal target, the abscissa λ (λ_{peak}, λ_{peak1}, λ_{peak2}) corresponding to the amplitude and the mean square response after optimizing the single variables ν, α_1, and α_2 respectively. From the perspective of system amplitude, the maximum amplitudes optimized by these three single variables are all higher than the optimization results of ξ under the same μ and β. The optimization of ξ can better minimize the maximum amplitude of the primary system under the single-parameter optimization. However, the mean square response of optimized ν is the best, and the difference between the abscissas corresponding to the two peaks is larger (as manifested in Appendix Table A1). It can be seen from Figure 9 that the amplitude curves of the analytical solution and numerical solution decrease at the initial position under the optimization of ν, which is why the mean square response is lower. Through the detailed analysis of the four single parameters in this chapter, the conclusions we drqaw can be multifaceted. For the purpose of suppressing the amplitude of the primary system, the optimization parameter ξ is a better choice. If we want to make the mean square response value of the system lower, we can choose the optimization parameter ν. Therefore, it is concluded that the influence of different parameters on the system must exist. The algorithm is further optimized based on the fixed-point theory to make the discussion of the vibration absorber more accurate.

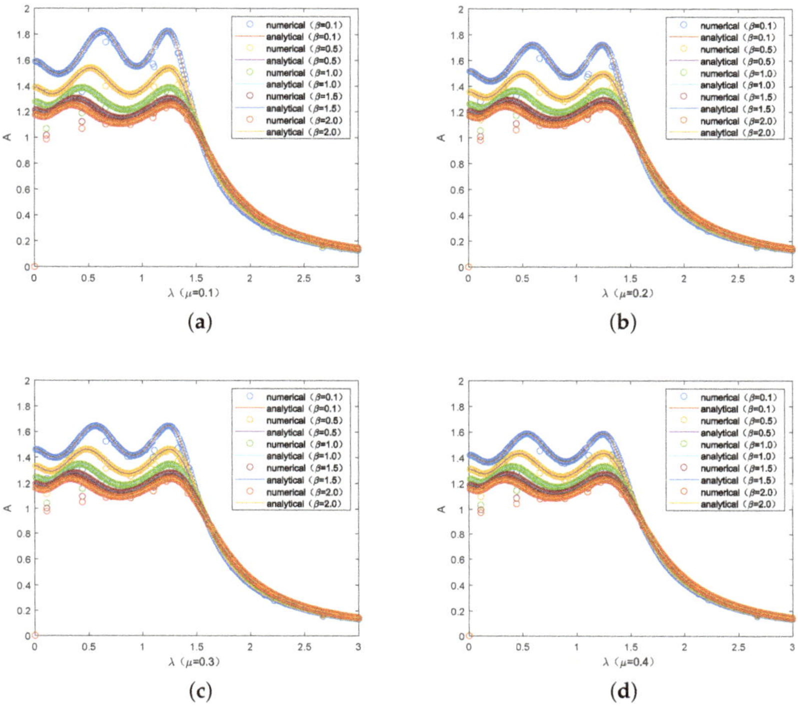

Figure 7. Comparison between the numerical solution and analytical solution when optimizing the single variable ξ ($\alpha_{2opt} = \alpha_{2b}$): (**a**) $\mu = 0.1$; (**b**) $\mu = 0.2$; (**c**) $\mu = 0.3$; (**d**) $\mu = 0.4$.

Table 3. The specific parameters of the system in different inerter-to-mass ratios when optimizing the other variables ($\alpha_{2opt} = \alpha_{2b}$, $\mu = 0.1$).

β	0.1	0.5	1.0	1.5	2.0
α_{1opt}	0.2428	0.6467	1.0072	1.2658	1.4591
A_{max}	1.9098	1.6181	1.4601	1.3744	1.3202
$\sigma^2_{opt}(\pi S_0/\omega_1^3)$	2.7754	2.1711	1.8560	1.6893	1.5853
λ_{peak}	1.142	1.099	1.061	1.034	1.013
β	**0.1**	**0.5**	**1.0**	**1.5**	**2.0**
α_{2opt}	−0.0981	−0.0733	−0.0302	0.0084	0.0424
A_{max}	1.8970	1.6372	1.4954	1.4175	1.3677
$\sigma^2_{opt}(\pi S_0/\omega_1^3)$	2.8039	2.2305	1.9323	1.7746	1.6764
λ_{peak1}	0.617	0.517	0.447	0.402	0.370
λ_{peak2}	1.209	1.195	1.182	1.174	1.168
$\lvert\lambda_{peak1} - \lambda_{peak2}\rvert$	0.592	0.678	0.735	0.772	0.798
β	**0.1**	**0.5**	**1.0**	**1.5**	**2.0**
ν_{opt}	1.2617	1.3753	1.3464	1.2903	1.2333
A_{max}	1.8373	1.5504	1.3971	1.3138	1.2607
$\sigma^2_{opt}(\pi S_0/\omega_1^3)$	2.7349	2.1274	1.8151	1.6516	1.5503
λ_{peak1}	0.588	0.459	0.368	0.309	0.268
λ_{peak2}	1.230	1.240	1.247	1.253	1.258
$\lvert\lambda_{peak1} - \lambda_{peak2}\rvert$	0.642	0.781	0.879	0.944	0.990

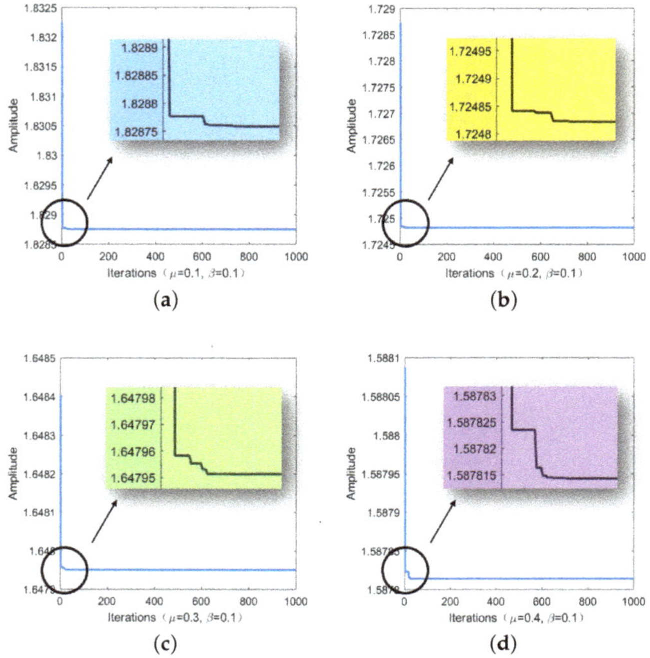

Figure 8. Iterations when optimizing the single variable ξ ($\alpha_{2opt} = \alpha_{2b}$, $\beta = 0.1$): (**a**) $\mu = 0.1$; (**b**) $\mu = 0.2$; (**c**) $\mu = 0.3$; (**d**) $\mu = 0.4$.

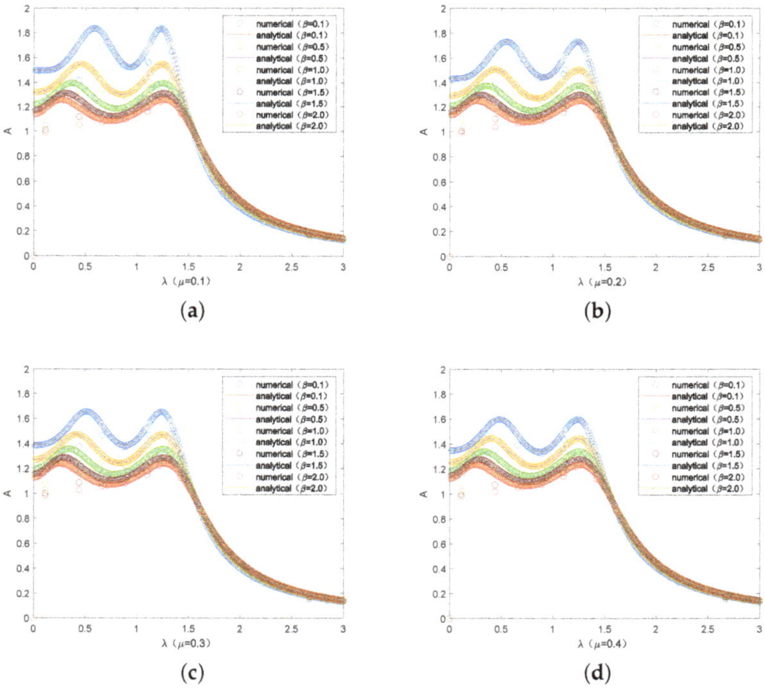

Figure 9. Comparison between the numerical solution and analytical solution when optimizing the single variable ν ($\alpha_{2opt} = \alpha_{2b}$): (**a**) $\mu = 0.1$; (**b**) $\mu = 0.2$; (**c**) $\mu = 0.3$; (**d**) $\mu = 0.4$.

3.2. Optimizing Four Variables: α_1, α_2, ν, and ξ

This section will simultaneously optimize four variables to observe the variation in the system amplitude curve and the degree of mean square response. The difficulty lies in the need to consider the value range of four parameter values at the same time. The optimized parameter value cannot be located at the endpoint value of the range, nor can the parameter value only meet part of the value range. The setting of the value range about the four parameter values is based on the range considered in the previous optimization of the single variable, which ensures that the optimal value obtained after the comprehensive optimization is comparable to the optimal value of the optimized single variable and further judges the iterative optimization efficiency of the PSO algorithm. The values of α_1 and α_2 (as shown in Table 4) are higher than those before optimization in Table 1. The values of ν and ξ are between the approximate optimal value before optimization and the optimal value after single optimization.

Table 4. The specific parameters of the system in different cases of inerter-to-mass ratio when optimizing four variables, α_1, α_2, ν, and ξ ($\alpha_{2opt} = \alpha_{2b}$).

Case 1:	$\mu = 0.1$							
β	α_{1opt}	α_{2opt}	ν_{opt}	ξ_{opt}	A_{max}	$A_{max(all-\xi)}$	$A_{max(all-\nu)}$	$\sigma^2_{opt}(\frac{\pi S_0}{\omega_1^3})$
0.1	0.2346	−0.1045	1.2346	0.6612	1.8151	−0.0137	−0.0222	2.7579
0.5	0.5898	−0.1010	1.3242	1.4165	1.5269	−0.0122	−0.0235	2.1360
1.0	0.9062	−0.0792	1.2712	2.0833	1.3821	−0.0044	−0.0150	1.8276
1.5	1.1576	−0.0664	1.2005	2.6207	1.2930	−0.0116	−0.0208	1.6546
2.0	1.3392	−0.0576	1.1368	3.0753	1.2375	−0.0154	−0.0232	1.5467
Case 2:	$\mu = 0.2$							
β	α_{1opt}	α_{2opt}	ν_{opt}	ξ_{opt}	A_{max}	$A_{max(all-\xi)}$	$A_{max(all-\nu)}$	$\sigma^2_{opt}(\frac{\pi S_0}{\omega_1^3})$
0.1	0.3249	−0.1047	0.9086	0.6224	1.7311	0.0063	−0.0037	2.5447
0.5	0.6497	−0.0968	0.9300	1.1182	1.4921	−0.0065	−0.0178	2.0559
1.0	0.9437	−0.0825	0.8868	1.5852	1.3520	−0.0144	−0.0248	1.7799
1.5	1.1789	−0.0666	0.8424	1.9237	1.2782	−0.0143	−0.0232	1.6288
2.0	1.3677	−0.0560	0.7942	2.2385	1.2290	−0.0157	−0.0233	1.5306
Case 3:	$\mu = 0.3$							
β	α_{1opt}	α_{2opt}	ν_{opt}	ξ_{opt}	A_{max}	$A_{max(all-\xi)}$	$A_{max(all-\nu)}$	$\sigma^2_{opt}(\frac{\pi S_0}{\omega_1^3})$
0.1	0.4079	−0.1030	0.7544	0.6267	1.6603	0.0123	0.0016	2.3830
0.5	0.7113	−0.0950	0.7547	1.0015	1.4545	−0.0097	−0.0210	1.9817
1.0	1.0262	−0.0754	0.7199	1.3287	1.3365	−0.0120	−0.0221	1.7424
1.5	1.2059	−0.0648	0.6802	1.6278	1.2671	−0.0143	−0.0229	1.6073
2.0	1.4099	−0.0507	0.6371	1.8823	1.2249	−0.0122	−0.0196	1.5177
Case 4:	$\mu = 0.4$							
β	α_{1opt}	α_{2opt}	ν_{opt}	ξ_{opt}	A_{max}	$A_{max(all-\xi)}$	$A_{max(all-\nu)}$	$\sigma^2_{opt}(\frac{\pi S_0}{\omega_1^3})$
0.1	0.4877	−0.1009	0.6595	0.6312	1.5985	0.0107	−0.0005	2.2532
0.5	0.7599	−0.0912	0.6441	0.9496	1.4289	−0.0058	−0.0169	1.9254
1.0	1.0724	−0.0694	0.6149	1.2030	1.3251	−0.0073	−0.0171	1.7141
1.5	1.2400	−0.0613	0.5801	1.4608	1.2584	−0.0127	−0.0211	1.5889
2.0	1.4140	−0.0528	0.5505	1.6637	1.2143	−0.0157	−0.0228	1.5020

From the perspective of amplitude, the amplitude amplification factor obtained by optimizing four variables at the same time is better than that obtained by optimizing single variables ν and ξ except for a few cases. From the perspective of the mean square response, it is better than optimizing the single variable ξ but inferior to the single variable ν. This conclusion holds in most cases and cannot be applied to all cases of μ and β. As can be seen from Figure 10 of the analytical and numerical solutions, the amplitude–frequency curves of the four variables optimized at the same time have a lower amplitude than ξ at the starting position, just like the single variable ν. At the trough between the two peaks, its steepness is less than that of the optimized single variable ν or ξ, and the stationarity looks smoother. In sum, whether optimizing a single variable or four variables, there are advantages and disadvantages. If four variables are selected to be optimized at the same time, the value range of each variable needs to be determined by optimizing the single variable, which increases the time cost of numerical simulation. In practical engineering applications, we need to combine the actual conditions and technical methods to select the appropriate optimization method. It is advisable to select a single variable or optimize several variables.

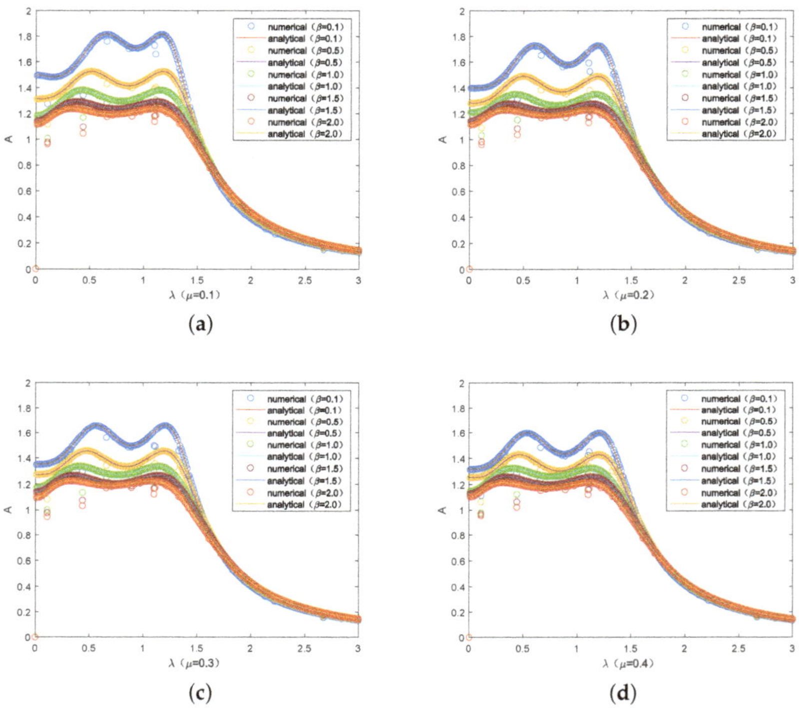

Figure 10. Comparison between numerical solution and analytical solution when optimizing four variables, α_1, α_2, ν, and ξ, at the same time: (**a**) $\mu = 0.1$; (**b**) $\mu = 0.2$; (**c**) $\mu = 0.3$; (**d**) $\mu = 0.4$.

3.3. Validity of Parameter Selection

Figure 11 shows the effectiveness of parameters after optimizing variable ξ according to the changes in different parameters in the system. When the value of μ and β are respectively increased, the corresponding amplitude curves not only show low resonance response peaks but also have a large impact on the vibration reduction bandwidth (as displayed in Figure 11a,b. On the premise of taking the optimal value as a reference, the numerical simulation is carried out by selecting its adjacent values to obtain the Figure 11c–f). The most obvious thing is that the orange line represents the curve at the optimal value and is consistent with the results obtained. Other curves have the following properties: (1) the left peak and the right peak are not at the same level; (2) the influence of the parameter value on the vibration reduction bandwidth exists; (3) different parameters affect the position of the initial point of the curve, which may be smaller or infinite; (4) the system will be over-damped, thus affecting the robustness under excitation.

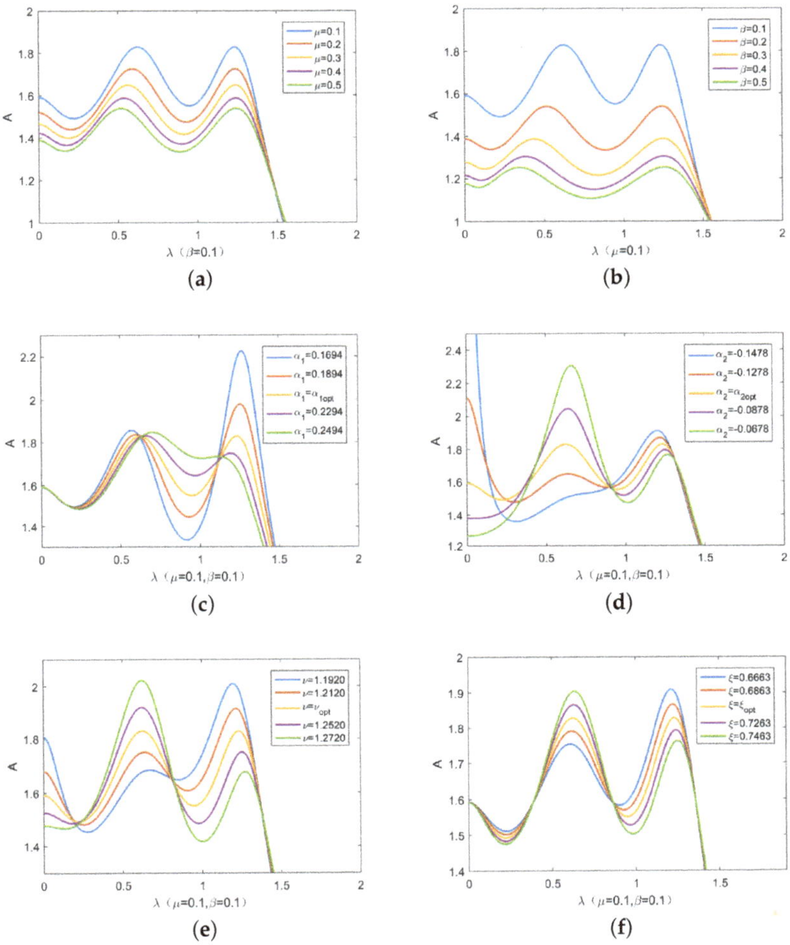

Figure 11. The optimal parameters verification when optimizing the single variable ξ: (**a**) change μ; (**b**) change β; (**c**) change α_1; (**d**) change α_2; (**e**) change ν; (**f**) change ξ.

4. The Mean Square Responses of the Primary System for Different DVAs

In nature and engineering, there is a class of vibration sources that cannot be described in a certain time and space, such as earthquakes, turbulence, noise, etc., which are called random vibration sources. Usually, the random vibration in structural dynamics is analyzed for stationary random processes. The difference between it and non-stationary random processes is whether the statistics such as mean and variance change with time. Due to the limitation of some necessary conditions, it is almost impossible for us to study the influence of the whole random process on the system, so we adopt the form of partial random vibration samples in the analysis process. This section explores the DVA under random excitation in more detail and uses comparisons to show how effective the design is. We determine the power spectral density functions $S(\omega)$ attached to various DVAs by considering the primary system under random excitation. The subscripts D, R, A, W, AN, WN, and M stand for the Voigt-type DVA, Ren model, Asami model, Wang model, Asami model with negative stiffness, Wang model with negative stiffness, and the DVA in this study. These models can be found in Figure 12. Based on the equations of each model, the mean square responses of the primary system under different DVAs can be calculated as follows.

$$
\begin{aligned}
\sigma_D^2 &= \int_{-\infty}^{+\infty} S_D(\omega)\mathrm{d}\omega = S_0 \int_{-\infty}^{+\infty} \|H_{Dx_1}(j\omega)\|^2 \,\mathrm{d}\omega = \frac{\pi S_0 Y_D}{2\omega_1^3 \mu \xi \nu} \\
\sigma_R^2 &= \int_{-\infty}^{+\infty} S_R(\omega)\mathrm{d}\omega = S_0 \int_{-\infty}^{+\infty} \|H_{Rx_1}(j\omega)\|^2 \,\mathrm{d}\omega = \frac{\pi S_0 Y_R}{2\omega_1^3 \mu \xi \nu^5} \\
\sigma_A^2 &= \int_{-\infty}^{+\infty} S_A(\omega)\mathrm{d}\omega = S_0 \int_{-\infty}^{+\infty} \|H_{Ax_1}(j\omega)\|^2 \,\mathrm{d}\omega = \frac{\pi S_0 Y_A}{2\omega_1^3 \mu \xi \alpha^2 \nu^3} \\
\sigma_W^2 &= \int_{-\infty}^{+\infty} S_W(\omega)\mathrm{d}\omega = S_0 \int_{-\infty}^{+\infty} \|H_{Wx_1}(j\omega)\|^2 \,\mathrm{d}\omega = \frac{\pi S_0 Y_W}{2\omega_1^3 \mu \xi \alpha^2 \nu^7} \\
\sigma_{AN}^2 &= \int_{-\infty}^{+\infty} S_{AN}(\omega)\mathrm{d}\omega = S_0 \int_{-\infty}^{+\infty} \|H_{ANx_1}(j\omega)\|^2 \,\mathrm{d}\omega \\
&= \frac{\pi S_0 Y_{AN}}{2\omega_1^3 \mu \xi \alpha_1^2 \nu^3 (1-\alpha_2\nu^2)^2 (1+\alpha_2+\mu\alpha_2\nu^2)} \\
\sigma_{WN}^2 &= \int_{-\infty}^{+\infty} S_{WN}(\omega)\mathrm{d}\omega = S_0 \int_{-\infty}^{+\infty} \|H_{WNx_1}(j\omega)\|^2 \,\mathrm{d}\omega \\
&= \frac{\pi S_0 Y_{WN}}{2\omega_1^3 \mu \xi \alpha_1^2 \nu^7 (1+\alpha_2+\mu\alpha_2\nu^2)} \\
\sigma_M^2 &= \int_{-\infty}^{+\infty} S_M(\omega)\mathrm{d}\omega = S_0 \int_{-\infty}^{+\infty} \|H_{Mx_1}(j\omega)\|^2 \,\mathrm{d}\omega \\
&= \frac{\pi S_0 Y_M}{2\omega_1^3 \mu \xi \alpha_1^2 \nu (\mu+\beta-\alpha_2)^2 [\alpha_2 + (1+\alpha_2)\mu\nu^2]}
\end{aligned}
$$

where

$$
\begin{aligned}
Y_D =& 1 + \left[4\xi^2(1+\mu) - \mu - 2\right]\nu^2 + (1+\mu)^2\nu^4 \\
Y_R =& 1 + \left(4\xi^2 + \mu - 2\right)\nu^2 + \nu^4 \\
Y_A =& 4\xi^2\{1 + (1+\alpha)\left[-2 + (1+\alpha)(1+\mu)\nu^2\right]\nu^2\} \\
&+ \alpha^2\nu^2\left[1 - (2+\mu)\nu^2 + (1+\mu)^2\nu^4\right] \\
Y_W =& 4\xi^2\{1 - 2(1+\alpha-\mu)\nu^2 + \left[(1+\alpha)^2 - (1+2\alpha)\mu + \mu^2\right]\nu^4\} \\
&+ \alpha^2\nu^2\left[1 + (\mu-2)\nu^2 + \nu^4\right] \\
Y_{AN} =& 4\xi^2\left(1+\alpha_2+\alpha_2\mu\nu^2\right)\{1 - 2(1+\alpha_1+\alpha_2)\nu^2 + \left[(1+\alpha_1+\alpha_2)^2 + \mu(1+\alpha_1)^2\right]\nu^4\} \\
&+ \alpha_1^2\nu^2\{1+\alpha_2 - \left[2(1+\alpha_2)^2 + \mu\right]\nu^2 + \left[(1+\alpha_2)^3 + 2(1+\alpha_2)\mu + \mu^2\right]\nu^4\} \\
Y_{WN} =& 4\xi^2\left(1+\alpha_2+\alpha_2\mu\nu^2\right)\{1 - 2(1+\alpha_1+\alpha_2-\mu)\nu^2 + [(1+\alpha_1+\alpha_2)^2 \\
&- (1+2\alpha_1+2\alpha_2)\mu + \mu^2]\nu^4\} + \alpha_1^2\nu^2\{1+\alpha_2 + [-2(1+\alpha_2)^2 \\
&+ \mu(1+2\alpha_2)]\nu^2 + \left[(1+\alpha_2)^3 - 2\alpha_2(1+\alpha_2)\mu + \alpha_2\mu^2\right]\nu^4\} \\
Y_M =& \alpha_1^2\left(\mu\nu^2+\alpha_2\right)^2\left[\alpha_2 + (\mu+\beta)^2 + \mu\nu^2(1+\mu+\beta)^2\right] \\
&+ \left[\alpha_2 + (1+\alpha_2)\mu\nu^2\right]\{4\xi^2\mu^2\nu^2(\mu+\beta)\left(\mu+\beta+\alpha_2^2\right) \\
&+ (1+\alpha_2)(\mu+\beta)\left[\alpha_1^2(\mu+\beta) - 8\xi^2\mu^2\nu^2\left(\mu\nu^2+\alpha_1+\alpha_2\right)\right] \\
&- 2(1+\mu+\beta)\left[\alpha_1^2(\mu+\beta)\left(\mu\nu^2+\alpha_2\right) - 2\xi^2\mu^2\nu^2\left(\mu\nu^2+\alpha_1+\alpha_2\right)^2\right]\}
\end{aligned}
$$

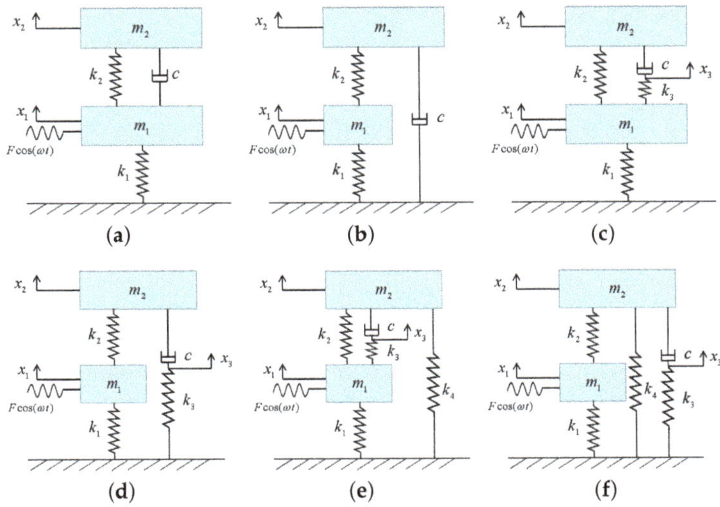

Figure 12. The DVA models: (**a**) Den; (**b**) Ren; (**c**) Asami; (**d**) Wang; (**e**) Asami with negative stiffness; (**f**) Wang with negative stiffness.

According to the optimal parameters in the literature [1,5,6,17,33,34], the mean square responses of the primary systems when $\mu = 0.1$ can be obtained as

$$\sigma_D^2 = \frac{6.401\pi S_0}{\omega_1^3}, \sigma_R^2 = \frac{5.780\pi S_0}{\omega_1^3}, \sigma_A^2 = \frac{6.039\pi S_0}{\omega_1^3}$$

$$\sigma_W^2 = \frac{7.065\pi S_0}{\omega_1^3}, \sigma_{AN}^2 = \frac{3.095\pi S_0}{\omega_1^3}, \sigma_{WN}^2 = \frac{3.090\pi S_0}{\omega_1^3}$$

In the previous section, we calculated the mean square responses by optimizing the single variable and four variables. It was found that the three cases studied in this paper are better than the above comparison models. This demonstrates that the model achieves better results than other DVAs under random excitation, and the inerter is crucial to the model. In addition, the model still outperforms the other DVAs when different mass ratios are selected. When random excitation is selected, 5000 normalized random numbers with zero mean value and unit variance are created as a 50 s random excitation (as shown in Figure 13). Firstly, we investigate three cases based on particle swarm optimization (ξ, ν, all) in this paper to select one for comparison with other models. As in Figure 14, three cases have roughly the same trend in the curve direction, and each section does not have the rule of periodic vibration. By locating the coordinates of the three curve peaks, the maximum peak appears the most times when the single variable ξ is optimized, and optimizing the single variable ν appears the fewest times. In the preliminary conclusion obtained in the previous section, the amplitude amplification factor obtained by optimizing the four variables simultaneously is better than that obtained by optimizing the single variables ν and ξ in most cases. From the perspective of mean square response, it is superior to the optimization of single variable ξ but inferior to the single variable ν. Therefore, the optimization of the single variable ξ is weaker than the other two cases according to the judgment. If it is selected to compare with the other models, it indicates that the three cases of optimization about this model are applicable.

It can be clearly observed from Figure 15a that the influence of the vibration absorber on the primary system is very great. The displacement can be considerably decreased with its help. In the meantime, raising the inerter coefficient can lessen the primary system's response for the model as shown in Figure 15b. According to the calculation of the model parameters in the existing literature, the fourth-order Runge–Kutta method is used to determine the amplitude responses under different DVAs conditions. These time history diagrams can be seen in Figure 16. Because the displacement variance of the primary system is frequently related to the vibration energy, the variances and decreasing ratios of the displacements for different systems are compiled in Table 5. Under random excitation, the DVA discussed in this work performs with better control performance than other DVAs. These results demonstrate that the proposed DVA can lower the mean square response of the system as well as the response peak.

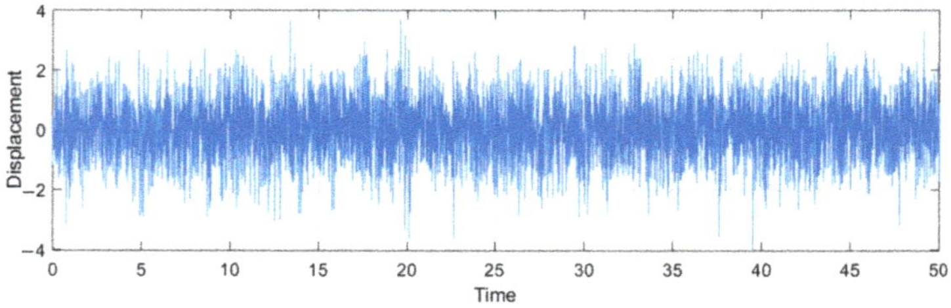

Figure 13. The time history of the random excitation.

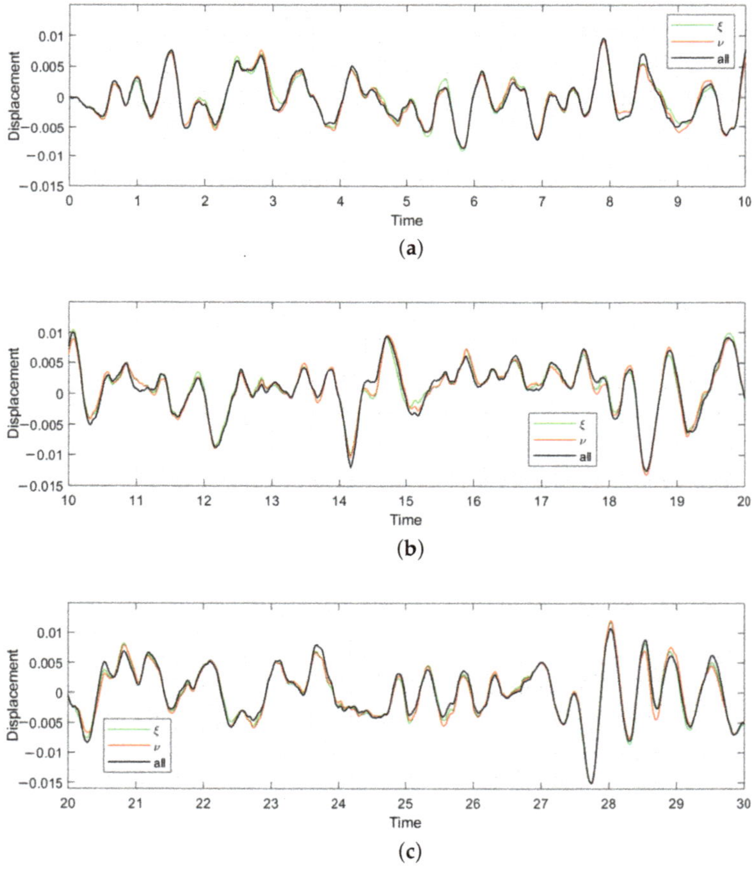

Figure 14. The time history of three cases based on particle swarm optimization (ξ, ν, all): (**a**) $t \subset [0, 10]$; (**b**) $t \subset [10, 20]$; (**c**) $t \subset [20, 30]$.

Table 5. The variances and decreasing ratios of the displacements in the primary system.

Models	Variances	Decrease Ratios (%)
Without DVA	2.57202×10^{-4}	/
DVA by Den Hartog	3.73465×10^{-5}	85.48
DVA by Ren	3.36063×10^{-5}	86.93
DVA by Asami	3.37462×10^{-5}	86.88
DVA by Wang	4.12604×10^{-5}	83.96
DVA by Asami with negative stiffness	1.83878×10^{-5}	92.85
DVA by Wang with negative stiffness	1.86308×10^{-5}	92.76
The presented model ($\mu = 0.1$, $\beta = 0.1$)	1.60176×10^{-5}	93.77
The presented model ($\mu = 0.1$, $\beta = 0.5$)	1.26826×10^{-5}	95.07
The presented model ($\mu = 0.1$, $\beta = 1.0$)	1.10374×10^{-5}	95.71
The presented model ($\mu = 0.1$, $\beta = 1.5$)	9.66774×10^{-6}	96.24
The presented model ($\mu = 0.1$, $\beta = 2.0$)	9.16522×10^{-6}	96.44

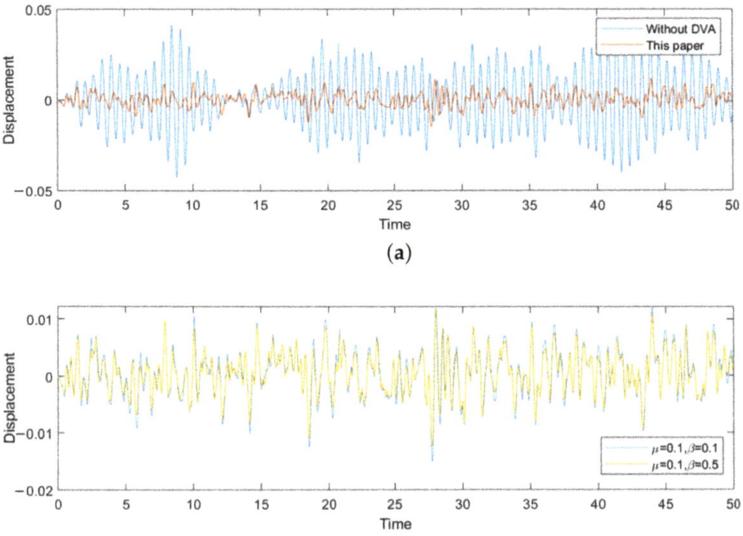

(a)

(b)

Figure 15. The time history of the primary system with models when $\mu = 0.1$: (**a**) comparison of this paper and without DVA; (**b**) comparison between different inerter-to-mass ratios ($\beta = 0.1$ and $\beta = 0.5$).

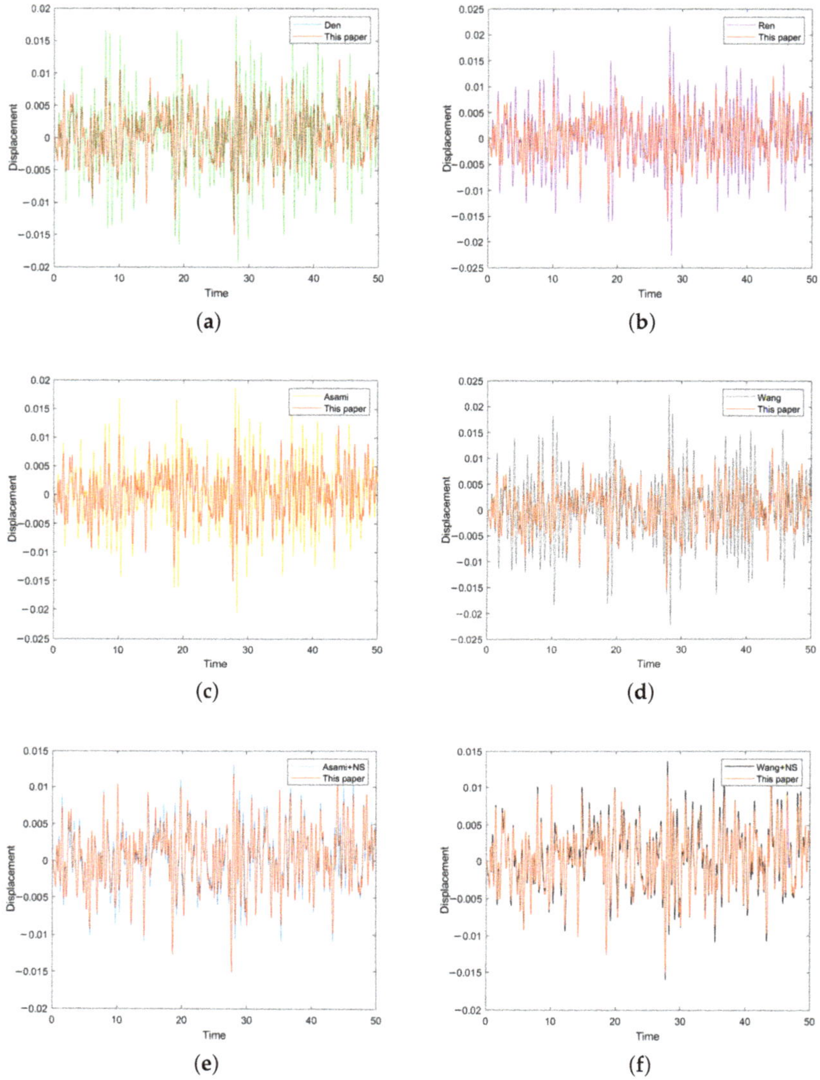

Figure 16. The time history of the primary system with models when $\mu = 0.1$: (**a**) Den; (**b**) Ren; (**c**) Asami; (**d**) Wang; (**e**) Asami with negative stiffness; (**f**) Wang with negative stiffness.

5. Conclusions and Prospects

Vibration phenomena can be found everywhere around us. Vehicles on the ground, aircraft in the air, and ships in the ocean are constantly generating vibration. Many academics concentrate on vibration reduction, vibration isolation, vibration absorption, and other control measures to design and optimize the structure of the vibration source or vibration transmission process because some vibrations may cause wear and consumption of objects. The introduction of DVAs provides an effective path to suppress the vibration of the primary system. The present paper discusses the viscoelastic Maxwell-type DVA model with an inerter and negative stiffness spring under the combination of traditional theory and the intelligent algorithm, which realizes the effect of equal resonance peaks and effectively reduces the amplitude response of the primary system.

On the basis of the H_∞ optimization criterion, the approximate optimal values of frequency ratio, stiffness ratio, and damping ratio are obtained by the fixed-point theory. Using the fourth-order Runge–Kutta method to simulate the analytical solution and the numerical solution, it is found that two peaks of the normalized amplitude–frequency curves are not equal and may be further optimized. Since there are many adjustable parameters in the model, we use the PSO algorithm to observe whether the maximum amplitude of the primary system can be minimized by optimizing the single variable and four variables. After continuously tracking and iterating the individual and global optimal values, the parameters of the final output make the optimized curves achieve equal peaks. For the three cases in which the algorithm is used for optimization in this paper, we obtained our conclusions. From the perspective of amplitude, the amplitude amplification factor gained by optimizing four variable was better than that obtained by optimizing single variables, except for a few cases. From the perspective of the mean square response, it falls between the two cases of optimizing the single variable. In addition, the benefit of all three cases is that the resonance frequency band is widened and the amplitude is suppressed. The analysis of the amplitude–frequency curves, the mean square responses, the variances, and the decreasing ratios of the displacements shows that the presented model is better than other typical DVAs under the optimization of the algorithm. The introduction of the algorithm can not only improve the efficiency of calculating the optimal parameters but also save the calculation time and ensure correctness. The integration of theoretical analysis and intelligent algorithms provides a solid reference for future research of DVAs in parameter optimization and structural design.

Author Contributions: Conceptualization, J.L.; Formal analysis, Y.C.; Funding acquisition, J.L.; Investigation, Y.C.; Methodology, J.L. and Y.C.; Project administration, J.L.; Supervision, J.L.; Validation, S.Z. and Y.C.; Visualization, Y.C. and H.Z.; Writing—original draft, Y.C.; Writing—review and editing, S.Z. and Y.C. All authors contributed equally to this research. All authors have read and agreed to the published version of the manuscript.

Funding: This research is supported by the National Natural Science Foundation of China (Grant No.12272011) and also supported by the National Key R&D Program of China (Grant No. 2022YFB3806000).

Institutional Review Board Statement: Not applicable.

Informed Consent Statement: Not applicable.

Data Availability Statement: The data presented in this study are available on request from the corresponding author.

Acknowledgments: The authors would like to thank all the peer reviewers and editors for their valuable contribution to this work.

Conflicts of Interest: The authors declare no conflict of interest.

Appendix A

Table A1. The specific parameters of the system in different cases of inerter-to-mass ratio when optimizing the single variable ν ($\alpha_{2opt} = \alpha_{2b}$).

Case 1: $\mu = 0.1$								
β	ν_{ori}	$\sigma^2_{ori}(\frac{\pi S_0}{\omega_1^3})$	ν_{opt}	$\sigma^2_{opt}(\frac{\pi S_0}{\omega_1^3})$	A_{max}	λ_{peak1}	λ_{peak2}	$\lvert\lambda_{peak1} - \lambda_{peak2}\rvert$
0.1	1.2320	2.7821	1.2617	2.7349	1.8373	0.588	1.230	0.642
0.5	1.3079	2.2072	1.3753	2.1274	1.5504	0.459	1.240	0.781
1.0	1.2516	1.9117	1.3464	1.8151	1.3971	0.368	1.247	0.879
1.5	1.1794	1.7570	1.2903	1.6516	1.3138	0.309	1.253	0.944
2.0	1.1124	1.6612	1.2333	1.5503	1.2607	0.268	1.258	0.990

Table A1. *Cont.*

β	ν_{ori}	$\sigma^2_{ori}(\frac{\pi S_0}{\omega_1^3})$	ν_{opt}	$\sigma^2_{opt}(\frac{\pi S_0}{\omega_1^3})$	A_{max}	λ_{peak1}	λ_{peak2}	$\lvert\lambda_{peak1}-\lambda_{peak2}\rvert$
Case 2: $\mu = 0.2$								
0.1	0.9063	2.5747	0.9354	2.5158	1.7348	0.547	1.234	0.687
0.5	0.9200	2.1280	0.9724	2.0436	1.5099	0.436	1.242	0.806
1.0	0.8749	1.8735	0.9446	1.7748	1.3768	0.354	1.249	0.895
1.5	0.8241	1.7344	0.9041	1.6278	1.3014	0.300	1.254	0.954
2.0	0.7778	1.6463	0.8644	1.5344	1.2523	0.261	1.259	0.998
Case 3: $\mu = 0.3$								
β	ν_{ori}	$\sigma^2_{ori}(\frac{\pi S_0}{\omega_1^3})$	ν_{opt}	$\sigma^2_{opt}(\frac{\pi S_0}{\omega_1^3})$	A_{max}	λ_{peak1}	λ_{peak2}	$\lvert\lambda_{peak1}-\lambda_{peak2}\rvert$
0.1	0.7523	2.4220	0.7818	2.3543	1.6587	0.513	1.236	0.723
0.5	0.7454	2.0613	0.7917	1.9732	1.4755	0.416	1.243	0.827
1.0	0.7059	1.8396	0.7649	1.7390	1.3586	0.341	1.250	0.909
1.5	0.6649	1.7138	0.7316	1.6059	1.2900	0.291	1.255	0.964
2.0	0.6281	1.6324	0.6996	1.5196	1.2445	0.255	1.259	1.004
Case 4: $\mu = 0.4$								
β	ν_{ori}	$\sigma^2_{ori}(\frac{\pi S_0}{\omega_1^3})$	ν_{opt}	$\sigma^2_{opt}(\frac{\pi S_0}{\omega_1^3})$	A_{max}	λ_{peak1}	λ_{peak2}	$\lvert\lambda_{peak1}-\lambda_{peak2}\rvert$
0.1	0.6548	2.3031	0.6847	2.2286	1.5990	0.484	1.238	0.754
0.5	0.6395	2.0043	0.6823	1.9129	1.4458	0.399	1.245	0.846
1.0	0.6040	1.8092	0.6567	1.7068	1.3422	0.330	1.251	0.921
1.5	0.5691	1.6948	0.6279	1.5858	1.2795	0.283	1.256	0.973
2.0	0.5380	1.6194	0.6006	1.5059	1.2371	0.248	1.260	1.012

Table A2. Symbols and nomenclature.

m_1	mass of the primary system	m_2	mass of the absorber system
k_1	stiffness of the primary system	k_2	stiffness of the absorber system
k_3	stiffness of the Maxwell structure	k_4	negative stiffness of the grounded spring
c	damping of the Maxwell structure	b	inerter
F_0	amplitude of the force excitation	ω	frequency of the force excitation
ξ	damping ratio ($\xi = \frac{c}{2m_2\omega_2}$)	μ	mass ratio ($\mu = \frac{m_2}{m_1}$)
α_1	ratio of spring constants ($\alpha_1 = \frac{k_3}{k_1}$)	α_2	ratio of spring constants ($\alpha_2 = \frac{k_4}{k_1}$)
β	inerter-to-mass ratio ($\beta = \frac{b}{m_1}$)	f	amplitude-to-mass ratio ($f = \frac{F_0}{m_1}$)
ν	natural frequency ratio ($\nu = \frac{\omega_2}{\omega_1}$)	λ	forced frequency ratio ($\lambda = \frac{\omega}{\omega_1}$)
x_1	displacement of the primary system	x_2	displacement of the absorber system
x_3	displacement of the division point about spring and damping in Maxwell structure		
ω_1	natural frequency of the primary system ($\omega_1 = \sqrt{\frac{k_1}{m_1}}$)		
ω_2	natural frequency of the absorber system ($\omega_2 = \sqrt{\frac{k_2}{m_2}}$)		
X_{st}	static deformation of the primary system ($X_{st} = \frac{F_0}{k_1}$)		
A	amplitude amplification factor of the primary system		
σ^2	mean square response of the primary system		

References

1. Ormondroyd, J.; Den Hartog, J.P. The theory of the dynamic vibration absorber. *ASME J. Appl. Mech.* **1928**, *50*, 9–22.
2. Hahnkamm, E. The damping of the foundation vibrations at varying excitation frequency. *Master Archit.* **1932**, *4*, 192–201.
3. Brock, J.E. A note on the damped vibration absorber. *ASME J. Appl. Mech.* **1946**, *13*, A284. [CrossRef]

4. Den Hartog, J.P. *Mechanical Vibrations*; McGraw-Hill Book Company: New York, NY, USA, 1947.
5. Asami, T.; Nishihara, O. Analytical and experimental evaluation of an air damped dynamic vibration absorber: Design optimizations of the three-element type model. *J. Vib. Acoust.* **1999**, *121*, 334–342. [CrossRef]
6. Ren, M.Z. A variant design of the dynamic vibration absorber. *J. Sound Vib.* **2001**, *245*, 762–770. [CrossRef]
7. Asami, T.; Sekiguchi, H. Fundamental investigation on air damper (1st report, theoretical analysis). *Trans. Jpn. Soc. Mech. Eng.* **1990**, *56*, 1400–1407. (In Japanese) [CrossRef]
8. Asami, T.; Sekiguchi, H. Fundamental investigation on air damper (2nd report, theoretical and experimental study). *Trans. Jpn. Soc. Mech. Eng.* **1990**, *56*, 3201–3209. (In Japanese) [CrossRef]
9. Asami, T.; Nishihara, O.; Baz, A.M. Analytical solutions to H_∞ and H_2 optimization of dynamic vibration absorbers attached to damped linear systems. *J. Vib. Acoust.* **2002**, *124*, 284–295. [CrossRef]
10. Asami, T.; Nishihara, O. H_2 optimization of the three-element type dynamic vibration absorbers. *J. Vib. Acoust.* **2002**, *124*, 583–592. [CrossRef]
11. Nishihara, O.; Asami, T. Closed-form solutions to the exact optimizations of dynamic vibration absorbers (minimizations of the maximum amplitude magnification factors). *J. Vib. Acoust.* **2002**, *124*, 576–582. [CrossRef]
12. Asami, T.; Nishihara, O. Closed-form exact solution to H_∞ optimization of dynamic vibration absorbers (application to different transfer functions and damping systems). *J. Vib. Acoust.* **2003**, *125*, 398–405. [CrossRef]
13. Lakes, R.S.; Lee, T.; Bersie, A.; Wang, Y.C. Extreme damping in composite materials with negative-stiffness inclusions. *Nature* **2001**, *410*, 565–567. [CrossRef] [PubMed]
14. Lakes, R.S.; Drugan, W.J. Dramatically stiffer elastic composite materials due to a negative stiffness phase? *J. Mech. Phys. Solids* **2002**, *50*, 979–1009. [CrossRef]
15. Wu, L.T.; Wang, K. Optimization design and stability analysis for a new class of inerter-based dynamic vibration absorbers with a spring of negative stiffness. *J. Vib. Control* **2022**, *0*, 1–15. [CrossRef]
16. Mantakas, A.G.; Kapasakalis, K.A.; Alvertos, A.E.; Antoniadis, I.A.; Sapountzakis, E.J. A negative stiffness dynamic base absorber for seismic retrofitting of residential buildings. *Struct. Control Health Monit.* **2022**, *29*, e3127. [CrossRef]
17. Shen, Y.J.; Wang, X.R.; Yang, S.P.; Xing, H.J. Parameters optimization for a kind of dynamic vibration absorber with negative stiffness. *Math. Probl. Eng.* **2016**, *2016*, 9624325. [CrossRef]
18. Shen, Y.J.; Peng, H.B.; Li, X.H.; Yang, S.P. Analytically optimal parameters of dynamic vibration absorber with negative stiffness. *Mech. Syst. Signal Pr.* **2017**, *85*, 193–203. [CrossRef]
19. Smith, M.C. Synthesis of mechanical networks: The inerter. *IEEE Trans. Automat. Contr.* **2002**, *47*, 1648–1662. [CrossRef]
20. Wang, F.C.; Liao, M.K.; Liao, B.H.; Su, W.J.; Chan, H.A. The performance improvements of train suspension systems with mechanical networks employing inerters. *Veh. Syst. Dyn.* **2009**, *47*, 805–830. [CrossRef]
21. Chen, M.Z.Q.; Hu, Y.L.; Huang, L.X.; Chen, G.R. Influence of inerter on natural frequencies of vibration systems. *J. Sound Vib.* **2014**, *333*, 1874–1887. [CrossRef]
22. Barredo, E.; Blanco, A.; Colin, J.; Penagos, V.M.; Abundez, A.; Vela, L.G.; Meza, V.; Cruz, R.H.; Mayen, J. Closed-form solutions for the optimal design of inerter-based dynamic vibration absorbers. *Int. J. Mech. Sci.* **2018**, *144*, 41–53. [CrossRef]
23. Barredo, E.; Larios, J.G.M.; Colin, J.; Mayen, J.; Flores-Hernandez, A.A.; Arias-Montiel, M. A novel high-performance passive non-traditional inerter-based dynamic vibration absorber. *J. Sound Vib.* **2020**, *485*, 115583. [CrossRef]
24. Wang, X.R.; Liu, X.D.; Shan, Y.C.; Shen, Y.J.; He, T. Analysis and optimization of the novel inerter-based dynamic vibration absorbers. *IEEE Access* **2018**, *6*, 33169–33182. [CrossRef]
25. Wang, X.R.; He, T.; Shen, Y.J.; Shan, Y.C.; Liu, X.D. Parameters optimization and performance evaluation for the novel inerter-based dynamic vibration absorbers with negative stiffness. *J. Sound Vib.* **2019**, *463*, 114941. [CrossRef]
26. Shen, Y.J.; Xing, Z.Y.; Yang, S.P.; Sun, J.Q. Parameters optimization for a novel dynamic vibration absorber. *Mech. Syst. Signal Pr.* **2019**, *133*, 106282. [CrossRef]
27. Zhu, X.Z; Chen, Z.B.; Jiao, Y.H. Optimizations of distributed dynamic vibration absorbers for suppressing vibrations in plates. *J. Low Freq. Noise Vib. Act. Control* **2018**, *37*, 1188–1200. [CrossRef]
28. Basta, E.; Ghommem, M.; Emam, S. Flutter control and mitigation of limit cycle oscillations in aircraft wings using distributed vibration absorbers. *Nonlinear Dyn.* **2021**, *106*, 1975–2003. [CrossRef]
29. Zhang, M.J.; Xu, F.Y. Tuned mass damper for self-excited vibration control: Optimization involving nonlinear aeroelastic effect. *J. Wind. Eng. Ind. Aerodyn.* **2022**, *220*, 104836. [CrossRef]
30. Wang, Q.; Zhou J.X.; Wang, K.; Gao, J.H.; Lin, Q.D.; Chang, Y.P.; Xu, D.L.; Wen, G.L. Dual-function quasi-zero-stiffness dynamic vibration absorber: Low-frequency vibration mitigation and energy harvesting. *Appl. Math. Model.* **2023**, *116*, 636–654. [CrossRef]
31. Gad, A.G. Particle swarm optimization algorithm and its applications: A systematic review. *Arch. Comput. Methods Eng.* **2022**, *29*, 2531–2561. [CrossRef]
32. Jain, M.; Saihjpal, V.; Singh, N.; Singh, S.B. An overview of variants and advancements of PSO algorithm. *Appl. Sci.* **2022**, *12*, 8392. [CrossRef]

33. Wang, X.R.; Shen, Y.J.; Yang, S.P. H_∞ optimization of the grounded three-element type dynamic vibration absorber. *J. Dyn. Contr.* **2016**, *14*, 448–453. (In Chinese)
34. Wang, X.R.; Shen, Y.J.; Yang, S.P.; Xing, H.J. H_∞ parameter optimization of three-element type dynamic vibration absorber with negative stiffness. *J. Vib. Eng.* **2017**, *30*, 177–184. (In Chinese)

mathematics

Article

CPPE: An Improved Phasmatodea Population Evolution Algorithm with Chaotic Maps

Tsu-Yang Wu, Haonan Li and Shu-Chuan Chu *

College of Computer Science and Engineering, Shandong University of Science and Technology, Qingdao 266590, China; wutsuyang@sdust.edu.cn (T.-Y.W.); lihaonan@sdust.edu.cn (H.L.)
* Correspondence: scchu0803@sdust.edu.cn

Abstract: The Phasmatodea Population Evolution (PPE) algorithm, inspired by the evolution of the phasmatodea population, is a recently proposed meta-heuristic algorithm that has been applied to solve problems in engineering. Chaos theory has been increasingly applied to enhance the performance and convergence of meta-heuristic algorithms. In this paper, we introduce chaotic mapping into the PPE algorithm to propose a new algorithm, the Chaotic-based Phasmatodea Population Evolution (CPPE) algorithm. The chaotic map replaces the initialization population of the original PPE algorithm to enhance performance and convergence. We evaluate the effectiveness of the CPPE algorithm by testing it on 28 benchmark functions, using 12 different chaotic maps. The results demonstrate that CPPE outperforms PPE in terms of both performance and convergence speed. In the performance analysis, we found that the CPPE algorithm with the Tent map showed improvements of 8.9647%, 10.4633%, and 14.6716%, respectively, in the Final, Mean, and Standard metrics, compared to the original PPE algorithm. In terms of convergence, the CPPE algorithm with the Singer map showed an improvement of 65.1776% in the average change rate of fitness value, compared to the original PPE algorithm. Finally, we applied our CPPE to stock prediction. The results showed that the predicted curve was relatively consistent with the real curve.

Keywords: chaotic-based PPE algorithm; meta-heuristic algorithm; chaotic maps

MSC: 90C26

Citation: Wu, T.-Y.; Li, H.; Chu, S.-C. CPPE: An Improved Phasmatodea Population Evolution Algorithm with Chaotic Maps. *Mathematics* **2023**, *11*, 1977. https://doi.org/10.3390/math11091977

Academic Editor: Jian Dong

Received: 18 March 2023
Revised: 20 April 2023
Accepted: 21 April 2023
Published: 22 April 2023

1. Introduction

The advancement of science and technology has led to the emergence of a multitude of meta-heuristic algorithms that address engineering problems across various fields [1,2]. These algorithms employ randomness and fall into the following two categories: trajectory-based meta-heuristics, which include well-known algorithms such as the Genetic Algorithm [3–6] and Differential Evolution [7]; and population-based meta-heuristics, such as Particle Swarm Optimization [8–10], the Whale Optimization Algorithm (WOA) [11–13], and the Butterfly Optimization Algorithm [14]. Meta-heuristic algorithms are particularly effective in avoiding local optima due to their random nature, which is also the most challenging aspect in their development.

In recent years, chaos theory has been increasingly applied to enhance the performance and convergence of meta-heuristic algorithms. Chaos theory deals with the randomness arising from deterministic systems and is extensively utilized in various fields, including meta-heuristics [15,16]. Several studies have combined chaos theory with meta-heuristics to enhance their performance, such as the following: Chaotic Particle Swarm Optimization [17], Chaotic Imperialist Competitive Algorithm [18], Chaotic Firefly Algorithm [19,20], Chaotic Bat Algorithm [21], Chaotic Genetic Algorithm [22], Chaotic Whale Optimization (CWO) Algorithm [23], Chaotic Dragonfly Algorithm [24], Chaotic Grasshopper Optimization (CGO) Algorithm [25], Chaotic Bird Swarm Algorithm [26], Chaotic Cloud Quantum

Bat Hybrid Optimization Algorithm [27], Chaotic Sparrow Search Algorithm [28], Chaotic GrayWolf Optimization Algorithm [29,30].

One of the more recent meta-heuristic algorithms is the Phasmatodea Population Evolution (PPE) algorithm [31,32], inspired by the evolution of phasmatodea populations. This population-based algorithm has strong convergence capabilities and a degree of local optima avoidance. In this study, we aimed to enhance the PPE algorithm's performance and convergence speed by combining it with chaos theory. We propose a new algorithm, the Chaotic-based Phasmatodea Population Evolution (CPPE) algorithm, which replaces the probabilistically-initialized population part of the original PPE with a chaotic map. Our main contributions are listed as follows:

- We combine chaos theory with the PPE algorithm for the first time to propose a new Chaotic-based PPE algorithm called CPPE.
- We select 12 different chaotic maps and 28 popular benchmark functions to evaluate the performance of the proposed CPPE algorithm. The experimental results demonstrate that the performance and convergence of CPPE are greatly enhanced.

The rest of the paper is organized as follows. We review related research on chaotic-based meta-heuristic algorithms and PPE algorithms in Section 2. Section 3 provides a detailed description of the CPPE algorithm. Experimental results are discussed in Section 4. Finally, Section 5 provides the conclusion.

2. Related Work

Previous studies have examined meta-heuristic algorithms that incorporate chaotic maps. In 2018, Kaur and Arora [23] proposed the CWO algorithm, which combines chaotic maps and the WOA. They utilized chaotic mapping to adjust the parameter p in WOA, comparing the effectiveness of 10 different chaotic mappings. Tent mapping was found to significantly improve the performance of WOA. In a similar vein, Arora and Anand [25] proposed the CGO algorithm, adjusting the parameters, c_1 and c_2, of the Grasshopper Optimization Algorithm (GOA) using chaotic maps and comparing the effectiveness of 10 different chaotic maps. They found that the Circle map significantly improved the performance of GOA.

Altay and Alatas [26] proposed the Bird Swarm Algorithm with Chaotic Mapping (CMBSA) in 2019, using chaotic mapping to initialize the population in the Bird Swarm Algorithm (BSA). The experimental results showed that CMBSA outperformed BSA. In 2021, Zhang and Ding [28] proposed the Chaotic Sparrow Search Algorithm, utilizing Logistic mapping to initialize the population in the Sparrow Search Algorithm (SSA). Xu et al. [29] proposed the Chaotic GrayWolf Optimization algorithm, which incorporated Chaotic Local Search (CLS) to adjust the radius of the algorithm's local search in the GrayWolf Optimization (GWO) algorithm. Similarly, Hao and Sobhani [30] proposed the Adaptive Chaotic GrayWolf Optimization algorithm, initializing the population using Logistic mapping in the population initialization phase.

In 2022, Gezici and Livatyalı [33] proposed the Chaotic Harris Hawks Optimization (CHHO) algorithm, utilizing 10 different chaotic maps to adjust various variables in the Harris Hawks Optimization (HHO) algorithm. They found that CHHO outperformed HHO. Gharehchopogh et al. [34] proposed the Chaotic Quasi-oppositional Farmland Fertility Algorithm (CQFFA), utilizing the CLS mechanism to adjust the radius of the local search using a chaotic map. Experimental results showed that CQFFA performed better than the Farmland Fertility Algorithm. In 2023, Chen et al. [35] proposed the Chaotic Satin Bowerbird Optimization Algorithm (CSBOA), utilizing the Bernoulli shift map initialization algorithm to initialize the population. Naik [36] proposed the Chaotic Social Group Optimization (CSGO) algorithm, replacing the parameter c in the Social Group Optimization (SGO) algorithm using a chaotic map. Experimental results showed that CSGO outperformed SGO.

In 2022, scholars primarily focused on improving and applying the PPE algorithm. Zhu et al. [37] proposed the Multigroup-based PPE algorithm with Multistrategy (MPPE), which divided the population into multiple groups in the initialization stage and incorporated the step size factor of the flower pollen algorithm into the population growth model of some groups. Similarly, Zhuang et al. [38] proposed the Advanced PPE (APPE) algorithm in 2022, which removed population competition and partial evolutionary trend updates and added jumping mechanisms, history-based searches, and population closure moves.

3. Chaotic-Based Phasmatodea Population Evolution (CPPE) Algorithm

3.1. Phasmatodea Population Evolution (PPE) Algorithm

The PPE algorithm simulates the way the phasmatodea population evolves. Three stages primarily make up the algorithm. The first stage is the initialization stage, the second stage is the population update stage, and the third stage is the selection of the population evolution trend. Figure 1 shows the flowchart of the PPE algorithm. In order to explain the PPE algorithm and CPPE algorithms, we define some symbols in Table 1.

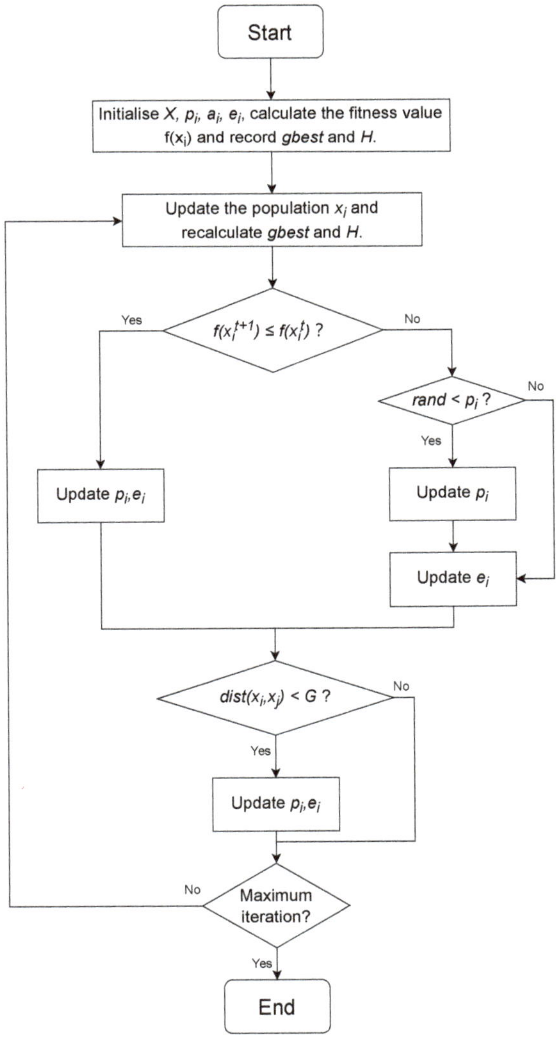

Figure 1. Flowchart of PPE algorithm.

Table 1. The symbols used in PPE and CPPE.

Symbols	Interpretation of Symbols
Np	The total population size
d	The dimensionality
x_i	i-th population
p_i	The size of x_i
a_i	The growth rate of x_i
e_i	The evolution trend of x_i
$f(x_i)$	The fitness value of x_i
m	Mutation factor
$rand$	A method to generate random numbers in the range (0, 1)
st	Impact factor
U, L	The upper and lower bounds
Max_gen	Total iterations
t	Current iteration count

In the initialization phase, we need to randomly initialize a $Np \times d$ matrix X, $X = [x_1, \ldots, x_i, \ldots, x_{Np}]$, where each element represents a population x_i, the dimension of each population is d, and there are a total of Np populations. Each population x_i has two attributes: (1) population size p_i. (2) growth rate a_i. The initial population size is $p_i = \frac{1}{Np}$, and the initial growth rate is $a_i = 1.1$. To initialize, the population evolution trend e_i is set to 0. After calculating the fitness value, use $gbest$ to present the current global optimal solution. In addition, set a $k \times d$ matrix H, $H = [x_{h1}, \ldots, x_{hi}, \ldots, x_{hk}]$, and use H to store the historical global optimal solution. The value x_{hi} represents the i-th global optimal solution, the number being set to k, $k = \lfloor \log(Np) \rfloor + 1$. Then, sort H from largest to smallest. The role of H is to guide the update of the surrounding populations.

In the population update phase, the t-th updated population is represented by x_i^t, and, then, the calculation formula of the $t+1$-th updated population is Equation (1).

$$x_i^{t+1} = x_i^t + e_i \tag{1}$$

After the population is updated, the fitness value needs to be recalculated, and $gbest$ and H need to be updated.

Finally, the third stage is the selection of the population evolution trend. Three cases are involved in this stage. First, we use $f(x_i^t)$ to represent the fitness value of the t-th update, and, then, the fitness value of the $t+1$-th update is represented by $f(x_i^{t+1})$. The first case is $f(x_i^{t+1}) \leq f(x_i^t)$. Use Equations (2) and (3) to update the p_i and e_i of the population.

$$p_i^{t+1} = a_i^{t+1} p_i^t (1 - p_i^t) \tag{2}$$

$$e_i^{t+1} = (1 - p_i^{t+1})[(x_{i,H}^t - x_i^t) \cdot c] + p_i^{t+1}(e_i^t + m) \tag{3}$$

For Equation (3), m is a mutation factor; $x_{i,H}^t$ is a historical optimal solution in H, and its fitness value is the closest to the fitness value of x_i^t in H, that is, $f(x_{i,H}^t) - f(x_i^t)$ is the smallest; c is the impact factor.The second case is $f(x_i^{t+1}) > f(x_i^t)$. However, there is a probability for the population to accept this update situation. We use the $rand$ method and p_i to make a probability judgment. If the number randomly generated by the $rand$ method is less than p_i, we accept the worse situation and use Equation (2) to update p_i. The second formula for updating e_i is Equation (4).

$$e_i^{t+1} = rand \cdot (x_{i,H}^t - x_i^t) + st \cdot B \tag{4}$$

Among them, st is the impact factor, and B is a randomly generated $1 \times d$ matrix that conforms to the standard normal distribution.The third case is the impact of competition before the population. First, to calculate the distance between the x_i and the x_j. If the distance is less than the defined threshold G, there is competition among populations. G is calculated as Equation (5). At this time, use Equations (6) and (7) to update the p_i and e_i of the population.

$$G = 0.1 \times (U - L)\frac{Max\_gen + 1 - t}{Max\_gen} \tag{5}$$

$$p_i^{t+1} = p_i^t + a_i^t p_i^t \left(1 - p_i^t - \frac{f(x_j^t)}{f(x_i^t)} p_j^t\right) \tag{6}$$

$$e_i^{t+1} = e_i^t + \frac{f(x_j^t) - f(x_i^t)}{f(x_j^t)}(x_j^t - x_i^t) \tag{7}$$

3.2. The Proposed CPPE Algorithm

Chaos is an unpredictable and random movement in a deterministic system. Given an initial value for a chaotic system, a chaotic sequence can be generated after chaotic mapping, which is random. This property can be used as an initialization method in the PPE algorithm to improve the convergence speed and the ability to find the global optimal solution. A random generator is used in the initialization phase in the standard PPE algorithm. Compared with the random generator, using chaotic maps to generate the initial population can make it more random and uniform.

The initialization of CPPE algorithm is described as follows.

- Initialize a matrix Z with dimension $Np \times d$, where all elements are zero, that is,
$$Z = \begin{bmatrix} z_{11} & \cdots & z_{1d} \\ \vdots & \ddots & \vdots \\ z_{Np1} & \cdots & z_{Npd} \end{bmatrix}, z_{11} = \cdots = z_{Npd} = 0;$$
- Using the *rand* method to randomly generate a $1 \times d$ vector, and replace the vector in the first row of the matrix Z;
- Traversing the second to Np-th rows of the matrix Z, and using the chaotic map to generate $Np - 1$ vectors, each of which is $1 \times d$;
- Traversing the first to Np-th rows of the matrix Z, and mapping each element to the (L, U) interval. The mapping formula is Equation (8), where z_{mn} represents an element in the matrix Z.

$$z_{mn} = L + (U - L) \times z_{mn} \tag{8}$$

Other initialization content is the same as that in the PPE algorithm. After the initialization phase is completed, the algorithm enters the iterative phase, which includes the population update phase and the population evolution trend update phase.

The flowchart of the CPPE algorithm is shown in Figure 2.

1. Use the chaotic map to initialize the $Np \times d$ matrix, in which each element represents a population, and initialize the two attributes p_i and a_i of the population. Initialize the evolution trend e_i is set 0. Calculate the fitness value, and use *gbest* to represent the global optimal solution, and use H to store k historical global optimal solutions;
2. Entering the iterative process, update each population, recalculate the fitness value, and update *gbest* and H;
3. For the updated fitness value, if $f(x_i^{t+1}) \leq f(x_i^t)$, then update p_i and use the first method to update e_i, if $f(x_i^{t+1}) > f(x_i^t)$, and, then, judge the first. The value generated by the *rand* method is compared with p_i. If it is less than p_i, the population size needs to be updated, otherwise it need not be updated. Then use the second method to update e_i;
4. Use the distance between x_i and x_j to compare with the threshold G. If it is less than G, this confirms that there is competition between the two populations, and the third method is used to update e_i;

5. Determine whether the maximum number of iterations has been achieved. If the maximum number of iterations is not reached, proceed to step 2 and repeat the process until the maximum number is attained.

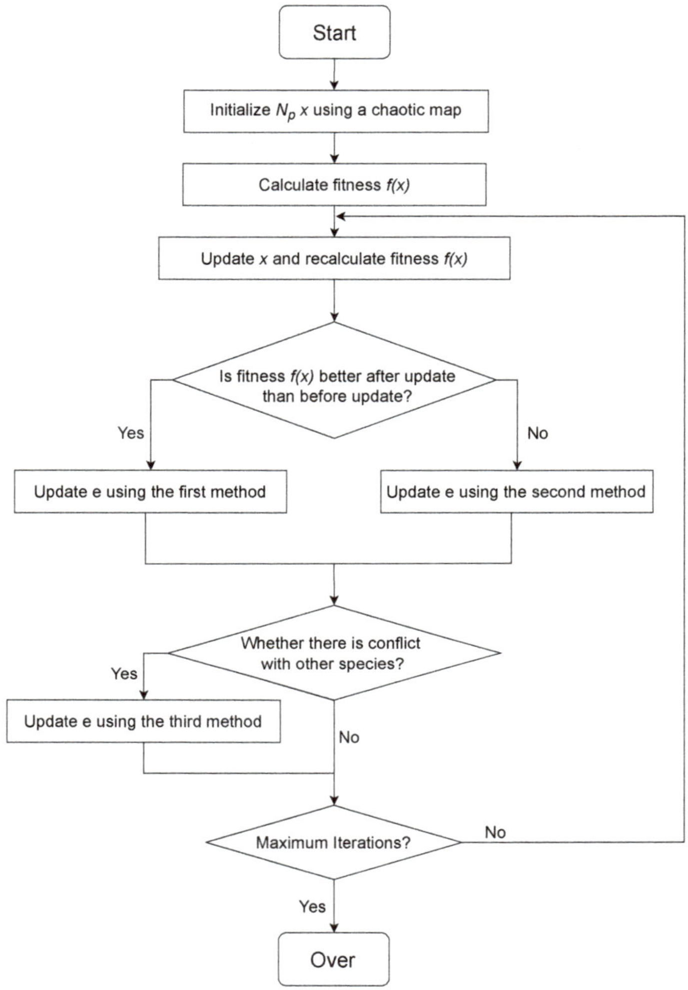

Figure 2. Flowchart of CPPE algorithm.

According to the above description, the pseudo-code of the CPPE algorithm is shown in Algorithm 1. The code for the algorithm has been uploaded to the website (https://github.com/Leon-paq/CPPE.git).

Algorithm 1: Pseudo-code of the CPPE algorithm.

```
Initialize Np populations using a chaotic map;
Initialize p_i = 1/Np, a_i = 1.1, e_i = 0;
Initialize k = ⌊log(Np)⌋ + 1;
Calculate fitness f(x_i), set gbest and H;
for t = 2 to Max_gen do
    Update each population x_i using Equation (1);
    Calculate new fitness f(x_i), update gbest and H;
    for i = 1 to Np do
        if f(x_i^{t+1}) ≤ f(x_i^t) then
            Update p_i using Equation (2);
            Update e_i using Equation (3);
        end
        else
            if rand < p_i then
                Update p_i using Equation (2);
            end
            Update e_i using Equation (4);
        end
        Calculate G using Equation (5);
        if dist(x_i,x_j) < G then
            Update p_i using Equation (6);
            Update e_i using Equation (7);
        end
    end
end
```

4. Experimental Results and Discussions

Three experiments were designed to verify the performance and convergence of the proposed CPPE algorithm. Specifically, these experiments aimed to compare the CPPE algorithm, which incorporates 12 different chaotic maps, with the unimproved PPE algorithm, in terms of performance and convergence. The 12 selected chaotic maps included the Logistic, Piecewise, Singer, Sine, Gauss, Tent, Bernoulli, Chebyshev, Circle, Cubic, Sinusoidal, and ICMIC maps. To facilitate comparisons between the CPPE algorithm and the unimproved PPE algorithm, the 12 different CPPE algorithms were labeled as CPP1 to CPPE12, as shown in Table 2.

Table 2. The notations of CPPE.

Symbols	Explains
CPPE1	PPE + Logistic map [39]
CPPE2	PPE + Piecewise map [40]
CPPE3	PPE + Singer map [41]
CPPE4	PPE + Sine map [42]
CPPE5	PPE + Gauss map [19]
CPPE6	PPE + Tent map [43]
CPPE7	PPE + Bernoulli map [44]
CPPE8	PPE + Chebyshev map [45]
CPPE9	PPE + Circle map [23]
CPPE10	PPE + Cubic map [46]
CPPE11	PPE + Sinusoidal map [47]
CPPE12	PPE + ICMIC map [48]

4.1. Benchmark Functions and Experimental Environments

For our experiment, we chose to utilize 28 benchmark functions from the widely-used CEC13 dataset [49]. These functions are commonly utilized for evaluating the efficacy of various algorithms. The CEC13 dataset is comprised of three types of benchmark functions: unimodal functions, basic multimedia functions, and composition functions. The mathematical expressions and attributes of these functions are presented in Table 3. Unimodal functions are represented by f_1 to f_5, basic multimedia functions are represented by f_6 to f_{20}, and composition functions are represented by f_{21} to f_{28}. The dimension of each function calculation is provided under the "Dimension" column, and the optimal value of each function is provided under the "Optimal" column.

Table 3. The twenty-eight benchmark functions used in this study.

Benchmark Function	Dimension	Optimal
$f_1(x) = \sum_{i=1}^{n} x_i^2$	10	0
$f_2(x) = \sum_{i=1}^{n} (10^6)^{\frac{i-1}{n-1}} x_i^2$	2	0
$f_3(x) = x_i^2 + 10^6 \sum_{i=2}^{n} x_i^2$	2	0
$f_4(x) = 10^6 x_i^2 + \sum_{i=2}^{n} x_i^2$	2	0
$f_5(x) = \sqrt{\sum_{i=2}^{n} \lvert x_i \rvert^{2+4\frac{i-1}{n-1}}}$	5	0
$f_6(x) = \sum_{i=1}^{n-1} (100(x_i^2 - x_{i+1})^2 + (x_i - 1)^2)$	5	0
$f_7(x) = (\frac{1}{n-1} \sum_{i=1}^{n-1} (\sqrt{x_i} + \sqrt{x_i} sin^2(50x_i^{0.2})))^2$	5	0
$f_8(x) = -20exp(-0.2\sqrt{\frac{1}{n} \sum_{i=1}^{n} x_i^2}) - exp(\frac{1}{n} \sum_{i=1}^{n} cos(2\pi x_i)) + 20 + e$	2	0
$f_9(x) = \sum_{i=1}^{n} (\sum_{k=0}^{k\ max} [a^k cos(2\pi b^k (x_i + 0.5))]) - n \sum_{k=0}^{k\ max} [a^k cos(2\pi b^k \cdot 0.5)]$	10	0
$f_{10}(x) = \sum_{i=1}^{n} \frac{x_i^2}{4000} - \prod_{i=1}^{n} cos(\frac{x_i}{\sqrt{i}}) + 1$	10	0
$f_{11}(x) = \sum_{i=1}^{n} (z_i^2 - 10cos(2\pi z_i) + 10), z = \Lambda^{10} T_{asy}^{0.2} (T_{osz}(\frac{5.12(x-o)}{100}))$	5	0
$f_{12}(x) = \sum_{i=1}^{n} (z_i^2 - 10cos(2\pi z_i) + 10), z = M_1 \Lambda^{10} M_2 T_{asy}^{0.2} (T_{osz}(M_1 \frac{5.12(x-o)}{100}))$	5	0
$f_{13}(x) = \sum_{i=1}^{n} (z_i^2 - 10cos(2\pi z_i) + 10), z = M_1 \Lambda^{10} M_2 T_{asy}^{0.2} (T_{osz}(y))$	5	0
$f_{14}(x) = 418.9829 \times n - \sum_{i=1}^{n} g(z), z = \Lambda^{10}(\frac{1000(x-o)}{100}) + 4.209687462275036e+002$	2	0
$f_{15}(x) = 418.9829 \times n - \sum_{i=1}^{n} g(z), z = \Lambda^{10} M_1(\frac{1000(x-o)}{100}) + 4.209687462275036e+002$	2	0
$f_{16}(x) = \frac{10}{n^2} \prod_{i=1}^{n} (1 + i \sum_{j=1}^{32} \frac{\lvert 2^j x_i - round(2^j x_i) \rvert}{2^j})^{\frac{10}{n^{1.2}}} - \frac{10}{n^2}$	10	0
$f_{17}(x) = min(\sum_{i=1}^{n} (\widehat{x_i} - \mu_0)^2, dn + s \sum_{i=1}^{n} (\widehat{x_i} - \mu_1)^2) + 10(n - \sum_{i=1}^{n} cos(2\pi \widehat{z_i})), z = \Lambda^{100}(\widehat{x} - \mu_0)$	5	0
$f_{18}(x) = min(\sum_{i=1}^{n} (\widehat{x_i} - \mu_0)^2, dn + s \sum_{i=1}^{n} (\widehat{x_i} - \mu_1)^2) + 10(n - \sum_{i=1}^{n} cos(2\pi \widehat{z_i})), z = M_2 \Lambda^{100}(M_1 \widehat{x} - \mu_0)$	5	0
$f_{19}(x) = g_1(g_2(x_1, x_2)) + g_1(g_2(x_2, x_3)) + \ldots + g_1(g_2(x_n, x_1)),$ $g_1(x) = \sum_{i=1}^{n} \frac{x_i^2}{4000} - \prod_{i=1}^{n} cos(\frac{x_i}{\sqrt{i}}) + 1,$ $g_2(x) = \sum_{i=1}^{n-1} (100(x_i^2 - x_{i+1})^2 + (x_i - 1)^2)$	10	0
$f_{20}(x) = g(x_1, x_2) + g(x_2, x_3) + \ldots + g(x_n, x_1), g(x, y) = 0.5 + \frac{(sin^2(\sqrt{x^2+y^2}) - 0.5)}{(1+0.001(x^2+y^2))^2}$	10	0

Table 3. *Cont.*

Benchmark Function	Dimension	Optimal
$f_{21}(x) = \sum_{i=1}^{n} \{\omega_i^* [\lambda_i g_i(x) + bias_i]\}, g_1 = f_6, g_2 = f_5, g_3 = f_3, g_4 = f_4, g_5 = f_1$	2	0
$f_{22}(x) = \sum_{i=1}^{n} \{\omega_i^* [\lambda_i g_i(x) + bias_i]\}, g_{1-3} = f_{14}$	2	0
$f_{23}(x) = \sum_{i=1}^{n} \{\omega_i^* [\lambda_i g_i(x) + bias_i]\}, g_{1-3} = f_{15}$	2	0
$f_{24}(x) = \sum_{i=1}^{n} \{\omega_i^* [\lambda_i g_i(x) + bias_i]\}, g_1 = f_{15}, g_2 = f_{12}, g_3 = f_9, \sigma = [20, 20, 20]$	2	0
$f_{25}(x) = \sum_{i=1}^{n} \{\omega_i^* [\lambda_i g_i(x) + bias_i]\}, g_1 = f_{15}, g_2 = f_{12}, g_3 = f_9, \sigma = [10, 30, 50]$	2	0
$f_{26}(x) = \sum_{i=1}^{n} \{\omega_i^* [\lambda_i g_i(x) + bias_i]\}, g_1 = f_{15}, g_2 = f_{12}, g_3 = f_2, g_4 = f_9, g_5 = f_{10}$	2	0
$f_{27}(x) = \sum_{i=1}^{n} \{\omega_i^* [\lambda_i g_i(x) + bias_i]\}, g_1 = f_{10}, g_2 = f_{12}, g_3 = f_{15}, g_4 = f_9, g_5 = f_1$	2	0
$f_{28}(x) = \sum_{i=1}^{n} \{\omega_i^* [\lambda_i g_i(x) + bias_i]\}, g_1 = f_{19}, g_2 = f_7, g_3 = f_{15}, g_4 = f_{20}, g_5 = f_1$	2	0

The experiment was conducted on a Windows 11 laptop, which had an AMD Ryzen 7 5800H CPU with a clock speed of 3.20 GHz and 16 GB of running memory. The experiment was implemented using MATLAB R2022b.

4.2. Performance Comparison between PPE and CPPEs

Before commencing the experiment, several parameters needed to be configured, as presented in Table 4. The "Population_Number" denotes the population counts for the CPPE algorithm and was set to 100 for this experiment. The maximum iteration count for the CPPE algorithm is denoted by the "Max_Gen" variable and was set to 100 for this experiment. In this experiment, the CPPE algorithm was run 50 times, as indicated by the "Run_Nums" variable.

Table 4. Parameters setting for performance experiments.

Parameters	Values
Population_Number	100
Max_Gen	100
Run_Nums	50

We ran PPE and CPPE1 to CPPE12 on 28 benchmark functions 50 times and recorded the respective results. We used the three criteria, Final, Mean and Standard, to compare algorithmic performance. Final represents the final optimal value of the algorithm, that is, the minimum result of running the algorithm 50 times. Mean is the average outcome of executing the algorithm 50 times and represents the method's average optimal value. Standard stands for the algorithm's total standard deviation, and the algorithm's degree of dispersion, after 50 iterations.

We displayed the results after running the experiment 50 times in a tabular form, as shown in Table 5. Where f_{1-28} represents the 28 benchmark functions, the first column represents different algorithms, and the second to fourth columns represent three comparison standards. We have put the data pertaining to results better than the PPE algorithm in bold in the table to improve the readability for readers. In addition, we made statistics on 28 benchmark functions in the experiment, and the number of CPPE superior to PPE is shown in Figure 3 and Table 6. In Figure 3, the horizontal coordinates indicate the different CPPE algorithms and the vertical coordinates indicate the number of times CPPE outperformed PPE on Final, Mean, and Std matrices. The data in the figure shows the number of times CPPE was superior to PPE on the 28 benchmark functions. The detailed benchmark functions are shown in Table 7.

Table 5. The experimental results of the 50 PPE and CPPE on 28 benchmark functions.

f_1	Final	Mean	Std	f_2	Final	Mean	Std	f_3	Final	Mean	Std
PPE	9.99E-02	3.89E-01	2.94E-01	PPE	2.33E-02	5.66E+01	1.11E+02	PPE	5.88E-03	4.08E+00	1.29E+01
CPPE1	**5.18E-02**	**2.64E-01**	**1.43E-01**	CPPE1	**1.26E-02**	1.68E+02	3.28E+02	CPPE1	**3.05E-03**	**2.69E+00**	**5.81E+00**
CPPE2	**6.39E-02**	**3.29E-01**	**2.40E-01**	CPPE2	3.10E-02	1.11E+02	2.08E+02	CPPE2	1.78E-02	**2.95E+00**	**4.41E+00**
CPPE3	**6.39E-02**	7.41E-01	3.97E-01	CPPE3	3.10E-02	3.47E+02	5.46E+02	CPPE3	1.78E-02	**1.36E+00**	**2.61E+00**
CPPE4	**4.41E-02**	**3.36E-01**	**2.05E-01**	CPPE4	**5.47E-03**	1.17E+02	2.76E+02	CPPE4	1.10E-02	4.52E+00	**7.25E+00**
CPPE5	**9.47E-02**	**3.63E-01**	**1.98E-01**	CPPE5	**1.15E-02**	1.41E+02	2.55E+02	CPPE5	**2.30E-03**	**3.50E+00**	**6.33E+00**
CPPE6	**2.69E-02**	**3.38E-01**	**2.01E-01**	CPPE6	6.13E-02	9.08E+01	2.35E+02	CPPE6	**5.43E-03**	**2.93E+00**	**6.14E+00**
CPPE7	**5.00E-02**	3.99E-01	**2.36E-01**	CPPE7	**4.03E-03**	7.59E+01	1.33E+02	CPPE7	1.61E-02	**3.66E+00**	**6.01E+00**
CPPE8	**9.46E-02**	3.90E-01	**2.36E-01**	CPPE8	**4.60E-03**	6.86E+01	1.19E+02	CPPE8	**4.52E-04**	4.61E+00	**9.50E+00**
CPPE9	**5.95E-02**	4.37E-01	**2.49E-01**	CPPE9	**1.83E-02**	**2.53E+01**	**5.59E+01**	CPPE9	**1.36E-03**	**3.07E+00**	**1.18E+01**
CPPE10	**4.74E-02**	3.89E-01	**2.08E-01**	CPPE10	**2.24E-02**	7.64E+01	1.56E+02	CPPE10	**4.93E-03**	**2.11E+00**	**3.52E+00**
CPPE11	**5.80E-02**	**3.29E-01**	**2.13E-01**	CPPE11	8.68E-02	1.64E+02	3.00E+02	CPPE11	6.02E-03	4.75E+00	1.37E+01
CPPE12	**2.87E-02**	3.95E-01	**2.34E-01**	CPPE12	2.95E-02	6.63E+01	1.11E+02	CPPE12	**4.11E-03**	7.05E+00	2.49E+0

f_4	Final	Mean	Std	f_5	Final	Mean	Std	f_6	Final	Mean	Std
PPE	4.44E-03	7.66E+01	2.44E+02	PPE	2.10E-04	3.00E-03	3.39E-03	PPE	3.22E-04	1.11E+00	1.77E+00
CPPE1	1.69E-02	9.47E+01	**1.63E+02**	CPPE1	**5.20E-05**	**2.97E-03**	**2.96E-03**	CPPE1	**5.27E-06**	1.14E+00	**1.75E+00**
CPPE2	2.36E-02	8.54E+01	**2.09E+02**	CPPE2	**5.47E-05**	3.80E-03	5.20E-03	CPPE2	**4.17E-05**	**7.00E-01**	**1.40E+00**
CPPE3	2.36E-02	**7.23E+01**	**1.90E+02**	CPPE3	**5.47E-05**	2.27E-02	2.85E-02	CPPE3	**4.17E-05**	4.10E+00	**1.19E+00**
CPPE4	1.83E-02	1.43E+02	**2.39E+02**	CPPE4	7.80E-04	5.00E-03	5.74E-03	CPPE4	**6.81E-06**	**7.04E-01**	**1.39E+00**
CPPE5	**9.05E-04**	**6.24E+01**	**1.85E+02**	CPPE5	3.20E-04	5.07E-03	7.87E-03	CPPE5	**3.02E-05**	**8.88E-01**	**1.58E+00**
CPPE6	1.65E-02	1.82E+02	3.43E+02	CPPE6	**1.53E-04**	3.24E-03	**2.58E-03**	CPPE6	5.39E-04	**9.89E-01**	**1.64E+00**
CPPE7	3.93E-02	8.55E+01	**1.95E+02**	CPPE7	**1.91E-04**	3.38E-03	**3.38E-03**	CPPE7	**1.34E-04**	**5.88E-01**	**1.26E+00**
CPPE8	1.45E-01	1.40E+02	2.65E+02	CPPE8	3.35E-04	4.99E-03	5.54E-03	CPPE8	2.02E-03	2.88E+00	1.93E+00
CPPE9	**3.82E-03**	**2.43E+01**	**5.28E+01**	CPPE9	5.43E-04	4.30E-03	**3.35E-03**	CPPE9	2.04E-02	**3.48E-01**	**6.07E-01**
CPPE10	4.69E-02	9.29E+01	**2.20E+02**	CPPE10	2.96E-04	7.14E-03	7.37E-03	CPPE10	1.31E-03	3.56E+00	**1.59E+00**
CPPE11	1.27E-01	1.65E+02	2.61E+02	CPPE11	**1.44E-04**	4.44E-03	5.40E-03	CPPE11	**3.02E-05**	**1.04E+00**	**1.68E+00**
CPPE12	**3.53E-04**	8.67E+01	**1.88E+02**	CPPE12	4.42E-04	7.36E-03	9.66E-03	CPPE12	2.19E-03	2.86E+00	1.97E+00

f_7	Final	Mean	Std	f_8	Final	Mean	Std	f_9	Final	Mean	Std
PPE	3.15E-02	7.70E-01	1.23E+00	PPE	6.42E-05	1.61E-03	8.21E-03	PPE	2.59E+00	5.21E+00	1.27E+00
CPPE1	3.61E-02	**7.08E-01**	**1.17E+00**	CPPE1	**5.00E-05**	**6.37E-04**	**6.79E-04**	CPPE1	**1.98E+00**	5.62E+00	**1.22E+00**
CPPE2	**2.70E-02**	8.54E-01	1.63E+00	CPPE2	**4.44E-05**	**4.20E-04**	**3.07E-04**	CPPE2	**2.53E+00**	5.26E+00	**1.25E+00**
CPPE3	**2.70E-02**	1.04E+00	1.36E+00	CPPE3	**4.44E-05**	2.06E+00	6.03E+00	CPPE3	**2.53E+00**	5.70E+00	1.74E+00
CPPE4	**2.93E-02**	1.06E+00	2.30E+00	CPPE4	**3.75E-05**	**4.17E-04**	**2.88E-04**	CPPE4	2.61E+00	5.22E+00	**1.20E+00**
CPPE5	**2.40E-02**	1.06E+00	2.11E+00	CPPE5	**3.42E-05**	**3.69E-04**	**3.63E-04**	CPPE5	2.95E+00	5.57E+00	**1.24E+00**
CPPE6	**1.08E-02**	**5.14E-01**	**1.16E+00**	CPPE6	**5.51E-05**	**4.14E-04**	**3.55E-04**	CPPE6	**2.52E+00**	5.49E+00	**1.14E+00**
CPPE7	**2.35E-02**	**7.07E-01**	1.55E+00	CPPE7	7.07E-05	4.00E-01	2.83E+00	CPPE7	2.95E+00	**5.09E+00**	**1.16E+00**
CPPE8	**1.43E-02**	1.35E+00	2.21E+00	CPPE8	**1.29E-05**	4.68E-01	2.83E+00	CPPE8	**2.35E+00**	**5.20E+00**	1.31E+00
CPPE9	**1.58E-02**	**6.38E-01**	**9.98E-01**	CPPE9	**1.58E-05**	**4.34E-04**	**3.91E-04**	CPPE9	2.61E+00	5.88E+00	**1.11E+00**
CPPE10	5.88E-02	1.82E+00	2.82E+00	CPPE10	**2.63E-05**	**4.90E-04**	**4.41E-04**	CPPE10	**1.88E+00**	5.46E+00	1.37E+00
CPPE11	**2.09E-02**	8.63E-01	1.70E+00	CPPE11	7.62E-05	3.92E-01	2.77E+00	CPPE11	**2.05E+00**	5.68E+00	1.46E+00
CPPE12	5.03E-02	1.11E+00	1.20E+00	CPPE12	**6.32E-05**	**8.56E-04**	**2.47E-03**	CPPE12	3.06E+00	5.54E+00	1.29E+00

f_{10}	Final	Mean	Std	f_{11}	Final	Mean	Std	f_{12}	Final	Mean	Std
PPE	1.02E+00	3.79E+00	3.15E+00	PPE	2.86E-04	8.57E-01	9.29E-01	PPE	1.00E+00	6.27E+00	3.20E+00
CPPE1	**3.41E-01**	**3.63E+00**	**2.19E+00**	CPPE1	**1.83E-04**	**6.00E-01**	**7.10E-01**	CPPE1	**2.07E-03**	**4.97E+00**	**2.77E+00**
CPPE2	**9.34E-01**	**2.81E+00**	**1.62E+00**	CPPE2	2.72E-03	**5.97E-01**	**6.04E-01**	CPPE2	1.99E+00	**5.52E+00**	**2.73E+00**
CPPE3	**9.34E-01**	2.37E+01	9.73E+00	CPPE3	2.72E-03	3.97E+00	2.47E+00	CPPE3	1.99E+00	1.49E+01	7.33E+00
CPPE4	1.13E+00	4.14E+00	3.52E+00	CPPE4	5.08E-04	**7.68E-01**	9.91E-01	CPPE4	**1.89E-03**	**5.28E+00**	**2.93E+00**
CPPE5	**8.46E-01**	**3.52E+00**	**2.46E+00**	CPPE5	**1.36E-04**	**6.13E-01**	**6.64E-01**	CPPE5	1.99E+00	**6.15E+00**	3.38E+00
CPPE6	1.03E+00	**3.30E+00**	**2.15E+00**	CPPE6	**2.08E-04**	**8.17E-01**	9.67E-01	CPPE6	1.99E+00	**5.66E+00**	**2.49E+00**
CPPE7	**8.74E-01**	**3.62E+00**	**2.08E+00**	CPPE7	**1.50E-04**	**5.80E-01**	**6.44E-01**	CPPE7	**9.95E-01**	**5.00E+00**	**2.80E+00**
CPPE8	1.41E+00	6.76E+00	3.81E+00	CPPE8	**9.87E-05**	1.13E+00	1.19E+00	CPPE8	**8.62E-03**	8.82E+00	5.06E+00
CPPE9	1.15E+00	**3.33E+00**	**1.66E+00**	CPPE9	3.76E-03	9.77E-01	**7.03E-01**	CPPE9	**9.96E-01**	7.97E+00	4.15E+00
CPPE10	1.11E+00	8.50E+00	5.68E+00	CPPE10	7.28E-04	1.25E+00	1.54E+00	CPPE10	**9.95E-01**	8.88E+00	4.92E+00
CPPE11	1.11E+00	4.84E+00	3.37E+00	CPPE11	1.06E-03	**6.36E-01**	**9.28E-01**	CPPE11	**9.96E-01**	**5.76E+00**	**3.10E+00**
CPPE12	1.04E+00	5.23E+00	**2.87E+00**	CPPE12	7.14E-04	9.17E-01	1.03E+00	CPPE12	**9.96E-01**	7.45E+00	3.61E+00

Table 5. *Cont.*

f_{13}	Final	Mean	Std	f_{14}	Final	Mean	Std	f_{15}	Final	Mean	Std
PPE	1.59E+00	8.17E+00	4.15E+00	PPE	3.60E-06	5.78E-02	1.21E-01	PPE	1.26E-05	1.17E+00	5.25E+00
CPPE1	**1.00E+00**	**6.89E+00**	**3.39E+00**	CPPE1	**1.09E-07**	**4.68E-02**	**1.09E-01**	CPPE1	**3.14E-06**	3.61E+00	1.73E+01
CPPE2	**5.17E-04**	**7.30E+00**	**3.59E+00**	CPPE2	**1.82E-06**	**5.34E-02**	1.31E-01	CPPE2	**7.14E-06**	**2.07E-01**	**2.32E-01**
CPPE3	**5.17E-04**	1.42E+01	8.33E+00	CPPE3	**1.82E-06**	7.94E-01	3.30E+00	CPPE3	**7.14E-06**	8.84E+00	2.87E+01
CPPE4	**1.39E+00**	**6.76E+00**	**3.73E+00**	CPPE4	**4.32E-07**	**5.09E-02**	**1.15E-01**	CPPE4	1.68E-05	1.78E+00	**4.60E+00**
CPPE5	**9.95E-01**	**8.12E+00**	**3.04E+00**	CPPE5	**2.99E-06**	6.56E-02	1.24E-01	CPPE5	**8.55E-07**	**8.92E-01**	**3.31E+00**
CPPE6	1.59E+00	8.20E+00	**3.17E+00**	CPPE6	**3.09E-08**	**5.22E-02**	**1.16E-01**	CPPE6	**5.26E-07**	1.19E+00	**3.98E+00**
CPPE7	1.59E+00	8.22E+00	**2.96E+00**	CPPE7	**2.78E-06**	**4.52E-02**	**1.09E-01**	CPPE7	**6.87E-07**	**5.42E-01**	**2.35E+00**
CPPE8	**1.39E+00**	8.63E+00	**3.80E+00**	CPPE8	**2.63E-06**	4.24E-01	2.36E+00	CPPE8	**1.80E-06**	4.97E+00	2.36E+01
CPPE9	2.19E+00	1.09E+01	4.30E+00	CPPE9	5.03E-06	**4.27E-02**	**1.03E-01**	CPPE9	**4.05E-06**	**1.40E-01**	**2.11E-01**
CPPE10	5.03E+00	9.67E+00	4.49E+00	CPPE10	**5.20E-08**	1.05E-01	1.49E-01	CPPE10	1.49E-05	4.95E+00	2.36E+01
CPPE11	**1.39E+00**	**8.00E+00**	4.33E+00	CPPE11	**2.82E-06**	7.64E-02	1.49E-01	CPPE11	**3.53E-06**	2.22E+00	5.46E+00
CPPE12	2.03E+00	**7.68E+00**	**3.37E+00**	CPPE12	**2.54E-08**	1.05E-01	1.43E-01	CPPE12	**3.05E-06**	3.43E+00	1.72E+01

f_{16}	Final	Mean	Std	f_{17}	Final	Mean	Std	f_{18}	Final	Mean	Std
PPE	5.62E-01	9.91E-01	2.55E-01	PPE	8.77E-01	6.14E+00	1.80E+00	PPE	1.82E+00	9.10E+00	3.13E+00
CPPE1	**4.44E-01**	**9.44E-01**	3.00E-01	CPPE1	**3.89E-01**	**5.59E+00**	2.06E+00	CPPE1	3.71E+00	**8.59E+00**	**2.28E+00**
CPPE2	**3.49E-01**	**9.59E-01**	**2.29E-01**	CPPE2	**4.94E-01**	6.32E+00	**1.67E+00**	CPPE2	**1.80E+00**	**8.87E+00**	**2.63E+00**
CPPE3	**3.49E-01**	**8.84E-01**	3.25E-01	CPPE3	**4.94E-01**	8.97E+00	1.87E+00	CPPE3	**1.80E+00**	1.48E+01	5.10E+00
CPPE4	**4.34E-01**	**9.02E-01**	2.77E-01	CPPE4	**1.49E-01**	**5.88E+00**	2.27E+00	CPPE4	2.58E+00	**8.54E+00**	**3.02E+00**
CPPE5	**5.00E-01**	9.96E-01	2.61E-01	CPPE5	1.08E+00	6.35E+00	**1.73E+00**	CPPE5	5.60E+00	**8.81E+00**	**1.80E+00**
CPPE6	**3.73E-01**	**9.02E-01**	2.92E-01	CPPE6	**6.76E-01**	6.16E+00	1.84E+00	CPPE6	1.87E+00	9.10E+00	**2.76E+00**
CPPE7	5.74E-01	**9.83E-01**	**2.51E-01**	CPPE7	**7.27E-01**	6.30E+00	1.81E+00	CPPE7	4.49E+00	1.02E+01	**2.76E+00**
CPPE8	**3.32E-01**	**9.01E-01**	2.89E-01	CPPE8	1.51E+00	7.00E+00	1.85E+00	CPPE8	3.38E+00	1.06E+01	3.97E+00
CPPE9	**2.60E-01**	**8.42E-01**	2.86E-01	CPPE9	5.31E+00	6.95E+00	**1.11E+00**	CPPE9	6.19E+00	1.07E+01	**3.00E+00**
CPPE10	**3.80E-01**	**9.45E-01**	**2.51E-01**	CPPE10	1.78E+00	7.14E+00	**1.51E+00**	CPPE10	5.39E+00	1.01E+01	**2.65E+00**
CPPE11	**3.74E-01**	**9.63E-01**	2.85E-01	CPPE11	**4.72E-01**	6.31E+00	2.18E+00	CPPE11	4.00E+00	9.81E+00	**2.77E+00**
CPPE12	**4.37E-01**	**8.80E-01**	2.57E-01	CPPE12	**3.55E-01**	6.42E+00	1.85E+00	CPPE12	5.95E+00	1.06E+01	3.22E+00

f_{19}	Final	Mean	Std	f_{20}	Final	Mean	Std	f_{21}	Final	Mean	Std
PPE	7.65E-01	2.67E+00	1.11E+00	PPE	2.27E+00	3.31E+00	3.97E-01	PPE	3.84E-04	7.86E-03	6.25E-03
CPPE1	1.19E+00	**2.20E+00**	**7.19E-01**	CPPE1	2.54E+00	3.33E+00	**3.59E-01**	CPPE1	**1.81E-04**	**6.24E-03**	**5.49E-03**
CPPE2	9.94E-01	**2.52E+00**	**8.09E-01**	CPPE2	**1.99E+00**	3.34E+00	4.42E-01	CPPE2	4.51E-04	2.01E+00	1.41E+01
CPPE3	9.94E-01	4.60E+00	2.51E+00	CPPE3	**1.99E+00**	3.78E+00	**1.86E-01**	CPPE3	4.51E-04	8.75E-03	8.53E-03
CPPE4	8.55E-01	**2.17E+00**	**8.48E-01**	CPPE4	**2.18E+00**	3.36E+00	4.21E-01	CPPE4	9.22E-04	2.01E+00	1.41E+01
CPPE5	8.06E-01	2.86E+00	**1.01E+00**	CPPE5	**2.20E+00**	3.37E+00	4.36E-01	CPPE5	**1.76E-04**	**6.36E-03**	**4.91E-03**
CPPE6	**7.53E-01**	**2.64E+00**	**9.52E-01**	CPPE6	2.50E+00	3.31E+00	**3.31E-01**	CPPE6	1.09E-03	**6.53E-03**	**5.99E-03**
CPPE7	1.12E+00	2.89E+00	1.27E+00	CPPE7	2.50E+00	**3.30E+00**	4.11E-01	CPPE7	4.56E-04	4.01E+00	1.98E+01
CPPE8	**5.88E-01**	2.74E+00	1.32E+00	CPPE8	2.35E+00	3.46E+00	**3.49E-01**	CPPE8	4.26E-04	**6.81E-03**	**4.90E-03**
CPPE9	1.78E+00	3.43E+00	**9.62E-01**	CPPE9	**2.02E+00**	**3.28E+00**	5.32E-01	CPPE9	4.45E-04	**6.16E-03**	**4.22E-03**
CPPE10	**7.16E-01**	3.03E+00	1.43E+00	CPPE10	3.07E+00	3.69E+00	**2.56E-01**	CPPE10	**2.10E-04**	**6.71E-03**	6.54E-03
CPPE11	**7.23E-01**	**2.23E+00**	**8.45E-01**	CPPE11	**1.54E+00**	**3.30E+00**	5.19E-01	CPPE11	**2.42E-04**	4.01E+00	1.98E+01
CPPE12	**5.20E-01**	3.35E+00	1.45E+00	CPPE12	2.58E+00	3.53E+00	**2.90E-01**	CPPE12	1.03E-03	**7.21E-03**	**5.00E-03**

f_{22}	Final	Mean	Std	f_{23}	Final	Mean	Std	f_{24}	Final	Mean	Std
PPE	9.26E-05	2.51E+00	1.24E+01	PPE	3.03E-04	7.19E-03	3.19E-02	PPE	2.79E-05	5.12E-01	2.72E+00
CPPE1	**6.80E-05**	**9.60E-04**	**7.66E-04**	CPPE1	**7.24E-05**	2.00E+00	1.41E+01	CPPE1	**6.98E-06**	1.88E+00	5.70E+00
CPPE2	1.14E-04	2.51E+00	1.24E+01	CPPE2	**9.60E-05**	6.43E-01	3.17E+00	CPPE2	**3.42E-06**	8.78E-01	3.75E+00
CPPE3	1.14E-04	9.59E+00	2.43E+01	CPPE3	**9.60E-05**	3.16E+01	4.78E+01	CPPE3	**3.42E-06**	2.22E+00	8.03E+00
CPPE4	**5.06E-05**	2.51E+00	1.24E+01	CPPE4	**1.19E-04**	6.50E-01	3.19E+00	CPPE4	**3.56E-06**	**5.02E-01**	**2.71E+00**
CPPE5	**6.93E-05**	**1.11E-03**	**8.06E-04**	CPPE5	**3.29E-05**	3.58E+00	1.78E+01	CPPE5	**1.21E-05**	9.46E-01	3.76E+00
CPPE6	**5.84E-05**	**1.21E-03**	**1.06E-03**	CPPE6	**1.72E-04**	1.60E+00	1.11E+01	CPPE6	**6.13E-06**	**5.02E-01**	**2.71E+00**
CPPE7	1.25E-04	**1.25E+00**	**8.86E+00**	CPPE7	**1.82E-04**	**2.33E-03**	**2.54E-03**	CPPE7	**7.00E-06**	8.39E-01	2.94E+00
CPPE8	**8.38E-05**	**1.25E+00**	**8.86E+00**	CPPE8	**9.04E-05**	4.33E+00	1.99E+01	CPPE8	**2.45E-05**	**1.89E-01**	**7.55E-01**
CPPE9	9.54E-05	**1.08E-03**	**8.44E-04**	CPPE9	**2.21E-04**	1.58E+00	1.11E+01	CPPE9	**6.21E-06**	8.15E-01	3.74E+00
CPPE10	**4.11E-05**	**1.20E-03**	**9.59E-04**	CPPE10	**2.19E-04**	5.11E+00	2.23E+01	CPPE10	**1.62E-05**	**4.40E-01**	**2.69E+00**
CPPE11	**3.67E-05**	**1.07E-03**	**9.33E-04**	CPPE11	**1.38E-04**	1.00E+01	3.03E+01	CPPE11	**9.83E-06**	5.71E-01	2.74E+00
CPPE12	1.38E-04	2.86E+00	1.26E+01	CPPE12	**9.71E-05**	3.68E+00	1.83E+01	CPPE12	**1.56E-05**	7.52E-01	3.72E+00

Table 5. *Cont.*

f_{25}	Final	Mean	Std	f_{26}	Final	Mean	Std	f_{27}	Final	Mean	Std
PPE	9.41E-05	9.72E-04	7.71E-04	PPE	2.07E-08	1.40E-01	2.04E-01	PPE	2.83E-03	3.95E+01	4.88E+01
CPPE1	**3.44E-05**	**8.99E-04**	**6.42E-04**	CPPE1	**1.81E-08**	2.26E-01	2.59E-01	CPPE1	1.82E-02	5.73E+01	4.91E+01
CPPE2	**7.25E-05**	**8.78E-04**	**6.66E-04**	CPPE2	8.16E-08	1.57E-01	2.38E-01	CPPE2	**6.27E-05**	**3.91E+01**	**4.86E+01**
CPPE3	**7.25E-05**	1.32E+01	3.33E+01	CPPE3	8.16E-08	4.81E-01	1.29E+00	CPPE3	**6.27E-05**	7.94E+01	**4.05E+01**
CPPE4	**3.03E-05**	2.09E+00	1.41E+01	CPPE4	2.51E-07	2.07E-01	2.60E-01	CPPE4	3.04E-03	4.89E+01	4.96E+01
CPPE5	**5.75E-05**	**8.96E-04**	7.81E-04	CPPE5	**1.58E-08**	1.66E-01	2.40E-01	CPPE5	3.27E-01	**3.56E+01**	**4.68E+01**
CPPE6	**7.88E-05**	**7.72E-04**	**6.25E-04**	CPPE6	**1.51E-08**	1.72E-01	2.23E-01	CPPE6	4.53E-03	**3.16E+01**	**4.58E+01**
CPPE7	**2.35E-05**	2.00E+00	1.41E+01	CPPE7	7.94E-08	**1.34E-01**	**1.83E-01**	CPPE7	**9.17E-04**	4.78E+01	4.93E+01
CPPE8	**8.98E-06**	**7.29E-04**	**6.83E-04**	CPPE8	**8.04E-09**	**1.19E-01**	**1.83E-01**	CPPE8	**1.30E-04**	5.54E+01	4.97E+01
CPPE9	**4.34E-05**	**6.38E-04**	**5.22E-04**	CPPE9	2.59E-08	**6.16E-02**	**1.52E-01**	CPPE9	9.76E-03	**2.15E+00**	**2.28E+00**
CPPE10	1.02E-04	**7.46E-04**	**6.38E-04**	CPPE10	**1.14E-08**	7.49E-01	4.45E+00	CPPE10	1.59E-02	5.37E+01	4.88E+01
CPPE11	**2.85E-05**	**8.42E-04**	**7.63E-04**	CPPE11	2.36E-08	2.10E-01	2.45E-01	CPPE11	**2.04E-03**	6.48E+01	**4.74E+01**
CPPE12	**5.87E-05**	4.00E+00	1.98E+01	CPPE12	7.30E-08	2.12E-01	6.17E-01	CPPE12	**6.20E-04**	5.47E+01	4.91E+01
f_{28}	Final	Mean	Std								
PPE	4.48E-04	4.42E-03	3.09E-03								
CPPE1	**4.15E-04**	**3.64E-03**	3.28E-03								
CPPE2	**1.16E-04**	**3.11E-03**	**2.50E-03**								
CPPE3	**1.16E-04**	2.00E+00	1.41E+01								
CPPE4	**2.94E-04**	**3.90E-03**	3.60E-03								
CPPE5	**3.60E-04**	**3.43E-03**	**2.30E-03**								
CPPE6	4.55E-04	**3.92E-03**	**2.85E-03**								
CPPE7	8.54E-04	**3.91E-03**	3.26E-03								
CPPE8	**3.09E-04**	**3.80E-03**	3.65E-03								
CPPE9	**7.55E-05**	**3.56E-03**	**2.56E-03**								
CPPE10	**2.70E-04**	**4.02E-03**	4.28E-03								
CPPE11	**2.77E-04**	**3.76E-03**	**3.03E-03**								
CPPE12	**1.23E-04**	**3.12E-03**	**2.27E-03**								

Table 6. The number of times CPPE is better than PPE.

	CPPE1	**CPPE2**	**CPPE3**	**CPPE4**	**CPPE5**	**CPPE6**	**CPPE7**	**CPPE8**	**CPPE9**	**CPPE10**	**CPPE11**	**CPPE12**
Final	22	19	19	16	21	17	15	20	14	15	20	15
Mean	18	16	3	14	16	18	15	8	17	9	11	5
Std	19	20	5	13	17	21	17	9	22	13	10	10

Table 7. The benchmark function of CPPE is better than PPE.

	Final	**Mean**	**Std**
CPPE1	$f_{1-3,5-6,8-17,21-26,28}$	$f_{1,3,5,7-8,10-14,16-19,21-22,25,28}$	$f_{1,3-14,18-22,25}$
CPPE2	$f_{1,5-10,13-18,20,23-25,27-28}$	$f_{1,3,6,8,10-16,18-19,25,27-28}$	$f_{1,3-4,6,8-19,22,25,27-28}$
CPPE3	f_1, f_{5-10}, f_{13-18}, f_{20}, f_{23-25}, f_{27-28}	$f_{3-4,16}$	f_{3-4}, f_6, f_{20}, f_{27}
CPPE4	$f_{1-2,6-8,12-14,16-17,20,22-25,28}$,	$f_{1,6,8,11-14,16-19,22,24,28}$	$f_{1,3-4,6,8-9,12-15,18-19,24}$
CPPE5	$f_{1-4,6-8,10-11,13-16,20-26,28}$	$f_{1,3-4,6,8,10-13,15,18,21-22,25,27-28}$	$f_{1,3-4,6,8-11,13,15,17-19,21-22,27-28}$
CPPE6	$f_{1,3,5,7-9,11,14-17,19,22-26}$	$f_{1,3,6-8,10-12,14,16,19-22,24-25,27-28}$	$f_{1,3,5-10,12-15,18-22,24-25,27-28}$
CPPE7	$f_{1-2,5-7,10-12,14-15,17,23-25,27}$	$f_{3,6-7,9-12,14-16,20,22-23,26,28}$	$f_{1,3-6,9-16,18,22-23,26}$
CPPE8	$f_{1-3,7-9,11-16,19,22-28}$	$f_{9,16,21-22,24-26,28}$	$f_{1,3,13,20-22,24-26}$
CPPE9	$f_{1-4,7-8,12,15-16,20,23-25,28}$	$f_{2-4,6-8,10,14-16,20-22,25-28}$	$f_{1-11,14-15,17-19,21-22,25-28}$
CPPE10	$f_{1-3,8-9,12,14,16,19,21-24,26,28}$	$f_{1,3,8,16,21-22,24-25,28}$	$f_{1,3-4,6,8,16-18,20,22,24-25,27}$
CPPE11	$f_{1,5-7,9,12-17,19-25,27-28}$	$f_{1,6,11-13,16,19-20,22,25,28}$	$f_{1,6,11-12,18-19,22,25,27-28}$
CPPE12	$f_{1,3-4,8,12,14-17,19,23-25,27-28}$	$f_{8,13,16,21,28}$	$f_{1,3-4,7-8,10,13,20-21,28}$

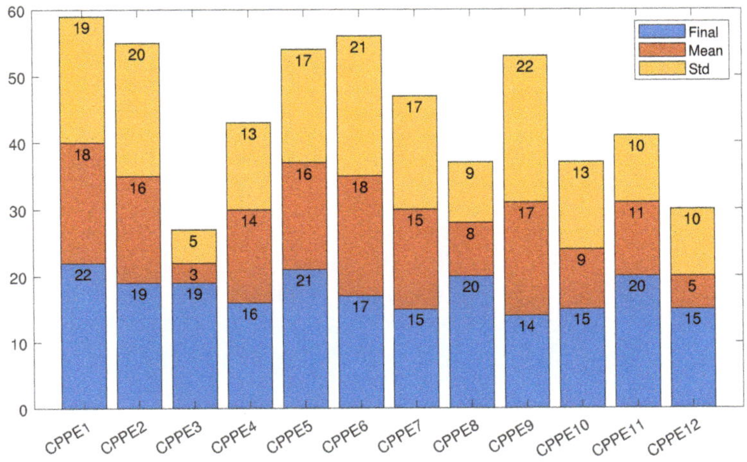

Figure 3. Number of times different CPPEs were superior to PPE.

Tables 5–7, and Figure 3 show that 12 CPPEs performed well in finding the final optimal value. In terms of average optimal value, CPPE3, CPPE8, CPPE10 and CPPE12 did not perform well, while CPPE1, CPPE6 and CPPE9 performed well. In terms of standard deviation, CPPE3 and CPPE8 performed slightly worse, while CPPE1, CPPE2, CPPE6 and CPPE9 performed very well. To sum up, the performances of CPPE3, CPPE8, CPPE10 and CPPE12 were not significantly better than that of PPE, that is, CPPE with Singer map, Chebyshev map, Cubic map and ICMIC map did not significantly improve the performance of the algorithm. However, CPPE1, CPPE2, CPPE4, CPPE5, CPPE6, CPPE7, CPPE9 and CPPE11 were obviously superior to PPE. That is, CPPE with the Logistic, Piecewise, Sine, Gauss, Tent, Bernoulli, Circle, and Sinusoidal maps significantly improved the algorithm's performance.

In addition to the initial evaluation, we also tallied the occurrences where the PPE algorithm and CPPE1 to CPPE12 attained optimal results on three metrics out of 28 benchmark functions. The statistical results are shown in Figure 4. In this chart, the horizontal axis represents 13 different algorithms, and the vertical axis represents the number of times that algorithm achieved the best results compared to the other algorithms across 3 metrics among 28 functions. The results show that CPPE9 achieved the best results 25 times, which was remarkable compared to other algorithms. CPPE9 is the CPPE algorithm with the Circle map.

Furthermore, to accurately calculate the improved percentage of CPPE compared to PPE, statistical analysis and calculations were performed on the experimental data. During the statistical process, we discovered that benchmark functions f_4, f_{21}, and f_{23} had outliers. As a result, we only calculated the results for the remaining 25 benchmark functions. Our approach was as follows: (1) First, the value of each CPPE was subtracted from the value of PPE on each indicator for each benchmark function, and, then, the resulting value was divided by the value of PPE and, finally, converted into a percentage. This provided the improved percentage of each CPPE over the PPE for each indicator of each benchmark function. For example, benchmark functions f_1, $f_1(PPE\_Final)$ and $f_1(CPPE1\_Final)$ indicate the value of PPE and CPPE1 in the Final indicator, respectively. Thus, the improved percentage of CPPE1 in the Final indicator compared with PPE is obtained by the following Equation (9).

$$\frac{f_1(PPE\_Final) - f_1(CPPE1\_Final)}{f_1(PPE\_Final)} \times 100\% \tag{9}$$

(2) After the obtained values were averaged, the average percentages of 12 CPPE in three indicators compared with PPE were obtained. The results are shown in Table 8. The first column indicates different CPPE algorithms, and the last three columns indicate the improved percentage of the CPPE algorithm compared with the PPE algorithm in the three indicators. In Table 8, it can be observed that CPPE1 (CPPE with Logistic map), CPPE6 (CPPE with Tent map), and CPPE8 (CPPE with Chebyshev map) showed improvements over PPE on the Final indicator. CPPE2 (CPPE with Piecewise map), CPPE6 (CPPE with Tent map), and CPPE9 (CPPE with Circle map) exhibited improvements over PPE on the Mean indicator. CPPE2 (CPPE with Piecewise map), CPPE5 (CPPE with Gauss map), CPPE6 (CPPE with Tent map), and CPPE9 (CPPE with Circle map) showed improvements over PPE on the Standard indicator. Therefore, the CPPE algorithm with Tent map performed the best compared to the PPE algorithm, with an increase of 8.9647%, 10.4633%, and 14.6716% in Final, Mean, and Standard indicators, respectively.

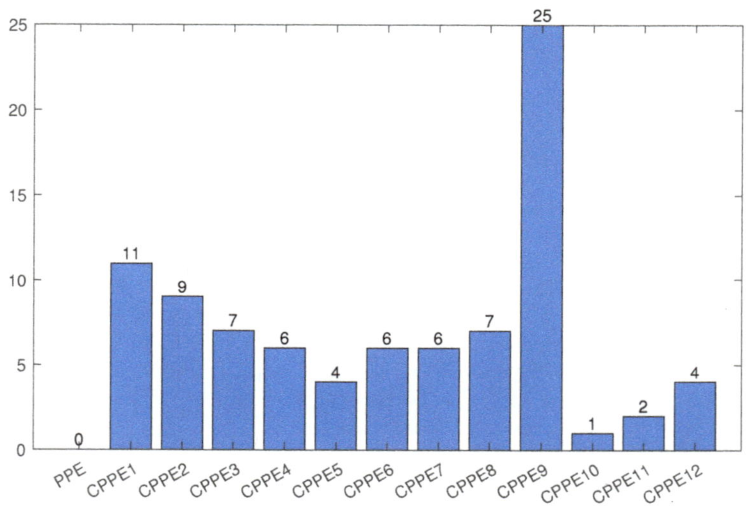

Figure 4. Optimal number of times for PPE and CPPEs on performance.

Table 8. The percentage of improved performance of CPPE compared to PPE.

	Final	**Mean**	**Std**
CPPE1	12.2222%	−16.1146%	−3.8127%
CPPE2	−28.3925%	6.0912%	10.2575%
CPPE3	−28.3925%	−61,464.2086%	−194,171.1520%
CPPE4	−33.2308%	−8601.8259%	−73,153.7043%
CPPE5	−447.3261%	−2.7712%	3.2219%
CPPE6	8.9647%	10.4633%	14.6716%
CPPE7	−6.9034%	−9211.8529%	−74,512.3505%
CPPE8	7.5525%	−1212.8028%	−1469.2995%
CPPE9	−329.5657%	16.9592%	26.3463%
CPPE10	−46.3178%	−56.9641%	−105.2342%
CPPE11	−0.1405%	−984.1307%	−1354.9638%
CPPE12	−35.6815%	−16,492.6669%	−102,746.3320%

4.3. Convergence Comparison between PPE and CPPEs

An experiment was designed to compare the convergence of the different algorithms. All parameters are shown in Table 9, where the number of population was set to 100, the number of iterations was set to 50, and the number of runs was set to 50 times.

Table 9. Parameters setting for convergence experiments.

Parameters	Values
Population_Number	100
Max_Gen	50
Run_Nums	50

In this experiment, an evaluation criterion was designed to compare the convergence of different algorithms, which we called the average change rate of fitness value. Our approach was as follows: (1) First, we ran PPE and 12 CPPE algorithms on each benchmark function once. To subtract the fitness values between the 50th generation and the initial generation. Finally, the result was divided by 50 to obtain the change rate of each generation. (2) We repeated this process 50 times and then calculated the average. The results yielded the average change rate of fitness value for the 28 benchmark functions. Table 10 shows the results between PPE and 12 CPPE algorithms .

Table 10. The experimental results of PPE and CPPE regarding iteration for 50 times on 28 benchmark functions.

	f_1	f_2	f_3	f_4	f_5	f_6	f_7	f_8	f_9	f_{10}	f_{11}
PPE	2.87E+02	3.94E+04	6.97E+04	2.16E+04	4.11E+01	2.86E+00	3.76E+00	3.51E-01	1.52E-01	3.79E+01	1.38E+00
CPPE1	4.43E+02	7.76E+04	1.13E+05	4.98E+04	6.85E+01	3.72E+00	3.29E+00	3.64E-01	1.48E-01	4.83E+01	1.74E+00
CPPE2	2.81E+02	1.92E+04	8.76E+04	2.68E+04	4.40E+01	2.70E+00	5.91E+00	3.51E-01	1.43E-01	3.30E+01	1.33E+00
CPPE3	4.73E+02	4.22E+04	1.85E+06	1.33E+05	7.26E+01	4.75E+00	3.02E+02	3.18E-01	1.39E-01	4.49E+01	1.94E+00
CPPE4	4.12E+02	2.77E+04	1.42E+05	1.90E+04	6.89E+01	3.37E+00	4.01E+00	3.81E-01	1.44E-01	4.86E+01	1.65E+00
CPPE5	2.91E+02	2.62E+04	5.02E+04	3.42E+04	4.34E+01	2.78E+00	3.94E+00	3.67E-01	1.43E-01	3.53E+01	1.35E+00
CPPE6	2.95E+02	2.48E+04	1.16E+05	2.69E+04	3.35E+01	2.80E+00	3.03E+00	3.59E-01	1.55E-01	3.42E+01	1.38E+00
CPPE7	2.79E+02	2.89E+04	4.08E+04	1.54E+04	3.52E+01	2.78E+00	3.07E+00	3.50E-01	1.45E-01	3.37E+01	1.34E+00
CPPE8	3.45E+02	6.47E+04	2.22E+05	4.06E+04	5.84E+01	4.01E+00	1.02E+01	3.68E-01	1.50E-01	4.11E+01	1.45E+00
CPPE9	2.08E+02	8.04E+03	2.44E+04	7.86E+03	7.14E+01	2.39E+00	1.26E+02	2.37E-01	1.25E-01	2.18E+01	1.23E+00
CPPE10	3.77E+02	3.05E+04	2.66E+05	2.91E+04	5.85E+01	3.62E+00	1.31E+01	3.65E-01	1.52E-01	4.12E+01	1.59E+00
CPPE11	3.90E+02	3.37E+04	1.34E+05	1.16E+04	5.04E+01	4.34E+00	3.05E+00	3.87E-01	1.45E-01	5.11E+01	1.63E+00
CPPE12	3.28E+02	4.05E+04	1.12E+05	2.69E+04	4.48E+01	2.59E+00	1.47E+01	3.75E-01	1.49E-01	4.00E+01	1.46E+00

	f_{12}	f_{13}	f_{14}	f_{15}	f_{16}	f_{17}	f_{18}	f_{19}	f_{20}	f_{21}	f_{22}
PPE	1.22E+00	1.29E+00	3.65E+00	3.79E+00	5.12E-02	1.84E+00	1.76E+00	2.40E+03	3.00E-02	3.60E+00	4.82E+00
CPPE1	1.80E+00	1.55E+00	4.54E+00	4.39E+00	4.66E-02	2.76E+00	2.66E+00	8.82E+03	2.80E-02	4.30E+00	5.34E+00
CPPE2	1.35E+00	1.28E+00	3.79E+00	3.97E+00	5.19E-02	1.71E+00	1.77E+00	2.66E+03	2.92E-02	3.37E+00	4.15E+00
CPPE3	2.04E+00	1.89E+00	4.37E+00	4.31E+00	5.20E-02	3.11E+00	2.63E+00	4.30E+04	2.00E-02	4.22E+00	5.17E+00
CPPE4	1.61E+00	1.66E+00	5.19E+00	3.91E+00	5.54E-02	2.86E+00	2.68E+00	8.39E+03	2.83E-02	4.06E+00	5.96E+00
CPPE5	1.26E+00	1.20E+00	4.03E+00	3.62E+00	5.15E-02	1.78E+00	1.81E+00	2.84E+03	3.09E-02	3.37E+00	4.87E+00
CPPE6	1.29E+00	1.26E+00	3.86E+00	3.73E+00	5.72E-02	1.78E+00	1.73E+00	2.61E+03	3.06E-02	3.54E+00	4.44E+00
CPPE7	1.37E+00	1.28E+00	3.96E+00	3.94E+00	4.86E-02	1.81E+00	1.70E+00	2.87E+03	2.89E-02	3.41E+00	5.37E+00
CPPE8	1.67E+00	1.46E+00	4.05E+00	4.54E+00	4.96E-02	2.31E+00	2.20E+00	1.38E+04	2.44E-02	3.80E+00	5.34E+00
CPPE9	9.29E-01	9.12E-01	2.81E+00	2.21E+00	5.61E-02	9.47E-01	8.61E-01	3.81E+02	2.38E-02	1.77E+00	3.30E+00
CPPE10	1.79E+00	1.72E+00	3.98E+00	4.48E+00	5.33E-02	2.46E+00	2.27E+00	1.62E+04	2.48E-02	3.95E+00	4.86E+00
CPPE11	1.69E+00	1.61E+00	5.19E+00	3.80E+00	5.07E-02	2.63E+00	2.73E+00	6.41E+03	2.65E-02	4.10E+00	6.83E+00

Table 10. *Cont.*

	f_{12}	f_{13}	f_{14}	f_{15}	f_{16}	f_{17}	f_{18}	f_{19}	f_{20}	f_{21}	f_{22}
CPPE12	1.48E+00	1.55E+00	4.19E+00	4.61E+00	4.78E-02	1.98E+00	2.19E+00	7.88E+03	2.63E-02	3.79E+00	5.18E+00
	f_{23}	f_{24}	f_{25}	f_{26}	f_{27}	f_{28}					
PPE	5.75E+00	1.71E+00	2.00E+00	1.77E+00	3.69E+00	2.23E+00					
CPPE1	6.35E+00	1.89E+00	2.20E+00	1.72E+00	3.72E+00	2.80E+00					
CPPE2	5.53E+00	1.59E+00	2.07E+00	1.53E+00	3.31E+00	2.23E+00					
CPPE3	5.99E+00	1.92E+00	1.94E+00	2.01E+00	2.73E+00	2.59E+00					
CPPE4	6.03E+00	1.91E+00	2.09E+00	1.87E+00	4.20E+00	2.73E+00					
CPPE5	5.16E+00	1.67E+00	2.07E+00	1.35E+00	4.28E+00	2.41E+00					
CPPE6	6.45E+00	1.54E+00	2.18E+00	1.42E+00	3.31E+00	2.24E+00					
CPPE7	5.99E+00	1.63E+00	2.18E+00	1.60E+00	3.60E+00	2.46E+00					
CPPE8	6.27E+00	1.81E+00	2.04E+00	1.71E+00	2.75E+00	2.62E+00					
CPPE9	3.90E+00	1.03E+00	1.45E+00	7.03E-01	3.62E+00	1.53E+00					
CPPE10	5.58E+00	1.87E+00	2.11E+00	1.72E+00	2.90E+00	2.60E+00					
CPPE11	7.08E+00	1.93E+00	2.28E+00	1.75E+00	3.25E+00	2.64E+00					
CPPE12	6.12E+00	1.70E+00	2.08E+00	1.41E+00	3.02E+00	2.47E+00					

Furthermore, to accurately calculate the improved percentage of CPPE compared to PPE, statistical analysis and calculations were performed on the experimental data. The same methods mentioned in Section 4.2 were used and the results are shown in Table 11. The first column indicates different CPPE algorithms and the last column indicates the improved percentages in the convergence of the CPPE algorithm compared with the PPE algorithm. In Table 11, it can be observed that CPPE1 (CPPE with Logistic map), CPPE3 (CPPE with Singer map), CPPE4 (CPPE with Sine map), CPPE6 (CPPE with Tent map), CPPE8 (CPPE with Chebyshev map), CPPE10 (CPPE with Cubic map), CPPE11 (CPPE with Sinusoidal map), and CPPE12 (CPPE with ICMIC map) increased the convergence. In addition, CPPE3 (CPPE with Singer map) had a significant effect, of about 65.1776%.

Table 11. The percentage of improved convergence of CPPE compared to PPE.

	The Average Change Rate of Fitness Value
CPPE1	3.1636%
CPPE2	−0.0739%
CPPE3	65.1776%
CPPE4	2.3946%
CPPE5	−1.1542%
CPPE6	1.1324%
CPPE7	−1.3921%
CPPE8	6.7471%
CPPE9	−2.8102%
CPPE10	7.2003%
CPPE11	2.2421%
CPPE12	1.7341%

4.4. Discussions

In Section 4.2, the performance of different CPPE algorithms and that of the PPE algorithm are compared. We performed three different analyses of the experimental data. Firstly, we counted the number of times that CPPE was better than PPE on three indicators in 28 benchmark functions. The statistical results showed that CPP1, CPPE2, CPPE4, CPPE5, CPPE6, CPPE7, CPPE9, and CPPE11 algorithms outperformed the PPE algorithm. Secondly, we counted the optimal times of all CPPEs and PPE on 3 indicators in 28 benchmark functions. The statistical results showed that CPPE9 was the most prominent among the 13 algorithms. Finally, the improved percentages of all CPPEs compared with PPE in the three indicators were counted. The statistical results showed that CPPE6 performed the best, with an increase of 8.9647%, 10.4633%, and 14.6716% compared with PPE in the three indicators of Final, Mean, and Standard, respectively. Based on the above analysis, we believe that, in terms of performance, CPPE6 is the best performing algorithm among all CPPEs, so the Tent map is the best choice to improve the performance of CPPE algorithms.

In Section 4.3, the convergence of different CPPE algorithms and PPE algorithm were compared. The experimental results showed that, compared with PPE, CPPE1, CPPE3, CPPE4, CPPE6, CPPE8, CPPE10, CPPE11, and CPPE12 increased the percentages of the average change rate of the fitness value. Among them, the improvement offered by CPPE3 was the most obvious, with an increase of 65.1776%. Based on the above analysis, we believe that, in terms of convergence, CPPE3 is the best performing algorithm among all CPPEs, so the Singer map is the best choice to improve the convergence of CPPE algorithms.

Though CPPE6 (CPPE with Tent map) had the best performance and CPPE3 had the best convergence, we found CPPE6 to be the best choice among all CPPEs in regard to both performance and convergence. It offered improvements of 8.9647%, 10.4633%, and 14.6716% in the three indicators and 1.1324% in convergence.

4.5. Real-Life Problem: Stock Prediction

We applied our CPPE to stock prediction. Here, Amazon stock and a commonly used prediction model, the LSTM neural network [50], were selected for our experiments. In our experiments, we used CPPE to optimize the three hyperparameters, "hidden_size", "batch_size" and "epochs", of the LSTM neural network to improve the effectiveness of LSTM, where "hidden_size" represents the dimension of hidden layers in LSTM, "batch_size" represents the number of inputs per batch in LSTM, and "epochs" represents the number of training sessions for LSTM. Note that, considering the best choice mentioned in Sections 4.2 and 4.3, we chose the CPPE algorithm with Tent map (CPPE6) to optimize LSTM.

Firstly, data processing was performed on the experimental data selected, which included the highest price, opening price, lowest price, closing price, and trading volume of Amazon's stock every day from 23 October, 2009, to 31 March, 2020. The data was divided into a training set and a test set, with a ratio of 9:1, and standardized.

The parameter settings for CPPE6 and LSTM model are shown in Table 12. In the CPPE6 algorithm, we set the population size to 10, the number of iterations to 10, and all dimensions to 3, because we needed to optimize the three hyperparameters of LSTM. The range of the solution was set to $[1, 300]$. In the LSTM model, the time step was set to 5, which meant using 5 days of data to predict the next day's data. The solver was set to "adam", and the initial learning rate was set to 0.005. After 100 rounds of training, we reduced the learning rate to 0.2 times the initial learning rate. Furthermore, in this experiment, the root mean squared error (RMSE) of the LSTM model was used as the fitness value of the CPPE6 algorithm.

After the experiment, we obtained three optimized hyperparameters: hidden_size = 179, batch_size = 110, and epochs = 181 with RMSE = 0.05762. Then, we input the three solutions into the LSTM model and obtained predicted results, as shown in Figure 5. The horizontal axis represents days sorted by time and the vertical axis represents stock value, where the red curve represents the predicted value, and the blue curve represents the real value. Thus, it can be seen that the predicted curve was relatively consistent with the real curve.

Table 12. Parameter settings for real application experiments.

Parameters	Values
Population_Number	10
Max_Gen	10
Dimension	3
L, U	1, 300
Time_step	5
Solver	"adam"
Learning_rate	0.005

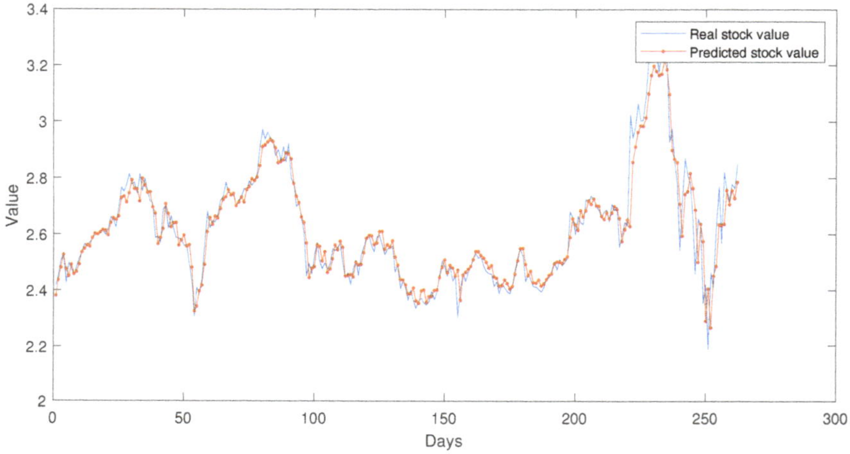

Figure 5. Prediction results on Amazon stock using CPPE6-LSTM.

5. Conclusions

This study proposes a Chaotic-based Phasmatodea Population Evolution (CPPE) algorithm by integrating chaotic mapping into the Phasmatodea Population Evolution (PPE) algorithm. To investigate the impact of various chaotic maps on the algorithm, 12 different chaotic maps were combined with CPPE, resulting in 12 CPPEs. The objective of this study was to determine whether CPPE outperforms PPE in terms of performance and convergence. To validate this claim, 28 benchmark functions were employed in the testing phase. Experimental results demonstrated that CPPE significantly improved both the performance and convergence speed of the algorithm. Among all chaotic maps, the Tent map is considered to be the best choice to improve the performance of the CPPE algorithm. Compared with PPE, CPPE with Tent map improved Final, Mean, and Standard by 8.9647%, 10.4633%, and 14.6716%, respectively. Moreover, the Singer map is considered to be the best choice to improve the convergence speed of the CPPE algorithm, and CPPE with Singer map was 65.1776% higher than PPE. Furthermore, we applied CPPE6 to stock prediction. Overall, this study contributes to the advancement of population-based optimization algorithms and provides insights into the impact of chaotic mapping on algorithmic performance.

Author Contributions: Conceptualization, T.-Y.W.; methodology, H.L.; software, S.-C.C.; validation, T.-Y.W.; investigation, H.L.; writing—original draft preparation, T.-Y.W., H.L. and S.-C.C. All authors have read and agreed to the published version of the manuscript.

Funding: This research received no external funding.

Institutional Review Board Statement: Not applicable.

Informed Consent Statement: Not applicable.

Data Availability Statement: The data are included in the article.

Conflicts of Interest: The authors declare no conflict of interest.

Abbreviations

The following abbreviations are used in this manuscript:

PPE	Phasmatodea Population Evolution
CPPE	Chaotic-based Phasmatodea Population Evolution
GA	Generic Algorithm
DE	Differential Evolution
PSO	Particle Swarm Optimization
WOA	Whale Optimization Algorithm
BOA	Butterfly Optimization Algorithm
GOA	Grasshopper Optimization Algorithm
CMBSA	Bird Swarm Algorithm with Chaotic Mapping
BSA	Bird Swarm Algorithm
SSA	Sparrow Search Algorithm
CLS	Chaotic Local Search
GWO	Gray Wolf Optimization
CHHO	Chaotic Harris Hawks Optimization
HHO	Harris Hawks Optimization
CQFFA	Chaotic Quasi-oppositional Farmland Fertility Algorithm
CSBOA	Chaotic Satin Bowerbird Optimization Algorithm
CSGO	Chaotic Social Group Optimization
SGO	Social Group Optimization
MPPE	Multigroup-based Phasmatodea Population Evolution Algorithm with Multistrategy
APPE	Advanced Phasmatodea Population Evolution Algorithm

References

1. Wu, T.Y.; Lin, J.C.W.; Zhang, Y.; Chen, C.H. A grid-based swarm intelligence algorithm for privacy-preserving data mining. *Appl. Sci.* **2019**, *9*, 774. [CrossRef]
2. Kang, L.; Chen, R.S.; Chen, Y.C.; Wang, C.C.; Li, X.; Wu, T.Y. Using cache optimization method to reduce network traffic in communication systems based on cloud computing. *IEEE Access* **2019**, *7*, 124397–124409. [CrossRef]
3. Leardi, R. Application of genetic algorithm–PLS for feature selection in spectral data sets. *J. Chemom.* **2000**, *14*, 643–655. [CrossRef]
4. Montazeri-Gh, M.; Poursamad, A.; Ghalichi, B. Application of genetic algorithm for optimization of control strategy in parallel hybrid electric vehicles. *J. Frankl. Inst.* **2006**, *343*, 420–435. [CrossRef]
5. Baldo, A.; Boffa, M.; Cascioli, L.; Fadda, E.; Lanza, C.; Ravera, A. The polynomial robust knapsack problem. *Eur. J. Oper. Res.* **2023**, *305*, 1424–1434. [CrossRef]
6. Zhang, F.; Wu, T.Y.; Wang, Y.; Xiong, R.; Ding, G.; Mei, P.; Liu, L. Application of quantum genetic optimization of LVQ neural network in smart city traffic network prediction. *IEEE Access* **2020**, *8*, 104555–104564. [CrossRef]
7. Pant, M.; Zaheer, H.; Garcia-Hernandez, L.; Abraham, A. Differential Evolution: A review of more than two decades of research. *Eng. Appl. Artif. Intell.* **2020**, *90*, 103479.
8. Saravanan, M.; Slochanal, S.M.R.; Venkatesh, P.; Abraham, P.S. Application of PSO technique for optimal location of FACTS devices considering system loadability and cost of installation. In Proceedings of the 2005 International Power Engineering Conference, Singapore, 29 November–2 December 2005; pp. 716–721.
9. Assareh, E.; Behrang, M.; Assari, M.; Ghanbarzadeh, A. Application of PSO (particle swarm optimization) and GA (genetic algorithm) techniques on demand estimation of oil in Iran. *Energy* **2010**, *35*, 5223–5229. [CrossRef]
10. Meng, F.Q.; Wei, S.; Wang, J.D.; Wang, P.F.; Li, B. An Information Feedback-based Particle Swarm Optimization Algorithm for Multi-regional Image Segmentation. *J. Netw. Intell.* **2023**, *8*, 194–210.
11. Mirjalili, S.; Lewis, A. The whale optimization algorithm. *Adv. Eng. Softw.* **2016**, *95*, 51–67. [CrossRef]
12. Mirjalili, S.; Mirjalili, S.M.; Saremi, S.; Mirjalili, S. Whale optimization algorithm: Theory, literature review, and application in designing photonic crystal filters. *Nat.-Inspired Optim.* **2020**, *811*, 219–238.
13. Liu, X.K.; Li, P.Q.; Zhang, Z.K.; Zen, J.J. Location and Capacity Determination of Energy Storage System Based on Improved Whale Optimization Algorithm. *J. Netw. Intell.* **2023**, *8*, 35–46.
14. Arora, S.; Singh, S. Butterfly optimization algorithm: A novel approach for global optimization. *Soft Comput.* **2019**, *23*, 715–734. [CrossRef]
15. Rezaee Jordehi, A. A chaotic artificial immune system optimisation algorithm for solving global continuous optimisation problems. *Neural Comput. Appl.* **2015**, *26*, 827–833. [CrossRef]

16. Chen, C.M.; Hao, Y.; Wu, T.Y. Discussion of "Ultra Super Fast Authentication Protocol for Electric Vehicle Charging Using Extended Chaotic Maps". *IEEE Trans. Ind. Appl.* **2023**, *59*, 2091–2092. [CrossRef]
17. Gao, J.M.L.Y.L. Chaos particle swarm optimization algorithm. *J. Comput. Appl.* **2008**, *28*, 322.
18. Talatahari, S.; Azar, B.F.; Sheikholeslami, R.; Gandomi, A. Imperialist competitive algorithm combined with chaos for global optimization. *Commun. Nonlinear Sci. Numer. Simul.* **2012**, *17*, 1312–1319. [CrossRef]
19. Gandomi, A.H.; Yang, X.S.; Talatahari, S.; Alavi, A.H. Firefly algorithm with chaos. *Commun. Nonlinear Sci. Numer. Simul.* **2013**, *18*, 89–98. [CrossRef]
20. Baykasoğlu, A.; Ozsoydan, F.B. Adaptive firefly algorithm with chaos for mechanical design optimization problems. *Appl. Soft Comput.* **2015**, *36*, 152–164. [CrossRef]
21. Gandomi, A.H.; Yang, X.S. Chaotic bat algorithm. *J. Comput. Sci.* **2014**, *5*, 224–232. [CrossRef]
22. Snaselova, P.; Zboril, F. Genetic algorithm using theory of chaos. *Procedia Comput. Sci.* **2015**, *51*, 316–325. [CrossRef]
23. Kaur, G.; Arora, S. Chaotic whale optimization algorithm. *J. Comput. Des. Eng.* **2018**, *5*, 275–284. [CrossRef]
24. Sayed, G.I.; Tharwat, A.; Hassanien, A.E. Chaotic dragonfly algorithm: An improved metaheuristic algorithm for feature selection. *Appl. Intell.* **2019**, *49*, 188–205. [CrossRef]
25. Arora, S.; Anand, P. Chaotic grasshopper optimization algorithm for global optimization. *Neural Comput. Appl.* **2019**, *31*, 4385–4405. [CrossRef]
26. Varol Altay, E.; Alatas, B. Bird swarm algorithms with chaotic mapping. *Artif. Intell. Rev.* **2020**, *53*, 1373–1414. [CrossRef]
27. Li, M.W.; Wang, Y.T.; Geng, J.; Hong, W.C. Chaos cloud quantum bat hybrid optimization algorithm. *Nonlinear Dyn.* **2021**, *103*, 1167–1193. [CrossRef]
28. Zhang, C.; Ding, S. A stochastic configuration network based on chaotic sparrow search algorithm. *Knowl.-Based Syst.* **2021**, *220*, 106924. [CrossRef]
29. Xu, Z.; Yang, H.; Li, J.; Zhang, X.; Lu, B.; Gao, S. Comparative Study on Single and Multiple Chaotic Maps Incorporated Grey Wolf Optimization Algorithms. *IEEE Access* **2021**, *9*, 77416–77437. [CrossRef]
30. Hao, P.; Sobhani, B. Application of the improved chaotic grey wolf optimization algorithm as a novel and efficient method for parameter estimation of solid oxide fuel cells model. *Int. J. Hydrog. Energy* **2021**, *46*, 36454–36465. [CrossRef]
31. Song, P.C.; Chu, S.C.; Pan, J.S.; Yang, H. Phasmatodea population evolution algorithm and its application in length-changeable incremental extreme learning machine. In Proceedings of the 2020 2nd international conference on industrial artificial intelligence (IAI), Shenyang, China, 23–25 October 2020; pp. 1–5.
32. Song, P.C.; Chu, S.C.; Pan, J.S.; Yang, H. Simplified Phasmatodea population evolution algorithm for optimization. *Complex Intell. Syst.* **2022**, *8*, 2749–2767. [CrossRef]
33. Gezici, H.; Livatyalı, H. Chaotic Harris hawks optimization algorithm. *J. Comput. Des. Eng.* **2022**, *9*, 216–245. [CrossRef]
34. Gharehchopogh, F.S.; Nadimi-Shahraki, M.H.; Barshandeh, S.; Abdollahzadeh, B.; Zamani, H. CQFFA: A Chaotic Quasi-oppositional Farmland Fertility Algorithm for Solving Engineering Optimization Problems. *J. Bionic Eng.* **2022**, *20*, 158–183. [CrossRef]
35. Chen, X.; Cao, B.; Pouramini, S. Energy cost and consumption reduction of an office building by Chaotic Satin Bowerbird Optimization Algorithm with model predictive control and artificial neural network: A case study. *Energy* **2023**, *270*, 126874. [CrossRef]
36. Naik, A. Chaotic Social Group Optimization for Structural Engineering Design Problems. *J. Bionic Eng.* **2023**. [CrossRef]
37. Zhu, Y.; Yan, F.; Pan, J.S.; Yu, L.; Bai, Y.; Wang, W.; He, C.; Shi, Z. Mutigroup-based phasmatodea population evolution algorithm with mutistrategy for iot electric bus scheduling. *Wirel. Commun. Mob. Comput.* **2022**, *2022*, 1500646. [CrossRef]
38. Zhuang, J.; Chu, S.C.; Hu, C.C.; Liao, L.; Pan, J.S. Advanced Phasmatodea Population Evolution Algorithm for Capacitated Vehicle Routing Problem. *J. Adv. Transp.* **2022**, *2022*. [CrossRef]
39. Pareek, N.K.; Patidar, V.; Sud, K.K. Image encryption using chaotic logistic map. *Image Vis. Comput.* **2006**, *24*, 926–934. [CrossRef]
40. Seyedzadeh, S.M.; Mirzakuchaki, S. A fast color image encryption algorithm based on coupled two-dimensional piecewise chaotic map. *Signal Process.* **2012**, *92*, 1202–1215. [CrossRef]
41. Ibrahim, R.A.; Oliva, D.; Ewees, A.A.; Lu, S. Feature selection based on improved runner-root algorithm using chaotic singer map and opposition-based learning. In Proceedings of the Neural Information Processing: 24th International Conference, ICONIP 2017, Guangzhou, China, 14–18 November 2017; Proceedings, Part V 24; Springer: Cham, Switzerland, 2017; pp. 156–166.
42. Belazi, A.; Abd El-Latif, A.A. A simple yet efficient S-box method based on chaotic sine map. *Optik* **2017**, *130*, 1438–1444. [CrossRef]
43. Li, C.; Luo, G.; Qin, K.; Li, C. An image encryption scheme based on chaotic tent map. *Nonlinear Dyn.* **2017**, *87*, 127–133. [CrossRef]
44. Chikushi, R.T.M.; de Barros, R.S.M.; da Silva, M.G.N.M.; Maciel, B.I.F. Using spectral entropy and bernoulli map to handle concept drift. *Expert Syst. Appl.* **2021**, *167*, 114114. [CrossRef]
45. Stoyanov, B.; Kordov, K. Image encryption using Chebyshev map and rotation equation. *Entropy* **2015**, *17*, 2117–2139. [CrossRef]
46. Mennis, J.; Viger, R.; Tomlin, C.D. Cubic map algebra functions for spatio-temporal analysis. *Cartogr. Geogr. Inf. Sci.* **2005**, *32*, 17–32. [CrossRef]

47. Jiteurtragool, N.; Ketthong, P.; Wannaboon, C.; San-Um, W. A topologically simple keyed hash function based on circular chaotic sinusoidal map network. In Proceedings of the 2013 15th International Conference on Advanced Communications Technology (ICACT), Pyeongchang, Republic of Korea, 27–30 January 2013; pp. 1089–1094.
48. Liu, W.; Sun, K.; He, Y.; Yu, M. Color image encryption using three-dimensional sine ICMIC modulation map and DNA sequence operations. *Int. J. Bifurc. Chaos* **2017**, *27*, 1750171. [CrossRef]
49. Liang, J.J.; Qu, B.; Suganthan, P.N.; Hernández-Díaz, A.G. *Problem Definitions and Evaluation Criteria for the CEC 2013 Special Session on Real-Parameter Optimization*; Technical Report; Computational Intelligence Laboratory, Zhengzhou University: Zhengzhou, China; Nanyang Technological University: Singapore, 2013; Volume 201212, pp. 281–295.
50. Huang, R.; Wei, C.; Wang, B.; Yang, J.; Xu, X.; Wu, S.; Huang, S. Well performance prediction based on Long Short-Term Memory (LSTM) neural network. *J. Pet. Sci. Eng.* **2022**, *208*, 109686. [CrossRef]

mathematics

Article

A Novel Discrete Differential Evolution with Varying Variables for the Deficiency Number of Mahjong Hand

Xueqing Yan [1] and Yongming Li [2,*]

[1] School of Computer Science, Shaanxi Normal University, Xi'an 710062, China; xueqingyan@snnu.edu.cn
[2] School of Mathematics and Statistics, Shaanxi Normal University, Xi'an 710062, China
* Correspondence: liyongm@snnu.edu.cn

Abstract: The deficiency number of one hand, i.e., the number of tiles needed to change in order to win, is an important factor in the game Mahjong, and plays a significant role in the development of artificial intelligence (AI) for Mahjong. However, it is often difficult to compute due to the large amount of possible combinations of tiles. In this paper, a novel discrete differential evolution (DE) algorithm is presented to calculate the deficiency number of the tiles. In detail, to decrease the difficulty of computing the deficiency number, some pretreatment mechanisms are first put forward to convert it into a simple combinatorial optimization problem with varying variables by changing its search space. Subsequently, by means of the superior framework of DE, a novel discrete DE algorithm is specially developed for the simplified problem through devising proper initialization, a mapping solution method, a repairing solution technique, a fitness evaluation approach, and mutation and crossover operations. Finally, several experiments are designed and conducted to evaluate the performance of the proposed algorithm by comparing it with the tree search algorithm and three other kinds of metaheuristic methods on a large number of various test cases. Experimental results indicate that the proposed algorithm is efficient and promising.

Keywords: Mahjong; differential evolution; deficiency number; combinatorial optimization

MSC: 68T20; 90C27

Citation: Yan, X.; Li, Y. A Novel Discrete Differential Evolution with Varying Variables for the Deficiency Number of Mahjong Hand. *Mathematics* **2023**, *11*, 2135. https://doi.org/10.3390/math11092135

Academic Editor: Jian Dong

Received: 20 March 2023
Revised: 27 April 2023
Accepted: 30 April 2023
Published: 2 May 2023

1. Introduction

Mahjong is a traditional, Chinese, tile-based game with a long history and is often played by four people [1,2]. In this game, each player is devoted to devising a proper strategy to win as soon as possible, with luck also playing an important role in this process. Due to its imperfect information, Mahjong has become a popular testbed for artificial intelligence (AI) research [3–9]. Nowadays, various variants of Mahjong with different rules for computing paybacks and/or the legality of actions have emerged due to the individual cultures of different regions and countries. However, they all have similar processes and can be easily extended by the basic version of Mahjong. Therefore, the basic version of Mahjong is just considered in the following without loss of generality.

In the basic version of Mahjong, four players are involved, and 108 tiles are used, consisting of 36 tiles of bamboo type, 36 tiles of character type, and 36 tiles of dot type. At the start of the game, each player in turn draws thirteen tiles from the tile wall, and then they each take one tile from the tile wall and discard one tile from their hand. When one player gets a winning hand or there are no tiles left in the tile wall, the game ends. So, all players need to continuously change their hands' tiles in order to ensure that their hands win quickly, and these processes involve a number of evaluations on the quality of various cases of tiles, i.e., calculating the minimum number of tiles needed to be changed to win, which is called the deficiency number [10]. Thereby, computing the deficiency number has an important role in Mahjong, and can promote AI development for the game. Moreover, the winning hand closely depends on the combinations of the tiles, and these combinations include a sequence of three or four identical tiles (called a pong or kong), a sequence of three consecutive tiles with the same type (called a chow), and a pair of identical tiles (called a pair or an eye). A pong or a chow is also called a meld, and a pseudomeld (abbr. pmeld) refers to a pair of tiles that can constitute a meld. Therefore, computing the deficiency number is in fact a combinatorial optimization problem, which is often not easily calculated due to its large search space.

As far as we know, there are very few studies on the calculation of the deficiency number at present [10–12]. Specifically, in the paper [10], Li and Yan presented a recursive method and a tree-based method for calculating the deficiency number. In the recursive method, for one hand with 14 tiles, all cases of 14 tiles with k deficiency must be known in advance before the deficiency number of one hand is determined to be $k+1$. In the tree-based method, all pseudo-decompositions of the tiles must be found and evaluated, and then the deficiency number is obtained by the minimum cost of these pseudo-decompositions. Herein, a pseudo-decomposition is a sequence π of five subsequences, $\pi[0], \pi[1], \ldots, \pi[4]$, where $\pi[i]$ for $0 \leq i \leq 3$ can be a meld, a pmeld, a single tile, or empty, and $\pi[4]$ can be a pair, a single tile, or empty. The cost of each pseudo-decomposition is the number of missing tiles compared to the current hand. Wang et al. [11] constructed a theoretical model of weighted restarting automaton to compute the deficiency number of 14 tiles, where the tiles are combined into melds and eyes during the process of simplification, and the number of changed tiles is counted using its weight function. Recently, Wang et al. [12] further proposed an efficient algorithmic approach, where the tiles in the player's hand are first divided into several groups, such as melds, pseudomelds, and isolated tiles, and then the deficiency number is computed based on the number of pseudomelds and that of the isolated tiles. Although these approaches can calculate the deficiency number of a Mahjong hand, the full searches are all implicit in them, which often take too much computational time and thus cannot meet the actual demand of response time in the game. Therefore, it is necessary to develop a more promising search approach for the deficiency number.

As is well known, because of the lower requirement on the problem to be solved, heuristic intelligent search/optimization methods have been regarded as the most important tools for solving real problems, especially complicated ones. In addition, various metaheuristic algorithms have been presented by simulating nature phenomena, animal behaviors, human activities, or physical criteria, such as the genetic algorithm (GA) [13], differential evolution (DE) [14], particle swarm optimization (PSO) [15], artificial bee colony algorithm [16], water cycle algorithm (WCA) [17], squirrel search algorithm [18], gravitational search algorithm (GSA) [19], teaching–learning-based optimization (TLBO) [20], gaining–sharing knowledge-based algorithm [21], and so on. In detail, more metaheuristic algorithms can be found in [22], and they have been widely researched and successfully applied in many scientific fields and practical problems up to now, including data clustering [23,24], stock portfolios [25], knapsack optimization problems [26], multitask optimization [27], and multimodal optimization [28].

As pointed out in [22], among the existing intelligent approaches, differential evolution (DE) [14] is one of the most popular population-based stochastic optimizers, and has been proven to be more efficient and robust on various problems. Due to its simplicity and simple implementation, DE always attracts more attention from researchers, and numerous DE variants have been put forward to strengthen its performance [29–34] and/or solve special practical problems [35–39]. For example, by dividing a population into multiple swarms and randomly selecting the solutions with better fitness values in each swarm to conduct mutations, Wang et al. [29] developed a novel adaptive DE algorithm. Through making full use of the information of the best neighbor, one randomly selected neighbor, and the current individual for each individual to predict the promising region, Yan and Tian [30] presented an enhanced adaptive DE variant, while, by adaptively combining the benefits of multiple operators, Yi et al. [34] developed a novel approach for continuous optimization problems. Moreover, by designing a Taper-shaped transfer function based on power functions to transform a real vector representing the individual encoding into a binary vector, He et al. [35] proposed a novel binary differential evolution algorithm for binary optimization problems. Meanwhile, for traveling salesman problems, Ali et al. [38] proposed an improved discrete DE version, where an enhanced mapping mechanism is devised to map continuous variables to discrete ones, a k-means clustering-based repairing method is devised to enhance the solutions in the initial population, and an ensemble of mutation strategies is used to maintain its exploration capability. In particular, a large number of numerical experiments were conducted in their papers, and the numerical results validated their effectiveness and superiority. Thereby, DE has a greater potential in a promising search performance. Following this, we adopt the framework of DE to calculate the deficiency number of the tiles in this paper, so as to obtain a promising performance. Specifically, more detailed research on the improvements and applications of DE can be further referred to in [40].

In this paper, a more efficient method is researched to calculate the deficiency number of a Mahjong hand, and the framework of DE is adopted to achieve this, based on its intrinsic advantages. In detail, in order to reduce the difficulty of computing the deficiency number, some pretreatment mechanisms are first devised to convert the original problem into a simple combinatorial optimization problem, where the dimensions of the search space are degraded to five, and each feasible solution may have different lengths. Noticeably, this makes the dealing problem significantly different to the existing studied discrete and/or combinatorial optimization problems, in which the size of every solution is fixed and consistent. Moreover, for this converted new problem, based on the basic framework of DE, a novel discrete DE (NDDE) algorithm is then specially presented by devising proper initialization, a mapping solution method, a repairing solution technique, a fitness evaluation approach, and mutation and crossover operations, which aim to meet the available search requirement of the discrete space and the characteristic of the varying sizes of different individuals. Then, the proposed NDDE algorithm is capable of computing the deficiency number of one hand efficiently and effectively. Finally, a large number of experiments are designed and conducted to verify the performance of the NDDE algorithm. Specifically, three representative data sets are employed and tested, including 118,800 hands with one type, 100,000 hands with two types, and 100,000 hands with three types, and the NDDE algorithm is compared with the tree search method in [10] and three other kinds of metaheuristic methods. The sensitivity of the parameters involved in the NDDE algorithm is also investigated. The experimental results show that the proposed algorithm has a promising performance for the deficiency number of the hand.

For clarity, compared with the existing works, the main contributions and novelties of this paper are described as follows.

(1) To our knowledge, the research presented in the paper is the first to utilize a heuristic intelligent algorithm for computing the deficiency number of a Mahjong hand. In fact, the works on computing the deficiency number of one hand are still rare up to now, and all of them adopt a deterministic approach. Thus, this study may provide a new alternative for devising more effective and efficient methods for calculating the deficiency number.

(2) The original problem of computing the deficiency number is converted into a more simple combinatorial optimization problem. This may effectively reduce the difficulty and computational costs of solving it.

(3) To solve the simplified problem above, a novel discrete DE (NDDE) algorithm is further specially proposed by devising proper initialization, a mapping solution method, a repairing solution technique, a fitness evaluation approach, and mutation and crossover operations. Significantly, the simplified problem has the characteristic that the feasible solutions may have various lengths, which is not involved in the previous discrete and/or combinatorial optimization problems. Therefore, the proposed algorithm has different and more rigorous design requirements.

(4) A large number of experiments are designed and conducted to verify the performance of the NDDE algorithm, where three representative data sets are employed and tested, including 118,800 hands with one type, 100,000 hands with two types, and 100,000 hands with three types. Moreover, the NDDE algorithm is compared with the tree search method in [10] and three other kinds of metaheuristic methods, and the sensitivity of the parameters involved in the NDDE algorithm is also investigated. Experimental results indicate that the NDDE algorithm is a more promising technique for the deficiency number of the hand.

Finally, it should also be mentioned that the reason the framework of DE is chosen to design the solver in this paper is solely because much of the research reported in the literature has proven its superiority on various problems, but other metaheuristic algorithms can also be adopted here, which we will further study in our future work.

The reminder of this paper is organized as follows. Some related works and basic notions on Mahjong are presented in Section 2. The proposed algorithm for computing the deficiency number of a Mahjong hand is introduced in Section 3, and the experimental tests are conducted and analyzed in Section 4. Finally, conclusions are drawn in Section 5.

2. Preliminaries

In this section, the related concepts and research on Mahjong and the classical DE algorithm shall be described.

2.1. Related Concepts on Mahjong

In this part, some related concepts in Mahjong are introduced to provide a foundation for the below descriptions. For simplicity, the basic version of Mahjong, denoted as M_0, is considered, which consists of tiles with bamboo type, tiles with character type, and tiles with dot type. Specifically, these tiles with bamboo, character, and dot type are represented as follows:

- Bamboos: $B_1, B_2, \ldots, B_9$.
- Characters: $C_1, C_2, \ldots, C_9$.
- Dots: $D_1, D_2, \ldots, D_9$.

Moreover, in M_0, each of the above tiles has four identical tiles; thus, there are 108 tiles in M_0 in total. Subsequently, some basic notions on Mahjong shall be provided, which mainly refers to the the literature [10,12].

Definition 1. *A* pong *is a sequence of three identical tiles, that is, a pong has the form of $X_iX_iX_i$ for $X \in \{B, C, D\}$ and $1 \leq i \leq 9$; A* chow *is a sequence of three consecutive tiles with the same type, that is, a chow has the form of $X_iX_{i+1}X_{i+2}$ for $X \in \{B, C, D\}$ and $1 \leq i \leq 7$; An* eye *(or* pair*) is a pair of identical tiles, that is, an eye has the form of X_iX_i for $X \in \{B, C, D\}$ and $1 \leq i \leq 9$. A* meld *is either a pong or a chow.*

Definition 2. *A* pseudochow (pchow) *is a pair of tiles X_iX_j with the same type, having $1 \leq |j - i| \leq 2$ and $X \in \{B, C, D\}$, which can become a chow if we add an appropriate tile with the same type in it. A* pseudomeld (pmeld) *is a pchow or a pair. We say a tile c* completes *a pmeld (ab) if (abc) (after reordering) is a meld. Similarly, a pair is completed from a single tile t if it is obtained by adding an identical tile to t.*

For example, $(B_1B_1B_1)$ is a pong, $(C_1C_2C_3)$ is a chow, (D_1D_1) is a pair, and (B_2B_3) and (C_3C_5) are two pchows.

Definition 3. *A* hand *is a set of 14 tiles, denoted by H, i.e., a sequence of 14 tiles from M_0, where every tile can not appear more than four times.*

Definition 4. *A hand H from M_0 is* winning *or* complete *if it can be decomposed into four melds and one pair. (For ease of presentation, we do not regard a hand with seven pairs as complete.) Given* *a complete hand H, a* decomposition *π of H is a sequence of five subsequences of H, where $\pi[i]$ is a meld for $0 \leq i \leq 3$ and $\pi[4]$ is a pair. If this is the case, we call $\pi[4]$ the* eye *of this decomposition.*

For example, the hand $H_1 = (B_1B_2B_3B_3B_3B_8B_8B_8)(C_4C_5C_6)(D_6D_7D_8)$ is a winning or complete hand, and its decomposition is $\pi = (B_1B_2B_3)(B_8B_8B_8)(C_4C_5C_6)(D_6D_7D_8)(B_3B_3)$.

As is well known, the hands involved in a Mahjong game are mostly incomplete. That is, there is no decomposition defined above for these hands. So, corresponding to the decomposition of a winning hand, another concept of predecomposition is further given here for the hands.

Definition 5. *Given a hand H, the predecomposition (abbr.* pDCMP*) of H is a sequence π of five subsequences, $\pi(1), \ldots, \pi(5)$, of H such that each $\pi(i)$ $(1 \leq i \leq 5)$ is a meld, pair, pchow, or empty.*

Noticeably, unlike the concept of pseudo-decomposition in [10], a single tile is not contained in the predecomposition and the position of the eye is no longer fixed. For example, with respect to the above hand H_1, the sequence $\pi_1 = (B_1B_2)(B_3B_3B_3)(B_8B_8)(C_4C_5C_6)(D_6D_7D_8)$ is one of its pDCMPs.

Definition 6. *Suppose π and π' are two* pDCMPs *for one hand H. We say π' is* finer *than π if $\pi(i)$ is identical to or a subsequence of $\pi'(i)$ for $1 \leq i \leq 5$. A* pDCMP *π is* completable *if there exists a decomposition π^* for H that is finer than π. If this is the case, we call π^* a* completion *of π. Moreover, the cost of a completable* pDCMP *π, written cost(π), is the number of missing tiles required to complete π into a decomposition, which consists of four melds and one eye.*

In particular, for one pDCMP π of one hand H, we say it has infinite cost if it is incompletable. Moreover, for the above pDCMP π_1 of H_1, its cost is 1 since it can be completed by one tile, B_3.

Definition 7. *For one hand H, the minimal number of necessary tile changes for making T a winning is called the* deficiency number (or simply *deficiency*) of H. If the deficiency of H is ℓ, we write $dfncy(H) = \ell$. Obviously, for a winning hand H, it holds that $dfncy(H) = 0$.

Based on the above notions, we can see that for one hand, H, its deficiency number can be obtained by finding all its possible predecompositions and then comparing their differences with the ideal decompositions.

2.2. Research on Mahjong Game

With the development of artificial intelligence (AI) techniques, games are continuously regarded as one of the most important test platforms. In particular, for games with perfect information, such as checkers [41], chess [42] and Go [43,44], AI has now even been able to beat the best human players. In contrast, for imperfect information games [45–49], there are still few works since players have to deal with some invisible information during the game, especially for Mahjong.

As stated in the Introduction, there have been various variants of Mahjong due to the unique cultures of each region and country. Among them, Riichi Mahjong is a popular version played in Japan, and most of the current research on Mahjong is based on it [5,8,9,49–52]. Specifically, Li et al. [51] proposed a Mahjong AI system, suphx, based on reinforcement learning, and the test results on the "Tenhou" platform showed its effectiveness. Kurita [5] abstracted the Mahjong process by defining multiple Markov decision processes, and then constructed an effective search tree for optimal decision-making. Mizukami and Tsuruoka [49] built a strong Mahjong AI by modeling opponent players and performing Monte Carlo simulations. Yoshimura et al. [50] proposed a tabu search method of optimal movements without using game records, while Sato et al. [52] presented a new method to classify the opponent players' strategy by analyzing Mahjong playing records. Additionally, for the version of bloody Mahjong, Gao and Li [8] developed a fusion model by using the deep learning and XGBoost algorithm to extract the Mahjong situation features and derive the card strategy, respectively. In particular, a more detailed review about the existing works on Mahjong AI can be further found in ref. [9], where the advantages and disadvantages of each method are analyzed.

Unlike the above works that aim to develop Mahjong AI players, there are still few studies to evaluate the quality of a Mahjong hand, which is more helpful for a player to devise an appropriate strategy during the game [10–12]. In [10], Li and Yan first introduced the notation of the deficiency number for measuring the quality of a hand, and developed two different calculation methods for it, namely, the recursive method and the tree-based method. After this, Wang et al. [11] presented a theoretical model of weighted restarting automaton for computing the deficiency number of 14 tiles. In the developed model, the tiles are combined into melds and eyes in the process of simplification, and the number of changed tiles is counted by its weight function. Moreover, by dividing the tiles into some groups, such as melds, pseudomelds, and isolated tiles, in advance and fully considering the relation between their numbers, Wang et al. [12] recently further proposed an efficient algorithm to calculate the deficiency number of 14 tiles. Even though these above methods have made some progress in measuring the quality of a hand, they all contains the idea of full searches, which might make their computational time too long to timely satisfy the actual demand of response time during a game. Therefore, it is necessary to devise a more promising technique for calculating the deficiency number.

2.3. Traditional DE Algorithm

For the convenience of later descriptions, the detailed operations of a classical DE is drawn as follows, including initialization, mutation, crossover, and selection [14]. Specifically, the minimization problem $\min\{f(\vec{x})|x_{min,j} \leq x_j \leq x_{max,j}, j = 1, 2, \ldots, D\}$ is considered here, where $\vec{x} = (x_1, x_2, \ldots, x_D)$ is the solution vector, D is the dimension of the search space, and $x_{min,j}$ and $x_{max,j}$ are the lower and upper bounds of the j-th component of the search space, respectively.

First, one population, P^0, consisting of NP solutions is randomly created in the search space. Each solution is denoted by $\vec{x}_i^0 = (x_{i,1}^0, x_{i,2}^0, \ldots, x_{i,D}^0)$ with $i = 1, 2, \ldots, NP$, and NP is the size of population. Concretely, the j-th component of $\vec{x}_i^0$ is generated by

$$x_{i,j}^0 = x_{min,j} + rand \cdot (x_{max,j} - x_{min,j}), \tag{1}$$

where $rand$ is a random number uniformly distributed in [0, 1].

After initialization of the population, for each solution $\vec{x}_i^g$ at g generation, the mutation operation is executed to create its mutation individual $\vec{v}_i^g$. The detailed process of operator 'DE/rand/1' can be provided as

$$\vec{v}_i^g = \vec{x}_{r1}^g + F \cdot (\vec{x}_{r2}^g - \vec{x}_{r3}^g), \tag{2}$$

where r_1, r_2, and r_3 are three random integers in $[1, NP]$ and have $r1 \neq r2 \neq r3 \neq i$, and F is a scaling factor.

Then, by combining the components of $\vec{v}_i^g$ and its corresponding target individual $\vec{x}_i^g$, one trial individual $\vec{u}_i^g = (u_{i,1}^g, u_{i,2}^g, \ldots, u_{i,D}^g)$ is created with the crossover operation. The rule of the binomial crossover method is just described here as:

$$u_{i,j}^g = \begin{cases} v_{i,j}^g, & \text{if } rand \leq Cr \text{ or } j = randn(i), \\ x_{i,j}^g, & \text{otherwise} \end{cases} \tag{3}$$

where $u_{i,j}^g$, $v_{i,j}^g$, and $x_{i,j}^g$ are, respectively, the j-th components of $\vec{u}_i^g$, $\vec{v}_i^g$, and $\vec{x}_i^g$, $Cr \in [0, 1]$ is the crossover rate, and $randn(i)$ returns a random integer within $[1, D]$, which ensures that $\vec{u}_i^g$ obtains at least one component from $\vec{v}_i^g$.

Finally, the selection operation is conducted to update the current population by comparing each target solution $\vec{x}_i^g$ with its trial vector $\vec{u}_i^g$ based on their fitness values. In particular, the greedy selection strategy can be expressed as follows.

$$\vec{x}_i^{g+1} = \begin{cases} \vec{u}_i^g, & \text{if } f(\vec{u}_i^g) \leq f(\vec{x}_i^g) \\ \vec{x}_i^g, & \text{otherwise.} \end{cases} \tag{4}$$

where $f(\cdot)$ is the objective function to be optimized.

Note that DE with (4) will either get better or remain at the same fitness status, but never deteriorate. Meanwhile, when DE is activated for one optimization problem, the mutation, crossover, and selection operations will in turn be executed until one satisfying solution is found or the prescribed termination criterion is met.

3. Proposed Algorithm

As described and discussed in the Introduction, the deficiency number evaluates the quality of a Mahjong hand and is helpful for a player to devise an appropriate strategy, which can facilitate the development of Mahjong AI. However, due to the fact that the tiles in one hand always have a large number of possible combinations, it usually cannot be easily calculated. To address this issue, several approaches have been presented, but they are very limited and always require too much computational time. Therefore, inspired by the advantages of DE, such as simplicity, easy implementation, strong robustness, and superior performance, we propose a novel discrete DE variant (NDDE) to compute the deficiency number of a Mahjong hand in this section. Specifically, the problem of computing the deficiency number is first converted to a simpler combinatorial optimization problem, and a new DE variant is presented for it by devising proper initialization, a mapping solution method, a repairing solution technique, a fitness evaluation approach, and mutation and crossover operations.

3.1. Simplified Problem of Deficiency Number

As stated in [10], the problem of computing the deficiency number is in fact an optimization problem and can be regarded as a combinatorial optimization problem to solve, i.e., finding one proper combination of the tiles that has minimal differences between it and its corresponding ideal winning hand. Recently, several approaches have been proposed to calculate the deficiency number of the tiles based on this [10–12]. However, there are often too many combinations in the search space, which might degrade the efficiency of these methods. To alleviate this demerit, we propose converting the problem of computing the deficiency number into a simpler one, where the dimension of the new search space is reduced to five. The details of the concrete processes are described in the following.

For one Mahjong hand H, we first search all its possible melds and pmelds and denote them by S. The reason for this is that the decomposition of a winning hand is constituted by four melds and one eye, and it can be completed by the predecomposition, which consists of melds and/or pmelds. Then, the problem of computing the deficiency number can be alternatively described as:

$$\min_{\pi \in \Pi} g(\pi) \tag{5}$$

where $\pi = (\pi(1), \pi(2), \pi(3), \pi(4), \pi(5))$ is the predecomposition of H with $\pi(i)$ $(1 \leq i \leq 5)$ being a meld, pair, or pchow from S or empty, Π is the set of all predecompositions of H, and $g(\pi)$ denotes the differences between π and its ideal decomposition, i.e., having $g(\pi) = cost(\pi)$, which will be further discussed in the next subsection.

According to the definition of Equation (5), all possible melds and pmelds of one Mahjong hand H must be found and contained in S, so as to ensure the completeness of all its predecompositions. Moreover, since the meld has the modes of chow and pong, the pmeld has the modes of pair and pchow, and the pchow always has two different modes, such as $(D_6 D_7)$ and $(D_6 D_8)$; then, S can be formed by considering each case above for each tile. Note that, to form a winning hand, the pchow must be able to constitute a chow, and thus, the number of tiles used to complete the pchow should be less than four in H. Thereby, for a Mahjong hand H, its related set S can be generated as follows. First, we find the distinct tiles of H and denote them by S_t, while initializing the set S to be empty. Then, for each tile $X_i \in S_t$, the following five cases are successively checked to create all possible melds and pmelds, which will be added into S.

Case 1. If $X_{i+1} \in H$ and the number of X_{i-1} or X_{i+2} in H is less than four, then add pchow $(X_i X_{i+1})$ into S;

Case 2. If $X_{i+2} \in H$ and the number of X_{i+1} in H is less than four, then add pchow $(X_i X_{i+2})$ into S;

Case 3. If $X_{i+1} \in H$ and $X_{i+2} \in H$, then add chow $(X_i X_{i+1} X_{i+2})$ into S;

Case 4. If the number of X_i in H is more than two, then add pair $(X_i X_i)$ into S;

Case 5. If the number of X_i in H is more than three, then add pong $(X_i X_i X_i)$ into S.

Particularly, Cases 1, 2, and 4 can provide all the possible pmelds, and Cases 3 and 5 can give all the possible melds involved in H.

In summary, from the above descriptions, all the possible melds and pmelds can be obtained for each Mahjong hand H, and then every predecomposition involved in it can be created by using S. Thus, the predecompositions obtained by the tree-based search algorithm will be contained in the search space Π of the new problem. Meanwhile, since the tree-based search algorithm is a full search approach, the legal solution for the new problem can also be obtained by it. So, the proposed operations cannot affect the deficiency number of one Mahjong hand, and the converted problem and its original one are equivalent. Moreover, it is easy to find that the dimension of this new problem is just five, and its search space is decided by the length of S. Additionally, the generation process of S is relatively cheap, and its size of S is often smaller; therefore, the new problem has a smaller search space and is easier to solve.

3.2. Proposed NDDE Algorithm

In this subsection, the special components of the NDDE algorithm shall be introduced, including the initialization, mapping solution method, repairing solution technique, fitness evaluation approach, and mutation and crossover operations.

3.2.1. Initialization of Population and Mapping Solution

According to the framework of DE, when DE is activated, an initial population with NP solutions will first be created. In this paper, since the objective function is a discrete one, the following special method is used to initialize the population P^0.

For convenience, we let N_S denote the size of the set S, each solution $\vec{x}_i^0$ denote a predecomposition π, and then have $\vec{x}_i^0 = (x_{i,1}^0, x_{i,2}^0, \ldots, x_{i,5}^0)$ with $i = 1, 2, \ldots, NP$. Specifically, for each element $x_{i,j}^0$ of $\vec{x}_i^0$, $j = 1, 2, \ldots, 5$, it will be created by

$$x_{i,j}^0 = randint(N_S), \tag{6}$$

where $randint(A)$ returns a random integer uniformly distributed in $[1, A]$.

Moreover, from Equation (6), one can easily find that each solution in P^0 is only represented by some integer values, and they are not compatible with the new problem described in Equation (5). Thus, a mapping method is further provided here for matching the solutions of the population with those of the new problem. In particular, for each solution $\vec{x}_i^0$ in P^0, its corresponding solution π_i^0 for the new problem can be obtained by

$$\pi_i^0 = (\pi_i^0(1), \pi_i^0(2), \pi_i^0(3), \pi_i^0(4), \pi_i^0(5)), \tag{7}$$

where $\pi_i^0(j)$ is the $x_{i,j}^0$-th element of S for $j = 1, 2, \ldots, 5$, which may be a meld or pmeld.

From the above descriptions, the solutions matching the DE algorithm and the new problem can all be obtained. Noticeably, the operations of initializing the population and mapping it are both simple and easy to implement. Thus, these operations will not add severe computational burdens.

3.2.2. Repairing Solution Technique

As described above, through the proposed mapping method, each individual in a population will generate a corresponding solution for the new problem. However, there is still a shortcoming in it, that is, the mapped solutions cannot be guaranteed to be feasible. In fact, for one Mahjong hand H and a mapped solution π_i, the number of some tiles in π_i may exceed that in H. Thereby, a repairing technique is also necessary to correct these infeasible solutions.

For the sake of saving the computational cost of the algorithm, the following simple repairing approach is used in this paper. For one Mahjong hand H and a mapped solution π_i, all distinct tiles of π_i are first found and recorded in one set, denoted by S_p. Then, for each tile X_i in S_p, we separately count its numbers in π_i and H, and if the number in π_i is larger than that in H, we gradually remove one meld or pmeld containing X_i from π_i until its number in π_i is less than or equal to that in H. At the same time, when one meld or pmeld is removed in π_i, its corresponding element in $\vec{x}_i^g$ will also be set to empty. Clearly, by this repairing method, each mapped solution will be changed to be feasible, and this correcting process is very easy to achieve.

3.2.3. Fitness Evaluation Approach

In order to determine which solutions will be selected in the next iteration, their fitness values should be evaluated as well. At each generation g, the fitness value of each individual $\vec{x}_i^g$ in population P^g is evaluated by the cost of its corresponding mapped solution π_i^g for the new problem. That is, we let $f(\vec{x}_i^g) = g(\pi_i^g)$ in this paper.

Concretely, for a mapped solution π^g, according to $g(\pi^g) = cost(\pi^g)$ and the definition of $cost(\pi^g)$, i.e., the number of missing tiles required to complete π^g into a decomposition, the fitness value of $\vec{x}_i^g$ can be calculated by

$$f(\vec{x}_i^g) = \begin{cases} 4 - m, & \text{if } m + n = 5 \text{ } and \text{ } p = 1, \\ 5 - m, & \text{if } m + n = 5 \text{ } and \text{ } p = 0, \\ 9 - 2 * m - n, & \text{if } m + n < 5. \end{cases} \tag{8}$$

Herein, m and n are the numbers of meld and pmeld in π_i^g, respectively, and p is the index of whether there is a pair in π_i^g. If there is a pair in π_i^g, then we have $p = 1$; otherwise, $p = 0$.

Moreover, it should be mentioned that there are still two other special cases in the evaluation of the solution. For one predecomposition π^g, the first case is that it has $m + n = 5$ and contains two identical pairs. In this case, one of the two pairs in π^g should have formed a meld, but the number of tiles in π^g will have increased to four. Thus, the actual cost should be added by one due to the invalid pmeld. Another case is that it has $m = 4, n = 0$, and the remaining two different tiles will have formed a pong in π^g. In this case, we further need to form a pair to complete π^g, but the remaining tiles cannot form a pair. Therefore, we need to change both of these two tiles to form a pair and the actual cost of π^g should be two.

For example, considering one Mahjong hand $H = (B_1B_2B_3B_3B_3B_3B_4B_8)(C_4C_5C_9)(D_6D_7D_8)$ and its three predecompositions $\pi_1 = (B_1B_2B_3)(B_3B_4)(B_3B_3)(C_4C_5)(D_6D_7D_8)$, $\pi_2 = (B_1B_2B_3)(B_3B_3B_3)(C_4C_5)(D_6D_7D_8)$, and $\pi_3 = (B_2B_3B_4)(B_1B_3)(B_3B_3)(C_4C_5)(D_6D_7)$, by using the above evaluation approach, we can find that for π_1, it has $m = 2, n = 3$, and $p = 1$; thus, $g(\pi_1) = 2$. While for π_2, it has $m = 3, n = 1$, and $p = 0$; thus, $g(\pi_2) = 2$. For π_3, it has $m = 1, n = 4$, and $p = 1$; thus, $g(\pi_2) = 3$.

In conclusion, from the above descriptions, the proposed fitness evaluation method can accurately assess the quality of each solution in the population.

3.2.4. Mutation and Crossover Operators

To fully search the decision space and ensure the computational efficiency of the algorithm, the mutation operator "DE/rand/1" and the binomial crossover operation are enhanced and employed to generate the mutant and trial individual, respectively, in the proposed NDDE algorithm.

Especially considering the fact that the search space involved in the NDDE algorithm is discrete and the lengths of different solutions may be various, a discrete version of "DE/rand/1" is devised and employed in this paper. In detail, for each individual $\vec{x}_i^g$ at g generation, its mutant individual $\vec{v}_i^g = (v_{i,1}^g, v_{i,2}^g, \ldots, v_{i,5}^g)$ can be generated by

$$v_{i,j}^g = \begin{cases} round(x_{r1,j}^g + F * (x_{r2,j}^g - x_{r3,j}^g)), & \text{if } x_{r1,j}^g \neq \varnothing \text{ and } x_{r2,j}^g \neq \varnothing \text{ and} x_{r3,j}^g \neq \varnothing, \\ randint(N_S), & \text{otherwise} \end{cases} \tag{9}$$

where $j = 1, 2, \ldots, 5$, r_1, r_2, and r_3 are three random integers in $[1, NP]$ with $r_1 \neq r_2 \neq r_3 \neq i$, F is a scaling factor, $round(A)$ denotes the nearest integer around A. In particular, we set $F = 0.5$ in this paper.

Similarly, based on the property of varying variables of individuals and to make full use of the information of the target individual, the following modified binomial crossover operation is developed and used to generate the trial individuals. Specifically, for each individual $\vec{x}_i^g$ and its mutant individual $\vec{v}_i^g$, the corresponding trial individual $\vec{u}_i^g = (u_{i,1}^g, u_{i,2}^g, \ldots, u_{i,5}^g)$ is obtained by

$$u_{i,j}^g = \begin{cases} x_{i,j}^g, & \text{if } x_{i,j}^g \neq \varnothing \text{ and } rand \leq Cr, \\ v_{i,j}^g, & \text{otherwise} \end{cases} \tag{10}$$

where $Cr \in (0, 1)$ is the crossover rate, and especially, we set $Cr = 0.5$ here.

As described above, the proposed mutation and crossover operator can broadly search the search space, fully utilize the acquired information, and have a simple implementing process. Consequently, they are capable of boosting the search ability of the algorithm for finding the deficiency number of one Mahjong hand.

Finally, after generating the trial individual for each target one, the population will be updated by comparing them based on their fitness values, and the best one among them will enter the new population. To achieve this process, the greedy selection strategy (see Equation (4)) is utilized in this paper. Overall, by integrating the proposed initialization, mapping solution method, repairing solution technique, fitness evaluation approach, and mutation and crossover operations, the framework of the proposed NDDE algorithm is shown in Algorithm 1. To improve the understanding of this paper, a flowchart of the proposed approach for computing the deficiency number is provided in Figure 1, where G and G_{max} denote the current number and maximum number of iterations, respectively.

It should be pointed out that, unlike the existing approaches for obtaining the deficiency number in [10–12], the proposed method simplifies the original problem of calculating the deficiency number and makes full use of the benefits of DE to improve the computational efficiency. Specifically, by previously finding all possible melds, pmelds, and pairs contained in one hand and constructing the form of the solution based on the structure of the decomposition, the problem of calculating the deficiency number is converted to a more simple combinatorial optimization problem. Meanwhile, according to the properties of discrete and varying variables of the new problem, a proper initialization, mapping solution method, repairing solution technique, fitness evaluation approach, and mutation and crossover operations are separately developed, and then a novel discrete DE algorithm is proposed. Thereby, the proposed method can effectively and efficiently compute the deficiency number of one Mahjong hand. It should also be mentioned that, for the hands with a larger deficiency number, the proposed approach might be less efficient than the tree-based deterministic algorithms. This is because the ones with a larger deficiency number always just contain a few melds, pmelds, and/or pairs, which might lead to few child nodes for each search step in the deterministic methods and then reduce the search cost, while the stochastic algorithms need to conduct the predefined searches for each hand at all times. Moreover, compared to the general discrete and/or combinatorial optimization problems, the simplified problem involved in this paper has a special characteristic that its feasible solutions may have various lengths. So, the previous discrete DE versions are not able to directly solve this problem. Meanwhile, for solving the simplified problem, other metaheuristic algorithms can be alternatively adopted instead of DE by designing some proper operations, which we will further study in our future work.

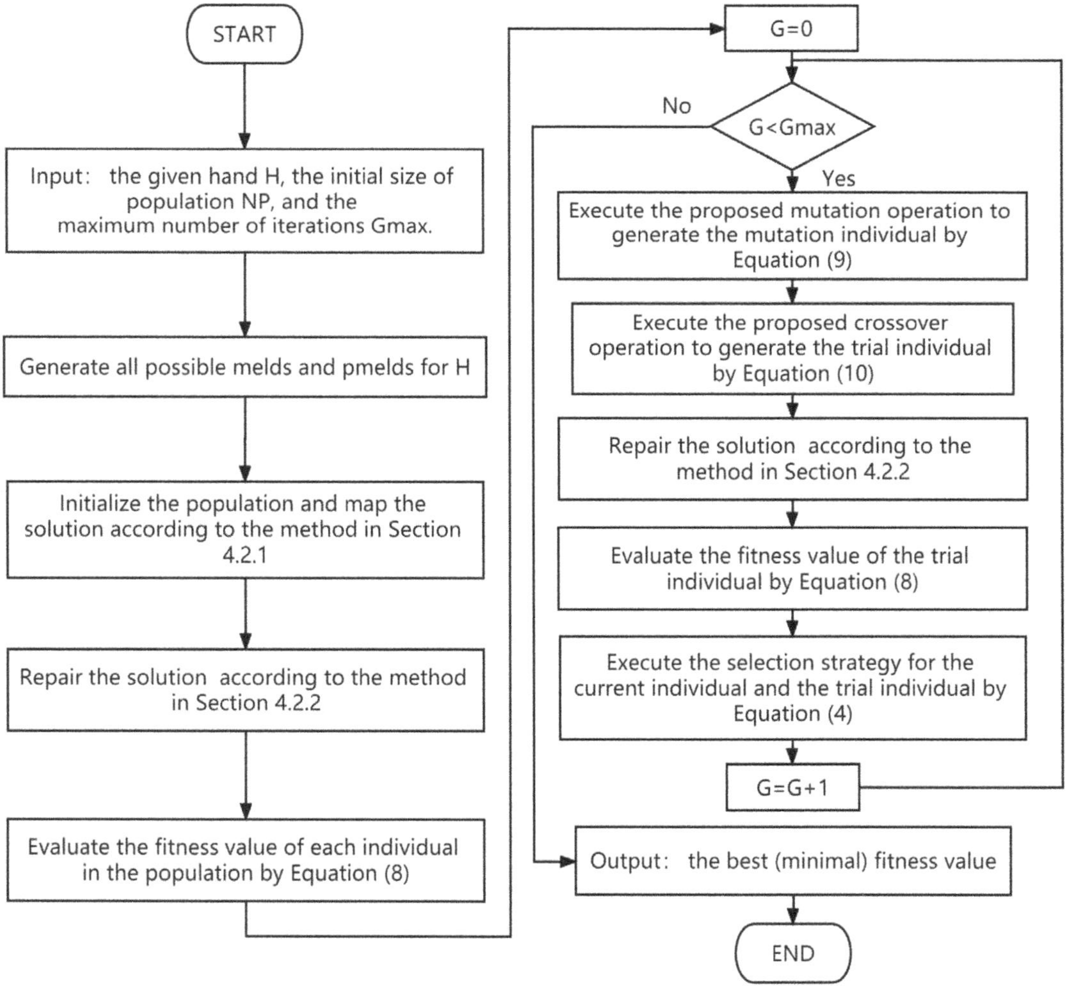

Figure 1. The flowchart of the proposed method in this paper for computing deficiency number.

Algorithm 1 (The framework of the proposed NDDE algorithm).

Input: the given hand H, the initial size of population NP, the maximum number of iterations G_{max}.
Generate the set S consisting of all possible melds and pmleds for H, and calculate N_S.
Set the current generation $g = 0$.
Initialize the population P^g by Equation (6), map and repair each individual in P^g by Equation (7) and the proposed repairing technique described in Section 4.2.2, respectively.
Evaluate the fitness value of each individual in P^g by Equation (8).
while $g \leq G_{max}$ **do**
  for $i = 1 : NP$ **do**
    Execute the proposed mutation operation to generate $\vec{v}_i^g$ by Equation (9);
    Execute the proposed crossover operation to generate $\vec{u}_i^g$ by Equation (10);
    Repair $\vec{u}_i^g$ by Equation (7);
    Evaluate the fitness value of $\vec{u}_i^g$ by Equation (8);
    Execute the selection strategy for the current individual $\vec{v}_i^g$ and its trial individual $\vec{u}_i^g$ by Equation (4);
  end for
  Set $g = g + 1$;
end while
Output: the best (minimal) fitness value.

4. Experimental Analyses

In this part, the performance of the proposed NDDE algorithm is evaluated by conducting a series of experiments on a large number of various, randomly generated test hands, including 118,800 hands with one type, 100,000 hands with two types, and 100,000 hands with three types. Meanwhile, the influence analyses of the parameters involved in the NDDE algorithm are investigated in terms of both search accuracy and running time, and the tree search algorithm (TSA) in [10] and three other metaheuristic algorithms, including PSO [15], GA [13], and TLBO [20], are also compared with the NDDE algorithm. Finally, the effectiveness of the NDDE algorithm is further demonstrated in a large number of Mahjong game battles.

In these experiments, the performance of each algorithm is measured by the accuracy rate and average running time. Moreover, in order to make fair comparisons and obtain statistical conclusions, each algorithm is run 30 times independently for each hand, and three widely used statistical tests, including the t test [53], Wilcoxon rank sum test [54], and Friedman test [55], are further adopted to distinguish the differences between the NDDE algorithm and each compared method. All algorithms are all implemented in Python 3.0 on a personal laptop with Intel i7-6700 CPU and 16 GB RAM.

4.1. Influence Analyses of NP and G_{max}

Herein, the influences of NP and G_{max} on the performance of the NDDE algorithm are analyzed. As stated in Algorithm 1, NP determines the number of solutions created at each iteration, while G_{max} decides the total iterations of the NDDE algorithm. Thus, various values for them might cause different performances of the NDDE algorithm. Specifically, in order to show the influence of each parameter, the full factorial design (FFD) [56] is used here, and NP and G_{max} are set to four and six different values, respectively, i.e., $NP \in \{10, 20, 30, 50\}$ and $G_{max} \in \{10, 30, 50, 100, 200, 500\}$. Tables 1 and 2 list the accuracy rate and average running time, respectively, of the NDDE algorithm on three kinds of test hands with one run. Note that when the actual deficiency number for a hand is found, the proposed NDDE algorithm will be terminated, and the corresponding running time is used just to measure its performance.

Table 1. Accuracy rates of NDDE algorithm with various NP and G_{max} on three kinds of test hands.

NP \ G_{max}		10	30	50	100	200	500
One type	10	40.246%	73.034%	85.332%	95.154%	98.879%	99.902%
	20	56.237%	85.348%	93.325%	98.337%	99.774%	99.988%
	30	65.250%	90.253%	96.000%	99.219%	99.927%	99.997%
	50	75.591%	94.689%	98.093%	99.751%	99.988%	100%
Two types	10	73.177%	92.509%	96.929%	99.407%	99.915%	99.998%
	20	84.632%	97.065%	99.044%	99.878%	99.992%	100%
	30	89.621%	98.464%	99.607%	99.955%	99.998%	100%
	50	93.979%	99.368%	99.873%	99.994%	100%	100%
Three types	10	87.124%	97.477%	99.146%	99.878%	99.982%	100%
	20	93.707%	99.154%	99.797%	99.977%	100%	100%
	30	96.130%	99.613%	99.930%	99.994%	100%	100%
	50	98.066%	99.863%	99.990%	99.999%	100%	100%

From Table 1, it can be seen that the accuracy rate of the NDDE algorithm is closely related to the values of NP and G_{max}, and gradually improves with their increase in all cases. Specifically, for the hands with one type, the accuracy rate of the NDDE algorithm exceeds 90% when G_{max} = 30 and NP = 30 and 50, G_{max} = 50 and NP = 20, 30, and 50, and every value for NP with G_{max} = 100, 200, and 500. The accuracy rate of the NDDE algorithm is 100% when $G_{max} = 500$ and $NP = 50$. Moreover, for the hands with two types, the accuracy rate of the NDDE algorithm exceeds 90% except when G_{max} = 10 and NP = 10, 20, and 30, while it reaches 100% when G_{max} = 200, NP = 50 and G_{max} = 500, NP = 20, 30, and 50. Moreover, for the hands with three types, the accuracy rate of the NDDE algorithm exceeds 90% except when G_{max} = 10 and NP = 10, while it reaches 100% when $G_{max} = 200$ and NP = 20, 30, and 50, and every value for NP with $G_{max} = 500$. In addition, from Table 2, one can further find that the average running time of the NDDE algorithm is also dependent on the values of NP and G_{max}, and it always gradually increases with their increase in all cases. Specifically, when the types of the hands increase, the average running time of the NDDE algorithm on them gradually decreases. The reason for this might be that as the types of the hands increase, the corresponding search space will be reduced. Hence, the proposed NDDE algorithm can always obtain the actual deficiency number for all hands with certain search costs.

Table 2. Average running time of NDDE algorithm with various NP and G_{max} on three kinds of test hands.

NP \ G_{max}		10	30	50	100	200	500
One type	10	4.97×10^{-3} s	1.01×10^{-2} s	1.20×10^{-2} s	1.48×10^{-2} s	1.56×10^{-2} s	1.72×10^{-2} s
	20	8.13×10^{-3} s	1.40×10^{-2} s	1.64×10^{-2} s	1.85×10^{-2} s	1.88×10^{-2} s	1.99×10^{-2} s
	30	1.11×10^{-2} s	1.81×10^{-2} s	1.98×10^{-2} s	2.07×10^{-2} s	2.22×10^{-2} s	2.11×10^{-2} s
	50	1.54×10^{-2} s	2.21×10^{-2} s	2.40×10^{-2} s	2.44×10^{-2} s	2.55×10^{-2} s	2.52×10^{-2} s
Two types	10	3.28×10^{-3} s	4.96×10^{-3} s	5.49×10^{-3} s	5.90×10^{-3} s	6.04×10^{-3} s	6.22×10^{-3} s
	20	4.94×10^{-3} s	6.39×10^{-3} s	7.22×10^{-3} s	7.21×10^{-3} s	7.22×10^{-3} s	7.36×10^{-3} s
	30	6.08×10^{-3} s	7.39×10^{-3} s	7.68×10^{-3} s	7.82×10^{-3} s	8.06×10^{-3} s	7.92×10^{-3} s
	50	7.95×10^{-3} s	9.00×10^{-3} s	9.28×10^{-3} s	9.61×10^{-3} s	9.74×10^{-3} s	9.57×10^{-3} s
Three types	10	2.31×10^{-3} s	3.08×10^{-3} s	3.12×10^{-3} s	3.22×10^{-3} s	3.25×10^{-3} s	3.27×10^{-3} s
	20	3.07×10^{-3} s	3.67×10^{-3} s	3.79×10^{-3} s	3.84×10^{-3} s	3.84×10^{-3} s	3.86×10^{-3} s
	30	3.73×10^{-3} s	4.24×10^{-3} s	4.34×10^{-3} s	4.35×10^{-3} s	4.38×10^{-3} s	4.34×10^{-3} s
	50	4.83×10^{-3} s	5.23×10^{-3} s	5.21×10^{-3} s	5.28×10^{-3} s	5.21×10^{-3} s	5.23×10^{-3} s

For the sake of clarity, Figures 2 and 3 further depict the accuracy rate and average running time of the NDDE algorithm on all kinds of hands. From Figures 2 and 3, it can easily be seen that whenever either NP or G_{max} increase, the accuracy rate of the NDDE algorithm improves for each type of hand. Meanwhile, with the increase in NP, the average running time of the NDDE algorithm increases in each case, while the NDDE algorithm has a minimal average running time on the hands with three types. Thus, it is essential to set suitable NP and G_{max} in the NDDE algorithm, and we let $NP = 20$ and $G_{max} = 50$ in the following experiments due to its promising performance in terms of both accuracy rate and average running time.

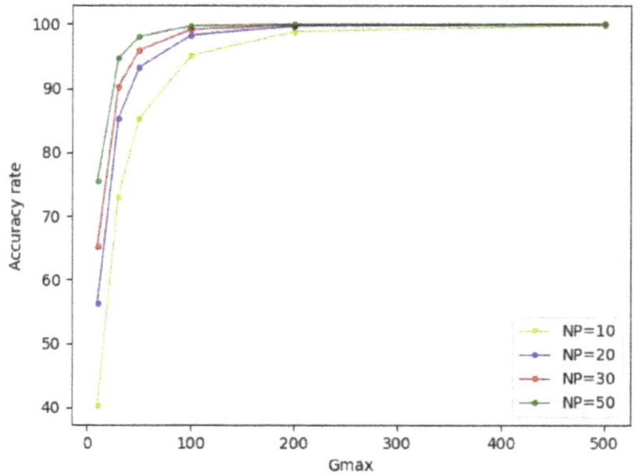

(**a**)

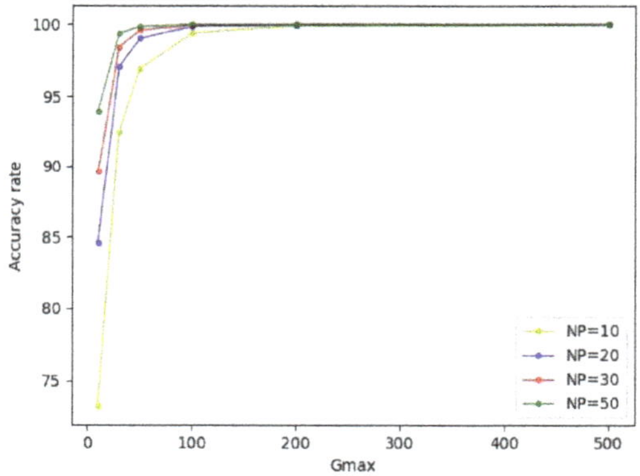

(**b**)

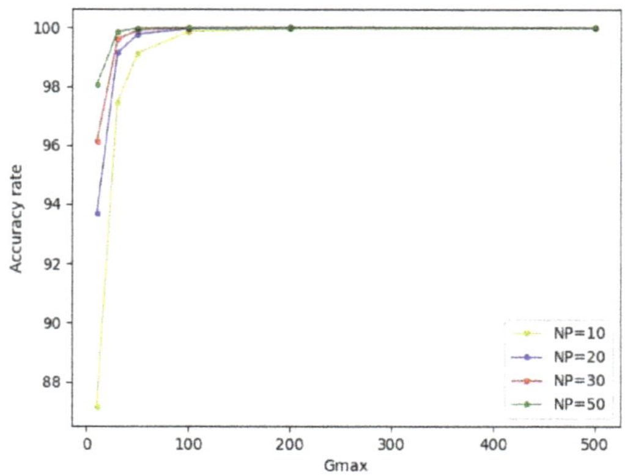

(**c**)

Figure 2. Accuracy rates of NDDE algorithm with various NP and G_{max} on three kinds of test hands. (**a**) Hands with one type, (**b**) hands with two types, and (**c**) hands with three types.

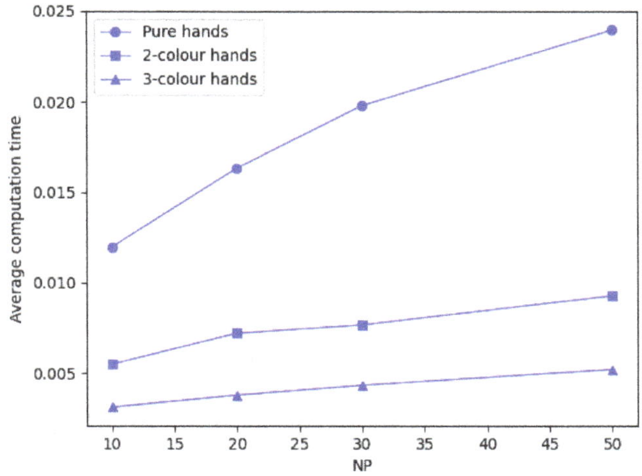

Figure 3. Average running time of NDDE algorithm with various NP and $G_{max} = 50$ on three kinds of test hands.

4.2. Comparisons and Discussions

In this subsection, in order to verify the performance of the NDDE algorithm, one typical deterministic method, namely TSA [10], and three other famous metaheuristic algorithms, including PSO [15], GA [13], and TLBO [20], are compared with it on all the above cases of hands. Specifically, to persuasively estimate the performance of these methods, each approach is run 30 times independently for each hand, and the average accuracy rate and running time of 30 runs on each kind of hand are employed to measure its performance. Moreover, t tests [53], Wilcoxon rank sum tests [54], and Friedman tests [55] are also utilized to show the differences between their performances.

It should be mentioned that PSO [15] is a famous swarm intelligent optimization algorithm, GA [13] is a typical approach belonging to evolutionary computation, and TLBO [20] is a promising metaheuristic method inspired by human activities. Meanwhile, the proposed NDDE algorithm is developed based on just the basic framework of DE. So, these methods are very representative and suitable and thus chosen as the compared ones here.

4.2.1. Comparisons of NDDE Algorithm with TSA

First, one typical deterministic method, namely TSA [10], is compared with the NDDE algorithm on all three kinds of hands. To clearly demonstrate the performance of the NDDE algorithm, its two versions, named $NDDE_1$ and $NDDE_2$, where NP and G_{max} are set to 20 and 50 and 50 and 500, respectively, are simultaneously employed here to compare with TSA. Tables 3 and 4 provide their average and statistical results of 30 runs on each kind of hand in terms of the accuracy rate and running time, respectively. Herein, p_t-value and p_w-value denote the p-values of the t test [53] and Wilcoxon rank sum test [54], respectively (the same below).

From Tables 3 and 4, it can be seen that $NDDE_1$ has the worst results among them in all cases, and $NDDE_2$ and TSA each obtain the actual deficiency number for all hands. Meanwhile, with respect to the average running time, TSA takes the longest time in each case, and $NDDE_1$ takes less time than $NDDE_2$. Moreover, according to the results of the t test and Wilcoxon rank sum test reported in both Tables 3 and 4, $NDDE_1$ has significant differences compared with TSA, and $NDDE_1$ and $NDDE_2$ are both significantly faster than TSA in all cases. Thus, the proposed NDDE is more effective and efficient than TSA for the deficiency number of one Mahjong hand.

Table 3. The average and statistical results of TSA, $NDDE_1$, and $NDDE_2$ on three kinds of hands in terms of accuracy rate.

Hands	Methods	Best Result	Worst Result	Median Result	Mean Result	Standard Deviation	p_t-Value	p_w-Value
One type	TSA	100%	100%	100%	100%	0.00	- -	- -
	$NDDE_1$	93.191%	93.503%	93.301%	93.308%	7.07×10^{-4}	<0.0001	<0.0001
	$NDDE_2$	99.999%	100%	100%	100%	3.19×10^{-6}	0.0192	0.0214
Two types	TSA	100%	100%	100%	100%	0.00	- -	- -
	$NDDE_1$	99.013%	99.129%	99.070%	99.070%	3.21×10^{-4}	<0.0001	<0.0001
	$NDDE_2$	100%	100%	100%	100%	0.00	1.0000	1.0000
Three types	TSA	100%	100%	100%	100%	0.00	- -	- -
	$NDDE_1$	99.760%	99.808%	99.788%	99.785%	1.21×10^{-4}	<0.0001	<0.0001
	$NDDE_2$	100%	100%	100%	100%	0.00	1.0000	1.0000

Table 4. The average and statistical results of TSA, $NDDE_1$, and $NDDE_2$ on three kinds of hands in terms of running time.

Hands	Methods	Best Result (s)	Worst Result (s)	Median Result (s)	Mean Result (s)	Standard Deviation	p_t-Value	p_w-Value
One type	TSA	1.88×10^{-1}	1.89×10^{-1}	1.88×10^{-1}	1.88×10^{-1}	1.66×10^{-4}	- -	- -
	$NDDE_1$	1.57×10^{-2}	1.59×10^{-2}	1.58×10^{-2}	1.58×10^{-2}	3.87×10^{-5}	<0.0001	0.0004
	$NDDE_2$	2.40×10^{-2}	2.43×10^{-2}	2.41×10^{-2}	2.41×10^{-2}	8.74×10^{-5}	<0.0001	0.0004
Two types	TSA	4.32×10^{-2}	4.41×10^{-2}	4.36×10^{-2}	4.36×10^{-2}	3.48×10^{-4}	- -	- -
	$NDDE_1$	7.05×10^{-3}	7.48×10^{-3}	7.09×10^{-3}	7.12×10^{-3}	9.04×10^{-5}	<0.0001	0.0004
	$NDDE_2$	7.95×10^{-3}	8.94×10^{-3}	8.03×10^{-3}	8.10×10^{-3}	2.10×10^{-4}	<0.0001	0.0004
Three types	TSA	1.72×10^{-2}	1.72×10^{-2}	1.72×10^{-2}	1.72×10^{-2}	4.46×10^{-6}	- -	- -
	$NDDE_1$	3.85×10^{-3}	4.91×10^{-3}	3.94×10^{-3}	3.97×10^{-3}	1.86×10^{-4}	<0.0001	0.0004
	$NDDE_2$	5.18×10^{-3}	5.30×10^{-3}	5.21×10^{-3}	5.21×10^{-3}	2.59×10^{-5}	<0.0001	0.0004

4.2.2. Comparisons of NDDE Algorithm with Three Other Famous Metaheuristic Algorithms

To further demonstrate the benefit of the NDDE algorithm, three other famous stochastic intelligent algorithms, including PSO [15], GA [13], and TLBO [20], are also compared with it in all cases of hands above. Specifically, in these chosen compared methods, the same mapping, repairing, and evaluation methods as in the NDDE algorithm are adopted, and the size of the population and the maximum number of iterations are also set to 20 and 50, which is consistent with the setting of the NDDE algorithm. Moreover, to show the differences between these compared methods and the NDDE algorithm, the three statistical tests above are further adopted to give statistical conclusions. Tables 5 and 6 list the average and statistical results of 30 runs on each kind of hand in terms of the accuracy rate and running time, respectively, and Table 7 reports their final comparison results based on the Friedman test [55].

As seen from Tables 5 and 6, the NDDE algorithm has a better accuracy rate than PSO, GA, and TLBO in all cases, and there are significant differences between them and the NDDE algorithm according to both the t test and Wilcoxon rank sum test. Meanwhile, in terms of running time, the NDDE algorithm also has the least time on all kinds of hands, and significantly performs best based on the statistical results. The reason for this might be because GA needs to calculate the selection probability for each individual at each generation, PSO always needs to record and update the personal best individual for each solution, and TLBO has to additionally compute the mean point of the whole population and compare the two target individuals based on their performances to determine the search direction. So, the NDDE algorithm has a more efficient search procedure than the others. Moreover, from Table 7, according to the Friedman test, the NDDE algorithm has the top performance among them on all three kinds of hands in terms of both the accuracy rate and running time. Thereby, the NDDE algorithm is the most promising solver for computing the deficiency number.

Table 5. The average and statistical results of NDDE algorithm, PSO, GA, and TLBO on three kinds of hands in terms of accuracy rate.

Hands	Methods	Best Result	Worst Result	Median Result	Mean Result	Standard Deviation	p_t-Value	p_w-Value
One type	PSO	80.900%	81.200%	81.100%	81.100%	6.05×10^{-4}	<0.0001	<0.0001
	GA	42.600%	43.000%	42.800%	42.800%	1.08×10^{-3}	<0.0001	<0.0001
	TLBO	67.300%	67.700%	67.500%	67.500%	8.29×10^{-4}	<0.0001	<0.0001
	NDDE	93.200%	93.500%	93.300%	93.300%	7.07×10^{-4}	- -	- -
Two types	PSO	94.300%	94.500%	94.400%	94.400%	5.71×10^{-4}	<0.0001	<0.0001
	GA	72.500%	72.900%	72.700%	72.700%	9.47×10^{-4}	<0.0001	<0.0001
	TLBO	91.100%	91.400%	91.300%	91.300%	6.50×10^{-4}	<0.0001	<0.0001
	NDDE	99.000%	99.100%	99.100%	99.100%	3.21×10^{-4}	- -	- -
Three types	PSO	97.800%	97.900%	97.800%	97.800%	3.09×10^{-4}	<0.0001	<0.0001
	GA	86.300%	86.700%	86.500%	86.500%	9.58×10^{-4}	<0.0001	<0.0001
	TLBO	97.000%	97.100%	97.100%	97.100%	3.28×10^{-4}	<0.0001	<0.0001
	NDDE	99.800%	99.800%	99.800%	99.800%	1.21×10^{-4}	- -	- -

Table 6. The average and statistical results of NDDE algorithm, PSO, GA, and TLBO on three kinds of hands in terms of running time.

Hands	Methods	Best Result (s)	Worst Result (s)	Median Result (s)	Mean Result (s)	Standard Deviation	p_t-Value	p_w-Value
One type	PSO	2.09×10^{-2}	2.20×10^{-2}	2.10×10^{-2}	2.10×10^{-2}	1.85×10^{-4}	<0.0001	<0.0001
	GA	2.85×10^{-2}	2.93×10^{-2}	2.86×10^{-2}	2.88×10^{-2}	2.41×10^{-4}	<0.0001	<0.0001
	TLBO	2.89×10^{-2}	3.52×10^{-2}	3.00×10^{-2}	3.03×10^{-2}	1.36×10^{-3}	<0.0001	<0.0001
	NDDE	1.57×10^{-2}	1.59×10^{-2}	1.58×10^{-2}	1.58×10^{-2}	3.87×10^{-5}	- -	- -
Two types	PSO	1.04×10^{-2}	1.05×10^{-2}	1.05×10^{-2}	1.05×10^{-2}	3.46×10^{-5}	<0.0001	<0.0001
	GA	1.68×10^{-2}	1.78×10^{-2}	1.70×10^{-2}	1.71×10^{-2}	3.00×10^{-4}	<0.0001	<0.0001
	TLBO	1.38×10^{-2}	1.55×10^{-2}	1.44×10^{-2}	1.44×10^{-2}	3.94×10^{-4}	<0.0001	<0.0001
	NDDE	7.05×10^{-3}	7.48×10^{-3}	7.09×10^{-3}	7.12×10^{-3}	9.04×10^{-5}	- -	- -
Three types	PSO	5.87×10^{-3}	6.17×10^{-3}	6.09×10^{-3}	6.08×10^{-3}	6.18×10^{-5}	<0.0001	<0.0001
	GA	9.68×10^{-3}	1.07×10^{-2}	9.81×10^{-3}	9.91×10^{-3}	2.15×10^{-4}	<0.0001	<0.0001
	TLBO	7.77×10^{-3}	1.09×10^{-2}	7.98×10^{-3}	8.10×10^{-3}	5.64×10^{-4}	<0.0001	<0.0001
	NDDE	3.85×10^{-3}	4.91×10^{-3}	3.94×10^{-3}	3.97×10^{-3}	1.86×10^{-4}	- -	- -

Table 7. The final comparison results of NDDE algorithm, PSO, GA, and TLBO on all kinds of hands according to Friedman test.

Algorithm	Accuracy Rate				Running Time			
	NDDE	PSO	GA	TLBO	NDDE	PSO	GA	TLBO
Rank	1.00	2.00	3.67	3.33	1.00	2.00	4.00	3.00

Furthermore, in order to clearly illustrate the performance of the NDDE algorithm, the convergence curves of the NDDE algorithm, PSO, GA, and TLBO are also depicted here on six different hands, including $H_1 = (B_4B_4B_6B_6B_6B_7B_7B_7B_7B_8B_9B_9B_9B_9)$, $H_2 = (B_3B_5B_5B_5B_5B_6B_6B_6B_7B_7B_8B_8B_9B_9)$, $H_3 = (B_1B_2B_4B_5B_5)(C_2C_3C_3C_3C_4C_4C_5C_7C_7)$, $H_4 = (B_4)(C_1C_1C_3C_4C_4C_4C_4C_5C_7C_8C_8C_9C_9)$, $H_5 = (B_4B_6)(C_5C_7C_8C_9)(D_1D_1D_2D_2D_3D_7D_7D_8)$, and $H_6 = (B_3)(C_9)(D_1D_4D_5D_6D_6D_6D_7D_7D_8D_8D_9D_9)$. Herein, H_1 and H_2 have just one color, H_3 and H_4 have two colors, and H_5 and H_6 have three colors. From Figure 4, one can easily find that the NDDE algorithm always has a better convergence performance than PSO, GA, and TLBO on each hand. Therefore, the NDDE algorithm has a more promising performance.

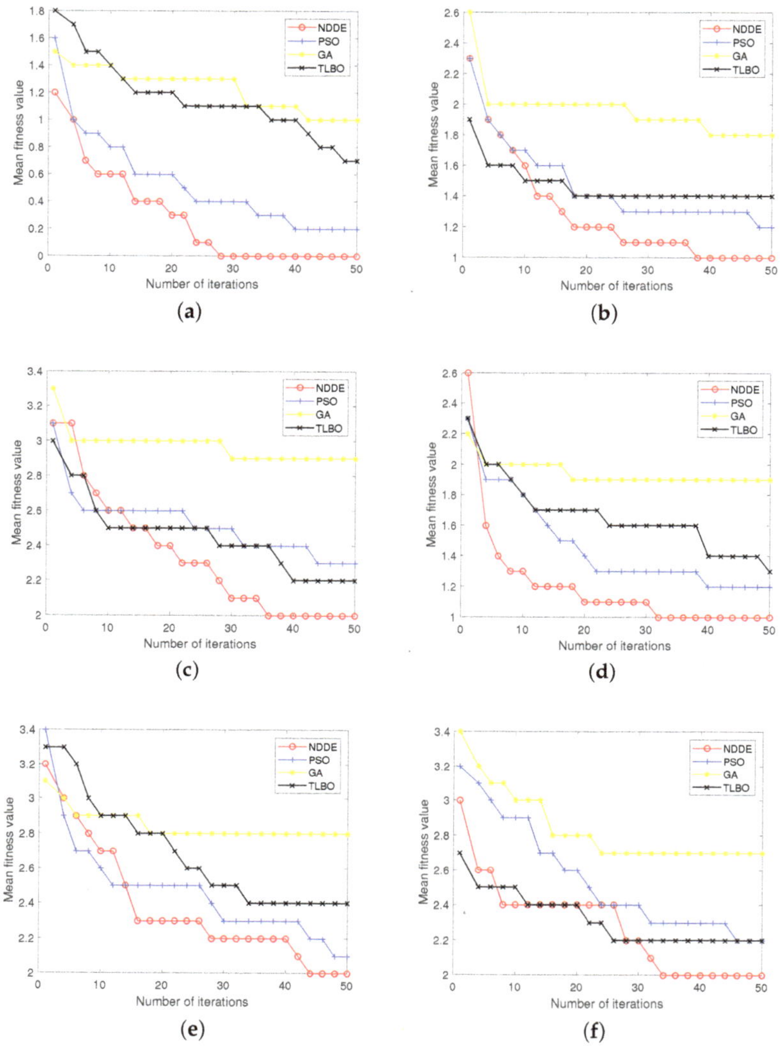

Figure 4. Convergence curves of NDDE algorithm and PSO, GA, and TLBO on six test hands. (**a**) H_1, (**b**) H_2, (**c**) H_3, (**d**) H_4, (**e**) H_5, and (**f**) H_6.

4.3. Effectiveness of NNDE on Mahjong Game Battles

In this part, the practicality of the NDDE algorithm is further evaluated by comparing it with the tree-based search method (TSA) [10] in a Mahjong battle with four players. In this test, 1000 randomly generated states of Mahjong are employed, where all players have drawn their hands and the order of tiles on the wall is fixed, and for each Mahjong game, two rounds are played. Moreover, all players adopt the same strategy to make the decisions for each action, such as pong, chow, and kong [10], except for the method employed to calculate the deficiency number. Specifically, for each state of the game, player 1 and player 3 use the NDDE algorithm to compute the deficiency number, while player 2 and player 4 adopt TSA in the first round. In contrast, player 1 and player 3 use TSA to compute the deficiency number, while player 2 and player 4 adopt the NDDE algorithm in the second round. The sum of the scores obtained by player 1 and player 3 in the first round and by player 2 and player 4 in the second round is recorded as the final score to evaluate the effectiveness of the NDDE algorithm. Herein, we set the basic score in game as 1, and let $NP = 20$ and $G_{max} = 50$ in the NDDE algorithm. After conducting these 1000 different games, the final score of the NDDE algorithm on them is -1.173. Importantly, it should be mentioned that the NDDE algorithm with $NP = 20$ and $G_{max} = 50$ has accuracy rates of 93.325%, 99.044%, and 99.797% on the hands with one, two, and three types, respectively, which can be found in Table 1. This result means that the NDDE algorithm has almost the same performance as TSA in the real battles. Thus, the NDDE algorithm is a promising approach for calculating the deficiency number of a Mahjong hand.

5. Conclusions

In this paper, a novel DE-based approach was presented to calculate the deficiency number of one Mahjong hand, which plays an important role in Mahjong and is helpful for boosting its AI development. Concretely, in order to decrease the difficulty of computing the deficiency number, some pretreatment mechanisms were first presented to convert the original problem into a simpler combinatorial optimization one, where the dimension of the search space of the new problem was reduced to five, and the feasible solutions might have various lengths. Meanwhile, inspired by the benefits of DE, such as simplicity, ease of implementation, a strong robustness, and a superior performance, a novel discrete DE (NDDE) variant was specially developed for solving this new problem by devising proper initialization, a mapping solution method, a repairing solution technique, a fitness evaluation approach, and mutation and crossover operations. Compared to the existing methods for calculating the deficiency number, where the full searches are all implicit in them, thus being very costly, the proposed algorithm employed the framework of the stochastic intelligent approach, and the problem of calculating the deficiency number was converted into a simpler one to solve in this paper. Thereby, the proposed approach is capable of more effectively and efficiently computing the deficiency number of one Mahjong hand. Finally, the performance of the proposed algorithm was evaluated by comparing with the tree search algorithm and three other kinds of metaheuristic methods on a large number of various test cases, and the sensitivity of the parameters involved in the NDDE algorithm was also investigated. The experimental results indicated that the proposed algorithm is more efficient and promising.

It should also be mentioned that this paper only adopted the framework of DE in the design of the algorithm due to its previous superior practical experiences, and the most simple version of DE only was used. Therefore, in our future work, we will focus on devising other solvers for calculating the deficiency number based on other metaheuristic algorithms, the existing enhanced DE variants, and discrete DE versions. Meanwhile, we will also focus on designing a hybrid method by properly integrating the merits of both the metaheuristic methods and the deterministic ones for calculating the deficiency number of a Mahjong hand.

Author Contributions: Conceptualization, X.Y. and Y.L.; methodology, Y.L.; software, X.Y.; validation, X.Y. and Y.L.; formal analysis, X.Y.; investigation, X.Y.; resources, Y.L.; data curation, X.Y.; writing—original draft preparation, X.Y.; writing—review and editing, X.Y.; visualization, X.Y.; supervision, Y.L.; project administration, Y.L.; funding acquisition, Y.L. All authors have read and agreed to the published version of the manuscript.

Funding: This research was funded by the National Natural Science Foundation of China No. 11671244 and 12071271.

Institutional Review Board Statement: Not applicable.

Informed Consent Statement: Not applicable.

Data Availability Statement: The datasets generated during and/or analyzed during the current study are available from the corresponding author on reasonable request.

Conflicts of Interest: The authors declare no conflict of interest.

References

1. The Origins of Mahjong. Available online: http://www.mahjongsets.co.uk/origins-mahjong.html (accessed on 15 December 2022).
2. Wikipedia. Mahjong. Available online: https://en.wikipedia.org/wiki/Mahjong (accessed on 15 December 2022).
3. Tang, J. Designing an Anti-swindle Mahjong Leisure Prototype System using RFID and ontology theory. *J. Netw. Comput. Appl.* **2014**, *39*, 292–301. [CrossRef]
4. Silver, D. Technical Perspective: Solving Imperfect Information Games. *Commun. ACM* **2017**, *60*, 80–80. [CrossRef]
5. Kurita, M.; Hoki, K. Method for Constructing Artificial Intelligence Player with Abstractions to Markov Decision Processes in Multiplayer Game of Mahjong. *IEEE Trans. Games* **2021**, *13*, 99–110. [CrossRef]
6. Wang, M.; Yan, T.; Luo, M.; Huang, W. A novel deep residual network-based incomplete information competition strategy for four-players Mahjong games. *Multimed. Tools Appl.* **2019**, *78*, 23443–23467. [CrossRef]
7. Gao, S.; Okuya, F.; Kawahara, Y.; Tsuruoka, Y. Building a Computer Mahjong Player via Deep Convolutional Neural Networks. *arXiv* **2019**, arXiv:1906.02146.
8. Gao, S.; Li, S. Bloody Mahjong playing strategy based on the integration of deep learning and XGBoost. *CAAI Trans. Intell. Technol.* **2022**, *7*, 95–106. [CrossRef]
9. Zheng, Y.; Li, S. A Review of Mahjong AI Research. In Proceedings of the RICAI 2020: 2020 2nd International Conference on Robotics, Intelligent Control and Artificial Intelligence, Shanghai, China, 17–19 October 2020; pp. 345–349.
10. Li, S.; Yan, X. Let's Play Mahjong! *arXiv* **2019**, arXiv:1903.03294.
11. Wang, Q.; Li, Y.; Chen, X. A Mahjong-Strategy based on Weighted Restarting Automata. In Proceedings of the MLMI '20: 2020 the 3rd International Conference on Machine Learning and Machine Intelligence, Hangzhou, China, 18–20 September 2020.
12. Wang, Q.; Zhou, Y.; Zhu, D.; Li, Y. A new approach to compute deficiency number of Mahjong configurations. *Entertain. Comput.* **2022**, *43*, 100509. [CrossRef]
13. Holland, J. *Adaptation in Natural and Artificial Systems: An Introductory Analysis with Applications to Biology, Control, and Artificial Intelligence*; MIT Press: Cambridge, MA, USA, 1975.
14. Storn, R.; Price, K. Differential evolution-a simple and efficient heuristic for global optimization over continuous space. *J. Glob. Optim.* **1997**, *11*, 341–359. [CrossRef]
15. Kennedy, J.; Eberhart, R. Particle Swarm Optimization. In Proceedings of the ICNN'95—International Conference on Neural Networks, Perth, Australia, 27 November–1 December 1995; pp. 1942–1948.
16. Karaboga, D.; Basturk, B. A powerful and efficient algorithm for numerical function optimization: Artificial bee colony (ABC) algorithm. *J. Glob. Optim.* **2007**, *39*, 459–471. [CrossRef]
17. Eskandar, H.; Sadollah, A.; Bahreininejad, A.; Hamdi, M. Water cycle algorithm-a novel metaheuristic optimization method for solving constrained engineering optimization problems. *Comput. Struct.* **2012**, *110–111*, 151–166. [CrossRef]
18. Jain, M.; Singh, V.; Rani, A. A novel nature-inspired algorithm for optimization: Squirrel search algorithm. *Swarm Evol. Comput.* **2019**, *44*, 148–175. [CrossRef]
19. Rashedi, E.; Nezamabadi-pour, H.; Saryazdi, S. GSA: A gravitational search algorithm. *Inf. Sci.* **2009**, *179*, 2232–2248. [CrossRef]
20. Rao, R.V.; Savsani, V.J.; Vakharia, D.P. Teaching-learning-based optimization: A novel method for constrained mechanical design optimization problems. *Comput.-Aided Des.* **2011**, *43*, 303–315. [CrossRef]
21. Mohamed, A.W.; Hadi, A.A.; Mohamed, A.K. Gaining-sharing knowledge based algorithm for solving optimization problems: A novel nature-inspired algorithm. *Int. J. Mach. Learn. Cybern.* **2020**, *11*, 1501–1529. [CrossRef]
22. Ma, Z.Q.; Wu, G.H.; Suganthan, P.N.; Song, A.J.; Luo, Q.Z. Performance assessment and exhaustive listing of 500+ nature-inspired metaheuristic algorithms. *Swarm Evol. Comput.* **2023**, *77*, 101248. [CrossRef]
23. Taib, H.; Bahreininejad, A. Data clustering using hybrid water cycle algorithm and a local pattern search method. *Adv. Eng. Softw.* **2021**, *153*, 102961. [CrossRef]
24. Chen, J.X.; Gong, Y.J.; Chen, W.N.; Li, M.; Zhang, J. Elastic Differential Evolution for Automatic Data Clustering. *IEEE Trans. Cybern.* **2021**, *51*, 4134–4147. [CrossRef]
25. Wang, J.Z.; Zhang, H.P.; Luo, H. Research on the construction of stock portfolios based on multiobjective water cycle algorithm and KMV algorithm. *Appl. Soft Comput.* **2022**, *115*, 108186. [CrossRef]
26. Sallam, K.M.; Abohany, A.A.; Allahi, R.M. An enhanced multi-operator differential evolution algorithm for tackling knapsack optimization problem. *Neural Comput. Appl.* **2023**.
27. Li, J.Y.; Zhan, Z.H.; Tan, K.C.; Zhang, J. A Meta-knowledge transfer-based differential evolution for multitask optimization. *IEEE Trans. Evol. Comput.* **2022**, *26*, 719–734. [CrossRef]
28. Liao, Z.W.; Mi, X.Y.; Pang, Q.S.; Sun, Y. History archive assisted niching differential evolution with variable neighborhood for multimodal optimization. *Swarm Evol. Comput.* **2023**, *76*, 101206. [CrossRef]
29. Wang, Z.; Chen, Z.; Wang, Z.; Wei, J.; Chen, X.; Li, Q.; Zheng, Y.; Sheng, W. Adaptive memetic differential evolution with multi-niche sampling and neighborhood crossover strategies for global optimization. *Inf. Sci.* **2022**, *583*, 121–136. [CrossRef]
30. Yan, X.; Tian, M. Differential evolution with two-level adaptive mechanism for numerical optimization. *Knowl.-Based Syst.* **2022**, *241*, 108209. [CrossRef]
31. Liu, D.; He, H.; Yang, Q.; Wang, Y.; Jeon, S.W.; Zhang, J. Function value ranking aware differential evolution for global numerical optimization. *Swarm Evol. Comput.* **2023**, *78*, 101282. [CrossRef]

32. Li, X.S.; Wang, K.Y.; Yang, H.C. PAIDDE: A permutation-archive information directed differential evolution algorithm. *IEEE Access* **2022**, *10*, 50384–50402. [CrossRef]
33. Li, Y.Z.; Wang, S.H.; Yang, H.Y. Enhancing differential evolution algorithm using leader-adjoint populations. *Inf. Sci.* **2023**, *622*, 235–268. [CrossRef]
34. Yi, W.C.; Chen, Y.; Pei, Z.; Lu, J.S. Adaptive differential evolution with ensembling operators for continuous optimization problems. *Swarm Evol. Comput.* **2022**, *69*, 100994. [CrossRef]
35. He, Y.; Zhang, F.; Mirjalili, S.; Zhang, T. Novel binary differential evolution algorithm based on Taper-shaped transfer functions for binary optimization problems. *Swarm Evol. Comput.* **2022**, *69*, 101022. [CrossRef]
36. Han, Y.; Yan, X.; Gu, X. Novel hybrid discrete differential evolution algorithm for the multi-stage multi-purpose batch plant scheduling problem. *Appl. Soft Comput.* **2022**, *115*, 108262. [CrossRef]
37. Gao, Z.; Zhang, M.; Zhang, L. Ship-unloading scheduling optimization with differential evolution. *Inf. Sci.* **2022**, *591*, 88–102. [CrossRef]
38. Ali, M.; Essam, D.; Kasmarik, K. A novel design of differential evolution for solving discrete traveling salesman problems. *Swarm Evol. Comput.* **2020**, *52*, 100607. [CrossRef]
39. Ali, M.; Essam, D.; Kasmarik, K. Novel binary differential evolution algorithm for knapsack problems. *Inf. Sci.* **2021**, *542*, 177–194. [CrossRef]
40. Opara, K.R.; Arabas, J. Differential evolution: A survey of theoretical analyses. *Swarm Evol. Comput.* **2019**, *44*, 546–558. [CrossRef]
41. Samuel, A.L. Some studies in machine learning using the game of checkers. *IBM J. Res. Dev.* **1959**, *3*, 211–229. [CrossRef]
42. Shannon, C.E.; Hsu, T.S. Programming a Computer for Playing Chess. *Philos. Mag.* **1950**, *314*, 256–275. [CrossRef]
43. Silver, D.; Huang, A.; Maddison, C.J.; Guez, A.; Sifre, L. Mastering the game of Go with deep neural networks and tree search. *Nature* **2016**, *529*, 484–489. [CrossRef]
44. Silver, D.; Schrittwieser, J.; Simonyan, K.; Antonoglou, I.; Hassabis, D. Mastering the game of Go without human knowledge. *Nature* **2017**, *550*, 354–359. [CrossRef]
45. Sandholm, T. Depth-Limited Solving for Imperfect-Information Games. *Science* **2018**, *347*, 122–123. [CrossRef]
46. Bowling, M.; Burch, N.; Johanson, M.; Tammelin, O. Heads-up limit hold'em poker is solved. *Science* **2015**, *347*, 145–149. [CrossRef]
47. Zhao, E.; Yan, R.; Li, J.; Li, K.; Xing, J. AlphaHoldem: High-Performance Artificial Intelligence for Heads-Up No-Limit Poker via End-to-End Reinforcement Learning. In Proceedings of the 36th AAAI Conference on Artificial Intelligence, Virtual, 22 February–1 March 2022; Volume 36, pp. 4689–4697.
48. Jiang, Q.; Li, K.; Du, B.; Chen, H.; Fang, H. DeltaDou: Expert-level Doudizhu AI through Self-play. In Proceedings of the Twenty-Eighth International Joint Conference on Artificial Intelligence (IJCAI-19), Macao, China, 10–16 August 2019.
49. Mizukami, N.; Tsuruoka, Y. Building a computer Mahjong player based on Monte Carlo simulation and opponent models. In Proceedings of the 2015 IEEE Conference on Computational Intelligence and Games (CIG), Tainan, Taiwan, 31 August–2 September 2015; pp. 275–283.
50. Yoshimura, K.; Hochin, T.; Nomiya, H. Searching optimal movements in multi-player games with imperfect information. In Proceedings of the 2016 IEEE/ACIS 15th International Conference on Computer and Information Science (ICIS), Okayama, Japan, 26–29 June 2016; pp. 1–6.
51. Li, J.; Koyamada, S.; Ye, Q.; Liu, G.; Hon, H.W. Suphx: Mastering Mahjong with Deep Reinforcement Learning. *arXiv* **2020**, arXiv:2003.13590.
52. Sato, H.; Shirakawa, T.; Hagihara, A.; Maeda, K. An analysis of play style of advanced mahjong players toward the implementation of strong AI player. *Int. J. Parallel Emergent Distrib. Syst.* **2017**, *32*, 195–205. [CrossRef]
53. Box, J. Guinness, Gosset, Fisher, and Small Samples. *Stat. Sci.* **1987**, *2*, 45–52. [CrossRef]
54. Wilcoxon, F. Individual comparisons by ranking methods. *Biom. Bull* **1945**, *6*, 80–83. [CrossRef]
55. Derrac, J.; Garca, S.; Molina, D.; Herrera, F. A practical tutorial on the use of nonparametric statistical tests as a methodology for comparing evolutionary and swarm intelligence algorithms. *Swarm Evol. Comput.* **2011**, *1*, 3–18. [CrossRef]
56. Lee, Y.; Filliben, J.J.; Micheals, R.J.; Phillips, P.J. Sensitivity analysis for biometric systems: A methodology based on orthogonal experiment designs. *Comput. Vis. Image Underst.* **2013**, *117*, 532–550. [CrossRef]

mathematics

Review

A Survey on Population-Based Deep Reinforcement Learning

Weifan Long [1], Taixian Hou [1], Xiaoyi Wei [1], Shichao Yan [1], Peng Zhai [1,2,3,*] and Lihua Zhang [1,4,5,*]

1 Academy for Engineering and Technology, Fudan University, Shanghai 200433, China
2 Ji Hua Laboratory, Foshan 528251, China
3 Engineering Research Center of AI and Robotics, Ministry of Education, Shanghai 200433, China
4 Institute of Meta-Medical, Fudan University, Shanghai 200433, China
5 Jilin Provincial Key Laboratory of Intelligence Science and Engineering, Changchun 130013, China
* Correspondence: pzhai@fudan.edu.cn (P.Z.); lihuazhang@fudan.edu.cn (L.Z.)

Abstract: Many real-world applications can be described as large-scale games of imperfect information, which require extensive prior domain knowledge, especially in competitive or human–AI cooperation settings. Population-based training methods have become a popular solution to learn robust policies without any prior knowledge, which can generalize to policies of other players or humans. In this survey, we shed light on population-based deep reinforcement learning (PB-DRL) algorithms, their applications, and general frameworks. We introduce several independent subject areas, including naive self-play, fictitious self-play, population-play, evolution-based training methods, and the policy-space response oracle family. These methods provide a variety of approaches to solving multi-agent problems and are useful in designing robust multi-agent reinforcement learning algorithms that can handle complex real-life situations. Finally, we discuss challenges and hot topics in PB-DRL algorithms. We hope that this brief survey can provide guidance and insights for researchers interested in PB-DRL algorithms.

Keywords: reinforcement learning; multi-agent reinforcement learning; self play; population play

MSC: 68T42

Citation: Long, W.; Hou, T.; Wei, X.; Yan, S.; Zhai, P.; Zhang, L. A Survey on Population-Based Deep Reinforcement Learning. *Mathematics* **2023**, *11*, 2234. https://doi.org/10.3390/math11102234

Academic Editors: Jian Dong and Marjan Mernik

Received: 31 March 2023
Revised: 7 May 2023
Accepted: 8 May 2023
Published: 10 May 2023

1. Introduction

Reinforcement learning (RL) [1] is a highly active research field in the machine learning community with decades of development. However, traditional RL methods have limited performance when it comes to complex, high-dimensional input spaces. Deep reinforcement learning (DRL) [2] addresses this issue by using deep neural networks as function approximators, allowing agents to use unstructured data for decision-making. DRL has shown impressive performance on a range of tasks, including game playing, robotics, and autonomous driving. There are many impressive research works from different fields which were achieved through DRL, such as gaming (AlphaGo [3], AlphaZero [4], AlphaStar [5]), nuclear energy (fusion control [6]), and mathematics (AlphaTensor [7]). While DRL has become increasingly popular due to its effectiveness and generality, there are many real-world applications that require multiple agents' cooperation or competition. A multi-agent system is usually employed to research problems that are difficult or impossible for a single agent. Multi-agent reinforcement learning (MARL) is one of the effective approaches to multi-agent system problems [8]; it has been used to address problems in a variety of domains, including robotics, distributed control, telecommunications, and economics [9]. However, many real-world applications can be described as large-scale games of imperfect information, which require a lot of prior domain knowledge to compute a Nash equilibrium, especially in a competitive environment. This can be a major challenge for traditional MARL methods. Population-based reinforcement learning (PB-DRL) has emerged as a popular solution, allowing for the training of robust policies without any prior domain knowledge that can generalize to all policies of other players.

Population-based approaches take advantage of the high parallelism and large search space typically found in optimization problems. This method has demonstrated remarkable performance in MARL, resulting in exceptional performance in games such as Pluribus [10] and OpenAI Five [11] without any expert experience. Czarnecki et al. [12] conducted research on the importance of population-based training techniques for large-scale multi-agent environments, which can include both virtual and real-world scenarios. According to their study, population-based methods offer several benefits for training robust policies in such environments, including diversity of strategies, scalability, and adaptability to changing conditions. The population diversity in PB-DRL allows for a more robust policy because it can handle a wider range of situations and scenarios. This can be particularly important in real-world applications where there may be plenty of variability and uncertainty. By using a population-based approach, the policy can be trained to be more robust and adaptable to different situations, which is crucial for success in real-world applications.

In contrast to prior surveys, the motivation of our survey lies instead in recent PB-DRL algorithms and applications specifically, which helps to achieve surprisingly outstanding performance. Accordingly, we also introduce general frameworks of PB-DRL. In this survey, we give an account of PB-DRL approaches and associated methods. We start with reviewing selected ideas from game theory and multi-agent reinforcement learning. Then, we move on to present several recent promising approaches, applications, and frameworks of PB-DRL. Here, we first give the idea of milestones and briefly describe others in each kind of PB-DRL; applications for how to use the corresponding methods will then be introduced. Finally, we finish by discussing challenges and hot topics of PB-DRL. Given the extensive literature from the MARL community and adjacent fields, we acknowledge that our survey is not exhaustive and may not cover all prior work. Specifically, in this survey, our focus is on PB-DRL algorithms including multi-agent reinforcement learning by using self-play-related technology, evolution-based training methods for reinforcement learning, and general frameworks. We conducted a comprehensive literature search following the guidelines for Systematic Literature Reviews (SLRs) [13] to conduct a comprehensive literature search on PB-DRL. We searched four databases that are widely used and recognized in the field of software engineering: Google Scholar, IEEE Xplore, ACM Digital Library, and DataBase Systems and Logic Programming. We used advanced search options to limit the results to peer-reviewed articles published in English from 2018 to 2023, as this survey is focused more on recent works and we used snowballing method to cover previous milestones. We used the following search string: ("population-based" AND "reinforcement learning") OR ("evolution algorithm" AND "reinforcement learning") OR ("self-play" AND "reinforcement learning"). The initial search yielded 200 papers from Google Scholar (capturing the first 20 pages of search results), 127 papers from IEEE Xplore, 381 papers from ACM Digital Library, and 80 papers from DataBase Systems and Logic Programming, resulting in a total of 788 papers before screening. We screened the titles and abstracts of these papers based on their relevance to our survey topic, which is PB-DRL methods and applications. We used the following inclusion criteria: (1) the paper must focus on PB-DRL or a related concept (e.g., evolutionary algorithm, self-play); (2) the paper must report novel approaches, significant results, or comparative evaluations related to PB-DRL. To ensure the high quality of the references, we also screened based on the publisher; famous conferences and journals such as Nature, Science, NeuralPS, ICML, and ICLR were included. After screening, we included nearly 30 papers for further analysis and excluded others for various reasons such as being out of scope, being duplicates, or being of low quality. We then used snowballing to complement our database search and ensure that we did not miss any relevant studies, i.e., we checked the references of the included papers to identify any additional relevant studies. Our aim is to provide an overview of recent developments in PB-DRL, and we hope that it can garner more attention and be applied in various industries.

2. Background

Population-based deep reinforcement learning is an approach that addresses the limitations of traditional reinforcement learning algorithms. PB-DRL algorithms maintain a population of agents that explore the environment in parallel and learn from each other to improve their collective performance. This approach has shown significant improvements in terms of sample efficiency and generalization in various applications. In this section, we start with necessary knowledge which may help to understand PB-DRL algorithms.

2.1. Game Theory

Game theory and MARL are closely related fields, as game theory provides a theoretical framework for analyzing and understanding strategic interactions between multiple agents, while MARL provides a practical approach for agents to learn optimal strategies through experience. Research in this survey usually considers a normal-form game or extensive-form game. A normal-form game refers to a game where players make decisions simultaneously without knowing the decisions made by other players, whereas an extensive-form game refers to a game where players make decisions sequentially and can observe the decisions made by other players before making their own decisions.

Normal-form games represent the game by way of a matrix, represented by a tuple $(\boldsymbol{\pi}, U, n)$, where n is the number of players, $\boldsymbol{\pi} = (\pi_1, \ldots, \pi_n)$ is a collection of strategies for all players, and $U : \boldsymbol{\pi} \to R^n$ is a payoff table mapping each joint policy to a scalar utility for each player. Each player aims to maximize their own payoff. Assume that π_i is a mixed strategy of player i and π_{-i} refers to the joint mixed strategies except π_i. $U_i(\pi_i, \pi_{-i})$ is the expected payoff of player i. Then, Nash equilibrium can be defined.

Definition 1 (Nash equilibrium). *A mixed strategy profile $\boldsymbol{\pi}^* = (\pi_1^*, \ldots, \pi_n^*)$ is a Nash equilibrium if for all player i:*

$$\max_{\pi_i'} U_i(\pi_i', \pi_{-i}) = U_i(\pi_i^*, \pi_{-i})$$

Intuitively, in a Nash equilibrium, no player has an incentive to change their current strategy unilaterally because doing so would result in no benefits or even negative returns. Therefore, the strategy profile remains stable. π_i^* is the best response (BR) of agent i.

In extensive-form games, players make decisions sequentially, with each player's action influencing the subsequent decisions of other players. These games generalize the normal-form game formalism for sequential decision-making scenarios. Every finite extensive-form game has an equivalent normal-form game [14], and an approximation of Nash equilibrium called ϵ-Nash equilibrium or approximate Nash equilibrium is typically considered. The corresponding BR is referred to as the ϵ-best response.

Definition 2 (ϵ-Nash equilibrium). *A mixed strategy profile $\boldsymbol{\pi}^* = (\pi_1^*, \ldots, \pi_n^*)$ is a ϵ-Nash equilibrium if for all player i:*

$$U_i(\pi_i^*, \pi_{-i}) \geq U_i(\pi_i', \pi_{-i}) - \epsilon, \quad \textit{for any policy } \pi_i' \textit{ of player } i$$

In the context of game theory, a real-life game can be incredibly complex, making it impractical to explicitly list out all the possible strategies. As a result, researchers often construct an "empirical game" that is smaller in size but still captures the essential features of the full game. This empirical game is built by discovering strategies and using meta-reasoning techniques to navigate the strategy space. In the general framework of PB-DRL algorithms, this empirical game is also known as the "meta-game." It starts with a single policy and grows by adding policies that approximate the best responses to the meta-strategy of the other players. In other words, the meta-game is a simplified version of the real game that captures its essential features, allowing PB-DRL algorithms to learn effective strategies in a computationally efficient manner.

2.2. Multi-Agent Reinforcement Learning

Reinforcement learning is a learning approach that aims to find the optimal way of mapping situations to actions to maximize a numerical reward signal [1]. It is often formalized as a Markov Decision Process (MDP) that addresses sequential decision-making problems in environments with discrete time-steps. Deep reinforcement learning combines RL with deep neural networks, resulting in improved performance compared to RL without neural networks. DRL can handle larger state spaces, enabling it to process larger input matrices such as images, and it can learn more complex policies with fewer hand-specified features to represent state information [15,16]. Some well-known DRL algorithms used in various applications include DQN [17], TD3 [18], and PPO [19].

Multi-agent reinforcement learning refers to sequential decision-making with multiple agents, which poses additional challenges due to the fact that taking action can influence the rewards of other agents. MARL tasks are commonly divided into cooperative (the agents work together to reach a common goal, like Overcooked), competitive (each agent has its own reward function and acts selfishly to maximize only its own expected cumulative reward, like Go), and mixed settings (each agent has an arbitrary but agent-unique reward function, like football). PB-DRL has shown good performance in applications with these settings [4,20,21].

MARL algorithms can be classified into six different learning paradigms, as outlined by Yang et al. [22]: (1) independent learners with shared policy, (2) independent learners with independent policies, (3) independent learning with shared policy within a group, (4) one central controller controlling all agents, (5) centralized training with decentralized execution (CTDE), and (6) decentralized training with networked agents. Types with independent learners (type 1-3) use independent reinforcement learning, where each agent treats the experience of other agents as part of its (non-stationary) environments [23,24]. This makes it a suitable approach for problems with a large number of agents or a high-dimensional action space. However, it may result in overfitting to the other agents during training and insufficient generalization during execution [25]. The fourth type of the learning paradigm can be seen as a single-agent RL method, which has a problem in large-scale strategy space. Type 5, CTDE, is a popular approach where agents can exchange information with others during training and act independently during execution [26,27]. This allows for efficient training but may suffer from communication overhead during execution. Decentralized training with networked agents, type 6, involves each agent learning its own policy based on local observations and communication with its neighbors in a networked structure [28]. This can improve scalability and adaptability but may require significant communication among agents.

PB-DRL algorithms belong to the CTDE paradigm and maintain a large, diverse population to train a robust policy that can generalize to non-communication situations. In PB-DRL, a population of agents explores the environment in parallel, allowing them to learn from each other to improve their collective performance. This approach has been shown to be more sample-efficient and to generalize better in various applications, including cooperative, competitive, and mixed settings, which makes it a promising technique for addressing the challenges in multi-agent reinforcement learning.

3. Population-Based Deep Reinforcement Learning

In recent years, PB-DRL has emerged as a promising research direction in the field of DRL. The key idea behind PB-DRL is to employ multiple agents or learners that interact with their environment in parallel and exchange information to improve their performance. This approach has shown great potential in achieving superior results compared to traditional single-agent methods. In this survey paper, we focus on several popular population-based methods, including naive self-play, fictitious self-play, population play, evolutionary-based methods, and the general framework. We will discuss the basic concepts, advantages, and limitations of each method to provide a comprehensive overview of the current state of the art in this field. For a brief overview of a selected subset of methods for PB-DRL, see also Table 1.

Table 1. A selected subset of research areas and recent algorithms or frameworks for PB-DRL.

Category	Algorithm	Advantages	Disadvantages	Descriptions
Naive Self-Play	Naive SP [29]	Simplicity, Effectiveness	Overfitting, Instability	Playing against a mirrored copy of the agent
Fictitious Self-Play	Fictitious play [30]	Flexibility	Exploration requirement	Players choose the best response to a uniform mixture of all previous policies at each iteration
	FSP [31]	Robust and efficient learning	Exploration requirement, Sensitive initialization	Extending FP to extensive-form games
	NFSP [32]	Handling complex environments, High scalability	Instability, Hyperparameter tuning	Combining FSP with neural network function approximation
	ED [33]	Efficient, No requirement of average strategies	Exploration requirement, Scalability issues	Directly optimizes policies against worst-case opponents
	δ-Uniform FSP [34]	Simplicity	Limited Exploration	Learning a policy that can beat older versions of itself sampled uniformly at random
	Prioritized FSP [5]	Simplicity	Limited Exploration	Sampling the policies of opponents by their expected win rate
Population-Play	PP [35]	Exploration, Diversity	Inefficiency	Training a population of agents, all of whom interact with each other
	FCP [20]	Zero-shot collaboration	Inefficiency, Prone to researcher biases	Using PP to train a diversity policy pool of partners which is used to train a robust agent in cooperative setting
	Hidden-Utility Self-Play [36]	Modeling human bias	Inefficiency, Domain knowledge requirement	Following the FCP framework and uses a hidden reward function to model human bias to human–AI cooperation problem
Evolution-based Method	PBT [37]	Efficient search, Dynamic hyperparameter tuning	Resource-intensive, Complex implementation	Online evolutionary process that adapts internal rewards and hyperparameters
	MERL [38]	No requirement for reward sharping	Computationally expensive	Split-level training platform without requiring domain-specific reward shaping
	CERL [39]	Efficient sampling	Resource-intensive	Using a collective replay buffer to share all information across the population
	DERL [40]	Diverse solution	Computationally expensive	Decoupling the processes of learning and evolution in a distributed asynchronous manner
General Framework	PSRO [25]	Robust learning, Zero-sum convergence	Low scalability, Computationally expensive	Using DRL to compute best responses to a distribution over policies and empirical game-theoretic analysis to compute new meta-strategy distributions
	PSRO_{rN} [41]	Open-ended learning, Non-transitive cycle	Low scalability, Computationally expensive	A framework based on PSRO but defines and uses the effective diversity to encourage diverse skills
	Diverse PSRO [42]	Open-ended learning, Low exploitability	Low scalability, Computationally expensive	Introducing a new diversity measure based on a geometric interpretation of games modelled by a determinantal point process to improve diversity
	Pipeline PSRO [43]	Scalability, High efficiency	Approximation errors	Maintaining a hierarchical pipeline of reinforcement learning workers to improve the efficiency of PSRO
	α-PSRO [44]	General-sum many-player game	Resource-intensive, Solver dependence	Using an α-Rank method as the meta-solver which is a critical component of PSRO

3.1. *Naive Self-Play*

Self-play (SP) is an open-ended learning training scheme that trains by playing against a mirrored copy of itself without any supervision in various stochastic environments. Compared with expert opponents, SP has shown more amazing performance in many complex problems. The simplest and most effective SP method is naive self-play, first proposed in [29]. As shown in Figure 1, the opponent (mirrored agent) uses the same policy network, i.e., the opponent downloads the latest policy network while the agent updates its policy network. Denote π as a policy being trained, $\boldsymbol{\pi}^{zoo}$ as a policy zoo, π' as the policy set of the opponents, Ω as the policy sampling distribution, and G as the gating function for π^{zoo} [45]. The policy sampling distribution Ω is

$$\Omega(\pi'|\pi^{zoo}, \pi) = \begin{cases} 1, & \forall \pi' \in \pi^{zoo} : \pi' = \pi \\ 0. & Otherwise \end{cases} \quad (1)$$

Since the policy zoo π^{zoo} only keeps the latest version of policy π, it always clears the old policies π^{zoo} and inserts π, $\pi^{zoo} = \pi$.

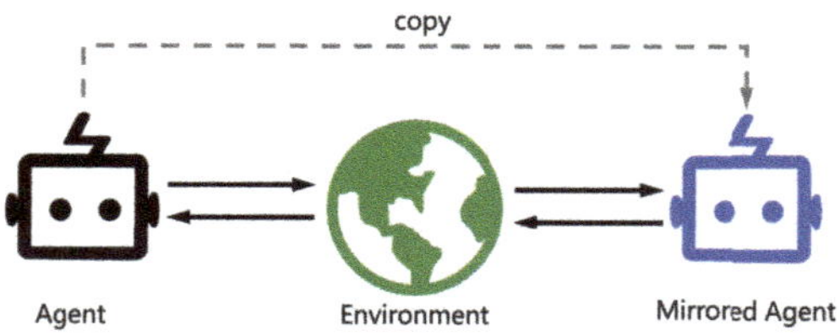

Figure 1. Overview of naive self-play.

A variety of works have followed this method since naive self-play is simple and effective. TD-Gammon [46] features naive SP to learn a policy by using TD(λ) algorithm. At that time, this work outperforms supervised learning with expert experience. AlphaGo [3] defeated the world champion of Go in 2017; it uses a combination of supervised learning on expert datasets and SP technology. SP is used to update the policy and to generate more data. SP-based applications have been developed rapidly in both academia and industry. One year after AlphaGo, AlphaZero [47] gained prominence. In contrast to AlphaGo, AlphaZero does not require domain-specific human knowledge but achieves outstanding performance. Instead, it learns the game policy by playing against itself, using only the game rules.

Naive SP is also a solution for handling many-to-many environments, as demonstrated by JueWu [48] which uses this approach for two players controlling five heroes in Honor of Kings during lineup and random lineup stages. Another study applied naive SP to an open-ended environment (hide-and-seek [49]), showing that it can lead to emergent auto-curricula with many distinct and compounding phase shifts in agent strategy.

Despite its effectiveness, naive SP may not be sufficient to learn a robust policy due to the lack of diversity in opponent policies. Fictitious self-play is a solution to this problem, where the agent plays against a mixture of its previous policies and fictional policies that are generated by sampling from a distribution over policies learned during training.

3.2. Fictitious Self-Play

Fictitious play, introduced by Brown [30], is a popular method for learning Nash equilibrium in normal-form games. The premise is that players repeatedly play a game and choose the best response to a uniform mixture of all previous policies at each iteration. As shown in Figure 2, fictitious self-play (FSP) [31] is a machine learning framework that implements generalized weakened fictitious play in behavioral strategies in a sample-based fashion. It can avoid cycles by playing against all previous policies. FSP iteratively samples episodes of the game from SP. These episodes constitute datasets that are used by reinforcement learning to compute approximate best responses and by supervised learning to compute perturbed models of average strategies.

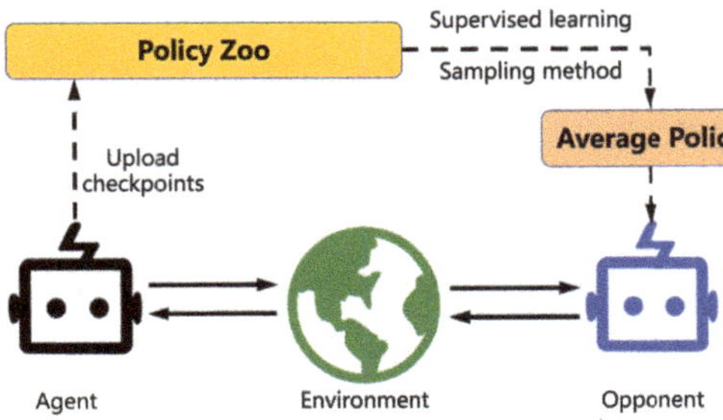

Figure 2. Overview of fictitious self-play.

Neural fictitious self-play (NFSP) [32] combines FSP with neural network function approximation. NFSP keeps two kinds of memories. One, denoted as $\mathcal{M}_{RL}$, was used for storing experience of game transitions, while the other, $\mathcal{M}_{SL}$, stored the best response behavior. Each agent computed an approximate best response β from $\mathcal{M}_{RL}$ and updated its average policy Π by supervised learning from $\mathcal{M}_{SL}$. In principle, each agent could learn the best response by playing against the average policies of other agents. However, the agent cannot get its best response policy β, which is needed to train its average policy Π, and its average policy Π is needed for the best response training of other agents. NFSP uses the approximation of anticipatory dynamics of continuous-time dynamic fictitious play [50], in which players choose the best response to the short-term predicted average policy of their opponents, $\Pi_t^{-i} + \eta \frac{d}{dt}\Pi_t$, where η is the anticipatory parameter. NFSP assumes $\beta_{t+1} - \Pi_t \approx \frac{d}{dt}\Pi_t$ as a discrete-time approximation. During play, all agents mixed their actions according to $\sigma = \Pi + \eta(\beta - \Pi)$. By using this approach, each agent could learn an approximate best response with predicted average policies of its opponents. In other words, the policy sampling distribution of all agents Ω is

$$\Omega(\pi) = \begin{cases} \beta, & \textit{with probability } \eta \\ \Pi. & \textit{with probability } 1-\eta \end{cases} \tag{2}$$

M_{RL} uses a circular buffer to store transition in every step, but M_{SL} only inserts transition while agent follows the best response policy β.

The Exploitability Descent (ED) algorithm [33] is a PB-DRL method that directly optimizes policies against worst-case opponents without the need to compute average policies. In contrast to NFSP algorithm, which requires a large reservoir buffer to compute an approximate equilibrium, ED focuses on decreasing the "exploitability" of each player, which refers to how much a player could gain by switching to a best response. The algorithm has two steps for each player on each iteration. The first step is identical to the FP algorithm, where the best response to the policy of each player is computed. The second step performs gradient ascent on the policy to increase the utility of each player against the respective best responder, aiming to decrease the exploitability of each player. In a tabular setting with Q-values and L2 projection, the policy gradient ascent update is defined by equation

$$\begin{aligned} \boldsymbol{\theta}_S^t &= P_{\ell_2}(\boldsymbol{\theta}_S^{t-1} + \alpha^t \langle \nabla_{\boldsymbol{\theta}_S} \boldsymbol{\pi}_{\boldsymbol{\theta}}^{t-1}(S), \boldsymbol{Q}^{\boldsymbol{b}}(S) \rangle) \\ &= P_{\ell_2}(\boldsymbol{\theta}_S^{t-1} + \alpha^t \boldsymbol{Q}^{\boldsymbol{b}}(S)), \end{aligned} \tag{3}$$

where $\boldsymbol{Q}^{\boldsymbol{b}}(S)$ is the expected return at state S with joint policy set $\boldsymbol{b}$, P_{ℓ_2} is the L2 projection, $\nabla_{\boldsymbol{\theta}_S} \boldsymbol{\pi}_{\boldsymbol{\theta}}^{t-1}(S)$ is an identity matrix, and α is the step size. In other words, the ED algorithm directly optimizes policies against worst-case opponents, making it a promising approach for addressing games with complex strategy spaces.

A related approach from another perspective is $\delta - Uniform$ FSP [34], which learns a policy that can beat older versions of itself sampled uniformly at random. The authors use a percentage threshold $\delta \in [0,1]$ to select the old policies that are eligible for sampling from the policy zoo π^{zoo}, i.e., the opponent strategy π' is sampled from

$$\Omega(\pi'|\pi^{zoo}, \pi) = Uniform(\delta|\pi^{zoo}|, |\pi^{zoo}|) \tag{4}$$

Significantly, the algorithm is the same as naive SP while $\delta = 1$. After every episode, the training policy is always inserted into the policy zoo π^{zoo}. Thus, π^{zoo} is updated with $\pi^{zoo} = \pi^{zoo} \cup \pi$.

While AlphaStar does use FSP as one of its learning algorithms, Prioritized FSP is actually a modification proposed by the AlphaStar team in their subsequent paper [5]. The authors argue that many games are wasted against players that are defeated in almost 100% of games while using regular FSP and propose Prioritized FSP which samples policies by their expected win rate. Policies that are expected to win with higher probability against the current agent have higher priority and are sampled more frequently. The opponent sampling distribution Ω can be written as

$$\Omega(\pi'|\pi^{zoo}, \pi) = \frac{f(P(\pi \text{ } beats \text{ } \pi'))}{\sum_{\Pi \in \pi^{zoo}} f(P(\pi \text{ } betas \text{ } \Pi))} \tag{5}$$

where f is a weighting function, e.g., $f(x) = (1-x)^p$. The policy zoo named league in the paper is complex; we will introduce the update method latter.

OpenAI Five also employs a similar method, as described in [11]. The method consists of training with a naive self-play approach for 80% of the games and using past sampling policies for the remaining 20%. Similar to the Prioritized FSP method, OpenAI Five uses a dynamic sampling system that relies on a dynamically generated quality score q. This system samples opponent agents according to a softmax distribution, where the probability of choosing an opponent p is proportional to e^q. If OpenAI Five wins the game, q is updated with a learning rate constant η as follows:

$$q = q - \frac{\eta}{Np} \tag{6}$$

where N is the size of policy zoo. At every 10 iterations, the policy of the current agent will be added to the policy zoo with an initial quality score equal to the maximum quality score in the zoo.

While self-play can bring remarkable performance improvements to reinforcement learning, it performs poorly in non-transitive games because it always plays against itself. Specifically, the opponent's policy only samples from one policy, which means the training agent only learns from a single type of opponent. This approach works well in situations where a higher-ranked player can always beat a lower-ranked player. Population-based training methods bring more robust policies.

3.3. *Population-Play*

Another population-based method for multi-agent systems is population-play (PP), which builds upon the concept of SP to involve multiple players and their past generations [5,35], as shown in Figure 3. With PP, a group of agents is developed and trained to compete not only with each other but also with agents from prior generations.

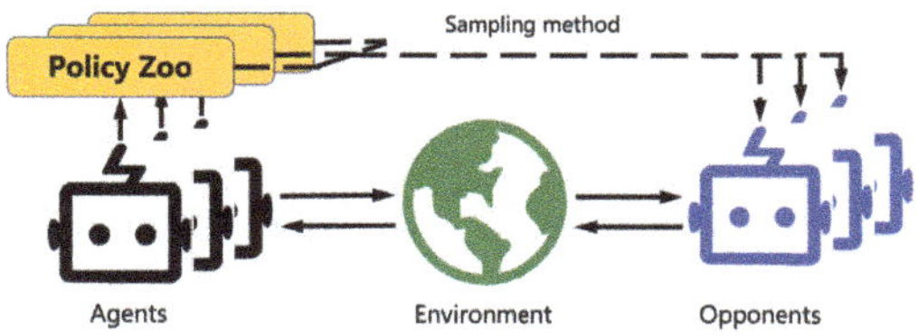

Figure 3. Overview of (naive) population-play.

To train an exceptional agent, AlphaStar [5] maintains three types of opponent pools: Main Agents, League Exploiters, and Main Exploiters. Main Agents are trained with a combination of 35% SP and 50% PFSP against all past players in the league, and the agent plays an additional 15% of matches against opponents who had previously been beaten but are now unbeatable, as well as past opponents who had previously exploited the weaknesses of the agent. League Exploiters are used to find a policy that league agents cannot defeat. They are trained using PFSP against agents in the league and added to the league if they defeat all agents in the league with a winning rate of more than 70%. Main Exploiters play against Main Agents to identify their weaknesses. If the current probability of winning is less than 20%, Main Exploiters employ PFSP against players created by Main Agents. Otherwise, Main Exploiters play directly against the current Main Agents.

For the Win (FTW) [35] is a training method designed for the game of Capture the Flag, which involves training a diverse population of different agents by having them learn from playing with each other. The training process involves sampling agents from the population to play as teammates and opponents, which is done using a stochastic matchmaking scheme that biases co-players to be of similar skill to the player. This ensures that a diverse set of teammates and opponents participate in training, and helps to promote robustness in the learned policies. A population-based training method is implemented to enhance the performance of weaker players and improve the overall ability of all players.

PP can accommodate a wide range of agents, making it also suitable for deployment in cooperative settings. However, Siu et al. [51] observed that in such scenarios, human players tended to favor rule-based agents over RL-based ones. This finding highlights the need to take into account human perceptions of AI when designing and developing systems intended for real-world adoption.

To address this issue, fictitious co-play (FCP) [20] aims to produce robust partners that can assist humans with different styles and skill levels without relying on human-generated data (i.e., zero-shot coordination with humans). FCP is a two-stage approach. In the first stage, N partner agents are trained independently in self-play to create a diverse pool of partners. In the second stage, FCP trains a best-response agent against the diverse pool to achieve robustness. Hidden-utility self-play [36] follows the FCP framework and uses a hidden reward function to model human bias with domain knowledge to solve the human–AI cooperation problem. A similar work for assistive robots learns a good latent representation for human policies [52].

3.4. Evolution-Based Training Methods

Evolutionary algorithms are a family of optimization algorithms inspired by the process of natural selection. They involve generating a population of candidate solutions and iteratively improving them by applying operators such as mutation, crossover, and selection, which mimic the processes of variation, reproduction, and selection in biological evolution. These algorithms are widely used in solving complex optimization problems in various fields, including engineering, finance, and computer science. Evolutionary-based DRL is a type of PB-DRL that approaches training from an evolutionary perspective and often incorporates swarm intelligence techniques, particularly evolution algorithms. In this subsection, we will focus on recent hybrid DRL algorithms that combine evolutionary approaches with deep reinforcement learning to accelerate the training phase. These algorithms can be used alongside SP or PP algorithms [35].

Population-based training (PBT) introduced in [37] is an online evolutionary process that adapts internal rewards and hyperparameters while performing model selection by replacing underperforming agents with mutated versions of better agents. Multiple agents are trained in parallel, and they periodically exchange information by copying weights and hyperparameters. The agents evaluate their performance, and underperforming agents are replaced by mutated versions of better-performing agents. This process continues until a satisfactory performance is achieved, or a maximum budget is reached.

Majumdar et al. [38] propose multi-agent evolutionary reinforcement learning (MERL) as a solution for the sample inefficiency problem of PBT in cooperative MARL environments where the team reward is sparse and agent-specific reward is dense. MERL is a split-level training platform that combines both gradient-based and gradient-free optimization methods, without requiring domain-specific reward shaping. The gradient-free optimizer is used to maximize the team objective by employing an evolutionary algorithm. Specifically, the evolutionary population maintains a variety of teams and uses evolutionary algorithms to maximize team rewards (fitness). The gradient-based optimizer maximizes the local reward of each agent by using a common replay buffer with other team members in the evolutionary population. Collaborative evolutionary reinforcement learning (CERL) [39] is a similar work which addresses the sample inefficiency problem of PBT. It uses a collective replay buffer to share all information across the population.

Deep evolutionary reinforcement learning (DERL) [40] is a framework for creating embodied agents that combines evolutionary algorithms with DRL, which aims to find a diverse solutions. DERL decouples the processes of learning and evolution in a distributed asynchronous manner, using tournament-based steady-state evolution. Similar to PBT [37], DERL maintains a population to encourage diverse solutions. The average final reward is used as a fitness function, and a tournament-based selection method is used to choose the parents for generating children via mutation operations. Liu et al. [53] demonstrated that end-to-end PBT can lead to emergent cooperative behaviors in the soccer domain. They also applied an evaluation scheme based on Nash averaging to address the diversity and exploitability problem.

3.5. General Framework

The policy-space response oracles (PSRO) framework is currently the most widely used general framework for PB-DRL. It unifies various population-based methods, such as SP and PP, with empirical game theory to effectively solve games [25]. As shown in Figure 4, PSRO divides these algorithms into three modules: meta strategy, best-response solution, and policy zoo expansion. The first module, meta strategy, involves solving the meta-game using a meta-solver to obtain the meta strategy (policy distribution) of each policy zoo. The second module, best-response solution, involves each agent sampling policies of other agents π_{-i} and computing its best response π_i with fixed π_{-i}. The third module, policy zoo expansion, involves adding the best response to the corresponding policy zoo. The process starts with a single policy. In each episode, one player trains its policy π_i using a fixed policy set, which is sampled from the meta-strategies of its opponents ($\pi'_{-i} \sim \pi^{zoo}_{-i}$). At the end of every epoch, each policy zoo expands by adding the approximate best response to the meta-strategy of the other players, and the expected utilities for new policy combinations computed via simulation are added to the payoff matrix.

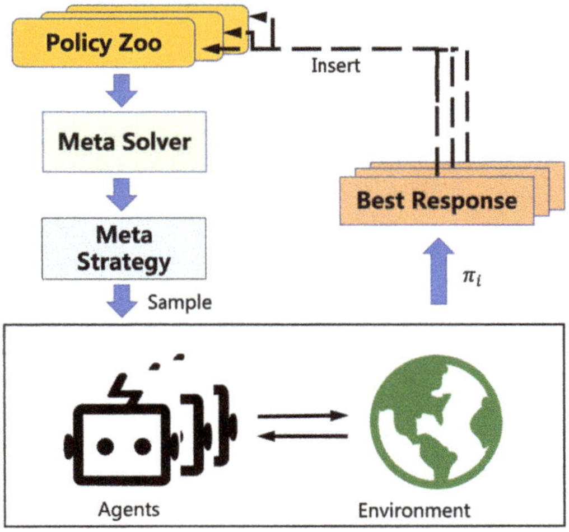

Figure 4. Overview of PSRO.

Although PSRO has demonstrated its performance, several drawbacks have been identified and addressed by recent research. One such extension is Rectified Nash response ($PSRO_{rN}$) [41], which addresses the diversity issue and introduces adaptive sequences of objectives that facilitate open-ended learning. The effective diversity of the population is defined as:

$$d(\pi^{zoo}) = \sum_{i,j=1}^{n} \lfloor \phi(w_i, w_j) \rfloor_+ \cdot p_i \cdot p_j \tag{7}$$

where $n = |\pi^{zoo}|$, $\phi(x, y)$ is the payoff function, $\boldsymbol{p}$ is the Nash equilibrium on π_{zoo}, $\lfloor x \rfloor_+$ is the rectifier, denoted by $\lfloor x \rfloor_+ = x$ if $x \leq 0$ and $\lfloor x \rfloor_+ = 0$ otherwise. Equation (7) encourages agents to play against opponents who they can beat. Perhaps surprisingly, the authors found that building objectives around the weaknesses of agents does not actually encourage diverse skills. To elaborate, when the weaknesses of an agent are emphasized during training, the gradients that guide its policy updates will be biased towards improving those weaknesses, potentially leading to overfitting to a narrow subset of the state space. This can result in a lack of diversity in the learned policies and a failure to generalize to novel situations. Several other works have also focused on the diversity aspect of PSRO frameworks. In [42], the authors propose a geometric interpretation of behavioral diversity in games (Diverse PSRO) and introduce a novel diversity metric that uses determinantal point process (DPP). The diversity metric is based on the expected cardinality of random samples from a DPP in which the ground set is the strategy population. It is denoted as:

$$Diversity(\pi^{zoo}) = E_{\pi' \sim \mathbb{P}_{L_{\pi^{zoo}}}}\left[|\pi'|\right] = Tr(\boldsymbol{I} - (L_{\pi^{zoo}} + \boldsymbol{I})^{-1}), \tag{8}$$

where a DPP defines a probability $\mathbb{P}$, $\boldsymbol{\pi'}$ is a random subset drawn from the DPP, and $L_{\pi^{zoo}}$ is the DPP kernel. They incorporate this diversity metric into best-response dynamics to improve overall diversity. Similarly, [54] notes the absence of widely accepted definitions for diversity and offers a redefined behavioral diversity measure. The authors propose response diversity as another way to characterize diversity through the response of policies when facing different opponents.

Pipeline PSRO [43] is a scalable method that aims to improve the efficiency of PSRO, which is a common problem of most of PSRO-related frameworks, in finding approximate Nash equilibrium. It achieves this by maintaining a hierarchical pipeline of reinforcement learning workers, allowing it to parallelize PSRO while ensuring convergence. The method includes two classes of policies: fixed and active. Active policies are trained in a hierarchical pipeline, while fixed policies are not trained further. When the performance improvement of the lowest-level active worker in the pipeline does not meet a given threshold within a certain time period, the policy becomes fixed, and a new active policy is added to the pipeline. Another work has improved the computation efficiency and exploration efficiency by introducing a new subroutine of no-regret optimization [55].

PSRO framework has another branch which optimizes the meta-solver concept. Alpha-PSRO [44] extends the original PSRO paper to apply readily to general-sum, many-player settings, using an α-Rank [56], a ranking method that considers all pairwise comparisons between policies, as the meta-solver. Alpha-PSRO defines preference-based best response (PBR), an oracle that finds policies that maximize their rank against the population. Alpha-PSRO works by expanding the strategy pool through constructing a meta-game and calculating a payoff matrix. The meta-game is then solved to obtain a meta-strategy, and finally, a best response is calculated to find an approximate optimal response. Joint PSRO [57] uses correlated equilibrium as the meta-solver, and Mean-Field PSRO [58] proposes newly defined mean-field no-adversarial-regret learners as the meta-solver.

4. Challenges and Hot Topics

In the previous section, we discussed several PB-DRL algorithms that have shown significant improvements in real-life game scenarios. However, the application of these algorithms also faces several challenges that need to be addressed to further advance the field of PB-DRL.

4.1. Challenges

One of the most significant challenges in PB-DRL is the need for increased diversity within the population. Promoting diversity not only helps AI agents avoid checking the same policies repeatedly, but also enables them to discover niche skills, avoid being exploited, and maintain robust performance when encountering unfamiliar types of opponents [22]. As the population grows, it becomes more challenging to maintain diversity and ensure efficient exploration of the search space. Without adequate diversity, the population may converge prematurely to suboptimal solutions, leading to the stagnation of the learning process. Overfitting to policies in the policy zoo is a significant challenge to generalization [25,59]. Although the diversity of a population has been widely discussed in the evolutionary algorithm community at the genotype level, phenotype level, and the combination of the previous two cases [60], which typically operate on a fixed set of candidate solutions, PB-DRL is often used in dynamic and uncertain environments where the population size and diversity can change over time. Additionally, since policies are always represented as neural networks, using difference-based or distance-based methods directly, which are widely used in evolutionary computations, are not suitable choices. Some heuristic algorithms have been proposed. Balduzzi et al. [41] design an opponents selection method to expand the policy game space to improve diversity. Another approach is to incorporate different levels of hierarchy within the population to maintain diversity [44]. An interesting work [42] models behavioral diversity for learning in games by using a determinantal point process as the diversity metric. Other techniques that improve the diversity of the policy pool can be found in [61–63].

The need for increased efficiency is a significant challenge in PB-DRL, as evaluating each individual within a growing population becomes computationally expensive, resulting in a reduced learning rate. PB-DRL is often applied to large-scale environments with high-dimensional state and action spaces, making the evaluation of each individual within a population even more computationally expensive. For instance, AlphaStar trained the league over a period of 44 days using 192 8-core TPUs, 12 128-core TPUs, and 1800 CPUs, which potentially cost more than 120 billion dollars in renting cloud computing services for training [5]. One promising approach to improving efficiency in PB-DRL is to develop more sample-efficient algorithms. This can be achieved through various means, such as monotonic improvement in exploitability [55], regret bound [64]. Another approach to improving efficiency in PB-DRL is to use distributed computing techniques [43,65]. These techniques can enable faster evaluation of individuals within a population, as well as better parallelization of the learning process. For example, some recent works named distributed deep reinforcement learning [66] are often used to accelerate the training process in PB-DRL, such as SEED RL [67], Gorila [68], and IMPALA [69]. In addition to the technical challenges of improving efficiency in PB-DRL, there are also practical challenges related to the cost and availability of computing resources. One possible solution to this challenge is to develop more energy-efficient algorithms that can run on low-power devices or take advantage of specialized hardware, such as GPUs or TPUs. Flajolet et al. [70] indicate that the judicious use of compilation and vectorization allows population-based training to be performed on a single machine with one accelerator with minimal overhead compared to training a single agent.

4.2. Hot Topics

Despite these challenges, it is essential to note that this field is rapidly evolving. Currently, there are several hot topics and future directions in PB-DRL worth exploring, and researchers are actively engaged in these endeavors.

Games: PB-DRL has demonstrated outstanding performance in many games, including board games [47], online games [5,11], and more. As a result, game manufacturers have become interested in exploring several directions. These include:

1. AI bots that can learn to make decisions like humans, making them suitable for use in tutorials, hosting games, computer opponents, and more.
2. AI non-player characters that train agents to interact with players according to their own character settings, which can be used for virtual hosts, open-world RPG games, and other applications.
3. AI teammates that are designed to help and support human players in cooperative games or simulations. AI teammates can provide assistance, such as cover fire, healing, or completing objectives, to human players in cooperative games or simulations.

Zero-shot coordination: The zero-shot coordination (ZSC) problem refers to the situation where agents must independently produce strategies for a collaborative game that are compatible with novel partners not seen during training [63]. Population-based reinforcement learning has been used for this problem, starting with FCP [20], and there is ongoing research using the keywords "zero-shot human-AI coordination." Researchers aim to identify a sufficiently robust agent capable of effectively generalizing human policies. Many methods have been used in this problem, such as lifetime learning [71], population diversity [62,63], and model human bias [36].

Robotics: Reinforcement learning has become increasingly prevalent in the robotics field [72–74]. The use of PB-DRL has also expanded to robots, including robotic manipulation [75], assistance with robots [52], multi-robot planning [76], and robot table tennis [77]. In a recent study, it was shown that PB-DRL could generate varied environments [78], which is advantageous for developing robust robotics solutions.

Financial markets: Population-based algorithms and concepts have immense potential for use in financial markets and economic forecasting [79]. Despite the widespread use of MARL in financial trading, the application of PB-DRL to financial markets appears to be underutilized in both academic and industry-related research. This is partly due to the high demands placed on simulation environments when working with PB-DRL. Once an environment that meets the requirements is created, PB-DRL will show its power.

5. Conclusions

In this paper, we have provided a comprehensive survey of representative population-based deep reinforcement learning (PB-DRL) algorithms, applications, and general frameworks. We categorize PB-DRL research into the following areas: naive self-play, fictitious self-play, population-play, evolution-based training methods, and general framework. We compare the main ideas of different types of algorithms by summarizing the various types of PB-DRL algorithms and describing how they have been used in real-life applications.

Furthermore, we introduce evolution-based training methods to expound on common ways to adjust hyperparameters or accelerate training. General frameworks for PB-DRL are also introduced for different game settings, providing a general training process and theoretical proofs. Finally, we discuss the challenges and opportunities of this exciting field. We aim to provide a valuable reference for researchers and engineers working on practical problems.

Author Contributions: Conceptualization, W.L. and P.Z.; methodology, W.L. and P.Z.; software, T.H.; validation, X.W. and S.Y.; formal analysis, X.W.; investigation, W.L. and X.W.; resources, W.L.; writing—original draft preparation, W.L.; writing—review and editing, T.H., X.W. and P.Z; visualization, S.Y.; supervision, L.Z.; project administration, P.Z. and L.Z.; funding acquisition, L.Z. All authors have read and agreed to the published version of the manuscript.

Funding: The work reported in this paper was supported by the National Key R&D Program of China (Grant Number: 2021ZD0113502, 2021ZD0113503), Shanghai Municipality Science and Technology Major Project (Grant Number: 2021SHZDZX0103), and China Postdoctoral Science Foundation (Grant Number: BX20220071, 2022M720769), and Research on Basic and Key Technologies of Intelligent Robots (Grant Number: KEH2310017).

Data Availability Statement: Not applicable.

Acknowledgments: Many thanks to FDU IPASS Group for taking the time to proofread this article.

Conflicts of Interest: The authors declare no conflict of interest.

References

1. Sutton, R.S.; Barto, A.G. *Reinforcement Learning: An Introduction*; MIT Press: Cambridge, MA, USA, 2018.
2. Mnih, V.; Kavukcuoglu, K.; Silver, D.; Graves, A.; Antonoglou, I.; Wierstra, D.; Riedmiller, M. Playing Atari with Deep Reinforcement Learning. *arXiv* **2013**, arXiv:1312.5602.
3. Silver, D.; Huang, A.; Maddison, C.J.; Guez, A.; Sifre, L.; Van Den Driessche, G.; Schrittwieser, J.; Antonoglou, I.; Panneershelvam, V.; Lanctot, M.; et al. Mastering the game of Go with deep neural networks and tree search. *Nature* **2016**, *529*, 484–489. [CrossRef] [PubMed]
4. Silver, D.; Hubert, T.; Schrittwieser, J.; Antonoglou, I.; Lai, M.; Guez, A.; Lanctot, M.; Sifre, L.; Kumaran, D.; Graepel, T.; et al. A general reinforcement learning algorithm that masters chess, shogi, and Go through self-play. *Science* **2018**, *362*, 1140–1144. [CrossRef]
5. Vinyals, O.; Babuschkin, I.; Czarnecki, W.M.; Mathieu, M.; Dudzik, A.; Chung, J.; Choi, D.H.; Powell, R.; Ewalds, T.; Georgiev, P.; et al. Grandmaster level in StarCraft II using multi-agent reinforcement learning. *Nature* **2019**, *575*, 350–354. [CrossRef] [PubMed]
6. Degrave, J.; Felici, F.; Buchli, J.; Neunert, M.; Tracey, B.; Carpanese, F.; Ewalds, T.; Hafner, R.; Abdolmaleki, A.; de Las Casas, D.; et al. Magnetic control of tokamak plasmas through deep reinforcement learning. *Nature* **2022**, *602*, 414–419. [CrossRef] [PubMed]
7. Fawzi, A.; Balog, M.; Huang, A.; Hubert, T.; Romera-Paredes, B.; Barekatain, M.; Novikov, A.; R Ruiz, F.J.; Schrittwieser, J.; Swirszcz, G.; et al. Discovering faster matrix multiplication algorithms with reinforcement learning. *Nature* **2022**, *610*, 47–53. [CrossRef]
8. Hernandez-Leal, P.; Kartal, B.; Taylor, M.E. A survey and critique of multiagent deep reinforcement learning. *Auton. Agents Multi-Agent Syst.* **2019**, *33*, 750–797. [CrossRef]
9. Buşoniu, L.; Babuška, R.; De Schutter, B. Multi-agent reinforcement learning: An overview. In *Innovations in Multi-Agent Systems and Applications-1*; Springer: Berlin/Heidelberg, Germany, 2010; pp. 183–221.
10. Brown, N.; Sandholm, T. Superhuman AI for multiplayer poker. *Science* **2019**, *365*, 885–890. [CrossRef]
11. Berner, C.; Brockman, G.; Chan, B.; Cheung, V.; Debiak, P.; Dennison, C.; Farhi, D.; Fischer, Q.; Hashme, S.; Hesse, C.; et al. Dota 2 with Large Scale Deep Reinforcement Learning. *arXiv* **2019**, arXiv:1912.06680.
12. Czarnecki, W.M.; Gidel, G.; Tracey, B.; Tuyls, K.; Omidshafiei, S.; Balduzzi, D.; Jaderberg, M. Real world games look like spinning tops. *Adv. Neural Inf. Process. Syst.* **2020**, *33*, 17443–17454.
13. Kitchenham, B.; Charters, S. *Guidelines for Performing Systematic Literature Reviews in Software Engineering*; Elsevier: Amsterdam, The Netherlands, 2007.
14. Kuhn, H. Extensive games and the problem of information. *Contributions to the Theory of Games*; Princeton University Press: Princeton, NJ, USA, 1953; p. 193.
15. LeCun, Y.; Bengio, Y.; Hinton, G. Deep learning. *Nature* **2015**, *521*, 436–444. [CrossRef] [PubMed]
16. Schmidhuber, J. Deep learning in neural networks: An overview. *Neural Netw.* **2015**, *61*, 85–117. [CrossRef] [PubMed]

17. Mnih, V.; Kavukcuoglu, K.; Silver, D.; Rusu, A.A.; Veness, J.; Bellemare, M.G.; Graves, A.; Riedmiller, M.; Fidjeland, A.K.; Ostrovski, G.; et al. Human-level control through deep reinforcement learning. *Nature* **2015**, *518*, 529–533. [CrossRef] [PubMed]
18. Fujimoto, S.; van Hoof, H.; Meger, D. Addressing Function Approximation Error in Actor-Critic Methods. In *35th International Conference on Machine Learning*; Dy, J., Krause, A., Eds.; PMLR: Cambridge, MA, USA, 2018; Volume 80, pp. 1587–1596.
19. Schulman, J.; Wolski, F.; Dhariwal, P.; Radford, A.; Klimov, O. Proximal policy optimization algorithms. *arXiv* **2017**, arXiv:1707.06347.
20. Strouse, D.; McKee, K.; Botvinick, M.; Hughes, E.; Everett, R. Collaborating with humans without human data. *Adv. Neural Inf. Process. Syst.* **2021**, *34*, 14502–14515.
21. Lin, F.; Huang, S.; Pearce, T.; Chen, W.; Tu, W.W. TiZero: Mastering Multi-Agent Football with Curriculum Learning and Self-Play. *arXiv* **2023**, arXiv:2302.07515.
22. Yang, Y.; Wang, J. An overview of multi-agent reinforcement learning from game theoretical perspective. *arXiv* **2020**, arXiv:2011.00583.
23. de Witt, C.S.; Gupta, T.; Makoviichuk, D.; Makoviychuk, V.; Torr, P.H.; Sun, M.; Whiteson, S. Is independent learning all you need in the starcraft multi-agent challenge? *arXiv* **2020**, arXiv:2011.09533.
24. Yu, C.; Velu, A.; Vinitsky, E.; Gao, J.; Wang, Y.; Bayen, A.; Wu, Y. The surprising effectiveness of ppo in cooperative multi-agent games. *Adv. Neural Inf. Process. Syst.* **2022**, *35*, 24611–24624.
25. Lanctot, M.; Zambaldi, V.F.; Gruslys, A.; Lazaridou, A.; Tuyls, K.; Pérolat, J.; Silver, D.; Graepel, T. A Unified Game-Theoretic Approach to Multiagent Reinforcement Learning. In Proceedings of the Advances in Neural Information Processing Systems 30: Annual Conference on Neural Information Processing Systems 2017, Long Beach, CA, USA, 4–9 December 2017; Guyon, I., von Luxburg, U., Bengio, S., Wallach, H.M., Fergus, R., Vishwanathan, S.V.N., Garnett, R., Eds.; Curran Associates Inc.: Red Hook, NY, USA, 2017; pp. 4190–4203.
26. Lowe, R.; Wu, Y.; Tamar, A.; Harb, J.; Abbeel, P.; Mordatch, I. Multi-Agent Actor-Critic for Mixed Cooperative-Competitive Environments. In Proceedings of the Advances in Neural Information Processing Systems 30: Annual Conference on Neural Information Processing Systems 2017, Long Beach, CA, USA, 4–9 December 2017; Guyon, I., von Luxburg, U., Bengio, S., Wallach, H.M., Fergus, R., Vishwanathan, S.V.N., Garnett, R., Eds.; Curran Associates Inc.: Red Hook, NY, USA, 2017; pp. 6379–6390.
27. Rashid, T.; Samvelyan, M.; Schroeder, C.; Farquhar, G.; Foerster, J.; Whiteson, S. QMIX: Monotonic Value Function Factorisation for Deep Multi-Agent Reinforcement Learning. In *35th International Conference on Machine Learning*; Dy, J., Krause, A., Eds.; PMLR: Cambridge, MA, USA, 2018; Volume 80, pp. 4295–4304.
28. Sukhbaatar, S.; Szlam, A.; Fergus, R. Learning Multiagent Communication with Backpropagation. In Proceedings of the Advances in Neural Information Processing Systems 29: Annual Conference on Neural Information Processing Systems 2016, Barcelona, Spain, 5–10 December 2016; Lee, D.D., Sugiyama, M., von Luxburg, U., Guyon, I., Garnett, R., Eds.; Curran Associates Inc.: Red Hook, NY, USA, 2016; pp. 2244–2252.
29. Al, S. Some studies in machine learning using the game of checkers. *IBM J. Res. Dev.* **1959**, *3*, 210–229.
30. Brown, G.W. Iterative solution of games by fictitious play. *Act. Anal. Prod. Alloc.* **1951**, *13*, 374.
31. Heinrich, J.; Lanctot, M.; Silver, D. Fictitious self-play in extensive-form games. In *International Conference on Machine Learning*; PMLR: Cambridge, MA, USA, 2015; pp. 805–813.
32. Heinrich, J.; Silver, D. Deep reinforcement learning from self-play in imperfect-information games. *arXiv* **2016**, arXiv:1603.01121.
33. Lockhart, E.; Lanctot, M.; Pérolat, J.; Lespiau, J.; Morrill, D.; Timbers, F.; Tuyls, K. Computing Approximate Equilibria in Sequential Adversarial Games by Exploitability Descent. In Proceedings of the Twenty-Eighth International Joint Conference on Artificial Intelligence, IJCAI 2019, Macao, China, 10–16 August 2019; Kraus, S., Ed.; pp. 464–470. [CrossRef]
34. Bansal, T.; Pachocki, J.; Sidor, S.; Sutskever, I.; Mordatch, I. Emergent Complexity via Multi-Agent Competition. In Proceedings of the International Conference on Learning Representations, Vancouver, BC, Canada, 30 April–3 May 2018.
35. Jaderberg, M.; Czarnecki, W.M.; Dunning, I.; Marris, L.; Lever, G.; Castaneda, A.G.; Beattie, C.; Rabinowitz, N.C.; Morcos, A.S.; Ruderman, A.; et al. Human-level performance in 3D multiplayer games with population-based reinforcement learning. *Science* **2019**, *364*, 859–865. [CrossRef]
36. Yu, C.; Gao, J.; Liu, W.; Xu, B.; Tang, H.; Yang, J.; Wang, Y.; Wu, Y. Learning Zero-Shot Cooperation with Humans, Assuming Humans Are Biased. *arXiv* **2023**, arXiv:2302.01605.
37. Jaderberg, M.; Dalibard, V.; Osindero, S.; Czarnecki, W.M.; Donahue, J.; Razavi, A.; Vinyals, O.; Green, T.; Dunning, I.; Simonyan, K.; et al. Population Based Training of Neural Networks. *arXiv* **2017**, arXiv:1711.09846v2.
38. Majumdar, S.; Khadka, S.; Miret, S.; Mcaleer, S.; Tumer, K. Evolutionary Reinforcement Learning for Sample-Efficient Multiagent Coordination. In *37th International Conference on Machine Learning*; Daumé, H., Singh, A., Eds.; PMLR: Cambridge, MA, USA, 2020; Volume 119, pp. 6651–6660.
39. Khadka, S.; Majumdar, S.; Nassar, T.; Dwiel, Z.; Tumer, E.; Miret, S.; Liu, Y.; Tumer, K. Collaborative Evolutionary Reinforcement Learning. In *36th International Conference on Machine Learning*; Chaudhuri, K., Salakhutdinov, R., Eds. PMLR: Cambridge, MA, USA, 2019; Volume 97, pp. 3341–3350.
40. Gupta, A.; Savarese, S.; Ganguli, S.; Fei-Fei, L. Embodied intelligence via learning and evolution. *Nat. Commun.* **2021**, *12*, 5721. [CrossRef]
41. Balduzzi, D.; Garnelo, M.; Bachrach, Y.; Czarnecki, W.; Perolat, J.; Jaderberg, M.; Graepel, T. Open-ended learning in symmetric zero-sum games. In *International Conference on Machine Learning*; PMLR: Cambridge, MA, USA, 2019; pp. 434–443.

42. Perez-Nieves, N.; Yang, Y.; Slumbers, O.; Mguni, D.H.; Wen, Y.; Wang, J. Modelling behavioural diversity for learning in open-ended games. In *International Conference on Machine Learning*; PMLR: Cambridge, MA, USA, 2021; pp. 8514–8524.
43. McAleer, S.; Lanier, J.B.; Fox, R.; Baldi, P. Pipeline psro: A scalable approach for finding approximate nash equilibria in large games. *Adv. Neural Inf. Process. Syst.* **2020**, *33*, 20238–20248.
44. Muller, P.; Omidshafiei, S.; Rowland, M.; Tuyls, K.; Perolat, J.; Liu, S.; Hennes, D.; Marris, L.; Lanctot, M.; Hughes, E.; et al. A Generalized Training Approach for Multiagent Learning. In Proceedings of the International Conference on Learning Representations, Addis Ababa, Ethiopia, 26–30 April 2020.
45. Hernandez, D.; Denamganai, K.; Devlin, S.; Samothrakis, S.; Walker, J.A. A comparison of self-play algorithms under a generalized framework. *IEEE Trans. Games* **2021**, *14*, 221–231. [CrossRef]
46. Tesauro, G. TD-Gammon, a self-teaching backgammon program, achieves master-level play. *Neural Comput.* **1994**, *6*, 215–219. [CrossRef]
47. Silver, D.; Schrittwieser, J.; Simonyan, K.; Antonoglou, I.; Huang, A.; Guez, A.; Hubert, T.; Baker, L.; Lai, M.; Bolton, A.; et al. Mastering the game of go without human knowledge. *Nature* **2017**, *550*, 354–359. [CrossRef]
48. Ye, D.; Chen, G.; Zhao, P.; Qiu, F.; Yuan, B.; Zhang, W.; Chen, S.; Sun, M.; Li, X.; Li, S.; et al. Supervised learning achieves human-level performance in moba games: A case study of honor of kings. *IEEE Trans. Neural Netw. Learn. Syst.* **2020**, *33*, 908–918. [CrossRef] [PubMed]
49. Baker, B.; Kanitscheider, I.; Markov, T.; Wu, Y.; Powell, G.; McGrew, B.; Mordatch, I. Emergent Tool Use From Multi-Agent Autocurricula. In Proceedings of the International Conference on Learning Representations, Addis Ababa, Ethiopia, 26–30 April 2020.
50. Shamma, J.S.; Arslan, G. Dynamic fictitious play, dynamic gradient play, and distributed convergence to Nash equilibria. *IEEE Trans. Autom. Control* **2005**, *50*, 312–327. [CrossRef]
51. Siu, H.C.; Peña, J.; Chen, E.; Zhou, Y.; Lopez, V.; Palko, K.; Chang, K.; Allen, R. Evaluation of Human-AI Teams for Learned and Rule-Based Agents in Hanabi. In *Advances in Neural Information Processing Systems*; Ranzato, M., Beygelzimer, A., Dauphin, Y., Liang, P., Vaughan, J.W., Eds.; Curran Associates, Inc.: Red Hook, NY, USA, 2021; Volume 34, pp. 16183–16195.
52. He, J.Z.Y.; Erickson, Z.; Brown, D.S.; Raghunathan, A.; Dragan, A. Learning Representations that Enable Generalization in Assistive Tasks. In Proceedings of the 6th Annual Conference on Robot Learning, Auckland, New Zealand, 14–18 December 2022.
53. Liu, S.; Lever, G.; Merel, J.; Tunyasuvunakool, S.; Heess, N.; Graepel, T. Emergent Coordination Through Competition. In Proceedings of the 7th International Conference on Learning Representations, ICLR 2019, New Orleans, LA, USA, 6–9 May 2019.
54. Liu, X.; Jia, H.; Wen, Y.; Hu, Y.; Chen, Y.; Fan, C.; Hu, Z.; Yang, Y. Towards unifying behavioral and response diversity for open-ended learning in zero-sum games. *Adv. Neural Inf. Process. Syst.* **2021**, *34*, 941–952.
55. Zhou, M.; Chen, J.; Wen, Y.; Zhang, W.; Yang, Y.; Yu, Y. Efficient Policy Space Response Oracles. *arXiv* **2022**, arXiv:2202.0063v4.
56. Omidshafiei, S.; Papadimitriou, C.; Piliouras, G.; Tuyls, K.; Rowland, M.; Lespiau, J.B.; Czarnecki, W.M.; Lanctot, M.; Perolat, J.; Munos, R. α-rank: Multi-agent evaluation by evolution. *Sci. Rep.* **2019**, *9*, 9937. [CrossRef]
57. Marris, L.; Muller, P.; Lanctot, M.; Tuyls, K.; Graepel, T. Multi-agent training beyond zero-sum with correlated equilibrium meta-solvers. In *International Conference on Machine Learning*; PMLR: Cambridge, MA, USA, 2021; pp. 7480–7491.
58. Muller, P.; Rowland, M.; Elie, R.; Piliouras, G.; Pérolat, J.; Laurière, M.; Marinier, R.; Pietquin, O.; Tuyls, K. Learning Equilibria in Mean-Field Games: Introducing Mean-Field PSRO. In Proceedings of the 21st International Conference on Autonomous Agents and Multiagent Systems, AAMAS 2022, Auckland, New Zealand, 9–13 May 2022; Faliszewski, P., Mascardi, V., Pelachaud, C., Taylor, M.E., Eds.; International Foundation for Autonomous Agents and Multiagent Systems (IFAAMAS), 2022; pp. 926–934. [CrossRef]
59. McKee, K.R.; Leibo, J.Z.; Beattie, C.; Everett, R. Quantifying the effects of environment and population diversity in multi-agent reinforcement learning. *Auton. Agents Multi-Agent Syst.* **2022**, *36*, 21. [CrossRef]
60. Črepinšek, M.; Liu, S.H.; Mernik, M. Exploration and exploitation in evolutionary algorithms: A survey. *ACM Comput. Surv. (CSUR)* **2013**, *45*, 1–33. [CrossRef]
61. Garnelo, M.; Czarnecki, W.M.; Liu, S.; Tirumala, D.; Oh, J.; Gidel, G.; van Hasselt, H.; Balduzzi, D. Pick Your Battles: Interaction Graphs as Population-Level Objectives for Strategic Diversity. In Proceedings of the AAMAS'21: 20th International Conference on Autonomous Agents and Multiagent Systems, Virtual Event, UK, 3–7 May 2021; Dignum, F., Lomuscio, A., Endriss, U., Nowé, A., Eds.; ACM: New York, NY, USA, 2021; pp. 1501–1503. [CrossRef]
62. Zhao, R.; Song, J.; Hu, H.; Gao, Y.; Wu, Y.; Sun, Z.; Wei, Y. Maximum Entropy Population Based Training for Zero-Shot Human-AI Coordination. *arXiv* **2021**, arXiv:2112.11701v3.
63. Lupu, A.; Cui, B.; Hu, H.; Foerster, J. Trajectory diversity for zero-shot coordination. In *International Conference on Machine Learning*; PMLR: Cambridge, MA, USA, 2021; pp. 7204–7213.
64. Bai, Y.; Jin, C. Provable self-play algorithms for competitive reinforcement learning. In *International Conference on Machine Learning*; PMLR: Cambridge, MA, USA, 2020; pp. 551–560.
65. Dinh, L.C.; McAleer, S.M.; Tian, Z.; Perez-Nieves, N.; Slumbers, O.; Mguni, D.H.; Wang, J.; Ammar, H.B.; Yang, Y. Online Double Oracle. *arXiv* **2021**, arXiv:2103.07780v5.
66. Yin, Q.; Yu, T.; Shen, S.; Yang, J.; Zhao, M.; Huang, K.; Liang, B.; Wang, L. Distributed Deep Reinforcement Learning: A Survey and A Multi-Player Multi-Agent Learning Toolbox. *arXiv* **2022**, arXiv:2212.00253.

67. Espeholt, L.; Marinier, R.; Stanczyk, P.; Wang, K.; Michalski, M. SEED RL: Scalable and Efficient Deep-RL with Accelerated Central Inference. In Proceedings of the International Conference on Learning Representations, Addis Ababa, Ethiopia, 26–30 April 2020.
68. Nair, A.; Srinivasan, P.; Blackwell, S.; Alcicek, C.; Fearon, R.; De Maria, A.; Panneershelvam, V.; Suleyman, M.; Beattie, C.; Petersen, S.; et al. Massively parallel methods for deep reinforcement learning. *arXiv* **2015**, arXiv:1507.04296.
69. Espeholt, L.; Soyer, H.; Munos, R.; Simonyan, K.; Mnih, V.; Ward, T.; Doron, Y.; Firoiu, V.; Harley, T.; Dunning, I.; et al. Impala: Scalable distributed deep-rl with importance weighted actor-learner architectures. In *International Conference on Machine Learning*; PMLR: Cambridge, MA, USA, 2018; pp. 1407–1416.
70. Flajolet, A.; Monroc, C.B.; Beguir, K.; Pierrot, T. Fast population-based reinforcement learning on a single machine. In *International Conference on Machine Learning*; PMLR: Cambridge, MA, USA, 2022; pp. 6533–6547.
71. Shih, A.; Sawhney, A.; Kondic, J.; Ermon, S.; Sadigh, D. On the Critical Role of Conventions in Adaptive Human-AI Collaboration. In Proceedings of the 9th International Conference on Learning Representations, ICLR 2021, Virtual Event, Austria, 3–7 May 2021.
72. Hwangbo, J.; Lee, J.; Dosovitskiy, A.; Bellicoso, D.; Tsounis, V.; Koltun, V.; Hutter, M. Learning agile and dynamic motor skills for legged robots. *Sci. Robot.* **2019**, *4*, eaau5872. [CrossRef] [PubMed]
73. Lee, J.; Hwangbo, J.; Wellhausen, L.; Koltun, V.; Hutter, M. Learning quadrupedal locomotion over challenging terrain. *Sci. Robot.* **2020**, *5*, eabc5986. [CrossRef] [PubMed]
74. Miki, T.; Lee, J.; Hwangbo, J.; Wellhausen, L.; Koltun, V.; Hutter, M. Learning robust perceptive locomotion for quadrupedal robots in the wild. *Sci. Robot.* **2022**, *7*, eabk2822. [CrossRef] [PubMed]
75. OpenAI, O.; Plappert, M.; Sampedro, R.; Xu, T.; Akkaya, I.; Kosaraju, V.; Welinder, P.; D'Sa, R.; Petron, A.; Pinto, H.P.d.O.; et al. Asymmetric self-play for automatic goal discovery in robotic manipulation. *arXiv* **2021**, arXiv:2101.04882.
76. Riviere, B.; Hönig, W.; Anderson, M.; Chung, S.J. Neural tree expansion for multi-robot planning in non-cooperative environments. *IEEE Robot. Autom. Lett.* **2021**, *6*, 6868–6875. [CrossRef]
77. Mahjourian, R.; Miikkulainen, R.; Lazic, N.; Levine, S.; Jaitly, N. Hierarchical policy design for sample-efficient learning of robot table tennis through self-play. *arXiv* **2018**, arXiv:1811.12927.
78. Li, D.; Li, W.; Varakantham, P. Diversity Induced Environment Design via Self-Play. *arXiv* **2023**, arXiv:2302.02119.
79. Posth, J.A.; Kotlarz, P.; Misheva, B.H.; Osterrieder, J.; Schwendner, P. The applicability of self-play algorithms to trading and forecasting financial markets. *Front. Artif. Intell.* **2021**, *4*, 668465. [CrossRef]

MDPI
St. Alban-Anlage 66
4052 Basel
Switzerland
Tel. +41 61 683 77 34
Fax +41 61 302 89 18
www.mdpi.com

Mathematics Editorial Office
E-mail: mathematics@mdpi.com
www.mdpi.com/journal/mathematics

www.ingramcontent.com/pod-product-compliance
Lightning Source LLC
Chambersburg PA
CBHW041015270926
51850CB00024B/168
9783036582542